CHILD DEVELOPMENT AND PERSONALITY

CHILD DEVELOPMENT AND PERSONALITY

Seventh Edition

Paul Henry Mussen
University of California, Berkeley

John Janeway Conger
University of Colorado School of Medicine

Jerome Kagan
Harvard University

Aletha Carol Huston
University of Kansas

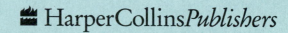
HarperCollinsPublishers

Sponsoring Editor: Laura Pearson	Cover Coordinator: Lucy Krikorian
Editorial Consultant: Carolyn Smith	Cover Design: Patchwork Studio
Project Coordination: Hockett Editorial Service	Photo Research: Inge King
Text Design: Marsha Cohen/Parallelogram	Production: Willie Lane

Cover credit: Edward Pothast, A *Holiday*, c. 1915, oil on canvas (77 × 103 cm). Friends of American Art Collection. Courtesy of the Art Institute of Chicago.

Photo Credits: Richard Dunkley, *ii;* **Roy Morsch**/Stock Market, *vi;* **George Ancona**/International Stock Photo, *vii,* (*xix,* 1983); **Tom Pollack** 1988/Monkmeyer, *viii;* **Renate Hiller**/Monkmeyer, *ix;* **Erika Stone** (1981, *x*), 126, 144 *left,* 155, 201, 225, 247, (306, 1987/Photo Researchers), (397 *left,* 1986), (407, 1981), 536; **Vandystadt**/Photo Researchers, *x;* **Blair Seitz**/Photo Researchers, *xi, xii,* (216, 1989); **Peter Tenzer**/International Stock Photo, *xiii;* **George Goodwin**/Monkmeyer, *xiv;* **Bill Stanton** 1983/International Stock Photo, *xv;* **Catherine Ursillo**/Photo Researchers, *xvi;* **Elizabeth Crews,** *xvii,* 8, 168, 233, 242, 269, 271, 304, 340, 366, 397 *right,* 424, 427, 434, 461, 493, 496, 519, 527, 533; **Ellis Herwig**/Picture Cube, *xviii,* Stock, Boston, *xxiv;* **James Kamp**/Black Star, *xx;* **Kevin Horan**/Picture Group, *xxi;* **Suzanne Szasz,** 3, 86, 124, 161, 169, 264; **Ray Ellis**/Photo Researchers, 4, 207; **Barbara Rios**/Photo Researchers, 7, 191, (502, 524, 1986); **Ulrike Welsch**/Photo Researchers, 11, 252, 564; **Lewis W. Hine**/Bettmann Archive, 12; **Michael Weisbrot**/Stock, Boston, 21; **Harlow Primate Laboratory, University of Wisconsin,** 24; **J. M. Steinlein**/Petit Format/Photo Researchers, 34; **Tim Davis** 1987/Photo Researchers, 36, 79; **Michael Grecco**/Stock, Boston, 48, 178; **Michael Tcherevkoff** 1988/Image Bank, 55; **Peter Vandermark**/Stock, Boston, 66, 119, 490; **Audrey Gottlieb**/Monkmeyer, 68; **Heggemann/Stern**/Black Star, 73; **Enrico Ferorelli,** 88; **Jean-Claude Lejeune**/Stock, Boston, 106; **Robert A. Isaacs** 1986/Photo Researchers, 134; **Michael Rizza**/Picture Cube, 137, 144 *middle;* **Julie O'Neil**/Picture Cube, 144 *right;* **Rick Friedman**/Black Star, 151; **Thomas McAvoy**/LIFE Magazine 1955 Time Inc., 158; **Carol Palmer**/Picture Cube, 185; **Hazel Hankin**/Stock, Boston, 188; **Renee Lynn** 1985/Photo Researchers, 197; **J. Guichard**/Sygma, 204; **Lynn McLaren**/Photo Researchers, 214; **Bill Stanton** 1983/International Stock Photo, 221; **Frank Siteman**/Picture Cube, (227, 1980), (389, 1988); **Barbara Alper**/Stock, Boston, 242; **Tom Cheek**/Stock, Boston, 260, 352; **Bill Anderson**/Monkmeyer, 266; **Gabor Demjen**/Stock, Boston, 275; **David Powers**/Stock, Boston, 281; **Sarah Putnam** 1982/Picture Cube, 282; **Ed Lettau**/Photo Researchers, 291, 664, 667; **Janice Fullman**/Picture Cube, 298, 635; **Mimi Cotter**/International Stock Photo, 302; **David S. Strickler**/Picture Cube, 307, 429, 466, 487; **Alice Kandell**/Photo Researchers, 314; **Thomas S. England**/Photo Researchers, 317; **Christopher Morrow**/Stock, Boston, 322, 612; **Spencer Grant**/Photo Researchers, 334; **American Museum of Natural History,** 337; **Andrew Brilliant**/Picture Cube, 348; **Arthur Sirdofsky**/Gamma-Liaison, 366; **Children's Television Workshop,** 371; **Vivienne della Grotta** 1987/Photo Researchers, 378; 1986 **Tom McCarthy**/Picture Cube, 380; **Elaine Rebman**/Photo Researchers, 383; **Miro Vintoniv**/Stock, Boston, 386; **Thomas Russell**/Picture Cube, 392; **Sam Sweezy**/Stock, Boston, 396; **Kindra Clineff**/Picture Cube, 416; **Bob Daemmrich**/Stock, Boston, 417, 673; **Gabe Palmer**/Stock Market, 448; **Michael Kienitz**/Picture Group, 449; **Michael Kagan,** Monkmeyer, 459; **Alexander Lowry** 1986/Photo Researchers, 474; **Meri Houtchens-Kitchens**/Picture Cube, 509, 652; **Stacy Pick**/Stock, Boston, 516; **David Strickler**/Monkmeyer, 535; **Gale Zucker**/Stock, Boston, 539, 544; **Herman Kokojan** 1986/Black Star, 553; **David R. Frazier**/Photo Researchers, 566; **Cindy Charles**/Gamma-Liaison, 573; **Bill Bachman** 1987/Photo Researchers, 570, 579; **Richard Pasley** 1985/Stock, Boston, 582; **Chris Brown**/Stock, Boston, 587; **Rhoda Sidney**/Stock, Boston, 593; **D. Fineman**/Sygma, 595; **Richard Hutchings**/Photo Researchers, 603; **Jeffry W. Myers**/Stock, Boston, 618; **Margot Granitsas**/Photo Researchers, 625; **NASA,** 629; **Addison Geary** 1984/Stock, Boston, 640; **Eugene Richards**/Magnum, 661; **Wide World,** 679; **Susan Rosenberg**/Photo Researchers, 683.

Child Development and Personality, Seventh Edition

Copyright © 1990 by HarperCollins*Publishers*

Library of Congress Cataloging-in-Publication Data

Child development and personality/
    Paul Henry Mussen . . . [et al.].—7th ed.
        p. cm.
    Includes bibliographical references.
    ISBN 0-06-044695-1
    1. Child psychology.   2. Personality in children.
    I. Mussen, Paul Henry.
    BF721.C5143 1990
    155.4—dc20   89-27797
                                            CIP #

    94 95   11 10 9 8

CONTENTS
in brief

Preface / xxii

1 Introduction / 1

Part One   35

THE PRENATAL PERIOD

2 Genetic and Prenatal Factors in Development / 37

Part Two   87

THE FIRST TWO YEARS

3 Perceptual and Cognitive Development in Infancy / 89
4 Emotional and Social Development in Infancy / 135
5 The Transition to Childhood: The Second and Third Years / 179

Part Three   215

THE CHILDHOOD YEARS:
LANGUAGE AND COGNITIVE DEVELOPMENT

6 Language and Communication / 217
7 Cognitive Development: Piaget and Beyond / 261
8 Cognitive Development: Learning and Information Processing / 299
9 Intelligence and Achievement / 325

Part Four   379

THE CHILDHOOD YEARS:
PERSONAL AND SOCIAL DEVELOPMENT

10 Identity and Individual Development / 381
11 The Development of Social Behavior / 425
12 Socialization in the Family / 475
13 Socialization Beyond the Family / 517

Part Five   565

ADOLESCENCE

14 Adolescence: Development and Socialization / 567
15 Adolescence: Identity, Values, and Vocational Choice / 613
16 Adolescence: Alienation and Problems of Adjustment / 653

References / R-1
Index of Names,
Index of Subjects / I-1

V

CONTENTS
in detail

PREFACE   xxii

Chapter 1   INTRODUCTION   1

What Is Development?/4
Theoretical Issues/5
  Box 1.1   Some Contrasting Early Views of Education/6
  Environmental vs. Biological Determinants of Behavior/7
  Active vs. Passive Nature of the Child/8
  Continuity vs. Discontinuity in Development/9
  Stability over Time/10
  Consistency Across Situations/11
Historical Perspectives on Developmental Psychology/12
  Box 1.2   Pioneers in Child Development/13
  Research in the Early Twentieth Century/14
  The Post-World War II Period/16
  The Past Twenty-five Years/17
Research on Child Development/18
  Applied and Basic Research/18
  The Research Process/18
Methods Used in Studying Children/20
  Cross-sectional and Correlational Studies/22
  Longitudinal Methods/23
  Experiments/23
  Field Experiments/25
  Cross-cultural Studies/26
  Cross-species Studies/26
  Summary of Research Methods/27
Ethical Issues in Research/27
  Box 1.3   Ethical Issues in Research/28
Organization of This Book/29
Summary/29
Review Questions/31
Glossary/32
Suggested Readings/32

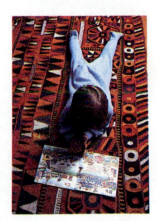

Part One
THE PRENATAL PERIOD/35

Chapter 2   GENETIC AND PRENATAL FACTORS IN DEVELOPMENT   37

The Beginnings of Life: Hereditary Transmission/38
  Chromosomes and Genes/39
  Genes and DNA/39
  The Mechanisms of Hereditary Transmission/42
  Is Sibling Identity Possible?/44
  The Sex Chromosomes/45
  Determining the Extent of Genetic Influences/46
    Physical Features/47
    Intelligence/47
    Developmental Disabilities/51
    Fragile-X Syndrome/51
  Box 2.1   Developmental Risk in Children with Sex Chromosome Abnormalities/52
    Mental Disorders/53
      Schizophrenia/54
      Depression/54
    Personality Characteristics/55
Prenatal Development/56
  Conception and Earliest Development/56
  The Germinal Period/59
  The Embryonic Period/59
    The Placental Barrier/59
    Growth of the Embryo/62
  The Fetal Period/64
    The Last Three Months/67
Prenatal Environmental Influences/67
  Age of the Mother/69
  Maternal Nutrition/69
  Box 2.2   What Is Amniocentesis?/70
  Drugs/73
    Fetal Alcohol Syndrome/74
    Nicotine/74
    Drugs Taken During Labor and Delivery/74
    Other Drugs/74
  Radiation/75
  Maternal Diseases and Disorders During Pregnancy/75
  The Rh Factor/76
  Maternal Stress/77
The Birth Process/77
  Anoxia and Other Complications/77
  Box 2.3   The Children of Kauai/78
  Prematurity/80
Summary/81
Review Questions/83
Glossary/83
Suggested Readings/85

Part Two
THE FIRST TWO YEARS/87

Chapter 3   PERCEPTUAL AND COGNITIVE DEVELOPMENT IN INFANCY   89

Theories and Assumptions/90
The Newborn/92
Sudden Infant Death Syndrome/92
Reflexes of the Newborn/94
Perception in the Newborn/95
Box 3.1   What Do We Learn from Infant Tests?/100
Physical Growth and Maturation in the First Year/103
Maturation of the Brain/104
Posture and Locomotion/104
Sitting/104
Crawling and Creeping/104
Box 3.2   Assessing Infant Intelligence/105
Standing and Walking/105
Cognitive Development in the First Year/107
Recognition of Information: The Schema/108
The Discrepancy Principle/108
Box 3.3   How Do We Know What the Baby Perceives?/111
Schemata Relating Different Sensory Modes/112
Categories/113
The Role of Memory/115
Enhancement of Recall Memory/117
Ability to Relate Past and Present/120
Learning Theory and Conditioning/121
Classical Conditioning/123
Instrumental Conditioning/123
Piaget's View of Infancy/125
Sensorimotor Schemes/125
The Sensorimotor Period/126
The Concept of Object Permanence/127
Piaget's Assumptions About Development/128
Summary/129
Review Questions/131
Glossary/131
Suggested Readings/132

Chapter 4   EMOTIONAL AND SOCIAL DEVELOPMENT IN INFANCY   135

The Meaning of Emotion/136
Emotions of Infancy/138
Inferring Emotions from Behavior/138
Fear of Strangers/139
Separation Fear/140
Other Fears/141
Inferring Emotions from Facial Expressions/143
The Smile/144

Temperamental Differences in Infants/147
  Activity Level/148
  Box 4.1 Living with a Difficult Baby/149
  Irritability/150
  Reaction to Unfamiliarity/150
  The Principle of Bidirectionality/151
Emotional and Social Relationships with Adults/153
  Theoretical Perspectives/153
  Box 4.2 Temperament and Early Experience/154
    Psychoanalytic Theory/154
    Social Learning Theory/156
    Ethology/157
  Attachment to Caregivers/158
  Measuring Attachment/162
    The Strange Situation/162
    Limitations of the Strange Situation/163
  Effects of Parental Practices/165
  Box 4.3 Early Bonding/166
    The Father's Behavior/167
  Consequences of Variations in Quality of Attachment/167
    Institutions and Depriving Environments/169
    Maternal Employment and Infant Day Care/170
  Common Themes in Theories of Infant Social Development/172
  Cultural Ideals and Child Rearing/172
Summary/173
Review Questions/175
Glossary/176
Suggested Readings/176

Chapter 5 **THE TRANSITION TO CHILDHOOD: THE SECOND AND THIRD YEARS**   **179**

Symbolic Functioning/180
  Symbolic Play/181
  Functions of Play/184
  Box 5.1 Does Play Promote Cognitive Development?/186
  Play with Other Children/187
Imitation/190
  The Development of Imitation/190
  Explanations of Imitation/192
    Imitation to Promote Social Interactions/193
    Imitation to Enhance Similarity to Another/194
    Emotional Arousal as a Basis for Imitation/194
    Imitation to Gain Goals/195
Standards and a Moral Sense/195
  Standards of Behavior/196
  Violations of Rules/197
Self-awareness/198
  Box 5.2 Are Children Innately Moral?/199
  Directing the Behavior of Others/200
  Describing One's Own Behavior/200

Self-recognition/200
A Sense of Possession/200
Box 5.3   The 2-Year-Old's Understanding of Self/202
Empathy/203
Family Interactions in the Second and Third Years/205
Processes of Socialization/206
Observation of Role Models/206
Love and Acceptance/206
Restriction vs. Permissiveness/206
Punishment/208
The Context Created by Siblings/209
Summary/210
Review Questions/211
Glossary/212
Suggested Readings/212

Part Three
THE CHILDHOOD YEARS: LANGUAGE AND COGNITIVE DEVELOPMENT   215

Chapter 6   LANGUAGE AND COMMUNICATION   217

The Functions of Language/220
Communication/220
Understanding Society and Culture/221
Social Relationships/221
Symbolic Categories/222
Reasoning/222
Components of Speech/222
Phonemes/222
Perceiving Phonemes/223
Producing Phonemes/223
Meaningful Sounds—Morphemes and Words/224
Semantics: Learning the Meanings of Words/226
Testing Hypotheses/228
Over- and Underextensions/228
Figurative Language/229
Syntax: Combining Words into Sentences/230
The First Sentences/231
Learning Syntactic Rules/231
Grammatical Morphemes/232
Complex Sentences/234
Box 6.1   The Wug Test/235
Questions/236
Deictic Words/236
Passive Sentences/237
Negatives/237
Language in the Deaf/237
Metalinguistic Awareness/238

Pragmatics: Language in Context/238
    Box 6.2 Humor/239
Theories of Language Acquisition/240
    Learning Theory/240
        Criticisms of Learning Theory/241
    Nativist Theory/243
    Box 6.3 Genie: Language Acquisition After Puberty/244
    Cognitive Theory/246
    Social Interaction Theory/247
Language and Cognition/248
    Cognition Precedes Language/248
    Language Influences Cognition/249
    Memory and Problem Solving/249
Environmental Influences on Language/250
    Adult Teaching and Language Learning/250
    Social-class Differences in Language/252
Communication and Conversation/253
    Early Verbal Exchanges/253
    Questions and Requests/254
Summary/256
Review Questions/258
Glossary/258
Suggested Readings/259

Chapter 7   COGNITIVE DEVELOPMENT: PIAGET AND BEYOND   261

Issues in Studying Cognitive Development/262
    Inferring Thought from Behavior/262
    Competence and Performance/263
    Broad vs. Narrow Competence/265
Piaget's Theory/265
    Box 7.1 A Brief Sketch of the Life of Jean Piaget/267
    Major Developmental Issues/268
        Maturation and Experience/268
        The Active, Constructive Child/268
    Organization and Adaptation/270
        Cognitive Structures/271
        Assimilation and Accommodation/272
    Developmental Stages/273
        The Sensorimotor Stage/273
        The Preoperational Stage/273
        The Stage of Concrete Operations/276
          Conservation/276
          Seriation/277
          Relational Thinking/278
          Class Inclusion/278
    Box 7.2 Children Reinvent Arithmetic/278
        The Stage of Formal Operations/280
Beyond Piaget—Empirical Findings and New Conceptions/283
    Maturational Limits and the Role of Experience/283
        Training in Concrete Operations/284

Number Skills/284
Class Inclusion/284
Egocentrism/285
Why the New Findings?/286
The Role of Activity in Learning/288
Is Cognitive Development Domain Specific?/288
Are Stages Universal?/289
The Nature of Developmental Change/290
Box 7.3   Playing, Pretending, and Cognitive Development/292
Evaluation of Piaget's Theory/293
Summary/293
Review Questions/295
Glossary/296
Suggested Readings/297

Chapter 8   COGNITIVE DEVELOPMENT: LEARNING AND INFORMATION PROCESSING

299

Learning Theory and Behaviorism/300
Experimental Analysis of Behavior/300
Cognitive Learning Theories/301
Critique of Learning Principles/302
Information Processing/303
Major Assumptions/303
Cognitive Units—How Information Is Represented/303
Schemata/304
Images/307
Concepts or Categories/308
Propositions/310
Comparison to Piaget/311
Cognitive Processes/311
Perception/311
Attention/313
Memory/314
Box 8.1   Attentional Inertia/315
Recognition and Recall/316
Developmental Changes in Memory/317
Memory Strategies/318
Box 8.2   Children's Eyewitness Testimony/318
Inference/320
Problem Solving/321
Metacognition/321
Knowledge About Cognition/323
Executive Processes/323
How Useful Is Metacognition?/325
A Critique of the Information-processing Approach/326
What Changes with Age?/326
Box 8.3   Children's Concepts About Where Babies Come From/327
Summary/329
Review Questions/331
Glossary/332
Suggested Readings/333

Chapter 9   INTELLIGENCE AND ACHIEVEMENT   335

Defining and Conceptualizing Intelligence/336
One Ability or Many?/337
What Are the Dimensions of Intelligence?/338
Crystallized and Fluid Abilities/338
Guilford's Structure of Intellect/338
Intelligence as Adaptation: A Triarchic Theory/339
Early Efforts to Measure Intelligence/341
The Wechsler Tests/341
Multidimensional Tests/341
Tests Based on Cognitive Processes/342
Limitations on Measures of IQ/343
How Should the IQ Test Be Used?/345
Motivation and School Achievement/346
Achievement Motivation/346
Attainment Value/347
Standards of Performance/348
Expectancies and Beliefs About One's Abilities/349
Attributions About Success and Failure/349
Changing Attributions and Achievement Behavior/351
Developmental Patterns/352
Test Anxiety/353
Summary/354
Cultural and Environmental Influences/355
Sex Differences/356
Differences Based on Nationality, Social Class, and Ethnic Group/356
Box 9.1   Why Do the Japanese Excel?/357
Difference vs. Deficit/358
Test Bias/360
Individual Differences in Intelligence and Achievement/360
Box 9.2   Should Intelligence Tests Be Used for Minority Children?/361
The Home Environment/361
The Physical and Social Aspects of the Home Environment/362
Affection and Involvement with the Child/362
Parents' Beliefs, Expectations, and Values/363
Parenting Styles and Discipline/363
Parents' Teaching Behavior/364
Implications/364
Early Intervention/365
Head Start/365
Box 9.3   How Long Does a Head Start Last?/367
Intervention in Infancy/368
Intervention with Television/369
Interaction Between Constitution and Environment/370
Summary/373
Review Questions/375
Glossary/376
Suggested Readings/376

Part Four
THE CHILDHOOD YEARS: PERSONAL AND SOCIAL DEVELOPMENT   379

Chapter 10 IDENTITY AND INDIVIDUAL DEVELOPMENT   381

Theories of Individual and Social Development/382
Theories of Social Cognition/382
Distinguishing People from Objects/383
Theories Based on Piaget/384
Information Processing: Schema Theory/384
Attribution Theory/385
Theories of Social Behavior: Social Learning/385
Conditioning/385
Observational Learning/385
Developing a Sense of Self/388
Self-concept/388
Developmental Changes/388
Concepts of Self vs. Others/390
Self-esteem/391
Measuring Self-esteem/391
Self-esteem Is Multidimensional/391
Sex Typing and Identity/392
Development of Sex Typing/394
Gender Identity/394
Preferences/395
Adoption of Sex-typed Behavior/396
How Does Sex Typing Come About?/398
Cognitive Development/398
Schemata/399
Gender Salience/399
Box 10.1   Nonsexist Child Rearing/400
Social-learning Theory/401
Ethnic Group and Identity/403
Children's Conceptions of Ethnic Groups/403
Group Identity and Self-esteem/404
Box 10.2   A Child Learns What It Means to Be Black in America/405
Emotion/407
Components of Emotion/408
Eliciting Context/408
Body States/410
Emotional Expression/410
Emotional Experience/410
How Children Acquire Emotions/411
Social Cognitions About Emotion/411
Attributions and Affect/413
How Emotions Are Learned/413
Problems in Individual and Social Development/414
Prevalence of Emotional Problems/414

Types of Emotional Disturbance/416
Depression/416
Social Withdrawal/416
Box 10.3   Children Teach Social Skills to Peers/418
Externalizing Syndromes/419
Duration of Emotional Disturbance over Time/419
Summary/419
Review Questions/421
Glossary/422
Suggested Readings/422

Chapter 11 THE DEVELOPMENT OF SOCIAL BEHAVIOR   425

Relationships with Peers/426
Peers and Play/426
Role Taking/430
Perceptions of Others/431
Box 11.1   Stages in the Development of Role-Taking Skills/432
Friendship/433
Concepts of Friendship/433
Forming Friendships/435
Parents as Models/435
Maintaining Friendships/437
Peer Relations and Group Structure/437
Acceptance and Rejection/438
Box 11.2   Training in Social Skills/440
Self-control and Moral Development/441
Measuring and Developing Self-control/442
Over- and Undercontrol/444
Moral Development/445
Moral Judgments/446
Kohlberg's Theory/447
Box 11.3   Democratic Atmosphere and Moral Judgment/454
Criticisms of Kohlberg's Theory/456
Moral Judgment and Behavior/456
Prosocial Behavior/458
Cultural Background/458
Empathy/459
Training for Prosocial Behavior/462
Modeling and Observation/462
Induction/462
Direct Instruction/464
Early Assignment of Responsibility/464
Aggression/464
Patterns of Aggressive Behavior/465
Determinants of Aggression/468
Biological Factors/468
Influence of the Family/469
Summary/470
Review Questions/472
Glossary/472
Suggested Readings/473

Chapter 12 SOCIALIZATION IN THE FAMILY   475

Determinants of Child-rearing Practices/478
Parental Characteristics and Beliefs/478
Children's Personality and Behavior/480
Social Contexts/481
Child-rearing Practices and Their Consequences/481
Box 12.1   Some Impacts of the Exosystem on Children/482
Reinforcement/484
Punishment/486
Negative Side Effects of Punishment/487
The Child's Role in Punishment/487
Inductive Techniques/488
General Comments on Disciplinary Techniques/489
Imitation and Identification/489
Influences on Family Socialization/491
Patterns and Styles of Parental Behavior/491
Siblings/495
Sibling Relationships/496
Sibling Influences/498
Only Children/498
Box 12.2   Only Children in China/499
Family Structure/500
Children with Single Parents/501
Divorce/502
Stepparent-stepchild Relationships/505
Maternal Employment/506
Child Abuse/507
A Systems Approach to Family Socialization/509
Box 12.3   The Family as a System/510
Summary/511
Review Questions/513
Glossary/514
Suggested Readings/514

Chapter 13 SOCIALIZATION BEYOND THE FAMILY   517

Day Care and School as Contexts for Development/518
Day Care and Preschool/519
Quality of Day Care/520
Box 13.1   Child Care Quality and Children's Behavior/521
School: The Physical Setting/522
Preschool Environments/522
Toys and Activities/523
Elementary School Buildings/523
Academic Organization of Schools/523
Open Education/523
Adult Structuring/525
Sex Differences/526
Teachers' Influences on Children/526
Praise and Criticism/528

      Teachers as Models/530
      Teachers' Expectancies/531
    Classroom Organization/531
      Cooperative Learning vs. Competition/531
      Desegregation and Integration/532
      Mainstreaming/534
Peers as Agents of Socialization/535
    Parents vs. Peers/536
    Social Learning from Peers/537
      Aggression and Prosocial Behavior/537
      Sex Typing/538
      Are Peer Reactions Effective Reinforcers?/539
      Social and Emotional Responses/540
      Peers as Teachers/540
Television as a Socializing Influence/542
    Time Spent Watching Television/542
    What Children Watch/542
    Parents' Influence on Children's Viewing/544
    Television vs. No Television/545
      Displacement of Other Activities/545
      Health and Physical Fitness/545
      School Achievement and Cognitive Processes/545
      Does Television Make Children Intellectually Passive?/547
    How Children Understand Television/547
      Attention to TV/547
      Cognitive Development/549
    What Is Learned from Television?/548
      Social Knowledge/548
      Stereotypes/548
Box 13.2 Changing Sex Stereotypes with Television/549
      Violence/550
      Prosocial Behavior/552
      Advertising/552
Government and Economic Influences/552
    Social Trends and Social Policy/553
      Poverty and Children/554
      Effects of Income Loss on Families/555
      Maternal Employment/555
      Single Parents/557
    Relations Between the Family and Other Social Systems/557
    Box 13.3 Family Policies in Other Countries/558
Summary/560
Review Questions/562
Glossary/562
Suggested Readings/562

Part Five

ADOLESCENCE   565

Chapter 14 ADOLESCENCE: DEVELOPMENT AND SOCIALIZATION   567

Growing Up: Physical Development of Adolescence/569
Hormonal Factors in Development/569
Hormonal Dimorphism/569
The Adolescent Growth Spurt/570
The Shape of Things to Come/572
Sexual Maturation/573
Sexual Development in Males/573
Sexual Development in Females/574
Normal Variations in Development/574
Psychological Aspects of Maturation/577
Onset of Menstruation/577
Erection, Ejaculation, and Nocturnal Emission/578
Early and Late Maturers/579
Early vs. Late Maturation in Males/579
Early vs. Late Maturation in Females/580
Cognitive Development in Adolescence/581
Hypothetical Thinking/583
Cognitive Aspects of Personality Development/584
Adolescent Sexuality/584
Sex Differences in Sexuality/585
Changing Sexual Attitudes and Behavior/586
Box 14.1   Sex Education/587
Premarital Sexual Intercourse/589
Homosexual Behavior and Orientation/590
Variations in Sexual Attitudes and Behavior/592
Pregnancy and Contraception/592
Box 14.2   Teenage Pregnancy in Developed Countries/594
Adolescent Mothers/595
Failure to Use Contraceptives/596
Box 14.3   Preventing Adolescent Pregnancy/596
Desire for Pregnancy/598
Parental Relations and the Development of Autonomy/598
Changing Perceptions of Parents/599
Variations in Parental Behavior/599
Authoritative Parents/599
Authoritarian and Autocratic Parents/600
Laissez-faire Parents/600
Family Communication/601
Adolescents and Their Peers/601
Conformity to Peer Culture/602
Parental vs. Peer Influences/603

Friendships and Identity Development/605
Relationships with Opposite-sex Peers/606
  Going steady/606
  Intimacy/607
  Adolescent Love/607
Summary/608
Review Questions/610
Glossary/611
Suggested Readings/611

Chapter 15 ADOLESCENCE: IDENTITY, VALUES, AND VOCATIONAL CHOICE   613

Identity/614
  Box 15.1   Erikson's Eight Stages of Development/615
  Developing a Sense of Identity/617
    Self-concept and Identity/619
    The Role of the Family/620
  Identity Foreclosure and Identity Confusion/621
    Identity Foreclosure/621
    Identity Confusion/621
  Achieved Ego Identity/622
  Variations in Identity Formation/622
  Gender Identity and Sex Role Identity/623
Vocational Choice in a Changing World/624
  Development of Vocational Goals/626
  Socioeconomic Influences/626
  Box 15.2   Employment in High School/627
  Women and Work/628
    Family Values, Sex Role Attitudes, and Vocational Goals/629
  Box 15.3   Marriage and Work: The Views of Today's High School Seniors/631
  Parental Influences/632
    Father's Occupation and Work Experience/633
    Maternal Employment/633
  School and Peer Group Influences/635
  Vocational Values and Social Change/635
  Vocational Prospects for Today's Youth/637
    College Graduates: Demand and Supply/640
Moral Development and Values/641
  Cognitive Growth and Moral Development/641
  Moral Values and Personal Conflicts/643
  Changing Religious Beliefs/643
    Sects and Cults/644
  Current Trends in Adolescent Values/644
    Personal and Moral Values/645
    The Blue-collar Revolution/646
  A Turning Point?/647
Summary/647
Review Questions/649
Glossary/650
Suggested Readings/650

Chapter 16 ADOLESCENCE: ALIENATION AND PROBLEMS OF ADJUSTMENT 653

The Roots of Alienation/654
 A "New" Alienation?/655
Adolescents and Drugs/655
 What Are the Facts?/656
 Prevalence of Adolescent Drug Use/656
 Box 16.1 Adolescents and Crack/660
 Why Do Adolescents Use Drugs?/662
  Peer Pressure/662
  Parent-child Relationships/662
  Escape from the Pressures of Life/662
  Emotional Disturbance/662
  Alienation or Societal Rejection/663
Adolescent Runaways/663
 Box 16.2 Runaway or Throwaway? One Runaway's Response to Abuse/665
Adolescent Delinquency/667
 Sex Differences/669
 Social Change and Poverty/669
  Gangs/670
 Personality Factors and Parent-child Relationships/670
  Personality Characteristics/671
  Family Relationships/671
 Prevention and Treatment of Delinquency/672
  Correctional Institutions/672
 Box 16.3 The Violent World of Peewee Brown/674
  Behavioral Methods/675
Psychological and Psychophysiological Disturbances/676
 Anxiety Reactions/676
 Adolescent Depression/677
 Suicide/678
  Reasons for Suicide Attempts/678
  Prediction of Suicide/680
  Treatment/680
 Adolescent Schizophrenia/681
  Causative Factors/681
  Prognosis/682
 Brief Reactive Psychosis/682
 Eating Disorders/682
 Treatment of Adolescents/685
Summary/685
Review Questions/687
Glossary/687
Suggested Readings/688

REFERENCES/R-1
INDEX OF NAMES,
INDEX OF SUBJECTS/I-1

PREFACE

Many students enter courses in child development expecting to learn how-to skills—how to raise children, how to teach young children, and how to deal with children's problems. They are often more aware of the questions raised by unusual development than of the issues surrounding normal development. For students early in their academic careers, psychological theory and research sometimes seem far removed from their practical interests and concerns. As instructors, our task is to help students understand the essential place of scientific knowledge, not only for the advancement of a field of inquiry, but for understanding the issues that concern them. We hope to do more than teach a body of information. We hope to build an appreciation for the importance of thinking analytically, asking questions, and recognizing that the obvious answer is not always the right one.

The field of child development has become more applied in the more than thirty years since the first edition of *Child Development and Personality* was published. Many basic researchers have become increasingly interested in generating knowledge that goes beyond the laboratory to real world settings and in putting their knowledge to work to improve parenting, schooling, day care, public policy, and many other domains of life that are critical to children's well-being. Throughout this edition, we have tried to incorporate bridges between basic knowledge and real world applications. For instance, in the discussion of basic memory processes, research on the reliability of children's testimony has been presented. Research on television and children has been used to shed light on basic processes of attention and story comprehension. Our purpose is not only to make the basic material more relevant for students, but to show that knowledge about basic principles is enhanced by learning how those principles operate, or fail to operate, in different contexts.

We have also tried to communicate some of the excitement of the science—the sense of curiosity and the thrill of devising rigorous and ingenious ways to get systematic information about complex and rapidly changing human beings. Studying children is even more a detective game than studying adults, because children often cannot or do not articulate their thoughts and feelings. The rapid growth of knowledge about infants' competence over the past twenty-five years has been due largely to scientific advancements in gaining access to infants' attention, memory, emotions, and social relationships.

At the same time we have continued our tradition of a thorough book that delves into the research literature. We firmly believe that enthusiasm and critical thinking are more likely to be generated when students are exposed to the questions, uncertainties, and processes of research than when they are confronted with a set of unsupported, dry generalizations.

Continuities and Changes in the Seventh Edition

As in previous editions of *Child Development and Personality*, material has been organized chronologically in four sections: prenatal development, infancy, childhood, and adolescence. Within each age, chapters are topical. Where possible, chapters about different age levels contain parallel topics. Theories have been introduced as they apply to the content instead of being restricted to an initial section labeled "theory" so that students can study the theory in context.

Several topics have new or considerably expanded coverage. We have tried to select those with lasting interest, not just the latest fads. In the section on prenatal development, new information about behavioral genetics and hazards in prenatal development is discussed. In the chapters on infants, we have presented recent knowledge derived from neuroscience about cognition and emotion, information about cross-modal perception, new knowledge about temperamental differences in sociability and inhibition, and a current assessment of infant daycare. We have devoted an entire chapter to the transition from infancy to early childhood, a period of development that has been virtually ignored until relatively recently.

In the domains of childhood cognition and language, many old controversies have given way to new syntheses. Social interaction approaches to language acquisition have avoided the nature-nurture conflicts of earlier theories. Piaget's theory has been challenged by demonstrations of preschool children's competence. Researchers from widely varying perspectives have adopted the view that cognitive skills are learned in context. Being able to remember phone numbers does not necessarily mean that you can remember Chinese characters. New topics include children's understanding of appearance and reality, Sternberg's triarchic theory of intelligence, and cross-national studies of achievement.

Social cognition is no longer relegated to a separate chapter, but has been woven throughout the chapters on social development and socialization. New information has been included on sex typing, ethnic group identity and minority children's self-concepts, behavior problems, peers as therapists, parents' beliefs about children, and the influences of television. We have given considerable emphasis to an ecological view that places children and families in the larger social context of school, neighborhood, parent work, and community. A new section on government policy and economic influences on family life was inspired by our concern about increasing poverty among American children and about public policy issues.

Some perennial themes of adolescence, including autonomy, identity formation, values, and going steady and dating, have also received a considerably updated treatment. Other issues have been given increased attention because they represent serious social problems. They include teen pregnancy and parenting, adolescent work, drug use, runaways, and serious emotional problems.

New Pedagogical Features   We have added a number of features designed to help students organize and learn the material, to stimulate thought about issues, and to encourage students to pursue some topics in depth. Each chapter has a **detailed outline** in the table of contents and at the beginning of the chapter. Chapter **summaries** are comprehensive and written to help students integrate the content. Every chapter has a **glossary** of terms that may be unfamiliar to students. **Review questions** at the end of each chapter are designed to help students think actively about the material presented. At the end of each chapter, a list of **suggested readings** describes books and articles that might be especially appropriate for further investigation of the topics discussed. Over 1400 **references** cited are assembled at the end of the text. This bibliography will be a valuable resource for student term papers.

In each chapter, there are three text **boxes** inserted to describe social issues, case studies, or particularly important research. They include such topics as the developmental risks of children with sex chromosome abnormalities, research on parent-infant bonding, a case study of a child who was isolated from human language until age 13, an autobiography of a black child growing up in the United States, research on only children in China, a comparison of family policies in the United States to those in other countries, and new research on the effects of employment in high school.

Acknowledgments   Even though four of us shared the work of writing, many other people have made essential contributions to the outcome. We thank Helen Cline, Alison Dishinger, Jeris Miller, Patricia Parker, and Dorothy R. Townsend for typing and retyping the manuscript. Even with word processing, their labors were considerable. Carolyn Smith made a major contribution with chapter-by-chapter editing, and she prepared many of the summaries, glossaries, captions, and outlines. We are grateful to each of our families for their support, understanding, and useful comments on the manuscript.

The following colleagues reviewed the book and offered valued insights: Terri D. Fisher, The Ohio State University-Mansfield Campus; Karen N. Haynes, University of New Mexico; Gwen Briscoe, College of Mount St. Joseph; Arden Miller, Southwest Missouri State University; Irwin W. Silverman, Bowling Green State University; Angela P. McGlynn, Mercer County Community College; Rosina Chia, East Carolina University; Jerome Small, Youngstown State University; Elizabeth Swenson, John Carroll University; Robert Stewart, Oakland University; Claire Kopp, University of California-Los Angeles; and Audrey Kast, Pittsburgh State University.

P. H. M.
J. J. C.
J. K.
A. C. H.

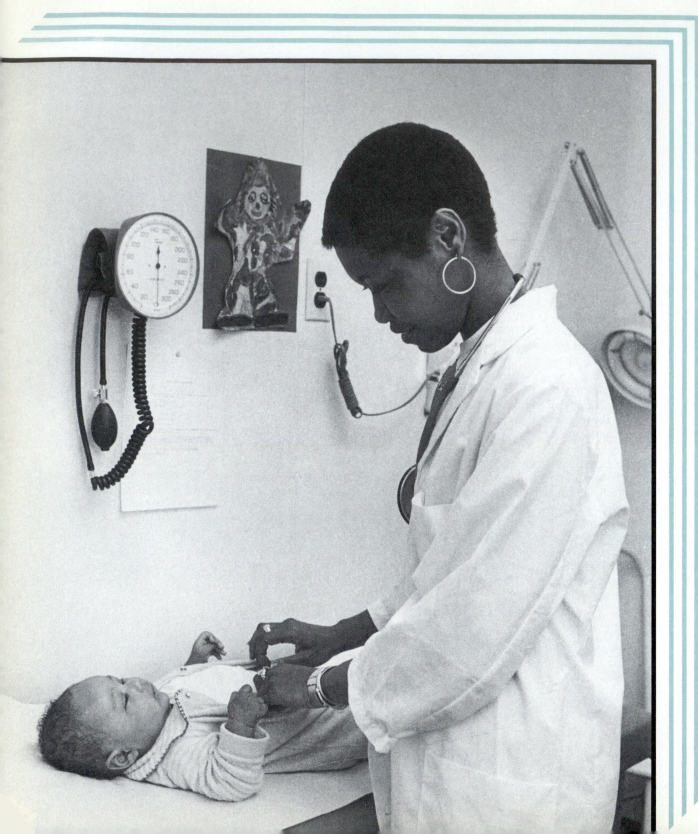

Chapter One

INTRODUCTION

What Is Development?

Theoretical Issues

Environmental vs. Biological Determinants of Behavior

Active vs. Passive Nature of the Child

Continuity vs. Discontinuity in Development

Stability over Time

Consistency Across Situations

Historical Perspectives on Developmental Psychology

Research in the Early Twentieth Century

The Post-World War II Period

The Past Twenty-five Years

Research on Child Development

Applied and Basic Research

The Research Process

Methods Used in Studying Children

Cross-sectional and Correlational Studies

Longitudinal Methods

Experiments

Field Experiments

Cross-cultural Studies

Cross-species Studies

Summary of Research Methods

Ethical Issues in Research

Organization of This Book

This book is about children's development—both what we have learned and what we still do not know. Child development is both a basic and an applied science. It is the study of how and why children develop perception, thought processes, emotional reactions, and patterns of social behavior. It also provides knowledge that is important for advising parents, forming educational programs, creating and defending government programs for children, making legal policies affecting children, and devising treatments for problem behavior.

People often ask experts in the field for information and advice. Here are some examples of such questions. Information pertaining to these topics can be found in the chapters indicated in parentheses.

"My two children are as different as they can be. One is quiet and mathematically inclined. The other one is a talker and likes to write poetry. How can they have inherited such different behavior from the same parents?" (Chapter 2)

"I plan to get pregnant next year. Should I stop smoking? Is it dangerous to drink alcohol while I'm pregnant? Is it really important to get along without painkillers during delivery?" (Chapter 2)

"Is it true that newborn babies can't see or hear very well?" (Chapter 3)

"Should I put my baby in day care? Will the baby get more attached to the day care personnel than to me? What qualities should I look for when I select a day care situation?" (Chapters 4 and 13)

"I want to teach my child the difference between truth and lies. Can she understand that difference at age 2?" (Chapters 5 and 11)

"My child used to use correct English but suddenly stopped. For instance, when she was 2 she said, 'I went to the store.' Now, at age 4, she says, 'I goed to the store.' Why?" (Chapter 6)

"Is it true that children can't understand another person's feelings before age 7?" (Chapters 7 and 10)

"I am an attorney handling a charge that a child was sexually abused. How reliable is the court testimony of young children? How can we know when they are telling the truth?" (Chapter 8)

"Congress is debating continued funding for Head Start. How effective is Head Start? Is it worth spending public money on?" (Chapter 9)

"How can I raise my daughter to avoid the trap of traditional sex roles?" (Chapter 10)

"The staff at the day care center say my 4-year-old hits other children a lot and is very aggressive. I think she'll grow out of it, but the teacher says she may have behavior problems later on if we don't do something now. Who is right?" (Chapter 11)

"My wife and I are getting a divorce. How will our kids be affected? What can we do to reduce the harm this may do them?" (Chapter 12)

"My neighbors just got rid of their television set, and they say this has done their kids a lot of good. Are kids better off without TV?" (Chapter 13)

During the 1980s increasing numbers of parents became concerned with the need to help their children realize their individual potential, regardless of gender.

"Our state requires every school to have sex education. What do junior and senior high school students know about sex? What should we teach them?" (Chapter 14)

"My 16-year-old has started to question her religion, the morality we have taught her, and practically everything else. Why? What have we done wrong?" (Chapter 15)

"What can be done to prevent drug addiction among young people? Does it do any good to tell them to 'just say no'?" (Chapter 16)

WHAT IS DEVELOPMENT?

Answers to questions like these arise from the scientific investigation of children's development. The study of development is the study of how and why the human organism grows and changes throughout life. **Development** is defined as orderly and relatively enduring changes over time in physical and neurological structures, thought processes, and behavior. In the first 20 years of life, these changes usually result in new, improved ways of reacting—that is, in behavior that is healthier, better organized, more complex, more stable, more competent, or more efficient. We speak of advances from creeping to walking, from babbling to talking, or from concrete to abstract thinking as instances of development. In each such instance we judge the later-appearing state to be a more adequate way of functioning than the earlier one.

One goal of studying development is to understand changes that appear to be *universal*—changes that occur in all children regardless of the culture in which they grow up or the experiences they have. For example, children all over the world

Children throughout the world learn to walk at about the same time.

smile at human faces during the second or third month of life, utter their first word at around 12 months, and walk alone at around 13 months. We try first to describe these changes. Then we attempt to explain why they occur—to understand what biological variables and experiences influence them. The knowledge we generate can be used to answer such questions as what behaviors are normal or natural for different ages, or whether parents' child-rearing practices have different effects at different ages.

A second goal of studying development is to explain *individual differences*. Some infants react by crying loudly when their mother leaves the room; others play happily. Some children learn mathematical concepts quickly; others find math more difficult. Information about individual differences can help answer questions about the possible effect of Head Start or about what characteristics of individual children should be considered in making decisions about schooling, custody, or placement outside the home.

A third goal is to understand how children's behavior is influenced by the environmental *context* or situation. A child may be friendly and outgoing to adults who come to her home, but shy when she meets adults at school. An adolescent is more likely to use marijuana if he attends a school where many others use it than if marijuana use is uncommon among his peers.

Context includes not only the immediate situation but also attributes of the larger settings in which people live—the family, neighborhood, cultural group, or socioeconomic group. Such settings are sometimes described as the *ecology* of the child's behavior. They can influence development by creating opportunities for different behaviors to occur or by affecting parents' behavior. For instance, children who live within walking distance of their school have more opportunity to play with classmates or participate in after-school activities than those who live at a distance and must leave immediately after school on a bus. Conscientious parents who live in dangerous urban neighborhoods often do not allow their children to play outdoors after school, encouraging them to watch television instead. In a safe neighborhood, the same parents may encourage their children to go to a local park or to another child's home.

Cultural and subcultural groups also value different behaviors. A middle-class girl who talks back to her parents may be viewed as articulate and assertive. In a working-class family, such behavior may be regarded as disobedient and insolent.

These three aspects of children's development—universal patterns, individual differences, and contextual influences—are all necessary for a full understanding of development. The emphasis placed on any one of them depends on the theoretical orientation guiding the investigator and the types of questions being studied.

THEORETICAL ISSUES

Anyone who studies children, whether as a scientist or as a practitioner, must confront certain fundamental issues. Some of these questions have been discussed for centuries by philosophers, theologians, and educators, as you can see from Box 1.1. There is no one "right" answer to most of them. Instead, different

BOX 1.1

Some Contrasting Early Views of Education

Almost all the major philosophers of the seventeenth and eighteenth centuries formed theories about the nature of childhood, the child's mind and development, and education. Each philosopher also offered advice to parents and teachers. John Locke, writing at the end of the seventeenth century, believed that children should be trained through rewards and punishment from the very earliest months onward; he was, in effect, a learning theorist. In contrast, Jean Jacques Rousseau, writing in the middle of the eighteenth century, believed that the child is by nature an active explorer who has enormous potentialities that would be actualized if adults did not interfere so much.

The contrasting points of view of these philosophers are evident in the following quotations from their major works. Here is what Locke believed:

> Rewards . . . *and* Punishments *must be proposed to Children, if we intend to work upon them. The Mistake . . . is, that those that are generally made use of, are* ill chosen . . . Esteem and Disgrace *are, of all others, the most powerful incentives to the Mind. . . . If you can once get into Children a love of Credit, and an apprehension of Shame and Disgrace, you have put into them the true Principle, which will constantly work, and incline them to the right. . . . If therefore the Father* caress and commend *them, when they do well; shew a cold and neglectful Countenance to them upon doing ill; And this accompanied by a like Carriage of the Mother, and all others that are about them, it will in a little Time make them sensible of the Difference; and this if constantly observed, I doubt not but will of itself work more than Threats or blows.*[1]

Rousseau, on the other hand, held a different view:

> *Leave childhood to ripen in your children. . . . It is the child's individual bent, which must be thoroughly known before we can choose the fittest moral training. Every mind has its own form, in accordance with which it must be controlled; and the success of the pains taken depends largely on the fact that he is controlled in this way and no other. Oh, wise man, take time to observe nature; watch your scholar well before you say a word to him; first leave the germ of his character free to show itself, do not constrain him in anything, the better to see him as he really is.*[2]

[1] From John Locke's *Some thoughts concerning education* (4th ed., enlarged). London: Churchill, pp. 54–66, 101–108, 118–121. The first edition was published in 1693.
[2] From Jean Jacques Rousseau, *Emile, or on education* (translated by Barbara Foxley). London: Dent, 1911. The first French edition was published in 1762; the first English edition in 1763.

points of view represent different assumptions about human nature, about how to interpret existing information, and about which approaches to advancing knowledge are most promising.

Environmental vs. Biological Determinants of Behavior

One of the most basic questions facing developmental psychologists is the relative importance of environmental versus biological determinants of behavior. This issue is the well-known "nature versus nurture" controversy. Some scientists believe that much of human behavior is guided by genetic makeup, physiological maturation, and neurological functioning. According to this view, the universals of development, such as the emergence of walking, speaking, and responding to other people, can be best explained as resulting from inborn biological factors, and individual differences are largely a result of genetic and physiological differences. A scientist taking this approach might argue, for example, that individual differences in performance on intelligence tests are due primarily to genetic factors and prenatal health. Accordingly, he or she might recommend government-supported prenatal care, but might also support a system of schooling in which children with high and low IQs are separated and receive different levels of instruction.

At the other end of the continuum, scientists emphasize the influence of the physical and social environment on development. They believe that children respond to the people and objects around them and that developmental changes result largely from experience. Individual differences in performance on intelligence tests, according to this view, are due primarily to differences in cognitive stimulation and opportunities to learn about the world. Therefore, schools that provide good learning experiences should lead to good performance for children at all IQ levels.

Both extremes of the nature-nurture controversy have obvious weaknesses. Most psychologists agree that both biological and environmental variables play a role in development. Biological factors are more important for some aspects of development (e.g., learning to walk), while environmental variables are more central for others (e.g., learning to read). The beginnings of speech depend heavily on biological maturation (though they do not occur in the absence of relevant experience). On the other hand, individual differences in altruism or generosity appear to depend primarily on children's experiences.

Many scientists contend that there is no way to separate or assign weights to biological and environmental variables because the two interact from the moment of birth (and probably before). These scientists sometimes speak of *transactions* between the organism and the environment. A child who is highly aggressive may have begun life with a biologically based tendency to be active or assertive; his parents may have responded to his aggression inconsistently or by spanking him, so that his tendency to be aggressive increased over time. A child with a different biological predisposition might be less likely to try hitting and pushing; a child whose parents used consistent and nonphysical forms of punishment might learn to inhibit biologically based aggressive tendencies. The behavior is a product of repeated transactions between biological and environmental determinants.

The age and speed at which a child learns to read are determined largely by environmental factors.

Active vs. Passive Nature of the Child

Some theorists view children as passive receivers of experience; others consider them active in organizing, structuring, and in some sense creating their worlds. A scientist who considers children to be passive does not think they are unresponsive, just that they enter the world ready to absorb whatever knowledge is provided by the environment. According to this view, children are molded by stimuli in the external environment and driven by internal needs over which they have little control. Theorists and educators who view the child as essentially passive often favor direct and carefully structured teaching methods. For example, some methods for teaching children to play the piano contain a series of specific steps, chords, and tunes to be learned in a prescribed order. The child must master each step before proceeding to the next one.

In contrast, an educator who believes that children are active assumes that they learn best when they explore and select their own learning materials and tasks. When teaching a child to play the piano, such an instructor might encourage the child to make up tunes or to select among different exercises. Human beings are assumed to have an inborn tendency to be curious, to explore their environment, and to organize the resulting experience in their own mental frameworks. Efforts to program learning too closely are likely to fail because they may not correspond to the child's interests. Instead, a relatively unstructured situation that offers opportunities for varied stimulation and exploration is optimal. What the child does and learns, then, depends mainly on interests that come from within and on his or her level of understanding.

Continuity vs. Discontinuity in Development

Do developmental changes occur in small, gradual, cumulative steps (i.e., continuously) or in jumps that produce qualitatively new and different abilities and patterns of behavior (i.e., discontinuously)? Consider an example from motor development. Babies typically begin to crawl sometime during the second six months of life. At first they creep on their stomach, then rock on hands and knees, then finally lurch forward and start to crawl. Over time they become better coordinated, faster, and more skilled at crawling. These changes are *continuous*—that is, they show a gradual improvement in skill. To stand on two feet and walk across the room, however, requires a completely different set of movements. The change from crawling to walking is not just a simple extension of crawling skills; it represents a qualitatively different behavior pattern. It is a *discontinuous* change.

Examples of continuous and discontinuous developmental curves appear in Figure 1.1. Discontinuous changes are sometimes called *stages* of development. The term *stage* is used in everyday speech to describe almost any behavior that is related to age (e.g., the "No" stage), but in developmental psychology it has a more specific meaning. Stages are *qualitatively different* from one another. The underlying structure of behavior or thought changes when a child moves from one stage to another. Stages of motor behavior include crawling and walking; stages of thought refer to different ways of thinking about the world. For example, Jean Piaget proposed that a new cognitive stage begins at around 18 months, when children become able to represent objects in thought (see Chapter 3).

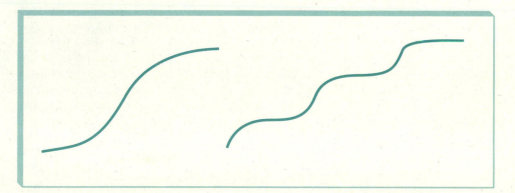

FIGURE 1.1 Examples of two types of growth curves. The curve on the left shows a continuous pattern of gradual change leveling off as the maximum level is reached. An example might be speed of crawling. The curve on the right shows discontinuous growth in which relatively sudden changes are interspersed with gradual change. An example might be speed of locomotion, which shows sudden changes when walking and running are mastered.

Stages occur in an *invariant order*. Crawling always precedes walking. Children may go through stages at different ages, but they all go through them in the same order.

All developmentalists agree that some changes occur continuously and gradually, but they do not agree about whether some changes are discontinuous. Some assert that all changes are cumulative, building on what went before. They might argue that walking is in fact an extension of what children have learned about moving in space and coordinating different body parts when they crawled. Others believe that some aspects of development are best regarded as discontinuous. For example, between 15 and 20 months of age children begin to show anxiety when they disobey a parent's request or violate a rule. Theorists who see development as discontinuous argue that this behavior represents a qualitative change in children's ability to comprehend and think about parental prohibitions.

Stability over Time

Is an aggressive 2-year-old likely to be an aggressive adult? Does early separation from the family produce long-term feelings of anxiety about separation? Does early education produce lasting changes in intelligence? Affirmative answers to these questions would mean that children's behavior is reasonably stable over time—that is, that early-formed behaviors and personal characteristics predict later behavior. A considerable amount of research has been devoted to studying the stability of children's behavior. Nevertheless, that evidence is open to different interpretations, depending on which findings are given the most emphasis. Some people stress the changes and malleability of the human organism; others emphasize its stability or sameness over time. This is a little like one person saying the glass is half empty and another saying it is half full.

One reason for these differing interpretations is that some behaviors and some periods of development are more stable than others. In general, children's behavior becomes more stable as they grow older. For example, IQ scores in the first few years of life are not good predictors of later IQ, but IQ at age 7 is a reasonably good predictor of IQ in adolescence and adulthood. Some kinds of behavior are more stable than others. For example, aggression is a reasonably stable behavior pattern; children who are aggressive in early and middle childhood are likely to be aggressive in adolescence and adulthood. Altruism and helpfulness are less stable from one time to another (Mischel, 1968).

The question of stability over time is further complicated by the fact that the same characteristics may be expressed in different ways at different ages. In such cases we say that the different behaviors are *functionally equivalent*. An aggressive nursery school child hits others; at age 12, insults and subtle hostility are more likely. A sociable 4-year-old offers toys and asks other children to play; at age 12, this child may show the same characteristic by spending hours on the telephone. Because all children's behavior changes with age, psychologists examine the question of stability by comparing the rank order of children at one age with their rank order at a later age. If a child who has a high rate of initiating play with others compared to other children in nursery school also ranks relatively high in the amount of time on the telephone at age 12, we infer that a trait like sociability is stable over time.

Consistency Across Situations

Is a child who is highly aggressive at home also aggressive at school? Is a child who is shy with peers also shy with adults? In other words, is children's behavior specific to particular situations, or do children have "traits" that are manifested in a wide range of settings? Is it the person—her traits and characteristics—or the situation that primarily directs the individual's behavior? Again, research on this question has produced evidence that both individual traits and situational variables influence behavior. Some theorists emphasize consistency across situations; others stress situational influences. In line with their general emphasis on external influences, strong environmentalists stress situational determinants of behavior. Therefore, they expect children to show little consistency across situations or stability over time unless the environment remains reasonably constant. People who stress biological bases for development and internal characteristics of the child tend to expect both consistency across situations and stability over time.

Many researchers have attempted to determine whether traits like aggressiveness are consistent across a variety of situations or whether they are manifested only in particular contexts.

These five issues—biological versus environmental bases of behavior, the passive versus active nature of the child, continuity versus discontinuity of development, stability over time, and consistency across situations—have affected the thinking and research of developmentalists for many years. Their influence can be demonstrated through a brief overview of the history of the field of child development during the twentieth century.

HISTORICAL PERSPECTIVES ON DEVELOPMENTAL PSYCHOLOGY

The systematic study of child development began early in the present century. Around the turn of the century, many reformers became concerned with children's welfare. Child labor laws, compulsory-education legislation, juvenile courts, and child welfare services were introduced. As professionals began to try to help children, they also began to recognize the need for knowledge about children so that they could assess developmental patterns and normal behavior. In the United States the scientific study of development was given a major boost by the establishment of research institutes for the study of child welfare on several university campuses using funds from one of the first private foundations (Sears, 1975). Some of the early research at one of these institutes, the Iowa Child Welfare Research Station, is described in Box 1.2.

Around the turn of the century, the long hours and dangerous conditions in which many children were forced to work generated concern about child welfare and led to the systematic study of child development.

BOX 1.2

Pioneers in Child Development

Marie Skodak Crissey and Ronald Lippitt participated in ground-breaking studies of children at the University of Iowa in the 1930s. In the following passages they describe what it was like.

Skodak: The first major center for the scientific study of child development was the Iowa Child Welfare Research Station at the State University of Iowa, established by the state legislature in 1917. A long, arduous struggle was needed in order to convince the legislators of that state that child study was as important as the study of corn or hogs. A grant from the Laura Spelman Rockefeller Memorial Fund in the mid-1920s enabled the Iowa Station to expand greatly its own research. . . .

From its inception, the emphasis at Iowa was on practical problems of children and the influence of environment on their development. . . .

The Station was located in a wing of the original hospital of the Medical School of the University. The quarters were very cramped and only senior staff had private offices. (A former supply closet housed the Marchand calculators, non-electric and actuated by hand-pulled levers.) Research assistants were paid $60.00 per month for halftime service and more than once an across-the-board cut was instituted due to financial austerity during the Depression.

Rich training experiences were available, including taking anthropometric measurements of infants and preschoolers, administering mental tests to infants and children of all ages, assisting in the nursery school, and working on publications with faculty members. While research at the Station on psychological development is probably the best known, there was ongoing research on just about every aspect of childhood—physical growth, preschool education, dental and nutritional problems, social and emotional development, etc.

In the 1930s a new research population became available. Harold Skeels opened the way for study in a state orphanage. . . . Facilities for the retarded and the delinquent as well as for orphans were used in various research projects. Perhaps the most significant contribution resulted from the study of children placed in adoptive homes in early infancy. Studies of their mental development as well as the development of children raised in institutions and less favored homes challenged the then prevailing attitude that intelligence is unaffected by environmental factors. Vigorous debate followed with Stoddard and the Iowans on the environmental side and researchers at Stanford and Minnesota on the other.

Lippitt: You need to visualize Kurt Lewin standing on a stepladder, peering with handheld camera over the burlap walls of the experimental clubrooms in the attic of old East Hall at the University of Iowa. The time was winter of 1939.

The camera's eye focused on two "clubs" of ten-year-olds, five in each club with an adult club leader.... The leaders rotated through the three roles of directive-structuring ("autocratic"), guiding-supportive ("democratic"), and permissive-unstructured ("laissez-faire"). Six observers recorded the content of all interaction, did interaction and group structure analysis by two minute units, and rated the relations between leaders and members....

There was no attempt to hide the camera, or the observers who sat in the shadow behind work tables. The initial curiosity elicited the response that the observers and camera were "trying to get a record of how clubs run in order to help club leaders run better clubs that would be more fun."...

The film stimulated a number of interesting activities:

1. The children in a summer camp, after viewing the film, decided they would like to experience the three types of leadership. Their leader arranged some meaningful contrasting experiences. Their reactions confirmed, very intensely, the results shown in the film. The leader reported, in her writings, that one consequence was that the children valued much more highly the customary democratic climate, took more responsibility for decision making, and became more sensitive to autocratic behaviors.

2. A colleague from Japan became very interested in replicating the experiment....

3. The film and study came to the attention of Ed Murrow, who had a CBS radio news series which did a dramatized replication of the studies....

By the standards of today, or even then, the film was of poor technical quality. The lighting in the attic was poor and varied, and Kurt Lewin's hand was not always steady as he stood on the ladder and got excited about some of the events being recorded. This was his first venture in the study of group phenomena.... This study can be called the birth of group dynamics.[1]

[1] From "Historical Selections from the 50th Anniversary Meeting," *Society for Research in Child Development*, 1983.

Research in the Early Twentieth Century

The approach that typified research during this early period began with G. Stanley Hall, a pioneer in the scientific study of children. Hall tried to investigate "the contents of children's minds" (Hall, 1891) using a new research technique, the questionnaire. Children were asked about their activities and interests. Hall's goal was to describe the sequence and timing of development, and he was one of the first to apply objective measures to large numbers of children.

During this period many psychologists assumed that developmental changes are largely a result of maturation. They assumed that the age differences they observed represented innate, universal patterns of development for all children. This approach led to descriptions of "normal" behavior for different ages, as illustrated in the following discussion by two psychologists at the Gesell Institute of Child Development:

> First of all, we have observed that 2 years of age, 5 years, and 10 years all constitute focal points at which behavior seems to be in good equilibrium, the child having relatively little difficulty within himself or with the world about him. Each of these relatively smooth and untroubled ages is followed by a brief period when behavior appears to be very much broken up, disturbed, and troubled, and when the child shows himself to be in marked disequilibrium. Thus, the smoothness of 2-year-old behavior characteristically breaks up at 2½; 5-year-old behavior breaks up at 5½ to 6; and 10 breaks up at 11, the 11-year-old child characteristically showing himself to be at definite odds with his environment and with himself. . . .
>
> All three of these ages are followed by periods of extreme expansiveness. Four, eight and fourteen are all times at which the child's behavior is markedly outgoing in most major respects. He is even in danger of expanding too much. He wanders from home and gets lost at 4, he demands to ride his bicycle in the street at 8 and may get hit, and he gets all tangled in his multiple and conflicting social plans at 14 (Ilg & Ames, 1955, pp. 10–11).

One major goal of research in the early part of the century was to collect descriptive information about normal development. For example, on the basis of extensive observations of children's language, information was published showing the average number of words that a 1-year-old child could say, the average age at which children use two-word combinations, and many other such "statistics" (McCarthy, 1946). Age changes in children's peer interactions from parallel play (e.g., one toddler builds a tower of blocks while another takes a doll for a ride in a wagon) to cooperative play (e.g., two children play house or build a road of blocks together) were described (Parten, 1932). And intelligence tests were designed on the basis of the average level of intellectual performance for each age level. Such descriptive research was intended to provide behavioral norms similar to the norms for height and weight that physicians use to determine when children's physical growth is normal.

Social practices having to do with children also were based on the assumption that developmental changes depend largely on maturation and heredity. For example, when babies became eligible for adoption they were placed in orphanages until they were 6 months old in order to determine whether they had normal intelligence. Most orphanages provided little intellectual stimulation. Children who showed delayed development under those circumstances were diagnosed as mentally retarded and were transferred to institutions for the retarded. The people making these decisions were not aware that the environment of the orphanage might have a significant influence on the intellectual development of young infants.

Two other movements in American and European psychology during this period had a strong influence on developmental psychology. First, Sigmund Freud's psychoanalytic theory became widely known. Freud suggested that children go through a series of "psychosexual" stages in which they encounter particular emotional conflicts that must be resolved if they are to become mature, emotionally healthy adults. He revolutionized many people's thinking about children by proposing that early childhood is a critical time for personality development and stressing the importance of early interactions between parents and children. Although most developmental psychologists no longer subscribe to the specifics of Freud's theory, current thinking on many issues owes a debt to his ideas.

Second, John B. Watson founded the behaviorist movement and conducted some pioneering experiments. He analyzed behavior into units called *stimuli* and *responses*, and studied learning as a process of conditioning (i.e., the association of stimuli with responses) (see Chapters 3 and 8). His work formed the basis for the dominant view in developmental psychology during the post-World War II years—the belief that children's development can be explained by stimulus-response learning processes and that environmental influences are primary. As Watson put it:

> Give me a dozen healthy infants, well-formed, and my own specified world to bring them up in and I'll guarantee to take any one at random and train him to become any type of specialist I might select—doctor, lawyer, merchant, chief, and yes, even beggar-man and thief, regardless of his talents, penchants, abilities, vocations, and the race of his ancestors. (1930/1967, p. 104)

The Post-World War II Period

Psychoanalysis and behaviorism formed the backbone of American child psychology in the period after World War II. A new brand of child psychologist emerged who approached the study of children as a branch of experimental psychology. Instead of merely describing developmental changes, these psychologists wanted to formulate and test theoretical explanations of children's behavior. They turned to both psychoanalytic theory and behavioral learning theory, often blending the two, in search of hypotheses about what processes and variables influence children's behavior. They were concerned with such questions as: How does early feeding experience affect dependency? How do different types of reward and punishment affect learning? What child-rearing practices are associated with the development of conscience? These psychologists were interested not just in describing behavior but also in predicting and explaining the reasons for children's actions. In their studies of children they emphasized overt behavior rather than unobservable mental events. The dominant view during this period was strongly environmentalist, and researchers were reluctant to assume that children's behavior was biologically determined. They became less interested than earlier psychologists in age changes or developmental stages, and correspondingly more concerned with situational, environmental influences.

Researchers in this period preferred laboratory experiments in which they could control all aspects of a situation. They argued that there were too many uncontrolled influences in natural situations to enable the researcher to draw any conclusions about which of those influences were important. For example, Albert Bandura (1969) conducted a classic set of experiments investigating children's imitative behavior. In one study he tested the theoretical hypothesis that children would imitate a warm, friendly adult more than a cool, distant one. He set up experimental situations in which some children had warm, friendly interactions with an adult while other children experienced a cool, detached adult. Then the children watched the adult model perform a series of actions, such as hitting a rubber doll, and subsequently had an opportunity to play in the same setting themselves. When they imitated the warm, friendly adult more than the cool adult, Bandura concluded that the hypothesis had been supported (Bandura & Huston, 1961).

The Past Twenty-five Years

In the early 1960s American psychology rediscovered Piaget's theory of cognitive development. His ideas brought about a major reorientation of our basic views about children. Piaget was interested in the universals of children's development rather than in individual differences, and he believed that development results from interactions between maturational changes and experience. His intensive observation of his own three children convinced him that children are active organisms who seek stimulation and organize their own experience without direct instruction or programming from people in the environment. He proposed four major stages of cognitive development, which are discussed in Chapters, 3, 7, and 14.

Partly as a result of Piaget's influence during the past 25 years, scientists have returned to the study of biological, genetic, and maturational influences on behavior. The field has not, however, simply returned to the assumptions of the early part of the century. Present-day investigations are typically designed to investigate transactions between the biological characteristics of the child and the experiences offered by the environment. For example, infants are biologically predisposed to form emotional attachments to their caregivers by about 1 year of age, but the quality of such attachments varies. Researchers studying this process have shown that individual differences in infants' temperaments and differences in caregivers' responsiveness to the infant both contribute to the quality of the infant's attachment to the caregiver (Crockenberg, 1981).

Another recent trend is the attempt to relate children's social behavior to their cognitive development. In earlier periods researchers tended to study cognitive changes as they affect learning, school performance, and the like. Social and emotional behaviors such as aggression, sex typing and morality were treated as a separate subject. Today it has become apparent that children's *social cognitions*, or ways of thinking about social situations and moral issues, help determine their social behavior (see Chapter 11). For example, whether a child retaliates when hurt by another child depends partly on whether the victim believes the aggressor inflicted the hurt intentionally or by accident—a social cognition.

Finally, the field has returned to a concern with practical and social applications of knowledge about children. During the 1950s and early 1960s, many developmental psychologists avoided applied questions; they felt that they did not know enough to give advice to parents and other people who deal with children. While we still lack knowledge in many areas, children growing up today cannot wait for science to progress. Decisions must be made even though the information available is incomplete. Developmental psychologists are in a better position than most others to offer some wisdom that can contribute to the welfare of children.

RESEARCH ON CHILD DEVELOPMENT

Answers to questions about children's development cannot be drawn solely from folk wisdom or informal experiences with children. They often require systematic research and careful collection, analysis, and evaluation of evidence. Because we do not know the answers, research is challenging and exciting. The process has elements of creating new ideas, solving puzzles, and making the most telling and logical arguments in a debate. Because scientific research is central to our knowledge of child development, we turn now to a discussion of how people do research.

Applied and Basic Research

Research is sometimes inspired by pressing social and practical issues concerning children. For example, as divorce in families with young children became increasingly common, psychologists and others began to study how children are affected by divorce, what helps children cope with divorce, and how different patterns of custody after divorce affect children's adjustment (see Chapter 12). Research designed to help parents, schools, and others who deal with children is called **applied research**.

The discovery of basic knowledge about child development is also an important scientific enterprise. Much of the research on child development is motivated by the desire to understand the most complex organism that exists—the human being. Investigators are concerned with explaining and predicting the processes of development as a means of advancing a science, even when there is no immediate social need for the knowledge they generate. Research intended to generate knowledge about the processes and sequences of development is called **basic research**.

Of course, the information generated by basic research is often used later in ways that were not originally anticipated. For example, some years ago a group of investigators studied infants' sucking patterns when different sounds were presented, in order to discover whether infants could discriminate among different speech sounds. Later, clinicians began to use this technique to determine whether a child is hearing-impaired. The original researchers did not plan this clinical application.

The Research Process

"Just when I knew all of life's answers, they changed all the questions," proclaims a Hallmark poster. In science, as in many other areas of life, the answers we get are only as good as the questions we ask. The first step in scientific research is to identify a good question. How do developmental psychologists decide what to study? How do they choose among the many questions that interest them?

Applied researchers in child development tend to be sensitive to urgent social issues; they often choose questions that address "hot" issues on the public agenda. Moreover, if a social issue becomes a national concern, government funds may be made available to study it. For example, in the late 1960s the outbreak of riots in urban ghettos and on college campuses stimulated concern about violence in American society. As a result, government funds were appropriated for a coordinated set of studies to determine the effects of television violence on aggression. In the late 1980s, increasing numbers of mothers were employed during their children's infancy; a government agency established funds for a set of coordinated investigations of the effects of infant day care on children.

Basic research questions sometimes arise from the need for descriptive information about what children can do at different ages (e.g., how many words children usually know at ages 2, 3, etc.). More often, such questions originate from prominent theories that generate testable hypotheses. A theory serves as a lens to help the researcher focus on particular aspects of development while ignoring others. For example, much of the research on child-rearing practices conducted during the 1950s and 1960s was based directly or indirectly on Freud's psychoanalytic theory, which asserts that early feeding and toilet training play a significant role in personality development. Psychologists therefore studied the effects of feeding practices and toilet training. They could just as easily have studied children's play patterns or interests, but Freud's theory did not emphasize those domains of children's behavior.

Whatever the initial source of a research question, generating knowledge is a continuous and dynamic process. The diagram in Figure 1.2 illustrates how issues arising from basic theory or from social concerns may be the initial impetus for a research question. As answers are provided, they feed back to stimulate further questions. Indeed, very often an applied social issue will lead to new theories and basic questions, or the results of basic research will suggest new ways of fostering children's development in the real world. For example, in the 1940s a psychiatrist named René Spitz wrote about severe intellectual and emotional problems among infants in institutions. His observations led others to do careful basic research on the conditions that are important for the development of visual perception, cognition, and emotional health in infancy. That research, in turn, led institutions and hospitals that served infants to provide mobiles and varied visual stimuli, opportunities to play with toys, and social interactions with adults.

The selection of both basic and applied questions is inevitably affected by contemporary social and cultural values. For example, because most people in the United States assume that infants should be cared for primarily by their mothers, investigators of day care for infants almost always ask whether such care has harmful effects. Investigators have rarely asked what benefits might accrue from day care. In China, all men and women are expected to be employed, and many children are in day care centers 12 hours a day, 6 days a week. A researcher in that culture might be more likely to study the beneficial effects of day care for teaching children cooperative values.

As social values change, new research questions often emerge. In the 1960s, psychologists who studied children's sex role development assumed that the emotionally healthy boy should be "masculine" and the healthy girl should be

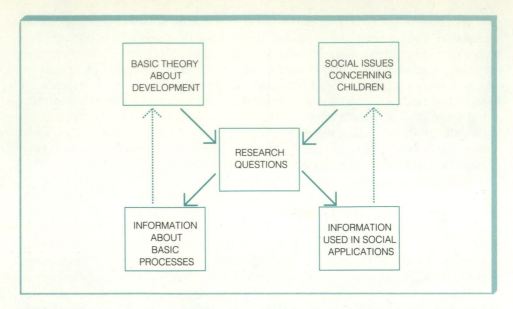

FIGURE 1.2   Sources of research questions. Questions arise from basic theory and from social issues. The answers to each type of question, in turn, contribute to the formation of additional problems for research.

"feminine." In the 1970s, when the women's movement raised doubts about the value of traditional sex roles, many people argued just the opposite—that traditionally defined femininity and masculinity were mentally unhealthy. Researchers then began to explore what experiences lead children to adopt nontraditional sex roles (see Chapter 10).

METHODS USED IN STUDYING CHILDREN

Many of us observe children every day. Teachers and parents know a great deal about children from these frequent contacts. What is different about the way a researcher observes children? What is required for the scientific study of their behavior?

The methods described here are alike in one way: all of them call for *controlled, systematic* observation of behavior. In some investigations, behavior is observed as it occurs in real-life settings like the home or school. In others, specific tasks or situations are created, often in laboratories, so that the reactions of different children can be observed in comparable circumstances. Sometimes children are interviewed; sometimes they are given tests; and sometimes observers use a prearranged set of categories and count the number of times each child displays behaviors in each category. In each case, however, the investigator tries to carry out similar procedures with all the children included in the study and tries to control or evaluate the situational variables that may affect the child's responses.

Objectivity is another fundamental feature of scientific research. No matter how a study is designed, its measuring techniques must be as free from subjective bias as possible. For example, in studying aggressive behavior, a researcher has to specify exactly and objectively what behaviors are to be called aggressive. Using such precise definitions, different observers can code the behavior of the same children. If these independent observers score a child's behavior similarly, the coding system is assumed to be objective. Objective measures are usually quantifiable—that is, they yield a set of numbers rather than just a verbal description of children's behavior. For example, the number of times a child hits other children might be counted and perhaps compared with the number of times other children hit the child being observed.

In the rest of this section we will examine different methods of research in the context of two related research problems: (1) Does aggression remain stable or does it change with age? (2) What is the effect of television violence on aggressive behavior? As the discussion will show, each of several methods can provide important information about a question, but no one method yields a definitive answer. Different ways of measuring the same attribute may produce different results. For example, if you want to know how aggressive a group of children are, you might get three quite different answers depending on whether you asked teachers for ratings, asked peers to nominate aggressive children, or observed the children's behavior directly. In general, we feel most confident in drawing conclusions when the results obtained using different methods are *convergent*—that is, when they agree.

Studies of the effects of televised violence on aggressive behavior have employed a variety of research methods.

Cross-sectional and Correlational Studies

Because much of developmental psychology is concerned with stability and change over time and with the impact of early experiences or characteristics on later behavior, researchers must have methods for studying children at different ages. They usually begin to study developmental changes with **cross-sectional investigations**, in which children of different ages are compared at one point in time. For example, if we compared groups of children aged 4, 8, 12, and 16, we might find that the amount of hitting and physical aggression is greater for younger children and the amount of verbal, insulting aggression is greater for older children.

Cross-sectional studies provide information about age differences, but they do not enable a researcher to determine whether individual children undergo a transition from physical to verbal aggression. Differences between different age groups at one point in time could reflect age changes, but they could also be a result of experiences associated with particular historical periods. For example, suppose that large amounts of television violence had been introduced within the two years preceding the study. The 4-year-olds might be responding to the television violence; their behavior might be quite different from that of 4-year-old children ten years earlier.

Correlational methods are used to test hypotheses about what variables may contribute to individual differences in development. In the simplest version of such a study, an investigator measures two variables for a particular group of people and determines whether there is a correlation between them. For example, information about how much violent television a large sample of elementary school children watched at home was obtained by asking the children to indicate which programs they viewed regularly. Their aggression at school was measured by peer nominations—asking each member of a class to name the children in the class who pushed, shoved, and fought most often. The investigators found that watching television violence was positively correlated with aggression—that is, children who watched more violence were more aggressive (Huesmann, Lagerspetz, & Eron, 1984).

A **correlation** is a measure of the relationship between two characteristics. A *positive correlation* means that high levels on one variable tend to be associated with high levels on the other, as in the preceding example. A *negative correlation* means that high levels on one variable tend to be associated with low levels on the other. For example, education is negatively correlated with the amount of television people watch. Highly educated people watch less television than people with little education. *No correlation* means that the two variables are not related. For example, height is not related to the amount of television people watch.

Correlations can range from +1.0 to −1.0. The + or − sign indicates the direction of the correlation (positive or negative), and the number describes the magnitude of the relationship. The greater the number, whether it is positive or negative, the more consistent the association. For example, the correlation between IQ at age 3 and age 10 is +.36; the correlation between IQ at age 8 and age 10 is +.88. We can predict IQ at age 10 with considerably more accuracy and confidence from IQ at age 8 than from IQ at age 3.

Both cross-sectional and correlational studies are sometimes called *field studies* because they measure naturally occurring conditions. One advantage of these methods is that the investigator measures the variables of interest as they exist in the real world, without tampering or intervening. The study described earlier measured aggression as it happens naturally in school and television viewing as it happens naturally at home.

Correlational data help determine whether or not a relationship exists between variables such as viewing violence and behaving aggressively, but they do not permit researchers to draw conclusions about *causes*. A positive correlation can be accounted for in three ways. First, watching violent television may instigate aggression. Second, highly aggressive children may select violent programs (that is, the child's aggression may "cause" the television viewing choices). Third, children's aggression and their preference for watching violent television may arise from a third variable associated with both, such as having an aggressive parent who turns on violent television programs often and whose aggression is imitated by the child.

Longitudinal Methods

In a **longitudinal investigation**, the same children are observed or tested at regular intervals over an extended period, sometimes a decade or longer. This approach overcomes some of the weaknesses of cross-sectional and correlational methods. It allows an investigator to study the stability of behavior over time. It is also useful for determining whether individual children undergo the developmental transitions suggested by cross-sectional investigations (e.g., from physical to verbal forms of aggression).

The questions about causal direction raised in correlational studies can be partly answered by longitudinal investigations. In the study of television violence and aggression described earlier, for instance, measures were collected initially for first- and third-graders; the same children were measured two years later when they were in the third and fifth grades. Children who watched heavy doses of television violence at a young age were more aggressive than their peers two years later. The reverse was also true: Children who were more aggressive at a young age watched more violence two years later. That is, viewing appeared to contribute to aggression, *and* aggressive personality characteristics appeared to contribute to a preference for TV violence (Huesmann, Lagerspetz, & Eron, 1984).

Experiments

Field studies and longitudinal investigations sample the richness of real-world events, but that very richness can be a drawback. So many factors contribute to naturally occurring events that it is difficult to know which of them are most important. For these reasons, field studies are often complemented by experimental investigations.

The essence of the experimental method is that the investigator systematically changes one variable (the **independent variable**) and collects objective measurements on another variable (the **dependent variable**). Meanwhile, all other factors that might affect the dependent variable are held constant. For example,

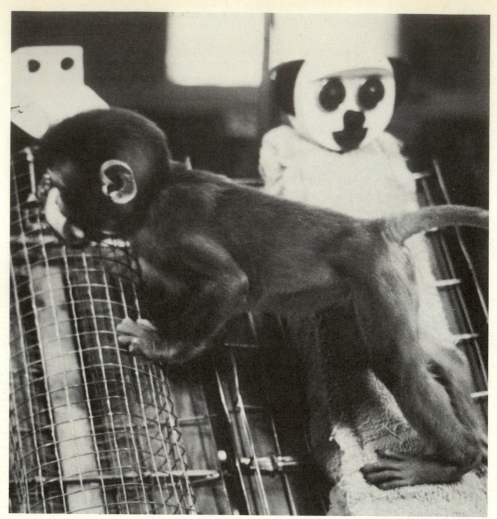

In Harry Harlow's classic experiments, the type of surrogate monkey "mother" (wire vs. terry cloth) was the independent variable and the behavior of infant monkeys was the dependent variable.

one experiment to test the effects of violent television on aggressive behavior was conducted by bringing individual children to a laboratory where they watched either a violent television program or a nonviolent travelog. Exposure to television violence was the independent variable. After viewing, the children were taken to a playroom containing aggressive toys such as inflated punching dolls and toy guns. Aggressive behavior in this play setting was the dependent variable (Liebert & Baron, 1972).

The children were randomly assigned to the violent-TV group or the travelog group; that is, they were placed in the experimental or control group by chance (e.g., by flipping a coin). Random assignment is a critical feature of experiments because it is the means of controlling individual differences among children. With a sufficiently large number of children in each group, we can assume that children who initially differed in level of aggression are evenly distributed in the violent and nonviolent viewing groups. Therefore, differences between the two groups after viewing are not due to predispositions or personality differences among individual children.

The experimental method permits inferences about the causal direction of effects. Because viewing of violent television was varied systematically and other variables were controlled by means of random assignment, we can conclude that the television viewing influenced the aggressive behavior. Because the control groups also watched television, we can also conclude that aggression is stimulated specifically by violent content and not simply by viewing television for a certain period. Thus, the experimental method enables the scientist to separate possibly important variables and to test hypotheses about the processes that account for the behavior of interest—in this case, aggression.

The experimental method also leaves some questions unanswered. Most experiments are necessarily short-term. For example, in the study described earlier the total time that the children watched television in the laboratory was about 10 minutes. We cannot be sure whether the many hours children spend watching television at home would have the same effect. Another problem with experiments is that one cannot be sure how well laboratory findings will generalize to natural settings. For example, the aggressive behavior measured in the study described here was not very violent, for ethical reasons. Children in a laboratory cannot be allowed to hit, kick, or bite each other. Naturally occurring aggression, such as interactions between siblings in the home, may be more hurtful. Moreover, the children did not choose the program they viewed, and this may have affected the results. The laboratory experiment provides precise and unique information about human development, but it must be considered in combination with observations of naturally occurring events, as occurs in a field study.

Field Experiments

A field experiment is an attempt to combine the advantages of the field-correlational and experimental approaches. In a field experiment children are randomly assigned to groups that undergo different experiences, as in a laboratory experiment. As in a field study, however, the groups are observed in naturally occurring situations and for a relatively long period. For example, adolescent males living in residential treatment facilities were randomly assigned to see violent or nonviolent movies every evening for a week. Trained observers rated their aggressive behavior in their residences before, during, and after the week of movies. The boys who had seen violent movies behaved more aggressively than those who had been shown nonviolent movies (Parke, Berkowitz, Leyens, West, & Sebastian, 1977).

The field experiment shows causal direction—the preceding one showed that violent movies affected aggressive behavior—and at the same time preserves the "real-life" quality of measurement in field settings. However, there is still the problem that the experimenter has *assigned* people to treatments; the effects of viewing something that someone has prescribed could be different from the effects of viewing one's own choices.

Cross-cultural Studies

It is tempting to make generalizations about trends in development after studying children who share a common cultural background, such as middle-class American children. Comparative studies in other cultures can serve as an antidote to overgeneralization. For example, observers in Western societies, particularly the United States, have often described adolescence as a period of "storm and stress" characterized by mood swings, rebellion, and conflict with parental authority. However, in many cultures adolescents become fully integrated, adult members of their societies, doing adult work and starting families.

Sometimes information from different cultures extends the range of variables that can be observed. For example, virtually every American child is exposed to television from birth onward, and television programming in every part of the country contains a great deal of violence. Therefore, the range of exposure to violent television in the United States is limited; there are almost no children who have grown up without it. However, television programming in many other countries is less violent. A group of investigators from Poland, Israel, Finland, and Australia conducted longitudinal studies that were parallel to the U.S. investigation of the relationship between television violence and aggressive behavior discussed earlier. Even though the rates of TV violence in the various countries were quite different, many of the results were similar (Huesmann & Eron, 1986).

"Universals" of development can also be evaluated in cross-cultural studies. For example, the first primitive sentences of English-speaking children contain names of concrete objects (e.g., *kitty*) and action words (e.g., *hit*). Is this due to certain characteristics of the English language and the language environments provided by English-speaking parents, or do infants learning to speak other languages also name concrete objects first? This question has been addressed by cross-cultural investigations of children's early speech in many languages. The results have shown that there are many common patterns among children in different cultures (see Chapter 6).

Cross-species Studies

Developmental questions are sometimes studied using animals instead of human beings because animals can be raised in highly controlled environments. For example, in a classic set of studies with monkeys, Harry Harlow investigated early deprivation of maternal care. Newborn monkeys were raised in isolation or with artificial mothers of various kinds, and the effects of the deprivation on their later behavior was measured (Harlow & Suomi, 1970). Human children cannot be deprived of mothering, nor can they be kept in a laboratory for lifetime observation as the monkeys were.

Although we must exercise caution in generalizing from other species to humans, cross-species studies can provide valuable information about developmental processes that are comparable to those that occur in human beings. For instance, the infant monkeys in Harlow's studies seemed to prefer a soft, terry-cloth "mother" that gave no food over a wire-mesh "mother" that dispensed food. This led Harlow to suggest that feeding was not the critical reason why human babies become emotionally attached to their mothers—an important developmental issue that is explored more fully in Chapter 4.

Summary of Research Methods

Each of the many methods used to study human development has strengths and weaknesses. Together, they complement and compensate for one another. We can feel more confident of conclusions obtained from studies using a variety of methods than of those obtained from only one type. In the case of television violence, the fact that correlational studies, laboratory experiments, field experiments, and longitudinal studies yield similar findings provides support for the conclusion that television violence contributes to aggressive behavior. Similarly, when longitudinal studies in the United States, cross-cultural studies, and cross-species studies all show that infants develop certain fears in a particular order, we feel confident that a universal developmental sequence has been identified (see Chapter 4).

ETHICAL ISSUES IN RESEARCH

Research in child development raises complex ethical dilemmas. The occasional horror story from medical research, such as prisoners being injected with cancer-producing drugs without their knowledge, has made researchers particularly aware of the need to establish ethical guidelines and to monitor research procedures. Gross violations of children's rights, such as deliberately depriving them of stimulation in early life, are recognized by everyone as unethical.

More subtle ethical problems also require careful consideration. If investigators ask children questions about their parents' child-rearing practices, are they invading the children's or the parents' right to privacy? Might the questions themselves lead to problems in parent-child relationships? Do parents have the right to be given information about things children have said in confidence? Is it ever morally justified to deceive children (e.g., by misleading them about their performance on a test or telling them that they will be alone in a room when they are being observed through a one-way mirror)? Is it ethical to subject a child to mild frustration or stress for experimental purposes? Is it permissible to observe people in public settings without their consent? These are difficult questions that have no absolute answers.

Both the American Psychological Association (1972) and the Society for Research in Child Development (1973) have formulated written guidelines and principles for research, particularly research with children. Some of the principles taken from the report of the Committee on Ethics in Research with Children (Society for Research in Child Development) are summarized in Box 1.3.

Of course, ethical problems in research with children cannot be solved simply by applying a set of rules. Investigators must weigh the advantages and disadvantages of conducting a particular study. Can the investigator's judgment about

BOX 1.3

Ethical Issues in Research

Research with human beings entails many ethical issues and responsibilities. The researcher's primary obligation is to safeguard the welfare, dignity, and rights of all participants in research, children and adults alike. Some of the ethical dilemmas encountered in developmental research are easy to solve, but others are more subtle.

To help psychologists in making ethical decisions, professional organizations like the American Psychological Association and the Society for Research in Child Development have formulated some broad principles for conducting research with children. Of course, ethical problems cannot be solved simply by applying a set of rules; investigators must continually weigh the advantages and potential contributions of research against the disadvantages that may be involved in conducting it.

The following is a sample of principles formulated by a committee of the Society for Research in Child Development:

1. No matter how young the child, he has rights that supersede the rights of the investigator. The investigator should measure each operation he proposes in terms of the child's rights, and before proceeding he should obtain the approval of a committee of [the investigator's] peers. . . .

5. The investigator should respect the child's freedom to choose to participate in research or not, as well as to discontinue participation at any time. . . .

6. The informed consent of parents or of those who act *in loco parentis* (e.g., teachers, superintendents of institutions) similarly should be obtained, preferably in writing. Informed consent requires that the parent or other responsible adult be told all features of the research that may affect his willingness to allow the child to participate. . . . Not only should the right of the responsible adult to refuse consent be respected, but he should be given the opportunity to refuse without penalty. . . .

9. The investigator uses no research operation that may harm the child either physically or psychologically. Psychological harm, to be sure, is difficult to define; nevertheless, its definition remains the responsibility of the investigator. When the investigator is in doubt about the possible harmful effects of the research operations, he seeks consultation from others. When harm seems possible, he is obligated to find other means of obtaining the information or to abandon the research.

possible harm to children or potential benefits of the research be trusted? Often it can be, but many feel that any individual's decisions about ethical problems need to be evaluated or monitored by some sort of jury. Therefore, many universities and other research facilities—as well as the U.S. Public Health Service, which supports a great deal of research in child development—require that an ethics advisory committee consisting of other researchers representing several disciplines review every research proposal that involves human subjects. This committee serves as a panel of judges, considers the objectives and potential benefits of the study, weighs these against the possible harmful effects on the children, and most important, guarantees that all possible steps are taken to safeguard the welfare and integrity of participants.

In the final analysis, neither codes nor committees can substitute for the investigator's moral integrity, maturity, honesty, sensitivity, and respect for the rights of others. Ultimately, the investigator is responsible for the conduct of the study and for applying the highest ethical standards in research.

ORGANIZATION OF THIS BOOK

Four age periods define the four sections of this book: (1) prenatal development (before birth), (2) infant and toddler development (birth to about age 3), (3) early and middle childhood (about age 3 to age 12), and (4) adolescence (about age 12 to age 20). Of course, the content discussed for different ages overlaps because most features of human development are not perfectly correlated with age.

Within each section, development in the domains of physical and biological growth, cognitive functioning, and social-emotional behavior are discussed. The universals of human development, as well as the bases for individual differences, are considered. Central influences—the family, school, peer group, and mass media—are considered as they apply to different age periods. Major theories and applied social issues are addressed as they apply.

When you have read some or all of the following chapters, it may be advisable to return to the introduction. Many of the general points presented here will take on added meaning as you apply them to the specific knowledge presented in later chapters.

SUMMARY

Development is defined as orderly and relatively enduring changes over time in physical and neurological structures, thought processes, and behavior. One goal of studying development is to understand changes that appear to be universal. Another is to explain individual differences among children, and a third is to understand how children's behavior is influenced by the context or situation.

A number of theoretical issues must be addressed when studying children's development. One of the most basic of these is the relative importance of environmental versus biological determinants of behavior ("nature" vs. "nurture"). Few scientists may be found at either extreme of the nature-nurture controversy; many believe that behavior is a product of repeated transactions between biological and environmental determinants.

Another basic issue is the active versus passive nature of the child. Some theorists view children as passive receivers of experience; others consider them active in organizing, structuring, and in some sense creating their worlds. Theorists also disagree on whether developmental changes occur continuously or discontinuously. Although all developmentalists agree that some changes occur continuously and gradually, they disagree on whether some changes are qualitative, that is, not extensions of previous development.

Still another issue on which researchers disagree is the stability of behavior over time. One reason for differing interpretations is that some behaviors and some periods of development are more stable than others. Another is the fact that the same characteristics may be expressed in different ways at different ages. In addition to stability over time, researchers study consistency of behavior across situations. There is evidence that both individual traits and situational variables influence behavior.

The systematic study of child development began early in this century. At first many psychologists assumed that developmental changes are largely a result of maturation and their task was to uncover innate, universal patterns of development. After World War II, the main themes in child psychology were psychoanalysis, pioneered by Sigmund Freud earlier in the century, and behaviorism, founded by John B. Watson. Research by Watson led to the view that children's development can be explained by learning process and that environmental influences are primary.

In the early 1960s American psychology rediscovered Piaget's theory of cognitive development and returned to the study of biological, genetic, and maturational influences on behavior. Present-day investigations are typically designed to investigate transactions between the biological characteristics of the child and the experiences offered by the environment. Another recent trend is the attempt to relate children's social behavior to their cognitive development.

Research on child development may be either applied or basic. Applied research is designed to help parents, schools, and others who deal with children. Basic research is intended to generate knowledge about the processes and sequences of development, even when there is no immediate social need for that knowledge. Basic research questions usually originate from prominent theories that generate testable hypotheses. The selection of both basic and applied questions is inevitably affected by contemporary social and cultural values.

A variety of methods are used in studying children. Cross-sectional investigations compare children of different ages at one point in time. Correlational methods are used to test hypotheses about what variables may contribute to individual differences in development. In a longitudinal study, the same children are observed or tested at regular intervals over an extended period. In experimental investigations the experimenter systematically changes one variable and collects objective measurements on another variable. Field experiments differ from laboratory experiments in that groups who are given different experiences are observed in naturally occurring situations over a relatively long period.

Comparative studies in other cultures can serve as an antidote to overgeneralization from studies of children who share a common cultural background. In addition, developmental questions are sometimes studied using animals instead of human beings.

Each of the many methods used to study human development has strengths and weaknesses. Together, they complement and compensate for one another. Researchers feel more confident of conclusions obtained from studies using a variety of methods than of those obtained from only one type.

Research in child development raises complex ethical dilemmas. Both the American Psychological Association and the Society for Research in Child Development have formulated written guidelines and principles for research. In addition to applying these rules, investigators must weigh the advantages and disadvantages of conducting a particular study. Many universities and other research facilities require that an ethics advisory committee review every research proposal that involves human subjects.

REVIEW QUESTIONS

1. What is meant by development? What are the goals of studying development?

2. Briefly discuss the nature versus nurture controversy.

3. List four other theoretical issues that must be addressed in the study of child development.

4. How has the systematic study of child development evolved in the twentieth century?

5. What are the fundamental concerns of research on child development today?

6. Distinguish between applied and basic research.

7. How do investigators select the questions on which they focus their research efforts?

8. Briefly describe several methods that are used in studying children's development.

9. What is a correlation? How is correlation related to causation?

10. What are some ethical issues that must be resolved by scientists who do research on child development?

GLOSSARY

development   The orderly and relatively enduring changes over time in physical and neurological structures, thought processes, and behavior.

applied research   Research designed to help parents, schools and others who deal with children.

basic research   Research intended to generate knowledge about the processes and sequences of development, even when there is no immediate social need for the knowledge.

cross-sectional investigation   Research in which children of different ages are compared at one point in time.

correlation   A measure of the relationship between two characteristics.

longitudinal investigation   Research in which the same children are observed or tested at regular intervals over an extended period.

independent variable   In an experiment, a variable that the investigator systematically changes.

dependent variable   In an experiment, the variable on which the investigator collects objective measurements.

SUGGESTED READINGS

Cairns, R. B. (1983). The emergence of developmental psychology. In W. Kessen (Ed.) & P. H. Mussen (Series Ed.), *Handbook of child psychology*: Vol. 1. *History, theory, and methods* (pp. 44–102). New York: Wiley. A thorough discussion of the history of developmental psychology, beginning with formative influences in the nineteenth century and summarizing the major advances in the twentieth century.

Review of child development research (Vols. 1–7). (1964–1984). Chicago: University of Chicago Press. These volumes contain reviews of the literature on selected topics. The reviews are designed to integrate available knowledge in a way that is useful for a broad spectrum of professionals who work with children.

Salkind, N. J. (1985). *Theories of human development* (2nd ed.). New York: Van Nostrand. A student who is interested in theory will find it useful to read a supplementary text devoted to a discussion of theory. This book organizes theories around the major issues discussed in the chapter, such as the passive versus active view of the child.

Sears, R. R. (1975). Your ancients revisited: A history of child development. In E. M. Hetherington (Ed.), *Review of child development research*: Vol. 5. Chicago: University of Chicago Press. Presents the history of child development, placing it in the context of concerns about children's social welfare that were prevalent in the early twentieth century.

Stevenson, H. W., & Siegel, A. (1984). *Child development research and social policy*: Vol. 1. Chicago: University of Chicago Press. Chapters in this book draw implications from child development research for public policies on such issues as divorce, child health, institutionalization of mentally retarded children, sex role socialization, and nutrition.

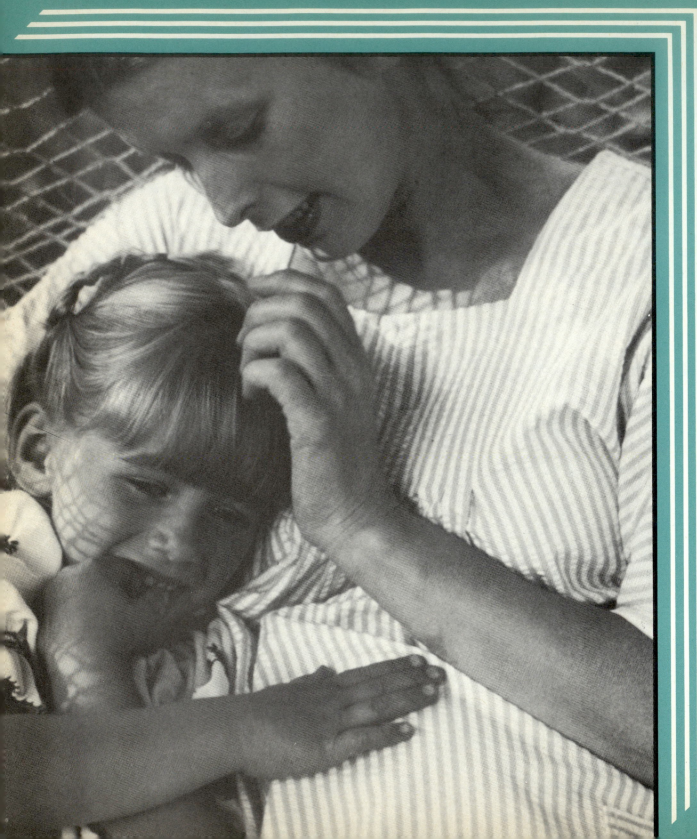

Part One

THE PRENATAL PERIOD

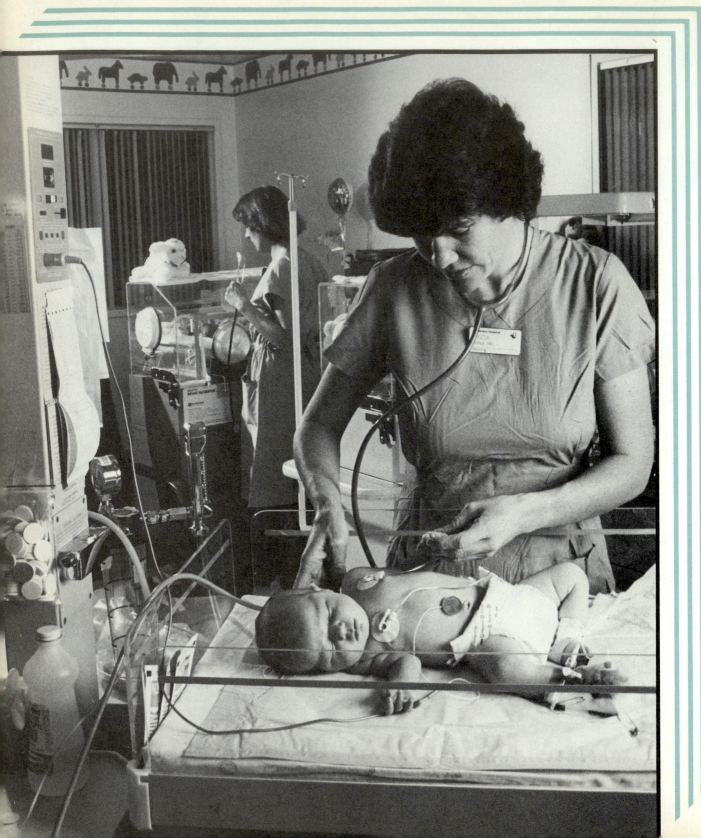

Chapter Two

GENETIC AND PRENATAL FACTORS IN DEVELOPMENT

The Beginnings of Life: Hereditary Transmission

  Chromosomes and Genes
  Genes and DNA
  The Mechanisms of Hereditary Transmission
  Is Sibling Identity Possible?
  The Sex Chromosomes
  Determining the Extent of Genetic Influences

Prenatal Development

  Conception and Earliest Development
  The Germinal Period
  The Embryonic Period
  The Fetal Period

Prenatal Environmental Influences

  Age of the Mother
  Maternal Nutrition
  Drugs
  Radiation
  Maternal Diseases and Disorders During Pregnancy
  The Rh Factor
  Maternal Stress

The Birth Process

  Anoxia and Other Complications
  Prematurity

Many factors must be considered in attempting to understand the behavior of the developing child. Even the simplest behavior may be a result of many different influences. These influences fall into five basic categories: (1) genetically determined biological variables, (2) nongenetic biological variables (e.g., malnutrition or lack of oxygen during the birth process), (3) the child's past learning, (4) the immediate sociopsychological environment (parents, siblings, peers, teachers), and (5) the general social and cultural milieu in which the child develops. As we noted at the beginning of this book, a child's behavior and personality at any one time are a product of the continual interaction of nature and nurture.

Although we consider biological and environmental influences separately, it is important to realize that they always act in unison. This is as true for the individual cell as it is for the whole person. Thus, the chemical action of the genetic material in a particular cell can be affected by the material outside the cell's nucleus. Indeed, the effect of a single gene depends on the constellation of other genes in that cell. Scientists try to discover the specific genetic and environmental forces that are controlling a specific behavior. They do not ask which influence is the cause, just as they would not ask whether moisture or cold produces a snowfall; both are important.

Recognition of the intimate interaction of genes and environment is relatively recent. As was pointed out in Chapter 1, even in the twentieth century many scientists still took dogmatic, one-sided views of the nature-nurture issue, attributing virtually all human behavior either to heredity or to environment. Consider, for example, this statement by J. B. Watson, the father of early behaviorism: "There is no such thing as an inheritance of capacity, talent, temperament, mental constitution, and characteristics" (Allport, 1937, p. 103). Or this one by another scientist: "The differences among men are due to differences in the gene cells with which they are born" (Allport, 1937, pp. 102–103).

In light of recent advances in biology and psychology, the extremes of environmentalism and genetic determinism are equally naive. Scientists must search for the ways in which the combined action of our inherited potentialities and the events we experience make us the way we are. The sciences of genetics and embryology have made dramatic progress during the past 25 years. This chapter will discuss current knowledge of human genetics (particularly as it affects behavior) and a variety of prenatal factors that affect the course of development.

THE BEGINNINGS OF LIFE: HEREDITARY TRANSMISSION

The development of every individual begins when a sperm cell from the father penetrates the wall of an ovum, or egg, from the mother. The fertilization of an ovum by a sperm sets in motion an intricate process called **mitosis**, in which the original fertilized ovum divides and subdivides until thousands of cells have been produced. Gradually, as the process continues, groups of cells begin to assume special functions as parts of the nervous, skeletal, muscular, and circulatory systems. The embryo, which at first resembles a gradually expanding ball, begins to take shape, and the beginnings of head, eyes, trunk, arms, and legs appear. Approximately nine months after fertilization, the fetus is ready for birth.

Chromosomes and Genes

Development begins at conception. But what are the forces that will influence that process throughout the individual's existence? When do they begin? The answer, again, is at conception. At the moment that the tiny, tadpole-shaped sperm penetrates the wall of the ovum, it releases 23 minute particles called **chromosomes**. At approximately the same time, the nucleus of the ovum breaks up, releasing 23 chromosomes of its own, so that the new individual begins life with 46 chromosomes.

This process is of great interest because the chromosomes, which are further subdivided into even smaller particles called **genes**, are the carriers of the child's heredity. (There are about 1 million genes in a human cell—an average of about 20,000 genes per chromosome.) The child's entire biological heritage is contained in these 23 pairs of chromosomes. Of these pairs, 22 are autosomes and are possessed equally by males and females. The twenty-third pair, the **sex chromosomes**, differ in males and females. Normal females have two X chromosomes (XX), while normal males have an X and a Y chromosome (XY) (see Figure 2.1).

Genes and DNA

For many years geneticists agreed that genes were the basic units of hereditary transmission, but the nature of the substances responsible for their action was in doubt. Few scientists suspected the importance of a critical component of the genes: deoxyribonucleic acid, or DNA. One reason that DNA's role was overlooked is that its chemical structure appeared too simple to account for the many complex tasks it would have to perform. However, in the 1940s Oswald Avery, a research physician at the Rockefeller Institute, produced evidence (overlooked at the time) that DNA played a critical role in genetic transmission (Borek, 1973). But how did it accomplish this?

Eight years after the discovery of DNA as the basic genetic material, James Watson and Francis Crick (1953), winners of the Nobel Prize in medicine, deduced that DNA is composed of not one but two molecular chains, which are coiled around each other to form a double-stranded helix. Perhaps the simplest way to visualize this is to imagine a rubber ladder twisted around its long axis as shown in Figure 2.2. Alternating sugar and phosphate molecules form the legs of the ladder. The cross steps are made up of the nitrogenous bases adenine, thymine, cytosine, and guanine. The nitrogenous bases, which are held together by hydrogen bonds, are always paired in a special way to form distinctive strands. By knowing the order of the nitrogenous bases in one strand of the helix, we can determine their order in the other (Fraser & Nora, 1986; Moore, K. L., 1982).

When DNA reproduces itself, the original strands first separate at the hydrogen bonds in the manner of a zipper. Bases from a pool of nucleotides in the cell nucleus attach themselves to the appropriate bases in the chain to form a complementary chain. The result is that two chains are constructed along the original

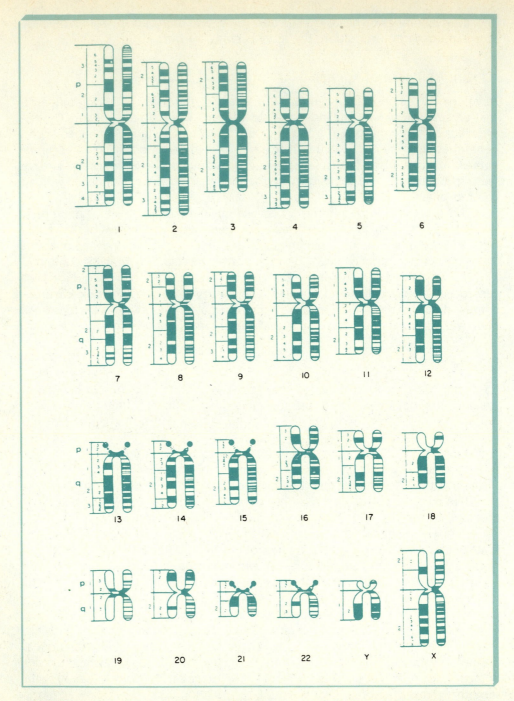

FIGURE 2.1   *Karyotype of the human male chromosomes, showing light and dark bands that help iden-tify the chromosome. (p) denotes the two upper arms of each chromosome; (q) denotes the two lower arms* (From J. J. Yunis, High resolution of human chromosomes. March 1976, *Science* 191. Copyright 1976 by the American Association for the Advancement of Science. By permission.)

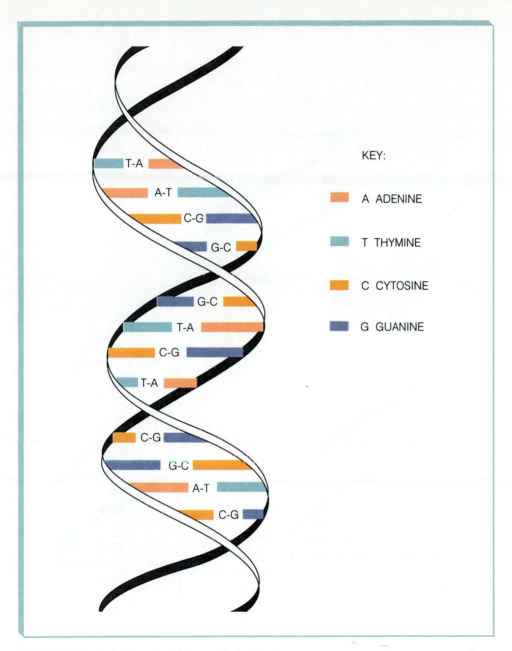

KEY:

■ A ADENINE

■ T THYMINE

■ C CYTOSINE

■ G GUANINE

FIGURE 2.2   The DNA double-stranded helix.

chains to form two new helixes, each one chemically identical to the helix from which it was derived (see Figure 2.3). When cells divide in this way, the genetic information they contain is preserved and transmitted unchanged to the daughter cells (Fraser & Nora, 1986; Whaley, 1974).

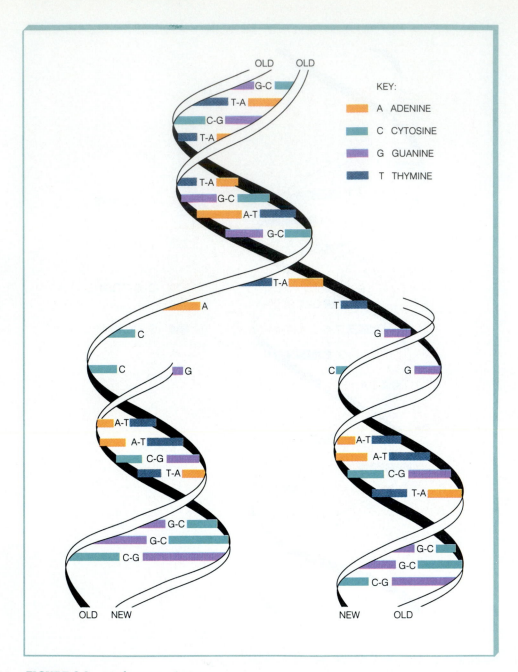

FIGURE 2.3   Replication of DNA.

The Mechanisms of Hereditary Transmission

One of the things that must have puzzled parents in prescientific days was how two children of the same parents can be so different physically. The answer lies in the mechanics of hereditary transmission.

If each child received all of both parents' genes, we could not explain genetic differences between siblings, as all brothers and sisters would have identical heredities. The fact is, however, that each child inherits only half of each parent's genes. Moreover, different children in a family inherit different combinations of their mother and father's genes. Thus, differences between them are not only possible but inevitable.

Before the fertilized ovum divides to form two new cells (through *mitosis*), each of its 46 chromosomes first divides in half, providing each of the new cells with the same number of chromosomes as the original cell (see Figure 2.4). But if this is true, why don't the sperm and ovum that combine to make up a new individual contain 46 chromosomes each instead of 23?

The answer is simple. The adult organism contains not one but two kinds of cells: body cells—which make up bones, nerves, muscles, and organs—and germ cells—from which the sperm and ova are derived. Throughout most of their history the germ cells develop in the same way as the body cells. But before they divide into recognizable sperm or ova the pattern changes. At this point a process called **meiosis** (from the Greek word meaning "to make smaller") results in cells whose nuclei contain only half the number of chromosomes present in the parent cell (see

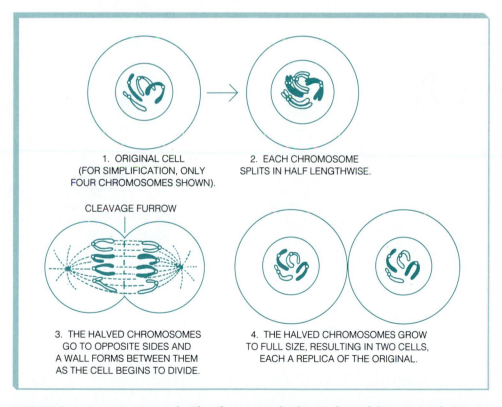

1. ORIGINAL CELL
(FOR SIMPLIFICATION, ONLY
FOUR CHROMOSOMES SHOWN).

2. EACH CHROMOSOME
SPLITS IN HALF LENGTHWISE.

CLEAVAGE FURROW

3. THE HALVED CHROMOSOMES
GO TO OPPOSITE SIDES AND
A WALL FORMS BETWEEN THEM
AS THE CELL BEGINS TO DIVIDE.

4. THE HALVED CHROMOSOMES GROW
TO FULL SIZE, RESULTING IN TWO CELLS,
EACH A REPLICA OF THE ORIGINAL.

FIGURE 2.4   Mitosis: How a fertilized ovum multiplies (Adapted from R. Rugh & L. B. Shettles. *From conception to birth: The drama of life's beginnings.* New York: Harper & Row, 1971. By permission.)

Figure 2.5). This explains why children of the same parents do not have to be alike. As can be seen in Figure 2.6, if sperm A unites with ovum D, the new individual will possess a different set of chromosomes than it would if sperm B united with it. (Ovum C is indicated in dotted lines because ordinarily only one ovum from the mother is ready for fertilization at any one conception.

Is Sibling Identity Possible?

We have seen how it is possible for individuals in the same family to be different in their genetic makeup. But is identity between siblings possible? The answer is no, except in the case of identical twins, who develop from a single fertilized ovum. If the 46 chromosomes in the germ cells divided the same way, with one combination going to one sperm or ovum and the rest to the other, identity would be possible; in fact, it would be frequent. But the chromosomes do not divide in this way. Except for the fact that half of each of the 23 pairs goes to one sperm or ovum and the other half to the other, the pattern of division is random. In other words, the way one pair of chromosomes separates does not influence the way another pair will split.

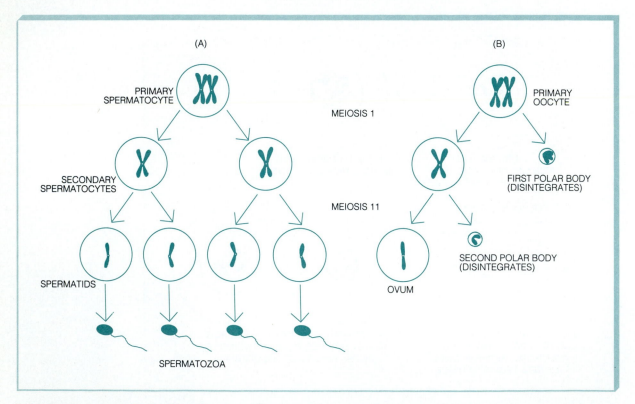

FIGURE 2.5   How male and female germ cells are produced. (*a*) Spermatogenesis results in four spermatozoa (sperm). (*b*) Oogenesis results in only one ovum. (From L. F. Whaley. *Understanding inherited disorders*. St. Louis: C. V. Mosby Company, 1974. By permission.)

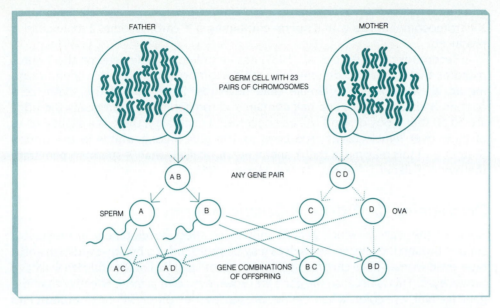

FIGURE 2.6 Schematic diagram showing possible gene combinations of offspring resulting from gene pairs of parents.

Moreover, in the formation of the germ cells a process called **crossing-over** increases the likelihood that each sperm or ovum will be unique and, therefore, that each individual will be unique (Scarr & Kidd, 1983). When the 23 pairs of chromosomes line up during meiosis, they can exchange blocks of corresponding genetic material much as if human beings facing each other were to exchange parts of their fingers. The likelihood that two genes will be exchanged together depends on how close to each other the gene sites are along the length of a chromosome. Genes that are located close to each other will usually be inherited together, while those located at opposite ends of one of the larger chromosomes are likely to be inherited independently (Scarr & Kidd, 1983).

If crossing-over did not occur, the total number of different combinations of sperm and ovum from one mother and father would be approximately 64 billion. Thus, one pair of parents could produce many more different kinds of children than the total number of people on the earth today. With crossing-over, the number of possible different offspring is many, many times that number. Except for identical twins, then, each human being is genetically unique and biologically different from every other person on earth.

The Sex Chromosomes

As we saw in Figure 2.1, one of the 23 pairs of chromosomes consists of the sex chromosomes and determines the sex of the child. In the normal female, both members of this pair are large and are called X chromosomes. In the normal male, one member of the pair is an X chromosome; the second is smaller and is referred to as a Y chromosome. Thus, the body cells of males contain one X chromosome and one Y chromosome. Half of the sperm cells contain an X chromosome; the remaining half contain a Y chromosome. When a female ovum (which contains an X chromosome) unites with a sperm containing a Y chromosome, a male child is produced.

Recent research (Page et al., 1987) has identified a single gene on the Y chromosome that appears to determine sex. When an ovum unites with a sperm carrying an X chromosome, a female child develops. Since half of the sperm cells contain X chromosomes and half contain Y chromosomes, theoretically the odds are 50:50 that a boy or a girl will be conceived. In actuality, there is a slight excess of male over female births (106 boys to 100 girls among whites in the United States), and this may mean that Y sperm are more likely than X sperm to penetrate the ovum (Falkner & Tanner, 1978a; Moore, 1982).

Determining the Extent of Genetic Influences

Some of the ways in which genetic influences affect development are relatively simple, though the effects themselves may be profound. If a brown-eyed man and a blue-eyed woman have children, it is likely that at least half of the children will have brown eyes. This is because the gene for brown eye color is more effective than the gene for blue eye color. When the two are paired, the former will be **dominant** and the latter will be **recessive**; that is, its effects will be masked. If the father happens to have two brown-eyed genes rather than one for brown eyes and one for blue, all of the couple's children will receive one brown eye-color gene and all will have brown eyes. If, however, the father has one blue eye-color gene, half of the children will probably have blue eyes.*

The relationship between genetic inheritance and behavioral characteristics can be seen in the case of phenylketonuria (PKU), a disorder that is caused by the presence of a particular pair of recessive genes. Many of the foods we eat contain a chemical called *phenylalanine*. Most people possess an enzyme that converts phenylalanine into a harmless by-product. However, a small number of children are born without the enzyme that converts the phenylalanine; they lack the gene that produces it. As a result, the concentration of phenylalanine rises above the normal level and the chemical is converted into phenylpyruvic acid. The cells of the central nervous system become damaged, and mental retardation results. Once scientists learned the nature of the specific metabolic disorder in PKU, they were able to devise a diet that was nutritious but contained very low levels of phenylalanine. When children with PKU followed this diet, the toxic acid did not accumulate and their mental development was almost normal.

Relatively simple genetic models like those for PKU are more the exception than the rule. Most behavioral traits are **multifactorial**; that is, they depend on more than one genetic or environmental factor (Scarr & Kidd, 1983; Vandenberg, Singer & Pauls, 1986). At the genetic level, a particular characteristic may require the presence of a number of genes, a situation that is termed **polygenetic**

---

*In actuality, the genetics of eye color are somewhat more complex than our description implies. More than one pair of genes may be involved in determining eye color; moreover, not all genes are dominant or recessive with respect to each other—sometimes there is a *blending*, as in the case of gray, green, or hazel eyes, or different shades of blue and brown. Generally, however, the genes for darker eye colors tend to be dominant over those for lighter colors (Fraser & Nora, 1986).

inheritance. Although progress is being made toward identifying the genes that affect polygenetic, multifactorial characteristics, we must still rely largely on incidence patterns among individuals who are genetically related to varying degrees and have been exposed to similar or different environmental influences. As we shall see in subsequent sections, a variety of techniques have been employed in studying such patterns, including "pedigree" studies of incidence within individual families, adoption studies, and studies comparing **monozygotic** ("identical") and **dizygotic** ("fraternal") twins.

PHYSICAL FEATURES.   Our physical features depend heavily on heredity. The color of our eyes, the pigmentation of our skin, and the color and curliness of our hair are determined by the genes we inherit. For the most part, variations in physical features within the American population bear little relation to an individual's biological ability to adapt to the demands of living. A person with brown eyes can see as well as one with blue eyes. The effects of such variations are more likely to be social and psychological. For example, adolescents whose appearance conforms to current social stereotypes about attractiveness are likely to be favored by their peers.

INTELLIGENCE.   To what extent are the kinds of abilities measured by intelligence tests influenced by heredity? This is a controversial topic. Some authorities assert that genetic influences play a dominant role in determining intellectual abilities; others claim that evidence for such an assertion is slight at most. How can these conflicting views be resolved?

If genetic factors do play a significant role in determining intellectual abilities, we would expect to find that a child or adolescent's IQ is more highly correlated with the IQs of his or her parents and other immediate relatives than with those of randomly selected nonrelatives. This is indeed the case. Unfortunately for investigators, however, the matter is not so simple. Parents who may have provided their children with a superior genetic endowment may be providing them with other advantages that are also related to intellectual ability, such as good health, a stimulating home environment, and superior educational opportunities. Thus, if we are to isolate the potential contributions of heredity, we must find a way to control the potential effects of other variables.

Investigation of the effects of heredity on intellectual ability is greatly aided by comparing *monozygotic* (MZ) twins with ordinary brothers and sisters and with *dizygotic* (DZ) twins. The latter are no more alike genetically than ordinary siblings. If genetic influences play an important role in the determination of intellectual ability, we would expect the IQs of monozygotic twins to be more highly correlated than those of dizygotic twins or nontwin siblings.

This turns out to be true. A review of 30 studies comparing the intelligence and abilities of monozygotic and dizygotic twins of the same sex found an average correlation* of .85 for monozygotic twins and .58 for dizygotic twins (Bouchard & McGee, 1981). The correlation for dizygotic twins is approximately the same as that

---

*Mathematically, a correlation coefficient of zero means that there is no relationship between two sets of measures. A coefficient of 1.0, on the other hand, indicates a one-to-one, or perfect, relationship. Partial relationships are expressed by coefficients ranging from zero to 1.0.

Studies of genetic factors in development often compare identical twins with fraternal twins and nontwin siblings.

for nontwin siblings reared in the same family. Both of these, in turn, are substantially higher than the correlation for unrelated individuals reared in the same family (Nichols, 1978; Scarr & Kidd, 1983; Segal, 1985; Wilson, R.S., 1977, 1983).

One fascinating investigation has found that even the patterns of developmental change at early ages may have a genetic component (Wilson, R. S., 1972, 1975, 1983; Wilson, R. S. & Harpring, 1972). Repeated measurements of mental and motor development were conducted during the first two years of life using techniques that will be described more fully in Chapter 3. When the scores of 261 monozygotic and dizygotic twins were analyzed, the profiles of the developmental spurts and lags were very similar, especially for MZ twins (see Figure 2.7). Apparently, "the developmental sequence is an expression of timed gene action which may produce spurts or lags between ages" (Wilson, R. S. & Harpring, 1972, p. 280).

Although twin studies comparing monozygotic and dizygotic twins can be extremely valuable in the search for genetic influences, some qualifications should be kept in mind. For one thing, it is frequently assumed that because they have the same genetic makeup, monozygotic twins are biologically identical at birth. This is not necessarily so. For example, one twin usually weighs slightly more than the other, perhaps because the two fetuses shared unequally in intrauterine blood circulation. It has been shown that even small differences between identical twins at birth can interact with the environment to produce larger differences in behavior (Smith, N. W., 1976).

Another inaccurate assumption is that the environmental influences to which DZ twins are exposed are as similar as those to which MZ twins are exposed (Plomin, 1986). It is true that both DZ and MZ twins grow up in the same family and

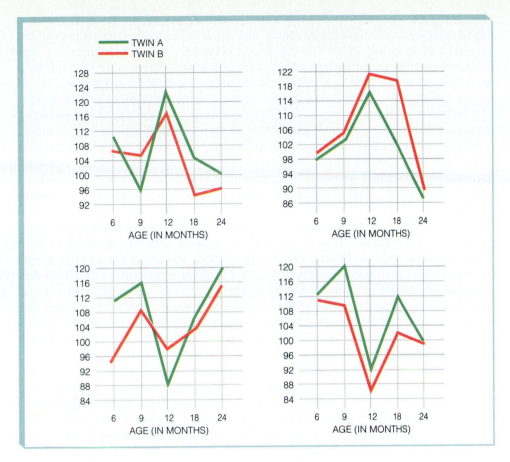

FIGURE 2.7 Bayley score profiles for four pairs of twins illustrating concordance in developmental status at each age and congruence for the pattern of changes over age. (Adapted from R. S. Wilson & E. B. Harpring. Mental and motor development in infant twins. *Developmental Psychology*, 1972, 7, 277–287. Copyright 1972 by the American Psychological Association. By permission.)

share many experiences. However, several studies have found that compared to fraternal twins, identical twins spend more time together, have more similar reputations, and are more likely to be in the same classrooms, have similar health records, and in many other respects share a nearly identical physical and social environment (Jones, H. E., 1946). MZ twins may also be treated in more similar ways by parents, siblings, peers, and others than DZ twins are, partly because they look alike and partly because their behavior is more similar to begin with (Loehlin & Nichols, 1976; Lytton, 1977; Plomin, Willerman, & Loehlin, 1976; Scarr & Carter-Saltzman, 1979; Willerman, 1979). Even in twin studies, then, environmental effects cannot be fully controlled.

Another useful way to investigate genetic influences on intelligence is to study children and adolescents who have been raised by adoptive parents from a very early age and compare their IQs with those of their biological and adoptive parents

(Plomin, 1986; Plomin & DeFries, 1985). Because these children have had little or no contact with their biological parents, any similarity to those parents is assumed to reflect genetic influences. The correlation between the IQs of children and their adopted parents is assumed to indicate environmental influences. In a comprehensive analysis of the best controlled investigations available in 1975, it was found that when all subjects from these studies were combined, there was a correlation of .19 between adoptive parents' intelligence test scores (obtained by averaging mother's and father's scores) and those of their adopted children (Munsinger, 1975). In contrast, the correlation between these children's scores and those of their biological parents was .48. However, for children raised by their biological parents, the correlation between parents' and children's scores was .58, suggesting that both heredity *and* environment were important contributors (Munsinger, 1975).

This conclusion is supported by more recent studies. These studies also found significant correlations between the IQs of biological parents and those of their adopted-away children (Horn, 1983; Plomin,1986; Plomin & DeFries, in press). Moreover, these correlations were higher than correlations between the IQs of children and those of their adoptive parents, confirming the influence of genetic factors. However, these and other studies also provide evidence of the important role that environmental influences can play in the development of intelligence (Horn, 1985; Huston, A. C., 1984; Schiff, Duyme, Dumaret, & Tomkiewicz, 1982; Skodak & Skeels, 1949; Walker & Emory, 1985).

In one major study of adopted-away children, intelligence tests were administered to both biological and adoptive mothers, as well as to the children themselves (Horn, 1983). Although the correlation in IQ between the children and their biological mothers (.24) was higher than between the children and their adoptive mothers (.15), separate analyses found that the average IQ of the adopted children was closer to that of their adoptive mothers than to that of their biological mothers (Huston, A. C., 1984; Walker & Emory, 1985). This was especially true when the biological mothers' IQs were below average (Huston, A. C., 1984).

In a French adoption study, children born to unskilled parents were reared by upper-income professional families (Schiff, Duyme, Dumaret, & Tomkiewicz, 1982). It was found that the IQs of the adopted children were similar to those of natural children from the same socioeconomically advantaged group, and 14 points higher than those of children of unskilled workers in general. Similar results were found in a study of black and interracial children adopted in infancy by middle-class white families (Scarr & Weinberg, 1976).

Similarities in IQ are highest between people who are most closely related genetically (i.e., monozygotic twins) and lowest between those who are unrelated. It seems clear that an individual's genetic inheritance is an important determinant of IQ. However, there are also similarities between adoptive parents and their adopted children. Although some of these similarities could be due to selective placement by adoption agencies, they also reflect the importance of the home environment (Scarr & Kidd, 1983; Munsinger, 1975; Willerman, 1979). Environmental as well as genetic factors are important in raising or lowering a child's level of intellectual performance, as we shall see in Chapter 9. Of course, environmental forces are effective only within the ultimate limits set by heredity.

DEVELOPMENTAL DISABILITIES.   There are more than 150 known gene defects that may result in mental retardation and other developmental disabilities, though fortunately most of these occur rarely (Scarr & Kidd, 1983; Vandenberg, Singer, & Pauls, 1986). In some instances, as in the case of PKU, genes fail to give the cells the proper instructions to produce enzymes needed for normal development, or they may give incorrect instructions. In other instances, abnormalities in the structure of the chromosomes may be responsible for mental retardation. These abnormalities may occur in either the autosomes or the sex chromosomes. A good example of the former is *Down's syndrome* (mongolism), a form of mental retardation that results from the presence of an extra chromosome at the twenty-first pair of autosomes (a normal pair is shown in Figure 2.1). Children with this disorder are born with an Oriental cast to their facial appearance and may have eye, heart, and other developmental defects. Most have IQs in the 25-to-45 range, though a few have IQs as high as 70, and about 4 percent can read. Generally, they are cheerful, have a faculty for mimicry, and enjoy music (Kopp & Parmelee, 1979; Reed, 1975; Scarr & Kidd, 1983).

Aberrant numbers of sex chromosomes are sometimes associated with behavioral problems and retarded intellectual development (Fraser & Nora, 1986; Vandenberg, Singer, & Pauls, 1986). For example, in *Klinefelter's syndrome*, which results from the presence of two X chromosomes in males (i.e., XXY rather than XY), secondary masculine characteristics fail to develop at puberty and there may be breast enlargement. Administration of the male hormone androgen promotes the development of male secondary sex characteristics, but the boy remains sterile. Boys with Klinefelter's syndrome are more likely than their peers to have behavioral problems and retarded intellectual development (Reed, 1975; Scarr & Kidd, 1983).

When retardation occurs among children with sex chromosome abnormalities, it is generally mild. Exceptions occur in the relatively rare conditions in which more than two X chromosomes are present (e.g., XXX or XXXXY). The degree of impairment is roughly proportional to the number of excess X chromosomes. Excess Y chromosomes may also adversely affect development, but their effect is significantly less than that of excess X chromosomes (Fraser & Nora, 1986; Vandenberg, Singer, & Pauls, 1986).

The study of children with sex chromosome abnormalities (SCA) provides an opportunity to observe the interplay of genetic and environmental influences. Recent research indicates that a nurturant home environment can reduce the effects of the more common, less extreme forms of SCA on development, while a stressful, nonsupportive home environment can increase these effects—in some instances dramatically (see Box 2.1).

FRAGILE-X SYNDROME.   Another sex chromosome abnormality, the *fragile*-X *syndrome* (Bregman, Dykens, Watson, Ort, & Leckman, 1987; Vandenberg, Singer, & Pauls, 1986), ranks second to Down's syndrome as the most prevalent

BOX 2.1

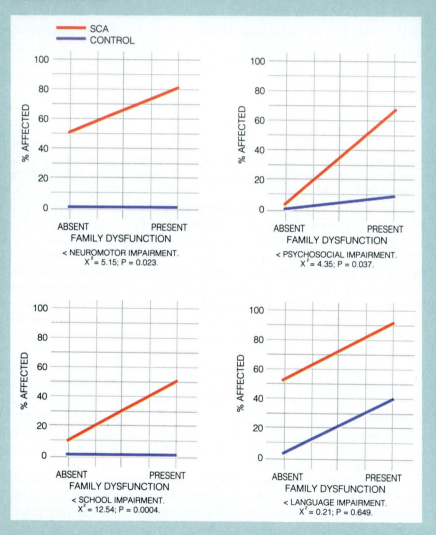

Developmental Risk in Children with Sex Chromosome Abnormalities

Percentages of SCA and control children from functional and dysfunctional families showing significant impairment. (Adapted from B. G. Bender, M. G. Linden, & A. Robinson. Environmental and developmental risk in children with sex chromosome abnormalities. *Journal of the American Academy of Child and Adolescent Psychiatry*, 1987, 26, 499–503. © 1987 by the American Academy of Child and Adolescent Psychiatry. By permission.)

Forty-six SCA infants—that is, infants with sex chromosome abnormalities (e.g., XXY, XYY, XXX)—were identified through the screening of 40,000 consecutive Denver newborns. These infants, together with a control group of non-SCA siblings, were followed annually through early adolescence (Bender, Linden, & Robinson, 1987). A relatively high percentage of children with significant neuromotor, learning, and psychosocial problems was found among SCA children (but not among control children) who were reared in "dysfunctional families," or families characterized by poor parent-child relationships and a high incidence of stressful life events (see chart). In contrast, in nurturant, relatively stress-free homes SCA children did not differ significantly from control children in school and psychosocial functioning, though they performed more poorly on neuromotor and language measures.

These findings indicate that SCA children have more limited resiliency and responses than normal children, and that "the damaging impact of an unsupportive environment is almost inescapable" (Bender et al., 1987, p. 502). On the positive side, it appears that good parenting skills and a nurturant, relatively stress-free home environment can serve as "protective factors" that minimize the adverse effects of SCA (Garmezy, 1985, 1987; Rutter, 1977, 1979).

chromosomal defect that may cause mental retardation, particularly in boys (Webb, Bundey, Thake, & Todd, 1986). In this condition an X chromosome has a pinched or constricted area near the lower tips that may result in breakage. About 80 percent of boys who inherit this genetic condition have mental impairment, which may range from severe retardation to low-normal intelligence (Bishop, 1986; Bregman, Dykens, Watson, Ort, & Leckman, 1987; de la Cruz, 1985). Many also have behavioral problems such as hyperactivity and emotional outbursts and, in some cases, *infantile autism* (a severe disorder characterized by rigid, ritualistic behavior, serious learning problems, and inability to communicate or form social and emotional relationships) (Brown, Jenkins, & Friedman, et al, 1982; Chudley, 1984; Largo & Schinzel, 1985). Girls are much less likely than boys to be affected by this condition, but about a third of all girls with a fragile-X chromosome have some degree of retardation or learning disability. Perhaps a girl's other X chromosome (which boys lack) may be able in some instances to mitigate or negate the damaging effects of the defective X chromosome.

MENTAL DISORDERS.   The role of genetic factors in causing mental disorders has been a source of much controversy. It has long been established that certain disorders are caused by infection or by the ingestion of various drugs or poisons. Some other, rather rare forms of mental disorder, such as Huntington's chorea, result from specific, clearly identifiable genetic defects.

There has been considerably less agreement until recently regarding the role of genetic factors in schizophrenia and the affective (depressive) disorders. Recently, however, a specific genetic marker located on chromosome 11 has been identified for at least one form of bipolar (manic-depressive) disorder (Egeland, 1987). There are also indications that other cases of this disorder may involve genetic markers near the tip of the X chromosome (Detera-Wadleigh et al., 1987; Hodgkinson et al, 1987). Nevertheless, most broad-based investigations of the potential role of genetic factors in major mental disorders are still dependent on studies of familial incidence (Cloringer, 1987).

Schizophrenia.   Schizophrenia, the most common form of major mental disorder, is characterized by severe defects in logical thinking and emotional responsiveness. Several generations ago, it was believed that traumatic experiences in childhood were the primary determinant of schizophrenia. However, recent research suggests that biological and hereditary factors frequently play a significant role (Gottesman & Shields, 1982; Plomin, 1986; Vandenberg, Singer, & Pauls, 1986). In a number of studies, the incidence of this disorder (or, perhaps, set of disorders with similar symptoms) among the relatives of schizophrenics has been shown to vary according to how closely they are related biologically (Gottesman & Shields, 1982; Plomin, 1986; Rosenthal, Wender, Schulsinger, & Jacobsen, 1975). For example, several well-controlled investigations have found that if one identical twin has schizophrenia, the chances are about 1 in 2 that the other twin will also develop it; among nonidentical twins the ratio is less than 1 in 10 (Kessler, 1975, 1980; O'Rourke et al, 1981; Rosenthal, 1970).

In an extensive study carried out in Denmark, schizophrenia occurred far more often among the biological relatives of adoptees who developed schizophrenia than among the relatives of those who did not. There were no differences in incidence among the adoptive parents of the two groups (Kendler, Gruenberg, & Strauss, 1981; Kety, Rosenthal, Wender, Schulsinger, & Jacobsen, 1975, 1978).

It may be more correct to speak of inheriting greater *vulnerability* to schizophrenia than to speak of inheriting schizophrenia per se (Freedman, Adler, Barker, Waldo, & Mizner, 1987). In that case, whether or not the disorder actually occurs would depend on two factors: how vulnerable a particular individual is and how much or what kind of stress he or she is subjected to. Certain life experiences, such as a highly disturbed family environment, may increase the chances that a person with a genetic susceptibility to schizophrenia will actually develop the disorder (Goldstein, M. J., 1987; Mednick, Parnas, & Schulsinger, 1987; Tienari et al., 1987).

Depression.   In many forms of depression, particularly those that are relatively minor and transient, psychological and social factors play the principal causative role. In such conditions the depressed feelings may be expected to recede when the problems that have brought them about—such as loss of a job, disappointment in love, or the death of a friend—are somehow resolved or worked through. In the case of severe depressive disorders, however, genetic factors, mediated by biochemical processes, appear to play a significant role (Puig-Antich, 1986; Klerman, 1988; Rutter, Izard, & Read, 1986; Weissman et al., 1984; Winokur, 1975).

Of the major mental disorders, bipolar or manic-depressive appears to have the strongest genetic component. This disorder is characterized by periods of excessive euphoria, grandiosity, hyperactivity, and poor judgment, alternating with periods of normality and periods of severe depression, loss of energy, and feelings of worthlessness (American Psychiatric Association, 1987). If one identical twin has bipolar disorder, the chances are 2 out of 3 (65 percent) that the other twin will also suffer from this disorder (Klerman, 1988; Nurnberger & Gershon, 1981; Plomin, 1986). In the case of nonidentical twins, the chances of the other twin also developing bipolar disorder are less than 1 in 6 (14 percent). Investigators have recently identified genetic markers for at least some forms of bipolar disorder (see page 54).

PERSONALITY CHARACTERISTICS.   Investigating the role of genetic factors in the development of personality presents special problems. Unlike some physical traits, mental disorders, or retardation, in which the characteristics to be studied are specific and clearly defined, aspects of personality can be difficult to define and measure. Personality characteristics are rarely all-or-nothing phenomena: They are present in different individuals in different degrees and blends. Nevertheless, progress is being made, most clearly through studies of monozygotic and dizygotic twins (Plomin, 1986; Scarr & Kidd, 1983). In general, it appears that genetic influences are strongest for basic temperamental characteristics (e.g., calm–easily distressed, passive–active, reflective–impulsive, shy–gregarious) that tend to be

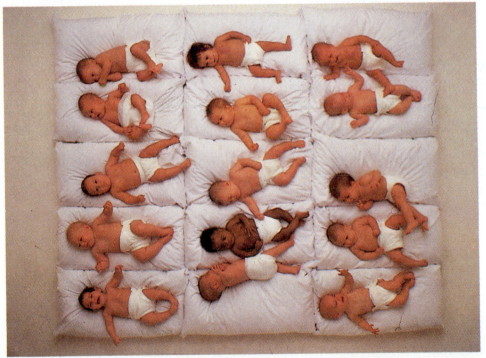

Genetic influences appear to be strongest for basic temperamental characteristics, which are evident even in very young infants.

relatively stable during development, and weakest for characteristics that are highly dependent on learning and social experience, such as ethical and social values (Buss & Plomin, 1984; Goldsmith & Campos, 1982; Kagan, Reznick, & Snidman, 1988; Matheny, 1983).

Studies of infants reveal that MZ twins are more alike than DZ twins in their responses to strangers, including smiling, playing, cuddling, and expressions of fear (Goldsmith & Campos, 1982; Matheny, Wilson, Dolan, & Krantz, 1981; Plomin, 1986; Scarr & Kidd, 1983). Identical twin babies also appear to be more alike in frequency of displays of temper, demands for attention, and amount of crying (Plomin, 1986; Wilson, R. S. & Harpring, 1972). From infancy to adolescence, MZ twins resemble each other significantly more than DZ twins do in many temperamental traits, including activity, attention, task persistence, irritability, emotionality, sociability, and impulsiveness (Buss & Plomin, 1984; Cohen, Dibble, & Grawe, 1977; Goldsmith, H. H., 1983, 1984; Matheny, 1983; Torgeson & Kringlen, 1978). At later ages, significant differences between MZ and DZ twins have also been found in such characteristics as introversion-extraversion and neuroticism (Floderus-Myrhed, Pederson & Rasmuson, 1980; Matheny, 1983; Plomin, 1986; Scarr & Kidd, 1983).

Although these studies suggest that genetic factors significantly affect temperament, it should be kept in mind that virtually all personality characteristics are influenced by both genes and environment. Further, genetic predispositions can frequently be "overridden" by environmental influences. Naturally shy individuals can often be helped to become more assertive, and punitive experiences can cause exuberant extraverts to become hesitant or withdrawn.

PRENATAL DEVELOPMENT

It is a curious fact that even though we recognize that development begins at conception, we reckon a person's age from the moment of birth. We seem to regard events that occur prior to birth as unimportant. Yet the environment in which the unborn child grows has a tremendous influence on its later development, both physical and psychological.

Conception and Earliest Development

Conception occurs when a sperm from the male penetrates the cell wall of an ovum, or egg, from the female. The occasions on which this is possible are strictly limited and quite independent of the vagaries of human impulse. Once every 28 days (usually around the middle of the menstrual cycle), an ovum ripens in one of the two ovaries, is discharged into the corresponding fallopian tube, or oviduct, and begins its slow journey toward the uterus, propelled by the small, hairlike cilia that line the tube (see Figure 2.8). In most cases it takes from 3 to 7 days for the ovum to reach the uterus. If the ovum has not been fertilized in the course of this journey, it disintegrates in the uterus after a few days.

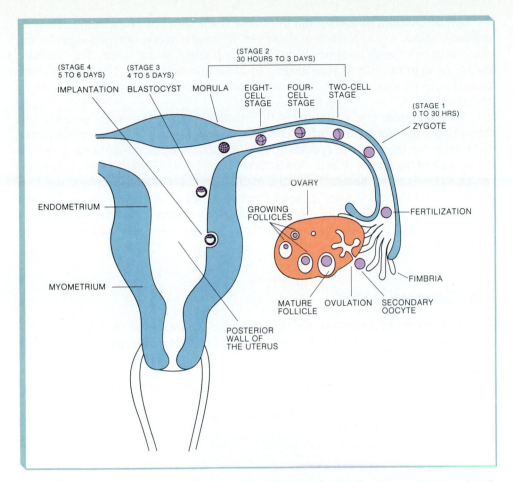

FIGURE 2.8   Diagrammatic summary of the ovarian cycle, fertilization and human development during the first week. Developmental stage 1 begins when the zygote forms. Stage 2 (days 2 to 3) comprises the early stages of cleavage (from 2 to about 16 cells, or the morula). Stage 3 (days 4 to 5) consists of the free, unattached blastocyst. In stage 4 (days 5 to 6), the blastocyst attaches to the center of the posterior wall of the uterus, the usual site of implantation. (Adapted from K. L. Moore. *The developing human: Clinically oriented embryology* [3rd ed.]. Philadelphia: W. B. Saunders, 1982. By permission.)

If, on the other hand, a mating has taken place, one of the many millions of sperm released by the male may find its way into the oviduct during the time that the ovum is making its descent. There, if it unites with the ovum, a new individual is conceived.

As indicated earlier, each sperm is a single cell that resembles a tadpole. The oval head of the sperm is packed with the 23 chromosomes. Behind the head are special structures that supply the energy required by the sperm to reach the ovum. It is estimated that the sperm travels at a velocity of about $\frac{1}{10}$ of an inch per minute.

At the moment of conception the ovum, the largest cell in the human body, is still only about $1/175$ of an inch in diameter. When the sperm enters the ovum, the nucleus of the sperm becomes fused with the nucleus of the ovum. The fertilized ovum, or **zygote**, immediately begins to grow and subdivide. The elapsed time from the sperm's penetration of the ovum to the first subdivision is usually from 24 to 36 hours.

The time from conception to birth is usually divided into three phases. The first phase, the **germinal period**, lasts from fertilization until implantation, the time when the many-celled zygote, now called a *blastocyst*, becomes firmly attached to the wall of the uterus. This period is about 10 to 14 days long. The second phase, which extends from the second to the eighth week, is the **embryonic** stage. It is characterized by cell differentiation as the major organs begin to develop. The last phase, from 8 weeks until delivery (which normally occurs at around 40 weeks), is the **fetal period**. It is characterized mainly by growth rather than by the formation of new organs.

The Germinal Period

The fertilized ovum continues to divide during its journey from the oviduct to the uterus. By the time the fertilized ovum reaches the uterus, it is about the size of a

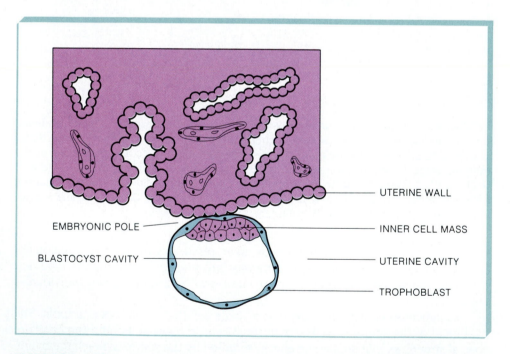

FIGURE 2.9   Schematic representation of an ovum at an early stage of implantation in the uterine wall.

pinhead and contains several dozen cells. A small cavity is formed within the mass of cells, resulting in an outer cluster of cells and a separate inner cluster (see Figure 2.9). The outer layer, called the *trophoblast*, will ultimately develop into accessory tissues that protect and nourish the embryo. The inner cluster will become the embryo itself.

While these developments are taking place, small burrlike tendrils have begun to grow around the outside of the trophoblast. In a few more days these tendrils will attach the ovum to the uterine wall. In the meantime the uterus itself has begun to undergo changes in preparation for receiving the fertilized ovum. At the time of implantation, extensions of the tendrils from the trophoblast reach into blood spaces that have formed within the maternal tissue. At this point the period of the ovum comes to an end and the second phase of prenatal development, the embryonic period, begins.

The Embryonic Period

When it enters the embryonic stage the new individual has ceased to be an independent, free-floating organism and has established a dependent relationship with the mother. Once the growing egg is successfully lodged in its new home, development is rapid. The inner cell mass, which will become a recognizable embryo, begins to differentiate into three distinct layers: (1) the *ectoderm* (outer layer), from which will develop the epidermis (the outer layer of the skin), the hair, the nails, parts of the teeth, skin glands, sensory cells, and the nervous system; (2) the *mesoderm* (middle layer), from which will develop the dermis (the inner skin layer), the muscles, the skeleton, and the circulatory and excretory organs; and (3) the *endoderm* (inner layer), from which will develop the lining of the entire gastrointestinal tract and the eustachian tubes, trachea, bronchia, lungs, liver, pancreas, salivary glands, thyroid glands, and thymus (Nilsson, Furuhjelm, Ingelman-Sundberg, & Wirsen, 1981; Moore, K. L., 1982; Rugh & Shettles, 1971).

While the inner cell mass is being differentiated into a recognizable embryo, the outer layers of cells are giving rise to two fetal membranes: the *chorion* and the *amnion*. These, together with a third membrane derived from the uterine wall, extend from the wall of the uterus and enclose the developing embryo (see Figure 2.10). They form a sac filled with a watery fluid (amniotic fluid) that acts as a buffer to protect the embryo from shocks experienced by the mother and helps maintain an even temperature for the embryo.

Simultaneously, other fetal sacs are formed; the most important of these becomes the umbilical cord. It extends from the embryo to the section of the uterine wall where the uterus and the chorion are joined. This area is called the **placenta**.

THE PLACENTAL BARRIER.   The umbilical cord is the lifeline of the embryo. Through it two arteries carry blood from the embryo to the placenta and a vein carries blood to the embryo from the placenta. However, the relationship between the

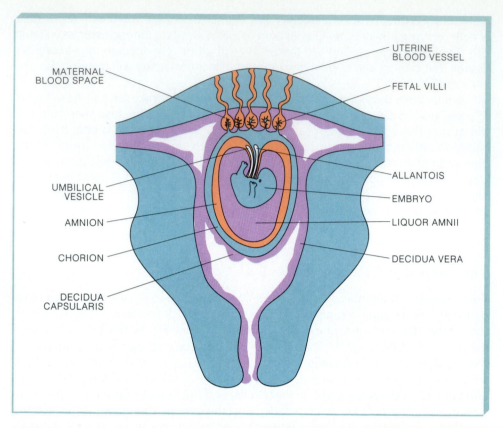

UTERINE
BLOOD VESSEL

MATERNAL
BLOOD SPACE

FETAL VILLI

ALLANTOIS

UMBILICAL
VESICLE

EMBRYO

AMNION

LIQUOR AMNII

CHORION

DECIDUA VERA

DECIDUA
CAPSULARIS

FIGURE 2.10   Diagram representing the relationship between the uterus, the membrane, and the embryo during early pregnancy. (Adapted from L. Carmichael. Origins and prenatal growth of behavior. In C. Murchinson [Ed.], A *handbook of child psychology* [2nd ed.]. Worcester, MA: Clark University Press, 1983, p. 50. By permission.)

child's bloodstream and the mother's is indirect. Both the child's and the mother's bloodstreams open into the placenta. But the two systems are always separated by semipermeable membranes that function as extremely fine screens, large enough to permit the passage of gases, salts, and other substances but too small to allow blood cells to get through.

Various nutrient substances from the mother's blood—sugars, fats, and some protein elements—permeate the placenta. Waste products from the infant, primarily carbon dioxide and other metabolites, can also pass through the placenta. In addition, some vitamins, drugs (including nicotine and alcohol), vaccines, and disease germs (e.g., diphtheria, typhoid, influenza, and rubella) may get through and affect the embryo's development. Thus, the health of the mother directly affects the health of the fetus.

There are no direct neural connections between the maternal and embryonic nervous systems; only chemicals can cross the placental barrier. Nevertheless, a mother's emotional state may indirectly influence the physiological functioning of

Steps in Prenatal Development

1 week	Fertilized ovum descends through fallopian tube toward uterus.
2 weeks	Embryo has attached itself to uterine lining and is developing rapidly.
3 weeks	Embryo has begun to take shape; head and tail regions discernible. Primitive heart begins to beat.
4 weeks	Beginnings of mouth region, gastrointestinal tract, and liver. Heart is developing rapidly, and head and brain regions are becoming more.clearly differentiated.
6 weeks	Hands and feet begin developing, but arms are still too short and stubby to meet. Liver is producing blood cells.
8 weeks	Embryo is about 1 inch long. Face, mouth, eyes, and ears have begun taking on fairly defined form. Development of muscle and cartilage has begun.
12 weeks	Fetus is about 3 inches long. It has begun to resemble a human being, though the head is disproportionately large. Face has babylike profile. Eyelids and nails have begun to form, and sex can be distinguished easily. Nervous system still very primitive.
16 weeks	Fetus is about 4½ inches long. The mother may be able to feel the fetus's movements. Extremities, head, and internal organs are developing rapidly. Body proportions are becoming more babylike.
5 months	Pregnancy half completed. Fetus is about 6 inches long and is able to hear and move about quite freely. Hands and feet are complete.
6 months	Fetus is about 10 inches long. Eyes are completely formed; taste buds appear on tongue. Fetus is capable of inhaling and exhaling and of making a thin crying noise should birth occur prematurely.
7 months	An important age. The fetus has reached the "zone of viability" (having a chance to live if born prematurely). It is physiologically capable of distinguishing basic tastes and odors. Pain sensitivity appears to be relatively absent. Breathing is shallow and irregular, and sucking and swallowing are weak.
7 months to birth	Fetus becomes increasingly ready for independent life outside the womb. Muscle tone increases; movement becomes sustained and positive; breathing, swallowing, sucking, and hunger cry become strong. Visual and auditory reactions are firmly established.

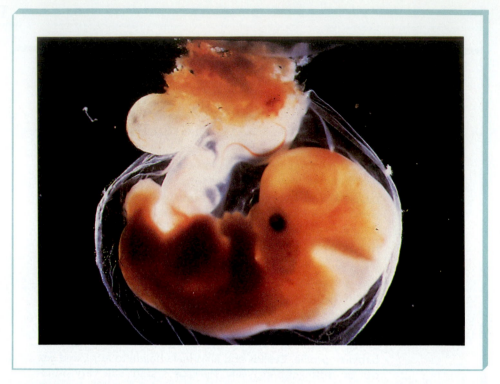

FIGURE 2.11   The human embryo at 5 to 6 weeks. The eye is seen as a dark-rimmed circle. (Copyright Petit Format/Nestle/Photo Researchers.)

her child. When the mother is emotionally aroused, a variety of physiological reactions occur and certain hormones, such as adrenaline, are released into the mother's bloodstream. Some of these substances may pass through the placenta and affect ongoing physiological processes in the unborn child (Apgar & Beck, 1974; Korones, 1986; Lubchenco, 1976).

GROWTH OF THE EMBRYO.   During the embryonic period the embryo develops extremely rapidly (see Table 2.1). By the eighteenth day it has begun to take shape. It has established a longitudinal axis; its front, back, left and right sides, head, and tail are discernible. By the end of the third week a primitive heart has developed and begun to beat.

By 4 weeks the embryo is about ¹/₅ of an inch long. It has the beginnings of a mouth region, a gastrointestinal tract, and a liver. The heart is becoming well developed, and the head and brain regions are becoming more clearly differentiated. At this stage the embryo is still a very primitive organism, however. It has no arms or legs, no developed features, and only the most elementary of body systems (see Figure 2.11).

By 8 to 9 weeks the picture has changed markedly. The embryo is now about 1 inch long. Face, mouth, eyes, and ears are fairly well defined. Arms and legs, hands

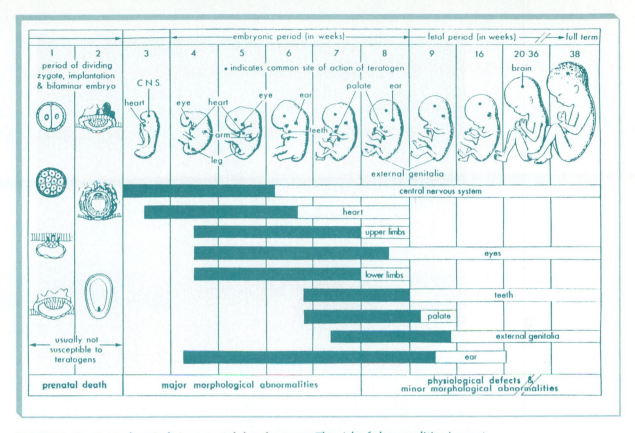

FIGURE 2.12 Critical periods in prenatal development. The risk of abnormalities is greatest (dark color) during the embryonic period, when organs are being formed and major structural (morphological) changes are occurring. (From K. L. Moore. *The developing human: Clinically oriented embryology* [4th ed.]. Philadelphia: W. B. Saunders, 1988. By permission.)

and feet, and even stubby fingers and toes have appeared; the sex organs are just beginning to form. The development of muscle and cartilage also begins, but well-defined neuromotor activity (activation of the muscles by impulses from the nerves) is still absent (Nilsson et al., 1981; Rugh & Shettles, 1971). The internal organs—intestines, liver, pancreas, lungs, kidneys—take on a definite shape and assume some degree of function. The liver, for example, begins to manufacture red blood cells.

The embryonic period is characterized by extremely rapid development of the nervous system (see Figure 2.12). During this period the head is large in relation to other parts of the body. This suggests that the first eight weeks constitute a sensitive period with respect to the integrity of the nervous system (see Figure 2.12). If there is any mechanical or chemical interference with development at this time (e.g., if the mother falls down stairs or takes an overdose of a drug), it is more likely to cause permanent damage to the nervous system than would be caused by a similar disruption at a later date. For example, if the mother contracts rubella (German

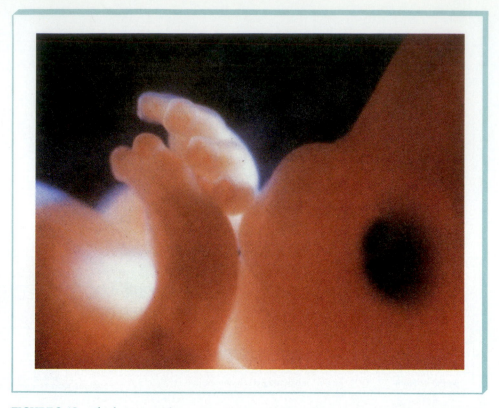

FIGURE 2.13   The human embryo at 10 weeks. Hands and fingers are now clear. (Copyright Petit Format/Nestle/Photo Researchers.)

measles) during this period, the child is more likely to be mentally deficient than if she were to have the illness during the last eight weeks of pregnancy (Lubchenco, 1976).

The Fetal Period

The third period of prenatal development, the fetal period, extends from the end of the second month until birth. During this time the various body systems, which were laid down in rudimentary form earlier, become quite well developed and begin to function. Up until about 8½ weeks the fetus has led a relatively passive existence, floating quiescently in the amniotic fluid. At this time, however, it becomes capable of responding to tactile stimulation. From this point on, motor functions become increasingly differentiated and complex (see Figure 2.13).

Toward the end of the eighth week, the reproductive system begins to develop. In both sexes the gonads (ovaries and testes) initially appear as a pair of blocks of tissue. It appears that the hormones manufactured by the male's testes are necessary to stimulate the development of a male reproductive system. If the testes are removed or fail to perform properly, the baby will possess a primarily

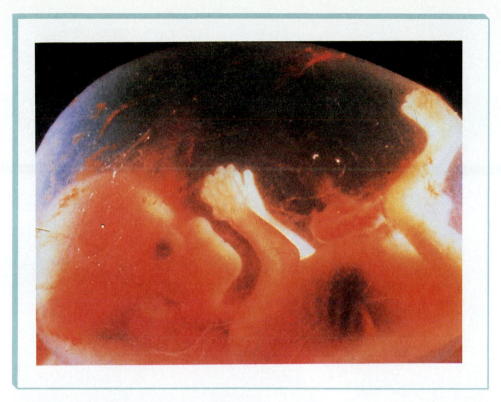

FIGURE 2.14   Human fetus at 16 weeks.
(Copyright Petit Format/Nestle/Photo Researchers.)

female reproductive system. Evidence from rabbits indicates that if the ovary is removed immediately after its formation, the female fetus develops normally. The anatomy of the female reproductive system thus can be considered basic; it is the form that will develop if either testes or ovaries are removed or do not function.

By the end of 12 weeks the fetus is about 3 inches long and weighs about ¾ ounce. It has begun to resemble a human being, though the head is disproportionately large. The muscles are becoming well developed, and spontaneous movements of the arms and legs may be observed. The eyelids and nails have begun to form, and the fetus's sex can be distinguished easily. The nervous system is still very incomplete, however.

During the next four weeks the fetus's motor behavior becomes more complex. By the end of 16 weeks the mother can feel the fetus's movements. (In popular language this is known as "the quickening.") At this point the fetus is about 4½ inches long. In the period from 16 to 20 weeks, the fetus grows to about 10 inches in length and 8 or 9 ounces in weight (see Figure 2.14). It becomes more human in appearance, and hair appears on the head and body. The mouth becomes capable of protrusion as well as opening and closing, and blinking of the eyes occurs, although the lids are still tightly fused. The hands become capable of gripping in addition to closing.

Much of the increase in the weight of the unborn baby occurs in the last three months of pregnancy.

After 20 weeks the skin begins to assume adult form, hair and nails appear, and sweat glands develop. By 24 weeks the eyes are completely formed and taste buds appear on the tongue. The fetus is now capable of "true inspiration and expiration, and of a thin crying noise" if born prematurely (Gessell, 1945, p. 71).

The fetal age of 28 weeks is an important time. It demarcates the zone between viability (ability to live if born) and nonviability. By this age the child's nervous, circulatory, and other bodily systems have become sufficiently mature to stand a chance of functioning adequately outside of the uterus, although special care is required. At this point the fetus's reactions to temperature changes approximate those of the full-term infant. Experimental studies of infants born at this age indicate that the fetus can differentiate among the basic tastes—sweet, salt, sour, and bitter—and among basic odors. Visual and auditory reactions occur, though not as clearly as in the full-term infant. On the other hand, sensitivity to pain seems to be slight or absent in the premature infant.

THE LAST THREE MONTHS.   The period from 28 weeks to birth at full term (38 to 42 weeks) is marked by further development of the basic body structures and functions. Gains in body weight and height continue to be rapid. By 7 months the average unborn baby weighs about 4 pounds and is 16 inches long. During the eighth month another 1⅓ pounds and 2 inches will be added. Much of the weight gain during these last three months comes from a padding of fat beneath the skin which will help to insulate the newborn baby from changes in temperature after birth (Apgar & Beck, 1974).

Each additional week that the fetus remains within the mother's uterus increases the likelihood of survival and normal development. As muscle tone improves, a good hunger cry and a strong sucking reflex develop, and mental alertness and perceptual and motor development increase. By the time the unborn infant weighs 3½ pounds, the chances of successful postnatal development are markedly improved; a baby born weighing at least 5 pounds will probably not need to be placed in an incubator (Apgar & Beck, 1974; Korones, 1986; Lubchenco, 1976).

By the beginning of the ninth month, the unborn baby, who once floated in weightless ease in the fluid of the amniotic sac, has grown so large that movement inside the uterus is quite constricted. Usually the fetus settles into a head-down position because this gives it the most room in the uterus, which is shaped like an inverted pear. Consequently, most babies are born head first, the easiest and safest way. However, about 10 percent of babies assume a feet-first position, which requires a breech delivery. A few maintain a crosswise position and may require delivery by means of a caesarean section. The average full-term baby is 20 to 21 inches long and weighs 7½ pounds, but a wide range of heights and weights are considered normal.

PRENATAL ENVIRONMENTAL INFLUENCES

There are many variations in prenatal environment, and the pressures to which one fetus is subjected may differ greatly from those exerted on another. Recent research suggests that the mother's physical and emotional state—and, consequently, the prenatal environment she provides—have important influences on fetal development and the subsequent health and adjustment of the child. Some of the more important prenatal environmental factors that have been investigated will be discussed in the following sections.

Infants born to teenage mothers are at greater risk than those born to mothers between the ages of 20 and 35.

Age of the Mother

With increasing numbers of adolescents becoming pregnant and many women in their thirties having children for the first time; there has been growing interest in the effects of age on fertility and on the health of both the infant and the mother. To place the issue in perspective, it should be noted that morbidity (disease or illness) and mortality risks at all ages have declined markedly in recent years. For example, in the United States the infant mortality rate has declined from 140 per 1000 live births at the turn of the century to 11 per 1000 today (U.S. Bureau of the Census, 1987). Despite our wealth as a nation, approximately 14 countries have lower infant mortality rates due to greater availability of proper health care and nutritional assistance for infants and their mothers (Conger, 1988; Schorr, 1988).

With good medical care, proper health practices, and adequate nutrition, most women of all ages will have healthy babies and will remain healthy themselves. Nevertheless, the years between 20 and 35 remain the most favorable ones for childbearing. As we shall see, the pregnancies of adolescents—particularly younger adolescents—are more likely than those of women in their twenties to endanger the health of both mother and child, although the risks are substantially reduced by adequate prenatal and postnatal care and good nutrition (Hayes, 1987; Menken, 1980). Currently, babies of teenage mothers are more likely to have low birth weights (a major cause of infant mortality) as well as neurological defects and childhood illnesses. The mothers themselves are more likely to have complications of pregnancy such as toxemia and anemia. Among very young teenagers (those under 15), pregnancy tends to inhibit the mother's growth as well as the child's (Gunter & LaBarba, 1980; Alan Guttmacher Institute, 1981; Hayes, 1987).

Women over 30 have a lower fertility rate than those in their twenties, and fertility continues to decline with age (Guttmacher & Kaiser, 1986). They are also more likely than younger women to experience illnesses during pregnancy and to have longer and more difficult labor. Mothers over 40 run a sharply increased risk of having a child with a chromosomal abnormality, particularly Down's syndrome. The average incidence of this disorder increases from less than 1 per 1000 through age 29 to 1.5 at ages 30-34, 6 at ages 35-39, 20 at ages 40-44, and 30 at ages over 45 (Guttmacher & Kaiser, 1986). Women over 35 are also more likely to have miscarriages and to give birth to underweight or stillborn babies (Kopp & Parmelee, 1979; Korones, 1986; Lubchenco, 1976). The older the woman, the greater the likelihood that these problems will arise; nevertheless, the absolute incidence of serious complications remains relatively small, especially for women who engage in good health practices and receive appropriate medical care. In cases in which there is reason to suspect the presence of a chromosomal or other abnormality, a procedure known as *amniocentesis* may be recommended (see Box 2.2).

Maternal Nutrition

An expectant mother should have an adequate diet if she is to maintain her own health during pregnancy and deliver a healthy infant. This appears entirely reasonable when we remember that the growing fetus's food supply comes from the

BOX 2.2

What Is Amniocentesis?

In the process known as amniocentesis a fine, hollow needle is inserted through the lower part of the abdominal wall into the amniotic sac that surrounds and protects the fetus, and a small amount of amniotic fluid (about two-thirds of an ounce) is removed (see figure). The procedure is usually carried out 16 to 18 weeks after pregnancy has begun. Amniotic fluid contains fetal cells that have been sloughed off in the normal course of events, just as we shed cells when we peel after a sunburn. These cells are cultured in a cytogenetics laboratory, and a chromosome analysis is performed. Because each cell in the body contains a replication of all the chromosomes that constitute our genetic inheritance, these cells can be examined for the presence of a number of chromosomal and metabolic disorders.

To date, over 75 different genetically based diseases—many of them extremely rare—can be detected by means of amniocentesis, and the number is growing. Included are abnormalities in the *autosomal chromosomes*, as in Down's syndrome, and *sex-chromosome* abnormalities, where there is an excess number of X or Y chromosomes. Amniocentesis can also detect a number of *metabolic diseases* (inborn errors of body chemistry that result in faulty production of enzymes) through excretions that appear in the amniotic fluid. Some of these metabolic diseases, such as Tay-Sachs disease (which leads to mental retardation and early death at age 2 or 3), are concentrated in particular races, religions, or geographic areas because of selective mating over long periods.

A number of genetic disorders are sex-linked—that is, their genes are carried on a sex chromosome. For example, *hemophilia*, a defect in the ability of the blood to clot properly, is carried on the X chromosome. The daughter of a woman who is a carrier of this disease will almost never have the disease, because it will be masked by the presence of a normal gene on her other X chromosome. Any sons, however, will have a 50 percent chance of developing the disease because they do not have a second X chromosome that can carry a normal gene to protect them. Because amniocentesis reveals the sex of the fetus, a mother who may be a carrier for hemophilia or another X-linked disorder can normally feel reassured if her unborn baby is a girl.

The risk from amniocentesis to mother and fetus is minimal. Harmless ultrasonic pictures (sonographs) are used to show the exact location of the baby and the placenta in the uterus. Nevertheless, the test is *not* indicated for every pregnant woman. It should be done only where there is a good medical reason for such prenatal diagnosis—not, for example, merely to determine the sex of the baby out of curiosity.

In general, amniocentesis is recommended when the family history of either the mother or father indicates that the fetus might have a genetic disease that can be detected—or ruled out—by this procedure. It is also useful for older women, particularly after age 40, largely because of the increased risk of Down's syndrome (from Moore, K. L., 1982; Rubin, S., 1980; Rugh & Shettles, 1971).

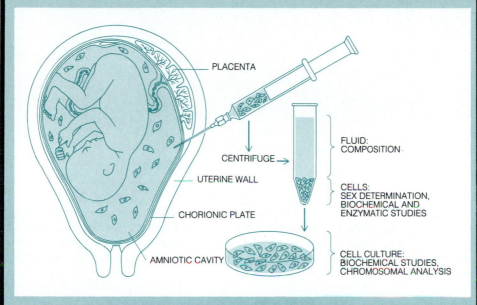

Amniocentesis. Amniotic fluid is removed from the amniotic sac and analyzed for chromosomal metabolic disorders. (Adapted from T. Friedman. Prenatal diagnosis of genetic disease. *Scientific American*, November 1971, 225, 34–42. Copyright © 1971 by Scientific American, Inc. All rights reserved. By permission.)

mother's bloodstream via the semipermeable membranes of the placenta and the umbilical cord. Babies born to mothers with nutritionally deficient diets are more likely to have low birth weights, to suffer from impaired brain development, to be less resistant to illnesses such as pneumonia and bronchitis, and to have a higher risk of mortality in the first year of life (Dobbing, 1976; Katz, Keusch, & Mata, 1975; Knoblock & Pasaminick, 1966; Kopp & Parmelee, 1979; Metcoff, 1978).

In one well-controlled study in Guatemala, the residents of two villages received nourishing supplemental diets for several years while the residents of two similar villages received soda pop supplements. Not only did infant mortality and morbidity go down and birth weight rise in the first two villages, but children from those villages scored somewhat better on mental tests at the end of seven years. These findings indicate that severe maternal malnutrition may impair the child's in-

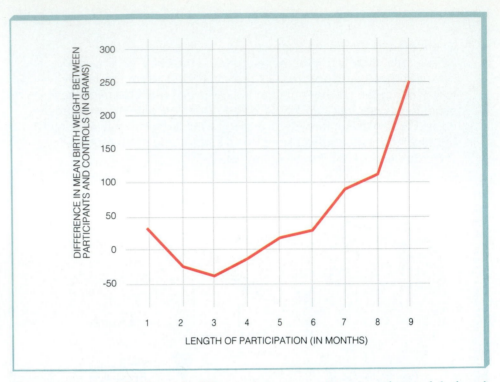

FIGURE 2.15   Mean birth-weight difference between participants and controls by length of participation in a federal nutrition program. (Adapted from M. Kotelchuck, J. Schwartz, M. Anderka, & K. Finison. 1980 *Massachusetts special supplemental food program for women, infants and children evaluation project.* Department of Public Health, Boston, 1983. By permission.)

tellectual development in addition to having adverse effects on physical development (Bhatia, Katiyar, & Apaswol, 1979; Cravioto & DeLicardie, 1978; Katz et al., 1975; Metcoff, 1978).

In a controlled study of the effectiveness of a federally funded nutritional supplement program for needy, high-risk pregnant women, mothers, and infants in Massachusetts, it was found that participation by pregnant women for at least four months resulted in infants with significantly higher birth weight, less prematurity, and decreased neonatal mortality (Kotelchuck, Schwartz, Anderka, & Finison, 1983). Moreover, the longer the subjects participated in the program, the more impressive the results were (see Figure 2.15). The relatively modest cost of adequate health care and nutritional programs for mothers and infants is clearly a good investment; it saves later medical and educational costs that are required for children who have birth defects, mental retardation, or other problems as a result of poor prenatal nutrition.

Nevertheless, funding for prenatal and postnatal medical care, disease prevention, counselling, and nutrition for poor families have declined steadily in the 1980s (Conger, 1988; Edelman, 1987; Schorr, in press). The United States' progress toward reducing infant mortality came to a halt in 1985; among black infants,

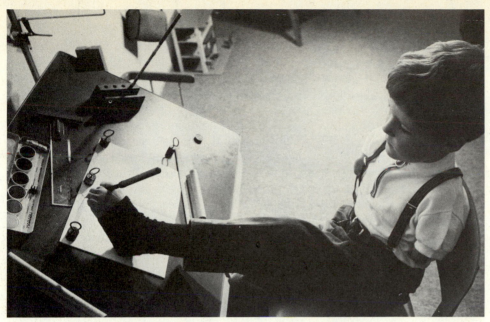

Some of the "thalidomide babies" born around 1960 have received extensive physical and rehabilitation therapy and can function remarkably well despite their severe handicaps.

neonatal mortality (death in the first 28 days of life) rose for the first time in twenty years (CDF Reports, 1988).

Drugs

During the past two decades physicians and parents have become increasingly concerned about the potentially harmful effects of drugs on the developing embryo and fetus. One of the most dramatic reasons for this concern was the discovery around 1960 that the gross anatomical defects of a certain group of babies had been caused by a drug, thalidomide, that had been taken by their mothers during pregnancy. Many other drugs are suspected of producing birth defects when taken during pregnancy; these include some antibiotics, hormones, steroids, anticoagulants, narcotics, tranquilizers, and possibly some hallucinogenic drugs (Apgar & Beck, 1974; Catz & Yaffe, 1978; Moore, K. L., 1982). Use of cocaine during the second half of pregnancy may result in separation of the placenta, which can cause fetal distress, premature labor, and death (Behrman & Vaughn, 1987; Madden, Payne, & Miller, 1986).

Many pregnant women who took the drug stilbestrol (an estrogenic compound) to prevent miscarriages had daughters who developed cancer of the vagina during adolescence (Moore, K. L., 1982). Industrial pollutants may also pose serious hazards (Illingworth, 1987). Even commonly used substances may adversely affect fetal development, particularly in the early months of pregnancy. For example, there is some evidence that aspirin taken in large doses may be harmful to the embryo or fetus (Catz & Yaffe, 1978; Corby, 1978; Moore, K. L., 1982).

FETAL ALCOHOL SYNDROME.   Drinking by pregnant women can produce *fetal alcohol syndrome* (Abel, 1980; Behrman & Vaughn, 1987; Jones, K. L., Smith, Ulleland, & Streissguth, 1973). The symptoms of this condition include retarded prenatal and postnatal growth, premature birth, mental retardation, physical malformations, sleep disturbances, and congenital heart disease. The heavier the pregnant woman's drinking, the greater the risk of fetal alcohol syndrome. One-third or more of the babies of heavy drinkers are born with this syndrome (Behrman & Vaughn, 1987). Although the incidence of fetal alcohol syndrome is far lower among the babies of moderate drinkers, it is still significantly higher than among the babies of abstainers. In one study, 12 percent of the babies of moderate drinkers (i.e., those who consume about 2 ounces a day of 100-proof alcohol) showed one or more signs of fetal alcohol syndrome (Hanson, 1977). Moderate drinking also increases the likelihood of low birth weight, developmental delays, physical difficulties (e.g., breathing and sucking problems), and spontaneous abortion (Moore, K. L., 1982; Streissguth, Barr, & Martin, 1983: Streissguth et al., 1984). It is estimated that each year at least 6000 infants born in the United States suffer from fetal alcohol syndrome.

NICOTINE.   Smoking by a pregnant woman retards the growth of the fetus and lowers the newborn's birth weight and resistance to illness (Korones, 1986; Moore, K. L., 1982; Page, Villee, & Villee, 1981). It also increases the chances of spontaneous abortion and premature birth, and may affect long-term physical and intellectual development as a consequence of the reduced capacity of the mother's blood to transport oxygen to the fetus (Behrman & Vaughn, 1987; Moore, K. L., 1982; Page, Villee, & Villee, 1981; *Smoking and health*, 1979).

DRUGS TAKEN DURING LABOR AND DELIVERY.   Drugs such as pentobarbital or meperidine (Demerol), that are taken just prior to delivery of a baby in order to ease a mother's distress or pain, may make the infant less attentive, at least temporarily. One study of the effects of anesthetic drugs on sensorimotor functions in newborns found lags in muscular, visual, and neural functioning (Brackbill, 1979; Conway & Brackbill, 1970). Although most such effects were greatest in the first few days of life, longer-term effects on cognitive functioning and gross motor abilities, particularly in cases of heavy drug dosages, have been found at 1 year of age (Brackbill, 1979; Goldstein, K. M., Caputo, & Taub, 1976; Standley, 1979).

OTHER DRUGS.   Pregnant women who are addicted to narcotic drugs such as heroin, methadone, and phenobarbital pass on their addiction to their unborn babies. Babies born to crack cocaine users are likely to have severe and persistent neurobehavioral problems (Behrman & Vaughn, 1987; Madden, Payne, & Miller, 1986). Withdrawal symptoms in an addicted newborn may emerge as early as 18 hours or as late as a week after birth. Addicted infants become irritable, tense, overactive, and fussy; they resist cuddling, sleep irregularly, and tend to cry in a high-pitched tone (Adamsons, 1987; Householder, Hatcher, Burns & Chasnoff, 1982; Kopp & Parmelee, 1979; Korones, 1986). When it is known that an infant is addicted, appropriate therapy can be instituted to replace the addicting drug with something less harmful and allow the infant to be withdrawn gradually.

Radiation

Another potential source of birth defects is radiation (X-ray) of the mother during pregnancy. This can result from treatment of pelvic cancer, from diagnostic testing, or from exposure to atomic energy sources, occupational hazards, or fallout (Brent & Harris, 1976; Illingworth, 1987; Kliegman & King, 1983). Although the hazards of radiation are not fully understood, it is clear that radiation can have a wide range of effects on unborn children, including death, malformation, brain damage, increased susceptibility to certain forms of cancer, shortened life span, and "mutations in genes whose effects may not be felt for generations" (Apgar & Beck, 1974, p. 107). Radiation that occurs between the time of fertilization and the time when the ovum becomes implanted in the uterus is thought to destroy the fertilized ovum in almost every case. The greatest danger of malformations comes between the second and sixth weeks after conception. Although the effects of X-rays may be less dramatic later in pregnancy, there is still some risk of damage, particularly to the brain and other body systems.

Maternal Diseases and Disorders During Pregnancy

In early pregnancy the placenta acts as a barrier against some harmful agents (e.g., larger organisms, such as syphilitic spirochetes and some bacteria). But even at this stage it allows many substances to reach the unborn child, and more can permeate it later. Some of these substances have positive effects. Antibodies produced by the mother to combat infectious diseases are transmitted to the fetus, usually producing immunity at birth and for some months thereafter. Other substances, including viruses, microorganisms, and various chemicals, may have extremely negative effects.

Viral diseases such as cytomegalovirus disease (which affects 5 to 6 percent of pregnant women), rubella (German measles), chicken pox, and hepatitis are particularly dangerous during the embryonic and early fetal periods (Behrman & Vaughn, 1987; Little, G. A., 1987). One of the most serious viral diseases during the first three months of pregnancy is rubella, which may produce heart malformations, deafness, blindness, or mental retardation. About 50 percent of babies whose mothers had German measles in the first month of pregnancy suffer birth defects; this figure falls to 22 percent in the second month, 6 percent in the third month, and only a small number thereafter (Babson, Pernoll, & Benda, 1980; Lubchenco, 1976; Moore, K. L., 1982). A pregnant woman can be tested to see whether she has already had rubella, but if she has not, she cannot be given vaccine for rubella because it contains live German measles viruses.

The rapid spread of the genital herpes virus among young adults poses another danger. Infection of the fetus with this virus usually occurs late in pregnancy—probably during delivery—and can result in severe neurological damage. When infection occurs several weeks prior to birth, a variety of congenital abnormalities can result. Prompt medical intervention is necessary if the presence of herpes during pregnancy is suspected (Dudgeon, 1976; Moore, K. L., 1982).

AIDS (acquired immune deficiency syndrome) currently threatens the lives of a growing number of unborn and newborn babies. Mothers with AIDS can pass the virus to their babies, either across the placental barrier during pregnancy or in some cases, by breast feeding (Curran et al., 1988; Koop, 1986). Typically, the course of AIDS in infants is much more rapid than in adults, averaging about four months from acquisition to death. The percentage of pregnant women who have developed AIDS or ARC (AIDS-related complex)—principally through intravenous drug use or from a bisexual or drug-using partner—is still relatively small. However, it is rising rapidly, especially among poverty-stricken inner-city blacks and Hispanics. A recent study of consecutive births in New York City found that 1 of every 60 babies born over a 30-day period tested positively for the presence of AIDS antibodies in the blood (Lambert, 1988). Although this does not establish that these babies will develop AIDS (probably about 40 percent will), it does indicate that their mothers were exposed to the AIDS virus.

Infection of the fetus with spirochetes from a syphilitic mother is not infrequent. Fortunately, however, the placental barrier does not permit passage of the spirochetes until after the fourth or fifth month of pregnancy. Consequently, transmission of the spirochetes (which otherwise would take place in about 24 percent of cases) may be prevented if treatment of a syphilitic mother begins early in pregnancy. When infection does occur, the spirochetes may produce miscarriage or a weak, deformed, or mentally deficient newborn. In some cases the child may not manifest symptoms of syphilis for several years.

Some general disturbances of the mother during pregnancy may also affect the fetus. One of the most common of these is *toxemia of pregnancy*, a disorder of unknown cause that affects about 5 percent of pregnant women in the United States. In its mildest form, toxemia is characterized by high blood pressure, rapid and excessive weight gain, and retention of fluid in the tissues. Prompt treatment usually ends the danger. However, if the disorder continues to progress, it can lead to convulsions and coma, resulting in death in about 13 percent of mothers and about 50 percent of their unborn infants. Children whose mothers had severe toxemia during pregnancy run a risk of lowered intelligence (Lubchenco, 1976).

The Rh Factor

The term R*h factor* refers to a chemical factor that is present in the blood of approximately 85 percent of the population, although there are racial and ethnic variations. In itself, the presence or absence of this factor makes no difference to a person's health. But when an Rh-positive man is married to an Rh-negative woman, there can sometimes be adverse consequences for their offspring. If their baby has Rh-positive blood, the mother's blood may begin to form antibodies against the "foreign" positive Rh factor. During the next pregnancy the antibodies in the mother's blood may attack the Rh-positive blood of the unborn infant. The resulting destruction may be limited, causing only mild anemia, or extensive, causing cerebral palsy, deafness, mental retardation, or even death.

Fortunately, a way of preventing these consequences has been developed. The blood of the newborn infant is tested immediately after birth, using a blood sample from the umbilical cord. If an Rh-positive child has been born to an Rh-negative mother, the mother is given a vaccine that will seek out and destroy the baby's Rh-positive blood cells before the mother's body begins producing many antibodies. The red cells of later children will not be attacked because the blood of the mother was never allowed to develop the antibodies (Apgar & Beck, 1974; Lubchenco, 1976).

Maternal Stress

Even though there are no direct connections between the maternal and fetal nervous systems, the mother's emotional state can influence the fetus's reactions and development. This is true because emotions like rage, fear, and anxiety bring the mother's autonomic nervous system into action, liberating certain chemicals (e.g., acetylcholine and epinephrine) into the bloodstream. In addition, under such conditions the endocrine glands, particularly the adrenals, secrete different kinds and amounts of hormones. As the composition of the blood changes, new substances are transmitted through the placenta, producing changes in the fetus's circulatory system.

These changes may be irritating to the fetus. One study noted that bodily movements of fetuses increased by several hundred percent while their mothers were undergoing emotional stress (Sontag, 1944). If the mother's emotional upset lasted several weeks, fetal activity continued at an exaggerated level throughout the entire period. When the upset was brief, heightened irritability usually lasted several hours. Prolonged emotional stress during pregnancy may have lasting consequences for the child. Infants born to upset, unhappy mothers are more likely to be premature or have low birth weights; to be hyperactive and irritable; and to manifest difficulties such as irregular eating, excessive bowel movements, gas pains, sleep disturbances, excessive crying, and excessive need to be held (David, DeVault, & Talmadge, 1961; Joffe, 1969; Sameroff & Zax, 1973; Sontag, 1944).

It is important to keep in mind that the great majority of babies are born healthy, including those of mothers who may have smoked, consumed alcohol in moderation, eaten a less than perfect diet, or received medication during delivery. Moreover, infants and young children have an immense capacity for recovering from all but severe prenatal and perinatal stress (see Box 2.3). Yet there can be no doubt that future mothers and fathers would be well advised to do everything they reasonably can to foster their baby's optimal development.

THE BIRTH PROCESS

Anoxia and Other Complications

The ease or difficulty with which a baby is born and how quickly it begins to breathe can affect its well-being. One major danger associated with birth is

BOX 2.3

The Children of Kauai

A massive longitudinal study of all pregnancies and births on the Hawaiian island of Kauai over more than a decade focused on later consequences of *perinatal stress* (problems that occur around the time of birth). With increases in the severity of such stress, there was a corresponding increase in the percentage of children who were rated below normal in physical and intellectual status by the age of 2. However, by age 10 the differences between children who had encountered varying degrees of perinatal complications were less than they had been at age 2. Most of the negative outcomes occurred in a small group of survivors of severe perinatal stress. The strongest relationships occurred in cases of physical handicaps related to central nervous system impairment and mental retardation or learning difficulties.

By age 18, the greatest number of physical, mental, social, and emotional problems were still found in the survivors of severe perinatal stress. Among the survivors of moderate perinatal stress, the rate of serious mental health problems, mental retardation, and teenage pregnancies was considerably higher than in 18-year-olds born without stress, but in both groups only a small minority were involved. In brief, the long-term consequences of mild or moderate perinatal stress appear to be modest. Even among those with severe stress, a clear majority are functioning adequately.

Furthermore, at ages 10 and 18 ten times more children had problems attributable to a poor childrearing environment than problems caused by the effects of severe perinatal stress (from Werner, Bierman, & French, 1971; Werner & Smith, 1982). Overall, the investigators found that

> perinatal complications were consistently related to later impaired physical and psychological development *only* when combined with persistently poor environmental circumstances (e.g., chronic poverty, family instability, or maternal health problem). Children who were raised in more affluent homes, with an intact family and a well-educated mother, showed few, if any, negative effects from reproductive stress, unless there was severe central nervous system impairment. (Werner & Smith, 1982, p. 31)

hemorrhaging, which is caused when very strong pressure on the head of the fetus breaks blood vessels in the brain. Another danger is failure of the infant to begin breathing soon after being separated from the maternal source of oxygen. Both hemorrhaging and failure to breathe affect the supply of oxygen to the nerve cells of the brain and produce a state called *anoxia*. The neurons of the central nervous system require oxygen; if they are deprived of it, some cells may die, and this can cause physical and psychological defects. If too many neurons die, the infant may suffer serious brain damage, or, in extreme cases, may die.

Anoxia in a newborn is more likely to damage the cells of the brain stem than those of the cortex, and to result in motor defects. The child may experience paralysis of the legs or arms, a tremor of the face or fingers, or inability to use the vocal muscles. In this last case, the child may have difficulty learning to speak. The term *cerebral palsy* describes a variety of motor defects associated with damage to the brain cells, possibly as a result of lack of oxygen during the birth process. It is estimated that about 30 percent of cerebral palsy cases involve problems that occurred during birth or immediately afterward (Apgar & Beck, 1974; Kopp & Parmelee, 1979; Lubchenco, 1976).

Anoxic infants are more irritable and show more muscular tension and rigidity than normal infants do during the first week (Graham, F. K., Matarazzo, & Caldwell, 1956; Korones, 1986; Voorhies & Vanucci, 1984). Infants with mild anoxia score lower on tests of motor development and attention during the first year and are more distractible (Corah, Anthony, Painter, Stern, & Thurston, 1965; Ernhart, Graham, & Thurston, 1960; Lubchenco, 1976). At age 3, they perform less well on tests of conceptualization. By age 7 or 8, behavioral differences between normal and mildly anoxic children are generally small, and their IQ scores are equal. In brief, the differences between mildly anoxic and normal children become smaller with age, and there is at present no firm evidence of serious and permanent intellectual damage. As indicated in Box 2.3, the same is true for children who suffer other stresses at the time of birth.

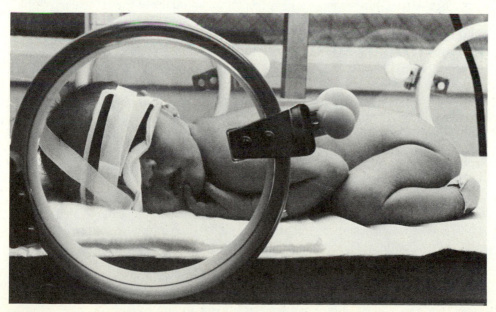

Premature infants must receive intensive care in the hospital for several weeks before they can be transferred to the home environment.

Prematurity

Infants born earlier than the thirty-eighth week of gestation and weighing less than 5 pounds are referred to as **premature**. Prematurity is more frequent among economically disadvantaged mothers than among the affluent. We have already noted that smoking, alcohol, and various drugs increase the likelihood that a baby will be born prematurely. Multiple births (twins, triplets, etc.) also tend to be premature.

There is a significant correlation between the birth weights of infants and the birth weights of their mothers, and there are also ethnic differences (even after controlling for the effects of such factors as maternal nutrition, smoking, and alcohol and drug use). This suggests that genetic factors play a role in determining birth weight (Klebanoff, Gronbard, Kessel, & Berendes, 1984; Shiono, Klebanoff, Gronbard, Berendes, & Rhoades, 1986).

The long-term effects of prematurity on development depend on how early the infant is born (gestational age), its birth weight, the type of postnatal care it receives, and the quality of its environment during early and middle childhood. Infants with gestation periods of less than 28 weeks ("extreme prematurity") or weights of less than 3.3 pounds have a reduced chance of survival. In contrast, those who are only slightly premature (34-38 weeks) and whose weight is appropriate for their gestational age resemble full-term babies in many ways. They are generally healthy, though they are less mature, more vulnerable to illness, and slower to gain weight, and they must be monitored carefully (Hack, 1983; Kopp & Parmelee, 1979; Korones, 1986; Lubchenco, 1976; Lubchenko, Searls, & Brazie, 1972).

Neonatal risk of mortality or handicap is a function of both gestational age and birth weight. An infant who is significantly premature *and* has a low birth weight for its gestational age faces a more serious risk than an infant of the same gestational age whose birth weight is age-appropriate. In general, risks appear highest for the small minority of infants that weigh less than 1500 grams (3.3 pounds) at birth (Allen, 1984; Battaglia & Simmons, 1978; Lubchenco, 1976). Recently, however, considerable progress has been made in caring for extremely premature infants and for "intermediate-term" infants, those that fall in the middle range of prematurity. These babies' gestational ages range between 30 and 33 weeks, and their birth weights are at least average for their age—around 1500 grams (3.3 pounds) or more at 30 weeks and 2000 grams (4.4 pounds) or more at 33 weeks. Premature babies that have received intensive, highly specialized care in university medical centers and major community hospitals have not only survived but gone on to develop normally (Allen, 1984; Battaglia & Simmons, 1978; Brandt, 1978).

Many treatment programs for premature infants provide sensory and tactile stimulation and encourage parents to participate in the child's care while the child is hospitalized. Some investigators have thought that children would benefit from rocking and gentle tactile stimulation that stimulates the conditions in the uterus. Others have provided visual, tactile, and auditory stimuli (such as mobiles and sounds) that are thought to facilitate development in newborn infants. Such programs appear to produce short-term benefits for premature children, but the differences that can be attributed to them decrease with age.

Like children who experience anoxia or complications during birth, premature children are particularly vulnerable to the effects of their environment. In homes with poor parental care and living conditions, premature babies are far more likely than full-term children to have both physical and psychological difficulties. Prematurity and perinatal complications are more frequent among economically disadvantaged families than among middle-class families, heightening the chances that a poor child will have to deal both with impairment at birth *and* a less favorable environment (Lubchenco, 1976; Richmond, 1982; Wilson, R. S., 1985). Premature children who are born into loving, nurturing homes where they receive competent physical and psychological care usually show little long-range impairment unless they were very premature or did not receive appropriate neonatal or postnatal care (Apgar & Beck, 1974; Battaglia & Simmons, 1978; Werner & Smith, 1982; Wilson, R. S., 1985).

SUMMARY

The development of every individual begins when a sperm cell from the father penetrates the wall of an ovum from the mother. At that time both the sperm and the ovum release 23 *chromosomes*, each of which is subdivided into many thousands of *genes*. The genes contain the child's biological heritage.

The basic mechanism of hereditary transmission is the replication of deoxyribonucleic acid (DNA). DNA is composed of two molecular chains coiled around each other to form a double-stranded helix. When DNA replicates itself the strands separate and reconstitute themselves to form two new helixes, each of which is chemically identical to the one from which it was derived. The process by which the original fertilized ovum multiples to form new cells is called *mitosis*.

The reason children of the same parents are not identical is that the germ cells, from which sperm and ova are derived, differ from other cells in the process by which they divide. That process, *meiosis*, results in cells whose nuclei contain only half the number of chromosomes present in the parent cell. This means that different sperm and ova contain different sets of chromosomes. In addition, a process called *crossing-over*, in which pairs of chromosomes exchange genetic material, increases the likelihood that each sperm or ovum will be unique.

One of the 23 pairs of chromosomes contains the *sex chromosomes* and determines the sex of the child. In females both members of the pair are X chromosomes; male body cells contain one X and one Y chromosome. However, as a result of meiosis sperm cells may contain either an X or a Y chromosome. When a sperm containing a Y chromosome unites with an ovum, which contains an X chromosome, a male child is produced.

Genes may be either *dominant* or *recessive*; if a dominant gene is present, the effect of a recessive gene for the same trait (e.g., eye color) will be masked. Most behavioral traits are *multifactorial*, meaning that they depend on more than one genetic or environmental factor. A particular characteristic may require the presence of a number of genes, a situation that is termed *polygenetic inheritance*.

Physical features depend heavily on heredity, but the extent to which intelligence (as measured by intelligence tests) is influenced by heredity is a subject of controversy. It is difficult to isolate the potential effects of heredity from those of other variables such as good health and superior educational opportunities. Twin studies have found a higher correlation between the IQs of monozygotic ("identical") twins than between those of dizygotic ("fraternal") twins or nontwin siblings. Even twin studies are not entirely definitive, though, since monozygotic twins may not be biologically identical and the environmental influences to which dizygotic twins are exposed may be less similar than those to which monozygotic twins are exposed. Moreover, there are similarities between adoptive parents and their adopted children, suggesting that environmental as well as genetic factors play an important role in a child's intellectual performance.

Numerous known gene defects may result in mental retardation and other developmental disabilities. In some instances, as in the case of phenylketonuria, genes fail to give the cells the proper instructions to produce enzymes needed for normal development; in others, abnormalities in the structure of the chromosomes may be responsible for mental retardation. Studies of children with sex chromosome abnormalities (SCA) indicate that a nurturant home environment can reduce the effects of less extreme forms of SCA on development.

Certain mental disorders are caused by infection, but others, such as schizophrenia and affective disorders, appear to be caused at least partially by genetic factors. It may be more correct to speak of inheriting vulnerability to these disorders than to speak of inheriting the disorders themselves. Certain personality characteristics also may be affected by genetic factors; in general, genetic influences are strongest on basic temperamental characteristics (e.g., activity-passivity). However, genetic predispositions can be overridden by environmental influences.

The time from conception to birth is usually divided into three phases: the *germinal period*, which lasts from fertilization until implantation; the *embryonic period*, in which the major organs begin to develop; and the *fetal period*, which is characterized mainly by growth. Throughout prenatal development the bloodstreams of the mother and child are separated by the placental barrier, but certain substances, including nutrients from the mother and waste products from the infant, pass through the barrier. Some vitamins, drugs, vaccines, and disease germs may also get through and affect the embryo's development. The fetus becomes viable (able to live if born) at 28 weeks.

Prenatal environmental influences can significantly affect the individual's development. These influences include the age of the mother (the years between 20 and 35 appear most favorable); maternal nutrition; drugs, including alcohol, nicotine, certain antibiotics, hormones, steroids, and narcotics, all of which can adversely affect fetal development; X-rays; maternal diseases and disorders, such as rubella and AIDS, chicken pox, genital herpes, and toxemia of pregnancy; and a negative Rh factor in the blood. The mother's emotional state also affects the fetus.

The ease or difficulty with which a baby is born and how quickly it begins to breathe can affect its well-being. Interruptions in the supply of oxygen to the nerve cells of the brain produce *anoxia*, which can cause serious brain damage or death. Another cause of problems for newborns is premature birth. Premature babies usually have low birth weights and, therefore, a higher risk of mortality. Considerable progress has been made in caring for extremely premature and "intermediate-term" infants. Premature children raised in favorable home environments usually show little long-range impairment.

Fortunately, the vast majority of all babies born in this country do not experience any of the problems discussed in this chapter. Most infants begin life well within the normal range. In addition, infants are surprisingly malleable, and many children apparently recover from early deficits, whether they are due to prematurity, anoxia, or other mild to moderate developmental problems.

REVIEW QUESTIONS

1. What is the basic unit of hereditary transmission? By what means does hereditary transmission occur?

2. Why is each human being genetically unique?

3. What is meant by the terms *dominant* and *recessive*? What is polygenetic inheritance?

4. Briefly describe the current state of research concerning the influence of heredity on intelligence.

5. What role do genetic factors play in the occurrence of mental disorders such as schizophrenia and bipolar (manic-depressive) disorders?

6. Describe the difficulties encountered in investigating the role of genetic factors in the development of personality. Is there evidence that they play any role at all?

7. Briefly describe the three major periods of development between conception and birth.

8. What aspects of the prenatal environment influence fetal development and the subsequent health and adjustment of the child?

9. What features of the birth process may affect the well-being of the infant?

10. What is meant by prematurity? What are its implications?

GLOSSARY

mitosis   A process in which a fertilized ovum divides and subdivides.

chromosomes   Particles within the cell that contain the individual's genetic inheritance; each cell contains twenty-three pairs of chromosomes.

genes   Particles within the chromosomes that contain the instructions that cause an individual to develop a specific inherited trait.

autosomes   Chromosomes that are possessed equally by males and females.

sex chromosomes   Chromosomes that differ in males and females; normal females have two X chromosomes, while normal males have an X and a Y chromosome.

meiosis   A process in which germ cells (from which sperm and ova are derived) divide to form cells whose nuclei contain half the number of chromosomes present in the parent cell.

crossing-over   A process in which chromosomes exchange blocks of corresponding genetic material during meiosis.

dominant   A term used to describe a gene whose effects will be expressed whenever it is present.

recessive   A term used to describe a gene whose effects will be masked whenever a dominant gene for the same trait is present.

multifactorial   A term used to describe traits that depend on more than one genetic or environmental factor.

polygenetic inheritance   A situation in which expression of a trait requires the presence of a number of genes.

monozygotic (identical) **twins**   Twins who develop from the same ovum.

dizygotic (fraternal) **twins**   Twins who develop from different ova that are fertilized at the same time.

zygote   A fertilized ovum.

germinal period   The period of prenatal development that extends from fertilization until implantation of the zygote in the wall of the uterus.

embryonic period   The period of prenatal development that extends from the second to the eighth week and is characterized by cell differentiation as the major organs begin to develop.

fetal period   The period of prenatal development that extends from 8 weeks until delivery and is characterized mainly by growth.

placenta   The section of the uterine wall to which the embryo is attached.

premature   A term used to describe an infant that is born earlier than the thirty-eighth week of gestation and weighing less than 5 pounds.

SUGGESTED READINGS

Apgar, Virginia, & Joan Beck (1974). Is *my baby all right?* New York: Pocket Books (paperback). An authoritative, well-written discussion of the factors that can affect prenatal development adversely, and how to avoid them.

Guttmacher, Alan F., revised by I. H. Kaiser (1986). *Pregnancy, birth, and family planning*. New York: New American Library (paperback).

Nilsson, Lennart (1986). *A child is born*. New York: Dell. An exciting account of development from conception to birth, beautifully illustrated with original color photographs by a prizewinning photographer.

Watson, James D. (1986). *The double helix*. New York: New American Library. A suspense-filled story of the competition to discover the structure of DNA, told by one of the discoverers.

Whaley, Lucille F. (1974). *Understanding inherited disorders*. St. Louis: Mosby. A clearly written, well-illustrated introduction to human genetics and the role of genetics in health and disease.

Part Two

THE FIRST
TWO YEARS

Chapter Three

PERCEPTUAL AND COGNITIVE DEVELOPMENT IN INFANCY

Theories and Assumptions

The Newborn

    Sudden Infant Death Syndrome

    Reflexes of the Newborn

    Perception in the Newborn

Physical Growth and Maturation in the First Year

    Maturation of the Brain

    Posture and Locomotion

Cognitive Development in the First Year

    Recognition of Information: The Schema

    Learning Theory and Conditioning

Piaget's View of Infancy

    Sensorimotor Schemes

    The Sensorimotor Period

    The Concept of Object Permanence

    Piaget's Assumptions About Development

In all societies the period of infancy is recognized as a special time and given a special name to distinguish it from later stages of life. Because the behaviors and abilities of the infant are so different from those of older children, infancy is often defined in terms of the *absence* of qualities that characterize the school-age child, such as the ability to speak, to reason, and to experience the emotions of guilt, empathy, and pride. But scientists face a serious problem of selection when they try to describe the qualities that infants *do* possess. Infants display a variety of behaviors: They eat, cry, move, babble, play, kick, and smile, among other things. Unfortunately, it is by no means obvious which of these reactions should be given special status in descriptions and inferences about the cognitive capacities of infants.

THEORIES AND ASSUMPTIONS

The terms that psychologists use to describe infants are influenced by deep, often unconscious beliefs. These beliefs, which are usually shared by the larger society, change over time. For example, nineteenth-century observers compared the human infant with infant calves and foals, which are born in a more mature state and can walk immediately after birth. Because the human infant appeared so helpless compared with most other newborn mammals, these observers called the infant incompetent. Now that recent research has demonstrated the impressive, though less obvious, psychological capacities of the human newborn, contemporary psychologists describe the infant as competent.

Each scholar approaches the study of the infant with certain biases about what qualities are important, and puts his or her observational "lens" closest to those qualities. Consider as an analogy two people visiting Los Angeles for the first time. One comes from a rural village in Indonesia, the second from London. To the Indonesian, the crowds of people, traffic, and tall buildings are the most unusual aspects of the city. After returning home, this traveler describes Los Angeles as a place with many people, cars, and buildings. But because these qualities are not unusual to the visitor from London, she ignores them and concentrates on the lack of public transportation and the high rate of street crime, both of which distinguish Los Angeles from London. The two visitors conceptualize Los Angeles in different ways because each came with different ideas of what cities are like.

The influence of a theorist's suppositions on the selection of descriptive terms is nicely illustrated by comparing three important theorists: Sigmund Freud, Erik Erikson, and Jean Piaget. Each highlighted a different aspect of the infant because each was loyal to assumptions that were part of the larger cultural context in which he lived.

When Freud was thinking and writing about the human infant, soon after the turn of the century, Darwinian evolutionary theory and the physical concept of energy were major sources of metaphors for human development. Scholars promoting Darwinian theory believed that the human infant was a link between apes and human adults; hence, infants should have the same basic biological drives as animals. Because hunger and sexuality were regarded as the two most important drives of animals, Freud assumed that they were also central to human psychological development. In a brilliant set of essays he suggested that each child is born with a fixed amount of energy—which he called *libido*—that, in time, becomes the basis for adult sexual motives. During the period of infancy, the libido's energy is bound up with the mouth, tongue, and lips and the activities of nursing. For this reason, Freud called this first period of development the *oral stage*. Although this bold hypothesis (which is discussed more fully in Chapter 4) may sound a little odd today, it was much more credible at the turn of the century because it was closely related to major ideas in the respected disciplines of evolutionary biology, physiology, and physics.

A half-century later, many American social scientists had come to believe that social experience, not biology, is responsible for the emergence of significant human qualities and for the obvious variations in adult talent, economic success, and character. Hence, theorists looking at the infant during the period between the two world wars focused on social interaction between mother and infant. In their view, Freud's hungry, nursing baby became a social being who is cared for by an adult. Hence, Erik Erikson (1963) regarded the first phase of development as one in which the baby learns whether adults could be relied on for care, love, and emotional security. Erikson called this first period the *stage of trust*. This idea had the same ring of validity in the 1950s that Freud's concept of the oral stage had a half-century earlier.

Although Piaget was also influenced by evolutionary theory, he differed from Freud in that he focused on changes in thought that permit successful adaptation rather than on neurotic symptoms of maladaptation. Piaget believed that the first structures of an infant's mind are created through the active manipulation of objects rather than through repeated cycles of frustration and gratification of the hunger drive. Thus, when Piaget looked at the infant he saw a baby playing with its mother's face, hair, and fingers.

Nursing, receiving love and nurture, and exploring the caregiver's fingers and face are all characteristics of the human infant. It is not obvious that one of these functions is more central than the other; only theory awards one class of events greater status than another. In our view, the infant's cognitive development provides the most comprehensive framework for the changes that may be observed during this period. Our approach to the study of infancy, therefore, emphasizes cognitive functions like memory, categorization, and detection of unfamiliar events. Although these concepts reflect the current views of a large segment of modern psychology, it should be borne in mind that in earlier times the words chosen to describe the infant were very different, and there is no doubt that new terms will be used in the next century.

THE NEWBORN

The average newborn infant weighs about 7½ pounds and is about 20 inches long; boys are slightly larger and a little heavier than girls. The young infant's psychological and physiological states vary a great deal during the opening weeks. They include the following: (1) a state of regular sleep in which the eyes are closed and respiration is regular; (2) a state of irregular sleep in which one sees limb movement and facial grimaces; (3) a state of drowsiness characterized by open eyes but general inactivity; (4) a state of alert inactivity in which the infant's eyes have a bright quality and pursue moving objects; (5) a state of waking activity in which the infant engages in diffuse motor activity involving the whole body; and (6) a state of distress characterized by crying. Of these, state 4 is optimal for learning and interacting with others.

Doctors and nurses often evaluate the state of the newborn by means of test procedures developed by a pediatrician, T. B. Brazelton. For example, in one procedure, the examiner moves a small, attractive object in front of the infant's face to see if the baby will attend to it and follow it as it passes from one side to the other. Healthy newborns will track the moving object.

The total amount of time spent sleeping decreases dramatically from about 18 hours a day during the first month of life to about 12 hours a day by the time the child is 2 years old. These early changes in sleep and other basic life functions occur because the infant's brain is immature at birth and much growth occurs during the initial years. The consequences of brain growth can be observed in changes in the states of sleep. One sleep state is called rapid eye movement, or REM, because it is accompanied by eye movements that can be observed under the infant's eyelids (see Figure 3.1). As the individual matures, there is a dramatic decrease in the proportion of time spent in REM sleep, from 50 percent of a sleep bout in the newborn to about 20 percent in an adult (see Figure 3.2). By 6 months, most infants follow the adult pattern, in which the first phase of sleep is non-REM and only after sleep becomes deep does REM sleep occur (Roffwarg, Muzio & Dement, 1966; Kligman, Smyrl & Emde, 1975).

Sudden Infant Death Syndrome

Although the parts of the brain that control the basic life functions, such as heart rate and breathing, are more mature at birth than most of the cortex (see Figure 3.3), in a small number of infants the brain centers controlling heart rate and breathing—located in the medulla—are less mature than they should be for normal functioning. As a result, a small proportion of these infants are at risk for a serious condition called sudden infant death syndrome (SIDS), in which the infant dies of asphyxiation, usually while sleeping. It is estimated that about 10,000 American infants die of SIDS each year. Such deaths are most common during the winter months, often following a cold. Because the brain centers that monitor breathing mature during the first half-year, death due to SIDS is most likely to occur during the first four months of life and rarely occurs after six months (Stratton, 1982; Steinschneider, 1975). Although doctors assess the integrity of the newborn

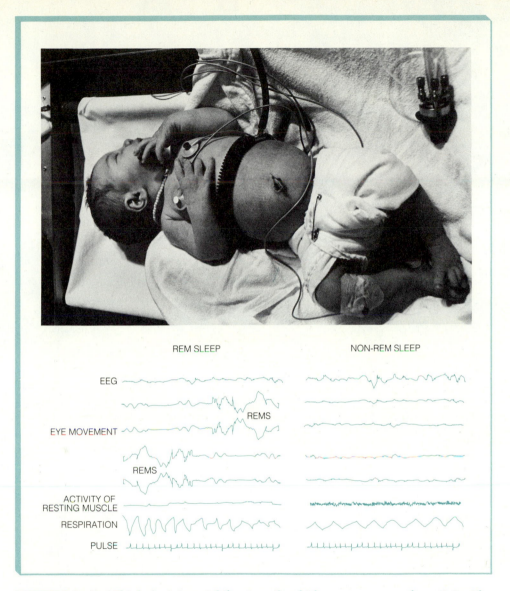

FIGURE 3.1   (*top*) This baby is in a stabilmeter crib, which measures muscular activity. The belt around the abdomen measures respiration, and the electrodes on the chest produce electrocardiographic records. When electroencephalographic recordings are made, electrodes are placed at the outer corners of the eyes. Although cumbersome, the apparatus is not uncomfortable for the baby. (*bottom*) Recordings showing the differences between 30 seconds of REM sleep and non-REM sleep in a newborn. Besides the heightened eye activity during REM sleep, note the absence of muscle activity, the rapid respiratory rate, and changing respiratory amplitude. (Photograph by Jason Lauré [Woodfin Camp & Assoc.]. Chart after H. P. Roffwarg, W.C. Dement, and C. Fisher. Preliminary observations of the sleep-dream pattern in neonates, infants, children, and adults. In E. Harms, Ed., *Monographs on Child Psychiatry*, No. 2. New York: Pergamon Press, 1964.)

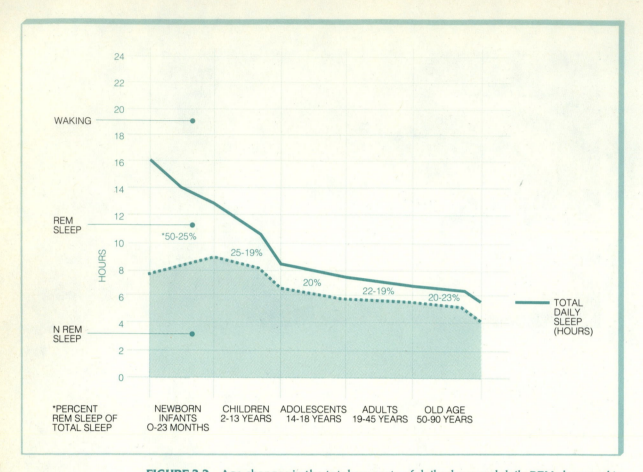

FIGURE 3.2   Age changes in the total amounts of daily sleep and daily REM sleep and in percentage of REM sleep. The percentage of REM sleep is indicated by the nonshaded area of the graph. The percentage of REM sleep drops from 50 percent in the newborn period to only 25 percent in the 2- to 3-year-old child. (Adapted from Roffwarg, Muzio, & Dement [1966]; revised since publication in *Science* by Dr. Roffwarg. By permission of the senior author.).

shortly after birth, babies who are at risk for SIDS do not always reveal their vulnerability on this examination.

Reflexes of the Newborn

On the day it is born, the normal infant displays a set of inherited reflexes, many of which are present in other primates such as monkeys and chimpanzees. Table 3.1 lists the major reflexes that are present during the opening days of life; Figures 3.4 and 3.5 illustrate some of these reflexes.

Some of the reflexes listed in Table 3.1, such as sucking and grasping, are useful as the infant adjusts to its new environment. Others, which are not

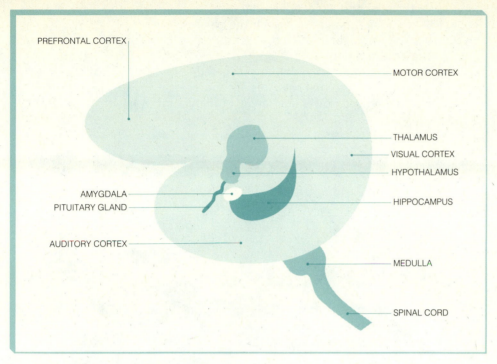

PREFRONTAL CORTEX

MOTOR CORTEX

THALAMUS

VISUAL CORTEX

HYPOTHALAMUS

AMYGDALA
PITUITARY GLAND

HIPPOCAMPUS

AUDITORY CORTEX

MEDULLA

SPINAL CORD

FIGURE 3.3   Schematic diagram of important brain areas discussed in this chapter.

obviously adaptive, are present because the cerebral cortex is not yet mature enough to control or monitor them. The Moro reflex (see Box 3.1) is a good example, for it does not seem to have an obvious advantage in human infants (who, unlike monkeys, are not carried upside down on their mother's belly for most of the day). However, by three months of age the more mature cortex inhibits the Moro response to a sudden loud noise.

Perception in the Newborn

The newborn also inherits a small number of perceptual biases that lead it to pay attention to some objects and events in its surroundings while ignoring others. The most important of these perceptual biases is the tendency to attend to stimuli that change in some way or that exhibit a great deal of variety. Thus, objects that move, objects that have black-white contrast, or sounds that vary in loudness, rhythm, and pitch are most likely to attract and hold an infant's attention.

Motion picture recordings reveal that when a newborn is placed in a dark room, it opens its eyes and looks around for subtle shadows or edges. For example, if an alert infant is shown a thick black bar on a white background, such as those in Figure 3.6, its eyes dart to the black contour and hover near it rather than wandering randomly across the visual field. One psychologist has suggested that newborns' attention seems to be guided by the following set of rules:

Rule 1: If awake and alert, open your eyes.

Rule 2: If you find darkness, search the environment.

Rule 3: If you find light but no edges, engage in a broad uncontrolled search of the environment.

Rule 4: If you find an edge, look near the edge and try to cross it.

Rule 5: Stay near areas that have lots of contour; scan broadly near areas of low contour and narrowly near areas of high contour (Haith, 1980).

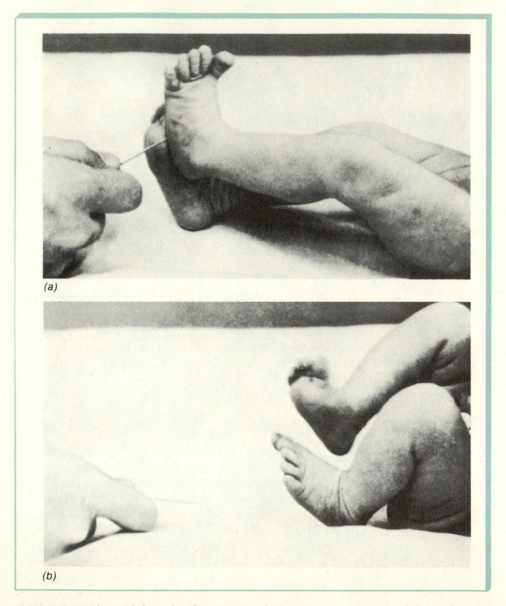

(a)

(b)

FIGURE 3.4 The withdrawal reflex: (*a*) Stimulation. The examiner gently scratches the infant's sole with a pin. (*b*) Response. The infant withdraws the foot.

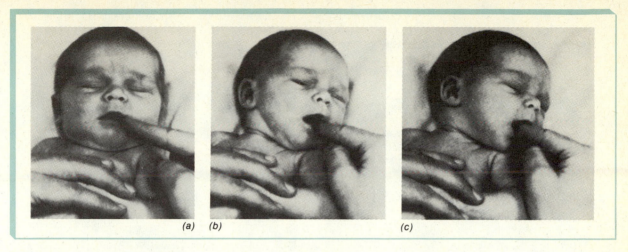

(a)   (b)   (c)

FIGURE 3.4 (continued)   The rooting response: (*a*) Stimulation. The examiner places finger on infant's chin and delivers short sharp tap to own finger. (*b*) Head turning. The infant turns his head in the direction of the finger. (*c*) Grasping with the mouth. The infant tries to suck the stimulating finger.

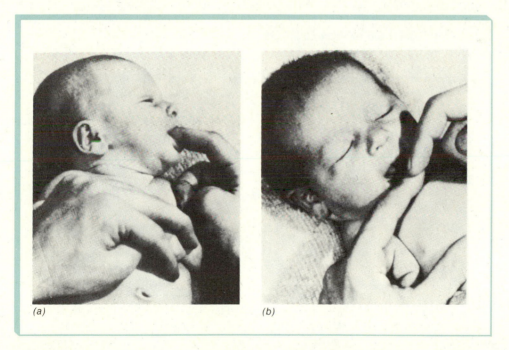

(a)   (b)

FIGURE 3.4 (continued)   (*a*) Testing sucking. The infant sucks the finger placed into his mouth. (*b*) Elicitation of the jaw-jerk. The examiner delivers a short, sharp tap to the chin; the infant's chin is lifted by contraction of masseteric muscles. (From H. Prechtl & D. Beintema. The neurological examination of the full-term newborn infant. *Little Club Clinics in Developing Medicine*, 1964, 12, 35, 40, 41, 42. London: Spastics Society Medical Information Unit and William Heinemann Medical Books, Ltd. By permission.)

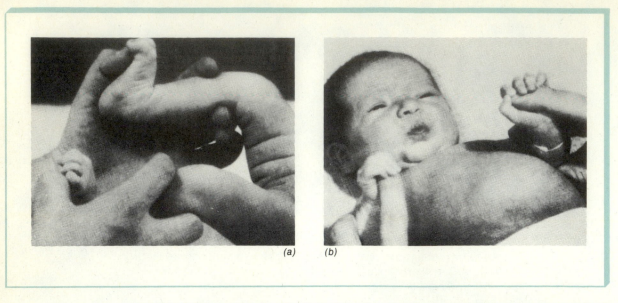

(a)   (b)

FIGURE 3.4 (continued)   (*a*) Elicitation of ankle clonus. The examiner presses both thumbs against the soles of the foot; the infant's toes flex around the thumbs. (*b*) Testing for the palmar grasp. The examiner presses his finger into the infant's palms; the infant's fingers flex around the examiner's fingers.

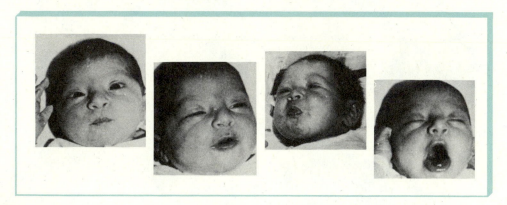

FIGURE 3.5   Although it was once believed that newborn infants are unable to tell the difference between lemon juice and sugar, research has shown that they respond to strong tastes much as adults do. The facial expressions of the neonate resemble those of an adult who has just tasted similar solutions, and the accompanying table shows how widespread such reactions were among a group of 175 babies whose ages ranged from several hours to a week. (From James M. Weiffenbach [Ed.], *The genesis of sweet preference*. National Institute of Dental Research, DHEW Publication No. (NIH) 77–1068, U. S. Department of Health, Education and Welfare, 1977. Photographs courtesy of Jacob E. Steiver.)

TABLE 3.1

Reflexes Present in the Newborn Infant

Reflex	Procedure used to elicit reflex	Description
Babinski Reflex	The examiner gently strokes the side of the infant's foot from heel to toe.	The infant flexes its big toe while extending the four smaller toes.
Moro Reflex	The examiner either produces a sudden loud noise (e.g., popping a balloon) or holds the infant and drops its head a few inches. If the baby is lying on its back in a crib, the examiner strikes the crib simultaneously on each side of the infant's head.	The infant throws its arms out and then brings them together in the midline.
Blink Reflex	A bright flash of light.	The infant closes both eyelids.
Grasp Reflex	The examiner puts a finger or pencil against the infant's palm.	The infant grasps the object.
Stepping Reflex	The infant is held upright and the examiner moves it forward and tilts it to one side.	The infant makes movements as if it were walking.
Rooting Reflex	The examiner stimulates the infant at the corner of the mouth or on the cheek.	The infant turns its head toward the finger, opens its mouth, and tries to suck.
Sucking Reflex	The examiner inserts an index finger into the infant's mouth.	The infant begins to suck.
Withdrawal Reflex	The examiner pricks the sole of the infant's foot with a pin.	The infant flexes the leg and withdraws from the pin.
Licking Reflex	The examiner puts sugar water on the infant's tongue.	The infant licks its lips and may suck.
Pursing Reflex	The examiner puts a sour substance on the infant's tongue.	The infant purses its lips and may blink.

BOX 3.1

What Do We Learn from Infant Tests?

Although the vast majority of babies are born with no defects, a small proportion, no more than 10 percent, are born either prematurely or with some difficulty and, hence, may suffer minor brain damage. For these reasons, parents often wish to have a pediatrician, neurologist, or psychologist test the baby to determine that it is normal. Several such tests have been devised, including a neurological test that checks the baby's reflexes (see Figure 3.4).

The presence of the Moro reflex in the first two months has long been regarded as useful in assessing the state of the infant's central nervous system. This reflex is a startle response in which an infant's arms spread wide and then slowly come together at the midline while the legs are brought up in a similar fashion. It is usually elicited by a loud noise, by letting the infant's head drop a few inches, or by banging the side of the baby's crib while it is lying on its back. If a one-month-old infant does not exhibit the Moro reflex, the examiner may apply further tests.

A second kind of test involves more molar behaviors. One such test, the Graham-Rosenblith behavioral test, assesses an infant's muscle strength and coordination, defensive responses to stimulation of the mouth and the nose, and reactions to rattles, bells, and visual stimuli. For example, the infant is placed face down in the crib and the examiner sees whether it turns its head to free its nose and mouth from the sheet.

In a third set of tests, developed by Joseph Fagan of Case Western Reserve University, infants 4, 5, and 6 months of age are tested to see whether they look longer at a novel stimulus after being exposed to a familiar one. Several studies have found that children who show long periods of fixation to the novel member of a pair of stimuli have higher IQs several years later. This provocative finding is attracting many investigators and is being used with increasing frequency to predict children's future IQs.

The infant's preference for contrast is used to test visual acuity. In one procedure a baby is presented with two stimuli alongside each other. One stimulus is a set of vertical black lines separated by only a few centimeters; the other is a blank field of equal brightness. Infants who can discriminate the stimulus with closely spaced lines from the stimulus without lines will look at the former stimulus longer because they prefer to look at the contrast created by the dark lines. Infants who cannot detect the lines as separate will look at both stimuli equally long. Using this

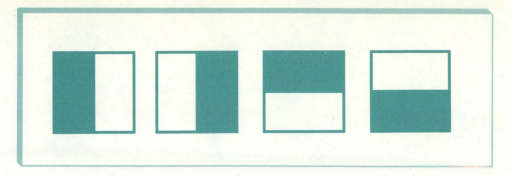

FIGURE 3.6   Stimuli shown to newborn infants, who tend to concentrate their scanning near the border of black and white. (Adapted from M. M. Haith. *Rules that babies look by*. Hillsdale, NJ: Erlbaum, 1980, p. 59. By permission.)

procedure, psychologists have found that young infants can detect the difference between a pattern composed of stripes only ⅛ inch wide and a patch that is completely gray.

Infants appear to be especially interested in changes in the size and spatial orientation of elements that are part of a larger pattern. In one experiment, infants first saw a pair of identical stimuli like design 1 at the top of Figure 3.7. They then saw one of the 12 different figures shown in the two columns in Figure 3.7, along with one of the original stimuli. Only the larger circles (design 2) and the vertically arranged circles (design 3) elicited prolonged attention compared to the original stimulus. It would be adaptive if infants were alerted by an increase in the size of objects, because in the real world an enlarging stimulus indicates that an object is approaching. It is more difficult to understand why the change from horizontal to vertical circles should be so attractive and why there was so little reaction to some of the other variations (Linn, Reznick, Kagan, & Hans, 1982).

Infants also perceive colors as belonging to discrete categories, just as adults do. The visible color spectrum (from red to purple) results from continuous differences in the wavelength of light, but we perceive the colors as if they belonged to separate categories. Thus, even though the differences in wavelength between two shades of blue, on the one hand, and a blue and a green, on the other, are equal, infants show a greater increase in attention to a change from blue to green than to a change from one shade of blue to another (Bornstein, Kessen, & Weisskopf, 1975).

In sum, young infants are prepared to orient themselves to particular aspects of the external world. The infant's attention is attracted and held by contrast, movement, curvilinearity, color, symmetry, and many other qualities, especially when they indicate a change in the immediate perceptual field. These biases, which appear to be inborn, might form the basis for our attraction to what are generally considered pretty, in contrast to plain or unattractive, female faces. The former tend to be curved rather than angular, and more symmetrical. Six-month-old infants look longer at female faces that both men and women judge to be attractive than at female faces that are judged unattractive—a fact that suggests that some criteria for attractive faces may be inborn.

FIGURE 3.7   Five-and-10-month-old infants were shown a pair of stimuli identical to stimulus 1. Then the pair of stimuli was removed, and the child saw stimulus 1 paired with one of the stimuli labeled 2 through 13. The infants showed an increase in attention to the changed stimulus 2 or 3 but did not show increased attention to the remaining stimuli. (Adapted from S. Linn, J. S. Reznick, J. Kagan & S. Hans. Salience of visual patterns in the human infant. *Developmental Psychology*, 1982, 18, 651–637. Copyright 1982 by the American Psychological Association. By permission.)

There are also perceptual biases in hearing. The newborn is more responsive to low-frequency (e.g., throaty) sounds than to high-frequency sounds such as whistles, and reacts more to sounds with a great deal of variety than to simple sounds. Therefore, it appears that the sounds adults make when they talk to babies are precisely those that are most likely to get their attention (Colombo, 1986).

PHYSICAL GROWTH AND MATURATION IN THE FIRST YEAR

The first year of life is characterized by rapid growth of the body and brain. Between birth and 1 year of age, healthy, well-fed children undergo a 50 percent increase in length and an almost 200 percent increase in height. However, not all parts of the body grow at the same rate, and there is no necessary correlation between the growth of one part (e.g., the head) and another (e.g., the muscles) (Johnston, F. E., 1978).

After 6 months, infants from economically advantaged homes grow faster than those from poorer families because of better nutrition, fewer illnesses, and higher standards of health. After the first birthday the growth rate slows, to be followed by a steady, almost linear increase in height and weight until adolescence (see Figure 3.8). It is not until 3 years of age that a child's height becomes a good predictor of his or her height at maturity.

To understand some of the changes that occur during the first two years of life, it is necessary to understand the concept of maturation. **Maturation** refers to a universal sequence of biological events occurring in the body and the brain that permit a psychological function to appear, provided that the infant is healthy and lives in an environment containing people and objects. The appearance of speech between 1 and 3 years of age in almost all children who are exposed to adult language is one of the best illustrations of this concept. The brain of a 3-month-old is not sufficiently developed to permit the infant to understand or speak a language. However, even though the brain of a 2-year-old is sufficiently mature, the child will

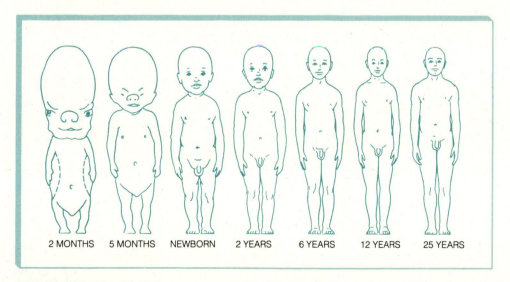

2 MONTHS   5 MONTHS   NEWBORN   2 YEARS   6 YEARS   12 YEARS   25 YEARS

FIGURE 3.8   Changes in form and proportion of the human body during fetal and postnatal life. (Adapted from C. M. Jackson. Some aspects of form and growth. In W. J. Robbins, S. Brody, A. F. Hogan, C. M. Jackson, & C. W. Green [Eds.], *Growth*. New Haven, CT: Yale University Press, 1929, p. 118. By permission.)

not speak unless he or she has been exposed to the speech of others. Thus, maturation alone cannot cause a psychological function to appear. It only serves to establish the earliest possible time of appearance of that function.

Maturation of the Brain

During most of the first year of life there is a rapid increase in the density of synapses being established in the brain (i.e., in the number of synapses per unit of brain tissue), continuing a process that began before birth. But at around 10 months the rate of increase levels off, and beginning with the first birthday it declines slowly through the rest of the person's life. (Rakic, Bourgeois, Eckennoff, Zecevic, & Goldman-Rakic, 1986). This implies that the skills and knowledge that young children learn are often accompanied by elaborating and strengthening some existing synapses (and eliminating some others), rather than adding new synapses. This is true even though new synapses are established throughout childhood. However, it is possible that in later childhood and adolescence the acquisition of new knowledge is accompanied by the addition of synapses (Greenough, Black & Wallace, 1987).

The first year is also marked by the establishment of firmer connections among various parts of the brain. For example, at around 6 months infants will reach for an object they see in front of them. It is likely that the appearance of this coordinated reaching requires the maturation of connections among the visual, parietal, and frontal lobes and special motor centers in the brain (see Figure 3.3).

At the same time that the infant begins to engage in coordinated reaching, it also displays a dramatic increase in spontaneous babbling while lying in a crib or playing with a toy. Although coordinated reaching and babbling appear to be very different reactions, the similarity in age of onset implies that both responses may be mediated by a common process (see Box 3.2).

Posture and Locomotion

The maturation of the brain and the establishment of connections with motor circuits in the spinal cord also permit the child to sit, crawl, and walk at specific stages of development.

SITTING.   Although the newborn cannot sit without support, this ability develops early (Gesell & Amatruda, 1941). Four-month-old babies are able to sit with support for a minute, and by nine months most can sit without support for 10 minutes or longer.

CRAWLING AND CREEPING.   Although there are individual differences in the age at which infants begin to crawl and creep, all who are allowed to locomote on the ground tend to go through the same sequence. The average age for crawling (moving with the abdomen in contact with the floor) is about 9 months; creeping on hands and knees occurs at about 10 months. An infant may skip one or two stages in development, but most children progress through most of the stages (Ames, 1937).

BOX 3.2

Assessing Infant Intelligence

Some early psychologists believed that intelligence could be measured in infancy. They created scales to measure infant intelligence in the hope that they would predict intelligence when the child is in school. In practice, these tests measure infants' relative progress on many behaviors that are influenced mainly by maturation, such as vocalizing, making a stack of blocks, and imitating an adult. Very few people still describe these scales as measures of intelligence, mainly because these scales are not good at predicting IQ at school entry, school grades, or any other popular index of intellectual ability in middle and later childhood.

Nevertheless, some psychologists still believe that infant development scales are useful for identifying potential developmental delays, particularly among high-risk infants. For example, among a group of premature and full-term infants, scores on the Bayley Scale were modestly related to later performance on intelligence and language tests in the preschool years (Siegel, 1979). Although children with serious mental retardation and delays in motor development would probably be identified without the test, it may detect less obvious problems, and detect them earlier, than a physician or parent might. If helpful interventions are begun early, they often are more effective than they can be later, when a problem has already become serious.

Psychologists who use infant scales now claim that they only assess infants' current developmental status, not their future intelligence. The Bayley Scale of Infant Development is the most fully standardized and widely used instrument for assessing infants' developmental status. It contains separate scales to measure mental and psychomotor development. The mental scales include vocalizing and imitating the action of an adult; the motor scales include grasping objects and rolling a ball. But for many children development proceeds at different rates in different domains. Thus, a child who is advanced in motor development may not be advanced in language development.

STANDING AND WALKING. The ability to walk is built on a series of earlier achievements. As in other aspects of development, the ages at which these achievements occur cover a wide range. The median age for pulling up to a standing position and standing while holding on to furniture is between 9 and 10 months. The average child stands alone at about 11 months, walks when led by one hand at 1 year, and can walk alone, although awkwardly, at about 13 months.

The average child can walk alone at about 13 months.

By 18 months, the child can get up and down stairs without help (and usually without falling) and can pull a toy along the ground. By the second birthday, the child can pick up an object from the floor without falling down and can run and walk backward (Gesell & Amatruda, 1941; Gesell, et al., 1940). Progress in motor development through the first year is illustrated in Figure 3.9.

Exactly when a child sits, stands, or walks depends both on the maturation of the neural and muscular systems and on opportunities to practice emerging motor skills. Specific training seems to lead to earlier appearance of motor skills (Super, C. M., 1976; Zelazo, Zelazo, & Kolb, 1972). African babies are often ahead of Caucasians in sitting, standing, and walking—and these are precisely the motor acts that African parents encourage in their infants. There are no differences between African and Caucasian infants in the time of appearance of responses that are not taught, such as rolling over or crawling (Super, C. M., 1976). By contrast, children growing up among the Ache in Paraguay are delayed in walking because adults restrain them from exploring their environment (Kaplan & Dove, 1987). Thus, the opportunity—or lack of it—to use motor skills as they emerge can speed up or slow down the development of universal skills in motor coordination.

1 MONTH	2 MONTHS	3 MONTHS	4 MONTHS
CHIN UP	CHEST UP	REACHES FOR OBJECT BUT USUALLY MISSES	SITS WITH SUPPORT

5 MONTHS	6 MONTHS	7 MONTHS	8 MONTHS
GRASPS OBJECT	SITS EASILY IN HIGH CHAIR; GRASPS DANGLING OBJECTS	SITS ALONE	GETS SELF INTO SITTING POSITION

9 MONTHS	9 MONTHS	10 MONTHS	10 MONTHS
STANDS HOLDING FURNITURE	CRAWLS ON ABDOMEN	WALKS IF BOTH HANDS ARE HELD	CREEPS ON HANDS AND KNEES

11 MONTHS	12 MONTHS	13 MONTHS	18 MONTHS
STANDS ALONE	WALKS WHEN LED BY HAND	WALKS ALONE	GOES UP AND DOWN STAIRS

FIGURE 3.9   The development of posture and locomotion in the infant.

COGNITIVE DEVELOPMENT IN THE FIRST YEAR

The important cognitive functions that appear in early childhood, including memory, language, and self-awareness, are not located in particular places within the brain but are derived from complex relationships among different parts of the brain. It is useful to think of the emergence of psychological processes during the first few years as derived from the growth of connections within the brain. This growth is due to maturation as well as experience. Maturation of the central nervous system, inborn perceptual biases, and postnatal experience act together to permit the infant to acquire two kinds of psychological structures: perceptual schemata and conditioned responses.

Recognition of Information: The Schema

From the first days of life, infants create representations of their experience; psychologists call these representations *schemata* (the singular form is *schema*). A **schema** is a representation of the salient elements in an event and their relationships to one another. Schemata exist in all sense modalities—visual, auditory, olfactory, and tactile. In each instance they preserve aspects of the original event, such as how the mother looks, the sound quality of her voice, or the smell of her skin. The infant's schema for a human face, for example, is likely to emphasize an oval frame containing two horizontally placed circular shapes.

It should be noted that schema is not an exact copy of any particular object or event, for the mind cannot register every feature, even of something as meaningful as the mother's face. Moreover, successive exposures to the same event are never truly identical. Because the infant relates the second experience to the first while simultaneously recognizing some differences between the two, it is assumed that the child creates a composite of similar experiences. The composite is called a **schematic prototype**.

These prototypes can represent not only static objects, such as a rattle or a cup, but also moving pictures. It may come as a surprise to learn that young infants are able to create a schema for a pattern as complex as that created by a person walking (Bertenthal, Proffitt, & Cutting, 1984). Infants 3 and 5 months old saw a moving pattern of 11 different lights on a screen (see Figure 3.10). The infants could tell the difference between the pattern of lights that corresponded to a person walking (stimulus A) and a random version of those lights (stimulus C). They could also tell the difference between the pattern of lights in stimulus A and an upside-down version (stimulus B). In addition, infants looked at stimulus C twice as long as they did at stimulus A, suggesting that they had more difficulty relating that stimulus to an existing schema. The fact that stimulus A was easier to recognize as familiar than stimulus C suggests that the infant had acquired a schema for a person walking and could relate stimulus A to that schema (Bertenthal, Proffitt, Kramer, & Spelner, 1987).

THE DISCREPANCY PRINCIPLE. We now pose an important question: If an infant creates a schematic prototype for a face, a sound, a moving person, or perhaps a pet cat, what *changes* in these events are most likely to alert the infant and lead it to devote prolonged attention to them? The answer is that infants are most likely to display prolonged attention to events that are "somewhat different" from those encountered in the past, and to attend somewhat less to either very familiar or very novel events. These "somewhat different" stimuli are called **discrepant events**.

The increase in attentiveness to discrepant events is part of a larger set of changes that occurs at 2 to 3 months of age. At this time the amount of spontaneous crying decreases, babbling and cooing increase, and new wave forms are seen

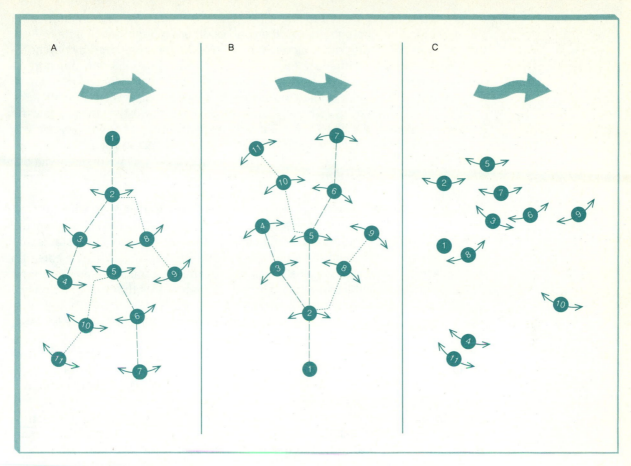

FIGURE 3.10 Seeing form from movement. (Adapted from B. I. Bertenthal, D. R. Proffitt, & J. E. Cutting. Infant sensitivity to figural coherence and biomechanical motions. *Journal of Experimental Child Psychology*, 1984, 37, 213–230. Copyright by Academic Press. By permission.)

in recordings from the infant's brain. The fact that these and other changes occur at the same time implies, but does not prove, the presence of a new stage of psychological organization resulting from maturational changes in the brain. These changes permit infants to relate an event in the perceptual field to their stored knowledge.

In order to understand the relationship between the schemata the infant has acquired and the degree of attentiveness it will show to a discrepant event, it is necessary to realize that the various dimensions of any particular schema are not equally important. They differ in what psychologists call *salience*. For most 1-year-olds, the head of a person is psychologically more salient than the arms and legs because of the frequent face-to-face interaction between infant and adult. However, when a 1-year-old looks at a dog, which is typically seen at a distance and has four legs rather than two, the limbs are likely to be more salient than the head.

In one study of the effects of discrepant stimuli, 1-year-old children were shown pictures of different adult women and of different dogs, one at a time. After they became bored with these pictures (or, to use the term preferred by psychologists, *habituated* to the stimulus), each child was shown three different transformations of either the woman or the dog: a woman or dog without a head, a woman or dog without limbs, and a woman or dog without a body. After seeing the pictures of women, the infants showed the greatest recovery of interest when they saw the picture of a woman without a head. But after seeing a series of dogs, they showed the greatest recovery of attention when they saw the picture of a dog without limbs. This pattern of attention suggests that the head was the more salient dimension for the schema of a person, while the limbs were more salient for the schema of a dog. (See Box 3.3.)

We now state a hypothetical principle, the *discrepancy principle*, which relates an infant's interest in an event to the extent to which the event differs from the schema the child has formed. For infants under 18 months, the principle states that events that contain transformations of noncentral dimensions (e.g., the ears of a human face or the whiskers of a cat), as well as events that transform all the central elements, usually elicit less sustained attention than events that transform one or two of the salient dimensions of a schema (e.g., the head of a person). Stated more plainly, very slight or very extreme transformations in a schema provoke less sustained attention than moderate transformations do.

An illustration of the discrepancy principle is provided by the pattern of change in an infant's preferences for human faces. Three-month-olds look longer at smiling faces than at neutral ones (Kuchuk, Vibbert, & Bornstein, 1986), but 7-month-olds look longer at fearful faces than at happy, smiling ones (Nelson, C. A. & Dolgin, 1985). One way to understand this fact is to suppose that for a 3-month-old an unfamiliar female face that is smiling may represent an optimal discrepancy from the face of a parent, but an unfamiliar face with a fearful expression may be optimally discrepant from the more mature 7-month old's schema for parents' faces.

Events that are slightly discrepant from a schematic prototype also produce distinct electrical changes in the brain (Nelson & Salapatek, 1986). A specific electrical potential, called the **event-related potential**, often occurs when a discrepant or unexpected event is encountered. Infants were exposed to a series of male and female faces presented at a rate of about one a second. When a male face occurred 80 percent of the time and a female face only 20 percent of the time, 6-month-old infants showed a larger event-related potential to the female face.

The discrepancy principle has several implications that are worth noting. We have seen that infants are most likely to be alerted by events that are a little different from their knowledge. But because each infant has a different set of schemata, the events that are most alerting will not be the same for all children. Moreover, at any one time an infant is maximally sensitive to a narrow band of events. As that set of experiences is understood and new schemata created or old ones modified, the child becomes receptive to a new "envelope" of events. Through this successive understanding of discrepant experience, the child's cognitive abilities grow.

Because variations in what is known are most likely to provoke an attempt at understanding and therefore to promote cognitive development, the intellectual

How Do We Know What the Baby Perceives?

When psychologists want to determine what infants hear, see, smell, or feel, they usually employ a method known as *habituation-dishabituation*. This procedure is based on the following reasonable assumptions: When infants become bored with a particular event because of repeated presentation or prolonged exposure, they will look at it for shorter and shorter intervals before looking away. When a changed stimulus appears, they will show increased attention (longer looks) if they detect the change. The decreased interest or boredom that accompanies the repeated presentation is called *habituation*; the recovery of interest in response to the new event is called *dishabituation*.

To cognitive psychologists, the increase in attention is important because it implies that the infant recognizes the new event as different from the original one. For instance, if infants are shown a picture of two identical red spheres until they look away out of boredom, and then are shown a picture of a red sphere alongside a red cube, most will look longer at the cube, implying that they detect the difference between the shapes of the two objects.

But we must be cautious in concluding that infants do *not* detect a difference between an old event and a new one simply because they do not look longer at the new stimulus. For example, when infants were shown a picture of a circle containing two dots, those who had become habituated to this stimulus did not look longer at a picture of two dots outside a circle, even though they should have been capable of perceiving the differences between the two stimuli (Linn et al., 1982). These observations reveal a common problem in inferring mental states in others. If a child looks longer at a new stimulus, we can conclude that she discriminated it from an older one. But if she does not look longer, we cannot conclude that she was unable to make the discrimination.

Because children do not always reveal their discrimination of a new stimulus by increased looking, it has proved valuable to record other behaviors besides fixation time when a dishabituation stimulus is presented. Changes in facial expression, increases or decreases in vocalization, or motor movements often occur. Some infants show a decrease in heart rate when they examine a new stimulus, suggesting that they are surprised by it.

Psychologists who are interested in the discrimination of auditory stimuli cannot use visual fixation time. If the baby is young, they record high-amplitude sucking. A rubber nipple is placed in the baby's mouth,

and every time the infant sucks with a specific pressure he hears a particular syllable—for instance, the syllable *pa*. When the baby becomes
bored, as indicated by less frequent and less intense sucking pressure,
the stimulus is changed—say, to *ba*. If the infant increases the rate and
pressure of sucking, the psychologist concludes that the child detected
a difference between the syllables *pa* and *ba*. Each of these changes in
behavior—looking time, vocalization, sucking, heart rate—is a valid indicator that the child has detected a new stimulus.

growth of infants living in environments with little variety should be a little slower
than that of infants living in environments that contain considerable change. This
prediction is confirmed by cross-cultural data on children living in isolated rural villages, as well as by information on children growing up in institutions with high ratios of infants to caregivers. Such children experience less variety each day and
attain the cognitive milestones of the first year at a slower rate (Kagan, Kearsley, &
Zelazo, 1978).

SCHEMATA RELATING DIFFERENT SENSORY MODES.   There is some evidence that infants can detect a similarity between two events when the events
originate in different sense modalities, such as vision and hearing or vision and
touch. If a 6-month-old baby is given a smooth or nubby nipple to suck on (see Figure 3.11) without being able to see the object, and later is shown both a smooth
and a nubby nipple, the infant looks longer at the nipple she explored with her
tongue. This surprising fact suggests that the infant may have created a schema for
"nubbiness" when sucking the nipple and used that schema in her visual search
(Meltzoff & Borton, 1979).

In a related experiment, babies first heard either a pulsing or a continuous
tone and subsequently were shown a set of short, discontinuous line segments and
a continuous line. The infants looked longer at the broken line after they had heard
the intermittent tone, and they looked longer at the continuous line after they had
heard the continuous tone (Wagner, Winner, Cicchetti, & Gardner, 1981). These
findings suggest that the infants were able to extract the dimension of "discontinuity" in both the auditory and visual modes; in other words, they had constructed a
cross-modal schema.

Infants only 5 months old are able to detect the relationship between the
shape of a person's mouth and the sound uttered (Kuhl & Meltzoff, 1982). Infants
first saw two silent films, each ten seconds long, one film right after the other. One
film depicted a woman's mouth with the shape it assumes when she repeats the
sound "A." The second film showed the shape of a woman's mouth as she repeats
the sound "E" (see Figure 3.12). After the infants had seen the films in succession,
they saw the same two films simultaneously but heard only the sound track corresponding to one of the films (either the "A" sound or the "E" sound). The infants
looked longer at the face that matched the sound they were hearing. Thus, these

FIGURE 3.11   Stimuli shown in demonstrating that infants can recognize similarities between objects across sensory modalities. Infants looked at the nubby form longer than at the smooth one after they had sucked the nubby form, but they looked at the smooth form longer after they had sucked that one, implying that they recognized that the object they were seeing was similar to the one they had sucked (but had not seen). (Adapted from A. M. Meltzoff & R. W. Borton. Intermodal matching by human neonates. *Nature*, 1979, 282, 403–404. Copyright © 1979 Macmillan Journals Limited. By permission.)

five-month-olds had created an association between the shape of a person's mouth and the vocal sound it produces.

In this case, the association between the shape of the person's mouth and the sound produced—a cross-modal schema—was *learned*. But some psychologists believe that infants can create cross-modal schemata when there is no possibility that they could have learned an association between the events in two different sensory modalities. We do not know whether the similarity between the two modalities is based on some shared quality of different modalities or on the degree of arousal generated by the events. For example, because an intermittent sound contains a great deal of change, it might produce greater physiological arousal than a continuous sound. Similarly, a discontinuous line with more contour would generate more arousal than a continuous line. As a result, the infant might match the discontinuous tone with the discontinuous line because both produced equivalent degrees of internal arousal, not because the infant generated an abstract schema of "interruptedness."

CATEGORIES.   The ability to create a schema for a dimension that is common to varied experiences, such as the dimension of continuity or discontinuity, implies that infants can create categories. A **category** is usually defined as a mental representation of the dimensions that are shared by a set of similar, but not identical, stimuli or events. The shared dimensions can be physical features like size and

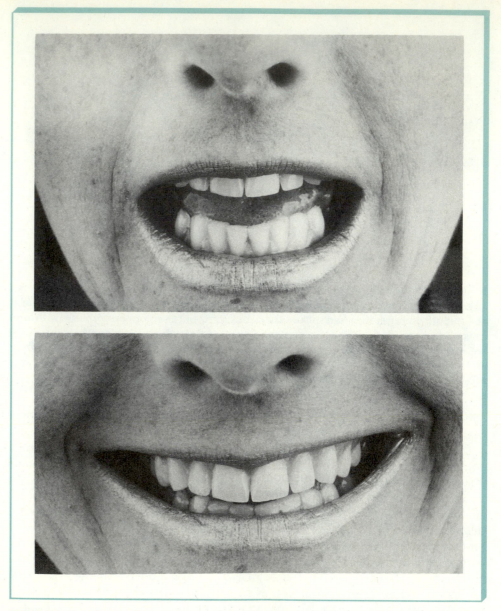

FIGURE 3.12   Photos of women repeating the sounds "A" and "E". (Photograph copyright Jack Deutsch.)

color, or actions like eating and throwing. Later in development the shared dimensions can be ideas like good, bad, justice, and beauty.

In order to create a category, the infant must be able to relate the few critical dimensions that characterize a class of objects or events, for example, the wings, beak and distinctive feet of a bird. When infants saw drawings of animals, 4-month-olds were much less proficient than 7-month-olds at relating these critical dimensions (Younger & Cohen, 1986). But by one year of age infants are able to create categories regularly and continually.

Although it is clear that a 1-year-old can create categories, the bases for the categories are less obvious. When a 1-year-old child playing with 20 toys that belong to different categories confidently picks up an oblong yellow banana and then a cluster of purple grapes, we wonder why those two toys were selected from the larger array. One hypothesis is that these two objects share the quality of being edible foods. Many 1-year-olds have formed categories for household furniture and animals as well as for edible foods. One-year-olds will even treat pictures of objects as belonging to categories. For example, after watching a series of slides depicting different women, infants responded with prolonged attention and excited facial expressions to a picture of a dog (Reznick, 1982), suggesting that the women and the dog belonged to different categories.

It is difficult to determine whether the young child's categories are concrete or abstract. For example, does the infant recognize that ducks and horses both belong to the category "animals," or is the category based only on perceptual similarities? In one study, ducks and flying birds were recognized as belonging to the same category because they are physically similar, but bears and horses were not regarded as belonging to the same category as ducks and birds because they are perceptually very different. However, a major change occurs between 2 and 3 years of age. Two- and three-year-olds were trained to place a three-dimensional toy on one of four pictures that belonged to the category of the toy the child was holding. After the children had been trained to understand that they were supposed to match the toy to the correct picture, they were tested (see Figure 3.13). Two-year-olds correctly matched the toy to a picture, but on the basis of perceptual similarity only. That is, they were able to match a toy duck to a picture of a flying bird (see Figure 3.13, row 2), but they would not match the duck to a picture of a bear or a horse (see rows 3 and 4). In contrast, 3-year-olds were more likely to understand the abstract concept "animal" and to place the toy duck on the picture of the bear or the horse (Fenson, Cameron, & Kennedy, 1987).

Infants appear to be innately prepared to detect qualities that are shared by different events. One-year-olds group objects even when they do not show signs of trying to communicate, and in the absence of external incentives or praise from adults. The act of grouping objects is spontaneous for a human infant, just as swooping down over a sandy spit is spontaneous for a well-fed seagull.

THE ROLE OF MEMORY. Memory processes help the infant create schematic prototypes and use them to guide action toward a goal. To appreciate this important cognitive process, imagine that every few seconds your mind went completely blank and whatever train of thought you were following was lost and you had to begin again. The process by which present experience is related to stored schemata over a period lasting 20 to 30 seconds is called **working memory**. Working memory is necessary for creating complex schemata and changing old ones on the basis of encounters with surprising or discrepant events.

If a 4-month-old infant sees an unfamiliar toy only once for about 15 seconds, it seems to forget that experience after a delay of only one minute (Albarran, 1987).

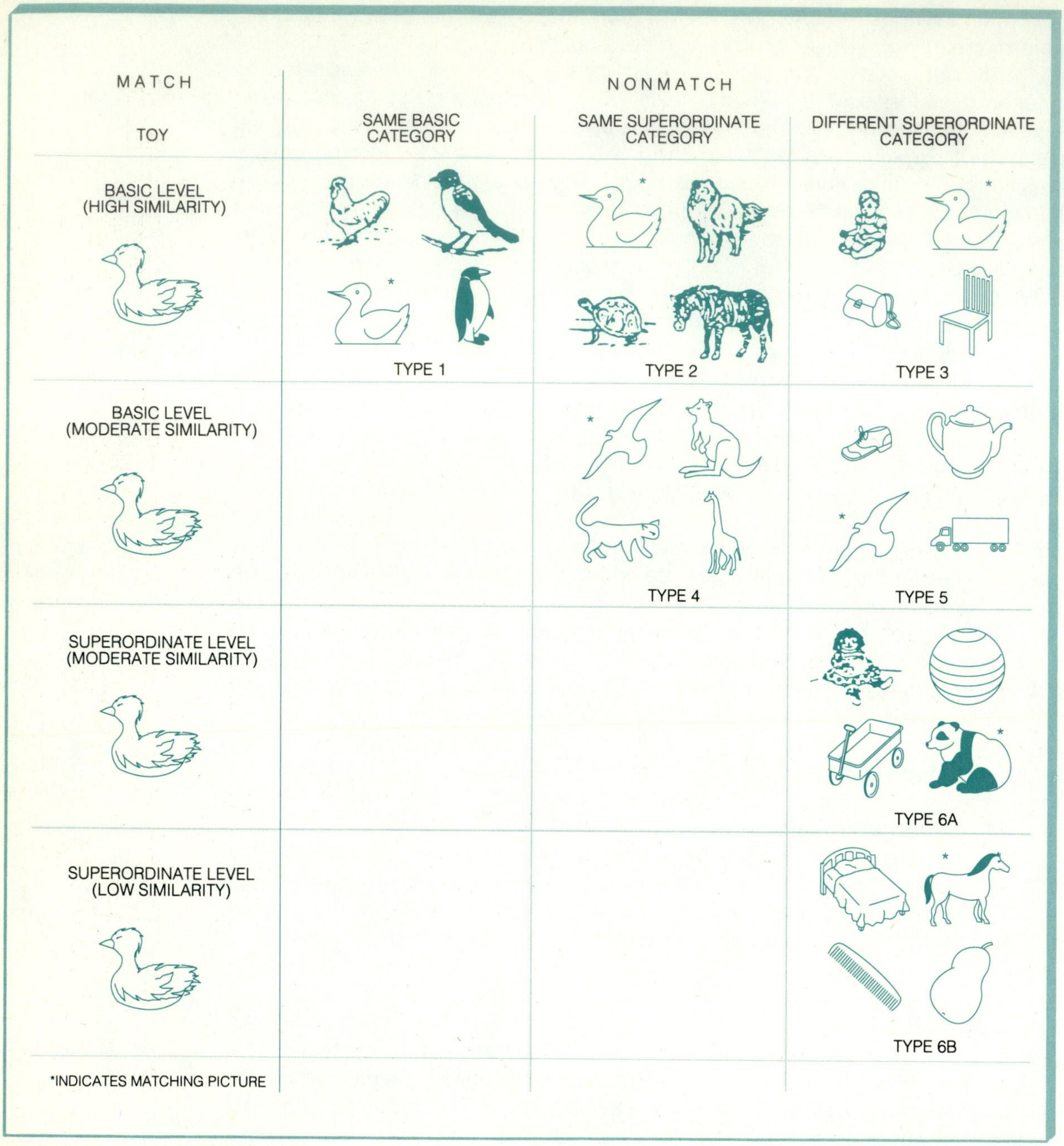

| MATCH | NONMATCH | | |
TOY	SAME BASIC CATEGORY	SAME SUPERORDINATE CATEGORY	DIFFERENT SUPERORDINATE CATEGORY
BASIC LEVEL (HIGH SIMILARITY)	TYPE 1	TYPE 2	TYPE 3
BASIC LEVEL (MODERATE SIMILARITY)		TYPE 4	TYPE 5
SUPERORDINATE LEVEL (MODERATE SIMILARITY)			TYPE 6A
SUPERORDINATE LEVEL (LOW SIMILARITY)			TYPE 6B

*INDICATES MATCHING PICTURE

FIGURE 3.13   **The Seven Types of Stimulus Arrays. The child is asked to select from the sets of four pictures the one that belongs to the category of the target toy. The picture marked with an asterisk is the correct answer.** (Adapted from L. Fenson,, M. S. Cameron, M. Kennedy. Role of perceptual and conceptual similarity in category matching at age two years. *Child Development*, 59, 1988, 900. By permission.)

Infants were visited at home every two weeks from 3 through 7 months of age. Each infant was first given a distinctive toy to play with for 15 seconds. The toy was then taken away gently, and after a delay of either 10 seconds, 1 minute, 3 minutes, 15 minutes, or 1 hour, the infant was shown a pair of toys simultaneously—the toy it had played with before and a new one. As noted earlier, infants have a natural tendency to look at unfamiliar objects. Therefore, if they had remembered the toy they had played with earlier, they should have looked longer at the new toy. Infants who were under 4 months of age would look longer at the unfamiliar toy if the delay was only 10 seconds. But if the delay was one minute, they behaved as if they had forgotten that they had played with the toy. It was not until after 6 months of age that infants remembered the toy after a delay of 15 minutes.

These results suggest that a single, brief exposure to an event may not be retained in working memory for more than 10 to 20 seconds in infants under 3 months old. A longer working memory may require the participation of limbic structures that are not yet mature in young babies (see Figure 3.3).

Working memory lasts longer if a motor response is involved and if the infant is given many opportunities to learn an association between a stimulus and a motor act. In one experiment, 3-month-old infants saw two different mobiles. One of the mobiles was tied to the infant's foot with a satin string. When mobile 1 was present, the mobile moved whenever the infant kicked. But if the infant kicked when mobile 2 was present, no movement of the mobile occurred. Gradually the infants learned to kick only when mobile 1 was present (see Figure 3.14).

Three weeks later the babies were visited again to see if they remembered the difference between the two mobiles. If an infant had not seen the mobiles during the three-week delay, it forgot that kicking made mobile 1 move but not mobile 2. However, if one day earlier (i.e., 20 days after the last exposure to the mobiles) the infant had watched mobile 1 move, on the next day it remembered to kick in response to mobile 1 but not in response to mobile 2 (Fagen, Yengo, Rovee-Collier, & Enright, et al., 1981).

A series of similar experiments suggests that the association between the stimulus of a mobile and the act of kicking is forgotten after one or two weeks. However, if the infant sees the mobile prior to being tested, the association appears to be reactivated and there is less forgetting (see Rovee-Collier, Sullivan, Enright, Lucas, & Fagen, 1980; Davis & Rovee-Collier, 1983).

Enhancement of Recall Memory.   Four-month-olds can recognize that a face in front of them is or is not similar to one they have seen before, but they are far less able to retrieve the schema for their father if the father is not in the room to prod their memory. This distinction between recognizing the father when he is present and retrieving the schema for the father when he is not present is similar to the difference between recognition and **recall memory** as applied to older children and adults (see chapter 8). In recognition, the person remembers that a present stimulus was experienced in the past. In recall, no relevant stimulus is present and the person must retrieve the schema. Thus, true-false questions on an examination require recognition, whereas essays require recall memory.

The capacity for recall appears to be enhanced after 8 months of age. Eight-month-old infants first watched a toy being hidden under one of two cloths—

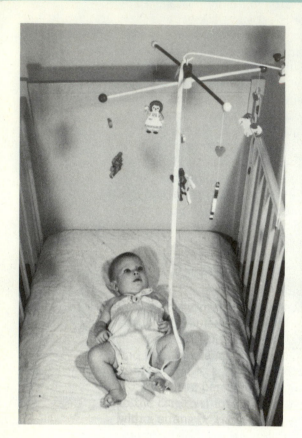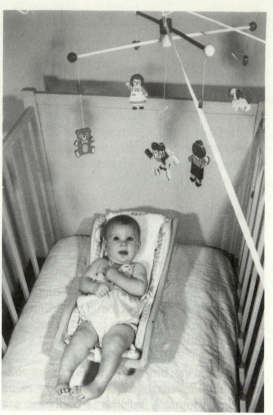

FIGURE 3.14 (*a*) An infant during a reinforcement phase with the ankle ribbon attached to the same suspension bar as that from which the mobile hangs. The empty mobile stand, clamped to the crib rail at the left, will hold the mobile during periods of nonreinforcement. (*b*) The same infant during a reactivation treatment. The mobile and ribbon are attached to the same suspension hook, but the ribbon is drawn and released by the experimenter (not shown), concealed from the infant's view at the side of the crib. Also not shown is the empty stand, positioned as before. The infant will be exposed to the reinforcer (the moving mobile) for only 3 minutes 24 hours before retention testing. (From C. K. Rovee-Colleir, M. Sullivan, M. Enright, D. Lucas, & J. Fagen. Reactivation of infant memory. *Science*, 208, 1980, 1159–1161. Copyright by the American Association for the Advancement of Science. Photograph by Breck P. Kent. By permission.)

cloth A—and retrieved it successfully (see Figure 3.15). After several successful retrievals of the toy, they watched the examiner hide the toy under the second cloth, cloth B. If the delay between seeing the toy being hidden and being allowed to reach for it was as long as 5 seconds, the infants went to cloth A and, of course, found no toy. If the delay was only a second or two, they would go to cloth B and retrieve the toy.

In the game of peek-a-boo the young child realizes that the parent's face exists even though it is temporarily hidden. This belief is one of the important competences that develop during the sensorimotor stage of development.

The experimenter then established the precise delay at which the infant would reach correctly—that is, go to cloth B rather than to cloth A. The delay was increased by several seconds, causing the infant to make the error and go to cloth A. As the infants approached 12 months of age, the length of the delay between hiding the toy under cloth B and permitting the child to reach for it had to be made

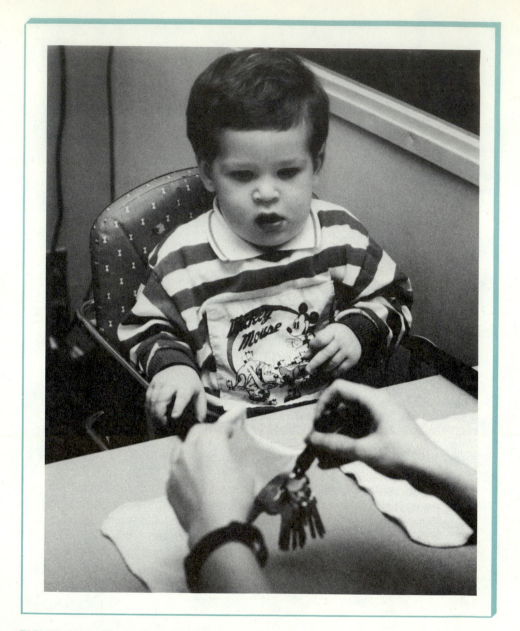

FIGURE 3.15   Illustration of discussion on page 118.

longer and longer in order to produce the error. This finding suggests that recall and working memory improve steadily during the second half of the first year of life (see Diamond, 1985).

Ability to Relate Past and Present.   With improvement in working memory comes the ability to relate an event in the environment to a past event. This competence is obvious when a toy is hidden under one of two cloths and the infant has to relate the schema of the toy to the schema of its location—that is, the cloth under which it has been hidden. Other evidence also shows that the ability to relate past and present events improves after 8 months of age. In one experiment a baby saw a particular object (a fur-covered cylinder) in one location, but the use of trick mirrors permitted the experimenter to place a totally different object (a smooth plastic object with protruding knobs) in that location. When the baby reached for the object, it might grasp either the object it saw or an entirely different one. Observers studied the baby's face and body to judge expressions of surprise when the object grasped was very different from the one that was visible. Eight-month-olds did not look very surprised, but babies only two to three months older (i.e., 9½ and 11 months old) were very surprised when they saw the fur-covered cylinder but grasped the smooth plastic object. Apparently the older infants were able to relate what they saw to what they felt and to evaluate the relationship between the two schemata.

Infants 8 to 9 months old can also connect a landmark (e.g., a picture on a wall) to an interesting event that occurred there. They show signs of anticipating that the event might occur again (Keating, McKenzie, & Day, 1986). This is also the age when infants begin to anticipate their mother's positive reaction when the two are in close face-to-face interaction, and to act so as to invite the mother to respond (Cohn & Tronick, 1987).

Learning Theory and Conditioning

We stated earlier that infants acquire two different classes of structures. One class consists of the schemata we have just discussed. The other consists of conditioned responses. **Conditioning** refers to the learning of the relationships between events (Rescorla, 1988). One set of relationships is between a particular stimulus, such as a tone, and another event that automatically produces a reflex—say, sucking movements in response to a sweet fluid. If a psychologist repeatedly sounds a tone and a second later places sugar water on an infant's lips, the infant will make sucking movements in response to the sweet taste. After a dozen repetitions of this sequence the infant will learn that the tone *predicts* that sugar water is about to be delivered, and will make sucking movements even if no sugar water were delivered.

A second set of relationships is between a response and an event that alerts, surprises, or gratifies the child. If the same psychologist arranged the experiment so that after the tone sounded the child had to turn its head to the right to get the sugar water, the infant would learn that *if* it turns its head to the right when the tone sounds, it will get the pleasure of the sweetness. The infant would have learned a relationship between turning its head in a particular direction and receiving a sweet taste. The first type of conditioning is termed *classical conditioning*; the second is referred to as *instrumental conditioning*.

An important reason for differentiating between perceptual schemata and conditioned responses is that monkeys who have lost their amygdala and hippocampus, and therefore cannot retrieve schemata for past events, nevertheless can learn over many trials to reach for a particular object that always leads to a reward (Mishkin & Appenzeller, 1987). Newborn infants also learn to turn their head toward a particular stimulus over many trials, even though their working memory of a schema for a particular stimulus is very fragile.

By 14 weeks infants are able to learn that an interesting stimulus will appear at a particular location, and will turn their eyes to anticipate the onset of that stimulus. Infants were placed in the apparatus illustrated in Figure 3.16. When they looked at the screen above them, they saw the following set of events: A picture (e.g., checkerboard) would appear first on either the right or the left side of the screen and move up and down for 0.7 second. The picture then went off, and after an interval of one second, during which nothing was on the screen, a different picture appeared on the other side of the screen. After only one minute of this alternation of pictures, some infants began to anticipate the appearance of the next picture and would move their eyes to the place where a picture was about to appear (Haith, 1987). They had learned a relationship between the appearance of a picture on one side and the later appearance of a different picture on the other.

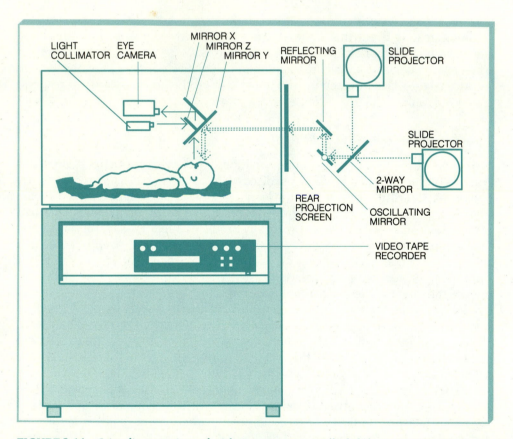

FIGURE 3.16 Stimuli are projected with computer-controlled slide projectors. The beam from one projector shows pictures on the right side of the screen; the beam from another shows pictures on the other side. The eye camera records where the infant is looking. (After M. M. Haith, C. Hazan, & G. S. Goodman. Expectation and anticipation of dynamic visual events by 3 to 5-month-old babies. *Child Development*, 1988, 59, 470. Copyright 1988 by the American Psychological Association. By permission.)

CLASSICAL CONDITIONING.   A newborn only two hours old is able to learn a classically conditioned response. The conditioned stimulus was stroking of the infant's forehead; the unconditioned stimulus was a sugar solution delivered to the infant's mouth with a pipette; and the unconditioned response consisted of orienting the head, puckering the lips, and sucking movements when the sugar solution was delivered (see Blass, Ganchrow, & Steiner, 1984). One group of infants received the sugar solution immediately after their foreheads were stroked. A second group received the sugar solution, but only after a much longer and more variable delay following the stroking. A third group received only the sugar solution and never received any stroking. After many trials, the stroking was administered *without* giving the baby any sugar solution. Only the first group of babies showed puckering of the lips and sucking movements when the examiner stroked their forehead, suggesting that these mouth responses had become classically conditioned to the tactile stimulus.

Despite almost three-quarters of a century of research, we still do not know how classically conditioned associations are established. Psychologists assume that infants (and older people as well) are prepared by their biological makeup to associate certain events with certain internal reactions or overt responses. Not all stimuli are capable of becoming conditioned stimuli for a particular response, and conditioned associations do not occur every time one event predicts another. A nursing baby, for example, is prepared to associate the fragrance of the mother's perfume with the feeling state that accompanies feeding, but is less prepared to associate the temperature of the room or the color of the walls with that feeling state.

INSTRUMENTAL CONDITIONING.   **Instrumental** or **operant conditioning** differs from classical conditioning in many respects. A 1-year-old cries when his mother tucks him into bed, turns out the light, and begins to leave the room. The child's cry provokes the mother to reenter the room, turn on the light, and return to the infant's side. This sequence increases the probability that the child will cry when put to bed the next day, because the mother's return is a reinforcing event. Another 1-year-old picks up her glass of milk by the top, causing it to spill. When she picks up the second glass and holds it by the side, it does not spill, and she drinks the contents. The successful outcome is referred to as the reinforcing event. Because the reinforcement—the return of the mother or being able to drink the milk—was attained by crying or holding the glass by the side, these responses have a higher probability of occurring again in response to these specific conditions.

The exact form of a young infant's sucking response can be modified by presenting or withholding milk, and babies can be instrumentally conditioned to turn their heads to certain sounds. They learn to *discriminate* cues in the environment that signal when they will be reinforced or which of several behaviors will be reinforced. One scientist (Papousek, 1967) presented 6-week-old infants with either a bell or a buzzer. When the bell sounded, the baby would receive milk only from the nipple on the left, not from the one on the right. When the buzzer sounded, milk was available on the right and not on the left. After about 30 days of such experiences, the infants learned to turn to the left when they heard the bell and to the right when they heard the buzzer. Papousek was even able to condition 4-month-

Some psychologists believe that if parents always return to a young child who cries every time he or she is put to bed, they will strengthen the child's tendency to behave in this way.

old infants to make two consecutive turns to one side or to alternate turns to the left with turns to the right. The kicking response to the sight of a mobile described earlier is another example of an instrumentally conditioned response.

Reinforcement increases the probability of recurrence of the instrumentally conditioned response in a particular context. When the reinforcing event reduces a biological drive like hunger or thirst, it is called a *primary reinforcer*. Any objects or people that were present when the biological drive was reduced may acquire reinforcing value and are called *secondary reinforcers*.

In the past, it seemed that the important thing about a reinforcement was its ability to provide pleasure. But this definition is too simple. We do not feel pleasure every time we engage in instrumental behavior—that is, in actions that attain a goal. Getting into a car to commute to school or work, for instance, is an instrumental behavior that may be performed daily even though it produces little if any pleasure. Some psychologists argue, therefore, that any change in experience can be reinforcing if it increases the probability that a response will recur, but changes in experience do not always increase the likelihood of a response. In addition, with repetition an event that is initially reinforcing seems to lose its reinforcing qualities. Consider the example of a baby who strikes a balloon full of plastic beads, causing it to move and make a noise. The baby laughs and repeats the action. The movement and interesting noise appear to be reinforcing, implying that the baby should repeat the act again and again. But after a few minutes the baby stops as if bored. This common phenomenon—boredom following attainment of a desirable goal—suggests that the child's state changes after he or she experiences reinforcements, and that the motivation for the reinforcing event is altered as a result.

As in the case of classical conditioning, we do not fully understand the mechanisms of instrumental conditioning. Nevertheless, this process is extremely useful in changing human behavior. It has been used to help retarded children learn basic skills such as how to tie their shoes or eat with silverware. It can also be used to help children overcome specific fears such as fear of large dogs.

PIAGET'S VIEW OF INFANCY

No discussion of cognitive development in infancy would be complete without some mention of the research of the Swiss psychologist Jean Piaget. Piaget is regarded as the most significant theorist of cognitive development in this century. When he died in 1980 at the age of 84, he had published over 40 books and more than 200 articles. Piaget's theory will be discussed in several parts of this book in association with various developmental stages (see Chapters 7 and 14). In the remainder of this chapter we deal with Piaget's view of cognitive development in infancy.

We have suggested that infants acquire two different forms of knowledge as a result of experience: perceptual schemata for stimulus events, and conditioned associations between two events or between an action and a subsequent event. The schemata permit the infant to recognize experience encountered in the past, while conditioned responses permit the child to use new behaviors to attain desired goals. Piaget suggested the existence of a third mental structure that combines schemata with actions. He called this structure a **sensorimotor coordination**.

Sensorimotor Schemes

The central unit of knowledge in Piaget's view of infancy is the *sensorimotor scheme*, best defined as a representation of a class of motor actions that is used to attain a goal. Piaget's term *scheme* is similar to the term *schema* used earlier in that it refers to the child's representation of the elements in several events, but Piaget emphasized the child's *actions* as the content of these early schemes. For example, the actions of holding, touching, and throwing become the child's scheme for balls or perhaps for round objects. Some important sensorimotor schemes are grasping, throwing, sucking, banging, and kicking. When these schemes are combined with appropriate actions they are *sensorimotor coordinations*.

Piaget claimed that infants acquire knowledge about objects through their actions with them. For example, children learn about their fingers by clasping and sucking them, and they learn about mobiles by tracking and kicking them. This knowledge is acquired through a sequence of stages, which together make up what Piaget termed the *sensorimotor period*.

The Sensorimotor Period

According to Piaget, the first major stage of intellectual development—the **sensorimotor period**—occupies the first 18 to 24 months of life. Throughout this period intelligence is manifested in action. Piaget divided the sensorimotor period into six stages. We will not describe each stage here; instead we will focus on the changes in infants' intelligence that take place during these stages.

During the first two years infants progress from automatic reflexes to inventing new ways to solve problems. They begin with reflexes, including crying, sucking, and orienting themselves toward sounds. Soon they go beyond these reflexes and develop *primary circular reactions*, in which they repeat actions that initially occur accidentally. For example, a hungry baby may accidentally brush his fingers against his lips and then repeat the action, a pattern that is not an inborn reflex. Around 6 months of age infants develop *secondary circular reactions*, in which they repeat actions that create interesting sights and sounds—making bells ring on a crib, for

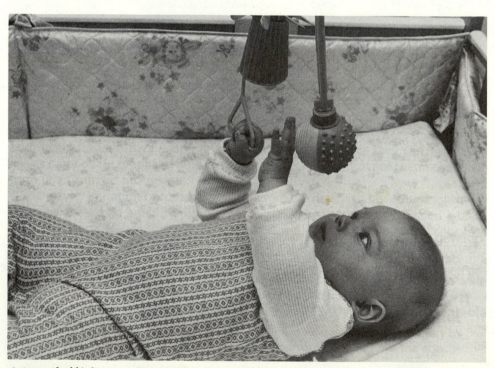

A 6-month-old infant may amuse itself for long periods by repeating actions that create interesting sights and sounds.

example. At this point they become interested in the effects of their actions on their environment rather than focusing just on their own bodily responses.

Near the end of the first year, children show increased ability to coordinate schemes to reach a goal. For instance, they will set aside an obstacle in order to reach a desired object, rather than picking up whatever they come to first. After about 12 months they form *tertiary circular reactions*, in which they vary their actions rather than repeating them, while observing their effects on the environment—almost as if they were systematically exploring the properties of objects. A 15-month-old will throw a ball, then push on it, then bang it on a surface, each time observing the sounds it makes or how soft it is.

In the last stage children invent new schemes through a kind of mental exploration in which they imagine certain events and outcomes. An 18-month-old who wants to reach a light switch that is too high will look back and forth between the light switch and a chair, then suddenly pull the chair over to the light switch, stand on it, and turn on the light. This behavior, which occurs later during the second year, represents the final stage of the sensorimotor period. For Piaget, the most significant feature of this stage is the development of a form of imagery that can be used to solve a problem or attain a goal for which the child has no habitual, available action. At this stage infants do not solve problems through trial-and-error explorations; instead they engage in "internal experimentation, an inner exploration of ways and means" (from Flavell, 1963). Piaget gives a vivid illustration:

> At one year, six months, for the first time Lucienne plays with a doll carriage whose handle comes to the height of her face. She rolls it over the carpet by pushing it. When she comes against a wall, she pulls, walking backward. But as this position is not convenient for her, she pauses and without hesitation goes to the other side to push the carriage again. She therefore found the procedure in one attempt, apparently through analogy to other situations but without training, apprenticeship, or chance.
> (quoted in Flavell, 1963)

The Concept of Object Permanence

Piaget made some ingenious observations of the development of what he called the concept of **object permanence**—the belief that objects continue to exist even when they are out of sight. During the first two or three months of life, children will follow an object visually until it passes out of their line of sight and then abandon their search for it. From 3 to 6 months, vision and movement of arms and hands become coordinated. At this age infants grab for objects they can see, but they do not reach for objects outside their immediate visual field. Piaget interprets the failure to search for hidden objects as indicating that children do not realize that the hidden objects still exist.

During the last three months of the first year, children advance a step further. They reach for an object that is hidden from view if they have watched it being hidden. Thus, a child who watches an adult place a toy under a blanket will search for the toy there. Ten-month-old infants show surprise if they first see an object being covered by a person's hand and discover later, when the hand is removed, that the object is missing. Their surprise suggests that they expected the object to be there; in other words, they believe in the permanence of the object (Charlesworth, 1966).

Piaget interpreted the development of the concept of object permanence as resulting from the child's prior interactions with objects. He believed that a 9-month-old's knowledge of the location of an object is contained in the actions necessary to retrieve it. In the experiment described earlier in which the child must retrieve an object that is hidden under a cover, Piaget would say that the child's knowledge of the location of the object is contained in the sensorimotor schemes that were used in reaching for it previously.

Piaget's Assumptions About Development

Over the course of history philosophers have disagreed on the bases for knowledge. Some, like John Locke, suggested that purely mental ideas (what we have called schemata and categories) are the most basic knowledge. On the other side is Piaget, who believed that knowledge is functional; its purpose is to aid adaptation in the real world. For Piaget, the deepest knowledge is that which can be applied in behaviors that accomplish something. Piaget believed that the infant's experience of acting on the world transforms the basic reflexes described in Table 3.1 into a series of complex adaptive behaviors that appear in a regular sequence. The fact that locomotion facilitates retrieval memory supports Piaget's ideas. In this case action is necessary for the maturational milestone to appear. But children who were born without arms because their mothers took thalidomide during pregnancy were able to develop sophisticated language skills and many normal cognitive abilities, suggesting that Piaget's insistence on the necessity of sensorimotor actions needs some correction. For this and other reasons, psychologists have questioned certain aspects of his theory. Some of these questions concern Piaget's basic assumptions about the nature of development during the first two years of life.

Piaget's view of the sensorimotor period of intellectual development contains four major assumptions. The first, with which most psychologists agree, states that interaction with the environment is an essential facilitator of development, though maturational changes affect *how* the child will use that experience to construct new knowledge. For Piaget, the central force for growth is the child's action on objects. Throwing, pushing, pulling, and sucking of balls, fingers, and cups change the sensorimotor schemes and create more sophisticated ways of dealing with them.

Second, Piaget viewed psychological growth during infancy as gradual or continuous rather than as discontinuous (see Chapter 1). For instance, the child's ability to know that objects are permanent grows slowly from the first days of life. Piaget proposed more qualitative or discontinuous changes between other major stages. However, some psychologists assert that there are qualitative changes during infancy, such as the emergence of working memory.

A third assumption is that there is a connection between successive periods of development. Connectivity means that each new advance in cognitive functioning is dependent on the preceding phase and includes some of the prior competences. Acquiring the ability to play the piano is a good example, for the growth of that skill is gradual and cumulative, each new improvement being built on earlier achievements. Most developmental theorists have assumed that the growth of mental structures during the early years is like learning to play the piano. This description is likely to be valid for many aspects of development, but perhaps not for all.

A fourth assumption in Piaget's theory of development during infancy is that increased intentionality is one of the major competences to develop during the first two years of life. Two-year-old children can make a plan, select the objects the plan requires, and implement the plan with a degree of resistance to distraction that is not possible in the opening weeks or months of life. Piaget believed that intentionality emerges gradually from the repetition of actions that produce change in the infant's world, but some psychologists argue that intentionality might appear in the repertoire late in the first year partly as a result of the maturation of parts of the brain.

SUMMARY

In all societies the period of infancy is recognized as a special time and distinguished from later stages of life. However, the terms that psychologists use to describe infants change over time as the fundamental beliefs of the larger society change. Today many psychologists believe that the infant's cognitive development provides a useful framework for describing the changes observed during this period.

The infant's brain is immature at birth, and many changes in the infant's behavior are a result of brain growth. Among those changes are a decrease in the proportion of time spent in REM (rapid eye movement) sleep. The risk of death from SIDS (sudden infant death syndrome) also decreases as the brain matures.

The normal infant displays a set of inherited reflexes, some of which are useful as it adjusts to its new environment; others are present because the cerebral cortex is not yet mature enough to control them. The newborn also inherits certain perceptual biases, of which the most important is the tendency to attend to stimuli that change in some way or exhibit a great deal of variety. Infants appear to be especially interested in visual events characterized by contrast, movement, curvilinearity, color, and symmetry.

Maturation refers to a universal sequence of biological events occurring in the body and the brain that permits a psychological function to appear. During most of the first year maturation of the brain occurs at a rapid rate. The first year is also marked by the establishment of firmer connections among various parts of the brain. Together, these changes permit the child to sit, crawl, and walk at specific stages of development.

Maturation of the central nervous system, inborn perceptual biases, and postnatal experience act together to permit the infant to acquire two kinds of psychological structures: perceptual schemata and conditioned responses. A *schema* is a representation of the original features of an event and their relationships to one another. Schemata exist in all sense modalities and can represent moving as well as static objects. Infants are most likely to display prolonged attention to events that are somewhat different from the schemata they have formed previously. Such attention-getting stimuli are referred to as *discrepant events*.

There is some evidence that infants can detect a similarity between two events when the events originate in different sense modalities; that is, they can construct cross-modal schemata. This implies that infants can also create *categories*, or mental representations of the dimensions that are shared by similar, but not identical, events. However, the bases for the categories created by infants are not clear, and it is difficult to determine how abstract they are.

Memory processes help the infant create schematic prototypes and use them to guide action toward a goal. The process of relating present experience to stored schemata over a period lasting 20 to 30 seconds is called *working memory*. In infants under 3 months old, a single, brief exposure to an event may not be retained in working memory for more than 10 to 20 seconds. Memory of a motor response usually lasts longer if the infant is given many opportunities to learn an association between a stimulus and a motor act.

Recall memory is the process of retrieving a stored schema when no relevant stimulus is present. The capacity for recall appears to be enhanced after 8 months of age. The infant also becomes better able to relate an event in the environment to a past event.

Conditioning refers to the learning of a relationship between two events or between an action and an external stimulus event. In *classical conditioning*, the child learns that a neutral stimulus predicts a biologically salient event that automatically produces a response. After repeated presentations of the neutral stimulus before the biologically salient one, the former is able to elicit the biological response.

In *instrumental* or *operant conditioning*, a response is modified by presenting or withholding *reinforcers* (rewards and punishments). A reinforcing event that reduces a biological drive is a *primary reinforcer*; objects or people that were present when the biological drive was reduced may become *secondary reinforcers*. An event that is initially reinforcing can lose its reinforcing qualities with repetition.

Jean Piaget suggested the existence of a mental structure—*sensorimotor coordination*—that combines a scheme with action. A *sensorimotor scheme* is a representation of a class of motor actions that is used to attain a goal. According to Piaget, infants acquire knowledge about objects through their actions with them, and this occurs through a sequence of stages that make up the *sensorimotor period*.

Early in the first year infants progress from automatic reflexes to *primary circular reactions*, in which they repeat actions that initially occur accidentally. Later they develop *secondary circular reactions*, in which they repeat actions that create interesting sights and sounds. After about 12 months they form *tertiary circular reactions*, in which they vary their actions rather than repeating them, while observing their effects on the environment. In the final stage of the sensorimotor period children invent new schemes by imagining events and outcomes.

Piaget also observed the development of the concept of *object permanence*—the belief that objects continue to exist even when they are out of sight. He believed that this concept develops as a result of the child's prior interactions with objects.

Piaget made four basic assumptions about the nature of development during the first two years of life: (1) Interaction with the environment is an essential facilitator of development; (2) psychological growth during infancy is continuous; (3)

there is a connection between successive periods of development; and (4) increased intentionality is one of the major competences to develop in the first two years of life. Other psychologists have questioned these assumptions, as well as Piaget's insistence on the necessity of sensorimotor actions for cognitive development.

REVIEW QUESTIONS

1. Describe psychological and physiological states seen in the newborn infant.

2. What perceptual biases in the newborn lead it to pay attention to some objects and events in its surroundings while ignoring others?

3. Define maturation. What role does maturation play in the appearance of specific psychological functions?

4. What is a schema?

5. Define and illustrate the discrepancy principle.

6. Infants appear to be able to create schemata that involve different sensory modes. What are some implications of this ability?

7. Describe the development of memory in the infant. Distinguish between recognition memory and recall memory.

8. Define conditioning and distinguish between classical and instrumental conditioning.

9. Compare Piaget's concept of a sensorimotor scheme to the concept of schematic prototypes.

10. What is meant by object permanence?

GLOSSARY

maturation   A universal sequence of biological events occurring in the body and the brain that permits a psychological function to appear, provided that the infant is healthy and lives in an environment containing people and objects.

schema   A representation of the salient elements in an event and their relationships to one another.

schematic prototype   A schema created on the basis of a composite of exposures to similar experiences.

discrepant events   Events that are somewhat different from those that have been encountered in the past (but not entirely novel).

event-related potential   An electrical discharge of the brain that occurs in response to discrepant or unexpected events.

category   A mental representation of the dimensions that are shared by a set of similar, but not identical, events.

working memory   The process by which present experience is related to stored schemata over a period lasting 20 to 30 seconds.

recall memory   Ability to retrieve a schema when no relevant stimulus is present.

conditioning   The learning of a relationship between two events or between an action and a subsequent event.

classical conditioning   The establishment of a relationship between a neutral event and a biologically salient event through repeated presentation of the former before the latter.

instrumental (operant) conditioning   The establishment of a relationship between a response and a subsequent event (called a reinforcement) that increases the probability that the response will recur.

sensorimotor coordination   A mental structure that combines a sensorimotor scheme with action.

sensorimotor scheme   A representation of a class of motor actions that attains a goal.

sensorimotor period   In Piaget's theory, the first stage of intellectual development, occupying the first 18 to 24 months of life.

object permanence   The belief that objects continue to exist even when they are out of sight.

SUGGESTED READINGS

Maurer, D. & Maurer, C. (1988). *The world of the newborn*. New York: Basic Books. Presents in a highly readable style what psychologists have learned about the prenatal and early postnatal periods. Also presents an exceptionally good summary of the infant's visual and auditory capacities.

Rosenblith, J. F., & Sims-Knight, J. E. (1985). *In the beginning: Development in the first two years*. Monterey, CA: Brooks Cole. Covers all the basic research on infancy, including excellent discussions of conditioning and memory in infants, sensory and perceptual abilities, Piaget's theory, and early communicative behavior.

Osofsky, J. D. (Ed.). (1987). *Handbook of infant development* (2nd ed.). New York: Wiley. One chapter, written by C. Rovee-Collier, contains an extensive and excellent discussion of conditioning in the infant. Another, written by S. A. Rose and H. A. Huff, provides an outstanding discussion of the concept of cross-modal schemata. A third, by T. B. Brazelton, J. K. Nugent, and B. M. Lester, discusses the validity of the Neo-natal Behavioral Assessment Scale, the most popular scale used to assess the relative maturity of newborn infants.

Wellman, H. L., Cross, D. & Bartsch, K. (1986). Infant search and object permanence. *Monographs of the society for research in child development*, 51 (serial No. 214). Analyzes all of the data on Piaget's object concept and concludes that the delay between hiding the object and permitting the child to reach is a critical determinant of the child's success. Presents a new theory of the child's performance in the object concept procedure.

Chapter Four

EMOTIONAL AND SOCIAL DEVELOPMENT IN INFANCY

The Meaning of Emotion
Emotions of Infancy
    Inferring Emotions from Behavior
    Inferring Emotions from Facial Expressions
Temperamental Differences in Infants
    Activity Level
    Irritability
    Reaction to Unfamiliarity
    The Principle of Bidirectionality
Emotional and Social Relationships with Adults
    Theoretical Perspectives
    Attachment to Caregivers
    Measuring Attachment
    Effects of Parental Practices
    Consequences of Variations in Quality of Attachment
    Common Themes in Theories of Infant Social Development
    Cultural Ideals and Child Rearing

In Chapter 3 we considered two important psychological systems that develop in infancy: perceptual schemata and conditioned responses. A third system involves emotional reactions and the behaviors associated with them. Emotions are important because they add perceptual salience to experience; as a result, conditioned responses and schemata that are associated with emotions are easier to retrieve. In addition, emotions can interrupt or influence ongoing behaviors. For example, a baby playing happily with a rattle may suddenly stop if it sees a stranger enter the room because of the emotional state created by the presence of the stranger.

Neuroscientists have discovered that these three systems have parallels in the structure and function of the central nervous system. The motor cortex, the cerebellum, and the basal ganglia are especially important for the initiation and control of actions. The sensory association areas of the cortex, the hippocampus, and the prefrontal cortex are especially important for the storage, retrieval, and transformation of schemata and categories. And the amygdala, hypothalamus, septum, and autonomic nervous system are especially critical in emotions.

Children's actions, knowledge, and emotions all influence their early social interactions, particularly with parents and other important adults. In this chapter we shall first consider what scientists have learned about the emotions of infants, then discuss differences among infants in their susceptibility to emotional states, and finally consider the emotionally based social attachments of infants to their caregivers.

THE MEANING OF EMOTION

In everyday conversation the word *emotion* refers to conscious awareness of a specific change in internal feeling tone, often accompanied by a set of thoughts about the quality of the feeling and the events that produced it. For example, a change in feeling tone might be due to the perception of an increased heart rate; the external event might be a charging dog; and the thought might be anticipation of being hurt. Most people would call the resulting emotional state *fear*. The same feeling might be produced by increased tension in the muscles after seeing a frown on the face of a friend and thinking that the friend might be angry because you refused him a favor. Some people would call this emotion *shame*.

However, young infants, especially those under 1 year old, have limited conscious awareness of their feelings and no extended set of thoughts about external events and bodily changes. Thus, a second meaning of **emotion**, one that is used more often by scientists, refers to changes in the brain and body, especially in the limbic and autonomic nervous systems, that follow encounters with pain, deprivation,

Many 8-month-old infants will react with fear to the presence of a stranger on some occasions.

novelty, danger, sensory gratification, challenge, play, social interaction, or separation from a familiar person. For example, most 8-month-old infants show a change in heart rate and facial expression when an unfamiliar person approaches them, but a different heart rate and facial expression if a jack-in-the-box suddenly pops up in front of them. Even though these infants probably have no conscious awareness of their facial expression or heart rate, psychologists would say that the infants were experiencing the emotional state of fear when the stranger approached and the emotional state of surprise when the jack-in-the-box popped up.

It is useful, therefore, to make a distinction between the emotions of infants, on the one hand, and those of older children and adults, on the other. The difference between the biological state of disease and the psychological state of illness furnishes an analogy. Very specific bodily states, such as cancer or tuberculosis, are regarded as diseases whether or not the patient has any conscious awareness of the changes that occur in his or her physiology. On occasion, however, people become aware of these biological changes, and if they evaluate the changes as due to a pathological process they regard themselves as having an illness. The conscious recognition that one is ill creates a new psychological state that could either exacerbate or reduce the symptoms of the disease. Some people may become depressed, irritable, or sad if they are aware that they have a serious disease. Similarly, when older children and adults become aware of their internal feeling states and the possible causes of these states, they evaluate that information and, in so doing, create complex emotional states that are not possible in the infant. Thus, it is unlikely that the emotional state of a 10-year-old when a peer threatens to grab a prized possession is the same as the emotional state of an 8-month-old whose bottle has been snatched away.

EMOTIONS OF INFANCY

During the first three to four months, infants display many reactions that suggest emotional states. One reaction consists of a quieting of motor activity and a deceleration of heart rate in response to an unexpected event. Psychologists might call this state "surprise in response to the unexpected." A second set of changes is characterized by increased movement, closing of the eyes, an increase in heart rate, and crying; these changes occur in response to pain, cold, and hunger. Scientists might name this combination "distress in response to physical privation." A third set, which includes decreased muscle tone and closing of the eyes after feeding, might be called "relaxation in response to gratification." A fourth pattern includes increased movement of the limbs, smiling, and excited babbling when a moderately familiar event or social interaction occurs. Psychologists might call this profile "excitement in response to assimilation of an event," although parents would be more likely to label it "joy" or "happiness." In each of these examples the name of the emotion contains a reference to its source or cause.

Infants respond to signs of anger and happiness in others (Kreutzer & Charlesworth, 1973). Mothers who kept records of their infants' reactions to the feelings of others reported that their 1-year-olds became upset and moved away when someone showed anger, but displayed either affection or jealousy when they saw affection between others (Zahn-Waxler, Radke-Yarrow, & King, 1979). However, mothers and fathers do not always agree in their interpretation of the infant's behavior (Adamson, Bakeman, Smith, & Walters, 1987).

Inferring Emotions from Behavior

During the period from about 7 to 12 months, infants develop new fears, possibly because of the improvement in recall memory and working memory that occurs during this period. Although a moderately unfamiliar event usually produces increased interest and, occasionally, excited babbling and smiling, it can also produce a state of uncertainty if the infant's efforts to relate it to previously formed schemata are unsuccessful. For example, an infant may cry if the mother is wearing a hat that makes her look different or if it hears for the first time a human voice coming from the speaker in a tape recorder. If, in addition, the infant has no behavior it can use to divert its attention from the state of uncertainty (such as playing with a toy or reaching for the mother), a more serious state is likely to arise. This state is often called *fear* or *anxiety*.

Fear is more likely to occur if an event is unpredictable than if it can be anticipated. One scientist varied the predictability of two noise-making mechanical toys (a cymbal-clapping monkey that produced a loud noise and a gun-shooting robot that lit up and made sounds). The predictable toys were active for 4 seconds and then inactive for 4 seconds on a regular schedule. When the toys were unpredictable, they could be on or off for 1 to 7 seconds. Each mother held her 1-year-old infant on her lap facing the toy until the toy had run through one cycle. After that the infants were free to move about the room. The infants who saw the predictable toys were much less fearful than those who were exposed to the unpredictable toys (see Figure 4.1).

FEAR OF STRANGERS.   One of the most common fears of the last part of the first year is *stranger anxiety*. An 8-month-old is showing stranger anxiety when she wrinkles her face as a stranger approaches, looks back and forth between the stranger and her mother, and after a few seconds begins to cry. Children do not always react to a stranger with fear. The fear is least likely to occur if the stranger approaches slowly, talks gently, and initiates play with the child; it is most likely if the stranger walks toward the child quickly, is quiet or very loud, and attempts to pick up the child. Although some children are more fearful than others, almost all infants show a fear reaction to a stranger on some occasion between 7 and 12 months of age.

One explanation of this fear is based on the assumption that infants compare the schemata for the faces of familiar people with their perception of the stranger. If they are unable to understand the discrepancy, they become distressed. Although

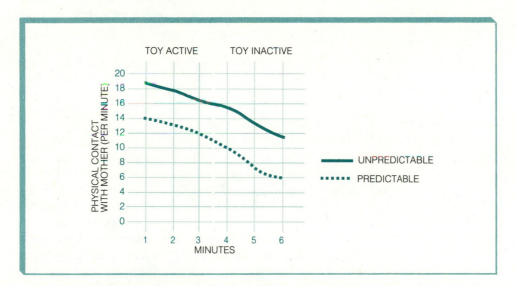

FIGURE 4.1   Infants who played with a toy that made unpredictable sounds and movements stayed closer to their mothers than those who played with predictable toys over a 6-minute interval. (Adapted from M.R. Gunnar, K. Leighton & R. Peleaux, The effects of temporal predictability on the reactions of one-year-olds to potentially frightening toys. *Developmental Psychology*, year 1984, 20, 452. Copyright 1984 by the American Psychological Association. By permission.)

this distress resembles the upset shown by 3-month-olds upon exposure to discrepant events, two important elements have been added to the competence of the 8-month-old. First, recognition of the discrepancy occurs much more quickly. The older child cries within the first 20 seconds of seeing the unfamiliar adult. More important, the older child does not have to be looking at the familiar person in order to become uncertain. The 8-month-old compares the stranger with her retrieved schema of the familiar person; when she cannot assimilate the former to the latter, she becomes uncertain and may cry.

SEPARATION FEAR.   The fear of temporary separation from a familiar caregiver shows up most clearly when the infant is left in an unfamiliar room or in the presence of an unfamiliar person. It is less likely to occur if the child is left at home or with a familiar relative or baby sitter. The mother tells her 1-year-old, who is playing happily, that she is leaving but will return shortly, and then departs. The child gazes at the door where the mother was last seen and a few seconds later begins to cry. Blind 1-year-olds who cannot see the mother are not protected against this distress, for they cry when they *hear* the mother leave the room (Fraiberg, 1975). Separation fear usually appears between 7 and 12 months of age, peaks between 15 and 18 months, and then gradually declines.

An explanation of separation distress similar to the one applied to stranger anxiety seems appropriate. Following the mother's departure, the infant generates from memory the schema of the mother's former presence and compares it with the present situation. If the child cannot resolve the discrepancy inherent in the comparison of the schemata for the present and past, he becomes uncertain and may cry. However, some children begin to cry as soon as their mother goes toward the door. Why?

One possibility is that the enhanced recall and working memory capacities of the maturing infant are accompanied by the ability to anticipate the future—mental representations of possible events. The child may think something like, "What will happen now? Will the parent return? What can I do?" If the child cannot answer such questions (and thus anticipate the parent's return) or make an instrumental response that might resolve the uncertainty, she becomes vulnerable to distress and may cry. If, however, the child can anticipate what might happen (say, that the parent will return soon with a treat for the child), she may laugh. Laughter in anticipation of a novel event becomes more frequent after 8 months of age.

This interpretation of separation distress differs from a more traditional one, which assumed that children cry after maternal departure because they anticipate pain or danger as a consequence of the mother's absence, that is, because of what psychologists call a conditioned fear reaction. Although this explanation seems reasonable, it does not explain why infants all over the world suddenly develop, between 8 and 12 months of age, the expectation that an unpleasant event will occur when the mother leaves (see Figure 4.2). Moreover, children whose mothers leave them in a day-care center each morning do not show separation distress earlier or with less intensity than those who are cared for by their mothers continually (Kagan et al., 1978). The age at which separation distress appears is very similar for children raised in nuclear families, kibbutzim in Israel, barrios in Guatemala, Indian villages in Central America, and American daycare centers. Although these settings

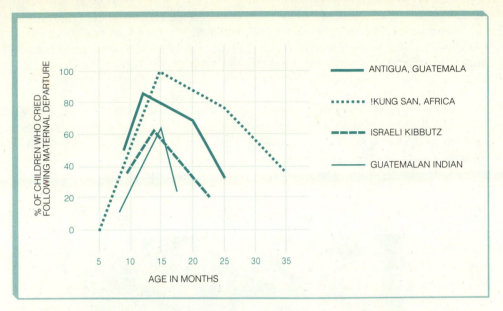

FIGURE 4.2 Separation anxiety in a variety of cultural settings. Children from widely different cultural backgrounds show fearful reactions when their mothers leave them, beginning around the first birthday. (Adapted from J. Kagan, R. Kearsley, & P. Zelazo, *Infancy: Its place in human development*. Cambridge, MA: Harvard University Press, 1978. By permission.)

provide different degrees and types of contact with the mother, separation anxiety appears at remarkably similar times in all of them.

The intensity of the child's distress over temporary separation may depend in part on the quality of the emotional relationship with the caregiver. The first appearance of separation anxiety, however, seems to be related to the emergence of the ability to retrieve the past, to compare past and present, and to anticipate events that might occur in the immediate future.

We are left with one final puzzle: The presence of a familiar person, such as a grandparent, or a familiar setting decreases the likelihood of crying in response to maternal departure, strangers, and unfamiliar toys. Why is this so? One possibility is that the presence of a familiar person or setting may make it easier for the child to make some response other than crying when the state of uncertainty is generated. Action often dispels anxiety in infants as it does in adults. When the mother leaves but the grandparent remains in the room, the grandparent's presence provides the infant with a potential target for particular behaviors. The child can approach if he wishes, vocalize, or simply turn toward the grandparent.

Separation distress recedes after 2 years of age because the older child is able to understand the event or predict the return of the mother. The child's experiences during the second year have created knowledge that makes it possible to solve the problem that engendered the anxiety in the first place.

OTHER FEARS.   Similar cognitive changes may account for other fears during infancy. One such fear is called avoidance of the visual cliff. An infant is placed on a narrow runway that rests on a large sheet of glass (see Figure 4.3). On one side of the runway is a checkerboard pattern placed directly under the glass; on the other, the checkerboard pattern is placed 1 to 2 feet below the glass, giving the appearance of depth on that side—hence the term *visual cliff*. Prior to 7 months, and before the onset of anxiety, most infants do not avoid the deep side of the glass. If their mother calls them from the deep side, they will cross to her. But after 8 months most infants avoid the side that has the appearance of a cliff and will cry if they are placed on that side. Why do these signs of fear appear at this time? They are not due to a new ability to perceive depth, for younger infants can perceive the difference between the deep and shallow sides, as evidenced by the fact that they show a distinct cardiac reaction when lowered face down on the deep side (Campos, Langer, & Krawitz, 1970).

FIGURE 4.3   *The visual cliff. The infant is on the shallow side and is approaching the deep side.* (Photograph by Enrico Ferorelli.)

One clue comes from the fact that only when infants begin to crawl or creep, usually around 8 months of age, do they begin to avoid the deep side of the visual cliff (Campos, Hiatt, Ramsey, Henderson, & Svedja, 1978). This self-produced locomotion is important, for if a baby who is unable to crawl on its own is given a "walker" so it can move around, it will begin to avoid the deep side of the cliff. Infants must have specific locomotor experiences before they will avoid the deep side, perhaps because locomotion crystallizes important cognitive abilities. In other words, when infants begin to crawl they encounter a broad range of new visual experiences and are confronted with continuous change in their visual perspective. These experiences may lead the infant to pay increased attention to its environment. The cognitive effort involved in attending to the environment facilitates the cognitive abilities that seem to be necessary if the infant is to avoid the deep side of the visual cliff.

The fear that appears in infants during the last part of the first year is also seen in monkeys that are placed in unfamiliar places. Each of six rhesus monkeys was raised alone with an inanimate toy (a hobbyhorse) in a restricted, confining environment. Each monkey was regularly placed in a novel environment, and the investigators noted two indexes of fear: a rise in heart rate and the occurrence of distress vocalizations. The highest heart rates and the most distress calls occurred when the monkeys were about 4 months old, and there was a dramatic increase in these two signs of fear between 2 and 4 months of age. The growth rate of the brain and body in monkeys is about three to four times the rate observed in human infants. Hence, the comparable period in the human child would be the interval between 7 and 15 months. This is precisely the time when fear reactions to unfamiliar people, to temporary separation, and to the visual cliff appear in human infants. Because the monkeys raised with the inanimate object had no opportunity to develop learned fears through interaction with other living creatures, it seems likely that their increased apprehension in response to discrepant events at 2 to 4 months was due in part to maturational changes in the central nervous system (Mason, 1978).

Inferring Emotions from Facial Expressions

It is impossible to measure a large number of separate physiological and bodily changes in infants; moreover, different types of biological changes do not necessarily occur together. A stranger entering a room might produce an increase in heart rate in one infant and an increase in muscle tension in another. This frustrating situation has motivated psychologists to seek a class of reactions that might be used as an index of different emotions in all children. Because changes in facial expression in response to emotionally charged events are universal and are accompanied by changes in the brain and autonomic nervous system, some scientists use facial expressions to infer the existence of specific emotions. For example, 3-month-old infants usually smile when an adult looks down and vocalizes to them; 8-month-olds display a facial expression resembling anger if an adult takes a cookie from them when they are about to eat it (Stenberg & Campos, 1983).

Infants display a range of facial expressions during the opening weeks of life, and many parents interpret these expressions as indicating that their 1-month-

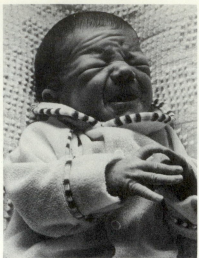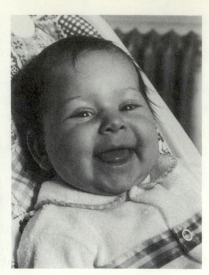

Changes in facial expressions are used to infer the presence of specific emotions in infants.

olds experience joy, anger, surprise, fear, sadness, or interest (Johnson, W. F., Emde, Pannabecker, Stenberg, & Davis, 1982). One psychologist (Izard, 1982) devised a coding scheme to measure brief changes in infants' facial expressions. Using this scheme, he found that the expressions corresponding to surprise and sadness are present by 4 months of age; the expressions of fear or anger do not appear until 5 to 7 months; and those reflecting shame and shyness do not emerge until 6 to 8 months. Expressions of contempt and guilt are not present until the second year of life.

Infants between 2 and 19 months old were videotaped as they received a painful inoculation that usually made them cry (Izard, Hembree, Dougherty, & Spizzirri, 1983). Two- to eight-month-olds showed a facial expression characterized by a round mouth and closed eyes while they were crying. This expression is termed *distress*. But 8-month-olds showed a facial expression characterized by a square mouth and open eyes while they were crying, an expression that is termed *anger*. However, many parents and some psychologists who saw an infant crying with a square mouth and open eyes after the mother had left the child alone in an unfamiliar room would probably call that child frightened or anxious, not angry. Thus, it is not clear that we can know the emotional state of an infant by looking only at its face.

THE SMILE.   The smile is the infant's most welcome facial expression. Although newborns will smile, this reaction is a reflex, often elicited by stroking of the lips or cheeks, even though the smile will occur in response to certain sounds during the first month of age (Wolff, 1987). By 2 months, however, the smile occurs in response to a wide range of stimuli, especially human faces and voices. The face of a person moving and speaking in front of a 6-week-old is the best way to generate a smile. During the first two months the mother's voice is much more effective than a high-pitched male voice (Wolff, 1987), and after 6 weeks the face is more effective than the voice (see Figures 4.4. and 4.5).

The smile may occur when the infant recognizes that an event resembles a previously acquired schema. The 3-month-old may smile in response to most human faces because it recognizes that the face is similar to a familiar face, perhaps that of a parent. This phenomenon is called the *smile of assimilation* or understanding. About one month later, at four to five months, infants begin to laugh (Sroufe & Wunsch, 1972), especially in response to social interaction, visual surprises, and tickling. During the first year infants are likely to laugh at events imposed upon them, for example, a mother playing peek-a-boo or tickling the child. But after the first birthday infants will smile and laugh at events that they themselves have caused. An 18-month-old puts on an animal costume and laughs, or acts in a mischievous manner and smiles. These reactions appear to be products of a sense of mastery. Because the state that accompanies assimilation of a schema or mastery of a motor skill may not be the same as the state that accompanies tickling, even though laughing and smiling occur in response to both, psychologists make a distinction between these two emotional states. The first might be called pride; the second, joy.

Although cognitive changes account for the onset of smiling and laughing, once children begin to smile, environmental contingencies and reinforcements influence the frequency of smiling. Gewirtz (1965) studied patterns of smiling in infants raised in three different environments in Israel. Institutionalized infants living in residential buildings rarely saw their parents and received routine institutional

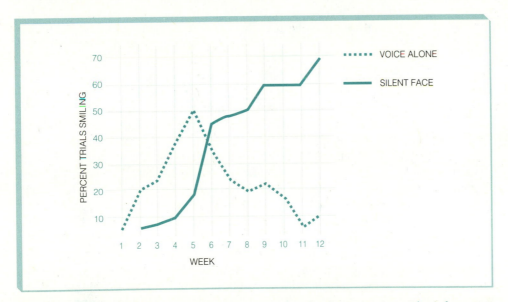

FIGURE 4.4 Infants 1 to 12 weeks old presented with a human voice with no face, or a face with no voice, smiled more often to the voice during the first 4 weeks, but thereafter smiled more often to the face. (Adapted from P. H. Wolff. *The development of behavioral states and the expression of emotions in early infancy.* Chicago: University of Chicago Press, 1987, p. 119. By permission.)

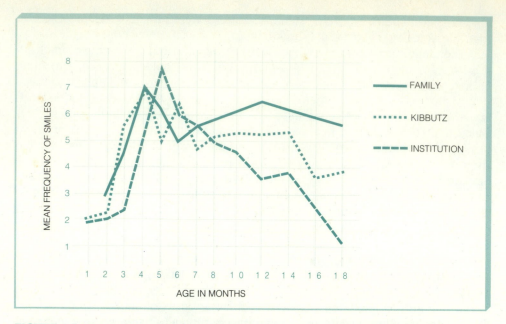

FIGURE 4.5   Frequency of smiling among infants raised in three different environments in Israel: families, kibbutzim, and institutions. Infants in all three environments began smiling at approximately the same time, but the smiling frequency of those in institutions declined over time, probably because they received fewer positive responses from adults. (Adapted from J. L. Gewirtz. The cause of infant smiling in four child-rearing environments in Israel. In B. M. Foss [Ed.], *Determinants of infant behavior* [Vol. 3]. London: Methuen, 1965. By permission of the publishers and The Tavistock Institute of Human Relations.)

care. Kibbutz infants were raised in large houses with professional caregivers but were frequently fed and cared for by their mothers during the first year. Family-reared children were raised in apartments by their mothers. Figure 4.5 graphs the frequency of smiling in response to a strange woman's face by infants in these three groups. Frequency of smiling reached a peak a few weeks earlier in the kibbutz- and family-reared infants than in the infants raised in the institution. But for all infants smiling was most frequent at about 4 months of age. During the following year, however, the children in the institution smiled less frequently, while those in family care maintained a high rate of smiling. The difference is probably due to the fact that family-reared children received more social feedback than those reared in institutions.

Although the similarity in the development of emotions in infants raised in different environments suggests that maturational factors are at work, emotional expression is also influenced by learning. As children mature, they begin to interpret and label their feeling states, often using concepts taught by other people. For example, two children are fighting over a toy; a parent takes the toy away, and the children scream loudly. One parent might tell the children they are angry, another might say they are afraid of the punishment that is imminent, and a third might tell them they feel shame for doing something wrong. The children might learn to associate their feelings and the situation with the label "anger," "fear," or "shame." The next time they have the same or similar feelings in a similar situation, they may apply the label they learned earlier.

TEMPERAMENTAL DIFFERENCES IN INFANTS

Any mother, father, or nurse in a newborn ward will tell you that there are obvious differences among infants that can be seen even from the first days of life. Some babies cry a lot, some are quiet; some sleep on a fairly regular schedule, others wake at irregular hours; some are constantly wriggling, others lie in their cribs quietly for long periods. It is possible, of course, to create excessively irritable or active babies through certain handling regimens. Nevertheless, there is good reason to believe that some babies are born with a bias toward certain moods and reaction styles. These inborn biases are called **temperament**.

Psychologists are interested in temperamental qualities for two reasons. First, if some qualities are based on inherited or prenatally acquired dispositions, these patterns might be resistant to change as the child grows. Second, children influence their parents as well as vice versa; thus, babies with different temperaments provoke different parental reactions and, even when they encounter similar experiences or child-rearing practices, react in different ways.

Experiments with three species of monkeys have shown that traumatic experiences have markedly different effects on infants with different temperamental predispositions, and the same could be true for human beings. For example, rhesus monkeys that are totally isolated during the first six months of life emerge from isolation with seriously deviant social behavior; crab eater monkeys show minimal disruption; and pigtail monkeys display intermediate levels of disturbed social behavior (Sackett, Ruppenthal, Fahrenbruch, Holm, & Greenough, 1981). Similar findings have been recorded for different species of dogs. The social behavior of beagles is seriously affected by 12 weeks of isolation, while terriers show little reaction to the same experience (Fuller & Clark, 1968). The genetic differences among species of dogs create dispositions that lead the animals to react to isolation in different ways. These dispositions are temperamental.

Infants vary in a large number of physiological and psychological characteristics. Two criteria have been used to assess which temperamental dimensions are most important: whether they are stable over time and whether they are based on inherited factors or on prenatal physiological factors. However, only a very small number of temperamental dimensions have been studied by scientists; these include activity, fussiness, fearfulness, sensitivity to stimuli, attentiveness, vigor of reaction, and the ability to regulate one's emotional state. These dimensions were selected in part because they are relatively easy to observe and seem likely to be related to the child's future adaptation.

The pioneering studies of temperament were carried out by Alexander Thomas and Stella Chess (1977), and their work remains very influential. They conducted detailed interviews with a sample of mothers every three months for the first two years of their infants' lives and less frequently until the children were 7 years old. The dimensions of temperament that emerged from the interviews were qualities that were most salient for the parents. These were activity level, rhythmicity (regularity of sleep and eating), fussiness, distractibility, attention span, intensity, response threshold, and readiness to adapt to new foods, new people, and changes in routine (Thomas & Chess, 1977).

Rating the infants on these temperamental qualities, the researchers classified the babies as *easy, difficult,* or *slow to warm up.* The easy children, who made up about 75 percent of the sample, were happy, adaptable infants who were not easily upset. The difficult children (about 10 percent) were often fussy, fearful of new people and situations, and intense in their reactions. The slow-to-warm-up babies (about 15 percent) were relatively inactive and fussy and tended to withdraw or to react negatively to novelty, but their reactions in new situations gradually became more positive with experience. By age 7, more of those children who were "difficult" infants had developed serious emotional problems than had children in the other two groups. It is likely that the parents of these hard-to-manage children sometimes responded to their behavior with frustration and hostility, thereby increasing the irritability that was an original characteristic of the infants' temperament.

It is not surprising that over time parents come to react in special ways to children with difficult temperaments. One group of mothers were asked to describe how difficult it was to take care of their infants. Later they were observed twice, once when their children were 12 months old and again at 18 months. On the first assessment each mother was given various assignments; for example, to get her child to give her an object when she named it (a set of keys or a spoon), and to get the child to manipulate toys in a desired manner without touching them (pounding a single peg). When the infants were 18 months old, the mothers were given different tasks; for example, to help the child place puzzle pieces correctly or stack a set of rings in the proper order.

When the infants were 12 months old the mothers behaved very similarly toward difficult and easy children. But six months later the mothers who had sons with difficult temperaments exerted far less effort during the tasks, as if they had developed a low expectation of success. The children with difficult temperaments apparently had influenced their mother's attitudes toward their competence (Maccoby, Snow, & Jacklin, 1984). Should such difficult children continue to frustrate their parents' standards and the parents continue to expect less of them, in time a spiral of self-defeating behavior could become established (see Box 4.1).

Activity Level

Squirmy, wiggly babies do not necessarily grow up to be the terrors of the schoolyard who run full tilt everywhere they go. Although very active newborns tend to be more active than most other children during the first year, there is only modest preservation of this quality in later childhood (Moss & Susman, 1980; Rothbart & Derryberry, 1981).

Genetic influences on temperament are best studied with twins. The rationale for this strategy is similar to the one set forth in Chapter 2 in discussing the genetic bases of intelligence. One of the largest groups of twins studied for this purpose was part of an investigation called the Collaborative Perinatal Project, in which 350

Living with a Difficult Baby

When parents realize that an infant's behavior is determined partly by the child's temperament rather than wholly by what the parents do, they can work more effectively toward a positive outcome for the child. One of the most difficult babies in Thomas and Chess's (1977) sample typically showed intense irritability and withdrawal when faced with new situations and was slow to adapt to anything unfamiliar. He showed this tendency with his first bath and his first solid foods. He also reacted negatively to the first days in nursery and elementary school and on his first shopping trip with his parents. Each of these experiences evoked stormy responses and much crying and struggling. However, his parents learned to anticipate his reactions. They learned that if they were patient and presented new situations gradually and repeatedly, eventually the boy adapted to them. The parents did not interpret their son's difficulties as reflecting on their effectiveness as parents. As a result, the boy never became a behavior problem, even though many children with this temperamental style are at risk for psychological problems.

During later childhood and adolescence, this boy was fortunate in being able to avoid many radically new situations. He lived in the same community and went through high school with the same friends. However, when he went to a college away from home he was confronted with new situations, new friends, and a complex relationship with a female student with whom he was living. In these circumstances his earlier temperamental tendencies to withdraw and show intense negative reactions were expressed once again. However, after a discussion with Dr. Thomas, who explained to the young man his temperamental history and some techniques he might use to adapt to college, the young man's difficulties disappeared, and by the end of the year he had adjusted again. When he was told that similar negative reactions might occur in the future, he said, "That's all right. I know how to handle them now" (Thomas & Chess, 1977, pp. 165-167).

pairs of twins were observed at birth, 8 months, 4 years, and 7 years of age. Half the twins were identical and half were fraternal. When the babies came into the hospital for testing, trained observers rated their behavior for activity level, sociability, irritability, and other dimensions of temperament. Analysis of the findings showed a moderate genetic contribution to activity level at 8 months, but at 4 or 7 years the difference between identical and fraternal twins disappeared. That is, at 8 months the identical twins were more similar to one another in activity level than the nonidentical twins were (Goldsmith, H. H. & Gottesman, 1981). Other scientists have also found only slight support for the notion that differences in activity level are genetically based (Plomin & Foch, 1980).

Irritability

Differences among infants in crying, fussiness, and general irritability during the first six months do not always predict that these differences will persist in older children, even though extreme irritability in infants over 7 months old is modestly preserved for the next year or two (Rothbart & Derryberry, 1981; Thomas & Chess, 1977). However, there is some evidence that extremely irritable newborns are a little less likely to become sociable 2-year-olds, for such infants are less likely to laugh and smile than typical infants are (Riese, 1987).

Reaction to Unfamiliarity

Two of the most stable temperamental qualities are the tendency to be shy, timid, and quiet in unfamiliar situations and the contrasting tendency to be sociable, bold, and spontaneous. These two qualities are obvious to parents: When several thousand mothers of infants 4 to 8 months old filled out questionnaires about their infants' behavior, they named the tendency to approach or avoid unfamiliar people and toys as the most striking quality (Sanson, Prior, Garino, Oberkaid, & Sewell, 1987).

About 10 percent of 2-year-olds are extremely quiet and shy and remain close to the caregiver for 10 or 15 minutes whenever they are in an unfamiliar place or with a stranger. These children are described as *inhibited*. A larger number of children, described as *uninhibited*, begin to play immediately and show no signs of initial timidity. Children in the former group resemble the prototypical adult introvert, while those in the latter group have the features of the future extravert. These two profiles reflect a more general quality, namely, the tendency to display restraint in speech and play, and to retreat to a familiar person, whenever the child encounters unfamiliar people or settings, or challenging situations. The words *restrained, watchful*, and *gentle* capture the essence of the inhibited child, while *free, energetic*, and *spontaneous* capture the style of the uninhibited youngster.

These qualities were the most stable in a longitudinal study of children observed from birth through 25 years of age (Kagan & Moss, 1962). The children who were extremely shy, timid, and fearful during the first three years of life displayed a coherent cluster during the early school years. They avoided dangerous activities, were minimally aggressive, conformed to parental requests, and avoided unfamiliar peer groups. When they were adolescents they avoided contact sports. The four boys who were most inhibited chose relatively solitary careers as adults (one music teacher and three university scientists). The four boys who had been least inhibited during the first six years chose traditionally masculine vocations that involved more social interaction with others (one athletic coach, one salesman, and two engineers). In another longitudinal study, two groups of children who showed these qualities to an extreme extent were observed regularly from the second or third

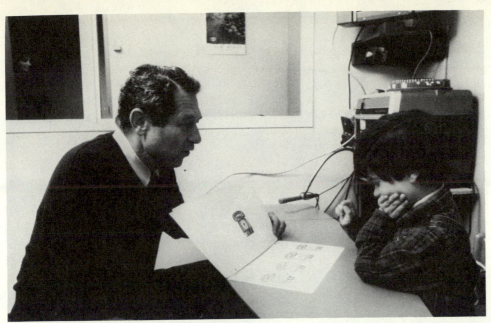

Jerome Kagan has conducted an extensive longitudinal study of shyness using observations in various contexts as well as interviews of subjects both as children and as adults.

year of life through the eighth year. About half of the children who were very shy and timid on the first assessment retained that quality; at 7½ years of age they had difficulty initiating play with unfamiliar children and were quiet and subdued when tested by adults or when playing with groups of nine or ten unfamiliar children. Moreover, the limbic system of persistently inhibited children is more easily aroused, for they have higher and more stable heart rates (see Figure 4.6), higher levels of cortisol, and greater muscle tension. Figure 4.7 shows that the children who had the highest level of limbic arousal when they were 5½ years old were the most inhibited two years later when they were 7½.

Child-rearing conditions can influence the degree to which a tendency to become inhibited will be actualized. If a child with this tendency is raised in an unusually benevolent environment that gently promotes an outgoing coping style, he or she will not develop into a shy, timid youngster. On the other hand, an overly stressful environment can create timid behavior even in children born with a temperamental disposition that favors spontaneous sociable behavior. Thus, only a small proportion of infants who are born with a temperamental disposition for shy behavior will become timid 3-year-olds. The presence of a biological predisposition toward shyness does not guarantee that the child will become shy (see Box 4.2).

The Principle of Bidirectionality

The reciprocal influence of parental behavior and infant temperament forms the basis for the principle of **bidirectionality** in development. This principle states

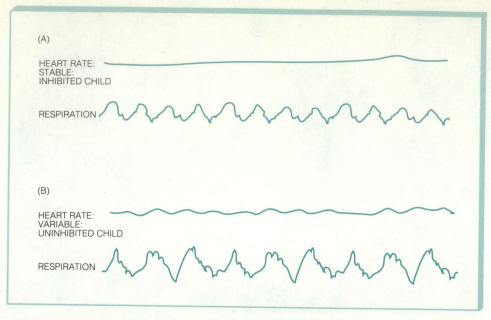

FIGURE 4.6   The heart rate and respiration patterns of an inhibited and an uninhibited child while looking at pictures. Both children have similar patterns of respiration. The inhibited child has a stable heart rate (top pattern), while the uninhibited child has a variable heart rate (bottom pattern). The peaks of the heart rate correspond to the peaks of the respiration cycles for the uninhibited child but not for the inhibited child. (Adapted from C. Garcia Coll, J. Kagan, & J. S. Reznick. Behavioral inhibition in young children. *Child Development*, 1984, 55, 1005–1019. Copyright by Society for Research in Child Development. By permission.)

that the parent-child relationship goes both ways: Parents influence children, and children influence parental behaviors. Another way to state this is to say that children's development is a product of the interaction between their own characteristics and those of the people who socialize them.

One example of this principle is a family that included two children born a little over a year apart. The older child, a boy named Elliott, was a cuddly baby who smiled readily and was very responsive. His mother and father smiled and talked to him a great deal. He was also very active. By 9 months he was walking, and soon he was getting into everything. He required a lot of attention just to ensure his safety. His younger sister, Susan, was a quieter, more sober baby. She watched people intently but did not smile readily. As a result, her parents talked to her less than they had to Elliott. Susan also was relatively inactive, seeming content to sit and watch others much of the time. She received less attention and less practice in social interaction, which may have contributed to her quiet manner.

Elliott and Susan had different patterns of behavior from the beginning, and as a result their parents treated them differently. The parents' behavior, in turn, encouraged different patterns of social response in their children.

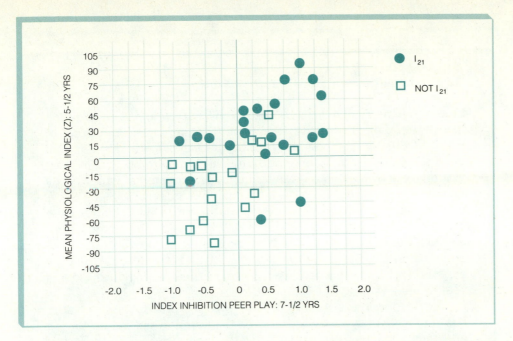

FIGURE 4.7 Children selected to be extremely inhibited (●, shy) at 21 months, compared with uninhibited children (□), showed higher levels of physiological arousal at 5½ years of age, and were more timid and quiet with a group of unfamiliar peers at 7½ years of age. J. Kagan (unpublished).

EMOTIONAL AND SOCIAL RELATIONSHIPS WITH ADULTS

Theoretical Perspectives

The temperamental qualities of the infant and the practices, attitudes, and personality of the parents combine to produce a characteristic pattern of social interaction between the infant and each parent. Almost every theorist has assumed that this pattern of interaction influences the infant's psychological growth in important ways. During most of this century, psychologists have regarded children's relationships with people who care for them as the major bases for emotional and cognitive development (Bowlby, 1969; Freud, 1964; Watson, 1928).

Until recently developmental theorists focused almost entirely on the mother as the person whose love, care, and attention were paramount in the baby's feelings of security and insecurity. Only during the past two decades have scientists studied the influence of fathers, siblings, and other caregivers on development. In addition, most theorists have emphasized the significance of pleasure and pain in the development of behavior. They assumed that human beings are motivated by the desire to obtain pleasure and to avoid pain. As a result, they awarded the greatest significance to the actions of caregivers who provide pleasure. Infants were

BOX 4.2

Temperament and Early Experience

Studies of the relationship between environmental stress and children's temperament must deal with the important question of whether a temperamental bias present at birth can produce a certain quality of behavior independent of the child's environment. The best guess at present is that certain kinds of environmental experiences must interact with the child's temperament in order to produce a particular behavioral profile. For example, it appears that children who are born with a temperamental bias that favors irritability and sleeplessness during the first year and shyness and timidity during the second and third years will develop the latter behaviors only if they experience some chronic environmental stress during the opening year of life.

Some possible stressors include prolonged hospitalization, the death of a parent, quarreling between the parents, and mental illness in a family member. These stressors do not appear with great frequency, however. On the other hand, a common source of stress is an older sibling who unexpectedly seizes a toy or teases or yells at an infant with a temperamental bias to become shy and timid. And it turns out that two-thirds of children who become inhibited have older siblings while two-thirds of children who are uninhibited and socially spontaneous are first borns without any older siblings. Thus, it is possible that in a child born with a temperamental bias favoring the development of shy, timid behavior, the presence of an older sibling can be the stress that acts as a catalyst for such behavior.

thought to develop positive feelings and close attachments to people who are frequent sources of pleasure, either because these people soothe and play with them or because they reduce the discomfort caused by pain, cold, hunger, or psychological distress.

PSYCHOANALYTIC THEORY.   Sigmund Freud's conception of social and emotional development was based on this assumption. Freud assumed that infants are born with biological instincts that demand satisfaction. A child's need for food, warmth, and reduction of pain represents a "striving for sensory pleasure." Freud described the biological basis for this striving as a kind of physical energy, which he termed *libido*.

As Freud saw it, the activities, people, and objects in which children invest libidinal energy change in predictable ways as the child grows older. During infancy, Freud argued, the events surrounding feeding are the most important sources of gratification. When children are being fed and cared for, their attention, derived from the energy of the libido, becomes focused on the person providing the gratification. Freud envisioned infants as continually investing libidinal energy not only in the people who care for them but also in the surfaces of the mouth, tongue, and lips. For this reason, Freud named the period of infancy the *oral stage*. Freud suggested that too much or too little gratification of oral needs could slow the child's progress into the next developmental stage; that is, a *fixation*, or resistance to transferring the libidinal energy to a new set of objects and activities, might occur. Freud proposed the bold hypothesis that a fixation at the oral stage, caused by excessive or insufficient gratification, could predispose an adult toward specific psychological symptoms. For example, infants who were undergratified might develop serious depression or schizophrenia, and those who were overly gratified might be excessively dependent on others.

According to Freud, the young infant's most important source of pleasure is being fed.

Freud suggested that the anal area and the activities surrounding defecation become important sources of libidinal gratification during the second year of life. Interactions with parents over toilet training assume special significance at this stage. Freud called this stage of development the *anal stage.* Fixation at this stage supposedly would produce either adults who are very neat, orderly, and concerned with their property, or else adults with the opposite qualities.

More recent theories derived from Freud's retain the assumption that early mother-child interactions have a special quality that is necessary for the infant's development (Ainsworth, Blehar, Waters, & Wall, 1978; Bowlby, 1969; Erikson, 1963). But they emphasize the psychological consequences of being cared for in an affectionate, consistent, reliable, and gentle manner, rather than the biological functions of feeding and toileting. Erik Erikson, for example, proposed that the critical developmental event during infancy is the establishment of a sense of trust in another person. Infants who have consistently satisfying experiences of nurturance traverse this stage successfully. Those who do not will lack a basic sense of trust in others as they grow older.

In the second year, Erikson suggested, children attempt to establish a sense of autonomy and independence from their parents. Children who fail to gain a sense of autonomy may be vulnerable to feelings of shame and doubt about their ability to function independently. In discussing these and later stages in the life cycle, Erikson retained the essence of the Freudian idea of fixation: He believed that failure to progress through one stage satisfactorily would interfere with progression through subsequent stages. His theory differed from Freud's because it emphasized *psychosocial* stages in contrast to *psychosexual* stages.

SOCIAL LEARNING THEORY.　A parallel theoretical approach appeared in the writings of behaviorists. These scientists also assumed that hunger, thirst, and pain are basic drive states that propel infants to action. But the behaviorists rejected the Freudian concept of libido because it cannot be measured. The impetus for psychological change, they believed, is not invisible feelings but biological drives and other measurable responses. An event that satisfies a child's biological needs (that is, reduces a drive) was called a *primary reinforcer.* For example, for a hungry infant, food is a primary reinforcer. People or objects that are present when a drive is reduced become *secondary reinforcers* through their association with the primary reinforcer. As a frequent source of food and comfort, an infant's mother is an important secondary reinforcer. The child therefore approaches her not only when hungry or in pain but on a variety of other occasions, displaying a generalized dependency on her. Social learning theorists assumed that the strength of the child's dependency is determined by how rewarding the mother is, that is, by how often she has been associated with pleasure and the reduction of pain and discomfort (Sears, Maccoby, & Levin, 1957).

The idea that infants' emotional ties and approach behaviors to the mother are based on the reduction of biological drives dominated American theories of infancy from World War I until the early 1960s. Because feeding was considered so important, child development experts as well as parents devoted a great deal of attention to whether a child was breast-fed or bottle-fed, whether it was fed on a schedule or on demand, and when and how the child should be weaned from breast to bottle or from bottle to cup. These important questions were investigated extensively, but no consistent relationships between feeding patterns and the child's subsequent social and emotional development were discovered. The results of this research cast some doubt on the utility of the concept of the oral stage. More recent evidence also indicates that the strength of a child's attachment to either parent is not related in any simple way to the frequency with which that parent feeds, changes, or cares for the physical needs of the child (Ainsworth et al., 1978).

But a fatal blow to theories emphasizing biological drive reduction was dealt by Harry Harlow and his colleagues in a series of experiments with infant monkeys. These researchers identified a new source of the mother-infant bond: *contact comfort*. In some of their experiments young monkeys were raised in a cage with two different kinds of inanimate "mothers" (Harlow & Harlow, 1966). One mother was made of wire, and the infant could nurse from a nipple mounted on this mother's chest (see Figure 4.8). The other mother was covered with soft terry cloth but did not provide the infant with any food. Contrary to the predictions of both psychoanalytic and behavioral theories, the infant monkeys spent most of their time resting on the terry-cloth mother. They went to the wire monkey only when they were hungry. When an infant monkey was frightened by an unfamiliar object, such as a large wooden spider, it ran to the cloth mother and clung to it as though it felt more secure there than clinging to the wire mother (see Figure 4.9). At least for these primates, the pleasure associated with feeding seemed not to be the foundation for the attachment bond between parent and infant.

ETHOLOGY.   At about the time that Harlow began his experiments with monkeys, the field of **ethology** was being created by a group of European naturalists, notably Konrad Lorenz (1981) and Nikko Tinbergen (1951). These scientists emphasized the need to study animals in their natural environments. In part, they were rebelling against the behaviorists' stress on conditioning and on research under strictly controlled laboratory conditions.

According to the ethologists, each species of animal is born with a set of *fixed action patterns*. A fixed action pattern is a stereotyped behavioral sequence that is set in motion when the proper environmental stimulus, called a *releaser*, occurs. Some fixed action patterns can be triggered only during a limited time span during the animal's development, called a *critical* or *sensitive period*. Releasers that occur before or after the critical period have little or no effect on the animal's behavior.

Imprinting is a fixed action pattern that takes place shortly after birth in ducks, geese, chickens, and some other species. A newly hatched duckling is innately prepared to follow the first moving object it sees. If that object is its biological mother, the duckling learns to follow the mother and to approach her when in distress. But if the moving object that the duckling sees during the critical period for imprinting is something else, such as a human being or an electric train, the young bird will follow that object instead of the mother duck.

The idea that human infants might be born into the world prepared to exhibit certain behaviors that are neither a result of prior learning nor based on drive reduction was attractive to a young British psychiatrist named John Bowlby, who was trained in psychoanalytic theory but receptive to the new ethological findings. Bowlby proposed that human infants are programmed to emit certain behaviors

Ethologist Konrad Lorenz has discovered the phenomenon of imprinting, which refers to a fixed action pattern that is released shortly after birth in many species of birds.

that will elicit caregiving from people around them and will keep adults nearby. These behaviors include crying, smiling, cooing, and crawling toward someone. From an evolutionary standpoint, these patterns have adaptive value because they help ensure that infants will receive the care necessary for their survival (Bowlby, 1969).

Attachment to Caregivers

A major result of mother-infant interactions, according to Bowlby, is the development in the infant of an emotional attachment to the mother. The function of the infant's attachment is to provide psychological security. **Attachment** has been defined as follows:

> The term *attachment system* refers to a regulatory system hypothesized to exist within a person. . . . The goal is to regulate behaviors that maintain proximity to and contact with a discriminated protective person, referred to as the attachment figure. From the psychological vantage point of the attached person, however, the system's set goal is felt security. (Bretherton, in Osofosky, 1987, p. 1063)

FIGURE 4.8 Wire and cloth mother surrogates used in studies investigating the effects of different types of mothering on infant monkeys. Wire mother had a nipple on her chest to feed the baby, but the cloth mother was padded and soft. Infants spent more time on the cloth mother and ran to her when frightened, suggesting that contact comfort rather than food was important for the infant's attachment to its "mother." (From H. F. Harlow & R. R. Zimmerman. Affectional responses in the infant monkey. *Science*, 959, 130, 422. By permission.)

The signs of an infant's attachment to a caregiver are evident in three phenomena. First, a target of attachment is better able than anyone else to placate and soothe the baby. Second, infants are much more likely to approach attachment targets for play or consolation than to approach others. Finally, infants are less likely to become afraid when in the presence of attachment targets than when these people are absent. For example, an unfamiliar woman visited the homes of 1-year-olds and showed the children objects and events that were likely to make them anxious

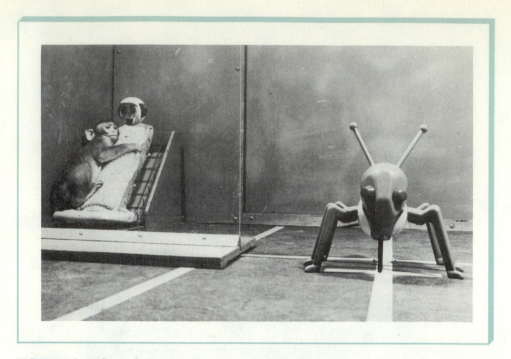

FIGURE 4.9   When a frightening object was introduced into a large open space (the open-field test), infant monkeys ran to the cloth mother and clung to her. This reaction was one indication that they were attached to the cloth mother rather than to the wire mother. (From H. F. Harlow & R. R. Zimmerman. Affectional responses in the infant monkey. *Science*, 1959, 130, 430. Copyright by the American Association for the Advancement of Science. By permission.)

(a large, frightening toy or an unusual sound coming from inside a chair). When the mother was in the room, the child was less likely to cry or show obvious signs of fear than when the mother was not there.

The attachment system and its set of specific responses are aroused by novelty, danger, or distress and are muted by the perception of safety. Infants display attachment behaviors—such as orienting toward or remaining near the parent—when they are anxious, tired, hungry, or otherwise distressed. The purpose of the attachment behavior is to reduce unpleasant feelings through interaction with the target of attachment. It has been suggested that after the first birthday children construct a schema or internal working model of the self and its relationship to its targets of attachment. This schema permits the infant to feel more secure, for the child knows that the target of attachment is potentially available even if he or she is not actually present.

Young children will ignore their parents and even prefer to play with a stranger as long as the target of attachment is present. But when infants feel threatened or experience uncertainty they will turn quickly to the mother, father, or other attachment figure, often to seek information about the degree of safety or danger in a

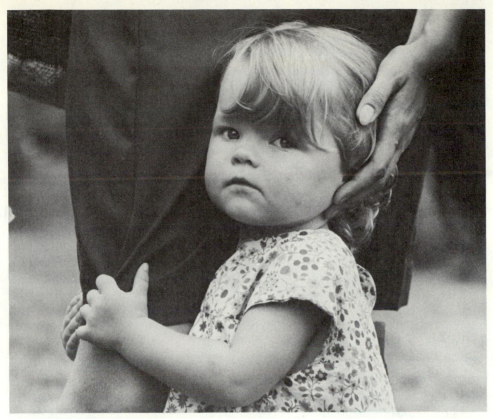

Attachment behaviors become evident when a young child feels threatened or experiences uncertainty.

particular situation. For example, if a 1-year-old is placed on the shallow side of the visual cliff while the mother is smiling and standing on the deep side, the child is likely to cross the deep side and approach her. But if the mother shows a fearful face the child is unlikely to approach her and may cry. Similarly, a child moving toward a novel toy will stop and crawl or run to the mother if she assumes a fearful face or utters a meaningless phrase in a frightened tone of voice. But the child will continue to approach the toy if the mother smiles or says something in a reassuring tone of voice (Klinnert, Campos, Sorce, Emde, & Svejda, 1983). This phenomenon, called *social referencing*, is one of the signs that the infant has developed an attachment to an adult.

Most infants form attachments, usually to more than one person. Many theorists propose that a strong attachment provides a basis for healthy emotional and social development during later childhood. Children with strong attachments are expected to become socially outgoing and curious about their environment, to be willing to explore, and to develop the ability to cope with stress. Serious disruptions in the attachment process are thought to produce problems in the child's later social development.

Measuring Attachment

Psychologists use two strategies in deciding whether a child possesses a certain psychological state or quality, such as secure attachment to an adult. On the one hand, they try to determine whether the environmental conditions that presumably produced the psychological state actually occurred. In the case of an attachment to an adult, this would mean frequently observing the parents and infant at home during the first year. Such observation is difficult and expensive to carry out. The other strategy, which is much easier and more economical, is to measure an aspect of the child's current state that might be a sign of the deeper quality the scientist wants to evaluate.

These two strategies do not always yield the same results. For example, the bodily state called "vulnerable to infectious disease" can be produced by many years of poor nutrition. However, it is difficult to determine whether a particular 10-year-old has a prior history of malnutrition. Therefore, many scientists use the child's current height and weight as a sign of a history of poor nutrition. A 10-year-old who is only as tall as a 7-year-old is assumed to have suffered chronic malnutrition during the early years of life. The problem with this conclusion is that many children who are below average in height did not suffer malnutrition. They are short for other reasons, including genetic factors and lower levels of growth hormone. Although these children are below average in height, they are not especially vulnerable to infectious disease.

THE STRANGE SITUATION.   The most popular procedure for assessing security of attachment was devised by Mary Ainsworth; it is called the Strange Situation. This procedure consists of a series of seven 3-minute episodes during which infants are observed with a parent, with a stranger, with a parent and a stranger, and alone, as shown in Table 4.1.

The two key episodes in the Strange Situation are 4 and 7, those in which the parent returns after being out of the room. The type of behavior shown when the parent returns is used as the principal index of the infant's attachment to him or her.

Three major patterns of attachment have been described. In general, children who seek the parent when he or she returns, and are easily comforted by the parent, are described as *securely attached*. They typically show mild protest following the parent's departure. Children who play contentedly and ignore the parent upon his or her return are usually classified as *avoidant and insecurely attached*. They often do not protest when the parent leaves the room. Finally, children who, after the parent returns, alternately cling to the parent and push him or her away are described as *resistant and insecurely attached*. These children are extremely distressed when the parent leaves. In samples of American 1-year-olds, about 65 percent are usually classified as securely attached, about 21 percent as avoidant, and about 14 percent as resistant (van IJzendorn & Kroonenberg, 1988).

Although the Strange Situation may seem artificial, classifications based on it do predict other qualities that theoretically should be related to the security of children's attachment. Children who were classified as securely or insecurely attached in the Strange Situation when they were 12 to 18 months old were observed

TABLE 4.1

Episodes in the Strange Situation

Episode	Event initiating episode	Persons present during episode
1	Parent and infant enter room	Parent and infant
2	Stranger joins parent and infant	Parent, infant, and stranger
3	Parent leaves room	Infant and stranger
4	Parent returns to room; stranger leaves	Parent and infant
5	Parent leaves	Infant alone
6	Stranger returns	Infant and stranger
7	Parent returns; stranger leaves	Parent and infant

at later ages ranging from 21 months to 5 years. Securely attached children were generally more socially outgoing with adults and with other children, more cooperative and compliant with their mothers and with strange adults, better able to cope with stress, and more curious than children who were classified as insecurely attached (Arend, Gove, & Sroufe, 1979; Londerville & Main, 1981; Pastor, 1981; Waters, Wippman, & Sroufe, 1979). Furthermore, when securely attached children were observed in their own homes, they sought physical contact with their mothers less often than did children who were classified as insecurely attached (Clarke-Stewart & Hevey, 1981).

LIMITATIONS OF THE STRANGE SITUATION. Although these findings indicate that the Strange Situation may be a sensitive index of quality of attachment, other information suggests caution in interpreting children's behavior in this situation as an indication of security or insecurity. First, many children change their attachment classifications during the period between 12 and 19 months. The changes are sometimes associated with changes in family circumstances, such as the mother's beginning employment outside the home, but children who experience such changes are just as likely to shift from insecure to secure attachment as the other way around (Thompson, R. A., Lamb, & Estes, 1982).

Second, a long-term study of mothers and children found no differences in the incidence of secure or insecure attachments at 1 year between children of normal mothers and children growing up with mothers who had serious mental and emotional disorders. Many of the emotionally disturbed mothers were not as lively or attentive to their infants as the normal mothers were, yet the children of these parents were not more likely to behave as if they were insecurely attached (Sameroff, Seifer, & Zax, 1982).

The primary basis for classifying a child as securely or insecurely attached is the child's reaction when the parent returns to the room. However, that reaction is determined partly by how upset the child became when the parent left the infant alone or with the stranger. Children who do not cry when the parent leaves because they are not especially anxious about the departure are also unlikely to approach the parent for comfort when he or she comes back. Such children are likely to be classified as avoidant and insecurely attached. Similarly, children who cannot be soothed easily (called resistant and insecurely attached) are likely to be those who become extremely upset by the maternal departure.

Some infants who are temperamentally vulnerable to becoming anxious and frightened by unexpected parental departure may also be more difficult to soothe in the Strange Situation. Many 1-year-old children who are classified as resistant and insecurely attached, compared with securely attached children, are very irritable, fearful, and difficult to care for from the first days of life through the first birthday (Miyake, 1986; Belsky & Rovine, 1987).

One-year-olds who are classified as resistant and insecurely attached may have been born with a nervous system that causes them to be unusually reactive to changes in stimulation. One indication of sensitivity is the infant's reaction to a change in the taste of liquids. Newborn infants were allowed to suck on a nipple that first delivered plain water. After 2 minutes the solution was changed to a mildly sweet liquid, and after 2 more minutes it was changed to an even sweeter liquid. Some newborns did not increase their rate of sucking very much despite the change from plain water to sweet liquid. However, other infants were very reactive to the change in taste and showed a large increase in sucking rate. When these children were seen at 18 months of age, those who had reacted to the sweet taste with an increase in sucking were more likely to be classified as resistant and insecurely attached; those who had shown minimal increases in rate of sucking were more likely to be classified as securely attached (Lipsitt & LeGasse, 1989). Thus, the temperamental characteristic called *inhibition* makes a substantial contribution to the attachment classification in the Strange Situation.

A second factor that may influence the child's behavior in the Strange Situation is the degree to which parents encourage their infants to control signs of fear during the first year. A child with an attentive and loving parent who encourages self-reliance and control of fear is less likely to cry when the parent leaves and, therefore, is less likely to approach the parent when he or she returns. Such a child is likely to be classified as avoidant.

Patterns of attachment differ in different cultures, suggesting that cultural values and child-rearing practices influence children's behavior in the Strange Situation. In Germany, about 35 percent of infants are classified as avoidant. The authors of one study wrote that their 1-year-old subjects may have received "a strong push in the direction of affective reserve" from their parents and other adults in the German culture (Grossmann, Grossmann, Huber, & Wartner, 1981, p. 179). In Japan and Israel, where parents are considerably more protective, higher percentages of children are classified as resistant. There are also large differences between samples from the same country, perhaps because of different parental practices and life experiences for children in those samples (van IJzendorn & Kroonenberg, 1988).

It may not be possible to determine the differential contribution of temperamental qualities, prior socialization, and the attachment bond to the baby's behavior in a single laboratory assessment of the Strange Situation. Thus, psychologists are faced with a dilemma. They believe that variation in the attachment of the infant to its caregivers is important, and they suspect that infants who are insecurely attached may be at some risk for later psychological problems. But they are not certain that they have a sensitive way to measure the security or insecurity of a child's attachment.

Effects of Parental Practices

Although the human infant appears to have an innate tendency to form attachments, the targets selected and the strength and quality of those attachments depend partly on the parents' behavior in relation to the child. Recent efforts to determine what parental qualities are important for attachment have shown that attachment does not result only from parental actions that satisfy the child's need for food, water, warmth, and relief from pain. Moreover, the sheer amount of time the child spends with the parent seems not to determine the quality of the child's attachment. For example, a group of Swedish children whose fathers had been their primary caregivers for some part of infancy showed no stronger attachment to their fathers than children whose fathers had been away working full time (Lamb, Hwang, Frodi, & Frodi, 1982). Similarly, infants with mothers who are employed full time seem to be as strongly attached to them as infants whose mothers are at home all the time. The old adage that the quality rather than the quantity of parenting is important seems to fit the facts in this case. Some theorists have proposed that the first step in attachment is a process of **bonding** that takes place immediately after birth. This process is discussed in Box 4.3.

What qualities of social interactions between parent and child are most important for the development of attachment? One major dimension has been variously described as sensitivity, synchrony, and reciprocity. Two components are involved. The first is sensitivity and responsiveness to the infant's signals, whether they are cries, glances, smiles, or vocalizations. Parents of strongly attached children generally respond quickly and positively to their children's social overtures and initiate playful, pleasant exchanges in ways that fit the baby's mood and cognitive abilities. A key dimension of sensitive interaction is the ability to act in harmony with the child's signals and behaviors (Ainsworth et al., 1978). Consider the following examples of two parents who show equal amounts of affection and interaction with their children but differ in their sensitivity:

Darcy, an 18-month-old, is playing with some toys on the floor. Her mother finishes some work at her desk and turns to watch her. She comments, "Those are nice blocks, Darcy. You are making a fine tower with them." Darcy smiles. Mother picks up a book and begins to read. In a few minutes, after finishing her tower, Darcy walks to Mother with a children's book in her hand, saying, "Book," and trying to crawl into Mother's lap. Mother takes Darcy in her lap, puts down her own book, and says, "Do you want to read this book?" Darcy says yes, and Mother reads.

Stacy, another 18-month-old, is playing on her living room floor when her mother finishes some desk work. Mother says, "Come here, Stacy. I'll read your

BOX 4.3

Early Bonding

In both popular and professional writing, some people have suggested that a critical process of "bonding" between mother and child takes place during the first hours after birth. The common practice in American hospitals, in which infants are placed in a separate nursery and taken to their mothers only for feeding, has been heavily criticized because it prevents the mother and infant from establishing an emotional bond during the first postnatal hours. Partly as a result, some hospitals now give the mother and infant some time together immediately after birth, encourage "rooming in" (in which the infant stays in the mother's room instead of in the newborn nursery), and have developed programs to involve parents in caregiving for premature babies.

We can ask two questions about early contact between parent and infant: (1) Does it foster attachment or bonding? (2) Is it critical for optimal development? The answer to the first question is a qualified yes, at least in the short run, but long-term effects are more difficult to demonstrate. The answer to the second question is no.

These questions were the subject of an experimental investigation in Germany in which some mothers had "early contact" with their infants. The babies were placed in the mother's arms on the delivery bed for at least 30 minutes after birth. The remaining mothers experienced the standard hospital procedure. Half of each group had "extended contact"—the mothers kept the babies in their rooms for about 5 hours a day in addition to regular feeding. The mothers without extended contact had their babies with them for feedings 5 times a day for about 30 minutes per feeding. The early-contact mothers showed more tender touching and cuddling toward their babies during the first 5 days than did the mothers without early contact. But these differences had disappeared by the time the babies were 8 to 10 days old. Furthermore, early contact was effective only for mothers who had planned pregnancies, suggesting that the effects depended on the mother's attitude toward the birth. There were no differences between the mothers who had extended contact and those who did not (Grossmann, Thane, & Grossmann, 1981). In another investigation, babies who were hospitalized after birth because of prematurity or illness showed patterns of attachment at twelve months that were similar to those found in earlier studies. Apparently the early separation of parents and children did not lead to long-term problems (Rode, Change, Fisch, & Sroufe, 1981).

Although early mother-child contact may not be critical for emotional bonding, placing the baby near the mother immediately after birth is emotionally satisfying to some parents and may contribute to a harmonious beginning for their relationship with the child. On the other hand, parents need not feel that they are depriving their newborn of a highly significant experience if they do not have early contact. Some mothers are exhausted after delivery and are relieved to have someone take care of them and the baby. Adopted infants have their first contact with their adoptive mothers days, months, or even years after birth, yet strong emotional bonds can be established between child and mother.

book to you." Stacy looks up but continues building a block tower in which she is apparently engrossed. Mother goes to Stacy and says, "Let's read now," picking her up and giving her a hug. Stacy squirms and whimpers. Mother puts her down, and Stacy returns to her tower. Later, having finished her tower, Stacy picks up the book and tries to crawl into Mother's lap, saying, "Book." Mother says, "No, you didn't want to read when I was ready. I'm busy now."

These two mothers provide their children with equal amounts of attention, but the first is more sensitive and responsive to the child than the second.

A second parental characteristic associated with strong attachment can be described as warmth, supportiveness, and gentleness. Parents of strongly attached children use warm tones and gentle commands when giving directions, and they support the child's behavior with positive comments when appropriate (Londerville & Main, 1981; Pastor, 1981).

THE FATHER'S BEHAVIOR.   Most infants develop clear attachments to fathers as well as to mothers, and some social critics have suggested that infants could benefit from receiving frequent care from their fathers as well as their mothers. Two questions about the role of fathers have been addressed in recent research: (1) Do fathers have the capacity to provide appropriate and sensitive care to infants? (2) What kind of interactions do fathers typically have with their infants?

Observations of fathers in standardized situations reveal that they show as much sensitivity, affection, and skill as their wives when feeding and holding their newborn infants (Parke & Tinsley, 1981). However, in American middle-class families fathers and mothers play with babies in different ways. The fathers are more likely to provide tactile and physical stimulation while the mothers are more verbal with their infants. This difference may be unique to American families; similar differences were not observed in Israeli or Swedish families (Sagi, Lamb, & Gardner, 1985; Lamb, et al., 1982).

Consequences of Variations in Quality of Attachment

Psychologists assume that the feelings of security produced by attachment to adults will vary with the regularity of that relationship and the degree to which it is

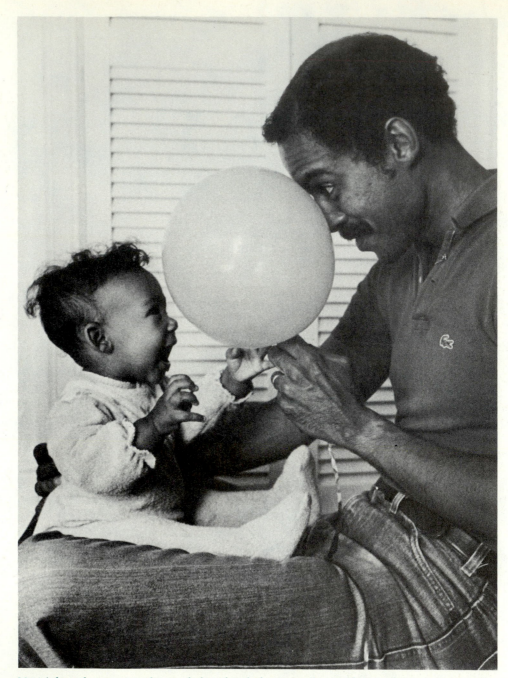

Most infants become strongly attached to their fathers as well as to their mothers.

satisfying. Thus, infants who experience irregular, unpredictable, or unsatisfying interactions with adults should show signs of anxiety and, perhaps, symptoms such as fears or antisocial behaviors when they are adolescents or adults.

INSTITUTIONS AND DEPRIVING ENVIRONMENTS.   Residential institutional care for young children (e.g., in orphanages or homes for children whose parents are unable to take care of them) is sometimes necessary in the United States and is common in poorer countries. Under these circumstances, the number of adults available to care for the child and the amount of intellectual stimulation provided are critical factors. Some children who have grown up in such institutions are more dependent, seek more attention from adults, and are more disruptive in school than children who have been reared at home (Rutter, 1979). However, it is not clear whether there will always be undesirable long-term consequences if a young child does not have a consistent attachment figure.

In one study, institutionally reared English girls were studied as adults. If they had married faithful, loving husbands, they did not show obvious signs of anxiety. However, many of the women had difficulty finding a satisfactory husband, and many had chosen a deviant man as a spouse. These women were anxious, but an important cause of their anxiety was an unsatisfactory marriage (Rutter, 1987).

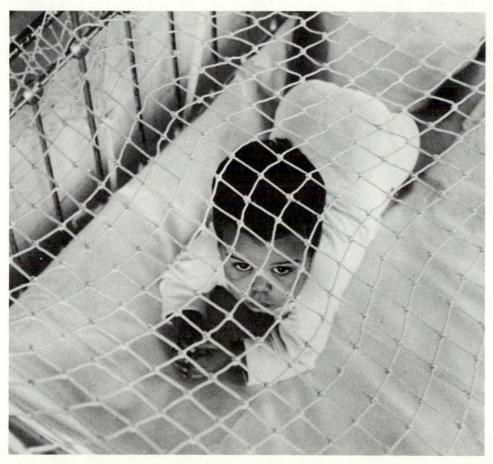

Children growing up in deprived environments are more likely to be dependent and disruptive than children reared at home.

MATERNAL EMPLOYMENT AND INFANT DAY CARE.   In the United States increasing numbers of women with young children are employed outside the home. By 1990 over half of women with children under age 3 will be employed, and more mothers join the work force each year. Similar trends are evident in most western European nations, and maternal employment is the norm in eastern European countries, the Soviet Union, and China. Because fathers rarely take primary responsibility for child rearing, maternal employment has created a need for new child care arrangements.

Many infants are cared for in family day care (group care in someone's home); a smaller number attend child care centers. As a result, considerable controversy has arisen about the effects of nonparental care on infants' development.

The controversy revolves around two issues. First, is the presence of one primary caregiver during infancy critical to children's emotional, social, and/or cognitive development? Theories stressing the importance of attachment lead some psychologists to predict that attachment to the primary caregiver may be disrupted if infants spend many hours a day in the care of someone other than their biological mother. We might call this the "one mother" hypothesis.

The effects of infant day care on attachment are not entirely clear, despite the fact that there have been many studies of the Strange Situation behavior of children in different child care arrangements. In most such studies the majority of children in day care show secure patterns of attachment. A few studies have found a higher percentage of insecure-avoidant attachment patterns to both mothers and fathers among infants in day care than among those raised only at home (Belsky, 1988; Gamble & Zigler, 1986), but other studies have found no differences (Roggman, 1988; Weinraub, Jaeger, & Hoffman, 1988).

The second, and more important, issue is the quality of the available care at home or away from home. Psychologically sound day care can create conditions for healthy development, just as some home environments do. What seems to be important is warm and frequent interactions between adults and children, verbal stimulation, opportunities for exploration and stimulation, space, and materials that are varied and age appropriate. Some signs that parents can use to evaluate quality of child care are a small adult/child ratio (e.g., 1/3), small group size, caregivers with training in child development or early-childhood education, and space designed for children (Phillips, 1987).

The long-term effects of infant care appear to depend on the type of care received. In one investigation Caucasian and Chinese-American children were studied from 3½ to 29 months of age. Half of the children in each ethnic group attended a high-quality day care center full time. The others, who were matched with the first group in social class and sex, were raised at home. The two groups showed similar patterns of development in language, cognitive skills, attachment to the mother, and fear of separation. Their patterns of separation anxiety are illustrated in Figure 4.10.

For a few children, high-quality day care enhances cognitive development. For instance, an experimental day care program was established for infants from poor families whose children were at "high risk" for developmental or learning problems. Follow-up studies demonstrated that children in the experimental program performed better on tests of intelligence, language development, and

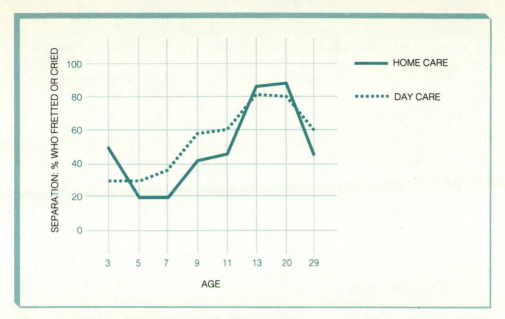

FIGURE 4.10   Percentage of children who attended infant day-care centers and infants who were raised at home full time who fretted or cried when their mothers left the room in a laboratory procedure. The similar patterns suggest that fear of separation from the mother is based on maturational, developmental changes that occur in similar ways for children with different histories of separation from their mothers. (Adapted from J. Kagan, R. B. Kearsley, & P. R. Zelazo, *Infancy: Its place in human development*. Cambridge, MA: Harvard University Press, 1978. By permission.)

school achievement than a matched control group (Ramey, Yeates, & Short, 1984).

The picture is not entirely positive, however, because much infant day care in the United States is not high in quality. The interactions of caregivers with children are less sensitive than parents' typical interactions with their own children. Most infants are in care settings that vary greatly in quality, and these settings are difficult to monitor.

Perhaps more important, changes in caregivers and settings are the rule rather than the exception for infants in day care. Personnel turnover is high because the pay is often set at the minimum wage. Family day care providers change, get "burned out," or go out of business. Many infants are cared for in two or three different settings. For instance, they may stay with a neighbor in the morning, then go to a relative's house in the afternoon. Frequent changes in people and places might be stressful for some of these children.

In sum, many infants in regular day care show healthy development. Quality of care, whether at home or elsewhere, is important for social and cognitive development, but high-quality care away from home is scarce and expensive. Unlike many other countries, the United States has not developed a system of quality child care at low cost to parents. Moreover, there are individual differences among children; some children do not adapt well to nonparental care.

In many European nations employed parents have an alternative to placing their infants in child care shortly after birth: They receive parental leaves of six to nine months at partial or nearly full pay. In the United States paid maternity leaves are unusual. Even unpaid leaves usually last only four to six weeks (Kamerman, Kahn, & Kingston, 1983).

Common Themes in Theories of Infant Social Development

All theories of infant social and emotional development emphasize the child's relationship to parents and other primary caregivers. One reason for this emphasis is the assumption that attachment to the parent has long-term consequences, providing a foundation of emotional security for the child and forming the basis for the parent's later influence on the child. As children grow, they will be reluctant to break the emotional bond with a parent to whom they are attached, and as a result, they will be willing to adopt the behaviors that fit the parent's values. Because in most instances parents encourage behaviors that are adaptive—that is, behaviors that help children get along well in the larger society—attachments usually serve children well. If, however, a parent encourages behavior that is maladaptive, the strongly attached child's efforts to conform to the parent's wishes may not be beneficial. For example, if a contemporary American mother taught her daughter to be passive, quiet, and uninterested in intellectual achievement, and if the daughter adopted those attitudes and behaviors because of her attachment to her mother, she might experience problems of adjustment during adolescence and adulthood (see Chapter 15). Hence, although attachment to parents is generally thought to produce benefits for the child, there are occasional exceptions to this generalization.

Cultural Ideals and Child Rearing

All theories about infants' social development and the child-rearing practices associated with healthy development must be considered within a cultural context. Different cultures have different conceptions of the ideal child, and these beliefs determine how parents rear their children. Puritan parents in colonial New England believed that infants were willful and had to be tamed. They punished young children severely, and the children were generally conforming. Contemporary parents in Calcutta believe that children are uncontrollable. Accordingly, they are more tolerant of tantrums in 2-year-olds, and their children are less obedient than Puritan children were.

The differences in behavior between Japanese and American mothers provide another contrast. American mothers conceive of their mission as molding their children into active, independent beings by stimulating them and teaching them self-reliance and social skills. Japanese mothers see their task as building a close loyalty to and dependence on the mother and other members of the family. In line with these values, American mothers put their children in rooms of their own, and they play with their infants to make them vocalize, smile, and laugh. By contrast, Japanese mothers remain very close to their young children; they respond quickly to crying by soothing and quieting more often than stimulating their babies. It is not surprising that American infants are more active, vocal, and spontaneous than Japanese infants.

Even within our own society there have been major differences in how mothers have handled their infants in the past 70 years. Government pamphlets published in 1914 containing advice to American mothers told them that because babies have extremely sensitive nervous systems, they should avoid excessive stimulation of the infant. By the 1960s such pamphlets instructed mothers to let their infants experience as much stimulation as they wished, because that is the way they can learn about the world. In 1914 mothers were told not to feed or play with the baby every time it cried, because those actions would spoil the infant. A half century later, mothers were told that they should not be afraid of spoiling their baby and that the child will feel trusting and secure if the mother always comes to nurture it when it cries.

Contemporary Americans believe it is essential to minimize anxiety in their 1-year-olds and to maximize the baby's comfort and security. These changes in advice reflect variations in philosophy and in the cultural concept of the ideal child. In spite of these variations, most children in each generation grow up to function well in their culture. Thus, it is clear that there are many paths to adaptive social development.

SUMMARY

In everyday conversation the word *emotion* is used to refer to conscious awareness of a specific change in internal feeling tone, often accompanied by thoughts about the quality of the feeling and the events that produced it. A second meaning of *emotion*, used more often by scientists, refers to changes in the brain and body that follow encounters with pain, deprivation, novelty, danger, and other events.

Infants display many reactions that suggest emotional states. Between 7 and 12 months of age, for example, a moderately unfamiliar event can produce a state of uncertainty. If the infant has no behavior it can use to divert its attention, the event may give rise to states that we call fear or anxiety. One of the most common emotions exhibited late in the first year is stranger anxiety. Infants also show fear of temporary separation from a familiar caregiver. These fears appear to be associated with the improvement in the infant's recall memory that occurs at about 8 months. They can be alleviated by the presence of a familiar person or a familiar setting.

Avoidance of the visual cliff also occurs at about 8 months, at the same time that infants begin to crawl or creep. It is believed that the infant's self-produced locomotion acts to crystallize cognitive abilities by causing the infant to pay increased attention to its environment.

Infants display a range of facial expressions that seem to indicate emotional states. However, because different observers may interpret an expression in different ways, psychologists are not certain that it is possible to know the emotional state of an infant simply by looking at its face.

Initially the infant's smile is a reflex, but by 2 months it occurs in response to human faces and voices. It may occur when the infant recognizes that an event resembles a previously acquired schema. Later, laughing occurs in response to social interaction, visual surprises, and tickling. Psychologists distinguish between the smiling or laughing that occurs in response to tickling and that which accompanies assimilation of a schema or mastery of a motor skill.

It appears that some babies are born with a bias toward certain moods and reaction styles, termed *temperament*. Scientists have studied a small set of temperamental dimensions, including activity, fussiness, fearfulness, sensitivity to stimuli, and attentiveness. Their research has shown that over time parents come to react to children with difficult temperaments in special ways that can affect the children's behavior and adjustment later in life.

Studies of infants' activity levels have found a moderate genetic influence at 8 months but not at later ages. On the other hand, differences among infants in irritability may be modestly preserved for the first two years. Two of the most stable temperamental qualities are shyness and sociability; they have been found to persist throughout childhood and adolescence. Child-rearing conditions can influence the degree to which these tendencies are actualized, however.

The reciprocal influence of parental behavior and infant temperament forms the basis for the principle of *bidirectionality*. This principle states that children's development is a product of the interaction between their own characteristics and those of the people who socialize them.

Most theorists assume that the pattern of social interaction between the infant and its caregivers influences the infant's psychological growth in important ways. Sigmund Freud proposed a theory of development in which the infant passes through a series of psychosexual stages; in each stage a particular source of gratification (e.g., feeding) becomes central, and too much or too little gratification can slow the child's progress into the next stage. Erik Erikson's developmental theory emphasized psychosocial as opposed to psychosexual stages. A parallel theoretical approach, social learning theory, was based on the idea that social development occurs as a result of the reinforcement of certain responses through the reduction of biological drives. Ethologists, in contrast, have studied the fixed action patterns exhibited by newborn animals and have attempted to find comparable patterns in humans.

A major result of parent-child interactions is the development in the infant of an emotional attachment to the caregiver, who is best able to soothe the baby and whom the baby approaches most often for play and consolation when aroused by novelty, danger, or distress. All normal infants form attachments, and many theorists propose that a strong or secure attachment provides a basis for healthy emotional and social development during later childhood.

Three major patterns of attachment have been described: Children who seek the parent when he or she returns after a brief separation in a laboratory setting are described as securely attached. Those who ignore the parent upon his or her return are classified as avoidant and insecurely attached. And children who alternately cling to the parent and push him or her away are described as resistant and insecurely attached. Securely attached infants have been found to be more socially outgoing and cooperative than insecurely attached infants at age 5. But it is likely that temperamental qualities contribute to the child's behavior in this context.

The targets of a child's attachments and the strength and quality of those attachments depend partly on the parents' behavior in relation to the child. In addition, psychologists assume that the feelings of security produced by attachment to adults will vary with the regularity of that relationship and the degree to which it is satisfying. Some children who have grown up in institutions are more dependent and disruptive than children who have been reared at home, but it is not clear whether lack of a consistent attachment figure will always have undesirable long-term consequences. Likewise, while it is often assumed that infants may be psychologically handicapped by group care, research on this issue has not produced conclusive findings.

It is generally believed that attachment to the caregiver provides a foundation of emotional security for the child and forms the basis for the parent's later influence on the child. When parents encourage behaviors that are adaptive, a strong attachment is beneficial; when they encourage maladaptive behaviors, it may create problems of adjustment. It should also be remembered that each child is reared within a particular cultural context, and that most children in each generation grow up to function well in their culture.

REVIEW QUESTIONS

1. Distinguish between the meaning of *emotion* in everyday conversation and the meaning of the term as it is used by scientists.

2. What conditions give rise to fear or anxiety in an 8-month-old infant? How is the emergence of these emotions explained by contemporary psychologists?

3. Describe the visual cliff. How has this device contributed to the understanding of infants' cognitive development?

4. What events cause the infant to smile or laugh at birth, 2 months, 4 months, and 1 year?

5. What is meant by a temperamental quality?

6. What temperamental qualities of infants have been found to be most stable?

7. Briefly discuss three theoretical perspectives on social and emotional development in infancy.

8. What is meant by *attachment*? What role does it play in social and emotional development?

9. How is attachment measured? Briefly describe the three major patterns of attachment that have been identified.

10. How do variations in the quality of children's attachment in infancy affect their later development?

GLOSSARY

emotion   Changes in the brain and behavioral disposition that follow encounters with pain, deprivation, novelty, danger, sensory gratification, challenge, play, social interaction, or separation from a familiar person.

temperament   An inborn bias favoring certain moods and reaction styles.

bidirectionality   A principle that states that children's development is a product of the interaction between their own characteristics and those of the people who socialize them.

ethology   An approach to the study of social development that emphasizes the presence of fixed action patterns in newborn animals and attempts to identify similar patterns in human infants.

attachment   An emotional relationship between an infant and a particular caregiver, who is better able than anyone else to soothe the baby and whom the baby approaches for play and consolation.

bonding   A process occurring immediately after birth in which the infant and its mother establish strong emotional ties to each other.

SUGGESTED READINGS

Ainsworth, M. D. S., Blehar, M. C., Waters, E., & Wall, S. (1978). *Patterns of attachment.* Hillsdale, NJ: Erlbaum. Summarizes the information that led to the use of the Strange Situation to classify children as securely or insecurely attached.

Averill, J. R. (1982). *Anger and aggression.* New York: Springer-Verlag. This insightful book examines the available knowledge on the emotion of anger and associated aggressive behavior.

Bowlby, J. (1969). *Attachment*, Vol. 1. New York: Basic Books. In this classic work Bowlby summarizes his theoretical ideas about the origins of attachment and its consequences.

Thomas, A., & Chess, S. (1977). *Temperament and development*. New York: Brunner Mazel. Summarizes the pioneering research of two psychiatrists who reintroduced the concept of temperament into discussions of development.

Kagan, J. (1984). *The nature of the child*. New York: Basic Books. A collection of essays that includes chapters on the meaning of emotion, the consequences of temperament, and the significance of the concept of attachment.

Chapter Five

THE TRANSITION TO CHILDHOOD: THE SECOND AND THIRD YEARS

Symbolic Functioning
> Symbolic Play
> Functions of Play
> Play with Other Children

Imitation
> The Development of Imitation
> Explanations of Imitation

Standards and a Moral Sense
> Standards of Behavior
> Violations of Rules

Self-awareness
> Directing the Behavior of Others
> Describing One's Own Behavior
> Self-recognition
> A Sense of Possession
> Empathy

Family Interactions in the Second and Third Years
> Processes of Socialization
> The Context Created by Siblings

During the six months that follow the first birthday, the child is transformed. Speech replaces gestures and babbling as a way of communicating desires and asking questions. Play becomes more spontaneous and often copies meaningful life experiences and imitates the behavior of parents, siblings, and other children. Behaviors that violate parents' standards about hitting, soiling, and destruction of property are followed by anxiety or shame. In short, speech, symbolism, imitation, and morality—some of the most distinctive characteristics of human nature—have become part of the child's profile. A few months later children use their own names and the personal pronouns I, *me*, or *my*, indicating that they have attained self-awareness or self-consciousness. At this time children also gain a capacity for empathy, reacting with sorrow and concern for the feelings of others, such as a dog whining in pain or a mother with tears on her cheeks. This chapter considers the emergence of all of these qualities except speech, which will be discussed separately in Chapter 6.

SYMBOLIC FUNCTIONING

Before the end of the first year, children can recognize and retrieve the past, categorize events, and generate ideas about what might happen in the immediate future. The next victory, which occurs around the first birthday, is the capacity to treat an object as if it were something other than it is—in other words, a talent for pretend play. It is likely that this is a uniquely human quality (Smith, P. K., 1982). No one has ever observed any animal engaging in pretend play without prior training.

As explained in Chapter 3, psychologists assume that during much of the first year children react to new events by creating schemata whose features correspond to those of the original event. But after the first birthday children transform experience and impose their own ideas on objects, rather than simply adjusting their actions to an object's physical properties. In the hands of a 10-month-old, a rubber ball is an object to squeeze and throw and a cup is something to hold and put to the mouth. However, by the second birthday children invent new and often original uses for these and other objects. They may treat a ball as a piece of food, a cup as a hat, a plate as a blanket, or a ball of yarn as a balloon. In other words, children are now capable of **symbolism**; they can both create and accept an arbitrary relationship between an object and an idea.

Consider the following example. A verbally precocious 26-month-old girl was playing with a set of toys that included two small dolls, a small bed, and a very large bed. After she had placed one of the small dolls on the small bed, she scanned the rest of the toys and noted that she needed another bed. She looked directly at the very large bed, touched it, but did not pick it up. After studying the available toys for almost 2 minutes, she finally selected a wooden sink about 4 inches long, placed the second small doll in it, and put this arrangement next to the other small bed. Apparently satisfied, she declared, "Now Mommy and Daddy are sleeping."

We can explain the child's rejection of the large bed (an appropriate object) in favor of the sink, which she knew was not a bed, by suggesting that she had an idea of the appropriate size for the two beds: Both had to be small, like the dolls. In order to have her behavior conform to that idea, the girl distorted reality a bit and used an object that belonged to another category because its size matched her idea of what was appropriate. In treating the sink as a bed, she revealed her talent for symbolism (Kagan, 1981).

Symbolic ability develops in phases. Around 12 months children will treat a toy cup as if it were a real cup and drink from it, or place a small wooden doll on a piece of wood as if the doll were a baby and the piece of wood a bed. Although the degree of distortion imposed on these objects is minimal, no 7-month-old would behave in this way. By the middle of the second year, children go one step further and impose new functions on objects. They might turn a doll upside down and treat it as a salt shaker or play with a wooden block as if it were a chair. Many 2-year-olds seem capable of simple metaphor. For example, they will treat two wooden balls that differ only in size as if they were a parent and child.

Once children become capable of imposing a symbolic meaning on events and the qualities they share, representations of experience become expanded. A woman with a bandaged eye is more than a physical event. She is a person in pain, someone to feel sorry for, and the bandaged eye is an event that has a cause to be discovered. This change in cognitive capacity is not due only to new experiences. Parents do not suddenly treat the child differently at the end of the first year, and they continue to feed, clean, talk to, and play with their children. Moreover, balls, bottles, and beds do not suddenly acquire new physical properties. The emergence of symbolic functioning in this period, like the improvement of recall memory at 8 months, is probably due to special changes in the central nervous system.

Symbolic Play

Although the concept of **play** is a familiar one, it is more difficult to define than most psychological ideas. Catherine Garvey (1977) lists the criteria that most observers use in defining play:

1.   Play is pleasurable and enjoyable.
2.   Play has no extrinsic goals. The child's motivations are subjective and serve no practical purpose.
3.   Play is spontaneous and voluntary, freely chosen by the player.
4.   Play involves some active engagement on the part of the player.

Like Garvey, most authors emphasize that play is a voluntary, spontaneous activity that does not have a real-world goal. Because our interest here is in children's ability to manipulate symbols, we will discuss only one type of play, a set of behaviors called *symbolic acts with objects* (see also Chapters 7 and 13).

Beginning in early infancy, children manipulate objects, usually small ones, for reasons that have nothing to do with biological needs like hunger, thirst, and warmth. During the second year these manipulations often reproduce acts that children have seen adults perform, such as talking on a telephone or drinking from a cup. These are early instances of symbolic acts.

An interesting change occurs late in the second year. At this time children begin to replace themselves with a toy as the active agent in play. For example, a child may put a toy bottle to a doll's mouth rather than to her own, or place a toy telephone beside an animal's head rather than her own. The role of these toys has changed. Instead of being mere participants in the child's sensorimotor schemes, they have become symbolic agents in a play that the child is both inventing and directing. This change in symbolic play with objects occurs at about the same time in American children, in children living on islands in the Fiji chain, and in children

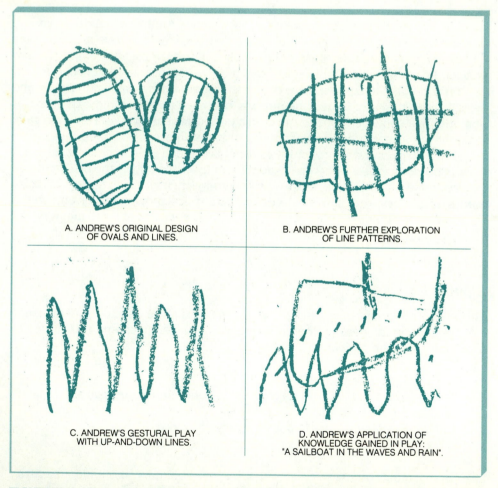

A. ANDREW'S ORIGINAL DESIGN
OF OVALS AND LINES.

B. ANDREW'S FURTHER EXPLORATION
OF LINE PATTERNS.

C. ANDREW'S GESTURAL PLAY
WITH UP-AND-DOWN LINES.

D. ANDREW'S APPLICATION OF
KNOWLEDGE GAINED IN PLAY:
"A SAILBOAT IN THE WAVES AND RAIN".

FIGURE 5.1   A spontaneous sequence of drawings by a 3-year-old boy. (Adapted from D. P. Wolf, Repertoire, style, and format. In P. Smith [Ed.], *Play in animals and humans*. Oxford: Basil Blackwell, 1984, pp. 175–193. By permission.)

living in Vietnamese families that have recently immigrated to the United States (Kagan, 1981).

Theorists have disagreed about both the causes and the purposes of play and have found it necessary to distinguish play that is *exploratory* (e.g., shaking a rattle) from play that is *constructive* (e.g., building a tower of blocks). However, on many occasions a play sequence can be both exploratory and constructive. For example, a 3-year-old boy, Andrew, had been drawing for almost 10 minutes, making what for him was a complicated design of ovals crossed by and encircled with lines (see Figure 5.1a). He then began to fool around with a large red marker and a stack of colored paper. In the next drawing he created an oval, which he crossed with closely spaced horizontal and vertical lines (see Figure 5.1b). In a set of four additional drawings, he simplified this pattern, one of which was nothing more than the quick up-and-down motion used earlier to create vertical stripes on the oval. The result was the jagged, wavelike line shown in Figure 5.1c. In a final drawing Andrew used this pattern by making another wavy line, adding a square form and some dots, and announcing that he had drawn "a sailboat in the waves and rain" (see Figure 5.1d) (Wolf, 1984).

Children's drawings become more symbolic during the second and third years, and they show a steady increase in complexity and sophistication. Sometime in the second year children begin to scribble, but they rarely try to draw familiar objects. Although their drawings do not portray specific objects, if they are asked to label a set of scribbles they may call it a dog, a cat, or a person. But by 3 years of age children create symbolic forms that look like animals or people (see Figure 5.2).

In one study, an examiner drew a schematic face on a piece of white paper, as illustrated in Figure 5.3. She then gave the child a piece of paper and told the child to make that drawing. The developmental sequence was very similar for children from different cultures. The first attempt to copy the face, around 16

(A)   (B)

FIGURE 5.2   Drawings of a "person" by a 2-year-old (*a*) and a 3-year-old (*b*). By age 3 children create symbolic forms that look like the objects they are depicting (After J. Kagan. *The second year*. Cambridge, MA: Harvard University Press, 1981.)

FIGURE 5.3   A picture of a face that an adult examiner drew on a piece of paper and showed to young children. (After J. Kagan. *The second year.* Cambridge, MA: Harvard University Press, 1981.)

months, usually resulted in a scribbling of parallel lines. During the next phase, which began to appear at about 20 months, children created an approximation of a crude circle but included no internal elements to represent the eyes, nose, or mouth. By the second birthday, most middle-class American children were able to draw a circle, and at 30 months most children attempted to place a few dots or lines inside the circle to represent parts of the face (Kagan, 1981) (see Figure 5.4).

A third type of symbolic play is pretending to be another person, usually the mother or father (McCall, Parke, & Kavanaugh, 1977). For example, a 20-month-old boy who had cut his forehead above the eye and had a Band-Aid over the stitches wanted to put on a bike helmet. His mother forbade him to do so because she was afraid the cut would start bleeding again. However, the boy was unhappy about having the Band-Aid on his eye. In order to placate him, the mother put a Band-Aid on a doll. Later that day the boy pointed to the Band-Aid on the doll and repeated what his mother had told him earlier, "Ouch, it hurts. Be better soon. Poor baby" (Rubin, S. & Wolf, 1979, p. 21).

Some young children prefer to use toys to act out scenes in which they play the role of another person. These children are referred to as *dramatists*. Other children—called *patterners*—are less likely to engage in role play. They often make designs and patterns with their toys. If these two kinds of children are given the same set of dolls and kitchen utensils, the patterners will arrange the dolls in a straight row while the dramatists will act out a family scene (Wolf, D. & Grollman, 1982).

Functions of Play

Some theorists believe that pretending to be another person is an attempt to cope with anxiety and conflict. For example, the child might act out in play an

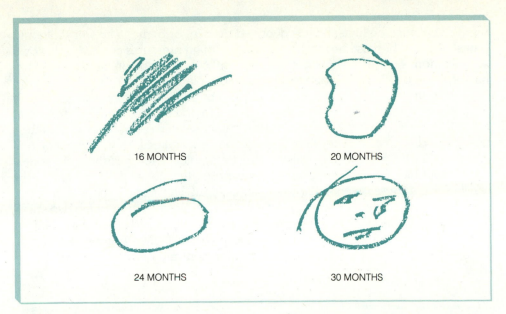

16 MONTHS   20 MONTHS

24 MONTHS   30 MONTHS

FIGURE 5.4   Drawings made by children of four different ages when they were asked to draw one like the examiner's picture in Figure 5.3. At 16 months children made scribbles of parallel lines; older children copied the circle; the oldest children tested added a few internal elements representing parts of the face. (After J. Kagan. *The second year*. Cambridge, MA: Harvard University Press, 1981.)

Some young children, referred to as dramatists, like to act out scenes in which they play roles like "doctor" and "nurse."

interaction between a mother and a doll. Perhaps he will take very good care of the doll because he himself feels deprived of love, or perhaps he will scold and punish the doll because he is trying to work through pressures created by his own socialization. Although acting out psychic conflicts can be one reason for play behavior, such conflicts do not account for most play.

Other investigators contend that play is a prerequisite for later skills. Jerome Bruner, for example, believes that play is crucial for the development of intellectual skills (Bruner, Jolly, & Sylva, 1976). In play, children can experiment without interference, and in so doing they may develop complex abilities. Playing with crayons and paper facilitates drawing skills; manipulating blocks teaches the child something about mechanics; playing with objects promotes the ability to generate new ways of using these objects. For example, children who had played with a set of sticks and colored chalk solved a "problem" that required them to clamp two sticks together to get the chalk out of a box. They were as quick and efficient as children who had watched someone else solve the problem (Sylva, Bruner, & Genova, 1976). The effects of play on cognitive development are discussed in Box 5.1.

BOX 5.1

Does Play Promote Cognitive Development?

A popular hypothesis in developmental psychology is that play facilitates intellectual development. The evidence for this claim comes from studies showing that children who have no toys and little opportunity to play with other children lag their age-mates in cognitive development. Moreover, children from economically disadvantaged families appear to engage in less pretend play at nursery school than middle-class children do. Thus, some psychologists believe that one reason many lower-class children have learning problems after they enter school is that their play experiences have been less frequent, less complex, and less varied than those of most middle-class children.

On the other hand, some anthropologists have reported on cultures in which no make-believe play occurs, even though in most cultures children do play symbolically. Hopi children conduct pretend rabbit hunts and make believe they are modeling pottery the way their parents do. Israeli children whose families came from Middle Eastern communities engage in much less make-believe play than do Israeli children whose families have emigrated from Europe. Thus, there are important cultural and class differences in the extent to which children play.

If play is important for full intellectual development, the introduction and stimulation of play may be one means of promoting cognitive development. Phyllis Levenstein has developed a program for bringing toys to economically disadvantaged children. Mothers are taught how to use the toys in playing with their children. The toys thus serve as a vehicle to promote pleasant, stimulating interactions between mothers and children. Because verbal stimulation and affectionate interactions are known to promote children's cognitive development, the beneficial effects of the program may be due to this feature rather than to the toys alone.

Appropriate toys can help slightly older children learn positive social behavior in preschool. Disadvantaged children attending Head Start programs watched television programs promoting positive behaviors such as helping, sharing, and cooperation. In some classrooms there were toys, puppets, records, and dolls that were similar to the characters and themes on the television program; other classrooms contained toys that were not related to the social themes of the TV program. When the toys supplemented the television messages, children adopted some of the social behaviors being taught; the toys apparently helped them practice the behaviors they had been taught.

Although these and other studies show that toys can be used effectively in combination with parents, teachers, or television programs to promote children's development, there is little evidence that the availability of toys alone contributes to the cognitive or social development of disadvantaged children.

Play with Other Children

As children play with objects in a more symbolic manner, their reactions to other children also change. Before the first birthday a meaningful interaction between two children is rare. Ten-month-olds treat other children as if they were animate toys; they pull at their hair, poke at their eyes, and babble to them. But by eighteen to twenty months children can cooperate and take turns with a playmate. In addition, they initiate play with each other, and arguments become more frequent and more intense.

Around the middle of the second year, there is a brief period of initial shyness with an unfamiliar child, which contrasts sharply with the spontaneous behavior of the ten-month-old. In one study, each child played in a pleasant room for 20 minutes while the mother sat nearby. Then an unfamiliar child of the same sex and age came into the room with his or her own mother. Children under 1 year continued to play happily with their toys and did not retreat to their mother when the unfamiliar child entered the room. Occasionally a ten-month-old would crawl to the other child and explore her hair, face, or clothes. But a few months after the first birthday the children showed signs of inhibition. They stopped playing, retreated, and clung to the mother while staring at the other child, although they rarely cried. By 2 to 2½ years of age, this inhibition had begun to decline (Kagan, 1981).

This brief period of apprehension in the presence of an unfamiliar child can be considered a counterpart to stranger anxiety, the distress infants begin to show at about eight months when confronted with an unfamiliar adult. The question of why it emerges five months later interests cognitive psychologists because it is related to infants' development of schemata and expectations. Since most infants are cared for by and interact most often with adults, perhaps they develop well-articulated schemata for adults, expectations about how adults will behave, and a set of responses they can make to adults early in the first year. The average infant has less regular contact with other infants and, therefore, may have less well developed schemata for them by the age of eight months. By thirteen months, however, the child may have matured enough to generate questions during an encounter with an unfamiliar child, such as "What should I do with her?" "What will she do to me?" "Will she take my toy?" If the child has no obvious answer to these self-generated inquiries, she becomes apprehensive, stops playing, and may retreat to the mother. After the second birthday the apprehension and uncertainty are resolved, partly because the child has learned how other children behave and how to behave toward them. At this point the child is able to enter into reciprocal play with another child and to use the other child as a model.

Frequent contact with other infants does not prevent timidity upon first meeting an unfamiliar child. Israeli infants who were raised in an infant house on a kibbutz showed the same degree of apprehension with an unfamiliar child early in the

Around the age of 2, children begin to play comfortably with other children who are not familiar playmates.

second year of life as Israeli infants who were raised in an apartment. By 29 months, the kibbutz-reared children showed less apprehension than apartment-reared youngsters when exposed to an unfamiliar child. The extensive daily interaction with other children hastened the decline of the inhibition (see Figure 5.5).

Two-year-olds will work together at a doll house, talk to each other on the telephone, and imitate each other in jumping off a couch. But they do not play games with rules, and their play episodes last only a few minutes. Nevertheless, interactive experiences with other children facilitate cooperate play later on (Kagan, 1981; Mueller & Brenner, 1977).

Although the play of boys and girls is basically similar, boys are more likely to engage in rough-and-tumble play with vigorous and aggressive behavior. Girls are more likely to act out social themes that are less vigorous or physically active. Note that these are average differences between the sexes as groups; individual girls who like very vigorous play and boys who enjoy social themes are not hard to find (Maccoby & Jacklin, 1974).

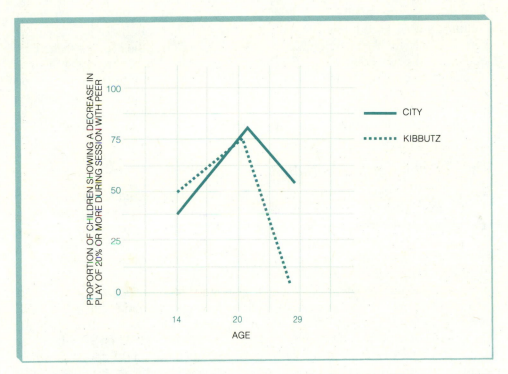

FIGURE 5.5   Changes in social inhibition with an unfamiliar peer. Children around 20 months old showed a decrease in play (suggesting inhibition when with an unfamiliar child in a playroom. The tendency to be inhibited with an unfamiliar peer appeared to decline at an earlier age for kibbutz children who had frequent experience in group settings with other children than for home-reared city children. (From M. Zaslow. Comparison of kibbutz and home-reared children. Unpublished doctoral dissertation, Harvard University, 1978. By permission.)

IMITATION

Imagine a scene in a typical home. A father is playing with his 3-month-old baby. The baby is propped in an infant seat and the father faces her. Father sticks out his tongue, and the baby sticks out hers. Father smiles, and the baby smiles back. Father then delightedly tells his friend, who is watching, that his daughter imitates everything he does. But is the infant really imitating the father?

Imitation has two defining characteristics. First, it must duplicate the behavior shown by the model. Second, it must be selective; that is, the imitative response must occur after a particular behavior by the model and not under a large number of other stimulus conditions. For example, if the baby just described also smiles in response to the father's voice or the shaking of his head, then her smiling in response to his smile is not selective.

Although some psychologists have claimed that newborns or babies in the first month will imitate adults' facial gestures such as opening the mouth, there is still controversy about whether these responses represent selective imitation (Kaitz, Meschulach-Safarty, Averbach, & Edelman, 1988; Meltzoff & Moore, 1977). Two-month-olds will stick out their tongue when a person sticks out his or her tongue at them, which looks like imitation, but they will also stick out their tongues when an adult moves a slender object like a pencil toward their mouth (Jacobson, 1979). Infants will also stick out their tongue when they are excited by an interesting mobile or sound. Thus, the fact that newborns stick out their tongue when an adult does so does not mean that they are imitating the adult. Rather, it means that they are highly aroused by the adult's actions and protruding the tongue accompanies the arousal.

The Development of Imitation

There is no doubt that selective imitation occurs by 7 or 8 months of age and becomes both more frequent and more complex during the next several years. One-year-old infants imitate novel gestures, sounds, and other behaviors that they see and hear, although they are more likely to imitate behaviors they can see themselves carry out (e.g., a hand movement) than acts they cannot see themselves perform (e.g., tongue protrusion).

Delayed imitation becomes possible before the first birthday. Nine-month-old infants watched an adult perform 2 simple acts; in one, the adult pushed a black button on top of a box and a sound occurred, while in another the adult shook an egg-shaped object containing small metal objects that rattled. When the infants returned to the laboratory one day later, many of them imitated the action they had seen on the previous day. Infants who had not watched the adult perform were much less likely to imitate those acts (Meltzoff, 1988).

Delayed imitation is very common after the first birthday. A 15-month-old stares quietly while her mother dials a telephone. A few minutes, hours, or perhaps weeks later, she repeats the essential form of that act. The motor coordinations necessary for dialing the telephone were in the child's repertoire long before the imitative act occurred. Similarly, a 20-month-old watches as a researcher puts a wooden block on a small slab of wood and says, "This doll is very tired, and we must put it to bed. Night-night, dolly." The child fails to imitate any part of that sequence during the next 20 minutes. But when she enters the same room one month later and sees the same set of toys, she immediately puts the wooden block on the slab of wood and says, "Night-night."

Imitation, especially of parental behavior, increases in frequency between 1 and 3 years of age, but the likelihood that a particular response will be imitated depends on the nature of that response. Children often imitate behavior's shown by their parents when the parents are cleaning or taking care of younger children, but they are less likely to imitate emotional expressions or behaviors that have no instrumental goal.

Even in laboratory situations children are very selective in the acts that they imitate. Children between 1 and 3 years of age were given an opportunity to imitate a variety of motor acts (for example, an adult moved a rectangular block along a table) and social behaviors (the adult placed a screen in front of her face and peeked around the side twice). A third kind of imitation required the coordination of two separate actions in one motor sequence (the adult lifted a small brass cup on a string and struck it three times with a metal rod). The frequency of imitation of each of the three classes of acts is shown in Figure 5.6. The motor behaviors were imitated most readily, with 2-year-olds imitating about 80 percent of all the acts modeled; imitations of the social behaviors were next most frequent. Imitation of

Young children imitate their parents more than they imitate other children.

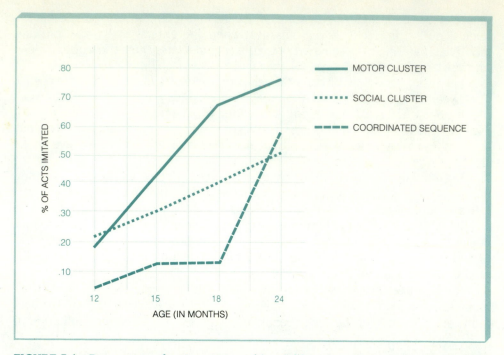

FIGURE 5.6   Percentage of actions imitated by children from 12 to 24 months. Actions were classified as motor, social, or coordinated behaviors. Children imitated motor actions earliest and most frequently, then social behaviors. Coordinated-action sequences were rarely imitated before 24 months. (Adapted from R. B. McCall, R. D. Parke, & R. D. Kavanaugh. Imitation of live and televised models by children one to three years of age. *Monographs of the Society for Research in Child Development*, 1977, 42, [No. 5]. © The Society for Research in Child Development, Inc. By permission.)

the coordinated sequences occurred rarely before 18 months, but increased between 1½ and 2 years.

Children are much more likely to imitate their parents than to imitate their brothers and sisters or even characters seen regularly on television. In one study, 71 percent of the imitative acts of 2-year-old children, as recorded by their mothers, were imitations of maternal acts (Kuczynski, Zahn-Waxler, & Radke-Yarrow, 1987). Most of these imitations occurred hours, days, or weeks after they had been seen, especially if the acts were punishments (see Figure 5.7).

Explanations of Imitation

The capacity to imitate another person is a major reason for the advanced intellectual and technological development of the human species, for imitation is an efficient way to perfect new actions. Two questions can be asked regarding imitation by young children. The first is: Why do children imitate at all? Contemporary theorists suggest that imitation is a universal maturational phenomenon, "a capacity that is built into the human species" (Yando, Seitz, & Zigler, 1978, p. 4). Indeed, imitation in

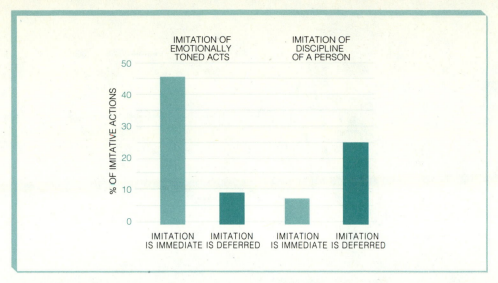

FIGURE 5.7   For 2-year olds emotionally toned acts are imitated immediately more often than after a delay (deferred), but disciplinary acts are more often imitated after a delay. (Adapted from L. Kuczynski, C. Zahn-Waxler, & M. Radke-Yarrow. Development and content of imitation in the second and third year of life. *Developmental Psychology*, 1987, 23, 276–282. Copyright by the American Psychological Association. By permission.)

the human child may be analogous to the swimming of fish and the flying of birds, both of which represent basic abilities that appear early in development.

The second question is: Why do children imitate some models more often than others and some behaviors more often than others? Children possess many more schemata for the behavior of other people than they ever duplicate in their own actions. Why do they imitate only a small number of the many acts they have observed? There are several hypotheses about the determinants of imitation. It is clear that several processes are involved and that imitation may serve different functions in infants, toddlers, and older children. For this reason, the bases for imitation at age 2 may be different from those that are most influential at age 10 or 20.

If 1- to 2-year-olds are only a little uncertain of their ability to perform a witnessed act, they will imitate. If they are too uncertain, they may show signs of distress. In one series of observations many 2-year-olds stopped playing, protested, clung to their mother, and even cried after having watched a researcher display actions that were a little too difficult to assimilate or to remember well (Kagan, 1981). The distress reactions did not occur when the actions displayed were either easy to imitate or far beyond the child's ability (see Figure 5.8). This means that 2-year-olds have some awareness of their ability to imitate an act, and become anxious if they are uncertain. If an act is very hard, they do not cry because they are not uncertain and will not try to imitate it.

IMITATION TO PROMOTE SOCIAL INTERACTIONS.   When an infant imitates a parent, the parent often smiles, tells the baby how wonderful and intelligent it is, and imitates the baby in return. The responsiveness of the parent may reinforce the

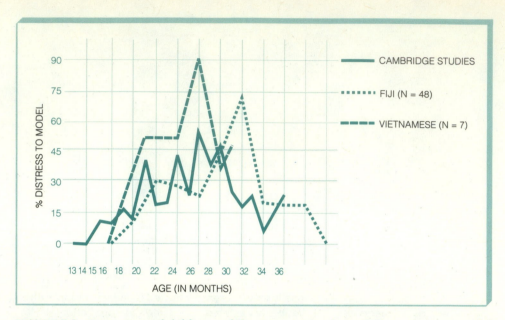

FIGURE 5.8   Percentage of children at different ages who showed distress when a model demonstrated a behavior that was moderately difficult for them to imitate. In three cultures children around 2 years old showed considerable distress, suggesting that they recognized a standard that they were not able to attain because they could not imitate the model successfully. (After J. Kagan. *The second year*. Cambridge, MA: Harvard University Press, 1981.)

baby's imitative behavior. Such social reinforcements increase the baby's general tendency to imitate as well as influencing which behaviors the baby chooses to imitate. Children are more likely to imitate an action that has received approval, such as eating with a spoon, than a response that is ignored, such as banging two forks together.

IMITATION TO ENHANCE SIMILARITY TO ANOTHER.   Another basis for imitation emerges as the child enters the third year and begins to imitate specific individuals rather than particular acts. By the second birthday most children are aware that they have qualities that make them more similar to some people than to others (for example, the boy recognizes that he and the father share the properties of short hair, trousers, and similar genital anatomy). The recognition of similarities to the father and other males leads the boy to assume that he belongs to the same category as other males. Correspondingly, girls assume that they belong to the same category as other females. This insight provokes each child to make an active effort to search for additional similarities to other people in order to firmly establish the category to which they belong. They do this by imitating the actions of those people (see Chapter 10 for further discussion).

EMOTIONAL AROUSAL AS A BASIS FOR IMITATING.   Children imitate their parents more often than other adults. One reason may be that parents are a more continuous source of emotional arousal—both pleasant and unpleasant—than most other people. Individuals who have the power to arouse the child emotionally—whether to joy, uncertainty, anger, or fear—recruit the child's attention, and as a result the child watches their actions more thoroughly than those of people who command less attention. A similar process occurs among children playing together. When pairs of unacquainted 2-year-olds play together, it is often the passive, quieter child who imitates the more dominant, active, loquacious one. The inhibited youngster appears to be apprehensive about losing a toy to the other and watches the dominant child closely. When the dominant one performs an action that the passive child might be able to master (e.g., jumping off a table), the latter is likely to imitate that act within the next few minutes.

IMITATION TO GAIN GOALS.   Imitation can be a self-conscious attempt to gain pleasure, power, property, or any of a number of other desired goals. For example, a child who is trying to build a house with blocks may watch carefully as another child or adult builds a similar structure, and may then imitate those actions. Or a 3-year-old may imitate the bullying behavior of another child because that behavior succeeds in getting desired toys away from other children. This basis for imitation typically emerges after the second birthday. At this point it is appropriate to say that children are *motivated* to imitate others, because they have an idea of a goal to be gained through the imitative act.

In summary, imitation may occur because of response uncertainty, social reinforcement, a desire to be more like another person, or a desire to attain particular goals. The behaviors imitated during the first three years of life depend partly on the child's level of cognitive development, which determines what behaviors the child perceives as challenging but not impossible. The motivation to be similar to another and the degree of emotional arousal induced by another person determine whom the child will imitate, and the motivation for certain goals determines what will be imitated.

STANDARDS AND A MORAL SENSE

During the last six months of the second year, children begin to create idealized representations of objects, events, and behaviors. Toys should not have cracks; shirts should have all their buttons; clothes should have no rips. These representations are termed **standards**. At the same time, children acquire standards about correct and incorrect behavior in specific situations, often dealing with cleanliness, control of aggression, and obedience to parents. These standards are the beginning of the child's understanding of right and wrong, good and bad; they are the first step in the development of a sense of morality.

If events match children's standards, they may smile, but events that violate a standard may produce signs of anxiety or distress. For example, children will point to broken objects, torn clothing, missing buttons, and the like, and show concern in their voice and face. They will point to a crack in a plastic toy and say, "Oh-oh," "Broke," or "Yukky." In one study, 14- and 19-month-olds were brought to a laboratory playroom containing a large number of toys, some of which were purposely flawed (a doll's face was marked with black crayon; the clothes on another doll were torn; the head of an animal was removed). None of the 14-month-old infants paid any special attention to the damaged toys, but over half the 19-month-olds were obviously preoccupied with them. They brought them to their mother, pointed to the damaged part, stuck their finger in the place where an animal's head had been removed, or, if they could talk, indicated that something was wrong by saying "fix" or "broke."

Parents often report that during the few months before the second birthday children suddenly show concern over dirty hands, torn clothes, and broken cups. Parents do not suddenly begin to punish destruction of property or dirty hands at 18 months; so why do the signs of concern appear at this age? It seems that children are developing the ability to infer that events have causes (even when they do not observe the cause). For example, a 21-month-old child sees a baby crying and immediately assumes that the baby is hungry or hurt. When children react emotionally to a broken toy or a shirt without a button, they are assuming that the flaw is not an inherent property of the object but has been caused by something or someone. For example, American 2- and 3-year-olds, as well as Mayan children living in villages in the Yucatan peninsula, looked longer at a picture of a human face with distorted features than at a normal face. The children's verbalizations—"What happened to his nose?" or "Who hit him in the nose?"—implied concern about the forces that might have damaged the face and inferences as to the events that might have produced the distortion. These observations suggest that by the second birthday children are ready to show concern about events that violate their standards and to assume that these events were produced by some external force (Kagan, 1981).

The fact that children not only notice flaws in objects but often become distressed about them suggests that their standards are ideal representations of the "right" or "correct" way things should be. In some cases they may have learned that breaking toys is followed by parental criticism or punishment. Signs of parental disapproval—a frown, a verbal chastisement, or a slap on the rear—produce an unpleasant state that probably resembles anxiety. This state could become associated with the child's mental representations of the acts that break toys or tear buttons from shirts. Hence, when a child guesses that the broken doll on the carpet resulted from someone's behavior, an emotional reaction is elicited. However, in many instances children's concern over broken toys and buttonless shirts does not seem to require any prior experience of parental disapproval. It seems to be an inherent part of the formation of standards.

Standards of Behavior

Also around the second birthday, children display distress if they are unable to meet standards of behavior imposed by others. As mentioned earlier, when a woman demonstrates acts that are hard to perform or remember, 2-year-old children from diverse cultural settings show distress. They may cry, throw toys around the room, or ask to go home. We suggested earlier that the children's upset was due to their recognition that they could not meet the standard represented by the model's behavior.

But why did the 2-year-olds feel that they should try to imitate the model? It is possible that past parental punishments for violations of standards regarding aggression or cleanliness lead 2-year-olds, but not younger children, to ask themselves, "What does the adult want?" and to infer that the adult model wants them to imitate her. In one study, 2-year-olds and 16-month-olds observed a model who, without using any toys, pretended she was talking on a telephone or drinking from a cup. After she left the room some of the 2-year-olds, but none of the 16-month-olds, imitated these behaviors. The response was in the younger child's repertoires, for the 16-month-olds imitated those acts when they were modeled with toys. But the younger children may not have been mature enough to infer that the adult wanted them to duplicate the behavior and therefore did not do so when no toys were available.

Another phenomenon implying that children possess standards of correct and incorrect performance is the appearance of a smile when they meet a self-imposed standard that requires the investment of effort. Children who take 5 minutes to complete a six-piece puzzle often smile when they finish the task. They do not look at the mother while smiling; rather, the smile is a private response reflecting the recognition that they have met the standard they set for themselves.

Children will also smile if they are about to do or are in the middle of a forbidden act that violates a standard, such as putting a hand in the toilet or threatening to spill some milk on the floor (Dunn, 1988). Consider the example of a pair of 2-year-olds, one of whom was playing the role of the mother and the other the role of the baby.

A: [Lying on her back]: Change my bottom, Laura. Change my bottom. Change my bottom.
B: Yes [pulls her pants off]. That's stinky [laughs]!
A: You're stinky!
B: Stinky! Stinky [laughs]!
A: Pull her pants up for her, Laura. Laura, pull her pants up.
B: Wee-wee.

Violations of Rules

As children grow from infancy into childhood, they become more likely to be amused by violations of adult rules and by events that will provoke disgust or disapproval in others. It is common to see 2-year-olds explore all the possible variations on acceptable behavior in the presence of siblings and parents in order to share laughter with them. Two-year-olds enjoy jokes that involve violations of standards about love relationships (e.g., "I don't love you, Mummy!") or about sex-appropriate behavior, disobedience, honesty, the mistakes of other people, and incongruities in family routines (e.g., eating in a bathrobe if that is not common in a particular family) (Dunn, 1988).

The age at which this appreciation of right and wrong behaviors appears is remarkably similar in children from many different cultures and families. One

investigator visited the homes of four children every two weeks when the children were 13 to 23 months of age, and recorded the children's behaviors on each occasion. Between 15 and 17 months every one of the children began to show a sudden increase in concern about objects that were broken or dirty and about violations in adult standards, as well as spontaneous smiles upon mastering a task. The age at which these reactions appeared was similar despite the fact that the children were growing up in different homes (see Figure 5.9).

In sum, at 2 years children begin to evaluate actions and events as good or bad, and they often show distress when events do not meet their standards. These capacities are common to children from many cultures, probably because they result from cognitive developmental changes that occur around the second birthday. Children's use of standards to evaluate events and behavior is the beginning of their moral sense of right and wrong (see also Chapters 9 and 11). The question of whether children are innately moral is discussed in Box 5.2.

SELF-AWARENESS

Each of us is familiar with the experience of reflecting upon our feelings and thoughts, knowing whether we are able to solve a particular problem, and initiating or inhibiting a goal-directed sequence of behaviors. In other words, we are conscious of our qualities and potentials for action.

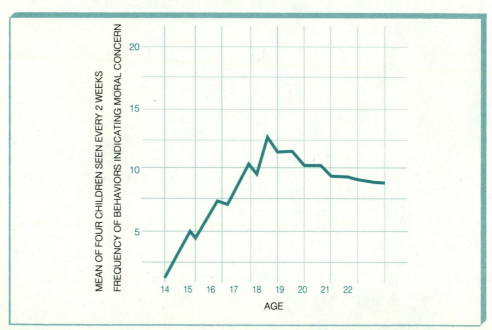

FIGURE 5.9   The frequencies of morally related behaviors at home for four children seen from 14 to 22 months of age. (Adapted from S. Lamb, A study of moral development. Unpublished doctoral dissertation, Harvard University, 1988. By permission.)

BOX 5.2

Are Children Innately Moral?

Must children learn a moral sense, or are they innately prepared to be sensitive to right and wrong? Mothers from many different cultures begin to hold their children responsible for their actions by the second or third birthday. For example, mothers living in the Fiji Islands comment that their children naturally become more responsible after the second birthday. At that time the children acquire a sense of right and wrong, which the Fijians call *vakayalo.*

At the end of the nineteenth century James Sully wrote that the child has an "inbred respect for what is customary and wears the appearance of a rule of life," as well as an "innate disposition to follow precedent and rule which precedes education" (1896, pp. 280-281). Sully, like most nineteenth-century observers, believed it was obvious, even to a child, that causing harm to another person is wrong and immoral. The child does not have to learn that hurting other people is bad; it is an insight that inevitably accompanies growth. How can this observation be explained?

Children seem to develop standards regarding aggressive behavior early in life. For example, many 2- and 3-year-olds are jealous and resentful toward younger siblings, yet they rarely do serious harm to a young infant. When they do, it makes headlines because it is viewed as a freak event. It appears that by the second birthday most children realize at some level that hurtful behavior is wrong.

Modern theorizing about developmental changes during the second and third years suggests that children develop many intellectual capacities that may make them sensitive or ready to absorb the rudiments of moral standards in their society. In this period children begin to understand that events have causes, even when the causes are not immediately observable, and they can hold an idea or plan of action over a longer time span. They often develop an appreciation for standards of behavior and begin to apply them.

Of course, moral standards are acquired from people around the child. In fact, initial inhibitions on aggression may be removed if the child is taught that aggression is acceptable. Nevertheless, even 3- and 4-year-olds distinguish "moral" wrongs that result in harm to people from violations that merely involve a social convention (e.g., eating with a spoon). The initial readiness to acquire those standards and the sensitivity to violations that hurt people or destroy objects appear to arise partly out of cognitive changes that have a maturational basis.

The last half of the second year is a time when children begin to be aware of their own qualities, states, and abilities. Observations of children in our own and other cultures reveal the appearance of a set of behaviors that invites the label **self-awareness**. The source and nature of self-awareness have long been subjects of debate among philosophers. Neurophysiologists believe they will eventually be able to account for it as a product of complex patterns of neuronal discharge in the central nervous system.

Directing the Behavior of Others

Two-year-old children begin to direct the behavior of others. The child may put a toy telephone to the mother's ear, indicate that he wants her to move to another chair, request help with a problem, or ask her to make a funny sound. These directives to adults are not aimed at obtaining a specific material object; the child does not want a cookie or a toy. Rather, the child's goal seems to be simply to influence the adult's behavior. Because children would not issue commands if they did not expect the parent to obey them, it is reasonable to assume that children are aware of their ability to influence other people.

Describing One's Own Behavior

When children being to speak three- and four-word sentences that contain verbs, they often describe their own actions as they are performing them. The 2-year-old says, "Go up" as he climbs up on a chair, "I fix" as he tries to rebuild a fallen tower of blocks, or "Want cookie" as he goes to the kitchen. Because children are more likely to describe their own activities than the behaviors of others, we assume that they are concerned with their own activities. When children first begin to speak, they are most likely to call out the names of objects whose meanings they are just learning, as if knowing the name of something is exciting. At this stage children are gaining a new insight, a new awareness of their own ability to act, to influence others, and to meet self-imposed standards. These ideas, like the realization that one knows the names of objects, are exciting. As a consequence, children describe their behaviors as they perform them (see Table 5.1).

Self-recognition

The emergence of self-awareness during the second year is also evident from children's recognition of themselves in a mirror (Lewis & Brooks-Gunn, 1979). Some of the research demonstrating self-recognition and self-awareness is described in Box 5.3.

A Sense of Possession

Social interactions between children provide additional signs of self-awareness. Consider the following example. Two 3-year-old boys, total strangers, were playing on opposite sides of an unfamiliar room with their mothers present. During the first

TABLE 5.1

Examples of Behaviors That Show Self-awareness

Behaviors that direct others	Statements describing child's own behavior
Child hands a doll and bottle to the mother, indicating that she wants her mother to feed the doll.	"My book." "I sit."
Child requests her mother to take her feet off the sofa and put them on the floor saying, "En ya shoe."	"Tina eat." "Me fix."
Child wants the examiner to move to the other side of the couch and points to the place where she wants the examiner to sit.	"Up chair." "I go." "I do."
Child wants the observer and the mother to hug a toy bear as the child had done moments earlier.	"I play."
Child wants the mother to bite a toy animal.	

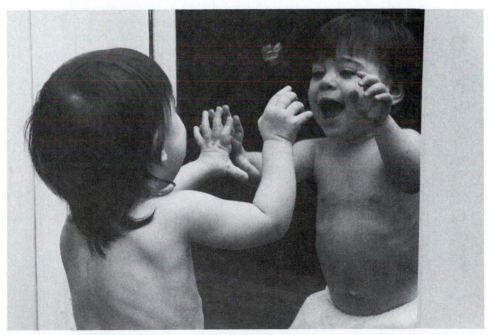

One sign of the emergence of self-awareness can be seen in a child's reactions to his or her reflection in a mirror.

BOX 5.3

The 2-Year-Old's Understanding of Self

By age 2 children acquire the beginnings of a concept of *self*. One facet of self-awareness during the second year was revealed in a simple experiment conducted by Michael Lewis and Jeanne Brooks-Gunn (1979). Children from 9 to 24 months of age were first allowed to look at themselves in a mirror. Then their mothers surreptitiously marked their noses with rouge, and the children were allowed to look at themselves in the mirror again. Children younger than about 18 to 21 months did not touch their nose or face when they saw the rouge in their reflected image, but by 24 months two-thirds of the children put their finger to their nose.

Soon after children point to their rouge-colored nose, they begin to use the pronouns I, *me*, and *you*, suggesting that they are now distinguishing clearly between the self and other people. Seymour Epstein (1973) describes an interesting episode:

> A little girl named Donna who was 2 years old was seated at the table with some relatives who were visiting. She was asked to point to Aunt Alice, and she did so correctly. Then there was a game in which they asked the little girl Donna to point to various people. Then someone said, "Point to Donna." The child was confused and initially pointed at random. Then her mother said, "You know who Donna is. Point to the little girl everybody calls Donna." Now Donna had a great insight, and she pointed unhesitatingly to herself. (pp. 412-413)

Three-year-old children may have a concept of a private, thinking self that is not visible to an outside observer. Here is an example of an exchange between an adult and a 3-year-old child:

> The examiner asks, "Can I see you thinking?" The child says, "No." The examiner says, "Even if I look in your eyes, do I see you thinking?" The child replies, "No." "Why not?" asks the examiner. The child says, "'Cause I don't have any big holes." The examiner says, "You mean there would have to be a big hole there for me to see you thinking?" The child nods. (Flavell, 1978, p. 16)

A strong argument for the contribution of maturation to the emergence of a sense of self is seen in the longitudinal study of a deaf child (born of deaf parents) who was learning to communicate with American Sign Language. In the middle of her second year, the same time that hearing children begin to describe their actions as they are performing them, the deaf child began to use signs that made reference to herself (Petitto, 1983).

20 minutes of play, Jack took toys from Bill on four separate occasions. On each occasion Bill did nothing. He did not protest, cry, whine, retaliate, or retreat to his mother for help. But after the fourth seizure Bill left his toys, walked across the room, took a toy that Jack had been playing with earlier, and brought it back to his own play area. Several minutes later, while Bill was playing with a wagon, Jack tried to take it. This time Bill held on and successfully resisted Jack's attempts at appropriation.

Why did Bill resist Jack on the fifth occasion when he had not done so on the first four? One reason may be that the continued experience of losing toys finally evoked in Bill an idea of personal possession, even though he was playing with these toys for the first time. When objects are lost or seized, the child may try to reaffirm his sense of possession by resisting or taking the other child's toys. These theoretical arguments are based on the assumption that the child has the concept of a "self" that can possess objects, even temporarily, and maintain control over them.

Two-year-old children who attain a sense of self-awareness a little earlier than other children are usually more possessive. In one study, 2-year-old boys were first tested for degree of self-awareness using the mirror test described in Box 5.3. They were also evaluated in terms of their understanding of the pronouns *my, you,* and *I* and their ability to adopt the perspective of another person. The boys were then observed in pairs in a free play session. The boys who had a firmer understanding of self were much more possessive of the toys, more often yelling and screaming, "my ball" when the other child came toward them (Levine, 1983).

These findings suggest that as children mature and become consciously aware of themselves they also become more possessive and more likely to become involved in quarrels. Perhaps this is the price humans pay for the gift of self-consciousness. However, the values of the society in which the child is raised can either amplify or mute this natural possessiveness. If adults discourage such behavior, as they do on Israeli kibbutzim or on communes in China, children will be less possessive with objects than they are in most American homes, where private property is highly valued.

Empathy

The emergence of self-awareness is accompanied by **empathy**; the ability to appreciate the perceptions and feelings of others. In one study, children 18, 27, and 36 months of age were visited at home and allowed to play with either a pair of ski goggles that they could see through or a pair of goggles that was opaque. A day later each child came to a laboratory and watched the mother put on the opaque goggles. The 2- and 3-year-old children who had previous experience with the opaque goggles behaved as if they believed their mothers could not see. They tried to remove the goggles and made no gestures toward the mother. These behaviors suggest that they were aware that the mother was experiencing the state they had experienced earlier (Novey, 1975).

The ability to infer the emotional state of another person is revealed in the behavior of children when they see a person who is hurt or in distress. Mothers who

With increased self-awareness comes greater possessiveness with toys.

kept diaries about their children's everyday behavior reported a major change in the children's actions during the last half of the second year. During this period children show an increased tendency to hug or kiss a person who has been hurt, or to give a victim a toy or food. These prosocial or helpful behaviors are relatively rare during the first part of the second year (Radke-Yarrow, Zahn-Waxler, & Chapman, 1983).

The following incident occurred when a 15-month-old boy, Len, was in the garden with his brother. Len was a stocky boy who often played a game with his parents that made them laugh. He would come toward the parents, walking in an odd way and pulling up his T-shirt and showing his stomach. On the day in question Len's brother had fallen and was crying vigorously. Len first watched solemnly and then approached his brother, pulled up his T-shirt, showed his tummy, and spoke to his brother as if he were trying to make him laugh and thus dilute his distress (Dunn & Kendrick, 1982).

The fact that most 2-year-olds are capable of inferring a psychological and emotional state in another person implies that children can recall their own earlier emotional experiences and act on that information. It seems reasonable to conclude that children are now conscious of their private experiences.

FAMILY INTERACTIONS IN THE SECOND AND THIRD YEARS

Although many of the competences of the second year—symbolism, imitation, standards, self-awareness—will emerge in any child who lives in a world of objects and people, their subsequent development depends on the individual's experiences. For young children, the most important experiences occur within the family. What are those experiences, and which of them facilitate or hinder the growth of these competences?

Many discussions of child rearing seem to be based on the premise that parents act on totally malleable young organisms and therefore bear most of the responsibility for their children's behavior and personality. However, some parents see themselves as holding the reins of a high-spirited animal charging through a forest. They try to monitor the speed and direction a little, but they believe that some of the child's growth is beyond their control. The latter view is consistent with current assumptions that children play an active role in their own development (see Chapter 1) and that parent-child influences are bidirectional (see Chapter 4).

Each phase of development leads to changes in children's surface behavior, and hence children of different ages present different sets of problems to their parents. During the first year, excessive irritability, sleeplessness, and feeding problems are likely to dominate parents' attention. During the second year, when the child has become mobile and self-aware, the possibilities of physical harm, destructiveness, and aggression overpower earlier worries. By the third year, disobedience, resistance to routine, poor social skills, and slow growth of verbal ability ascend to the top of the hierarchy of parental preoccupations in many American families. To the extent that each type of behavior provokes a different pattern of corrective action by parents, the changing profile of parental behavior is partially controlled by the child.

The child-rearing techniques that parents choose depend in part on their beliefs about development and on the qualities they regard as most important for children to acquire. In modern America, parental ideals for 3-year-olds include cognitive skills, sociability, emotional security, self-confidence, obedience, and control of aggression. A little later, parents hope to see gains in independence, autonomy, motivation for mastery, capacity for solitude, and willingness to compete with others and to defend the self against attack and domination.

Parents believe that early development of these qualities will help their children adapt to the social and cognitive challenges they will confront as adolescents and young adults. Hence, when a 2-year-old's behavior violates the parent's standards for children of that age, the parent moves into action. If the 2-year-old is too timid with other children, the mother may initiate a play group or enroll the child in nursery school. If the child is too dependent on the mother, she will encourage him or her to play alone.

There are, therefore, two complementary bases for parental socialization practices. One is the changing profile of behavior in the child; the other is the parents' view of the ideal behaviors for the child at that stage of development, which depends in part on the parents' ideals for the future.

Processes of Socialization

Socialization is the process by which children learn the standards, values, and expected behaviors of their culture and society. In the toddler years, the parents are the principal *agents of socialization*. Socialization occurs through the parents serving as models of behavior, expressing acceptance and warmth, providing restrictions or freedom, and punishing unacceptable behavior.

OBSERVATION OF ROLE MODELS.   As discussed earlier, children begin to imitate others in the second year of life. Hence, observation becomes one means of socialization. Adults assume that if young children simply see what others do, they will learn what is correct and practice it. This is true for many standards. But for some standards observation alone, without some sign from parents indicating that the behavior is approved or disapproved, may not work. For example, it is difficult to learn through observation alone that honesty, persistence, and loyalty to one's beliefs are desirable standards.

Observation is most effective when people display the desirable behavior consistently. If a parent sometimes uses harsh physical punishment and sometimes controls this form of aggression, the child is unlikely to accept control of aggression as the proper way to behave since the child sees how effective aggression is in controlling others. But if a child never sees physical aggression at home, nonaggressive ways of handling frustration will be learned as the appropriate standard. Of course, the child is likely to observe physical aggression elsewhere, among playmates or perhaps on television. In societies like ours, where there is so much behavioral diversity, observation of the parents alone is not always sufficient to override the influence of other agents of socialization. Parents try to deal with this problem by adding other strategies to their use of modeling; for example, they express approval or disapproval of the child's behavior (see Chapter 12 for further discussion of these techniques).

LOVE AND ACCEPTANCE.   The attachment relationship that began in the first year (see Chapter 4) forms an important basis for socialization in the toddler years. As we noted earlier, a strong attachment is facilitated by parents who are sensitive and responsive to the child's needs and who are generally warm and accepting. Parents may communicate their belief in the child's value, goodness, and ability in many ways. Physical affection, delight in the child's accomplishments, and playful interaction are frequent in our culture; other means of communicating the same basic message prevail in some other cultures.

Parents' acceptance of the child's value may be particularly important for the self-image the child forms during the initial period of self-awareness. If children feel valued and loved, their self-images are apt to be positive and they are likely to feel confidence in their emerging abilities.

RESTRICTION VS. PERMISSIVENESS.   For many parents, the issue of restricting their children's actions arises for the first time during the toddler period. As children become physically mobile, they run, climb, poke their fingers into strange places, spill things, pull objects out of cupboards and drawers, and put almost anything into their mouths, to name only a few possibilities. Many of these behaviors can be dangerous to the child or destructive to property, so parents must find a way of dealing with them. At the same time, as children develop the rudiments of standards and empathy, parents begin to feel that they can expect or demand that children learn to control their behavior. The toddler period is one in which parents often set the pattern for the amount and kinds of control they will exert over their children's behavior.

The issue of restriction or control poses a dilemma for many American parents because they are afraid that curbing children excessively will make the children overly fearful of them or of authority in general. They value the child's freedom to exercise his or her own will and occasionally rebel. At the same time, they want their children to obey them. As a result, they may be inconsistent in responding to disobedience and aggression, with the result that these behaviors are encouraged.

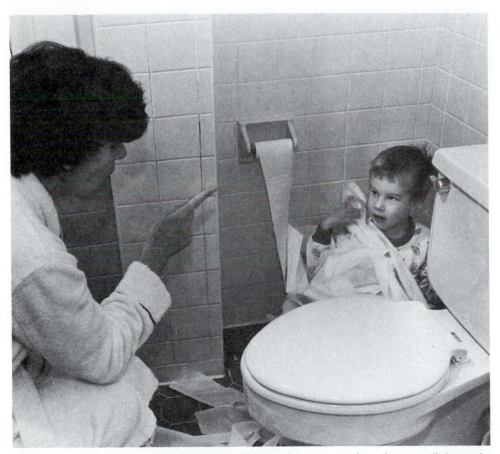

Many parents face a dilemma: They value their child's freedom to exercise his or her own will, but at the same time they want the child to obey them.

The dilemma about restriction grows partly out of the Western, particularly American, celebration of individual freedom. During the last part of the nineteenth century, American and European scholars urged parents to give their children some freedom to disobey and develop independence from the family. James Sully, who wrote toward the end of the century, reminded readers of John Locke's declaration that "children love liberty, and therefore they should be brought to do the things that are fit for them without feeling any restraint laid upon them." Sully declared that children resent any check on their impulses, and many parents took his recommendations to heart.

The effects of restriction on very young children depend on the context and the domains of behavior in which it is exercised. Most parents restrict some kinds of behavior but not others. Some of the domains in which parents may attempt to curb behavior include aggression, destruction of property, messiness at the table, toileting, sexual habits such as masturbation, exploring new places without adequate supervision, and lack of cleanliness. Although some parents make and enforce rules about many of these areas, few are highly restrictive across all of them. More typically, parents restrict and prohibit only behaviors that they care about, that is, those that violate their ideal of child behavior. For example, some may be highly restrictive about matters involving physical safety yet be permissive about sexual and aggressive behavior. Therefore, though we often speak of restrictive parents, it is more accurate to examine the areas in which the parent is restrictive or permissive.

The effects of restrictiveness vary with other components of the parent-child relationship, particularly the level of acceptance and affection. As we noted in Chapter 4, the attachment generated in an affectionate parent-child relationship provides a strong motive for the child to obey the parent in order to maintain that bond. Hence, a child with a strong attachment to the parent may respond more readily to restrictions, even during the toddler period. The long-term impact of restriction imposed in an affectionate context is seen in reminiscences of Japanese adults who grew up in highly restrictive families in which there were strong attachments and bonds of loyalty. The president of a Japanese automotive company recalls his feelings about his father: "Once his anger was over he did not nag or complain, but when he was angry I was really afraid of him. His scolding was like thunder. . . . I learned from my father how to live independently, doing everything on my own. He was the greatest model for my life" (Wagatsuma, 1977, p. 199).

Restrictiveness does not necessarily imply that a parent is punitive. A parent may patiently, but consistently, stop a young child from opening the refrigerator or putting her hand into a light socket with a gentle "no." Even though 1- and 2-year-old children often do not understand elaborate explanations, some brief verbal reason may be helpful in teaching the child (e.g., "Hitting hurts Mommy"). In many cases the child learns as well or better from these mild "punishments" as from more severe yelling or slapping.

PUNISHMENT.   Harsh punishment may have other consequences beyond those of restriction, and it may be relatively ineffective in producing behavior control in the child. For example, some behaviors that concern parents during the toddler period are likely to decline if they are ignored. Children between 1 and 3 years old often throw temper tantrums. They lie down on the floor, cry, beat against objects, and the like. In many cases they will stop this behavior in a few moments if adults ignore it. If a parent becomes harshly punitive, the behavior often escalates.

Although harsh punishment has many potential negative effects on children and is not a recommended disciplinary method, it does not always generate hostility or feelings of insecurity. Particularly as children grow older, their interpretation of the punishment and the social context in which they live affect how they respond to punitive parents. For example, working-class parents appear to be somewhat harsher when they scold their children than middle-class parents, but their behavior may be seen as appropriate in their social milieu. The resilience of some children with punitive parents is suggested by interviews with adults who had been studied throughout their childhood. Observers had described some children's parents as excessively punitive—they spanked their children a lot and imposed heavy penalties for small misdeeds. Twenty years later those children were productive, happily married adults without symptoms, and they considered their parents' practices to have been in their own best interest (Kagan & Moss, 1962).

In sum, the most effective and beneficial methods of socializing the toddler include acting as a consistent model of desired behavior and establishing a warm, affectionate relationship with the child during the first two years. As children begin to exhibit behavior that parents want to change, parents need to think carefully about what behaviors they want to socialize. Then they can use verbal disapproval and provide reasons for restrictions. Physical punishment may be less effective than consistent reprimands and gentle interventions such as pulling the child's hand away from a hot stove. The effects of any of these child-rearing practices depend, however, on the social context in which they occur.

The Context Created by Siblings

One of the most important social contexts in a family is defined by the number of children in the home. A 2- or 3-year-old with no brothers or sisters has less opportunity to become entangled in quarrels and therefore is less likely to be punished by parents. By contrast, a 3-year-old with a younger sibling will experience more restriction and punishment as a result of quarrels with the younger child (Kendrick & Dunn, 1983). Moreover, a toddler without siblings does not have to share the parents' attention with a younger child. After the birth of another child such sharing is necessary, for parents interact much less with the older child after another infant appears (Dunn, 1983). As a result, many firstborns, especially boys, show sleep disturbances and an increase in temper tantrums after the birth of a sibling. Of course, the child's temperament is also important; children who are irritable and vulnerable to stress will be more upset by the arrival of a sibling than temperamentally calm children.

When both siblings are of the same sex the rivalry between them tends to be more intense; thus, later-born brothers are more jealous of first-born brothers than of first-born sisters. It is also more likely that the younger sibling will imitate the older one. Boys with older sisters are less aggressive and more likely to display traditional female behavior than boys with older brothers (Brim, 1958; Koch, 1960). Children who have older siblings experience attacks from the stronger, older child and are continually compared with the older child with respect to maturity, responsibility, and skill. As a result, the younger child is a bit more likely to conclude that life is unfair and that the authority of older people, represented by the parents and the older sibling, is not totally benevolent and, therefore, not deserving of unquestioned obedience and loyalty.

SUMMARY

Around the first birthday children become able to treat an object as if it were something other than it is; they are now capable of symbolism. Once they have gained this competence, their representations of experience become expanded.

Important evidence for the development of symbolism is seen in play with objects. During the second year children manipulate objects in ways that reproduce acts that they have seen adults perform. Children begin to replace themselves with a toy as the active agent in play, and they may pretend to be another person. Children's drawings also become symbolic during the second and third years. Some theorists believe that play is a prerequisite for the development of other skills; but this idea is controversial.

As children play with objects in a symbolic manner, their reactions to other children also change. At about 18 months they become inhibited in the presence of another child, but by age 2 this reaction begins to disappear; 3-year-old children engage in reciprocal play and use other children as models.

Imitation is selective duplication of the behavior of a model. It begins at 7 or 8 months and becomes increasingly frequent and complex thereafter. Delayed imitation appears before the first birthday and is common during the second year. Children often imitate behavior that has an instrumental goal, but are less likely to imitate emotional expressions. They are much more likely to imitate their parents than to imitate anyone else.

Imitation is a universal maturational phenomenon. However, children imitate some models and behaviors more than others. There are several hypotheses about the determinants of imitation. It is suggested that children engage in imitation to promote social interactions and to enhance similarity to another person, and that children are most likely to imitate people who arouse them emotionally. In addition, imitation can be a self-conscious attempt to gain pleasure, power, property, or other desired goals.

During the last six months of the second year, children begin to create standards—idealized representations of objects, events, and behaviors. Events that violate a standard may produce signs of anxiety or distress. This reaction may be due to the development of the ability to infer that events have causes, even when the causes are not observed. Children's concern about violations of standards suggests that they have developed ideal representations of the "right" or "correct" way things should be.

Around the second birthday children display distress if they are unable to meet standards of behavior imposed by others, but they show pleasure when they meet standards they have set for themselves. In addition, they are amused by violations of adult rules and by events that will provoke disgust or disapproval in others. The age at which this appreciation of right and wrong behavior appears is similar in children from different cultures and families.

During the last half of the second year, children begin to be aware of their own qualities, states, and abilities. Children indicate this self-awareness by directing the behavior of others, describing their own behavior as they perform it, recognizing themselves in a mirror, and affirming personal possession of objects. The emergence of self-awareness is accompanied by an improvement in the ability to appreciate the perceptions and feelings of others.

The development of symbolism, imitation, standards, and self-awareness depends on experiences with other people. The most important experiences occur within the family and are directly related to the parents' beliefs about the qualities children should acquire. The process by which children learn the standards, values, and expected behaviors of their culture is termed *socialization*. Parents socialize their children by serving as models of behavior, expressing acceptance and warmth, providing restrictions on freedom, and punishing unacceptable behavior.

The issue of restriction poses a dilemma for many American parents because, although they want their children to obey them, they value the child's freedom to exercise his or her own will. As a result, they are inconsistent in responding to certain behaviors.

One of the most important social contexts in a family is defined by the number of children in the home. Children with no siblings have less opportunity to become entangled in quarrels and do not have to share the parents' affection. It is also more likely that younger siblings will imitate older ones and that they will be continually compared with the older child.

REVIEW QUESTIONS

1. What is symbolism and when do children first display this competence?

2. In what ways does play contribute to the development of symbolism?

3. Describe the ways in which children react to and interact with other children in the first two years.

4. What are the defining characteristics of imitation?

5. Why do children imitate some models and behaviors more often than others?

6. What are standards? How do children indicate that they have begun to use standards to evaluate events and behavior?

7. In what ways do children indicate that they have become aware of their own qualities, states, and abilities?

8. How is self-awareness related to the appearance of empathy?

9. Who are the principal agents of socialization in the toddler years? What are the primary processes of socialization?

10. How do birth order and the presence or absence of siblings affect development?

GLOSSARY

symbolism   The ability to create and accept an arbitrary relationship between an object and an idea.

play   A voluntary, spontaneous activity that does not seem to have a real-world goal.

imitation   Behavior that selectively duplicates the behavior shown by a model.

standards   Idealized representations of objects, events, and behaviors that are evaluated as good or bad.

self-awareness   Awareness of one's own qualities, states, and abilities.

empathy   The ability to appreciate the perceptions and feelings of others.

socialization   The process by which children learn the standards, values, and expected behaviors of their culture and society.

SUGGESTED READINGS

Dunn, J. (1988). *The beginnings of social understanding*. Cambridge, MA: Harvard University Press. Presents information based on observations in the home during the second year that reveal the effects of social interaction on empathy with others.

Garvey, C. (1977). *Play*. Cambridge, MA: Harvard University Press. Discusses the meaning of play, types of play, and the significance of play in children's lives.

Kagan, J. (1981). *The second year*. Cambridge, MA: Harvard University Press. Summarizes a longitudinal study of children in the second year that focused on the emergence of a moral sense and the first signs of self-awareness.

Kagan, J., & Lamb, S. (Eds.) (1988). *The emergence of morality in young children*. Chicago: University of Chicago Press. Contains essays by leading scholars on the development of standards and discusses the role of cultural setting, biology, and family experience on the emergence of morality.

Lewis, M., & Brooks-Gunn, J. (1979). *Social cognition and the acquisition of self*. New York: Plenum. Discusses the emergence of a self-concept in young children and some of the evidence supporting the idea that self-awareness appears in the second year.

Part Three

THE CHILDHOOD YEARS: LANGUAGE AND COGNITIVE DEVELOPMENT

Chapter Six

LANGUAGE AND COMMUNICATION

The Functions of Language

Communication

Understanding Society and Culture

Social Relationships

Symbolic Categories

Reasoning

Components of Speech

Phonemes

Meaningful Sounds—Morphemes and Words

Semantics: Learning the Meanings of Words

Testing Hypotheses

Over- and Underextensions

Figurative Language

Syntax: Combining Words into Sentences

The First Sentences

Learning Syntactic Rules

Grammatical Morphemes

Complex Sentences

Questions

Deictic Words

Passive Sentences

Negatives

Language in the Deaf

Metalinguistic Awareness

Pragmatics: Language in Context

Theories of Language Acquisition

Learning Theory

Nativist Theory

Cognitive Theory

Social Interaction Theory

217

Language and Cognition
   Cognition Precedes Language
   Language Influences Cognition
   Memory and Problem Solving
Environmental Influences on Language
   Adult Teaching and Language Learning
   Social-class Differences in Language
Communication and Conversation
   Early Verbal Exchanges
   Questions and Requests

Every animal species possesses a small number of special abilities in addition to those that are necessary for reproduction and survival. Among birds, the ability to sing and to fly are two such unique talents. Among humans, two significant competences are a moral sense, discussed in the preceding chapter, and language—the ability to communicate with others using words and sentences. Language is a powerful component of the human biological heritage. Perhaps this is one reason why children acquire it with such rapidity.

In the short span of 2½ or 3 years, children progress from uttering their first word to speaking grammatically correct sentences. Consider the case of Eve, a little girl whose speech was carefully recorded and studied.

When she was 18 months old Eve produced many two-word sentences, for example:

"Right down."
"Mommy read."
"Look dollie."

Just nine months later, at the age of 27 months, she communicated with much more complete and complex sentences, for example:

"I go get a pencil 'n' write."
"We're going to make a blue house."
"How 'bout another eggnog instead of cheese sandwich?"
(R. Brown, 1973).

The contrast between Eve's utterances at 18 months and the sentences she spoke at 27 months highlights the speed with which language skills are acquired and improved. In this chapter we will encounter many other examples of the remarkably fast progress young children make in learning language and in communicating (see Table 6.1).

TABLE 6.1

A Brief Overview of Language Development

Ages	Language characteristics	Examples
4–8 months	Babbling	baba dada gagaga
12 months (approximately)	First understandable words	Mommy dog dirty yes
18 months	Two-word combinations	Mommy soup[a] my pencil drink juice
24–30 months	Longer, more complex utterances with elaboration of different parts of sentence	That why Jackie cried.[a] Put my pencil in there. What is that on the table?
	Children converse, talking to each other in simple sentences, taking turns, but not always responding to each other directly	(Conversation between Susie, 35 months old, and Jackie, 38 months, each playing with a can of play-dough.)[b] (*Jackie hums.*) Susie: Very bad, Jackie, you're very bad. Jackie: My singing wasn't bad! Susie: No, *you* are bad. Jackie: Me? Susie: Mm-hmm. (*puts her can of play-dough next to Jackie's*) We have the same things. Jackie: Mm-hmm. (*takes Susie's can*) Susie: No! Mine! Jackie: (*gives can back*) Look at funny. (*reaching can*) Susie: You're funny. Jackie: I'm funny.

TABLE 6.1 *continued*

Ages	Language characteristics	Examples
4 years	Utterances longer and more complex; conversation in which utterances are related to each other, more adultlike	(Jane & Kate are playing "tea party")[b]
		Jane: Let's pretend when mommy's out.
		Kate: Oh, yeah. Well, I'm not the boss around here. . . . My mom is. Pretend we are the bosses.
		Jane: Yeah.
		Kate: Us children aren't the bosses.
		Jane: When I grow up and you grow up, *we'll be the bosses!* Hoah!
		Kate: Mm-hmm. But maybe we won't know how to punish.
		Jane: I will.
		Kate: How?
		Jane: I'll spank 'em. That's what my mom does.
		Kate: My mom does sometimes too.

[a]These are samples of the speech of Eve, one of the children Brown (1973) studied, recorded at ages 18 months and 27 months.
[b]The conversations of the 3- and 4-year-olds are taken from videotapes of peer interactions, courtesy of Susan Ervin-Tripp and Nancy Budwig.

THE FUNCTIONS OF LANGUAGE

Although the most obvious function of language is to communicate ideas, language has four additional functions. It allows users to understand their society and culture; helps in establishing and maintaining social relationships; permits users to classify events in linguistic categories; and aids in reasoning.

Communication

Children use language to communicate their needs, internal states, and attitudes. By the first year some children will say simple words like *milk* or *cookie* when they are hungry. Upon returning home from the child care center, a child may report to her parents what happened during the day or explain why she does not want to go to bed early or have string beans for dinner. Among primates, facial expressions and gestures as well as shrieks and calls serve the function of influencing the behavior of others. However, by simply saying "It hurts," a child can induce a parent to alleviate his distress.

Understanding Society and Culture

Language also helps children understand their society and culture. Before there were schools, books, or newspapers, listening to adults and peers gave children the worldly knowledge they needed and told them what moral rules were to be obeyed. A young baboon has to learn the hard way to avoid fights with larger animals or to remember where food is located. For humans, much of this information is packaged in words. During this century, as technical knowledge has become more critical to occupational success, the ability to use printed language has become essential for adaptation.

Social Relationships

Language helps children establish and maintain relationships with others. Conversations at the dinner table, between friends and associates, and of course, between lovers and spouses are analogous to the dances of flamingos preparing for mating or the grooming of one adult chimpanzee by another. Each animal species relies on ritual actions with others to bond the members of a group together. Talk serves this function in our species.

A basic function of language is communication with others.

Symbolic Categories

As indicated in Chapter 3, animals and human infants represent the world around them in the form of perceptual structures called *schemata*. Language, however, makes possible more symbolic and abstract ways of representing the world. A person walking in a Maine forest in May, for example, experiences an extraordinary variety of trees, shrubs, and flowers of varied colors, forms, and smells. The scene experienced by the person is rich and complex. Yet the simple phrase "a Maine forest in spring" captures the elements of the scene symbolically.

Language permits one to classify objects into symbolic, linguistic categories, which are efficient modes of representation. The word *tree* summarizes the variety of forms that belong to that type of plant, just as the world *aggression* covers a large number of very different actions. Thus, language enables a person to categorize diverse events that share some common features.

Reasoning

The use of language to classify experience into symbolic categories is related to another use of language: as an aid in inference and deduction, which comprise the essence of human reasoning. Consider a 4-year-old who has learned that her cat is also called a *pet*. When she learns that her cousin has a pet goldfish, she tries to figure out why a cat and a fish are both called by the same name. After inferring the correct meaning of *pet*, she may come to appreciate a new idea, namely, that children can have relationships to any of a large number of animals. Later in the chapter we will consider the relationship between thoughts and words in more detail.

COMPONENTS OF SPEECH

Scientists have learned much more about the child's use of language for communication than about the other four functions of language; hence, we will deal first with how the child learns to speak words and sentences in order to communicate his or her desires, knowledge, and feelings.

After the third birthday most of the child's communications consist of sentences or partial sentences. Hence, linguists regard the sentence as the primary unit of communication. But sentences can be analyzed into three smaller units. These units, beginning with the smallest, are phonemes, morphemes, and words.

Phonemes are the basic sounds that are combined to make words. Most languages have about 30 phonemes. In English, the phonemes correspond roughly to the sounds of the spoken letters of the alphabet. For example, one phoneme in English is the sound *t* as it is pronounced in words like *tap*, *step*, or *later*. Even though the sounds of *t* in these three words are slightly different, *t* is regarded as a single phoneme by speakers of English. English contains some phonemes that are rare in other languages; one example is the *th* sound in *this*. On the other hand, many African languages contain unique phonemes in the form of click sounds. In some languages, such as Chinese, a rising or falling vocal tone applied to a word is a phoneme.

Every language has rules governing the combination of two or more phonemes to make words. These rules permit some combinations and prohibit others. For example, in English there are no words that begin with the phonemes that correspond to *ng*, *zb*, or *tn*, although these can begin words in some other languages. The young child readily learns that a particular phoneme remains the same even though adults from different regions of a country do not always pronounce the phoneme in the same way. The *a* sound in the word *baby*, for instance, differs in subtle ways each time we say it, and we can recognize that sound despite differences in the pronunciation of *baby* by people from Maine, Mississippi, or Australia.

PERCEIVING PHONEMES.   Infants only a few days old can discriminate between similar phonemes; for example, they can discriminate *ba* from *bu* or *da* (Eimas, 1975; Bertoncini et al., 1988). This ability has been demonstrated using the habituation method described in Chapter 3. A nipple is placed in an infant's mouth; when she sucks on the nipple at a particular rate, a loudspeaker emits a particular syllable, such as *ba*. When the infant's rate of sucking begins to slow because she is becoming habituated to the sound *ba*, the syllable emitted by the loudspeaker is changed by switching channels on a tape recorder. As Figure 6.1 shows, if infants continue to hear the same syllable, they do not show an increase in sucking rate. But if they hear a new syllable—either *bu*, *du*, or *da*—they show an increase in sucking rate, indicating that they perceive a difference between the original syllable and each of the three new syllables.

Human infants can make many more phonemic discriminations than are required by their language. However, if a particular phonemic discrimination is not part of their language, they will eventually lose the power to make that discrimination (Werker & Tees, 1984). For example, although infants can discriminate between the phonemes *ra* and *la*, this distinction does not occur in Japanese, and Japanese adults do not make this discrimination easily.

PRODUCING PHONEMES.   Although 1-month-old infants can discriminate among phonemes, they are unable to produce them. Newborns cry, burp, cough, and sneeze, but the speech areas of the brain and their connections to the vocal cords are not yet mature enough to produce the phonemes of their language. It is not until the third month that infants begin to coo and make vowel sounds while playing alone or with others. These sounds represent the infant's first phonemes. At 5 or 6 months of age, all infants spontaneously begin to babble by combining vowel and consonant sounds in strings of syllables that sound like *ba-ba-ba* or *da-da-da*. These babbling sounds often sound like real speech because of their rising and falling intonations. The fact that babbling appears in all infants around 6 months of age suggests that maturation of the brain as well as growth of the vocal system has made it possible for the infant to babble when it is excited. Although babbling has no symbolic meaning, it increases in frequency until infants are about

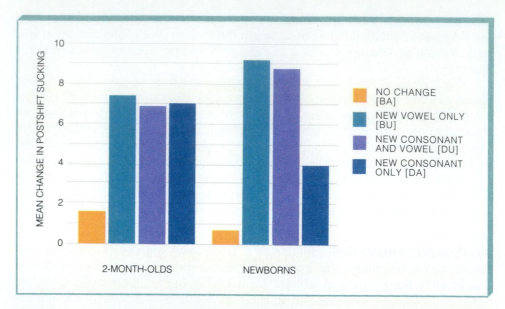

FIGURE 6.1   Results of an experiment showing that infants can discriminate between phonemes. Sucking rates were measured before and after a shift from hearing one phoneme to hearing another. The change in postshift sucking when the syllable changes indicates discrimination. (Adapted from J. Bertoncini, B. Bijelac-Babic, P. W. Jusczyk, L. J. Kennedy, & J. Mahler. An investigation of young infants perceptual representations of speech sounds. *Journal of Experimental Psychology: General*, 1988, 117, 21–33. Copyright by the American Psychological Association. By permission.)

1 year old and speak their first meaningful words. From then on, babbling decreases.

The frequency of babbling before the first birthday does not predict how early or late normal children will begin to speak words or the size of their vocabulary when they enter school. Babbling reflects the child's degree of excitability and tendency to express excitement in vocal sounds. Support for this conclusion is provided by the fact that deaf children who cannot hear their own voice or the voices of others also begin to babble at about 6 months of age, and their babbling is very similar to that of hearing children. However, the babbling of deaf children quickly declines after a month or two, suggesting that in order to continue vocalizing infants need to hear themselves babble as well as receive feedback from other people.

Meaningful Sounds—Morphemes and Words

Around the first birthday most children begin to speak their first meaningful sounds, usually in the form of single words called morphemes. A **morpheme** is the smallest unit of meaning in a language; it cannot be broken into any smaller parts that have meaning. However, linguists make a distinction between **words** and two kinds of morphemes. An **unbound morpheme** is a word that can stand alone. The

Most infants begin to babble spontaneously at about 5 or 6 months.

words *cat, milk,* and *danger* each consist of one unbound morpheme. Other morphemes, called **bound morphemes,** cannot stand alone and are always parts of words. Prefixes, suffixes, plurals, and possessives are all bound morphemes that are connected to other morphemes. Thus, the bound morpheme *-ness,* when added to the unbound morpheme *happy,* produces the word *happiness;* the bound morpheme *s* following the unbound morpheme *dog* becomes the word *dogs.* Bound morphemes also indicate the tense of a verb and the possessive case.

It should be clear from this discussion that words can be composed of one morpheme or many. For example, while the word *cat* consists of one morpheme and *cats* contains two, the word *retyping* consists of three morphemes: *re* + *typ(e)* + *ing.*

The single words that children utter most of the time during the second year stand for things—*socks, shoes, milk*—or people—*mama, dada, baby.* Occasionally children use words for actions, such as *bye-bye, go,* and *sit.* They quickly learn the names for toys, familiar objects in the home, articles of clothing, animals, and body parts, as well as words that tell their parents what they want—such as *up*, *down*, *open*, *more*, and *no*. The first words are usually names for people with whom the baby interacts and for objects that change or that the child plays with often. Names for animals and vehicles, both of which move, are more common than names of rooms and plants, which do not move. Words for food, toys, and articles of clothing that children can remove easily (e.g., *juice*, *cookie*, *ball*, *sock*) are common in children's early vocabulary; words for immovable objects and those that are not easily acted upon (e.g., *wall*, *table*, *window*, *mitten*) occur less frequently.

Unless the context is very clear, we do not usually know what 2-year-olds intend when they say a single word. A child in a high chair who says *milk* could mean "I see the milk," "I want the milk," "I want a glass," or (watching the mother drink a glass of milk) "I see that you are drinking milk." Moreover, children will typically guess at a word for a new event if they do not know the correct word. For example, a child who happens to know the word *dog* and sees a cow for the first time (and does not know the word *cow*) may call the cow *dog*. But this does not mean that the child does not recognize the obvious differences between dogs and cows. It means that the only word the child knew that seemed appropriate to the new animal was *dog*.

Children understand many more words than they actually speak (Bates, Bretherton, & Snyder, 1988). (In technical terms, psychologists say that children's *receptive* language abilities are usually more complete than their *productive* abilities.) Infants who are not yet saying words will often respond to questions like "Where is your bottle?" or "Pat the doggy" with appropriate actions. In one experiment a group of 1-year-olds, many of whom were not saying words, were brought to a laboratory. The infants sat on their mothers' laps facing a screen on which slides were projected. A pair of pictures appeared on the screen—say, a dog and a frog—and the mother asked, "Where is the dog?" The infants often looked at the correct picture, indicating that they knew the word *dog* (Reznick, 1987).

During the period from 1 to 3 years of age, children comprehend about five times as many words as they use in everyday speech. By the time children are 6 years of age, they will have learned about 13,000 different words (Benedict, 1979; Kagan, 1981).

SEMANTICS: LEARNING THE MEANINGS OF WORDS

When language is used for communication, it has three interrelated aspects: semantics, syntax, and pragmatics. **Semantics** refers to the meanings of words; **syntax** refers to the grammatical rules that specify how words should be combined in sentences; and **pragmatics** refers to the relationship between the meaning of an utterance and the context in which the utterance occurs.

Many new words are acquired through elaborate "naming rituals" that parents indulge in from the time their babies first utter something that sounds like a word (Ninio & Bruner, 1976). Parents point to objects, name them, and correct the child's attempt to repeat the names. Often young children establish effective

Parents teach their children many new words by pointing to objects and naming them.

routines for eliciting the names of objects from their parents. For instance, they repeatedly say, "What's that?" Simply hearing a word used to label an object a few times is often sufficient for a child to learn its meaning and begin using it (Carey, 1977; Leonard, 1976).

As adults, we can label objects at several different levels of generality. A pet is Prince, a Dalmation, a dog, a mammal, or an animal. Most of the terms of reference that young children learn are at an intermediate level of generality. Children between 1 and 3 years old are likely to call a beagle a *dog* rather than a *beagle* (more specific) or an *animal* (more general).

Testing Hypotheses

A single word in a child's vocabulary may refer to both object and action. Some children say "door" as a door opens or closes, while others say "open" to refer to these actions. When children hear a new word they make a preliminary hypothesis about its meaning and test the hypothesis as they use the word. If necessary, they gradually modify their original ideas about the meaning of the word to make them coincide with those of adults (Clark & Anderson, 1979).

Under the right conditions, older children can often figure out the meaning of a word. In one experiment children 2 to 4 years old were asked to help the experimenter. They were asked to retrieve one of two objects from a chair in a corner of the room. One of the objects was a familiar one for which the child had a word; the other object was unfamiliar, and the child did not know the correct name for it. For example, when the experimenter wanted the child to learn a new color word she might say to the child, "There is something that you could do to help me. Do you see those two books on the chair? Could you bring me the *chartreuse* one? Not the red one, the chartreuse one." Often the child ignored the red object and brought the chartreuse object. A child who is being taught a word for a shape might be asked, "Could you bring me the parallelogram, not the round one?" A child who is being taught a word for a texture might be asked, "Could you bring me the fleecy box, not the smooth one?"

About ten minutes later the children were tested to see whether, on the basis of a single experience with the new word, they would spontaneously name the new colors, shapes, or textures encountered just a few minutes earlier. For example, the child who was being taught a new shape word would be shown an array of objects with various shapes. The experimenter would say, "Now I am going to ask you some questions about these trays on the table. See this tray? What is it? What does it look like?" Children readily learned new words for shapes and colors but less often learned new words for textures. However, even though the children learned new words for shapes and colors they did not use those words often in their spontaneous speech (Heibeck & Markman, 1987).

Over- and Underextensions

The meanings children attribute to words are often quite different from adult meanings for those words. Some are *overextensions*. *Doggie* may be used to refer to cats, cows, horses, rabbits, and other four-legged animals as well as to dogs. Many mothers have been embarrassed when their toddlers greeted strange men as *Daddy*. *Moon* or *ball* may designate many objects that are round, such as cakes, oranges, and the letter *o*. Overextensions are usually based on perceptual similarities in shape, size, sound, texture, or movement (Bowerman, 1976; E. Clark, 1973), although some are based on similarities in function (K. Nelson, 1975). When a child uses the word *moon* to refer not only to the moon in all of its phases but also to a slice of lemon and a shiny leaf, he may be saying that the word *moon* means anything that is small or shiny. When a child calls an oven a mouth, she is announcing that she recognizes the fact that the human mouth and the oven have a similar function; that is, they receive food.

Children also overextend the meanings of words that do not refer to objects and cannot be generalized on the basis of perceptual or functional similarities, such as *more, all gone, off, there*. They use these words in a wide variety of contexts and in relation to many different objects and activities. For example, one child used *on* and *off* in getting her socks off, getting on or off a toy horse, pulling beads apart and putting them together, unfolding a newspaper, pushing hair out of her mother's face, opening and closing boxes with lids, and putting lids on jelly jars or caps on bottles. Apparently the meanings of these prepositions were generalized to virtually any act involving the separation or coming together of objects or parts of objects.

Some words are *underextended*, that is, defined too narrowly. For example, one 9-month-old used the word *car* to refer to cars moving on the street below but not to cars standing still or to pictures of cars (Bloom, 1973). For some children the word *kitty* at first refers only to the family's pet cat. Later the word may be extended to include other cats and possibly overextended to dogs or cows as well (E. Clark, 1973; Kessel, 1970). When asked, "Where are the shoes?" one 8-month-old crawled to his mother's closet and played with her shoes, but only with *her* shoes and only when the shoes were in the closet. When the shoes were placed in a different location or the child was in front of his father's shoes, he would still crawl to the shoes in his mother's closet. Thus, for this young child the original meaning of *shoes* was limited to mother's shoes in the closet (Reich, 1977).

Overextensions are more common in the production of speech than in comprehension. A child who overgeneralizes *apple*, applying that word to balls, tomatoes, and other round objects, has no difficulty pointing to the apple in a set of pictures of round objects (Gruendel, 1976; Thompson & Chapman, 1975). Overextended definitions usually last only a short time, fading out as new words enter the child's vocabulary. When the child learns the word *cow* and understands that this animal has features such as moo sounds and horns, the meaning of *cow* is differentiated from the meaning of *dog* (E. Clark, 1973).

Figurative Language

Until about the third birthday children use language literally to name real events in the world, and they understand that when other people speak they intend a literal meaning. But between the third and fourth birthdays children begin to understand the figurative or nonliteral meanings of phrases like "My dresses are friends" or "Clouds are like ice cream cones." The ability to understand these nonliteral, figurative expressions, and later metaphors, is enhanced as the child prepares to enter school. By the age of 6 some children are rather expert at understanding metaphors and similes. This is also the age at which irony appears (Winner, 1988). A 6-year-old will understand his father's intended meaning if the father comments on a stormy day, "Boy, is this a nice morning."

When a 5-year-old knows that the meaning of a metaphorical sentence spoken by an adult is obviously incorrect, the child assumes that the adult must intend a nonliteral meaning. For example, when a mother says, referring to two tired 5-year-olds playing in a sandbox, "There sure isn't any pepper in the soup," the two children may understand that because there is no soup in the vicinity of the sandbox, the mother's remark must have been intended as a metaphor to suggest that the children are tired. However, when their father, sitting at a table at a restaurant, is served heavily seasoned soup and says, "There sure isn't any pepper in the soup," such a sentence could be appropriate in that context. As a result, the 5-year-olds might be confused and not understand that the father intended the statement to be ironic.

Irony requires advanced cognitive development, especially the ability to appreciate that an adult might say the opposite of what he or she intends. (This ability to infer the thoughts of another person will be relevant again when we consider concrete operations in Chapter 7.) In both metaphor and irony the child displays the fundamental human ability to go beyond what is given and, in some cases, to contradict the given. The ability to recognize that a statement is false on one level but true on a deeper level emerges in most children by the time they are 7 years old. Children can now appreciate that an action or a remark can be understood from two perspectives—how it appears on the surface and the private intention of the person who acted. It is at this age that the idea of sincerity takes on meaning for children

SYNTAX: COMBINING WORDS INTO SENTENCES

The First Sentences

As children reach the middle of the second year, when their speaking vocabulary is about 50 words, they begin to put two words together and speak their first sentences. Typical of these two-word sentences are "See doggy," "Where daddy?" "All gone," "Throw ball," and "More car." The last sentence, "More car," might mean "Drive around the block some more," or it might communicate the fact that the child has seen a long line of cars.

A few months before the second birthday, there is a major increase in the size of the child's vocabulary and in the variety of two- and three-word combinations the child will speak. One boy spoke his first two-word sentence at 19 months and used 14 different two-word combinations during that month. During the next six months the number of different two-word combinations spoken by that boy increased dramatically; the totals for those months were 24, 54, 89, 250, 1,400, and over 2,500, respectively (Braine, 1963).

The child's first two-word sentences are like telegrams or abbreviated versions of adult sentences, because they consist primarily of a noun or verb and an adjective. Like a telegram, these sentences contain only essential words; they lack prepositions (*in, on, by*), conjunctions (*and, but, or*), and articles (*a, the*). These short sentences also omit auxiliary verbs like *have* and *may* and morphemes like the plural s or the morpheme that indicates the tense of a verb. Children will even utter such telegraphic sentences when they are asked to imitate a longer sentence. For example, if an adult asks a 3-year-old child to repeat a sentence like "I can eat a cookie," the child is likely to say, "Eat cookie." Table 6.2 lists some important classes of sentences that are produced in two-word utterances. The relationships listed in the table occur in all languages, which suggests that they are based on concepts that are acquired by children as a result of cognitive maturation.

Learning Syntactic Rules

Children's speech typically preserves correct word order for their language. For example, in imitating the sentence "I can eat a cookie," children will say "Eat cookie," not "Cookie eat." Almost all of children's two-word sentences place words in the appropriate order. In other words, children follow the rules of syntax or grammar when they speak.

Children learn syntactic rules with very little explicit instruction or tutoring from adults. Parents often teach their children new words or correct them when they use words with incorrect meaning. They less often teach grammar or correct children's grammatical mistakes. Parents are more concerned with the accuracy of children's remarks than with their grammatical form.

Much of what we have learned about the development of syntax comes from studying tape recordings of children's speech when they are playing or in social interaction. As children grow older, their sentences become longer. The length of sentences is a good indicator of the level of a child's syntactic development, at least during the period from 1 1/2 to 4 years of age. Psychologists compute the

TABLE 6.2

Meanings Expressed in Telegraphic Speech

Locate, Name:	see doggie, book there
Demand, Desire:	more milk, want candy
Nonexistence:	allgone milk
Negation:	not kitty
Possession:	my candy
Attribution:	big car
Agent-Action:	mama walk
Action-Object:	hit you
Agent-Object:	mama book
Action-Location:	sit chair
Action-Recipient:	give papa
Action-Instrument:	cut knife
Question:	where ball?

Source: Slobin, 1972.

average length of 50 to 100 utterances by a particular child and call that index the *mean length of utterance*, or MLU. The MLU is based on the average number of morphemes in a set of utterances, not on the number of words. You will recall that morphemes include not only simple words like *cat* and *dog* but also prefixes, suffixes, plurals, tense endings, and possessives. Thus, the sentence "The dogs ran" contains four morphemes but "The dog ran" contains only three. It takes about a half-hour of recorded conversation to calculate the MLU of an average child. Figure 6.2 shows the increase in MLU for three children from 18 through 44 months of age.

As is clear from Figure 6.2, there are dramatic differences among children in mean length of utterance between the ages of 2 and 4. One group of investigators who studied children from 10 to 28 months old found that the 28-month-olds with the greatest MLU scores were those who had uttered a large number of nouns when they were 1 year old and a large number of verbs when they were 2 years old. These facts suggest that the differences in language ability of preschool children can be predicted and that the use of nouns by 1-year-olds to name objects in the environment, rather than words like *bye-bye* or commands to others, is a particularly sensitive sign of later language precocity (Bates, Bretherton, & Snyder, 1988).

Grammatical Morphemes

Children master the grammatical morphemes of their language in a particular order. Roger Brown of Harvard University discovered this order for English by studying three children who were called Adam, Eve, and Sarah. The order in which 14 English grammatical morphemes were mastered by these children is shown in Table 6.3.

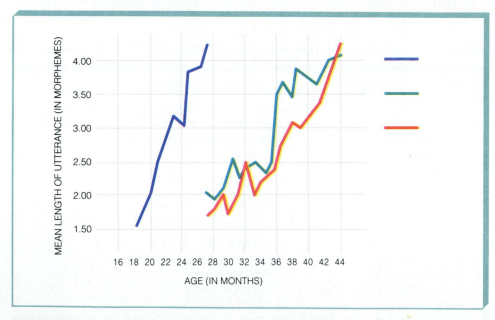

FIGURE 6.2   Mean length of utterance and chronological age for three children. (*Adapted from* R. Brown. A *first language*. Cambridge, MA: Harvard University Press, 1973. By permission.)

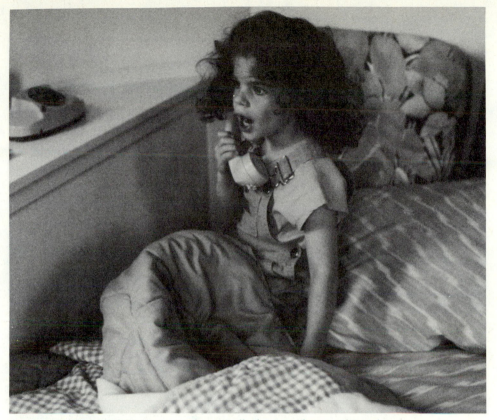

Children's language ability increases dramatically between the ages of 2 and 4.

Most children first learn the present progressive ending *-ing* (as in *walking, eating, singing*), followed by correct use of the prepositions *in* and *on*, the plural, the irregular past tense (*he went, she ate*), the possessive (*Mary's, dog's*), the correct use of *are* and *is*, articles like *the* and *a*, and the regular past tense (*he walked, she stopped*). These victories are followed by mastery of the third person present tense (*she walks*), the third person present tense irregular (*she does*), auxiliary verbs that are not contracted (I *am walking, she is singing*), the contractible form of the verb *to be* (*That's a book*), and finally, the contractible form of auxiliary verbs (*I'm walking*).

The first few morphemes that are mastered—for example, adding *-ing* to a verb or adding *s* to a noun to form the plural—are produced early because these sounds are perceptually distinctive. The order of mastery is different in other languages. For example, in languages in which the plural is not perceptually distinctive, it appears at a later age. (Box 6.1 describes a procedure used by psychologists to determine the child's understanding of grammatical morphemes.)

Children learn general rules for syntactic morphemes, rather than specific endings for words. Thus, a child who uses the word *went* correctly may say "I wented" when she intends to use the past tense because she has learned the rule that one should add *-ed* to indicate an event that happened in the past. Similarly, a child

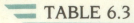

TABLE 6.3

Average Order of Acquisition of 14 Grammatical Morphemes by Three Children Studied by R. Brown (1973)

1. present progressive
2/3. prepositions (*in/on*)
4. plural
5. irregular past tense
6. possessive
7. copula, uncontractible
8. articles
9. regular past tense
10. third person present tense, regular
11. third person present tense, irregular
12. auxiliary, uncontractible
13. copula, contractible
14. auxiliary, contractible

who uses the word *feet* correctly may say *feets* to indicate the plural because he has learned that one should add *s* to indicate more than one.

Complex Sentences

When simple sentences about four words long have become frequent and grammatical inflections like the plural and possessive are being mastered—generally between the ages of 2 and 3—complex sentences begin to appear spontaneously in children's speech. These sentences may consist of two or more simple sentences joined by the conjunction *and* (e.g., "You call and he comes") or one thought embedded in another (e.g., "I hope I don't hurt it"). Some complex sentences contain *wh* clauses (those that begin with *what, who, where,* or *when*), such as "I know where it is" and "When I get big, I can lift you up."

To construct complex sentences, children have to learn the rules for combining larger groups of words (phrases, clauses, and even sentences) and using connective words (e.g., *and, but, because*). *And* is generally the first and most frequently occurring connective in a child's vocabulary during the third year. *Because, what, when,* and *so* are also used frequently; *then, but, if,* and *that* appear less frequently (Bloom, Lahey, Hood, Lifter, & Fiess, 1980).

Children's early complex sentences express a number of different meanings. The order of appearance of semantic relationships is fairly constant, although some children begin the sequence earlier and move through it faster than others. Additive relationships (e.g., "You can carry that and I can carry this") are expressed first, followed by temporal and causal statements ("You better look for it when you

BOX 6.1

The Wug Test

Jean Berko invented a procedure in which children are shown drawings of unfamiliar animals or actions, each of which is given a nonsense name. The children are then provided with a linguistic context that is appropriate for adding the plural or possessive *s* to the noun or the progressive third person present or past tense to the verbs. (Two examples are shown in the chart.) The child is shown the drawing of the single animal as well as the two animals below it. The examiner points to the single animal and says, "This is a wug." Then, pointing to the two animals, she says, "Now there is another one. There are two of them. There are two _____." The child is then invited to say the correct form of the plural, which would be *wugs*.

The second example is a drawing of a man swinging an unfamiliar object. The examiner says, "This is a man who knows how to rick. He is ricking. He did the same thing yesterday. What did he do yesterday? Yesterday he _____." If the child understands the past tense, he or she should say, "Yesterday he ricked" (from Berko, 1958; see Gleason, 1985, p. 153).

THIS IS A WUG.

NOW THERE IS ANOTHER ONE.
THERE ARE TWO OF THEM.
THERE ARE TWO _____.

THIS IS A MAN WHO KNOWS HOW TO RICK.
HE IS RICKING.
HE DID THE SAME THING YESTERDAY.
WHAT DID HE DO YESTERDAY?
YESTERDAY HE _____.

Two items from the "Wug" test designed to test children's knowledge of rules for generating plurals and verb tenses. (From J. Berko, The child's learning of English morphology. *Word*, 1958, 14, 50–177. By permission.)

get back home," "She put a Band-Aid on her shoe and it maked it feel better"). Contrast or opposition ("I was tired but now I'm not tired"), object specification ("The man who fixes the door"), and notice ("Watch what I am doing") appear still later. During the third year progress in the use of complex sentences is usually slow and steady, with no sudden leaps forward or abrupt changes from one form to another (Bloom et al., 1980).

Questions

Advances in linguistic development are also reflected in a gradual but regular improvement in the production and comprehension of questions. Two-year-olds understand *yes* and *no* as well as *where*, *who*, and *what* questions, and generally answer appropriately. These questions pertain to people, objects, and locations—precisely the things that children are interested in and talk about in their first sentences. At this age *when*, *how*, and *why* questions are answered as though they asked *what* or *where*. (Q: When are you having lunch? A: In the kitchen. Q: Why are you eating that? A: It's an apple.). However, at about age 3 children begin to respond to *why* questions appropriately (Ervin-Tripp, 1977). The frequency of correct answers to all types of *wh* questions increases between the ages 3 and 5.

When children begin to construct more complex sentences, they also properly invert the auxiliary verb and noun in yes-no questions ("Are you going to help me?). However, they still fail to make this inversion in *wh* questions ("Sue, what you have in your mouth?" "Why kitty can't stand up?"). *Wh* questions are more complex grammatically than yes-no questions because they require two operations: inserting the question word and inverting the subject and verb. At this stage the child can perform each of these operations separately but cannot yet combine them in the same sentence.

Deictic Words

Deictic words are words like *here*, *there*, *this*, *that*, *mine*, and *yours*, all of which refer to the location of objects in relation to the speaker. Children's comprehension and production of these words shows that they are capable of taking the point of view of others. Two-year-olds clearly understand the perspective of the speaker when interpreting the words *here* and *there*. If a mother says to a child on the other side of the room, "Your toy is over here," the child moves to the mother's side of the room to get it. Moreover, *this*, *that*, and *there*—often pronounced *dis*, *dat*, and *dere*—are used with appropriate meaning by infants in their second year. Yet findings from laboratory studies indicate that full understanding of these terms is not achieved until some years after they first appear in the child's speech—a case of production occurring prior to complete comprehension (de Villiers & de Villiers, 1978).

In one study, a child between 2 and 5 years of age sat at a table opposite the experimenter. Facing a low wall across the center of the table, the child and the experimenter played a game together. Each player had an overturned cup. While the child's eyes were closed, the experimenter hid a piece of candy under one of the cups. The experimenter then gave the child clues such as "The candy is on *this* side of the wall" (or "under the cup" or "here" or "in front of the wall"). To obtain the candy the child had to translate the experimenter's viewpoint into his or her own—"*this* (the experimenter's) side of the wall" was, from the child's perspective, *that* side. All the children readily distinguished between *mine* and *yours*, but 2-year-olds had difficulty when a shift of perspective was required. Three-year-olds are adept at taking the speaker's perspective, since they correctly interpret *this* and *that*, *here* and *there*, and *in front of* and *behind* (de Villiers & de Villiers, 1974).

Passive Sentences

The passive voice (e.g., "The window was broken by the dog") is rarely used by children under 4 years of age, but after that time children begin to master this syntactic form. By age 5 children will act out, with toys, a passive sentence such as "The boy was kissed by the girl" or "The truck was hit by the car." Although 4-year-olds do not ordinarily use passive sentences when they talk, they can understand them if the context is unusual. For example, an animal attacking a person is an unusual and salient event. Therefore, upon seeing that event, schoolchildren will spontaneously utter a passive sentence like "He is being bitten by the dog" (Lempert, 1984).

Negatives

There is also a regular sequence in children's acquisition of the ability to speak grammatically correct negative sentences. At first, many children put the word *no* at the beginning of the sentence—"No sit down," "No go bed." A little later, the child moves the word *no* inside the sentence—"I no like it," "I no want bed." Finally, the child masters the correct form (Gleason, 1985). The many changes in children's language during the first four years are illustrated in Table 6.1.

Language in the Deaf

Deaf children who live with deaf parents and are learning sign language express in their signs the same ideas that are expressed in speech by children who hear. Further, both deaf and hearing children show similar rates of language development. Among deaf children, the first signs are for objects; later they display signs for ideas like "Mommy eat" or "Daddy coat" (trying to persuade the father to take off his coat). Deaf children often produce their first sign by 8 or 9 months, a few months before the average hearing child utters his or her first words. Utterances composed of two signs occur at about 17 to 18 months, the same time that hearing children begin to combine two words in their first sentences.

One reason deaf children's first signs occur earlier than hearing children's first words is that the motor skills required for the display of signs may be more mature than the centers of the brain that mediate the production of speech. Thus, it may be easier to express symbolic ideas with the hands than with the vocal cords, mouth, and tongue. This explanation implies that there is no difference in comprehension between deaf and hearing children; they differ only in expression.

Metalinguistic Awareness

The speech of 4- or 5-year-olds demonstrates a remarkable mastery of complex rules of grammar and meaning. To what extent are children conscious of those rules? We call this ability **metalinguistic awareness**. Language itself becomes a topic that the child reflects on, seeks to understand, and talks about.

Preschool children differentiate between sounds that are real words and those that are not; for example, they regard *apple* as a word and reject *oope*. However, young children do not understand that words are assigned to objects arbitrarily, by custom rather than by necessity. If you ask a preschooler, "Could you call a *dog* a *cow* and a *cow* a *dog*?" the child is likely to reply, "No. Dogs bark and cows give milk." The attributes of the object are thought to be inherent in the word (Vygotsky, 1962).

Two-year-olds can recognize some grammatically incorrect sentences. When presented with a series of sentences like "Eat the cake" and "Lock the open," they can tell the difference between well-formed and deviant ones, though their discrimination is far from perfect (Gleitman, Gleitman, & Shipley, 1972). When asked to correct a deviant sentence, many youngsters suggested changes in meaning rather than just grammar, changing *house a build* to *live in a house*, for example. With increasing linguistic maturity, the children shifted from corrections that change meaning to corrections of word order (de Villiers & de Villiers, 1974).

"Spontaneous repairs"—instances in which a child makes a speech error, recognizes it, and spontaneously corrects it—provide further evidence that the child is thinking about grammatical rules. A 3-year-old girl said, "She—he didn't give her any food." She began her sentence with the wrong word, giving the object the action, and then corrected herself (E. Clark & Anderson, 1979).

With greater metalinguistic awareness comes appreciation of ambiguity and comprehension of the fact that certain words, phrases, or sentences can mean different things in different contexts. Ambiguities in language and understanding of the different meanings of words underlie the ability to create metaphors and jokes (see Box 6.2).

PRAGMATICS: LANGUAGE IN CONTEXT

To communicate effectively, children must know more than word meanings and grammatical rules. They must learn to relate language to the physical and social context in which it is used. This is the pragmatic aspect of language. Consider the sentence "Yeah, let's do it." It has one meaning if the speaker is a pitcher in a baseball game talking to the catcher and quite another meaning if the speaker is holding a stone above his head and aiming it at a window.

Even young children speaking one-word utterances have different pragmatic aims. They can use single words to ask for something they want, to label something, or to describe an event that has happened. The mother who has just heard her child say "milk" has to use the context as well as the tone of voice and facial

BOX 6.2

Humor

As their metalinguistic awareness advances, children begin to think about, talk about, and "play with" words and language forms. Much of our appreciation of humor depends on comprehension of linguistic ambiguities and our awareness that many words have more than one meaning and can be used in different ways.

Children under the age of 7 or 8 tend to regard words as having only one meaning; consequently, they do not find jokes based on word play to be funny. In one study, first- and second-grade children were asked to indicate which answer to a riddle was funnier, a joking answer or a factual one. Consider the riddle "Why did the old man tiptoe past the medicine cabinet?" A joking answer is "Because he didn't want to wake up the sleeping pills"; a serious one is "Because he dropped a glass and didn't want to cut his foot." First-graders chose the serious answer as funny just as often as the joking answer, but second-graders preferred the joking answer (McGhee, 1974).

The humor in riddles and jokes may be based on several kinds of linguistic ambiguity. The kind of jokes and riddles that children first consider funny, beginning at age 6 or 7, depends on *phonological ambiguity*, that is, situations in which the same sound can be interpreted in different ways:

Waiter, what's this?
That's bean soup, Ma'am.
I'm not interested in what it's been; I'm asking what it is now.

Appreciation of the humor in lexical ambiguity, involving double meaning, develops soon afterwards. Most 7- and 8-year-olds enjoy jokes like the following:

Order! Order in the court!
Ham and cheese on rye, please, Your Honor.

Not until the ages of 11 or 12 do children understand jokes based on ambiguities in grammatical structure or on different semantic interpretations, such as these:

I saw a man-eating shark in the aquarium.
That's nothing. I saw a man eating herring in a restaurant.

Call me a cab.
You're a cab. (McGhee, 1979; Schultz & Horibe, 1974)

expression to decide whether the child wants some milk, saw a quart of milk and named it, or has just spilled some milk. The same utterance can have at least three different meanings.

Pragmatic skills also involve knowledge about the social context. The use of polite forms is part of pragmatics. A child who is a dinner guest at another child's house may say, "Please pass the potatoes" or, "May I have some potatoes?" When eating in the school cafeteria, it may be more socially appropriate to say, "Give me the potatoes." Children who want a favor from their parents will often adopt a special tone of voice and a particular rate of speech if they are uncertain about the parents' response. Children use different tones and words when speaking to their peers, to their younger siblings, or to their parents, indicating that they recognize that there are social and cultural rules for the content and tone of speech that vary with the social context.

THEORIES OF LANGUAGE ACQUISITION

What accounts for the rapid improvement in children's comprehension and use of complicated grammatical structures and rules? What role, if any, do innate mechanisms play? Is the child *active* in the process of language acquisition, searching for rules and regularities, formulating and testing hypotheses about grammar and meaning? Are reinforcement and modeling important? To what extent is progress in language dependent on the growth of cognitive capacities? Do parents and other people interacting with the child influence the course of linguistic development?

These are critical questions, for which there are at present no fully satisfactory answers. However, a number of rich and interesting—as well as controversial—theories about these issues have been proposed. No single theory provides a sufficient or adequate explanation of all the processes underlying the acquisition of language; each represents a different approach to the issues, and each basically deals with a different aspect of language development.

Learning Theory

During the first half of this century, learning theory dominated American psychological thinking and research. Learning theorists viewed reinforcement (reward) and imitation of models as the principal mechanisms governing the acquisition and modification of most behavior, including language. Learning theory stresses *nurture* rather than *nature* as the most powerful influence on development. Partly for this reason, it does more to explain language *performance* (speech production) than to explain the competencies underlying *comprehension*. For example, according to learning theory, the change from babbling to saying words is the outcome of parents and others selectively rewarding the child for producing sounds that resemble words; words therefore become prominent in the child's vocalizations. Analogously, children learn to speak grammatically because they are reinforced when they utter correct sentences and not when they speak ungrammatically. In short, learning theorists held that children speak in ways that increasingly conform with adult speech because this is the behavior that environmental reinforcers shape and maintain.

Learning theorists emphasize the roles of observation, modeling, and imitation in language acquisition. Certainly children imitate what they hear their parents (models) say, and thus add new words and ways of combining words to their language repertoires. Children cannot acquire a vocabulary or the grammatical structure of their language without exposure to models: Children in the United States learn English; children in China learn Chinese. They gather information about their own language by hearing others speak it.

Children can also be taught to use complex grammatical forms—for example, correct and incorrect inflections for plurals and verbs, correct ways to order words in sentences—through modeling. In experimental studies demonstrating this aspect of imitative learning, young children have been taught to produce difficult constructions such as sentences with passive verbs, prepositional phrases, adverbs, correct tenses, and conjunctions (Sherman, 1971). After observing a model, children produced responses similar to the ones they had observed but not exactly the same; that is, they generalized the responses they acquired through observation to new linguistic responses.

CRITICISMS OF LEARNING THEORY. Developmental psycholinguists point out that learning theory does not describe or explain the underlying capacities that enable a child to acquire linguistic knowledge and skills. Reinforcement alone cannot account for the astonishing rate of language development in young children; we can hardly imagine what an enormous number of utterances would have to be rewarded if progress depended on that alone. Nor, they argue, can reinforcement fully explain the acquisition and use of the rules or principles of grammatically correct speech. When an utterance is not reinforced, the child has no way of knowing what was wrong or how to correct the error. When it is reinforced, the child has no information about what was correct. The real problem, the psycholinguists argue, is to determine how children come to understand the principles for ordering words and parts of words so that they make sense (Slobin, 1971).

Moreover, observational studies have cast serious doubt on the assertion that parents and other adults reinforce grammatically correct statements. Apparently parents are much more interested in the truth, cleverness, or appropriateness of what children say than in the correctness of their grammar. When a child in one study said, "Her curl my hair," her comment was approved (rewarded) because her mother was curling the little girl's hair. But another child's grammatically impeccable "There's the animal fun house" was disapproved (punished) because she was looking at a lighthouse.

Developmental psycholinguists also argue that observation and imitation do not fully explain language acquisition. For one thing, some of a child's first two-word utterances are unique and creative combinations of words that adults are unlikely to use (e.g., "allgone bye-bye"). Similarly, when children overregularize (e.g., "The mouses runned"), they use language forms that they are unlikely to have

Observation and imitation of others clearly play a role in language acquisition, since children everywhere learn the language of the people around them.

heard from adults. When children are observed at home, some children imitate the utterances of other people a great deal and some do not, but amount of imitation is not correlated with rate of language acquisition (Bloom, Hood, & Lightbown, 1974). Clearly, imitation and observation of others play a role in language production, but simple imitation of the speech of others cannot be the principal means of acquiring language (see Figure 6.3).

Nativist Theory

The nativist view of language acquisition stresses innate biological determinants of language—the influence of *nature* rather than *nurture*. This view is concerned with explaining children's *competence* or ability to understand and use language rather than with influences on *performance* (how and when they speak). Many

FIGURE 6.3 Although a blind child cannot observe the actions of others, she can still learn the meanings of sentences that refer to actions. The blind child lifts her hands in response to the request "Look up." (From B. Landau, & L. R. Gleitman. *Language and experience.* Cambridge, MA: Harvard University Press, 1985, p. 57–58.)

developmental psycholinguists argue that young children are not taught grammar; rather, they hear words and sentences, from which they somehow infer grammatical rules. This task is so complex that it could not be accomplished unless the child's mind were somehow predisposed or "set" to process linguistic input (the language the child hears) and derive grammatical rules from it.

Noam Chomsky, a leading proponent of this point of view, maintains that humans possess an inborn brain mechanism that is specialized for the job of acquiring language. Chomsky has called this mechanism a *language acquisition device* (LAD) (Chomsky, 1957, 1959). The evidence cited for an innate language mechanism includes the universality and regularity of trends in children's production of sounds, which we discussed earlier. Also, regardless of the language they are learning, children progress through the same sequence: babbling, saying their first word at 1 year, using two-word combinations in the second half of the second year, and mastering most grammatical rules of their language by the age of 4 or 5. First words and sentences in all languages express the same basic set of semantic relationships.

Some nativist theorists believe that the brain is especially "ready" for language acquisition between the age of 18 months and puberty; that is, they believe there is a *sensitive period* for language acquisition. "Within this period language acquisition is expected to proceed normally but outside it language acquisition is difficult if not impossible" (Elliott, 1981, p. 23). Informal evidence for this view includes the observation that adult immigrants generally find learning a new language difficult and almost always retain a foreign accent. Their preadolescent children, in contrast, learn the new language quickly, make few errors, and speak without an accent (Labov, 1970).

To test the sensitive-period hypothesis directly, we would need to determine whether a person who had not learned any language before puberty could do so later on. But where could one find such a person except among the severely retarded? Amazingly, Genie, a girl of 13 who had been isolated by her parents and knew very little language was discovered in Los Angeles in 1970. Box 6.3 presents an account of her history and language learning. Genie's case provides partial support for the sensitive-period hypothesis. Genie did not acquire language in the same way that a preschool child would. But her progress demonstrated that a great deal of language learning can occur after puberty.

BOX 6.3

Genie: Language Acquisition After Puberty

When Genie was brought to the attention of the authorities, she was 13½ years old and past puberty, but she was so malnourished that she weighed only 60 pounds and looked like a young child. She was mute, incontinent, and unable to stand erect. The story of her life was incredible.

Her tyrannical father believed she was retarded because she was slow in learning to walk (actually this was due to a hip deformity). When she was 20 months old he locked her into a small, closed room, keeping her tied to a potty chair or lying in a covered crib. She remained imprisoned there until she was discovered almost 12 years later. Her mother, who was almost blind, came into the room only a few minutes a day to feed her. No one spoke to Genie, and she heard few sounds, although her father and older brother occasionally barked at her like dogs. Her father beat her if she made noises or sounds.

After her rescue she went to live in a foster home, where she heard normal language, although she had no special speech training at first. Within a short time she began to imitate words and learn names, at first speaking in a monotone or a whisper but gradually raising her voice and using more varied tones. Her language development was in many ways similar to that of a young child, although in some respects she progressed at a faster rate. She began to produce single words spontaneously about 5 months after she went to live in the foster home, and began to use two-word utterances about 3 months after that. Her earliest two-word combinations expressed the same relationships that young children express first, for example, agent-action, action-object, possession, and location. Gradually she produced longer sentences.

Genie's conceptual development appeared to be more advanced than her language development. From the start, she generalized words appropriately from specific objects to the class (e.g., generalizing the label *dog*, first applied to a household pet, to all other dogs), and she did not overextend or underextend her early words. Words for colors and numbers, which generally appear relatively late in the normal child's language acquisition, were parts of Genie's early vocabulary.

Nevertheless, Genie's language development was deficient in some respects. Five years after she began to acquire language and extensive speech training, her speech was essentially telegraphic. She was still unable to use negative auxiliaries (such as *haven't, isn't, hadn't*) correctly, had difficulty forming past tenses (using *-ed* endings), asked no spontaneous questions (although she asked questions that she was specifically trained to ask), could not combine several ideas in a sentence, and confused opposite words such as *over* and *under*. In addition, she performed poorly on tests of comprehension (Curtiss, 1977).

Clearly, Genie was able to acquire some basic language after puberty, that is, after the end of the so called "sensitive period" for language acquisition. She failed to master some important features of grammar, and "her development [was] laborious and incomplete, but the similarities between it and normal acquisition outweigh the differences" (de Villiers & de Villiers, 1977, p. 219).

Cognitive Theory

Other theorists, though they may not subscribe to the idea of an inborn mechanism specialized for language acquisition, nevertheless maintain another kind of nativistic view. For them, language development is dependent on certain cognitive, information-processing, and motivational predispositions that are inborn. These theorists assume that children are inherently active and constructive and that internal forces rather than forces in the external environment are chiefly responsible for creativity, problem solving, hypothesis testing, and children's efforts to identify regularities (rules) in the speech they hear.

Dan Slobin has proposed that children in all societies are equipped with certain information-processing abilities or strategies that they use in learning language. His cross-cultural studies of language acquisition convinced him that children formulate and follow a set of "operating principles." One operating principle is "Pay attention to the ends of words." Children find ends of words more salient than beginnings and middles, perhaps for reasons of attention and memory. Ways of marking (indicating) place or position that come after the noun, such as suffixes, are easier for children to learn than markers placed before the noun. In Turkish, for example, a suffix marks place (the equivalent of *pot stove on*), whereas in English the preposition comes before its object (*pot on stove*). Turkish-speaking children learn these place markers before English-speaking children do (Slobin, 1979).

Another operating principle is "Pay attention to the order of words." Word order in children's early speech reflects word order in the adult speech the child hears. Children also seem to have strong preferences for consistent and regular systems; a third operating principle, thus, is "Avoid exceptions." As a result, overregularization is common in children's early speech (e.g., *bringed*, *goed*, *deers*).

"These operating principles are, of course, only a sketch of what might be a theory of language acquisition," Slobin points out (1979, p. 110). The important point is that infants appear to possess strategies for analyzing and interpreting events in the world around them, including speech. By means of these strategies, they acquire knowledge of the structure of language, which is then used in the process of learning to speak and understand.

Piaget and his followers maintain that cognitive development *directs* language acquisition—that the development of language depends on the development of thought rather than vice versa (Piaget, 1967). To support their view, they point out that infants show sensorimotor intelligence before any aspect of language appears (Sinclair, 1971). Language acquisition does not begin until a number of important cognitive abilities, such as object permanence, have emerged. Moreover, infants interpret the world about them, form mental representations, and categorize objects and events before they utter their first words. They identify regularities in the environment and construct a system of meanings before they have acquired productive language (Bowerman, 1981).

By and large, children's earliest utterances pertain to things they already understand. Children talk about what is interesting to them and attracts their attention (Greenfield, 1979) and about what they know about people, objects, events, and relationships (R. Brown, 1973). In other words, children's cognitions—their thoughts, perceptions, and modes of interacting with others—develop first.

Children quickly learn the names of things that interest them and attract their attention.

"Linguistic development is, in good part, learning how what you already know is expressed in your native language" (Flavell, 1977, p. 38). "The meanings expressed in children's earliest word combinations and the rules for combining words must be explained in terms of the child's knowledge of real world objects, i.e., that objects exist, cease to exist, recur, can be acted upon, and are associated with people's activities" (Rice, 1983, p. 9). Language, according to this line of argument, is "mapped onto" the child's existing cognitive categories and knowledge.

Social Interaction Theory

A major dimension that differentiates theories of language acquisition from one another is the relative emphasis on abilities that accompany the maturation of the brain as opposed to abilities and knowledge that depend primarily on social interaction. A theory that attempts to establish a compromise between these two extremes is social interaction theory. This approach accepts some of the arguments of both camps. The theory assumes that biological factors influence the course of language acquisition, but it insists that interaction between children and adults is absolutely necessary if language skills are to develop.

Those who believe in the importance of social-interaction theory argue that the structure of human language probably arose from the fact that language plays an important role in human social interaction. Children give their parents clues that provoke them to supply the language experience the child needs. Social-interaction theory regards the adult-child dyad as a dynamic system, in which each party requires the other.

Social-interaction theorists tend to be cautious about the inferences they draw from a child's language. They are less likely than nativists to attribute abstract linguistic competence to the child if the child has just issued a one- or two-word sentence. Proponents of this view emphasize the fact that the way parents speak to children is extremely important, especially their tendency to emphasize the important content words in a sentence, to slow the rate of their speech, to repeat themselves if the child does not seem to understand, and to add critical nonverbal information like pointing or frowning in order to help the child understand what it is they are saying. Some linguists have said that parents supply a *scaffold* for the child to build upon in learning language.

In general, social-interaction theorists recognize both the role of experience and the role of biology. But they claim that one must look at the specific environmental experiences of the child in order to understand the emergence of language. Innate mechanisms alone cannot explain the child's mastery of language, and that mastery involves more than conditioning and imitation. It includes turn taking, joint attention, and a social context as well. As might be expected, those who favor social-interaction theory give a central role to the mother's interaction with the child, in contrast to other children and adults with whom the child communicates.

These theories of language acquisition adopt different positions on two important issues: (1) the relationships between language and other cognitive processes, such as thinking, forming concepts, remembering, and problem solving, and (2) the influence of the environment on language. Each of these is discussed further in the following sections.

LANGUAGE AND COGNITION

Although most theories recognize important links between language and cognitive processes, a question of priority arises: Do cognitive achievements stem from advances in linguistic ability? Or are cognitive achievements *prerequisite* to higher competence in language? Certainly words and sentences play significant roles in our everyday reasoning, in problem solving, and in coding and storing knowledge. However, Einstein did much of his scientific thinking by means of visual images and mathematical symbols. Composers think by means of musical notes and auditory images, and painters often think in abstract visual modes.

Cognition Precedes Language

Piaget and other cognitive psychologists maintain that language development is an aspect of cognitive development and hence reflects, rather than directs, cognitive progress (Sinclair, 1971). For them, language is not a necessary forerunner of cognitive growth; on the contrary, it is cognitive development that guides language acquisition.

For example, a young child cannot master the meaning of the word *gone* until he or she has first grasped the concept of object permanence, together with a nonlinguistic understanding of the disappearance of objects, both of which usually occur by the first birthday. In addition, children do not begin to learn the morpheme for the plural until they understand the concept "greater than one." Similarly, the child must grasp the idea that something can happen in the past before he or she begin to talk about past events in language.

Language Influences Cognition

Although progress in language usually depends on cognitive growth, occasionally language can aid cognition. For example, the form in which a verbal instruction is given to children can influence their categorizations of objects or pictures. Three-year-old children often have difficulty creating a superordinate class from the different members of that class—for example, realizing that cats, cows, and horses belong to the superordinate category *animals*, or recognizing that shoes, trousers, and hats belong to the superordinate category *clothing*. Even if the experimenter gives the child a hint by showing him or her some typical examples of a category—for example, a dog, a horse, and a duck as representatives of the category *animal*—the child still will not put all of the animals into one group. However, if the experimenter speaks a nonsense word while pointing to the different members of the category—saying, for example, "These are *dobutsus*"—the child is much more likely to group all the animals together.

The use of a noun like *dobutsu*, even though it is an unfamiliar word, helps the child create the superordinate class. The use of an adjective leads the child to form subordinate categories. Thus, if the experimenter, pointing to different dogs, says, "These are *dobish* ones," the child is likely to put the collies into one group and the terriers into another. Thus, the language adults use with children provides them with information about the proper way to categorize events. In this sense, there is a reciprocal relationship between language and cognition (Waxman, 1987).

Memory and Problem Solving

Experiences are often represented mentally by means of words and sentences; they may also be retrieved from memory through language cues. This was demonstrated in a classic experiment in which two groups of individuals were shown figures but were given different labels for them. For one group, the figure was labeled *beehive*; for the other, it was labeled *hat*. Later the subjects were asked to draw the figures from memory. Those who had coded the figure as a *beehive* tended to distort the figure so that it looked like one. Those who had been given the label *hat* tended to draw it like a hat. The participants' memory of the image was strongly affected by the word or label assigned to it. Apparently the verbal label was remembered (stored and retrieved), and the figure was reconstructed to conform to that label (Carmichael, Hogan, & Walter, 1932).

Complex problems may be solved more easily if the child labels the component parts and uses labels to guide actions. In a Russian study, children were shown pictures of butterfly wings and told to match them with similar ones in a large display. The matches were to be made on the basis of the patterns of wing markings. The children found this task perplexing at first because they had trouble separating the pattern from the color of the wings. An experimental group was then taught labels (the words for *spots* and *stripes*) to describe the various patterns, while a control group was not given any descriptive labels. After learning the labels, the experimental group made more accurate matches than they had earlier. Younger members of the experimental group even performed better than the older members of the control group (Liublinskaya, 1957). Attaching labels to these stimuli gave them a degree of distinctiveness that made the matching task easier.

ENVIRONMENTAL INFLUENCES ON LANGUAGE

The major theories of language development lead to different hypotheses about the importance of environmental influences on children's language development. Learning theories suggest that opportunities for reinforcement and observation of models should be important determinants of language development. Nativist and cognitive-developmental theories suggest that opportunities to hear spoken language and to be active in exploring and learning about the environment are important, but that specific reinforcements or training are not essential to successful learning of language. Social-interaction theorists stress the importance of interaction between parent and child. Research on environmental influences has investigated how parents talk and respond to their young children, as well as differences among social-class and cultural groups.

Adult Teaching and Language Learning

Children learn language in social settings—by communicating with other people, usually the mother, father, siblings, and other adult caregivers. Many theorists have assumed that it is the mother who shapes the child's early linguistic environment. Does the way a mother talks influence her child's language development? This question has theoretical importance because it relates to the impact of environmental influences on language development.

As social-interaction theorists have noted, when talking to their babies mothers usually use a language that is different from the one they use in adult discourse. A special vocabulary (including words like *tummy* and *choo-choo*) and several other distinctive features characterize mothers' talk to babies, which is referred to as *motherese*. The pitch of the voice tends to be higher, and intonation is exaggerated. Sentences are short, simple, and grammatically correct; they contain fewer verbs and modifiers, function words, subordinate clauses, and embeddings. There are more questions, imperatives, and repetitions, and speech is more fluent and intelligible (Newport, 1977; Snow, 1974; Vorster, 1974).

A number of studies indicate that motherese may facilitate early language development. In one study, the speech of mother-child pairs in their homes was recorded twice, first when the babies were 18 months old (at the one-word stage) and again 9 months later, after the children had begun talking in sentences. If a mother used relatively simplified language when speaking to her 18-month-old (e.g., many yes-no questions and a high proportion of nouns relative to pronouns), her child was likely to show a high level of linguistic competence at 27 months (longer sentences and more verbs, noun phrases, and auxiliary verbs). The children of mothers who used longer and more complex sentences during the first observation progressed more slowly. The investigators concluded that motherese may be an effective teaching language for very young children (Furrow, Nelson, & Benedict, 1979).

Another investigator, working with somewhat older children, compared the speech of mothers whose children showed accelerated speech development with that of mothers whose children were making normal progress in language. Although the sentences that the two groups of mothers used in talking to their children did not differ in simplicity or length, mothers of accelerated children spoke more clearly, made fewer ambiguous or unintelligible statements, let their children lead in conversation, and responded to the children's utterances with related contributions. In effect, they tailored what they said to what the child said, often repeating or expanding the child's statement. For example, if Sally drops a ball and says, "Ball fall," her mother replies with the correct expanded sentence: "The ball fell down." And if Sally says correctly, "The ball fell down," her mother says, "Yes, the ball fell down because you dropped it" (Penner, 1987).

The effects of different kinds of maternal speech undoubtedly vary with the age and language ability of the child. The data do suggest, however, that the mother's sensitivity to the child's language ability, intentions, and meanings—and her adjustment of her responses to take account of these factors—can accelerate the child's linguistic progress.

Mothers speak differently to firstborn than to later-born children. They ask fewer questions of later-borns and are less likely to say to later-borns, "Tell me what these colors are" or "Say hello" or "Is that a horse or a dog?" This may be one reason most firstborns have more advanced language than later-borns (Jones & Adamson, 1987).

A well-controlled experimental study shows how specific training can accelerate children's acquisition of complex grammatical forms. Before the experiment began, the 28-month-olds in the study did not spontaneously use either tag questions (e.g., "I found it, didn't I?") or negative questions (e.g., "Doesn't it hurt?"). They also did not use future or conditional verbs (e.g., "He will eat it," "He could find it"). One group of children was given five training sessions demonstrating the use of questions, while another group had five sessions emphasizing verb forms. The training consisted of recasting or rewording the child's sentences in the form to be acquired. For instance, when a child in a question training session said, "You can't have it," the experimenter would reply, "Oh I can't have it, can I!" In a verb training session, the experimenter would answer a question like "Where it go?" with "It will go there."

The training proved to be effective. All the children who were exposed to tag and negative questions acquired the ability to frame and produce such questions, but they made no progress in the use of future or conditional verbs. Similarly, all the children in the verb training group produced new verb constructions, but they did not add tag or negative questions to their language repertoires. The two groups of children showed the same degree of progress on other measures of language development, such as length of utterances and number of words used. Training by means of rephrasing or recasting sentences apparently had very specific, selective effects (Nelson, 1975).

The findings of these studies may be interpreted as supporting the learning theory and social-interactionist view that environmental input is important in language development. At the same time, it should be noted that these studies dealt only with the *facilitation* of linguistic development after children had acquired some basic language skills. The studies do not show that special environmental input (such as motherese and training) is *necessary* for language acquisition, nor do they provide any evidence that contradicts the nativists' assertion of a biological basis of language development.

Social-class Differences in Language

Children from middle-class well-educated families generally score higher than those from parents who did not complete high school on practically all standard measures of linguistic ability—vocabulary, sentence structure, sound discrimination, and articulation (Templin, 1957). One basis for these differences may be the different types of speech used by mothers in these social-class groups. In some early work on this issue, an English educational sociologist described two patterns of verbal interaction (Bernstein, 1970). Lower-class mothers, he reported, typically use a *restricted language code*, talking to their children in short, simple, easily understood sentences that refer primarily to here-and-now events. Middle-class mothers, on the other hand, use an *elaborated code* in disciplining their children, teaching them moral standards, and communicating feelings and emotions. Although the simpler codes might be useful to

Children raised in an economically disadvantaged environment often hear speech patterns that are different from those heard by children from more affluent, middle-class families.

very young children, the more complex codes used by middle-class mothers could enable older children to be more oriented toward abstractions.

COMMUNICATION AND CONVERSATION

One of the most important functions of language is communication. Effective communication requires not only knowledge of the rules of grammar (syntax) and the meanings of words (semantics) but also the "ability to say the appropriate thing at the appropriate time and place to the appropriate listeners and in relation to the appropriate topics" (Dore, 1979, p. 337). In this section we expand our earlier discussion of the pragmatic aspect of language to examine how children learn to use language in social contexts to converse and communicate.

As we have seen, babies communicate before they speak, using actions and gestures to express emotional states and to get help in gratifying their needs. Babies will reach toward an object they want, hand a mechanical toy to an adult so that the adult will start it, and shake their heads or make pushing gestures to indicate refusal (Pea, 1980). The child's earliest intentional vocal communication may accompany these gestures. Other early communicative sounds draw attention to objects or events or serve as part of a ritual game such as waving goodbye or playing peek-a-boo. These actions and vocalizations may be the precursors of communication through language (Bruner, 1975).

With words and sentences, children can communicate much more efficiently and converse more effectively. Competence in conversation draws upon many social, speaking, and listening skills: taking turns; recognizing one's own turn to speak; taking account of the listener's competence, knowledge, interests, and needs; refraining from dominating the interaction or interrupting one's conversational partners; recognizing when a message is not understood and clarifying ambiguous statements; signaling attention and willingness to continue the interaction by nonverbal means such as eye contact; and more (Dore, 1979).

Do young children possess the cognitive capacities needed to develop these communication skills? Piaget's observations led him to conclude that they do not; he stated that early speech is essentially noncommunicative or *egocentric* (Piaget, 1926). Children of this age, Piaget said, are not aware that a listener's point of view may be different from their own. They talk as if they were thinking aloud, often describing their own actions, and they engage in "collective monologues" in which two children each follow a line of conversation with little evidence that they are responding to the other's comments. (Sara: "Here goes my train." Sally: "The horse is hurt." Sara: "It's going faster.") Not until the age of 6 or 7 is egocentric speech replaced by "socialized" speech, which takes into account the viewpoint of the listener and thus makes real dialogue possible (Piaget, 1926).

Early Verbal Exchanges

It is now generally agreed that Piaget grossly underestimated young children's competence in communicating. Two-year-olds speak directly to each other and to adults, usually in staccato utterances referring to familiar objects in the immediate environment. Most such messages bring adequate responses; if they do not, the communicator is likely to repeat the message. Short utterances are typical, but longer, more elaborate communications occur in some play situations, for example, when children try to cooperate in moving a piece of furniture from one place to another.

In conversations initiated by adults, 2-year-olds often simply repeat what the adult says. Three-year-olds take turns with an adult conversational partner, and about half of their responses add new and relevant information to what the adult has said. The conversation is short, however, seldom continuing for more than two turns (Bloom, Rocissano, & Hood, 1976). In talking with other 3-year-olds, children sometimes sustain much longer turn-taking sequences. One pair of 3-year-olds took 21 turns, asking and replying to questions about a camping trip (Garvey, 1975, 1977).

By the age of 4, children know how to make major adjustments in their conversational strategies when their audience requires it. The 4-year-olds in one study were observed talking to 2-year-olds, to peers, and to adults during spontaneous play and while explaining how a toy works. When talking to 2-year-olds they used simpler, shorter sentences and more attention-getting words like *hey* and *look* than they did when talking to adults or other 4-year-olds. Sentences addressed to adults and peers were longer and more complex, containing more coordinate and subordinate clauses (Shatz & Gelman, 1973).

Questions and Requests

Beginning at about age 3, children's spontaneous conversations include *contingent queries*, that is, questions about what another child has said or done. These questions are frequently requests for elaboration, clarification, or explanation, the most common being "what?" or its synonym "Huh?"

Lenny: Look it, we found a parrot in our house.
  Phil: A what?
Lenny: A parrot. A bird.
  Phil: Wow!

In this conversation—a representative interaction between 3-year-olds—the query "A what?" (spoken with rising intonation) was clearly a request for repetition. After making his inquiry, the listener gave the speaker his turn to respond, and the speaker gave the expected response plus an expansion. The listener then responded, acknowledging that the speaker's initial statement had been clarified (Garvey, 1975).

Researchers often study children's communication by having pairs of children play a game that requires an exchange of information. For example, the children may sit opposite each other at a table with a barrier across it so that they cannot see each other. In one such study, each child was given a peg and a set of blocks that could be stacked on the peg. The blocks contained distinctive but hard-to-describe drawings like those shown in Figure 6.4. The task of one child, the speaker, was to pick up a block, describe the drawing on it to the other child, and put it on the peg. The listener's task was to choose the block that matched the speaker's description and put it on the peg, so that at the end of the game the blocks would be stacked on both pegs in the same order.

All the children played the game eight times. The first time, all performed poorly. The older children improved rapidly, however, performing without error by the eighth game. Kindergarten children continued to make many mistakes throughout the series. Young children's messages often showed little awareness of the kind of information the other player might find meaningful. For example, they might describe the drawing on a block by saying "Mommy's dress" or "Daddy's shirt." If the listener asked for more information, a young speaker was likely to repeat the description already given or to remain silent. Older speakers gave fuller, more informative descriptions. They also reacted more appropriately to feedback from the listener. If the listener said, "I don't know which one you mean," an older speaker was likely to give a new description or add more details (Glucksberg & Krauss, 1967; Krauss & Glucksberg, 1969).

Compared with preschoolers, older children consider what the speaker says more carefully and are better able to evaluate whether they understand, that is, whether the speaker's statements are adequate, informative, or ambiguous. They do a better job of asking for information to reduce ambiguity and uncertainty. This skill can be augmented simply by instructing children to ask questions freely whenever a message is not entirely clear (Patterson, Massad, & Cosgrove, 1978).

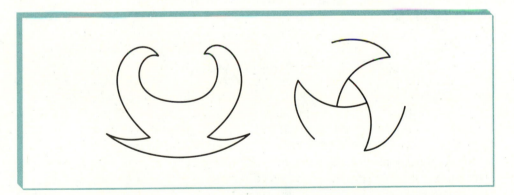

FIGURE 6.4 Drawings used in a study in which one child had to describe a drawing to another who could not see it. By age 7 or 8, children provided descriptions that were clear and specific enough for the listener to choose a matching drawing from an array. (Reprinted from S. Glucksberg & R. M. Krauss. What do people say after they have learned how to talk? *Merrill-Palmer Quarterly*, 1967, 13, 309–316. By permission of the Wayne State University Press. Copyright 1967. The Merrill-Palmer Institute of Human Development and Family Life.)

SUMMARY

Language has five basic functions. It makes it possible to communicate ideas, allows the user to understand his or her society and culture, helps in establishing and maintaining social relationships, permits the user to classify events in linguistic categories, and aids in reasoning.

Phonemes are the basic sounds that are combined to make words. In English, the phonemes correspond roughly to the sounds of the spoken letters of the alphabet. Every language has rules governing the combination of two or more phonemes to make words.

Infants only a few days old can discriminate between similar phonemes, and in fact can make many more phonemic discriminations than are required by their language. However, they cannot produce phonemes themselves. At five or six months of age, all infants spontaneously begin to babble by combining vowel and consonant sounds in strings of syllables. This babbling has no symbolic meaning.

Around the first birthday most children begin to speak their first meaningful sounds, usually in the form of single words, or morphemes. (A *morpheme* is the smallest unit of meaning in a language.) Most of the words used by children in the second year stand for things or people. Children understand many more words than they actually speak. Many of their new words are acquired through "naming rituals" that parents engage in with their children from the time the infant first utters something that sounds like a word.

According to Clark, when children hear a new word they make a hypothesis about its meaning and test the hypothesis as they use the word, gradually modifying their original ideas about its meaning. Under the right conditions, older children can often figure out the meaning of a word.

The meanings children attribute to words are often quite different from adult meanings for those words. Some are overextensions, in which a word is used to refer to objects that are similar to the one the word actually designates. Others are underextensions, in which the meaning of the word is defined too narrowly. Between the third and fourth birthdays children begin to understand the figurative or nonliteral meanings of words and phrases. Around age 6 children become able to recognize that a statement may be false on one level but true on a deeper level; in other words, they become able to appreciate irony.

About the middle of the second year, children begin to put two words together and speak their first sentences. The variety of children's two- and three-word combinations increases greatly as they approach their second birthday. Typically, children's speech preserves correct word order for their language.

As children grow older, their sentences become longer. Mean length of utterance (MLU) increases dramatically between the ages of 2 and 4. At the same time, children master the grammatical morphemes of their language—the present progressive ending *-ing*, correct use of *in* and *on*, the plural, and so forth. They also begin to utter complex sentences consisting of two or more simple sentences joined by *and* or of one thought embedded in another. To construct such sentences, children have to learn the rules for combining larger groups of words and using connective words. They thus become able to produce questions; use deictic words like *here*, *there*, *this*, and *that*; construct passive sentences; and use negatives.

As their cognitive competence advances, children's metalinguistic awareness expands; that is language itself becomes a topic that the child reflects on, seeks to understand, and talks about. Two-year-olds can recognize some grammatically incorrect sentences, and sometimes make "spontaneous repairs." With greater metalinguistic awareness comes appreciation of ambiguity and the ability to create metaphors and jokes.

To communicate effectively, children must know more than word meanings and grammatical rules. They must learn to relate language to the physical and social context in which it is used. This is the pragmatic aspect of language. Even young children speaking one-word utterances have different pragmatic aims. Pragmatic skills increase throughout childhood with increased awareness of the social context of speech.

There are a number of theories about how language is acquired. According to learning theory, the principal mechanisms governing the acquisition of language are reinforcement (reward) and imitation of models. Certainly children imitate what they hear others say; they cannot acquire a vocabulary or the grammatical structure of their language without exposure to models. However, observation and imitation do not fully explain language acquisition. The nativist view of language acquisition stresses innate biological determinants. Chomsky, for example, maintains that humans possess an inborn brain mechanism that is specialized for the job of acquiring language. A related view is that language development is dependent on certain cognitive, information-processing, and motivational predispositions.

Social-interaction theory attempts to establish a compromise between the learning theory and nativist approaches. It assumes that biological factors influence the course of language acquisition, but it insists that interaction between children and adults is necessary if language skills are to develop.

Are cognitive achievements a prerequisite for language competence, or vice versa? Piaget and other cognitive psychologists maintain that language development reflects, rather than directs, cognitive processes. However, occasionally language can aid cognition. The language adults use with children provides them with information about the proper way to categorize events. Thus, it appears that there is a reciprocal relationship between language and cognition.

One of the most important functions of language is communication. Babies communicate before they speak, and the infant's earliest intentional vocal communication may accompany nonverbal gestures. Piaget believed that children's early speech is noncommunicative or egocentric, but it is now generally agreed that Piaget underestimated children's competence in communicating. Beginning at about age 3, children's spontaneous conversations include questions and requests. By the age of 4, children know how to make major adjustments in their conversational strategies when their audience requires it.

REVIEW QUESTIONS

1. What are the five basic functions of language?

2. What are phonemes? Briefly discuss the infant's ability to perceive and produce phonemes.

3. What is meant by bound morphemes and unbound morphemes?

4. How do children learn the meanings of new words?

5. When do children begin to use figurative language and become able to appreciate irony?

6. Briefly describe the process through which children learn to combine words into simple and complex sentences.

7. What is meant by metalinguistic awareness?

8. What is meant by the ability to employ pragmatics in speech?

9. Briefly discuss the three main theories of language acquisition.

10. What is the relationship between language and cognition?

GLOSSARY

phonemes   The basic sounds that are combined to make words.

morpheme   The smallest unit of meaning in a language.

word   A morpheme or combination of morphemes.

unbound morpheme   A morpheme that can stand alone.

bound morpheme   A morpheme that cannot stand alone and is always part of a word.

semantics   The meanings of words.

syntax   The grammatical rules that specify how words should be combined in sentences.

pragmatics   The relationship between the meaning of an utterance and the context in which the utterance occurs.

metalinguistic awareness   Awareness of language as a topic that one can reflect on, understand, and talk about.

SUGGESTED READINGS

de Villiers, J.G., and de Villiers, P. A. (1978). *Language acquisition*. Cambridge, MA.: Harvard University Press. Presents in easily comprehended form the basic principles and facts about language development.

Gleason, J. B. (1985). *The development of language*. Columbus, OH: Charles E. Merrill. Contains an excellent summary of language development in children, including phonemic, semantic, and syntactic development, as well as chapters on individual differences in language acquisition and the role of language in society.

Labov, W. (1972). *Sociolinguistic patterns*. Philadelphia: University of Pennsylvania Press. Discusses social-class and ethnic differences in language expression and development.

Winner, E. (1988). *The point of words*. Cambridge, MA.: Harvard University Press. This excellent essay describes in depth the young child's understanding of metaphor and irony.

Chapter Seven

COGNITIVE DEVELOPMENT: PIAGET AND BEYOND

Issues in Studying Cognitive Development
    Inferring Thought from Behavior
    Competence and Performance
    Broad vs. Narrow Competence
Piaget's Theory
    Major Developmental Issues
    Organization and Adaptation
    Developmental Stages
Beyond Piaget—Empirical Findings and New Conceptions
    Maturational Limits and the Role of Experience
    The Role of Activity in Learning
    Is Cognitive Development Domain Specific?
    Are Stages Universal?
    The Nature of Developmental Change
    Evaluation of Piaget's Theory

During the first few years of life children make remarkable progress in their ability to think about and understand their world. The processes of thinking and knowing, called **cognition**, include attending, perceiving, interpreting, classifying, and remembering information; evaluating ideas; inferring principles and deducing rules; imagining possibilities; generating strategies; and fantasizing. Consider the boy just past his sixth birthday who sat next to one of the authors on an airplane. As he looked around the plane (attending), he asked where the seatbelt and exit signs were (perceiving); then he read the signs that said "aisle," "center," and "window" (recognizing). He talked about his recent trip to Florida—where he went, what he saw, and the date on which he came home (remembering). He described his family—mother, stepfather, father, stepmother, stepgrandmother, two brothers, no sisters—seeming to understand their relationships to one another (classifying). He described an incident in which his 1-year-old brother had spontaneously brought his mother a blanket for his infant brother. "Wasn't that helpful?" he said (interpreting). He saw a river below the plane and said it was the Mississippi. When he was told it was the Missouri, he said, "How do you know?" (evaluating information).

Developmental psychologists are concerned with describing how cognitive functioning changes with age and with understanding the maturational and environmental factors that account for those changes. To achieve these goals, they must find ways to observe and measure cognitive processes. Before discussing what we know about children's cognitive development, therefore, we will consider three basic dilemmas facing scientists who wish to measure and conceptualize cognitive processes.

ISSUES IN STUDYING COGNITIVE DEVELOPMENT

Inferring Thought from Behavior

Obviously, we cannot observe thought processes directly. We can observe only overt behavior or performance on a task. Theorists disagree about whether and to what extent we can infer unobservable thoughts from observed behavior.

At one extreme are the radical or strict behaviorists, most of whom adhere to the tenets of B. F. Skinner (Bijou & Baer, 1961; Skinner, 1938). They assert that observable behavior is psychologists' only legitimate concern. The influence of strict behaviorism has waned in the past 20 or 30 years, but the caution against excessive dependence on inference should be kept in mind.

By contrast, many psychologists theorize about children's thought processes with the aim of describing and understanding those nonobservable processes. Piaget and his followers are included in this group. Most developmental psychologists fall between these two extremes. They are comfortable making inferences about cognition, but they base those inferences on careful observations of what children do. They constantly refine their ideas and test them by predicting particular behaviors as precisely as possible.

Consider the case of children's attention to television. The simplest and most frequently used way of measuring attention is to observe where children are looking. If they are looking at the TV screen, they are "attending"—or are they? It is possible to stare blankly at a TV screen while thinking about something else. If children look away from the screen, they are said to be "inattentive." Yet they might be attending to the program by listening. A researcher who believes that fixation on the screen indicates attention might test this inference by obtaining physiological measures or by asking children questions about the content of the program. If the physiological measures correspond to eye fixations or if children recall the content that appeared while they were looking at the screen better than that which occurred while they were looking away, the researcher may conclude that visual fixation is a good measure of attention. In short, observable behavior (including what children say) is the main criterion for testing theories.

Competence and Performance

A second, related, issue is the distinction between the knowledge and skills that a child possesses, which we call **competence**, and the demonstration of knowledge and skills in observable problem-solving situations, which we call **performance**. Children may possess knowledge that they do not use, even when the occasion calls for it. For example, although on a particular occasion a person may forget the name of an old friend, we would not conclude that the person does not know the friend's name or that he or she lacks the ability to recall people's names.

Consider a 2-year-old girl who was playing with some plastic rods that were brown, red, and orange. She and her mother met an adult friend, who asked her what colors her toys were. She looked a little blank and then said, "Yellow, blue." A few minutes later she and her mother encountered another adult friend. The child spontaneously said, "Look what I've got. This one's brown, and this one's red, and this one's orange."

This example shows that one cannot conclude that a child does not know something (i.e., lacks a particular competence) simply because she does not demonstrate her knowledge (performance). If individuals perform or demonstrate a skill, we can conclude with reasonable confidence that they possess that particular competence. However, the reverse is not true. If they fail to perform the skill, we do not know whether they have the competence or not. If you correctly answer all but a few of the questions on the midterm for this course, you have demonstrated that you know the material. If you do poorly on the test, an outsider cannot be sure whether you have not learned the material or whether you failed to demonstrate your knowledge because of fatigue, anxiety, or a host of other reasons.

A child may possess knowledge and skills that are not always demonstrated in observable problem-solving situations.

One reason children's performance may fail to reveal their actual competence is that children occasionally misunderstand the problems they are asked to solve. Much of our knowledge about cognitive development is based on children's answers to questions posed by adult examiners. However, children often interpret questions in a way that the examiner did not anticipate. An answer that is viewed as incorrect by the examiner may be correct from the child's perspective.

Consider the following example: A 4-year-old child was shown an array containing four toy garages and three toy cars. Each of the cars was in a garage, leaving one garage empty. The examiner asked the child, "Are all the cars in the garages?" The child said "No," and the examiner concluded that the child did not know the meaning of *all*. But when the examiner first asked several questions that involved only three cars, the child answered correctly. The child had initially assumed that if there were four garages, there must be four cars. After all, why would there be a garage if there were no car for it? The child inferred that a fourth car was missing. He understood the meaning of *all* perfectly well, but he brought to the problem an assumption that the examiner did not anticipate.

A different form of competence is the ability to acquire a new skill or bit of knowledge; this is often called **aptitude** or **potential competence**. Suppose that a group of 5-year-olds do not know the meaning of the words *artisan*, *waft*, and *viola*; that is, they lack a specific competence. Are they able to learn those words? If so, we say that they have the aptitude or potential competence for understanding those words. We might test for aptitude by teaching them the words and testing their knowledge afterward. If they pass the test of word knowledge that we devise (i.e., performance), we can conclude that they had the potential competence for learning those words. If they fail the test, however, we do not know whether or not they had the potential competence. Maybe our teaching was not good enough or long enough, or maybe our test did not assess what the children had actually learned.

Broad vs. Narrow Competence

Suppose that the 5-year-olds perform correctly on the test of new words. How broad a name should we give to their competence? It seems a bit grandiose to conclude that these children have the aptitude for learning language in general, and just as ridiculous to say that their competence is limited to learning the words *viola*, *waft*, and *artisan*. Between these two extremes lies an enormous range within which to define the children's potential or actual competence.

Most psychologists favor defining competences somewhat narrowly, partly because this approach permits more precise comparisons between different groups of children. Mayan 8-year-olds living in an isolated village in the highlands of northwestern Guatemala had great difficulty remembering a list of eight words and the order of a series of eight pictures laid side by side on a table. American children of the same age recalled all eight words and the series of pictures quite easily. This evidence might lead us to conclude that the Mayan children lacked the potential competence to memorize information. But when those children were required to memorize the unique associations between 20 pairs of geometric designs and meaningful ideas, they learned all of them after only a few trials (Kagan, Klein, Finley, Rogoff, & Nolan, 1979). Apparently this particular memory task was easier for them than remembering a list of eight unrelated words. Hence, it seems wise to conceive of a child's competence as "domain-specific," that is, as applying to particular content domains rather than to very broad ones (Brown, Bransford, Ferrara, & Campione, 1983).

PIAGET'S THEORY

Two major theoretical approaches guide the study of cognitive development. The first is represented most clearly by Piaget's theory, in which cognitive development is related to maturation. The second is usually called the information-processing

Jean Piaget was known for his careful observation of children's behavior.

approach. Piaget's theory and similar views of cognitive development will be discussed in this chapter; information-processing approaches are presented in Chapter 8.

Piaget vies with Freud for the title of "most influential developmental theorist of the twentieth century." He has been described as a "giant of the nursery" (Elkind, 1981). Piaget initially approached the study of children from the point of view of a biological scientist with an interest in describing naturally occurring processes of growth and change. He was a meticulous and careful observer. His observations of his own three children, which formed the basis for many elements of his theory, were not simply the pastime of a doting father but a systematic, detailed record of children's spontaneous behavior. Here is an example of his daughter's early symbolic play:

> At 21 months, Jacqueline saw a shell and said "cup." After saying this, she picked it up and pretended to drink. . . . The next day, seeing the same shell, she said "glass," then "cup," then "hat," and finally "boat in the water." Three days later she took an empty box and moved it to and fro saying "motycar." . . . At 24 months and 22 days, she moved her finger along the table and said: *finger walking . . . horse trotting.* (Piaget, 1962, p. 124)

Box 7.1 presents a brief sketch of Piaget's life and career.

BOX 7.1

A Brief Sketch of the Life of Jean Piaget

Jean Piaget was born in 1896 in Neuchatel, Switzerland. As a child he was fascinated by biology. He collected birds, fossils, and seashells. A precocious child, at the age of 10 he published a one-page scientific note on an albino sparrow he had observed in a public park. During his teenage years he worked as a volunteer laboratory assistant in the local natural-history museum. He became a specialist in mollusks, publishing several papers about them before he was 21. His early training and interest in biology was reflected in his psychological theories. The concepts of organization, adaptation, and equilibrium all draw heavily upon biological concepts.

Piaget completed a doctorate in natural sciences in 1918. But his scholarly reading and interests covered philosophy, religion, biology, sociology, and psychology. He pursued his interest in psychology by studying for brief periods at several laboratories and clinics in Europe.

Two events in Piaget's early professional life had enduring significance. When he was studying psychology, Piaget worked at the laboratory of Binet, the founder of the modern intelligence test. He was assigned to administer test items to grade-school children in Paris, a task that appeared dull until he began to notice the processes by which children arrived at their answers. Often he was more interested in their reasoning about wrong answers than in why they gave the right ones. He began questioning his young subjects about their thinking, and on the basis of the results he developed the "clinical method" that became the hallmark of his later studies of children.

The second significant event of Piaget's early career was a series of studies of his own children that he conducted with the assistance of his wife, Valentine Chatenay. Their detailed observations of Lucienne, Jacqueline, and Laurent were meticulous and original. They bear the stamp of Piaget's training in natural science and are well worth reading today.

Piaget returned to Switzerland to found a program of child study at the Institut J. J. Rousseau in Geneva and to teach at the University of Neuchatel. He remained in Geneva for his entire career, directing a long and productive program of research and writing. He carried out innumerable empirical studies of children's thought, language, perception, and memory. In addition to conducting basic research, he spent a great deal of time translating developmental theory into educational practice (Flavell, 1963).

When Piaget died in 1980, he left an extensive and vital legacy. Major work in developmental psychology throughout the world continues to revolve around his ideas.

Major Developmental Issues

Although Piaget began writing early in the twentieth century, his work was rediscovered in the United States in the early 1960s. His ideas radically changed the direction of developmental psychology in this country. In 1960 the dominant view, based on learning theory, was strongly environmentalist; little attention was given to maturation or heredity. Children were viewed as passive recipients of environmental stimuli. Developmental change, when it was discussed at all, was described as gradual and continuous, and learning was thought to be specific to particular tasks or situations. Piaget's theory thus was not just another theory but a challenge to prevailing opinions on each of the fundamental issues described in Chapter 1.

MATURATION AND EXPERIENCE.   Piaget's natural-science orientation led him to assume that the biological characteristics of the human child place some limits on the order and speed at which particular cognitive competences emerge. At the same time, he believed that active experience with the world is critical to cognitive growth. That is, he was a strong interactionist (see Chapter 1): He believed that maturation and experience cannot be assigned separate roles in development; both are required. For example, infants come to understand the permanence of objects because their neurological systems mature *and* they have experience with objects in their world (see Chapter 3). That knowledge would not be gained simply through maturation, nor could a child without the appropriate neurological structures profit from that experience.

Piaget insisted that some cognitive ideas, operations, and structures are universal, not because they are inherited but because all children's ordinary experiences in the world of objects and people force them to come to the same conclusions. Piaget believed that all children eventually learn to group categories like *dog* into more abstract categories like *pets* or *mammals*. All children come to realize that any category can be divided into at least two smaller sets. The category *animals*, for example, can be separated into two smaller classes: dogs and animals that are not dogs. Similarly, all children come to realize that events can be ordered by their magnitude, from smallest to largest or lightest to heaviest. These rules as well as a great many others develop, Piaget claims, as a result of the everyday interactions that occur between children and other people and between children and objects.

THE ACTIVE, CONSTRUCTIVE CHILD.   Piaget's central thesis is that people are active, curious, and inventive throughout life. Moreover, knowledge is assumed to have a specific goal: to aid the individual in adapting to the environment. Human beings spontaneously seek contact and interaction with the environment and actively look for challenge. When left to their own devices, children explore, learn, and discover.

According to Piaget, children *construct* their world by imposing order on the raw material provided by sights, sounds, and smells. The major focus of Piaget's theory is to understand the transformations that humans impose on the information they receive through the senses. "It is the interpretation, not the event itself, which

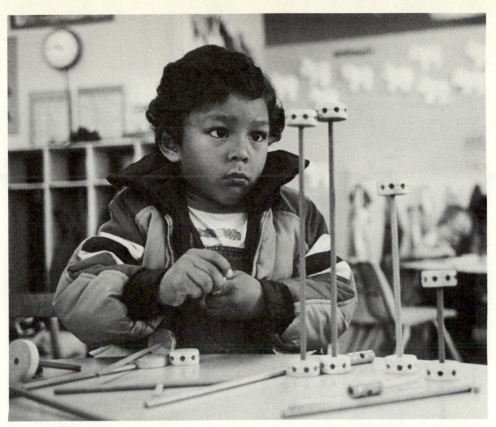

According to Piaget, children actively construct their world, continually trying to organize their knowledge more coherently.

affects behavior" (Ginsburg & Opper, 1979, p. 67). Children and adults continually construct and reconstruct their knowledge of the world, trying to make sense of their experience and attempting to organize their knowledge more efficiently and coherently. This effort is apparent in one of Piaget's observations:

> At 25 months and 13 days, Jacqueline wanted to see a little hunchbacked neighbor whom she used to meet on her walks. A few days earlier she had asked why he had a hump, and after I had explained she said: *Poor boy, he's ill, he has a hump.* The day before Jacqueline had also wanted to go and see him, but he had influenza, which Jacqueline called "being ill in bed." We started out for our walk and on the way Jacqueline said: *Is he still ill in bed?*—"No. I saw him this morning, he isn't in bed now."—*He hasn't a big hump now.* (Piaget, 1962, p. 231)

The assumption that children are active constructivists has important implications for education, especially in early childhood. Piagetians assume that cognitive growth will occur best when children are allowed to explore and act on their environment. They sometimes argue that when you teach children specific skills, you remove the opportunity for them to invent knowledge on their own.

If a child when he is counting pebbles happens to put them in a row and to make the astonishing discovery that when he counts them from the right to the left he finds the same number as when he counts them from left to right, and again the same when he puts them in a circle, etc., he has thus discovered experimentally that the sum is independent of the order. But, this is a logicomathematical experiment and not a physical one, because neither the order nor even the sum was in the pebbles before he arranged them in a certain manner (i.e., ordered them) and joined them together in a whole (Piaget, 1970, p. 721).

Organization and Adaptation

The two basic principles guiding human development, in Piaget's view, are organization and adaptation. In order to appreciate the human capacity for organization, consider the drawings shown in Figure 7.1. In the left-hand figure, many people see a vase or a goblet, but you can also see profiles of two people. In the right-hand figure, you see a child with a toy duck, but if instructed, you can find in her skirt the triangle that matches the figure above the child's head. What you see depends on how you organize the stimulus. Piaget proposed that the tendency to organize experience is a basic human characteristic. With development, children form cognitive "structures" as a result of the interaction between maturation and experience.

FIGURE 7.1   Two figures that can be perceived in different ways. The left-hand figure can be seen as a vase or as two people facing each other (From D. Hothersall. *History of psychology*. Philadelphia: Temple University Press, 1984, p. 168). In the right-hand figure the triangle above the child's head can be found in the picture of the child (Adapted from Preschool Embedded Figures Test by Susan Coates. Consulting Psychologists Press, Inc., Palo Alto, CA 94306, Copyright 1972. By permission.)

COGNITIVE STRUCTURES.   As described in Chapter 3, the sensorimotor schemes formed in infancy are the child's initial organizational structures. But after about age 2, according to Piaget, the child's cognitive structures are internal—or mental—structures. For instance, most 2-year-olds have concepts, or structures, for dog, cat, boy, and girl, to name just a few. In the course of development these structures become organized in hierarchies. Children learn that both dogs and cats are furry; that both girls and boys are human; and that they are all living things.

One important cognitive structure is the operation, an action that the child performs mentally and that is reversible (Ginsberg & Opper, 1979). An **operation** is a manipulation of ideas that can be performed in reverse, allowing the person to return mentally to the beginning of the thought sequence. Planning a series of moves in a game of checkers or chess and then mentally retracing one's steps to the beginning of the sequence is an operation. Squaring the number 2 to get 4 is an operation; so is extracting the square root of 4 to obtain 2. Similarly, eight stones can be divided into subgroups of various sizes—for example, four and four, seven and one, or six and two—and recombined into a single set.

A series of moves in a game like checkers is an operation—a manipulation of ideas that can be performed in reverse.

ASSIMILATION AND ACCOMMODATION.   Piaget viewed human cognition as a specific form of biological adaptation in which a complex organism adapts to a complex environment (Flavell, 1985). Humans continuously interact with the environment, organizing what they experience and forming new organizational structures in response to new experiences. This process of adaptation occurs through two complementary processes: assimilation and accommodation.

Assimilation refers to the individual's "efforts to deal with the environment by making it fit into the organism's own existing structures—by incorporating it" (Donaldson, 1978, p. 140). New objects or ideas are understood by interpreting them with ideas or concepts that were previously acquired. A 5-year-old who has a concept of birds as living things that fly and have beaks and wings will assimilate an ostrich that she sees at the zoo to her concept of bird. She may, however, be a little bothered by the size of the ostrich (larger than her concept of bird) and by learning that the ostrich does not fly. Her discomfort about whether or not the ostrich is a bird puts her in a state of *disequilibrium.*

Accommodation, the complement of assimilation, occurs when the qualities of the environment do not fit existing concepts well. Through accommodation, concepts are changed in response to environmental demands. The 5-year-old may accommodate to her new information about the ostrich by changing her concept of bird—for instance, she may decide that not all birds fly. She may also form a new concept, ostrich, that is different from her concept of bird.

As a result of accommodation, our 5-year-old will be in a temporary state of *equilibrium* or cognitive balance. Her concepts and her experience match reasonably well. Piaget assumed that all organisms strive for equilibrium. When cognitive balance is disturbed—for example, when something new is encountered—the processes of assimilation and accommodation function to reestablish it. Establishing equilibrium is sometimes called *equilibration.*

Assimilation and accommodation almost always occur together. The child first attempts to understand a new experience by using old ideas and solutions (assimilation); when these do not work, the child is forced to change his or her structure or understanding of the world (accommodation).

Although all adaptive behavior contains some elements of assimilation and accommodation, the proportions of each vary from one activity to another. The *make-believe play* of young children is an example of behavior that is almost entirely assimilative because the children are not very much concerned with the objective characteristics of their playthings. A piece of wood may be used as a doll, a ship, or a wall, depending on the game being played. By contrast, *imitation* is mainly accommodation; children shape actions to fit a model in their environment.

The processes of equilibration and adaptation function throughout our lives as we adapt our behavior to changing circumstances. For example, students who are beginning to study Spanish typically assimilate words and rules in that language to the words and grammatical rules of the language they already know. In other words, they translate. In Spanish, however, there are two words for "to be," *ser* and *estar*, which are used in different ways. Accommodation occurs as new rules about when to use *ser* and *estar* are learned.

The extremes of disequilibrium become less frequent over time because people have more concepts and structures in their repertoires and confront completely new situations less often. Adults are unlikely to encounter a zoo animal that does not fit into some category they already know. An unfamiliar animal will be similar to some familiar ones; only minor modifications of the existing categories for animals are required.

Developmental Stages

Piaget proposed that development proceeds *discontinuously* (see Chapter 1) in a sequence of four qualitatively distinct stages: the sensorimotor stage (0 to 18 months), the preoperational stage (18 months to 7 years), the concrete operational stage (7 to 12 years), and the formal operational stage (12 years and over). The transition from one stage to the next entails a fundamental reorganization of the way the individual constructs (or reconstructs) and interprets the world. That is, when children pass from one stage to another they acquire qualitatively new ways of understanding their world. For example, an infant in the sensorimotor stage may have a scheme for balls—they are round objects that you can hold, throw, and bounce. The child of 5 or 6 may conceive of balls as part of a game, such as T-ball, or he may pretend that a ball is some other object, such as an airplane. He can arrange six balls in order from small to large or from light to dark.

The sequence of stages is invariant; that is, all normal children go through the stages in the same order. No child skips from the preoperational stage to the formal operational stage without going through the stage of concrete operations. This is because each stage builds on, and derives from, the accomplishments of the previous one. At each stage new, different, more adaptive cognitive capabilities are added to what has previously been achieved.

Although the order in which the stages emerge does not vary, there are wide individual differences in the speed with which children pass through them. Hence, the ages associated with the various stages are approximations or averages. Some children reach a particular stage early, others considerably later.

THE SENSORIMOTOR STAGE.   Cognitive growth during the sensorimotor stage is based primarily on sensory experiences and motor actions. Beginning with actions that are primarily reflexes, the infant advances through six substages in which behavior becomes increasingly flexible and goal oriented. The sensorimotor stage was discussed in Chapter 3; you should reread that section now.

THE PREOPERATIONAL STAGE.   Between about 18 months and 2 years, the transition from the sensorimotor stage to the preoperational stage occurs. The hallmark of this transition is mental representation: The child acquires the ability to think about objects and events that are not present in the immediate environment—to represent them in mental pictures, sound, images, words, or other forms. The new ability allows children to move beyond the here and now, for example, to understand fully that objects still exist when you cannot see them.

Delayed imitation demonstrates the preoperational child's newly acquired representational ability. Piaget described his daughter, Jacqueline, who watched in awe as a little boy visiting her house had a temper tantrum in which he screamed, stamped his feet, and shook the playpen. The next day Jacqueline, who was not prone to tantrums, screamed, stamped her feet, and shook the playpen. A sensorimotor infant might have imitated the boy immediately; the deferred imitation demonstrated that Jacqueline had stored some representation of the boy's behavior that she could imitate (Piaget, 1951).

Mental representation also enables children to search for objects after a delay. When asked where her shoes were for example, a 2-year-old disappeared up the stairs of her house. She went directly to her parents' room and returned with the shoes which had been left there the previous day. A younger child might have looked in the usual place for the shoes; a mental representation of some kind was required to find them in a place where they were not usually kept. The child's behavior demonstrated the ability to form and use mental representations. (However, as most parents know only too well, children's performance in finding lost objects does not always match their competence in forming mental representations.)

The preoperational stage also marks the beginning of the ability to use and manipulate symbols. Children now understand that a mental image or idea can be a symbol for an object or experience. Symbolic ability is demonstrated in pretend play in which one object is used to symbolize another. A box may be used as a bed, table, chair, automobile, airplane, or baby carriage. Children also use toys as symbols for people and are able to take on make-believe roles. Consider the symbolic use of words and objects in the following conversation between two 4-year-old boys:

Joe: (putting an empty suitcase on his bed): Let's use this for a train.

Al: Can I get on it?

Joe: Yeah. You're gonna ride on it. Sit here (points to one end of the suitcase). I'm the engineer and I sit here (gets on the other end of the suitcase).

Al: (sitting at the end of the suitcase he has been assigned): O.K. Let's go to my Grandma's house in Milwaukee.

Words are, of course, an important form of symbolic representation. As noted in Chapter 6, however, Piaget believed that children often acquire an understanding of a concept or idea at a nonlinguistic level and then attach language to their understanding. Piaget placed relatively little emphasis on language as a vehicle for acquiring basic concepts in the early years. For example, teaching a child the words *more, less, one, two,* and so on does not help the child learn to count. Once the child understands the basic principles of counting, the words can be attached to that understanding.

Despite these major achievements, preoperational children lack some important forms of logical understanding, according to Piaget. Their thought and speech are often *egocentric*. Egocentrism does not mean that young children are selfish. Instead, Piaget proposed that they do not understand that other people have a different perspective or point of view than they do. One form of egocentrism was demonstrated by asking children about the "three mountains task." A three-dimensional scale model of three mountains of different shapes was shown to the child. The child was then asked what the model would look like to people sitting in other places around the table. Young children (before age 6) said that the other

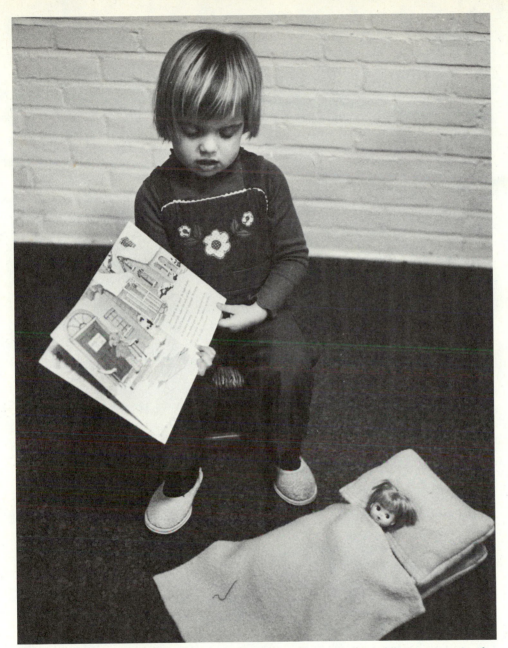

Piaget believed that young children do not understand that other people have a different perspective than they do. More recent research has shown that this is not always the case.

person would see the same view of the mountains that they did. They apparently did not understand that the scene would look different to a person sitting in a different place.

THE STAGE OF CONCRETE OPERATIONS. Some time between 6 and 8 years of age, children enter the stage of concrete operations. You will recall that the operation is a basic cognitive structure that is used to transform information, or "operate" on it. One achievement that is characteristic of this stage is the ability to engage in mental operations that are flexible and fully *reversible*. For example, children understand that subtracting a few pennies from a jar of pennies can be reversed by adding the same number of pennies to the jar.

Second, concrete operational thinkers are capable of **decentration**; that is, they can focus their attention on several attributes of an object or event simultaneously and understand the relationships among dimensions or attributes. They understand that objects have more than one dimension—for example, weight and size—and that these dimensions are separable. A pebble is both small and light; a bowling ball is both small and heavy; a balloon may be both large and light; a car is both large and heavy.

Third, children shift from relying on perceptual information to using logical principles. One important logical principle is the *identity principle*, which states that basic attributes of an object do not change. If a box of Lincoln logs contains 32 pieces, a house built using all of those logs will also contain 32 pieces. The *equivalence principle* is closely related to the identity principle. It states that if A is equal to B in some attribute (e.g., length) and B is equal to C, then A must be equal to C. For example, if Mary wears the same size shoe as Denise and Denise wears the same size shoe as Valerie, can Mary wear Valerie's shoes? Concrete operational thinking enables the child to answer "Yes."

Conservation. Piaget's famous conservation experiments demonstrate three features of concrete operational thinking: reversibility of mental operations, decentration, and change from perceptual to logical judgments. In one type of experiment, shown in Figure 7.2, the child is shown two identical glasses, both of which contain the same quantity of colored liquid. After the child agrees that both glasses contain the same amount of liquid, the interviewer pours the liquid from one of the glasses into a taller, thinner glass and asks, "Does this glass (the taller one) have the same amount, more, or less liquid than this one (the shorter one)?" Preoperational children often say that the taller glass contains more. Concrete operational children understand that the amount of liquid has not changed despite the change in its appearance.

A critical part of the experiment is questioning the child about *why* the amount is the same or different. A child in the concrete operational stage may say, "If you poured it back into the original glass, it would look (be) the same again" (reversibility), or, "The second one is taller, but it is also thinner" (decentration, relations among dimensions), or, "You didn't take any away, so it must be the same" (logical identity rule).

The experiments with liquid and clay shown in Figure 7.2 demonstrate **conservation of substance** (understanding that the amount of a substance does not change just because its shape or configuration changes). **Conservation of number** is also illustrated. In a typical number-conservation experiment, the child is shown two identical rows of buttons. After the child agrees that the number of buttons in the two rows is the same, the buttons in one row are spread out. Preoperational

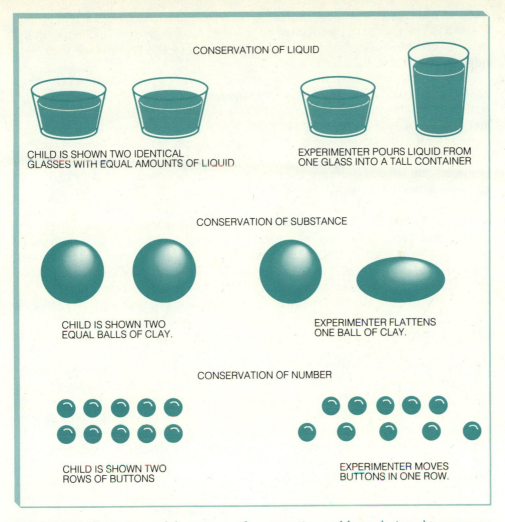

FIGURE 7.2 Illustrations of three types of conservation problems designed to measure concrete operational thinking.

children are likely to say that the longer row has more buttons because they focus on one dimension (length) and use perceptual cues rather than logical principles. Concrete operational thinkers can mentally reverse the operation (move the buttons back to their original positions), decenter (consider both length and density), and use the identity principle to conclude that rearrangement does not change the number of buttons in a row.

Seriation. Another characteristic of the concrete operational stage is the ability to arrange objects according to some quantified dimension such as weight or size. This ability is called **seriation**. An 8-year-old can arrange eight sticks of different lengths in order from shortest to longest. Seriation illustrates the child's grasp of another important logical principle, *transitivity*, which states that there are certain fixed relationships among the qualities of objects. For example, if A is longer than B and B is longer than C, then it must be true that A is longer than C. Children in the stage of concrete operations recognize the validity of this rule even if they have never seen objects A, B, and C.

Seriation can be demonstrated in the card game known as War, a favorite of children in the early years of the concrete operational stage. The players each play one card, and the card with the higher value wins the trick. Children must understand the sequence of the numbers 2 through 10, and they must learn that kings are worth more than queens and jacks. Seriation is critical to understanding the relationships of numbers to one another, and therefore it is essential in learning arithmetic. In fact, an arithmetic curriculum based on Piaget's theory uses card games like War in the early grades (see Box 7.2).

Relational Thinking.   The concrete operational child appreciates the fact that many terms, such as *taller, shorter,* and *darker,* refer to relationships rather than to absolute qualities. Younger children tend to think in absolute terms and thus interpret *darker* as meaning "very dark" rather than "darker than another object." If they are shown two light objects, one of which is slightly darker than the other, and asked to pick the darker one, they may not answer or may say that neither object is darker. Relational thinking illustrates the ability to consider more than one attribute simultaneously because it requires comparison of two or more objects.

Class Inclusion.   Children's understanding of class inclusion illustrates the logical principle that there are *hierarchical relationships* among categories. If 8-year-olds are shown eight yellow candies and four brown candies and asked, "Are there more yellow candies or more candies?" they will usually say that there are more candies. However, when given the same problem 5-year-olds are likely to say that there are more yellow candies, even though they are capable of counting the candies and understand what yellow candies and all candies are. Their difficulty, Piaget believed, reflects their lack of understanding of hierarchical relationships as well as the inability to reason about a part and the whole simultaneously.

Concrete operational children appreciate the fact that some sets of categories nest or fit into each other. For example, all oranges belong to the category *fruits,* all fruits belong to the larger category *foods,* and all foods belong to the larger category *edible things.* Moreover, the child can perform an operation and mentally take apart

BOX 7.2

Children Reinvent Arithmetic

Piaget's theory can be translated into educational practice. Sometimes the result is a radical departure from the methods typically used in schools in the United States. To take one example, Constance Kamii, a developmental psychologist, and Georgia DeClark, a first-grade teacher, created an arithmetic curriculum based on Piaget's theory (Kamii, 1985). Several assumptions guided their work. First, arithmetic is based on the fundamental principles of logical thinking that children acquire in their everyday activities. Second, mathematical knowledge is *constructed* by each child; every child "invents" addition, subtraction, and the like. In other words, such knowledge cannot be imposed from the environment. Third, social interaction is important to children's thinking and their construction of knowledge. Teaching should encourage group interactions rather than individual exercises.

In their first-grade curriculum, Kamii and DeClark eliminated all traditional instruction (especially worksheets) and replaced it with two kinds of activities: situations from everyday life and group games. For example, children in each of several reading groups were asked to vote on a name for their group. As they voted, they kept track of the number of votes and discussed how many votes were needed to win. In another activity a child was asked to distribute letters from the office to be taken home. There were three letters left over. The teacher asked how many letters the office had sent altogether. The children could add the number of students plus 3, or they could count.

The group games included card games, such as War, Double War, and Go Fish, and board games. One of the board games, Benji, includes instructions like "Move any player back or forward to 18." Children often argue about whether "any player" includes themselves. On the board, the square for 18 has only a picture on it; the child must infer that it is 18 from the surrounding numbers.

In Piaget's view, the goal of education is to encourage moral and intellectual autonomy. In this curriculum, therefore, children's arguments and exchanges of views are important learning experiences. The teacher encourages the children to think in their own ways rather than to recite correct answers. When the curriculum was put into practice, the children adjusted to the opportunities for autonomy gradually; they became involved in the games and activities and spontaneously selected materials appropriate to their level of competence. Many, but not all, also performed well on conventional tests of addition.

A second-grade teacher of our acquaintance once said, "Math is just work for children. There's no way to make it any fun." The methods in this Piagetian curriculum prove that she was wrong. Some questions remain unanswered, however. For example, does a curriculum like this one help prevent later distaste and anxiety about math? Is it more important to help children learn that math is fun and an integral part of their lives than to teach them calculation skills? These and other questions may form the basis for further research on the implications of Piaget's theory.

every category of objects and put them back together. The class of foods, therefore, consists of all edible things that are fruits and all edible things that are not fruits.

Second, the concrete operational child realizes that objects can belong to more than one category or more than one relationship at any one time, a principle called the *multiplication of classes or relationships.* Children appreciate the fact that bananas can belong simultaneously to the category of natural foods and the category of sweet foods; bread can belong to the category of manufactured foods and the category of starchy foods; a person can be both a computer programmer and a mother. Similarly, a snowball can be both light in weight and light in color; a rock can be heavy and dark.

Although concrete operational children have advanced beyond children at the preoperational stage in reasoning, problem solving, and logic, much of their thinking continues to be restricted to the here and now of concrete objects and relations. At this stage children conserve quantity and number and can order and classify real objects and things, but they cannot reason as well about abstractions, hypothetical propositions, or imaginary events. Moreover, although they can arrange a series of boxes by size, they have difficulty solving abstract verbal problems such as "Edith is taller than Susan. Lily is shorter than Susan. Who is tallest?"

THE STAGE OF FORMAL OPERATIONS.   In the most advanced stage of cognitive development, which begins at about age 12 and extends through adulthood, the limitations of the concrete operational stage are overcome. The child uses a wider variety of cognitive operations and strategies in solving problems, is highly versatile and flexible in thought and reasoning, and can see things from a number of perspectives or points of view (Ginsburg & Opper, 1979).

One of the most striking features of this stage is the development of the ability to reason about hypothetical problems—about what *might* be—as well as about real ones, and to think about possibilities as well as actualities. The concrete operational child mentally manipulates objects and events; in the stage of formal operations, the child can manipulate ideas about hypothetical situations. For example, an older child can reach a logical conclusion when asked, "If all Martians have yellow feet and this creature has yellow feet, is it a Martian?" A 7-year-old has difficulty reasoning about improbable or impossible events and is likely to say, "I never saw a Martian" or "Things don't have yellow feet."

Another hallmark of problem solving in the stage of formal operations is systematic searching for solutions. Faced with a novel problem, an adolescent attempts to consider all possible means of solving it and checks the logic and effectiveness of each one. When planning to drive to the seashore, for example, adolescents can mentally review all the possible routes, systematically assessing which one is safest, shortest, and fastest (though they may not employ this competence in a specific instance).

In formal operational thought, mental operations are organized into higher-order operations. **Higher-order operations** are ways of using abstract rules to solve a whole class of problems. For example, in solving the problem "What number is 30 less than 2 times itself?" concrete operational children are likely to try first one number and then another, using addition and multiplication until they finally

The concrete operational child can order and classify real objects but is not yet ready to engage in abstract reasoning.

arrive at the correct answer. An adolescent combines the separate operations of addition and multiplication into a single, more complex operation that can be expressed as an algebraic equation, $x = 2x - 30$, and quickly finds the answer: 30.

During the stage of formal operations, individuals think about their own thoughts, evaluating them and searching for inconsistencies and fallacies. A 14-year-old may brood about the following two propositions:

1. God loves humanity.
2. There are many suffering human beings.

These two beliefs seem incompatible, causing the adolescent to look for ways of resolving the tension created by the inconsistency.

In Piaget's investigations of formal operations, which he conducted in collaboration with his longtime colleague Barbel Inhelder, children were asked to solve a variety of logical and scientific problems. The problems called for conclusions about the behavior of floating objects, oscillating pendulums, balance beams, and chemical mixtures. For example, in one experiment children were given five bottles containing colorless liquids and instructed to find a way of combining them that would produce a yellow liquid. In attempting to solve this problem, children in the stage of concrete operations use a trial-and-error approach, trying out a number of

In the stage of formal operations, the adolescent considers all the possible solutions to a problem, formulating hypotheses and systematically testing them.

solutions, generally in an inefficient way. They often test each chemical individually with one or two others but fail to consider all the possible combinations. In contrast, adolescents act more like adult scientists or logicians, considering all the possible solutions in an exhaustive way, formulating hypotheses about outcomes, and systematically designing tests of the hypotheses. They try out all the possible combinations of chemicals and draw accurate conclusions through deductive, logical reasoning.

Formal operational thought can also be observed in games like Twenty Questions. If they are told that the thing they are to guess is an animal, concrete operational children are likely to ask questions like "Is it a dog?" When children reach the stage of formal operations, they ask "constraint-seeking" questions like "Is it smaller than a goat?" These questions provide information regardless of whether the answer is yes or no. The concrete operational thinker starts with an unsystematic selection of concrete possible answers. The formal operational thinker considers the hypothetical universe of possible answers, divides it into approximately equal sections, and uses an efficient strategy to eliminate possibilities. Adolescents' cognitive development is discussed more fully in Chapter 14.

BEYOND PIAGET—EMPIRICAL FINDINGS AND NEW CONCEPTIONS

Every great scholar generates revisions, extensions, and outright dispute. Piaget was no exception. In fact, he himself revised and extended his views until his death in 1980, and his associates in Geneva continued the process (Bullinger & Chatillon, 1983). A great strength of Piaget's theory is its capacity to stimulate research. As a result of that research, by the end of the 1970s serious questions had been raised about some of its statements. Even when parts of the theory were rejected, however, it served an important purpose in stimulating studies that produced new knowledge about children's cognitive development.

At the beginning of the chapter we listed some basic assumptions of Piaget's theory. We will now examine some criticisms and revisions of that theory in the framework of those assumptions.

Maturational Limits and the Role of Experience

Years ago, while teaching a class about Piaget's concept of egocentrism, one of the authors made the statement that preschool children could not take other people's perspectives. After class a woman came forward and asked how that statement fit with her observation that her 2-year-old daughter would respond to her mother's crying by patting and comforting her. It was observations like this one that led psychologists to do research demonstrating that preschool children know a great deal more than Piaget gave them credit for.

These recent studies raise questions about Piaget's assertions that maturation places limits on how quickly children can move through developmental stages and that efforts to train children in a skill before they are "ready" are likely to fail. Some studies also contradict the notion that children benefit more from unstructured exploration of the environment than from structured training because they can se-lect the experiences for which they are ready. Finally, the new studies indicate that preschool children can use some concrete operations (e.g., reversibility, decenter-ing, using hierarchical classes) if the tasks are designed appropriately.

TRAINING IN CONCRETE OPERATIONS.   According to Piaget, training in basic cognitive skills like conservation is not likely to be effective because true acquisi-tion requires interaction between a "ready" organism and an appropriate environ-ment. He predicted that training might be helpful for children during the transition to concrete operations because they would be developmentally ready for such training. Neither of these predictions has been supported by research findings. By now, many studies have shown that preoperational children can benefit from train-ing in conservation and other types of concrete operational thinking. Moreover, children who are deemed "ready" on the basis of their current level of functioning do not learn more easily than those who do not appear to be ready (Brainerd, 1983).

NUMBER SKILLS.   Very young children demonstrate conservation of number when given a simplified task. In the "magic game," children were shown two plates, each of which contained a row of toy mice. On one plate were two mice; on the other were three, arranged in rows of the same length. Children then played a game in which the plates were covered and they had to guess which plate was the winner on a series of trials. Three mice always won. Then the experimenter began to change one of the plates surreptitiously, either by adding or subtracting mice or by lengthening or shortening rows. Even children 2½ or 3 years old responded cor-rectly to the changes in number and ignored changes in row length (Gelman & Baillargeon, 1983). Not only do these findings contradict Piaget's notion that preoperational children do not conserve number, but they suggest that very young children have numerical concepts.

Preschool children use counting principles. Ask a 3-year-old to count eight blocks. You may hear, "1, 2, 3, 4, 6, 10, 13, 20." You rarely hear a sequence like "10, 6, 20, 13." When you ask the child how many there are, the answer will probably be 20. If you then ask her to count eight sandwiches, she will go through a similar se-quence. What does this child know about the principles of counting? First, she knows one-to-one correspondence—a number label goes with each object. Sec-ond, she uses the number labels in a stable order—larger ones always come after smaller ones; this is the *ordinal principle*. Third, she knows that the final label in a se-quence represents the total number of objects; this is the *cardinal principle*. Fourth, she knows that number labels can be applied to any object—the *abstraction principle*. Fifth, she knows that the order of the objects does not matter—she can count any one of the blocks first or second, and so on (Gelman & Gallistel, 1978). Thus, even though she does not count many objects accurately, this 3-year-old has a consid-erable amount of basic number knowledge.

CLASS INCLUSION.   In one of Piaget's tests, children are given sets of objects such as four red flowers and two white ones and asked, "Are there more red flowers or more flowers?" Preoperational children often say that there are more red flowers, a response that Piaget attributed to their inability to decenter, or think simultaneously of a subclass and a class. Other experiments with 4-year-olds, however, demonstrate that they can use class inclusion to draw inferences. For example, the children were asked questions like the following: "A yam is a kind of food, but not meat. Is a yam a hamburger?" "A pawpaw is a kind of fruit, but not a banana. Is a pawpaw food?" In one study, children answered such questions correctly 91 percent of the time. Clearly, they had some understanding of classes and subclasses (Gelman & Baillargeon, 1983).

EGOCENTRISM.   Contrary to Piaget's theory, preschool children can take other people's perspectives. In one study, for example, children between 1 and 3 years old were given open wooden cubes with photographs pasted on the inside back surface. They were told to show the picture to the adult sitting across from them. Almost all children age 2 or older turned the cube toward the adult and away from themselves (Lempers, Flavell, & Flavell, 1978). They understood that the adult saw something different than what they were seeing.

Slightly older preschool children can discern other people's perspectives in more complicated situations. Margaret Donaldson (1978) showed children problems like the one illustrated in Figure 7.3. Initially the children were shown two

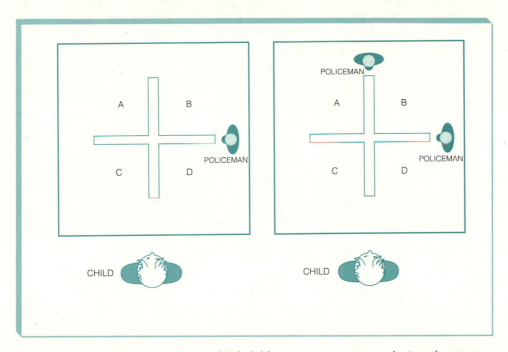

FIGURE 7.3   Scenes shown to preschool children in an experiment designed to assess whether they are egocentric. Children were asked whether a child standing in positions A, B, C, and D could be seen by one policeman or two policemen. (Adapted from M. Donaldson. *Children's minds.* New York: Norton, 1978, pp. 14–15. By permission.)

dolls—a police officer and a boy—standing near two walls that formed a cross. The police doll could "see" the areas marked B and D but not those marked A and C. The examiner placed the boy doll in section A and asked, "Can the policeman see the little boy?" The question was repeated for sections B, C, and D. A second police doll was introduced, and the two police dolls were placed at different locations. The children were asked to hide the boy so that neither police officer could see him. Among children between 3½ and 5 years of age, 90 percent placed the doll correctly. These young children were capable of taking another person's perspective.

WHY THE NEW FINDINGS?   Why do psychologists investigating similar topics reach opposite conclusions? Is it simply a case of experts who do not agree, or the courtroom phenomenon in which one can find an expert to take any position? We do not think so. Both Piaget's original theory and the newer research contradicting some of its conclusions have made important contributions to our understanding of children's thought. In fact, careful examination of the differences between Piaget's earlier studies and the newer ones shed light on developmental differences between preschool-age children and those in middle childhood.

First, Piaget's studies relied on children's understanding of abstract language, for example, the words *more*, *less*, and *same*. Preschool children are often confused by these words, but they can understand a game in which they are to pick a winner or carry out a simple instruction to show a picture to someone. Children in middle childhood not only understand the basic principle but can apply it in the context of instructions using abstract words.

Second, Piaget's tasks were often more complex than those that were later used successfully with preschool children, even though they required the child to use the same basic principle. For example, children's egocentrism was tested by placing on a table arrangements of blocks that differed in height, shape, and breadth (see Figure 7.4). When there were only a few blocks, fairly young children (5-year-olds) could accurately decide what the array looked like from another side of the table. But as the number of blocks was increased, only older children gave correct answers. For arrays containing large numbers of blocks, even some adolescents had difficulty deciding how they appeared from another side of the table (Flavell, Botkin, Fry, Wright, & Jarvis, 1968). In sum, both younger and older children understood the basic principle that another person would see something different than what they saw. What changed with age was the complexity of the task in which children could apply that knowledge accurately.

Finally, studies of preschoolers have included clever ways to test children's *implicit* knowledge. When a person can use a principle but cannot explain it, we say that his or her knowledge is implicit. For example, preschool children can use the rule to form the past tense, but they cannot explain that the rule is to add −*ed* to the verb (see Chapter 6). In the research just discussed, ingenious ways were found to get children to demonstrate their implicit knowledge of number, class inclusion, and other principles that Piaget believed required concrete operations. What is added in middle childhood is the ability to *explain* the principles, that is, *explicit* knowledge about number, class, relationships, and logic.

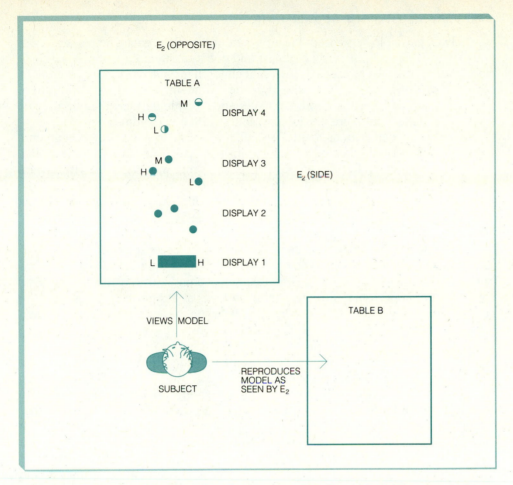

FIGURE 7.4   Arrays of blocks used to demonstrate the effects of stimulus complexity on children's responses to tests of egocentrism. Children were seated in the position indicated, looking at an array of blocks. They were told to arrange the blocks on Table B so that they looked the way the model on Table A looked to the experimenter seated at one side or opposite the child. Young children (second-graders) performed well on the simple displays, but even adolescents sometimes had difficulty with the complex displays.

Display 1 comprised a single blue-colored block of wood 6 in. long and 1 in. thick. It was 6 in. high at one end and 4 in. high at the other, and thus its upper edge was diagonal rather than parallel to the ground. It was always placed so that its higher side (H) was on S's right and its lower side (L) on his left, as he faced the model.

Display 2 consisted of three identical blue wooden cylinders, 4 in. high and 1 in. in diameter, standing on end in the spatial arrangement shown in the figure.

Display 3 also consisted of three blue wooden cylinders of 1 in. diameter. Their heights, however, were 6 in. (H), 4 in. (M), and 2 in. (L).

Display 4 included three cylinders identical in size to those of Display 3. However, each was painted red for half its circumference (including top and bottom cross sections, and white for the other half. (Adapted from J. H. Flavell, P. T. Borkin, C. L. Fry, Jr., J. W. Wright, & P. E. Jarvis. *The development of role-taking and communication skills in children.* New York: Wiley, 1968. By permission.)

The Role of Activity in Learning

Virtually all psychologists accept Piaget's dictum that children are active seekers of knowledge who spontaneously organize and construct their experience. This notion is sometimes interpreted to mean that children must *do* something in order to benefit from their interactions with their environment. For instance, preschool teachers often believe that hands-on experience, manipulation of materials, and interactive participation are crucial to young children's learning.

However, activity can be mental as well as physical. In one set of experiments pairs of preschool children were tested. In each pair one child was an active "learner-model"; the other was an observer. The learner-model played with several pairs of toys while the other child watched. Then both children were tested to see if they could recall which toys had been paired. The observing children remembered as well as the learner-models did, even after a delay of one day (Zimmerman, 1984).

Television is often criticized as a passive activity because children do not do anything visible while viewing. Their parents see them staring at the tube like zombies. Yet there is often mental activity taking place under that bland surface. One sign of active processing is the fact that the level of attention changes with the comprehensibility of the content. For example, when the sound track is in a foreign language, the level of attention drops; when the sound track is understandable, the level of attention increases (Anderson, D. R., Lorch, Field, & Sanders, 1981).

At a more subtle level, children use their knowledge about television production conventions to decide how closely they will attend. In one investigation young children saw two public-service announcements about nutrition that were identical except for format. One was animated and used production features that are typical of children's programs; the other used live actors in a format that is typical of adult programs. Young children attended more to the child-oriented format *and* learned more of its content than they did in the case of the adult-oriented format (Campbell, Wright, & Huston, 1987). Clearly, children think, evaluate, and make judgments while watching television.

Do these findings suggest that preschool teachers are wrong about the importance of hands-on experience? Probably not. It is much easier to maintain young children's interest and attention when they are manipulating materials or participating in a learning activity. But we should probably not go so far as to argue that active participation is the only way to learn. Even young children can be cognitively active while they are physically inactive.

Is Cognitive Development Domain Specific?

In Piaget's theory developmental stages cover broad domains of thought; Piaget believed that children use the same cognitive structures across a wide range of tasks. Once children understand the use of hierarchical classification for foods, for example, they should be able to use hierarchies of classes for animals, people, motor vehicles, and so on. However, cognitive skills appear to be more domain specific than Piaget thought. For example, children who respond egocentrically when asked how three mountains look from another perspective do not necessarily show egocentrism when asked what their sister would like to eat.

One reason cognitive skills are domain specific is that knowledge of information within a content domain is important. Children and adults perform at "higher" cognitive levels when they know a lot about a topic. In fact, some people have argued that most changes that occur with age are primarily a result of the fact that individuals accumulate knowledge about many diverse topics as they grow older. This argument can be tested by comparing children who are experts in a particular knowledge area with adults who are novices in that area. Children who were recruited from a chess tournament, for example, recalled the positions of chess pieces on a board and could carry out complex hypothetical moves better than adults who knew little about chess (Chi, 1978). The children could use more complex thinking than the adults because they knew more about chess. They would not necessarily use such complex processing on topics with which they were less familiar.

People use different problem-solving strategies for material that is very familiar to them than for material that is less familiar. Here is an example: Multiply 3 times 5. How long did it take you? What problem-solving strategy did you use? You probably did it quickly, and you probably needed no strategy because you memorized the answer long ago. Now multiply 347 times 79. Answer the same questions. It probably took you longer, and you probably had to apply some rules for multiplying, using pencil and paper. Bookkeepers who worked in the days before computers used to do these calculations as quickly in their heads as you do when you multiply 3 times 5.

Robert Siegler (1986) observed the same process when children were given arithmetic problems. On familiar problems (ones that they had encountered frequently), children answered quickly from rote memory. When problems were unfamiliar, children used overt strategies such as holding up their fingers and counting aloud. As those problems became more familiar, the children had less need for problem-solving strategies.

Are Stages Universal?

Piaget believed that his principles of logical thinking are universal because they are based on children's interactions with the physical world. This assumption may be partially true for the logical principles described in our discussion of the stage of concrete operations, but it becomes questionable as the individual moves into the stage of formal operations. Many adolescents and adults apparently have difficulty solving some problems involving formal operations; between 40 and 60 percent of college students and adults are unsuccessful at such tasks (Neimark, 1975a).

Patterns of cognitive development also differ across cultures. The principles of Western logic are not necessarily universal. For example, in Western logic the statement "The sky is blue" is equivalent to the double negative "It is not true that the sky is not blue." In one form of Indian philosophy, these two statements do not have the same meaning.

The Nature of Developmental Change

Stages are a central part of Piaget's theory. The term *stage* is sometimes used loosely to describe almost any change that occurs with age, but in most developmental theories it has a more restricted meaning. Stages have two defining attributes: (1) Thinking at different stages is qualitatively different, (2) Stages occur in an *invariant order*; preoperational thinking, for example, always precedes concrete operations.

Although many psychologists no longer accept the notion that children move from one form of thought to a completely different form between the ages of 18 months and 2 years or between age 4 and age 7, they do accept the notion that some qualitative changes in thinking occur between the preschool and school years. It is probably not a coincidence that in virtually all societies children begin their formal education sometime around age 6 or 7.

There may be qualitative changes in the brain at the ages identified by Piaget as transitions between stages. There is a change in the coherence of the EEG (electroencephalogram) in the left hemisphere between the ages of 4 and 6 (the transition from preoperational thought to concrete operations), and another change occurs between the ages of 12 and 14 (the transition to formal operations). They are illustrated in Figure 7.5. These neurological changes may provide a basis for the ability to use qualitatively different thought processes (Thatcher, Walker, & Giudice, 1987).

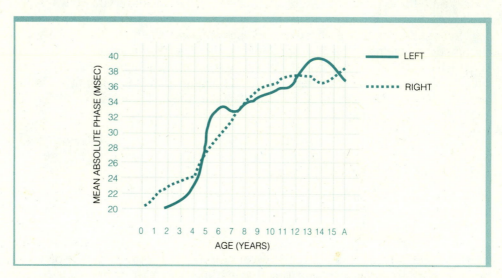

FIGURE 7.5 Development of the mean absolute phase of the EEG from the left and right frontal-occipital areas from infancy through adulthood. The dotted line represents the right hemisphere; it shows a relatively smooth, continuous pattern of development. The solid line represents the left hemisphere; it shows more abrupt developmental changes, with spurts of growth between ages 4 and 6 and again between ages 12 and 14. These age periods correspond to the transitions between stages in Piaget's theory. (Adapted from R. W. Thatcher, R. A. Walker, & S. Giudice. Human cerebral hemispheres develop at different rates and ages. *Science*, 1988, 236, 1110–1113. By permission.)

Rejection of Piaget's broad stages of development does not mean that developmental sequences or regular patterns of change are no longer of interest. In some cases those changes appear to be gradual rather than sudden. As you might guess from our earlier discussion, changes also tend to be specific to particular content domains. Recent theorists have set themselves a more modest goal than Piaget's: to delineate developmental sequences in particular cognitive domains. For example, Flavell (1986) and his associates have identified developmental changes in children's understanding of appearance vs. reality.

In Chapter 5 we discussed the emergence of pretend play. During the second year of life children begin to use objects as though they were something different (object substitution) and to use themselves or toys as pretend people (self-other substitution). The development of pretend play is described in Box 7.3. Pretending is one manifestation of the ability to use symbols, an important development in early childhood. In many respects preschool children understand the difference between pretending and reality—even a 2-year-old knows that his teddy bear is not really eating.

Yet 3- and 4-year-olds do not completely understand a more fundamental difference: the distinction between appearance and reality. Consider the following dilemmas, which were presented to a series of children. First the children were shown a very realistic looking fake rock made of sponge rubber. They were allowed to handle and squeeze it. Then they were asked, "Is this *really* and *truly* a sponge, or is it *really* and *truly* a rock?" "When you look at this with your eyes right now, does it *look like* a rock or does it *look like* a sponge?" Other children were shown a white piece of paper, which was then placed behind a blue filter; they were asked about its real color and its apparent color. These tasks are among those used by John Flavell

BOX 7.3

Playing, Pretending, and Cognitive Development

In all cultures children play and pretend. Psychoanalysts have long used play as an avenue to understanding the child's unconscious. Cognitive developmentalists view play as a window on the workings of the child's mind, an external manifestation of cognitive processes.

What is play? Play is spontaneous. It is fun. It is usually initiated by a child. It often has no apparent goal; the activity itself is the goal. And it is pretending—imagining that objects are something else, taking imaginary roles and identities. Between the ages of 1 and 2, children begin to pretend (see Chapter 5). From age 2 to age 6 or 7, children spend an increasing percentage of their time in fantasy play. Consider the following example:

Girl: This is a train (putting suitcase on the sofa). We're eating dinner on the train. This is steak and this is cake (pointing to empty places on a plate). You be the conductor.
Boy: I'm the conductor. Where is your ticket?
Girl: (Holds out her hand with imaginary ticket.)
Boy: (Pretends to punch the ticket, then points to her toy dog.) You can't have dogs here.
Girl: It's not a dog; it's my baby.

When children pretend, they transform objects (e.g., sofa = train) or invent them out of thin air (e.g., the "ticket"). With age, children become increasingly free from the actual properties of objects, although they often use toy objects in realistic ways. For example, a toy telephone is usually used as a "real" telephone.

Children engaging in pretend play take on new identities and roles (e.g., conductor). With age, children are more likely to instruct their companions (e.g., "You be the conductor") and to combine role taking with object transformations. Very young children typically do one or the other but not both.

In play, children practice cognitive skills, imagination, social roles, and language. For example, children who spontaneously engage in a lot of fantasy play are more socially competent, assertive, and skilled in understanding other people's perspectives than children of comparable intelligence and sociability who indulge in less fantasy play. An old saying sums up the importance of play: "Play is the work of childhood" (Connolly, Doyle, & Ceschin, 1983; Garvey, 1977; Rubin, K. H., Fein, & Vandenberg, 1983).

(1986) and his associates to test children's understanding of the difference between appearance and reality. You can see that understanding this distinction is one aspect of understanding conservation. Three- and four-year-old children have difficulty with these questions, but by age 6 or 7 most children get them right.

Why should young children have so much difficulty with these tasks? They understand that the "sponge" rock is a "pretend rock." What seems to be difficult for them to understand is that something can have two identities simultaneously; one identity is its appearance and another is its reality. When an object is "pretend," it is just that—a pretend rock or spoon or astronaut. But if children think an object is a real sponge, they tend to say it looks like a sponge. If it looks blue, it is blue.

Evaluation of Piaget's Theory

What is left of Piaget's theory? Many of its basic assumptions are now so widely accepted that we take them for granted. Most psychologists agree that human organisms function according to general principles of organization and adaptation. They agree that children *actively* construct their world rather than being passive registers for external stimuli, and that cognitive development is a product of continual interactions between the child and the environment. Moreover, they point out the great contribution made by Piaget's own empirical studies for our understanding of children's development, although they often consider children more malleable and less subject to maturational limits than Piaget did.

On the other hand, many psychologists now reject Piaget's notions of discontinuous broad stages of development in favor of more narrowly defined advances in cognitive skills. Although qualitative changes in thought can be identified, many skills appear to develop more gradually and continuously than Piaget's theory suggests.

SUMMARY

Scientists who wish to measure and conceptualize cognitive processes face three basic dilemmas: the extent to which thought can be inferred from behavior, the distinction between competence and performance, and broad versus narrow definitions of competence. Theorists disagree on whether and to what extent we can infer unobservable thoughts from observed behavior. Strict behaviorists assert that observable behavior is psychologists' only legitimate concern. On the other hand, many psychologists want to know about the events that take place inside children's heads. Most researchers use observable behavior as the main criterion for testing theories.

Competence refers to the knowledge and skills that a child possesses; the demonstration of knowledge and skills in observable problem-solving situations is called *performance*. Children may possess knowledge that they do not use, even when the occasion calls for it. Sometimes children's performance does not reveal their actual competence because they misunderstand the problems they are asked to solve. Most psychologists favor defining competences somewhat narrowly, partly because this approach permits more precise comparisons between different groups of children.

Piaget assumed that the biological characteristics of the child place some limits on the order and speed at which particular cognitive competences emerge. At the same time, he believed that active experience with the world is critical to cognitive growth. His central thesis is that people are active, curious, and inventive throughout life. Thus children *construct* their world by imposing order on the information they receive through their senses.

The two basic principles guiding human development, according to Piaget, are organization and adaptation. Children organize their experience into cognitive structures such as the *operation*, a manipulation of ideas that can be performed in reverse. In interacting with the environment, they adapt those structures in response to new experiences. The process of adaptation occurs through the processes of *assimilation* (using previously acquired ideas or concepts to understand new ones) and *accommodation* (modifying existing concepts in response to environmental demands). The result of these processes is a temporary state of *equilibrium* or cognitive balance.

Piaget proposed that development proceeds discontinuously in a sequence of four stages. The transition from one stage to the next entails a fundamental reorganization of the way the individual constructs and interprets the world. The sequence of stages is invariant because each stage builds on the accomplishments of the previous one. There are, however, individual differences in the speed with which children pass through the stages.

During the sensorimotor stage cognitive growth is based primarily on sensory experiences and motor actions. Between about 18 months and 2 years, the transition to the preoperational stage occurs. The hallmark of this transition is *mental representation*, or the ability to think about objects and events that are not present in the immediate environment. The preoperational stage also marks the beginning of the ability to use and manipulate symbols. Despite these achievements, the child's thought and speech are often *egocentric*.

Sometime between 6 and 8 years of age, children enter the stage of concrete operations. They become able to engage in mental operations that are flexible and fully reversible, and they can *decenter*; that is, they can focus on several attributes of an object or event simultaneously. In addition, they shift from relying on perceptual information to using *logical principles* such as the identity principle and the equivalence principle.

Other characteristics of the concrete operational stage are *seriation*, the ability to arrange objects according to a quantified dimension; *relational thinking*, the ability to appreciate the fact that many terms refer to relationships rather than to absolute qualities; and *class inclusion*, the ability to appreciate the fact that some sets of categories fit into each other, as well as the realization that objects can belong to more than one category or relationship at a time.

Upon reaching the stage of formal operations, the child uses a wider variety of cognitive operations and strategies in solving problems, is highly versatile and flexible in thought and reasoning, and can see things from a number of perspectives. The child can now manipulate ideas about hypothetical situations and engage in a systematic search for solutions. In formal operational thought, mental operations are organized into higher-order operations, or ways of using abstract rules to solve a whole class of problems.

Recent studies have raised questions about Piaget's assertions that maturation places limits on how quickly children can move through developmental stages and that efforts to train children in a skill before they are ready are likely to fail. They also contradict the notion that children benefit more from unstructured exploration of the environment than from structured training. Preoperational children can benefit from training in conservation and other types of concrete operational training, demonstrate conservation of number when give a simplified task, and use class inclusion to draw inferences. In addition, studies have shown that preschool children can take other people's perspectives.

Although psychologists accept Piaget's dictum that children are active seekers of knowledge, they believe that activity can be mental as well as physical. They also believe that cognitive skills are more domain specific than Piaget thought. Knowledge of information within a content domain is important, and people use different problem-solving strategies for material that is very familiar to them than for material that is less familiar. Finally, the assumption that the principles of logical thinking are universal becomes questionable as the individual moves into the stage of formal operations.

Although many psychologists no longer accept the notion that children move from one form of thought to a completely different form at various points in development, they do accept the notion that some qualitative changes in thinking occur between the preschool and school years. In addition, they believe that developmental changes are gradual rather than sudden, and that they tend to be specific to particular content domains.

REVIEW QUESTIONS

1. Briefly describe three basic dilemmas facing scientists who wish to measure and conceptualize cognitive processes.

2. According to Piaget, how do biological maturation and active experience influence cognitive development?

3. What is meant by organization and adaptation? By assimilation and accommodation?

4. Briefly describe the four stages of Piaget's theory of cognitive development.

5. What is an operation?

6. What is meant by conservation of number? Of substance?

7. What is seriation? What is relational thinking?

8. In what ways has recent research challenged Piaget's assertion that maturation places limits on children's ability to move through developmental stages?

9. Is it necessary for children to manipulate materials and actively interact with their environment in order to learn something?

10. Psychologists today believe cognitive skills are more domain specific than Piaget thought. Why is this the case?

GLOSSARY

cognition   The processes of thinking and knowing, including attending, perceiving, interpreting, classifying, and remembering information; evaluating ideas; inferring principles and deducing rules; imagining possibilities; generating strategies; and fantasizing.

competence   The knowledge and skills that an individual possesses.

performance   The demonstration of knowledge and skills in observable problem-solving situations.

aptitude (potential competence)   The ability to acquire a new skill or bit of knowledge.

operation   A manipulation of ideas that can be performed in reverse.

assimilation   The individual's efforts to deal with the environment by making it fit into his or her own existing structures.

accommodation   The process of changing existing concepts in response to environmental demands.

decentration   The ability to focus attention on several attributes of an object or event simultaneously and understand the relationships among dimensions or attributes.

conservation of substance   The ability to understand that the amount of a substance does not change just because its shape or configuration changes.

conservation of number   The ability to understand that the number of objects in a set does not change just because the objects are rearranged.

seriation   The ability to arrange objects according to some quantified dimension such as weight or size.

higher-order operation   A way of using abstract rules to solve a whole class of problems.

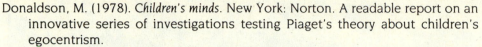

SUGGESTED READINGS

Donaldson, M. (1978). *Children's minds*. New York: Norton. A readable report on an innovative series of investigations testing Piaget's theory about children's egocentrism.

Flavell, J. H. (1985). *Cognitive development* (2nd ed). Englewood Cliffs, NJ: Prentice-Hall. An excellent text by one of the major translators of Piaget's theory. Covers many aspects of cognitive development, with particular emphasis on memory.

Gelman, R, & Gallistel, C. R. (1978). *The child's understanding of number*. Cambridge, MA: Harvard University Press. A ground-breaking set of investigations showing that very young children understand many of the basic principles of number. This work was important for demonstrating that young children can use some of the principles of concrete-operational thinking.

Ginsburg, H., & Opper, S. (1979). *Piaget's theory of intellectual development* (2nd ed). Englewood Cliffs, NJ: Prentice-Hall. A good basic text explaining Piaget's theory.

Kamii, C. K. (1985). *Young children reinvent arithmetic: Implications of Piaget's theory*. New York: Teachers College Press. A description of a radically different curriculum for teaching arithmetic in the early grades, written from the vantage point of the teacher as well as that of the researcher. Contains many examples and direct observations that make fascinating reading.

Chapter Eight

COGNITIVE DEVELOPMENT: LEARNING AND INFORMATION PROCESSING

Learning Theory and Behaviorism
    Experimental Analysis of Behavior
    Cognitive Learning Theories
    Critique of Learning Principles
Information Processing
    Major Assumptions
    Cognitive Units—How Information Is Represented
    Cognitive Processes
    Metacognition
    A Critique of the Information-processing Approach
What Changes with Age?

P iaget and other stage theorists follow one set of assumptions about the growth of cognitive abilities and skills. They believe that children's cognitive talents are reorganized periodically as a result of the maturation of new abilities in interaction with active exploration of the environment. They search for mental structures and processes, and they assume that those structures change dynamically just as cells and other biological structures do.

Learning theorists, who have been a major influence in American psychology, follow a different set of assumptions. Developmental psychologists in this tradition strive "to chart the child's increasing ability to discriminate or encode various classes of stimuli on the one hand, and to induce the correlations or associations among them on the other. . . . They are united in their view that learning and development are essentially equivalent" (Case, 1986, p. 57). In recent years this view has been advocated primarily by followers of B. F. Skinner, who describe themselves as behavior analysts. They are interested in applying behavioral principles to help children with learning or behavior problems, as well as in doing basic research on learning processes.

Assumptions from both of these positions are represented in information-processing approaches to understanding children's cognitive development. Psychologists who take this approach believe that children are active in interactions with their environment and that neurological and biochemical changes are important, but they often reject the notion of discontinuous stages.

LEARNING THEORY AND BEHAVIORISM

Learning theorists conceptualize learning as a set of associations between *stimuli* and *responses*. *Conditioning* is the process by which learning takes place. The two types of conditioning, which were discussed in Chapter 3, are *classical* or *respondent* conditioning and *instrumental* or *operant* conditioning. As we shall see in Chapter 10, learning can also occur through observation of other people's behavior. B. F. Skinner (1938) founded a radical behaviorist system of psychology based on these fundamental learning principles. His work forms the basis for modern **behavior analysis**.

Experimental Analysis of Behavior

To understand this approach, let us consider an applied problem: how to teach basic number skills to 6-year-old Sharon. In behavior analysis learning is defined by behavior. (Recall the debates about cognition versus behavior and competence versus performance discussed at the beginning of Chapter 7.) Because behavior analysts consider only observed behavior, Sharon's competence in number skills is defined by her observable performance. Therefore, the first step in training is to define behavioral objectives in detail. What behaviors constitute number skills? Our teacher outlines the following goals: (1) selecting a specified number of objects from an array of ten when the teacher says the numeral, (2) counting aloud from 1 to 10, (3) recognizing the written symbols for the numbers 1 to 10, and (4) writing the symbols for the numbers 1 to 5.

Next Sharon is given a series of learning trials in which difficulty levels are increased in very small increments. First she is shown three blocks and the teacher says, "Hand me three blocks." When she performs correctly, the teacher praises her (positive reinforcement). Then she is shown three blocks and asked, "Give me one block," and then, "Give me two blocks." Praise follows correct performance. When Sharon's performance is nearly perfect, a larger number of blocks is presented and the procedure is repeated. For each new task, trials are continued over several days until the child's performance is nearly perfect. The rate of correct responding is recorded daily, usually on a graph. If Sharon is not making progress, easier problems are repeated or a different method is tried. Learning is accomplished when the child can select any number of blocks (from one to ten) from a larger array. At that point *generalization* to stimuli other than blocks is tested. Can Sharon perform similar behaviors for toy trucks, dolls, and other objects?

Two important features of behavior analysis are illustrated in this example. First, a **reinforcing stimulus** is defined as an event that increases the probability of behavior. We assume that a teacher's praise is reinforcing, but if the desired response does not increase in frequency, we may try other consequences, such as gold stars or an opportunity to play with an attractive toy, in an effort to find events that are reinforcing to Sharon. Second, the child's responses guide the teacher's choice of a next step. Training proceeds to new levels only when the child performs the current level correctly. If the child is not improving, a different stimulus or method is tried. In a very real sense, the customer is always right. Failure to learn is blamed on the teaching method, not on the child (Sherman, 1982).

Cognitive Learning Theories

Some psychologists use concepts from learning theory but are willing to consider internal, unobservable mental processes as well as observable behavior. Often they conceptualize thought processes as internal associations between stimuli and responses (e.g., Gagne, 1965). Learning theorists share three basic assumptions that contrast with Piaget's approach: (1) They are strong environmentalists, placing little emphasis on maturation. (2) Children are viewed primarily as passive receivers of environmental inputs rather than as active organizers or initiators of their experiences. As a result, teaching is highly structured and organized, in contrast to methods based on Piaget's theory, which emphasize exploration and discovery. (3) They reject concepts of development that imply an unfolding maturational process. Instead, they emphasize gradual and continuous change that is due primarily to accumulated experience. Therefore, they do not consider age to be an important variable; the rate at which a child can gain new skills is assumed to depend largely on the kinds of experience the child has, not on some internal timetable (Baer, 1970).

Critique of Learning Principles

Learning principles have been applied successfully in many contexts. They are useful in teaching many academic skills, particularly to children who have difficulty learning when conventional teaching methods are used. Some of the most successful forms of intervention and therapy are based on behavior analysis and cognitive learning theory. For example, Wolf and his associates have developed the Teaching Family Model, a system of residential treatment for adolescent delinquents in which youths live in groups of six to ten with two teaching parents. The homes are run like democratic families in which expected behaviors are clearly spelled out and reinforcements (e.g., praise and privileges) are based on appropriate behavior (Braukmann, Ramp, Tigner, & Wolf, 1984).

Although behavior analysis is widely used in applied settings, learning theory has declined from its early prominence among psychologists interested in understanding developmental processes. No one disputes the fact that basic conditioning processes occur, but these processes have proved inadequate to explain many of the most fascinating aspects of children's intellectual development. For example, conditioning cannot adequately explain children's language development (see Chapter 6). Therefore, many American psychologists who want to describe and understand children's intellectual development have moved away from learning theory toward an information-processing approach.

Rewards such as gold stars may be used to reinforce appropriate behaviors.

INFORMATION PROCESSING

The major goals of psychologists in the information-processing tradition are similar to those of Piaget. First, they want to describe the nature of thought—to analyze how the human mind represents and manipulates information. They are less interested in documenting exactly what children know than in finding out how their knowledge is organized and processed. A 5-year-old laughs while watching a television show in which a dog moos and a cow barks. The psychologist is concerned not with the fact that the child knows what dogs and cows sound like, but with identifying the mental structures and processes the child uses to decide that the combinations portrayed are incongruous.

Second, these psychologists try to specify how cognitive processes change with age and experience. For example, when asked to search for a lost baseball glove a 10-year-old goes about the task more systematically than a 4-year-old. With age, children become more planful, better able to monitor their own thoughts and cognitive activities, and better aware of what they do and do not know.

Major Assumptions

To some extent, information-processing approaches base their models of human intellectual functioning on computer operations. They often use flowcharts and diagrams similar to those used in computer programming.

Most psychologists who favor this approach assume an *interaction between maturation and experience*. They believe that biological factors set important limits on human cognition, but that experience provides factual information and opportunities to acquire specific skills. They typically assume that children are *active* in selecting, constructing, and interpreting the information they receive. But they do not share Piaget's emphasis on the need for children to initiate encounters with their environment or to manipulate objects in their environment. Children can think and develop by perceiving objects and events, remembering them, and drawing inferences about them.

Advocates of information-processing theories believe that whether developmental change is continuous or discontinuous is an empirical question rather than a theoretical given. In general, they propose that developmental changes are gradual and continuous, although they recognize some qualitative changes in functioning. Psychologists in this tradition generally opt for relatively specific, narrow definitions of cognitive domains. In fact, one of the major thrusts of some research is to determine the effects of task domain on children's processing. Finally, like learning theorists, information-processing theorists use carefully controlled observations and experiments to test their ideas.

Cognitive Units—How Information Is Represented

It is helpful to think of cognitive functioning as a set of *processes* for working with different *units* of knowledge. What are those units? We will describe four types: schemata, images, concepts, and propositions (Kagan, 1984).

Most psychologists believe that both maturation and experience play important roles in children's cognitive development.

SCHEMATA.   The **schema**, discussed in Chapter 3, is not identical to Piaget's *scheme*. It is a composite of the typical and distinctive characteristics of a scene or sequence of events. To understand a schema, think for a moment about your livingroom, visualizing the furniture, the pictures, the windows and doors. Now think about livingrooms in general—about what they typically contain. You will probably say that most such rooms have chairs, a sofa, small tables, at least one door, and a few windows. You have a schema of livingrooms in general that is not simply an image of a particular room but a composite of the typical and distinctive characteristics of livingrooms. Like a cartoonist's caricature, it preserves the essential aspects of the thing it represents.

Children's schemata for scenes contain information about the objects in a scene and about the relationships among them. Such a schema can serve as the basis for ordinary spatial knowledge. A child who easily finds her way to school and to several friends' houses probably has a schema of her neighborhood. She can visualize the layout of streets and houses. When she goes somewhere, she is not merely following a route learned for that particular location; she is walking through a "map" of her neighborhood.

Schemata make memory efficient because they preserve the essence of a scene without requiring the person to remember all the details. An investigation of children and adults' memories for simple and complex pictures illustrates how people use schemas to remember things (see Figure 8.1). The simple pictures contained basic information; the complex versions contained added details and shading. Subjects were shown a series of these pictures and told to try to remember them. A few minutes later they were shown another set of pictures in which some were identical to the previous set but others were different. For example, if the subjects had seen picture A in Figure 8.1, the different version was B; if they had seen picture D, the different version was C. People detected additions to simple pictures

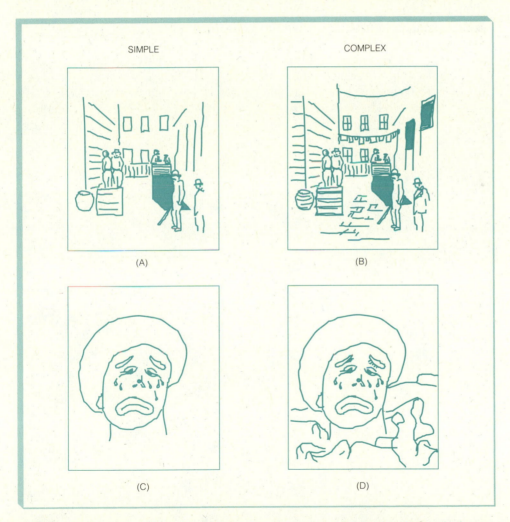

FIGURE 8.1   Examples of simple and complex pictures used to test the effects of schemata on memory. Simple pictures contain information that is crucial; complex versions have additional details and shading. (Adapted from K. Pezdek. Memory for pictures: A life-span study of the role of visual detail. *Child Development*, 1987, 58, 810. By permission.)

(e.g., they recognized that B was not the version they had seen before), but they were less likely to detect subtractions from complex pictures (e.g., they did not recognize that C was not the version they had seen before). What they had stored in memory was a schema representing the essentials of the picture, so they did not notice when details were omitted (Pezdek, 1987).

Children can form schemata for temporal sequences of events as well as for scenes. An event schema "can be defined as a temporally organized representation of a sequence of events or as a set of expectations about what will occur and when it will occur in a given situation" (Mandler, 1983, p. 456). Some concrete event schemata are called *scripts*. Ask ten people to describe the sequence of events involved in getting up in the morning or going to a class. You will find a good deal of agreement on the events involved *and* the sequence in which they occur. The common components constitute the "getting up in the morning" script or the "going to class" script.

Young children know the scripts for the events they experience repeatedly. For example, children accurately described going to the grocery store. "You get a cart. Then you put some lettuce and some cereal in your cart. You stand in line and pay." Preschool children (4- and 5-year-olds) sometimes had difficulty describing these events, but they recognized events that fit scripts accurately. For instance, when asked whether taking off your shoes and socks is part of going to the grocery store they said no (Adams & Worden, 1986).

Children learn "scripts" for events that they experience repeatedly, such as going to the grocery store.

Why are schemata and scripts important? Some people argue that they are among the first cognitive units used by children because they represent groupings of objects or events from everyday experience (Mandler, 1983). A blackboard, desks, bulletin boards, and a teacher are grouped in a schema for a classroom because they occur together in experience, not because they share any abstract similarities.

Schemas and scripts help us function efficiently because they allow us to anticipate and predict. They produce expectancies. You expect to see things that are consistent with a schema, so you are likely to notice those things. You may fail to note something that is inconsistent, and you may even distort what you see or what you remember in order to make your experience consistent with your schema. Thus, children recalling a preschool classroom may remember the play areas and the rug for "group time," but they may not remember a large filing cabinet in the room or may recall it as a prop associated with play activities.

IMAGES.   An **image** is a sensory impression—a picture, sound, or smell—that is re-created mentally. Images are often created from schemata, but are consciously elaborated. The difference is like the difference between a schematic wiring diagram for an electrical appliance and a picture of the insides of the appliance itself. When you imagined your livingroom, you generated an image.

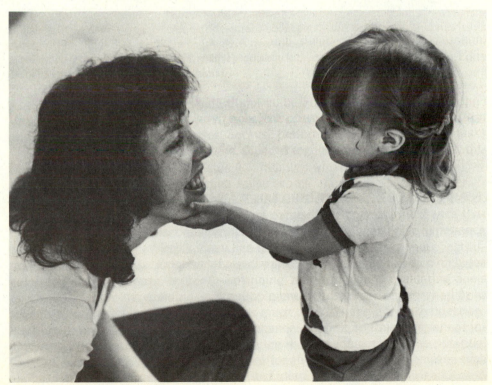

An image—like that of the mother's face—is a sensory impression that is re-created mentally.

We all use images sometimes, but some psychologists have suggested that young children rely on images to solve problems more than older children and adults do.

CONCEPTS OR CATEGORIES.   As they grow older, children acquire abstract concepts, the third major unit of cognition. Schemata and images are faithful to the physical characteristics of the scenes or events they represent; **concepts** are not. A concept is a symbolic representation of a group of objects or events. Language is one major form of symbolic representation. Words do not have any physical similarity to the objects they represent; the word *food*, for example, is arbitrarily assigned to things we eat.

Symbolic concepts are often **categories** that represent shared abstract qualities of a group of objects. We group together carrots, beef, milk, and lemon pie in the category "food" because they share the property of being edible. We could also group carrots with basketballs and orange cars because they are all the same color.

Children begin to group objects into categories very early. For instance, children between 12 and 24 months old who were given a set of black and white blocks spontaneously grouped them by color. A child may know and use a category without knowing a word for it; these toddlers, for example, probably did not know the words *black*, *white*, or *color*. This is another illustration of young children's implicit knowledge, which we discussed in Chapter 7.

Symbolic concepts increase our ability to understand the world because we can apply conceptual knowledge to new situations. We do not have to begin anew in learning about each person or situation we encounter. For example, preschool children readily use "boy" and "girl" as categories for people; they apply what they know about these categories to new boys and girls whom they encounter. In one investigation, children were shown pictures of three children like the example in Figure 8.2. They were given information about the two children at the top, such as "This boy has little seeds inside; this girl has little eggs inside." Then they were told, "This [the figure at the bottom] is a boy. Does he have little eggs or little seeds inside?" Even though the bottom figure looked more like a girl than a boy, the children used the symbolic concept of "boy" to infer the correct answer (Gelman, Collman, & Maccoby, 1986).

How can we tell whether children are using images or symbolic concepts to represent information? One technique that is often used by information-processing psychologists is to test *how long* it takes to process information. For example, children and adults were told to think about different animals such as cats or birds. Sometimes they were instructed to use imagery—to visualize the animal; at other times they were told not to use imagery. Then they were asked about a small part of an animal; for example, "Does a cat have claws?" Stop for a moment to consider how you would answer this question if you visualized a real cat or if you did not. With a mental image, you must scan the picture for the answer. Without imagery, you rely on your symbolic knowledge about cats and birds, so you can answer more quickly. In fact, children and adults took longer to answer such questions when they were instructed to use images than when they were not (Kosslyn, 1980).

FIGURE 8.2   Pictures of boys and girls used to test children's ability to use concepts such as "girl" or "boy" to make inferences about individual girls and boys. (Adapted from S. Gelman, P. Collman, & E. E. Maccoby. Inferring properties from categories versus inferring categories from properties: The case of gender. *Child Development*, 1986, 57, 398. By permission.)

As they grow older, children's symbolic concepts change in three respects. First, the dimensions that define the concept come to match those that most adults agree are critical. To a 2-year-old, the concept "dog" may stand for a set of stuffed animals he owns. By 5 years of age, most children understand that the concept "dog" refers to animals that live on farms, in houses, or in apartments, have certain sizes and shapes, and make barking sounds.

Second, symbolic concepts become more readily available for use in thought. For example, a 3-year-old's concept of "hour" or "day" is vague, so she does not have a sense of how long she will have to wait when her mother says she will be back in an hour. Older children are better able to think about units of time.

Third, children become better able to describe their symbolic concepts in words. A 4-year-old cannot say very much about his understanding of the concept "love," although he knows that it has to do with a close relationship between two people. A 15-year-old can write a 1000-word essay on love because the attributes of love have become linked to language and differentiated from similar concepts like attraction, friendship, and loyalty.

Concepts do not remain static; they are dynamic and constantly changing. Children continually transform their conceptual knowledge and, without conscious effort, detect dimensions shared by two ideas that were originally separate and unrelated. An example appears in a psychologist's diary recording her daughter's speech. At 2 years of age, the girl used the words *put* and *give* correctly. A year later, she began to make occasional errors in which *put* was used when *give* was proper and vice versa. She said, "You put me bread and butter" and "Give some ice in here." It seemed that the two words became closer in meaning and that as a result of recognizing this shared dimension the child began to make substitution errors. It is unlikely that she was taught the shared dimension or was even conscious of it. Rather, she detected it unconsciously as her mind continually worked on its knowledge base (Bowerman, 1978).

PROPOSITIONS.   When two or more concepts are related to one another, a **proposition** is constructed. "Cats are mammals" is a proposition. Rules like "The speed of a car is found by dividing the distance traveled by the time" are propositions. As children grow older, they become able to perform increasingly complex cognitive manipulations on propositions; they also become able to coordinate two or more propositions while solving a problem.

Robert Siegler (1983) has analyzed in detail the age changes in the rules children use to make judgments about problems in which two dimensions must be considered. One example is a task known as the balance beam, illustrated in Figure 8.3. The examiner places individual weights on one peg on each side of the fulcrum and asks the child to predict whether the beam will tip to the right, tip to the left, or remain balanced when its ends are released. Before reading on, stop for a moment to see whether you know the rule that applies to this "teetertotter" task.

Siegler (1983) identified a developmental sequence consisting of four types of rules. Rule 1, which is characteristic of 5- or 6-year-olds, is to use only one dimension, usually weight. Children predict that the side with more weights will tip down; if the number of weights is equal, they predict that the beam will balance. Rule 2,

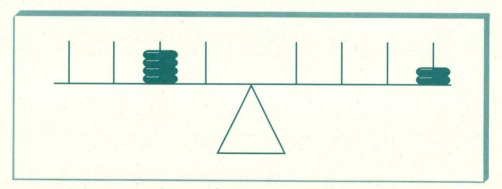

FIGURE 8.3 An illustration of the balance beam used to measure children's use of rules. At the most mature level, children must consider both the distance from the fulcrum and the number of weights on a peg to decide whether the scale will tip to the left, tip to the right, or remain balanced.

which is characteristic of slightly older children, is to use a second dimension, distance, but only when the number of weights is equal. If the number of weights is the same, the children predict that the side with weights that are more distant from the fulcrum will tip down. If the weights are unequal, they predict that the side with more weights will tip down regardless of distance.

Rule 3 is a transition in which children recognize that the earlier simple rules do not work on some problems, but they do not know the correct rule, so they guess. The final level, rule 4, involves knowing that one multiplies the number of weights by the distance on each side to predict which way the beam will tip. Similar developmental sequences have been described for other tasks involving the relationships between two dimensions. For instance, distance is a product of time and speed; area is a product of length and width.

COMPARISON TO PIAGET.   The four types of cognitive units just discussed are similar in some ways to Piaget's organizational structures. Schemata and images, like Piaget's schemes, represent the physical properties of objects fairly faithfully. Symbolic concepts, like Piaget's hierarchical classes, represent abstract categorical groupings. Propositions are similar in some ways to Piaget's operations because they represent relationships among objects. However, Piaget's operations are also processes—mental actions on information. We turn now to the cognitive processes described by information-processing psychologists.

Cognitive Processes

Cognitive *units* are the building blocks of cognition. Cognitive *processes* describe how those blocks are created, manipulated, and transformed. Figure 8.4 shows one way to conceptualize some cognitive processes and their relationships to one another. You may recognize the similarity of this diagram to the flowcharts used in computer programming. Obviously, such diagrams do not represent the brain in any physiological or anatomical sense, but they do show how various functions are interrelated.

The processes shown in Figure 8.4 may be summarized as follows: Environmental events impinge on the sensory register, but only to the extent that they receive attention. Sensations are transformed by perception and enter working memory (sometimes called short-term memory). Working memory has a limited capacity—it is what you can hold in conscious or active thought at any one time. Long-term or permanent memory includes knowledge and skills that have been accumulated over much of an individual's lifetime. Information is centrally processed using schemata, concepts, or other cognitive units. Cognitive processes control the flow of information, and they structure and transform information. In the rest of this section we will discuss each of these processes in more detail.

PERCEPTION.   **Perception** can be defined as the detection, recognition, and interpretation of sensory stimuli. A child looks out the window and sees a pattern of light, dark, and colors. From this mosaic of sensation the child extracts or constructs information; the pattern is perceived as trees, cars, and people. One way to appreciate the difference between raw sensation and perception is to compare a

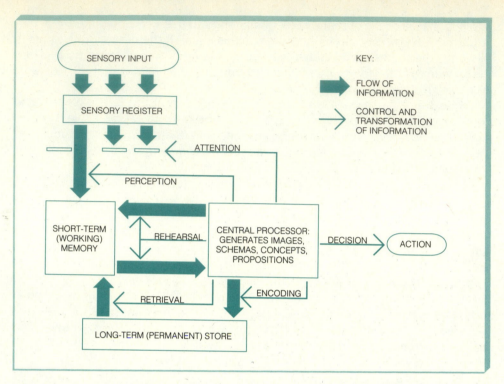

FIGURE 8.4   Some cognitive processes and their relationships to one another. Synthesis of several information-processing models. (Courtesy of John C. Wright, University of Kansas.)

scene in a meadow as registered by a camera and the same scene as registered by a person. The camera records all the colors, shadows, and lines in one plane; the person organizes the scene, often selecting some aspects and ignoring others. The person may concentrate on the delicate dogwood blossoms, seeing the dark evergreens as background. Or consider wearing a hearing aid that amplifies all sounds equally. People who use such devices often complain that they cannot "hear," even though they are receiving plenty of sound, because they are inundated with background noise.

Growing children learn to focus on the most informative aspects of objects and scenes and to ignore uninformative aspects. They learn, for example, to fix their attention on their mother's eyes and voice in order to detect her mood. Or they search for the presence of a plus or minus sign beside a row of numbers to decide whether they should add or subtract them.

The specific dimensions used to distinguish one event from another depend on the question the perceiver is trying to answer and the expectations or mental set he or she has developed for a particular situation. A boy walking in a forest who sees a moving object wonders whether it is a bear or a person and searches for a critical feature, such as clothing or fur. But when seeing a moving object in a game of hide and seek, the boy will search for cues about who the person is (e.g., hair color or height) and the direction in which the person is going. The specific problem that the child is trying to solve generates a specific mental set, which in turn sensitizes the child to certain dimensions.

The role of selection and mental set in perception is exemplified in a procedure used by neurologists that is called the face-hands test. The child, whose eyes are closed, is touched simultaneously on one cheek and on the opposite hand. The examiner asks the child to indicate where he or she was touched. Typically, children under 6 years of age report that they were touched on the face and do not mention the hand. Some neurologists have concluded that this failure indicates an immaturity on the central nervous system that causes sensations from the face to block sensations from the hand. In fact, young children's failure to mention the hand is due to a mental set that leads them to expect that they will be touched in only one place. If the examiner says, "Sometimes I'm going to touch you only on the cheek, sometimes I'm going to touch you only on the hand, and sometimes I'm going to try to fool you and touch you in two places," young children respond accurately to being touched in two places simultaneously.

As we mentioned in Chapter 3, people not only select elements of incoming sensation but also relate what they are perceiving to what they perceived a moment ago and to what may come next. Thus, a child who sees a dog run behind a fence will watch the other end of the fence to see the dog emerge. Most basic perceptual competences are complete by the end of infancy. Therefore, many of the changes that occur throughout childhood are largely changes in attentional patterns.

ATTENTION.   We frequently hear instructions like "Turn your attention to the picture on the south wall" or "Jeremy, pay attention to what I'm telling you." The notion of attention is implicit when we talk about perception. **Attention** acts as a filter or gatekeeper—we selectively orient our perceptual activity toward certain inputs and ignore other inputs. However, attention involves more than simply pointing one's eyes at a particular object; it is a central cognitive process through which information is admitted or focused upon for further processing. Attention often shifts quickly from one input to another, but the longer one attends to one thing, the more likely one is to continue attending. This phenomenon, called *attentional inertia*, is discussed in Box 8.1.

Imagine a 5-year-old attending a three-ring circus for the first time. The multitude of colorful costumes, circus acts, music, clowns, and popcorn sellers is overwhelming. The child's attention is likely to shift quickly from one thing to another in an unsystematic way. She looks at a clown in front of her until she is attracted by a loud fanfare introducing the lion act in the center ring; then she notices people on the high trapezes and looks at them. If the circus comes to town every year, by the time our child is 10 she'll be much more familiar with the circus and will guide her attention more planfully. She will watch for the high-wire act because she especially likes it; she'll ignore the dogs riding bareback but attend quickly when the dancing bears appear.

This example illustrates several developmental changes. First, children become better able to *control* the deployment of attention—to "decide" what they will and will not attend to. Second, children's attentional patterns become more *adaptive* to the situation; for instance, they can scan several areas broadly if that is called

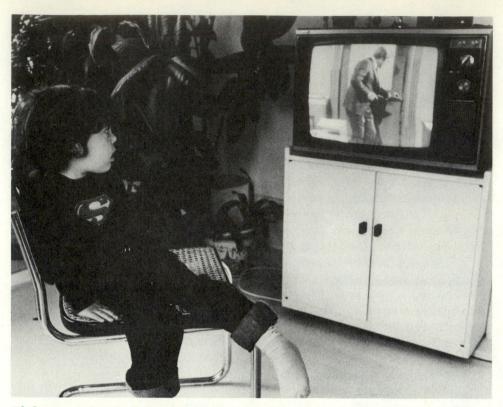

The longer a person attends to one thing, such as a television program, the more likely he or she is to continue attending to it.

for, or they can focus narrowly if that is appropriate. Third, children become more *planful*. Rather than simply selecting from what is available, they anticipate what they want to see or hear and search accordingly. Fourth, children become increasingly able to extend their attention, sometimes dividing it among different activities over time. For example, they might attend sporadically to a baseball game on television while playing a game of Monopoly.

   The circus example illustrates another important point: When we use the term *developmental change*, we do not mean just maturational changes that occur with age. We also refer to changes that occur over time as a result of experience. Part of the reason the 10-year-old can control her attention adaptively and planfully at the circus is because she has seen it before. Another 10-year-old attending her first circus would probably show more attentional control than the 5-year-old but less than the experienced 10-year-old.

MEMORY.   Memory is in some ways the core of cognition. Without memory, cognition would have little meaning because none of its products would be lasting. Psychologists distinguish among three types of memory: sensory, short-term, and long-term (see Figure. 8.4).

BOX 8.1

Attentional Inertia

For the last 15 minutes Colin has been watching a television program without looking away from the set. In another room his brother Gus has been watching a program for 30 seconds. Which of them is most likely to still be looking 1 minute from now? The correct answer is Colin.

These boys' TV-watching patterns illustrate a phenomenon called *attentional inertia*. It can be described in simple terms as follows: "The longer a viewer continuously maintains an episode of visual attention, the more likely it becomes that he or she will continue to do so" (Anderson, D. R., Choi, & Lorch, 1987, p. 798).

Why should attentional inertia occur? Anderson and his associates propose that it indicates a progressive engagement of attention over time. As you look at something longer and longer, you become more engrossed in it. In fact, the researchers found that children are less easily distracted when they have been looking for a long time than when they have been looking for just a few seconds. Children who have been looking for a long time are also less likely to look away during scene or commercial breaks. Attentional inertia appears to carry them across a break in content that might otherwise cause them to look away.

Attentional inertia occurs in activities other than TV viewing. When children look away from the television screen and play with toys, they become progressively more involved in playing with the toys and less likely to look back at the television set.

Attentional inertia is a good illustration of a psychological phenomenon that goes beyond common sense. Most people would probably guess that people will become increasingly bored and subject to distraction the longer they have been looking at a single stimulus. It is satisfying to find that commonsense predictions are not always right. Our challenge is to explain why.

Sensory memory (or the sensory register) is very brief. If a picture or sound is not stored or in some way related to existing knowledge within about 1 second, it vanishes. Thus, as you drive down a highway the trees along the road are registered in your sensory memory but are not retained unless you think about them or process them in some way.

Short-term memory, sometimes called *working memory*, holds information for a maximum of about 30 seconds. If you look up a phone number, for example, you will remember it for about 30 seconds unless you repeat it to yourself or otherwise make an effort to retain it.

Long-term memory, sometimes call *permanent memory*, refers to knowledge that is potentially available for a long time, perhaps forever. Information is stored in long-term memory by being integrated with already existing knowledge—for instance, with existing schemata, images, or concepts.

Having information in memory is not sufficient to make it usable; the information must be organized if it is to be accessible. Perhaps this is one reason why most people recall little from their early years. Organization occurs when information is transferred from working memory to long-term memory through the process of *encoding*, in which the information is interpreted with available schemata and concepts. For example, suppose Sara is asked to learn the opinions about labor unions held by all the Presidents of the United States in the twentieth century. Rather than memorizing all of them separately, she clusters them as Democrats or Republicans because she knows that Democrats are generally more favorable toward unions than Republicans are.

Organization also influences the process of *retrieval*, or recovering information from memory. If Sara is later asked to recall the opinions about labor unions held by Franklin Roosevelt, Dwight Eisenhower, John Kennedy, and Richard Nixon, she will be able to retrieve that information by remembering which political party each President belonged to.

Each time you transfer information from long-term memory to working memory, you rehearse, interpret, elaborate, and recode it. This is one reason why you are more likely to remember information that has been frequently and extensively rehearsed—you have integrated it into your system of schemata and concepts in more ways, so there are many ways to retrieve it.

Permanent memory is a little like a giant filing cabinet. When you put an item in, you file it under certain headings (encoding). When you want to find information in the cabinet, you need to know which headings to look under (retrieval). When you rehearse or elaborate the information, you refile it with cross-references. The more organized your filing system and the better your system of cross-referencing, the more likely you are to find information when you want it. Your existing cognitive units at any one time constitute your filing system.

Recognition and Recall.   It may now be apparent why recognition is usually better than recall. It is easier to recognize a person's name than to remember it. In a recognition test people are shown a set of pictures or objects, some of which they have seen before, and asked to identify the ones they have seen. Even very young children perform well on recognition tasks. For example, 4-year-old children were shown 60 pictures cut from magazines. They looked at each picture for about 2 seconds. The next day they were shown 120 pictures—the 60 they had seen the previous day and 60 new ones—and asked to point to the ones they had seen before. The children were correct an average of 80 percent of the time. Recognition tasks like this one provide cues for retrieval. In effect, the child is asked to compare each picture with a specific schema or concept in long-term memory.

In studies of recall, children are asked to describe or reproduce information—for example, "Tell me what pictures you saw yesterday." In this task children must select the appropriate cues for retrieval. Moreover, they must be able to communicate what they remember, usually in words. It is more difficult to describe or draw a picture to show what you remember than it is to point at one.

Developmental Changes in Memory.   Recogition is better than recall at all ages, but the difference is greatest for young children. Another way of stating the same thing is to say that recall improves with age more than recognition does. A 10-year-old who has seen 12 pictures can usually recall about 8 of them and recognize all 12. A 4-year-old also recognizes all 12 pictures but recalls only 2 or 3. Memory abilities improve with age partly because the knowledge base used to encode and retrieve information improves. Children acquire more schemata and general knowledge, and they have more complex and organized concepts.

A second change that occurs with age is an improvement in the speed and capacity of working memory. As children grow older, they can search their memory for information more quickly. For example, in one experiment people from 8 to 21 years of age were shown series of digits (e.g., 4, 7, 3, 1, 8) on a computer screen for 2 seconds; then they were shown one digit (e.g., 5) and told to decide whether it was part of the set they had just seen. This task requires people to search their memories of the set they just saw. Although subjects of all ages could perform the task, there was a regular increase with age in the *speed* of performance. In fact, similar changes in speed occur for many cognitive tasks (Kail, 1988).

Pascual-Leone (1970) proposed that there is also an increase in the amount of information that can be held in working memory or what he calls M space. One can regard M space as the number of discrete cognitive units (schemata, concepts, images) that can be operated upon in working memory simultaneously. A 3-year-old can deal with one unit of information; a 15-year-old can deal with seven units. For example, Pascual-Leone asked children of different ages to learn different motor responses to different visual stimuli. The children had to clap their hands when they saw the color red, but they were to open their mouths when they saw a large cup. Once the children had learned these simple associations, they were presented with two or more visual stimuli simultaneously and asked to respond (a variation on the old game of rub your stomach and pat your head). The number of correct responses performed simultaneously increased with age among preschool and school-age children, confirming the idea that M space increases with development.

Still another developmental change in memory is selectivity. With age, children become more skilled at selecting important items to remember, that is, at distinguishing central from incidental information. Children (and even some college students) sometimes study inefficiently because they do not actively distinguish important material from less important information. For example, when given an extra period to study, a majority of children in grades 5, 6, and 7 merely reread their books. A minority underlined some passages or took notes. Not only did they select important information for encoding, but they actively restructured and grouped the information in their own ways. Not surprisingly, those children performed better on a subsequent test (A. W. Brown, Bransford, Ferrara, & Campione, 1983).

Young children *can* select central information for recall when the material is well within their cognitive capacities. For example, 4-, 5-, and 6-year-old children

saw story segments from *Sesame Street*, each of which was 1 to 3 minutes long. All of the children recalled parts of the segments that were important to the theme or plot better than parts that were incidental (Lorch, Bellack, & Augsbach, 1987).

The limitations on young children's memory capabilities make it difficult for adults to evaluate children's recollections of events. For example, when a 4-year-old tells her father that Steven was mean to her today, her father may not be sure how to interpret her report. Questions about the reliability of children's memories are especially critical when they report that adults have abused them violently. These questions are discussed in Box 8.2.

Memory Strategies.   Suppose a preschool teacher says to her class of 4-year-olds, "I'm going to read you a story. I want you to listen very carefully because I'm going to ask you questions about it." In all likelihood those children will not remember any more than a group of children who hear the story without instructions to remember. By the age of 8 or 10, however, performance improves considerably if children are told to try to remember. One reason seems to be that the older children have learned *strategies* for remembering.

With age, children acquire increasingly efficient strategies for encoding, rehearsal, and retrieval. When tasks are cleverly designed, we can observe children's strategies without having to rely on their verbal skills to explain them. For example, children were shown a board with two rows of six doors on it (see Figure 8.5). Half of the doors had cages on them and covered drawings of animals; the other half had houses on them and covered pictures of household objects. The children were given two different tasks: (1) to decide whether the pictures in the top row were the same as or different from those in the bottom row or (2) to remember all the animals (or household objects). Before each trial they were told to open the doors one at a time and study the pictures. The most efficient strategy for the same-different judgment is to open a door in the top row and then a door below it, comparing

BOX 8.2

Children's Eyewitness Testimony

In Miami, Florida a few years ago, a woman and her husband were accused of sexually abusing preschool children in a day care center they operated in their home. After several parents noticed that their children acted oddly when they came home, one parent asked law enforcement authorities to conduct an investigation. The children were interviewed repeatedly by two developmental psychologists, who often used leading questions. Although the children initially denied that they had engaged in any sexual activity, they eventually began to recount sexual acts and demonstrate them with anatomically correct dolls. Experts for the defense argued that the children's testimony was unreliable because the children had not spontaneously described sexual abuse. They had only agreed to describe it after they had been asked leading questions.

How accurate are children's memories for events like child abuse? Are children reliable witnesses? Jurors do not think so. They are likely to discount the testimony of a child if it contains inconsistencies, even though they will accept similarly inconsistent testimony by an adult.

Young children produce less information through spontaneous recall than adults do. Therefore, they require more probing questions, often raising the possibility that the questioner may influence the child's report. However, when young children respond to questions they are about as likely to be accurate as older children and adults. In fact, in one study 6-year-old children gave fewer incorrect responses than adults did (Goodman, Aman, & Hirschman, 1987).

When interviewers ask probing questions, they may suggest things that did not happen. Do children later incorporate such suggestions into their memories of the event? Not usually. Preschool children are suggestible in the sense that they will agree with an adult's suggestion that *x* or *y* happened. However, they do not usually include the suggestion in later reports.

Critics have been concerned that traumatic stress could affect children's memories. Some experiments have tested children after they have experienced a mild stress, such as going to the dentist or being inoculated. The children's memories of these stressful events were no less accurate than their memories of nonstressful events.

Some developmental psychologists have suggested using interviewing techniques designed for young children. First, reconstruction of events using props such as dolls and furniture helps children provide accurate information. Second, when children are reporting repeated events, as is often the case with child abuse, they may have formed scripts for those events. Their memory for scripts is sometimes more accurate than their memory for specific events. Questions such as "What happens when Daddy puts you to bed?" may be better than "What did Daddy do last Tuesday?" Finally, sample tasks help children answer questions accurately. For example, if the child is asked to identify an adult molester from a photo lineup, she might first be given practice on the photo identification task by being asked to identify the examiner's picture (King & Yuille, 1987).

The children in Miami were proved correct when their woman babysitter confessed, corroborating their testimony, but not all trials have such a clear resolution. Often children are the only eyewitnesses. In many cases they are accurate witnesses whose testimony should not be dismissed (from Ceci, Toglia, & Ross, 1987).

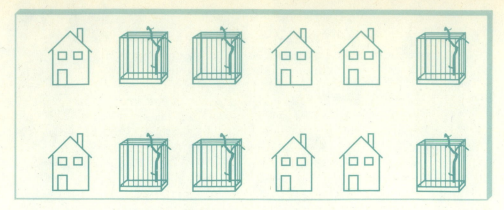

FIGURE 8.5   A test of children's memory strategies. Children could open doors that concealed animals (cage on door) or household objects (house on door). The doors they chose to open and the order in which they opened them were different when the task was to decide whether the top and bottom rows were identical than when the task was to memorize all the household items. (Based on P. H. Miller, V. F. Haynes, D. DeMarie-Dreblow, & J. Woody-Ramsey. Children's strategies for gathering information in three tasks. *Child Development*, 1986, 57, 1429–1439.)

pairs of pictures. For the recall task, it is more efficient to open only the doors for the category you need to remember. Eight- and 10-year-old children used these different strategies more consistently than 6-year-olds did. The younger children tended to open all the doors or to open them in an unsystematic order (Miller, P. H., Haynes, DeMarie-Dreblow, & Woody-Ramsey, 1986).

Strategies for retrieval allow a child to search for something systematically. A 12-year-old who cannot find his jacket will think systematically about where he last had the jacket and then proceed through the places he has been since then in a fairly systematic fashion. A 6-year-old will try to think about where the jacket is without making a systematic search of her memory.

INFERENCE.   Inference is the process by which children use their cognitive structures to go beyond what is immediately observable and generate expectations about what may occur in the future or hypotheses about past events and causal relations. Three-year-old Mark asked his mother, "Where does the sun go when it goes into the ground at night?" He had already learned that all objects that move have a resting place, permanent or temporary. Because the sun appeared to be an object that moves, he inferred that it, too, must come to rest (Kagan, 1984). Inferences are based on a perceived similarity between two events and on existing concepts. Mark placed the sun in a category, "things that move," because it was similar to other objects in that category.

Young children make simple inferences readily, often by using schemata for everyday events. In one study, 4-year-olds were shown short animated films containing cuts from one action to another. For instance, a doll was shown getting out of bed in pajamas; the film then cut to a scene showing the doll in play clothes eating breakfast. The children were given similar dolls and props and asked to reenact the story they had just seen. They regularly filled in the gap by showing the doll changing its clothes and walking down the stairs (R. Smith, Anderson, & Fischer, 1985). A script for "getting up in the morning" could easily be used to fill the gaps in the film.

Young children can also make inferences on the basis of logical rules, though that ability improves considerably after age 6. Take the following example: Clara (age 7) and her parents go to a restaurant with Aunt Vera. Aunt Vera feels cold in the air-conditioned restaurant and asks Clara to get a sweater from her blue car. If there is only one blue car in the parking lot, Clara has no difficulty inferring that it is Aunt Vera's. But if she sees three blue cars she cannot decide which is the right car, and she goes back to ask for more information. A younger child might choose one of the blue cars without realizing that she had insufficient information. By the age of 6 children can make inferences of this type and can tell when they need more information (Fabricius, Sophian, & Wellman, 1987).

PROBLEM SOLVING.   Problem solving occurs when children figure out how to use available materials or resources to achieve a goal. For example, children of different ages were given a tall cylinder containing a small amount of water with a bead floating on the surface. Beside the cylinder was a tray containing scissors, string, gum, tongs, a block, and a glass of water. The children were told to try to get the bead out of the cylinder without turning it over, but the tongs and the string were too short to reach the bead. What is the solution? You can fill the cylinder with the water in the glass to raise the level of the floating bead. Very few first-graders solved the problem.

One important feature of this problem is that it requires a person to go beyond the obvious first solution. Tongs and string with gum are obvious tools for retrieving an object. Most people try them first. With age, young children become better able to think of unusual ways of using materials when the obvious ways do not work.

Experience as well as age contributes to problem-solving ability. For instance, children were presented with a problem that involved reaching a lure. To solve the problem, they had to clamp two long sticks together. Children who had an opportunity to play with the materials before being given the problem solved it better than those who had no past experience with the materials. Careful observation of their spontaneous play showed that some children made constructions with large numbers of sticks and connectors; when they were given the goal of reaching the lure, the solution was readily available to them (Cheyne & Rubin, 1983).

Metacognition

Suppose Joshua and Brian are both going to a new school for the first time. As Joshua's father drives him to school, he says, "Try to remember the names of all the kids in your class so you can tell me about them after school." Brian's father says "Be good," but he does not mention remembering names. Which child will recall more names? If the children are younger than about 7 or 8, they will probably remember about the same number of names. If they are 11 or 12, Joshua will probably recall more names.

Both maturation and experience contributed to these children's ability to build and operate a small business enterprise.

When children respond to instructions to remember, they are using **metacognition**; that is, they are using knowledge about their own cognitive processes, and they are using executive processes to control their cognitive activities.

KNOWLEDGE ABOUT COGNITION.   With development, children gradually acquire knowledge about human cognitive processes. Flavell and his associates (1985) demonstrated children's knowledge about memory (**metamemory**). For example, children were asked who would learn the names of all the birds in their city faster—a boy who had learned them last year and then forgotten them, or a boy who had never learned them. By the third grade, the children knew that relearning was likely to be faster than new learning. In another study, children were asked, "If you wanted to phone your friend and someone told you the phone number, would it make any difference if you called right away after you head the number or if you got a drink of water first?" Fifth-graders were aware that they would remember the phone number for only a brief time, but kindergarteners were not.

One can also have metacognitive knowledge about people, tasks, and strategies (Flavell, 1985). Knowledge about people includes accurate assessment of one's own cognitive abilities in relation to particular tasks. As children grow older they gain a more accurate picture of their own abilities, and they become more accurate in predicting individual differences among other people. They also know that some tasks are more difficult than others (e.g., that recognition is easier than recall). By late childhood children can articulate strategies for remembering. When asked how they would go about remembering a name or a phone number, they may suggest rehearsal, writing it on your sleeve, associating it with something familiar, and other such strategies.

In general, children gain competence in cognitive processes earlier than they gain metacognitive knowledge about those processes. To put it more simply, children can do something before they can explain it. For example, 4- and 6-year-olds sat with an adult, Angelika, for the following task: The children and Angelika were shown a bowl of green balls; then the bowl was placed behind a screen and the tester told them that he was putting one ball from the bowl in a bag. What color is the ball in the bag? The children could make the inference that the ball was green even when they had not seen it moved from bowl to bag, but the 4-year-olds often argued that Angelika did not know its color because she had not seen the ball placed in the bag. The children's metacognitive knowledge about how other people draw inferences was less advanced than their own ability to infer (Sodian & Wimmer, 1987).

EXECUTIVE PROCESSES.   Metacognition also refers to children's ability to regulate their own cognitive processes—to plan, search, monitor, and control their attention, memory, and other cognitive processes. These abilities are sometimes called **executive processes** to indicate that they are analogous to the activities of an executive in an organization, who directs and plans the activities of other employees.

A frequently used executive process is *planning*. Although preschool children can use plans to guide their behavior, older children are more likely to plan activities prior to carrying them out. Two 6-year-olds setting up a lemonade stand will go back and forth to the house, gradually collecting what they need. Two 12-year-olds can think ahead to anticipate what they will need for a car wash to raise money for their Girl Scout troop.

The first step in planning is *formulating the problem*. Asking the right question is one of the most important steps in this process. There is a story, which may or may not be true, about the people gathered around the famous poet Gertrude Stein as she lay on her deathbed. Someone asked her, "You wrote of the mysteries of life. Tell us before you go, what is the answer?" She replied, "What is the question?"

As children grow older, they become increasingly able to define a problem and generate possible solutions. A pair of 4-year-olds trying to build a snow fort may give up when the snow will not pack properly. A pair of 8-year-olds are more likely to identify the problem—snow that is too powdery—and propose possible solutions, such as pouring water on the snow.

Planning enables a child to go about a task systematically, exhausting most of the possible solutions. A child asked to find her lost book bag may go systematically through each room in her house or she may look haphazardly in a few rooms, then return to places she has already looked. With increasing age, the child's search becomes more systematic and thorough.

Another important executive process is *activating cognitive rules and strategies*. Children who know rules and strategies may not always use them when they are needed. We have already pointed out that older children are more likely than younger ones to improve their performance when they are instructed ahead of time to remember what they see and hear. Older children respond to those instructions by activating the strategies they know. For example, an adult who is attending a party as part of a job interview will probably try to remember everyone's name by rehearsing (e.g., calling each person by name a few times), creating associations (e.g., this woman is named Karen and looks like your sister Sharon), and other strategies.

Monitoring learning is a frequently used executive process. Consider Stacey, an eighth-grader, who is preparing for a geography test by reading a chapter in her social studies book. After reading each section she tests herself by closing her eyes and trying to remember or by trying to answer the review questions at the end of the chapter. When she does not remember some information, she returns to that section and reviews it, possibly using new strategies to learn the information. If she does not understand some of the vocabulary, she looks it up in the glossary. All of these behaviors are examples of monitoring learning—keeping track of one's own performance and adjusting one's learning strategies accordingly.

In the preschool and early school years, children do not monitor their performance well, partly because they sometimes do not realize what is required for good performance. For example, 4-, 6-, 8-, and 10-year-olds played a game in which they sat opposite an adult with a divider between them. The child held a card with four objects pictured on it; the adult described one of those objects. In some cases the descriptions did not give enough information to enable the child to decide which object was being described. For instance, the adult said that the object was a rabbit, but there were two rabbits among the child's choices. Older children detected the inadequate messages more often, asking questions to help determine which choice was correct. Younger children made choices apparently without realizing that they did not have enough information. Subsequent research demonstrated, however, that younger children could be trained to detect inadequate messages and to ask for more information—another example in which experience affected an ability that also changes with age (Patterson, C. J., Massad, & Cosgrove, 1978).

Ability to control distraction and anxiety also increases with age. A young child doing a puzzle may be distracted when someone comes into the room and speaks to her. If the puzzle is difficult, she may become upset and give up. As children grow older, they learn to screen out distraction and (sometimes) to control their anxious reactions when they begin to fail. Young children can, however, be taught to use plans and strategies to resist distraction. For example, in a series of studies children were given a routine task to complete. As they worked, a clown in a box did tricks and talked. Children who were previously trained in ways to resist distraction were better able to stick to their task than those who had no such instruction (Mischel & Patterson, 1978).

As children grow older, they not only monitor the learning process but become more likely to determine when they have reached a solution or learned what they set out to learn; that is, they *evaluate the product*. They have an increasing desire to achieve an "elegant solution." The Matching Familiar Figures test illustrates this desire. Children are shown a picture (the standard) and told to select one exactly like it from an array of six like the ones shown in Figure 8.6. All six are quite similar, but only one is exactly like the standard. With age, children make fewer errors, often taking more time to scan the array and make sure they have made the correct choice. It appears that older children evaluate a solution more carefully before settling on it.

HOW USEFUL IS METACOGNITION?   The notion of metacognition has an immediate appeal because it seems to describe some of the higher-order cognitive

FIGURE 8.6   Items from the Matching Familiar Figures test.

processes that are uniquely human. But after the first blush of enthusiasm you may ask, as many psychologists do, whether it is a useful notion. In many respects it is. Understanding what children know about knowing is of considerable interest in its own right. And many of the executive processes are central to advanced cognitive processing.

There are, however, two criticisms that merit some attention. First, although it is clear that there are changes with age in children's knowledge about cognition, it is less clear that such knowledge is critical for advanced cognitive processing. For example, there are only moderate correlations between children's knowledge about memory and their performance on memory tasks (Brown et al., 1983). Second, many of the executive processes sound much like the "ordinary" cognitive processes, such as strategies and problem solving, described earlier. It is important to identify and study such processes, but it is not always apparent how to decide whether a process is "meta" or "executive."

A Critique of the Information-processing Approach

Psychologists working within the general framework of information processing have generated a great deal of knowledge about how children's cognitive structures and processes work. Because they are not guided by one clear-cut theory, their explanations are not subject to disproof in the same sense that learning theory and Piagetian theory are. A few reservations are in order, however. There is some danger that models that are based on computer terminology and look like flowcharts will be interpreted at a more concrete level than they deserve to be. The boxes in Figure 8.4 are convenient ways of summarizing psychological processes; they should not be interpreted as models of the brain. Arrows from one box to another suggest one-way processes; we know, however, that most human thought involves complex interactions among the structures and processes shown. Finally, these models have been criticized for being static, that is, for failing to describe how changes in cognitive units and processes occur. Although developmental change is often described, the models tell us little about how it comes about.

WHAT CHANGES WITH AGE?

Despite their different theoretical assumptions and methods, the Piagetian and information-processing approaches have converged in the past several years. Researchers from both groups have attempted to learn how children develop conceptual knowledge in a wide variety of content domains. One such domain, children's concepts about the origin of babies, is described in Box 8.3.

There is some consensus about what cognitive processes are important and what changes occur as a result of development. The following list is a partial summary of those changes. As you read it, keep in mind that changes may result from maturation, experience, or some combination of both.

We will illustrate the list by discussing why 14-year-old Leslie might be able to design and build a backyard playhouse while 6-year-old Chris probably could not do so.

BOX 8.3

Children's Concepts About Where Babies Come From

Both Piagetian and information-processing theorists agree that children actively construct their conceptual knowledge base. They interpret what they are told and what they observe within the framework of their existing knowledge and skills. This constructive quality of children's thought is illustrated by age changes in concepts about where babies come from.

Anne Bernstein and Philip Cowan (1981) interviewed children at three age levels (3-4, 7-8, and 11-12), asking them questions like "How do people get babies?" They identified six levels of thinking. At level 1, "The Geographers," children replied with locations: "You go to the baby store and buy one" (p. 14). At level 2, "The Manufacturers," children recognized that babies arise from some cause, but they interpreted the process according to events in their own experience: "You just make the baby first. You put some eyes on it. You put the head on, and hair, some hair all curls. . . . Well, they get it, and they put it in the tummy and then it goes quickly out" (p. 14). Most preschool children responded at one of these two levels.

At level 3, "In Transition," children explained procreation with processes that are technically feasible, but they were sometimes misled by common metaphors, such as planting a seed. For example: "Like a flower, I think, except you don't need dirt" (p. 15). At this level children understood that procreation results from a social relationship between a man and a woman and that a sperm and an egg are brought together by sexual intercourse. At level 4, "Reporters," children described the processes of conception without recourse to notions of mechanics or manufacturing, but they lacked the knowledge that the baby results from a union of genetic materials. When asked why the seed and egg have to come together, one girl replied: "Or else the baby, the egg won't really get hatched very well. The seed makes the egg grow" (p. 16).

At level 5, "Theoreticians," children speculated on the processes involved, but they assumed that the baby is preformed in either the sperm or the egg. "I guess the egg just has sort of an undeveloped embryo and when the sperm enters it, it makes it come to life" (p. 16). Level 6, "Putting It All Together," was reached by only some of the 11- and 12-year-olds. They understood that the embryo is a result of the genetic combination of an egg and a sperm.

Because children assimilate this information according to their existing levels of understanding and processing capabilities, they go through these stages even when parents attempt to provide accurate information about conception and birth early in life. Misconceptions can be increased, however, by indirect means of teaching children about sex and procreation. Books often attempt to teach about procreation by referring to other animals. When asked how a woman would get a baby to grow in her tummy, a child answered, "Get a duck. 'Cause one day I saw a book about them, and they just get a duck or a goose and they get a little more growed and then they turn into a baby" (p. 24).

Because children's concepts of procreation change with cognitive development, it is not enough to teach them once. For example, one 10-year-old girl showed an adult friend of her mother a "Visible Woman" doll that contained separable parts of the human anatomy, asking many questions about sex and reproduction. Upon hearing about her questions, her mother said, "She already knows that. I've told her all those things." The mother may have told her "those things," but she didn't "know" them completely. Children cycle back to questions on a subject as their conceptual abilities improve, often reaching new levels of understanding through new sets of questions.

KNOWLEDGE BASE   (factual content and organization). Leslie has learned about building materials and principles from her parents and from a course, "World of Construction," that she took in the seventh grade.

ACCESSIBILITY OF SKILLS ACROSS DOMAINS   (ability to apply skills learned in one domain to another). Leslie not only has more advanced math skills than Chris does but is probably better at applying them to a new situation such as figuring out the dimensions needed to build the playhouse.

USE OF TASK-APPROPRIATE STRATEGIES.   Leslie will probably make drawings of the house before beginning to build it; Chris might just begin to nail boards together.

FLEXIBILITY IN APPROACHING TASKS.   If the wood that Leslie planned to use will make the house too heavy, she will try to obtain some other material that is lighter.

SPEED OF INFORMATION PROCESSING.   Leslie can plan, measure, and figure more quickly than Chris can.

CAPACITY TO DEAL WITH LARGE AMOUNTS OF INFORMATION.   Leslie will be able to deal with the designs for several parts of the house, keeping in mind how they will fit together.

ABILITY TO CONSIDER MORE THAN ONE DIMENSION OR FACTOR IN MAKING A JUDGMENT.   Leslie will be able to consider height (tall enough to stand up in), weight (light enough to move), and floor area simultaneously in deciding on the final product.

ABILITY TO COMPREHEND SUCCESSFULLY HIGHER-ORDER RELATION-
SHIPS.   Leslie can consider the length and width of rectangles and then
think of them as units in a three-dimensional structure.

FAITH IN THOUGHT (belief that it is useful to stop and think when having difficulty solving a problem). When the roof will not attach to the house
properly, Leslie sits down to think again about how it was supposed to
work.

DESIRE FOR AN ELEGANT SOLUTION (ability to evaluate an outcome or
product in relation to a standard). When the house is built, Leslie will
judge how well its parts fit together and how suitable it is for playing. She
will be unhappy if it is crooked and pleased if it is straight and tight.

METACOGNITIVE KNOWLEDGE. Leslie can describe how she should go about
figuring out dimensions and remembering to follow the steps in the right
order.

ABILITY TO PLAN. Leslie thinks ahead to the final product, then decides what
intervening steps are needed.

ABILITY TO RESIST DISTRACTION, TO GUIDE ATTENTION AND CONCEN-
TRATION TO ACCOMPLISH A GOAL. When Leslie is working on her playhouse, she ignores the television, her brothers and sisters, and her
mother's demand that she take out the trash.

ABILITY TO BE EXHAUSTIVE AND SYSTEMATIC IN SOLVING PROBLEMS.
Before Leslie begins construction, she double-checks her plans to make
sure she has considered all the parts of the house and that she has all the
materials she needs. (Based on Brown, A. L. et al., 1983; Kagan, 1984;
Sternberg, 1985.)

In sum, cognitive development involves much more than simply accumulating
information about the world. Children develop an extraordinary set of capabilities
that enable them to use and manipulate the information they encounter for many
different purposes. These remarkable accomplishments occur as a result of maturational changes that interact with children's active selection and processing of experience.

SUMMARY

Learning theory, behaviorism, and information-processing approaches are all important strands in cognitive-developmental psychology. In traditional stimulus-
response theory, learning is conceptualized as a set of associations between
stimuli and responses. It takes place through conditioning and through observation of other people's behavior. These fundamental learning principles are applied
in modern behavior analysis, in which reinforcing stimuli are used to increase the
probability of desired behaviors.

Learning theorists are strong environmentalists and view children as passive receivers of environmental inputs. They emphasize gradual and continuous change that is due primarily to accumulated experience. Because stimulus-response theory fails to explain many aspects of children's intellectual development, many psychologists have moved toward an information-processing approach. This perspective assumes an interaction between maturation and experience and views children as active in selecting, constructing, and interpreting the information they receive.

The four basic cognitive units are schemata, images, concepts, and propositions. A *schema* is a composite of the typical and distinctive characteristics of a scene or sequence of events. It preserves the essence of a scene or sequence without requiring the person to remember all the details. An event schema is sometimes referred to as a script. Schemata and scripts help people function efficiently because they make it possible to anticipate and predict.

An *image* is a sensory impression—a picture, sound, or smell—that is re-created mentally. Images are often created from schemata, but images are consciously elaborated.

Symbolic *concepts* represent abstract qualities of objects, events, or ideas. Often they are categories such as shape or color. They increase our ability to understand the world because we can apply conceptual knowledge to new situations. As they grow older, children's symbolic concepts come to match those that most adults agree are critical and become more readily available for use in thought. Children also become better able to describe their symbolic concepts in words.

When two or more concepts are related to one another, a *proposition* is constructed. As children grow older, they become able to perform increasingly complex cognitive manipulations on propositions.

Whereas cognitive units are the building blocks of cognition, cognitive processes describe how those blocks are created, manipulated, and transformed. One such process is *perception*, or the detection, recognition, and interpretation of sensory stimuli. Growing children learn to focus on the most informative aspects of objects and scenes and to ignore uninformative aspects.

Since most basic perceptual competences are complete by the end of infancy, many of the changes that occur throughout childhood are largely changes in attentional patterns. Attention acts as a filter or gatekeeper to orient perceptual activity selectively toward certain inputs. As they grow older, children become better able to control the deployment of attention. In addition, their attentional patterns become more adaptive to the situation and they become more planful and able to extend their attention over time.

Psychologists distinguish among three types of memory. *Sensory memory* lasts less than a second. *Short-term memory* holds information for a maximum of about 30 seconds. *Long-term memory* refers to knowledge that is potentially available for a long time. Information is stored in long-term memory by being integrated with already existing knowledge. Information is transferred from working memory to long-term memory through the process of *encoding*, while the process of *retrieval* recovers information from memory.

Recognition is better than recall at all ages, but recall improves with age more than recognition does. A second change that occurs with age is an improvement in the speed and capacity of working memory. Children also become increasingly skilled at selecting important items to remember. One reason for the improvement in children's memory is that older children have learned strategies for remembering.

Inference is the process of using cognitive structures to go beyond what is immediately observable and generate expectations or hypotheses. Young children can make some inferences on the basis of logical rules, but that ability improves considerably after age 6. Children's problem-solving ability also improves with age and experience.

The term *metacognition* refers to knowledge about one's own cognitive processes. For example, knowledge about memory is termed *metamemory*. One can have metacognitive knowledge about people, tasks, and strategies. In general, children gain competence in cognitive processes earlier than they gain metacognitive knowledge about how those processes work.

Metacognition also refers to *executive processes*—planning, searching, monitoring, and controlling one's own cognitive processes. The most important executive processes are planning, activating cognitive rules and strategies, monitoring learning, controlling distraction and anxiety, and evaluating the product.

REVIEW QUESTIONS

1. What are the basic principles of learning theory?

2. Why have psychologists tended to move away from learning theory toward information-processing approaches?

3. Briefly describe the four basic cognitive units.

4. How do children's symbolic concepts change as they grow older?

5. What is perception? Attention?

6. Distinguish among the three types of memory. How does memory change with age?

7. How do children's abilities to make inferences and solve problems change over time?

8. What is metacognition?

9. Briefly describe the abilities known as executive processes.

10. Summarize the basic changes in cognitive processes that occur as a result of development.

GLOSSARY

behavior analysis   An approach, based on the theory of B. F. Skinner, in which learning is conceptualized as the association of observable events (stimuli) and observable responses.

reinforcing stimulus   An event that increases the probability that a particular behavior will recur.

schema   A composite of the typical and distinctive characteristics of a scene or sequence of events.

image   A picture, sound, smell, or sensory impression that is re-created mentally.

concept   A symbolic representation of a group of objects or events.

category   A symbolic concept that represents the shared abstract qualities of a group of objects.

proposition   A statement that relates two or more concepts to one another.

perception   The detection, recognition, and interpretation of sensory stimuli.

attention   The process of selectively orienting perceptual activity toward certain inputs and ignoring other inputs.

sensory memory   Memory that vanishes within 1 second if it is not stored in short- or long-term memory.

short-term (working) **memory**   Memory that holds information for a maximum of 30 seconds unless an effort is made to retain it.

long-term (permanent) **memory**   Knowledge that is potentially available for a long time, perhaps forever.

inference   The process by which one uses cognitive structures to go beyond what is immediately observable and generate expectations and hypotheses.

metacognition   Knowledge about one's own cognitive processes; includes executive processes.

metamemory   Knowledge about memory.

executive processes   The processes by which one plans, searches, monitors, and controls one's own cognitive processes.

SUGGESTED READINGS

Bryant, J., & Anderson, D. R. (Eds.). (1983). *Children's understanding of television: Research on attention and comprehension.* New York: Academic Press. Contains chapters describing attention and information processing as they apply to children's most frequent pastime: watching television. Can help students understand basic cognitive processes as they operate in an important context.

Ceci, S. J., Toglia, M. P., & Ross, D. F. (Eds.). (1987). *Children's eyewitness memory.* New York: Springer-Verlag. Contains a variety of interesting essays on how children's memory processes operate in important situations, particularly those in which strong emotions may occur.

Collins, W. A. (Ed.). (1984). *Development during middle childhood: The years from six to twelve.* Washington, DC: National Academy Press. Contains chapters that integrate cognitive development with children's experiences in the family, school, and peer group during middle childhood.

Daehler, M. W., & Bukatko, D. (1985). *Cognitive development.* New York: Knopf. Covers in depth most of the topics discussed in this chapter. A good source for students who want to pursue questions about attention, perception, memory, and other cognitive processes.

Kagan, J. (1984). *The nature of the child.* New York: Basic Books. The essays in this book describe features of children's thought that recur across a wide range of topics, including morality, emotion, and understanding of the physical environment.

Chapter Nine

INTELLIGENCE AND ACHIEVEMENT

Defining and Conceptualizing Intelligence
One Ability or Many?
What Are the Dimensions of Intelligence?
Early Efforts to Measure Intelligence
The Wechsler Tests
Multidimensional Tests
Tests Based on Cognitive Processes
Limitations on Measures of IQ
How Should the IQ Test Be Used?
Motivation and School Achievement
Achievement Motivation
Changing Attributions and Achievement Behavior
Developmental Patterns
Test Anxiety
Summary
Cultural and Environmental Influences
Sex Differences
Differences Based on Nationality, Social Class, and Ethnic Group
Difference vs. Deficit
Individual Differences in Intelligence and Achievement
The Home Environment
Early Intervention
Interaction Between Constitution and Environment

In the last two chapters we described developmental patterns in children's cognitive processes with a focus on the universals, or common features, of children's thinking and learning. In this chapter we take a different perspective and examine individual differences in intellectual functioning. For many years psychologists and educators have searched for ways to predict which children will learn more quickly and which ones will learn more slowly in standard educational programs. The intelligence test and the notion of IQ were invented in the early 1900s to help meet this need. IQ tests are widely used today, but their use has generated a great deal of controversy about *why* individuals differ in IQ. To what extent is intelligence genetically determined? How do family, school, and culture affect IQ? Why are there differences in IQ among different groups in society?

One major reason for measuring intelligence is to predict school performance. School is, after all, the major arena in which our society expects children to use their cognitive abilities. School performance depends partly on intelligence, but it also depends on motivation, expectancies regarding success, socialization experiences, and the social context of the classroom. In this chapter we examine how intelligence and school achievement are affected by these factors. First, however, it is necessary to have a thorough understanding of how intelligence is defined and measured.

DEFINING AND CONCEPTUALIZING INTELLIGENCE

Among the many definitions of **intelligence**, the following seems most sensible to us: Intelligence is the capacity to learn and use the skills that are required for successful adaptation to the demands of one's culture and environment. Different cultures may require skills in social interaction, language, mathematics, memory, fine motor coordination, sports, or many other domains. Because widely diverse abilities are required for adaptation in different cultures, it follows that people who are regarded as intelligent in one culture will have different talents than people who are regarded as intelligent in another culture. Thus, modern Americans emphasize speech, reading, and mathematics. Children and adults who excel in these skills are described as intelligent. By contrast, the !Kung San of the Kalahari Desert in southern Africa prize superior hunting skills; South Pacific islanders value outstanding navigational ability.

The specific talents that are valued depend on the society's requirements for survival and on the beliefs of its population. Even societies that value mental ability do not necessarily prize the same intellectual talents. The prerevolutionary

The people who are regarded as intelligent in a particular culture are those who have skills that are valued in that culture.

Chinese valued mastery of written language; the Sophists of Athens celebrated mastery of oratorical skill; and the Indians of modern Guatemala value alertness to opportunity. For several centuries Chinese artists were praised for copying the style of established masters, while European painters were given recognition for innovation and imaginative departures from earlier works.

One Ability or Many?

Initially, intelligence was defined as a general competence—an ability that could be displayed across a wide variety of tasks. Before long, however, this view was challenged by those who argued that different intellectual skills do not necessarily occur together. This issue—whether intellectual ability is a general quality that applies to many task situations or a set of specific cognitive abilities—has been debated for years. You will recognize it from our discussion in Chapter 7 of general versus specific competences.

Although the issue is not entirely settled, most psychologists agree that patterns of abilities differ from one individual to another. Some children are especially good at learning verbal skills; others are good at visualizing spatial relations; still others are talented at mathematics. The same principle applies across cultures. Among Quechua-speaking children in Peru and Mayan Indian children from Guatemala, there is little relationship between the ability to remember a pattern of pictures and the ability to remember words or sentences. Children who do well on one of these tasks are not necessarily proficient on the others (Kagan, et al., 1979;

Stevenson, Parker, Wilkinson, Bonnaveaux, & Gonzalez, 1978). Thus, averaging a child's performance across a variety of tasks may make it impossible to detect the child's particular strengths and weaknesses.

Intellectual skills are also specific to the particular environmental *contexts* in which they are learned and practiced. For example, Kpelle rice farmers in Nigeria perform better than American adults when asked to estimate the amounts of rice in bowls of different sizes, but less well when asked to estimate the lengths of objects. In the Kpelle culture there is a standardized system for measuring volume that is used in buying and selling rice; there is no standard system for measuring length (Laboratory of Comparative Human Cognition, 1983).

What Are the Dimensions of Intelligence?

Although many experts agree that intelligence is multidimensional and includes several abilities, they do not always agree on the nature of these abilities. Some divide abilities according to the *content* of the task, for example, verbal comprehension, number comprehension, spatial relations, social skills, and musical ability (Anastasi, 1987). Others emphasize cognitive *processes* like memory, inference, and problem solving, which were described in Chapter 8.

CRYSTALLIZED AND FLUID ABILITIES.   One important theory distinguishes between crystallized and fluid abilities (Horn, 1968). **Crystallized abilities** refer to the knowledge a person has accumulated. Vocabulary tests measure crystallized ability because they measure how much knowledge about word meanings one has acquired. **Fluid abilities** refer to the processes we use in solving problems and dealing with new information. They require some knowledge, but they also entail reasoning, memory, logical thinking, seeing connections, and inference. Analogies like "Doctor is to patient as lawyer is to_____" measure fluid abilities. As people grow older, their fluid abilities decline faster than their crystallized abilities.

GUILFORD'S STRUCTURE OF INTELLECT.   J. P. Guilford (1979) has proposed another model to describe different types of intellectual ability. After examining people's performance on a wide variety of tests, he suggested that intellectual abilities can be classified along three dimensions. First, there are different kinds of task *content*. For instance, a person might be thinking about pictures of toys (figural content) or words in a song (symbolic content). Second, different types of processing or *operations*, such as memory, evaluating information, and divergent production, may be required. For instance, a child might try to remember what toys were on the shelf in a store or might try to produce variations on the verses of a song (divergent production). The third basis for classifying intellectual abilities is the *product*. One product might be a transformation such as imagining what a model plane would look like upside-down. Another might be a prediction about what color will result when red paint is mixed with blue.

In Guilford's structure of intellect, the three dimensions are crossed as illustrated in Figure 9.1. Guilford devised tests to represent the different combinations of contents, operations, and products that appear as cubes in the diagram. For example, a child might be asked, "Name as many objects as you can that are both

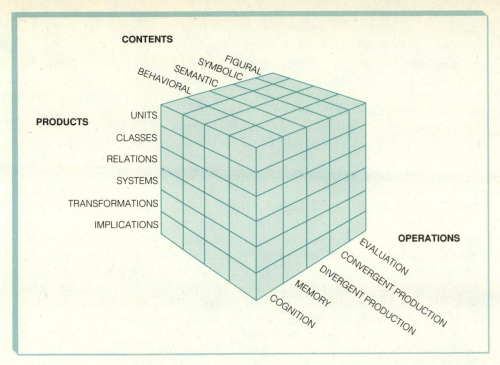

CONTENTS

FIGURAL
SYMBOLIC
SEMANTIC
BEHAVIORAL

PRODUCTS

UNITS
CLASSES
RELATIONS
SYSTEMS
TRANSFORMATIONS
IMPLICATIONS

OPERATIONS

EVALUATION
CONVERGENT PRODUCTION
DIVERGENT PRODUCTION
MEMORY
COGNITION

FIGURE 9.1 Guilford's structure of intellect showing three major dimensions by which intellectual tasks can be classified: operations, contents, and products. The model is designed to show that intelligence involves multiple abilities and to classify those abilities. (Adapted from J. P. Guilford. *Cognitive psychology with a frame of reference.* San Diego: Edits Publishers, 1979, p. 22. By permission.)

white and edible." The content is symbolic; the operation is divergent production; and the products are units in classes. Because performance on some of these tasks did not predict performance on others, Guilford argued that they represented different facets of intelligence.

INTELLIGENCE AS ADAPTATION: A TRIARCHIC THEORY.   Sternberg (1985; Sternberg & Suben, 1986) has proposed an expanded theory of intelligence that incorporates cognitive skills but also includes the individual's wider life experience and adaptive skills. His *triarchic theory* has three major components.

The first component consists of *cognitive processes and knowledge*. It also includes *metacognitive processes* (see Chapter 8)—planning, monitoring, and evaluating one's task performance. For example, in a multiple-choice test one decides whether to read for detail or general ideas, plans how much time to devote to each question, and develops strategies for optimal performance. In addition, this component includes *problem-solving skills*. For instance, during the test you compare the potential answers for critical differences, and you look for giveaways to wrong answers, such as the use of "always" or "never." Third, it includes *knowledge acquisition*, or adding to one's store of knowledge. In the test example, you study for the test by deciding what information in the reading and lectures is relevant; then you relate it to what you already know.

The second component refers to how easily and quickly individuals deal with new *experiences*, that is, how rapidly they learn. Behavior is intelligent if a person applies cognitive processes to new situations *and* if such applications become automatic fairly quickly. For example, when a child sees a sign in a store saying that the price of tennis racquets is 25 percent off, she will figure out what mathematical operations are required to calculate the price, then do the calculation. After a few similar shopping experiences, she will know automatically to multiply the price by 0.75.

The third component refers to the ability to adapt to one's social and cultural environment. A*daptation* does not consist merely of changing yourself or your ways of thinking. It also involves shaping your environment to fit your needs or selecting a new environment. For example, a child who learns how to ask the teacher good questions will get answers that help him learn—he is shaping his environment. When he reaches junior and senior high school, he can select teachers and courses to a limited extent; that is, he can select his own learning environments. Intelligence in the broad sense can be manifested by all of these ways of adapting to and influencing the environmental context in which one performs everyday skills.

One might expect that tests of intelligence would be created to fit these various theories. Historically, however, efforts to measure intelligence have sometimes preceded the development of theories about intelligence.

A child who learns how to ask questions well is shaping his or her environment and will learn more as a result.

Early Efforts to Measure Intelligence

The first intelligence tests were created in the early 1900s by a Frenchman, Alfred Binet. He had a practical purpose: to predict which children would succeed or fail in school. The research strategy was *empirical*. The researchers administered a variety of questions to children who were doing well in school and to children who were not doing well. The questions finally selected for the intelligence test were those on which the high achievers performed better than the poor achievers. The quality the researchers were trying to measure was not an abstract, theoretical entity; it was the children's potential for performance in the specific situation of school.

The test that resulted was eventually called the Stanford-Binet because it was modified for use in the United States by Lewis Terman and Maude Merrill at Stanford University. It contained a large number of items designed to measure everyday information, verbal ability, memory, perception, and logical reasoning. To standardize the test, items were administered to a representative sample of children of different ages. Then the items were assigned to age levels. For example, the items assigned to the 3-year level were those that were passed by about half of the 3-year-olds; the items placed at the 6-year level were those that were passed by about half of the 6-year-olds; and so on. The IQ (intelligence quotient) was calculated by comparing the child's score with averages for other children of the same age.

Figure 9.2 shows the distribution of IQ scores for the population used in standardizing the Stanford-Binet. The test was constructed so that the distribution of scores would closely resemble the normal bell-shaped curve, with the center or mean of the curve at IQ=100 and higher and lower IQs about equally common. Table 9.1 shows the percentage of individuals in different IQ ranges and the interpretive label for each range.

The Wechsler Tests

The early Stanford-Binet provided only a summary IQ score; the authors assumed that intelligence is a generalized quality. The Wechsler Intelligence Scales, which are widely used today, include subtests for many dimensions of intelligence. The items were selected in much the same way as those included in the early Stanford-Binet, but they are arranged in subtests measuring particular skills such as vocabulary, discerning similarities and differences, memory for numbers, and constructing designs with colored blocks. The subtests can be scored separately, but they are also grouped into two scales: the Verbal IQ, which is based on items using language (e.g., vocabulary) and numbers, and the Performance IQ, which is based on subtests that do not require language (e.g., assembling parts of a puzzle). The Full Scale IQ is an average of the Verbal and Performance IQs.

Multidimensional Tests

Some other tests of intelligence are even more clearly based on the multidimensional view. For instance, the Primary Mental Abilities Test, designed for elementary school children, and the Differential Aptitude Test, designed for older children

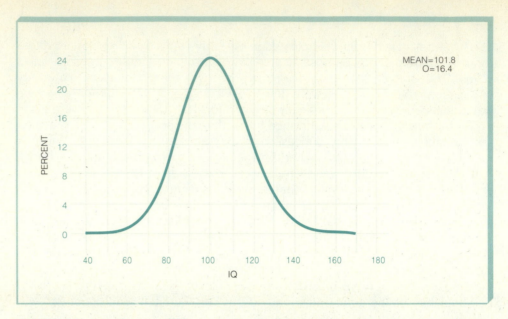

FIGURE 9.2   Distribution of IQs on the Stanford-Binet in the 1937 Terman-Merrill standardization group. (Adapted from L. M. Terman & M. A. Merrill. *Stanford-Binet Intelligence Scale: Manual for the third revision of Form* L-M. Boston: Houghton Mifflin, 1973, p. 18. Copyright, © 1973 by Houghton Mifflin Company, reproduced by permission of the publisher, The Riverside Publishing Company.)

and adolescents, both contain separate tests for skills such as verbal reasoning, number facility, spatial relations, and perceptual speed. The child obtains scores on each subtest but is not given an average or overall score. Although many of these tests correlate with the Stanford-Binet and the Wechsler, multidimensional tests are especially useful when one has questions about specific abilities, such as "Does this child have difficulty visualizing spatial relationships?" (Anastasi, 1987).

Tests Based on Cognitive Processes

The intelligence-testing movement and the development of theories about cognitive development occurred separately. The testing movement had a practical goal that was approached through a trial-and-error process. Psychologists studying cognitive development, on the other hand, were concerned with generating theory and knowledge about children. They usually had little interest in applying their work to the measurement of individual differences. Recently these two groups have approached each other: Theories of intelligence have incorporated what we know about cognitive processing, and intelligence tests are increasingly based on those theories.

The fourth major revision of the Stanford-Binet (Thorndike, Hagen, & Sattler, 1986) and the Kaufman A-B-C tests are both recent examples of a theory-based approach (Anastasi, 1987). The authors of the Stanford-Binet still assume that some aspects of intelligence are generalized. They propose that general

TABLE 9.1

Percent of Children at Different Levels of IQ in the 1937 Standardization Group of the Stanford-Binet

IQ	Percent	Classification
160–169	0.03	
150–159	0.2	Very superior
140–149	1.1	
130–139	3.1	Superior
120–129	8.2	
110–119	18.1	High average
100–109	23.5	Normal or average
90–99	23.0	
80–89	14.5	Low average
70–79	5.6	Borderline defective
60–69	2.0	
50–59	0.4	Mentally defective
40–49	0.2	
30–39	0.03	

Source: L. M. Terman & M. A. Merrill: *Stanford-Binet Intelligence Scale: Manual for the third revision of Form L-M.* Boston: Houghton Mifflin, 1973, p. 18. Copyright © 1973 by Houghton Mifflin Company, reproduced by permission of the publisher, The Riverside Publishing Company.

intelligence probably involves the metacognitive and executive processes described in Chapter 8—the ability to decide what is needed for solving new problems and to mobilize the appropriate strategies. However, items are grouped to represent three components of intelligence: crystallized abilities (e.g., vocabulary and mathematical calculations), fluid-analytic abilities (e.g., constructing block designs and identifying missing parts in a picture), and short-term memory (e.g., remembering a string of digits). A person receives scores for each component as well as an overall score. As on virtually all intelligence tests, scores are calculated by comparing the individual's performance to others of the same age from the same country on a scale with a mean of 100 and a standard deviation of 16 (see Figure 9.2). However, the score is called a Standard Age Score (SAS), not an IQ. Before reading further, stop to consider why the test authors made this change.

Limitations on Measures of IQ

The public and many professionals have imbued the IQ with almost mystical qualities. Many people seem to believe that the tester can peer into the mind and discover a number that is predetermined by heredity, fixed for life, and determined by one's innate potential. None of these assumptions is correct.

Is IQ a "pure" index of innate potential? No. An IQ score measures how much you know about certain topics and how well developed certain skills are at the time that the test is given. Your score is influenced by your past experiences and familiarity with the skills and information contained in the test as well as by your genetic and biological make-up. Just as your performance on a reading test depends partly on your previous experience with reading, your performance on an intelligence test is affected by your opportunities to learn and use vocabulary, information, arithmetic, memory, and spatial skills. Your genetic endowment plays a role in how quickly you learn from experience, but that is true for any kind of cognitive achievement, not just IQ.

Is IQ fixed for life? No. Intelligence test scores are among the most stable human qualities that psychologists measure, but a person's score does not remain the same throughout life. Even over a few weeks, test scores can vary by as much as 10 points because of changes in motivation, variations in attention, or fatigue. Over longer periods there is some stability in intelligence test scores after about age 2; that is, a score at one age predicts scores at later ages.

Evidence for this statement comes from two longitudinal studies in which the same children were tested from ages 2 to 18 (Honzik, MacFarlane, & Allen, 1948; Sontag, Baker, & Nelson, 1958). Two generalizations describe the trends in these studies: (1) As children advance in age, their test scores become increasingly better predictors of later performance. For instance, the correlation between IQs at ages 3 and 5 is lower than the correlation between scores at ages 8 and 10. (2) The shorter the interval between tests, the higher the correlations between them; that is, the more similar the scores.

Nevertheless, some children show marked changes in IQ as they grow older. In a longitudinal study that followed children between the ages of 2½ and 17, the difference between the average child's highest and lowest scores was 28.5 points (McCall, Appelbaum, & Hogarty, 1973). Even after age 6, when IQ scores are relatively stable, the scores of some children show large changes, increasing as well as decreasing. The average changes between the ages of 6 and 18 for children in two groups studied at the University of California are shown in Table 9.2. The scores of the majority of the children shifted 15 points or more, and in over one-third of the cases they shifted 20 points or more.

Larger changes in IQ are less common. It would be rare (though not impossible) for a child's score to shift from 70 to 130 or from 130 to 70. For practical purposes, we can predict that a child with a high score is unlikely to change to a very low score and vice versa, but we cannot predict with any precision what score a child will have a few years from now.

Does IQ measure aptitude or achievement? **Aptitude** refers to the ability to learn a new skill or to do well in some future learning situation. For example, the Scholastic Aptitude Test, which is given to high school students throughout the United States, is designed to predict their academic performance in college. **Achievement**, on the other hand, describes how much a person has learned in a particular course or school subject. The standardized achievement tests given in most public school systems are used primarily to measure how well students have learned

TABLE 9.2

Changes in IQ Between Ages 6 and 18

Change in IQ	Guidance N = 114(%)	Control N = 108(%)	Total N = 222(%)
50 or more IQ points	1	—	.5
30 or more IQ points	9	10	9
20 or more IQ points	32	42	35
15 or more IQ points	58	60	58
10 or more IQ points	87	83	85
9 or fewer IQ points	18	17	15

Source: Adapted from M. P. Honzik, J. W. Macfarlane, & L. Allen. The stability of mental test performance between two and eighteen years. *Journal of Experimental Education*, 1948, 17. A publication of the Helen Dwight Reid Educational Foundation. By permission.

reading, math, and other academic subjects. Aptitude tests often cover a wide range of content, whereas achievement tests measure a specific set of information or skills (Anastasi, 1987). In fact, however, there is no clear separation between aptitude and achievement. Performance on intelligence tests depends on what one knows, and conversely, achievement tests can be used to predict future academic success. Therefore, intelligence tests measure both aptitude and achievement.

Does performance reflect competence? People who interpret test scores must constantly remind themselves of the difference between competence and performance (see Chapter 8). If children perform well on a test, one can be reasonably confident that they have the competences measured by the test. However, if a child does not answer the questions correctly, one cannot be sure that those competences are lacking—only that they were not demonstrated. When children do not perform correctly, we must be cautious about saying that they cannot do so.

How Should the IQ Test Be Used?

All of these cautions about the meaning of the IQ score raise questions about its use. Two of the points made earlier in the chapter are pertinent to this issue. First, because intelligence is multidimensional, it is probably more useful to examine tests of specific skills than to rely solely on a single IQ score. Rather than saying that a child is intelligent, we might say that he is good at language, math, spatial reasoning, creative writing, or artistic composition.

Second, because intelligence tests are basically tests of achievement across a wide range of cognitive domains, the label "IQ" could be replaced by a term like "school ability," "academic aptitude," or "Standard Age Score" (Reschly, 1981; Thorndike et al., 1986). These labels might avoid the implications that test scores are an index of innate potential or a fixed entity that the person carries throughout life. They might better convey the notion that tests of cognitive performance can be useful for educational diagnosis, while reducing the possibility that children will be stigmatized with a label that says they are unable to learn.

Even with these restrictions, we must recognize that IQ is not the only determinant of success in school, work, or other life situations. Intelligence accounts for only part of individual variations in school performance (Anastasi, 1987). Existing tests do not measure all aspects of intelligent behavior. For instance, most tests do not measure all the components defined in Sternberg's triarchic theory. They rarely measure children's ability to learn from experience or to adapt to new environments. Moreover, qualities other than intelligence are important for achievement. In short, we need to look beyond IQ and consider such factors as motivation and expectancies.

MOTIVATION AND SCHOOL ACHIEVEMENT

Achievement in school and in adult life depends not only on people's abilities but also on their motivation, attitudes, work skills, and emotional reactions to school and other achievement situations. The diagram in Figure 9.3 illustrates the contributions of ability and motivational variables to achievement.

Achievement Motivation

Achievement motivation is "an overall tendency to evaluate one's performance against standards of excellence, to strive for successful performance, and to experience pleasure contingent on successful performance" (Feld, Ruhland, & Gold,

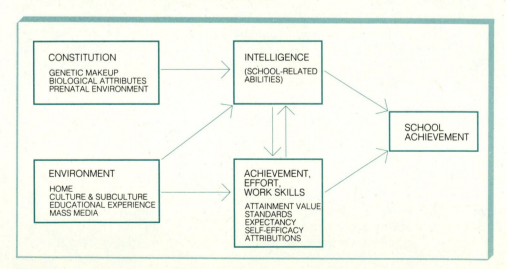

FIGURE 9.3 The major influences on intellectual functioning and school achievement.

1979, p. 45). It is the desire to do well in a particular domain (e.g., football or music), together with a tendency to evaluate one's own performance spontaneously. We often infer achievement motivation from *achievement behaviors* such as persisting at a difficult task, working intensely or striving for mastery, and selecting challenging but not impossibly difficult tasks, that is, setting a moderate *level of aspiration*.

It is easy to see that these achievement behaviors could contribute to school success. Consider two children whose IQs are both 100 in the first few grades of school. Sara begins learning to read with enthusiasm. She concentrates on the books and worksheets that the teacher provides, and she persists in attempting to solve problems that are difficult for her. When she goes to a learning center where there is a choice of activities, she selects a book that has some difficult words as well as some words that she knows. Linda begins with the same level of skill but is inclined to be distracted from assignments when a teacher is not working with her. When she encounters difficult words, she gives up easily. At the learning center she chooses a very easy book. Over time Sara will probably learn more reading skills than Linda will, and she will be better liked by her teachers.

Like intellectual abilities, achievement motivation and behavior vary across tasks and situations. Even if we restrict the discussion to school achievement, children's levels of motivation may vary from one subject area to another or from one time period to the next. One child may be very persistent and involved when working on art projects but make little effort in math. Another may read avidly, selecting challenging books, but seek the easiest position in a team sport. Of course, the greatest social concern arises when children show less than optimal motivation in hard-core school subjects, especially reading and math.

What determines a child's level of motivation or effort in a particular task area? Some of the factors involved are *attainment value* (the value the child attaches to success); *standards of performance; expectancies and beliefs about one's abilities*; and *attributions* about the reasons for success or failure.

ATTAINMENT VALUE.   Questions like "How important is it to you to do well in music?" "How important do you think math will be in your future work?" and "How much would you like to be good at leadership?" are efforts to assess attainment value, that is, how much value a person attaches to attainment in a particular area. Attainment value influences children's selection of achievement activities.

Jacquelynne Eccles and her colleagues at the University of Michigan investigated achievement in mathematics among a group of 668 students in grades 5 through 12 using a large battery of questions about motivations and attitudes. All of the students were assessed on two occasions a year apart so that comparisons over time could be made. The investigators were interested in two outcomes: math grades and selection of advanced math courses as electives. Course choices were particularly important because students who stop taking mathematics in junior or senior high school are effectively disqualified from later courses of study and college majors that require advanced math. One reason that males perform better than females on math tests during high school and college is that more males take advanced math courses (Fennema & Peterson, 1985).

Girls rarely encounter female role models like this one, and as a result they are likely to consider math less useful and important than boys do.

The attainment value attached to math was the best predictor of students' intention to take advanced math. Students who considered math important and thought it would be useful to them in the future were most likely to say that they intended to take elective math courses. Girls considered math less useful and important for their future lives than boys did. Boys' higher attainment value for math was a major reason that boys took more elective math courses than girls did (Eccles, Adler, & Meece, 1984).

STANDARDS OF PERFORMANCE.   Evaluating performance means comparing it with a standard of excellence. You may evaluate how well you do something on the basis of your own past performance (e.g., I ran a mile in less time than I have run it before), on the basis of a goal that you have selected for yourself (I set a goal of reading 20 books this summer, and I did it), or on the basis of comparisons with others (e.g., I was fifth highest in my class on that test). When the standards you adopt are personal or are based on comparisons with your own past performance, they are **autonomous standards**. When they are based on comparisons with other people's performance, they are described as **social-comparison standards** (Veroff, 1969). Children begin to use social-comparison processes to evaluate their performance around age 5 or 6, in part because the advent of concrete-operational thought enables them to compare their performance with that of others and to consider a standard that orders performances on a continuum. In American society the emphasis on competition and individual achievement contributes to increasingly heavy reliance on social comparison as a basis for evaluating performance during the school years.

EXPECTANCIES AND BELIEFS ABOUT ONE'S ABILITIES.   As children progress through school, they form beliefs about their abilities in different subject areas, such as reading, math, and music. When they encounter a specific task, such as a math test, they have expectancies about how well they will perform that are based partly on their *self-concepts of ability* in math and partly on their own past performance in that particular course (e.g., algebra). Expectancies of success not only result from previous success; they also contribute to effective performance. Children who believe they have good math ability are likely to select advanced math courses as electives (Eccles, 1983).

One's self-concept of ability is an example of **perceived self-efficacy**, a characteristic described by Albert Bandura (1981; 1982). "Perceived self-efficacy is concerned with judgments of how well one can execute courses of action required to deal with prospective situations" (Bandura, 1982, p. 122). A sense of efficacy influences achievement behavior—what kinds of activities you choose to try and how much effort and persistence you exhibit (Bandura, 1981).

Some people have concluded that school achievement can be improved by raising children's self-esteem or sense of efficacy. However, training programs designed to raise children's self-esteem have generally failed to change their school performance (Scheirer & Kraut, 1979). One reason is the failure of such programs to realize that self-concepts are specific to particular domains. In a group of fifth-graders, for instance, achievement in reading and math were associated with high academic self-concepts but were not related to self-concepts in nonacademic domains (Marsh, Smith, & Barnes, 1985). In other words, making children feel good about their athletic skills or their general worth as people does not usually have much effect on their reading skills. Interventions that focus on self-concepts about particular domains of achievement are more likely to be effective.

ATTRIBUTIONS ABOUT SUCCESS AND FAILURE.   Expectancies of success and concepts of one's abilities are not simply a result of past successes. Children with the same levels of performance often have different perceptions of their abilities, different expectations about future success (Vollmer, 1986). For example, across a wide range of achievement areas boys often have higher expectancies than girls, even when their average past performance is similar or lower (Crandall, 1969; Eccles, 1983; Stein & Bailey, 1973).

Children's expectancies may differ because they interpret their successes and failures differently. That is, they make different attributions about the reasons for their successes and failures. **Attributions** are inferences about the causes of one's own or someone else's behavior. Whether or not we are aware of it, we are constantly making attributions. Mary must be grouchy today because she didn't get enough sleep. Joe is usually a poor student; if he got an A, it must be an easy course.

Attributions about the reasons for successes and failures affect achievement behavior and expectancies about future performance (Bar-Tal, 1978; Dweck & Elliot, 1983). Four major causes of success or failure have been defined: (1) ability (or lack of it), (2) effort (or lack of it), (3) task difficulty (or ease), and (4) luck (good or bad). Examples of each are shown in Table 9.3.

As you can see, the four attributions are classified along two dimensions. One dimension is *internal/external*. Ability and effort are internal causes because they originate within the individual and are, to some degree, within that person's control. Task difficulty and luck are external causes because they arise outside the individual and are often beyond his or her control. This internal/external dimension is sometimes called *locus of control*.

The second dimension is *stable/unstable*. Ability and task difficulty are stable characteristics that are not easily changed, while effort and luck are unstable and can change readily. Attributing success or failure to stable causes is more likely to affect future expectancies than attributing them to unstable causes. For example, a person who believes that a good tennis score reflects ability will probably expect to do well in the next game. One who thinks that the score was due to extraordinary effort or to luck will not expect to do as well.

Consider the case of Jennifer, a 12-year-old who is trying to become a good swimmer:

> Every day she counts the number of laps she swims and times how long it takes her. Like most of us, she does well on some days and less well on others. If she considers her good days an index of her ability and interprets her bad days as

TABLE 9.3

Examples of Attributions About Success and Failure

Internal		External	Effect on expectancy
Stable	**Ability**	**Task Difficulty**	
Success	"I'm good at math."	"It was an easy test."	Expect future success.
Failure	"I'm lousy at math."	"It was a hard test."	Expect future failure.
Unstable	**Effort**	**Luck**	
Success	"I studied hard."	"I guessed right."	Don't know.
Failure	"I didn't study enough."	"I guessed wrong."	Future could be different.

times when she is not trying as hard as she might, she will probably feel good about her swimming ability. She will also redouble her efforts after a setback or a string of poor performances. On the other hand, if she thinks that her good days are flukes or a result of superhuman effort, but that her bad days show that she really does not have the ability to become a high-powered swimmer, she will probably become discouraged.

A pattern of maladaptive attributions—believing that your successes do not reflect ability and that your failures cannot be reversed by effort—has been labeled **learned helplessness** (Dweck & Elliot, 1983). Some children believe that the causes of failure are lack of ability, task difficulty, or bad luck—reasons that are outside their control or cannot be changed. As a result, they feel helpless and give up easily when they fail (Diener & Dweck, 1978; 1980). Such children do not necessarily experience any more failures or successes than other children do, but they interpret them differently.

Changing Attributions and Achievement Behavior

People who are easily discouraged by failure can sometimes be helped by being taught new attributions and coping strategies. In some experimental programs children and adults were taught to attribute their failure on a task to lack of effort. For example, when children failed on a set of math problems, an adult told them that they should have tried harder. Children who received this form of "attribution retraining" after failure performed better on math tests than children who had been given easy problems on which they succeeded 100 percent of the time (Dweck, 1975). In general, attribution retraining leads not only to changes in attribution but also to improved expectancies of success, perceptions of self-efficacy, task persistence, and task performance *in the task domain on which training is focused* (Forsterling, 1985). However, a few cautions are in order.

Teaching children that their failures are due to lack of effort may be harmful if they lack the appropriate skills for the task. A child who tries very hard and fails may conclude that the failure resulted from low ability (Covington & Omelich, 1979). In these instances it is more useful to teach strategies for approaching problems. For example, children's self-efficacy, achievement effort, and performance improved most when they were taught strategies for solving math problems as well as "adaptive" attributions. The most effective strategy was modeling and practice—the children watched an adult talking about how to solve problems as he did them, and they practiced verbalizing to themselves as they did problems (Schunk & Cox, 1986).

Clearly, a careful diagnosis of the basis for children's failure is important in deciding what interventions are appropriate. A child who lacks certain skills should be taught those skills and perhaps provided with a graded series of successes that will build expectancies of success and feelings of self-efficacy. Such teaching can be especially effective if the child sets small goals and achieves them. If the child has skills but is inclined to give up very quickly when faced with difficult problems, attribution training may be appropriate.

Developmental Patterns

Perceptions of self-efficacy, attributions, and attainment values develop gradually throughout childhood. As they grow older, children develop more refined abilities to think about and adopt standards of performance and to use information about

In their early school years children may develop strong feelings of anxiety about being tested.

the performance of others in their self-evaluations (Ruble, Boggiano, Feldman, & Loebl, 1980) (see Chapter 5). Preschool children show achievement behavior: They persist at tasks and make efforts to master new skills, and there is some correspondence between their expectancies of success and their efforts to achieve (Crandall, 1978). Compared to elementary school children, however, they more often choose easy rather than challenging tasks (Stein & Bailey, 1973).

During the first few years of school, several changes occur: (1) Children's stated expectancies become more realistic, that is, more closely related to their actual performance (Ruble, Parsons, & Ross, 1976; Nicholls, 1978). (2) Children increasingly use social comparison in evaluating their own performance (Feld et al., 1979; Ruble, Boggiano, Feldman, & Loebl, 1980). (3) Children set higher levels of aspiration for themselves; that is, they choose more difficult tasks (Feld et al., 1979). (4) Children express more anxiety about failure when responding to questionnaires designed to measure test anxiety (Sarason, Hill, & Zimbardo, 1964; Rholes, Blackwell, Jordan, & Walters, 1980).

With age, children differentiate the causes of success and failure along the lines described in Table 9.3. Younger children sometimes do not distinguish clearly among effort, ability, and luck. In one study, 5- and 6-year-old children did not see the difference between tasks requiring luck and skill. In the "luck" task, they were asked to match pictures that they could not see because the cards were turned face down; in the "skill" task, they could see the pictures to be matched. Clear differentiation between the two tasks occurred only for children in the 9-to-14 age range (Nicholls & Miller, 1985).

The distinction between ability and effort is even more subtle and is not well understood by young children. For instance, kindergarten and first-grade children assume that people who try harder are smarter—even if they fail. Even 7- to 9-year-olds do not conclude that a lazy child who succeeds has more ability than one who works hard and does not succeed. It is not until the ages of 10 to 13 that most children clearly distinguish effort from ability (Shantz, 1983).

Whether these age-related changes are due to cognitive development, school experience, or both, we do not know. Cognitive growth is probably important in enabling children to compare themselves with a standard and to understand different types of attributions. At the same time, for most American children elementary school serves as their initiation into the world of grades, evaluations, failures, competition, and clear comparisons with peers. Beginning in the first grade, children in most schools are placed in reading and arithmetic groups according to "ability" (i.e., current level of skill). They are evaluated on report cards; their papers are graded; and they are tested. These school experiences may teach children to evaluate themselves, to compare themselves with peers, to make attributions about their successes and failures, and to be anxious about failure.

Test Anxiety

American schools increasingly rely on tests—standardized achievement tests, minimum-competency tests, and entrance examinations—to make decisions about educational placement and judgments about students' achievement. During the first few years of school, many children develop a pattern of anxiety over testing that interferes with their performance. Consider an example supplied by Kennedy Hill (1980). Mark gets nervous before a standardized test. As the teacher reads complicated instructions, he has trouble concentrating. He is nervous about the time limit because he has trouble finishing timed tests. (Nobody bothered to tell him that children are not expected to finish standardized tests.) He notices that some other children are farther along than he is. He starts to rush. He manages to finish but gets few answers right. Mark is a child with high test anxiety. He does not perform as well on tests as his teachers think he can.

In one longitudinal study, 713 elementary school children were followed for four years. Children with high test anxiety performed more poorly than those with low test anxiety. The differences between high- and low-anxiety children became more pronounced as the children grew older (Hill, K. T. & Sarason, 1966). How do we know whether the anxiety caused the poor test performance or the history of poor performance led to anxiety? Of course, we cannot be sure, but it is most likely that some of each occurred.

One reason to believe that anxiety affects performance adversely is that the performance of highly anxious children changes when testing conditions are altered. Children were given math problems under four testing conditions: standard instructions stating that the test measured the children's ability; "diagnostic" instructions stating that the test would tell where they needed help; "expectancy reassurance" instructions, in which they were told that no one gets all the answers right; and "normative" instructions, in which they were told that individual scores were not important. The performance of children with high, medium, and low test anxiety is shown in Figure 9.4. The highly anxious children performed much better when the instructions provided reassurance or removed the threat of individual evaluation (Hill, K. T., 1980).

A research program conducted by Kennedy Hill at the University of Illinois is designed to find ways of reducing the negative effects of text anxiety on children in their everyday school experiences. Children are taught about test formats, how to deal with timed tests, and the purposes of testing. Report cards contain specific feedback about strengths and weaknesses instead of letter grades. Children's own accomplishments are emphasized; comparison with others is minimized. The evaluations suggest that this approach is particularly helpful to children with high test anxiety (Hill, K. T., 1980).

Summary

Children's achievement in school depends not only on their intellectual abilities but also on their motivations and their interpretations of achievement situations. Achievement behaviors such as task persistence and setting moderate levels of aspiration can facilitate learning. Attainment value, realistic standards of performance, expectancy of success, positive self-concepts about one's abilities, and appropriate attributions about the reasons for success and failure are all factors that affect children's selection of achievement activities and the amount of effort they expend when they are involved in such activities. Anxiety about failure can

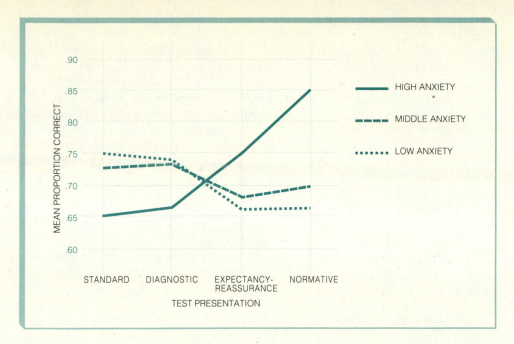

FIGURE 9.4 Test performance of children with different levels of anxiety under four types of test instructions. The diagnostic, expectancy-reassurance, and normative instructions were intended to reduce children's debilitating anxiety, while standard instructions were thought to increase it. (Adapted from K. T. Hill, Motivation, evaluation, and educational testing policy. In L. J. Fyans [Ed.], *Achievement motivation: Recent trends in theory and research*. New York: Plenum, 1980, p. 65. By permission.)

interfere with performance, but its effects can be alleviated through training and by reducing situational cues for anxiety.

One theme that emerges from this research will be familiar by now: Skills, motivations, and beliefs about achievement are specific to particular task situations. It is not usually useful to talk about generalized achievement motivation or a general self-concept, to mention only two examples. Instead, one must examine a child's self-concept and motives for reading, math, football, or basket weaving in order to predict behavior within any one of those domains.

CULTURAL AND ENVIRONMENTAL INFLUENCES

We are now ready to ask what accounts for individual differences in intelligence and achievement behavior. The diagram in Figure 9.3 provides an overview of different types of influences. Intelligence is partly a function of genetic and constitutional influences, as discussed in Chapter 2. In this chapter we discuss group differences in ability and achievement in relation to environmental influences—culture and subculture, home environment, and planned learning experiences.

Sex Differences

Among American children there are consistent sex differences in intellectual performance and school achievement. When the Stanford-Binet and other intelligence tests were constructed, items were discarded if the average performance of boys and girls differed. That is, the tests were constructed so as to avoid particular types of content or skills on which males and females differed. Nevertheless, girls have slightly higher IQs in the early years than boys do (Broman, Nichols, & Kennedy, 1975). Girls also earn higher grades than boys do throughout the school years, but the difference decreases in high school and college.

Males and females, on the average, have different patterns of performance in different intellectual domains. In childhood, females perform a little better than males on standardized tests of verbal ability—reading, verbal fluency, and verbal comprehension. During elementary school males and females perform about equally well in mathematics, but males begin to do better in high school and clearly excel in college. Males also perform better, on the average, on tasks that require visual-spatial reasoning, such as imagining how a cube constructed of black and white blocks would look from another side, or reading a map (Halpern, 1986; Huston, A. C., 1983; Maccoby & Jacklin, 1974).

Of course, the average scores do not represent any individual; there are many boys who perform well on tests of verbal skills and many girls who do very well at math and spatial reasoning. Nevertheless, the reasons for the average differences have been hotly debated by scientists.

The patterns of achievement for males and females are consistent with cultural stereotypes about appropriate behaviors for men and women. American children learn early that reading, art, and verbal skills are stereotyped as feminine while mechanical, athletic, and mathematical skills are socially defined as masculine (Stein & Bailey, 1973). Males and females also learn different attribution patterns. Males are more likely to show adaptive attributions; that is, they attribute their successes to ability and their failures to luck. Females more often attribute their failures to lack of ability, a maladaptive pattern (Hansen & O'Leary, 1986).

The socialization that boys and girls receive from family, school, peers, and the mass media all contribute to the differences in patterns of intellectual development and ultimate occupational achievement shown by males and females. Although there are genetically-based neural differences between the sexes, to date studies have not demonstrated a physiological basis for sex differences in visual-spatial, mathematical, or verbal abilities (Halpern, 1986; Wittig & Petersen, 1979).

Differences Based on Nationality, Social Class, and Ethnic Group

Some cultural groups emphasize intellectual achievement in the socialization of children more than others do. Children in Japan, Taiwan, and the United States were compared in an extensive investigation described in Box 9.1.

Many of the environmental factors that exert the greatest impact on the child's IQ and achievement are associated with the social class and ethnic group of the family. Social class typically correlates with IQ and school grades (the average correlation is about .50). For example, in a study that followed 26,760 children

BOX 9.1

Why Do the Japanese Excel?

Thirty years ago, if a product was made in the United States most people assumed that it represented the best workmanship and quality available. Foreign products were suspect. Today, by contrast, American engineering and craftsmanship are often maligned, and Japanese products are praised. Educators sometimes attribute Japan's superior technology and engineering to a superior educational system.

Do Japanese children accomplish more in school than American children? Are they more intelligent? These questions guided a carefully designed comparison of achievement levels and cognitive development among first- and fifth-grade children in Japan, Taiwan, and the United States. By the fifth grade Chinese and Japanese children had higher levels of performance in math and some areas of reading than American children. The three groups did not differ on various tests of general intellectual ability, suggesting that the difference is not due to genetic or constitutional differences among nationalities.

Instead, the differences appear to result from differences in educational systems and in parents' socialization practices. Children in Japan and Taiwan spend more time in school than children in the United States; they have longer school days and longer school years. When they are in school they spend more time in math instruction, and they are less likely to spend that time in irrelevant "off-task" activity. Teachers in those societies spend more time in group instruction than American teachers do. In addition, they are more enthusiastic and better trained in math. Within the three countries, these features of the classroom are correlated with children's math achievement (Stigler, Lee, & Stevenson, 1987). Another important contributor to the superior performance of Chinese and Japanese children may be the emphasis placed on achievement by parents and other people in the culture (Stevenson et al., 1985).

The United States cannot import a system of education and cultural values from another nation. However, we can benefit from the experiences of those nations in attempting to improve learning among our children.

from before birth to age 4, the best predictor of IQ at age 4 was the mother's education and social status. Neither the child's prenatal and birth history nor the child's performance on an infant intelligence scale predicted IQ as accurately (Broman et al., 1975).

Children from economically disadvantaged minority groups in both the United States and Europe, many of whom are nonwhite, obtain lower IQ scores and perform less well in school than the average child from the majority group in the same country (Scarr, Caparulo, Ferdman, Tower, & Caplan, 1983). For instance, black children in the United States, who often come from economically impoverished homes, have average IQ scores 10 to 15 points below the average for white children (Broman et al., 1975; Hall & Kaye, 1980).

Periodically during the twentieth century, certain scholars (e.g., Jensen, 1969) have claimed that the differences in IQ between blacks and whites are a result of genetic factors. Like many other psychologists, we disagree. The available evidence does not support the conclusion that one race is genetically inferior to another; rather, it suggests that black children have lower IQ scores because of experiences in their families, neighborhoods, and schools, as well as the events associated with economic disadvantage and racial discrimination (Scarr, 1981).

The importance of family environment is demonstrated by studies of black children who have been adopted by middle-class white or black families. The IQs of adopted black children are above average and are similar to those of adopted white children. Children who were adopted as infants have higher averages than those who were adopted when they were 1 year old or older. In an early study biracial adopted children (those with one black and one white biological parent) scored higher than children with two black biological parents, probably because the biracial children had been adopted at an earlier age (Scarr & Weinberg, 1976). A more recent comparison, in which the age of adoption for the two groups was similar, showed no differences between biracial and other black children (Moore, 1986). However, black children who had been adopted by white parents performed better than those who had been adopted by black parents.

Observations of the mothers with their children demonstrated that the white adoptive parents more often taught their children the strategies and skills needed for high performance on tests (Moore, 1986). Current research supports the conclusion that "the social environment plays a dominant role in determining the average IQ level of black children and that both social and genetic variables contribute to individual variation among them" (Scarr & Weinberg, 1976).

Genetic explanations have also been suggested for social-class differences in average IQ, and similar arguments against such explanations can be offered. Children who were born to lower-class families in France and were adopted by upper-middle-class families had average IQ scores of 110, 18 points higher than those of siblings who had remained in their lower-class homes. The proportion of school failure was 12 percent for the adopted children and 70 percent for the brothers and sisters who remained with their original families (Schiff et al., 1978). In a second French sample, the proportion of school failures for adopted children was similar to that for other children in the social class of their adoptive families, not to that for children in the social class of their biological parents (see Figure 9.5) (Duyme, 1988). Thus, social class and ethnic group differences in school achievement and test performance are not due primarily to genetic factors.

Difference vs. Deficit

Although we have argued that social experience makes a major contribution to ethnic and class differences in IQ, we must avoid the trap of assuming that minority

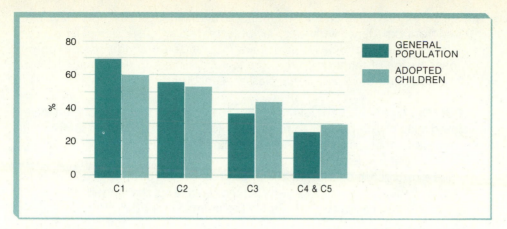

FIGURE 9.5 Percentages of school success by social class. (C1 = professionals, higher management; C2 = middle management; C3 = craftsmen, tradesmen, or lower management; C4 and C5 = skilled and unskilled workers. Ns for each social class [light columns] are as follows: C1 = 1,764, C2 = 2,463, C3 = 1,859, C4 and C5 = 8,865. Ns for each adoptees social class [dark columns] are as follows: C1 = 25, C2 = 13, C3 = 14, C4 and C5 = 35.) (Adapted from M. Duyme. School success and social class: An adoption study. *Developmental Psychology*, 1988, 24, 203–209. Copyright 1988 by the American Psychological Association. By permission.)

and lower-class children have deficient intelligence when intelligence is defined according to the broad definitions offered at the beginning of the chapter. That approach is sometimes called the *deficit* model.

It is more accurate to say that nonwhite and lower- class children often learn *different* skills; what they sometimes lack are the school-related skills that are valued in white middle-class society (Boykin, 1983). They learn what is adaptive in their subcultures. Consider the children in Trackton, a lower-class black community in the Carolina hills. When Trackton children go to school, they do not understand indirect requests from the teacher, such as "It's time for everyone to put away your crayons," because such requests are not part of their home experience. They sometimes fail even to answer the question "What is your name?" because they are used to nicknames like Frog and Red Girl, which teachers sometimes refuse to use (Sternberg & Suben, 1986).

Middle-class parents often ask children questions to which the adult knows the answer. "What is this picture, Jennifer?" In some subcultures children are not accustomed to such questions. For example, during a study of the speech of Oakland black youngsters a psychologist asked one child, "Where do you live? "How do you get there from here?" The child's answer was vague. "A little later the psychologist's husband asked the same question. The answer he got was, "You go down the stairs, turn left, walk three blocks . . ." What was the difference? Her husband had never been to the child's house, but she had picked the child up there (Erwin-Tripp, 1972, p. 145).

When assessments are properly designed, children from different racial and social-class groups show cognitive skills acquired from common experiences. Preschool and kindergarten boys from middle- and lower-class black and white families were tested on their understanding of mathematical concepts that can be acquired from experience with everyday objects. Tasks were designed to measure the children's understanding of "more," addition and subtraction, basic counting, and conservation of number. There were few differences in performance among children of different races or social classes (Ginsburg & Russell, 1981).

TEST BIAS.   One implication of the "difference" model is that tests of intelligence are biased against lower-class and minority children. That is, the tests sample skills and information that are part of middle-class culture, not the skills and information that minority children learn. This problem has been recognized for many years, but there was a resurgence of concern about it during the 1970s and 1980s, partly because of a number of court cases in which minority parents challenged the use of IQ tests to place their children in classes for the mentally retarded. This issue is discussed in Box 9.2.

The content of most IQ tests is probably more familiar to middle-class white children than to many minority children. For example, a middle-class white child might be more familiar with the word *lecture* than a lower-class black child would be. Although some content bias of this kind undoubtedly occurs, it is not as simple as it appears. When Anglo, Hispanic, and black college students rated items on an IQ test for bias, there was very little agreement among members of each group about which items were biased. Still more disconcerting was the fact that the items the adults thought were biased were not those on which minority children performed poorly (Sandoval & Millie, 1980).

More general differences in life experience probably do make IQ tests difficult for minority children. For many ethnic minorities in the United States, standard English is a second language that is less familiar than the language spoken at home or in their neighborhoods. In addition, minority children may have less opportunity to learn test-taking skills or to become familiar with the process of testing. Finally, fear of failure (test anxiety) and low concepts of their own abilities appear to be especially severe among lower-class and minority children.

One group of researchers tried to arrange testing conditions so as to reduce children's anxiety about failure and make them feel confident and comfortable in the testing situation. The average IQ in these "optimal" testing conditions was about six points higher than that for a comparison group tested in the standard way (Zigler, Abelson, & Seitz, 1973; Zigler, Abelson, Trickett, & Seitz, 1982). There is some basis for believing that IQ tests do not measure all of the cognitive competences of lower-class and minority children as well as they do those of middle-class white children.

INDIVIDUAL DIFFERENCES IN INTELLIGENCE AND ACHIEVEMENT

Within nations and cultural groups, there are obviously large individual differences among children. Some of those differences may be due to their experiences at home and in school (see Figure 9.3).

BOX 9.2

Should Intelligence Tests Be Used for Minority Children?

In the 1979–1980 school year, two court cases regarding the use of intelligence tests were decided—in opposite directions. A California judge ruled that standardized tests could not be used to identify or place black children in special classes for the mentally retarded. Meanwhile an Illinois judge ruled that using tests for placement did not discriminate against black children (Bersoff, 1981).

Should IQ tests be used to make educational decisions for any child, particularly a member of a minority group? On the one hand, some people argue that an IQ test measures the skills needed to achieve in school, even though such tests may also have a middle-class bias. That is, a test may indicate how much a minority child has learned about the requirements for achievement in the middle-class society represented by schools. In fact, among college students test scores predict academic performance about as well for minority students as for those from the majority culture (Cleary, Humphreys, Kendrick, & Wesman, 1975; Cole, 1981). Moreover, an "objective" test may provide an opportunity for academically talented minority students to be identified even when biased teachers fail to recognize their ability.

On the other hand, there is considerable danger that teachers and parents will label a child who scores low on an IQ test as stupid and incapable of learning, particularly if that child is black or Hispanic. It is difficult to escape from the widely held misconceptions about IQ, the notion that a person's IQ is innate or that it is immutable. Teachers might convey low expectancies for success and fail to put forth their best efforts to teach a child with a low IQ. Once children are placed in a special class for retarded children, they may be further labeled and have little chance of making normal progress in school.

The Home Environment

What elements of the environment are important for promoting intelligence and achievement? One way to answer this question is to study the environments of children who achieve at different levels and try to identify factors that correlate with performance. This method has one major flaw, which is summarized in an adage that is taught to all introductory psychology students: Correlations do not imply causation. If we find that parents of brighter children behave differently than parents of children who do not perform well, we do not know whether the parents' behavior stimulated the child or the parents responded to certain characteristics of their children. For example, in the United States the amount of time parents spend helping their children with homework is negatively correlated with the children's school achievement. That is, the poorer students get more help. Does parental help interfere with school achievement? Probably not. It is more likely that poor achievers need or ask for help more often. With these cautions in mind, let us examine the evidence.

Some psychologists have tried to evaluate the influence of environment by examining the correlation between the IQs of adoptive parents and those of their children. Although adopted children as a group perform at levels similar to those at which other children in the parents' social class perform, there is relatively little association between individual parents' and children's IQs. That is, highly intelligent adoptive parents have children whose IQs are only slightly higher than those of children with less intelligent adoptive parents (Horn, 1983). It appears that parental IQ is not a good indicator of the environmental stimulation affecting children's intellectual development, such as the presence of books, magazines, stimulating toys, and parental involvement.

THE PHYSICAL AND SOCIAL ASPECTS OF THE HOME ENVIRONMENT. A systematic evaluation of both the physical and social qualities of children's homes is provided by the Home Observation for Measurement of the Environment (HOME). It includes six features of the home environment: (1) how emotionally and verbally responsive the mother is to the child; (2) the mother's acceptance of the child; (3) the mother's involvement or interest in the child; (4) the degree of organization in the household—whether there are regular times for meals, going to bed, and the like; (5) whether appropriate play materials are available, and (6) the variety of daily stimulation—changes in activities, opportunities to go places, and the like.

The HOME was used in several investigations of low-income families, many of which were black. The qualities of the home environment when children were quite young (age 2) predicted performance on the Stanford-Binet at age 3 and school achievement several years later (Bradley & Caldwell 1984; Bradley, Caldwell, & Elardo, 1977; Van Doorninck, Caldwell, Wright, & Frankenburg, 1981). Children with high IQs and achievement levels had mothers who were involved with them, were affectionate and verbally responsive, and avoided restriction and punishment. There were predictable routines, such as regular times for naps and meals, but there was also some variety in daily activities. Of particular importance was the availability of appropriate play materials.

One feature of the physical environment that can interfere with intellectual functioning is excessive noise and disorganization. For example, in a group of 39 children who were studied between the ages of 12 and 24 months, the presence of noise from television, other children, traffic, or appliances was consistently associated with relatively poor performance on tests of intellectual functioning (Wachs, 1979).

AFFECTION AND INVOLVEMENT WITH THE CHILD. In general, high-achieving children have parents who are at least moderately affectionate and involved with them. In one investigation the researchers defined "affective quality" by observing mothers' responsiveness to the child's activities, flexibility (e.g., allowing the child to change activities), concern for the child's feelings (e.g., asking why the child does not want to do something), and acceptance (e.g., "I let her do things at her own pace"). Affective quality at age 4 predicted children's school readiness at ages 5–6, IQ at age 6, and school achievement at age 12 (Estrada, Arsenio, Hess, & Holloway, 1987).

A positive parent-child relationship can affect achievement because it forms a basis for the child to accept the parent's expectations and demands. If the parent does not expect achievement but encourages dependency, affection does not lead to high levels of achievement effort (Stein & Bailey, 1973). Parental affection may also increase the child's social competence and willingness to explore and take risks. Rejection, on the other hand, leads to a variety of antisocial, aggressive, or maladaptive behaviors that conflict with achievement (Huesmann & Eron, 1986).

PARENTS' BELIEFS, EXPECTATIONS, AND VALUES.   Children's achievement efforts are affected by their attainment values, expectancies of success, concepts about their abilities, and attributions. They get those beliefs and values partly from their parents. In the University of Michigan study of math achievement, the value that parents attached to different areas of achievement influenced their children's values. For example, parents considered math more important for their sons' future than for that of their daughters. The children's attainment values reflected those priorities.

Parents' perceptions of their children's abilities appear to have a direct influence on the children's sense of efficacy and their expectancies of success. An investigation of third-graders who were doing well in school but had low academic self-concepts (an "illusion of incompetence") suggests that these self-concepts resulted from their parents' low evaluation of their abilities (Phillips, 1987). In the University of Michigan study, students' expectancies of success were more closely related to their parents' expectancies than to their own past performance (Parsons, Adler, & Kaczala, 1982).

PARENTING STYLES AND DISCIPLINE.   One way in which parents communicate confidence in their children's abilities is to set high standards and demand mature behavior. When they do, they convey the message, "I think you are capable of doing this."

Achievement and task persistence are associated with a parenting style that is sometimes termed **authoritative** (Baumrind, 1973). Authoritative parents are moderately affectionate, but they have clear standards and expect children to behave maturely. Obviously, such demands need to be appropriate to the child's developmental level. When the child is 2, a parent might expect her to use a spoon for eating, to indicate when she needs to go to the bathroom, or to learn to recognize colors and simple shapes. When the child is 5, a demanding parent might expect her to eat neatly, ask before interrupting, and learn reading skills.

Authoritative parents enforce rules firmly, sometimes using punishment, but they explain the reasons for rules and involve their children in decision making about rules. For example, if a child repeatedly runs into the street, an authoritative parent might stop him each time and explain why he should not go into the street. If the child continues, the parent might make him go to his room. Although authoritative parents are fairly strict, they encourage their children to "talk back"; that is, they encourage verbal give-and-take and communication.

A contrasting style is termed **authoritarian**. Authoritarian parents are also strict, but they emphasize unquestioning obedience and respect for authority. They discourage talking back or verbal give-and-take, and they are not very affectionate. A second contrasting style is termed **permissive**. The parents use little punishment, but they also make few demands on the child for obedience or for mature behavior. They have few rules and allow their children to regulate themselves. These parenting styles are discussed further in Chapters 12 and 14.

Both cross-sectional and longitudinal studies show that high achievement in school is associated with authoritative parenting. In one large sample, high school students with the highest grades had parents who were authoritative. The lowest grades occurred among students with authoritarian parents (Dornbusch, Ritter, Leiderman, Roberts, & Fraleigh, 1987).

In another investigation mothers' behavior with their preschool children was observed and the children were followed up in kindergarten and sixth grade. High achievers had mothers who had high expectations for mature behavior and achievement, communicated effectively with their children, and were affectionate (Hess, Holloway, Dickson, & Price, 1984). Mothers of high achievers controlled their children's behavior with explanations of reasons and consequences. For example, when the child refused to eat, the mother said, "If you don't eat, you won't be healthy and get bigger" (Hess & McDevitt, 1984, p. 2020). Mothers of low achievers more often used authoritarian methods such as threatening to spank the child if she did not eat.

PARENTS' TEACHING BEHAVIOR.   When parents play with young children, they can teach at the same time. Direct observation of parents working with their children on problem-solving tasks helps us understand what parents do and how different teaching methods affect children's skills and motivation.

Mothers of high achievers praise the child's efforts (e.g., "That's an interesting idea") rather than criticizing (e.g., "You know that doesn't look right") (Moore, E. G. J., 1986). They ask the child to think of different possible answers. They give suggestions that provide guidance about strategies for solving problems (e.g., "Why don't you try turning the pieces around to see if some of them fit that way") rather than giving the child the answer (e.g., "Try this piece here") (Hess & McDevitt, 1984). The parent's strategy suggestions provide guidance without solving the problem for the child. In earlier studies of Dutch and American families, parents were especially likely to tell girls the answers while encouraging boys to solve problems independently (Block, 1984; Hermans, Ter Laak, & Maes, 1972).

IMPLICATIONS.   Both the home environment and parental behavior can influence children's intellectual skills, school achievement, and achievement efforts. Some of the differences among ethnic and social-class groups discussed earlier are probably due to differences in these environmental variables (Hess et al., 1984; Moore, E. G. J., 1986). For example, among low-income families the environmental variables measured by the HOME index predicted children's IQs better than did the family's social status, particularly for black families (Bradley, Caldwell, & Elardo, 1977).

The home environment appears to be particularly important during the preschool years. Parents' behavior predicted children's school readiness when they entered school; differences in readiness accounted for later differences in achievement (Hess et al., 1984). Children's skills and abilities change more readily in the early years than in middle childhood and adolescence. In addition, the home environment may be especially important in these years because many children do not have other educational experiences; after the age of 6 school becomes an important influence and children spend more time with peers and adults outside the home.

Early Intervention

HEAD START.   In the 1960s a large number of intervention programs were established with the goal of enhancing the intellectual achievement of preschool and elementary school children. The best known of these is Project Head Start. The first Head Start programs were established during the summer of 1965 for 500,000 children. One goal of Head Start was to provide economically deprived children with the skills they would need when they entered public school. Although the program was also intended to contribute to children's physical, social, emotional, and cognitive development, most of the evaluations of Head Start's success have focused on school-related skills, particularly IQ (Zigler & Valentine, 1979).

Extensive evaluations were conducted in the early years of Head Start. The results were scrutinized by educators and legislators to determine whether the benefits of the program were sufficient to merit continued support by the federal government. These evaluations consistently showed that children in Head Start programs made significant gains in IQ, vocabulary, and school readiness skills such as understanding letters, numbers, and concepts. The gains were especially large for children with initially low IQs (Horowitz & Paden, 1973; Zigler & Valentine, 1979).

A few years after Head Start began, evaluations of the program began to be less optimistic—they suggested that short-term gains tended to fade out during the early school years. In many cases, however, these evaluations were faulty because all Head Start programs were grouped together without attention to the quality of the program, the skills of the teachers, and the like. More important, there usually were no appropriate control groups with which Head Start children could be compared. Often they were compared to other children in their neighborhoods or in their schools. We now know that the children selected for Head Start were significantly more deprived than others in their neighborhoods. That is, they began with fewer skills and lower test scores. Their parents were less well educated; they were more often black; their homes were more crowded; they had larger families but fewer had fathers at home; and their mothers read to them less in comparison to children who attended other kinds of preschools or did not go to preschool (Lee, Brooks-Gunn, & Schnur, 1988). Follow-ups using appropriate control groups have shown that Head Start children perform better in school and have fewer academic problems than comparable children without Head Start experience, even several years after entering school (Zigler & Valentine, 1979).

Well-controlled studies of preschool intervention programs show clear long-term effects. Children enrolled in 14 experimental preschool programs were tested in elementary and high school. The participants in preschool programs had fewer school failures and finished high school more often than children in control groups. The results of these studies are described in Box 9.3.

Preschool programs like Head Start have been shown to have positive long-term effects.

BOX 9.3

How Long Does a Head Start Last?

Economically disadvantaged children can gain lasting academic benefits from participation in a carefully designed early-education program during their preschool years. In 1976, eleven investigators in different parts of the country who had directed experimental early-education programs in the 1960s formed a consortium to follow up their graduates, who were then 10 to 17 years old. Many of the programs had been the models on which Project Head Start was based. The programs were selected because they all were initially evaluated with control groups of children selected to be comparable to the children participating in the educational program. (Most other Head Start evaluations were difficult to interpret because they lacked such control groups.) All of the children were from low-income families, and over 90 percent were black. Each investigator collected information on grade levels, special class placements, achievement test scores, and IQ.

In 1976 the experimental groups (those who had participated in the preschool programs) more often fulfilled the achievement requirements of their schools than did children in the matched control groups. They less often repeated a grade or were assigned to special classes for slow learners. They also performed better on reading and mathematics achievement tests during much of elementary school and on intelligence tests for three or four years after they left preschool.

In a few programs students were followed through the high school years. Those who had participated in preschool programs more often completed high school and were more likely to be employed after high school. Female students from the experimental groups were as likely as females in the control groups to become pregnant before completing high school, but they more often returned to school after having their babies. Of the experimental group, 25 percent were enrolled in some form of post-high school education, compared with 3 percent of the control group (Lazar & Darlington, 1982).

These findings contradict earlier reports that Head Start programs produce no long-term effects on children's intellectual development. They suggest that carefully designed early-education programs can produce lasting benefits for economically disadvantaged children.

The long-term effects of intervention may reflect lasting changes in home environments as well as changes in the children themselves. Parents whose children participate in such programs appear to learn new ways to convey skills and encouragement to their children. For instance, in the follow-up study described in Box

9.3, mothers of children who had participated in an early-intervention program had higher aspirations for their children and were more positive about their children's school performance than mothers in a control group. One program attempted to teach mothers how to provide cognitive stimulation for their children; in follow-up evaluations the children's younger sisters and brothers showed some improvement even without attending preschool, presumably because the mothers were practicing the skills they had learned in the program (Klaus & Gray, 1968).

A second reason why a "head start" can have long-term effects is that children who enter school with reasonably good academic skills, ability to attend, and high motivation to learn are viewed favorably by teachers, who in turn have higher expectations regarding achievement by those children. Such early advantages in school may lead to greater achievement, which leads to more self-confidence and more positive school experiences. Contrast this cycle with what might occur for a child entering school who does not know the alphabet, has trouble sitting still, and does not pay attention to directions. Children from early-intervention programs thus may "create" different school environments for themselves.

INTERVENTION IN INFANCY.   Although poor children who have experienced preschool intervention have improved chances to achieve, their intellectual performance still tends to be below average. More intensive intervention, beginning in infancy, can lead to IQs in the average range for high-risk children. The Carolina Abecedarian Project, for example, provides educational day care for children beginning at 3 months and continuing throughout the preschool years. During infancy the major emphasis is on verbal stimulation. Teachers talk to infants and play games with them, much as middle-class mothers do with their infants at home (see Chapter 6). After age 3 the curriculum includes math, music, science, and prereading skills.

Children receiving this intensive educational day care were compared to comparable children in a control group. All the children in both groups received nutritional supplements and health care. The results of intelligence tests administered during the first four years of life are illustrated in Figure 9.6. Although both groups performed in the average range during infancy, the scores of the control group declined. Apparently early intervention can reverse the decline in intellectual functioning that characterizes children from intellectually and materially impoverished environments (Ramey, Yeates, & Short, 1984).

We can sum up the results of experiments in early intervention with a few conclusions:

1.   Early educational intervention can produce an increase in school-related intellectual skills, IQ, and language use. Children who experience early-intervention programs enter school with more skills than they would otherwise have.

2.   Some positive effects of well-planned programs last for many years. Early intervention provides a partial counterweight to the downward trend in school performance that frequently occurs among poor children.

3.   Early and intensive intervention can reduce the tendency of children from impoverished homes to drop behind during the preschool years.

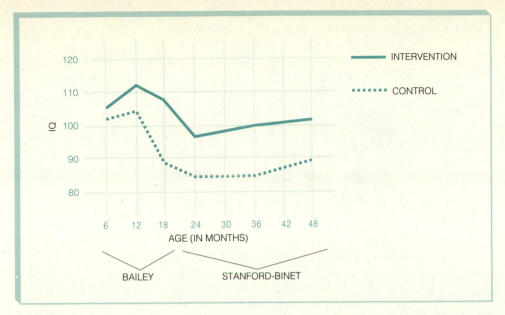

FIGURE 9.6 Performance on intelligence tests for children who received educational day care (intervention) from early infancy through age 4 and a control group of children who did not receive the intervention. The drop for both groups at 24 months is probably due to a change in the tests used. (Adapted from C. T. Ramey, K. O. Yeates, & E. J. Short. *The plasticity of intellectual development: Insights from preventive intervention. Child Development*, 1984, 55, 1913–1925. By permission.)

INTERVENTION WITH TELEVISION.   The late 1960s also witnessed a major effort to use television in teaching disadvantaged children. A group of educators, psychologists, television writers, and producers combined their talents to create "Sesame Street" and "The Electric Company." Production techniques from advertising and cartoons were used to package information about reading, cognitive skills, self-esteem, and prosocial behavior. Since that time other educational programs designed to teach science ("3-2-1 Contact") and math ("Square One") have been created. These programs reach a large number of children in a wide range of social groups. Evaluations have demonstrated that children learn letters, numbers, and other cognitive skills from these programs.

"Sesame Street" was evaluated in several parts of the country during its first two years. In the first of these evaluations, children who watched the program frequently were compared with children who did not. In the second, the researchers used a field experimental design in which children were randomly assigned to view or not to view the program at home. The experimental group was given cable connections or UHF sets (necessary to receive the program), and their mothers were asked to encourage the children to watch the program. The control group did not receive extra TV reception aids or encouragement to watch the program. Both groups of children took a test of cognitive skills before and after the viewing season (about six months). The results of the two evaluations are shown in Figure 9.7. As

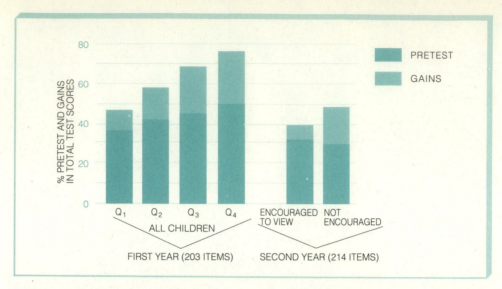

FIGURE 9.7   Pretest and gain scores on the test measuring skills taught by "Sesame Street." In the first year, different frequencies of viewing were compared. Viewing quartiles were defined as follows: Q_1, once a week or less; Q_2, two or three times per week; Q_3, three or four times per week; Q_4, five or more times per week. In the second year, experimental "encouraged to view" children were compared with a control group who were not specially encouraged. (Adapted from S. Ball & G. A. Bogatz. *The first year of "Sesame Street": An evaluation.* Princeton, N.J.: Educational Testing Service, 1970, and G. A. Bogatz & S. Ball. *The second year of "Sesame Street": A continuing evaluation.* Princeton, N.J.: Educational Testing Service, 1971. Copyright, Children's Television Workshop.)

you can see, the children who watched most often gained significantly more than those who watched infrequently. Children learn most from "Sesame Street" when their parents encourage them and watch with them, but they can learn vocabulary, letters, numbers, concepts, and information about the world even when they watch without adult intervention (Bogatz & Ball, 1971; Cook et al., 1975; Rice, Huston, Wright, & Truglio, 1988).

Interaction Between Constitution and Environment

In Figure 9.3 the child's constitution (genetic and biological attributes) and the environment are shown as the two major influences on intellectual development. Most psychologists agree that both are important. Each contributes to a child's intellectual skills and academic accomplishments.

We sometimes say rather glibly that there is an *interaction between constitution and environment*. By this we mean more than "both contribute." We mean that the effects of the child's constitution depend on the environment *and* the effects of the environment depend on the child's constitution. Consider the following example: In the Carolina Abecedarian Project discussed earlier, children were classified as high or low risk at birth on the basis of their Apgar scores. As you will recall from Chapter 2, the Apgar score is an index of the child's basic responsiveness at birth; a low

Children can learn numbers, letters, vocabulary, and other information from "Sesame Street" even when they watch the program alone.

Apgar score suggests some constitutional vulnerability. The children were randomly assigned to educational day care or to a control group; that is, they experienced two types of environment.

The intelligence test scores of the children with two types of constitution in two environments are shown in Figure 9.8. Children who received educational day care performed well regardless of their Apgar scores. That is, in a stimulating environment constitutional vulnerability made little difference. In the control group, however, the high-Apgar-score children performed better than the low-Apgar-score children. In the control environment constitutional vulnerability did make a difference. One can also read Figure 9.8 to say that children with optimal constitutional attributes were less affected by poor environments than children with signs of constitutional vulnerability.

A model for understanding one type of interaction between organism and environment is shown in Figure 9.9 (F. D. Horowitz, 1987). In this model, organisms are placed on a continuum from constitutionally vulnerable to invulnerable and environments are classified on a continuum from facilitative to nonfacilitative. Children with relatively invulnerable constitutions are expected to develop normally even in environments that are not highly stimulating or facilitating. Children in facilitative environments are expected to develop normally even when they have

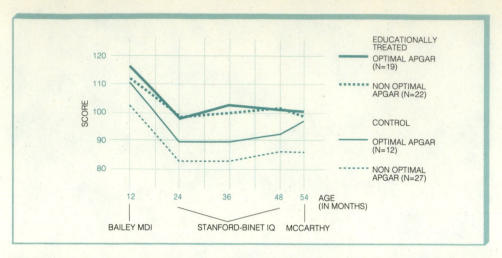

FIGURE 9.8   Mental test performance of high-risk children during the first 4½ years as a function of educational history (environment) and Apgar status (constitution). (Adapted from B. J. Breitmayer, & C. T. Ramey. Biological nonoptimality and quality of postnatal environment as codeterminants of intellectual development. *Child Development*, 1986, 57, 1151–1165. By permission.)

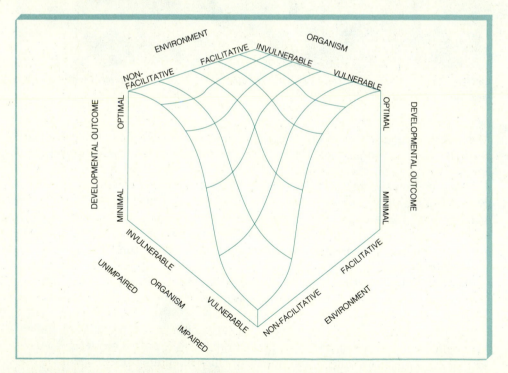

FIGURE 9.9   *The structural behavioral model* to account for developmental outcome illustrates the interaction between constitution and environment. (Adapted from F. D. Horowitz. *Exploring development theories: Toward a structural/behavioral model of development.* Hillsdale, N.J.: Erlbaum, 1987. By permission.)

vulnerable constitutional attributes. The model is not intended to suggest that any child is completely invulnerable; a sufficiently bad environment can affect even a constitutionally strong child. Instead, it is intended to show that the greatest risk occurs for children who are biologically vulnerable *and* experience nonfacilitative environments.

This general model can be applied to understanding particular aspects of children's intellectual development. For instance, children with low birthweight or neurological problems in infancy are vulnerable to developing poor cognitive and academic skills (see Chapter 2). However, when these constitutionally vulnerable children grow up in supportive, stimulating environments, they do not usually develop achievement problems in school. One group of psychologists followed all the children born in one year on the Hawaiian island of Kauai from before birth to adulthood. In stable, supportive middle-class families, by age 10 the school performance of children with neurological problems in infancy was indistinguishable from that of children with no signs of vulnerability in infancy. By contrast, early biological problems were exacerbated for children who lived in poverty in unstable homes with poorly educated parents (Werner & Smith, 1982). In the United States children living in poverty are at higher risk than children in affluent families for both biological vulnerability (e.g., low birthweight) and nonfacilitative environments.

================================ **SUMMARY** =====

Intelligence is the capacity to learn and use the skills that are required for successful adaptation to the demands of one's culture and environment. Initially, it was defined as a general competence, but today most psychologists agree that patterns of abilities differ from one individual to another. Intellectual skills are also specific to the particular environmental contexts in which they are learned and practiced.

Although many experts agree that intelligence includes many abilities, they do not always agree on the nature of those abilities. One theory distinguishes between *crystallized abilities*, or the knowledge a person has accumulated, and *fluid abilities*, or the processes we use in solving problems and dealing with new information. Another approach, the *structure of intellect* model, classifies intellectual abilities along three dimensions: task content, operations, and the product or outcome of intellectual activity. Yet another approach is a *triarchic theory* with three major components: cognitive processes and knowledge, ability to deal with new experiences, and the adaptation to the environment.

The first intelligence tests were created in the early 1900s to predict which children would succeed or fail in school; they provided only a summary IQ score. The Wechsler Intelligence Scales, which are widely used today, include subtests for several dimensions of intelligence; the subtests can be scored separately but are also grouped into verbal and performance scales. Some other tests of intelligence contain separate tests for various abilities and do not yield an average or overall score. Recent tests are increasingly based on theories about cognitive processes.

Popular assumptions about the nature of IQ and the value of IQ tests are incorrect. IQ is not a pure index of innate potential and is not fixed for life. Intelligence tests measure both aptitude and achievement, but performance on an IQ test does not necessarily reflect competence. Many experts believe it is more useful to examine tests of specific skills than to rely solely on a single IQ score.

Achievement motivation is an overall tendency to evaluate one's performance against standards of excellence, to strive for successful performance, and to experience pleasure contingent on successful performance. It can be inferred from achievement behaviors such as persisting at a difficult task or setting a moderate level of aspiration. The factors that determine a child's level of motivation include attainment value (the value the child attaches to success), standards of performance, expectancies about one's abilities (an aspect of perceived self-efficacy), and attributions about the reasons for success or failure.

Perceptions of self-efficacy, attributions, and attainment values develop gradually throughout childhood. During the first few years of school children's expectancies become more realistic; they increasingly use social comparison in evaluating their own performance; they set higher levels of aspiration for themselves; and they express more anxiety about failure. Many children develop a pattern of anxiety over testing that interferes with their performance.

Among American children there are consistent sex differences in intellectual performance and school achievement. On the average, males and females have different patterns of performance in different intellectual domains. These patterns are consistent with cultural stereotypes about appropriate behaviors for men and women. Intellectual achievement also differs among different cultural groups, social classes and ethnic groups. The claim that differences in IQ between blacks and whites are a result of genetic factors is not supported by the available evidence.

Although social experience makes a major contribution to ethnic and class differences in IQ, this does not mean that minority and lower-class children have deficient intelligence. It is more accurate to say that nonwhite and lower-class children often learn different skills than white middle-class children. One implication of this "difference" model is that intelligence tests are biased against lower-class and minority children. It is probably true that general differences in life experience make IQ tests difficult for minority children: Among other factors, such children are less familiar with standard English, they have less opportunity to learn test-taking skills, and they are especially prone to fear of failure and low concepts of their own ability.

Various aspects of the home environment contribute to individual differences in intelligence and achievement. Among these are features of the physical and social environment, such as whether parents are affectionate and verbally responsive and the level of noise and disorganization in the home. A positive relationship between parent and child can affect achievement because it forms a basis for the child to accept the parent's expectations and demands. Parents' beliefs, expectations, and values affect the achievement efforts of their children, as do parenting styles, discipline, and parents' teaching behavior. These differences in home environment and parental behavior are probably responsible for some of the differences in IQ among ethnic and social-class groups.

Intervention programs designed to enhance the intellectual achievement of preschool and elementary school children were established in the 1960s and are collectively known as Head Start. Well-controlled studies of such programs show that they have positive long-term effects, probably reflecting changes in the child's environment as well as in children themselves. More extensive intervention, beginning in infancy, can lead to IQs in the average range for high-risk children.

The 1960s also witnessed a major effort to use television in teaching disadvantaged children through such programs as "Sesame Street" and "The Electric Company." Such programs have been shown to have a positive effect on children's academic skills.

Psychologists often say that there is an interaction between constitution and environment. By this they mean that the effects of the child's constitution depend on the environment and vice versa. In a stimulating environment, constitutional vulnerability makes a relatively small difference; conversely, children with optimal constitutional attributes are less affected by poor environments than are more vulnerable children. This general model can be applied to understanding particular aspects of children's intellectual development.

REVIEW QUESTIONS

1. What is intelligence?

2. Briefly describe three theories about the dimensions of intelligence.

3. When were the first intelligence tests created? How have intelligence tests evolved since that time?

4. What are some limitations on measures of IQ?

5. What is meant by achievement motivation? What factors determine a child's level of motivation in a particular task area?

6. Briefly describe developmental patterns in achievement motivation.

7. How do the patterns of intellectual performance differ for males and females?

8. Contrast the "deficit" and "difference" models of ethnic and class differences in IQ.

9. What elements of the home environment are important for promoting intelligence and achievement?

10. Discuss the effects of intervention programs designed to enhance the intellectual achievement of preschool and elementary school children.

GLOSSARY

intelligence   The capacity to learn and use the skills that are required for successful adaptation to the demands of one's culture and environment.

crystallized abilities   The knowledge a person has accumulated.

fluid abilities   The processes used in solving problems and dealing with new information.

aptitude   The ability to learn a new skill or to do well in some future learning situation.

achievement   The amount a person has learned in a particular course or school subject.

achievement motivation   An overall tendency to evaluate one's performance against standards of excellence, to strive for successful performance, and to experience pleasure contingent on successful performance.

autonomous standards   Standards based on comparisons with one's own past performance.

social-comparison standards   Standards based on comparisons with other people's performance.

perceived self-efficacy   One's judgments of how well one can execute courses of action required to deal with prospective situations.

attributions   Inferences about the causes of one's own or someone else's behavior.

learned helplessness   The belief that one's successes do not reflect ability and that one's failures cannot be reversed by effort.

authoritative   A parenting style in which parents are moderately affectionate but have clear standards and expect children to behave maturely.

authoritarian   A parenting style in which parents are strict and emphasize unquestioning obedience and respect for authority.

permissive   A parenting style in which parents use little punishment but also make few demands on the child for obedience or for mature behavior.

SUGGESTED READINGS

Gould, S. J. (1981). *The mismeasure of man*. New York: Norton. A critical analysis that views the mental testing movement in a broad societal context.

Howe, M. J. A. (Ed.). (1983). *Learning from television: Psychological and educational research*. New York: Academic Press. Contains chapters by several authors describing how children and adults learn from television programs designed for education.

Scarr, S. (1981). *Race, social class, and individual differences in* IQ. Hillsdale, NJ: Erlbaum. A collection of essays by one of the most prominent investigators of genetic and environmental contributions to intelligence.

Spence, J. T. (Ed.) (1983). *Achievement and achievement motives: Psychological and sociological approaches*. San Francisco: W. H. Freeman. Contains chapters by several authors who have investigated achievement motivation. Most of the important views on this topic are represented.

Werner, E. E., & Smith, R. S. (1982). *Vulnerable, but invincible: A longitudinal study of resilient children and youth*. New York: McGraw-Hill. A report on a longitudinal study of children on the Hawaiian island of Kauai. All of the children were followed from birth to adulthood.

Part Four

THE CHILDHOOD YEARS: PERSONAL AND SOCIAL DEVELOPMENT

Chapter Ten

IDENTITY AND INDIVIDUAL DEVELOPMENT

Theories of Individual and Social Development
    Theories of Social Cognition
    Theories of Social Behavior: Social Learning
Developing a Sense of Self
    Self-concept
    Self-esteem
Sex Typing and Identity
    Development of Sex Typing
    How Does Sex Typing Come About?
Ethnic Group and Identity
    Children's Conceptions of Ethnic Groups
    Group Identity and Self-esteem
Emotion
    Components of Emotion
    How Children Acquire Emotions
Problems in Individual and Social Development
    Prevalence of Emotional Problems
    Types of Emotional Disturbance
    Duration of Emotional Disturbance over Time

The preceding four chapters have been concerned largely with intellectual and cognitive aspects of children's development; with this chapter, we begin a new section dealing with personal and social developments in early and middle childhood (roughly ages 2-12). In this chapter we discuss the "personal" or individual side of development: characteristics of the inner child, the development of self-concept and self-esteem, the acquisition of identities as a female or male and as a member of a sociocultural group, and the elaboration and development of feelings and emotions. We conclude with a brief discussion of emotional problems, which occur both in individual thoughts and feelings and in social interactions with others. In the next chapter the "social" aspects of development are discussed: children's relationships with peers, their friendships, and their moral development, aggression, and prosocial behavior.

THEORIES OF INDIVIDUAL AND SOCIAL DEVELOPMENT

Over the past 30 years we have come to believe that children's personal and social development is heavily influenced by their concepts and thoughts about themselves and other people; these are collectively known as **social cognition**. Personal qualities and social behavior are also affected by the people surrounding the child—the child's social environment. When we talk about what and how children learn from their social environment, we are discussing **social learning**. Not surprisingly, the two major sets of theories emphasize these two aspects of development: cognitive influences and social learning.

Theories of Social Cognition

The study of social cognition has emerged in recent years as psychologists have realized that children's social and emotional reactions depend partly on how they think. Consider the following example: A 4-year-old takes a bowl of oatmeal away from her 1-year-old brother. She does not like oatmeal, so she assumes that she is doing him a favor. He screams, and her father scolds her for being mean to her brother.

The problem in this example is the 4-year-old's failure to take into account her brother's preferences and to recognize that they are different from her own. If her father understood her social-cognitive processes, he might praise her for her efforts to be kind but also point out that her brother likes oatmeal.

Broadly defined, social cognition refers to perception, thinking, and reasoning about humans and human affairs (Flavell, 1985). Investigations of social-cognitive development focus on children's knowledge and understanding of the social world—of people, including themselves, and of social relationships.

DISTINGUISHING PEOPLE FROM OBJECTS. Although many principles of cognitive development apply to understanding both the physical and social worlds, children know very early that living things are different from inanimate objects. Young infants appear to expect interactions from people but not from objects. They become distressed—grimacing, thrashing, and crying—if a person faces them without speaking or moving (Gelman & Spelke, 1981; Trevarthen, 1977). By 5 months of age they react to other people's expressions of positive emotions with smiles and cooing but become upset by expressions of anger, fear, and sadness (Kreutzer & Charlesworth, 1973). When an 8-month-old sees another person gazing in a particular direction, the infant is likely to look in the same direction (Scaife & Bruner, 1975).

The qualities that distinguish people from inanimate objects—such as the ability to move independently and the possession of feelings—are recognized early. Two-year-olds are surprised when a chair seems to move by itself but not when it is moved by a person. Three-year-olds agree that a sentence like "The girl is sorry" is sensible while the sentence "The door is sorry" is not (Keil, 1979).

Even at age 5 or 6, however, children are uncertain about whether computers are alive, since computers can think and respond, qualities that children consider

Young children sometimes believe that computers are alive.

part of the animate world. During the early elementary school years, children refine the distinction between people and objects. At this point they recognize that computers do not have feelings or volition of the kind that people and animals have (Turiel, 1984).

Theories designed to explain how social cognition functions and how it affects individual and social development have been drawn from the basic cognitive theories described in earlier chapters: Piaget's theory, information processing, and attribution theory.

THEORIES BASED ON PIAGET.   Piaget's theory of cognitive development inspired much of the initial research on social cognition. Researchers adopted Piaget's assumption that children's concepts and reasoning about people pass through qualitatively distinct levels or stages that emerge in an invariant order, though at varying rates, in different children.

Piaget's concept of egocentrism formed the backbone of social-cognitive theorizing in this tradition. As you know from Chapter 7, Piaget regarded preoperational children as egocentric, unable to understand that their own perspectives, points of view, thoughts, motives, intentions, and attitudes are different from those of others. He maintained that egocentrism begins to decline sharply at age 6 or 7, when children enter the stage of concrete operations and recognize that other people have their own thoughts, points of view, and intentions. However, recent evidence demonstrates that even very young children are not as egocentric as Piaget supposed. They are frequently aware that other people do not see things the way they do, and they often modify their behavior to take account of the needs and interests of others (see Chapter 7).

INFORMATION PROCESSING: SCHEMA THEORY.   Information-processing concepts, such as the schema (described in Chapter 8), have also been applied to social cognition. Researchers using this perspective have proposed four types of social schemata:

1. A *person schema* is a set of notions about personality traits and attributes of people. For example, you may classify people as curious, sophisticated, or stupid.
2. A *self schema* is your set of concepts about yourself. Are you kind, outgoing, original, assertive?
3. A *role schema* is a set of beliefs about people in social groups or social roles—for example, concepts about women and men, people in different ethnic groups, occupational groups, and the like.
4. An *event schema* or *script* (see Chapter 8) describes a sequence of typical events in an everyday situation such as going to the supermarket or getting ready for a party (Fiske & Taylor, 1984).

According to schema theory, schemata guide perception, memory, and inferences about social events. People are more likely to perceive and remember information that fits a schema than information that does not fit. For instance, when children heard a story about going to the grocery store, they remembered the incidents that were part of the "grocery store script," such as pushing the shopping cart around the store. They were less likely to recall incidents that were not part of the script, such as a balloon floating on the ceiling (Adams & Worden, 1986).

ATTRIBUTION THEORY.   In Chapter 9 we discussed attributions about success and failure; however, people make causal attributions about many other events as well. Any time a person makes a judgment about what causes an action, that is an attribution. Social psychologists pointed out many years ago that we are all "naive psychologists." We make hypotheses and assumptions about the reasons not only for our own actions but also for the actions of other people.

People make attributions about the causes of other people's actions; those attributions often determine their reactions. We make assumptions about whether behavior is accidental or intentional. For example, if someone dumps a plate of food on your lap, you will probably react differently depending on whether you think they did it deliberately or accidentally. Attributions affect our perceptions of an individual's responsibility for his or her actions; if a child has been medically diagnosed as hyperactive, we may not hold him responsible for failing to sit still in school.

Theories of Social Behavior: Social Learning

Social-learning theories offer hypotheses about how environmental conditions affect social behavior as well as social cognition. Two major processes have been proposed: conditioning and observational learning.

CONDITIONING.   *Classical conditioning* (see Chapter 3) can be a means of learning social behavior and self-control. For example, if a father says "hot" just before a child touches a stove, the word is paired with the resulting pain. On another occasion the word *hot* acts as a conditioned stimulus that will stop the child from touching a hot pair of tongs. Ultimately, children may use conditioned words to aid in self-control. One little girl was observed starting to reach for an electric wall socket; as her hand moved, she said "no, no" and stopped.

Operant conditioning results from contingent reinforcement and punishment. Sharing, helping, aggression, sex-typed behavior, and many other personal and social behaviors are influenced by the rewards and punishments they produce.

OBSERVATIONAL LEARNING.   Children acquire a wide range of social and emotional qualities without going through a cumbersome trial-and-error process; they accomplish this simply by observing others. Children are great imitators, sometimes in ways that do not please their parents. A mother of our acquaintance was inspired to give up smoking when her 2-year-old daughter began to puff on an imaginary cigarette. Albert Bandura (1977) articulated a widely held theory describing the variables that affect observational learning and imitation. It is illustrated in Figure 10.1. You will note that cognitive concepts from information processing are incorporated along with environmental influences.

The steps shown in Figure 10.1 can best be understood through an example. Suppose that a group of children are exposed to a woman doing origami (making delicate figures by cutting and folding paper). Their *attention* will depend on how

Children can learn skills like ice skating by observing and imitating others.

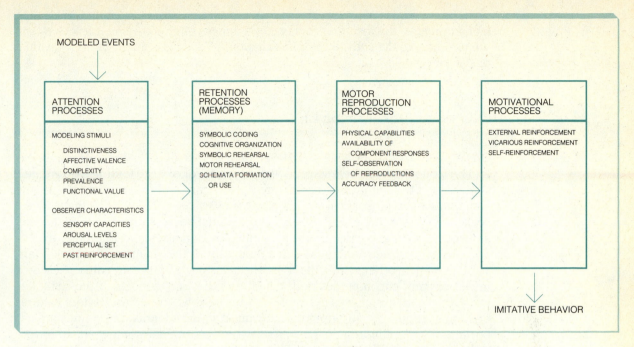

MODELED EVENTS

ATTENTION PROCESSES	RETENTION PROCESSES (MEMORY)	MOTOR REPRODUCTION PROCESSES	MOTIVATIONAL PROCESSES
MODELING STIMULI DISTINCTIVENESS AFFECTIVE VALENCE COMPLEXITY PREVALENCE FUNCTIONAL VALUE OBSERVER CHARACTERISTICS SENSORY CAPACITIES AROUSAL LEVELS PERCEPTUAL SET PAST REINFORCEMENT	SYMBOLIC CODING COGNITIVE ORGANIZATION SYMBOLIC REHEARSAL MOTOR REHEARSAL SCHEMATA FORMATION OR USE	PHYSICAL CAPABILITIES AVAILABILITY OF COMPONENT RESPONSES SELF-OBSERVATION OF REPRODUCTIONS ACCURACY FEEDBACK	EXTERNAL REINFORCEMENT VICARIOUS REINFORCEMENT SELF-REINFORCEMENT

IMITATIVE BEHAVIOR

FIGURE 10.1   Component processes proposed as governing observational learning in a social learning analysis. (Adapted from A. Bandura, *Social learning theory*. Englewood Cliffs, NJ: Prentice-Hall, 1977, p. 23. © 1977 Prentice-Hall, Inc. By permission.)

distinctive her actions are and on how interested they are in origami. An involved child will encode the woman's actions in a schema (e.g., a spiral pattern of cutting) and will rehearse her sequence of actions mentally or even with his fingers in order to *remember* what she did. Imitation then depends on the child's ability to cut and to visualize what the paper figure will look like (*motor reproduction*) and on how much praise from others, vicarious reinforcement (praise to the model), or self-satisfaction (*reinforcement*) he receives for making a successful copy.

Sometimes the process stops after retention; children remember what the model did but do not reproduce it. When this happens, we say that learning is *acquired* but not *performed*. However, the learned behavior may be imitated long after the child has observed the model. This capacity for delayed imitation means that the effects of observational learning may be difficult to detect. A 10-year-old may watch a roller derby on television; a few years later, on his first visit to a roller rink, he may call upon that knowledge and imitate the behavior of the television performers.

Imitation is not necessarily an exact copy of the model's behavior. Children who have acquired knowledge through observation may adapt what they have seen, and they may generalize from the principles they infer. For instance, children who observed a model making sentences with passive verb constructions (e.g., "The toy was played with by the baby") showed an increase in passive constructions even for sentences that were not performed by the model (Bandura, 1977).

These theories of social cognition and social behavior have guided research in many domains; the resulting concepts will appear often in the next few chapters. We turn now to the substance of this chapter—the development of the individual or the inner child.

DEVELOPING A SENSE OF SELF

One of the "tasks" of growing up is developing a sense of self, a sense of who one is and how one fits into one's society. William James, one of the founders of psychology, divided the self into two components, the "me" and the "I." The "me" is "the sum total of all a person can call his" (James, 1892/1961, p. 44), including abilities, social and personality characteristics, and material possessions. The "I" is the "self as knower." This aspect of the self "continually organizes and interprets experience, people, objects, and events in a purely subjective manner" (Damon & Hart, 1982, p. 844). In other words, the "I" is reflective, aware of its own nature. Research in self-concept encompasses both the "I" and the "me" aspects of the self.

Not all cultures give as much primacy to the sense of self as Western cultures do. To us, people are autonomous individuals whose identity and privacy are important. We give children their own rooms and accord them some rights to private thoughts and activities. Our self-descriptions emphasize such traits as kindness, assertiveness, or athletic talent. In many cultures, however, people are defined in relation to their social and group contexts—as part of a larger whole. People in those cultures emphasize their social roles (e.g., mother, community builder) and social contexts (e.g., member of the Miranda family) (Shweder & Bourne, 1984).

Self-concept

As explained in Chapter 5, the beginnings of self-awareness appear during the second year of life. At around 18 months of age children recognize their own face and point to pictures of themselves when someone says their name (Damon & Hart, 1982). During the childhood years the rudimentary sense of self grows into an elaborated and relatively stable network of self-perceptions and feelings.

Self-concepts are usually measured by asking people to describe themselves or to tell how they are different from others. For example, a child might be asked to tell how he would describe himself in a diary that no one else would see, or how he would be different if he were his best friend. A teenager might reveal her self-concept if she were asked to write to a new roommate whom she had never met. These measures of self-concept are intended to identify the attributes that the person considers most important. One person might focus on how kind (or unkind) he is, while another might emphasize how interesting (or dull) he is.

DEVELOPMENTAL CHANGES.   There are regular developmental changes in the categories children use when asked to describe themselves. Until about age 7 children tend to define themselves in physical terms. They name concrete, observable features of themselves, such as hair color, height, or favorite activities ("I like to

play ball"). They are less likely to name comparative qualities such as reading ability or bravery. Inner psychological experiences are not described as being separate
from overt behavior and physical characteristics (Selman, 1980).

During middle childhood descriptions of self shift gradually to more abstract
statements of facts ("I don't get into fights") and psychological traits (Damon &
Hart, 1982; Harter, 1983; Selman, 1980). Distinctions are made between mind and
body, between the private, subjective self and external events, and between mental and motivational characteristics and body parts. As a consequence, children
begin to think about themselves, to realize that they can monitor their thoughts
and deceive others about their ideas. At this age a child feels distinct from others
because she realizes that she possesses unique thoughts and feelings. Children of
this age seem to be particularly concerned with their own competencies, especially
in comparison with others ("I can ride my bike better than my brother can").

These general trends are shown by the responses of children in the first, third,
and sixth grades to questions about what would change if they become their own
best friends or when they grew up, or what had changed since they were babies
(see Table 10.1). First-graders most often named external characteristics, such as
name, age, and possessions. Older children described their typical behavior. Some
sixth-graders also referred to their feelings and thoughts (Mohr, 1978). Because the
information is based on children's verbal reports, the developmental trends could
be partly a function of changes in verbal abilities. For example, in early childhood children may have words for physical characteristics but not for psychological attributes.

*In the early school years children become concerned with their own competencies and often compare them
with those of siblings and other children.*

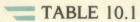

TABLE 10.1

Self-concept at Different Ages

Responses to the question "What would you have to change about yourself for you to become your best friend?" Numbers are percent of children who gave each category of response.

Type of characteristic described	GRADE LEVEL		
	First	Third	Sixth
External (physical attributes, name, possessions, age)	85	36	8
Behavioral (regular behavior or traits)	5	56	76
Internal (thoughts, feelings, knowledge)	10	8	16

Source: Adapted from D. M. Mohr. Development of attributes of personal identity. *Developmental Psychology*, 1978, 14, 427–428. Copyright 1978 by the American Psychological Association. By permission.

CONCEPTS OF SELF VS. OTHERS.   Children form self-concepts at least partly by accepting what other people say about them and judging how others react to them. They also compare themselves to others. You might expect, therefore, that the dimensions of self-concept would be similar to the dimensions used in thinking about other people. In many ways they are, as you will see when concepts of peers are discussed in Chapter 11. Subjectively, however, we know ourselves better than we know other people, and children sometimes use different modes for describing themselves and others. For example, children sometimes attribute their own behavior to situational conditions like the place they are in or the people they are with, but they attribute the behavior of other children to personality traits (see Chapter 9). For example, when John was scolded for hitting other children in preschool, he said he did it because they teased him. When asked why Sam fought a lot, John said Sam was mean.

In one study, children from the first through twelfth grades were asked to tell about themselves, their family, and school. They described themselves concretely, by what they did; they described others more abstractly, with trait labels. They focused more on emotion when describing their own inner states and more on ideas when describing other people's thoughts. They described themselves as more dynamic and changing; others were perceived as more static (McGuire & McGuire, 1986). We cannot be sure whether these responses reflect true differences between the children's ways of knowing themselves and others or they simply indicate differences in what the children were willing to say; nevertheless, the findings suggest that the subjective perspective on oneself is in some ways unique.

Self-esteem

As children form identities and concepts about themselves, they implicitly assign positive or negative values to their own attributes. Collectively, these self-evaluations constitute their self-esteem. Self-esteem differs from self-concept because it involves evaluation. The **self-concept** can be a set of ideas about oneself that is descriptive but not judgmental. The fact that one has dark hair and a soft voice can be part of one's self-concept, but those qualities are not judged as good or bad; they are neutral. **Self-esteem**, on the other hand, refers to one's evaluations of one's own qualities. Consider an 8-year-old boy who views himself as someone who fights a lot. If he values his ability to fight and stand up for himself, that quality may add to his self-esteem. If he is unhappy about his tendency to get into fights, this behavior might detract from his self-esteem.

MEASURING SELF-ESTEEM.   When children are asked questions about how much they like themselves or how they evaluate their abilities, there is a risk that the responses will be biased. For children under age 7, it is difficult to measure self-esteem in any meaningful way. If you ask preschool children how good they feel about themselves or their abilities, they almost always say they are satisfied and happy with themselves, accompanying their comments with a slightly mystified look. By age 9 or 10, children more often report low self-evaluations, and they probably have a more clearly formulated sense of their worth and competence in different areas (Harter, 1983).

Even older children, however, may not want to admit that they have undesirable qualities or may be unaware that certain qualities are considered undesirable by others. In one investigation children's self-evaluations were compared with those of teachers and peers. Many children's self-evaluations were consistent with those of others, but almost one-third of the children whose peers and teachers rated them as unpopular or incompetent rated themselves as popular and competent. Either these children's self-esteem was inflated compared to the opinions of others, or they were reporting more positive self-images than they really felt (Kagan, Hans, Markowitz, & Lopez, 1982).

One measure designed to reduce response bias is the Self Perception Profile for Children. For each question, descriptions of two types of children are presented and the child is asked which group he or she belongs to. Typical descriptions are "Some kids feel there are a lot of things about themselves that they would change if they could" versus "Other kids would like to stay pretty much the same" (Harter, 1985). This scale succeeds in measuring children's self-perceptions more accurately than earlier measures, partly because it includes questions about different types of behavior.

SELF-ESTEEM IS MULTIDIMENSIONAL.   Although individuals seem to have a general sense of self-worth, self-esteem varies for different domains of behavior. For example, on the Perceived Competence Scale there are scores for three content areas: cognitive, social, and physical skills. Children rate themselves differently in the three areas. An even finer distinction was demonstrated for children in grades 2 through 6 using a questionnaire containing items like "I am good at sports." The children received separate scores for four nonacademic areas—physical ability, physical appearance, peer relations, and parent relations—and three academic areas—reading, math, and general school ability (Marsh, H. W., 1985).

This fact—that self-evaluations vary for different content domains—is parallel to the point made in Chapter 9 that achievement motivation varies across task areas. It is an important point for parents and teachers to remember. Adults may be able to help children by emphasizing areas in which the children are competent and building self-esteem in those areas. On the other hand, they should not expect positive self-evaluations in one domain to carry over directly into another.

SEX TYPING AND IDENTITY

A child's sense of self consists partly of the individual attributes included in the self-concept, but it also includes an identity based on the social categories or groups to which the child is assigned by his or her culture. One of the most basic social categories in almost every society is gender. Often the first question asked about a baby is "Is it a boy or a girl?" Our culture and most others define a host of

Gender is a basic social category in almost every society and affects the way children are raised from birth.

interests, personality attributes, and behaviors as "feminine" or "masculine." Children learn and adopt many of these cultural standards at a remarkably early age.

The process of **sex typing** describes the ways in which biological gender and its cultural associations are incorporated into the child's self-perceptions and behavior. Like almost everything else you have encountered in this book, sex typing is multifaceted. Table 10.2 illustrates one way of describing its components. Across the top of the table are four features of sex typing. The first is *identity or self-perception*. **Gender identity** is acceptance of one's basic biological nature as female or male—

TABLE 10.2

A Taxonomy of Sex Typing

CONTENT AREA	CONSTRUCT			
	Identity (how you perceive yourself)	Concepts (knowledge about gender and social stereotypes)	Preference (what you would like)	Adoption (what you do; how other people see you)
Biological Gender	Gender identity Sex role identity	Gender constancy	Wish to be male or female	Clothing, hair, surgical sex change
Activities and Interests	Perception of your own interests	Concepts about sex typing of toys, activities, interests	Preferred toys, games, interests	Spending time with toys, games, interests
Personality Attributes, Social Behavior	Perception of your own personality	Concepts about sex typing of aggression, kindness, and the like	What attributes you value, would like to have	Observed aggression, kindness, and the like
Gender-based Social Relationships	Perception of your patterns of friendship, sexual orientation	Concepts about norms for same-sex friends, opposite-sex lovers, and the like	Preference for male or female friends, lovers, models to emulate	Selecting others for social or sexual contact on the basis of gender (e.g., same-sex peer choices)

the fundamental sense of being a girl or a boy. **Sex role identity** is a sense of being feminine or masculine—that is, a feeling that one's interests, personality, and behavior conform to one's own definitions of femininity or masculinity.

The second facet is *concepts or knowledge* about what society defines as masculine or feminine. We all know many of the social stereotypes and expectations for males and females, whether or not we agree with them or adopt them for ourselves.

Sex role preferences, the third facet, represent what a person values or would like to be. *Sex role adoption*, the fourth facet, involves acting in ways that are culturally defined as feminine or masculine. Each of these facets is somewhat independent. For example, sex role identity describes children's personal and private definition of self; sex role adoption refers to their overt behavior.

The vertical divisions in Table 10.2 show different content areas that are part of sex typing. Femininity or masculinity is defined not only by biological gender but also by activities and interests (e.g., playing with dolls or guns), personality characteristics (e.g., being sensitive or independent), and gender-based social relationships (e.g., playing mostly with girls or with boys).

Masculine and feminine qualities are not mutually exclusive. A woman may enjoy cooking and may also be interested in repairing cars; she may have a firm sense of her identity as a female even though she has interests that are culturally defined as both feminine and masculine. A man may be both independent and kind; he may regard both of these qualities as consistent with his masculine identity even though others define kindness as a feminine trait. A man may enjoy cooking and knitting while also preferring heterosexual relationships. In each case the person's basic gender identity as female or male remains solid. It is a rare person who conforms to all of his or her society's sex role expectations.

A person who combines feminine psychological qualities with masculine attributes is sometimes described as psychologically **androgynous** (Bem, 1974; Spence & Helmreich, 1978). When the concept of androgyny was introduced in the early 1970s, many people believed that it represented a healthier pattern than traditional sex typing because a person with the capacity to be kind, gentle, and nurturant as well as assertive and independent could adapt to many situations. Thus, a girl in a science class may find verbal assertiveness more adaptive than traditional feminine kindness and gentleness. A boy who can be gentle and kind may be better able to establish a close relationship than one who is dominant and unemotional.

Development of Sex Typing

GENDER IDENTITY.   Children develop at least a rudimentary gender identity sometime between 18 months and 3 years of age. They learn to label themselves and others correctly as females or males. Nevertheless, during the preschool years understanding of gender is limited. One 3-year-old boy upset his parents by announcing that he was going to be a mommy when he grew up. Another child became alarmed when she saw her mother dressed in a man's business suit for a Halloween party. Children make these mistakes because they have an imperfect understanding of biological gender; they lack what cognitive theorists call gender constancy (see Table 10.2).

Gender constancy refers to a child's understanding that gender does not change. Gender constancy is acquired in three steps. First, children acquire gender identity. Next, they learn (around age 4) that gender does not change over time. By age 5 or 6, most children also understand that gender remains the same regardless of changes in appearance, clothing, or activities. Before that age, children may say that a boy who wears a dress or plays with a doll is a girl. Such confusion is due partly to the wording of the questions. If children are asked whether the boy is really a girl or is just pretending, they often answer correctly. However, some genuine confusion may exist for children who do not know that genitals are the critical basis for deciding whether a person is male or female. Children who are aware of genital differences are also likely to understand that gender does not change with new clothing or haircuts (Bem, 1988).

By the time American children reach their third birthday, they not only classify people correctly as female or male but also have a remarkable amount of information about social expectations for the two sexes. They know that girls are supposed to play with dolls and dress up like women, while boys are supposed to play with trucks and pretend to be firemen. By the age of 4 or 5 they know most of the stereotypes for adult occupations. They expect women to be teachers and nurses and men to have a variety of occupations such as pilot and police officer. A young child may adamantly assert that "women can't be doctors" or "men don't change diapers."

Preschool children often assume that sex stereotypes are absolute prescriptions for correct behavior, and they sometimes enforce them more rigidly than older people do. By around age 5 children begin to learn stereotypes about personality and social behavior. Boys are believed to be big, loud, aggressive, independent, and competent; girls are thought to be small, quiet, nurturant, obedient, and emotional. Stereotypes for personality traits are probably learned later than those for play activities and interests because personality attributes are abstractions. In addition, sex differences in related behaviors are less pronounced and therefore are less likely to be observed by children than differences in dress, play activities, and jobs.

In middle childhood children continue to refine their understanding of social expectations for females and males. At the same time, their thinking becomes less rigid. They seem more ready than younger children to recognize that people can combine behaviors that are stereotyped as masculine and feminine, and better able to accept departures from sex role prescriptions. For example, girls aged 7 to 11 were questioned about whether they thought various activities, qualities, and occupational goals were more appropriate for a man, a woman, or both. Younger children gave more stereotyped answers than older children did. Older children more often acknowledged that both men and women could perform a job (Marantz & Mansfield, 1977). The patterns appear in Figure 10.2.

PREFERENCES.   Children often prefer the activities and roles that are expected for members of their own sex, but not always. Boys are more attracted to masculine interests and activities than girls are to feminine activities. In fact, many young girls consider themselves tomboys and enjoy "masculine" games and activities, particularly during the elementary school years. Because the male role has higher

In middle childhood children's social expectations for females and males become less rigid.

status than the female role in most societies, children of both sexes are often attracted to activities and interests that are defined as masculine.

ADOPTION OF SEX-TYPED BEHAVIOR.   Children's behavior is sex typed very early. By age 2 children select toys and activities that fit sex stereotypes. Children in a toddler day care center were observed during periods when a specially selected set of toys was arranged in their play area. The toys were either masculine, feminine, or neutral, according to adult stereotypes. The amount of time that girls and boys played with each group of toys is shown in Figure 10.3. Even these very young children, particularly boys, selected sex-typed toys (O'Brien & Huston, 1985). The same pattern occurred when 2-year-old children were observed at home. Girls more often played with soft toys and dolls, asked for help, and dressed up in adult clothes. Boys more often played with blocks and manipulated objects or toys (Fagot, 1974).

Children also begin to select same-sex playmates during the preschool years. If you observe a typical preschool, you are likely to see groups of girls, often playing in the housekeeping area, and groups of boys, often playing with blocks or trucks. In elementary school sex segregation becomes extreme (Maccoby & Jacklin, in press). In a one-room day camp attended by 8- to 10-year-old children, boys interacted with other boys almost three times as much as they socialized with girls; girls interacted primarily with other girls (Huston, A. C., Carpenter, Atwater, & Johnson, 1986).

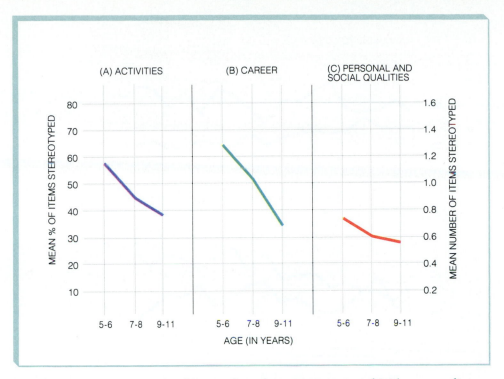

FIGURE 10.2   Mean percent of items viewed as sex-stereotyped (either masculine or feminine) in three domains: (a) activities (e.g., fixing a car or doing dishes), (b) careers (wanting to be a teacher or an engineer), and (c) qualities (kindness or dominance). Stereotypes decline from age 5 to 11 because older children view more characteristics as appropriate for both sexes. (Adapted from S. A. Marantz & A. F. Mansfield. Maternal employment and the development of sex-role stereotyping in five- to eleven-year-old girls. *Child Development*, 1977, 48, 672. By permission.)

At a very early age children begin to select sex-typed toys and activities.

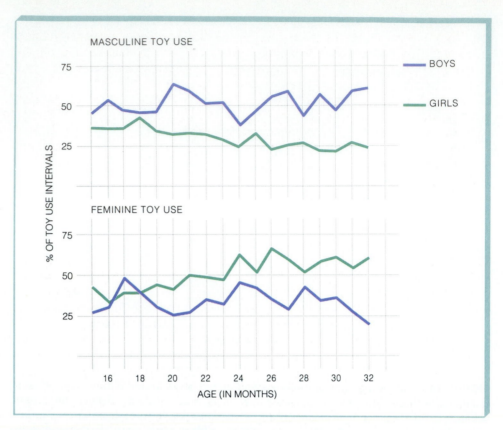

FIGURE 10.3   Percent of play time that toddler boys and girls spent with stereotypically masculine and feminine toys. (Adapted from M. O'Brien & A. C. Huston. Development of sex-typed play behavior in toddlers. *Developmental Psychology*, 1985, 21, 866–871. Copyright 1985 by the American Psychological Association. By permission.)

Although there are early and clear sex differences in games, activities, and peer selection, sex typing in personality and social behavior is less pronounced, even in middle childhood. Boys are, on the average, more aggressive than girls, but there are no reliable differences between the sexes in dependency, altruism, independence, or most other personal qualities (Huston, A. C., 1983; Maccoby & Jacklin, 1974; Shipley-Hyde & Linn, 1986).

How Does Sex Typing Come About?

Several explanations of sex typing have been suggested. They are based on theories of cognitive development, schemata, and social learning.

COGNITIVE DEVELOPMENT.   In 1966 Lawrence Kohlberg proposed that sex typing results from cognitive-developmental changes, a view that departed radically from the accepted wisdom of the time. He suggested that children achieve gender identity (i.e., classify themselves as girls or boys) as part of the general tendency to think in categories. Once gender identity is established, children actively look for information about the activities, values, and behaviors that distinguish boys from girls. They do not need to be given direct instruction or encouragement by adults; they acquire information about sex typing spontaneously, by constructing knowledge about the roles assigned to each gender in their surroundings. It is then a natural step for children to value the patterns associated with their own gender. In effect, a boy says, "I am a boy. Therefore, I want to do 'boys' things." Kohlberg proposed that this process is completed when children achieve gender constancy—an accomplishment that accompanies concrete-operational thought.

Some parts of this theory are well supported by evidence, but others are not. Children acquire gender identity and knowledge about gender roles spontaneously, without direct teaching, as Kohlberg proposed. They absorb information about male and female behavior by observing parents, teachers, neighbors, siblings, television characters, and anyone else they encounter. However, evidence does not support the prediction that gender constancy is important for sex typing; children who acquire gender constancy early are no more likely to be sex typed than those who acquire it later. Moreover, not all children value the role prescribed for their gender, even though they understand it. Finally, the theory accounts for the fact that sex role concepts appear early in life and are almost universal, but it does not explain individual differences in the strength and nature of sex typing.

SCHEMATA.   Information-processing theorists also propose that children's cognitions about gender—their gender schemata—explain sex typing (Liben & Signorella, 1987; Martin & Halverson, 1981). According to this theory, once children have acquired gender role schemata, they interpret events in their world according to those schemata. When events violate sex stereotypes, the child may fail to notice or remember. For example, children saw a large number of pictures showing men and women in sex-stereotyped roles (e.g., a female nurse, a male judge) and counter-stereotyped roles (e.g., a female dentist, a male typist). A few minutes later they were asked to select the pictures they had seen from a larger set containing similar pictures. The children recognized more pictures that were consistent with sex stereotypes than pictures that were inconsistent (Cann & Newbern, 1984).

In extreme cases memory is distorted. Groups of 6-year-olds saw one of four short films about a doctor and a nurse. The only difference between the films was the gender of the two actors (two males; two females; male doctor, female nurse; female doctor, male nurse). Children who saw the traditional version (male doctor, female nurse) remembered the actors and their roles correctly. Those who saw female doctors or male nurses often remembered incorrectly. Some thought the male nurse was a doctor (Cordua, McGraw, & Drabman, 1979).

GENDER SALIENCE.   Schema theory explains individual differences in sex typing by proposing that gender may be more salient or important to some children than to others (Bem, 1981). Although all members of a society are well aware of the social expectations for males and females, gender may be a particularly salient category for some people. They interpret the world through gender-based glasses. Others may judge people and situations according to different categories. Consider Sue, who goes to a picnic in a park where a lot of people are playing frisbee. She is trying to decide whether to join the game. If gender schemata are salient to her, she might consider whether it is feminine to play frisbee. She will probably notice whether other girls are playing, or think about whether she will be attractive to boys if she plays. Tammy, for whom gender schemata are not very salient, might consider whether she has enjoyed playing frisbee in the past, whether she is so uncoordinated that she will look foolish if she plays, or whether she sees another activity that she prefers. She is basing her decision on criteria unrelated to gender. Both girls might make the same decision, but for different reasons.

Children for whom gender is especially salient show strong sex-typed preferences and behavior. They choose games and activities that are socially prescribed for their gender, and they are especially likely to play with same-sex peers (Serbin & Sprafkin, 1986). They are also more likely to remember events that fit sex stereotypes and forget those that do not (Signorella & Liben, 1984). Some socialization experiences that may encourage or discourage gender salience are discussed in Box 10.1.

BOX 10.1

Nonsexist Child Rearing

Using her theory of gender salience, Sandra Bem presented a series of proposals for socializing children in a nonsexist manner. She suggested first that gender as a category has assumed too much significance in our culture. It is used even when it is irrelevant. For example, in an elementary school classroom the monitors are one boy and one girl each day; boys and girls are put on opposing teams or are selected alternately for teams. Teachers do not use race, eye color, or other categories to sort children. As a result of the attention gender receives from adults, it becomes highly salient in children's thinking and takes on more importance than it otherwise might.

Bem suggests that one way to counteract this pattern is to teach children early that gender is a biological fact defined by reproductive capacities and anatomy. Parents can stress that genitals, not clothes or behavior, define a person as a girl or a boy. Many parents, even those who teach their children labels for everything around them, avoid labeling genitals or talking directly about biological sex. Yet such labels and discussion enable the child to understand what is critical to being a girl or a boy and what is not. Bem illustrates this point by describing her son Jeremy's experience when he wore barrettes to nursery school at age 4. On several occasions another boy told Jeremy he was a girl because "only girls wear barrettes." Jeremy explained that "wearing barrettes doesn't matter. Being a boy is having a penis and testicles." Jeremy finally pulled down his pants to make his point more convincing. The other boy was not impressed. He simply said, "Everybody has a penis; only girls wear barrettes" (Bem, 1983, p. 607).

In addition to teaching that biology defines gender, parents can counteract and try to alter some of the messages about sex stereotypes that children receive from the larger culture. Television programs and storybooks for very young children can be selected carefully. When children encounter traditional themes in books or television, parents can discuss them with the children. Parents can point out that it is strange that in fairy tales women so often need rescuing and men so often go on adventures. Parents can also select schools that share and support their values, and they can make their views known to teachers and administrators.

In discussions with children, Bem suggests that parents stress individual differences—that some boys like to play football and others do not—and point out that people have different opinions about what is right or appropriate. Just as people differ on politics or religious values, they also differ on ideas about sex-appropriate behavior. Children can gradually acquire and understand the value system that their parents hold—that women and men are fundamentally alike in most respects (from Bem, 1983).

SOCIAL-LEARNING THEORY.   Social-learning theorists believe that sex-typed behavior is learned through the same processes that operate for other forms of behavior: instrumental conditioning and observation. They propose that boys and girls are reinforced and punished for different behaviors from early childhood on, and that children learn to expect certain roles for females and males by observing others (Mischel, 1970).

Careful observational studies in homes and preschools support the assertion that parents, teachers, and peers reinforce different kinds of behavior in girls and boys. Parents of children between 20 and 24 months of age more often reacted favorably when the children engaged in activities that were "sex appropriate" than when they performed behaviors that were deemed appropriate for the other sex. For instance, they responded positively when girls played with dolls, asked for help, followed an adult around, and helped with an adult task. They reacted positively when boys played with blocks, manipulated objects, and were physically active (see Table 10.3). When interviewed, many of these parents said that they treated children of both sexes similarly. There was little correlation between their observed behavior and the attitudes they expressed in the interviews.

Children also have many opportunities to observe sex-typed behavior in their daily lives. Parents are not the only models, but they are extremely important because of children's strong attachments to them. Children are especially likely to imitate parents who are warm and powerful (i.e., are dominant and decisive and exercise control over the child's life). Parental example does influence children's

TABLE 10.3

Parents' Reactions to Behavior of Toddler Boys and Girls

| | Parent reaction | | | |
| | Positive | | Negative | |
Child behavior	To boys	To girls	To boys	To girls
Masculine Behavior				
Block play	.36	.00*	.00	.00
Manipulates objects	.46	.46	.02	.26*
Transportation-toy play	.61	.57	.00	.02
Rough-and-tumble play	.91	.84	.03	.02
Aggression: hit, push	.23	.18	.50	.53
Running and jumping	.39	.32	.00	.07
Climbing	.39	.43.	.12	.24*
Riding trikes	.60	.90	.04	.06
Feminine Behavior				
Play with dolls	.39	.63*	.14	.04*
Dance	.00	.50	.00	.00
Ask for help	.72	.87*	.13	.06*
Play dress up	.50	.71	.50	.00
Help adult with task	.74	.94*	.17	.06*
Follow parent around	.39	.79*	.07	.07

Note: The proportions in this table represent the percentage of occasions on which parents responded positively (by praising, guiding, comforting, explaining, or joining the child's activity) or negatively (by criticizing, restricting, punishing, or stopping play) when their children engaged in each of the behaviors listed. The information was obtained by observing parents and their 20- to 24-month-old children at home. The asterisks indicate that the difference between treatment of boys and girls was statistically significant.

Source: B. I. Fagot. The influence of sex of child on parental reactions to toddler children. *Child Development*, 1978, 49, 459–465. By permission.

sex typing. For instance, children of employed mothers have less traditional sex role concepts than children whose mothers work at home full time; daughters of employed mothers also have higher educational and career aspirations than daughters of nonemployed mothers (Huston, A. C., 1983). However, parents' attitudes about their roles are also important. For instance, having a father who participated in household work did not change children's sex stereotypes unless their mothers adopted nontraditional attitudes about the male role. If mother thinks it is consistent with masculinity for father to cook and change diapers, the child's sex role schemata incorporate father's nontraditional behavior (Baruch & Barnett, 1986).

Children also learn the social expectations of their culture by observing other adults, peers, teachers, and the mass media. Television may be an especially potent source because children spend many hours each week watching TV and because the portrayal of women and men on television is often highly stereotyped. Television women cook, clean, care for children, and try to look beautiful (often while managing a demanding job); television men are aggressive, adventurous, and successful (Calvert & Huston, 1987).

Cognitive and social-learning theories can be integrated to explain sex typing. Children learn social expectations for the sexes through direct reinforcement and by observing others. They process that information actively, integrating it with other knowledge that they have acquired to construct concepts of gender appropriateness. Knowledge of social stereotypes alone, however, does not lead individuals to acquire sex-typed identities and preferences. If gender becomes a salient basis for thinking about everyday life, children are likely to act in accordance with social expectations for their gender. Their preferences and behavior also depend on the social value and reinforcement they receive from important people in their surroundings.

ETHNIC GROUP AND IDENTITY

Children's identities include the racial, ethnic, and religious groups to which they belong. Many of the principles that govern acquisition of sex-typed identity probably also apply to other social categories. This is especially true in the case of ethnic identity.

Virtually all of the research on ethnic identity has been carried out with black children. As early as age 3, both black and white children classify people according to skin color, just as they classify people by gender or by age. They may recognize different racial groups before that, but children younger than age 3 have not been studied (Katz, 1976; Powell, 1985).

Children's Conceptions of Ethnic Groups

The group differences recognized by very young children (through about age 6) are based on obvious physical characteristics such as skin color and facial features. During middle childhood black children develop a complex concept of race that includes social cues that differentiate blacks from whites, such as style of dress, speech patterns, culinary tastes, musical preferences, history, and ancestry (Alejandro-Wright, 1985). Young children are also more likely to understand ethnic distinctions that are emphasized in their culture than ones that are not considered important. In the United States, white children are relatively unaware of differences between light- and dark-skinned Afro-Americans, even though their physical appearance is quite different, but they classify light-skinned Afro-Americans as different from Caucasians, despite the physical similarity between the two groups.

Minority children are aware of ethnic differences earlier than non-minority children. Such differences have more profound social consequences for them, and in the formation of self-concept there is a general tendency for distinctive qualities to be salient. (For example, very short people mention height when they define themselves more often than people of average stature [McGuire, McGuire, Child, & Fujioka, 1978].) Even in adulthood, being black is probably a more salient aspect of one's identity than being white, at least in a predominantly white culture like ours. This is illustrated by one survey of black adolescents. In response to the question "Who are you?" 95 percent mentioned being black or Negro. It would be most surprising to find white teenagers mentioning being white in response to the same question (Powell, 1973).

Group Identity and Self-esteem

In the 1940s and 1950s many researchers concluded that black children had negative self-images because they preferred white people to black people in a variety of tests. It appeared that black children had accepted the devaluation of their group by the majority culture. More recent studies have been contradictory—black children sometimes express positive and sometimes negative attitudes toward their own group. At the same time, black children report high self-esteem on questionnaires like those described earlier, perhaps because the measures are based on self-reports (Harter, 1983; Katz, 1976; Rosenberg, 1985).

The contradiction between self-esteem and group attitudes may reflect the difference between group identity and personal identity. Group identity includes both ethnic-group awareness (e.g., "I am Cuban" or "I am Afro-American") and attitudes (e.g., "Black people help each other"). Personal identity includes both self-concept (e.g., "I am tall," "I am shy") and self-esteem (e.g., "I am a good athlete"). Group identity might contribute to personal identity, but many factors other than one's ethnic-group identity could influence self-concept and self-esteem. A black child might have a strong positive academic self-concept and think of himself as smart even if he believes that many black children are poor students. Conversely, he might consider himself a poor athlete even though he thinks blacks are generally superior athletes. In fact, when measures of both group identity and personal identity are given to children and adolescents, there is little relationship between the two (Cross, 1985).

The social changes that have taken place in the past 40 years may also have produced changes in group attitudes among black people. Studies conducted before 1960 consistently showed that black children had negative attitudes about their racial group. The 1953 school desegregation decision, followed by the civil rights movement and the Black Power movement in the 1960s, produced a new group image for black people. Studies conducted between 1968 and 1977 suggest that children's attitudes reflected that change; the majority of those studies found that black children had positive attitudes toward blacks. Although in the 1980s black children faced reduced opportunities, more poverty, and less social support than had been available in the previous two decades, positive changes appear to have been maintained, particularly when parents have taught pro-black attitudes (Cross, 1985).

Almost no information exists about ethnic identity for other minorities, such as Asian-Americans, American Indians, or Hispanics. We might expect that children's awareness of these groups would depend on visible physical cues and on the social importance of group distinctions, just as it does for black Americans. We need more information, however, particularly as increasing numbers of children in these groups become part of the American population. (Box 10.2 illustrates the process of gaining an ethnic identity as it was experienced by one black child.)

BOX 10.2

A Child Learns What It Means to Be Black in America

Richard Wright's autobiography, *Black Boy* (1945), contains many perceptive recollections of a child's efforts to understand racial distinctions. Some especially telling passages from Wright's book are presented here.

I soon made a nuisance of myself by asking far too many questions . . . It was in this manner that I first stumbled upon the relations between whites and blacks, and what I learned frightened me. Though I had long known that there were people called "white" people, it had never meant anything to me emotionally. I had seen white men and women upon the streets a thousand times, but they had never looked particularly "white.". . .It might have been that my tardiness in learning to sense white people as "white" people came from the fact that many of my relatives were "white"-looking people. . . . And when the word circulated among the black people of the neighborhood that a "black" boy had been severely beaten by a "white" man, I felt that the "white" man had had a right to beat the "black" boy, for I naively assumed that the "white" man must have been the "black" boy's father. . . . A paternal right was the only right, to my understanding, that a man had to beat a child. But when my mother told me that the "white" man was not the father of the "black" boy, was no kin to him at all, I was puzzled.

"Then why did the 'white' man whip the 'black' boy?" I asked my mother.

"The 'white' man did not *whip* the 'black' boy," my mother told me. "He *beat* the 'black' boy."

"But why?"

"You're too young to understand." (pp.30-31)

At last we were at the railroad station . . . and for the first time I noticed that there were two lines of people at the ticket window, a "white" line and a "black" line. During my visit at Granny's a sense of the two races had been born in me with a sharp concreteness that would never die until I died. When I boarded the train I was aware that we Negroes were in one part of the train and that the whites were in another. Naively I wanted to go and see how the whites looked while sitting in their part of the train.

"Can I go and peep at the white folks?" I asked my mother.

"You keep quiet," she said. . . .

I had begun to notice that my mother became irritated when I questioned her about whites and blacks, and I could not quite understand it. I wanted to understand these two sets of people who lived side by side and never touched, it seemed, except in violence. Now, there was my grandmother. . .Was she white? Just how white was she? What did the whites think of her whiteness?

"Mama, is Granny white?" I asked as the train rolled through the darkness.

"If you've got eyes, you can see what color she is," my mother said.

"I mean, do the white folks think she's white?"

"Why don't you ask the white folks that?" she countered.

"But you know," I insisted. . . . "Granny looks white," I said, hoping to establish one fact, at least. "Then why is she living with us colored folks?". . .

"Don't you want Granny to live with us?" she asked, blunting my question. . . .

"Did Granny become colored when she married Grandpa?"

"Granny didn't *become* colored," my mother said angrily. "She was *born* the color she is now."

Again I was being shut out of the secret, the thing, the reality I felt somewhere beneath all the words and silences. . . .

"What has Papa got in him?" I asked.

"Some white and some red and some black," she said.

"Indian, white, and Negro?"

"Yes."

"Then what am I?"

"They'll call you a colored man when you grow up," she said. She turned to me and smiled mockingly and asked: "Do you mind, Mr. Wright?"

I was angry and I did not answer. I did not object to being called colored, but I knew that there was something my mother was holding back. She was not concealing facts, but feelings, attitudes, convictions which she did not want me to know; and she became angry when I prodded her. All right, I would find out someday. Just wait. All right, I was colored. It was fine. I did not know enough to be afraid or to anticipate in a concrete manner. True, I had heard that colored people were killed and beaten, but so far it all had seemed remote. There was, of course, a vague uneasiness about it all, but I would be able to handle that when I came to it. (pp. 55-56)

EMOTION

Identity, self-concept, and attitudes about oneself are individual matters; they are part of the inner child. Another central facet of the inner self is emotion. The terms *feeling*, *emotion*, and *affect* are all used to describe a domain of human experience that is subjectively clear and vivid to most adults. However, psychologists do not find emotion easy to understand.

It is clear from children's speech and behavior that emotions like happiness and sadness are central to their experiences.

Children's everyday conversations make it clear that happiness, sadness, fear, and many other emotions are central to their experiences and to their relationships with others. Consider the following examples of 6- and 7-year-olds' spontaneous remarks. After his mother praised him for good behavior, one child said, "Yes, I like it when I'm good. It feels good." Another child said in a low voice, "It scared me very much when you and Dad were fighting." During a phone conversation with Grandma: "Aw, Grandma, . . . don't be sad on your birthday. I love you" (quoted in Bretherton, Fritz, Zahn-Waxler, & Ridgeway, 1986, pp. 540-541).

Components of Emotion

One framework for understanding emotions is illustrated in Figure 10.4. It has four components: eliciting context, body states, emotional expression, and emotional experience.

1. ELICITING CONTEXT.   One component of any emotional response is its *eliciting context* (see Chapter 4). Events in one's environment, such as getting a new bike or seeing a horror movie on television, can elicit emotions. Thoughts and memories, and even previous emotional experiences, can also elicit feelings, particularly as children get older (Lewis & Saarni, 1985).

In one investigation, 4- to 7-year-old children were asked what things make them happy, sad, angry, afraid, and surprised. The reasons named fell into seven categories: material goods (e.g., getting a new toy), fantasy (monsters), interpersonal events (being teased), environmental events (going to Disneyland), achievement (getting straight A's), food (having to eat vegetables), and animals (a dog dying). The results are shown in Figure 10.5.

Interpersonal and environmental events were named often as elicitors of all types of emotion. Interactions with other people were especially important in stimulating sadness and anger. Material goods were frequently named as reasons for happiness and surprise. Fantasy was associated primarily with fear.

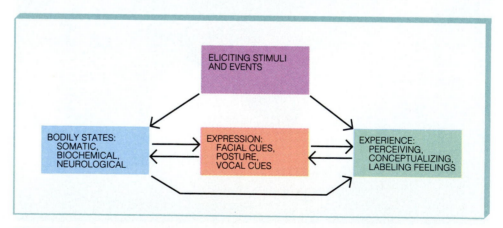

FIGURE 10.4   Four components of emotion. (Based on M. Lewis & C. Saarni (Eds.) *The socialization of emotions.* New York: Plenum, 1985.

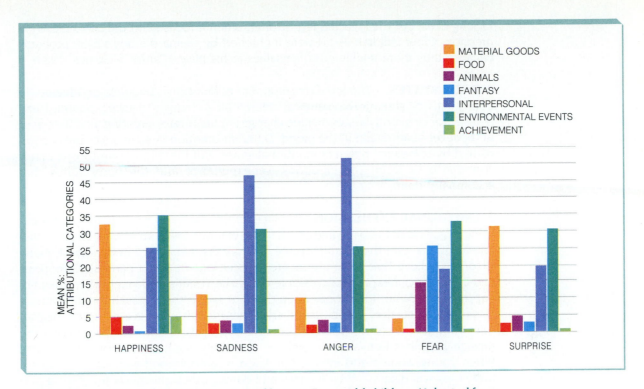

FIGURE 10.5 Causes of emotion as reported by 4- to 7-year-old children. (Adapted from J. Strayer. Children's attributions regarding the situational determinants of emotion in self and others. *Developmental Psychology*, 1986, 22, 649–654. Copyright 1986 by the American Psychological Association. By permission.)

As they grow older, children's understanding of the social world changes, and they enter new settings, such as school, that provide new contexts for emotion. The stimuli that elicit emotion also change. In the study just described, 7-year-olds cited interpersonal events and achievement as reasons for emotions more often than 4-year-olds did; younger children more often referred to fantasy (Strayer, 1986).

Age changes are partly due to cognitive-developmental changes. Joanne Cantor and her associates at the University of Wisconsin used Piaget's theory to predict what types of television stimuli would elicit fear in preschool and elementary school children. They expected that physical transformations like the change from a man to a green monster shown on "The Incredible Hulk" would frighten preoperational children because such children do not yet know that underlying reality does not change with appearance (see Chapter 7). In contrast, concrete-operational children were not expected to react with fear. This prediction was confirmed by the children's reactions.

The researchers' second prediction was that concrete-operational children would respond with more fear than preoperational children when the stimulus required them to be empathic, that is, to take the perspective of a television character. In one experiment children saw a film of a boy being attacked by a swarm of bees. Children from 3 to 5 years old were frightened when the camera focused on the attacking bees, but they reacted less strongly when it focused on the boy's facial expression. Older children (9-11) were frightened by seeing the boy's face, probably because they more readily put themselves in his place (Cantor & Sparks, 1984).

2. BODY STATES.   The second component of emotion is *body state*, or "changes in bodily activity: somatic, biochemical, neurological changes" (Lewis & Saarni, 1985, p. 6). Emotional body states include changes in heart rate, sweating, and increases in the level of adrenalin in the blood. Different emotional experiences are accompanied by somewhat different emotional states, but there is no one-to-one correspondence between the emotions we experience and the body states that accompany them.

3. EMOTIONAL EXPRESSION.   Facial expressions, body movements, and vocalizing (e.g., screaming or crying) are all forms of emotional expression. They are visible to others, and they communicate feelings. As mentioned in Chapter 4, many theorists believe that there are innate associations between particular emotions and certain facial expressions. People everywhere smile and laugh when they are happy and frown or look sober when they are sad. Although such innate connections may exist, they can be modified. Different cultures have different "display rules" about what forms of expression are appropriate. For example, among the Kipsigis people in Kenya it is considered extremely inappropriate for adults to cry. When young women and men are initiated into adulthood with painful puberty rites, they will disgrace their families and damage their prospects for respect and leadership if they cry (Harkness & Super, 1985).

4. EMOTIONAL EXPERIENCE.   Conscious emotional experience occurs when a person perceives or labels feelings. Many people think language is critical for emotional experience because it provides a means of identifying vague internal sensations and distinguishing among feelings. Before language is acquired, infant emotional experience may not be comparable to the experience of older children and adults (see Chapter 4). Cross-cultural comparisons reveal cultural differences in the types of emotions for which there are words. For example, the language of Ifaluk Atoll contains the word nguch, which has no direct translation in English. Its meaning is a mixture of being bored, tired, and slightly disgusted. Children and adults describe their emotional experience as "nguch" often; the word defines an emotional concept for that culture (Lutz, 1985).

An emotion, therefore, is a combination of an eliciting condition, a bodily state, facial and body expression, and a conscious perception. When psychologists say a person is afraid, all of these components are included. Sandra, a 9-year-old, is waiting outside the principal's office after having been sent there for misbehaving (an eliciting stimulus). She may have perspiration on her face and hands (body state), and her face may look frightened as she bites her fingernails (expression). When you ask her how she feels, she says, "I'm scared" (emotional experience).

Some of the arrows in Figure 10.4 go in both directions in order to illustrate the fact that different components can affect each other. One might assume that elicitors lead to body states, which in turn lead to expression and experience.

However, other possibilities have been proposed. For example, some psychologists argue that facial expressions and actions can affect body states or experience. If you smile and laugh, you will experience happiness. Running away from a charging bull generates the experience of fear. Conversely, if one's culture and family do not acknowledge or label a particular emotion and do not permit its expression, one's ability to experience that emotion may be affected. For instance, most young children discover a vague feeling of pleasure when they touch their genitals, but many American parents forbid them to express those feelings and refuse to label or discuss them. As a result, children may have difficulty understanding their bodily states or knowing how to express the feelings involved.

How Children Acquire Emotions

Both cognitive-developmental and social-learning theories provide some understanding of how children move from infant to adult emotions. Children's increasing cognitive and linguistic sophistication permits them to acquire concepts about emotions, to learn the rules of their culture for emotional expression, and to label and sometimes regulate body states. Social-cognitive theories focus primarily on what children understand about emotion.

SOCIAL COGNITIONS ABOUT EMOTION.   By the age of 2 many children have a vocabulary describing basic emotions, and they connect emotions to eliciting stimuli in their conversations. Here are some samples from 28-month-olds: "I give a hug. Baby be happy." "It's dark. I'm scared." "You sad Mommy. What Daddy do?" (Bretherton et al., 1986, p. 534).

Between the ages of 2 and 5, children learn to recognize and label situations and facial expressions denoting different feelings. The distinction between positive and negative feelings is acquired earliest, and it remains fundamental. Young children and adults were asked which of a set of pictures of facial expressions were similar or different. They grouped the pictures along two dimensions: degree of pleasure (e.g., happy and excited vs. bored and sad) and degree of arousal or intensity (e.g., contented vs. elated) (Russell & Bullock, 1986).

By age 5 children can differentiate among emotions within the broad categories of positive and negative. For example, children were asked to describe the feelings displayed in each of the six photographs in Figure 10.6. Most 5-year-olds labeled the happy, sad, and angry expressions correctly but did not describe the surprised, fearful, or disgusted expressions accurately. However, when an adult used the labels and asked the children which face went with each, the 5-year-olds performed well on all emotions except disgust (Michalson & Lewis, 1985).

Developmental changes occur in children's understanding of several aspects of emotion. One of those is the source of emotions: Children increasingly understand that the source of feelings can be internal as well as situational. For instance, they know that memories can produce feelings and that the sources of feelings may endure for a while. When George says, "Mom is irritable with me because she found out this morning that she lost $2,000 on the stock market," he is acknowledging that the causes of feelings can last over a period of time.

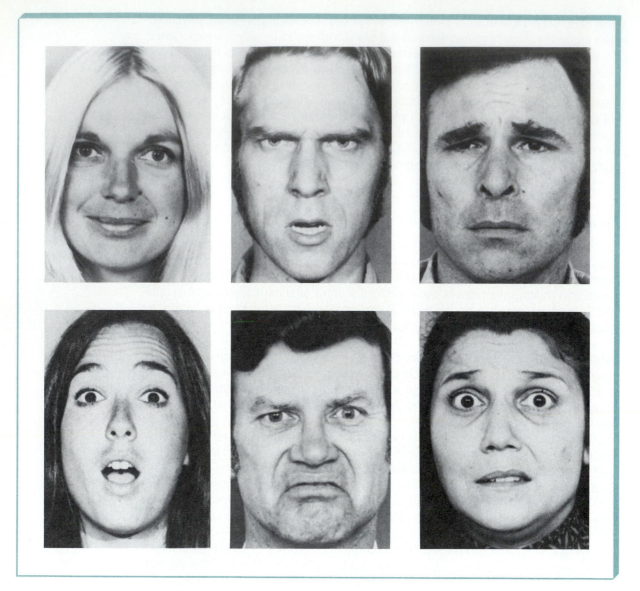

FIGURE 10.6   Facial expressions for six emotions (happiness, anger, sadness, surprise, disgust, and fear). (From P. Eckman & W. V. Friesen, Pictures of facial affect. Consulting Psychologists Press, Palo Alto, CA, 1976).

Children also increasingly understand that multiple and sometimes conflicting feelings can occur. Before about age 6 or 7, they are likely to name either positive or negative emotions. Ambivalence, or feeling a mixture of negative and positive emotions, is not clearly understood until age 9 or 10 (Harris, 1985). For instance, boys and girls heard a story about a child (named Mike or Molly) whose favorite puppy wrecks a toy that he/she likes a lot. By the age of 9 or 10, children could articulate the mixture of love and anger that is implied by the story (Donaldson & Westerman, 1986).

As they grow older, children increasingly understand that real feelings may be different from those that can be observed (i.e., that emotional experience may not match emotional expression). They learn that one can disguise one's emotions. Exactly when this change occurs is not entirely clear. In studies in which children heard stories and were asked to describe the feelings of the person in the story, 4-year-old children had limited understanding of the possibility that a person might look one way and feel another; 6- and 10-year-olds understood the distinction clearly (Harris, Donnelly, Guz, & Pitt-Watson, 1986). However, in everyday conversation even 2-year-olds "pretend" emotions and show some rudimentary understanding that internal feelings are not always what they appear to be on the surface (Bretherton et al., 1986).

ATTRIBUTIONS AND AFFECT.   Cognitive-developmental theory deals primarily with what children know about emotion; attribution theory is concerned with how cognitions influence emotional reactions. Consider this example: Jennifer asks Stacey to come over to her house. Stacey says no. Jennifer's emotional reaction will depend on her attribution about why Stacey refused. If she thinks Stacey does not want to come, she will feel hurt; if she thinks Stacey's mother won't let her come because Stacey has to clean her room, she probably will not feel hurt. Children understand the effects of attributions on feelings as early as age 5. However, as they progress through elementary school they become more likely to disguise the causes of their behavior in order to reduce other people's hurt or angry reactions. For example, 10- to 12-year-olds are more likely than younger children to tell Jennifer that their mother won't let them come even if it is not true (Weiner, B. & Handel, 1985).

HOW EMOTIONS ARE LEARNED.   Human beings are probably "prewired" for a small set of emotional responses. People in several cultures have similar facial expressions and words to describe six basic emotions: happiness, surprise, fear, anger, sadness, disgust (Campos, Barrett, Lamb, Goldsmith, & Stenberg, 1983). Nevertheless, much of our emotional responding depends on learning. Direct learning probably occurs through conditioning, both classical and instrumental. John B. Watson demonstrated many years ago that a young child could be made afraid of a rabbit by pairing the rabbit with an unconditioned stimulus for fear (e.g., a loud noise).

Most emotional training, however, probably results from parents' labels and interpretations of children's behavior. The following passage illustrates how parents teach children to label their emotional expressions:

> Douglas, a 13-month-old, sits quietly playing with blocks. Carefully, with a rapt expression, he places one block on top of another until a tower of four blocks is made. As the last block reaches the top, he laughs out loud and claps his hands. His mother calls out, "Good, Doug. It is a ta-l-l-l tower. Don't you feel good!" Returning to the tower, Doug tries one more block, and as he places it on top, the

tower falls. Doug bursts into tears and vigorously scatters the blocks before him. His crying brings his mother, who, while holding him on her lap and wiping his tears, says softly, "Don't feel bad. I know you're angry. It's frustrating trying to build such a tall tower. There, there, try again." (Lewis, 1978, p. 3).

Observational learning is also a potent means of acquiring cultural and family norms for situations that elicit emotion, modes of expressing emotion, and labels for emotional experience. Children observe emotional behavior in their families from infancy on; they also learn schemata for emotions from observing others outside their families, either directly or on television (Dorr, 1985; Potts & Collins, in press).

Observation can be used therapeutically to help children learn to cope with stressful situations. For example, a film called *Ethan Has an Operation* shows a young boy going through a surgical procedure with some initial apprehension but no ill effects. Children who see the film are less frightened of surgery than those who do not see it. Contrast that film with the following common procedure: Before a cavity is filled, the dental assistant gives the child a detailed description of the whole procedure. The child becomes increasingly wide-eyed and frightened. Merely giving preparatory information does not enable children to cope with stress or pain, but films showing peers or puppets going through the process and overcoming fear are helpful (Miller, S. M. & Green, 1985).

PROBLEMS IN INDIVIDUAL AND SOCIAL DEVELOPMENT

Most children develop a healthy concept of self, an identity that incorporates their gender and ethnic identities, and an adaptive pattern of emotional responses. However, children can be depressed, self-deprecating, or dissatisfied with themselves; they can also be hyperactive, aggressive, and cruel. In this section we shift from "normal" emotional and behavioral development to some of the emotional problems and behavior disorders of childhood. Anticipating Chapter 11, we include problems in social relationships as well as problems in individual development.

Disturbed or pathological behavior is not, in most instances, qualitatively different from "normal" behavior. Typically, it represents an extreme of behaviors that are discussed throughout this book. The causes of disturbed behavior can best be understood by knowing the causes of normal behavior. We can understand depression by examining what leads to sadness and anxiety among children in general. We can understand social withdrawal by knowing how children gain social skills and confidence in general. Therefore, this section highlighting a few deviant behaviors should not be considered in isolation. You can learn about both normal and abnormal behavior in each section of this book.

Prevalence of Emotional Problems

How many children show serious emotional disturbance at some time during childhood? Disturbance is defined as deviance from behavior that is normal or usual *for the child's age*. For instance, it is not unusual for a 2-year-old to cling to her mother in a strange place, but it is unusual for a 12-year-old to do so. We always define psychopathology in the context of what we know about normal development.

Most researchers estimate that 6 to 10 percent of all children have serious emotional or behavioral problems for some period of their childhood (Kauffman, 1985). These estimates are obtained primarily from reports by teachers and other adults. For instance, in one longitudinal investigation teachers were asked which of the children in their classes had behavior problems. The majority of children were thought to have a behavior problem by at least one teacher at some time in their school career. However, slightly over 10 percent were considered a problem by every teacher who rated them over three years.

More specific information about the kinds of behavior that adults consider disturbed comes from checklists like the Child Behavior Checklist. This list includes a large number of behavior problems; parents and teachers can check any that characterize a particular child. The behavior problems that differentiate children who are referred for emotional problems from those who are not are shown in Table 10.4 (Achenbach & Edelbrock, 1981).

TABLE 10.4

Items from the Behavior Problems Checklist that Differentiate Children Referred to Professional Help for Emotional Problems from Children Who Are Not Referred

Acts too young	Is teased
Argues a lot	Hangs around with children
Can't concentrate	who get into trouble
Obsessions	Impulsive
Hyperactive	Lying or cheating
Too dependent	Nervous
Lonely	Not liked
Confused	Too fearful or anxious
Cries a lot	Feels too guilty
Cruel to others	Stomachaches, cramps
Daydreams	Attacks people
Demands attention	Poor schoolwork
Destroys own things	Refuses to talk
Destroys others' things	Screams a lot
Disobedient at home	Secretive
Disobedient at school	Stubborn, sullen, or irritable
Poor peer relations	Moody
Lacks guilt	Sulks a lot
Easily jealous	Swearing
Feels unloved	Temper tantrums
Feels persecuted	Threatens people
Feels worthless	Unhappy, sad, or depressed
Fighting	Withdrawn, worrying

Types of Emotional Disturbance

The many specific problems of children fall into two broad categories: **internalizing** *and* **externalizing syndromes**. Internalizing syndromes involve excessive internal distress, anxiety, depression, social withdrawal, and self-deprecation. Externalizing syndromes include hyperactivity, poor behavior control, aggression, and delinquency. Two internalizing syndromes have generated particular concern in recent years; they are childhood depression and social withdrawal.

DEPRESSION.   Depressed children look sad and say they feel sad, cry easily, feel lonely and pessimistic, are moody and irritable, and often have negative thoughts about themselves. Cognitive and social-learning processes are sometimes used to explain why children become depressed. In Chapter 9 we discussed learned helplessness, a pattern of attributions in which people believe that they have no control over events in their world, especially negative or aversive events. Some psychologists have proposed that depression results from these feelings of helplessness. Depression is associated with family disruption and loss or unpredictability of important people in the child's life (Petti, 1983). However, many other factors may contribute to childhood depression, including genetic and temperamental attributes. Psychologists do not yet know which of these factors contribute most to the incidence of depression in childhood.

SOCIAL WITHDRAWAL.   Children who are socially withdrawn—who do not interact with other children—often lack social competence. They may also lack

Depressed children look and feel sad and lonely.

A child who does not interact with others may lack social competence.

social-cognitive knowledge, such as how to detect the intentions of others (Dodge, Murphy, & Buchsbaum, 1984).

A number of methods have been successful in helping shy children gain social skills and become more sociable. Placing them in situations with younger peers, small groups, and/or structured activities is sometimes helpful (Kendall, Lerner, & Craighead, 1984). Peers can be trained to help withdrawn children increase their levels of interaction, as discussed in Box 10.3. Peer encouragement and reinforcement often work better than adult interventions. When adults become involved in children's interactions, even to praise them for playing well together, child-to-child interaction tends to decline and the children direct their attention toward the adult.

≡ BOX 10.3

Children Teach Social Skills to Peers

Children with handicaps such as mental retardation, physical disabilities, or severe emotional problems often lack basic social skills for relating to peers. They are frequently rejected by other children. Integrating handicapped children in regular classes is not enough to make them fully participating members of the peer group; sometimes it simply confronts them more directly with their handicap (see Chapter 13).

Philip Strain and his associates (1985) have developed a successful program of intervention for children with social handicaps. The core of the intervention is training peers as intervention agents. The researchers first observed interactions among normally developing preschool children to find out what types of social initiatives are most common and most successful in getting another child involved in play. They then trained normally developing peers to "help the teacher" by getting handicapped children to play with them. The peer helpers were taught to use the following behaviors: statements that might organize play (e.g., "Let's play house"), sharing toys, physically helping another child with a task, showing affection, and rough-and-tumble play.

Peer helpers received role-playing training in which the teacher pretended to be another child. Every other time the child tried to initiate play, the teacher turned away or failed to respond, simulating the behavior of a socially withdrawn peer. At the same time, the child was encouraged to keep trying. After the training, the peer was assigned a handicapped child. Over the course of a month, the target handicapped children went from near-zero levels of social responding to levels that were normal for their age group. Similar peer intervention has been successful in reaching children with severe emotional problems, visually impaired children, and retarded adults.

Peer interventions work better than adult interventions for teaching social behavior to peers. When adults reinforce or intervene in children's social behavior, the behavior tends to stop. For instance, if a child shares a toy with another child, the second child may respond by taking the toy and getting involved in play. If the teacher says, "I'm glad you are sharing," or makes some similar comment, the play tends to stop as the children attend to the teacher.

Children who participate as trainers benefit from the experience, too. They learn specific techniques for drawing out a child who is shy or withdrawn. They learn to be concerned about such children and to try to help them rather than rejecting them.

EXTERNALIZING SYNDROMES.   As noted earlier, externalizing syndromes involve behavior that is hyperactive, aggressive, and/or delinquent. Children with these syndromes lack behavior control and frequently have immature moral judgment. They misinterpret other people's intentions, often seeing hostility where other children would not see it (Dodge et al., 1984). We discuss some of the family patterns that contribute to excessive aggression, and some of the treatments for such behavior patterns, in the section on aggression in Chapter 11.

Duration of Emotional Disturbance over Time

Parents whose children show disturbed behavior are intensely interested in knowing whether emotional problems in childhood portend long-term difficulties. Do children "grow out of" emotional problems? Although many children have minor problems that do not endure, serious behavioral and emotional problems in childhood are likely to continue in later life. Problems that arise during the preschool years are less likely to persist over several years than problems that are manifested in the elementary school years; school-age children's emotional and behavioral disturbances have a moderately high probability of persisting (Campbell, 1983; Fischer, Rolf, Hasazi, & Cummings, 1984). However, even preschool children's disturbances should not be ignored on the grounds that they will eventually disappear; early intervention has a better probability of success than intervention after several years of difficulty.

Externalizing problems are particularly persistent over time. When children with these patterns were followed into adulthood, they had higher rates of antisocial behavior, illegal behavior, marital problems, and alcoholism than a control sample from the same neighborhood (Robins, 1966). Internalizing problems also continue over time, but there is less evidence that they persist into adulthood, perhaps because symptoms like anxiety, depression, and withdrawal are less obvious to other people than externalizing behaviors (Campbell, 1983; Fischer et al., 1984).

SUMMARY

The two major sets of theories of individual and social development emphasize cognitive influences and social learning. Investigations of social-cognitive development focus on children's knowledge and understanding of the social world, which begin with the ability to distinguish people from objects. Theories explaining how social cognition functions have been drawn from Piaget's theory, information-processing concepts, and attribution theory.

Piaget's theory of cognitive development inspired much of the initial research on social cognition. Piaget regarded preoperational children as unable to understand that their own perspectives are different from those of others. However, recent research has shown that young children are frequently aware that other people do not see things the way they do, and they often modify their behavior to take account of the needs of others.

Researchers using information-processing concepts have proposed four types of social schemata: person schemata, self schemata, role schemata, and event schemata or scripts. According to schema theory, these schemata guide perception, memory, and inferences about social events. Attributions also affect perceptions and inferences about social events.

According to social-learning theories, social behavior is learned through conditioning and observation. Social-learning theorists point out that children acquire a wide range of social and emotional qualities by observing and imitating others. Imitation may be delayed and is not necessarily an exact copy of the model's behavior.

An important task of growing up is developing a sense of self. The beginnings of self-awareness appear during the second year of life. Until about age 7 children tend to define themselves in physical terms. During middle childhood descriptions of self shift to behavior patterns and psychological traits. People evaluate themselves more subjectively than they evaluate others.

The positive or negative values one assigns to one's own attributes constitute one's self-esteem. Self-esteem is difficult to measure in children under 7. Even older children may give biased responses. Self-esteem varies for different domains of behavior.

The process of sex typing describes the ways in which biological gender and its cultural associations are incorporated into the child's self-perceptions and behavior. It has four facets: gender and sex role identity, concepts or knowledge about what society defines as masculine and feminine, sex role preferences, and sex role adoption. A person who combines feminine and masculine attributes is sometimes described as psychologically androgynous.

Children develop at least a rudimentary gender identity by age 3. Later they acquire gender constancy, the understanding that gender does not change. Preschool children often assume that sex stereotypes are absolute prescriptions for correct behavior. In middle childhood, children's understanding of social expectations for females and males is refined and their thinking becomes less rigid.

Children's behavior is sex-typed very early: By age 2 they select toys and activities that fit sex stereotypes, and they begin to select same-sex playmates during the preschool years. According to Kohlberg, sex typing is based on cognitive-developmental changes; for example, gender identity is related to the tendency to think in categories. Information-processing theorists explain sex typing in terms of schemata—once children have acquired gender role schemata, they interpret events according to those schemata. Schema theory explains individual differences in sex typing by proposing that gender may be more salient to some children than to others. Social-learning theorists believe that sex-typed behavior is learned through the same processes that operate for other forms of behavior.

Children's identities include the racial, ethnic, and religious groups to which they belong. The group differences recognized by very young children are based on obvious physical characteristics. During middle childhood children develop a complex concept of ethnic group that includes social as well as physical cues. Minority children are aware of ethnic differences earlier than non-minority children.

The components of emotions are eliciting context, body states, emotional expression, and emotional experience. Each of these components can affect the others. Both cognitive-developmental and social-learning theories provide some understanding of how children move from infant to adult emotions.

By the age of 2 many children connect emotions to eliciting stimuli in their conversations. Between the ages of 2 and 5, children learn to recognize and label situations and facial expressions denoting different feelings. In subsequent years developmental changes occur in children's understanding of several aspects of emotion: They increasingly understand that the source of feelings can be internal as well as situational, that multiple and sometimes conflicting feelings can occur, and that real feelings may be different from those that can be observed.

According to attribution theory, children's emotional reactions depend on their attributions about the behavior of others. Learning theorists believe that human beings are predisposed to make some emotional responses, but that much of our emotional responding depends on learning. Most emotional training probably results from parents' labels and interpretations of children's behavior. Observational learning is also a potent means acquiring norms for situations that elicit emotion, modes of expressing emotion, and labels for emotional experience.

Emotional disturbance is defined as deviance from behavior that is usual for the child's age. The emotional problems of children fall into two broad categories: internalizing and externalizing syndromes. Internalizing syndromes include depression and social withdrawal; externalizing syndromes involve behavior that is hyperactive, aggressive, and/or delinquent. Problems that arise during the preschool years are less likely to persist over several years than problems that are manifested in the elementary school years. Externalizing problems are particularly persistent over time.

REVIEW QUESTIONS

1. Briefly describe the three main social-cognitive theories of individual and social development.

2. Discuss the processes of social development described by social-learning theorists.

3. What regular developmental changes occur in the development of self-concept?

4. Distinguish between self-concept and self-esteem.

5. What are the four facets of sex typing? What is gender constancy?

6. Describe the various explanations of sex typing that have been proposed by cognitive and learning theorists.

7. How do children's conceptions of ethnic groups and ethnic identity develop?

8. What are the components of emotion?

9. How do children acquire emotions?

10. What are the main types of emotional disturbances experienced by preschool and school-age children?

GLOSSARY

social cognition   People's concepts and thoughts about themselves and other people.

social learning   The process by which children learn from their social environment.

self-concept   A set of ideas about oneself that is descriptive but not judgmental.

self-esteem   One's evaluations of one's own qualities.

sex typing   The processes by which biological gender and its cultural associations are incorporated into the child's self-perceptions and behavior.

gender identity   Acceptance of one's basic biological nature as female or male.

sex role identity   A feeling that one's interests, personality, and behavior conform to one's own definitions of femininity or masculinity.

androgynous   A term used to describe a person who combines feminine and masculine psychological qualities.

gender constancy   A child's understanding that gender does not change.

internalizing syndromes   Emotional disturbances that involve excessive internal distress, anxiety, depression, social withdrawal, and self-deprecation.

externalizing syndromes   Emotional disturbances that involve hyperactivity, poor behavior control, aggression, and delinquency.

SUGGESTED READINGS

Cicchetti, D. & Schneider-Rosen, K. (Eds.). (1984). *New directions in child development*: Vol. 26. *Childhood depression*. San Francisco: Jossey-Bass. Contains four papers on the developmental patterns and causes of childhood depression. Depression is discussed in relation to cognitive and social development. Relationships between maternal depression and children's emotional disturbance are described.

Harter, S. (1983). Developmental perspectives on the self-system. In E. M. Hetherington (Ed.) & P. H. Mussen (Series Ed.), *Handbook of child psychology*:

Vol 4. *Socialization, personality, and social development* (4th ed.). New York: Wiley. A readable but highly scholarly review of the literature on self-concept and self-esteem, useful for students who wish to explore this domain in depth. The volume contains other review chapters on topics covered in Chapters 10-13.

Lewis, M., & Saarni, C. (Eds.). (1985). *The socialization of emotion*. New York: Plenum. Chapters in this book cover many aspects of emotional development in childhood, including cross-cultural comparisons. The authors take a perspective that emphasizes learned aspects of emotion, particularly the influence of language on emotional experience and expression.

Liben, L. S., & Signorella, M. L. (Eds.). (1987). *New directions in child development*: Vol. 38. *Children's gender schemata*. San Francisco: Jossey-Bass. Six chapters address the formation and effects of gender schemata. Basic developmental patterns are described, and individual differences are examined. Effects of family, school, and television on children's gender schemata are discussed. One chapter reviews interventions designed to change children's gender schemata.

Spencer, M. B., Brookins, Geraldine K., & Allen, W. R. (Eds.). (1985). *Beginnings: The social and affective development of black children*. Hillsdale, NJ: Erlbaum. An edited collection of recent psychological studies of black children. Contains several articles about self-esteem and identity, socialization, and academic development. The authors present a well-rounded, perceptive, and sympathetic picture of black children.

Chapter Eleven

THE DEVELOPMENT OF SOCIAL BEHAVIOR

Relationships with Peers
 Peers and Play
 Role Taking
 Perceptions of Others
Friendship
 Concepts of Friendship
 Forming Friendships
 Maintaining Friendships
 Peer Relations and Group Structure
 Acceptance and Rejection
Self-control and Moral Development
 Measuring and Developing Self-control
 Over- and Undercontrol
 Moral Development
 Prosocial Behavior
 Training for Prosocial Behavior
Aggression
 Patterns of Aggressive Behavior
 Determinants of Aggression

Chapter 10 focused on the development of internal psychological attributes, that is, children's feelings, motives, and emotions, their conceptions of themselves and others, and their standards and ideas about the behaviors appropriate to their sex. From the earliest years, however, these personal attributes are vital in shaping children's relationships with others; their social orientations and attitudes, their moral values and behavior, and their expression or inhibition of aggression. These are the topics of this chapter.

How do children's interactions with peers develop and change over time? What determines a child's social status or popularity? How do children make moral judgments and how are those judgments modified with increasing age? How do children's play activities contribute to their social, emotional, and cognitive development? These are some of the questions we will be asking as we explore the development of social behavior in children.

RELATIONSHIPS WITH PEERS

Peers and Play

The primary vehicle for the development of relationships with peers is play with other children. Such play does not occur with any frequency before age 2. During the toddler years children's play shifts from primarily sensorimotor responses, such as running around or pounding with a hammer, toward more symbolic, solitary play, such as pretending to drive a car or diapering a doll (see Chapter 5). During this period toddlers typically show more interest in toys and objects than in other children in the room, although they will often approach each other and, in brief encounters, touch, smile, ruffle hair, imitate one another, and exchange toys (Bronson, 1975; Garvey, 1977; Mueller & Lucas, 1975). After the age of 2, peers become an increasingly important part of children's social life. Interactions between children increase and become more positive, and many children can initiate play, cooperate, and take turns (Bronson, 1975; Eckerman, Whatley & Kutz, 1975; Mueller & Lucas, 1975). Generally, it is play that brings children together and provides a setting for the formation and maintenance of social relationships, including friendships.

Direct observations show that between the ages of 2 and 5 children's interactions become more frequent, more sustained, more social, and more complex. In the earliest preschool years, children engage mostly in *solitary* play, in which they pay no attention to their peers, or in *parallel* play, in which they play next to each other without interacting. A higher proportion of play after age 3 is either *associative*, in which children play together but not in a coordinated manner, or *cooperative*, in

During the preschool years children tend to engage in parallel play, in which they play next to each other without interacting.

which children interact helping each other achieve a shared goal and/or taking different roles (Parten, 1932; Barnes, 1971; Rubin, Watson, & Jambor, 1978). As one research team describes it,

> Solitary play did not appear to be gradually *replaced* by group play during the preschool years; rather, the shift was in the *relative predominance* of social modes of play as children developed. Among children ages 3 and 4, solitary play was the predominant mode, shifting to group play as the predominant mode for the 5-year-olds, although solitary play remained a common form of play for fours and fives. (Monighan-Nourot, Scales, Van Hoorn, & Almy, 1987, p. 78) (see Figure 11.1)

With increasing age, children's solitary or parallel play becomes more mature from a cognitive standpoint. For example, in their parallel play older preschoolers engage less in *functional* sensorimotor play (simple, repetitive muscle movements, such as repeatedly pouring sand through a funnel) and significantly more in *constructive* or *dramatic* play (creating something, such as building a tower of blocks or depicting imaginary situations and acting out roles). Constructive play is probably the most common form of activity during the preschool and kindergarten years, ranging from 40 percent of all activity at 3½ years to approximately 51 percent at 4, 5, and 6 years (Rubin, K. H., Fein, & Vandenberg, 1983). Such play may serve to increase the cognitive competence of the child (Forman & Hill, 1980). In many cases it is combined with imaginative activity, as in the following example:

> Four-year-old Miguel has built a three-tiered structure from playdough and has placed smaller pieces of dough around it, like stepping stones. Using a cookie cutter shaped like a man, he walks it around the structure, chanting,

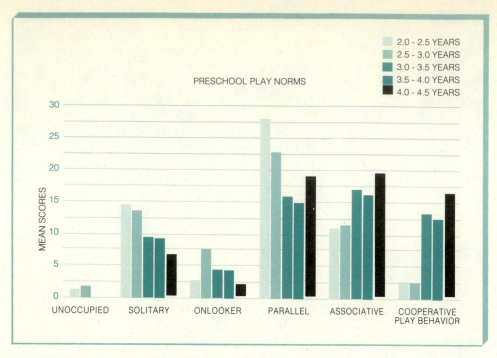

FIGURE 11.1   Mean unoccupied, solitary, onlooker, parallel, associative, and cooperative scores for 2-, 3-, and 4-year-olds. (Adapted from K. E. Barnes, Preschool play norms: A replication. *Developmental Psychology*, 1971, 5, 99–103. Copyright 1971 by the American Psychological Association. By permission.)

> "I'm walking on the sidewalk!" Then he hops the cutter up and down in front of the structure. In a low, gruff voice he says, "Little pig, little pig, let me come in. I'll huff and I'll puff and I'll come in." Then he changes to a high voice, "Not by the hair of my chinny-chin-chin!" In a normal voice he says, "Whoa! B-r-ck!" and crushes the playdough structure with the cutter. (Monighan-Nourot et al., p. 27)

Pretend play may be a solitary or a group activity. Group dramatic play generally emerges by the age of 3, although it is not yet well coordinated (Fein, 1981). The proportion of pretend or dramatic group play rises steadily between the ages of 3 and 6 or 7; over time this form of play gradually becomes more elaborate. Pretend play is based on the players' "shared imaginations" (Garvey, 1977) and involves the integration of complementary or reciprocal actions and role relationships (e.g., doctor-patient; mother-child) (Rubin, K.H. et al., 1983).

Note the differences in coordination and reciprocity in the following episodes. The first illustrates the social play of 3-year-olds:

Molly (playing mother):	Here's some food, baby.
Joe (playing baby):	I want my ball.
Molly:	This cereal is good for you. (Joe crawls on the floor after the ball.)

By age 5 or 6, the following interaction would be more typical:

Michael (playing teacher):	Show me the yellow balloon.
Mindy (playing pupil):	That's the yellow one and that's the red one.
Michael:	Very good. Now go wash your hands.
Mindy:	No, my hands are clean.

Pretend play serves many functions in the child's development. Social skills, patterns of effective interaction, and various social roles and rules are thought about, tested, and practiced. In addition, empathy, cooperation, and competence in role taking are enhanced; communication skills improve; reciprocal roles are more realistically related to each other; self-confidence and self-control increase (Singer, 1973); and boredom is alleviated (Ellis, 1973). (See also Chapter 5, pages 180–189.) Imaginativeness in play is associated with humorous and playful attitudes, emotional expressiveness, creativity in other activities, curiosity, openness in communication, self-control, and low aggression (Rubin, K.H. et al., 1983; Singer & Singer, 1980). In sum, "social play is an enjoyable and self-conscious exercise in mutuality, and it offers children a chance to explore patterns of social interaction that they would rarely experience in real life" (Damon, 1983, p. 109).

Games with rules require greater cognitive ability—understanding, acceptance of, and conformity to constraints or rules, as well as competitiveness. Consequently, they do not become part of the child's play repertoire until later. Participation in

Games with rules require greater cognitive ability than pretend play.

simple group games and board games generally begins between the ages of 4 and 7, but participation in games with more abstract rules is more likely during the period from age 7 to age 12, that is, the period of concrete operations (Eifermann, 1970; Rubin, K. H. et al., 1983). As we will see in the next section, the ability to play such games depends on the development of role-taking skills.

Role Taking

Age-related changes in social interaction and play are to some extent a function of increasing skill in *role taking*, that is, the ability to put oneself mentally in someone else's position. It has been hypothesized that underlying role-taking ability is **empathy**, the recognition, understanding, and vicarious feeling of another person's emotions—in brief, "shared emotional responses which the child experiences on perceiving others' emotional reactions" (Feshbach, 1978). Many psychologists regard empathy and role taking as central processes in social cognition, interaction, and communication. These processes have a profound effect on the individual's perceptions of others, as well as on their friendships, social status, moral judgment, and moral behavior (see pages 435–464).

As noted in Chapter 5, some 2- and 3-year-olds show rudimentary awareness of other people's feelings and desires, recognizing such states as happiness, sadness, and anger; however, they cannot yet assume someone else's perspective. Thus, after seeing another child fall and hurt herself, a toddler may react with intense crying or agitation; she may not know how to help the distressed child effectively, but she may give him attention and affection, express sympathy, or offer him a toy in an attempt to comfort him (Dunn & Kendrick, 1979; Rheingold, Hay, & West, 1976).

Skills in perspective or role taking are manifested much more clearly in the early elementary school years. According to Piaget, this change is attributable to older children's more extensive social experiences, specifically the increased frequency, intensity, and duration of their interactions with peers. The findings of a recent study support Piaget's hypothesis. Children in the third grade were asked to nominate classmates who were high or low in sociability (i.e., "someone who makes friends easily" or "someone who likes to play with others rather than alone"). They were also questioned about a series of cartoons depicting characters in emotional situations. On the basis of their responses the investigators assessed the children's perspective-taking ability, that is, their understanding of the thoughts and reactions of the cartoon characters. As predicted, the children who were very low in sociability performed significantly more poorly on the perspective-taking test than classmates who were rated as average or high in sociability (LeMare & Rubin, 1987).

To trace the development of role-taking skills from the preschool period through adolescence, Robert Selman presented children of various ages with story dilemmas designed to elicit reasoning about social or moral situations. He then asked them some probing questions. Here is an example:

Holly is an 8-year-old girl who likes to climb trees. She is the best tree climber in the neighborhood. One day while climbing down from a tall tree, she

falls off the bottom branch but does not hurt herself. Her father sees her fall. He is upset and asks her to promise not to climb trees any more. Holly promises.

Later that day, Holly and her friends meet Shawn. Shawn's kitten is caught up in a tree and can't get down. Something has to be done right away, or the kitten may fall. Holly is the only one who climbs trees well enough to reach the kitten and get it down, but she remembers her promise to her father. (Selman, 1980, p. 36)

The role-taking questions included the following: "Does Holly know how Shawn feels about the kitten? Why?" "How will Holly's father feel if he finds out she climbed the tree?" "What does Holly think her father will think of her if he finds out?" The responses were coded for the child's explanation of the thoughts and feelings of each individual in the story and the relationships among their various perspectives.

The data indicated that role-taking skills develop through a series of qualitatively distinct stages; these are described in Box 11.1. In reviewing these stages, keep in mind that children's responses reflect their ability to reason about abstract social situations and to explain their reasoning. It must not be inferred that younger children are not empathic or have no understanding of other people's perspectives simply because they do not respond to hypothetical verbal measures in the same way that older children do.

Role-taking ability is correlated with general intelligence (Shantz, 1983) and with moral behavior, including altruism, helping, sharing, and consideration for others (see pages 459–462). Deficiencies in role-taking skills are characteristic of juvenile delinquents, and training in perspective taking may sometimes help reduce their problem behaviors. In one training study, delinquent preadolescent boys wrote and videotaped skits about people their own age, repeating the skits until every boy had played the role of every character. Those who received this training performed better on role-taking measures than members of control groups who received no training or simply watched movies instead of performing in skits. More important, those who received the training had significantly lower levels of delinquent behavior during an 18-month follow-up period (Chandler, 1973).

Perceptions of Others

With more extensive social experience and advances in cognitive abilities, particularly role-taking skills and the ability to conceptualize thoughts and feelings, children's conceptions of others become more abstract, more complex, and more focused on psychological (rather than external) characteristics. In fact, developmental trends in conceptions of others are strikingly parallel to the changes in self-concept and self-description reviewed in Chapter 10. When asked, "Tell me about Bill" or "What sort of person is Edna?" children younger than age 7 usually refer to external, concrete attributes such as physical characteristics, appearance, possessions, and overt behavior. Although they frequently use global evaluative adjectives like *good*, *bad*, *mean*, and *nice*, they do not usually refer to psychological attributes.

BOX 11.1

Stages in the Development of Role-taking Skills

The examples given here are responses to questions about the story dilemma in which Holly promises her father that she will not climb trees any more, but soon afterward encounters a friend whose kitten is caught in a tree (see page 430).

At stage 0, the *egocentric viewpoint*, young children fail to distinguish between their own interpretation of an event and someone else's. Children at this stage do not realize that others can see a social situation differently than they do. For example, in response to the question, "How will Holly's father feel when he finds out?" the child says, "Happy, he likes kittens."

At stage 1, *social informational role taking* (ages 5–8), children are aware that other people have different perspectives, thoughts, or feelings about things because they are in different situations or have different information. A child might say, "Holly's father will be mad because he doesn't want her to climb trees."

Self-reflection is the essence of stage 2 (ages 8–10), in which children recognize that each individual is aware of other people's thoughts and feelings and knows that the other person is also aware of the child's perspective. Moreover, the child is conscious of the fact that this mutual awareness influences each person's view of the other. For example, a child who was asked, "Will Holly's father punish her?" replied, "She knows her father will understand why she climbed the tree, so he won't punish her."

In stage 3, *mutual role-taking* (ages 10–12), children can consider an interaction simultaneously from their own point of view and from that of another person, and recognize that the other person can do the same. The child can take the perspective of a disinterested third person—an onlooker, parent, or mutual friend—and anticipate how each participant (including herself) will react to the viewpoint of the partner. A question about her father might be answered in this way: "Holly and her father trust each other, so they can talk about why she climbed the tree."

Finally, in stage 4, *social and conventional system role-taking* (ages 12–15+), children realize that there are integrated networks of perspectives that are shared by the members of a group, such as an "American" or a "Catholic" point of view. "The subject realizes that each self considers the shared point of view of the social system in order to facilitate accurate communication with and understanding of others" (Selman, 1976, p. 306).

In middle childhood, beginning around age 8, there are major changes in person perceptions specifically, increased use of abstract adjectives referring to traits, motives, beliefs, values, and attitudes (Livesley & Bromley, 1973; Peevers & Secord, 1973). The child "becomes less bound to the surface aspects of people and increasingly abstracts regularities across time and situations and infers motives for behavior" (Shantz, 1983, p. 506). However, descriptions given at this age are often poorly integrated and sometimes inconsistent. Consider a 10-year-old's description of a classmate:

> He smells very much and is very nasty. He has no sense of humour and is very dull. He is always fighting and he is cruel. He does silly things and is very stupid. He has brown hair and cruel eyes. He is sulky and 11 years old and has lots of sisters. I think he is the most horrible boy in the class. He has a croaky voice and always chews his pencil and picks his teeth and I think he is disgusting. (Livesley & Bromley, 1973, p. 217)

The descriptions given by children age 12 to 14 are generally better organized and show greater sensitivity to the complexity (and sometimes contradictory nature) of personality characteristics and behavior. Qualifying terms like *sometimes* and *quite* are used frequently, and explanations of behavior are common. At this age children seem to understand that an individual's behavior depends not only on personality traits but also on situations and cognitive factors (Shantz, 1983). The following is a 15-year-old's description of a friend:

> Andy is very modest. He is even shyer than I am when near strangers and yet is very talkative with people he knows and likes. He always seems good tempered and I have never seen him in a bad temper. He tends to degrade other people's achievements, and yet never praises his own. He does not seem to voice his opinions to anyone. He easily gets nervous. (Livesley & Bromley, 1973, p. 221)

FRIENDSHIP

Concepts of Friendship

Outside the family circle, the child's most significant social relationships are with friends. As would be expected, children's ideas of friendship change as they mature. To investigate children's conceptions of friendship, researchers use interview techniques ("Who is your best friend?" "Why is Nancy your best friend?") (Damon, 1977; Selman, 1980; Youniss, 1980) or present children with hypothetical dilemmas and ask questions about them (Selman, 1976). For example, in one dilemma two girls, Kathy and Debbie, have been friends since they were 5. A new girl, Jeanette, moves into their neighborhood. Jeanette invites Kathy to go to the circus with her on a day that Kathy has promised to play with Debbie. What will Kathy do? Questions about friendship and social relationships follow.

According to some theorists, there are stages in the development of conceptions of friendship that parallel the stages in the development of role-taking skills (Selman, 1981). Thus, although many preschool children form friendships with each other, they are not concerned with lasting relationships and characteristically view friends as "momentary physical playmates"; to them, a friend is whomever one is playing with at the time (Rubin, Z., 1980). Older children, however, think of friendships as relationships that continue beyond single, brief interactions. Between the age of 5 and adolescence, children's conceptions of friendship evolve through three major levels (Damon, 1977). At the first level, which is typical of 5- to 7-year-olds, friends are the playmates whom the child sees most frequently, usually neighbors or schoolmates. They share things such as food and toys, "act nice," and are "fun to be with." Friendships have no permanent status and are easily established and terminated; there is no sense of liking or disliking the stable personal traits of another child. One 5-year-old reported that "when I don't play with them they don't like me" (Damon, 1977, p. 156).

Between the ages of 8 and 11, children regard friends as people with whom they cooperate, exchange good deeds, and share. Mutual trust, shared interests, reciprocity, response to each other's needs, and possession of desirable attributes such as kindness and considerateness are also critical features of friendships. Thus, Betty, age 10, likes Karen "because she's nice; she gives me jewelry and candy, and I give her things, too" (Damon, 1977, p. 158).

Friendships become more enduring between the ages of 8 and 11.

Beginning at about 12 years of age, friendships are judged in terms of mutual understanding and sharing of thoughts, feelings, and other secrets, and they are usually stable over long periods. Friends help each other handle psychological problems such as loneliness and fear, and they avoid upsetting each other. According to one 13-year-old boy, "You need someone you can tell anything to, all kinds of things that you don't want spread around. That's why you are someone's friend" (Damon, 1977, p. 163).

Forming Friendships

If you ask children how to make friends, their answers will reflect their conceptions of friendship. Thus, for young children the way to form a friendship is simply to play with another child. Older children view the process as more complicated and gradual; friendships become deeper as people gain greater insight into one another's traits, interests, and values. A 13-year-old said, "You don't really pick your friends, it just grows on you. You find out that you can talk to someone, you can tell them your problems, when you understand each other" (Rubin, 1980, p. 35).

The social processes involved in becoming friends were investigated in two complementary studies in which the conversations of pairs of children between the ages of 3 and 9 were tape-recorded while they were playing together. In the first study, the interactions of children playing with their best friends were compared with those of children playing with strangers their own age. Six social processes related to friendship formation were examined: (1) *connectedness and communication clarity*, (2) *information exchange*, (3) *establishing common ground*, (4) *resolution of conflict*, (5) *positive reciprocity*, and (6) *self-disclosure*. These are defined in Table 11.1. Children playing with friends surpassed those playing with strangers in the manifestation of all six of these social processes.

In the second study, the investigator attempted to trace children's progress toward friendship by pairing previously unacquainted children for three sessions and recording their conversations. Among these children, those who "hit it off" and were likely to become friends scored higher on each of the six social dimensions than children who did not become friendly with each other. The researcher concluded that

> when two strangers meet, they need to interact in a connected fashion, exchange information successfully, establish a common ground activity, and manage conflicts successfully. As the relationship proceeds, communication clarity becomes more important; so does information exchange, the establishment of common ground activity, the exploration of similarity and differences, the resolution of conflict, and self-disclosure. (Gottman, 1983, p. 44)

PARENTS AS MODELS.   A parent's style of interacting with his or her child may serve as a model for the child's approach to strangers who are potential friends. Children in the first grade were observed as they played a game with their mothers and as they played with agemates whom they had not met before. Children of disagreeable, demanding, and highly controlling mothers were characteristically preoccupied with themselves and with getting their own way when interacting with

TABLE 11.1

Social Processes in Friendship Formation

Process	Definition	Example
1. Communication clarity and connectedness	Request for clarification of a message followed by appropriate clarification.	"Which truck do you want?" "The dumpster."
2. Information exchange	A question-answer sequence; one child asks a question and the other answers.	"Hey, you know what?" "No, what?" "Sometime you can come to my house."
3. Establishing common ground	Finding something to do together or exploring similarities and differences.	"Let's play house." "We're both 4."
4. Conflict resolution	Successfully resolving arguments and disagreements.	"Give me the green crayon." "No, I'm using it; here, try the blue one." "O.K. That's just as good."
5. Positive reciprocity	One child responds to the other's positive behavior and extends a positive interchange, as in chains of gossip, joking, or fantasy.	"Katie's too bossy." "Yeah, and she's mean, too."
6. Self-disclosure	One child asks about the other's feelings, and the other expresses her feelings.	"Are you scared of taking swimming lessons?" "Yeah, I'm scared of the water. You scared?" "Not any more."

Source: Adapted from Gottman, 1983.

other children—behavior that hardly made them attractive as friends. The results of this study are consistent with what one might expect when certain behaviors are modeled by an adult: "Children in their social interactions with peers seem to display affective behavior similar to that of their mothers. Positive, agreeable mothers have positive, agreeable children; mothers who focused on feelings had children who focused on feelings; and disagreeable mothers had disagreeable children" (Putallaz, 1987, p. 336).

Maintaining Friendships

As we have seen, early friendships are often fragile; they are quickly formed and easily terminated. Yet even in the preschool years some children maintain strong bonds of friendship. Such friendships are generally formed with children who live nearby, share interests and favorite activities, and have interesting playthings; however, there is no single basis for these friendships (Hayes, 1978). The friendships of preschool children have many functions. According to one researcher, "Friends are security givers, standards against whom one can measure oneself, partners in activities that cannot be engaged in alone, guides to unfamiliar places, and apprentices who confirm one's own developing sense of competence and expertise" (Rubin, 1980, p. 69).

Schoolchildren tend to select friends of their own age, sex, and race. Even in integrated classrooms there are usually relatively few close friendships between children of different races (Asher, Singleton, & Taylor, 1982; Kandel, 1978; Singleton & Asher, 1979). In middle childhood, friends tend to share interests, attitudes, social orientations (e.g., the tendency to seek or avoid social participation), and values, but they do not generally resemble each other closely in intelligence or personality characteristics (Byrne & Griffitt, 1966; Challman, 1932; Davitz, 1955). In adolescence, college-bound children are likely to have college-bound friends, while those who are not planning to go to college choose friends whose educational goals are similar to their own (Duncan, Featherman, & Duncan, 1972).

As children grow older, their friendships become more stable and enduring. The fourth- and eighth-graders in one study answered questionnaires about their friendships at both the beginning and the end of the school year. Over two-thirds of those who were close friends at the beginning of the year were still close friends at the end. Enduring friendships were characterized by frequent interactions and a high degree of liking for each other, whereas unstable friendships were relatively lacking in intimacy at both times measured. Not surprisingly, the children who were involved in weaker friendships reported less intimacy and less similarity to their friends—and more disloyalty or unfaithfulness—in the spring than they had in the fall. In evaluating their friendships, eighth-graders emphasized intimacy and stimulation more than fourth-graders did, and girls stressed intimacy, loyalty, and faithfulness more than boys did (Berndt, Hawkins, & Hoyle, 1986).

Peer Relations and Group Structure

Children's interpersonal relations are not restricted to friendship pairs. Most preschool children seek out and enjoy their peers, and if they find themselves alone they are likely to try to join ongoing activities with others (Corsaro, 1981). During the preschool years there are sharp increases in the strength of children's attachment to peers generally (Almy, Monighan, Scales, & Van Hoorn, 1983), and social relationships—primarily between playmates of the same sex—become closer, more frequent, and more sustained. Communication improves as children accommodate their language to that of their peers. Also, as they become older children are more willing to participate in joint efforts, coordinate their activities more effectively, and often collaborate successfully in solving problems (Cooper, C.R., 1977).

Compared with younger children, school-age children engage in more task-related interactions, which tend to be better organized as they grow older (Smith, 1977). Cooperation and other kinds of prosocial behavior, such as sharing and altruism, increase throughout the school years, while aggression and quarreling decrease. With greater understanding of other people's motivations and intentions and improved use of feedback from others, communication among peers becomes more effective and more highly valued (Hartup, Brady, & Newcomb, 1981). By adolescence, time spent with peers exceeds time spent with adults, including parents (Hartup, 1970; Medrich, Rosen, Rubin, & Buckley, 1982).

The structure of social groups changes with age. Between the ages of 6 and 8, the predominant group is the informal *gang*, formed by children themselves. The gang has few formal rules, and there is a rapid turnover in membership. Later, between the ages of 10 and 14, children's groups are likely to become more formal, highly structured, and cohesive, with special membership requirements and elaborate rituals for conducting meetings. Even so, the membership of such groups may change frequently, and the group itself may not last long.

Acceptance and Rejection

Within any classroom or social group, some children are popular with their peers and some are not. For research purposes, social status may be evaluated by means of observation, particularly in nursery school, but more commonly sociometric techniques are used. Children respond to questions such as "Who in the class is your best friend?" and "Who are the ones that aren't liked by others?" by listing the names of classmates. On the basis of such peer nominations, children can be classified as *popular*, *rejected* (receiving many "don't like" nominations), or *ignored* (receiving neither positive nor negative nominations). During the school years the statuses of "popular" and "ignored" are fairly stable over a five-year period, and the status of "rejected" is highly stable (Coie & Dodge, 1983). Children who have poor relationships with peers are at risk for later problems such as dropping out of school and criminal behavior (Achenbach & Edelbrock, 1981; Parker & Asher, 1987; Roff, Sells, & Golden, 1972).

What determines whether children are popular or unpopular, accepted or rejected by their peers? Clearly, many factors—including social and cognitive skills, personality, and social attributes—are influential. Among the cognitive attributes associated with popularity are well-developed role-taking skills (ability to recognize the needs and emotions of companions and respond appropriately) (Kurdek & Krile, 1982) and friendly, outgoing, sympathetic orientations toward others (Renshaw & Asher, 1983). Moreover, compared with unpopular children, those with high social status have greater social knowledge and understanding of effective ways of interacting. When asked how they would react in several hypothetical social situations (e.g., entering a new group at recess or observing a child being teased), popular first-, second-, and third-graders are more likely than less popular children to suggest solutions that are active, assertive, and likely to maintain and advance positive relationships (Asher & Renshaw, 1981; Putallaz, 1987).

In general, personal characteristics that are highly valued by the culture in which a child is raised, such as physical attractiveness, foster popularity, while negative traits, such as immaturity, are related to rejection (Cavior & Dokecki, 1973; Lerner & Lerner, 1977). Some handicapped children who are mainstreamed into regular classrooms so that they can be taught along with normal children find that they are stigmatized in the classroom and have relatively fewer social interactions with classmates than handicapped children in special classes do. Such experiences may lead to diminished self-esteem and a sense of inadequacy, which may also adversely affect the child's ability to learn (Caparulo & Zigler, 1983).

Popular children are rated as friendlier, more outgoing, more adept at initiating and maintaining social interactions, more enthusiastic and helpful, kinder, and more cooperative than unpopular children. Rejected children are not necessarily less sociable or friendly than others, but they are more frequently the initiators or targets of teasing, fighting, and arguing, and they act in immature, antisocial, disruptive, inappropriate, or deviant ways (Asher & Hymel, 1981; Gottman, 1977). In short, "the interaction of unpopular children might be summarized as disagreeable and bossy" (Putallaz & Gottman, 1981, p. 143).

Moderately high self-esteem is more likely to lead to acceptance by peers than either very high or very low self-esteem. Exaggerated reports of self-esteem may be inaccurate; in addition, children who say they are wonderful may be perceived as arrogant and thus turn others away (Cook, Goldman, & Olczak, 1978).

These correlational findings must, of course, be interpreted cautiously: What is cause and what is effect? Friendliness and helpfulness may augment a child's popularity; being disgruntled and uncooperative may lead to rejection. But it is also possible that popularity reinforces, and thus enhances, a child's friendliness, and that rejection may make a child more disagreeable or uncooperative.

Styles of interacting with peers may be acquired in—and generalized from—children's relationships within their families. When interacting with their mothers, unpopular first-graders (as measured by peer nominations) talked more about themselves and were more disagreeable than children of high social status, and their mothers were more negative and controlling. In contrast, mothers of high-status children were more likely to interact in positive, agreeable ways and showed more concern with their own and their children's feelings (Putallaz, 1987).

The strategy used in attempting to become part of a new group strongly influences the likelihood of a youngster's being accepted or rejected by the group. Among second- and third-graders, those who approached a new group by joining the ongoing conversation or activity, and contributing relevant comments about what the group was doing, were readily accepted. In contrast, those who called attention to themselves by hovering around the edge of the group, stating their own opinions or expressing disagreements with others, were generally unsuccessful, being either rejected or ignored by the group (Putallaz & Gottman, 1981).

Fortunately, isolated and rejected children can sometimes be coached in the kinds of skills that are effective in establishing better social relationships. Box 11.2 describes a program designed to improve the social skills of preschool and kindergarten children. In another study, some socially isolated third- and fourth-grade children gained greater acceptance after they had participated in five sessions of instruction and practice in social skills such as cooperation (e.g., taking turns and sharing things) and communication (conversing with another child). A year later these children showed further gains in popularity (Oden & Asher, 1977; Shantz, 1983).

BOX 11.2

Training in Social Skills

Myrna Shure and George Spivak of the Hahnemann Community Mental Health Center in Philadelphia believe that the difficulties experienced by children in their social relationships are due at least in part to lack of understanding of others and lack of skill in social problem-solving. They therefore developed extensive training programs to teach preschool children better ways of dealing with interpersonal relationships; they evaluated these programs for two years.

Children were randomly assigned to an experimental group that received training or to a control group that did not. Three types of skills were taught. One skill was *finding alternatives*—generating as many different solutions to a problem situation as possible. For example, children were shown some pictures and were told, "Johnny wants a chance to play with this shovel, but Jimmy keeps on playing with it. What can Johnny do so he can have a chance to play with the shovel?" The children were encouraged to think of as many different possibilities as they could. A second skill was *anticipating the consequences* of actions. For instance, a child character was described as having taken an object, such as a flashlight, from an adult without asking. The children were asked to anticipate how the adult might react. The third skill was *understanding cause and effect.* In one story the children were told, "Debbie is crying. She is talking to her mother." They were encouraged to speculate about why the events in the story were happening, that is, to suggest that someone may have hit Debbie or that she might have fallen.

Children were tested in cognitive problem-solving skills at the beginning and end of each year. Those who received the training performed significantly better than the untrained control group in all three skill areas. The scores are shown in the accompanying chart.

Teachers also rated the behavioral adjustment of children before and after the training. Among the children who were initially poorly adjusted, those who received the training were rated as better adjusted afterwards, whereas those who did not receive the training had not improved. The children who learned cognitive problem-solving skills showed more appropriate levels of emotional expression and assertiveness,

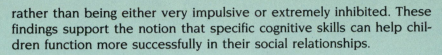

rather than being either very impulsive or extremely inhibited. These findings support the notion that specific cognitive skills can help children function more successfully in their social relationships.

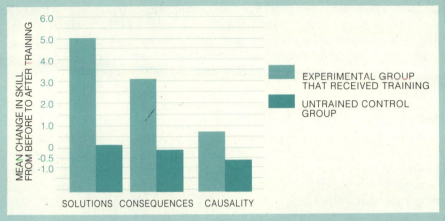

Mean change in children's interpersonal cognitive problem-solving skills for children who received training in preschool and kindergarten and for a control group who did not receive training. Three types of skills were measured: finding alternative solutions in social situations; understanding the consequences of people's actions; and understanding cause-and-effect relationships between actions and outcomes. Children who received training improved significantly more than untrained children in all three skills. They were also rated as better adjusted by their teachers. (Adapted from M. B. Shure & G. Spivak. Interpersonal problem solving as a mediator of behavioral adjustment in preschool and kindergarten children. *Journal of Applied Developmental Psychology*, 1980, 1, 37. By permission.)

SELF-CONTROL AND MORAL DEVELOPMENT

One of the prerequisites for establishing and maintaining satisfactory social relationships is the ability to regulate and control one's own behavior in ways that take other people's needs and feelings into account and, at the same time, conform to the standards of one's society or culture. As children grow older, they become more able to do this; they gradually become more skilled in role taking and adopt their culture's rules and restrictions. Some of these rules are *prescriptive* (referring to what one *should* do) while others are *proscriptive* (referring to what one should *not* do). In American society, the proscriptive rules require that one control one's impulses, resist temptation, tolerate frustration, inhibit acts that violate moral values, and refrain from hurting others or destroying property when angry. Individuals must also learn to resist distraction while working and to sacrifice attractive immediate rewards in order to obtain larger or more important rewards later on.

Many hypotheses about self-control originated in psychoanalytic theory. Freud suggested that the personality has three components: the *id*, which represents unconscious drives and impulses; the *superego*, which incorporates conscience or sense of right and wrong; and the *ego*, which is responsible for balancing or modulating the conflicting demands of one's own needs and impulses, one's conscience, and reality. Ego processes are the rational components of the personality that help people devise means of satisfying some of their basic needs (or obtaining pleasure) without incurring punishment—including social disapproval—or violating their own moral standards. This often entails suppressing certain impulses, delaying gratification, or finding socially acceptable ways of expressing impulses.

Consider this simple example. An 8-year-old wants an expensive doll displayed in a toy store, and she would love to have it immediately. Because she does not have enough money to buy the doll, she may be tempted to try to steal it from the counter. But ego processes help her resist that temptation and devise acceptable strategies for getting enough money to buy the doll. Perhaps she can save several weeks' allowance or find ways to earn money. In either case, she will have to delay gratification of her desire.

Social-learning theorists do not explain self-control, resistance to distraction, and delay of gratification as functions of ego processes. Rather, they see them as outcomes of reinforcements and observational learning (modeling and imitation). If a child is rewarded for delaying gratification or controlling impulses, these responses are strengthened and therefore are more likely to occur on future occasions. On the other hand, if children are exposed to models who display these responses, they are likely to emulate the models' behavior (see page 443).

Measuring and Developing Self-control

In many developmental studies, self-control is measured in terms of the child's ability or willingness to postpone immediate gratification of a desire in order to obtain something more valuable later on. Children are given a choice between two alternatives, one of which is immediately available but less desirable while the other is more attractive but available only after a delay. For example, in one laboratory study children were left alone for 15 minutes in a room with a relatively unattractive pretzel and a highly attractive marshmallow. They were told that they could eat only one of them; they could eat the pretzel at any time or, if they were willing to wait 15 minutes, they could have the marshmallow. Presented with this choice, older children were more likely than younger ones to delay gratification, that is, to choose the more valuable alternative, for which they would have to wait, over the less valuable, but immediately available, alternative (Mischel & Metzner, 1962). When the delay is very long or the delayed reward is not much more valuable than the alternative, children are more likely to choose the immediately available reward (Mischel, 1966, 1974; Schwarz, Schrager, & Lyons, 1983). Also, if rewards are visible, children are less likely to delay gratification. Apparently, waiting for a visible desirable object is so frustrating that many children choose the less desirable, immediately available reward (Mischel & Ebbesen, 1970).

Children who are generally self-controlled and able to delay gratification are more responsible and mature than other children. They are also higher in achievement motivation, more intelligent, better students, and more likely to follow rules, even when they are working alone without supervision (Mischel, 1966). Training techniques may enhance children's cognitive controls and, hence, their ability to delay gratification. One such technique is distracting attention from the desirable qualities of the delayed incentive—essentially, learning not to think about those qualities. In one study, one group of children were instructed to think about the taste and feeling of the relatively undesirable pretzel and the desirable marshmallow in front of them, whereas another group were told to imagine that the marshmallows were fluffy white clouds and the pretzels were logs for a cabin. The children in the second group, distracted from thinking about the positive qualities of the delayed reward, waited almost twice as long as those who were thinking about the taste of the candy (Mischel & Patterson, 1978).

Even very young children can use self-instruction to regulate self-control (Patterson, G. R., 1982). Preschool children were offered an attractive reward for completing a long, repetitive task (copying letters of the alphabet) but were warned that a talking "clown box" might try to distract them while they worked. Some of the children were instructed to repeat to themselves short sentences or "plans," such as "I'm not going to look at Mr. Clown," when this occurred. These children were less distracted and did more work than children in control groups who were not given these instructions.

Older children can learn to monitor themselves so as to resist distraction (Pressley, 1979). For example, sixth-graders in an individualized math curriculum were trained to record instances of "off-task behavior" (e.g., talking to others, fooling around) and to use them as signals to return to work. These children spent more time concentrating on their work and performed better on mathematics tests than children in control groups who did not receive this training (Sagotsky, Patterson, & Lepper, 1978).

Positive labeling is another strategy that may increase the ability to delay gratification. Before playing a "candy game," girls in the first and second grades chatted briefly with the experimenter. During the chat, the experimenter told half of the participants, "I hear you are very patient because you can wait for nice things when you can't get them right away" (positive label); the other half were told, "I hear that you have some very nice friends here at school" (irrelevant label). In the game, a machine dispensed one M&M every 60 seconds, and all the accumulated candies belonged to the child. However, as soon as she took any of them the machine stopped and the game was over. The results showed that the experimenter had created a self-fulfilling prophesy: The children who had been labeled "patient" showed significantly greater ability to delay gratification, waiting about twice as long as the others (Toner, Moore, & Emmons, 1980).

Observation of a model who defers gratification can also alter a child's level of self-control. In one study, 9- and 10-year-olds who consistently chose a small immediate payoff in a game, rather than waiting for larger delayed payoffs, observed a model who always chose to delay and get richer rewards. In contrast, children who generally delayed gratification observed a model who preferred immediate, though smaller, rewards. The effects of observing the model were apparent both immediately and a month later: The initially impulsive children who observed a model who delayed gratification subsequently tended to delay immediate gratification; those who were initially inclined to delay gratification chose more immediate, less attractive rewards (Bandura & Mischel, 1965). Thus, parents and other agents of socialization may successfully promote a tendency to delay immediate gratification in order to achieve more desirable long-range objectives by training children in techniques of cognitive control such as self-monitoring, or by serving as models of self-control.

General readiness to work hard is another ingredient of self-control; it can be augmented by training children to expend greater effort to achieve worthwhile goals. To study this issue, investigators assessed second- and third-graders' original or baseline willingness to work hard by offering them repeated choices between earning three cents for doing a tedious task (copying nonsense words) for a minute or earning two cents for "simply sitting here" for a minute. After all the children had experienced ten such trials, they were randomly assigned to one of three groups of equal size. In the high-effort training group, children were paid on several occasions for doing some relatively difficult object-counting, picture memory, and shape-matching tasks; those in the low-effort group were rewarded with the same amount for doing much easier tasks of the same sort; and a third group, the control, did not receive effort training. After the training sessions, the children were retested in the original situation. As Figure 11.2 shows, those in the high-effort group showed strikingly greater readiness to work hard than those in either the low-effort or the control group. The investigators concluded that reward for high effort increases a person's tendency to choose high effort and large rewards in preference to low effort and small rewards (Eisenberger, Mitchell, & Masterson, 1985).

Children's perceptions of their classroom environment are significantly associated with their level of self-control. Specifically, students in the fourth and fifth grades who were rated high in self-control described their classes as well organized, possessing clear rules of behavior, and encouraging independent and active involvement in tasks (Humphrey, 1984).

Over- and Undercontrol

Although self-control is a key component of social adjustment, extremes of control may be maladaptive, a conclusion that is well documented in a longitudinal study of ego control (a concept that is similar to self-control as defined earlier). The 3-year-old participants in the study were observed in free play in preschool, tested, interviewed, and rated by parents and teachers. Using data from all these sources, the investigators classified some youngsters as *overcontrollers* and some as *undercontrollers*. The former showed strong tendencies toward conformity, planfulness, inhibition, perseverance, resistance to distraction, undue delay of gratification, and reluctance to explore new situations. They also showed minimal emotional expression, had narrow, unchanging interests, and manifested their needs indirectly rather than directly. In sharp contrast, the undercontrollers were emotionally expressive and spontaneous, nonconforming, distractible, exploratory, and unable to delay gratification of desires.

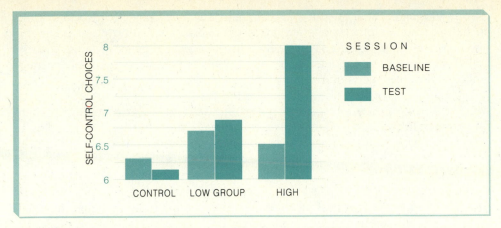

FIGURE 11.2   The number of hard-working choices in the baseline session and in the test session by the control group, the low-effort group, and the high-effort group. (Adapted from R. Eisenberger, M. Mitchell, and F. A. Masterson. Effort training increases generalized self-control. *Journal of Personality and Social Psychology*, 1985, 49, 1294–1301. Copyright 1985 by the American Psychological Association. By permission.)

It is often adaptive to shift from greater to less control as circumstances change. For this reason, the investigators also assessed **ego resilience**, an index of flexibility or adaptability. Highly resilient children can exercise strong control when it is called for; they can also "let go," acting spontaneously and expressively in other situations (Block & Block, 1980).

The behavioral manifestations of ego control and ego resilience remain relatively stable throughout early childhood. Four years after the initial classification (at age 3), undercontrollers were more energetic, curious, restless, and expressive of impulses than more controlled children were, and in their relationships with peers they exhibited more teasing, manipulativeness, and aggression. Those who were overcontrollers at age 3 were shy and inhibited at age 7.

Early ego resilience was associated with empathy, social responsiveness, and caring. Lasting consequences of variations in ego processes were also discerned. The combination of high ego control and high ego resilience at age 3 was predictive of excellent adjustment at age 7—specifically, a high degree of socialization and a relative absence of anxiety. However, children who were high in ego control but lacking in ego resilience at age 3 were poorly adjusted at age 7; they suffered from anxiety and feelings of inadequacy, and they viewed the world as threatening and unpredictable (Block & Block, 1980).

Moral Development

The quality of children's interpersonal behavior is not only a function of self-control and conformity to socially accepted standards. That is, behavior does not depend solely on the adoption of proscriptive rules and restrictions. Of at least equal importance are social actions based on prescriptive moral rules—standards regarding what members of the culture *should* do, what responses are acceptable and valued. Included in this category are both cognitive responses—such as making judgments that are fair and just—and a wide variety of prosocial actions such as sharing, helping, cooperating, and expressing sympathy. Moral judgments and prosocial behavior often entail self-control because they may require that the child suppress, or at least defer gratification of his or her own desires and interests while serving the needs of others.

MORAL JUDGMENTS. Piaget laid the groundwork for research on developmental changes in children's cognitions about moral issues—their understanding of rules, their beliefs and judgments. He observed children of different ages at play, participated in games with them, and interviewed them about the rules of games, the nature of justice, and the morality of characters in stories. For instance, he would ask, "Why shouldn't you cheat in the game?" Or, after telling a story about a mother who gave the biggest piece of cake to her most obedient child, he questioned the child about the justice of her action.

Piaget found that preschool children play in idiosyncratic ways rather than by following rules. "The child will invent his or her own rules, will change these rules at will, and in general will conduct the game according to his or her own private desires and fantasies" (Damon, 1983, p. 185). However, beginning at about age 5 the child enters the first of two stages of moral development, the stage of *moral realism* (also called the stage of *heteronomous autonomy*). During this stage the child believes that rules are handed down by authorities (e.g., parents and teachers) and therefore are fixed, absolute, and sacred. Ideas about right and wrong are also inflexible, and justice is subordinate to adult authority. The young children whom Piaget interviewed did not think it was ever right to tell a lie, and when asked about a story in which the commands of a parent conflicted with justice or equality, they usually chose obedience to adults as the correct course of action.

Related to their strong respect for rules and adult authority is the moral realists belief in *immanent justice*, the notion that breaking rules or disobeying authority will surely result in punishment. For example, a child may believe that if he tells a lie he is likely to fall or to be hit by a falling branch.

Also at this stage, actions are judged more by their consequences than by the intentions of the actor. Piaget asked children who was naughtier, a boy who was trying to help his mother and accidentally upset a tray and broke 15 glasses, or another boy who, while trying to sneak a cookie out of a cupboard, broke one glass. Most moral realists said that the first boy was naughtier because he broke more glasses (Piaget, 1932/1965).

Recent research shows that youngsters' understanding of intentions is more complex than Piaget thought. The difference between deliberate and accidental wrongdoing is clear even to preschoolers (Karniol, 1978), and they take intentions into account when judging another's actions (Costanzo, Coie, Grumet, & Farnill, 1973). "I did it on accident, Mom," said one preschooler when she had done something wrong. In fact, when evaluating an individual's actions young children consider many factors, including whether the results are positive or negative and whether the object of an action is an inanimate object, an animal, or a person (Rest, 1983).

According to Piaget, children attain the second stage, *moral relativism* (also referred to as *autonomous morality* or the *morality of reciprocity*), at the age of 10 or 11.

During this stage ideas of reciprocity in human interactions and the belief that everyone has an equal right to justice and consideration predominate in moral thinking. The second stage is built upon, and replaces, the first; no child achieves the stage of moral relativism without first passing through the stage of moral realism.

During the stage of moral relativism, children realize that many social rules, including the rules of games, are simply statements of convention and can be changed by agreement or consensus. Blind obedience to authority is rejected, and moral rules are regarded as the products of cooperation, reciprocity, and interaction among peers. Consequently, children at this stage are more flexible in their moral judgments, taking into consideration the circumstances of an individual's actions as well as the actor's point of view, emotions, and feelings. Disobedience, lying, or violation of rules are sometimes justified, and not all wrongdoing will inevitably be punished. Children now believe in equal justice for all, and their judgments about transgressions take into account the intentions of the actor and the nature and extent of the harm done.

Piaget maintained that progress from moral realism to moral relativism is a joint function of the child's greater cognitive abilities *and* more extensive social experiences. The most significant cognitive changes, he believed, are a decline in egocentrism and an increase in the ability to take roles and assume another person's perspective. Also, as a result of more numerous and more enduring contacts with peers, children learn to work cooperatively—and often make compromises—with others of equal status. Unilateral respect for adult authority is thereby reduced, and respect for peers and their points of view increases. Piaget suggested that parents can help their children achieve higher levels of moral thinking by being less authoritarian and maintaining egalitarian relationships with them (Piaget, 1932).

KOHLBERG'S THEORY.   About 30 years after Piaget published his studies of moral development, Kohlberg began to extend and amplify Piaget's work. Kohlberg and his associates presented children and adolescents with a series of moral dilemmas and asked them to resolve them, stating their reasoning. An example is the situation of Heinz, a man whose wife is dying. He does not have enough money to buy a drug that will save her life. The druggist refuses to lower the price or delay the payment, so Heinz breaks into the drugstore and steals the drug. Should Heinz have done that? Why or why not? The individual's level of moral judgment is assessed on the basis of the structure or kind of reasoning used, not the content of the judgment. In other words, a person could receive a high score for saying that Heinz was right or for saying that he was wrong; the score depends on the reasons for the judgment (Kohlberg, 1963, 1964).

Analyses of the responses to these dilemmas led Kohlberg to propose three levels of moral judgment, each of which is further subdivided into two stages. At the *preconventional level*, children judge right and wrong primarily by the consequences of actions. In the earliest stage (stage 1), right and wrong are judged in terms of obeying rules in order to avoid punishment. In stage 2, a simple doctrine of reciprocity develops. People should act to meet their own needs and let others do the same; doing what is "fair" constitutes an equal exchange. The saying, "You scratch my back and I'll scratch yours" fits this stage. The child's moral orientation

Conventional morality takes account of the intention behind an action.

is still primarily individualistic, egocentric, and concrete, although the rights of others are seen as coexisting with the child's rights (Colby, Kohlberg, Gibbs, & Lieberman, 1983; Kohlberg, 1976).

At the second level, *conventional morality*, the focus is on interpersonal relationships and social values; these take precedence over individual interests. Initially, at stage 3, a child may put strong emphasis on being "a good person in your own eyes and those of others" (Kohlberg, 1976, p. 34), which means having worthy motives and showing concern about others. Typically, conformity to stereotyped images of natural behavior (i.e., the behavior of the majority) is emphasized. The intention behind an action acquires major importance; one seeks approval by "being good." At stage 4, a *social* or *member of society perspective* takes precedence. The child shows concern not only with conformity to the social order but also with maintaining, supporting, and justifying this order. "Right behavior consists of doing one's duty, showing respect for authority, and maintaining the given social order for its own sake" (Kohlberg & Gilligan, 1972, p. 160).

At the *postconventional* and *principled* levels (stages 5 and 6), moral judgments are based on broad abstract principles, principles that are accepted because they are believed to be inherently right rather than because society considers them right. At stage 5, the individual willingly participates in the social order and, in effect, enters into a social contract with others in which equal distribution of power and protection of each person's liberties and rights are ensured. The emphasis at this stage is on democratic processes, impartiality in applying the laws of society, and opposing laws if they violate the principles of equality, liberty, and justice. Stage 6, the highest (and most ideal) stage of moral development, is characterized by a rational moral perspective and involves the application of universal, absolute principles of justice, equality, and respect for human life and human rights. When Martin Luther King said that disobeying segregation laws was morally right because he was obeying a higher law, he was making a postconventional moral argument. This level is characterized by a "major thrust toward abstract moral principles which are universally applicable,

Postconventional morality involves accepting broad abstract principles because they are inherently right rather than merely because society considers them right.

and not tied to any particular social group" (Kohlberg & Gilligan, 1972, p. 159). (A detailed explanation of each stage appears in Table 11.2.)

Like Piaget, Kohlberg believed that moral development depends on advances in general cognitive abilities and that, like those advances, moral stages emerge in an invariant sequence, each stage evolving from, and replacing, the preceding one. Piaget believed that egalitarian relationships with peers stimulate progress from moral realism to moral relativism. Similarly, Kohlberg asserted that participation in a democratic institution leads to greater moral maturity (see Box 11.3 on p. 454).

Most adults are at stage 3 or 4 of Kohlberg's sequence. Although stage 5 responses appear with increasing frequency in late adolescence and during the college years, only a small percentage of the population reaches this stage. Stage 6

TABLE 11.2

Six Stages of Moral Judgment

	Content of Stage		
Level and stage	What is right	Reasons for doing right	Social perspective
LEVEL I—PRECONVENTIONAL			
Stage 1: Heteronomous morality	Not breaking rules backed by punishment, obedience for its own sake, avoiding physical damage to persons and property.	Avoidance of punishment, the superior power of authorities.	*Egocentric point of view.* Doesn't consider the interests of others or recognize that they differ from the actor's; doesn't relate two points of view. Actions are considered physically rather than in terms of psychological interests of others. Confuses authority's perspective with one's own.
Stage 2: Individualism, instrumental purpose, and exchange	Following rules only when it is to someone's immediate interest; acting to meet one's own interests and needs and letting others do the same. Right is also what's fair, an equal exchange, a deal, an agreement.	To serve one's own needs or interests in a world where one must recognize that other people have interests, too.	*Concrete individualistic perspective.* Is aware that everybody has his or her own interest to pursue and that these may conflict, so that right is relative (in the concrete individualistic sense).

reasoning is found so rarely that it has been dropped from the scoring system (Kohlberg, 1978). Apparently, this stage is reserved for such extraordinary humanists as Gandhi, Martin Luther King, and Mother Theresa!

Level and stage	Content of Stage		Social perspective
	What is right	Reasons for doing right	
LEVEL II—CONVENTIONAL			
Stage 3: Mutual interpersonal expectations, relationships, and interpersonal conformity	Living up to what is expected by people close to you or what people generally expect of people in your role as son, brother, friend, etc. "Being good" is important and means having good motives and showing concern about others. It also means maintaining mutual relationships, such as trust, loyalty, respect, and gratitude.	The need to be a good person in one's own eyes and those of others. Caring for others. Belief in the Golden Rule. Desire to maintain rules and authority that support stereotypical good behavior.	*Perspective of the individual in relationships with other individuals.* Aware of shared feelings, agreements, and expectations that take primacy over individual interests. Relates points of view through the concrete Golden Rule, putting oneself in the other person's shoes. Does not yet consider generalized system perspective.
Stage 4: Social system and conscience	Fulfilling the actual duties to which one has agreed. Laws are to be upheld except in extreme cases in which they conflict with other fixed social duties. Right is also contributing to society, the group, or an institution.	To keep the institution going as a whole, to avoid the breakdown in the system that would occur "if everyone did it," or the imperative of conscience to meet one's defined obligations. (Easily confused with stage 3 belief in rules and authority.)	*Differentiates societal point of view from interpersonal agreement or motives.* Takes the point of view of the system that defines roles and rules. Considers individual relations in terms of place in the system.

TABLE 11.2 *continued*

| | Content of Stage | | |
Level and stage	What is right	Reasons for doing right	Social perspective
LEVEL III—POSTCONVENTIONAL or PRINCIPLED			
Stage 5: Social contract or utility and individual rights	Being aware that people hold a variety of values and opinions, that most values and rules are relative to one's own group. These relative rules should usually be upheld, however, in the interest of impartiality and because they are the social contract. Some nonrelative values and rights like *life* and *liberty*, however, must be upheld in any society and regardless of majority opinion.	A sense of obligation to law because of one's social contract to make and abide by laws for the welfare of all and for the protection of all people's rights. A feeling of contractual commitment, freely entered upon, to family, friendship, trust, and work obligations. Concern that laws and duties be based on rational calculation of overall utility, "the greatest good for the greatest number."	*Prior-to-society perspective.* Perspective of a rational individual aware of values and rights prior to social attachments and contracts. Integrates perspectives by formal mechanisms of agreement, contract, objective impartiality, and due process. Considers moral and legal points of view; recognizes that they sometimes conflict and finds it difficult to integrate them.

Kohlberg's theory has had considerable influence and has stimulated a great deal of research as well as controversy. Evidence from research supports the hypothesis that the moral stages represent an orderly, universal, and invariant progression in moral development. As predicted from this hypothesis, preconventional reasoning (stages 1 and 2) declines sharply with age, accounting for 80 percent of 10-year-olds' moral judgments, 18 percent of 16- to 18-year-olds', and only 3 percent of 24-year-olds'. The proportion of conventional moral judgments (stages 3 and 4) increases from 22 percent at age 10 to almost 90 percent at age 22. Similar trends have been found in cultures as divergent as those of Taiwan, Turkey, Central America, India, and Nigeria (Edwards, 1981; Kohlberg, 1969; Magsud, 1979; Turiel, Edwards, & Kohlberg, 1978).

Level and stage	Content of Stage		Social perspective
	What is right	Reasons for doing right	
Stage 6: Universal ethical principles	Following self-chosen ethical principles. Particular laws or social agreements are usually valid because they rest on such principles. When laws violate these principles, one acts in accordance with the principle. Principles are universal principles of justice: the equality of human rights and respect for the dignity of human beings as individuals.	Belief as a rational person in the validity of universal moral principles, and a sense of personal commitment to them.	*Perspective of a moral point of view* from which social arrangements derive. Perspective is that of any rational individual recognizing the nature of morality or the fact that persons are ends in themselves and must be treated as such.

Lawrence Kohlberg (1976) proposed six stages of moral judgment. This table lists those stages and gives some examples and definitions for each.

Source: Adapted from J. Rest. Morality. In P. H. Mussen, J. Flavell, & E. Markman, (Eds.), *Handbook of child psychology*: Vol. 3. *Cognitive development* (4th ed.). New York: Wiley, 1983. By permission.

A 20-year longitudinal study of a group of American men who were tested at four-year intervals between preadolescence and their mid-30s provides further evidence that successive moral stages are attained in the predicted order (see Figure 11.3). None of the subjects skipped any stage. Their judgments at any period tended to be remarkably consistent; that is, the vast majority of an individual's responses in a testing session were at the same level of moral reasoning (Colby et al., 1983). Longitudinal studies in other cultures have yielded similar results (White, Bushnell, & Regnemer, 1978; Nisan & Kohlberg, 1982).

Research findings have also confirmed Kohlberg's hypothesis that advances in moral judgments are related to changes in general cognitive abilities. For example, conventional reasoning (levels 3 and 4) is said to depend on the individual's ability to assume the perspectives of others. In one study, 11-year-old girls who were good at role taking were at the conventional level of moral reasoning, whereas poor role takers were generally at stage 2 (Moir, 1974). Also as predicted, formal operations and abstract thinking are prerequisites for postconventional moral reasoning (level 5): Preadolescent girls and college women who reasoned at the postconventional level in response to the Kohlberg dilemmas used formal operational thinking in cognitive tests. However, not all those who had achieved the level of formal operations on the general cognitive tests were at the postconventional level in moral judgment (Tomlinson-Keasy & Keasy, 1974). Formal operations apparently are necessary, but not sufficient, for the development of postconventional morality.

BOX 11.3

Democratic Atmosphere and Moral Judgment

Lawrence Kohlberg believed that people's moral judgments and actions are significantly influenced by the moral atmosphere of groups or institutions in which they participate. "Individual moral decisions in real life are almost always made in the context of group norms or group decision-making processes" (Higgins, Power, & Kohlberg, 1984, p. 75). Kohlberg and his colleagues hypothesized that if the moral atmosphere of a social institution were improved, individuals associated with that institution would gain greater moral maturity. They tested this hypothesis by comparing the moral judgments of students in traditional high schools with those of comparable students in special high schools where issues of fairness were discussed and rules enforced in weekly meetings based on participatory democracy (i.e., one person, one vote, whether teacher or student). Participation in such a democracy, the investigators reasoned, would give the students a greater sense of community and collective norms as well as a greater sense of responsibility for what happened in the school.

The moral dilemmas used in the study included standard justice situations like the Heinz dilemma (see page 447), but the emphasis was on practical situations and particularly on students' prosocial thinking and sense of responsibility for others. For example, in one of the dilemmas a student, Harry, needs someone to drive him 40 miles on a Saturday morning for an interview at a college that he has applied to; a classmate has a car, but to help Harry he would have to get up very early on Saturday, the only day he can sleep late. In another dilemma students have agreed not to use drugs on a field trip. During the trip, some of the students light up a joint and offer it to Bob. Should Bob refuse to smoke? Students were asked what they would think and do in each dilemma and how their peers would reason and act.

Comparisons of the responses of students in the traditional and democratic schools provided substantial support for the investigators' hypothesis. Although a majority of the students in both kinds of schools said that they would make, and act upon, prosocial choices, the proportion of such choices was higher among those in the democratic schools. There were striking differences between the two groups' beliefs about how their classmates would think and act. In the democratic schools, over 80 percent of the students' responses indicated that they believed their peers felt that they *should* act prosocially, whereas in the regular high schools this was true of only about 40 percent of the responses. In the words of the researchers,

> In predicting their peers' *behavior*, about 60 percent of the democratic school students' responses indicated that they felt their peers would act consistently with their prosocial choice. In the regular high schools, about 30 percent of the responses showed that students believed their peers would act prosocially ... In the democratic schools, most children report that they themselves would make the prosocial choice and act on it. They also report that most of their peers would do the same. (Higgins et al., 1984, p. 104)

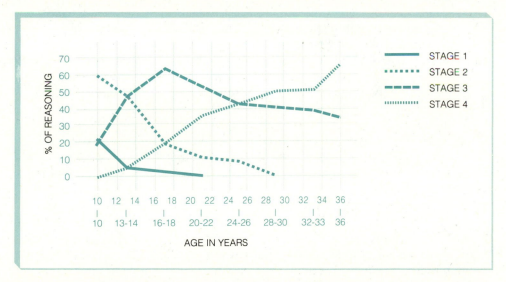

FIGURE 11.3 Percentage of moral reasoning at each stage for each age group. (Adapted from A. Colby, L. Kohlberg, J. Gibbs, & M. Lieberman. A longitudinal study of moral development. *Monographs of the Society for Research in Child Development*, 1983, 48, Serial No. 200. By permission.)

CRITICISMS OF KOHLBERG'S THEORY.   Kohlberg's work has been criticized on grounds of both theory and method. Some critics argue that all morality is culturally relative and that it is ethnocentric to view one kind of moral thought as "higher" than another. Principled judgments that oppose the laws of a society might not be considered the most advanced form of moral thinking in another culture or at another time (Baumrind, 1978). Kohlberg's conclusion that young children's moral judgments are based exclusively on rewards, avoidance of punishment, and deference to authority has also been challenged. According to some investigators, children have more profound knowledge and understanding of morality than they are able to articulate; they have "an intuitive moral competence that displays itself in the way they answer questions about moral rules and in the way they excuse their transgressions and react to the transgressions of others" (Schweder, Turiel, & Much, 1981, p. 288).

Young children recognize **moral issues** (general principles relating to justice, fairness, and the welfare of others), distinguishing these from **social conventions** (arbitrary rules of conduct sanctioned by custom and tradition). In one study, children between 5 and 11 years of age were asked about school policies that permit children to hit each other or to take off their clothes in school. The majority of children of all ages said that a school should not permit hitting but could allow children to undress (Weston & Turiel, 1980).

Children will argue that it is wrong to hit or steal (moral issues) even in the absence of rules or laws against such acts, and they often react spontaneously to their peers' violations of moral rules by citing reasons for obeying those rules (Nucci & Nucci, 1982; Nucci & Turiel, 1978; Smetana, 1981). Thus, it is clear that social-conventional thinking and morality are distinct conceptual systems in children's thinking (Turiel, 1983).

Because the Kohlberg sequence of stages is based on responses to hypothetical situations rather than responses to issues and dilemmas that people actually confront, some critics are doubtful about its meaningfulness and the extent to which it can be generalized (Baumrind, 1978). Furthermore, it has been maintained that Kohlberg's scoring system is biased in favor of males because high scores in moral maturity depend on an orientation toward justice. Such an orientation is stressed in the socialization of males, whereas females are socialized to be nurturant, empathic, and caring. A recent review of relevant studies concludes that in fact males do not score higher on Kohlberg's dilemmas than females do (Walker, 1985; Rest, 1986). Nevertheless, it is probably true that if women were presented with dilemmas about personally relevant issues, such as how to deal with an unwanted pregnancy, they would very likely give responses that differ considerably from men's and from their own responses to the Kohlberg dilemmas.

MORAL JUDGMENT AND BEHAVIOR.   Can children's moral behavior be predicted on the basis of their reasoning about moral issues? This question has not been answered adequately. Young children's moral judgments are not related to resistance to cheating or violation of social norms (Santrock, 1975; Blasi, 1980, 1983), and their actions may be inconsistent with their stated beliefs about fairness and justice. Thus, in one study children worked in groups of four, making bracelets. The situation was arranged so that some children made more and prettier bracelets than others; for example, one child was younger and less skilled, so she worked more slowly than the others. In individual interviews about the fairest way to divide the reward among the participants, many children said that all should share equally because they had all worked hard and contributed to the best of their ability. However, when they were actually distributing the rewards, children often "acted in ways that were as much tied to their self-interest as their notions of justice. For example, children at all ages studied tended to favor themselves somewhat more than others" (Damon, 1983, p. 137; Gerson & Damon, 1978). The children's reasoning had "only a partial influence on their actual social conduct" (Damon, 1983, p. 137).

The moral behavior of older children, adolescents, and adults is more likely to be consistent with their moral judgments. Given opportunities to cheat, only 15 percent of college students at the postconventional level of moral development actually did so, in contrast to 55 percent of those at the conventional level and 70 percent of those at the preconventional level. Similarly, during the 1965 Berkeley Free Speech Movement some students acted consistently with their strong moral position and "sat in" at the administration building to protest the university's rules prohibiting political activity on the campus. They did this at great personal risk, for many were forcibly evicted or arrested. Yet 73 percent of the students who were at stage 5 on the Kohlberg scale became active protesters, in contrast to only 40 percent of those at stage 4 and 10 percent of those at stage 3 (Haan, Smith, & Block, 1968).

Judging from available evidence, we can make only tentative predictions from moral judgments to social behavior because the relationship between the two is at best a moderate one and is closer among older individuals than among younger ones. Perhaps this is what we should expect, because beliefs about what is right, fair, or just are only one of many factors that determine how an individual will act in any particular situation.

Nevertheless, knowing children's level of moral judgment may help parents and others reason with them persuasively. Consider the following anecdote:

> Teddy, 10, had promised to attend a movie with his grandmother. Then his friend called to ask him to go skating. He wanted to go skating, but his mother thought that he should keep his promise to his grandmother. She tried first pointing out that Grandma's feelings would be hurt if he did not go with her, but he continued to protest that he wanted to go skating. Mother then said, "You know, Grandma has given you a lot of things and done a lot of nice things for you recently. It's your turn to do something nice for her." Teddy's face suddenly cleared, and he said, "Oh yeah, I guess you're right."

Teddy was persuaded by a line of reasoning that emphasized an obligation of reciprocity resembling Kohlberg's stage 2, his own stage of moral judgment. In general, when parents' explanations of rules and disciplinary actions fit the child's cognitive level and level of moral judgment—that is, when they represent the type of reasoning the child uses himself or herself—children are more likely to internalize those rules and comply with them.

Prosocial Behavior

The term **prosocial behavior** refers to positive social actions, including altruism, helping, sharing, caring, and sympathizing. The development of such behavior is a topic of utmost importance from both a theoretical and a practical standpoint, and it has been the focus of many investigations. Infants occasionally offer toys to others (Hay, 1979; Leung & Rheingold, 1981), but sharing and other altruistic acts generally occur relatively infrequently during the early years; such acts are far outnumbered by selfish and aggressive responses (Murphy, 1937; Whiting & Whiting, 1975; Yarrow & Waxler, 1976). However, the incidence of sharing, helping, sympathy, and empathy increases dramatically during the elementary school years (Emler & Rushton, 1974; Rushton & Weiner, 1975; Ugurel-Semin, 1952). Similarly, although 2-year-olds play some games that require taking turns, indicating a rudimentary understanding of cooperation, spontaneous cooperative responses are much more common among preschool children who work together to achieve common goals or engage in fantasy play taking reciprocal roles such as mother and baby (see pages 427–429).

Is there a general prosocial trait; that is, are cooperative children also more generous and helpful to others? The findings of a number of observational studies conducted in naturalistic settings suggest that the answer is yes. For example, among preschool children observed during free play there were substantial associations among different types of prosocial interactions, including sharing, helping, and cooperating; some children were consistently more generous and also more helpful than others (Strayer, Waring, & Rushton, 1979). Other studies have yielded more modest, although generally positive, relationships among different types of prosocial behavior (e.g., Krebs & Sturrup, 1982; Payne, 1980). Closely related types of behavior, such as sharing and donating, are most highly correlated (Moore, B. S. & Eisenberg, 1984).

Longitudinal studies demonstrate that prosocial tendencies are fairly stable over time (Bar-Tal & Raviv, 1979; Block & Block, 1973). In one study, the correlations between measures of prosocial behavior taken during nursery school and agin five or six years later were substantial (.60 for boys and .37 for girls) (Baumrind, 1971).

Even casual observation demonstrates that children differ markedly in tendency toward prosocial behavior. In the last two decades many investigators have attempted to discover the determinants of these individual differences. Among the most significant determinants are cultural background and empathy.

CULTURAL BACKGROUND.   A child who is reared in a culture whose economy and way of life are based on cooperation among members of the family and the community will be trained for cooperation, whereas a child who is brought up in a competitive society will be socialized in different ways. When playing a game like the one illustrated in Figure 11.4, in which they must work together to win prizes, children from traditional subcultures and small agricultural communal settlements in Mexico and Israel are much more cooperative—and far less competitive—than their conterparts in middle-class urban areas (Madsen, 1967; Madsen & Shapira, 1970; Shapira & Madsen, 1974). The differences in the children's behaviors are

Spontaneous cooperative responses are more common among preschool children who spend time together in play and other activities.

undoubtedly related to the values and economic systems of the communities in which they were raised. Competitiveness is punished in societies where it threatens to undermine the culture but is encouraged in societies in which it is advantageous in the struggle for survival.

EMPATHY.   According to one influential theory, empathy is a universal, biologically based response that changes with cognitive development and environmental influences (see pages 203 and 430). Infants seem to recognize and react to the distress of others; for example, they may cry when they see another child crying. Their attempts to help are generally inappropriate and ineffective, however. With advances in cognitive ability—specifically, the ability to assume the perspective

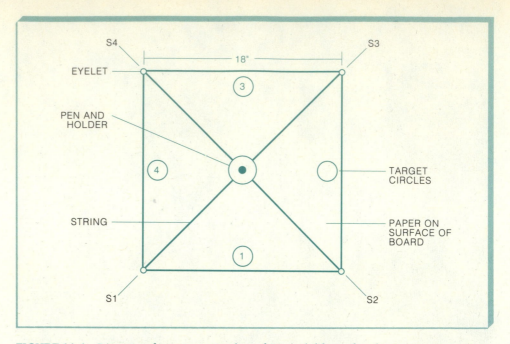

FIGURE 11.4   Diagram of a cooperation board. Four children play the game. A pen is suspended at the center, and strings attached to the pen pass through the eyelets at the four corners of the board. The object is to pull the pen through the circles on the board. Because each child controls one string, all must cooperate or work together to move the pen to any of the circles. (Adapted from A. Shapira & M. C. Madsen. Cooperation and competitive behavior of urban Afro-American, Anglo-American, Mexican-American, and Mexican village children. *Developmental Psychology*, 1970, 3, 16–20. By permission.)

of others and to take roles—children acquire a more complete and accurate understanding of other people's feelings and emotions. As a consequence, they become more compassionate and more likely to assist others in appropriate ways (Hoffman, M. L., 1981).

Individual differences in level and pattern of empathic responses are apparent from very early childhood, and these differences tend to be quite stable. Some toddlers react to the distress of peers with loud crying or agitation, whereas others respond in calmer, more cognitive ways (e.g., exploring and asking questions); some behave aggressively (e.g., hitting a child who hit another child) or in an anxious or avoidant manner (e.g., turning and looking away). In one longitudinal study, two-thirds of the children made responses at age 7 that were similar to those they had made at age 2 (Radke-Yarrow & Zahn-Waxler, 1984).

As social-learning theorists would predict, environmental factors and social experiences contribute significantly to the development of empathy and to individual differences in children's predispositions toward empathy. It has been hypothesized that secure early attachment to the caregiver promotes the development of high levels of empathic response. Compared with infants who lack secure attachments, those who are judged to have secure attachments to their

With increased cognitive ability comes a more complete and accurate understanding of other people's feelings and emotions.

mothers at 1 year show greater concern with distressed adult playmates nine months later, and at 3 years of age they are more sympathetic with peers in distress (Main, Weston, & Wakeling, 1979; Waters et al., 1979).

The caregiver's child-rearing practices and disciplinary techniques—especially reactions to the toddler's hurting or frustrating another child—also contribute to the development of empathy. According to the results of one study, the reactions that are most likely to lead to high levels of empathy are clear cognitive messages stressing the consequences of the child's behavior, accompanied by displays of emotion and statements of principles (e.g., "Look what you did! Don't you see you hurt Amy? Don't *ever* pull hair!") (Zahn-Waxler, Radke-Yarrow, & King, 1979). In the words of one researcher,

> The mother's highly emotional reaction may indicate the importance of the situation to the child as well as model emotional responsiveness to the other's distress. The content . . . may . . . provide additional information to the child about how to feel and act in the situation. Thus it appears that in the caregiver's response to the child . . . the interaction of cognitive and affective components is essential. (Barnett, 1987, p. 154)

The relationship between empathy and prosocial behavior increases with age. Among preschool children, the association is weak but positive; empathy with another child's sadness and worry is correlated with prosocial behavior, but empathy with happiness or anger is not (Feshbach, 1978; Lennon, Eisenberg, & Carroll, 1986). However, among older children, adolescents, and adults there are stronger associations between indices of empathy and prosocial responses such as helping others in distress (Eisenberg & Miller, 1987). For example, 5- and 6-year-old children who showed great empathy (judged from facial expressions) with a child who had lost a marble collection subsequently worked harder to replace the other child's loss than did children who showed no empathic reaction (Leiman, 1978).

Experiences in role taking may raise the level of empathy with others and, consequently, the level of altruism. Six-year-olds who practiced taking roles—often switching roles—in a series of skits and who answered questions about the motives and feelings of characters they were portraying were more likely to share candies with needy children than were children who had no role-playing experience (Iannotti, 1985).

Training for Prosocial Behavior

In their efforts to promote their children's prosocial behavior, parents use a variety of techniques, including rewarding altruistic actions, modeling, reasoning, and assigning responsibility to the child.

MODELING AND OBSERVATION.   In an ingenious experimental study, one group of children observed a model exhibiting "symbolic" altruism. Using toy animals and people and three-dimensional plastic settings, the model portrayed scenes in which someone needed help, for example, a monkey trying to get a banana that was outside its cage and beyond its reach. The model helped the toy person or animal, at the same time expressing awareness of the distress and sympathy, using the word *help* to highlight what she had done. The child, using a duplicate set of toys, then emulated the model's altruism, and the model pointed out how helpful the child had been (Yarrow, Scott, & Waxler, 1973). Another group of children observed this symbolic modeling and, in addition, witnessed the model in an act of real altruism: A second woman came into the room, tried to retrieve something under a table, and "accidentally" banged her head and acted as if she were in pain. The model responded warmly, putting her hand on the woman's shoulder and saying, "I hope you aren't hurt. Do you want to sit down a minute?" The victim responded appreciatively. With half the children in each modeling condition, the model was nurturant, helpful, and supportive; with the other half of the children, she was nonnurturant, aloof, and only minimally helpful.

The differential effects of the two kinds of modeling were apparent two weeks later in tests involving other imaginary or symbolic situations as well as actual opportunities to help in real-life situations. Symbolic modeling alone—in effect, giving "lessons"—resulted in increased helping, verbalizations, and actions *only* in symbolic or imaginary situations. However, observing a nurturant adult modeling real altruism produced an increase in real-life altruism (e.g., helping a mother by picking up a basket of spools that had spilled or retrieving toys that a baby had dropped out of its crib). Drawing upon these findings, the investigators concluded that if parents want to socialize their children to high levels of altruism, they should not only try to inculcate the principles of altruism in the children but also exhibit altruism in their everyday interactions (Yarrow, et al., 1973).

The personal histories of unusually altruistic adults provide impressive evidence of the contribution of parental modeling and identification to prosocial behavior. Non-Jews who risked their lives trying to rescue Jews from the Nazis during Workd War II tended to be strongly identified with parents who held strong moral convictions and acted in accordance with them (London, 1970). When interviewed in depth, fully committed workers in the civil rights movement of the 1960s—those who made extensive sacrifices to work for equal opportunities for people of all races—described their parents as vigorous workers in the cause of justice and human welfare, and as warm, loving, and willing to express their feelings about moral issues. In contrast, workers who were only partially committed to the movement—those who did some work, but without making great sacrifices—did not regard their parents as good models of altruistic behavior. Their parents, they reported, gave lip service to humane causes but did not actually work for those causes and they were cool, aloof, and avoidant in their relationships with their children—behavior that was hardly likely to promote strong identification with them (Rosenhan, 1969).

The prosocial participants in another recent study were volunteers at a crisis counseling center who underwent rigorous training and worked very hard, making major investments of time and effort. Among the volunteers, those who had had warm, positive relationships with altruistic parents during childhood completed their six-month commitment to this prosocial work even if they found the training difficult and unrewarding. However, those who had had poor relationships with nonaltruistic parents sustained their crisis work only if they found the training situation personally rewarding (Clary & Miller, 1987).

INDUCTION.   If caregivers use *induction* in disciplining their young children—that is, if they reason with them and point out the painful consequences of misbehavior—the children are more likely to make prosocial responses to the distress of others (Zahn-Waxler et al., 1979). In studies of elementary school children, parents answered questionnaires about their disciplinary methods; in addition, sociometric techniques were used to assess the children's prosocial tendencies (Hoffman, M. L., 1970; Hoffman, M. L., & Saltzstein, 1967). Parental use of induction was associated with children's helpfulness and consideration. By contrast, more assertive, power-based techniques—control by means of power or material resources (including physical punishment, withdrawal of privileges, and threats)—led to socially negative outcomes, lack of consideration for others, stinginess in donations, and self-centered values (Dlugokinski & Firestone, 1974). The disciplinary pattern that is most likely to enhance prosocial behavior consists of frequent use of induction and infrequent use of power.

Induction is viewed as an effective technique for eliciting the child's natural tendency toward empathy (Hoffman, M. L., 1970), which may then lead to attempts to help. Parents who make extensive use of techniques based on power, on the other hand, may communicate to children that following rules established by authorities yields better results than considering the possible effects of their actions.

DIRECT INSTRUCTION.   Parents often lecture their children about the virtues of prosocial behavior, and according to some research evidence such moral preaching may have some generalized positive effects. For example, when children were told that they ought to donate some of their winnings in a game to poor children, they exhibited greater generosity than children in a control group who were not told what they ought to do; these effects were discerned both immediately and eight weeks later (Rushton, 1975). The effects of such instructions about expected behavior may produce as much immediate and enduring generosity as is produced by modeling (Grusec, Saas-Kortsaak, & Simutis, 1978; Rice & Grusec, 1975).

EARLY ASSIGNMENT OF RESPONSIBILITY.   Children who are given responsibility for household chores, taking care of siblings, or contributing to the economic wellbeing of the family are more likely than others to develop high levels of prosocial responsiveness. Children reared in cultures in which they are routinely assigned such responsibilities are more prosocial than children reared in cultures in which this is not done (Whiting & Whiting, 1973, 1975). Within our own culture, parental demands for mature behavior—pressure to assume responsibility and to achieve in accordance with one's abilities—also promote the development of high levels of altruism and nurturance toward others (Baumrind, 1971).

In summary, the development of high levels of altruism and other prosocial behavior depends on all the major processes of socialization in the family—identification, modeling and imitation, explaining, assigning responsibility, and moral preaching. Each of these processes reinforces the effects of the others. (The contributions of school and the media to the development of prosocial behavior are discussed in Chapter 13.)

AGGRESSION

All societies must find ways of preventing their members from injuring, killing, and doing serious harm to one another, but they vary enormously in the extent to which they regulate aggression. For example, among American Indian tribes, the Comanche and the Apache raised their children to be warriors, whereas the Hopi and the Zuni teach peaceful, nonviolent behavior. In some American subcultures aggression and toughness are highly valued, whereas among the Hutterites and Amish pacifism is a way of life and children are trained to be nonaggressive.

Much research on aggression was stimulated by the formulation of the *frustration-aggression hypothesis* in the late 1930s (Dollard, Doob, Miller, Mowrer, & Sears, 1939). This hypothesis asserts that frustration serves to instigate aggression. It is assumed that there is an innate connection between frustration and aggressive behavior. The sources of frustration may be deprivation, punishment, barriers that prevent or delay the achievement of important goals, feelings of inadequacy or anxiety that inhibit the pursuit of desirable outcomes, or threats to self-esteem.

Two types of aggression have been identified. **Instrumental aggression** is aggresive behavior that is directed toward a goal, such as acquiring a toy or other desirable object; **hostile aggression** is action that is intended to harm another person either physically (hitting or kicking), or verbally (teasing, name calling, or expressing disapproval).

There is abundant evidence that frustration often, though not always, elicits aggressive responses; in other words, aggression is a prominent and frequent reaction to frustration. The evidence also shows that aggression is not the only possible reaction to frustration; moreover, not all aggressive responses are motivated by frustration (Feshbach, 1970).

Patterns of Aggressive Behavior

As children develop, their patterns of aggressive behavior change. Two- and three-year-olds frequently fight and quarrel, usually over possession of toys or other desirable objects (i.e., instrumental aggression); the total amount of aggression displayed peaks at about 4 years of age. As children reach elementary school age, aggressive acts become less frequent and instrumental, and more often hostile. Verbal aggression, such as teasing or name calling, increases during the preschool and early elementary school years. Because older children are better able to understand other people's intentions, more of their aggression, both physical and verbal, is retaliatory, consisting of responses to frustration or attacks by others (Hartup, 1974).

Sex differences in aggression are evident from the age of 2 or 3 on. In nursery school, boys instigate aggression—both verbal and physical—more often than girls do and are more likely to retaliate after being attacked. Boys are also more frequently the targets of aggression (Darville & Cheyne, 1981; Maccoby & Jacklin, 1980). Sex differences in aggressive behavior are found in all social classes and all cultures (Parke & Slaby, 1983) and at almost all ages, although the differences are most marked during puberty and early adulthood (Cairns, 1983). (See Figure 11.5.)

What accounts for these consistent sex differences? Both biology and learning are involved. Some argue that the prevalence of sex differences across human cultures, and in almost all species, is strong evidence for biological determinants. There may indeed be a biological foundation that gives some male children a particularly high potential for learning aggressive behavior, but at present scientists cannot describe such a biological system.

The social experiences of boys and girls with respect to aggression are very different. Aggressive behavior is part of the masculine stereotype in our culture; it is expected and often implicitly encouraged in boys. For instance, in one study preschool boys received more attention for their aggressive actions than girls did both from adults and from peers (Fagot & Hagan, 1982). The attention was sometimes positive (e.g., smiling or joining the child's play) and sometimes mildly negative (e.g., moving the child to another activity); either form of attention can encourage aggression more than simply ignoring it will.

For both males and females, aggressiveness is stable over time. Highly aggressive nursery school children are likely to become highly aggressive kindergarteners. The amount of physical and verbal aggression expressed at ages 6 to 10 is

American culture tends to encourage aggressive behavior in boys.

correlated with aggression toward peers at ages 10 to 14 (Emmerich, 1966; Kagan & Moss, 1962; Olweus, 1979). The most impressive evidence of the stability of aggression comes from a 22-year longitudinal study that began with a large number of 8-year-olds in the third grade. At that time the children were asked to name classmates who behaved in certain ways, including aggression (e.g., "Who pushes or shoves children?") (Huesmann et al., 1984). Aggression was measured several times in the ensuing years. Children who were rated as aggressive by their peers when they were 8 years old tended to be rated as aggressive by their peers ten years later. Moreover, those who were rated as aggressive by their peers tended to rate themselves as aggressive, to rate others as aggressive, and to see the world as an aggressive place (Eron, 1987; Huesmann et al., 1984; Lefkowitz, Eron, Walder, & Huesmann, 1977). In addition, those who were rated as highly aggressive at age 8 were three times more likely to have police records by the time they

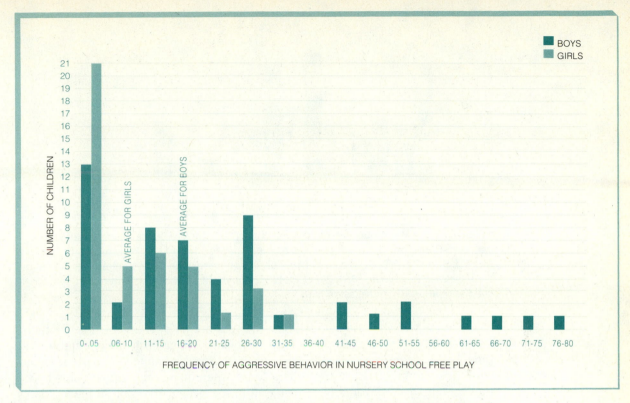

FIGURE 11.5 Frequency of interpersonal aggressive behavior for 4-year-old boys and girls in a preschool classroom. (Adapted from data reported in L. K. Friedrich & A. H. Stein. Aggressive and prosocial television programs and the natural behavior of preschool children. *Monographs of the Society for Research in Child Development*, 1973, 38 [4, Serial No. 151].)

those who were not so rated, and at age 30 signifcantly more of them had been convicted of criminal behavior, were aggressive toward their spouses, and tended to punish their own children severely.

By contrast, children who were regarded by their classmates as highly prosocial at age 8 (i.e., those who were frequently named as "never fighting when picked on" and "being polite to others") showed very little antisocial behavior in subsequent years. Figure 11.6 illustrates these findings, showing that both males and females who were high in aggression at age 8 had a relatively high number of criminal convictions by age 30, while those who were high in prosocial behavior had very few. One of the investigators therefore concluded" that

aggression and prosocial behavior represent opposite kinds of interpersonal problem-solving strategies that are learned early in life. If a child learns one mode well, he or she does not tend to learn the other well. Thus, an important factor in the control of aggressive behavior is the learning of nonaggressive behaviors." (Eron, 1987, p. 440; Eron, Walder, & Lefkowitz, 1971; Goldstein, 1981; Patterson, G. R., 1982)

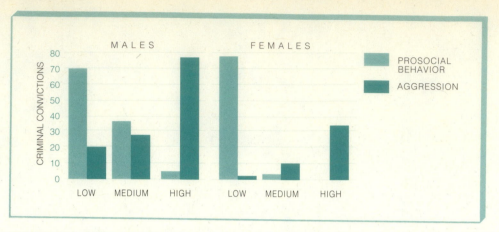

FIGURE 11.6   Mean number of criminal convictions by age 30 as a function of levels of aggression and prosocial behavior at age 8. (Adapted from L. R. Huesmann, L. D. Eron, M. M. Lefkowitz, & L. O. Walden. The stability of aggression over time and generations. *Developmental Psychology*, 1984, 20, 1120–1134. Copyright 1984 by the American Psychological Association. By permission.)

The aggressive child's cognitions, interpretations of the behavior of others, and ways of processing information help explain why aggressiveness is stable over time. Highly aggressive boys are more ready than their nonaggressive peers to perceive hostility in the actions of others. Thus, when questioned about some hypothetical ambiguous events (e.g., being hit in the back with a ball or having one's toys knocked to the ground by a peer), aggressive boys are likely to assume hostile intent. When they view the peer as acting in a hostile way toward them, they are inclined to retaliate with what they feel is justified aggression. In this way an ambiguous, possibly accidental act by a peer may lead to an intentional aggressive act by the aggressive child (Dodge, 1980, 1985, 1986).

This view of the world as hostile is based at least in part on actual experience, for aggressive boys are in fact likely to be the targets of aggression by their peers. In this way a spiral of aggression and counteraggression is created and perpetuated. When unacquainted 7-year-old boys were brought together to play freely for several sessions, those who were highly aggressive in their early interactions frequently became the targets of aggression in later sessions, and those who were initially the targets of aggression became more aggressive in later sessions. These findings support the notion that aggressiveness develops from reciprocal influences. Aggressive boys "will become rejected by peers, who will then treat them in antisocial ways. The antisocial treatment will serve to perpetuate and exacerbate the reciprocal aggression" (Dodge, 1986, p. 296).

Determinants of Aggression

BIOLOGICAL FACTORS.   What are the roots of individual differences in aggressiveness? Biological factors undoubtedly play a role. For example, the testosterone levels of adolescent boys are significantly correlated with self-reports of physical and verbal aggression, tolerance for frustration, and irritability. Temperament may also have a lasting impact: children who had been irritable and hard to soothe as infants were anxious, hyperactive, and hostile when they were 3 years old (Bates, 1982). Moreover, infants who are very active, irregular, distractible, and low in adaptability ("hot-headed") are more likely than others to develop aggressive behavior in subsequent years (Olweus, 1980; Thomas, Chess, & Birch, 1968).

INFLUENCE OF THE FAMILY.   Clearly, these biological influences interact with social experiences. Conditions in the child's environment may serve both to facilitate and to restrain the expression of biological tendencies (Parke & Slaby, 1983). Among those conditions, the most significant is the influence of the family.

Both parental rejection and permissiveness are conducive to high levels of aggression in children. In rejecting their children, parents ". . . may ignore the young child's expressions of discomfort and thwart his needs for nurturance. Also, nonacceptance probably means that the parent is a poor source of positive reinforcements or rewards, which should result in the parent being less effective as a teacher of self-restraint whether for the control of aggression or for any other socially disapproved behavior" (Martin, 1975, p. 511). Also, if parents are overly permissive and accepting in the early years and fail to set clear limits on the child's aggressiveness, the child's aggressive responses become strong and persistent (Olweus, 1980). Children of both sexes who do not identify closely with their parents tend to express more aggression than those with a strong identification with their parents (Eron, 1987).

Physical punishment, especially if it is used frequently, erratically, and inconsistently, may result in enduring high levels of aggression and hostility (Eron et al., 1971; Eron and Huesmann, 1984; Lefkowitz et al., 1977; Patterson, G. R., 1982). The effects of punishment vary with the child's general level of aggression; relatively nonaggressive children are likely to suppress their hostile responses if they are punished, but highly aggressive children who are punished will persist in, or even increase, their aggressive behavior (Eron et al., 1971).

Family interactions frequently take the form of an escalating pattern of coercion that serves to maintain and increase aggression in the family. When a child is hostile, other family members are likely to do something that increases the probability of further aggression. For example, a brother yells at his sister; she in turn yells back, calling him names; he then hits her; she hits him back; and so on. A similar pattern of escalation may develop between parent and child—the child reacts defiantly and the parent makes stronger threats and punishes the child more severely. Aggressive children usually are unresponsive to social disapproval and unlikely to react to mild verbal discipline.

To study the socialization of aggression in the family, Gerald Patterson and his associates (1976, 1980) observed children with aggressive behavior problems both at home and at school. The parents of these children were generally hostile and lax in their enforcement of rules and standards. The mothers sometimes reacted positively to both deviant and prosocial behaviors; on other occasions they ignored or punished similar kinds of behavior.

Patterson and his colleagues developed a comprehensive program of behavior modification for retraining parents of highly aggressive children. First the parents study techniques of child management, such as how to notice and reinforce desirable behavior and how to enforce rules consistently. Next they are taught to observe and record their children's deviant and prosocial actions, the events that elicit them, and their consequences. Modeling and role playing are used to teach the parents how to reinforce appropriate behaviors with warmth and affection and to reduce deviant behavior by not giving in to the child's aggression and not allowing their own coercion to escalate. Techniques of control using rewards for desirable responses and calm forms of punishment such as "time out" (removing the child from an activity until she stops using coercive tactics) are substituted for more severe forms of punishment.

Detailed observations demonstrate that this program is very successful in reducing aggressive behavior, and observations a year later show that the beneficial effects of the treatment generally persist. Clearly, parents can learn more effective, nonpunitive ways of interacting with their aggressive children, and this can be accomplished in a relatively short period (Patterson, G. R., 1976, 1980).

Of course, the child's level of aggressiveness is also affected by many other factors. For example, frequent exposure to television violence may lead to increases in aggression, whereas some school experiences may reduce the expression of hostility. These influences are discussed in Chapter 13.

SUMMARY

The primary vehicle for the development of relationships with peers is play, beginning around age 2. Between the ages of 2 and 5 children's interactions become more frequent, more sustained, more social, and more complex. A higher proportion of play after age 3 is either associative (children play together but not in a coordinated manner) or cooperative (children help each other achieve a shared goal and/or take different roles).

Group dramatic play, which generally emerges by the age of 3, contributes to the development of social skills, patterns of effective interaction, empathy, cooperation, and competence in role taking. Games with rules require greater cognitive ability and consequently do not become part of the child's play repertoire until later.

Age-related changes in social interaction and play are to some extent a function of increasing skill in role taking. Role-taking ability appears to develop through a series of qualitatively distinct stages and is correlated with general intelligence and moral behavior.

With more extensive social experience and advances in cognitive abilities, children's conceptions of others become more abstract, more complex, and more focused on psychological characteristics. Beginning around age 8, children make increased use of abstract adjectives referring to traits, beliefs, values, and attitudes. The descriptions given by children age 12 to 14 are generally better organized and show greater sensitivity to the complexity of personality characteristics and behavior.

Children's ideas about friendship change as they mature. Whereas preschool children are not concerned with lasting relationships, older children think of friendships as relationships that continue beyond single, brief interactions. Between the age of 5 and adolescence, children's conceptions of friendship evolve from a stage in which friends are the playmates whom the child sees most frequently, through one in which friends are the people with whom they cooperate and share, to one in which friendships are judged in terms of mutual understanding.

Many factors influence the social status of children. Among the cognitive attributes associated with popularity are well-developed role-taking skills and friendly, outgoing, sympathetic orientations toward others. Children with high social status also have greater social knowledge and understanding of effective ways of interacting. Moderately high self-esteem is more likely to lead to acceptance by peers than either very high or very low self-esteem.

Children's self-control increases as they grow older. According to psychoanalytic theory, ego processes (the rational components of the personality) balance the conflicting demands of the individual's needs and desires, conscience, and reality. In contrast, social-learning theorists see self-control and delay of gratification as outcomes of reinforcements and observational learning.

Children who are generally self-controlled and able to delay gratification are more responsible and mature than other children. Training techniques can be used to enhance children's cognitive controls and, hence, their ability to delay gratification. Positive labeling and observation of a model can also increase children's ability to delay gratification.

The groundwork for research on moral development was laid by Jean Piaget who proposed that at about age 5 children enter a stage of *moral realism*, in which they believe that rules are handed down by authorities and therefore are fixed and absolute. At age 10 children attain the state of *moral relativism*, in which ideas of reciprocity and the belief that everyone has an equal right to justice predominate. Piaget's work was extended by Lawrence Kohlberg, who proposed three levels of moral judgment that are achieved in an orderly progression. At the *preconventional* level, children judge right and wrong primarily by the consequences of actions. At the *conventional* level, interpersonal relationships and social values take precedence over individual interests. At the *postconventional* level, moral judgments are based on broad abstract principles.

In early childhood, prosocial behaviors are far outnumbered by selfish and aggressive responses. However, the incidence of sharing, helping, sympathy, and empathy increases dramatically during the elementary school years. Longitudinal studies demonstrate that prosocial tendencies are fairly stable over time. Individual differences in prosocial tendency are influenced by cultural background and empathy. Infants with more secure attachment to their caregivers appear to develop higher levels of empathic response.

A variety of techniques have been used in efforts to socialize children to engage in prosocial behaviors. They include modeling and observation, induction (reasoning with the child), direct instruction, and early assignment of responsibility.

According to the frustration-aggression hypothesis, aggression is instigated by frustration due to deprivation, punishment, barriers to the achievement of goals, feelings of inadequacy or anxiety, or threats to self-esteem. However, frustration does not always lead to aggression, and not all aggressive responses are motivated by frustration.

As children develop, their patterns of aggressive behavior change. The total amount of aggression displayed peaks at about 4 years of age. In elementary school, aggressive acts are more likely to be hostile than instrumental; also, verbal aggression increases during the preschool and early elementary school years. Sex differences in aggression are evident from the age of 2 or 3 on. For both males and females, aggressiveness is stable over time.

Among the determinants of aggression are biological factors such as testosterone level and family influences such as parental rejection and permissiveness. Parents of highly aggressive children can be retrained to break the escalating pattern of coercion that serves to maintain and increase aggression in the family.

REVIEW QUESTIONS

1. How does children's play contribute to the development of peer relationships?

2. What is meant by role taking? How is skill in role taking related to empathy?

3. In what ways do children's perceptions of others change as they grow older?

4. What social processes are involved in the formation of friendships? What factors play a role in the maintenance of friendships?

5. What factors determine the social status of children among their peers?

6. How is children's self-control measured? How can their ability to delay gratification be increased?

7. Compare Piaget's and Kohlberg's theories of moral development. On what grounds has Kohlberg's work been criticized?

8. What is meant by prosocial behavior and what are its most significant determinants?

9. What techniques are used in attempting to socialize children to engage in prosocial behaviors?

10. How do patterns of aggressive behavior change as children develop?

GLOSSARY

empathy   The recognition, understanding, and vicarious feeling of another person's emotions.

ego resilience   An index of flexibility or adaptability.

moral issues   General principles relating to justice, fairness, and the welfare of others.

social conventions   Arbitrary rules of conduct sanctioned by custom and tradition.

prosocial behavior   Positive social actions, including altruism, helping, sharing, caring, and sympathizing.

instrumental aggression   Aggressive behavior that is directed toward a goal.

hostile aggression   Action that is intended to harm another person either physically or verbally.

SUGGESTED READINGS

Eisenberg, N., & Mussen, P. (1990). *Roots of prosocial behavior*. New York: Cambridge University Press. An up-to-date, comprehensive survey of the biological, social, familial, cultural, and cognitive factors that influence the development of prosocial behavior (caring, sharing, and helping) in children.

Hartup, W. W. (1983). Peer relations. In E. M. Hetherington (Ed.), *Socialization, personality, and social development* (Vol. 4). *Handbook of Child Psychology* (P. Mussen, general editor). New York: Wiley. An in-depth, insightful, and evaluative discussion of developmental patterns of peer interaction (including friendship, popularity, and social status); the formation, structure, and processes of children's groups; and the role of peers in socialization.

Higgins, E. T., Ruble, D. N., & Hartup, W. W. (Eds.) (1983). *Social cognition and social development*. New York: Cambridge University Press. In this stimulating set of essays, a broad sociocultural perspective is applied to a wide range of theories and studies of the development of social cognition. Among the issues examined are stages in the development of social cognition, attributional processes, the relationship between social cognition and social behavior, and the directions of future research.

Monighan-Nourot, P., Scales, B., & Van Hoorn, J., with Almy, M. (1987). *Looking at children's play: A bridge between theory and practice*. New York: Teachers College Press. A rich mixture of descriptions and analyses of many types of children's play, based largely on the observations of the authors, all of whom are experienced nursery school teachers and administrators. Included are many realistic examples of play with peers, with parents, and with teachers, as well as many practical suggestions about how to stimulate play that promotes cognitive and social development.

Olweus, D., Block, J., & Radke-Yarrow, M. (1986). *Development of antisocial and prosocial behavior*. Orlando, FL: Academic Press. This thought-provoking volume consists of seventeen essays, each by an expert in the field, focused on research, theory, and issues in the domains of aggression, delinquency, cooperation, and altruism. The principal themes are biosocial approaches, early developmental patterns, impulse control, socialization in the family and peer groups, and continuities in social development.

Chapter Twelve

SOCIALIZATION IN THE FAMILY

Determinants of Child-rearing Practices
    Parental Characteristics and Beliefs
    Children's Personality and Behavior
    Social Contexts
Child-rearing Practices and Their Consequences
    Reinforcement
    Punishment
    Inductive Techniques
    General Comments on Disciplinary Techniques
    Imitation and Identification
Influences on Family Socialization
    Patterns and Styles of Parental Behavior
    Siblings
    Family Structure
    Child Abuse
A Systems Approach to Family Socialization

Consider two healthy, attractive 6-year-old girls, Nancy and Tracy, both of whom are above average in intellectual ability (IQs around 115). They attend the same first-grade class in a medium-sized American community. Nancy is energetic, eager, outgoing, and cheerful, and is doing well in school. Her teacher regards her as one of the brightest children in the class (although she isn't). When a question is asked, Nancy frequently raises her hand or calls out, "I know, I know," even though she may guess at the answer. When faced with a difficult problem, Nancy is persistent, trying one solution after another; if she cannot solve the problem herself, she is comfortable asking the teacher for help. She is popular with her classmates, a leader in group activities, considerate of her peers, and generally helpful.

Tracy is a much different kind of child, slow-moving, quiet, and shy. She is doing poorly in school and is considered unintelligent by her teacher (although she isn't). She never volunteers answers to the teacher's questions, and she gives up quickly when faced with a difficult problem—"I just can't do it." Tracy has few friends, shows little interest in group games or activities, and seldom shares things with others or helps peers in any way.

What accounts for the vast differences between the two girls in personality and social behavior? Obviously, the determinants are many and varied. The contributions of heredity, temperament, and variations in early attachments were reviewed in earlier chapters. However, in any discussion of social and personality development the concept of socialization also looms large. As we saw in Chapter 5, **socialization** is the process through which children acquire the behavior, skills, motives, values, beliefs, and standards that are characteristic, appropriate, and desirable in their culture. The **agents of socialization** are the individuals and institutions that participate in the process—parents, siblings, peers, teachers, members of the clergy, television, and other media. Although all of these agents may influence the child in important ways (see Chapter 13), ordinarily the family is the most salient part of the child's environment. For this reason, it is generally regarded as the primary or most powerful agent of socialization, playing the key role in shaping personality, characteristics, and motives; guiding social behavior; and transmitting the values, beliefs, and norms of the culture.

The goals of socialization—that is, the attributes and social responses to be acquired by the child—vary from one culture to another, as do the techniques used to socialize the child. In American culture independence, self-reliance, intellectual ability, considerateness, popularity, self-confidence, assertiveness, and standing up for one's rights are generally valued (Kagan, Reznick, Davies, et al., 1986). Parents promote these characteristics through verbal encouragement, reward, and punishment. However, in Japanese culture the most important values are a sense of dependence on the group and community, emotional control, obedience, willingness to work hard and persevere to achieve long-range goals, courteous behavior, and self-effacement (Caudill & Frost, 1973; Goodnow, 1985; Werner, 1979). Japanese parents frequently use shame as a technique to control nonconforming behavior; for example, they may ask the child questions like, "What will other people think?" (Harrison et al., 1984).

Although the process of socialization begins in infancy, it becomes much more vigorous and intense in the second year of life, when children's cognitive abilities improve and they become more mobile, autonomous, and self-aware. Parents then find it necessary to teach the child restrictions: Certain impulses must be inhibited; some things must not be touched; some places must be avoided. Toilet training is likely to begin at this time, and some degree of self-control is expected. As the child develops and his or her cognitive abilities are augmented, the process of socialization becomes more complex.

Much socialization takes place through observation and imitation as well as through reward and punishment. For example, 3-year-old children watch their parents using knives and forks at the dinner table and try to imitate them; the parents, in turn, reward their children by praising them when they handle the silverware in appropriate ways. Through further demonstration, explanation, or criticism, they help the children modify undesirable responses. But many significant personal and social attributes, motives, and attitudes—for example, kindness toward others, placing a high value on intellectual achievement, and self-confidence—are not simply consequences of imitation, reward, or punishment. Instead, they are strongly influenced by general features of the family environment, child-rearing practices, and identification with family members.

What kinds of family environments and experiences enhance children's learning, emotional and social development, competence, and happiness? What family experiences are detrimental to personality and well-being? Have the radical changes in the structure of the family that have occurred during the last few decades—for example, the enormous increases in divorce rates, single parenthood, and maternal employment outside the home—adversely affected children's behavior and development? What roles do brothers and sisters play in shaping the child's behavior and personality? This chapter deals with these and related questions.

DETERMINANTS OF CHILD-REARING PRACTICES

Every parent's style and techniques of child rearing are a function of many interacting factors. As noted earlier, cultural background is one of these—Japanese parents are much more likely than Americans to use shame as a disciplinary technique. Within American culture, parents in some subcultures and social-class groups are prone to punish children physically for misbehaving, whereas parents in other groups seldom resort to physical punishment. Another factor that affects disciplinary techniques is the child's developmental level. In general, parents' use of physical punishment declines as children grow older, and physical displays of affection such as caressing tend to be replaced by other ways of expressing affection and approval. As the child's language skills improve, parents can make greater use of verbal guidance, explanations, and reasoning. "The more the child can speak intelligibly, the more efficient the parent becomes in responding to the child's bids for attention and help" (Maccoby, 1984, p. 322).

According to one well-known student of socialization, other factors that influence parents' child-rearing practices fall into three major categories: (1) forces emanating from within the parent (personality; expectations; beliefs about the goals of socialization, the nature of children, and effective socialization techniques); (2) attributes of the child (personality characteristics and cognitive abilities); and (3) "the broader social context in which the parent-child relationship is embedded—specifically, marital relations, social networks, and occupational experiences of parents" (Belsky, 1984, p. 84). A model illustrating the impacts of these factors on parenting is presented in Figure 12.1.

Parental Characteristics and Beliefs

Styles of parenting and disciplinary techniques inevitably reflect the caregiver's personality characteristics and belief systems. Mature, well-adjusted parents are more likely to react with sensitivity and nurturance to their children's signals and needs than immature, maladjusted parents are, and this kind of parenting promotes emotional security, independence, social competence, and intellectual achievement (Belsky, Lerner, & Spanier, 1984). Parents' self-confidence, trusting attitudes toward others, and belief that they can control what happens to them are associated with warmth, acceptance, and helpfulness in their relationships with their children (Mondell & Tyler, 1981). Not surprisingly, assertive and impatient fathers have been found to react very differently than passive, patient ones to low-key children (Bates & Petit, 1981), and depressed mothers provide disruptive, hostile, and rejecting home environments that have adverse effects on their children's development (Coletta, 1983; Orvaschel, Weissman, & Kidd, 1980).

In addition to their personality characteristics, parents' cognitions and beliefs about children's motivations and abilities are significant in shaping disciplinary practices (Dix & Grusec, 1985). As they attempt to socialize their children to become accepted, well-functioning, happy members of society, parents generally evaluate their children's actions as good or bad, mature or immature, to be

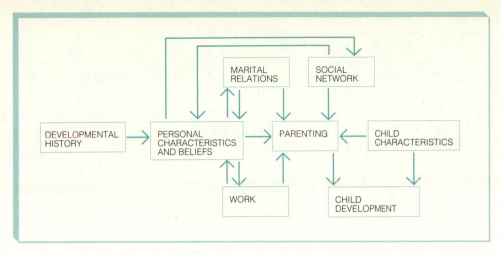

FIGURE 12.1   A process model of the determinants of parenting. (Adapted from J. Belsky The determinants of parenting: A process model. *Child Development*, 1984, 55, 83–96. By permission.)

encouraged or to be eliminated (Bacon & Ashmore, 1986). Thus, a mother who believes that her 3-year-old daughter pushed another child accidentally is not likely to be upset or to reprimand her. But if she believes the act was intentional, she may punish the child or try to modify her behavior in other ways. Similarly, a mother is not likely to react punitively to her 3-year-old son's temper tantrums if she considers him too young to control his behavior or if the tantrum was a reaction to some temporary frustration; under these circumstances she will probably be sympathetic and comforting. However, if she thinks the child's tantrum was a reflection of a self-centered, impatient disposition, she is likely to try to eliminate this response (Dix & Grusec, 1985).

Some parents believe that children are constructive, self-regulating learners who acquire knowledge through experimentation. They discuss issues with their children and ask them many questions, thereby stimulating them to think and reason. In contrast, parents who think children are primarily passive learners use directives and commands that are less likely to promote cognitive development (Sigel, 1986). Furthermore, those who perceive children as naturally capable, rapid learners "believe that they should not be rigidly directive and restrictive . . . whereas those who have a low opinion of the child's natural abilities tend to believe that they should be directive and restrictive" (Scheintuch & Levin, 1981, cited in Goodnow, 1985).

Parents' social orientations—their general conceptions of others—also affect their interactions with their children. Parents who stress psychological characteristics, motives, and feelings—in contrast to those who think primarily in terms of concrete features such as physical appearance, occupation, or position in society—tend to use person-centered disciplinary techniques. They call their children's attention to the feelings and motives of others and encourage them to reflect on their own behavior and emotions. This approach contributes to the development of the child's understanding, sense of personal responsibility, and autonomy (Applegate, Burke, Burleson, Delia, & Klein, 1983).

In sum, parents' cognitions—their inferences about children's behavior and motivations, their beliefs, opinions, and social orientations—are significant determinants of their child-rearing practices and disciplinary techniques. However, ideas about childhood and parenting are not fixed and immutable. Beliefs about child rearing may change in fundamental ways as a result of the experience of raising a child, noticing the differences between siblings, getting advice from more experienced parents about how to handle new situations (e.g., preparing the child to enter school), and consulting with experts, especially when children have health or psychological problems (Goodnow, 1985).

Parents' socialization goals, as well as their ideas about children and parenting, are largely the products of their culture (Goodnow, 1985). For instance, obedience and respect for authority have traditionally been highly valued by members of the working class. Consequently, parents in this class tend to be controlling, authoritarian, and arbitrary, seldom asking their children's opinions or giving reasons for rules or requirements. In contrast, middle- and upper-class parents are more concerned with their children's happiness, creativity, achievement, independence, curiosity, and self-control. Therefore, they are generally more democratic and permissive in dealing with their children, show more warmth and affection, reason with them more, and explain the reasons for rules and regulations (Bacon & Ashmore, 1986; Hess, 1970; Hoffman, L. W., 1984; Maccoby, 1980).

Social-class differences in child-rearing practices reflect the parents' social experiences. At work, working-class adults are often required to follow instructions that seem arbitrary; their supervisors seldom explain the reasons for the rules and requirements of the job. The lower-class parent therefore "is less involved in making, changing and bending rules in society, so that the existence of rules and authority structures seems more compelling than their rationale. As a parent, the mother may know the hygienic basis for the requirement that the child brush his teeth but the real answer to 'Why?' is 'Because you are supposed to' or 'Because I said so'" (Hoffman, L. W., 1984, p. 233). (For further discussion of social-class differences in child rearing, see page 356.)

Children's Personality and Behavior

The principle of bidirectionality is clearly illustrated in parent-child interactions: The child's temperament and attributes influence the quality and quantity of the care he or she receives, just as the parents' child-rearing practices influence the child's characteristics. An irritable and sleepless infant is likely to be very frustrating to its caregivers, eliciting hostile reactions that, in turn, serve to increase the infant's irritability (Thomas & Chess, 1975). Mothers who consider their infants "difficult" interact with them less and respond less sensitively to their cries than other mothers do (Campbell, 1979). Hyperactive, restless children between 4 and 8 years of age are relatively lacking in self-control, ask more questions, and comply less readily with instructions than normal children do. In response, their mothers are more controlling and give more instructions and criticisms. Some of these mothers' behavior is probably due to their children's initial tendency toward hyperactivity; the children's behavior, in turn, is probably influenced by their mothers' reactions (Mash & Johnston, 1982).

One way of thinking about the mutual influence of parents and children is to suppose that parents have upper and lower limits for acceptable behavior. When the child's behavior is above or below those limits, the parents respond with efforts to change the behavior. For example, if a very aggressive child exceeds the parent's upper limit of tolerance for aggression, the parent may punish her and attempt to restrain her aggressive impulses. The same parent might respond to a timid child by encouraging him to act more assertively. Many studies demonstrate that parents of highly aggressive children tend to use physical punishment frequently. This pattern could indicate either that parents react to aggressive behavior in their children by becoming punitive or, conversely, that children learn aggressive behavior from parental punishment (Bell, R. Q., 1979; Bell, R. Q. & Harper, 1977).

Social Contexts

Satisfactory, supportive marital relationships facilitate adaptation to parental roles (Grossman, Eichler, Winickoff, & Associates, 1980), and secure, satisfying husband-wife relationships are associated with sensitive parenting, which, in turn, is related to secure attachments between parent and child (Goldberg & Easterbrooks, 1984). For example, while instructing their school-age children, fathers who were discontented in their marriages gave less positive feedback and intruded more in the children's efforts to learn than did fathers who were satisfied with their marriages. In contrast, mothers who were discontented in their marriages used more positive teaching techniques than either their husbands or mothers who were contented with their marriages. Perhaps those mothers were trying to compensate for an unsatisfactory marriage through greater involvement with their children, or perhaps they wanted to provide better parenting than their husbands did (Brady, Pillegrini, & Sigel, 1986).

Family functioning, including child-rearing practices, may also be affected by environmental conditions outside the family setting. Urie Bronfenbrenner is concerned with such conditions, which he has labeled "exosystems" (Bronfenbrenner, 1979, 1986). These include the parents' work place, social networks, and community influences. Box 12.1 briefly summarizes the findings of some research on relationships between social-environmental conditions and parenting behavior.

CHILD-REARING PRACTICES AND THEIR CONSEQUENCES

Almost all parents have implicit or explicit ideals regarding what their children should be like, that is, what knowledge, moral values, and patterns of behavior their children should acquire as they develop. In their efforts to achieve these ideals, parents ordinarily try a variety of strategies, since different techniques are useful for different purposes. Rewards and punishments are likely to be effective in teaching children particular skills and socially desirable responses such as dressing oneself and saying "Please" when asking for something. But many

BOX 12.1

Some Impacts of the Exosystem on Children

The Work Place

Working-class men whose jobs typically require compliance with authority stress obedience and conformity in socializing their children. Middle-class men whose work involves greater initiative, competitiveness, and risk-taking attempt to train their children to be independent and self-directing (Kohn & Schooler, 1978, 1983).

Men in occupations that make high demands on their physical and mental energy have little time for other activities, including spending time with their children. This may generate feelings of guilt, increased irritability, and impatience in dealing with the children, with adverse affects on the children's emotional and social adjustment (Heath, 1977).

Parental Support Systems

Mothers (especially single, poor, teenage mothers) who have relatively strong social support from relatives and friends feel less stress in parenting, have more positive attitudes toward themselves and their children, are more responsive and less rejecting, and provide better care than mothers who have relatively little social support. The latter tend to be more restrictive and punitive in their relationships with their children (Coletta, 1981, 1983; Crockenberg, 1981). Social support networks seem to play a particularly significant role under conditions of stress; stress is more debilitating and support more beneficial for single mothers than for married ones (Weinraub & Wolf, 1983).

The Community

Rates of childhood psychiatric disorders and juvenile delinquency are much higher in urban areas than in rural areas, and the problems most characteristic of city children begin early, last a long time, and are accompanied by many other problems in the family (Rutter, 1981). Although it is not clear why children who live in the city are at greater risk for emotional disturbances than their peers in rural areas, research seems to indicate that the main adverse effects of city life result from tension and disruption in urban families. A careful longitudinal investigation demonstrated that delinquency rates among boys in London decreased after their families moved out of the city (West, 1982).

Although living in the city may have adverse effects on social and emotional adjustment, it may be advantageous for cognitive development among older children. The intelligence and achievement test scores of 11-year-olds in a large city were found to be higher than those of peers in smaller communities, probably because the city offered a richer cultural environment and better educational facilities (e.g., libraries, and other learning opportunities outside the home and school) (Vatter, 1981).

Homelessness

An American tragedy of increasing proportions, and one that will inevitably affect children's social, emotional, and cognitive development, is homelessness. It is virtually impossible to obtain an accurate census of homeless people, but it is estimated that there are more than 2 million in the United States; the vast majority of these are families with children. The average homeless family includes one parent and two or three children. Many live in temporary shelters or long-term hotels provided by civic, federal, or private agencies. Family life as it is generally known is virtually destroyed; fathers are frequently separated from their families, and in large cities the families are shifted from one shelter or hotel to another. In the words of an official New York City report, "the seemingly endless shuttling between hotels and shelters can come to resemble a game of 'human pinball.'" Two-thirds of the "pinballs" are dependent children.

Living conditions in these hotels and shelters are deplorable—cramped, filthy, noisy, and unsanitary. The children are inadequately nourished and often hungry; their parents are desperate and depressed; drugs and violence abound in their surroundings; and the children attend school sporadically, if at all. One school principal in New York estimates that one-quarter of the children in hotels and shelters for the homeless are two or three years behind their peers in academic skills, which makes them even more reluctant to attend.

A keen observer of homeless families highlighted the devastating effects of homelessness on children:

> All but a few of the children [in hotels for the homeless] will fail to thrive in any meaningful respect. Early death or stunted cognitive development are not the only risks these children face. Emotional damage may be expected, too . . . A psychiatrist . . . speaks of interviewing children who are more depressed than those she would expect to find in psychiatric clinics. She describes a 19-month-old baby who had started having nightmares and stopped eating, and a 10-year-old who, ridden with anxiety, has begun to mutilate himself: he has pulled out his permanent teeth.
>
> Anger that does not turn in upon the child frequently turns out to vent itself on society. Children at [these] hotels . . . live with a number of good reasons for intense hostility and with very few for acquiescence in those norms by which societies must live. Such children, if they do not cause disruption in the streets and the hotels, may do so in school. (Kozol, 1988a, p. 80; see also Kozol, 1988b)

complex behaviors and personality characteristics, such as altruism or high levels of achievement motivation, are acquired through more subtle processes such as imitation and identification.

Parents are pleased when they observe their children cleaning their rooms, sharing their toys, or concentrating on their homework. They are likely to reward or reinforce these behaviors by praising the child or giving her something she wants, thereby strengthening the desired responses and increasing the probability that they will be repeated in the future. When a child is observed engaging in undesirable or unacceptable behavior—such as eating candy before supper, hitting another child, or failing to help a younger brother who needs help—a parent may punish him or reason with him, attempting to suppress or eliminate the undesirable behaviors.

In using these disciplinary techniques, parents are attempting to promote compliance with their own and/or society's values and standards of acceptable behavior, not only at home or under the surveillance of adults but also when the child is alone. "Indeed, it is the shift from initially external forms of control to later internalized . . . mechanisms that is the hallmark of successful socialization" (Lepper, 1983, p. 295). The ultimate goal of disciplinary techniques is the achievement of intrinsic motivation in which the child has a personal desire to behave in socially acceptable ways.

Reinforcement

Reinforcers or rewards can be social (praise, affection) or nonsocial (material goods, special privileges) in nature. The effectiveness of social reinforcements like praise depends partly on the child's relationship with the adult. Praise from a warm, accepting parent usually is more effective than praise from a cold, rejecting one, although rare praise from the latter may have special significance.

B. F. Skinner, one of the founders of modern behaviorism, argued that parents can rely entirely on positive reinforcement in socializing their children and never have to punish them. Indeed, careful application of the principles of reinforcement can lead to highly effective and humane child rearing (see Hawkins, 1977). However, parents' attempts to use reinforcement do not always yield the intended result because parents do not always know what their children consider the best rewards. For example, a parent may give a child money for doing a chore when the child would rather have a different reward, such as going to a baseball game with her father.

For young children, reinforcements are most effective when they are given immediately after the desired behavior has occurred, so that the connection between the action and the reward is obvious (Millar & Watson, 1979). Immediate rewards probably are less important for older children, who are more capable of delaying gratification and of understanding the relationship between their behaviors and rewards that come later (Maccoby & Martin, 1983).

Extrinsic rewards must be administered cautiously, especially for spontaneous, intrinsically motivated behavior, because under certain circumstances such rewards may actually diminish the child's interest in the rewarded behavior. This was demonstrated in an experiment in which children were rewarded with prizes for drawing with felt pens, an activity they were highly motivated to engage in and that they found very interesting; they subsequently manifested much less interest in this activity. Similarly, a parent may sometimes administer overly generous rewards when a child acts in desirable ways. For example, if a 6-year-old receives a large reward—say, permission to watch television for an extra hour—for spontaneously sharing a toy with another child, he may perceive the reward as more salient than the behavior that led to it. If he subsequently complies with parental wishes simply to get a reward, his motivation to share is less likely to be internalized; on later occasions he may not share unless he believes he will be rewarded.

Perhaps the most appropriate rewards are those that fit the minimum-sufficiency principle (Lepper, 1983), which states that the most effective means of changing a child's behavior over the long term are those that are applied with just enough coercion or reward to engage the child in the new behavior. In other words, "External incentives provided by the adult must be minimally sufficent to change the child's behavior without being more salient in themselves than the standards that the adult is trying to promote. Under these conditions . . . the child's attitudes and behavior will be permanently transformed because the child will internalize the new standards" (Damon, 1983, p. 182).

If children are praised highly for everything they do, they are unlikely to interpret praise as a valid sign of achievement or approval. A child who is striving for autonomy may regard rewards for helping her sister as attempts to control her, and therefore may fail to internalize the motivation to help a younger sibling. A simple statement of approval that emphasizes the child's intrinsic motivation and initiative (e.g., "It's really nice that you like to help others") may achieve more than too much praise or a material reward.

Reinforcement is sometimes given unintentionally, as when children get attention for misbehaving. Consider the following example:

> Sally is playing with her friend in one room of the house while her mother works in another room. Sally and her friend decide to play a chase game, running through the room where Sally's mother is working. Mother looks up from her work and tells them not to run through there. They run through the room again, and Mother tells them a little more firmly to stop it. They repeat the action, and Mother gets up from her work, takes them back to the room where they were playing, and suggests that they play with some puzzles there. Just as Mother settles back to her work, they run through again.

What has happened here? It appears that the mother's attention is serving as a positive reinforcer for running through the room and interrupting her. What could this mother do differently? One technique that sometimes works is **extinction**. If attention is reinforcing, then ignoring the behavior may stop it. The mother might pay no attention to the running children. After a few tries, they might stop running because that behavior is not being reinforced. In this way the undesirable behavior is extinguished.

If the mother finds it impossible to ignore the behavior (e.g., if the children are about to knock over a good lamp), she could try reinforcing an alternative behavior. She could take the children to their quiet game and pay attention to them while they play it. Probably a better strategy would be to tell them she will play with them after a specified time *if* they stop running.

Punishment

If all the strategies just described fail, this mother may need to use punishment to get the children to stop running through forbidden areas. In fact, most parents believe that they have to resort to punishment in some situations, especially when they are trying to teach their children to avoid dangerous objects or when they wish to inhibit activities such as running out into the street. Punishment may have some negative consequences, but it can be applied effectively to reduce or inhibit undesirable responses and to promote the development of self-control and appropriate social behavior. To accomplish these goals, punishment must be administered in accordance with some well-established principles.

First, timing is of the utmost importance; the shorter the delay between the undesirable behavior and the punishment, the more effective the punishment will be. The ideal time to stop an unacceptable act is just before it occurs or as it is beginning (Aronfreed, 1968; Parke, 1977). For example, if a young child repeatedly runs into the street, the best time to administer punishment is when he is just about to step off the curb. Second, punishment from a nurturant, affectionate parent is more likely to produce the desired result than punishment from a cold or hostile parent. Third, if the goal is to inhibit or extinguish unacceptable actions, consistency in punishment is essential. Inconsistent or erratic punishment—punishing a particular behavior on some occasions and ignoring it on others—is likely to cause the behavior to persist. The parents of juvenile delinquents and highly aggressive boys are more inconsistent in their use of rewards and punishment than are parents of nondelinquents (Parke, 1977). (See also pages 465–470.)

In accordance with the minimum-sufficiency principle, the punishment for a prohibited action should be just severe enough to induce compliance (Lepper, 1981). Severe punishments may bring future compliance with rules but may also generate resentment and fear, which, in turn, may lead the child to resist accepting and internalizing those rules. Prohibitions and punishments are most likely to have their intended effects if they are accompanied by explanations of the underlying reasons (LaVoi, 1973; Parke, 1977). The child is more likely to obey a prohibition like "You should stay out of the street because cars can hurt you" than the rule "Don't play in the street!" Explanations should be short and should be phrased in ways that are appropriate to the child's vocabulary and level of cognitive development. A child who is told in a calm way why she should stop running through the house acquires some understanding of her behavior as well as gruidance for future behavior.

These principles are applied in many homes and schools in a disciplinary strategy known as "time out," in which a prohibited activity is prevented by having the child sit on the sidelines for a short time without any attention from adults or other children. This form of discipline can be administered quickly and calmly; the reasons underlying it can be explained clearly; and it is not physically or emotionally harmful to the child (Hawkins, 1977; Parke, 1977).

The minimum-sufficiency principle is illustrated by the "time out" technique, in which the child is temporarily deprived of attention from others.

NEGATIVE SIDE EFFECTS OF PUNISHMENT.   Punishment must be used cautiously because it can have undesirable side effects. Severe punishment may generate such anxiety in children that they do not learn the lesson the punishment was designed to teach. Moreover, as a reaction to punishment that they regard as unfair, children may avoid punitive parents, who therefore will have fewer opportunities to teach and guide the child.

In addition, punitive parents provide aggressive models. A child who is regularly slapped, spanked, shaken, or shouted at may learn to use these forms of aggression in interactions with peers. In one investigation preschool children were shown videotapes of parent-child conflicts and asked what they would do if they were the parent. They advocated methods of discipline similar to those that their own parents applied (Wolfe, Katell, & Drabman, 1982). It may be inferred that parents who use severe punishment are also training their children to become punitive parents, and indeed many abusing parents were abused themselves as children (Parke & Collmer, 1975).

THE CHILD'S ROLE IN PUNISHMENT.   As would be expected on the basis of the principle of bidirectionality, the child's personality and past behavior influence the level and type of punishment administered by the adult. For example, highly aggressive preschool children are punished by teachers for aggressive acts more often than other children who exhibit the same aggressive responses. Perhaps because they are expected to be more aggressive and disobedient, boys are punished by parents and teachers more frequently than girls are (Maccoby & Jacklin, 1974). In one study, sons received more parental punishment for failure in a learning task than daughters did, even when their patterns of success and failure were identical (Mulhern & Passman, 1981).

In addition, aggressive and nonaggressive children react differently to punishment. Nonaggressive children are likely to respond to parental punishment by inhibiting the actions for which they were punished, whereas highly aggressive boys often escalate their undesirable behavior following punishment (Patterson, G. R., 1982). If a child is defiant or continues a prohibited action, parents often become more punitive (Mulhern & Passman, 1981; Parke, 1977; Passman & Blackwelder, 1981). (This point is discussed more fully in Chapter 11.)

Inductive Techniques

Although parents sometimes decide that punishment is necessary, psychologists generally agree that nonpunitive disciplinary strategies are preferable. As noted earlier, punishment accompanied by reasoning is more effective than punishment used alone in bringing about lasting improvements in children's behavior.

Nonpunitive strategies for modifying children's behavior—referred to as **inductive** or *information internalization* **techniques**, include reasoning, pointing out the consequences of undesirable actions, and appealing to the child's pride or desire for mastery (Damon, 1983; Hoffman, M. L., 1970). Examples of other-oriented inductive statements are "Don't yell at me; that hurts my feelings" and "Don't push him or he'll fall and cry." These strategies "lead children to focus on the actual standards that their parents are trying to communicate rather than on the disciplinary means by which the parents enforce these standards" (Damon, 1983, p. 180). Successful application of inductive techniques depends on good communication between parent and child, as well as on the child's understanding of and ability to internalize the reasons for rules and directives.

A series of studies by Martin Hoffman and his colleagues (1967, 1970, 1975, 1981, 1983) demonstrated that parents whose principal disciplinary techniques are inductive enhance their children's moral maturity, moral reasoning and behavior, and ability to feel guilt and shame. In contrast, *power assertive* techniques (e.g., threats, withholding of privileges, or physical punishment) do not promote the internalization of moral values and may actually inhibit moral development. Inductive discipline that orients the child toward the feelings of others is particularly effective in motivating compliance with rules and regulations, as the following experiment demonstrates.

Nine- and ten-year-olds first played with some highly attractive toys for 10 minutes and then were informed that these were to be put aside while they worked with an uninteresting crank-turning mechanism. Some of the children were given a simple prohibition ("Don't look at those toys again until I let you"). With others, a *self-oriented inductive technique* was used ("You'll be unhappy if you look at them. . . . If you don't work hard enough you'll have to do some of this work later and you'll have little time to play with those toys"). A third group received *other-oriented induction* ("You'll make me unhappy if you look at them now. If you don't work hard enough I'll have to do some of this work later and I'll have little time to do what I want to do"). The children who received other-oriented induction worked harder with the uninteresting toy and spent much less time gazing at the forbidden toys than did those who received self-oriented induction or simple prohibition. Clearly, other-oriented induction proved most effective in persuading the children to resist temptation and internalize rules (Kuczinski, 1983).

These positive and long-lasting consequences may be attributable to the cognitive and affective (emotional) processes activated by the use of inductive techniques. Inductions, particularly those that are other-oriented, are often centered on other people's feelings and emotions, thereby eliciting the child's empathy and concern for others. At the same time, these techniques provide the child with information about the standards and values the parents wish him or her to internalize. Children can apply these standards in evaluating their own actions and in guiding their future behavior and interactions with peers and adults (Damon, 1983; Hoffman, M. L., 1970, 1983). (See also the discussion of prosocial behavior in Chapter 11.)

General Comments on Disciplinary Techniques

It is difficult to evaluate the effects of different methods of discipline for several reasons. First, disciplinary techniques work best in the context of a warm, supportive parent-child relationship. Second, most parents use a combination of methods; families differ, for instance, in the extent to which they rely on power assertion versus induction, but it is a rare family that does not use some of each. Third, the type of discipline used depends partly on the child's initial responses. Mild reprimands and explanations are likely to be used first, but if the child is unresponsive, parents may gradually escalate to more intense, power-assertive methods. Consider the following example:

> Deborah and Sharon are playing, and both want to ride the one available bicycle. Their mother tells Sharon, who is riding the bicycle, that she and Deborah should take turns. Mother explains that it is fair to share the bicycle and that Deborah will feel bad if she does not get a turn (induction). If Sharon gives Deborah a turn, no further discipline is necessary. If Sharon does not give Deborah a turn, Mother may repeat her instructions. If Sharon still does not comply, however, Mother will probably resort to power assertion by telling her to get off the bike or else. If Sharon still refuses, Mother will probably punish her.

Imitation and Identification

Direct training techniques such as rewards, punishments, and reasoning are intentionally employed by parents in their attempts to enforce rules and to regulate or modify their children's responses. But these are not the only means by which children are socialized. Parental example obviously is also extremely important.

Children acquire many of their parents' behavior patterns through imitation.

Children acquire many of their parents' behavior patterns, idiosyncracies, motives, attitudes, and values through the processes of imitation and identification. These processes operate without the parents deliberately teaching or attempting to influence the child and without the child intentionally trying to learn. In fact, children often imitate behavior that parents would rather not teach them. A 4-year-old who swears when he hits his finger with a hammer is demonstrating the power of imitative learning.

Identification can be differentiated from imitation on theoretical grounds. **Imitation** may be defined simply as copying someone else's specific behaviors. **Identification**, a concept derived from psychoanalysis, refers to a more subtle process in which a person incorporates the characteristics and global behavior patterns of another person. Identification depends on the presence of a strong emotional tie to the person whose behavior is adopted; imitation does not. Freud maintained that by identifying with parents, particularly the parent of the same sex, a child acquires his or her superego or conscience, moral values, and standards as well as the responses and attitudes appropriate to his or her sex. Thus, through identification a young girl may adopt her mother's behavior patterns, attitudes, values, interests, mannerisms, and standards.

Another critical feature of identification is the child's perception of himself or herself as similar to the model and, consequently, as sharing the model's attributes and reactions. Warmth, dominance, competence, and social status are valuable resources, and according to one theory the child can share them by identifying with a model who has these qualities. One implication of this view is that identification can lead to antisocial as well as desirable values; for example, if a parent is a successful criminal, the child may adopt criminal values and behavior through identification with that parent.

Research findings support the theoretical prediction that children identify most strongly with warm, nurturant, dominant, and powerful parents. For example, children with warm parents were rated as more similar to their parents and showed a greater tendency to imitate them than did children with relatively cold parents. In marriages in which power was unbalanced—one partner made decisions and led the other most of the time—children were more likely to imitate the dominant parent (Hetherington, 1967; Lavine, 1982).

Identification and imitation can have long-delayed effects. A child may observe parents' behavior or internalize a moral principle but have no occasion to use that learning until months or even years later. For instance, young children learn many adult rules and principles by watching their parents and others, and they can apply those rules and principles in many situations and settings. In fantasy play, they often rehearse being a mommy or a daddy or a train conductor or some other role. But the end product of this identification may not be apparent until the child grows up and becomes a parent or takes a job.

INFLUENCES ON FAMILY SOCIALIZATION

Patterns and Styles of Parental Behavior

Parental disciplinary techniques and the strength of the child's identification are rooted in broad patterns of parent-child interaction or child-rearing styles. These patterns or styles may be described in terms of many different dimensions, such as acceptance, affection, control, nurturance, warmth, permissiveness, restrictiveness, and demandingness. The approach to child rearing that is considered most effective differs from one culture to another and, within any culture, from one family to another; in addition, views of proper child-rearing techniques change over time. In some eras—and in some cultures and some families—strict control and authoritarian patterns, characterized by many rules and close supervision of children, are common. During other historical periods, and in other cultures and families, the prevailing patterns are predominantly nurturant, permissive, and accepting of the child, with few restrictions and demands.

No single dimension fully describes the patterns or styles of parental behavior. Thus, a dimension like control (i.e., high or low parental control over the child) is meaningful only in combination with other factors, such as the extent to which a parent communicates openly with the child, the warmth of the home environment, and the severity of punishment. "It is the particular patterns or combinations of these factors that have predictable influences on the child-rearing process" (Damon, 1983, p. 152).

The longitudinal studies conducted by Diana Baumrind at the University of California at Berkeley are concerned primarily with the connections between patterns of parental behavior and children's behavior. Baumrind's first study compared the parents of three groups of preschool children characterized by very different personality characteristics and social behavior. The first group, which consisted of competent children, were those whom observers and interviewers rated high in independence, maturity, self-reliance, activity, self-control, exploration, friendliness, and achievement orientation (pattern I). Moderately self-reliant but discontented, withdrawn, and distrustful children (pattern II) constituted another group, and the third group was made up of the least self-reliant, explorative, self-controlled children (pattern III).

To assess parental behavior, the investigators used a variety of procedures, including home visits, observations in specially designed situations, and interviews. Four aspects of parents' behavior toward their children were evaluated: (1) *control*, or efforts to influence the child's goal-oriented activity, modify the expression of dependent, aggressive, and playful behavior, and promote internalization of parental standards; (2) *maturity demands*, or pressures on the child to perform at a high level intellectually, socially, or emotionally; (3) *clarity of parent-child communication*, for example, using reason to obtain compliance, asking the child's opinions and feelings; and (4) *parental nurturance*, including both warmth (love, caretaking, and compassion) and involvement (praise and pleasure in the child's accomplishments).

The scores of the parents of the three groups of children on these four child-rearing dimensions are shown in Figure 12.2. The parents of mature competent children (pattern I) scored uniformly high on all four dimensions. Compared with the other parents, they were warmer, more loving, more supportive, more conscientious, and more committed to their role as parents. They understood their

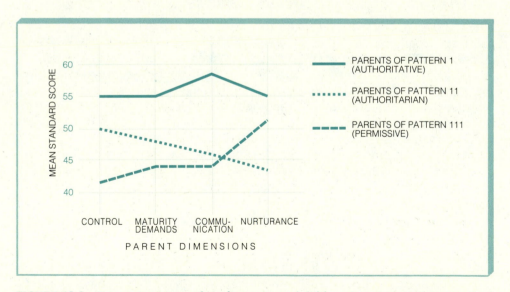

FIGURE 12.2   Parents' scores on four dimensions of child rearing. Parents were grouped according to their children's pattern of behavior. Pattern I children were socially competent and mature; pattern II children were moderately self-reliant but somewhat withdrawn; pattern III children were immature. The child-rearing patterns of parents of the three groups of children were called authoritative, authoritarian, and permissive. (Adapted from D. Baumrind. Child care practices anteceding three patterns of preschool behavior. *Genetic Psychology Monographs*, 1967, 75, 43–88. By permission.)

Authoritative parents may require that their children help with household tasks.

children's personality characteristics, points of view, interests, and motives, and they communicated well, encouraging frank discussions of parental decisions. At the same time, they were controlling and demanded mature behavior, guiding their children's activities consistently and requiring them to help with household tasks. They respected their children's independence and opinions but generally held firm in their own positions, providing clear reasons for them. This combination of parental control, inductive discipline, and positive encouragement of the child's autonomous and independent strivings was termed *authoritative* parental control.

The parents of pattern II children used rational control less and relied more heavily on power-assertive, coercive discipline. They were also less warm, nurturant, affectionate, and sympathetic with their children, and they did not encourage discussion of parental decisions or rules. These parents were termed *authoritarian* because they were highly controlling and used power freely, attempting to instill in their children conventional values such as respect for authority, work, and the preservation of order and tradition.

The parents of the least mature children (pattern III) were permissive, noncontrolling, and warm, and they were lax both in disciplining their children and in rewarding them. They made few demands on their children for mature behavior, allowed them to regulate their own activities as much as possible, avoided the exercise of control, and did not insist on obedience (Baumrind, 1967, 1973).

In two subsequent studies Baumrind used an alternative approach, first identifying parents who fit the authoritative, authoritarian, and permissive patterns and then evaluating the personal and social characteristics of their preschool children. Children of authoritative parents proved to be consistently and significantly more competent than children of authoritarian parents. Compared with girls from authoritarian homes, the daughters of authoritative parents were more independent, purposive, dominant, and achievement oriented. Boys in authoritative families showed social responsibility and friendly, cooperative behavior, whereas those from authoritarian households were more hostile and resistant. Both sons and daughters of permissive couples showed relatively little achievement motivation, and the girls in these families were much less socially assertive than girls from authoritative homes (Baumrind, 1971).

These children and their parents were reassessed when the children were 9 years old (Baumrind, 1988). As in the earlier studies, a wide array of parent and child variables were assessed by means of interviews, questionnaires, psychological tests, and observations in both natural and experimental situations. This study focused on combinations of two basic parental parameters: demandingness and responsiveness (see Figure 12.3). Four prototypes of parental patterns were derived from these combinations: authoritative, authoritarian, permissive-indulgent, and rejecting-neglecting. Each family was assigned to one of these patterns.

The major dimensions of children's behavior that were targeted for assessment were social competence (social assertiveness, social confidence, and social ascendance) and social responsibility (friendliness, cooperation, and sensitivity to others). Competent children were those who were rated high on both of these dimensions; incompetent children were those who were rated low on both of them.

The consequences of these differences in parenting style for the 9-year-olds were essentially parallel to those found during the preschool period. Authoritative

	ACCEPTING, RESPONSIVE, CHILD-CENTERED	REJECTING, UNRESPONSIVE PARENT-CENTERED
DEMANDING CONTROLLING	AUTHORITATIVE-RECIPROCAL HIGH IN PARENT-CHILD COMMUNICATION	AUTHORITARIAN POWER-ASSERTIVE
UNDEMANDING LOW IN CONTROL ATTEMPTS	PERMISSIVE-INDULGENT	REJECTING-NEGLECTING, IGNORING, INDIFFERENT, UNINVOLVED

FIGURE 12.3   A two-dimensional classification of parenting patterns. (Adapted from E. E. Maccoby & J. A. Martin. Socialization in the context of the family: Parent-child interaction. In P. H. Mussen [Series Ed.] and E. M. Hetherington [Ed.], *Handbook of child psychology* (Vol. 4): *Socialization, personality, and social development*. New York: Wiley, 1983. By permission.)

child rearing—the pattern combining high demandingness with high levels of warmth and responsiveness—had the most positive consequences for the children. The children who experienced an authoritative upbringing were the most socially competent, responsive, and intellectually able, as well as more achievement oriented and planful than children in any of the other categories.

The daughters of authoritarian parents who were highly demanding but not responsive were socially assertive, whereas both permissive and rejecting-neglecting parents produced daughters who were lacking in social competence. The sons of rejecting parents tended to be domineering but deficient in leadership skills and lacking in social competence.

These studies make it clear that children's behavior depends on the entire pattern of parental practices rather than on a single dimension like warmth or control. The authoritative pattern stands out as the one that is most likely to have enduring benefits for the child's personality and social behavior. Baumrind concludes that

> there are only a few ways to be an optimally competent parent whereas departures from competence may take many forms. Permissive parents give too much room, asking too little and leaving too many decisions up to the child. Authoritarian parents give too little room, asking too much and leaving too few decision up to the child. . . . Authoritative . . . parents are more ideal and rejecting-neglecting parents are less ideal than most parents in most areas. (Baumrind, 1988, p. 223)

Again the principle of bidirectionality must be considered. Perhaps temperamentally "easy" children, who are more obedient, socially outgoing, and independent from the start, are most readily disciplined in authoritative ways, whereas such methods are impractical or ineffective in dealing with temperamentally "difficult" children. Although the value of authoritative child-rearing practices seems well established, it may not be possible to apply such practices successfully to all children.

Siblings

More than 80 percent of American children have one or more sisters or brothers. These siblings may be highly significant agents of socialization. One-year-olds spend as much time in interaction with their siblings as they do with their mothers (and far more than they do with their fathers); 4- to 6-year-olds spend over twice as much time in the company of brothers and sisters as they do with their parents (Bank & Kahn, 1975).

Sibling interactions are reciprocal and are more egalitarian than parent-child relationships. From these interactions children learn patterns of loyalty, helpfulness, and protection as well as conflict, domination, and competition. "Siblings set and maintain standards, provide models to emulate and advice to consider . . . and serve as confidants and sources of social support in times of emotional stress" (Lamb, 1982, p. 6).

Parents usually treat their firstborn child differently than they treat later-born children; their attitudes, expectations, and skills in child rearing—as well as their

Children may learn patterns of loyalty, helpfulness, and protection from sibling interactions.

anxieties—are modified as a result of their experience with the first child. In general, parents are more involved with firstborns, pay more attention to them, and stimulate and talk to them more; they are also likely to be highly demanding, expecting a great deal from their oldest child.

For these reasons, it is hardly surprising that compared with younger siblings, firstborns tend to be more strongly motivated toward achievement; more outgoing; more dependent on others for support; more adult oriented and conforming to authority; more conscientious; more prone to guilt feelings; more cooperative, responsible, and helpful; and less aggressive (Glass, Neulinger, & Brim, 1974; Sampson & Hancock, 1967; Sutton-Smith & Rosenberg, 1970). A disproportionate percentage of eminent scientists and scholars are firstborns, and because they are oriented to authority, they are likely to resist ideas that challenge a prevalent theoretical position; younger siblings are more likely to be receptive to new ideas, even unpopular ones. For example, the majority of the biological scientists who opposed the theory of evolution when it was first presented in the nineteenth century were firstborns. In contrast, over 90 percent of those who favored the new theory, including Charles Darwin and Alfred Wallace, were later-borns (Sulloway, 1972a).

SIBLING RELATIONSHIPS.   When a second child is born, the older sibling's power is inevitably usurped to some extent, and she must now compete, often unsuccessfully, for parental attention, rewards, and satisfaction of dependency needs. When mothers are with two of their children, they tend to pay more attention to the younger one (Bryant & Crockenberg, 1980; Bryant, 1982).

Although rivalry or aggression often seem to predominate in sibling relationships, young siblings at home spend a great deal of time playing together; cooperating in games; showing concern, understanding, and physical affection; and attempting to help and comfort each other (Pepler, Abramovitch, & Corter, 1982; Dunn, 1983; Dunn & Kendrick, 1982). The frequency of positive social responses from younger siblings to older ones increases with age, and younger siblings continue to imitate older ones, especially those of the same sex, more than older ones imitate the younger ones. In general, playful responses—for example, pretending to be a monster, pointing a cane like a gun—rather than new skills are imitated, but imitative sequences demonstrate the siblings' interest in each other, the rapport between them, and the capacity of the older child to serve as a model for the younger one. Typical examples of imitative behavior are climbing on a chair to reach a high shelf in a cupboard, reciting the ABCs, and repeating various words and phrases (Pepler et al., 1982).

In relationships between preschool-age siblings, the older one tends to be dominant, initiates more interactions (both helpful and cooperative and interfering and aggressive), and gives more orders and suggestions (Berndt & Bulleit, 1985). Firstborn males tend to use more techniques based on physical power with their younger siblings, whereas firstborn females are more likely to explain, ask, and take turns with their younger brothers and sisters (Sutton-Smith & Rosenberg, 1970). Younger siblings are not completely submissive, however. As they grow older, they become equal partners in interactions with their older siblings; they initiate more positive actions and also become less compliant and more aggressive (Pepler, et al., 1982; Dunn, 1983). Apparently, interactions with older siblings are intellectually and socially stimulating, for compared with other preschoolers, younger siblings talk more about their fantasies, ask and answer more questions, and engage in more cooperative play (Berndt & Bulleit, 1985). Ambivalent feelings toward siblings are also very common. For example, an older child, although she may feel hostility toward her baby brother, might side with him against their mother.

During middle childhood older siblings, particularly older brothers, are perceived as powerful and "bossy", but this may be welcomed, for older siblings may use their power to help younger ones (Bigner, 1974; Sutton-Smith & Rosenberg, 1968). In the middle childhood years girls are likely to help care for younger siblings, often providing help and advice. As a result, the majority of secondborn children feel strong attachment to their older siblings (Bryant & Crockenberg, 1980).

Siblings' responses to each other are regulated partially by their relationships with their mother. For example, mothers who talk frankly about the new baby's needs and feelings and invite participation in discussions and decisions about the infant's care (e.g., asking questions such as, "What do you think he wants?") stimulate close, friendly relations between the siblings. Mothers who do not discuss the baby in this way produce siblings who are less likely to make positive approaches to each other. Firstborn girls who have particularly intense and playful relationships with their mothers are likely to become hostile toward a new baby, who, in turn, is likely to develop negative attitudes toward the older sibling (Dunn & Kendrick, 1981).

Longitudinal data indicate that siblings' interactions are quite stable over time. Children who were friendly to their new baby sibling were still friendly toward that sibling three or four years later; those who initially withdrew from a newborn sibling were more aggressive toward that sibling at later ages (Dunn & Kendrick, 1982; Stilwell, 1983).

SIBLING INFLUENCES.   Older siblings, especially those of the same sex, can serve as models for sex-typing behavior. Boys with older brothers have more masculine interests than boys with older sisters, and among boys reared without a father, those with an older brother tend to be more masculine, less dependent, and higher in academic aptitude than those with older sisters only (Santrock, 1970; Sutton-Smith, Rosenberg, & Landy, 1968; Wohlford, Santrock, Berger, & Liberman, 1971). Girls with older brothers are more intellectually competent, ambitious, aggressive, and tomboyish than girls with older sisters (Sutton-Smith & Rosenberg, 1970).

As early as preschool, older siblings can serve as effective teachers for younger ones, instructing and guiding them, monitoring their behavior, and modifying their own directives to help the younger child (Stewart, 1983). Older sisters appear to be more acceptable and more skillful as teachers of academic subjects than older brothers, using more directive and deductive methods, offering more explanations, and providing better feedback (Cicirelli, 1972, 1973, 1975).

The quality of early sibling interactions may have lasting consequences for the child's later behavior. Hostile sibling relationships in 3- and 4-year-olds are associated with antisocial behavior five years later (Richman, Graham, & Stevenson, 1982). In contrast, close, affectionate sibling relationships augment the development of desirable characteristics and responses, including role-taking and communication skills, social sensitivity, cooperation, and understanding of social rules and roles (Dunn & Kendrick, 1982).

ONLY CHILDREN.   The only child is frequently described in negative terms, for example, "maladjusted, self-centered and self-willed, attention-seeking and dependent on others, temperamental and anxious, generally unhappy and unlikeable, and yet somewhat more autonomous than a child with siblings" (Thompson, V. D., 1974, pp. 95–96). The validity of such descriptions has been tested in many studies. The findings have been mixed and, in some cases, contradictory. A systematic analysis of over 100 relevant studies led to the conclusion that only children do not generally suffer any developmental disadvantage. In fact, only children surpass those with many siblings in intelligence and achievement motivation, and they resemble firstborns and those from two-child families not only in these respects but also in measures of sociability, character, and adjustment. Compared with children in large families, only children, firstborns, and children in two-child families probably receive more parental attention, which helps the child acquire more sophisticated intellectual skills, such as vocabulary, as well as more mature behavior patterns (Falbo & Polit, 1986).

This general finding does not preclude the possibility that many only children are "spoiled." This possibility is a matter of concern in China, where there is an established tradition of large families together with a powerful national policy of attempting to limit families to a single child (see Box 12.2).

BOX 12.2

Only Children in China

China has the largest population of any nation in the world—it is home to over a billion people. But it is a technologically backward and economically impoverished country, and although all the members of Chinese society are adequately nourished and housed, their standard of living is low compared to that of people in Western nations. The rate of population growth in China is rapid, primarily because in the decades since the establishment of the People's Republic in 1949 infant mortality has declined sharply and average life expectancy has increased enormously (from 35 before 1949 to almost 70 in 1980). The Chinese economy simply cannot support this kind of population growth, let alone modernize China, raise living standards, and increase educational and economic opportunities for all citizens. In 1970 the Chinese government initiated a vigorous program to encourage one-child families, offering strong incentives such as salary bonuses to families who have only one child, together with disincentives (fines) for having larger families. Large billboards in downtown Peking and other Chinese cities pictured a happy one-child family and announced in large letters that "Parents need only one child and we don't need sons!"

Large families have traditionally been highly valued in China, for such families were thought to bring happiness and to assure parents that someone would care for them when they became old. Moreover, males were more highly valued than females, and no family considered itself complete until it had at least one male child. Given this tradition, the one-child policy is indeed revolutionary. And although it has met with opposition in rural areas, the program has had remarkable results in the cities—it is estimated that 98 percent of Chinese children between the ages of 3 and 6 living in cities are only children.

The structure of Chinese families has been radically altered as a result of the one-child policy. Whereas fifty years ago the norm was a large extended family, including grandparents and many children, the typical Chinese urban family today is, in the words of two Chinese developmental psychologists, "structured in a 4:2:1 fashion, i.e., there are four grandparents, two parents, and one child in a family. This single child is the center of affectionate care of six elders: he or she is said to be the 'little sun,' the 'little emperor or empress,' in the family. Adults in the family try to satisfy all the child's demands, including unreasonable ones . . . . Proper discipline is often neglected" (Ching, 1982). All Chinese young women work outside the home, and as a result many children are reared primarily by doting grandparents who "spoil" them.

The implications of onliness are understandably of great concern to the Chinese people, as well as to government and educational authorities, whose highest values are the promotion of discipline, collectivism, cooperation, and consideration. Can these values be perpetuated in a society that consists primarily of only children? "A widely held view about only children is that they are more egocentric, less cooperative, less affiliative, and more maladjusted than sibling children" (Jiao, Ji, & Jing, 1986, p. 357).

The consequences of being an only child in China have not yet been thoroughly investigated, but the results of one systematic study indicate that there is, indeed, reason to be concerned about the future adjustment and orientation of Chinese youngsters. In this study of 1000 children between 4 and 10 years of age, both urban and rural, only children were matched in age, sex, and socioeconomic status with children who had siblings. Sociometric techniques were used to assess such characteristics as independent thinking, persistence, control, tolerance for frustration, cooperation, prestige and leadership, and egocentrism. Only children were rated as more egocentric, whereas children with siblings were better liked and more often leaders and, at the same time, manifested higher levels of persistence and cooperation—all highly valued attributes in China.

Assuming that these findings are reliable and can be replicated in other studies, the Chinese people and government face a monumental problem: How can the one-child policy be maintained if young children are expected to develop the characteristics that are most highly valued in Chinese society?

Family Structure

The traditional family in the United States is the nuclear family, which consists of a mother and father living in one household with their children. However, over the last three or four decades increasing numbers of American children have grown up in family settings that are quite different from the traditional family. At present, one out of every five children in the United States lives in a single-parent family, and 90 percent of these families are headed by a mother who is separated, divorced, widowed, or never married. Each year over a million children experience the divorce or separation of their parents, and it is estimated that by 1990, 60 percent of the children in this country will spend part of their childhood in a single-parent household (U. S. Bureau of the Census, 1986a) (see Figure 12.4).

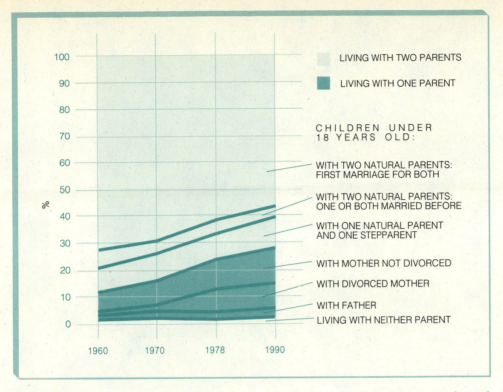

FIGURE 12.4 Living arrangements for children under 18 in the United States. (Adapted from P. C. Glick. Children of divorced parents in demographic perspective. *Journal of Social Issues*, 5 1979, 35[4], 172. By permission.)

CHILDREN WITH SINGLE PARENTS. The consequences of growing up in a mother-only household depend on the child's sex, age, and temperament; also significant are the mother's attitudes; the reason for the absence of the father (e.g., divorce or death), and whether other adults or siblings can fill in for the father in some ways. Single mothers ordinarily experience more stress than mothers in nuclear families. They have more financial problems, a greater work load, stronger feelings of isolation and loneliness, and greater difficulty in rearing their children.

For children in a single-parent family, living with the parent of the same sex seems to be an advantage. Boys make better adjustments in father-custody homes while girls benefit from being in mother-custody homes (Santrock & Warshek, 1979). Boys in father-absent homes tend to be more aggressive, anxious, and lacking in self-control, less interested in "masculine" toys and activities, and more impulsive and antisocial than boys in nuclear families. However, girls in single-parent households do not differ consistently from girls in nuclear families in these respects (Biller, 1971; Guidubaldi, Perry, & Cleminshaw, 1983; Hetherington, Cox, & Cox, 1982; Huston, A. C., 1983; Zill, 1985). The impact of the absence of the father is particularly strong if it begins during the first few years of the child's life. Two-year-old Israeli boys whose fathers had been killed before they were born and who were living with widowed mothers showed more dependency, more anxiety about

The experience of growing up in a single-parent family is influenced by a variety of factors, such as the reason for the other parent's absence and the presence of older siblings.

separation, more aggression, and less autonomy than comparable boys who were living with both parents (Levy-Shiff, 1982).

Both boys' and girls' cognitive abilities, particularly their problem-solving and quantitative skills, appear to be adversely affected by the absence of the father. Children reared in mother-only households perform less well in school and on tests of intelligence and achievement than do children reared in two-parent families, and they are more likely to be inattentive and disruptive in class (Guidubaldi et al., 1983; Hetherington, Camara, & Featherman, 1983). Verbal skills are less influenced by father absence than quantitative skills, and deficits in the quantitative area appear to be partially alleviated by having a substitute or stepfather at home (Chapman, 1977; Shinn, 1978). Perhaps this is because math and number skills tend to be stereotyped as masculine in our society.

DIVORCE.   It seems safe to state that no one in a family escapes entirely from the adverse effects of divorce. This is the conclusion of an extensive longitudinal study in which divorcing parents and their 4-year-old children were followed for six years after the divorce and compared with a matched group of children in intact families who were studied for the same period (Hetherington et al., 1982).

The first year after the divorce proved to be the most stressful one for the parents because they encountered many new and difficult problems in managing their households, finances, and working arrangements. After a divorce the income of mother-only families (the most common kind) often drops appreciably. Families often sell their home when a divorce occurs and move to a new neighborhood; in many cases the move leads to further disruption and problems of adjustment in addition to those directly related to the divorce itself. Under these circumstances, it is not surprising that parents' self-concepts deteriorate and that feelings of anxiety, depression, anger, rejection, and incompetence and inadequacy in establishing meaningful relationships are common at this time.

As might be expected, the stress and insecurity of the divorced parents are reflected in their relationships with the children. Compared with other parents, those who had divorced recently were less affectionate and more restrictive, made fewer demands for mature behavior, communicated less well, were inconsistent in their discipline, and lacked control over their children. Mother-son relationships were particularly poor at this time. In the first two months after the divorce, fathers, eager to maintain contact with their children, typically initiated many interactions. However, this changed rapidly; after the first few months most divorced fathers have little contact with their children.

Two years after the divorce parents coped with their problems more adequately; their self-concepts were better; and there were marked improvements in parent-child relationships. Mothers became more nurturant and consistent in their disciplinary practices, better able to control their children, and more demanding of mature behavior; they communicated better and used more explanation and reasoning in dealing with their children. Divorced fathers also became more demanding of mature behavior, communicated better, and were more consistent in their disciplinary techniques. With time, however, they became less nurturant and affectionate and more detached from their children.

As would be predicted from these parental reactions, the major adverse impact of divorce on children was evident during the first year, and the effects appeared to be more severe and enduring for boys than for girls. After their parents have divorced, boys often show more problems in cognitive, emotional, and social areas; they are more likely than girls to become unruly, aggressive, and impulsive, yet at the same time to be dependent, anxious, and lacking in task orientation.

Preschoolers seem to be most vulnerable to these negative effects, perhaps because their level of cognitive development does not enable them to understand what is happening and may lead them to misinterpret the reason for their parents' separation. In the immediate post-divorce period, many children in this age group manifest such symptoms as nightmares, depressed play, eating disturbances, bedwetting, and guilt over having "caused" the separation (Hetherington, Cox, & Cox, 1979). When observed in interactions with their peers in nursery school, children of divorced families smiled and hugged other children less but cried, whined, and complained more than other children. These trends increased from two months to one year after the divorce. In brief, preschool children of divorced parents seemed more immature and poorly adjusted than children in intact families, even families in which there was a great deal of marital discord.

School-age children may be better able to cope with divorce than preschoolers are because they have a better understanding of their parents' problems and the reasons for the divorce. In addition, they are far more aware of their own feelings and more open about expressing their reactions to stress and sadness. Nevertheless, children in this age group often feel abandoned by their parents and angry at them after they divorce. In many cases, especially among boys, the children's school performance deteriorates and behavior problems increase both at school and at home (Wallerstein & Kelly, 1980).

As the parents' psychological well-being and adjustment improve during the second year after the divorce, so do the children's. In the study described earlier, the adverse consequences had dissipated substantially and, in the case of girls, practically disappeared two years after the divorce. According to the investigators.

> **These findings suggest that in the long run it is not a good idea for parents to remain in a conflicted marriage for the sake of the children if the alternative is a stable one-parent household. In the long run, marital discord may be associated with more adverse outcomes for children than is divorce. However, the short-run picture appears to be quite different. In the transition period of family disequilibrium and reorganization in the first year following a divorce, children's problems may be exacerbated before they begin to decline. (Hetherington et al., 1982, p. 262)**

The detrimental effects of divorce on children may be reduced if household routines are well organized and discipline is authoritive and consistent (Hetherington et al., 1982). Living with a happy, well-adjusted parent with whom she has a warm relationship and good communication enables a child to cope better with her parents' divorce. A boy who lives with his mother after divorce benefits from a good relationship with his father. Boys who maintain such relationships exercise greater self-control and get better school grades, especially in math, and higher scores on achievement tests (Guidubaldi et al., 1983).

The interactions between the divorced parents also play a significant role in children's adaptation. "Low conflict and absence of mutual denigration, high support and agreement on childrearing and discipline, and frequent contact with the other parent if that parent is not extremely deviant or destructive are associated with positive adjustment in children" (Hetherington & Camara, 1984, p. 417). Summarizing the findings of many relevant studies, one authority concluded that "adjustment problems in the areas of cognitive, emotional, and social development are *unlikely* to occur for children *if* there is: minimal depletion of financial resources; low interparent conflict and hostility preceding and following the divorce; high agreement between parents on child-rearing and discipline; approval and love from both parents; authoritative discipline from the custodial parent; cordial and supportive relations between ex-spouses and regular visitation by the noncustodial parent; and an emotional climate that facilitates children's discussing divorce-related concerns" (Kurdek, in press).

Almost all studies of divorce have involved white middle-class parents and children originally living in nuclear family groups (i.e., father, mother, and children). Generalizations from these studies must be made very cautiously. For example, the organization and economic status of black families may be quite different from that of most middle-class white families. A much higher proportion of black than of white families are single-parent families, families in which the parents have divorced, and/or extended families (including grandparents and other relatives), and many more black than white families have incomes below the official poverty line. In addition, black family structure is more likely to fluctuate as a result of frequent changes in family composition and membership, as well as frequent changes in living quarters and arrangements. Any or all of these factors can be expected to influence parents' and children's reactions to divorce when it occurs.

STEPPARENT-STEPCHILD RELATIONSHIPS.   Approximately 75 percent of parents who divorce remarry. This means that 35 percent of the children born in the United States in the early 1980s will spend part of their lives living with a stepparent (Glick, 1984). Because in 90 percent of divorce cases custody of the child is given to the mother, many more children live with stepfathers than with stepmothers.

After a period of adjustment to living with only one parent (often an unsettling experience), many children must cope with another major change: living in a new nuclear family with a stepparent. Young children and adolescents appear to adjust to this situation better than children between the ages of 9 and 13. Problems may be aggravated if both parents bring children to the new marriage (Hetherington et al., 1982).

In fiction, stepparents are often depicted as cruel and evil, and as making life miserable for their stepchildren, but research shows that the opposite is often true: Boys often benefit from having a stepparent, particularly a stepfather. Thus, 6- to 11-year-old boys with stepfathers tended to be more mature, better adjusted, and more socially competent than boys living with single mothers (Santrock & Warshak, 1979). These positive outcomes are probably due to the fact that many young boys are excited about having a new stepfather and rapidly become attached to him (Wallerstein & Kelly, 1980); moreover, stepfathers are often attentive, competent parents. In addition, remarried mothers are generally happier and more secure than those who are single, and because their work loads, financial worries, and loneliness are reduced, they can devote more time and energy to their children. Thus, remarried mothers exercise firmer control over their children than single mothers do, and they are more intellectually stimulating and expressive, particularly with their sons (Santrock, Warshak, Lindbergh, & Meadows, 1982).

Girls with stepfathers fared less well, however; they expressed more anxiety than girls in intact families. There is likely to be more friction between a girl and her remarried mother than between a boy and his remarried mother (Santrock et al., 1982). On the other hand, an accepting and nurturant stepmother may enhance a young girl's adjustment. Stepmother-stepdaughter relationships generally improve over time, and girls develop more positive perceptions of their families, less aggressive behavior, and fewer inhibitions (Furstenberg, Nord, Petersen, & Zill, 1983). Frequent contact with their biological mothers may have some adverse effects for these girls, leading to a poorer self-concept and a less positive relationship with the stepmother (Clingenpeel & Segal, 1986; Furstenberg, Nord, Petersen, & Zill, 1983).

Successful stepparenting—that is, stepparenting that benefits the child—is not simply a function of the stepparent's gender or residence in the home but, rather, of his or her personality characteristics, interest in the child, attitudes, and child-rearing practices, as well as the quality of the new marriage. In addition, remarriage may improve the natural parent's emotional adjustment and self-concept, and these factors, in turn, may lead to better interactions between parent and child, with beneficial effects on the child's personal and social adjustment.

MATERNAL EMPLOYMENT.   The proportion of American mothers with children under 18 who work outside the home has increased enormously in the last two decades; by 1985 over 63 percent were employed, an increase of 20 percent since 1975. Half of all mothers with children under 5 are in the work force. Most of these women work because they need to earn money to support their families, but more than 75 percent say that they would work even if they did not need the money (U. S. Department of Labor, 1986).

In families in which the mother is employed full-time, the father is usually more involved in housework and child rearing than fathers in more traditional families, although domestic responsibilities are seldom divided equally. Nevertheless, children who live in a home where both parents are employed experience a more egalitarian relationship between the parents, more care by people outside the family, and more responsibility for household chores than children in other types of family (Hoffman, L. W. & Nye, 1974).

Although it is often assumed that children suffer if their mother works, there is ample evidence that maternal employment can have positive effects on both mothers and children, especially girls. Employed mothers typically are more satisfied with themselves and their roles than nonemployed mothers are (Gold, D. & Andres, 1978a, 1978b, 1978c), and on the average they give their children as much attention and affection. Often they spend as much or more time doing things with their children, but they enjoy this time more because they are not with the children all day every day (Hoffman, L. W., 1979).

Toddlers with employed mothers are less dependent on adults, more self-sufficient, and more sociable than those whose mothers do not work outside the home (Schacter, 1981). Compared with other nursery school and elementary school children, children of working mothers are more independent, score higher on tests of social and personal adjustment and have less stereotyped ideas about sex roles (Gold, D. & Andres, 1978b, 1978c; Gold, D., Andres, & Glorieux, 1979; Hoffman, L. W., 1979; Huston, A. C., 1983; Lamb, 1982).

The enhancing effects of maternal employment are more clearly discernible among girls than among boys. Mothers who happily combine employment and child rearing serve as successful models for their daughter in the areas of achievement and education. They also tend to orient their daughter toward careers that are not traditionally feminine (Hoffman, L. W., 1979).

Although some studies suggest that boys' academic and cognitive skills may suffer if their mothers are employed, these differences are typically small and inconsistent (Gold, D. & Andres, 1978a, 1978b, 1978c; Hoffman, L. W., 1979). Perhaps working mothers pay more attention to their daughters and less to their sons (Stuckey, McGhee, & Bell, 1982). Also, many working mothers and their husbands have more favorable attitudes toward their daughters, regarding the daughters as self-reliant and the sons as noncompliant and aggressive (Bronfenbrenner, Alvarez, & Henderson, 1984).

Some women are better parents if they are employed outside the home; others are happier and more effective if they are full-time homemakers. Consistency between a woman's beliefs about parenting and her employment situation appears to be more important than employment or nonemployment per se. Nonemployed mothers who believe that babies need to be cared for exclusively by their mother are likely to have securely attached babies; the same is true for working mothers who believe that babies can be satisfactorily cared for by others and who do not need guidance from others about parenting practices (Hock, 1980).

Child Abuse

Raising children is one of the most difficult and demanding responsibilities a person can take on, and it is one for which most people have little preparation or training. Some adults have emotional problems or life stresses that make it difficult for them to be good parents, and as a result some of them subject their children to violence, sexual abuse, or extreme neglect.

Although precise data are virtually impossible to obtain, it is estimated that over a million children are abused each year—maimed, injured, severely beaten, sexually molested, starved, stabbed, whipped, kept in isolation, or subjected to other extreme forms of maltreatment. Child abuse is reported more often in lower-class than in middle-class families, but it occurs in all social classes, races, and ethnic groups. Abusive treatment, like other disciplinary practices, is a function of interactions among the parents' personal and cognitive attributes, the child's behavior and attitudes, and the social context.

Many abusive parents experienced abuse and rejection themselves as youngsters and seem to be perpetuating this pattern, especially when they are under stress and lack social supports (Conger, Burgess, & Barrett, 1979). Only 10 percent of child abusers have serious mental illnesses, but many more manifest personality and behavioral characteristics associated with poor parenting and inability to handle stress adequately (Kempe & Kempe, 1978). Compared with mothers who take excellent care of their children, abusive mothers are less intelligent and more aggressive, defensive, anxious, irritable, and immature. They have relatively low expectations about their relationships with their children, and their attempts at discipline are erratic and unpredictable; they may make equally positive (or negative) responses to desirable and undesirable behavior (Brunnquell, Crichton, & Egeland, in press; Egeland, Breitenbucher, & Rosenberg, 1980; Mash, Johnston, & Kovitz, 1982).

Children who are victims of abuse may inadvertently contribute to their own maltreatment because they are difficult to deal with and place strain on family relations. Irritable, unresponsive, highly demanding infants, as well as physically unattractive, hyperactive, disobedient children, are more likely to be targets of abuse than children who are responsive, attractive, quiet, undemanding, and compliant (Johnson, B. & Moore, 1968; Parke & Collmer, 1975).

Child abuse is frequently part of a pattern of family violence, and it has been hypothesized that anger at a spouse is often displaced onto the relatively defenseless child. Threats, physical punishment, criticism, sarcasm, disapproval, and anger are characteristic of the reactions of abusive and severely neglecting parents;

smiles, praises, and expressions of affection occur much less frequently in abusive families than in nonabusive families (Burgess & Conger, 1978) (see Figure 12.5). In addition, siblings in abusive families are more hostile toward each other than are siblings in nonabusive families (Parke & Slaby, 1983).

Social and economic stress increases parents' potential for abusing children. The incidence of abuse is highest among adolescent, poor, uneducated, and socially isolated parents, particularly those with large families. When unemployment rates in a community rise, the incidence of child abuse also increases in the next few months, suggesting that the stresses of unemployment build up over time (Steinberg, Catalano, & Dooley, 1981). However, some poor neighborhoods are "high risk" for child abuse whereas others that are equally poor are "low risk." Families in the "high risk" neighborhoods tend to regard themselves as under stress, socially isolated, and in need of support; they hardly ever use available community services such as child-care and recreational centers. In contrast, families in "low risk" areas have greater pride in their neighborhood, engage in more neighborly exchanges, and make more use of available community resources (Garbarino & Sherman, 1980).

The consequences of child abuse may become apparent very early. In interactions with their mothers, abused infants show much more avoidant, resistant, and noncompliant behavior than nonabused children do (Egeland & Sroufe, 1981). In day-care centers, toddlers who have been abused tend to be more aggressive toward their peers and more wary and ambivalent toward their caregivers, whom they seem to distrust and sometimes threaten or attack. Abused toddlers who were observed in a day-care center sometimes reacted to others' distress with fear, aggression, or anger, and no abused toddler ever showed concern or an empathic response, although more than half of the nonabused children showed sadness or

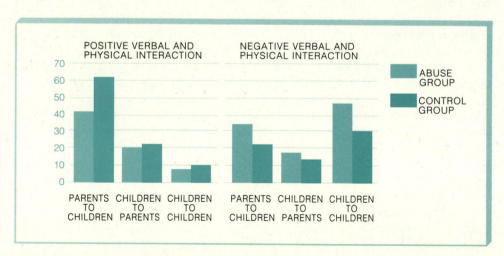

FIGURE 12.5   Rates of positive and negative verbal and physical interactions directed by different family members to one another in families with abused children as compared to control-group families without a history of abuse. (Adapted from R. L. Burgess & R. D. Conger. Family interaction in abusive, neglectful, and normal families. *Child Development*, 1978, 49, 1170. By permission.)

Parent support groups can help alleviate the stress that sometimes leads to child abuse.

empathy under these circumstances (Main & George, 1979). Clearly, many abused children learn to distrust adults and to react aggressively to others, a pattern that they may maintain and use when they become parents. Nevertheless, many abused children develop into well-functioning, empathic, kindly individuals who become excellent parents (Conger et al., 1979).

Several treatment programs have been effective in teaching abusive parents new, less violent methods of discipline through role playing, modeling, and home visits (Zigler, 1980). The incidence of child abuse can be reduced if the community provides adequate resources and support systems for families that are under stress, including employment and educational opportunities for mothers and children, support groups for parents, child-care facilities, homemaker services, public service programs on television, and hotlines (Parke & Slaby, 1983).

A SYSTEMS APPROACH TO FAMILY SOCIALIZATION

Most of the studies we have reviewed center on one significant dyadic (two-person) relationship, usually that between a mother and her child, and they tend to examine unidirectional (one-way) influences such as the consequences of the mother's employment outside the home on the development of the child's personality or the effects of authoritarian parenting on children's social behavior. However, we have stressed the principle of bidirectionality in discussions of how children's personality, temperament, and behavior affect parents' child-rearing practices and the child's relationships with others (see pages 487 and 495).

If you think about your own family and other families you have known, you will recognize that each family constitutes a complex system that is made up of many subsystems (e.g., mother-father, mother-child, brother-sister, mother-father-brother, grandmother-grandchild, etc.) that interact and influence one another. Thus, as noted earlier, the quality of the relationship between the mother and father (the mother-father system) may affect the mother-child and father-child systems: A stable, happy marital relationship is likely to be associated with warm, nurturant parenting, whereas unsatisfactory husband-wife relationships may generate parental tensions and anxieties that are reflected in poor parenting. On the other hand, some parents, most often mothers, may become more involved and supportive in their parenting in order to compensate for unhappy marital situations. Or a young boy who is treated harshly by his parents may avoid social and emotional maladjustment because he finds warmth and nurturance in his relationships with an older sister or an understanding grandparent.

In a systems approach, each family member is seen as an active participant in a number of interacting subsystems. To understand an individual child's development and personality, the whole family system and its subsystems must be considered and investigated. This approach is advocated by family therapists; they work with entire family units; observing many interactions within the family network, in order to help resolve a child's problems and reduce conflicts. Patricia Minuchin, a developmental psychologist who is also a family therapist, has given a lucid, succinct account of the systems point of view and has spelled out the implications of this view for research (Minuchin, 1985). A summary of her ideas is presented in Box 12.3.

Unfortunately, psychologists do not yet have adequate methods for investigating and evaluating, either complex interacting subsystems such as child-parent-sibling subsystems or the family as an integrated unit. When such methods are devised, research in socialization will yield richer and more meaningful findings that can be applied not only in the practice of therapy but also in making wise decisions about public policy.

BOX 12.3

The Family as a System

Family therapists base their work on systems theory, viewing the family as an integrated system and each family member as a contributing participant. "The family system is a complex one composed of interdependent subsystems; each individual is a subsystem as are each parent-child pair, siblings, husband-wife, and grandparents-grandchildren. The interactions of people within and between subsystems are regulated by implicit rules and patterns that are recurrent and stable and that are maintained as well as created by all participants" (Minuchin, 1985, p. 291). From this perspective, a particular dyadic relationship like the mother-child relationship is never independent and can be understood only in the context of the family and its various subsystems.

The family is an "open" system, which means that it undergoes periods of stability and periods of change. Many features of the family system and patterns of interaction among its members that have become well established keep the family functioning in stable, adaptive, and reasonably smooth ways. But sometimes situations change radically—perhaps the family inherits a great deal of money, the father loses his job, the mother becomes critically ill or is seriously injured, a grandparent moves into the home, or an adolescent daughter becomes pregnant. Under such conditions the established patterns are disrupted, precipitating changes in emotional reactions and restructuring of relationships. New and different individual, as well as family, goals may be generated. Alternatives to the established family system must be explored and tried, and the family system, as well as its various subsystems, is likely to become reorganized and considerably changed.

Systems theory and the experiences of family therapists challenge traditional ways of thinking about child development and research in socialization. If children are regarded as interdependent, contributing participants in systems and subsystems that control their behavior, they must be studied in the context of the organization and functioning of their natural families; they cannot be studied meaningfully in isolation from the family and its subsystems.

This argument implies that dyads such as mother-child are not the only salient units for research; rather, a variety of naturally occurring systems—mother-father-child and mother-father-grandparents-child, for example—must be viewed as units and be the targets of systematic developmental studies. This kind of research is needed to determine how *patterns* of relationship are established and changed and how each subsystem relates to the child's personality and social behavior.

In sum, "The experience of family therapists is an invitation to study the complexity of . . . development in context, with particular attention to those aspects therapists seldom see and do not highlight: the conditions and parameters of healthy . . . functioning in the family" (Minuchin, 1985, p. 297).

SUMMARY

Parental child-rearing techniques are a function of many interacting factors. These include cultural and social-class background, the child's developmental level, personal attributes of both parent and child, and the social context in which the parent-child relationship is embedded, especially the relationship between the parents.

Among the parental characteristics that affect parenting styles and disciplinary techniques are maturity and emotional adjustment. Parents' cognitions and beliefs about children's motivations and abilities are also significant in shaping disciplinary practices. Parents are more likely to react punitively to misbehavior if they believe it was intentional and that the child is old enough to control his or her behavior. Parents who believe children are constructive, self-regulating learners have different parenting styles than those who believe children are primarily passive learners.

The techniques that are most commonly used in child rearing are rewards, punishments, and reasoning or induction. Rewards (reinforcers) can be social (e.g., praise) or nonsocial (e.g., special privileges). Attempts to use reinforcement do not always yield the desired result because parents do not always know what their children consider the best rewards. Also, the effectiveness of social reinforcements depends partly on the child's relationship with the adult.

Reinforcement is sometimes given unintentionally, as when children get attention for misbehaving. Under such conditions the parent may attempt to *extinguish* the undesirable behavior by ignoring it.

If reinforcement strategies fail, parents may feel that they must use punishment. For punishment to be applied effectively, however, it must be administered as soon as possible after the undesirable behavior. Punishment is more effective if it comes from a nurturant, affectionate parent, and consistency is essential if it is to inhibit unacceptable actions.

In accordance with the minimum-sufficiency principle, the punishment for a prohibited action should be just severe enough to induce compliance. Prohibitions and punishments are most likely to have their intended effects if they are accompanied by explanations of the reasons underlying them. If punishment is severe or unfair, it can have negative side effects.

Nonpunitive disciplinary strategies, which are referred to as inductive techniques, include reasoning, pointing out the consequences of undesirable actions, or appealing to the child's pride or desire for mastery. Successful application of these techniques depends on good communication between parent and child, as well as on the child's understanding of the reasons for rules and directives.

Children are socialized not only by direct training techniques but also by parental example, that is, through the processes of imitation and identification. *Imitation* is copying someone else's specific responses. *Identification* is a more subtle process in which a person incorporates the characteristics and global behavior patterns of another person. Identification depends on the presence of a strong emotional tie to the person whose behavior is adopted and on the child's perception of himself or herself as similar to the model.

Child-rearing styles vary from one culture to another and from one historical era to another; they also differ from one family to another. Researchers have identified four general patterns of parental control: authoritative, authoritarian, permissive-indulgent, and rejecting-neglecting. The authoritative pattern, which combines high demandingness with high levels of warmth and responsiveness, appears to have the most positive consequences for the child.

Birth order is also important in socialization: Parents usually treat their firstborn child differently than later-born children, with the result that firstborns tend to be more achievement oriented, outgoing, and dependent on others for support. The birth of additional children leads to competition among siblings, but young siblings also play together and attempt to help and comfort each other. Older siblings serve as models for sex-typing behavior and as effective teachers.

Children with single parents grow up in a different environment than children in traditional families. Those who live with the parent of the same sex seem to have an advantage over those who live with the parent of the opposite sex. For children of both sexes, cognitive abilities appear to be adversely affected by the absence of the father.

For children of divorced parents, the first year after the divorce is the most stressful one. The stress and insecurity felt by the parents are reflected in their relationships with the children. Preschool-age children seem to be most vulnerable to the negative effects of divorce. School-age children may be better able to cope with divorce because they have a better understanding of their parents' problems and the reasons for the divorce. The interactions between the divorced parents play a significant role in children's adaptation to divorce.

Maternal employment has been found to have positive effects on children. Toddlers with employed mothers are less dependent and more sociable, and nursery and elementary school children are more independent and score higher on tests of social and personal adjustment. Mothers who happily combine employment and child rearing serve as successful models for their daughters.

Child abuse occurs in all social classes, races, and ethnic groups. It is a function of interactions among the parents' personal and cognitive attributes, the child's behavior and attitudes, and the social context. Many abusive parents experienced abuse and rejection themselves as youngsters and seem to be perpetuating this pattern. Child abuse is frequently part of a pattern of family violence, and increases in situations of social and economic stress.

A family can be viewed as a complex system made up of many subsystems that interact and influence one another. In a systems approach to family socialization, each family member is seen as an active participant in a number of interacting subsystems. To understand an individual child's development and personality, therefore, the whole family system and its subsystems must be considered and investigated.

REVIEW QUESTIONS

1. What factors interact to shape each parent's style or techniques of child rearing?

2. What is a reinforcer? Under what conditions are reinforcements most effective?

3. What general principles govern the effectiveness of punishment?

4. Give some examples of inductive or nonpunitive strategies for modifying children's behavior.

5. Distinguish between imitation and identification.

6. Researchers have identified four general patterns or styles of parental behavior. Name them and describe each briefly.

7. What effects do birth order and the presence or absence of siblings have on a child's development?

8. How do the consequences of growing up in a single-parent family differ from those of growing up in a traditional family?

9. Describe the impacts of divorce and remarriage on preschool and school-age children.

10. Do children suffer if their mother works outside the home?

GLOSSARY

socialization   The process through which children acquire the behavior, skills, motives, values, beliefs, and standards that are characteristic, appropriate, and desirable in their culture.

agents of socialization   The individuals and institutions that participate in the socialization process.

reinforcer   A reward for desired behavior.

extinction   The process of eliminating undesired behavior by not reinforcing it.

inductive techniques   Nonpunitive strategies for modifying children's behavior; also referred to as information internalization techniques.

imitation   Copying specific behaviors of another person.

identification   A process in which a person incorporates the characteristics and global behavior patterns of another person.

SUGGESTED READINGS

Brooks, J. (1987). *The Process of Parenting*. (2nd ed.). Palo Alto: Mayfield. A well-written, practical guide to child-rearing techniques and ways of dealing with everyday problems, based on developmental research and theory.

Damon, W. (1983). *Social and Personality Development*. New York: Norton. A lucid, comprehensive account of the social, familial, and cognitive determinants of a wide range of personal characteristics and social behaviors, including attachment, prosocial behavior, sex typing, aggression, and self-development.

Dunn, J. (1985). *Sisters and Brothers*. Cambridge, MA: Harvard University Press. A broad survey of sibling relationships and their impact on development, illustrated with many realistic examples.

Lamb, M. (1982). *Nontraditional Families: Parenting and Child Development*. Hillsdale, NJ: Erlbaum. A summary of research and theory on a variety of nontraditional family arrangements and their impact on the development of children. Included are discussions of day care, shared-caregiving families, divorce, and father custody families.

Maccoby, E., & Martin, J. (1983). *Socialization in the Context of the Family: Parent-Child Interaction*. In E. M. Hetherington (Ed.), *Handbook of child psychology*: (Vol. 4). *Socialization, Personality, and Social Development*. New York: Wiley. A review and evaluation of experimental and naturalistic studies of the influences of child-rearing techniques on personality and social behavior.

Parke, R. D. (Ed.). (1984). *The Family. Review of Child Development Research*, 7. Chicago: University of Chicago Press. A set of thorough and insightful reviews of the family from biological, psychological, cross-cultural, historical, and sociological perspectives. Included are discussions of the effects of parental work on socialization of the child, the family as an educational institution, relationships between the family and the community, ethnic families, and families in the process of dissolution and reconstitution.

Chapter Thirteen

SOCIALIZATION BEYOND THE FAMILY

Day Care and School as Contexts for Development

Day Care and Preschool

School: The Physical Setting

Academic Organization of Schools

Teachers' Influences on Children

Classroom Organization

Peers as Agents of Socialization

Parents vs. Peers

Social Learning from Peers

Television as a Socializing Influence

Time Spent Watching Television

What Children Watch

Parents' Influence on Children's Viewing

Television vs. No Television

How Children Understand Television

What Is Learned from Television?

Government and Economic Influences

Social Trends and Social Policy

Relations Between the Family and Other Social Systems

Letifa is a 10-year-old girl whose parents immigrated to the United States from Saudi Arabia. She is the youngest of six children. Her mother wears traditional Saudi dresses, keeps her head covered in public, and generally retreats quietly to the kitchen when a stranger enters the house. She rarely speaks to adults whom she does not know, perhaps because her English is not very proficient. Letifa's father wears western clothes but speaks English with a heavy accent. The family are practicing Moslems, and they speak Arabic at home in an attempt to maintain their culture.

Letifa and her older sisters dress in the standard garb of American children and adolescents—blue jeans and sweatshirts. They speak English fluently with no trace of an Arabic accent. The older girls drive cars, go to college, and readily greet visitors to their home. The Americanization that is superficially evident in their dress and manner pervades these girls' values, beliefs, and expectations about human relationships at deeper levels.

Conflicts between family and peer values can arise, however. For example, one Sunday afternoon Letifa wanted to go to a roller skating party with her friends, but her parents wanted her to attend Arabic school. Because Moslems observe a different sabbath than Christians do, their schedule of religious and cultural events is different from the standard pattern in the midwestern community where Letifa lives.

Letifa attends a school where she is the only Saudi student; her friends are all middle-class white Americans. The family owns a Betamax videorecorder, and all the children watch American television. The VCR also permits the family to watch Arabic language tapes that may help them preserve their original culture.

Children like Letifa illustrate the importance of socialization beyond the family. Although the family is central to the socialization of children, children are also influenced by the schools they attend, the peers with whom they associate, and the mass media they encounter. Less direct, but important, are the effects of economic conditions and government policies. In this chapter we discuss the effects of day care, school, peers, media, government policies, and the family's economic circumstances on children's development.

DAY CARE AND SCHOOL AS CONTEXTS FOR DEVELOPMENT

"The school is a social institution reflecting the culture of which it is part, and transmitting to the young an ethos and a world view" (Minuchin & Shapiro, 1983, p. 1). In industrialized societies children begin formal schooling sometime between the ages of 5 and 7. The school is a small social system in which children learn rules of morality, social conventions, attitudes, and modes of relating to others, as well as academic skills.

Day Care and Preschool

For many children, experience in group settings begins well before age 5. For years many middle-class children have attended preschools designed to provide them with social and intellectual stimulation for a few hours a week. Early-education programs like Head Start have been available to some children from low-income families since the 1960s, although in the late 1980s only about 16 percent of eligible children were served by such programs (Children's Defense Fund, 1987). In addition, in recent years mothers of young children have entered the labor market in increasing numbers, and many of their children have been placed in day care arrangements of various kinds.

Although the term *day care* is sometimes viewed as equivalent to baby-sitting, there is no clear delineation between a day-care center and an early-childhood education program. Indeed, good-quality day care centers strive to promote social and intellectual development of children just as other early childhood programs do. Similarly, family day care (group care in the home of the caregiver) exposes

Many children begin learning how to get along in groups well before age 5.

children to regular contacts with other children and can be organized so as to achieve specific educational and developmental goals.

We have already discussed the controversy over infant day care (Chapter 4). Day care for preschool children (age 3 and older) has generated less controversy, although information about its effects is just beginning to accumulate.

Efforts to study day care began with a simple question: Does day care have any effects on children's social, emotional, or cognitive development? This question does not have a simple answer, however. In some studies children who have participated in day care are more socially skilled, cooperative, and task oriented than children who have spent their preschool years at home (Phillips, McCartney, & Scarr, 1987). Moreover, the longer children are in day care, the more time they spend in social participation and constructive play rather than being unoccupied or watching others play (Schindler, Moely, & Frank, 1987).

In some studies children with day care experience are considered less compliant and more aggressive when they reach elementary school (Haskins, 1985). One reason for lower rates of compliance may be that children in day care have learned to distinguish rules based on social convention from those based on moral principles (see Chapter 11). In one investigation, 4-year-olds who had been in day care for 18 months or more rated violations of social convention (e.g., not sitting in the correct place at story time) as less naughty than did children who had recently entered the same day care centers. The two groups considered moral violations (e.g., taking another child's apple) equally naughty (Siegal & Storey, 1985). A second reason for the difference between the two groups may be that children with peer group experience have learned to be more aggressive or assertive with other children in order to protect themselves or their property.

QUALITY OF DAY CARE.   The effects of day care are not uniform; the care provided varies greatly in both form and quality. The quality of day care has been shown to have important effects on the short- and long-term development of children. But how can we define quality? One important component is *adult-child interaction*, particularly verbal interaction. Children in centers with frequent adult-child interaction learn language earlier, gain better communication skills, and acquire more social skills than children in centers with low rates of interaction (McCartney, Scarr, Phillips, & Grajek, 1985). The smaller the group of children and the higher the ratio of adults to children, the more adults talk to children. Caregiver training is also important; caregivers with specialized training in working with young children often provide a richer experience than that provided by untrained caregivers. The *physical setting*, toys and educational materials, and play space are also important (Phillips et al., 1987). The long-term effects of high- versus low-quality day care are discussed in Box 13.1.

The attributes of quality day care are not unique to day care settings. We noted in Chapter 9 that parent-child interaction, appropriate toys and materials, and freedom to explore in a context of organized routines are important aspects of children's home environments. Some of these attributes are also important in schools throughout the age span from preschool through high school. We turn now to an examination of school characteristics that affect children's development.

BOX 13.1

Child Care Quality and Children's Behavior

Many infants and preschool children spend a large part of their time in child care while their parents are working. The quality of the care those children receive ranges from excellent to very poor. Evidence has accumulated that quality of care has long-term effects on children's social and academic development.

What is quality care? Most professionals in the field define quality according to several criteria: a small ratio of children to adults, a small total number of children in a group, ample physical space, materials that are appropriate to the children, and experienced caregivers with training in early child development. In high-quality care, adults frequently express positive emotion and respond positively to children; they provide opportunities for learning and conversation; and they rarely express negative emotion or respond negatively to children.

Howes and Stewart (1987) studied a group of children from 11 to 30 months old who were in family day care, that is, group care in someone's home. They evaluated both the quality of the child care and characteristics of the children's homes. The children's peer interactions were rated for competence, defined by the extent of complementary and interactive interchanges with peers. Play with objects was rated for complexity and originality. Both the quality of child care and the attributes of the home contributed to the children's peer interactions and competent play. Children in high-quality child care played more competently than those in low-quality care. These differences existed even when family characteristics were equated. Families that were nurturant and had strong support systems had children who played more competently than children from families that were restrictive and were experiencing high levels of stress.

Howes (1988) also conducted a longitudinal investigation of children who had entered high- and low-quality care during their infant and preschool years. Children who had experienced low-quality care were less compliant and less likely to show self-regulation as toddlers; they were less competent with peers as preschoolers; and they were more hostile and less task oriented in kindergarten. These effects were more pronounced for children who entered low-quality care before their first birthday, but they were also observed for children who entered child care between ages 1 and 4.

Deborah Lowe Vandell and her associates conducted a follow-up study of children who had been observed at age 4 in high- and low-quality child care. At age 8, children from better-quality day care "had more friendly interactions and fewer unfriendly interactions with peers, were rated as more socially competent and happier, and received fewer 'shy' nominations from peers" (Vandell, Henderson, & Wilson, 1988, p. 1286).

Policy debates about child care have been vigorous since the early 1970s. Two issues are paramount: how to provide enough child care to meet the increasing demand and how to assure quality. Many professionals in the field advocate federal minimum standards regarding adult/child ratios, space, and cleanliness to ensure that the basic ingredients of quality child care are provided. Many states have such standards, but they vary widely and often are not enforced. The mounting evidence that quality of care has long-term effects only emphasizes the importance of providing sufficient funds and establishing effective policies to assure quality care for every child.

School: The Physical Setting

PRESCHOOL ENVIRONMENTS.   Preschools are found in church basements, old houses, unused elementary school classrooms, and many other physical settings. Most states have regulations about minimum amount of space per child and other aspects of the physical environment. Some researchers have tried to determine whether children's behavior changes as a result of environmental variables such as crowding, number of children in a class, and amount and kinds of equipment available.

In a series of studies carried out in Sheffield, England, classroom physical environments were varied experimentally. Children in different play groups were randomly assigned to classes with different environmental characteristics, and their behavior was observed over the course of an entire school year. The researchers tried to separate three factors involved in "crowding" or density of people: (1) group size, (2) amount of space per child, and (3) amount of equipment per child.

The results, which are consistent with those of other studies, showed that children in large groups spent more time doing "table activities," did more chasing and rough-and-tumble play, and spent more time in same-sex interactions than did children in small groups. When groups were small, children engaged in more fantasy and imaginative play. Density, or space per child, did not have many effects on behavior except when spaces were very crowded (15 square feet per child). In such cases there was a decrease in cooperative play and some increase in aggression.

Amount of equipment was more important than amount of space. When classes had several of each type of plaything, children were less aggressive and less likely to cry than they were when there were only one or two of each item. But in settings with scarce equipment children shared equipment and played together more (Smith & Connolly, 1980). Because these studies were experiments with random assignment, the differences can be confidently attributed to the classroom characteristics studied rather than to other differences among the children or their families.

These findings suggest that a preschool classroom that is crowded or inadequately equipped may produce aggression and other kinds of stress for children. On the other hand, small spaces can be carefully organized, and children can learn to share when equipment is limited. In addition, the effects of space and equipment may depend on the child's culture and other experiences. For instance, in Holland, where living quarters are typically small, children displayed positive social interactions and little solitary play in preschools with only 12.5 square feet of space per child (Fagot, 1977).

TOYS AND ACTIVITIES. Toys and activities also affect the nature of play and social interaction among children. Blocks often elicit aggression and, not surprisingly, constructive play. Art and fine motor activities (e.g., playing with Lego blocks) tend to reduce social interaction; children often participate in these activities by themselves. Housekeeping and dramatic play centers stimulate cooperation and role taking (Pellegrini, 1985; Stoneman, Cantrell, & Hoover-Dempsey, 1983).

The fact that children play differently with different types of toys seems fairly obvious, but its implications are often ignored. One of the major tools for influencing children's behavior in a home or preschool context may be the selection of toys and activities. The effects of toys on behavior are often pronounced. In one experiment pairs of preschool boys participated in two play sessions. In one, they were given toys designed to facilitate aggression (e.g., an inflated clown and a "Rock Em Sock Em" game); in the other, they were given toys designed to encourage prosocial cooperation and turn taking (e.g., a nurf basketball that required one boy to hold the basket while the other threw the ball). The rates of behavior in each session are shown in Table 13.1. Children were much more likely to hit each other and to attack the toys when aggressive toys were provided. When they were given toys designed to promote prosocial behavior, they cooperated, took turns, and made up rules to guide their play (Potts, Huston, & Wright, 1986).

ELEMENTARY SCHOOL BUILDINGS. Open-space schools without interior walls enclosing each classroom became the new look in school construction during the 1960s. Part of the rationale for such construction was to permit "open" educational programs, in which children could work individually or in small groups, move from one area to another, and follow flexible schedules. Open architecture by itself, however, appears to have little effect on the behavior of children. The types of educational practices that fill the building are more important than the physical arrangement per se (Gump, 1980; Gump & Ross, 1977).

Academic Organization of Schools

OPEN EDUCATION. "Open education" was introduced as an alternative to "traditional" instruction during the 1960s and 1970s. The programs that are referred to as open education differ widely from one setting to another, but they all subscribe to at least some of the following principles: giving students some choices of

The types of toys available affect the nature of play and social interaction among children.

activity, providing individualized and small-group instruction, encouraging students to guide their own learning, providing rich learning materials, deemphasizing grades and competition, teaching respect for peers, and viewing the teacher as a facilitator rather than a director of learning (Weinstein, 1979).

Children in open and traditional programs show about equal levels of academic achievement, but children in open schools have more positive attitudes toward school and are more independent, creative, intellectually curious, and cooperative (Horwitz, 1979; Minuchin & Shapiro, 1983). However, these differences could reflect the values held by the families that select open education rather than

TABLE 13.1

Frequencies of Social Behavior When Pairs of Preschool Boys Played with Aggressive or Prosocial Toys

| | Type of Toys | |
Social Behavior	Aggressive	Prosocial
Prosocial Behavior		
Helping/sharing	1.15	1.50
Cooperation	0.31	20.45
Turn taking	2.09	3.09
Stating rules	7.34	9.04
Aggressive Behavior		
Interpersonal aggression	4.87	1.89
Fantasy aggression	16.71	0.17
Object aggression	12.84	0.64

Source: From C. R. Potts, A. C. Huston, & J. C. Wright. The effects of television form and violent content on boys' attention and social behavior. *Journal of Experimental Child Psychology*, 1986, 41, p. 11. Copyright 1986 by Academic Press. By permission.

an effect of the program itself. More precise information about program effects can be gained by systematically examining some of the variables associated with open education. These include the amount of structure or direction provided by the teacher and the degree of emphasis on cooperative or group learning as opposed to individual competition.

ADULT STRUCTURING.   Teachers' methods can be classified along a continuum from teacher-directed to learner-directed. High levels of adult structuring or teacher-direction occur when the teacher tells children which activity or task they should carry out, gives them directions about how to do the task, provides written instructions, or offers specific praise or criticism for their performance. Low levels of structure occur when children choose their own activities and tasks and decide how they should be carried out without adult direction. Of course, there are many points on this continuum, and some people argue that intermediate levels of structure provide opportunities that do not occur at either extreme. Variations in structure can also exist within a classroom. Some activities may be closely supervised while others are relatively unsupervised.

Observations and experimental studies in preschool classrooms show that children in highly structured classes or activities attend well during learning tasks, comply with teachers' directions, and turn to the teacher for approval and recognition. They also follow classroom rules and procedures, such as putting away materials after using them, with relatively few reminders from teachers. They spend a lot of time interacting with the teacher and relatively little time in peer interactions.

Low structure, by contrast, encourages positive interactions with peers— helping, cooperation, empathy—as well as aggression, assertiveness, and leadership. Children in less structured classes and activities also spend more time in fantasy and imaginative play (Huston, A. C. & Carpenter, 1985; Huston-Stein, Friedrich-Cofer, & Susman, 1977; Smith, P. K. & Connolly, 1980; Thomas, N. G. & Berk, 1981). One author concludes that low levels of structure encourage children to create their own structure in play activities, while high levels of structure encourage them to adopt or fit into structures offered by others (Carpenter, 1983).

SEX DIFFERENCES.   Structure is not always imposed on children; both in classrooms and at home children can often choose among different activities. From the early preschool years on, girls are more likely to select activities structured by adults, while boys more often select less structured activities. This sex difference was evident in observations of preschool children in a number of classrooms over the course of several months. Although different activities were structured by adults in different classrooms, girls chose structured activities more often than boys did (Carpenter, 1983). This difference was even more striking in observations of 8- to 10-year-olds in a day camp where identical activities were available with and without adult structuring. Girls participated in the adult-structured activities 60 percent of the time, whereas boys did so 35 percent of the time (Huston, A.C. et al., 1986).

Children's responses to structure illustrate an important principle: Although environments influence behavior, children also choose their environments. One group of psychologists refer to this process as "niche building" (Scarr & McCartney, 1983). Figure 13.1 illustrates this process. It shows how individual or personal characteristics influence the choice of an environment, but it also indicates that once children have placed themselves in an environment, the qualities of that setting affect behavior. As children grow older, they have more freedom to select their own environments, and as a result their individual preferences may play an increasingly important role in determining what they learn about interacting with people.

In sum, we do not know why girls more often prefer adult structure and boys frequently avoid it, but we do know that structure influences behavior for both genders. Both highly structured and less structured activities teach children useful skills, so it may be helpful for teachers and parents to encourage both girls and boys to enter both structured and unstructured activities.

Teachers' Influences on Children

Teachers influence children through the processes of reinforcement and modeling described in social-learning theory, but their influence also depends on the child's cognitive construction of the teacher's behavior and the school situation. Teachers reward, punish, and serve as models; they convey expectancies and attributions. However, children interpret their actions within the framework of more general social and moral understandings.

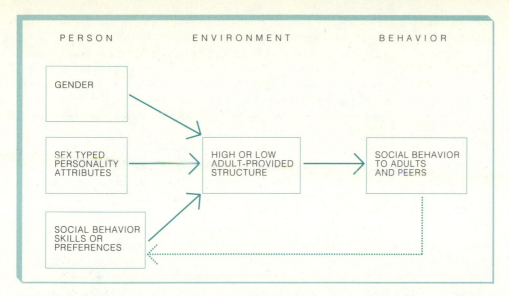

FIGURE 13.1   A theoretical model of the relations among individual "person" attributes, environmental structure, and social behavior in middle childhood. This model illustrates that children choose environments and those environments then influence their behavior. (Adapted from A. C. Huston, C. J. Carpenter, J. B. Atwater, & L. M. Johnson. Gender, adult structuring of activities, and social behavior in middle childhood. *Child Development*, 1986, 57, 1201. By permission.)

Praise is not an effective social reinforcer unless it is contingent on good performance.

PRAISE AND CRITICISM.   Teachers offer praise and criticism for students' academic accomplishments and for their behavior. However, the effectiveness of social reinforcement depends on how it is used. For example, praise for academic performance is most likely to raise a student's expectancies when it is contingent on good performance. If teachers praise children indiscriminately (in an effort to make them feel good, for instance), children discount the praise (Parsons et al., 1982). These and other guidelines for the effective use of praise are presented in Table 13.2.

When teachers do offer praise or criticism, what behaviors do they encourage? One might expect that most teachers would praise good academic performance, but in most classrooms the rates of praise and criticism for academic performance are quite low. Instead, teachers reward quiet, conforming, and obedient behavior, and generally punish disruptive, aggressive, or overly dependent behavior.

Because girls more often conform to adult demands, they are less often punished, scolded, or criticized than boys are. Surprisingly, however, girls do not necessarily receive more praise and positive feedback from teachers. Some teachers take girls' "good" behavior for granted and give relatively little attention to quiet, conforming children; others actively praise and interact with the girls in their classes more than they do with the boys (Huston, A. C., 1983; Maccoby & Jacklin, 1974).

Teachers and other adults are sometimes accused of encouraging sex-stereotyped behavior, but the opposite is often the case. In one set of careful observational studies, activities were classified as "female-preferred" if girls spent more time in them than boys did and as "male-preferred" if boys played in them more than girls did. Female-preferred activities generally include dolls, housekeeping play,

TABLE 13.2

Guidelines for Effective Praise

Effective praise	*Ineffective praise*
1. Is delivered contingently.	1. Is delivered randomly or unsystematically.
2. Specifies the particulars of the accomplishment.	2. Is restricted to global positive reactions.
3. Shows spontaneity, variety, and other signs of credibility; suggests clear attention to the student's accomplishment.	3. Shows a bland uniformity, which suggests a conditioned response made with minimal attention.
4. Rewards attainment of specified performance criteria (which can include effort criteria, however).	4. Rewards mere participation, without consideration of performance processes or outcomes.

5. Provides information to students about their competence or the value of their accomplishments.

5. Provides no information at all or gives students information about their status.

6. Orients students towards better appreciation of their own task-related behavior and thinking about problem solving.

6. Orients students toward comparing themselves with others and thinking about competing.

7. Uses students' own prior accomplishments as the context for describing present accomplishments.

7. Uses the accomplishments of peers as the context for describing students' present accomplishments.

8. Is given in recognition of noteworthy effort or success at difficult (for *this* student) tasks.

8. Is given without regard to the effort expended or the meaning of the accomplishment (for *this* student).

9. Attributes success to effort and ability, implying that similar successes can be expected in the future.

9. Attributes success to ability alone or to external factors such as luck or easy task.

10. Fosters endogenous attributions (students believe that they expend effort on the task because they enjoy the task and/or want to develop task-relevant skills).

10. Fosters exogenous attributions (students believe that they expend effort on the task for external reasons—to please the teacher, win a competition or reward, etc.).

11. Focuses students' attention on their own task-relevant behavior.

11. Focuses students' attention on the teacher as an external authority figure who is manipulating them.

12. Fosters appreciation of and desirable attributions about task-relevant behavior after the process is completed.

12. Intrudes into the ongoing process, distracting attention from task-relevant behavior.

Source: J. Brophy. Teacher praise: A functional analysis. *Review of Educational Research*, 1981, 51, 26. Copyright 1981, American Educational Research Association, Washington, DC. By permission.

arts and crafts, and table activities. Boys more often preferred blocks, rough-and-tumble games, and outdoor activities. Teachers gave more attention and positive reinforcement to both boys and girls who participated in female-preferred activities, not because the activities were "feminine" but because such activities are part of the curriculum of the preschool. Quiet intellectual games, arts and crafts, and activities in which children manipulate and assemble small objects are important educational experiences for young children, and they often require more adult guidance than blocks and large-motor activities such as riding a tricycle or climbing. Therefore, teachers spend more of their time with children in those activities (Fagot, 1978).

Teachers can deliberately modify many aspects of children's behavior in the classroom by giving a child attention when the desired behavior occurs and not attending to the child when the behavior is absent. In "time out," for example, a child who hits other children can be asked to sit quietly for a specified length of time. When that child behaves appropriately, the teacher can praise her or give her attention.

Teachers often counteract children's tendencies to play in gender-segregated groups by structuring play or activities. For instance, a teacher can enforce a rule that everyone is allowed to participate in a particular activity. In one series of studies, teachers were trained to reinforce children for playing in cross-gender activities, that is, activities that are usually preferred by members of the other sex. The children increased their rates of play in cross-gender activities and with peers of the other gender, but returned to their earlier patterns when the teachers discontinued the reinforcements (Serbin, Tonick, & Sternglanz, 1977) (see Figure 13.2).

TEACHERS AS MODELS.   Teachers' actions can be models for students' behavior. For example, in one experiment preschool teachers participated in different classroom activities on a preassigned schedule. Children joined teachers in activities that they had previously ignored, and they imitated the teachers' behavior. For example, when a teacher began building with blocks, children joined the teacher and often imitated the things she was building (Serbin, Connor, & Citron, 1981).

Teachers also serve as models for sex-typed behavior. Most teachers of young children are female, and most college teachers are male. Throughout school, men

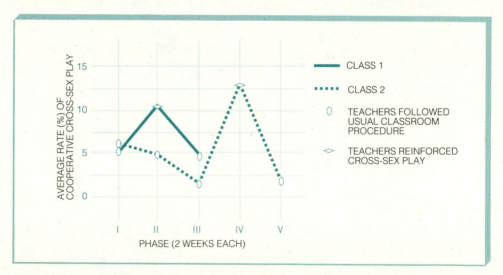

FIGURE 13.2   Frequencies of cross-sex play when teachers reinforced such play and when they did not. (Adapted from L. A. Serbin, I. J. Tonick, & S. H. Sternglanz. Shaping cooperative cross-sex play. *Child Development*, 1977, 48, 927. © The Society for Research in Child Development, Inc. By permission.)

more often teach math and science and are more likely to be administrators. Women more often teach English and social studies. Efforts to recruit more men into preschool teaching and more women into college and university teaching are sometimes based on the notion that women and men treat students differently. In fact, however, they do not. Numerous observational studies show that male and female teachers value and reinforce similar behavior in the classroom (Brophy, 1985). However, it is probably easier for children to use teachers of their own sex as role models. Young boys may view the behavioral demands of school as more compatible with masculinity if they see adult men meeting those demands. For instance, they may think that sitting quietly and reading a book is a masculine activity if some of their teachers are men. Conversely, adolescent females may develop more motivation to pursue math and science if they see women teaching those subjects in high school and college.

TEACHERS' EXPECTANCIES.   In the late 1960s both educators and the public were startled by the publication of *Pygmalion in the Classroom*, which proposed that teachers' beliefs about a child's IQ could affect that child's performance. The authors argued that children would learn more when teachers expected high performance than when they did not (Rosenthal, R. & Jacobson, 1968). Since then a large body of research has accumulated showing that teachers' expectancies *can*, under some circumstances, affect learning independently of the child's abilities (Minuchin & Shapiro, 1983; Rosenthal, R., 1976). For example, a teacher may decide that a child who is a little dirty and poorly dressed probably is not very smart; the teacher may then demand less from the child or ignore him. As a result, that child may show lowered performance and have low expectations of success, low motivation, and low self-esteem.

How are teacher expectancies communicated to children? For one thing, teachers are friendlier, smile more often, and show more positive feelings toward the students they consider bright than toward those they think are less able. Also, when a student for whom a teacher has high expectancy fails to answer a question, the teacher often asks the question again, perhaps giving clues and pressing the student to try again. When a low-expectancy student fails to answer the question, the teacher asks someone else, possibly to avoid embarrassing the student. Through these actions teachers unintentionally teach attributions: The high-expectancy student's failure is due to insufficient effort, but the low-expectancy student's failure is due to lack of ability (Cooper, H. M., 1979).

Classroom Organization

COOPERATIVE LEARNING VS. COMPETITION.   In the traditional American classroom individual learning is stressed. Children are forbidden to look at another person's paper or talk to other children; they take tests individually; and they receive an evaluation (a grade) that tells them not only how well they did but how their performance compares with that of their classmates. The goal is to promote learning by encouraging individual effort and competition.

Encouraging cooperation among students can also promote learning and better interpersonal relationships among pupils (Slavin, 1987). Cooperative learning programs are based on two critical elements: group interaction or discussion and a group reward structure. For example, in one method children are placed on study teams of about five people; the teams are matched on the basis of previous achievement. Group members study together, discuss the material, and quiz one another. Sometimes each child is given different parts of the material that all members of the group must learn. Then each member of the team is tested to see how well they know the information, and the team whose members do best wins an award. Each student is individually accountable for the material, so the weaker students cannot goof off while the better students do all the work. At the same time, each team member benefits from the successes of the others, so there is a strong incentive to work together (Aronson, Blaney, Stephan, Sikes, & Snapp, 1978; Slavin, 1987).

Cooperative learning structures not only improve learning in some instances but also contribute to positive attitudes toward other students and concern for the welfare of others. In one investigation children in cooperative learning classrooms showed improved self-esteem, and they liked their classmates better than those in comparison classrooms (Aronson et al., 1978).

DESEGREGATION AND INTEGRATION. School desegregation was originally ordered by the Supreme Court to provide all children in the nation with an equal opportunity for a good education. However, the effects of desegregation on students' self-perceptions, aspirations, and intergroup relations may be at least as important as its potential effects on academic achievement. Nevertheless, official desegregation does not necessarily lead to social or academic integration. Minority students are often resegregated into different classrooms within a school or different groups within a classroom on the basis of ability and in other ways. Social segregation in lunchrooms and on playgrounds is also common.

In general, friendly relations among members of different ethnic groups are most likely when the school organization promotes cooperation rather than competition and when individual achievement is deemphasized. Children in classes using cooperative learning structures have better intergroup relations than children in comparable classes organized more conventionally (Aronson et al., 1978; Minuchin & Shapiro, 1983; Slavin, 1987). In a survey of northern California classrooms, white children were most friendly to black children in classrooms that deemphasized achievement differences and competition and instead emphasized cooperation and judging one's performance independently of that of others. Black children were generally more friendly toward peers of other races than white children were (Hallinan & Teixeira, 1987).

Meaningful contact among members of different ethnic groups may be more likely in elementary school, where children spend most of their time in a single classroom, than in junior and senior high school, where they move from class to class. In a longitudinal study of children who entered integrated schools in kindergarten, both black and white children had generally positive attitudes toward members of each group. Children were asked how much they would like to play with and work with each of their classmates. The average ratings are shown in Figure 13.3. In the third,

Desegregation alone does not automatically lead to friendly relations among members of different ethnic groups; an atmosphere of cooperation is also necessary.

seventh, and tenth grades, the children's cross-race and own-race ratings were fairly similar. When they were asked who their best friends were, however, their choices were overwhelmingly members of their own race (see Figure 13.3). In the seventh and tenth grades, the students also knew more members of their own group than of the other racial group (Asher, Singleton, & Taylor, 1982).

In sum, school integration alone does not automatically improve self-esteem or intergroup relations, but cooperative, equal-status interactions among children do lead to increased self-esteem and positive intergroup attitudes. Although intergroup relations are often positive in integrated schools, friendships tend to form along ethnic lines. Positive intergroup relations are most likely in classrooms where students are similar in level of achievement and social status. Where the

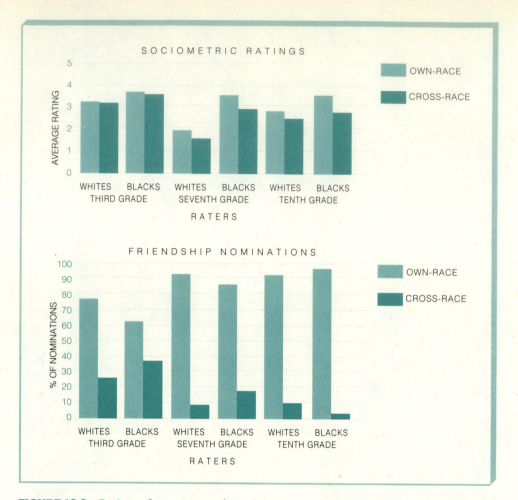

FIGURE 13.3   Ratings of own-race and cross-race peers in integrated classes of black and white children at three grade levels. Sociometric ratings reflect general ratings for how much peers are liked; friendship nominations are for peers selected as good friends. (Adapted from S. R. Asher, L. C. Singleton, & A. R. Taylor. *Acceptance versus friendship: A longitudinal study of racial integration.* Paper presented at the Annual Meeting of the American Educational Research Association, New York, 1982. By permission.)

backgrounds of children are quite different, mutual respect can be fostered by placing them in cooperative structures in which each person has a valued role to play.

MAINSTREAMING.   The integration of children with physical and mental handicaps into regular classrooms is called **mainstreaming.** Proponents of mainstreaming argue that it provides handicapped children with the best possible opportunities for educational advancement and normal social relations with other children. Like school integration, however, mainstreaming does not always achieve these goals. A number of studies have shown that nonhandicapped children in both preschool and elementary school classes interact more with other nonhandicapped peers than with

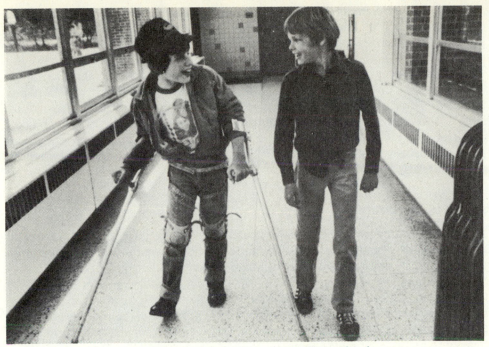

Children with physical disabilities are often "mainstreamed" into regular classrooms.

handicapped children (Ipsa, 1981). Even mildly retarded children were rejected by peers, were anxious and dissatisfied in their peer relationships, and displayed disturbed behavior. Some were shy and withdrawn; others were aggressive and disruptive (Taylor, Asher, & Williams, 1987). The self-esteem of handicapped children does not necessarily improve in mainstreamed classes; in some instances mentally retarded children may feel less confident in classes with normal children than they do in special classes.

PEERS AS AGENTS OF SOCIALIZATION

Schools are important in socialization not only because of the teachers, the buildings, and the organization of learning environments but also because the children who attend school constitute a miniature society. In Chapter 11 we discussed the development of peer relations and friendships. In this section we examine the ways in which peers socialize and influence one another. (It would be wise to reread the first part of Chapter 11 at this point in order to gain a more complete picture of peer relations and influences.)

Peers (agemates) contribute in unique and major ways to the shaping of a child's personality, social behavior, values, and attitudes. Children influence one another by acting as models, reinforcing or punishing behavior, and interpreting behavior. The world of peers is a subculture, influenced in many ways by the larger culture but also having its own history, social organization, and means of transmitting its customs from one generation to the next. Much of the child's understanding of social behavior and how to relate to others is transmitted by peers, not by adults.

The peer group instructs or trains children in critical social skills that cannot be learned in the same way from adults: how to interact with agemates, how to relate to a leader, how to deal with hostility and dominance. In later childhood peers can help one another deal with personal problems and anxieties. Sharing problems, conflicts, and complex feelings may be reassuring. For instance, discovering that peers are also angry at their parents or are worried about masturbation may reduce a child's tension and guilt.

Parents vs. Peers

Which are more influential, parents or peers? This question cannot be answered in any general way. Quite often the values and behavior of parents and peers are similar. Children's peer groups are determined largely by their neighborhoods and schools, and many parents choose to live in areas where the neighbors and schools fit their own values and aspirations. Moreover, parents and peers often influence different aspects of children's behavior. Children may acquire their values about religion and education from their parents, but their choices of music and clothing are heavily influenced by their peers.

The power of peers as socializers varies from one culture to another and from one historical era to the next. Contemporary American culture is highly peer oriented. Children are encouraged to interact with peers very early and are strongly

Peer groups teach children social skills that they are unlikely to learn from adults.

influenced by them. In contrast, in the nineteenth century many children lived on isolated farms where they had infrequent contact with children from other families.

Social Learning from Peers

The social-learning principles of reinforcement, punishment, and modeling are useful in understanding how children influence each other. Positive and negative responses from peers are potent sources of feedback for children from a very early age.

Children may consider peers to be more appropriate models than adults because they perceive other children as similar to themselves. For example, 2-year-old Sara and 3-year-old Ian were playing when Ian told Sara's mother that he had to "wee." Sara followed him to the bathroom, watched him using the toilet, and then announced that she had to wee, too. After that event she achieved toilet control fairly quickly. She might have used an adult model, but another child, especially one slightly older than herself, may have seemed more appropriate to her.

AGGRESSION AND PROSOCIAL BEHAVIOR. Peers are particularly important influences on aggressive and prosocial behavior. As we noted in Chapter 11, aggressive behavior can be instrumental—a means of reaching a goal or getting something the child wants—or hostile, that is, based on anger or intended to hurt someone. Prosocial behaviors, such as helping, sharing, and expressing sympathy, also are often directed at other children, and they seem to have somewhat different meanings for children when they are directed toward peers than when they are directed toward adults. A child helping another child has equal competence, whereas a child helping an adult is almost always in a subordinate position.

Although most children do not approve of aggressive behavior, they often reinforce it through their actions (or inaction), just as parents sometimes accidentally reinforce behavior by giving children their attention (see Chapter 12). Detailed observations of preschool groups indicated that approximately 75 percent of the aggressive actions—attacks, grabbing others' toys, invasion of territory—were reinforced because the other children yielded, withdrew, or gave up something such as a desired toy or a place in line (Patterson, Littman, & Bricker, 1967). When a child yields to aggression, the aggressor is likely to repeat the behavior on a subsequent occasion. Aggression often succeeds as a response to aggression; assertive or prosocial reactions can also be effective, but they may require more self-control and social-cognitive understanding than simply hitting back.

Consider an example. Nathan is riding a Big Wheel around the playground. Chris comes up behind him and pushes him off. Nathan stands up and walks away while Chris rides the Big Wheel. Chris's aggressive action has succeeded; it has been reinforced. The next day Nathan is again riding the Big Wheel. Chris pushes him, but this time Nathan hits Chris and rides away. Now Nathan's aggressive action has been reinforced; he kept the Big Wheel. This example illustrates why aggression is learned in peer groups. It often succeeds in achieving goals, and it is an effective way of countering other children's aggression. Nathan has other alternatives, though. Suppose he tells Chris to leave him alone, pulls his arm out of Chris's grasp, and rides away. This time Chris's aggression was not reinforced, but Nathan achieved his goal in an assertive but nonaggressive way.

Peers are particularly important in socializing aggression because most aggressive actions are aimed at other children. Adults in preschool classrooms do not even see most of the children's aggressive acts; therefore, relatively few aggressive behaviors receive any response, positive or negative, from teachers (Patterson et al., 1967). Adults are even less likely to know about the aggression that occurs among older children because those children are less closely supervised than preschoolers are.

Peers can teach aggression through modeling as well as reinforcement. Laboratory experiments have demonstrated that children imitate child models who make aggressive responses (e.g., hitting bobo dolls, striking toys with a mallet, or throwing things), sometimes more than they imitate adult models (Bandura, 1969). Moreover, vicarious reinforcement—reinforcement of a model—increases the likelihood of imitation. Suppose that Stefanie watches the exchanges between Nathan and Chris. A few days later she is riding a Big Wheel and Chris tries to push her off. She hits him and rides away. She learned that hitting is effective by watching Nathan (vicarious reinforcement), and she imitated Nathan's behavior.

Prosocial responses—friendliness, cooperation, generosity, sharing, helping—can also be augmented by means of peer reinforcement and modeling. In preschool classrooms children who are friendly, helpful, and kind to other children receive more positive responses than children who do not exhibit these traits (see Chapter 11). In laboratory situations children imitate generosity and helpful behavior when they see other children demonstrating such behavior. Repeated exposure to prosocial peer models can produce prosocial dispositions in the same way that repeated exposure to adult prosocial models does.

SEX TYPING.   Preschool children reinforce sex-stereotyped behaviors and punish cross-sex behaviors more stringently than adults do. We noted earlier that preschool teachers often reinforce female-preferred behavior for both boys and girls. Peers, on the other hand, reinforce male-preferred behavior for boys and female-preferred behavior for girls. Boys who play with masculine toys and girls who play with feminine toys are more likely to find friendly playmates and to receive positive reactions from their peers. A boy who engages in doll or dress-up play is likely to be teased, or at least ignored, by both boys and girls (Fagot, 1977; Langlois & Downs, 1980).

Many parents who want their children to avoid rigid sex stereotyping worry that teaching nonstereotyped behavior will subject the child to ostracism and peer rejection. Observations of young children (age 5 or younger) show that children who like both feminine and masculine play activities are likely to receive some criticism from peers, but they also receive frequent positive reactions. That is, androgynous patterns do not lead to consistent rejection. However, children who play *predominantly* with toys and activities that are stereotyped for the other sex are not well accepted.

When children reach middle childhood they can conceptualize sex roles as flexible—they are better able to understand that individuals can have attributes associated with both femininity and masculinity. In addition, older girls' peer groups place considerably less value on "feminine" attributes than preschoolers do. In fact, in the elementary school years many girls consider themselves tomboys

In middle childhood sex roles become much more flexible and children are able to understand that a person can have both "masculine" and "feminine" attributes.

and are well accepted by their peers. Boys with exclusively feminine interests, however, are severely rejected by other children (Huston, A. C., 1983).

Peers can be agents of social change as well as bastions of conservatism. Peer rejection for violating sex stereotypes can be reduced by placing children in group settings that foster non-sex-stereotyped behavior. When schools encourage non-sex-typed behavior children play in a wide variety of activities and in groups made up of both girls and boys.

ARE PEER REACTIONS EFFECTIVE REINFORCERS?   Peers reinforce sex-stereotyped behavior, but are children aware of the norms of their peer group, and do they respond to the demands of their agemates?

Childrens' awareness of peer opinions about sex-typed behavior was illustrated when they were observed in a playroom alone, with a same-sex peer, or with a peer of a different sex. Six toys were available, three of them stereotypically masculine (plastic soldiers, miniature fire trucks, toy airplanes), and three of them feminine (small dolls and doll furniture, a plastic tea set, an ironing board and iron). The children were much less likely to play with "sex-inappropriate" toys when peers were present than when they were playing alone. "In many instances, . . . a child who picked up an inappropriate toy merely looked over at the peer who was busily engaged in drawing and then switched back to an 'appropriate' activity even when the peer gave no overt indication of disapproval" (Serbin et al., 1979, p. 308). If children do play with cross-sex toys, they may be uncomfortable about others knowing it. One little boy played happily with a plastic make-up set when he was alone;

when it was time to return to the classroom, he anxiously asked the adult to be sure that there wasn't "any of that stuff" remaining on his face.

One clever observational study demonstrated that by the age of 2 children's behavior is influenced by peer reinforcement and punishment, but primarily when the peer is of the same gender. Children were observed in groups of 12 to 15. Peers' and adults' positive and negative reactions to each child's behavior were recorded. Then the probability that the child would continue the same behavior or switch to another activity was calculated. Boys were more likely to continue activities when they received positive reactions from other boys than when they received negative reactions. They were especially likely to get teased or punished for "feminine" behavior such as doll play and to leave such play quickly. However, boys' behavior was influenced less by the reactions of girls or adults. Girls continued an activity more often after positive reactions from teachers or other girls, but they were influenced less by boys. (These patterns are illustrated in Figure 13.4.) These observations indicate that very young children are affected by the social consequences provided by same-sex peers (Fagot, 1985).

Children teach sex typing by responding differently to peers of their own gender than to those of the other gender. In one investigation pairs of children who were not yet 3 years old were brought to a playroom. Even though there were few obvious cues regarding gender, boy-girl pairs of children interacted less than same-sex pairs. Such self-imposed segregation of boys and girls begins by age 2 or 3 and increases as children get older, peaking in the 9-12 age range (Maccoby & Jacklin, 1988). It sometimes erupts as active hostility or exclusion, as in a boys' hideout with a hand-lettered sign saying "No girls allowed." This segregation of peer groups encourages sex-stereotyped behavior: All-girl groups are likely to play feminine games; all-boy groups tend to play masculine games.

SOCIAL AND EMOTIONAL RESPONSES.   Children's emotional reactions and social interactions may also change as a consequence of observing peers. For example, children are more likely to laugh and smile in response to humor if they are with others who react in these ways (Brown, Wheeler, & Cash, 1980). We described in Chapter 10 how children's fears can be reduced by watching a peer model who is calm during an experience such as having a cavity filled. Peers can also be trained to help other children overcome shyness and social withdrawal, as can be seen in Box 10.3 (p. 418).

PEERS AS TEACHERS.   As indicated in our earlier discussion of cooperative learning, peers can be effective teachers of school subjects. Children who have been tutored by other children show improvement in reading and quantitative skills, and they perform better on standard tests. The greatest benefits accrue when the tutor is somewhat older than the pupil and when the tutoring is conduced on a long-term, one-to-one basis (East, 1976; Linton, 1973).

Some educators maintain that the tutors gain as much from peer tutoring as the children who are being tutored, if not more. The tutor's own motivation and involvement in the subject matter appears to increase, improving his or her academic

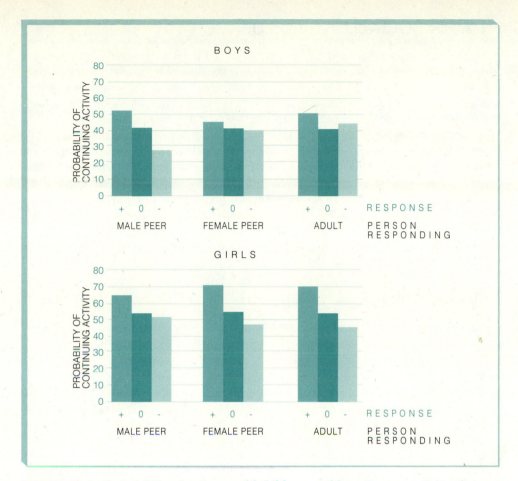

FIGURE 13.4   Probabilities that 2-year-old children would continue an activity after receiving a positive (+), neutral (0), or negative (−) reaction from a peer or a teacher. Responses by male peers had a significant effect on the behavior of boys. Responses by teachers and female peers had a significant effect on the behavior of girls. (Adapted from Table 2 in B. I. Fagot. Beyond the reinforcement principle: Another step toward understanding sex role development. *Developmental Psychology*, 1985, 21, 1097–1104. Copyright 1985 by the American Psychological Association. By permission.)

performance. "Tutor benefits are also thought to include increases in self-esteem, prosocial behavior, and (positive) attitudes toward school (both toward teachers and subject matter) since the tutor carries social status, attention from adults, and deference from other children" (Hartup, 1983, p. 158).

Peers can also serve as models for effective studying. Children who had observed a peer learning fractions through a gradual process in which different strategies were tried showed improved skill and a greater feeling of self-efficacy when they approached the task themselves. The peer who learned gradually was a more effective model than one who had already mastered the task (Schunk, Hanson, & Cox, 1987).

TELEVISION AS A SOCIALIZING INFLUENCE

From the beginning of most children's lives, television is an important socializing influence. Television is an "early window" on the outside world, conveying information and values from the broader society in which children live long before they are exposed to formal schooling or to peers (Liebert & Sprafkin, 1988).

American children spend more time watching television than engaging in any other single activity except sleeping. Even when children view television merely for amusement, they learn from it. For the child, all television is educational television.

Children begin watching television in infancy. Many parents report that they place their babies in front of the television set, propped in an infant seat, because television quiets or interests the baby. Six-month-olds show signs of distress when the audio or video transmission is distorted, suggesting that they notice changes in the kind of stimulation emanating from the "magic box" (Hollenbeck & Slaby, 1979).

Time Spent Watching Television

Popular media often report that children watch an average of 25 to 35 hours of television a week, but most systematic investigations lead to estimates of 12 to 20 hours a week—2 or 3 hours a day. Individual differences are large. Some children watch 6 or more hours a day; others watch very little. Viewing increases with age until the child enters school; then it drops slightly. It rises again until age 10 to 13; then it declines, probably because adolescents are more mobile and spend more time away from home. Children in families of lower socioeconomic-status watch more than children in middle-class families do; within social classes, black children watch more than white children do.

For research purposes, "viewing television" is sometimes defined as being in the same room with an operating television set. Because sets are usually in central living spaces, children may often be present but uninvolved in what others are watching. A group of investigators at the University of Massachusetts videotaped more than 100 families during all of their viewing for ten days. They calculated the percentage of time that each person in the room looked at the set. They found that attention rose rapidly during the preschool years, reaching a peak in middle childhood (Anderson, D. R. & Field, 1983) (see Figure 13.5). Clearly, young children become attuned to the television set well before they reach school age.

What Children Watch

Television is sometimes discussed as though all TV programs were alike. They are not. Two distinctions are particularly important: (1) the intended audience—whether the program is designed for children or for adults—and (2) informative content—whether the program is designed to educate and inform about the world or merely to entertain.

In a longitudinal study conducted at the University of Kansas, parents of children between the ages of 3 and 7 kept diaries of the family's viewing for one week

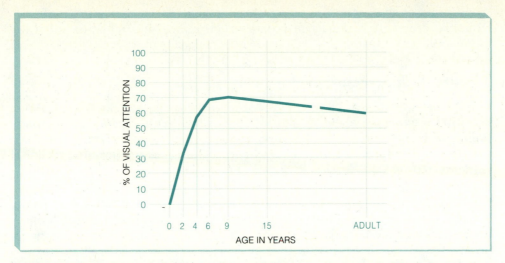

FIGURE 13.5   Percent of time that children of different ages looked at the television set when it was turned on in their home environment. (Adapted from D. R. Anderson & D. E. Field. Children's attention to television: Implications for production. In M. Meyer [Ed.], *Children and the formal features of television*. Munchen: K. G. Saur, 1983, By permission.)

every six months for two years. The amount of time the children spent viewing different types of programs is shown in Figure 13.6. Two points are especially noteworthy. Young children spend a large amount of time watching programs that are not designed for children and that they probably do not understand fully. Second, viewing of informative children's programming drops with age while viewing of car-

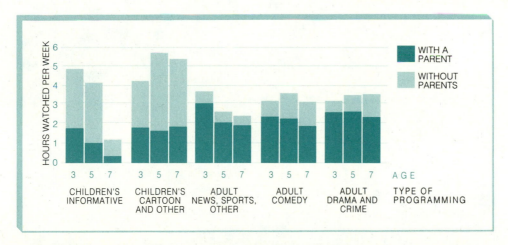

FIGURE 13.6   Number of hours per week that children from ages 3 to 7 watched different categories of television programs with and without their parents. (Adapted from A. C. Huston, J. C. Wright, M. L. Rice, D. Kerkman, & M. St. Peters [1987, April]. *The development of television viewing patterns in early childhood: A longitudinal investigation*. (Paper presented at the meeting of the Society for Research in Child Development, Baltimore.)

toons increases, at least until age 5. One reason that older children watch fewer informative programs is that such programs are scarce once children outgrow "Sesame Street" (Huston, A. C., Wright, Rice., Kerkman, & St. Peters, 1987).

Parents' Influence on Children's Viewing

It is often suggested that poor viewing habits arise from lack of parental supervision. Critics envision "latchkey" children as glued to the television set when no adult is at home. Contrary to this view, research suggests that children develop their viewing habits as a result of being with their parents. In the University of Kansas study, a parent was present during most (67%) of the adult programs watched by 3- to 7-year-olds (see Figure 13.6). Preschool children who stay at home with their mothers watch more television than those whose mothers are employed (Pinon, Huston, & Wright, 1989). Once children reach school age, they watch similar amounts of television whether their mothers are employed or not (Massaris & Hornik, 1984). Thus, it may be true that unsupervised children watch a lot of television, but supervised children do, too. Most parents impose few if any restrictions on their children's viewing.

When parents and children watch television together, the parents can make the experience more profitable for the children, though they do not always take advantage of this opportunity. For example, children learn more from educational television when an adult watches with them than they do by themselves (Salomon, 1977). With very young children, programs like "Sesame Street" can be treated as

Although children often watch television alone, their viewing habits develop as a result of being with their parents.

"talking picture books" that parents and children discuss (Lemish & Rice, 1986). Parents of older children can use television as an occasion to discuss values, morality, and factual information with their children. Increases in the availability of multiple channels on cable and the spread of videotape players give parents a greater range of choices in selecting programs to suit their children's needs and level of understanding.

Television vs. No Television

Some critics and theorists suggest that television as a medium, regardless of its content, can affect thought, social activity, and other aspects of life (e.g., Postman, 1977; Winn, 1987). They argue that television replaces family interaction, play, and other activities; that it has negative effects on health and physical fitness and on school achievement; and that it induces passive approaches to learning.

These claims are difficult to evaluate with carefully collected evidence because virtually everyone is exposed to television. The small groups of nonviewers cannot be studied for comparison to viewers because they probably differ from television users in many characteristics other than exposure to television. In British Columbia and Australia, however, two different groups of investigators were able to conduct "natural experiments." Each group located a town that did *not* have television reception as well as towns that were similar in other respects and *did* receive television (Murray & Kippax, 1978; Williams, 1986). In the remainder of this section we discuss their results, along with correlational studies, in relation to the criticisms just noted.

DISPLACEMENT OF OTHER ACTIVITIES   Television affects the structure of leisure time, displacing some activities much more than others. When television is introduced, children reduce their use of radio, records, movies, and similar media, but the effect on the time they spend reading is small. Television does lead to reduced participation in some community activities, particularly sports, clubs, dances, and parties (Williams, T. M., 1986). For adults, there is a corresponding increase in time spent on home hobbies like needlepoint and carpentry, which may be combined with television viewing (Murray & Kippax, 1978). Television does not reduce the time families spend together, but it may reduce their level of interaction (Dorr, 1986).

HEALTH AND PHYSICAL FITNESS.   The British Columbia study showed that television viewing leads to reduced participation in sports, which might well affect physical fitness. Large-scale studies in the United States also show a correlation between amount of time spent watching television and obesity. Longitudinal analyses show that childhood viewing predicts adolescent obesity, even when childhood obesity is taken into account (Dietz & Gortmaker, 1985). Children who spend a lot of time watching television are inactive and snack often; both may contribute to obesity.

SCHOOL ACHIEVEMENT AND COGNITIVE PROCESSES.   Large-scale correlational studies consistently show a small relationship between heavy television viewing and low levels of achievement in school. In a review of 23 studies including thousands of children, the pattern shown in Figure 13.7 emerged. For children who watched more than about 10 hours a week, more television viewing was generally associated with lower achievement. However, achievement actually improved with increased television viewing up to about 10 hours a week (Williams, P. A., Haertel, Walberg, & Haertel, 1982).

Several researchers have tried to determine whether the relationship between television viewing and low achievement may be due to the fact that both are associated with other factors, such as social class and intelligence. Although children from lower-class homes watch more television and perform less well in school than those from middle-class homes, the association between viewing and achievement holds true even within social classes. However, when children are of equivalent intelligence there is little association between the total amount of television viewed and most types of school achievement or cognitive functioning (Anderson, D. R. & Collins, 1988).

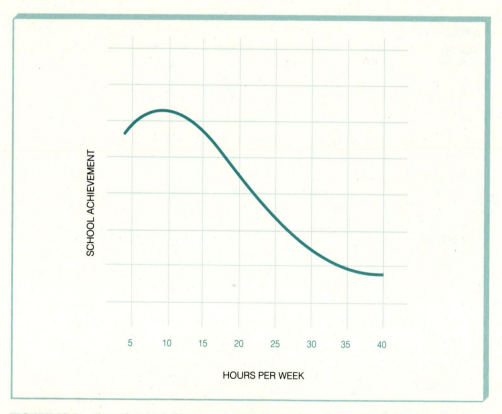

FIGURE 13.7   The relationship between average amount of television viewing and school achievement, based on a summary of 23 large-scale studies. (Adapted from P. A. Williams, E. H. Haertel, H. J. Walberg, & G. D. Haertel. The impact of leisure-time television on school learning: A research synthesis. *American Educational Research Journal*, 1982, 19, 19–50. By permission.)

Reading is the one subject that may be negatively influenced by television, but the effects are small. In the British Columbia study, for example, young children in the town without television reception performed better on reading tests than comparable children in the towns that received television. Two years later, after television was introduced in the "no TV" town, children in the early elementary school grades had poorer reading skills (Williams, T. A., 1986). Among children in the United States who have grown up with television, heavy viewing of entertainment television is slightly associated with poor reading skills. However, reading skill is much more directly affected by practice and by attitudes toward print. Children who watch television and also become familiar with books are likely to become good readers (Morgan & Gross, 1982; Ritchie, Price, & Roberts, 1987).

Different types of television programs have different effects on achievement and cognitive functioning. We have already pointed out that children learn vocabulary, letters, and number skills from programs like "Sesame Street" and "The Electric Company" (see Chapter 9). Documentaries and instructional television can be used effectively to teach a wide range of information (Liebert & Sprafkin, 1988).

Television can also teach cognitive skills through example. A camera can demonstrate visual analysis (i.e., finding parts of a complex stimulus) by zooming in on sections of the stimulus and zooming out to show the whole thing. In one series of studies children who watched several demonstrations of such zooms performed better than a control group on a test of visual analysis (Salomon, 1979).

DOES TELEVISION MAKE CHILDREN INTELLECTUALLY PASSIVE?   Because children usually watch television for entertainment rather than for educational reasons, they often treat it as an occasion to relax and put forth minimal mental effort (Salomon, 1983). On the other hand, children are not passive receivers of stimuli from the TV tube. From a very early age they make choices about what, when, and how attentively to watch. Their attention is attracted by vivid, rapidly moving productions that contain many audiovisual gimmicks and special effects, but such production features alone are not enough to maintain their interest (Huston, A. C. & Wright, 1983). They attend to content that they can understand (Anderson, D. R. & Lorch, 1983) and to content that is funny or interesting (Zillmann, Williams, Bryant, Boynton, & Wolf, 1980). They think actively about what they are viewing, perhaps more than adults do.

How Children Understand Television

ATTENTION TO TV.   Certain features of television programs hold children's attention. These include humor, character movement, sound effects and auditory changes, children's and women's voices, and animation. Children tend to lose interest when programs contain men's voices, complex speech, live-animal photography, and long zooms (Anderson, D. R. et al., 1981; Huston, A. C. & Wright, 1983). For the most part, violence and aggression do not increase attention to a program that has other attractive features (Potts et al., 1986). Violence is not necessary to hold children's interest; they like nonviolent programs with humor, animation, and other attention-getting features.

COGNITIVE DEVELOPMENT.   The extent to which children understand what they see on television depends partly on their level of cognitive understanding. Although children watch many programs that are specifically designed for children, most of what they view is intended for adult audiences. The plots, characters, and situations they encounter in adult programs are often unfamiliar to them. Until age 9 or 10 they have difficulty understanding adult programs because they lack some of the relevant cognitive skills. As a result, they may obtain different messages from those programs than most adults do.

Young children sometimes have difficulty discriminating central, important content from content that is tangential to the main point. An incidental sight gag (Fat Albert falling flat on his face, for instance) may seem at least as important as the central theme (he and his gang are trying to help a girl who is unhappy about her parents' divorce).

Children may also fail to integrate different elements of a story that occur at different times. For example, a child may not connect the scene of a masked man holding up a bank with a scene occurring half an hour later in which a man is arrested and taken to jail.

Children also have difficulty making inferences about events that are not explicitly shown and about the feelings and intentions of characters. For instance, when the camera cuts from a scene with soldiers attacking a village to a view of the village in ruins, children may not infer the intervening events (Collins, 1982).

What Is Learned from Television?

It is sometimes said that television serves three major functions for children: teaching intellectual skills and information, providing social learning, and selling products. In Chapter 9 we discussed intentional efforts to educate through television. Most of children's social learning from television is not intended, however; it occurs as children watch programs designed primarily for entertainment.

SOCIAL KNOWLEDGE.   Children acquire some of their knowledge about social relationships and behavior from television. They learn "scripts" for many real-life situations (see Chapter 8), such as what people are expected to do on dates, on a military base, at a royal wedding, and in many other settings with which they have little direct contact. In fact, many adolescents, particularly those from poor and minority families, say that they use television deliberately to find out how to act in social situations. The glamorous, adventurous life of many people shown on television looks attractive, and many young people consider it a better guide than the humdrum everyday existence of their parents (Comstock & Cobbey, 1978).

STEREOTYPES.   Children also learn social stereotypes of women, men, minorities, elderly people, and many other groups, including children themselves, from television. The typical lead character on commercial television is a white, middle-class, young or middle-aged man, as are most news and sports broadcasters and most adults on children's programs. Children and elderly people are seldom shown, and many minority groups are virtually absent from the screen. When such groups are shown, they are often portrayed as having unfavorable attributes and little power. These stereotypes are exaggerated on children's programs, where many villains have dark skin and foreign accents and the male characters take the lead in coping with situations while females remain passive or helpless. Moreover, when there are historical changes in American society, television images typically lag far behind. For instance, as women entered the labor force during the years from 1950 to 1980 the percentage of employed women in television fiction increased, but it remained considerably lower than the percentage of employed women in the United States population (Calvert & Huston, 1987).

Children learn from these portrayals, particularly when they have little contact with the group being portrayed. For example, white children who knew few black people derived many of their ideas about blacks from television (Berry & Mitchell-Kernan, 1982; Greenberg, 1972; 1986; U.S. Commission on Civil Rights, 1977). Perhaps more important, portrayals that run counter to prevalent stereotypes can make a significant change in children's views about a group of people. One television series, called "Freestyle", was specifically designed to counteract gender and ethnic stereotypes that might influence children's career interests. It is described in Box 13.2.

BOX 13.2

Changing Sex Stereotypes with Television

Television can be used to change children's sex stereotypes. In 1977 the U.S. Office of Education funded the production of a television series called "Freestyle" aimed at children between the ages of 9 and 12. The major purpose was to reduce children's stereotypes about the careers that are appropriate for men and women and for people of different ethnic groups.

Planning and production were done by a team that included television production personnel, writers, career education experts, child psychologists, and media evaluation specialists. Thirteen half-hour programs were made to be shown on public television and in school classrooms. Most of the programs were dramatic stories about children. For instance, "Grease Monkey" was about a girl who loved working on cars. Her experiences getting and keeping a job in a service station made a good story. Another story was about two boys who became volunteers in a nursing home for the elderly and learned that they could not just go in and impose their ideas on the residents.

A few programs were magazines composed of vignettes. In one, a Chicano man and his son are in the kitchen when the mother calls to say she has gotten a promotion and has to work late. Father and son decide to prepare an omelette. "The first thing you do," the father says, "is close the shade so the neighbors can't see what is going on in here."

Then the father surprises his son with his cooking skill. They enjoy the process, and the vignette ends with the father throwing up the shade and waving the frying pan in front of the window to let all the neighbors know what he has done.

Children's responses to the programs were evaluated in classrooms where additional materials for reading and discussion were supplied and in classrooms without the additional materials. The children generally liked the series, and many of them chose to watch it at home. The program was successful in reducing children's stereotypes about what girls and boys (or women and men) should do. They became more accepting of nontraditional activities, occupations, and family roles. However, when they were asked what they planned to do themselves, there was less change. Girls said that they intended to do more mechanical and athletic activities, but boys' intentions were not influenced by the program. The most pronounced changes occurred when supplemental materials and discussion were used in the classroom (Johnston, J. & Ettema, 1982).

Portrayals of women on commercial television changed during the 1980s. Women were more often shown in "masculine" careers such as police officer, lawyer, or newspaper reporter. The attitudes of children who were interviewed in 1987 reflected this change. Girls expressed positive attitudes and aspirations to enter careers in which women are shown on television (e.g., lawyer, police officer). For example, one intellectually gifted girl from a black family said she wanted to be like Claire Huxtable of the *Cosby Show* because she wanted to be a lawyer. Girls did not, however, aspire to traditionally male jobs that they see in everyday life (e.g., dentist, insurance agent) (Wroblewski & Huston, 1987). In sum, television can influence children's beliefs and attitudes about appropriate behavior for women and men; expanded portrayals of family roles and careers can extend the range of options that children will consider.

VIOLENCE.   Violent scenes abound on American television, and violent crime is widespread in American society. The rates of both homicide and television violence are considerably higher in the United States than in many other countries (see Figure 13.8). The effects of television violence on viewers have been studied more extensively than any other aspect of television. The evidence accumulated from a wide variety of sources indicates that television violence *can* cause aggressive behavior (Liebert & Sprafkin, 1988).

Laboratory experiments, field experiments, and longitudinal correlational studies have been used to study television violence (see Chapter 1). One group of investigators conducted parallel longitudinal studies in five countries: Poland, Israel, Australia, Finland, and the United States. Children's aggressive behavior in

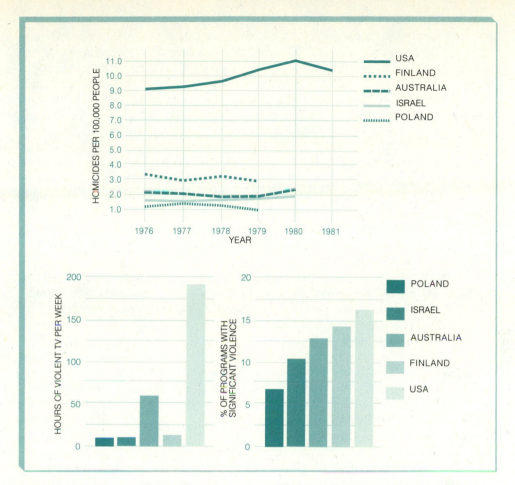

FIGURE 13.8 Rates of homicide and amounts of violent television broadcast in five countries. [Adapted from L. R. Huesmann & L. D. Eron (Eds.). *Television and the aggressive child*: A *cross-national comparison.* Hillsdale, N.J.: Erlbaum, 1986. By permission.]

school and the amount of television violence they watched were measured on three occasions over a two-year span. The findings varied slightly from one nation to another, but in general the children who watched a lot of television violence became more aggressive over time than those who did not. It was also true that those who were initially aggressive developed an increasing taste for TV violence, indicating a self-perpetuating circle (Huesmann & Eron, 1986).

Although many people may not be inspired to physical violence by television, their attitudes and reactions to other people's violent actions may be influenced. People who watch a lot of violence on television are more likely to approve of aggressive behavior. They also become desensitized—they are less likely to respond to real-world violence with horror or to make an effort to help a victim (Liebert & Sprafkin, 1988).

PROSOCIAL BEHAVIOR.   Prosocial interactions such as altruism and sympathy are also shown often on television. Children can learn prosocial approaches to problem solving (e.g., negotiation) when they see them on television. Programs, such as "Mr. Rogers' Neighborhood", that are deliberately designed to teach positive social behavior—cooperation, helping, understanding others—influence children's behavior in their everyday interactions (Stein & Friedrich, 1975). In fact, in a review of a large number of studies Hearold concluded that prosocial portrayals have a greater effect on behavior than antisocial portrayals do (1986).

ADVERTISING.   Commercials for foods, toys, and other products are an integral part of American children's television-viewing experiences. Young children are particularly susceptible to persuasion by advertising because they lack the cognitive skills to understand its purposes. Until about age 5, children have considerable difficulty telling programs and ads apart. Even at age 6, they use concrete perceptual cues. For example, they often say that you can tell a commercial from a program because it is short.

Children's ability to understand the purposes of advertising have been studied using Piaget's theory. Researchers proposed that concrete-operational thought and advanced perspective-taking skills would enable children to comprehend that advertisements are made by someone who has a purpose (i.e., to sell), who may not be truthful, and who intends the message for a particular audience. Their findings demonstrated that children gradually develop these concepts between the ages of 6 and 11 (Liebert & Sprafkin, 1988).

Young children often take an ad at face value; they are persuaded to want the latest doll or action figure. One 4-year-old boy persuaded his mother to buy him a brand of shoes that he had seen advertised on TV. When they got home he put then on, tried a running jump across the living room, and burst into tears. The explanation for his disappointment was that when the boys on TV wore those shoes, they were able to jump a six-foot fence—and in slow motion, too. By the age of 10 or 11 most children are skeptical of advertising messages, but they are still vulnerable to subtle forms of deception (Wartella & Hunter, 1983).

GOVERNMENT AND ECONOMIC INFLUENCES

So far our discussion of socializing influences on children has dealt primarily with the *direct* effects of children's interactions with people (family and peers) and institutions (schools and media). But children live within a culture and a society, and these also affect children's development; often the effects are *indirect*. For example, the nature of parents' jobs affects the amount of time they can spend with their children, their levels of psychological stress, and the city and neighborhood in which they choose to live. These factors in turn influence parent-child interactions and the types of peers and schools to which the child is exposed, to give just a few examples.

At the end of the last chapter we discussed *systems* within the family. We now consider the family in relation to larger systems in the society. Urie Bronfenbrenner articulated the importance of these systems in his ecological theory of human development. He conceptualized development as the "progressive, mutual accommodation between an active, growing human being and the changing properties of the immediate settings in which the developing person lives, as this process is affected by relations between these settings, and by the larger contexts in which the settings are embedded" (Bronfenbrenner, 1979, p. 21).

The "larger contexts" referred to by Bronfenbrenner are created by social policies and programs and by the economic policies of the workplace. Government policies affect family income (e.g., tax exemptions for dependents or tax credits for child care); the types of services available to families (e.g., free immunizations, Head Start), and many aspects of family life. Economic policies affect parental employment, wage rates, working hours, health benefits, and the like. In this section we consider a few of the many ways in which economic events and government policies influence families and children.

Social Trends and Social Policy

Three social trends gained attention in the 1980s: an increase in the number of children living in poverty, the large-scale migration of mothers into the paid labor force, and an increase in the number of single-parent families headed by mothers. These trends have produced major changes in the functioning of many families; they highlight the role of support systems for families.

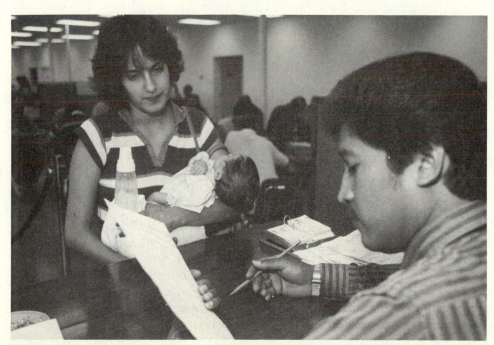

Government programs like Aid to Families with Dependent Children affect the contexts in which children grow up.

POVERTY AND CHILDREN.   By the late 1980s approximately 25 percent of all children under age 6 in the United States lived in families with incomes below the poverty line. The median incomes for different types of families from 1970 to 1986 are shown in Figure 13.9. Although income declined in the early 1980s for most types of families, the most drastic and lasting drop occurred for single mothers with children and young two-parent families: "While families as a whole were markedly better off in 1986 than they had been 16 years earlier, some types of families, particularly low-income, single mothers with children and families with heads under age 25, became worse off during the period. These income patterns resulted in greater inequality of incomes among families in 1986 than in 1970" (Congressional Budget Office, 1988).

Three interrelated factors account for the increasing number of children living in poverty. The first is the nature of the economy, including both the types and the number of jobs available. The recession of the early 1980s led to unemployment or partial job loss for many parents. Many of the new jobs created during the decade paid low wages and had few if any benefits like health insurance. Young workers in particular often could not earn enough to rise out of poverty or support a family (Children's Defense Fund, 1987).

The second factor is a decline in government-sponsored income support for poor families. Major support programs, such as Aid to Families with Dependent Children (AFDC) and child care funding, were reduced at the same time that the need for them increased. In 1973, 84 percent of the children living in poverty received AFDC. In 1985, slightly over 57 percent of poor children received benefits, and the amounts received were worth about 30% less than they were in 1970 (Stipek & McCroskey, 1989).

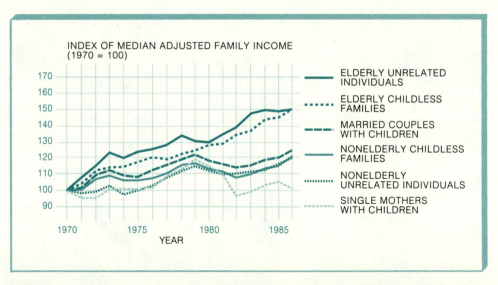

FIGURE 13.9   Median family income (adjusted for inflation) for different types of families from 1970 to 1986. (Adapted from Congressional Budget Office. *Trends in family income:* 1970–1986. Washington, D.C.: U.S. Government Printing Office, 1988.)

The third factor is increases in the divorce rate and in the number of single-parent families, most of which are headed by women. Such families are especially vulnerable to poverty because in the majority of cases there is only one wage earner. That wage earner is usually a woman, and women's average wages are about two-thirds of the average earned by men.

EFFECTS OF INCOME LOSS ON FAMILIES.   Many families are not chronically poor, but they may experience periods of poverty or major fluctuations in income. A University of Michigan study found, for instance, that over a span of ten years 25 percent of an adult sample had incomes below the poverty line for at least one year, but fewer than 3 percent were chronically poor (i.e., poor for eight years or more). The major cause of income loss for men was losing a job; the major cause for women was dissolution of a marriage through divorce or death (Duncan, 1984).

When a parent loses a job, severe stresses occur within the family. We noted earlier the association between unemployment and child abuse (Chapter 12). The effects of income loss on families have been studied for two periods of high unemployment: the Great Depression of the 1930s and the recession of the early 1980s. Longitudinal data on families with children collected during the 1930s permitted comparisons of families that experienced major income loss (reductions of more than 35%) with families that did not. When a family's income dropped, there were increases in the children's behavior problems—specifically, temper tantrums and uncontrolled outbursts. The cause appeared to be the father's behavior: Fathers who were experiencing economic stress became more punitive, and the children reacted with tantrums and angry outbursts (Elder, & Caspi, 1988).

Men who were unemployed in the 1980s spent more time with their children than employed men did, partly so that their wives could work at jobs outside the home, but they were less nurturing toward their children than employed fathers were. Once they returned to work, their involvement with the children returned to the same level as that of continuously employed men (Goldsmith & Radin, 1987).

A systems analysis of the effects of income loss on families is shown in Figure 13.10. Children in families that have experienced serious income loss manifest socioemotional problems, somatic symptoms (e.g., stomachaches), and reduced aspirations and expectations for higher education and job success. The father's response to income loss and his behavior toward the child are among the primary causes of these effects. In families in which fathers maintain a nurturant relationship with the child and in which the mother can provide support, income loss has relatively small effects on children (McLoyd, 1989).

Because our society emphasizes the importance of work for men, most studies of unemployment focus on fathers. However, unemployment for a mother may also produce family stress, particularly if she is single or provides an important proportion of the family's income. Investigations of maternal unemployment are just beginning.

MATERNAL EMPLOYMENT.   Because maternal employment has increased dramatically, economic and workplace policies have become an important direct influence on children's development. Sometimes the demands of jobs and parenting are at odds with one another. Such conflicts were well illustrated in *Kramer vs.*

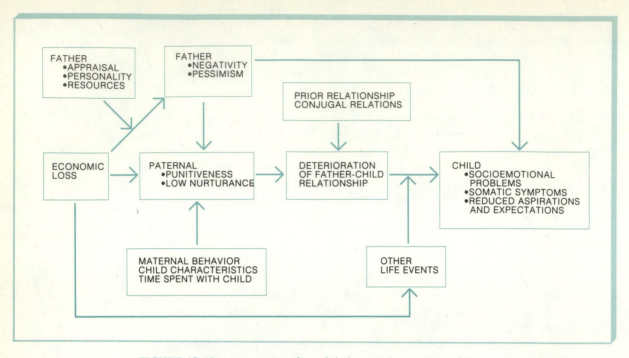

FIGURE 13.10 A conceptual model showing how paternal income loss affects parental behavior, which in turn influences children's behavior problems. (Adapted from V. C. McLoyd. Socialization and development in a changing economy: The effects of paternal job and income loss on children. *American Psychologist*, 1989, 44, p. 294. By permission.)

Kramer, a film about a single father who lost his high-level advertising job when he had to leave a critical conference to pick up his sick child at school.

Several work place policies have potential effects on families and children, but little careful research has been conducted to evaluate those effects. When a child is born, the mother must go through a period of physical recovery, and both parents face intense demands on their time when they care for the infant. Employers' policies toward *parental leave* can influence family income during an expensive set of events, and they also affect the level of stress experienced by the parents. If both parents return to work, their employers' willingness to allow part-time work and flexible working hours may affect the amount of time they spend caring for their child as well as the degree of stress and exhaustion they feel when they are with the child. As their children grow older, the parents' work schedules determine whether they can easily talk with teachers, take children to the doctor, or attend a special event at the child care center (Zigler & Frank, 1988).

Earlier in the chapter we discussed the direct effects of child care and the importance of the quality of child care for children's development (see also Chapter 4). But indirect effects also occur as a result of parental concern and worry about the care their children are receiving. In surveys conducted in several countries, employed women's most frequent source of worry was the kind of care their children were receiving while they worked (Cook, 1978). The cost of good child care is prohibitive for many families; as a result, the quality of the care received by many children depends on government and work place policies. Government can influence the availability and quality of child care by providing subsidies and by establishing minimum standards for safety, caregiver/child ratios, and the like.

SINGLE PARENTS.   Many of the long-term consequences of divorce and single parenting for children's development are partly due to income loss and poverty (Garfinkel & McLanahan, 1986). The incomes of families headed by women typically are about half of the family's income before a divorce. Government policies determine the types of services and financial aid that are available to single-parent families that are experiencing economic strains. Programs that provide medical care and nutritional supplements for infants and pregnant women are generally approved and have well-documented benefits for children (Schorr, 1988). However, programs that provide income to single mothers carry the social stigma of "welfare." Despite the intense public interest in these programs, psychologists know little about their effects on family processes or on children's development.

Government policies also define the legal obligations of a nonresident parent, whether or not the parents were originally married. Lax enforcement of child support obligations, which was typical in the United States until recently, leaves many single-parent families entirely dependent on maternal earnings or welfare. In the 1980s enforcement of support obligations was improved and awards were increased in many areas (Garfinkel & McLanahan, 1986). Psychologists are now beginning to examine how these policies affect relationships among family members. For example, do parents who are forced to pay child support give their children more attention, or do they express hostility and resentment toward them?

Relations Between the Family and Other Social Systems

Relations between families and other social systems occur within a context of cultural values and beliefs about children and families. In the United States the underlying ideology is highly individualistic: Children are considered to be the sole responsibility of their parents. We view government actions as intrusions into the privacy of the family, justified only when the parents fail to fulfill their obligations, for example, in cases of child abuse and neglect (Grubb & Lazerson, 1988). The one clear exception is education; government is expected to provide schools and educational opportunities for all.

In societies with a more communal ideology, there is a somewhat different division of responsibility between parents and other social institutions. For instance, in some Israeli kibbutzim (agricultural communities based on a communal ideology) children are raised in a children's house by a specially trained caregiver. They see their parents each day, but their parents are not solely responsible for their upbringing.

Even in societies with a less clear communal ideology than the kibbutzim, the responsibility for socializing children is shared by individuals, communities, and institutions outside the family. For instance, an American psychologist living in Paris was struck by observing that adults other than parents felt free to correct children playing in a public park. It seemed to be taken for granted that any adult had the right, and perhaps the responsibility, to intervene in children's behavior. In the United States, an adult who corrected another person's child would be considered a busybody or worse.

Perhaps because of our individualistic ideology, government policies affecting children in the United States are quite different from those in most other industrialized countries. This can be seen in Box 13.3. The United States could benefit from the experience of other nations in finding ways to provide for the welfare of children, even though particular solutions must be adapted to different cultural contexts.

 BOX 13.3

Family Policies in Other Countries

Most industrialized countries, including Canada and almost all the European countries, have evolved family policies designed to facilitate the health and development of children by providing assistance and services to families. We can illustrate these policies by following a hypothetical French mother, Nicole, and her husband Pierre through pregnancy, childbirth, and child rearing.

Because France has universal, state-supported medical care, Nicole's prenatal care and delivery and medical care for the baby will cost very little. If she is poor, she may receive income support during her pregnancy, but she must get regular prenatal checkups in order to qualify. If Nicole has a job, when the baby is born she will entitled to 16 weeks of maternity leave (six months if it is a third child) at 90 percent of her salary (up to a certain limit). She will be guaranteed the opportunity to return to the same job or a comparable one, and will retain her seniority and pension rights. She or her husband may also be eligible for unpaid leave for up to two years to take care of the child (Allen, 1988).

Regardless of their income, Nicole and Pierre, like parents in 67 other countries, will receive a child allowance—a monthly cash payment to help meet the expenses of raising their child. If Nicole is single during part of the child's developing years and has no earnings, she will receive between 50 and 90 percent of the average wage for all workers in the nation. If she gets a job, state-supported child care will be available. If her family income is low, she will be eligible for a housing allowance (Kahn & Kamerman, 1983; Kamerman et al., 1983).

France is not atypical. Some countries, such as Sweden, have more extensive benefits for parents; others have slightly fewer. In all cases the benefits are justified on the ground that it is in the best interest of society to promote the healthy development of children. Parents deserve help because they are contributing to the general welfare by bringing up children.

In the United States Nicole and Pierre would receive much less support from most employers and from government. If they have health insurance (which many people do not), the costs of prenatal care, delivery, and postnatal care will be partially covered. In some instances, if Nicole is poor enough she will be eligible for publicly supported medical care. But if Nicole and Pierre fall into the large category of young adults who work at jobs with few benefits, Nicole may get little prenatal care. If she works for a large employer with a policy allowing leaves for physical disability, she will get a 6- to 8-week unpaid parental leave when the baby is born, and will retain rights to her job and seniority; however, many young workers in the United States are not eligible even for these minimal benefits.

Because of the general lack of family policies, Nicole and Pierre may have little time to establish confidence in their parenting or enjoy interactions with their baby. It is also difficult to breast feed an infant when the mother works full time, and the physical benefits of breast feeding are well established (Stipek & McCroskey, 1989) (see Chapter 2).

If Nicole and Pierre both have jobs, they will need child care. However, they will discover that high-quality child care is difficult to find and expensive, particularly for an infant. They can subtract 20 to 30 percent of child care costs from their income tax, but they have to pay the rest. If they are very poor, they may receive some government-subsidized child care, but not necessarily. In California, a state with extensive government support for child care, fewer than 10 percent of eligible children are served by state-subsidized child care (Stipek & McCroskey, 1989).

The United States has fewer family benefits than other industrialized countries. When assistance is provided to parents, it is often justified on grounds other than the welfare of children. Parental leave, for example, came about when pregnancy was defined as a temporary physical disability, not because it is good for children's development. Subsidized child care is often defended because it enables mothers to be employed rather than being on welfare, not because the society has a responsibility to provide for its children.

Many children in the United States are suffering from poor health care, lack of education, and poverty. In 1980-1985 there were 16 industrialized nations with lower infant mortality rates than the United States (Hughes, Johnson, Rosebaum, Simons, & Butler, 1987). Reports on the poor educational performance of American children have been issued almost annually for some time. Policies that would provide medical care, nutrition, housing, and basic sustenance to families might go a long way toward improving the lot of the nation's children.

SUMMARY

Many children attend preschools and early-education programs, and many more are in day care. There is no clear answer to the question of whether day care has any effects on children's social, emotional, or cognitive development, but the quality of child care does have important effects on development. Components of quality include the amount of adult-child interaction and the physical setting (available materials and space).

The physical environment of the preschool affects social interaction and play patterns. Group size is more important than density (number of square feet per child). An inadequately equipped classroom may produce increased aggression and other kinds of stress, but children also learn to share when equipment is limited. Toys and activities can affect behavior by encouraging aggression, prosocial behavior, high levels of activity, and the like.

The academic organization of schools—that is, "open" versus "traditional" education—does not seem to affect children's levels of academic achievement, but children in open schools have more positive attitudes toward school and are more independent, creative, intellectually curious, and cooperative. Another school variable is adult structuring of children's activities. Children in highly structured classes attend well, comply with directions, and turn to the teacher for approval. They interact almost exclusively with the teacher and relatively little with peers. Low structure, in contrast, encourages positive interactions with peers as well as aggression, assertiveness, and leadership. Girls are more likely to participate in adult-structured activities than boys are.

Teachers influence children through the processes of reinforcement and modeling, but their influence also depends on how children interpret their actions. The effectiveness of social reinforcement, such as praise for academic performance, depends on how it is used; indiscriminate praise is likely to be discounted. Although teachers are sometimes accused of encouraging sex-stereotyped behavior through their praise and criticism, the opposite is often the case. However, teachers can serve as models for sex-typed behavior.

Recent research has shown that teachers' expectancies can, under some circumstances, affect learning independently of the child's abilities. Expectancies are communicated to children through behaviors such as smiling and showing positive feelings toward students who are considered to be bright.

Cooperative learning programs are based on group interaction and a group reward structure. They improve learning in some instances and also contribute to positive attitudes toward other students and concern for the welfare of others. Racial integration is more successful when the school organization promotes cooperation rather than competition and when individual achievement is deemphasized. Mainstreaming, or integrating children with physical and mental handicaps into regular classrooms, is less successful than its advocates originally hoped, but programs stressing peer interaction and cooperation can make mainstreaming more effective.

Peers influence one another by acting as models, reinforcing or punishing behavior, and interpreting behavior. The peer group instructs or trains children in critical social skills that cannot be learned in the same way from adults. In later childhood peers can help one another deal with personal problems and anxieties. Sometimes children consider their peers to be more appropriate models than adults.

Peers are particularly important influences on aggressive and prosocial behavior. Although most children do not approve of aggressive behavior, they often reinforce it through their actions. Peers can teach aggression through modeling as well as reinforcement. Prosocial responses such as friendliness, generosity, and sharing can also be augmented by means of peer reinforcement and modeling. Peer reinforcement is especially effective in the case of sex-typed behaviors. Peers can also be effective teachers of school subjects and can serve as models for good study habits.

An important socializing influence within the home is television; on the average, children watch two or three hours of television a day. Young children often watch programs that are not designed for children. Television viewing is sometimes thought to replace family interaction, play, and other activities; to have negative effects on health and physical fitness and on school achievement; and to induce passive approaches to learning. Researchers have found that television does affect the structure of leisure time and that it leads to reduced participation in sports, which may affect physical fitness. Television viewing is associated with lower achievement in school for children who watch more than about 10 hours a week. It does not appear to make children intellectually passive. In fact, children think actively while viewing, and if the program content is informative, they learn a great deal from television.

The extent to which children understand what they see on television depends partly on their level of cognitive understanding. Young children sometimes have difficulty discriminating central, important content from content that is tangential to the main point. They may also fail to integrate different elements of a story that occur at different times, and may have difficulty making inferences about events that are not explicitly shown.

Children acquire much of their knowledge about social relationships and behavior from television. They also learn social stereotypes. In addition, television violence can cause aggressive behavior. Children can also learn prosocial approaches to problem solving when they see them on television.

Children are affected by governmental policies and programs and by the economic policies of the work place, in part because their parents are affected. Government policies affect family income, the types of services available to families, and many aspects of family life. Such workplace policies as parental leave for childbirth, wage rates, working hours, health benefits, and the like affect parental enployment and the quality of family life. Major social trends such as high rates of poverty, maternal employment, and single-parent families have long-term consequences for the development of the current generation of children.

REVIEW QUESTIONS

1. How do preschool and day-care environments affect social, emotional, and cognitive development?

2. What effects do the physical and academic organization of schools have on children's development?

3. How do teachers influence children?

4. Briefly discuss cooperative learning, desegregation and integration, and mainstreaming in terms of their effects on children.

5. In what ways do peers act as socializing agents?

6. How do preschool and school-age children contribute to sex typing of children's behavior?

7. How much time do children spend watching television and what kinds of programs do they watch?

8. What are the effects of television viewing on family interaction, physical fitness, school achievement, and learning?

9. What kinds of knowledge do children acquire from television?

10. In what ways do social and economic policies influence the lives of children?

GLOSSARY

mainstreaming   The integration of children with physical and mental handicaps into regular classrooms.

SUGGESTED READINGS

Elder, G. H., Jr. (1977). *Children of the great depression: Social change in life experience.* Chicago: University of Chicago Press. An analysis of families that experienced severe income loss during the depression of the 1930s. Longitudinal data are examined to compare children whose families lost income with those whose families did not.

Hartup, W. W. (1983). Peer relations. In E. M. Hetherington (Ed.) & P. H. Mussen (Series Ed.), *Handbook of child psychology*: Vol. 4. *Socialization, personality, and social development.* New York: Wiley. A comprehensive review of the theory and literature regarding peer influences, and an excellent reference source.

Liebert, R. N., & Sprafkin, J. N. (1988). *The early window: Effects of television on children* (3rd ed.). New York: Pergamon. A readable review of the literature on the effects of television. Provides a historical examination of the research in relation to changes in the industry and government policy over the 40 years since television was introduced in the United States.

Minuchin, P. P. & Shapiro, E. K. (1983). The school as a context for social development. In E. M. Hetherington (Ed.) & P. H. Mussen (Series Ed.), *Handbook of child psychology*: Vol. 4. *Socialization, personality, and social development*. New York: Wiley. Reviews what is known about the effects of schools on children's social development. It is an excellent summary of research findings and theory.

Scarr, S. (1984). *Mother care/other care*. New York: Basic Books. Presents a popularized summary of the research on day care, taking the position that day care is not harmful to children and in many cases can be beneficial.

Schorr, L. B. (1988). *Within our reach: Breaking the cycle of disadvantage*. New York: Anchor Press. The author argues that we know a great deal about how to help disadvantaged children and families break out of persistent poverty. She reviews interventions that have been successful in producing long-term change in such domains as child health, education, and adolescent pregnancy, and draws clear implications for national policy.

Part Five

ADOLESCENCE

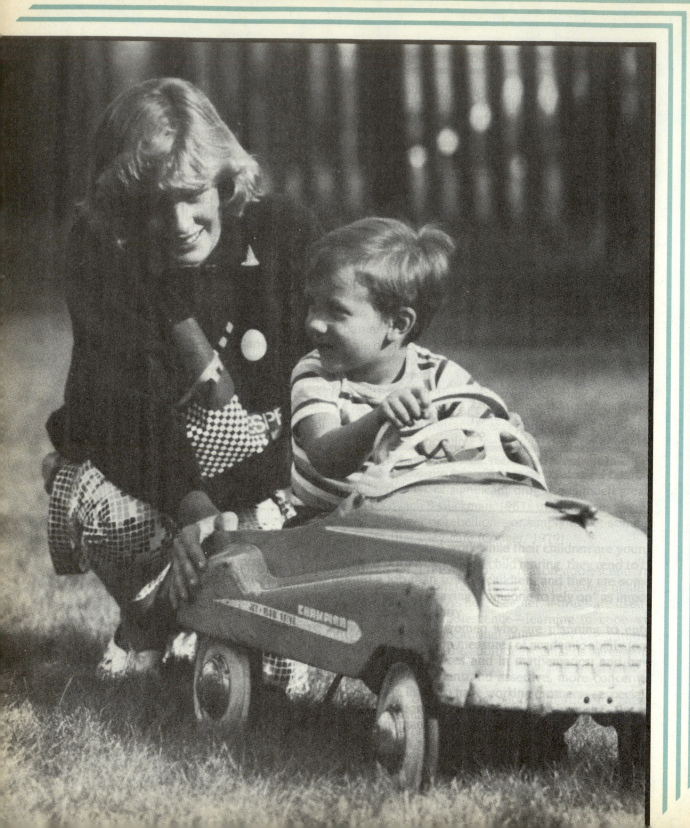

Chapter Fourteen

ADOLESCENCE: DEVELOPMENT AND SOCIALIZATION

Growing Up: Physical Development in Adolescence
    Hormonal Factors in Development
    Hormonal Dimorphism
    The Adolescent Growth Spurt
    The Shape of Things to Come
Sexual Maturation
    Sexual Development in Males
    Sexual Development in Females
    Normal Variations in Development
Psychological Aspects of Maturation
    Onset of Menstruation
    Erection, Ejaculation, and Nocturnal Emission
    Early and Late Maturers
Cognitive Development in Adolescence
    Hypothetical Thinking
    Cognitive Aspects of Personality Development
Adolescent Sexuality
    Sex Differences in Sexuality
    Changing Sexual Attitudes and Behavior
    Premarital Sexual Intercourse
    Homosexual Behavior and Orientation
    Variations in Sexual Attitudes and Behavior
    Pregnancy and Contraception
Parental Relations and the Development of Autonomy
    Changing Perceptions of Parents
    Variations in Parental Behavior
    Family Communication

Adolescents and Their Peers
Conformity to Peer Culture
Parental vs. Peer Influences
Friendships and Identity Development
Relationships with Opposite-sex Peers

Adolescence has traditionally been considered a more difficult developmental period than the middle-childhood years, both for children and for their parents. Some 300 years before the birth of Christ, Aristotle complained that adolescents are "passionate, irascible, and apt to be carried away by their impulses" (Kiell, 1967, pp. 18–19). Plato advised that boys not be allowed to drink before the age of 18 because of their excitability: "Fire must not be poured on fire" (Plato, 1953, p. 14). And in a funeral sermon a seventeenth-century clergyman compared youth to "a new ship launching out into the main ocean without a helm or ballast or pilot to steer her" (Smith, S. R., 1975, p. 497).

Early in this century, G. Stanley Hall, founder of the American Psychological Association and originator of the scientific study of adolescence, introduced the notion of adolescence as a period of great "storm and stress" as well as immense physical, mental, and emotional potential. A number of prominent clinicians and psychoanalytic theorists still view adolescence as a psychologically disturbed state. However, empirical investigations of typical adolescents indicate that the extent of adolescent—and parental—turmoil during this period has been greatly exaggerated (Conger, 1977a; Offer, 1975).

Nevertheless, it cannot be denied that adolescence is a challenging and sometimes difficult stage of life. Why should this be so? Adolescence, particularly early adolescence, is above all a period of change—not only physical, sexual, psychological, and cognitive changes in the adolescent, but also changes in the social demands made by parents, peers, teachers, and society itself. It seems almost unfair that so many socialization demands—for independence, for changing relationships with peers and adults, for sexual adjustment, for educational and vocational preparation—are made at the same time that the young person is experiencing an almost unprecedented rate of biological maturation. Besides coping with all these developmental changes, adolescents are struggling to achieve identities of their own—personal answers to the age-old question "Who am I?"

In this chapter we will examine in some detail the maturational changes of adolescence and their effects on psychological development. We will also explore the basic socialization tasks confronting adolescents and the role played by parents and peers in making those tasks easier or harder.

GROWING UP: PHYSICAL DEVELOPMENT IN ADOLESCENCE

The term **adolescence** comes from the Latin verb *adolescere*, which means "to grow into adulthood." It begins with the onset of puberty and ends with the assumption of adult responsibilities; as one philosopher remarked, adolescence begins in biology and ends in culture. Thus, the period we call adolescence may be brief, as it is in some simpler societies, or relatively prolonged, as it is in our own relatively advanced society. Its onset may involve abrupt changes in social demands and expectations, or a gradual transition from previous roles. Despite such variations, one aspect of adolescence is universal and separates it from earlier stages of development: the physical and physiological changes of puberty that mark its beginning.

The term **puberty** refers to the first phase of adolescence, in which sexual maturation becomes evident. Strictly speaking, puberty begins with hormonal increases and their manifestations, such as gradual enlargement of the ovaries in females and testicular cell growth in males. But because these changes are not outwardly observable, the onset of puberty is often measured by such events as the emergence of pubic hair, the beginning of elevation of the breasts in girls, and an increase in the size of the penis and testes in boys. Sexual maturation is accompanied by a "growth spurt" in height and weight that usually lasts about four years.

Hormonal Factors in Development

Of critical importance in the regulation of pubertal growth is the pituitary gland. This gland is located at the base of the brain, to which it is connected by nerve fibers. When the cells of the hypothalamus "mature" (an event that occurs at different times in different individuals), signals are sent to the pituitary gland to begin releasing previously inhibited hormones (Grumbach, 1978). The hormones released by the pituitary have a stimulating effect on most other endocrine glands, including the thyroid and adrenal glands and the testes and ovaries, which in turn begin releasing hormones that affect growth and sexual development. These include *androgens* (masculinizing hormones), *estrogens* (feminizing hormones), and *progestins* (pregnancy hormones). They interact with other hormones in complex ways to stimulate an orderly progression of physical and physiological development.

Hormonal Dimorphism

In the early days of sex-hormone research, when sex differences were viewed as dichotomous and absolute, it was assumed that females produce only female sex hormones and males only male sex hormones; indeed, the sex hormones were named accordingly. Actually, however, there is some *dimorphism* or overlap; the hormones of both sexes are present in both men and women (Gupta, Attanasio, & Raaf, 1975; Marshall, 1978). The hormonal difference between the sexes is a difference in the *proportions* of masculinizing and feminizing hormones present in males and females. As may be seen in Figure 14.1, as puberty proceeds, the ratio of estrogen levels to testosterone levels increases in females and decreases in males.

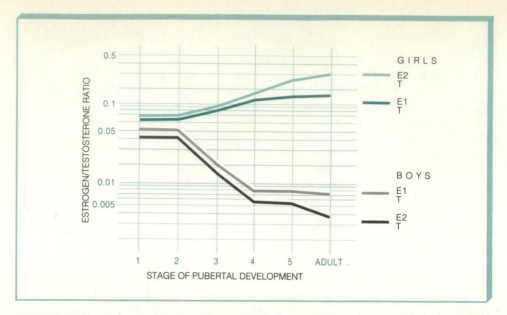

FIGURE 14.1 Mean trends in estrogen/testosterone ratios during pubertal development for girls and boys. Two measures of estrogen level are shown, estrone (E1) and the more potent estradiol (E2). (Adapted from D. Gupta, A. Attanasio, & S. Raaf. Plasma estrogen and androgen concentrations in children during adolescence. *Journal of Clinical Endocrinology and Metabolism*, 1975, 40, 636–643. By permission.)

The Adolescent Growth Spurt

The term *growth spurt* refers to the accelerated rate of increase in height and weight that occurs at puberty. This increase varies widely in intensity, duration, and age of onset from one child to another, even among perfectly normal children—a fact that is often poorly understood by adolescents and their parents and consequently is a source of needless concern.

In both sexes, the adolescent growth spurt lasts about 4½ years (Boxer & Petersen, 1986; Faust, 1984; Marshall, 1978). For the average male, the growth rate peaks at age 13; in females this occurs about two years earlier, at age 11. In the average boy, the growth spurt begins a few months before his eleventh birthday, though it may begin as early as age 9; similarly, the growth spurt is usually completed shortly after age 15 but may continue until age 17. In girls, the growth spurt usually begins and ends about two years earlier. Further slow growth may continue for several years after the growth spurt is completed (Faust, 1983; Falkner & Tanner, 1978b). Because the onset of the growth spurt is so variable, some young people complete the pubertal growth period before others have begun it (see Figure 14.2); clearly, *normal* does not mean "average."

Many parents have the feeling that rapidly growing adolescents, particularly boys, are "eating us out of house and home." Indeed, the nutritional needs of young people increase considerably during the years of rapid growth, although there are wide individual variations, depending on such factors as body size and

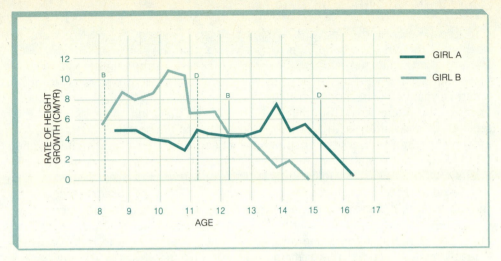

FIGURE 14.2   Differences in timing of the pubertal growth period in height. The early-developing girl (A) reached the end (d) of the pubertal period before the late-developing girl (B) reached onset (b). (Adapted from M. S. Faust. Somatic development of adolescent girls. *Monographs of the Society for Research in Child Development*, 1977, 42 [1, Serial No. 169]. © The Society for Research in Child Development, Inc. By permission.)

activity level. As can be seen in Table 14.1, on the average boys need more calories at every age than girls do. However, a large, very active girl obviously will have greater nutritional needs than a small, inactive boy. Similarly, late maturers need fewer calories than early maturers of the same age.

TABLE 14.1

Recommended Daily Dietary Allowances

	Age	Weight (pounds)	Height (inches)	Calories
Boys	11–14	97	63	2800
	15–18	134	69	3000
	19–22	147	69	3000
Girls	11–14	97	62	2400
	15–18	119	65	2100
	19–22	128	65	2000

Source: National Academy of Sciences, National Research Council, *Recommended dietary allowances, revised*, 1974. Washington, D.C.: National Academy of Sciences, National Research Council, 1974.

The Shape of Things to Come

Changes in height and weight are accompanied by changes in body proportions in both boys and girls. The head, hands, and feet reach adult size first. The arms and legs grow faster than the trunk, which is completed last. As the English pediatrician James Tanner has written, "A boy stops growing out of his trousers (at least in length) a year before he stops growing out of his jackets" (1971, p. 94). These differences in the rate of growth in different parts of the body largely account for the feelings of awkwardness that some adolescents feel, especially those who are growing fastest. For brief periods some young people may feel that their hands and feet are too big or that they are "all legs." Of course, thoughtless comments by adults may intensify the adolescent's feelings of awkwardness.

Sex differences in body shape also are magnified during early adolescence. Although even in childhood girls have wider hips than boys do, the difference becomes more pronounced at puberty. Conversely, males develop thicker as well as larger bones, more muscle tissue, and broader shoulders (see Figure 14.3). Partly as a result, males become, and remain, stronger than females (particularly in the upper body) as adolescence proceeds. Other reasons for males' greater physical strength relative to their size are that they develop larger hearts and lungs, higher systolic blood pressure, a greater capacity for carrying oxygen in the blood, and a lower heart rate while resting. They are also more resistant chemically to fatigue from exercise (Forbes, 1978; Tanner, 1970, 1971).

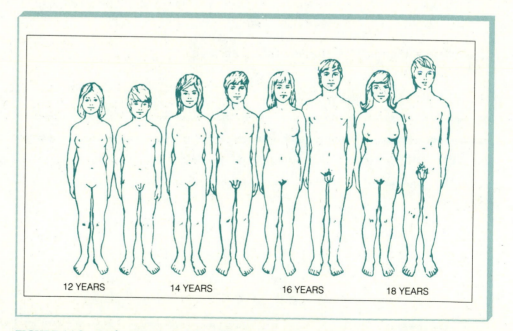

| 12 YEARS | 14 YEARS | 16 YEARS | 18 YEARS |

FIGURE 14.3   Body growth and development from ages 12 years to 18 years. (From P. H. Mussen, J. J. Conger, & J. Kagan, *Essentials of child development and personality.* New York: Harper & Row, 1980.)

SEXUAL MATURATION

As in the case of the growth spurt, there are marked individual differences in the age at which sexual maturation begins. While there is some variation within developmental sequences—for example, breast development in girls may appear before or after the development of pubic hair—physical development during puberty and adolescence generally follows a rather orderly progression (Boxer & Petersen, 1986; Faust, 1984). Thus, a male who has an early growth spurt is more likely to develop pubic hair and other attributes of sexual maturation early; a female who shows early breast development is likely to have early **menarche** (onset of menstruation). Preadolescents with advanced skeletal development will probably have an early growth spurt and early sexual maturation (Roche, 1978; Tanner, 1970, 1971).

Sexual Development in Males

Although testicular cell growth and secretion of male sex hormone begin earlier—typically about age 11½—the first outward sign of impending sexual maturity in males is usually an increase in the growth of the testes and scrotum (the baglike structure enclosing the testes) beginning at about age 12½. There may also be some growth of pubic hair. Approximately a year later, an acceleration in growth of the penis accompanies the beginning of the growth spurt in height. Axillary (body) and facial hair usually make their first appearance about two years after the

There are often large differences in the age at which adolescents begin the growth spurt and attain sexual maturity.

beginning of pubic-hair growth, although in a few children axillary hair appears first (Marshall & Tanner, 1970).

A definite lowering of the voice usually occurs fairly late in puberty. In some young men this change is abrupt and dramatic, while in others it is so gradual that it is hardly perceptible. During this process the larynx (Adam's apple) enlarges significantly and the vocal cords (which it contains) approximately double in length, with a consequent drop in pitch of about an octave.

During adolescence the male breast also undergoes changes. The diameter of the areola (the area surrounding the nipple) increases considerably (although not as much as in girls) and is accompanied by elevation of the nipple. In some males (perhaps 20 to 30 percent) there may be a distinct enlargement of the breast about midway through adolescence. Usually this disappears within a year or so (Bell, 1980). Prepubescent boys may also show a tendency toward adiposity of the lower torso, which, again, may suggest feminine body contours to the apprehensive adolescent or adult. Although these bodily configurations typically disappear with time, they may represent a source of needless anxiety for both adolescents and parents who are preoccupied with "masculinity" (Conger & Petersen, 1984). There is no evidence that (in the absence of specific pathology) either of these conditions is related to any deficiency in sexual functioning.

Sexual Development in Females

The appearance of unpigmented, downy pubic hair is usually the first outward sign of sexual maturity in girls, although the so-called bud stage of breast development may sometimes precede it (Faust, 1984). Budding of the breasts is accompanied by the emergence of downy, unpigmented axillary hair and increases in the secretion of estrogen (female sex hormone). In the following year the uterus and vagina show accelerated growth; the labia and clitoris also enlarge. Menarche occurs relatively late in the developmental sequence (about age 12½), almost always after the growth spurt has begun to slow down (Faust, 1977, 1983; Tanner, 1970).

There is frequently a period of a year or more following the beginning of menstruation during which the adolescent female is not yet able to conceive. Similarly, males are able to have intercourse long before they produce live spermatozoa. Obviously, however, because of significant individual differences younger adolescents should not assume that they are "safe" because of their age. Some young women are able to conceive within the first year after menarche (Boxer & Petersen, 1986; Zabin, Kantner, & Zelnik, 1979). The typical sequences of sexual maturation for boys and girls are summarized in Table 14.2.

Normal Variations in Development

Even in today's somewhat more tolerant climate, deviance from group norms in rate of development and physical appearance are agonizing for many adolescents and can impair their self-esteem (Simmons, Blyth, & McKinney, 1983; Simmons & Rosenberg, 1975; Tobin-Richards, Boxer, & Petersen, 1983). It should be emphasized that the average developmental sequences discussed here are just that—

TABLE 14.2

Maturation in Boys and in Girls

Although there may be some individual—and perfectly normal—variations in the sequence of events leading to physical and sexual maturity in boys, the following sequence is typical:

1. Testes and scrotum begin to increase in size.
2. Pubic hair begins to appear.
3. Adolescent growth spurt starts; the penis begins to enlarge.
4. Voice deepens as the larynx grows.
5. Hair begins to appear under the arms and on the upper lip.
6. Sperm production increases, and nocturnal emission (ejaculation of semen during sleep) may occur.
7. Growth spurt reaches peak rate; pubic hair becomes pigmented.
8. Prostate gland enlarges.
9. Sperm production becomes sufficient for fertility; growth rate decreases.
10. Physical strength reaches a peak.

Although, as in the case of boys, there may be normal variations in the sequence of physical and sexual maturation in girls, a typical sequence of events is as follows:

1. Adolescent growth spurt begins.
2. Downy (nonpigmented) pubic hair makes its initial appearance.
3. Elevation of the breast (the so-called bud stage of development) and rounding of the hips begin, accompanied by the beginning of downy axillary (armpit) hair.
4. The uterus and vagina, as well as labia and clitoris, increase in size.
5. Pubic hair grows rapidly and becomes slightly pigmented.
6. Breasts develop further; nipple pigmentation begins; areola increases in size; axillary hair becomes slightly pigmented.
7. Growth spurt reaches peak rate and then declines.
8. Menarche (onset of menstruation) occurs.
9. Pubic hair development is completed, followed by mature breast development and completion of axillary hair development.
10. Period of "adolescent sterility" ends, and girl becomes capable of conception (up to a year or so after menarche).

average. Among perfectly normal adolescents there are wide variations in the age of onset of the developmental sequence (and sometimes in the order of the events in the sequence). For example, while maturation of the penis may be complete by age 13½ in some boys, in others it may not be complete until age 17 or even later. The bud stage of breast development may occur as early as age 8 in some girls, as late as age 13 in others. Age at menarche may vary from about 9 to 16½. The

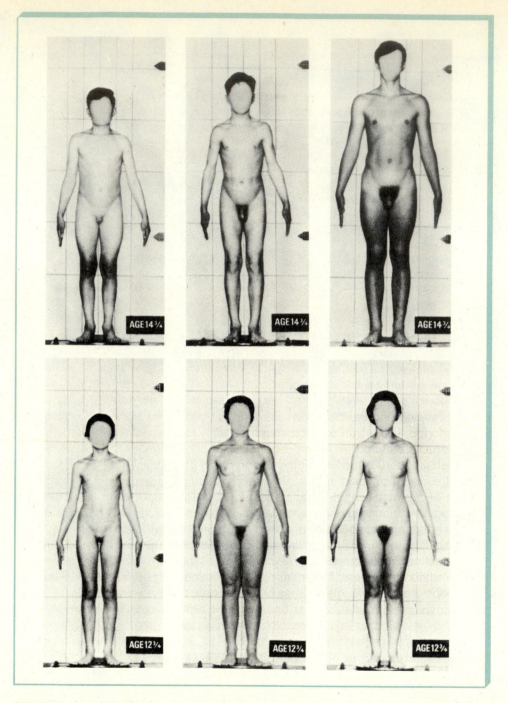

FIGURE 14.4   Different degrees of pubertal development at the same chronological age. Upper row: three boys, all aged 14¾ years. Lower row: three girls, all aged 12¾ years. (From J. M. Tanner, Growth and endocrinology of the adolescent. In J. L. Gardner [Ed.], *Endocrine and genetic diseases of childhood.* Philadelphia: W. B. Saunders, 1969. By permission.)

marked differences that occur among normal adolescents in their rates of development are illustrated in Figure 14.4, which shows the differing degrees of pubertal maturity among three normal males, all aged 14¾ years, and three normal females, all aged 12¾ years.

PSYCHOLOGICAL ASPECTS OF MATURATION

Many adults have suppressed their more anxiety-laden memories concerning the physical changes of adolescence; even college students are better at remembering events from earlier years than those surrounding the onset of puberty (Conger & Petersen, 1984). Consequently, adults are likely to have only a vague understanding of how acutely aware the average adolescent is of the growth process (Bell, R., 1980). The adolescent's awareness is hardly surprising, however. A clear sense of identity as a person requires, among other things, a feeling of consistency and stability of the self over time (see Chapter 15). This is not an easy feeling for adolescents to maintain, faced as they are with the many rapid internal changes that take place during puberty. Unlike younger children, whose physical growth is gradual and orderly, rapidly changing adolescents are likely at times to feel like strangers to themselves. Time is needed to integrate these dramatic changes into an emerging sense of a stable, self-confident identity. This is particularly true in connection with changes related to sexual functioning—onset of menstruation in girls and erection and ejaculation in boys.

Onset of Menstruation

Menstruation is much more to the adolescent girl than a physiological readjustment. It is a symbol of sexual maturity—of the girl's future status as a woman (Brooks-Gunn & Ruble, 1983; Greif & Ulman, 1982; Ruble & Brooks-Gunn, 1982). Because a girl's reaction to menstruation may generalize so broadly, her initial experiences should be as favorable as possible. Increasing numbers of contemporary girls view the onset of menstruation calmly and look forward to "becoming a woman." In the words of one older adolescent, "It seemed that all my friends had gotten their period already, or were just having it. I felt left out. I began to think of it as a symbol. When I got my period, I would be a *woman*." Unfortunately, many other girls view this normal—and inevitable—development negatively. In several studies (Boxer & Petersen, 1986; Brooks-Gunn & Ruble, 1982, 1984; Greif & Ulman, 1982), a majority of preadolescent and adolescent American girls saw the effects of menstruation as negative or at best neutral; most felt that menstruation "is something women just have to put up with." Its most positive aspect was as a sign of maturity; its most negative aspect was "the hassle" of needing to be prepared for its occurrence (Ruble & Brooks-Gunn, 1982).

Why do so many adolescent girls react negatively to the onset of menstruation? One reason is the negative attitudes of others. If a girl's parents and friends act as though she requires sympathy for her "plight"—an attitude indicated by such labels as "the curse"—she is likely to react in a similar fashion. Negative initial reactions to menstruation may also stem from physical discomfort, including headaches, backaches, cramps, and abdominal pain. In a recent national health survey, a majority of American adolescent females (aged 12 to 17 years) reported experiencing at least mild pain before or during menses. However, only 14 percent of those reporting cramps or other pain described it as severe, and relief is now available from several drugs (including aspirin) that inhibit the primary biochemical substance that produces pain (Klein & Litt, 1984). Regular exercise, proper diet (including avoidance of excessive amounts of salt, sugar, and caffeine), and sufficient rest can also be helpful.

Negative psychological reactions to menstruation can be avoided or alleviated if parents employ a wise and understanding approach (Bell, R., 1980). By preparing their child for menarche, seeking medical care for significant physical or psychological side effects, explaining the naturalness of the phenomenon, and showing pride and pleasure in her greater maturity, parents—particularly the mother but also the father—can help make the onset of menstruation a welcome rather than a feared or hated event. Wardell Pomeroy, a clinical psychologist and coauthor of the Kinsey reports, describes one father "who observed the occasion of his daughter's first menstruation by bringing her flowers and making a little ceremony of the fact that she had now become a young woman. That daughter could not help feeling proud and good about becoming an adolescent" (Pomeroy, 1969, p. 47).

Erection, Ejaculation, and Nocturnal Emission

Just as the onset of menstruation may cause concern to adolescent girls, uncontrolled erection and initial ejaculation may surprise and worry adolescent boys. Although genital stimulation, like other forms of bodily stimulation, is pleasurable for children, erection and genital stimulation usually carry a greater sense of sexual urgency after puberty. During this period the penis begins to tumesce very readily, either spontaneously or in response to a variety of stimuli: "provocative sights, sounds, smells, language, or whatever—the [younger] male adolescent inhabits a libidinized life-space where almost anything can take on a sexual meaning" (Stone & Church, 1973, p. 424). Although males may be proud of their capacity for erection as a symbol of emerging virility, they may also be worried or embarrassed by their apparent inability to control this response. They may become apprehensive about dancing or even having to stand up in a classroom to give a report. They may wonder if other males experience a similar apparent lack of control (Bell, R., 1980; Conger & Petersen, 1984).

The adolescent male's first ejaculation is likely to occur within a year after the onset of the growth spurt (around age 14, although it may occur as early as 11 or as late as 16). First ejaculation may occur as a result of masturbation or nocturnal emission (ejaculation of seminal fluid during sleep, often accompanied by erotic dreams). A boy who has previously masturbated, with accompanying pleasant sensations but without ejaculation, may wonder if the ejaculation of seminal fluid is harmful or an indication that something is physically wrong with him. Others have no such concern. As one 15-year-old put it, "I think a first wet dream is a powerful moment. It marks becoming a man. I was really excited about it" (Bell, R., 1980, p. 15).

Early and Late Maturers

As we have already seen, young people vary widely in the age at which they reach puberty. At age 15 one boy may be small, with no pubertal development of reproductive organs or pubic hair. At the same age another boy may appear to be virtually a grown man, with broad shoulders, strong muscles, adult genitalia, and a bass voice (Tanner, 1970, 1971). Even though such variations are perfectly normal and do not either help or interfere with the eventual achievement of full physical and sexual maturity, they can affect the way adolescents view themselves—and the way they are viewed by others.

EARLY VS. LATE MATURATION IN MALES.   In general, the psychological effects of early or late maturation appear to be greater among males than among females and are easier to understand. Adults and other adolescents tend to think of the 14- or 15-year-old who looks 17 or 18 as older than he actually is. They are likely to expect more mature behavior from him than they would from a physically less developed male of the same age (Conger, 1979, in press; Steinberg & Hill, 1978). Because there is less discrepancy in height between an early-maturing boy and most girls his own age (who typically experience an earlier growth spurt), the boy may become involved in boy-girl relationships sooner and with more self-confidence. Moreover, a physically more developed male has an advantage in many activities, especially athletics. Although a boy who matures much faster than most of his peers may feel somewhat different, he is not likely to feel insecure about the difference. After all, with his more rugged physique, increased strength, and greater sexual maturity, he can assure himself that he is simply changing in the direction society expects and approves (Blyth et al., 1981; Conger, in press; Petersen, 1988; Simmons et al., 1979, 1983).

In contrast, the late-maturing male is more likely to be "treated like a child." He is likely to have a harder time excelling in athletics and other activities and establishing relationships with females. He may wonder when, if ever, he will reach full physical and sexual maturity.

Not surprisingly, all of this results, on the average, in personality differences between early and late maturers. Extensive long-term research at the University of California found that males who matured late tended to be less poised, more tense and talkative, and more self-conscious and affected than males who matured early. They were also likely to be "overeager" and more restless, impulsive, bossy, and "attention seeking." Though obviously there are exceptions to these patterns, late maturers tended to be less popular with peers, and fewer of them were leaders. Early maturers, on the other hand, appeared more reserved, self-assured, and matter-of-fact, and were more likely to engage easily in socially appropriate behavior. They were also more likely to be able to laugh at themselves. Later studies have obtained similar results (Clausen, 1975; Jones, H. E., 1954, 1957; Mussen & Jones, 1957; Simmons et al., 1979, 1983).

While early-maturing boys generally have an advantage over those who mature late, the picture is not entirely one-sided. When early- and late-maturing groups were compared at or after (but not before) puberty, late-maturing boys emerged as more intellectually curious and higher in exploratory behavior and

social initiative (Peskin, 1967; Livson & Peskin, 1980). In contrast, early maturers tended to avoid problem solving or new situations unless urged. "The early maturers appeared to approach cognitive tasks cautiously and timidly, with a preference for rules, routines, and imitative action" (Livson & Peskin, 1980, p. 73).

A far-ranging follow-up study of the participants in the University of California studies, conducted when the subjects were 38 years old, demonstrated that differences between early and late maturers—both positive and negative—can easily persist into adulthood (Clausen, 1975; Jones, M. C., 1957; Livson & Peskin, 1980). As adults, the early-maturing males were more responsible, cooperative, sociable, and self-contained but also more conventional, conforming, moralistic, humorless, and concerned with making a good impression. On the other hand, the late maturers remained less controlled, less responsible, and more impulsive and assertive but also "more insightful, perceptive, creatively playful, and able to cope with the ambiguity of new situations" (Livson & Peskin, 1980, p. 71).

Much can be done by parents, teachers, and others to minimize the anxiety and other negative psychological effects of late maturation. Adults can make a conscious effort to avoid treating a late maturer as younger than he actually is. They can help him realize that his slower maturation is normal—that he will indeed "grow up" and be just as physically and sexually masculine as his peers. And they can help him achieve success in activities in which his smaller size and strength are not a handicap. For example, while immaturity and smaller size can be a handicap for a football player, they may be assets for a diver or a tumbler.

Conversely, parents and others can assist early maturers by not forming unrealistic expectations of maturity based on physical appearance. They can also encourage early-maturing boys—and, as we shall see, girls—to take time to catch up psychologically and socially instead of rushing headlong into adult activities.

EARLY VS. LATE MATURATION IN FEMALES.   Although early or average maturation is generally advantageous to boys, among girls the differences are generally less extensive and more variable (Crockett & Petersen, 1987; Faust, 1960, 1977, 1984; Livson & Peskin, 1980; Simmons et al., 1979, 1983). Initially, early-maturing girls tend to be less satisfied with their body image; more easily disorganized under stress; more restless, listless, moody, and complaining; and less popular with same-sex peers than late-maturing girls (Blyth et al., 1981; Faust, 1960, 1977; Peskin, 1973; Petersen, 1988). They are more likely to perform poorly in school, score lower on achievement tests, exhibit problem behaviors in school, and have lower academic aspirations (Simmons et al., 1979, 1983). However, they also emerge as more independent, more popular with opposite-sex peers, and more interested in dating.

Of particular interest is the clear difference in body image between early-maturing boys and girls. While the early-maturing boy is steadily developing in the direction of favored adult norms, this is not typically the case for early-maturing girls, who tend initially to be bigger, heavier, and fatter than their more petite late-maturing peers (Simmons, Blyth, & McKinney, 1983; Simmons et al., 1983; Tobin-Richards, Boxer, & Petersen, 1984). The exaggerated emphasis our society places on being tall and slim may help explain the finding that the heavier a girl is—or thinks she is—the more dissatisfied she is with both her weight and her body shape. In contrast, late-maturing girls initially are more gregarious, socially poised, assertive, and active; more popular with peers; and more satisfied with their body image. They also do better academically, exhibit fewer behavior problems in school, and have higher academic aspirations (Faust, 1960, 1984; Petersen, 1988; Peskin, 1973; Simmons et al., 1983; Stolz & Stolz, 1985).

By late adolescence and adulthood, however, the picture changes significantly. The formerly stress-ridden early-maturing girl has become more popular with peers of both sexes than the late-maturing girl, as well as more self-possessed, better at coping, and more self-directed cognitively, socially, and emotionally (Faust, 1960; Livson & Peskin, 1980; Peskin, 1973).

How can we explain this change, as well as the fact that early maturation is clearly a more favorable event for boys than for girls? First, early-maturing adolescents are in a minority among their peers; this is no longer the case when all of their peers have also matured (Simmons et al., 1983). Second, society favors early maturity in males more clearly and less ambiguously than in females. In boys, early maturation means greater strength and physical prowess and, eventually, active sexual behavior. Among girls, early maturation may mean being temporarily bigger and heavier than one's female peers and taller than boys one's own age. In our society it may also mean being subjected to more conflicting sexual messages than is the case for males.

In the case of an early-maturing female, parents and others should be careful to avoid pushing her into having sexual relationships too early. They can help her develop her own interests and maintain her friendships with peers her own age, assuring her that they will soon catch up with her physically. At the same time, parents and others need to assure the late-maturing female of her ultimate physical and sexual maturity. If they can help her realize that there is no need to rush things along, that gradual maturation can even be useful in allowing her to devote her energies to other important developmental tasks, many unnecessary concerns can be alleviated (Conger, 1979; in press).

COGNITIVE DEVELOPMENT IN ADOLESCENCE

In Piaget's stage theory, which was explained in Chapter 7, early adolescence is characterized by a transition from the concrete operations of middle childhood to formal operational thinking. Recent research indicates that the reality is more complicated than Piaget's formulation suggests. Not only is the age of onset of formal operational thinking more variable than Piaget envisaged, but this change occurs less suddenly and is less universal and more specific to particular areas in which the individual is especially competent, such as physics or politics (Flavell, 1985; Keating, 1980). Thus, investigators have found some aspects of formal thinking in highly intelligent younger children (Keating, 1975, 1980). Conversely, some adolescents and adults never acquire true formal operational thought because of limited ability or cultural limitations, both in our own and in other countries (Flavell, 1985; Keating, 1980; Neimark, 1975a; Ross, 1973). Even very bright adolescents and adults do not always employ their capacity for formal operational thinking—for example, when a problem seems too far removed from reality, or when they are bored, tired, frustrated, or overly involved emotionally (Conger & Petersen, 1984; Neimark, 1975a, 1975b).

Nevertheless, in our society adolescents are more likely than younger children to develop and refine a variety of capabilities that are characteristic of formal operational thinking. As we saw in Chapter 7, these include ability to reason about hypothetical problems, about what *might* be as well as what is; awareness of the need to explore alternative possibilities in a systematic search for solutions (much as a scientist would), rather than simply accepting the first plausible answer that comes to mind; ability to think abstractly and to use abstract rules to solve a whole class of problems (what Piaget called "higher-order operations"); and ability to think about one's own thought, almost, at times, like a spectator.

In addition to developing formal operational thinking to varying degrees, adolescents are more likely than younger children to be aware of the distinction between simply perceiving something and storing it in memory. They are also more likely to use sophisticated strategies as aids to memory, such as dividing a long number into "chunks" to make it easier to remember (Flavell, 1985; Keating, 1980; Neimark, 1975b). Their future-time perspective is considerably greater than that of younger children, and they are more likely to have what Flavell calls "a sense of the game": an awareness that much of life consists of anticipating, formulating, and developing strategies for dealing with problems, whether the problem is planning a

Adolescents have attained the stage of cognitive development known as formal operations, in which they can reason about hypothetical problems and explore alternative possibilities in a systematic search for solutions.

household budget or estimating the motivations and probable behavior of other people (Flavell, 1985; Flavell & Ross, 1981; Ford, 1982).

From an information-processing perspective, adolescents are generally able to process more, and more complex, information than younger children, and to do so more quickly and efficiently (see Chapter 8). They appear to be able to accomplish this in part because of their increased ability to pay careful attention and to remember, and partly because they have developed a variety of information-processing strategies (e.g., increasingly powerful rules for solving problems) and are able to employ them selectively in accordance with the demands of a particular task (Brown, A. L., 1975; Brown, A. L. et al., 1983; Flavell, 1985; Sternberg, 1984).

Cognitive changes play a critical role in helping adolescents deal with increasingly complex educational and vocational demands. It would be virtually impossible to master such academic subjects as calculus or the use of metaphors in poetry without a high level of abstract thinking or the ability to think about statements that are unrelated to real objects in the world.

Hypothetical Thinking

One of the most important characteristics of adolescent thinking is the ability to entertain hypotheses or theoretical propositions that depart from immediately observable events. In contrast to younger children, who are preoccupied with the here and now, adolescents are likely to grasp not only the immediate state of things but also the state they might or could assume. The implications of this change alone are vast. For example, many adolescents show a new-found and frequently wearing talent for discovering a previously idealized parent's feet of clay— questioning the parent's values, comparing them with other, more understanding or less conservative parents, and accusing them of hypocritical inconsistencies between professed values and behavior. All of these changes appear to be at least partly dependent on changes in the adolescent's cognitive ability: "The awareness of the discrepancy between the actual and the possible also helps to make the adolescent a rebel. The [adolescent] is always comparing the possible with the actual and discovering that the actual is frequently wanting" (Elkind, 1968, p. 152).

The tendency of some adolescents to criticize existing social, political, and religious systems and to attempt to construct alternative systems is similarly dependent on the emerging capacity for formal operational thought. An adolescent's apparently passionate concern with the deficiencies of the social order and the creation of viable alternatives frequently turns out to be more a matter of word than of deed. Sometimes it seems that the young person is exercising new-found cognitive abilities for their own sake.

At the same time, however, it is important to recognize the positive aspects of the adolescent's newly acquired ability to conceptualize and reason abstractly about hypothetical possibilities. While younger adolescents may seem to be playing a game of ideas, this is nevertheless a vitally important and productive exercise. What may appear to an adult "to be vain rehashing or sterile questioning of old worn-out problems corresponds in reality, for the youngster, to youthful explorations and true discoveries" (Osterrieth, 1969, p. 15).

Cognitive Aspects of Personality Development

As noted earlier, a preoccupation with thought itself, particularly with one's own thoughts about oneself, is characteristic of formal operations. An adolescent girl or boy is likely to become more introspective and analytical. In addition, thought and behavior may appear to be egocentric (Elkind, 1968; Enright, Lapsley, & Shukla, 1979). Because adolescents think about themselves a lot, they are likely to conclude that other people, too, are subjecting their thoughts and feelings, personality characteristics, behavior, and appearance to critical scrutiny. This idea may well increase the adolescent's already strong feelings of self-consciousness.

Cognitive development also plays an important role in the emergence of a well-defined sense of identity:

> By getting away from the concrete, by reasoning, by "concentrating," by trying out hypotheses, he meets up with himself. Who is he, this person who thinks, who adopts an attitude, who speaks his opinion? What is he? What is it in him, what is this center where his ideas are shaped, where his thoughts are produced, where his assumptions are formulated? Is it not himself? (Osterrieth, 1969, pp. 15–16)

Some adolescents may employ intellectualization as a psychological defense to deal with troubling feelings. *Intellectualization* involves casting issues that are of immediate personal concern in an abstract, impersonal, philosophical form as a way of dealing with them. Thus, apparently impersonal, highly intellectual discussions of human sexuality, the role of aggression in human affairs, responsibility versus freedom, the nature of friendship, and the existence of God may reflect deep-seated personal and emotional concerns. While much of the motivation for the use of intellectualization may be to avoid anxiety, it nevertheless may give the adolescent important practice in thinking abstractly and formulating and testing hypotheses. In general, intellectualization as a defense is most likely to be employed by bright, well-educated middle- and upper-class youth.

ADOLESCENT SEXUALITY

Among the many developmental events that characterize puberty and the onset of adolescence, none is more dramatic than the physical and psychological changes associated with sexual development. These changes require many new adjustments on the part of the young person and contribute significantly to a changing self-image. As one 16-year-old expressed it, "When I was 14, my body started to go crazy" (Bell, R., 1980, p. 73).

Although sexuality in the broadest sense is a lifelong part of being human (even babies love to be held and may fondle their genitals), the hormonal changes accompanying puberty lead to stronger sexual feelings. These feelings are manifested differently in different individuals; even in the same person they may be expressed differently at different times. Some adolescents find themselves thinking more about sex and becoming sexually aroused more easily; others are less aware of sexual feelings and more excited by other interests. At the same age, one adolescent may be in love and going steady, another may be involved in sexual experimentation, and a third may feel that it is much too early for such activities (Bell, R., 1980; Conger, 1980; Conger & Petersen, 1984).

Sex Differences in Sexuality

For most boys, the rapid increase in sexual drive that accompanies puberty is difficult to deny and tends to be genitally oriented (Miller, P. Y. & Simon, 1980). Males perceive their sex drive as reaching a peak during adolescence. The frequency of total sexual outlet also reaches a peak in adolescence—primarily through masturbation, except for the minority of adolescents who are married or living together (Chilman, 1983).

Among adolescent girls, there appears to be a much wider range of individual differences. Some experience sexual desire in much the same way as the average male. But for the majority, sexual feelings are more diffuse and more closely related to the fulfillment of other needs, such as self-esteem, reassurance, affection, and love (Bell, R., 1980). There is a significant increase in sexual interests and behavior among members of both sexes during adolescence. Although sexual activity in general—and masturbation in particular (see page 586)—is greater among males than among females, the extent of the difference has decreased in recent years (Chilman, 1983; Conger, 1980, in press).

Young women still display more conservative attitudes toward sex than young men do. For example, in 1984, among American first-year college students nearly two-thirds of the males but less than one-third of the females agreed with the statement, "Sex is okay if people like each other" (Astin, Green, & Korn, 1987). On the other hand, when there is deep involvement, as in living together prior to marriage, differences are much smaller. Among American adolescents, only 32 percent of females and 21 percent of males said that they would not be willing to have intercourse in such circumstances (Norman & Harris, 1981).

In contrast to their Victorian forebears, a majority of today's adolescent females believe that women enjoy sex as much as men do, and only one in ten believes that women have less innate capacity for sexual pleasure than men do—a view that is clearly supported by recent research (Conger, 1980; Masters & Johnson, 1970; Masters, Johnson, & Kolodny, 1988). The female's physiological capacity for sexual response is greater than that of males (Masters & Johnson, 1970). In addition, sexual behavior (e.g., frequency of orgasm) varies much more widely among females than among males; even for a particular female such behavior may vary greatly at different times (Chilman, 1983; Conger, 1980).

Whether for biological or psychological reasons or both, sexuality appears to be more intimately bound up with other aspects of personality in the case of females. Erotic stimulation that cannot be related to oneself as a total person—because it is perceived as threatening, because it conflicts with existing values, because it is impersonal, or because it is aesthetically offensive—is more likely to "turn off" the average adolescent female than her male peer (Conger & Petersen, 1984; Katchodourian, 1985; Schmidt, 1975). Fantasies reported by both male and female college students during sexual arousal were most likely to concern petting or intercourse with "someone you love or are fond of" (Miller, P. Y. & Simon, 1980). However, fantasies of sexual activity with strangers for whom they had no particular emotional attachment were ranked a close second for males (79 percent) but not for females (22 percent). In contrast, "doing nonsexual things with someone you are fond of or in love with" ranked second for females (74 percent) but not for males (48 percent). For females, "the investment of erotic meaning in both explicitly sexual and nonsexual symbols appears to be contingent on the emotional context" (Miller, P. Y. & Simon, 1980, p. 403).

It may be that the greater sexual aggressiveness generally manifested by adolescent males is related, at least in part, to vastly greater increases in testosterone levels at puberty. It has been demonstrated that this hormone increases sexual and aggressive behavior in members of both sexes under experimental conditions (Hamburg & Trudeau, 1981; Katachourian, 1985; Petersen, 1988).

Changing Sexual Attitudes and Behavior

Today's adolescents are more open and honest about sex than their predecessors, and increasingly tend to base decisions about appropriate sexual behavior on personal values and judgment rather than conformity to institutionalized social codes (Conger, 1980, in press). This change has manifested itself in a variety of ways, ranging from greater freedom in sexual relations to a desire for more and better sex education, including access to birth control information (see Box 14.1). At the same time, however, most young people clearly oppose "exploitation, pressure or force in sex; sex solely for the sake of physical enjoyment without a personal relationship; and sex between people too young to understand what they are getting into" (Conger & Petersen, 1984, p. 283). What many adolescents seem to be saying is that the morality of sexual behavior can often be judged not so much by the nature of the act itself as by its meaning to the individuals involved.

In 1986, for example, American high school seniors were asked their reactions to the idea of a man and woman living together without being married. About one in four said that such couples were experimenting with "a worthwhile alternative lifestyle." Smaller minorities felt either that they were violating a basic principle of human morality or that they were living in a way that is destructive to society. In contrast, half expressed the view that the couples were "doing their own thing and not affecting anyone else" (Johnston, L. D., Bachman, & O'Malley, 1986, p. 194). Approximately three-fourths of contemporary adolescents believe that "it's all right for young people to have sex before getting married if they are in love with each other" (Conger & Petersen, 1984; Sorensen, 1973).

How are continuing changes in sexual attitudes and values among adolescents reflected in their behavior? The answer depends on *what* behaviors one is referring to, and among *which* adolescents. Available information indicates that among males, the number who have engaged in masturbation by age 19 has remained fairly stable at 85 to 90 percent since their parents' generation (Chilman, 1983; Conger & Petersen, 1984). But the number who masturbate at younger ages is increasing significantly—about 65 percent report masturbating by age 13, compared with 45 percent in the 1940s. Among females, there has been an increase in

Today adolescents increasingly base their decisions about appropriate sexual behavior on personal values rather than on institutionalized social codes.

BOX 14.1

Sex Education

Even though 85 percent of American parents favor sex education and think it fosters a healthy attitude toward sex (L. Harris, 1987), the subject remains highly controversial. A militant minority view sex education, even at the high school level, as dangerous and premature for "impressionable" adolescents, and as likely to lead to promiscuity and higher rates of adolescent pregnancy. Others believe sex is something that should be taught only by parents in the privacy of the home (Conger, 1988).

In the light of current statistics on adolescent premarital intercourse, pregnancy, and abortion, as well as the general social climate, it is difficult to see how sex education for adolescents could be viewed as premature (Hofferth, Kahn, & Baldwin, 1987; Zelnik & Kantner, 1980). Indeed, a recent nationwide study found that among young women who first had sex at age 15, only 58 percent had already taken or were currently taking a sex education course; for young men the comparable figure was even lower—only 26 percent (Marsiglio & Mott, 1986).

Moreover, while greater participation by parents is clearly desirable, the fact is that despite greater openness about sex in contemporary society, many parents still are not providing the knowledge their children need (Bell, R., 1980; Conger, 1987; Harris, 1987).

Interestingly, however, adolescents who report that they *are* able to discuss sex freely and openly with their parents are less, rather than more, likely to engage in premarital intercourse (Conger, 1988; Sorensen, 1973); of this group, those who are sexually active are less likely to become pregnant (see chart). In addition, recent research indicates that sex education programs are associated with better

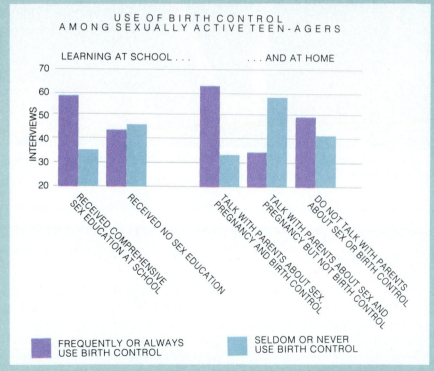

USE OF BIRTH CONTROL
AMONG SEXUALLY ACTIVE TEEN-AGERS

LEARNING AT SCHOOL . . .   . . . AND AT HOME

INTERVIEWS

RECEIVED COMPREHENSIVE SEX EDUCATION AT SCHOOL

RECEIVED NO SEX EDUCATION AT SCHOOL

TALK WITH PARENTS ABOUT SEX, PREGNANCY AND BIRTH CONTROL

TALK WITH PARENTS ABOUT SEX AND PREGNANCY BUT NOT BIRTH CONTROL

DO NOT TALK WITH PARENTS ABOUT SEX OR BIRTH CONTROL

FREQUENTLY OR ALWAYS USE BIRTH CONTROL

SELDOM OR NEVER USE BIRTH CONTROL

Source: Planned Parenthood Federation of America, 1986. Based on 350 in-person interviews among sexually active 12- to 17-year-olds, conducted during September and October 1986 by Louis Harris and Associates for Planned Parenthood.

communication with parents about pregnancy and conception (*Sex education*, 1986; Dawson, 1986).

The notion of some adults that adolescents have nothing left to learn about sex also is not supported by the facts. Many adolescents think they cannot become pregnant from their first intercourse, or if they do not have an orgasm or do not want to become pregnant (L. Harris, 1987; Kantner & Zelnik, 1973; *Teenage pregnancy*, 1981; Zelnik & Kantner, 1977, 1980). In one representative study, only 40 percent of 15- to 19-year-old adolescent American girls clearly understood the time in the menstrual cycle when the risk of pregnancy is highest (Kantner & Zelnik, 1973).

Finally, there is no consistent evidence that sex education, including information about contraception, increases the likelihood of becoming sexually active. On the other hand, there is considerable evidence that active adolescents who have had sex education are more likely to use effective contraceptive methods. In addition, teenagers who have had sex education courses are, if anything, less likely to become pregnant (Dawson, 1986; Marsiglio & Mott, 1986; *Sex education*, 1986.

masturbation at all ages; by age 13, the incidence is about 33 percent (in contrast to 15 percent in their mothers' generation); by age 20, it is about 60 percent (compared to about 30 percent for their mothers) (Conger, 1980; Haas, 1979; Kinsey, Pomeroy, & Martin, 1948; Kinsey, Pomeroy, Martin, & Gebhard, 1953). Masturbation is about three times as likely among adolescents who have engaged in sexual intercourse or petting to orgasm as among the sexually inexperienced (Conger, in press; Sorensen, 1973).

It seems that these changes in the incidence of masturbation are due largely to more tolerant social attitudes and a decline in myths about the harmful effects of masturbation. Masturbation itself is a normal developmental phenomenon. It becomes a problem only when it serves as a substitute for social and other activities in which the young person feels inadequate. But in such instances masturbation is not a cause of the individual's problems so much as response to them.

Petting appears to have increased somewhat in the past few decades, and it tends to occur slightly earlier. The major change, however, has probably been in the frequency of petting, the intimacy of the techniques involved, the frequency with which petting leads to erotic arousal or orgasm, and certainly, frankness about this activity (Chilman, 1983; Conger, 1980, in press; Haas, 1979).

Premarital Sexual Intercourse

A source of heated social, political, and personal controversy is the extent of premarital sexual intercourse among adolescents. Until recently opinions on this subject were rife, but comprehensive data (except in the case of college students) were scarce. Consequently, as late as the mid-1970s some social observers were proclaiming a "sexual revolution" while others asserted that young people were actually no more sexually active than their parents had been, just more open and honest about sex.

Recent national studies have made it clear that the youth revolution of the late 1960s did indeed lead to a transformation, not only in sexual attitudes and values but in sexual behavior as well (Hayes, 1987; Hofferth, Kahn, & Baldwin, 1987; Zelnik & Kantner, 1980). For example, among American women who were teenagers in the late 1950s and early 1960s, slightly over 7 percent reported having had premarital sexual intercourse by age 16 and less than one-third reported having done so by age 19 (Hofferth, Kahn, & Baldwin, 1987). By 1971 the picture had changed significantly, with almost one in four 16-year-olds and about half of 19-year-olds reporting premarital intercourse (see Table 14.3).

In the intervening years, rates of intercourse among all 15- to 19-year-old female teenagers have continued to increase, so that by 1982 (the last year for which representative national data are available) 30 percent of 16-year-olds and nearly three-fourths of 19-year-olds acknowledged having been sexually active (Hofferth et al., 1987).

Data for males are more sketchy, but overall changes are less dramatic for boys than for girls, and absolute incidence is consistently higher, especially at younger ages (Chilman, 1983; Conger, 1980). Thus, a limited national survey conducted in the early 1970s found that among teenage boys, 44 percent reported having had intercourse by age 16 and 72 percent had done so by age 19 (Sorensen, 1973). By 1979 a clear majority (56 percent) of 17-year-olds and more than three-fourths (77 percent) of 19-year-olds reported having been sexually active (Zelnik & Kantner, 1980). Comparable results were obtained in 1980 in another large, but somewhat less systematically controlled, national sample of adolescents aged 13 to 18. Among 13- to 15-year-olds, 41 percent of boys reported having had sexual intercourse; among those aged 16 to 18, 70 percent of boys had done so (Norman & Harris, 1981).

Homosexual Behavior and Orientation

Although over 90 percent of young people develop an exclusively heterosexual orientation by the end of adolescence, a minority develop an exclusively or predominantly homosexual orientation. Contrary to some popular conceptions, the incidence of homosexuality in our society does not appear to have increased in the last 40 years, although openness about homosexuality has increased dramatically (Bell, A. P., Weinberg, & Hammersmith, 1981; Chilman, 1983; Conger, 1980, in press; Hunt, 1974; Kinsey, Pomeroy, & Martin, 1948, 1953).

Why some young people become homosexual while most become heterosexual is still unclear. Some theorists have stressed the potential importance of social and psychological influences (e.g., disturbances in parent-child relationships); others emphasize genetic, hormonal, or other biological factors (Beach, 1977; Bell,

TABLE 14.3

Percentage of U.S. Teenage Women Who Had Ever Had Premarital Sexual Intercourse, by Race and Age, 1971–1982; Calculated from the 1982 National Survey of Family Growth

Race and Age	Year			
	1971	1976	1979	1982
TOTAL				
15–19	**31.7**	**39.0**	**43.4**	**45.2**
(Standardized)	(31.7)	(38.6)	(42.7)	(44.0)
15	14.6	10.8	21.9	18.6
16	23.5	26.4	27.1	30.0
17	30.7	37.4	47.0	41.8
18	36.9	54.0	54.4	57.8
19	54.0	65.8	64.8	73.4
WHITE				
15–19	**29.2**	**36.2**	**40.8**	**43.1**
(Standardized)	(29.2)	(36.0)	(40.0)	(42.0)
15	13.5	8.9	20.1	16.8
16	20.8	24.7	24.0	28.1
17	27.9	34.2	5.3	38.6
18	33.2	50.1	49.5	55.4
19	51.6	62.7	62.1	71.8
BLACK				
15–19	**51.2**	**56.1**	**61.2**	**56.5**
(Standardized)	(51.2)	(54.8)	(59.6)	(54.9)
15	22.7	23.2	33.1	27.9
16	45.1	37.3	45.2	40.0
17	51.9	57.1	58.1	56.4
18	68.1	78.3	85.7	73.7
19	73.3	85.0	81.8	82.5

Source: S. L. Hofferth, J. R. Kahn, & W. Baldwin. *Family Planning Perspectives*, 1987, 19, No. 2, 46–53. By permission.

A. P. & Weinberg, 1978; Green, 1980, 1988; Luria, Friedman, & Ross, 1987). It may well be that a complex interaction of biological, psychological, and social factors beginning early in life is involved, and that the nature of the interaction may vary from one individual to another (Bell, Weinberg, & Hammersmith, 1981). What is clear, as Alan Bell and his colleagues at the Kinsey Institute have observed, is that neither homosexuals nor heterosexuals are what they are by design. Homosexuals, in particular, cannot be dismissed as persons who simply refuse to conform. There is no reason to think it would be any easier for homosexual men or women to reverse their sexual orientation than it would be for heterosexual [individuals] to become predominantly or exclusively homosexual. (Bell, A. P. & Weinberg, 1978, p. 222)

With additional research, we may gain a better understanding of the genesis of sexual orientation. In the meantime, however, it should be possible, with greater self-understanding and understanding of others, for both homosexuals and heterosexuals to enjoy mature, constructive, and rewarding lives (Conger, in press).

Variations in Sexual Attitudes and Behavior

Although adolescents from families of lower socioeconomic status tend to initiate sexual activity at earlier ages (Hayes, 1987), it is among economically privileged, highly educated adolescents and youth, especially females, that the greatest changes in sexual attitudes and behavior have occurred. Before the mid-1960s the incidence of premarital intercourse among college seniors was about 55 percent for males and 25 percent for females. But by the beginning of the 1980s these figures had increased to a high of 82 percent for males and 76 percent for females (Chilman, 1983; Conger, 1980, in press). Black adolescents are more sexually active than whites; interestingly, however, the percentage of sexually active black adolescent females declined between 1979 and 1982, while it continued to rise for whites (see Table 14.3).

It is important to keep in mind that despite the "sexual revolution," many adolescents have not engaged in premarital sexual intercourse, including a majority of girls age 17 and under (Hofferth et al., 1987). Although a majority of nonvirgins report that sex has made their lives more meaningful, others report feelings of conflict and guilt, find themselves exploited or rejected, or discover belatedly that they have gotten in over their heads emotionally (Conger, 1980, in press). Especially after the first experience of intercourse, females are far more likely than males to have negative feelings about sex. While males are most likely to report being excited, satisfied, and happy, females most frequently report being afraid, guilty, worried, or embarrassed (Bell, R., 1980; Sorensen, 1973).

There are obviously dangers—particularly for females, who generally have stronger affiliative needs—in assuming that sexual involvement is "okay as long as you're in love" (Chilman, 1983). Encouraged by such a philosophy among their peers, adolescents may become involved in deeper emotional relationships than they can handle responsibly at a particular stage of maturity. Young people may also believe that their attitudes are more liberal than they actually are, with the result that sexual involvement may lead to unanticipated feelings of guilt, anxiety, or depression.

Pregnancy and Contraception

Certain practical problems are associated with adolescent sexuality, including the possibility of pregnancy and of sexually transmitted diseases, including those for which there is currently no cure, such as genital herpes and acquired immune deficiency syndrome (AIDS). Despite significant progress during the past decade, among female adolescents who were sexually active in 1982 only about half consistently used some form of contraception—up from approximately one-third in 1976. Compared to younger adolescents (age 15), older adolescents (age 19) are twice as likely to have used contraceptives in their most recent intercourse, including first intercourse (Zelnik & Kantner, 1977, 1980; Shah & Zelnik, 1981).

As a result of the widespread lack of proper contraceptive measures and the continuing increase in premarital intercourse among adolescents, in the United States alone well over 1 million 15- to 19-year-old girls (i.e., about 11 percent of this age group) become pregnant each year (Hayes, 1987). Two-thirds of these pregnancies are conceived out of wedlock. In addition, 125,000 girls under the age of 15 become pregnant each year (Edelman, 1987). More than one-third of sexually active adolescent girls become pregnant at some time during their adolescent years (Hayes, 1987; Jones et al., 1987; Zelnik & Kantner, 1980). (See Box 14.2.)

The consequences of this epidemic of adolescent pregnancies are serious indeed. In 1984, 47 percent of pregnant adolescents gave birth, while 40 percent had induced abortions; the remainder miscarried (Jones, E., Forrest, Goldman, Henshaw, Lincoln, Rosof, Westoff, & Wolf, 1985). Even in the 27 percent of adolescent pregnancies that occur postmaritally each year, problems are more frequent than in pregnancies of older women. (See Chapter 2 for a discussion of the health risks associated with teenage pregnancy.)

The rate of teenage pregnancy has increased dramatically and created an increased need for birth control counseling.

BOX 14.2

Teenage Pregnancy in Developed Countries

A recent study by the Alan Guttmacher Institute has found that the United States leads nearly all the developed countries in the incidence of adolescent pregnancy and childbearing—including other western industrialized nations with comparable levels of sexual activity. Pregnancy rates for white adolescents alone are higher than those in most other industrialized countries. Particularly troubling is the fact that the maximum difference in birthrates between the United States and other countries occurs among the most vulnerable adolescents, girls under 15; also, the United States is the only developed country in which adolescent pregnancy has *increased* in recent years (see chart).

Opponents of such preventive measures as sex education and access to counseling and contraceptive services for sexually active adolescents assert that such measures would further increase already high rates of adolescent pregnancy, abortion, and childbearing. Ironically, however, this comprehensive study found just the opposite. The countries with the most open and straightforward attitudes

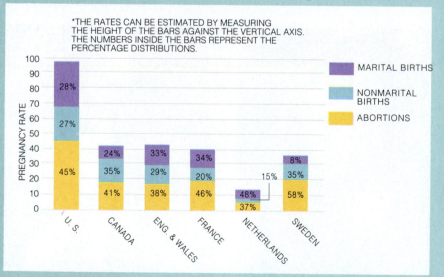

*THE RATES CAN BE ESTIMATED BY MEASURING THE HEIGHT OF THE BARS AGAINST THE VERTICAL AXIS. THE NUMBERS INSIDE THE BARS REPRESENT THE PERCENTAGE DISTRIBUTIONS.

Percentage distribution of pregnancies, pregnancy rates and outcomes for women aged 15–19, 1980/1981. (Adapted from E. F. Jones, J. D. Forrest, N. Goldman, S. K. Henshaw, R. Lincoln, J. J. Rosoff, C. F. Wertoff, and D. Wulf. Teenage pregnancy in developed countries: Determinants and policy implications. *Family Planning Perspectives*, 1985, 17, 53–63. By permission.)

toward sex, the most effective formal and informal sex education programs, and the most accessible counseling and contraceptive services for adolescents have the *lowest* rates of teenage pregnancy, abortion, and childbearing.

ADOLESCENT MOTHERS.   In addition to the risks of pregnancy, teenage mothers—90 percent of whom decide to keep their babies—generally face significant problems in other areas. They are twice as likely as their peers to drop out of school, less likely to gain employment, and more likely to end up on welfare (Burt, 1986; Edelman, 1987; Furstenberg, 1976; Furstenberg, Brooks-Gunn, & Morgan, 1987). Many still need mothering themselves and are ill prepared to take on the psychological, social, and economic responsibilities of motherhood; their knowledge of an infant's needs and capabilities is often unrealistic, leading to expectations and demands that their infants cannot meet (Conger, 1980, 1988). Moreover, single adolescent mothers have less chance of getting married than their peers, and a much greater chance of divorce if they do marry (Furstenberg & Brooks-Gunn, 1986). Even adolescents who are already married when they become pregnant, or who marry prior to the birth of their child, are far more likely to divorce than those who become mothers after age 20. Nevertheless, with adequate social

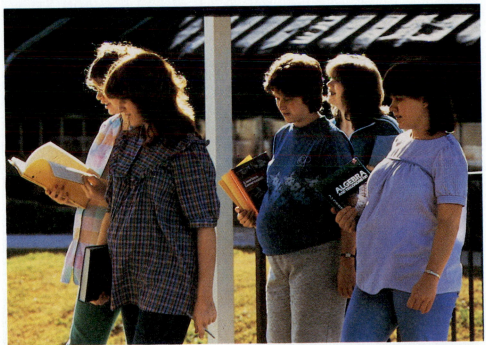

Special programs for pregnant teenagers like these in Fort Worth, Texas, help adolescent mothers complete high school and find regular employment.

support substantial numbers of adolescent mothers do go on to complete high school, become effective parents, escape public assistance, and find fixed regular employment (Furstenberg, Brooks-Gunn, & Morgan, 1987b).

FAILURE TO USE CONTRACEPTIVES. In recent surveys the major reasons given by teenagers for not using contraceptives were that they (usually mistakenly) thought they could not become pregnant—because of time of month, age, or infrequency of intercourse—or that contraceptives were not available when they needed them. As the Planned Parenthood Federation notes, the first set of reasons could be remedied with better education, the second with more adequate service programs (Conger, 1988; *Teenage pregnancy*, 1981). (See Box 14.3.)

BOX 14.3

Preventing Adolescent Pregnancy

Although there are no quick fixes, much can be done to reduce the rate of adolescent pregnancy, but only if the problem is approached realistically. First, we need age-appropriate family-life education, including sex education from the early school years through adolescence. Adolescents in particular need to be told the facts about sexuality and parenthood; even more important, they need help integrating that information into their thinking about themselves and their futures (Edelman, 1987). And we need to encourage much greater parental participation in these efforts.

Sexually active adolescents also need access to contraceptive methods. In many instances these needs can best be met in the context of adolescent clinics, in or out of the school setting, that provide comprehensive, high-quality, easily accessible health services for adolescents and preadolescents (*Adolescent pregnancy*, 1986; Conger, 1988; Schorr, 1988.) At four of the oldest school-based clinics, located in St. Paul, Minnesota, the overall annual rate of first-time pregnancies has been reduced from 80 per 1000 to 29; repeat pregnancies have been reduced to only 1.4 percent, compared to 33 percent nationally (*Adolescent pregnancy*, 1986; Edelman, 1987; Kirby, 1985). One of the great advantages of adolescent clinics is that sexuality in all its aspects can be dealt with in the context of overall health care by a staff that is attuned to the special needs and concerns of this age group.

Better sex education and family planning services alone will not solve the problem of adolescent pregnancy, however, particularly for high-risk adolescents. Motivation to avoid pregnancy is essential. And such motivation can come only when young people feel good about themselves and have a "clear vision of a successful and self-sufficient future" (Edelman, 1987, p. 58). This requires opportunities to build academic and work-related skills, job opportunities, life-planning assistance, and comprehensive health and mental health services.

An excellent example of the kind of approach that is needed is provided by the Children's Defense Fund (CDF) in their Agenda for Adolescent Pregnancy Prevention and Youth Self-Sufficiency (Edelman, 1987; *Adolescent pregnancy*, 1987). This program calls on federal, state, and local governments to provide more comprehensive sex education and life-planning programs in the schools. But it also advocates establishing or strengthening vocational scholarships, community learning centers, job creation programs, dropout prevention programs, adolescent health services, and after-school care for 10- to 15-year-olds. According to Marian Wright Edelman, president of CDF, "We need investments in young people that will enable them not only to make responsible decisions but to move along a steady path toward self-sufficiency" (*Adolescent pregnancy*, 1987, p. 4).

Psychological studies comparing sexually active adolescent girls who do and do not use contraceptives (or use them rarely) have found that those who do not use contraceptives are more likely to have fatalistic attitudes: to feel powerless to control their own lives, to have a low sense of personal competence, and to have a passive, dependent approach to male-female relationships. They are also more inclined to take risks and to cope with anxiety by attempting to deny dangers rather than face up to them. In contrast, consistent contraceptive use is more likely among female adolescents who are older, are in love and involved in an ongoing relationship, have high levels of self-esteem and self-confidence, are making normal progress in school, have positive attitudes toward their parents, and received sex education early and at home, rather than from an acquaintance (Chilman, 1983).

Some adolescents avoid using contraceptives because they fear that it would spoil the spontaneity of the relationship or because they think it would indicate that they *expect* to have intercourse. One sign that the double standard persists in some circles is that frank pursuit of sexual relations is still considered more acceptable for boys than for girls (Goodchilds & Zellman, 1984; Santrock, 1987). For a significant number of adolescents, it is more acceptable for a girl to be swept away by the passion of the moment than to take contraceptive precautions (Morrison, 1985). Interestingly, girls who frankly accept their sexuality and girls who are able to discuss sexual matters easily with their parents are more likely to use contraceptives than those who deny it to themselves or others (Chilman, 1983; Conger, 1987; Hornick, Doran, & Crawford, 1979).

Among male adolescents, those who are most likely to employ contraceptive measures are older, more experienced in dating, and more organized and responsible in their general approach to life. They also tend to have parents who approve of their sexual involvement. Males who are least likely to employ contraception tend either to be sexually naive or to be permissively reared and "exploitive," believing that contraception is the female's responsibility (Goldfarb et al., 1977; Kelley, 1979).

DESIRE FOR PREGNANCY.   Contrary to frequently expressed opinions on the subject, only one in fifteen pregnant adolescents in a national sample stated that she did not use contraceptives because she was trying to have a baby, and only one in eleven indicated that she "didn't mind" getting pregnant. However, among adolescents who either seek or do not object to pregnancy, a common theme is emotional deprivation. In the words of one pregnant 15-year-old, "I guess for once in my life, I wanted to have something I could call my own, that I could love and that would love me." Other, related motivations may include being accepted as an adult, getting back at one's parents, "holding" a boyfriend, gaining attention from peers, escaping from school, or just looking for some change in an unrewarding existence (Chilman, 1983).

Of all the changes brought about by the youth culture of the late 1960s and early 1970s, greater sexual freedom and openness appear to be the most enduring. There has been a shift toward premarital intercourse as an accepted practice, and especially toward a steady relationship with only one partner as the most frequent and the most socially approved pattern among sexually experienced adolescents, that is unlikely to be reversed. What one must hope is that adolescents who do become involved in sexual relationships can be helped to become mature, informed, responsible, and sure of their own identities and value systems, as well as concerned about the welfare of others. If this can be achieved, the casualties of the sexual revolution can be reduced to a minimum and sex, as a vital part of human relationships, can promote growth toward maturity and emotional fulfillment.

PARENTAL RELATIONS AND THE DEVELOPMENT OF AUTONOMY

During adolescence parents and their sons and daughters must learn to establish new kinds of relationships with each other. Parents must be able to recognize—and encourage—the adolescent's needs for increased, age-appropriate independence. Young people require sufficient freedom from parental control to express themselves as individuals with needs and feelings of their own, to make decisions about their own lives, and to take responsibility for the consequences of those decisions (Conger, 1979, in press; Steinberg & Hill, 1978; Youniss & Smollar, 1985).

When parents continue to think of an adolescent as "our darling baby" or "our little boy" and treat him or her accordingly, they create a prescription for later problems in the form of explosive rebellion or inappropriate dependence. However, adolescents also need their parents' guidance and support, especially in early adolescence. The need for dependence continues to exist, often in an uneasy and fragile alliance with the need for greater independence. Partly because so many things are changing in the adolescent's world, the young person urgently needs a base of security and stability—something to take for granted while other, more immediate concerns are worked out (Conger, 1979; in press).

Contrary to the arguments of some theorists, the development of age-appropriate autonomy does not require that the adolescent abandon family ties. Indeed, under favorable circumstances the development of age-appropriate autonomy is a dual process, providing *both* for separateness, individuality, and self-exploration *and* for continuing family connectedness, encouragement, and mutual support (Cooper, C. R., Grotevant, & Condon, 1983; Youniss, 1983; Youniss & Smollar, 1985).

As adolescence proceeds, there is a gradual shift away from unilateral parental authority toward more cooperative interactions. Although parents can—and do—continue to assert unilateral authority at times, particularly with respect to basic social obligations like schoolwork, in other matters (e.g., personal problems or concerns) they act as advisors who are willing to listen and seek to understand (Youniss & Smollar, 1985). In addition, adolescents spend much of their social and personal life outside the family circle, particularly with peers. Consequently, they are able to gain independence from parental authority in many more areas of their lives than is true for younger children (Hill, J. P. & Holmbek, 1987; Wright & Keple, 1981; Youniss & Smollar, 1985).

Changing Perceptions of Parents

As adolescents gain in cognitive ability, their perceptions of their parents undergo a corresponding shift (Youniss, 1980). Younger children are likely to perceive their parents as "*figures* who have knowledge and power to get things done, especially those things children need or want" (Youniss & Smollar, 1985, p. 75). In contrast, adolescents are better able to differentiate parents as *persons* (with unique needs and feelings) from the *roles* parents play in carrying out their responsibilities as mothers and fathers. As one older adolescent girl said about her current relationship with her mother, "I'm more independent of her. Also, I am more free with my opinions even when I disagree. I realize she's not only my mother but an individual herself and I take her more on that level now. We still turn to each other when we have problems. We're still close" (Youniss & Smollar, 1985, p. 80). Similarly, a 15-year-old girl said of her mother: "She respects me more and lets me be on my own more. Treats me like a person, consults my opinion. I am a voice that is heard. Five years ago she was just a mother, now she's a person" (Youniss & Smollar, 1985, p. 80).

Variations in Parental Behavior

AUTHORITATIVE PARENTS. For parents to be perceived as persons and not simply as parental authority figures, they must act accordingly. As indicated in Chapter 12, parents like those described here tend to be *authoritative* or *democratic* (Baumrind, 1968, 1975; Elder, 1980). They value both autonomous will and disciplined behavior. They encourage verbal give-and-take, and when they exercise parental authority in the form of demands or prohibitions, they explain their reasons for doing so (Block, 1987; Cohler & Boxer, 1984; Lesser & Kandel, 1969). The following description by a 16-year-old girl is typical of such parents:

> I guess the thing I think is great about my parents, compared to those of a lot of kids, is that they really listen. And they realize that eventually I'm going to have to live my own life—what I'm going to do with it. A lot of the time when I explain what I want to do, they'll go along with it. Sometimes, they'll warn me of the consequences I'll have to face if I'm wrong, or just give me advice. And sometimes, they just plain tell me no. But when they do, they explain why, and that makes it easier to take. (Conger, 1979, p. 49)

Research has shown that such parents are most likely to foster the development of confidence and self-esteem, responsibility, social competence, autonomy, and close, positive relations between parent and child (Bachman, 1970; Elder, 1980; Lesser & Kandel, 1969; Santrock, 1984).

AUTHORITARIAN AND AUTOCRATIC PARENTS.   Authoritarian and autocratic parents do not feel an obligation to explain the reasons for their directives, and they view unquestioning obedience as a virtue (Baumrind, 1968, 1975; Elder, 1980). Some parents may take this stance out of a feeling of hostility or because they cannot be bothered with explanations and arguments. Others, however, do so because they think this is the way to develop "respect for authority." One mistake that they make is that although they may suppress dissent, they usually do not eliminate it; indeed, they are likely to encourage resentment. Adolescents with autocratic parents are less likely to be self-reliant and able to think and act for themselves, probably because they are not given enough opportunities to test their own ideas or take independent responsibility and because their opinions have not been viewed as worthy of consideration (Elder, 1980; Lewis, 1982). They also are likely to be less self-confident, less independent, less creative, less intellectually curious, less mature in their moral development, and less flexible in approaching intellectual, academic, and practical everyday problems than adolescents with authoritative parents. And they are more likely to view their parents as unaffectionate, rejecting, and unreasonable or wrong in their expectations and demands (Baumrind, 1968, 1975; Conger & Petersen, 1984; Elder, 1980; Lesser & Kandel, 1969, Santrock, 1984).

LAISSEZ-FAIRE PARENTS.   Parents who are permissive or neglecting, or who assume a false and exaggerated egalitarianism, also do not provide the kind of support that adolescents need. Neglecting parents let adolescents "do their own thing," either because they are not involved or do not care. Other parents have distorted notions of parental responsibility. Among middle-class adolescents, high-risk drug use and other forms of socially deviant behavior occur most frequently among those whose parents say they value individuality, self-understanding, readiness for change, maximization of human potential, and egalitarianism in the family, but actually use these proclaimed values to avoid assuming parental responsibility (Blum, 1972; Conger, 1979, in press; Jessor & Jessor, 1975, 1977). Such parents allow their children to drift without offering them dependable models of responsible adult behavior. Moreover, no matter how much children and adolescents may protest at times, they do not really want their parents to be equals. They want and need them to be *parents*—friendly, understanding parents, but parents nonetheless, models of adult behavior.

In brief, it appears that democratic, authoritative parental practices, with frequent explanations of expectations and rules of conduct, foster responsible independence in several ways. First, they provide opportunities for increasing autonomy under the guidance of interested parents who communicate with the young person and exercise appropriate degrees of control. Second, they promote positive identification with the parents, based on love and respect for the child rather than rejection or indifference. Finally, they show by example that autonomy is possible within the framework of a democratic order (Conger, in press).

Family Communication

Changing long-established patterns of parent-child interaction in order to adapt to the changes brought on by puberty and adolescence is seldom easy, either for parents or for their children. But transitional difficulties and conflicts can be greatly reduced by effective communication and openness within the family (Barnes, H. & Olson, 1985; Grotevant & Cooper, 1983; Youniss, 1983). In a recent large study of essentially normal families, it was found that families with better communication between parents and adolescents were also higher in family cohesion, adaptability, and satisfaction (Barnes, H. & Olson, 1986). Indeed, effective communication plays a vital role in helping family members strike a balance between separateness from and connectedness to one another (Barnes, H. & Olson, 1985; Grotevant & Cooper, 1983). Recent research indicates that effective family communication fosters adolescent identity formation and mature role-taking ability (Cooper, Grotevant, & Condon, 1983). In contrast, studies of parent-child interaction in troubled families, or in families with a mentally ill parent or child, have often found distortions in the capacity of parents and child to communicate effectively with one another (Goldstein, Baker, & Jamison, 1980; Rutter, 1980; Wynne, Singer, Bartko, & Toohey, 1976).

ADOLESCENTS AND THEIR PEERS

Peers play a crucial role in the psychological and social development of most children and adolescents. This is especially true in age-segregated technologically based societies like our own, in which entry into the adult world or work and family responsibility is increasingly delayed. The role played by peers in adolescence is especially critical. Relations with both same- and opposite-sex peers during the adolescent years serve as prototypes for adult relationships—in social relations, at work, and in interactions with members of the opposite sex. A young man or woman who has not learned how to get along with others of the same sex and to establish satisfactory heterosexual relationships by the time he or she reaches adulthood is likely to face serious obstacles in the years ahead (Conger, 1979).

Adolescents also are more dependent on peer relationships than younger children are, simply because their ties to parents become progressively looser as they gain greater independence. In addition, relations with family members are likely to become charged with conflicting emotions in the early years of adolescence—dependent yearnings exist alongside of independent striving; hostility is mixed with love; and conflicts occur over cultural values and social behavior. Consequently, it becomes difficult for the adolescent to share many areas of his or her inner life and outward behavior with parents.

In several related studies, more than two out of three adolescents said that a close friend understood them better than their parents did; that they felt more "themselves" with their friend; and that at this time in their life they could learn more from their friend than from their parents (Youniss & Smollar, 1985). Parents, in turn, having managed to repress many of the painful emotional ups and downs of their own adolescence, may have difficulty understanding and sharing their own adolescent sons' and daughters' problems, even though they make an effort to do so and are truly interested in the welfare of their children (Conger & Petersen, 1984).

If parents are hostile, neglecting, or exploitative, interested and competent peers may sometimes provide a physical and psychological escape from a difficult family situation and a source of understanding and support as well. They may also serve as alternative role models for achieving mutually rewarding interactions with others (Conger, 1971, 1979; Hartup, 1970, 1983). For example, a girl whose father has acknowledged her worth only when she has accomplished some socially approved external goal, such as high grades in school, may learn from a male peer that it is possible to be appreciated for herself alone—for who she is rather than for what she can do. An egalitarian male friend may demonstrate to the son of a competitive, authoritarian father that not all relationships between males need to be characterized by competition or by patterns of domination and submission.

Of course, there is another side to the coin. Relations with peers during this vulnerable stage can sometimes be harmful. For example, a boy or girl who is put down, laughed at, or rejected in his or her initial efforts to establish heterosexual relationships or to join a high school clique may acquire anxious, avoidant responses to such situations that will prove difficult to extinguish. Moreover, adolescents may be pressured by their peers into suspending their own judgment and engaging in behaviors that they may later regret (Conger, in press; Conger & Petersen, 1984).

Obviously, it is desirable that the majority of an adolescent's experiences with peers be positive, for more than at any other time of life, the young person needs to be able to share strong and often confusing emotions, doubts, and dreams (Kniesel, 1987). Adolescence is typically a time of intense sociability, but it is also often a time of intense loneliness (Avery, 1982; Bennan, 1982; Moore, D. & Schultz, 1983). Consequently, being accepted by peers in general, and especially by one or more close friends, may make a great difference in the young person's life.

Conformity to Peer Culture

Because of the heightened importance of the peer group during adolescence, the motivation to conform to the values, customs, and fads of the peer culture

Conformity to the values, customs, and fads of the peer group increases during adolescence.

increases during this period. Although evidence of a need for conformity to the peer group is clearly observable in middle childhood (see Chapter 11), there is a rather rapid rise in conformity needs and behavior during the preadolescent and early adolescent years, followed by a gradual but steady decline from middle through late adolescence (Berndt, 1979; Hartup, 1983; Steinberg & Silverberg, 1986).

The need to conform to peers may vary with socioeconomic background, relationships with parents and other adults, school environment, and personality factors (Brownstone & Willis, 1971; Clasen & Brown, 1985; Cooper, C. R. & Ayers-Lopez, 1985; Costanzo & Shaw, 1966; Steinberg & Silverberg, 1986). For example, children and adolescents with a strong tendency toward self-blame scored significantly higher in conformity than those who were low or medium in self-blame, and young people with low status among their peers are more conforming than those with high status (Coleman, 1980; Costanzo, 1970). Adolescents with high self-esteem and strong feelings of competence are less conforming than their peers (Cooper, C. R. & Ayers-Lopez, 1985; Hartup, 1983).

Parental vs. Peer Influences

Many people believe that parental and adolescent peer group values are mutually exclusive and that heightened peer group dependence and conformity lead to a sharp decline in parental influence. This is not the case, however, at least for most adolescents. In the first place, there is usually a considerable overlap between the values of parents and those of peers because of similarities in their cultural backgrounds (Conger, 1971, 1975; Lerner & Knapp, 1975). In addition, neither parental nor peer influence is monolithic, extending to all areas of adolescent decision making and behavior (Clasen & Brown, 1985; Larson, 1972a, 1972b; Wilks, 1986). The weight given to a parent or peer's opinion depends to a large extent on the adolescent's appraisal of its relative value in a specific situation. For example, peer influence (especially that of same-sex peers) is more likely to dominate in such matters as tastes in music and entertainment, fashions in clothing and language, patterns of same- and opposite-sex peer interaction, and the like. Parental influence is more likely to dominate in such areas as underlying moral and social values and understanding of the adult world (Brittain, 1966, 1969; Conger, 1971; Sebald & White, 1980; Wilks, 1986).

Studies that measure conformity to parents and peers separately have found that, on the average, conformity to parents tends to decline during preadolescence and early adolescence while conformity to peer influence rises (Berndt, 1979; Steinberg & Silverberg, 1986). Not until middle and late adolescence do increases in *overall* autonomy occur, for only then does conformity both to parents *and* to peers decline for a majority of young people—most dramatically in the case of antisocial behavior (see Figure 14.5).

Finally, we tend to overlook the important fact that the need for rigid conformity to *either* parents or peers varies enormously from one adolescent to another (Berndt, 1979; Conger, 1971, 1979; Larson, 1972a, 1972b; Steinberg & Silverberg, 1986). Thus, more self-confident, democratically (authoritatively) reared adolescents may be able to profit from the views and learning experiences provided by both parents and peers without being strongly dependent on either or unduly

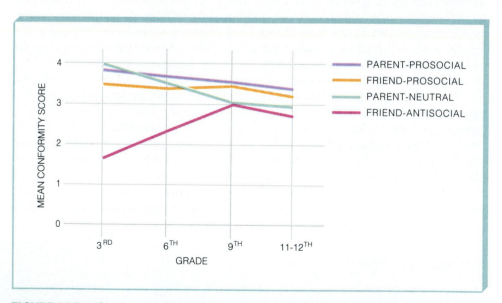

FIGURE 14.5   Changes in conformity to peers and to parents during adolescence. (Adapted from L. Steinberg, *Adolescence*. New York: Alfred A. Knopf, 1985. Adapted from T. J. Berndt, Developmental changes in conformity to peers and parents. *Developmental Psychology*, 1979, 15, 606–616.)

troubled by differences between them (Cooper, C. R. & Ayers-Lopez, 1985; Hartup, 1983; Stone & Church, 1973). Ironically, the adolescent who has gained the most confidence (as a result of such child-rearing techniques) and who is least concerned with popularity and most individualistic, may find that peers flock around him or her as a tower of strength.

Friendships and Identity Development

Friendships hold a special place among adolescents' peer relationships. Compared to other peer interactions, friendships typically are more intimate, involve more intense feelings, and are more honest and open and less concerned with self-conscious attempts at role playing in order to gain popularity and social acceptance (Berndt, 1982; Douvan & Adelson, 1966; Youniss & Smollar, 1985).

In one intensive study, middle-class adolescents of both sexes selected "close friend" as the person with whom they were most likely to "talk openly" and share "true feelings." The relationship was viewed as reciprocal; close friends "are not afraid to talk about . . . doubts and fears"; they "depend on each other for advice"; and even when they disagree, they listen to each others' reasons for thinking as they do (Youniss & Smollar, 1985, p. 103).

In view of the sensitivity of adolescents to the potential dangers involved in revealing their inner feelings, it is not surprising that they place particular emphasis on the need for security when they discuss the requirements of friendship: They want the friend to be loyal, trustworthy, and a reliable source of support in any emotional crisis (Berndt, 1982; Cooper & Ayers-Lopez, 1985). Indeed, untrustworthy behavior is cited by adolescents as the primary cause of serious conflict between close friends (Hartup, 1983; Youniss & Smollar, 1985). In the words of a 14-year-old girl from an urban ghetto, "A friend don't talk behind your back. If they are a true friend they help you get out of trouble and they will always be right behind you and they help you get through stuff. And they never snitch on you. That's what a friend is" (Konopka, 1976, p. 85).

Owing to the freedom of close friends to criticize each other, an adolescent can learn to modify behavior, tastes, or ideas without the painful experience of rejection. At their best, friendships help young people learn to deal both with their own complex feelings and with those of others. They can serve as a kind of therapy by allowing free expression of suppressed feelings of anger or anxiety and by providing evidence that others share many of the same doubts, hopes, fears, and seemingly dangerous feelings. As one 16-year-old girl expressed it, "My best friend means a lot to me. We can talk about a lot of things I could never talk about with my parents or other kids—like hassles we're getting or problems we're worried about, and like ideals and things. It really helps to know you're not the only one that has things that bother them" (Conger, 1979, p. 70).

Finally, and most broadly, close friendships may play a crucial role in helping young people develop a sense of their own identity. By sharing their experiences, their plans, their hopes and fears—in brief, by explaining themselves to each other—adolescent friends are also learning to understand themselves. There is an implicit awareness that self-definition and a coherent view of external reality cannot be achieved solely through reflection, that without the corrective functions of an external voice, one "risks self-delusion or egoism" (Youniss & Smollar, 1985, p. 167). In the words of one adolescent, "You can't always decide what you want to do yourself. You need a second opinion" (Youniss & Smollar, 1985, pp. 164–165). There is also awareness that mutual understanding is a reciprocal process: "You have to give a friend advice when he has a problem because a lot of times when a person is involved in a problem, he can't see it too well" (Youniss & Smollar, 1985, p. 164).

In addition, when a friend who "really understands" you still likes you and values you, your own confidence and self-esteem are bolstered (Bell, R., 1980; Erikson, 1968). In short, under favorable circumstances friendships may help the adolescent define his or her identity and gain greater confidence and pride in it.

Relationships with Opposite-Sex Peers

In our society the traditional vehicle for fostering individual heterosexual relationships has been the institution of dating. Although dating is much less formal and structured today than it was in earlier generations, the characteristics adolescents say they look for in a prospective date, the "rules of the game" that they anticipate or desire, and the personal doubts and anxieties they share are not nearly as new and different as one might expect (Bell, R., 1980). Young people are still concerned with such questions as "Does he like me?" "If I ask her to go out with me, will she turn me down?" "Will he call?" "Will I know what to say and how to act if I go out with her?" "What about making out?"

Many contemporary adolescents, like their peers of an earlier day, are concerned about what kinds of sexual activity are or are not appropriate at various stages of the dating process, and about how to initiate or respond to sex-related behavior. Although sexual standards are generally more liberal, most adolescents still expect the boy to take the lead in "making out": Nearly two out of three adolescent girls said that they prefer the boy to take the lead, although fewer than one out of four boys would be "turned off" by the girl taking the lead. (Bell, R., 1980; Bell, R. & Wildflower, 1983; Lindsay, 1985; Johnston, L. D., Bachman, & O'Malley, 1987).

GOING STEADY.   In a national survey adolescents were asked if they were going steady at the present time. Eleven percent of 13- to 15-year-old boys and 31 percent of 16- to 18-year-old boys said that they were going steady. Among girls, the comparable figures were 22 percent for 13- to 15-year-olds and 40 percent for 16- to 18-year-olds (Conger, in press; Gallup, 1979).

An adolescent who begins restricting his or her peer relations to one member of the opposite sex at too early an age is likely to miss a number of important developmental experiences. For one thing, the young person may never achieve the benefits of like-sex friendships, which can be very important in adult life, even after marriage. For another, when young people begin going steady at an age when they are both emotionally and socially immature, their relationship is likely to have these qualities; moreover, their further development toward becoming mature, self-reliant individuals may be jeopardized. They may tend to use their relationship as a way of avoiding other important developmental tasks, such as gaining autonomy and a clear sense of their own identity. Finally and most obviously, they may miss the invaluable opportunity adolescence provides to get to know, understand, and enjoy a wide variety of acquaintances of both sexes.

INTIMACY. Among girls, the capacity for emotional intimacy in relationships with both opposite- and same-sex peers usually develops sooner and more intensely than is true for boys (Blyth, Hill, & Thiel, 1982; McCabe & Collins, 1979; Sharbany, Gershoni, & Hoffman, 1981; Steinberg, 1988) (see Figure 14.6). Moreover, adolescent girls tend to place somewhat greater emphasis on the intimate, emotional, interpersonal aspects of boy-girl relationships, while boys are more likely to emphasize shared activities and interests. Even in late adolescence, however, most dating relationships tend to be rather stereotyped and superficial, and do not involve a high degree of intimacy (Hodgson & Fisher, 1979; Kacerguis & Adams, 1980; Orlofsky, Marcia, & Lesser, 1973).

ADOLESCENT LOVE. In some cases adolescent romances evolve gradually into stable, committed, long-term relationships; more frequently they involve an "intense emotional experience that lasts a while and then changes" (Bell, R., 1980, p. 68). Nevertheless, during the relationship the feelings can be just as vital, and the capacity for joy or despair just as great, as in adult love affairs. To be in love with someone who does not reciprocate is painful; it is "even more painful when you are still in love with someone who's no longer in love with you" (Bell, R., 1980, p. 69). For adults to dismiss adolescent "puppy love" as not serious (or even as amusing) indicates lack of sensitivity—as well as a short memory.

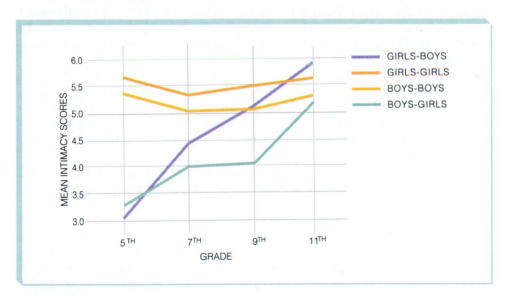

FIGURE 14.6 Age differences in reported intimacy in same- and opposite-sex relationships. (Adapted from R. Sharabany, R. Gershoni, and J. Hofman, Girlfriend, boyfriend: Age and sex differences in intimate friendship. *Developmental Psychology*, 1981, 17, 800–808. By permission.)

Overall, it appears that the young person who is best prepared for both social and vocational responsibilities in adult life, and also for the intimate, emotional demands of marriage, will be one who has been able to try out a variety of social and personal roles. Optimally, this means involvement both with opposite-sex peers and with close friends of the same sex in the early years of adolescence. In the later years, it also means opportunities to develop meaningful, trusting, and mutually supportive relationships with an opposite-sex peer.

SUMMARY

Adolescence has long been considered a more difficult stage of development than the middle-childhood years. However, the concept of adolescence as a psychologically complex stage worthy of scientific study did not emerge until the end of the nineteenth century.

Adolescence is a period of rapid physical, sexual, psychological, cognitive, and social change. It begins with puberty, the developmental phase in which sexual maturation becomes evident. At this time the pituitary gland begins releasing previously inhibited hormones, which in turn stimulate other glands to begin releasing hormones that affect growth and sexual development. The hormonal difference between the sexes is a difference in the proportions of masculinizing and feminizing hormones present in males and females.

A growth spurt—an accelerated rate of increase in height and weight—occurs at puberty. In both sexes the growth spurt lasts about 4½ years, but it peaks about two years earlier in girls than in boys. Changes in height and weight are accompanied by changes in body proportions. Sex differences in body shape also are magnified during early adolescence.

In males, sexual maturation begins with an increase in the growth of the testes and scrotum, followed by an acceleration in growth of the penis, the appearance of axillary hair, and a lowering of the voice. In females, the first sign of sexual maturity is the appearance of pubic hair and "budding" of the breasts. These changes are followed by accelerated growth of the reproductive organs and finally by menarche (onset of menstruation).

For adolescent girls, the onset of menstruation is a symbol of "becoming a woman." However, a majority of American adolescent girls react negatively to menarche, partly because of the negative attitudes of others and partly because of the associated physical discomfort. For adolescent boys, uncontrolled erection and initial ejaculation may be a source of worry and embarrassment.

Early-maturing males face higher expectations of mature behavior and have an advantage in many activities, especially athletics. Late-maturing males are more likely to be "treated like children" and are likely to have more difficulty excelling in athletics and other activities. These differences result in personality differences that tend to favor early-maturing boys, who are likely to be more self-assured and able to engage easily in socially appropriate behavior.

The effects of early versus late maturation are generally less extensive and more variable for girls than for boys. Initially, early-maturing girls tend to be less satisfied with their body image, more restless and moody, and less popular with same-sex peers than late-maturing girls. However, by late adolescence early-maturing girls have become more popular with peers of both sexes as well as more self-possessed and self-directed.

Continuing cognitive development, including the advent of the stage of formal operations, allows adolescents to think more abstractly, to formulate and test hypotheses, and to consider what might be, not merely what is. These abilities often lead adolescents to criticize parental and social values. Adolescent thought and behavior may also appear *egocentric*; young people may conclude that others are as preoccupied with their behavior and appearance as they themselves are. Adolescent cognitive development also plays an important role in personality development and in the formation of a clear sense of identity.

Perhaps the most dramatic changes associated with adolescence have to do with sexuality. Boys experience a rapid increase in sexual drive, whereas for many girls sexual feelings are more diffuse and more closely related to the fulfillment of other needs. Although there is a significant increase in sexual interests and behavior among members of both sexes, young women display more conservative attitudes toward sex than young men do.

Today's adolescents are more open and honest about sex than their predecessors, and increasingly tend to judge the morality of sexual behavior not so much by the nature of the act itself as by its meaning to the individuals involved. Recent national studies have shown that there has been a transformation not only in sexual attitudes and values but in sexual behavior as well. Rates of premarital intercourse have increased among teenagers, especially girls.

Among the problems associated with adolescent sexuality are the possibility of pregnancy and sexually transmitted diseases. Only about half of female adolescents who are sexually active consistently use some form of contraception; as a result, more than one-third of sexually active adolescent girls become pregnant during their adolescent years. Those who decide to keep their babies are twice as likely as their peers to drop out of school, less likely to gain employment, and more likely to end up on welfare.

Teenagers who do not use contraceptives either believe (usually mistakenly) that they cannot become pregnant or are unable to obtain contraceptives when they need them. Compared with those who use contraceptives, they are more likely to have fatalistic attitudes and are more inclined to take risks. Among those who seek or do not object to pregnancy, a common theme is emotional deprivation.

Variations in parental behavior affect the ease with which adolescents make the transition from dependent child to independent adult. Authoritative parents, who value both autonomous will and disciplined behavior, are most likely to foster the development of confidence, responsibility, and autonomy. Authoritarian parents, in contrast, tend to suppress dissent but they cannot eliminate it, and their adolescent children are less likely to be self-reliant and able to think and act for themselves. Parents who are permissive or neglecting also fail to provide the kind of support that adolescents need; they allow their children to drift without offering them dependable models of responsible adult behavior.

Peers play a crucial role in the psychological and social development of most adolescents. Relations with peers serve as prototypes for adult relationships. Adolescents also are more dependent on peer relationships than younger children are. Motivation to conform to the peer culture increases during early adolescence; however, conformity to peer group values does not cause a sharp decline in parental influence.

Friendships are especially important in adolescence. They provide emotional support and allow the adolescent to modify behavior, tastes, or ideas without experiencing rejection; they also play a crucial role in helping adolescents develop a sense of their own identity. Relations with opposite-sex peers are especially significant in adolescence. However, adolescents who begin going steady at too early an age may never achieve the benefits of like-sex friendships, and their further development toward becoming mature, self-reliant individuals may be jeopardized.

REVIEW QUESTIONS

1. Briefly describe the role of hormonal factors in adolescent physical development.

2. How does sexual development progress in adolescent males and females?

3. What effects does maturation, particularly early versus late maturation, have on the psychological well-being of adolescent boys and girls?

4. Name four cognitive capabilities that are likely to develop during adolescence. What are some implications of these cognitive changes?

5. Briefly describe the effects of recent social changes on sexual attitudes and behavior in males and females. How do these vary among different sectors of the population?

6. Why do sexually active adolescents often fail to use contraceptive measures?

7. How do children's relationships with their parents change during adolescence?

8. What effects do variations in parental behavior (e.g., authoritative vs. authoritarian) have on adolescents' ability to develop an appropriate degree of autonomy?

9. Why do peer relations play a crucial role in the psychological and social development of adolescents?

10. What do we know about the relative influence of parents and peers on the adolescent?

GLOSSARY

adolescence   The period of development that extends from puberty to adulthood.

puberty   The initial phase of adolescence, in which the reproductive system matures and secondary sex characteristics develop.

menarche   The onset of menstruation.

SUGGESTED READINGS

Bell, R. (1987). *Changing bodies, changing lives: A book for teens on sex and relationships*. New York: Random House (paperback). A valuable source of information on physical and sexual development in adolescence and the effects of these changes on feelings and relationships.

Flavell, J. (1985). *Cognitive development* (2nd ed.). Englewood Cliffs, NJ: Prentice-Hall, (paperback). A sophisticated but readable discussion of cognitive development, including excellent chapters on middle childhood and adolescence.

Hartup, W. W. (1983). The peer system. In P. H. Mussen (Series Ed.) & E. M. Hetherington (Ed.), *Handbook of child psychology*: Vol. 4. *Personality and social development* (4th ed.). New York: Wiley. A comprehensive review of research on the development of peer relations from infancy through adolescence.

Hayes, C. D. (Ed.). (1987). *Risking the future*: (Vol. 1). *Adolescent sexuality, pregnancy, and childbearing*. Washington, DC: National Academy Press (paperback). A comprehensive summary of current knowledge about causes, incidence, and consequences of adolescent sexuality, pregnancy, and childbearing.

Youniss, J., & Smollar, J. (1985). *Adolescent relations with mothers, fathers, and friends*. Chicago: University of Chicago Press. An informative study of the role of parents and friends in helping adolescents become autonomous adults. Does an excellent job of integrating theory and empirical data.

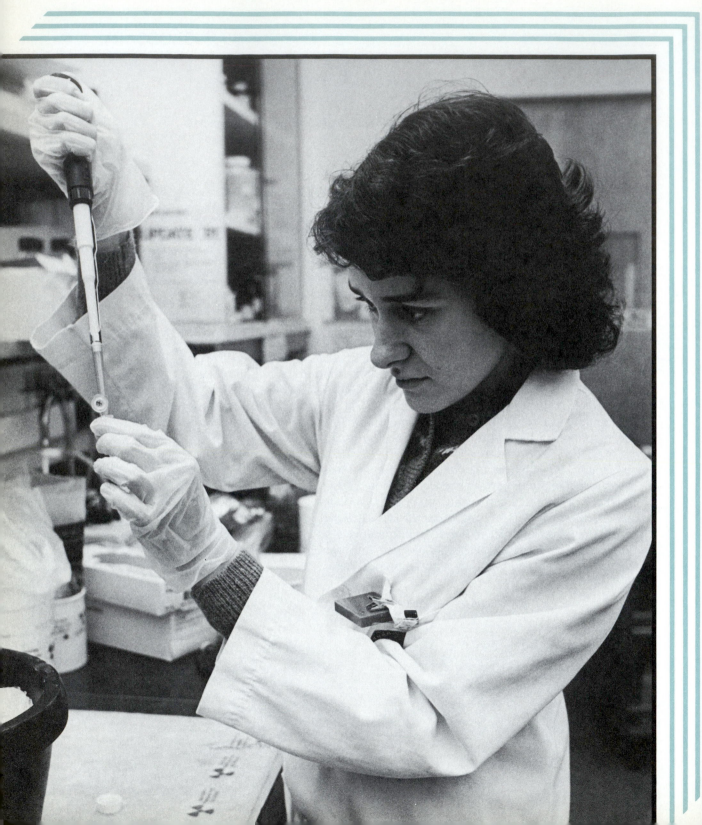

Chapter Fifteen

ADOLESCENCE: IDENTITY, VALUES, AND VOCATIONAL CHOICE

Identity

Developing a Sense of Identity
Identity Foreclosure and Identity Confusion
Achieved Ego Identity
Variations in Identity Formation
Gender Identity and Sex Role Identity

Vocational Choice in a Changing World

Development of Vocational Goals
Socioeconomic Influences
Women and Work
Parental Influences
School and Peer Group Influences
Vocational Values and Social Change
Vocational Prospects for Today's Youth

Moral Development and Values

Cognitive Growth and Moral Development
Moral Values and Personal Conflicts
Changing Religious Beliefs
Current Trends in Adolescent Values
A Turning Point?

613

W. H. Hudson, the author of *Green Mansions*, spent an idyllic childhood in the back country of Argentina. It was a time to be lived close to nature rather than thought about. But as he writes in his autobiography, there came a critical moment in which he realized that such times come to an end.

Fifteen years old! This was indeed the most memorable day of my life, for on that evening I began to think about myself, and my thoughts were strange and unhappy thoughts to me—what I was, what I was in the world for, what I wanted, what destiny was going to make of me!... It was the first time such questions had come to me, and I was startled at them. It was as though I had only just become conscious; I doubt that I had ever been fully conscious before. (W. H. Hudson, 1918, cited in Conger, 1979, p. 9)

As Hudson's experience illustrates, a central task of adolescence is finding a workable answer to the question, Who am I? Although this question has preoccupied humankind for many centuries and has been the subject of innumerable poems, novels, and autobiographies, only in recent decades has it become a focus of systematic psychological concern, initially through the writings of the psychoanalyst and psychologist Erik Erikson. In Erikson's view, before adolescents can successfully abandon the security provided by their childhood dependence on others, they must have some idea of who they are, where they are going, and what are the possibilities of getting there (Erikson, 1968; Waterman, 1984).

IDENTITY

Adolescents and adults with a strong sense of their own identity see themselves as separate, distinctive individuals. The very word *individual*, when used as a synonym for *person*, implies a universal need to perceive oneself as somehow separate from other people, no matter how much one may share with them. Closely related is the need for self-consistency, a feeling of wholeness. When we speak of the *integrity* of the self, we imply both separateness from others and unity of the self—a workable integration of the person's needs, motives, and patterns of responding.

In order to have a clear sense of ego identity, the adolescent or adult must also have a sense of *continuity* of the self over time. In Erikson's words, "The younger person, in order to experience wholeness, must feel a progressive continuity between that which he has come to be during the long years of childhood and that which he promises to become in the anticipated future" (1956, p. 91).

Finally, for Erikson a sense of identity requires *psychosocial reciprocity*—consistency "between that which he conceives himself to be and that which he perceives others to see in him and expect of him" (1956, p. 94). Erikson's assertion that one's sense of identity is tied at least partly to social reality is important; it emphasizes the fact that societal or individual rejection can seriously impair a child or adolescent's chances of establishing a strong, secure sense of personal identity. (Erikson's theory of development is explained further in Box 15.1.)

Developmental influences that help establish confident perceptions of oneself as separate and distinct from others, as reasonably consistent and integrated, as having continuity over time, and as being similar to the way one is perceived by others contribute to an overall sense of ego identity. By the same token, influences that impair these self-perceptions foster identity confusion (or diffusion), "failure to achieve the integration and continuity of self-images" (Erikson, 1968, p. 212).

BOX 15.1

Erikson's Eight Stages of Development

Erik Erikson, a psychoanalytic theorist, proposed major revisions in Freud's ideas about stages of development. Erikson thought that Freud had overemphasized the biological and sexual determinants of developmental change and underemphasized the importance of child-rearing experiences, social relationships, and cultural influences on the development of ego or self. He also believed that important developmental changes occur after childhood. He proposed a series of eight stages of development stretching over the entire lifespan. Erikson's theory has stimulated little research on young children. However, it has been influential in generating research on adolescent and adult development.

The eight stages proposed by Erikson are presented in the accompanying chart. Each stage is defined by a developmental task or crisis that needs to be resolved if the individual is to continue a healthy pattern of development. As noted in Chapter 5, the major concern of the first stage is establishment of trust. Erikson believed that infants develop trust when their world is consistent and predictable—when they are fed, warmed, and comforted in a consistent manner.

The second stage is described as a conflict between autonomy and shame and doubt. In the toddler period children begin to assert independence—they say no, and they can walk and run where they choose. Toilet training, often begun during this period, can become a battlefield where the child refuses to do what the parent wishes. Erikson believed that it is important to give children a sense of autonomy and not to be harsh or punitive during this period. Parents who

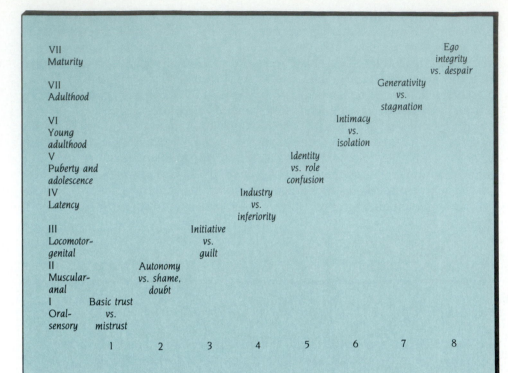

The eight stages of development in Erikson's theory. At the left side, the approximate ages or Freudian psychosexual stages corresponding to each stage are listed. The conflicts central to each stage in Erikson's theory are shown on the diagonal. (From E. Erikson. *Childhood and society* [2nd ed.]. New York: Norton, 1963, p. 273.)

shame their children for misbehavior could create basic doubt about being independent.

The third stage entails a conflict between initiative and guilt. The child in this stage begins to be task oriented and to plan new activities. It is a period when masturbation and sexual curiosity are often noticed by parents. The danger in this period, according to Erikson, is that the child may develop excessive guilt about his or her actions.

During middle childhood children need to solve the conflict between industry and inferiority. Children enter school, begin to perform tasks, and acquire important skills. Achievement and a sense of competence become important; a child who has no particular competences or experiences repeated failure may develop strong feelings of inferiority.

The major conflict in adolescence is between identity formation and role confusion. The young person solidifies many elements of childhood identity and forms a clear vocational and personal identity. Failure to solve this conflict can result in role confusion or diffusion of identity. Erikson acknowledged that identity formation might proceed somewhat differently for males than for females because society emphasizes different adult roles for men and women. He thought that career identity is particularly important for males but that females' identity might center on their future spouse and their role as wife and mother. The changes in women's roles in recent years have led many psychologists to revise this portion of the theory to include career goals as part of females' identity as well.

In young adulthood the major conflict is between intimacy and isolation. Deep, enduring personal relationships need to be formed. A person who does not form such relationships may be psychologically isolated from others and have only superficial social relationships. The most important intimate relationship, according to Erikson, is a committed sexual relationship with a partner of the other sex. Again, this view has been challenged as unnecessarily narrow; some people have argued that many kinds of intimate relationships are important and rewarding.

In middle adulthood the conflict is between generativity and stagnation. One form of generativity is having children, but being productive and creative in one's work or other activities can also be important. Without a sense of producing or creating, Erikson argued, an adult stagnates and ceases to grow.

The final conflict is between ego integrity and despair. People with ego integrity have a sense of order and meaning in life and a feeling of satisfaction with what they have accomplished. There is a sense of being part of a larger culture or world. Despair can occur when people become afraid of death or do not accept the life they have led as satisfying or worthy (Erikson, 1963).

Developing a Sense of Identity

The development of a sense of identity does not begin or end in adolescence. The child's ultimate identity is already being shaped during earlier periods of life, beginning, in Erikson's view, with the establishment of basic trust or mistrust of the people and the world around the infant (see Box 15.1). Nor does identity development always end in adolescence. Some men and women, once they have grown up, gone to work, and gotten married, seem to become caricatures of their former selves; instead of finding themselves, they become more like everybody else. Many others—including Eleanor Roosevelt, Mahatma Gandhi, and Erikson himself, as well as many lesser-known individuals—become more genuinely individual as they grow older (Conger, 1979; Lynd, 1966).

Many young people establish a strong, secure sense of personal identity during adolescence.

Even though identity development may be a lifelong process, the search for a sense of identity is especially relevant during adolescence, partly because change is the order of the day. As we have already noted, during adolescence the young person is confronted with a host of psychological, physiological, sexual, and cognitive changes, as well as by new and varied intellectual, social, and cognitive demands. Not surprisingly, at times adolescents may feel like spectators observing their changing selves. In the words of an adolescent poet,

Standing in front of the mirror,
I'm wondering what that person is all about . . .
—Tony Hall, age 16

Adolescents need time to integrate the rapid changes occurring in their bodies and minds into a unified sense of identity. When one young adolescent was asked why she had three distinctly different handwriting styles, she replied, "How can I have just one style till I know who I am?" (Conger, 1979, p. 11).

Achieving a clear sense of identity also depends partly on cognitive skills. The young person must be able to conceptualize herself or himself in abstract terms. The capacities for abstract and hypothetical thinking and for taking a future time perspective (discussed in Chapters 7 and 13) aid the adolescent in the search for an individual identity. At the same time, they make the search more difficult because they open up a wider range of possibilities to choose among.

SELF-CONCEPT AND IDENTITY.   Adolescents have a much more sophisticated view of what a sense of one's self encompasses than younger children do. While the self-descriptions of younger children tend to center on concrete characteristics, those of adolescents are likely to be more abstract and to include psychological characteristics, interpersonal relationships, self-evaluations, and conflicting feelings (Harter, 1983; Hill & Palmquist, 1978; Montemayor & Eisen, 1977; Selman, 1980). Self-conceptions also become more differentiated and better organized during adolescence (Chandler, Boyer, Ball, & Hala, 1985).

For example, note the concrete flavor of this 9-year-old boy's self-description, emphasizing his age, sex, address, physical characteristics, and likes and dislikes:

> My name is Bruce C. I have brown eyes. I have brown hair. I have brown eyebrows. I'm nine years old. I LOVE! Sports. I have seven people in my family. I have great! eye site. I have lots! of friends. I live on 1923 Pinecrest Dr. I'm going on 10 in September. I'm a boy. I have a uncle that is almost 7 feet tall. My school is Pinecrest. My teacher is Mrs. V. I play Hockey! I'am almost the smartest boy in the class. I LOVE! food. I love freash air. I LOVE School.

Now consider the self-description of this 11½-year-old girl. Although she, too, speaks of her likes, she stresses psychological characteristics and interpersonal relationships:

> My name is A. I'm a human being. I'm a girl. I'm a truthful person. I'm not pretty. I do so-so in my studies. I'm a very good cellist. I'm a very good pianist. I'm a swimmer. I try to be helpful. I'm always ready to be friends with anybody. Mostly I'm good, but I lose my temper. I'm not well-liked by some girls and boys. I don't know if I'm liked by boys or not.

Finally, note how this 17-year-old twelfth-grader is preoccupied with describing her identity in terms of her psychological characteristics, moods, and ideological concerns:

> I am a human being. I am a girl. I am an individual. I don't know who I am. I am a Pisces. I am a moody person. I am an ambitious person. I am a very curious

person. I am not an individual. I am a loner. I am an American (God help me). I am a Democrat. I am a liberal person. I am a radical. I am a conservative. I am a pseudoliberal. I am an atheist. I am not a classifiable person [i.e., I don't want to be].

The authors of the study from which these descriptions are taken add the following comment:

> Children describe where they live, what they look like, and what they do. Their self-concept seems somewhat shallow and undifferentiated, both from other people and from their environment. Adolescents, however, describe themselves in terms of their beliefs and personality characteristics, qualities which are more essential and intrinsic to the self and which produce a picture of the self that is sharp and unique. (Montemayor & Eisen, 1977, p. 318)

THE ROLE OF THE FAMILY.   An adolescent's freedom to explore a variety of possibilities in pursuit of an individual identity is significantly influenced by relationships within the family (Cooper, C. R., Grotevant, & Condon, 1983; Marcia, 1980; Youniss & Smollar, 1985). In one study of family interactions, adolescents who scored high on a measure of *identity exploration* were more likely to come from families in which self-assertion and freedom to disagree ("separateness") were encouraged along with "connectedness" to the family, including openness or responsiveness to the views of others ("plurality") and sensitivity to and respect for the ideas of others ("mutuality"). In the words of one high-scoring participant in the study, "I have a say but not a deciding vote in family decisions" (Cooper, C. R. et al., 1983, p. 54).

In contrast, adolescents who scored lower in identity exploration were more likely to come from families in which individuality was not encouraged and mutual support and agreement were emphasized. It is not surprising that a low-scoring young woman commented with respect to career choice, "I'm having a hard time deciding what to do. It would be easier if they would tell me what to do, but of course I don't want that" (Grotevant & Cooper, 1983, p. 55).

Other studies have shown that opportunities for separateness in family interactions appear to be especially important for girls' development, while connectedness in family relations, particularly with the father, appears to be especially important for boys (Cooper & Grotevant, 1987; Grotevant & Cooper, 1985; Huston, 1980). Perhaps the greater importance of separateness for females "reflects the effort needed to overcome the greater restrictiveness they experience relative to males in domains such as play, peer relations, and career development" (Cooper & Grotevant, in press). Boys, on the other hand, are more likely to be pressured by society to be autonomous and assertive in identity exploration. Consequently, their greatest need in family interaction may be for mutual understanding, respect, and support, particularly from their fathers, who serve as gender-role models (Cooper & Grotevant, 1987; Hauser et al., 1987; Huston, T. & Ashmore, 1986; Youniss & Ketterlinus, 1987).

The findings of these studies are consistent with Erikson's view that people with a strong sense of identity perceive themselves as separate, distinctive individuals. They also support the idea that openness and responsiveness to the views of others are important "because identity function requires the consideration, selection, and interpretation of possible sources of information about the self and others" (Cooper, et al. 1983, p. 53); such information is more readily available when people can communicate in an atmosphere of openness.

Identity Foreclosure and Identity Confusion

Erikson (1968) pointed to two important ways in which the search for identity can go wrong: It may be *prematurely foreclosed* (i.e., crystallized too early), or it may be *indefinitely extended*.

IDENTITY FORECLOSURE.   **Identity foreclosure** is an interruption in the process of identity formation. It is a premature fixing of one's self-image that interferes with the development of other potentials and possibilities for self-definition. Youth whose identities have been prematurely foreclosed are likely to be highly approval oriented. They base their sense of self-esteem largely on recognition by others, usually have a high degree of respect for authority, and tend to be more conforming and less autonomous than other youth. They are also more interested in traditional religious values, less thoughtful and reflective, less anxious, and more stereotyped and superficial, as well as less close and intimate in both same-sex and opposite-sex relationships.

Although they do not differ from their peers in overall intelligence, young people whose identity has become fixed have difficulty being flexible and responding appropriately when confronted with stressful cognitive tasks; they seem to welcome structure and order in their lives. They tend to have close relationships with their parents (especially in the case of sons and their fathers) and to adopt their parents' values with few questions. Their parents, in turn, generally appear to be accepting and encouraging while at the same time exerting considerable pressure for conformity to family values (Bourne, 1978a, 1978b; Donovan, 1975; Marcia, 1980; St. Clair & Day, 1979).

IDENTITY CONFUSION.   In contrast, other adolescents go through a prolonged period of **identity confusion.** Some never develop a strong, clear sense of identity; these are adolescents who cannot "find themselves," who keep themselves loose and unattached (Douvan & Adelson, 1966). Such a person may exhibit a pathologically prolonged identity crisis, never achieving any consistent loyalties or commitments.

Young people who experience identity confusion often have low self-esteem and immature moral reasoning. They are impulsive; their thinking is disorganized; and they have difficulty taking responsibility for their own lives. They tend to be focused on themselves, and their relationships are often superficial and sporadic. Although generally dissatisfied with their parents' way of life, they have difficulty fashioning one of their own (Adams, G. R., Abraham, & Markstrom, 1987; Donovan, 1975; Marcia, 1980; Orlofsky, 1978; Waterman & Waterman, 1974).

Achieved Ego Identity

Searching and confusion may sometimes be beneficial. Individuals who have achieved a strong sense of identity after a period of active searching are likely to be more autonomous, creative, and complex in their thinking than those whose identities were formed without a period of confusion. They also show a greater capacity for intimacy, a more confident sexual identity, a more positive self-concept, and more mature moral reasoning. While their relationships with their parents are generally positive, they have typically achieved considerable independence from their families (Hodgson & Fischer, 1978; Orlofsky, 1978; Orlofsky, Marcia, & Lesser, 1973; St. Clair & Day, 1979).

Research comparisons show that young women who have achieved a clear sense of identity weighed a variety of occupational and ideological options and arrived at conclusions to which they are committed. They also yielded less to pressure for conformity and were less uncomfortable in resisting such pressure than other women (Toder & Marcia, 1973). They chose relatively difficult college majors, and they manifested few negative feelings, such as anxiety, hostility, or depression, than women who lacked a firm identity (Marcia, 1980).

Variations in Identity Formation

So far we have been discussing identity formation as though it were a single task at which a young person either succeeds or fails. In reality, the matter is more complex. Patterns of identity formation may vary widely as a result of influences that range from parent-child relationships to cultural pressures and social change. In a simple society, where the number of possible adult roles is limited and there is little social change, identity formation may be a relatively straightforward task that is quickly accomplished. But in a rapidly changing, complex society like our own, where there is so much choice, the search for identity can be difficult and prolonged (Conger & Petersen, 1984; Erikson, 1968; Marcia, 1980; Waterman, 1982, 1984).

Within a particular society, identities may be typical or deviant: An individual may seek personal, social, and vocational roles that are expected and approved by society, or may adopt more idiosyncratic roles. Some unusual roles are positive and constructive, as in the case of the artist or poet who "marches to a different drummer"; others are negative, as in the case of the long-term drug addict or "career criminal" (Conger, 1977a; Douvan & Adelson, 1966).

There are many variations in the process of identity formation. The popular stereotype of an acute and prolonged adolescent "identity crisis" is probably exaggerated. Indeed, Erikson himself was moved at one point to ask, "Would so many of our youth act so openly confused and confusing if they did not *know* they were supposed to have an identity crisis?" (1968, pp. 18–19). The belief of some clinical psychologists and psychiatrists that the absence of a period of intense adolescent turmoil portends later emotional disturbance is not supported by research findings (Conger, in press; Petersen, 1988; Offer & Offer, 1975). In short, many adolescents form an ego identity without serious "storm and stress."

Gender Identity and Sex Role Identity

As noted in Chapter 10, most people acquire gender identity, an awareness and acceptance of one's biological nature as a male or female, early in life. With the notable exception of transsexuals (who typically report having felt, even as children, that they were trapped in a body of the wrong sex), the great majority of people, including most homosexuals, appear to be content with being male or female and have no desire to change their sex (Green, 1974, 1987; Stoller, 1980).

But for those who resent their biological identity (e.g., who resent their sexual nature and their procreative capabilities or are hostile to their own or the other sex), adolescence can be a particularly stressful and confusing period. Rapid sexual maturation calls attention to the fact that gender is a biological fact. Conflicts about gender identity are difficult to deal with and are likely to create significant problems in the development of a confident, secure *overall* identity (Conger, in press; Conger & Petersen, 1984).

As explained in earlier chapters, a secure sex role identity means that one perceives oneself as masculine or feminine according to one's own definition of these terms. This does not require rigid conformity to sex role stereotypes. Rather, in the words of Jeanne Block, a pioneer in sex role research, "Sexual identity means, or will mean, the earning of a sense of self that includes a recognition of gender secure enough to permit the individual to manifest human qualities that our society, until now, has labeled unmanly or unwomanly" (1984, p. 1). Thus, two young women may both have clear and confident sex role identities but may define them quite differently. One may view being a highly independent, competitive corporate executive in a traditionally male business as entirely consistent with a feminine sex role identity, while the other may feel that her feminine identity is best expressed by devoting herself primarily to the roles of wife, mother, and homemaker.

The pattern that has been labeled androgyny—a combination of socially valued "masculine" and "feminine" characteristics in the same individual—has recently come to be viewed as socially adaptive (Bem, 1981; Huston, A. C., 1983; Spence & Helmreich, 1978). In one study, four groups were compared. One consisted of adolescents and youth who scored high on both socially valued masculine characteristics (e.g., independence, assertiveness) and socially valued feminine characteristics (e.g., nurturance, understanding); this was the androgynous group. The other three groups consisted of: youth who scored high only on masculine items; those who scored high only on feminine items; and those who scored low on both, referred to as "undifferentiated." As may be seen from Table 15.1, relatively few males or females were "cross-typed"; that is, few males scored highest on feminine items and few females scored highest on masculine items.

Androgynous individuals of both sexes scored highest on measures of self-esteem, followed by the masculine, the feminine, and lowest of all, the undifferentiated group. Androgynous individuals also reported receiving more academic and extracurricular honors than undifferentiated individuals did. Female athletes and scientists are more likely to score high on androgyny or on masculinity rather than femininity alone. Masculine and androgynous self-perceptions characterize young people of both sexes who value and expect to do well in mathematics, formal logic, and spatial skills (Huston, A. C., 1983; Nash, 1979; Spence & Helmreich, 1978).

TABLE 15.1

Percentage of Students Falling into Each of the Four Personal Attributes Categories for College and High School Samples

	College Sample Undifferentiated	Feminine	Masculine	Androgynous
Males	25	8	34	32
Females	28	32	14	27
	High School Sample Undifferentiated	Feminine	Masculine	Androgynous
Males	23	8	44	25
Females	18	35	14	35

Source: J. T. Spence. *Traits, roles, and the concept of androgyny.* Paper presented at the Conference on Perspectives on the Psychology of Women, Michigan State University, May 13–14, 1977. By permission.

Androgyny in these studies is defined by socially valued attributes of both sexes. Negatively valued feminine attributes (e.g., being gullible, servile, whiny, or nagging) have also been measured. Males and females who have such characteristics do not fare well. They generally have low self-esteem, and they face adjustment problems because they are vulnerable, insecure, and hypersensitive. Men or women with negative masculine attributes tend to be overly aggressive and critical of others (Block, 1973, 1984; Spence, Helmreich, & Holahan, 1979).

It would seem to be socially and personally desirable to permit males and females alike to be "both independent and tender, assertive and yielding, masculine and feminine, allowing people to cope more effectively with diverse situations" (Bem, 1975, p. 62). And indeed, from one situation, task, or setting to another many people do vary in the extent to which they exhibit one or another gender-related psychological characteristic (Spence, 1985). A young corporate executive may act quite differently in the office and at home. However, positive masculine attributes, such as independence and self-confidence, are the most important and adaptive components of androgyny, especially for females (Huston, 1983).

VOCATIONAL CHOICE IN A CHANGING WORLD

For most people, young and old alike, vocational identity forms an important part of their overall identity (Erikson, 1968; Marcia, 1980; Osipow, 1986). Having a job that society values—and doing it well—enhances self-esteem and facilitates the development of an increasingly secure, stable sense of identity. Conversely, being told by society that one is not needed and that meaningful employment is not available (a message that is being given to large numbers of disadvantaged minority youth today) can foster self-doubt, resentment, and loss of self-esteem. It increases the likelihood of identity confusion or even, as in some cases of delinquency or "dropping out," a negative identity (Borow, 1976; Conger, in press).

Opportunities for adolescents to gain constructive and appropriate work experiences can give them a sense of purpose and responsibility, help generate a feeling of meaningful participation in the broader society, and reduce the communication barrier between adults and young people. Such work experiences may also provide young people with a chance to learn about vocational possibilities, develop their interests, and test their skills and talents against the demands of the so-called real world.

A limited number of programs around the country are currently providing high school (and college) students with well-planned exposure to the kinds of work actually involved in a variety of careers in health care, industry and business, the arts, and local government and social-service agencies. In Denver, for example, a joint program sponsored by a high school and a building-trades union enabled students to gain on-the-job experience in house building while learning related academic skills in the classroom (Conger, in press). Other students may work with research scientists in their laboratories or with business executives; tutor younger students

Having a job that society values enhances self-esteem and facilitates the development of a stable sense of identity.

who are having problems in school; provide services to children, the elderly, or the handicapped; or work in business-funded training programs at such tasks as renovating buildings in the community (Greenberger & Steinberg, 1986; Hamilton & Crouter, 1980; Bacas, 1986; William T. Grant Foundation, 1988).

If such programs are to be of value in helping adolescents make the transition to the adult world of work, the experiences provided should be meaningful and relevant to their goals. Recent studies suggest that the kinds of jobs that are most frequently available to adolescents attending school, such as working at drive-in fast-food outlets, washing cars, or packing groceries, may promote greater understanding of money matters, increased work orientation, and a somewhat greater feeling of independence, but they do little to encourage educational and vocational aspirations and planning (Greenberger & Steinberg, 1981, 1986). Indeed, for some young people, especially those who work long hours and are poorer students to begin with, such employment may interfere significantly with school performance (see Box 15.2).

Development of Vocational Goals

As adolescents approach the time when they must support themselves, they become progressively more realistic about their vocational goals. During this period they attempt to match their aspirations and capabilities with available opportunities (Ginzberg, 1972; Herr & Cramer, 1979; Osipow, 1986; Super, D. E., 1967, 1980).

In our society the actual requirements of most jobs and their availability in the labor market are not matters of common knowledge, and young people need help to make intelligent choices. Knowledgeable, skilled assistance is rarely available, however. Consequently, a young person's vocational interests usually develop in a rather unsystematic fashion, guided by such influences as parental desires, the suggestions of school counselors (some of whom are poorly informed), accidental contact with various occupations, and the kinds of jobs their friends are finding. And as we will see shortly, social class and sex-typed expectations also play a role.

Socioeconomic Influences

Social class influences vocational goals in a variety of ways. For one thing, it helps determine the kinds of occupations the young person will be familiar with and, hence, likely to consider in setting occupational goals (Conger & Petersen, 1984). In addition, it plays an important role in determining the social acceptability of various occupations. Certain types of occupations are considered appropriate for the members of a particular social class; others are considered inappropriate. For example, becoming a truck driver, a clerk in a grocery store, or an automobile mechanic may be considered an appropriate choice in a lower-middle-class group but not in an upper-class group.

In one pioneering study, all graduating seniors in Wisconsin high schools were asked to state the occupations that they hoped eventually to enter. Their choices were then assigned "prestige scores." Very few students whose families were in the lower third of the socioeconomic-status scale aspired to high-prestige occupations; many students in the upper third did so. Moreover, in subsequent years the

BOX 15.2

Employment in High School

Part-time employment for high school students is far more common in the United States than in other industrialized countries. The difference is due partly to scheduling conflicts (longer school days and shorter business hours) in those countries and partly to the fact that opportunities for part-time employment are not as readily available elsewhere as they are in the United States. In considerable measure, however, it is a function of the much more extensive after-school demands placed on students in other countries. Many European and Japanese students, for example, are assigned four to five hours of homework nightly (Steinberg, 1985). In contrast, in one survey less than one-third of American students reported spending an hour or more on homework, while 40 percent said they spend no time at all (National Assessment of Educational Progress, 1981).

In its report on the quality of education in America, *A Nation at Risk: The Imperative for Educational Reform*, the National Commission on Excellence in Education asserted that "the educational foundations of our society are being eroded by a rising tide of mediocrity" (National Commission, 1983, p. 5). The Commission noted that American students as a group perform relatively poorly on a wide variety of academic achievement measures when compared to students from many other industrialized countries. One reason may be the large amount of time and energy Americans spend in paid employment.

Currently, well over 50 percent of high school seniors hold at least the equivalent of a half-time job (Greenberger & Steinberg, 1986). If we are to achieve the kinds of goals set for American education in reports like *A Nation at Risk*, and if our students are to be able to compete successfully with students from other developed countries, the whole question of how much time even our brightest, most promising young people can afford to spend in academically unproductive part-time employment may need to be readdressed (Greenberger & Steinberg, 1986).

actual occupational attainments of students of lower socioeconomic status were close to their expectations (Little, 1967).

Some researchers argue that the relative values assigned by adolescents to different occupations vary by social class and that these variations largely account for social-class differences in vocational goals (Caro, 1966). Others argue that both middle-class and working-class youth agree on the relative desirability and prestige of various occupations. Differences in goals, they say, stem less from values than from perceptions of differences in opportunities and general life chances (Borow, 1976; Stephenson, 1979). A girl whose parents are unable or unwilling to help her go to college is not very likely to aspire to be a doctor. Similarly, a boy whose parents expect him to go to work after completing high school is not likely to spend much time contemplating a career as an engineer.

Women and Work

One of the most significant changes in American society since World War II has been the rapid rise in the number of women entering the labor force. In 1947, only one-third of all women over age 16 were employed outside the home; in 1984, for the first time a majority of married women from intact families with children under the age of 6 were employed outside the home, and their numbers continue to grow (see Table 15.2). It is estimated that in 1990 two out of every three married women, and—somewhat surprisingly—three out of every four married women with children living at home, will be in the job market. The stereotype of a wife as someone

TABLE 15.2

Labor Force Status of Married, Separated, and Divorced Women, by Presence and Age of Children: 1960 to 1985 (in Percent)

ITEM	Participation Rate[a]			
	1960	1970	1980	1985
Married, husband present, total	30.5	40.8	50.2	54.2
No children under 18	34.7	42.2	46.1	48.2
Children 6–17 yr only	39.0	49.2	61.8	67.8
Children under 6 yr	18.6	30.3	45.0	53.4
Separated, total	(NA)	52.3	59.4	61.3
No children under 18	(NA)	52.3	58.7	60.0
Children 6–17 yr only	(NA)	60.6	66.4	70.9
Children under 6 yr	(NA)	45.4	51.8	53.7
Divorced, total	(NA)	70.9	74.5	75.0
No children under 18	(NA)	67.7	71.4	77.9
Children 6–17 yr only	(NA)	82.4	82.3	83.4
Children under 6 yr	(NA)	63.3	68.0	67.5

Source: **U.S. Bureau of the Census,** *Statistical abstract of the United States,* 1986 (106th ed.). Washington, D.C.: U.S. Government Printing Office, 1986.
Note: NA = Not available.
[a]Percent of women in each specific category in the labor force.

who stays home to look after children will fit only about one-quarter of American wives (Smith, R. E., 1979; U.S. Department of Labor, 1984; U.S. Bureau of the Census, 1987).

Despite the dramatic increase in women's participation in the labor force and decreases in sex role stereotyping in recent decades, members of both sexes still tend to have relatively traditional, sex-related occupational aspirations (e.g., skilled worker for boys; office worker, nurse, or teacher for girls). However, many more young women are seeking and gaining entrance into jobs, both professional and nonprofessional, that previously were largely reserved for men. Nearly equal numbers of male and female high school seniors aspire to managerial and professional occupations such as office manager, lawyer, physician, dentist, or college professor (Bachman, Johnston, & O'Malley, 1981, 1987). Similar trends are occurring at the college level (see Table 15.3). The reasons for these profound social changes are both economic and social. They include a sharply declining birthrate, increased employment opportunities and higher salaries for women, changing social and sex roles, and a family's desire to keep up with the cost of living by having two wage earners (Conger, in press).

FAMILY VALUES, SEX ROLE ATTITUDES, AND VOCATIONAL GOALS. Young women with high-status occupational expectations, typically in full-time careers and often in traditionally male fields, are more likely to have less traditional sex role attitudes. If they are among the more than 90 percent who are planning to marry, they are more likely than those without such expectations to plan to marry

Astronaut Sally Ride was the first woman to travel in space.

TABLE 15.3

Sex Differences in Probable Career Occupations of First-Year College and University Students, 1986

Probable Career Occupation	All Men	All Women
Accountant or actuary	5.1	6.5
Architect or urban planner	2.3	.7
Business executive	13.9	12.1
Business owner or proprietor	5.3	2.3
Clinical psychologist	.6	2.1
Computer programmer or analyst	4.6	2.5
Engineer	17.4	2.8
Law enforcement officer	1.7	.6
Lawyer or judge	4.1	4.0
Military service or career	2.0	.3
Nurse	.2	5.1
Physician	4.1	3.4
Social, welfare, or recreation worker	.4	2.3
Therapist (physical, occupational, speech)	.9	3.2
Teacher (elementary)	.6	7.9
Teacher (secondary)	2.6	3.1
Writer or journalist	1.6	2.9
Skilled trades	2.6	.3

Source: A. W. Astin, K. C. Green, W. S. Korn, and M. Schalit. *The American freshman: National norms for fall, 1986.* Los Angeles: Higher Education Research Institute, University of California at Los Angeles, 1986.

later, to have relatively fewer children, and to work while their children are young. Although most want to experience both a career and child rearing, they tend to be somewhat more oriented toward a job than toward children, and they are somewhat less likely to view having children and having "someone to rely on" as important needs or satisfactions in deciding to marry.

Other studies have shown that young women who are planning to enter nontraditional careers typically score higher on measures of academic ability (particularly in the physical and biological sciences and in mathematics) and have higher grades. They are also more independent and assertive, more concerned with exhibiting competence, and more likely to have working mothers—especially mothers who have a positive orientation toward working (Areshansel & Rosen, 1980; Cerra, 1980; Farmer, 1985; Hoffman, L. W., 1973, 1980, 1984, 1986; Marini, 1978).

In contrast, the minority of young women who are planning to become full-time homemakers tend to strongly endorse traditional values with respect to the occupational and domestic roles of men and women, and to have more traditional perceptions of male and female behavior in general. They also plan to marry earlier and have more children, have lower educational aspirations, and view children and "having someone to rely on" as important family values (Areshansel & Rosen, 1980; Tittle, 1980, 1981).

Occupying a middle ground between these two extremes are adolescents who plan to stay at home while their children are young but to work before having children and when their children are older. On most variables (e.g., desired family size, relative importance of children and jobs, occupational and domestic values, sex role attitudes), their scores fall between those of full-time homemakers and high-status career seekers. Not surprisingly, perhaps, these young women are more likely to have relatively traditional occupational expectations.

With the new variety of options for women comes uncertainty among high school seniors about how to coordinate job and child-rearing roles (Areshansel & Rosen, 1980; Bachman, et al., 1981, 1986; Smith, R. E., 1979; Lerman, 1986) (see Box 15.3). This uncertainty reflects a genuine dilemma, as increasing numbers of career women, particularly those on the corporate ladder, are discovering. Finding workable solutions to the problems of combining children and a career is not easy in today's society (Kantrowitz, 1986; Taylor, 1986; Wessel, 1986).

BOX 15.3

Marriage and Work: The Views of Today's High School Seniors

In a continuing national survey, the attitudes of high school seniors toward various working arrangements between husband and wife were investigated (Bachman, Johnston, & O'Malley, 1981, 1987; Herzog, Bachman, & Johnston, 1979). For couples without children, the most widely preferred arrangements are those in which the husband is employed full-time and the wife is employed either full-time or half-time—with slightly more females preferring that both partners work full-time and slightly more males preferring that the wife work half-time (Bachman et al., 1987). Only 10 percent of the males and less than 5 percent of the females viewed as desirable the traditional pattern in which the husband is employed full-time and the wife is not employed outside the home. (Except for a very small minority, neither males nor females considered a reversal of this traditional sex role pattern desirable or even acceptable.)

The presence of preschool children changes the picture dramatically, however. Under these circumstances the most preferred arrangement is for the husband to work full-time while the wife remains at home; indeed, only 9.9 percent of those surveyed considered it unacceptable. In contrast, 56 percent of the males and 46 percent of the females considered unacceptable an arrangement in which the wife, as well as the husband, works full-time. While only 14 percent think it desirable for a wife with young children to work half-time if the husband is working, most (especially females) feel that they could at least accept this arrangement.

Interestingly, regardless of their preferred pattern of husband-wife working arrangement, both males and females showed the greatest preference for an equal division of labor in child care, although many considered a somewhat greater proportion of care by the female acceptable, particularly when the male is working full-time.

The results of this study reflect an interesting mixture of egalitarianism and traditionalism among today's high school seniors. Although in the case of childless couples both males and females prefer to have the wife work part- or full-time, and although both also believe in sharing child care (and other household duties) when young children are present, a majority oppose arrangements in which the wife works full-time—a view that is shared by both males and females. (Unfortunately, this study did not include attitudes toward wives working when the children are of school age or older, although it seems likely that under these circumstances the wife's working would be considered more acceptable or desirable.)

In the final analysis, despite a significant liberalization of attitudes toward male and female roles in marriage, it appears that for the majority of young people the ultimate responsibility for the financial stability of the family still rests more with the husband, while the ultimate responsibility for child care rests more with the wife.

But the picture is not static. For example, in 1980 nearly two-thirds (63.4 percent) of seniors considered it unacceptable for both parents to work full-time when there are preschool children in the home; by 1985 this figure had declined to 56 percent. Similarly, the percentage of seniors considering half-time work acceptable or desirable for wives with preschool children increased from 60 percent to 70 percent between 1980 and 1985 (Bachman et al., 1981; Johnston, L. D. et al., 1986). Further changes may well occur as the number of working women continues to grow.

Parental Influences

In general, if parents set high educational and occupational goals and reward good schoolwork, their children have high levels of aspiration. Working-class adolescents are more likely to seek advanced education and occupational mobility if their parents urge them to do so than if their parents do not exert pressure in this direction (Hoffman, L. W., 1984, 1986). In one study, *ambitious middle-class males* reported the highest percentage of parental support and encouragement for educational and vocational achievement. *Upwardly mobile working-class males* ranked a close second (Simpson, 1962). In contrast, *unambitious middle-class males* and *nonmobile working-class males* ranked far behind in percentage of parental support. A major reason for the superior academic success of many Asian students, including children of recent immigrants, lies in the great importance their families attach to education and hard work, together with the high credibility of parental values in the eyes of their children (Brand, 1987).

FATHER'S OCCUPATION AND WORK EXPERIENCE.   Parents' occupations and the way parents view their work can significantly influence the career choices of their children. Up to now most research dealing with the influence of parental occupation on adolescent career choices has involved fathers. The father's occupation exerts a significant influence on the career choices of sons, though generally not directly on those of daughters (Hoffman, L. W., 1984, 1986; Mortimer, 1976).

Some of the reasons that sons often choose the same work as their fathers seem obvious: more opportunities to become familiar with the father's occupation compared with others, easier access to that occupation, and in some cases, strong parental motivation—and sometimes pressure—to enter that occupation. However, it appears that more subtle factors also play a part. For instance, a father may communicate certain values to his son that relate to the father's vocation. A physician might encourage his son to value health, the power of science, service to others, intellectual satisfaction, and high income. Such a process is most probable when the father's job has high prestige, the son has a close relationship with his father, and the father provides a generally strong and positive role model (Bell, A. P., 1969; Mortimer, 1976).

More broadly, several theorists have maintained that "through one's job one develops notions of what qualities and values are important for success, and these ideas are embodied in child-rearing patterns" (Hoffman, L. W., 1986, p. 184). For example, investigators have found that fathers in middle-class, white-collar occupations that involve manipulation of ideas, symbols, and interpersonal relations and require considerable flexibility, thought, and judgment place a high value on self-direction and independence (Kohn, 1959a, 1959b, 1969; Kohn & Schooler, 1978, 1982). Accordingly, in child rearing they emphasize achievement, independence, and self-reliance. In contrast, lower-class or blue-collar fathers whose occupations are more standardized, less complex, and more closely supervised—and more likely to require manipulation of physical objects than of ideas or interpersonal relationships—are more likely to value obedience and conformity in their child-rearing practices.

MATERNAL EMPLOYMENT.   Studies of the father's influence have tended to focus on the idea that the father's occupation affects the child because the traits required for success in that occupation are valued and passed on to the child (Hoffman, L. W., 1984). In contrast, in studies of the mother's influence the focus has been primarily on her employment status per se (Bronfenbrenner & Crouter, 1982; Hoffman, L. W., 1986). Moreover, until recently it was assumed that maternal employment outside the home is likely to have an adverse effect, not merely on vocational orientation but on child and adolescent development generally.

Recent research suggests, however, that maternal employment is more likely to have positive effects, particularly for female adolescents. Maternal role models influence daughters' career choices and both sons' and daughters' attitudes regarding appropriate sex and vocational roles for women (see Chapter 11). Female adolescents and youth whose mothers are employed outside the home also are more likely to view work as something they will want to do if and when they themselves become mothers (Banducci, 1967; Hoffman, L. W., 1974; Huston, A. C., 1983; Smith, 1969). Compared to sons and daughters of nonemployed mothers, young people, especially young women, with employed mothers consider male-female differences in such generally sex-stereotyped attributes as competence and warmth or expressiveness to be smaller (Vogel, Broverman, Broverman, Clarkson, & Rosenkrantz, et al., 1970). Adolescent daughters of employed mothers admire and want to be like their mothers more often than daughters of nonemployed mothers do (Hoffman, L. W., 1974; Huston, A. C., 1983). Employed mothers appear to be more likely to encourage independence in their children and indeed, daughters of working mothers tend to be more autonomous, active, self-reliant, and achievement oriented (Almquist & Angrist, 1971; Gold & Andres, 1978a; Hoffman, L. W., 1974, 1986).

Finally, young women's vocational attitudes and aspirations are influenced not just by whether their mother is employed but also by the mother's attitudes toward employment. If the mother is satisfied and involved in her work, and if she succeeds at combining the roles of worker, mother, and wife, her daughter is more likely to emulate her. A father who supports and accepts his career-oriented wife also contributes to his daughter's vocational attitudes (Baruch, 1972).

In sum, high-achieving women have high-achieving daughters because they provide appropriate role models for combining achievement and family roles, encourage independence in their daughters, and have husbands who also encourage independence and achievement by women (Hoffman, L. W., 1973, 1984, 1986).

Maternal employment does not appear to have as favorable an effect on adolescent boys, who are somewhat more likely to have academic and adjustment problems (Gold & Andres, 1978a; Hoffman, L. W., 1980, 1986; Montemayor, 1985). Some theorists have suggested that the sons of working mothers, perhaps because of their greater independence, may be more likely to become involved in peer groups that undermine adult socialization (Bronfenbrenner & Crouter, 1982; Montemayor, 1985). Conversely, in early adolescence sons of full-time homemakers are more inhibited and conforming but also perform better in school (Moore, T. W., 1975). It may be that employed mothers place too much pressure for independence on their adolescent sons, while nonemployed middle-class mothers unwittingly encourage oversocialization and conformity and place too little emphasis on independence (Hoffman, L. W., 1986).

It has also been found that working mothers (and their husbands) have more positive views of their daughters than of their sons, while the reverse is true for nonworking mothers (Bronfenbrenner, et al., 1984). While working mothers tend to view their daughters as self-reliant and helpful, they are more likely to complain about their sons' noncompliance and aggressiveness. In turn, adolescent sons (but not daughters) report more frequent, longer, and more intense conflicts with employed mothers than with nonemployed mothers (Montemayor, 1985).

In brief, full-time involvement of mothers in careers that they enjoy and in which they succeed appears to have positive effects on the educational and vocational aspirations of adolescent girls, particularly when the father provides encouragement and support. However, thus far the picture does not appear either as clear or as positive in the case of sons of middle-class working mothers.

School and Peer Group Influences

Teachers, school counselors, and peer values also affect adolescents' career choices. Boys from lower-class homes have higher educational and vocational aspirations if they attend a largely middle-class school and associate frequently with middle-class boys than if they attend a school in which the students come primarily from lower-class homes. Increased contact with middle-class peers appears to foster "anticipatory socialization" into middle-class values (Simpson, 1962). Even these school influences may be related to parental values; upwardly mobile lower-class parents often choose a neighborhood for its middle-class schools. In general, parental influence is stronger than that of peers.

Vocational Values and Social Change

The vocational values and attitudes of young people in the 1980s differ in a number of important respects from those of their counterparts in the late 1960s and

The advice of school counselors is a significant influence on many students' career choices.

early 1970s. In the intervening years there have been profound changes in social values, rapid—often unpredictable—shifts in patterns of occupational demand, and perhaps most significant, declining productivity and a dramatic rise in the cost of goods and services. In contrast to earlier periods, even a "good," reasonably well-paying job no longer provides assured access to such elements of the American Dream as a home of one's own, a college education for one's children, or financial security during retirement.

Consequently, it is hardly surprising that the percentage of strongly "career-minded" college students has increased steadily in recent years, while the number of students who view their college experience as a period of self-discovery and change has declined considerably (Astin, Green, & Korn, 1987; Astin, Green, Korn, & Schalit, 1986; Yankelovich, 1974, 1981). Between 1969 and 1986 the percentage of first-year college students in the United States who cited "being very well off financially" as an "essential or very important objective" increased from slightly less than half to over seven out of ten (three-fourths for males and two-thirds for females) (Astin et al., 1986, 1987). In contrast, while "developing a philosophy of life" was cited as a very important objective by 86 percent of females and 78.5 percent of males in 1969, by 1986 these figures had declined to 43 percent for both males and females (see Figure 15.1).

Among high school seniors, too, there have been parallel but less dramatic increases in the number for whom "the chance to earn a good deal of money" and to have "a predictable, secure future" was rated as very important in a job (Bachman & Johnston, 1979; Bachman et al., 1981, 1987). In accordance with these changing concerns and values, the percentages of college students enrolling in the arts and humanities and the sciences have declined steadily, while the percentages

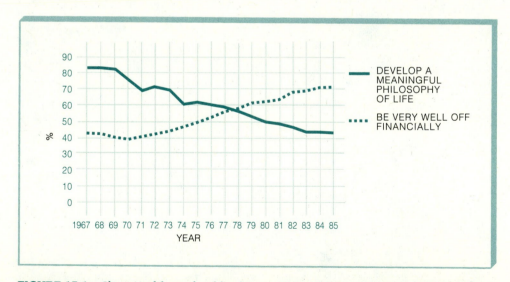

FIGURE 15.1   Changing life goals of freshmen, 1967–1985 (percentages). (Adapted from A. W. Astin, K. C. Green, & W. S. Korn. *The American freshman: Twenty year trends.* Los Angeles: Higher Education Research Institute, University of California at Los Angeles, 1987. By permission.)

enrolling in such fields as business and preprofessional programs have increased (Astin et al., 1986, 1987).

These changes have been particularly evident among women students. For example, while the number of first-year college women aspiring to be teachers declined by more than two-thirds in the past decade and a half (from 38 to 9.5 percent), the number planning to become business executives more than tripled (from less than 4 percent to nearly 14 percent (Astin et al., 1986, 1987).

Do these changes mean, as some observers have suggested, that contemporary adolescents and youth are engaged in a return to pre-1960s vocational values and goals? The answer is no. A study of college students in the late 1950s found them to be "models of the status quo," with few real commitments and a rather uncritical acceptance of the values and practices of social institutions generally, including those of government and big business (Goldsen, Rosenberg, Williams, & Suchman, 1960; Wolensky, 1977). In contrast, today's adolescents and youth, though they are generally more willing to adjust to the demands of the work place and more ready to accept compromise than their 1960s predecessors, are far less willing than 1950s youth to suppress their own individuality and need for self-expression, on or off the job. Nor are they as ready or willing to accept a sharp dichotomy between their private lives and their work. And they do not see as much need to do so. Although they acknowledge an increased interest in economic security and "getting ahead," they are also more concerned that their work be personally rewarding (Conger, 1981, in press; Bachman et al., 1988).

Nor do today's youth share the unquestioning faith in big business (and other social institutions) that characterized their 1950s counterparts, although their views are somewhat more favorable in the late 1980s than they were at the beginning of the decade. For example, in 1986 over 60 percent of high school seniors agreed that there is at least moderate dishonesty and immorality in the leadership of large corporations, and less than half believed that corporations are doing a good or very good job for the country (Bachman et al., 1987). One-third thought that corporations should have less influence on people's lives (down from 55 percent in 1980).

In brief, today's young people want to combine challenging work, self-expression, and free time for outside interests with at least a moderately high income, economic security, and the chance to get ahead (Conger, in press; Conger & Petersen, 1984; Yankelovich, 1981). How successful they will be in achieving these combined goals remains to be seen.

Vocational Prospects for Today's Youth

What, then, are the prospects for today's adolescents and young adults, in terms of the overall numbers and kinds of jobs that are likely to be available? Between 1960 and 1980 an increase of nearly 50 percent in the number of youth of working age, combined with a dramatic increase in the participation of women in the labor force, severely strained the ability of the labor market to absorb new workers (Smith, R. E., 1979; U.S. Department of Labor, 1984). Teenage unemployment increased accordingly, reaching a high of over 20 percent by 1980.

Since 1980, however, the number of young people has been decreasing steadily, and it will continue to do so for the remainder of this century (U.S. Bureau of the Census, 1987). As a consequence, young people aged 16 to 24, who made up nearly a quarter of the total work force only six years ago, account for only 21 percent today, and this figure will drop further, to 16 percent, by 1995 (Bacas, 1986; see Figure 15.2). Whereas the postwar baby-boom generation faced a growing shortage of jobs, the employers of the "baby-bust" generation are encountering a growing shortage of entry-level workers.

It would appear that these population trends augur well for the vocational prospects of the generation of young people who are now coming of age, and this may be generally true. However, a number of qualifications are necessary. It has become increasingly apparent in the last 20 years that automation and rapid technological change (especially in the development and application of computer technology), the consolidation of small businesses and farms into larger ones, and increased urbanization are producing significant shifts in employment patterns. The number of jobs available to unskilled industrial workers and farm workers declined during the 1970s; those for professional and technical workers, and for workers engaged in service occupations and clerical and sales positions, rose significantly. These trends are expected to continue well into the 1990s (see Figure 15.3).

It is clear that poorly educated youth with few skills will find themselves increasingly penalized in the years ahead. For example, in 1984, among 16- to 21-year-olds who were seeking work and not in college, more than twice as many dropouts as high school graduates were unemployed (27.7 percent versus 13.4 percent) (U.S. Bureau of the Census, 1986b).

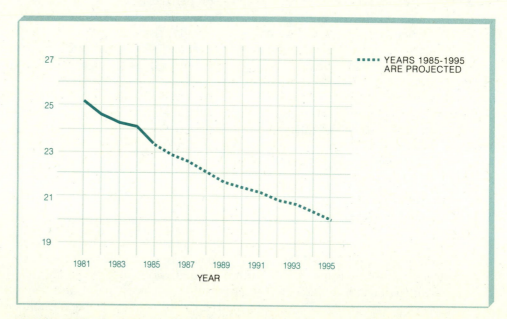

FIGURE 15.2   Youth in the Civilian Labor Force Aged 16–24 (in millions). (Adapted from Department of Labor, Bureau of Labor Statistics, 1986.)

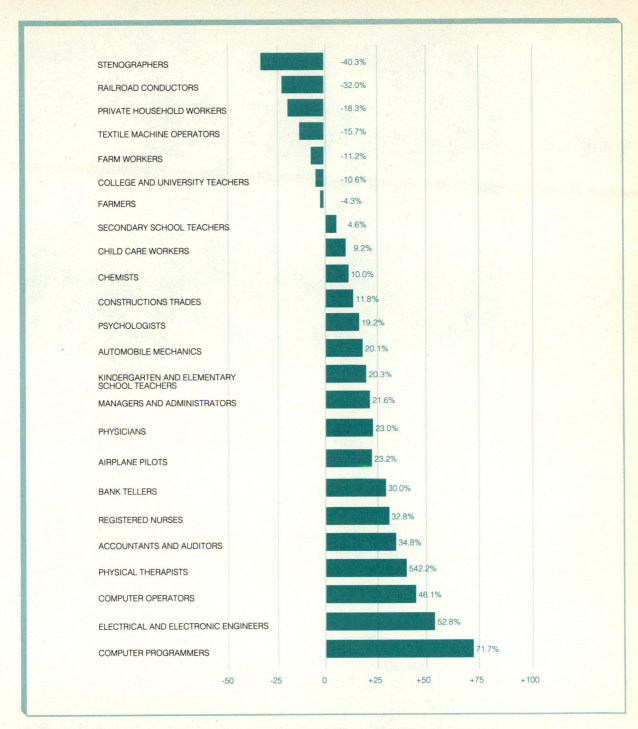

FIGURE 15.3   Job requirements and growth, 1984–1995. (Adapted from U.S. Department of Labor, Bureau of Labor Statistics. *Occupational projections and training data*, April 1986. Bulletin 2251. Washington, DC: U.S. Government Printing Office, 1986.)

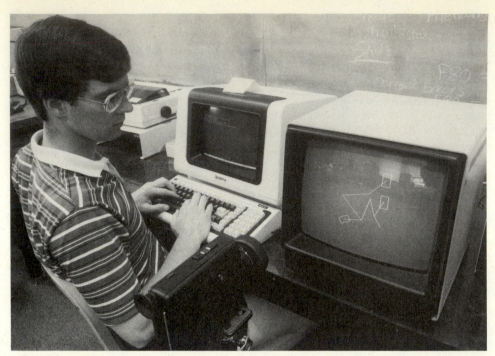

The number of jobs for professional and technical workers is expected to continue to increase in the 1990s.

Most critically, however, large segments of poor and minority youth have become increasingly isolated not only from participation in the economy but from the mainstream of American society (Conger, in press). Although the current economic recovery and a shrinking youth population have contributed to a decline of more than 10 percent in the unemployment rate among black youth since 1983, in mid-1986 the rate was still nearly 40 percent, sharply higher than the 15 percent rate for white teenagers. In some inner-city areas, the teenage minority unemployment rate remains as high as 70 percent or more. Our society is in real danger of creating a permanent underclass of poor minority youth who are excluded from any meaningful form of participation in society (Freeman, 1986; Lemann, 1986). For many inner-city youth, their only realistic chance of breaking out of the cycle of poverty and depression is likely to be through specifically targeted, adequately funded educational and training programs and accessible initial employment opportunities (Bacas, 1986; Brannigan, 1986; Conger, in press).

COLLEGE GRADUATES: DEMAND AND SUPPLY.   Although in the decade ahead opportunities will be much greater for youth with more skills and education, this does not mean that graduation from college will guarantee a high-level job—even with smaller numbers of young people coming into the job market. A major reason for this is the unprecedented rise in the number of college graduates, which more than doubled between 1960 and 1985 (U.S. Bureau of the Census, 1986b;

1987). Roughly one out of five college graduates who entered the labor market between 1970 and 1984 took a job that does not usually require a degree.

The oversupply of college graduates is likely to continue through the mid-1990s. Not all occupations that require a college degree will be overcrowded, however. For example, there will be good opportunities for systems analysts, nurses, elementary school teachers, and electrical engineers. Despite the generally competitive job market for college graduates, a college degree is still needed for most high-paying and high-status jobs. Moreover, unemployment rates are consistently lower for college graduates (U.S. Department of Labor, 1986).

MORAL DEVELOPMENT AND VALUES

At no time in life are people more concerned about moral values and standards than they are during adolescence. The increased cognitive capacities of adolescents foster greater awareness of moral issues and values and more sophistication in dealing with them. At the same time, the demands placed on adolescents by society are changing at an accelerated rate, and this in itself requires a continuing reappraisal of moral values and beliefs—particularly in a society as filled with conflicting pressures and values as our own. Under such circumstances the problem of developing a strong sense of identity cannot be separated from the problem of values. In short, "if individuals are to be able to maintain some stability in their conception of self and in internal guides to action in a changing world, they must be faithful to some basic values" (Conger, 1977a, p. 516), although they may have to adapt new ways of implementing those values to meet changing circumstances.

Cognitive Growth and Moral Development

The stages of moral judgment postulated by Kohlberg were discussed in Chapter 11. As indicated there, adolescent thinking about moral issues has usually advanced at least to the level of *conventional morality* (stages 3 and 4 in Kohlberg's system). At this level societal needs and values take primacy over individual interests. In stage 3, this means a strong emphasis on being "a good person in your own eyes and those of others" (Kohlberg, 1976, p. 34), that is, having socially desirable motives and showing concern for others. The intention behind behavior, not simply the behavior itself, is of major importance; one seeks approval by "being good." In stage 4, this approach is expanded to include concern with conforming to the social order and maintaining, supporting, and justifying it. Many adolescents do not advance beyond this level to postconventional stages of moral judgment (Colby et al., 1983; Kohlberg, 1976, 1984; Rest, 1983, 1986).

With more advanced cognitive and moral development, adolescents begin to question the social and political beliefs of their parents and other adults. Their personal values and opinions become less absolute and more relative. Political thought also becomes more abstract and less authoritarian. For example, when asked the purpose of laws, a 12-year-old replied, "If we had no laws, people could go around killing people" (Adelson, 1971, p. 1015). In contrast, by 15 or 16 years of age, and certainly by age 18, laws tend to be viewed as codes for guiding human conduct ("something for people to go by," "to set up a standard of behavior") (Adelson, 1982).

Maturity of moral judgment is positively related to level and quality of formal education, extent of exposure to the arts and humanities, breadth of cultural and intercultural experiences, assumption of real-world responsibilities and decision making, and such personal qualities as tolerance of diversity and open and trusting relationships with others (Rest, 1986; Schomberg, 1978; Spickelmier, 1983).

Both as high school students and later as young adults, students who score high in moral development are more likely than those who score low to display "growing awareness of the social world and one's place in it" (Rest, 1986, p. 57). They emerge as people who enjoy intellectual stimulation, seek challenges, make plans and set goals, and take responsibility for themselves and their environs (Deemer, in press; Spickelmier, 1986). Not surprisingly, they are more likely to "come from stimulating and challenging environments, and from social milieus that support their work, interest them, and reward their accomplishments" (Rest, 1986, p. 57).

Like an adult, an adolescent may be able to conceptualize moral issues with considerable sophistication and to formulate the proper moral course to take, yet may not always act in accordance with this formulation (Blasi, 1980; Hoffman, M. L., 1970, 1980; Rest, 1986; Weiss, 1982). In other words, as pointed out in Chapter 11, moral judgments do not relate to moral behavior in a simple way. In one study, subjects were asked, "Why should people follow rules?" (Tapp & Levine, 1972). They were then asked, "Why do you follow rules?" Most middle-school children and adolescents showed more "primitive" moral reasoning in answering the second question than in answering the first. For example, only 3 percent of older adolescents said that people *should* follow rules "to avoid negative consequences," but 25 percent said that they personally *would* do so.

Another study demonstrated that having to wrestle with real-life moral choices (such as whether or not to terminate an adolescent pregnancy) fosters development of a higher level of moral reasoning in some individuals but apparently leads to regression to a lower level in others. Young women who reached a higher level of moral reasoning when they made a decision about abortion showed better subsequent adjustment than those who regressed (Gilligan & Belenky, 1982).

Some adolescents show a reasonable degree of adherence to moral principles, even under duress. Others yield rather quickly to temptation or to group pressure to engage in thoughtless or antisocial behavior. Still others appear to be guided in their behavior solely by the threat of punishment. Whether moral standards will be internalized and serve as strong guides to behavior depends to a considerable extent on the nature of parent-child relationships. Parents who are warm and whose disciplinary practices are based primarily on induction (reasoning and explanations for rules or standards) are most likely to have children who reach mature levels of moral development, as evidenced by internalized moral standards (Hoffman, M. L., 1970, 1980). Inductive techniques are particularly important for adolescents. They "help foster the image of the parent as a rational, nonarbitrary authority. They provide the child with cognitive resources needed to control his own behavior" (Hoffman, M. L., 1970, p. 331).

Moral Values and Personal Conflicts

Adolescents' values do not always represent rational decisions arrived at in a logical fashion. Values are often chosen by adolescents for reasons having to do with personal conflicts and motives, many of which are unconscious (Conger, in press; Conger & Petersen, 1984; Douvan & Adelson, 1966). Preoccupation with the moral issues of war and peace, for example, may stem from perfectly rational concern about these important matters, or it may reflect uncertainty about being able to handle the strong aggressive impulses that are likely to accompany adolescence, particularly in boys. Conflicts with parents about morality or politics may reflect efforts to establish an independent identity or to express deeply felt resentment toward hostile or indifferent parents. Intimate, often unconscious motivations and conflicts have much to do with the increased preoccupation with moral values and beliefs that characterizes many adolescents.

Changing Religious Beliefs

A young person's religious beliefs are likely to become more abstract and less literal between the ages of 12 and 18 (Elkind, 1978; Farel, 1982; Fowler, 1981). For example, God comes to be seen more frequently as an abstract power and less frequently as a fatherly human being. Religious views also become more tolerant and less dogmatic.

Cultural as well as age-related changes in religious values appear to be at work) Caplow & Bahr, 1979). Although most young people still express a general belief in God or a universal spirit, during the 1960s and 1970s there was a steady erosion in the percentage of young people who viewed religion as "a very important personal value" (Yankelovich, 1974). This trend has continued through the 1980s. In 1980, 32 percent of American high school seniors stated that religion was very important in their lives; by 1986, this figure had declined to 26 percent (Bachman et al., 1981, 1987).

At least part of the decline in interest in religion is related to changes in values among young people and a perception on the part of many of them that religion—at least formal, institutionalized religion—is failing to reflect those changes (Conger & Petersen, 1984; Farel, 1982; Sorensen, 1973). For example, rightly or wrongly, approximately half of all adolescents believe that churches are not doing their best to understand young people's ideas about sex. Many more contemporary adolescents attribute an understanding attitude about sex to God than to institutionalized religion. A number of young people, particularly in the women's movement, also feel that the Catholic church and some Protestant denominations are not according full status and recognition to women, and a majority of Catholic youth disagree with the church's position on birth control, annulment and divorce, and the right of priests to marry.

At the same time, there has been an increase in interest in fundamentalist religious traditions among a significant number of youth. Nearly half of all Protestant teenagers and 22 percent of their Catholic peers report having had a "born-again" experience—a turning point in their lives achieved by making a personal commitment to Christ (Gallup, 1978; Norback, 1980). These figures are similar to those obtained among adults.

SECTS AND CULTS.   Another development among young people in the past two decades was the emergence of a number of new religious sects like the Jesus Movement, Hare Krishna, Children of God, and the Unification Church (Galanter, 1980; Gallup & Polling, 1980; Swope, 1980). Some of these groups are informal and loosely structured. They are held together principally by concern for others, disillusionment with materialistic values (or the apparent absence of strong personal values), and a belief—often simple and direct, and sometimes fundamentalist—in personal salvation. Other groups tend to be highly authoritarian in structure. They may require the surrender of all individual autonomy and complete conformity, in both behavior and belief, to the dictates of the leader.

Some young people enlist in such groups as a result of sudden and total conversion experiences following a period of rootlessness and identity confusion. There is often a prior history of difficulties in parent-child relationships, extensive drug use, sexual exploration, and life "on the road" (Adams & Gullota, 1983; Conger & Petersen, 1984; Dean, 1982). Other young people, particularly in less authoritarian movements, seem to be expressing a satisfying and, for them, workable set of simple, straightforward values in an otherwise chaotic society.

Current Trends in Adolescent Values

The greatest danger in discussing trends in adolescent values and behavior and their relationship to social change is the risk of overgeneralization. In the middle and late 1960s much was made of a so-called revolution in the values of young people, who were said to be developing a "counterculture." There is no question that the troubled decade of the 1960s brought major changes in the values and behavior of many American adolescents. A significant minority of young people became increasingly disillusioned by a society that they viewed as unjust, cruel, hypocritical, overly competitive, or, in the broadest sense of the term, immoral (Conger, 1973, 1981). In response, some, like the hippies, became social dropouts, while others initiated vigorous efforts to institute social change—efforts that ran the gamut from conventional political activity "within the system" to extreme "revolutionary" tactics.

By no means all adolescents joined the counterculture of the 1960s and early 1970s. Its values were most strongly held and expressed by a conspicuous, often highly articulate minority of young people on high school and college campuses, in the streets, and in films and the arts. Although the values of the *average* adolescent of that period did change in important respects, they changed less than popular stereotypes suggested (Conger, 1973; Harris, L., 1971; Yankelovich, 1974).

As America entered the 1980s, the risk of overgeneralization again became great. Some critics interpreted the marked decline in political and social activism that occurred during the 1970s as the beginning of an across-the-board return to more conservative and conformist pre-1960s attitudes and values. Again, however, the reality has proved considerably more complex than such a simplistic interpretation would lead us to expect (Conger, 1988, in press).

As we noted in discussing vocational choice, it is true that the social and economic values of adolescents have become more conservative. There is increased concern among adolescents and young adults for personal well-being and financial success. In addition, there is diminished concern for the welfare of others—particularly the disadvantaged—and of society itself (Astin, 1980; Astin et al., 1986, 1987; Bachman, & Johnston, 1979, Bachman et al., 1981, 1987). Less than one-fifth of contemporary high school seniors consider "making a contribution to society" or "working to correct social and economic inequities" a very important value (Bachman, et al., 1987). And among students entering college in 1986, record lows were recorded for interest in "participating in community action programs," "participating in programs to clean up the environment," and "promoting racial understanding." Even at a more personal level, the number of college students who considered "helping others in difficulty" to be a very important objective declined in the past decade, from 58 percent to 53.4 percent among males and from 75 percent to 70 percent among females.

This shift in emphasis from social to personal concerns has been accompanied by a decline in political liberalism (despite a recent modest reversal) and an increase in the proportion of people who view themselves as "middle-of-the-road" or "conservative" (see Figure 15.4). A further reason for this shift may be a general skepticism about ideologies and social institutions. Unlike their 1950s counterparts, today's young people have reservations about the infallibility, or even at times the morality, of major institutions like big business, big labor, Congress, the executive branch of government, the courts, the schools, and law enforcement agencies (Astin, et al., 1986, 1987; Bachman, J. G., Johnston, & O'Malley, 1987).

PERSONAL AND MORAL VALUES.   In their personal and moral values, too, today's young people show little resemblance to those of the 1950s. In the area of sexual values, not only has there not been a return to traditional sexuality morality but previous trends have accelerated, at least until recently (the impact of the AIDs epidemic on youth remains to be determined). The predominant view among both high school seniors and college students is that heterosexual behavior should be more a matter of personal decision than a subject for socially imposed moral codes (Bachman, J. G., et al., 1987; Astin et al., 1986, 1987).

More broadly, the desire to fulfill oneself as a person and to have opportunities for self-expression has also remained strong. The ideals of freedom, self-determination, and gender equality received increasingly broad support in the 1970s and 1980s. In accordance with the continuing emphasis on "freedom to be me," many young people showed heightened interest in physical well-being, as evidenced in jogging, conditioning programs, and concern for nutrition. Others

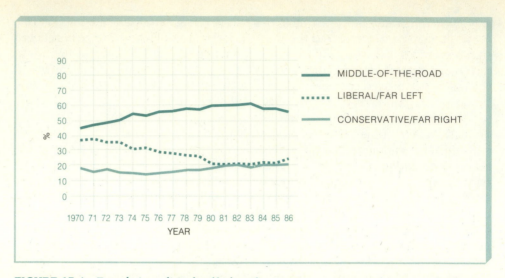

FIGURE 15.4   Trends in political self-identification (percentages of entering freshmen). (Adapted from A. W. Astin, K. C. Green, & W. S. Korn. *The American freshman: Twenty year trends.* Los Angeles: Higher Education Research Institute, University of California at Los Angeles, 1987. By permission.)

became involved in self-improvement programs and a variety of psychological therapies ranging from assertiveness training and support groups to meditation and relaxation programs. Self-realization—physical, psychological, spiritual, or material—was a central theme (Conger, 1981, 1988).

The appropriate question, in our view, is not whether the adolescents and young adults of the 1980s are engaged in a general retreat from the values of the 1960s and early 1970s. Rather, it is whether the extension and expansion of such values as self-fulfillment and self-expression is psychologically growth-enhancing in the absence of a corresponding sense of commitment to the welfare of others and of society itself.

THE BLUE-COLLAR REVOLUTION.   One of the more remarkable aspects of the changes in values that have taken place since the late 1960s is the extent to which the values of noncollege, working-class youth have become more like those of their more economically favored, college student peers. In 1969 the attitudes and beliefs of noncollege youth were markedly more conservative than those of college youth. This generalization held for a wide range of issues, from sexual freedom, drug use, and conformity in dress to views on the Vietnam War, minority rights, and the actions of business and government. Clearly, in the late 1960s young people, like adults, had their own "silent majority" (Yankelovich, 1969).

In the intervening years, however, there appears to have been a rapid transmission of values from a minority of college youth to youth generally (Conger, 1981, in press; Yankelovich, 1974, 1981). By the early 1980s differences between coilege or college-bound young people and their noncollege peers were much less extensive than they had been in the late 1960s. For example, both groups currently share similar views with respect to sexual morality, religion, the work ethic, race relations, the role of women in the work force, and the importance of marriage and family life (Bachman et al., 1981, 1987; Yankelovich, 1974, 1981).

Are today's young people—and adults—ready for a shift toward greater concern and compassion for others and away from self-absorption and a one-sided preoccupation with material rewards? Although it is too early to be sure, there are some encouraging signs (Conger, 1988). For example, three out of four Americans now believe that the problems of children and adolescents are serious and getting worse, and that government needs to take more responsibility in dealing with these problems—a complete reversal of popular sentiment in only four years (Harris, 1987).

One thing appears certain. Unless such a shift occurs, we will all be the losers. "The most obvious victims will continue to be those whose need is greatest and whose power is least; poor children, adolescents, and families" (Conger, 1988, p. 299). In a larger sense, however, all of us, young and old alike, will be victims. For the fact is that preoccupation with "self-realization," untempered by an abiding concern for others, is ultimately self-defeating. Without love and concern for others or for some transcendental purpose, it is not possible to realize one's self except in the most superficial sense (Conger, 1981, 1988; Erikson, 1980, 1983).

SUMMARY

A central task of adolescence is developing a sense of one's own identity, that is, a sense of oneself as a separate, distinctive individual. A sense of identity requires a perception of oneself as separate from others, a feeling of self-consistency or wholeness, and a sense of continuity of the self over time. It also requires psychosocial reciprocity—consistency between one's own and other people's perceptions of one's identity.

Although identity development is a lifelong process, the search for identity is especially relevant during adolescence. Achieving a clear sense of identity takes time and depends partly on cognitive skills. The search for identity is significantly influenced by relationships within the family; adolescents who feel free to explore a variety of possibilities come from families in which individuality is encouraged.

The search for identity can go wrong in either of two ways: It can be prematurely foreclosed or indefinitely extended. Identity foreclosure is a premature fixing of one's self-image that interferes with the development of other potentials and possibilities for self-definition. For example, it may result in lack of flexibility and inability to respond appropriately to stressful cognitive tasks. Identity confusion, on the other hand, results from a long, inconclusive search for identity; individuals who are unable to transcend identity confusion are likely to be immature and to have low self-esteem.

Individuals who have achieved a strong sense of identity after a period of active searching are likely to be more autonomous, creative, and complex in their thinking than those whose identities were formed without a period of confusion. They also show a greater capacity for intimacy and a more positive self-concept.

Gender identity is one major component of identity formation. Different individuals may define different characteristics as part of their gender identity. One female may consider a career to be central to her feminine identity, while another may think motherhood is a major component. *Androgyny* is a combination of culturally defined and valued masculine and feminine traits. Adolescents who are androgynous have high self-esteem and high levels of academic achievement, particularly in areas such as mathematics and formal logic.

Vocational identity is an important part of a person's overall identity. Opportunities for adolescents to gain constructive and appropriate work experiences can give them a sense of purpose and responsibility, help generate a feeling of meaningful participation in the broader society, and reduce the communication barrier between adults and young people. However, this is not generally true of the types of jobs that are most frequently available to adolescents attending school, and other employment may interfere with school performance.

Most young people's vocational interests develop in a rather unsystematic fashion and are subject to a variety of influences. Social class helps determine the kinds of occupations the young person will consider. Gender also affects occupational aspirations, although less so today than in previous generations. Family values and sex role attitudes are especially important in determining whether a young woman will seek a nontraditional career. More generally, if parents set high educational goals and reward good schoolwork, their children will have high levels of aspiration.

The father's occupation exerts a significant influence on the career choices of sons, not only because sons have more opportunities to become familiar with the father's occupation but also because the father is likely to communicate values that relate to his vocation. Maternal employment influences both sons' and daughters' attitudes regarding appropriate sex and vocational roles for women. Other influences on adolescents' career choices include teachers, school counselors, and peers.

In the 1980s the percentage of strongly career-minded college students has increased while the number of students who view college as an opportunity for self-discovery and change has declined. Parallel changes have occurred among high school students. These changes do not signal a return to pre-1960s values and goals, however. Today's young people want to combine challenging work, self-expression, and time for outside interests with a moderately high income and the chance to get ahead.

Although the labor market was hard pressed to absorb new workers in the past, the number of young workers is decreasing, a trend that augurs well for the vocational prospects of the generation that will come of age in the 1990s. Jobs will not be available in all areas, however; unskilled industrial workers and farm workers will have difficulty finding employment, while professional and technical workers and workers engaged in service occupations will have more opportunities.

The increased cognitive capacities of adolescents foster greater awareness of moral issues and values and more sophistication in dealing with them. Adolescent thinking about moral issues has usually advanced at least to the level of conventional morality. Adolescents begin to question the social and political beliefs of adults. Their personal values and opinions become less absolute, and their political thought becomes less authoritarian. They do not, however, always act in accordance with their moral values.

Religious beliefs are likely to become more abstract between the ages of 12 and 18. In general, there has been a decline in interest in religion among young people, although there has been an increase in interest in fundamentalist religious traditions and in new religious sects.

Although it is dangerous to generalize about adolescent values, it is true that the social and economic values of adolescents have become more conservative. There is increased concern for personal well-being and financial success, and diminished concern for the welfare of others and of society itself. The shift in emphasis from social to personal concerns has been accompanied by a decline in political liberalism.

In the area of sexual values, the predominant view among young people is that heterosexual behavior should be more a matter of personal decision than a subject for socially imposed moral codes. More broadly, the desire to fulfill oneself as a person and to have opportunities for self-expression has remained strong. On the other hand, there are indications that the nation may be ready for a shift toward greater compassion and concern for others.

REVIEW QUESTIONS

1. Describe the three main characteristics of a fully developed identity.

2. What role does the family play in the development of identity?

3. What is meant by identity foreclosure and identity confusion?

4. How is sex role identity related to overall identity?

5. What factors influence the vocational choices of adolescents?

6. In what ways do parents' occupations influence the vocational choices of their children?

7. How have the vocational values and attitudes of young people changed since the early 1970s?

8. What are the vocational prospects for today's youth?

9. How is moral development related to cognitive growth?

10. Briefly describe current trends in adolescent political, religious, personal and moral values.

GLOSSARY

identity foreclosure   A premature fixing of an individual's self-image that interferes with the development of other potentials and possibilities for self-definition.

identity confusion   A prolonged period in which an individual is unable to develop a strong, clear sense of identity.

gender identity   Awareness and acceptance of one's biological nature as a male or female.

sex role identity   One's perception of oneself as masculine or feminine according to one's own definition of these terms.

androgyny   A combination of socially valued "masculine" and "feminine" characteristics in the same individual.

SUGGESTED READINGS

Block, J. H. (1984). *Sex role identity and ego development*. San Francisco: Jossey-Bass. This book brings together the important contributions of the late Jeanne Block to our understanding of gender differences, their causes, and their effects on cognitive and emotional development.

Erikson, E. H. (1968). *Identity: Youth and crisis*. New York: Norton (paperback). A classic series of essays on identity development, with applications to the problems facing contemporary youth, women, and minorities.

Greenberger, E., & Steinberg, L. (1988). *When teenagers work: The psychological and social costs of adolescent employment*. New York: Basic Books. This well-researched book argues convincingly that much current teenage employment is of questionable value and, in some instances at least, may actually interfere with optimal educational, psychological, and even social development.

Grotevant, H. D., & Cooper, C. R. (Eds.) (1983). *Adolescent development in the family*. San Francisco: Jossey-Bass. The various studies described in this book indicate that adolescent development involves not an abandonment but, rather, a transformation of parent-child relationships. Continued "connectedness" to the family is needed even as the young person pursues the goals of autonomy and individuality.

Hoffman, M. L. (1980). Moral development in adolescence. In J. Adelson (Ed.), *Handbook of adolescent psychology*. New York: Wiley. A well-organized, clearly written summary of theory and research on moral development in adolescence.

Chapter Sixteen

ADOLESCENCE: ALIENATION AND PROBLEMS OF ADJUSTMENT

The Roots of Alienation
   A "New" Alienation?
Adolescents and Drugs
   What Are the Facts?
   Prevalence of Adolescent Drug Use
   Why Do Adolescents Use Drugs?
Adolescent Runaways
Adolescent Delinquency
   Sex Differences
   Social Change and Poverty
   Personality Factors and Parent-Child Relationships
   Prevention and Treatment of Delinquency
Psychological and Psychophysiological Disturbances
   Anxiety Reactions
   Adolescent Depression
   Suicide
   Adolescent Schizophrenia
   Brief Reactive Psychosis
   Eating Disorders
   Treatment of Adolescents

In their attitudes toward their own lives, most young people are reasonably optimistic. Although fewer noncollege youth than college youth feel that they are in control of their future (largely for economic reasons), nearly two-thirds of noncollege youth do feel that way. And among both groups three-quarters feel that, all in all, "my own life is going well." Nearly 70 percent say that they are "pretty happy," and another 18 percent say that they are "very happy." Six out of ten state that they anticipate "no difficulty in accepting the kind of life society has to offer." When asked whether they thought their lives would be better in five years, almost nine out of ten American high school seniors said yes—although only about one-third expected things to get better for the country during that period (Bachman et al., 1987).

Although young people generally feel reasonably happy, positive about themselves, and optimistic about their future, there remain significant minorities for whom life is not going well. As we will see in this chapter, these include young people who for one reason or another are alienated from society and its values, emotionally isolated, dependent on drugs, or delinquent. It also includes the growing number of young people who have attempted suicide, are runaways or "throwaways," or suffer from serious psychological or psychophysiological disturbances.

THE ROOTS OF ALIENATION

Alienation is a profound rejection of the values of society or an isolation from other people that goes well beyond the skepticism of the average adolescent. Lower-class minority and poor white youth who have suffered economic deprivation and ethnic discrimination clearly have reason to feel alienated from society. However, in the turbulent decade of the 1960s and early 1970s another kind of alienation became increasingly apparent—among privileged middle- and upper-class youth.

There were significant variations in the sources of these privileged youths' alienation and the ways in which it was manifested. For some, alienation was derived from certain developmental experiences, such as disturbed parent-child relationships, that would be likely to result in alienation in most societies (Conger, 1976; Keniston, 1968; Seeman, 1975). For others, specific social concerns played a dominant role: racial oppression, economic discrimination, violations of personal freedom, the bitterly opposed war in Vietnam, and the dangers of nuclear war. In still other instances, alienation was both deep and pervasive, amounting to a rejection of society as a whole. Society was viewed as inimical to these young people's most deeply held values: intimacy, individuality, autonomy, and honesty (Conger, 1976, 1981; Yankelovich, 1969, 1974).

Levels of political and social alienation have declined markedly since the early 1970s, although small but significant minorities of today's young people (10 to 20 percent) express strong disenchantment with major social institutions. They remain highly critical of government, business, labor, the military, the courts, the police, and the judicial system, and they feel that these institutions have too much influence in our society (Bachman et al., 1981, 1987).

Among the current generation of adolescents and youth, there seems to be an increasing pragmatism and a greater substitution of private for public concerns. Though not enchanted by the state of society and its institutions, these young people appear less inclined to view issues as one-sided, less likely to believe that social changes can occur quickly, and more skeptical of the ability of the individual to contribute significantly to them.

A "New" Alienation?

Although it is difficult to define with precision, a newer form of alienation has been noted in a minority of adolescents. This alienation is more subtle, elusive, and private than the highly public, multifaceted, intense, and strongly articulated alienation and dissent of the 1960s. It is characterized by increased feelings of loneliness; desire for—but difficulty in achieving—intimacy; feelings of rootlessness; a decreased sense of purpose and direction in life; and a diffuse sense of self (Conger, 1981, in press; Lasch, 1979; Yankelovich, 1981).

Achieving the capacity for intimacy is the developmental task that follows the attainment of identity, according to Erikson's theory (1968, 1983). Intimacy is a true sharing of oneself that involves caring, trust, and sustained commitment. This is especially true in love, but it is also true in friendship. The alternative to intimacy is isolation, and it appears to be quite common. A representative national survey found that 70 percent of Americans "now recognize that while they have many acquaintances they have few close friends—and they experience this as a serious void in their lives" (Yankelovich, 1981, p. 25). Moreover, two out of five stated that they have fewer close friends now than they did in the past. Whether these trends will be reversed, and whether current efforts to develop a greater sense of community (e.g., mutual support groups, neighborhood coalitions) will succeed, is still unclear (Conger, 1987, in press).

ADOLESCENTS AND DRUGS

Until recently, American adults tended to view increased drug use as an isolated adolescent phenomenon, one that was almost exclusively a product of the youth culture of the latter 1960s. However, the picture is changing. More and more, excessive drug use is being viewed as a major problem not only of adolescents and youth but also of society as a whole (Conger, in press; Kerr, 1986, Lamar, 1986). Reports of extensive drug use among professional athletes, stockbrokers, young executives, actors—even physicians and nurses, train crews, pilots, and air traffic controllers—have alarmed parents, politicians, and the public, as has the mounting use of cocaine, especially its most lethal form, "crack." In recent national polls 50 percent of Americans said that increased drug use reflects a "fundamental breakdown" in morals, while 42 percent said that the problem is "serious, but not a moral breakdown" (Clymer, 1986, p. 16). Not surprisingly, these percentages were higher for people age 45 and older than for those between the ages of 18 and 44.

What Are the Facts?

Widespread drug use and abuse are not restricted to adolescents and did not begin with the advent of the youth culture in the 1960s. Although there have been, and to some extent still are, significant differences between generations in patterns of drug use, the fact is that American society has been developing into a drug culture for many years. For example, one-quarter to one-third of all prescriptions written in the United States are for pep or diet pills (amphetamines) or tranquilizers like Valium (which is now the most widely prescribed drug in the nation). Also, adult use of a number of drugs has increased as members of the baby-boom generation and their immediate successors have aged, replacing older adults who, although they were frequent users of alcohol and tobacco, were infrequent users of many other drugs, such as marijuana, cocaine, and hallucinogens (Brinkley, 1986; Johnston, L. D. et al., 1987).

Prevalence of Adolescent Drug Use

It is important to note that although far too many adolescents become serious, high-risk drug users, the majority do not. Despite predictions in the late 1960s of an all-out epidemic of indiscriminate adolescent drug use that would spread to most young people, to date an epidemic of this magnitude has not occurred. Although use of marijuana, alcohol, and tobacco is widespread among young people, and one-quarter have tried amphetamines (stimulants) at one time or another, other substances have never been used by more than one person in five in the United States (fewer in most other Western countries), and many occasional users appear to have quit, as indicated by the response "no use in the past year" (see Figure 16.1).

The overall rate of drug use by adolescents, which reached a peak in 1978, declined from 1979 through 1987 (Johnston, L. D., 1988; Johnston, L. D. et al. 1984, 1987). Regular use of marijuana, particularly daily use, which had been rising steadily among high school students for fifteen years, declined by half from 1978 through 1987, reaching its lowest level in over a decade. Peer disapproval of marijuana use—particularly steady use—and the perceived risk associated with the drug reached its highest levels in the same period (Bachman, Johnston, O'Malley, & Humphrey, 1988; Johnston, L. D., 1988). Decreases also occurred in the use of barbiturates, tranquilizers, and cigarettes, while use of alcohol and other drugs leveled off.

Perhaps most important, in 1987 cocaine use showed a significant drop for the first time in eight years (see Table 16.1). At the same time, the percentage of high

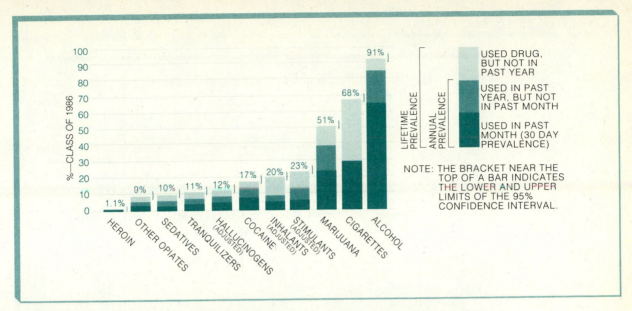

FIGURE 16.1 Prevalence and recency of use: eleven types of drugs, class of 1986. (Adapted from L. D. Johnston, P. M. O'Malley, & J. G. Bachman. *National trends in drug use and related factors among American high school students and young adults, 1975–1986.* U.S. Department of Health [DHHS Publication No. ADM 87–1535] Washington, DC: National Institute on Drug Abuse, U.S. Government Printing Office, 1987.)

school seniors who perceived "great risk" in occasional cocaine use increased to 67 percent (from 54 percent in 1986). Undoubtedly, the tragic deaths of sports stars Len Bias and Don Rogers as a result of cocaine use served to get the attention of many young Americans. The message was clear: No one is invincible. Personal attitudes and peer norms are also changing: In 1987, 87 percent of seniors disapproved of even trying cocaine, a 7 percent jump in one year. Fully 97 percent disapprove of regular cocaine use (Johnston, L. D. et al., 1988).

Despite these trends, there is little reason for complacency. Over 15 percent of seniors, and nearly 40 percent of high school graduates in their late twenties, have at least tried cocaine. Moreover, drug use is higher among school dropouts than among those who remain in school (Johnston, L. D., 1988). The rapid spread of "crack" or "rock," an extremely potent and addictive form of cocaine, has created major problems for drug treatment centers and law enforcement officials in New York, Los Angeles, Chicago, Detroit, and other cities (see Box 16.1). For most drugs other than cocaine, between 40 and 50 percent of eventual users initiate use during or prior to the ninth grade (Johnston, L. D. et al., 1987). Almost 10 percent of 14-year-olds are already heavy drinkers.

In the minds of most people who work with adolescents, the young person in greatest danger is not the one who has occasionally had a few drinks or smoked marijuana with friends "for fun"; it is the adolescent or youth who repeatedly turns to drugs in order to cope with insecurity, stress, low self-esteem, feelings of rejection or alienation, or problems of daily living. One of the important tasks of adolescence is

TABLE 16.1

Trends in Thirty-Day Prevalence of Sixteen Types of Drugs

	Percent who used in last thirty days						
	Class of 1975	Class of 1976	Class of 1977	Class of 1978	Class of 1979	Class of 1980	Class of 1981
Approx. N =	(9400)	(15400)	(17100)	(17800)	(15500)	(15900)	(17500)
Marijuana/Hashish	27.1	32.2	35.4	37.1	36.5	33.7	31.6
Inhalants[a]	NA	0.9	1.3	1.5	1.7	1.4	1.5
Inhalants Adjusted[b]	NA	NA	NA	NA	3.2	2.7	2.5
Amyl & butyl nitrites[c,h]	NA	NA	NA	NA	2.4	1.8	1.4
Hallucinogens	4.7	3.4	4.1	3.9	4.0	3.7	3.7
Hallucinogens Adjusted[d]	NA	NA	NA	NA	5.3	4.4	4.5
LSD	2.3	1.9	2.1	2.1	2.4	2.3	2.5
PCP[c,h]	NA	NA	NA	NA	2.4	1.4	1.4
Cocaine	1.9	2.0	2.9	3.9	5.7	5.2	5.8
"Crack"[g]	NA	NA	NA	NA	NA	NA	NA
Other cocaine[c]	NA	NA	NA	NA	NA	NA	NA
Heroin	0.4	0.2	0.3	0.3	0.2	0.2	0.2
Other opiates[e]	2.1	2.0	2.8	2.1	2.4	2.4	2.1
Stimulants[e]	8.5	7.7	8.8	8.7	9.9	12.1	15.8
Stimulants Adjusted[c,f]	NA	NA	NA	NA	NA	NA	NA
Sedatives[e]	5.4	4.5	5.1	4.2	4.4	4.8	4.6
Barbiturates[e]	4.7	3.9	4.3	3.2	3.2	2.9	2.6
Methaqualone[e]	2.1	1.6	2.3	1.9	2.3	3.3	3.1
Tranquilizers[e]	4.1	4.0	4.6	3.4	3.7	3.1	2.7
Alcohol	68.2	68.3	71.2	72.1	71.8	72.0	70.7
Cigarettes	36.7	38.8	38.4	36.7	34.4	30.5	29.4

NOTES: Level of significance of difference between the two most recent classes: s = .05, ss = .01, sss = .001. NA indicates data not available.

[a]Data based on four questionnaire forms. N is four-fifths of N indicated.

[b]Adjusted for underreporting of amyl and butyl nitrites. See text for details.

[c]Data based on a single questionnaire form. N is one-fifth of N indicated.

[d]Adjusted for underreporting of PCP. See text for details.

[e]Only drug use which was not under a doctor's orders is included here.

[f]Based on the data from the revised question, which attempts to exclude the inappropriate reporting of non-prescription stimulants.

[g]Data based on two questionnaire forms. N is two-fifths of N indicated.

[h]Question text changed slightly in 1987.

Source: L. D. Johnston, J. G. Bachman, & P. M. O'Malley (in press). National trends in drug use and related factors among American high school students and young adults, 1975–1987. U.S. Department of Health and Human Services. Washington, D.C.: National Institute on Drug Abuse.

	Percent who used in last thirty days						
	Class of 1982	Class of 1983	Class of 1984	Class of 1985	Class of 1986	Class of 1987	'86–'87 change
Approx. N =	(17700)	(16300)	(15900)	(16000)	(15200)	(16300)	
Marijuana/Hashish	28.5	27.0	25.2	25.7	23.4	21.0	−2.4s
Inhalants[a]	1.5	1.7	1.9	2.2	2.5	2.8	+0.3
Inhalants Adjusted[b]	2.5	2.5	2.6	3.0	3.2	3.5	+0.3
Amyl & butyl nitrites[c,h]	1.1	1.4	1.4	1.6	1.3	1.3	0.0
Hallucinogens	3.4	2.8	2.6	2.5	2.5	2.5	0.0
Hallucinogens Adjusted[d]	4.1	3.5	3.2	3.8	3.5	2.8	−0.7
LSD	2.4	1.9	1.5	1.6	1.7	1.8	+0.1
PCP[c,h]	1.0	1.3	1.0	1.6	1.3	0.6	−0.7s
Cocaine	5.0	4.9	5.8	6.7	6.2	4.3	−1.9sss
"Crack"[g]	NA	NA	NA	NA	NA	1.5	NA
Other cocaine[c]	NA	NA	NA	NA	NA	4.1	NA
Heroin	0.2	0.2	0.3	0.3	0.2	0.2	0.0
Other opiates[e]	1.8	1.8	1.8	2.3	2.0	1.8	−0.2
Stimulants[e]	13.7	12.4	NA	NA	NA	NA	NA
Stimulants Adjusted[c,f]	10.7	8.9	8.3	6.8	5.5	5.2	−0.3
Sedatives[e]	3.4	3.0	2.3	2.4	2.2	1.7	−0.5s
Barbiturates[e]	2.0	2.1	1.7	2.0	1.8	1.4	−0.4
Methaqualone[e]	2.4	1.8	1.1	1.0	0.8	0.6	−0.2
Tranquilizers[e]	2.4	2.5	2.1	2.1	2.1	2.0	−0.1
Alcohol	69.7	67.2	65.9	65.3	2.1	66.4	+1.1
Cigarettes	30.0	30.3	29.3	30.1	29.6	29.4	−0.2

learning to cope with stress, conflict, and frustration; other key tasks include the development of cognitive, social, and vocational skills and the establishment of rewarding interpersonal relationships. Failure to meet these essential demands because of repeated escapes into the world of drugs leaves the young person ill prepared to meet the additional demands of responsible adulthood.

A significant minority of adolescents who may think that they are trying drugs only for fun or to experiment find that drug use becomes a psychological crutch. In addition, an extremely addictive drug like crack produces such an intense rush (high), and such a powerful subsequent crash, that it may lead to compulsive repetitive behavior, even among first-time users (Lamar, 1986). While addiction to regular cocaine typically develops over several years, crack users usually are hooked after six or eight weeks or less (Conger, in press). In the words of one expert, "There is no such thing as the recreational use of crack" (Morganthau, 1986, p. 58).

BOX 16.1

Adolescents and Crack

Since crack first emerged on the drug scene in 1983, this relatively inexpensive, highly addictive form of cocaine has had a devastating effect on the already torn social fabric of poor urban neighborhoods, and its use is spreading into middle-class areas (Lamar, 1986, 1988). Most of the recent rapid rise in youth gang violence and murder is related to drugs, especially crack (see chart). In part, this has resulted from the effects of drugs on users; in larger measure, it stems from disputes over potentially enormous profits for dealers. Unlike their predecessors in the heroin trade, crack dealers (many of whom are part of a nationwide network of Jamaican gangs) are likely to be far more violent, impulsive, and ready to kill at the slightest provocation.

Young people are heavily involved in all aspects of the processing and sale of crack—far more than any other drug, including heroin. For poor ghetto adolescents with no other skills, the lure of easy money can be hard to resist; "many have grown up in fatherless homes, watching their mothers labor at low-paying jobs or struggle to stretch a welfare check" (Lamar, 1988, p. 20). With unemployment rates exceeding 50 percent in many ghetto areas, these largely unskilled, poorly educated youth find little work available, and what there is usually pays

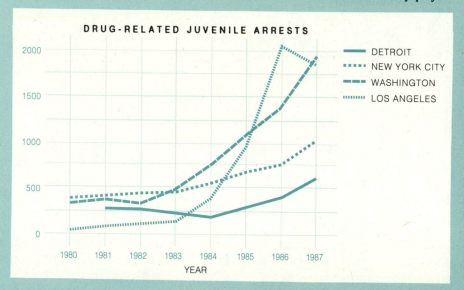

Cocaine-related juvenile arrests in major cities, 1981–1987. (Adapted from J. V. Lamar. Kids who sell crack. *Time*, May 9, 1988, pp. 20-33. By permission.)

only a minimum wage—"chump change," in street language—hardly enough to pay for food and clothing, much less a decent place to live.

In contrast, dealers in such areas can often make $3000 or more a week, and even 9- and 10-year-olds may make $100 a day as lookouts. For those higher up in the drug trade, a major advantage of employing young adolescents is that they are rarely imprisoned for long; consequently, "they provide a uniquely recyclable labor pool" (Lamar, 1988, p. 22).

To date, police crackdowns have had little effect on the drug trade. In addition, prisons and juvenile facilities in most major cities are already severely overcrowded, as are most treatment centers for youthful victims of crack. For example, the treatment program in the borough of Queens in New York City is currently able to treat only one in every twenty prospects. Moreover, graduates of even the best programs have a 50 percent relapse rate (Lamar, 1988).

Unless major steps are taken soon to institute workable, cost-effective programs in the areas of employment and education, as well as expanded prevention and treatment programs, it appears likely that increasing numbers of urban youth will end up as criminals, burned-out addicts, or casualties of drug wars before the age of 20.

The rapid increase in the use of crack has created serious problems for many adolescents as well as for society as a whole.

Why Do Adolescents Use Drugs?

The reasons that adolescents use drugs vary widely, as does the seriousness of their drug use. One reason that adolescents may try a drug is simply because it is easily available (Johnston, L. D. & O'Malley, 1986; Johnston, L. D. et al., 1987). Adolescents are curious about their expanding world. In addition, they are far more inclined to take risks than most adults. They probably do so partly to prove their boldness ("not being chicken") and sense of adventure, and partly because they do not really believe, at least initially, that anything disastrous can really happen to *them* (Conger, 1979, in press).

PEER PRESSURE.   Peers play an important part in adolescent drug use (Brook, Lukoff, & Whiteman, 1980; Brunswick & Boyle, 1979; Elliott, Huizinga, & Ageton, 1985). Indeed, one of the best predictors of whether an adolescent will use a drug is use of that drug by friends, especially the young person's best friend (Jessor & Jessor, 1977; Kandel, 1980).

Overall disapproval of the use (especially regular use) of drugs, including marijuana, has risen steadily in recent years, at least among in-school adolescents (Bachman et al., 1988; Johnston, L. D., 1988). However, among out-of-school youth in socially disintegrating urban areas current trends are far more ominous. It is in these areas that the use and sale of crack and other dangerous drugs has risen most rapidly, along with related gang violence and homicides.

PARENT-CHILD RELATIONSHIPS.   Whether adolescents become involved in serious drug use appears to depend a good deal on their relationships with their parents. For children of democratic, authoritative, accepting parents (especially those with relatively traditional values) who allow the gradual development of independence, the risk of serious drug involvement is generally low. For children whose parents have not been loving, and who are either neglectful (overly permissive) or authoritarian and hostile, the risk of significant drug use is much greater (Barnes, G. M., 1984; Jessor, 1984; Kovach & Glickman, 1983). In such cases a young person may use drugs as a form of anger or rebellion—or simply to get some response from the parents as a sign that they care (Conger, 1979).

ESCAPE FROM THE PRESSURES OF LIFE.   Another reason adolescents frequently give for using drugs is to escape from tension and the pressures of life or from boredom (Johnston, L. D., et al., 1987). As noted earlier, if drugs are used to escape from the developmental tasks of adolescence—learning to cope with stress and acquiring cognitive, social, and vocational skills—they may interfere with the young person's preparation to meet the additional demands of responsible adulthood.

EMOTIONAL DISTURBANCE.   For other young people, particularly heavy multiple-drug users, reliance on drugs may reflect emotional disturbance. In some such cases we need to look to disturbances in family relationships during the course of development for clues to the young person's difficulties. Among adolescents in residential treatment centers and halfway houses for alcohol and drug users, common themes acknowledged both by staff members and by recovering users are feelings of parental rejection or indifference; lack of acceptance by peers; emotional isolation; and low self-esteem, which the young person attempts to conceal by appearing "cool" (Brook, et al., 1980; Conger, 1979; Kandel, 1980).

Some young people who have been using alcohol or drugs steadily since pre-adolescence acknowledge that they have never known any other way to cope with anxiety, boredom, depression, fear of failure, or lack of purpose. Poignantly, an important aim of one treatment program, in addition to helping young people learn to deal with their personal problems and establish genuine friendships with peers, was simply to teach them something many did not know: how to have fun without drugs (Conger, in press; Conger & Petersen, 1984).

ALIENATION OR SOCIETAL REJECTION. In some instances, adolescent drug use may reflect alienation and a turning inward to the self-preoccupied world of mind-altering drugs (Conger & Petersen, 1984; Pittel & Miller, 1976). In other instances, an indifferent society does the rejecting. Too many young people face the future without hope. Many are confronted with economic, social, or racial discrimination, impossible living conditions, untreated physical ailments, and broken homes. As a result, they may give up the search for ego identity and a meaningful life and seek escape in the oblivion of hard narcotics, or what one adolescent addict called "death without permanence, life without pain" (Luce, 1970, p. 10).

In sum, there are many reasons that adolescents may take drugs, with varying outcomes. Drugs may produce oblivion, temporary escape, or even a greater appreciation of beauty. But there is little evidence that they produce a long-term sense of well-being, true creativity, or the ability to cope successfully with the demands of living; in fact, there is considerable evidence that theses qualities are impaired by drug use (Conger & Petersen, 1984).

ADOLESCENT RUNAWAYS

Each year more than 1 million young people run away from home (Garbarino, Wilson, & Garbarino, 1986; Senate Committee, 1977, 1981). Of these, perhaps half return after a few days or weeks. Most of the rest become, for all intents and purposes, homeless (House Committee, 1984; Janus, McCormack, Burgess, & Hartman, 1987). Although those who return home after a brief interval are more likely than nonrunaways to have adjustment problems and difficulties in family relationships, it is those who do not return who are of greatest concern to youth workers. These adolescents are in jeopardy for a variety of reasons: They are more likely to come from dysfunctional homes, to have significant adjustment problems, and to be victims of exploitation, neglect, or even death on the streets (Garbarino, et al., 1986).

Studies of the families of "serious" runaways typically reveal chronic patterns of family conflict and lack of communication. Often, however, the problems in these children's homes are much worse. They may include parental alcoholism, family violence, physical and sexual abuse (including incest), chronic neglect, and

These teenagers, who were abandoned by their parents, formed a club called Nobody's Children.

outright rejection (Adams & Munro, 1979; Brennan, 1980; Garbarino et al., 1986; Janus, McCormack, Burgess, & Hartman, 1987). In a recent study of homeless runaways in Toronto, for example, 73 percent reported having been physically beaten and 51 percent reported sexual abuse (Janus et al., 1987). Clearly, many "runaways" could more aptly be described as "throwaways," even when parental mistreatment has not included actual ejection of the young person from the home (see Box 16.2).

In some cases, running away from home may constitute a healthy response to an impossible situation (Silbert & Pines, 1980). More often, however, the young person already carries the psychological scars of prior mistreatment. These may include low self-esteem, mistrust, lack of social competence, suicidal impulses, emotional isolation, fear of sex, feelings of going crazy, and psychophysiological problems (Brennan, Huizinga, & Elliott, 1978; Edelbrock, 1980; Garbarino et al., 1986; Janus et al., 1987). Runaways who have been subjected to extremely stressful events, such as rape and assault, may show symptoms of *post-traumatic stress disorder* similar to those found among combat veterans. These symptoms include denial of the traumatic event or obsessive preoccupation with it; unpredictible flashbacks; fears both of social involvement and of being alone; crying spells, suicidal thoughts, sleep problems, and self-deprecating feelings (Janus et al., 1987).

Ironically, "the personal maladjustment, family conflict, and parental mistreatment that often precipitate running away also make the adolescent especially vulnerable to the risks that running away itself produces" (Garbarino et al., 1986, p. 45). Lacking money, food, or shelter, adolescent runaways who flock to major cities are ready candidates for exploitation. In one year alone, over 400 runaway teenage girls from the Minneapolis area were entrapped into prostitution by New York City

BOX 16.2

Runaway or Throwaway? One Runaway's Response to Abuse

Marie is a sixteen-year-old, black female; 5 feet, 5 inches tall and weighing 110 pounds; with black, curly hair and a pretty, if overly made-up face. At the beginning of the interview, Marie appeared shy and nervous. She rarely raised her eyes; she spoke in a quiet, somewhat mumbled voice, and she twisted two fingers of her left hand with her right hand.

Marie first ran away from home at age fifteen and has run away twice. She last left home about a month before our interview and has been on her own for the last week.

The earliest that Marie remembers being physically abused is at age six. She says that both her mother and her father beat her at that time. When asked to recall that specific first instance, Marie is unable to do so and says that she thinks she was beaten because she did not do her chores. She recalls that her brother was being hit with a stick and dragged down stairs, and she remembers knowing she was hurt. Marie explains that she has trouble remembering things, as there were so many incidents that she cannot separate them. She was beaten every day that she can remember until she ran away from home.

When questioned about whether she had ever been sexually abused, Marie initially said she had not. However, during the discussions of her relationship with her father, it becomes apparent that her father molested her frequently, often during the physical beatings. Marie remembers his "always pinching my buttocks and touching my breasts." She says that her grandmother once told her that her father had raped his sister and that Marie should try to stay away from him.

When Marie was fifteen years old, she told her friends that she could not stand it any more and that she was leaving. Without saying anything to her parents, she left for a babysitting job, called a girlfriend, and after getting permission from her girlfriend's parents, took a bus to her friend's home. She says that being physically abused was the most important reason for running away.

Her girlfriend's parents called the Children's Aid Society, and Marie told them about the abuse. She said that they didn't believe her and that they brought her back home. Her parents were angry with her when she returned home because "I left and because they said I made up stories."

The parental physical abuse continued during her final year at home, and when she could stand it no longer, Marie ran again to the same girlfriend's home. Her father and mother, when contacted by her girlfriend's parents, were angry. Sometime in the next few weeks her mother told her father that Marie was sleeping with a boy at the girlfriend's home. The father became enraged, went to the friend's home, and beat Marie. He "grabbed me by the breasts and threw me into a chair and then a wall." Marie ran away from her friend's home and traveled from her province to Toronto. Marie had arrived at the shelter the day before our interview.

Marie reports suffering from headaches, dizzy spells, and sleep problems (nightmares) during childhood and at present. She has always felt lonely and has always been afraid of adult men and women. She admits to shyness, nervousness, self-mutilation, and suicidal feelings. (From M-D Janus, A. McCormack, A. W. Burgess, and C. Hartman. *Adolescent Runaways: Causes and Consequences*. Lexington, MA: Lexington Books, pp. 50–51. Copyright © 1987. By permission.)

pimps (*New York Times*, 1977). Indeed, a fifteen-block stretch of Eighth Avenue pornography parlors, strip joints, cheap bars, and fleabag hotels became known as the Minnesota Strip to the young hookers (male and female), as well as drifters, pimps, and addicts, who populated it. Although current redevelopment projects in the area have led to shifts in locale, the activities themselves continue to expand.

Thousands of adolescent runaways, male and female, have become involved in prostitution, including homosexual prostitution, and the production of pornographic films and magazines, especially in large metropolitan areas like Los Angeles and New York. The average age at which adolescent girls enter prostitution is 14, and the great majority are under 16 (Weisberg, 1985). In addition, many runaways are robbed, physically assaulted, underfed, or lured into drug use and small-time pushing. Their need for adequate human services—health care, shelter, protection, and counseling—is often desperate (Janus et al., 1987). Each year more than 5000 young people are buried in unmarked graves because nobody has identified or claimed them (NBC Monitor, 1983).

Temporary shelters, such as Under 21 (run by Covenant House), Independence House, and The Door: A Center of Alternatives in New York City, make a valiant effort to protect and assist young runaways, but they are typically understaffed and underfunded in relation to the increasing size of the problems they face, and many young people have had to be turned away from these shelters (Janus et al., 1987; Scott, 1980). It is estimated that no more than one in twelve of the runaway and homeless youth who have actually been identified and counted are currently receiving shelter, and no more than one in three are receiving services of any kind. When the large number of such youth who escape the attention of youth workers or police is taken into account, the figures become even more alarming (House Committee, 1984; Janus et al., 1987). The need for our society to assume a far

Among the best-known shelters for runaways is Under 21, operated by Covenant House in New York City under the leadership of Father Bruce Ritter.

greater burden of responsibility for abused and exploited children and adolescents is urgent.

ADOLESCENT DELINQUENCY

In our society the term **juvenile delinquent** refers to a young person, generally under 18 years of age, who engages in behavior that is punishable by law. Some delinquent acts, such as robbery, aggravated assault, rape, homicide, or illegal drug use, would also be considered crimes if they were committed by adults. Others are **status offenses**—acts like curfew violations, truancy, "incorrigibility," running away, and underage drinking—that are illegal only when committed by young people. Delinquency itself is a legal rather than a psychological term; what is considered delinquent at one time and place may be lawful at another time or in another place.

After rising rapidly in the 1960s and 1970s, the delinquency rate in this country reached a peak in 1980; it then declined slightly (see Figure 16.2). Whether this relatively steady rate will persist (albeit at a distressingly high level), only time will tell. At current levels, it is estimated that at least 22 percent of boys and 10 percent of girls are likely to turn up in juvenile-court records before they reach adulthood (Elliott, Ageton, Huizinga, Knowles, & Canter, 1983; Farrington, 1981, 1987; Shannon, 1981).

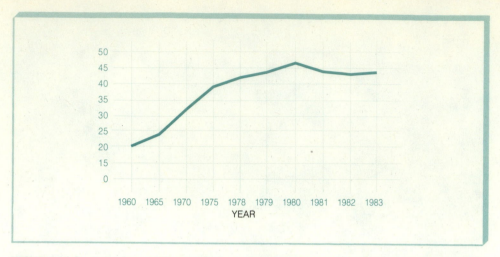

FIGURE 16.2   Rate (per 1000 population) of delinquency cases disposed of by juvenile courts involving children and adolescents 10 through 17 years of age. (Adapted from U.S. Bureau of the Census, *Statistical abstract of the United States*, 1987 [107th ed.]. Washington, D.C.: U.S. Government Printing Office, 1986.)

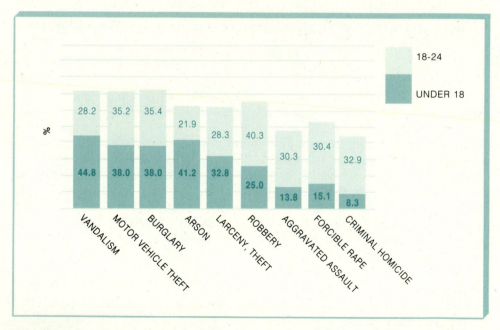

FIGURE 16.3   Arrests of persons under 18 years of age, and of persons between 18 and 24 years of age, as a percentage of all arrests. (Adapted from Federal Bureau of Investigation, *Crime in the United States*, annual; and U.S. Bureau of the Census, *Statistical abstract of the United States*, 1987 [107th ed.]. Washington, D.C.: U.S. Government Printing Office, 1986.)

Since 1960 the incidence of serious offenses by young people has been rising at a faster rate than the rate of delinquency in general. Although in 1985 people aged 14–17 comprised only 26 percent of the total population, they accounted for a far higher percentage of many offenses (see Figure 16.3).

Sex Differences

There are clear sex differences in the incidence of recorded delinquency. Although the male:female ratio has declined in the last half-century both in the United States and in England, boys still outnumber girls in juvenile arrests, particularly for serious offenses (Farrington, 1987; U.S. Bureau of the Census, 1986b; Visher & Roth, 1986). For example, boys outnumber girls in rates of burglary and robbery by approximately 15 to 1; in contrast, sex ratios are lowest for offenses like theft and shoplifting (less than 3 to 1). Because girls also tend to become involved in delinquency at later ages than boys, the male:female ratio is highest in early adolescence (Elliott et al., 1983; Farrington, 1987). A number of factors may contribute to sex differences in delinquency. These include opportunity (boys are more likely to "hang out" in groups on street corners, girls in shopping malls); differences in aggressiveness and physical strength; and socialization differences, including less parental supervision of boys (Elliott et al., 1985; Farrington, 1987).

Social Change and Poverty

Both social conditions and individual experiences contribute to juvenile delinquency. Poverty and associated living conditions are one set of factors, together with major changes that disrupt the structure and functioning of societies. Thus, in the United States and other highly industrialized nations current high rates of delinquency appear to be related at least in part to changes in the structure of society. Increased geographic mobility has disrupted well-established cultural patterns and family ties, as have social disorganization and population shifts in large metropolitan areas. In addition, unemployment and cutbacks in social programs for the poor have intensified the frustration and financial need of people at or below the poverty line (Conger, 1987; Edelman, 1987).

Research has indicated that economic deprivation is most likely to lead to crime and delinquency when it is associated with marked inequality in the distribution of society's resources. In one study, a number of indexes of inequality were used to predict average crime rates in 193 cities over a six-year period. The income gap between the poor and the average income earner was shown to be a significant predictor of crime rates (Braithwaite, 1981).

Increases in delinquency, as well as other adolescent difficulties, appear to be most likely in situations in which a sense of community solidarity and the integrity of the extended family have been most seriously disrupted (e.g., in urban ghettos and in some affluent suburban communities). They are least likely in situations in which these ties have been preserved, as is the case in some small, stable, relatively isolated towns and cities (Conger, in press). In recent years the greatest increase in the juvenile crime rate has occurred in the suburbs. Within the suburbs, increases appear to be greatest in communities and among families characterized by a high degree of social and geographic mobility and a lack of stable ties to other people and social institutions (National Center, 1979; U.S. Bureau of the Census, 1987; U.S. Federal Bureau of Investigation, annual).

Nevertheless, absolute rates of delinquency are still highest in deteriorated neighborhoods near the centers of large cities (Braithwaite, 1981; Gold, 1987; Rutter & Giller, 1984). In such areas, which are characterized by poverty, rapid population turnover, and general disorganization, there are many opportunities to learn antisocial behavior from delinquent peers, individually or in gangs. Immigrant families and families that have only recently moved to crowded cities are more likely to produce delinquent children than families that have lived in the city for a long time. Parents in families that have recently arrived may lack the knowledge and skills needed to deal successfully with their difficult environment and hence may serve as inadequate role models for their children. They may also be too preoccupied or defeated by their own problems to give their children adequate attention and guidance (Conger & Petersen, 1984).

GANGS.   Lower-class youth in urban ghettos are more likely than middle-class youth to join delinquent gangs. Although many of these groups encourage delinquency, in the past the better organized and less violent gangs also helped meet needs that are common to all young people—a sense of personal worth, a meaningful social life, peer group acceptance, and self-preservation (Campbell, 1984; Cloward & Ohlin, 1968; Gold & Mann, 1972). Since the 1970s, however, inner-city gangs have become increasingly disorganized and violent. Gang members in major cities have terrorized, wounded, or killed scores of teachers, elderly citizens, and nongang youth. They have also attacked each other: 60 percent of the victims of gang violence are other gang members (Conger & Petersen, 1984; Miller, 1976). In 1986 there were an estimated 50,000 gang members in Los Angeles County alone, and about 300 of them were murdered. A 14-year-old summed up the situation as follows: "The human race stinks, man. I'm glad I ain't in it."

Personality Factors and Parent-child Relationships

Even in high-poverty neighborhoods, many adolescents do not become delinquent. Why does one child from a particular neighborhood, school, social class, and ethnic background become delinquent while another, apparently subject to the same environmental influences, does not? In approaching this problem, investigators have typically used a research design in which delinquents and nondelinquents from the same general background are compared with respect to personality characteristics and parent-child relationships at various ages.

As a group, delinquents, especially recidivists (those with repeated convictions), score somewhat lower than average on IQ tests and have a slightly higher-than-average incidence of mental retardation (Grace & Sweeney, 1986; Rutter & Giller, 1984). However, most delinquents are at least average in IQ, and low intelligence itself does not appear to be a primary factor in delinquency (Hirschi & Hindelang, 1977; Quay, 1987a). Among children who were adopted shortly after birth, delinquency and adult criminality are more closely related to the behavior of their biological parents than to that of their adoptive parents. This suggests that genetic factors may play some indirect role in increasing an individual's predisposition to engage in delinquent behavior, perhaps through greater impulsiveness or distractibility (Hutchings & Mednick, 1974; Robins, 1978; Trasler, 1987). However, family and peer relationships, together with other psychological and social influences, appear to play a far more critical role.

PERSONALITY CHARACTERISTICS.   Delinquents have been found to be more likely than nondelinquents to be socially assertive, defiant, lacking in achievement motivation, hostile, suspicious, destructive, and lacking in self-control (Farrington, Biron, & LeBlanc, 1982; West & Farrington, 1973). They are also more likely to be lacking in sympathy, sociomoral reasoning, and interpersonal problem-solving ability (Arbuthnot, Gordon, & Jurkovic, 1987). Many of these traits appear to be defensive in nature, reflecting impaired self-concepts and feelings of inadequacy, emotional rejection, and frustration of the need for self-expression (Gold & Mann, 1972).

Indeed, numerous longitudinal studies suggest that efforts to defend against low self-esteem and an uncertain, poorly integrated sense of self are important in the development of delinquency. Some investigators maintain that delinquency can serve to improve self-esteem, while others contend that delinquents continue to have a negative self-concept and view themselves as undesirable people (Arbuthnot et al., 1987; Armstrong, 1980; Bliss, 1977; Brynner, O'Malley, & Bachman, 1981; Fitts & Hammer, 1969; Kaplan, 1980; Quay, 1987b; Zieman & Benson, 1983).

Differences between nondelinquents and delinquents in social behavior and personality characteristics show up early, even though clearly defined delinquent behavior may not begin until later. Several studies have found future delinquents, especially boys, to differ significantly from nondelinquents by age 10 in peer ratings of honesty, troublesomeness, daring, and unpopularity. They also differ in teacher ratings of "aggressive maladjustment," in behavioral problems, and in attentional problems and school difficulties (Conger & Miller, 1966; Farrington et al., 1982; Gold & Petronio, 1979; Snyder & Patterson, 1987).

In one extensive longitudinal study, future adolescent delinquents were viewed by their teachers as more poorly adapted than their classmates by the end of the third grade. This was true regardless of the child's social class, intelligence, parents' occupations, and residential neighborhood (Conger, 1977a; Conger & Miller, 1966). Future delinquents of both sexes were rated as less considerate and fair in dealing with others, less friendly, less responsible, more impulsive, more distractible and less persistent in their schoolwork, and more antagonistic to authority. They were also less well liked and less accepted by their peers. These social and academic problems appeared to reflect underlying emotional problems; moreover, in the opinion of their teachers future delinquents more often came from a disturbed home environment.

FAMILY RELATIONSHIPS.   Within a social-class group, family relationships are the best single predictor of delinquency. The early disciplinary techniques to which delinquents have been subjected are likely to be lax, erratic, or overly strict and to involve physical punishment rather than reasoning with the child about misconduct (Olweus, 1980; Pulkkinen, 1983; Rutter & Giller, 1984; West & Farrington, 1973). Recent research indicates that a critical factor may be lack of parental supervision. In one study in England, the family variable that was most strongly associated with delinquency was weak parental supervision, as indicated by such items as not requiring children to say where they are going and when they will return home, or not knowing where a child is much of the time (Wilson, H., 1980). Families of aggressive and delinquent children and adolescents also seem to have few if any "house rules." The parents do not monitor the young person's activities, respond inconsistently to unacceptable behavior, and lack effective ways of dealing with family conflict (Patterson, G. R., 1981a, 1981b; Snyder & Patterson, 1987).

Delinquents' relationships with their parents often lack intimate communication, mutual understanding, and affection. Instead, there is mutual hostility and parental rejection, indifference, dissension, or—not infrequently—abuse and family violence (Canter, 1982; Hirschi, 1969; Rutter & Giller, 1984; West & Farrington, 1973). Parents of delinquents are more likely to have minimal aspirations for their children, to avoid engaging in leisure activities as a family, to be hostile or indifferent toward school, to have personal and emotional problems of their own, and to have police records (Cressey & Ward, 1969; Robbins, 1966, 1978). One longitudinal study found that 39 percent of boys with criminal fathers became delinquent, compared to 16 percent of those whose fathers had no criminal record; other studies have yielded similar results (Farrington et al., 1982).

Broken homes are associated with a high incidence of delinquent behavior. However, it has also been shown that the likelihood of adolescent delinquency is far higher in nonbroken homes characterized by hostility, indifference or apathy, and lack of cohesiveness than in broken (usually mother-only) homes in which there is cohesiveness, mutual affection and support (Ahlstrom & Havighurst, 1971; Garbarino & Plantz, 1986; Rutter & Giller, 1984).

Prevention and Treatment of Delinquency

Although a wide variety of approaches have been employed in efforts to prevent or treat delinquency, the results have not been particularly encouraging (Lorian, Tolan, & Wahler, 1987; Rutter & Giller, 1984; Sheldrick, 1985). Counseling and psychotherapy, transactional analysis, treatment in "therapeutic communities," family casework, foster home placement, recreational programs, educational and vocational programs, youth service bureaus, and combinations of these and other approaches (e.g., health care, legal aid) have not had widespread success. However, most approaches—even those that use a combination of techniques—have concentrated largely on young people with already serious problems and have tended to do too little, too late (Klein, M. W., 1979; Quay, 1987c; Sechrest & Rosenblatt, 1987).

CORRECTIONAL INSTITUTIONS.   There is considerable evidence that imprisonment in traditional "correctional" institutions does little to solve the problem of delinquency. It subjects the young person to traumatic and embittering experiences, frequently including sexual and physical abuse, while providing little or no psychological, educational, or vocational help. Moreover, such institutions often serve as "finishing schools" for future criminals (Kaufman, 1979; Prescott, 1981; Wooden, 1976). Not surprisingly, reconviction rates among previously institutionalized youth generally run between 60 and 70 percent (Rutter & Giller, 1984).

In view of these facts, it is unfortunate that juvenile courts in many states are permitted to institutionalize adolescents who have committed only status offenses (actions that are illegal for minors but not for adults, as explained earlier). In a national survey conducted in the mid-1970s, two-thirds of the females and one-third of the males in correctional institutions had been confined solely because of status offenses; many of the females were committed only for sexual activity (Wooden, 1976). In the view of Irving R. Kaufman, chief judge of the U.S. Court of Appeals in New York, "Children whose actions do not amount to adult crimes should be dealt with outside the judicial system" (Kaufman, 1979, p. 58).

Ironically, the judicial system sometimes fails to institutionalize adolescents who repeatedly commit serious crimes. Because of the organizational chaos, underfunding, and understaffing of the juvenile court systems in large metropolitan areas (and in some instances because of peculiarities in the laws regarding juveniles), many adolescents and youth who have repeatedly committed violent offenses—including homicide—serve little or no time in correctional institutions (Kaufman, 1979). The treatment received by one such youth is summarized in Box 16.3.

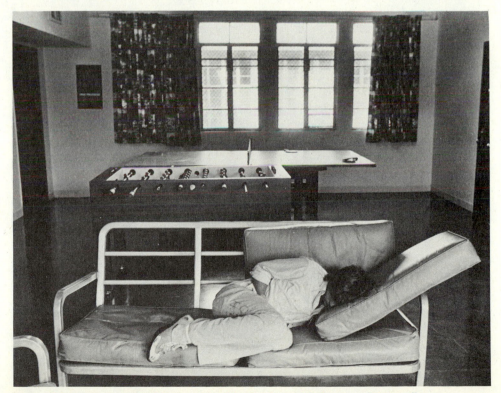

Many adolescents are confined in correctional institutions solely because of status offenses.

BOX 16.3

The Violent World of Peewee Brown

Harold (Peewee) Brown was born on September 24, 1961, the son of an unemployed alcoholic who left his wife when Peewee was 7 months old and who died when the boy was 14. Peewee's mother, Louise, an articulate woman with a high school education, always worked to support herself and her three sons. She had to be at her job by 8 a.m., so she left them alone at home at 7 a.m. and did not return until 5 p.m. Often, she conceded, she did not know what they were doing while she was gone.

"I told them at school, 'When he gets bad, get your stick,'" Mrs. Brown recalled. "I'd tell them, 'You're the kid's mother and father when you're in school. I can't be there. Whomp his behind. . . .'"

There were many at school who tried to help Peewee. He saw psychologists, was assigned to dedicated teachers, and eventually was sent to a special public school. But his violence only increased. He said it was not uncommon for him to stab someone who had inadvertently hurt his feelings and that he once negotiated the price of a sandwich with one of his many guns. In the very beginning, there was a tug of war between the world of school and that of the streets.

"We knew when he was here he was going to kill somebody and that there was nothing we could do to help him," said Coy Cox, the principal of Public School 369, the special school to which Peewee was sent in the sixth grade.

Over a 4-year period, from the age of 11 to 15, Peewee was arrested fifteen times on charges ranging from sodomy to assault, although the school system—for reasons of confidentiality—was never informed.

He now admits that those arrests were for only a small number of his crimes. For example, he said, when he was 13 he shot and killed a man on a deserted street corner in Brooklyn, but was never caught. He added that he seriously wounded at least six others and committed countless other robberies.

But even those few times he was caught, Peewee went free. Each time he was arrested, Family Court routinely dismissed the charge or put him on probation, releasing him back into his mother's custody in an absurd cycle of crime, capture, and release that continued until, at the age of 15, Peewee shot and killed a Brooklyn grocer.

Just 3 weeks before, according to court and school records, Peewee had been arrested for having taken a loaded revolver to school.

Because Family Court records are sealed, it is impossible to know the court's rationale in disposing of the gun case or any of the others.

"All they would do is send him back," said Mrs. Brown, a 41-year-old framemaker who to this day remains confused by the leniency with which her son was repeatedly treated. "They didn't punish him. I told them: 'He keeps getting into trouble. There should be somewhere he can go.' All they did was send him back to me."

The last time, however, Peewee didn't come back home. Now 20, he has been in prison 5 years for the murder of the Brooklyn grocer. (From D. Kleiman. The violent world of Peewee Brown. *New York Times*, February 28, 1982, p. 22. © 1982 by The New York Times Company. By permission.)

BEHAVIORAL METHODS.   Currently, behavioral methods appear to show the greatest promise for the treatment of delinquency (Garrett, 1984, 1985; Quay, 1987c; Rutter & Giller, 1984). In this approach, appropriate behavior is systematically rewarded, perhaps with tokens that can be exchanged for special privileges. Inappropriate behavior earns the person no reward and may have unpleasant consequences, such as a temporary loss of privileges. Behavorial methods may be applied in an institutional setting such as a residential treatment center or correctional institution, in school or community programs, or in the family (Burchard & Harig, 1976; Kirigin, Wolf, Braukman, Fixsen, & Phillips, 1979; Rutter & Giller, 1984; Sarason, 1978; Snyder & Patterson, 1987).

In one institutional project the principal focus was on training in social skills (e.g., those needed in applying for a job, resisting peer pressure to engage in delinquent behavior, personal problem solving, and planning ahead) (Sarason, 1978; Sarason & Ganzer, 1973). Strong emphasis was placed on developing behavorial skills that would be widely applicable in everyday life. Modeling, role playing, and rehearsing future behaviors in problem situations were among the techniques used. Five years later, youth who had participated in the project had a recidivism rate of 23 percent, compared to 48 percent—or more than double—for youth who had not been part of the program while they were in the institution.

Recent research findings have several implications. One is that in the long run prevention or intervention efforts have little chance of success unless they include efforts to change the child or adolescent's home environment and existing patterns of parent-child relationships. Another is that in most instances efforts to help the delinquent directly must be concerned with improving his or her social problem-solving skills and social competence generally, rather than just seeking to suppress deviant behavior (Rutter & Giller, 1984). Such efforts have their best chance of success if they begin early in life and are part of a larger program of comprehensive psychological and physical care, education, and training directed toward optimal development—a commitment our society appears to be unwilling to make.

Although there are clearly some instances in which institutionalization may be the only practical alternative, particularly for violent or "professional" offenders, in many instances suspended sentences, official and unofficial probation, and formal police warnings are at least as effective in terms of recidivism rates. Indeed, several studies have indicated that for first offenders such noncustodial alternatives result in somewhat lower reconviction rates (Dixson & Wright, 1975; Rutter & Giller, 1984).

PSYCHOLOGICAL AND PSYCHOPHYSIOLOGICAL DISTURBANCES

During periods of physical, cognitive, or social change, people often develop psychological and psychophysiological disturbances that temporarily disrupt their equilibrium. Early adolescence is a time of rapid change in all of these dimensions, and psychological and psychophysiological disturbances of varying degrees of severity do occur in a significant minority of young people. For some adolescents, the disturbance may be relatively minor and transient; for others, it may be severe and resistant to treatment.

The limited number of available epidemiological studies suggest that the rate of incidence of significant psychological disturbance in adolescents is between 15 and 20 percent (Graham, P. & Rutter, 1985; Rutter & Garmezy, 1983). Most frequently encountered are anxiety reactions, depression (or other affective disorders), personality and conduct (antisocial) disorders, psychophysiological disturbances, and psychoneuroses (Graham, P. & Rutter, 1985; Weiner, I. B. & del Gaudio, 1976). In contrast, only about 1 percent of adolescents suffer from schizophrenia or other severe mental disorders (Steinberg, 1985). It is not possible to review here the full range of adolescent disturbances, with their causes and specialized treatment requirements, but we will consider a few of the most significant ones. These include anxiety, depression, suicide, and schizophrenia.

Anxiety Reactions

An adolescent with an acute anxiety reaction feels a sudden surge of fearfulness, as if something bad were about to happen. He or she may become agitated and restless, startle easily, and experience physical symptoms like dizziness, headache, nausea, or vomiting. Attention span may be limited, and sleep disturbances are common; the anxious adolescent may have difficulty falling asleep, and sleep itself may be limited and restless, with much tossing and turning, perhaps accompanied by nightmares or sleepwalking (Nemiah, 1988).

If there is no obvious external reason for an acute anxiety reaction, the young person may be puzzled about its source or may attribute it to relatively trivial external circumstances. Upon more careful examination, however, it usually becomes clear that far more extensive and fundamental factors are involved—factors of which the adolescent may not be consciously aware, such as disturbed parent-child relationships, concern about the demands of growing up, or fear and guilt regarding sexual or aggressive impulses.

In cases of acute anxiety in adolescence, therapeutic intervention should begin early, while the relevance of these causative factors is still apparent. Then the anxiety can be dealt with before it becomes chronic and before the individual's responses to it—psychological withdrawal, impairment of schoolwork, or continuing physical symptoms such as pains, diarrhea, shortness of breath, or fatigue— become a way of life.

Adolescent Depression

Depressive disorders cover a wide spectrum, ranging from mild, temporary states of sadness, often in response to a specific life event, to severely disturbed conditions that may involve cognitive as well as affective disturbances (Emde, Harmon, & Good, 1986; Klerman, 1988; Shaffer, 1985). Until recently it was widely assumed that children and younger adolescents rarely exhibit depression (Klerman, 1988; Rutter, 1986). However, recent clinical and research studies have demonstrated that this is not the case. Both major and minor forms of depression have been found during childhood, puberty, and adolescence (Kovacs, Feinberg, Crouse-Novak, Paulauskas, & Finkelstein, 1984; Puig-Antich, 1986; Rutter, Izard, & Read, 1986).

One of the reasons that significant depression in childhood and early adolescence tended to be overlooked is that clinical depression is less common at younger ages (Pearce, 1978; Rutter, 1986; Rutter, Tizard, & Whitmore, 1970/1981). Another reason is that depression may be manifested in different ways at different ages, for a variety of reasons—cognitive, psychological, social, or biological (Carlson & Cantwell, 1980b; Graham, P. & Rutter, 1985; Shaffer, 1985). In early adolescence young people are unlikely to express their feelings openly, and they tend to deny negative and self-critical attitudes. They do not generally exhibit the gloom, hopelessness, and self-deprecation that characterize adult depressives. Many adolescents mask depressive feelings with disguises ranging from boredom and restlessness to hypochondriacal complaints or acting-out behavior such as sexual, aggressive, or delinquent activity (Achenbach & Edelbrock, 1981; Carlson & Cantwell, 1980a; Nicholi, 1988).

Investigators have shown that the incidence of depressive feelings rises rapidly during and after puberty (Rutter, 1986; Rutter, et al., 1970/1981). Up to 40 percent of postpubertal adolescents report having had significant, though usually temporary, feelings of sadness, worthlessness, and pessimism about the future. As many as 8 to 10 percent report having experienced suicidal feelings (Nicholi, 1988; Rutter, 1980; Rutter et al., 1986).

Interestingly, although psychiatric disorders with depression are more frequent among boys before puberty, they are more frequent among girls after puberty (Pearce, 1982; Rutter, 1986; Weissman & Boyd, 1983). Similarities between adolescent and adult symptoms of depression tend to be greater in the case of major affective disorders than in less severe cases of depression (Ryan & Puig-Antich, 1986).

As we saw in Chapter 2, biological—primarily genetic—factors appear to play a more significant part in the etiology of the major depressive disorders, such as manic-depressive (bipolar) disorder, than in that of less severe, seemingly less intractable instances of depression (Puig-Antich, 1986; Klerman, 1988). Psychological factors, on the other hand, seem to play a primary role in two frequently encountered forms of adolescent depression (Conger, in press; Josselyn, 1971; Nicholi, 1988). The first is expressed as lack of feeling and a sense of emptiness. It is as though the childhood self had been abandoned and no growing adult self had replaced it; the resulting vacuum engenders a high level of anxiety. This kind of depression resembles a state of mourning and tends to be the least persistent and most resolvable form of depression.

A second type of adolescent depression often is more difficult to resolve. It has its basis in repeated experiences of defeat over a long period. The adolescent may actually have tried hard to solve problems and achieve personally meaningful goals, but without success (Beck et al., 1979; Garmezy, 1986; Seligman & Peterson, 1986). Perhaps other people fail to accept or understand what the adolescent is trying to do, or perhaps personal inadequacies make the goals impossible to achieve. Many—probably a majority—of adolescent suicide attempts are a result not of a momentary impulse but of a long series of unsuccessful attempts to find alternative solutions to difficulties. Frequently, the final straw in this type of depression is likely to be the loss of a meaningful relationship, whether with a parent, a friend, or a boy- or girlfriend (Curran, 1987; Easson, 1977; Inamdar, Siomopoulos, Osborn, & Bianchi, 1979).

Suicide

Suicide is rare in children and almost as infrequent among young adolescents. Beginning at about age 15, however, the reported suicide rate increases rapidly. It reaches a level of over 20 per 100,000 for ages 15 through 24 among white males; rates for blacks and females are significantly lower (see Figure 16.4). The overall suicide rate among older adolescents has tripled since 1950, although it has decreased slightly in recent years (Holinger, 1978; U.S. Bureau of the Census, 1981, 1987).

Females are more likely than males to use passive methods of suicide, such as ingestion of drugs or poisons, and less likely to use active methods, such as shooting or hanging. Among both sexes, firearms or explosives account for the greatest number of *completed* suicides, whereas drugs or poisons account for greatest number of *attempted* suicides. Although males outnumber females in completed suicides, attempted suicides are far more common among females (Curran, 1987; Holinger, 1978; Shaffer, 1986).

REASONS FOR SUICIDE ATTEMPTS.   In considering adolescent attempts at suicide, it is important to distinguish between immediate precipitating factors and longer-term predisposing factors. Precipitating events may include the breakup or threatened breakup of a romance; pregnancy (real or imagined); school failure; conflicts with parents; rejection by a friend; being apprehended in a forbidden or delinquent act; loss of a parent or other loved person; and fear of serious illness or imminent mental breakdown (Curran, 1987; Jacobs, 1971; Miller, M. L., Chiles, & Barnes, 1982). On closer examination, however, it becomes clear that the

The reported suicide rate increases rapidly after age 15. Fortunately, this young woman was prevented from jumping to her death.

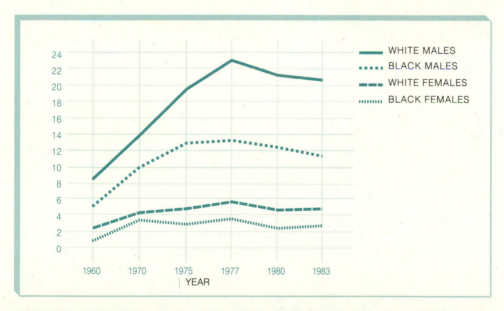

FIGURE 16.4   Death rates (per 100,000) from suicide among 15- to 24-year-olds, 1960–1983. (Adapted from U.S. Bureau of the Census. *Statistical abstract of the United States, 1987* [107th ed.]. Washington, DC: U.S. Government Printing Office, 1986.)

adolescent's reaction to such events is generally the culmination of a series of difficulties. One study of 154 adolescents who had attempted suicide found that hopelessness, rather than depression resulting from immediate situations, was most often the critical factor (Wetzel, 1976).

Adolescents who attempt suicide frequently have a long history of escalating family instability and discord. They have reached a point at which they feel unable to communicate with their parents or turn to them for support. Early parental loss is also more common among suicidal adolescents (Brown, Harris, & Bifulco, 1986; Curran, 1987; Shaffer, 1986). Typically, suicidal adolescents have fewer close friends, but their relationships with them are much more intense: "Their relationships become supercharged with a degree of desperation and need that is often not shared by their friends and lovers" (Curran, 1987, p. 30).

PREDICTION OF SUICIDE.   There is a dangerous myth, not only among the public but also among some clinicians, that a person who talks about committing suicide will not do so. The tragic fact, however, is that many adolescents (and adults) who have threatened suicide and been ignored or dismissed as attention seekers *do* subsequently take their own lives. Moreover, in talking about suicide adolescents are conveying a message that something is wrong and that they need help, even though they may not yet be seriously intent on suicide as the only remaining solution to their problems.

Talk of suicide should always be taken seriously (Parry-Jones, 1985; Resnick, 1980; Teicher, 1973). It is not easy to predict suicide, but there are a number of warning signals that can alert the careful observer to the possibility. They include the following:

1. A persistently depressed or despairing mood (or frantic activity alternating with intolerable boredom and listlessness).
2. Eating and sleeping disturbances.
3. Declining school performance.
4. Gradual social withdrawal and increasing isolation from others.
5. Breakdown in communication with parents or other important people in the young person's life.
6. A history of previous suicide attempts or involvement in accidents.
7. Seemingly reckless, self-destructive, and uncharacteristic behavior, such as serious drug or alcohol use, reckless driving, sexual acting out, delinquency, or running away.
8. Statements like "I wish I were dead" or "What is there to live for?"
9. Inquiries about the lethal properties of drugs, poisons, or weapons.
10. Unusually stressful events in the young person's life, such as school failure, breakup of a love affair, or loss of a loved one.

TREATMENT.   Prompt treatment is necessary for potentially suicidal adolescents as well as for those who have already made suicide attempts. Many communities have hotlines that people who are considering suicide or who feel desperate can call for immediate help. More extended treatment should deal not only with the current circumstances that are troubling the young person but also with long-standing problems and conflicts (Curran, 1987; Tabachnick, 1986).

Adolescent Schizophrenia

Among adolescents, schizophrenia is by far the most frequently occurring psychotic disorder. Its incidence, though still relatively rare (under 1 percent) increases dramatically from age 15 onward and reaches a peak during late adolescence and early adulthood, leveling off toward the end of the third decade (Cancro, 1983; Graham, P. & Rutter, 1985). Boys are more likely than girls to develop schizophrenia in childhood and adolescence; adult onset is more frequent among women than among men (Lewine, 1980). Like its adult counterpart, adolescent schizophrenia is characterized by disordered thinking; distortions of, or lack of contact with, reality; limited capacity for establishing meaningful relationships with others; and poor emotional control (Graham, P. & Rutter, 1985; Steinberg, L., 1985; Weiner, I. B., 1970, 1980).

In its fully developed form, adolescent schizophrenia can usually be identified without much difficulty: The young person's speech is likely to seem peculiar—stilted, overelaborate, disconnected, or even incoherent. He or she may make odd facial grimaces or movements; appear distracted, withdrawn, or confused; and show inappropriate emotional reactions—either failing to respond with appropriate feeling or overreacting in a poorly controlled fashion. Hallucinations—usually auditory and typically reflecting control by others (e.g., outside voices telling one what to do)—and intense, bizarre delusions may also be present (Steinberg, L., 1985).

Proper diagnosis may be difficult in the early stages of adolescent schizophrenia, partly because the symptoms may be far less obvious or dramatic than they will become later, and partly because some characteristics that might suggest incipient schizophrenia in adults are more likely to occur among nonschizophrenic as well as schizophrenic adolescents (Weiner, I. B., 1970, 1982). These include circumstantial thinking, abstract preoccupation, and conscious awareness of sexual and aggressive imagery, as well as ideas of reference (the belief that others are talking about one). All of these symptoms tend to occur more frequently among nonschizophrenic adolescents than among nonschizophrenic adults (Rutter, Graham, Chadwick, & Yule, 1976).

CAUSATIVE FACTORS.   Several generations ago it was believed that traumatic experiences in childhood are the primary determinants of schizophrenia (Steinberg, 1985). However, as we saw in Chapter 2, recent research indicates that biological and hereditary factors frequently play a major role in the development of this disorder. As noted previously, it may be more accurate to speak of inheriting an increased *vulnerability* to schizophrenia than of inheriting schizophrenia per se. In that case, "whether or not the disorder is precipitated would depend on two factors: how vulnerable a particular individual is and how much of what kind of stress he or she is subjected to" (Conger, in press). Recent longitudinal studies have found that vulnerable individuals are more likely to develop schizophrenia or to suffer relapses after treatment if their families are characterized by high levels of stress, negative expressed emotions, and disturbed communication patterns (Goldstein, M. J., 1987; Marcus et al., 1987; Mednick et al., 1987; Tienari et al., 1987).

PROGNOSIS.   Among hospitalized adolescent schizophrenics "it can be anticipated that about one-quarter will recover, one-quarter will improve but suffer residual symptoms or occasional relapses, and the remaining 50 percent will make little or no progress and require continuing residential care" (Weiner, I. B. & Elkind, 1972, p. 220). In general, the older the adolescent is when schizophrenia appears, the better the prognosis is likely to be. Other favorable indications include sudden onset of the disturbance; clear-cut precipitating factors; above-average intelligence; previously good personal, academic, and social adjustment; and early response to treatment (Eggers, 1978; King & Pitman, 1971; Steinberg, L., 1985; Weiner, I. B., 1980). Finally, the outlook for improvement is better if the family is able to accept the disturbance and if there is adequate planning for future treatment and school, work, and living arrangements (Doane, Goldstein, Miklowitz, & Falloon, 1986; Falloon, Boyd, & McGill, 1984; Goldstein, M. J., 1987; Vaughn, Snyder, Freeman, Jones, Falloon, & Libeman, 1982).

Brief Reactive Psychosis

It is important to distinguish between brief psychotic episodes and schizophrenia (American Psychiatric Association, 1987; Feinstein & Miller, 1979). Although during the episode the individual may exhibit some psychotic symptoms, such as incoherence, disorganized associations or behavior, delusions, or hallucinations, these symptoms appear suddenly and are short-lived (lasting from a few hours to at most a couple of weeks). The psychotic symptoms typically appear immediately after a severe and recognizable "psychosocial stressor," such as loss of a loved one or a life-threatening event, that would evoke significant symptoms of distress in almost anyone (Conger, in press). Invariably there is emotional turmoil, manifested by rapid, generally depressed, and anxious mood swings. This disorder, which usually appears first in adolescence or young adulthood, may be followed by feelings of mild depression or loss of self-esteem. But with psychological assistance and support, the young person or adult may be expected to return fully to his or her previous level of functioning.

Eating Disorders

Many adolescents go through brief periods in which their weight deviates upward or downward from generally accepted norms. Once their growth has stabilized, most adolescents will correct their weight by regulating their diet; some, however, will not. In some cases, sustained overeating may lead to serious *obesity* (Rodin, 1985; Stunkard, 1980). In others, pathologically prolonged and extreme dieting may lead to serious, sometimes life-threatening degrees of weight loss. This latter condition, known as *anorexia nervosa*, is most likely to occur during adolescence and

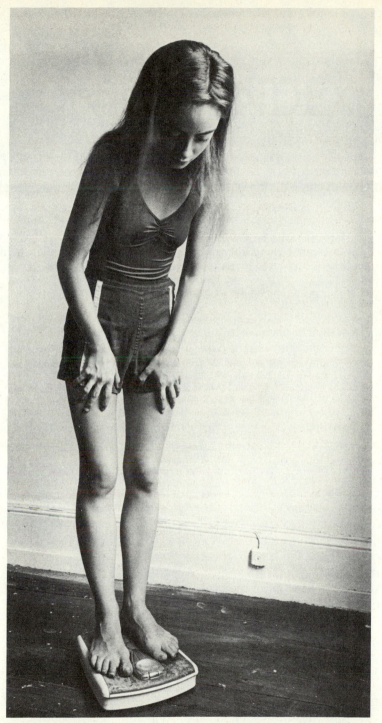

Anorexia nervosa is characterized by a pathological concern with body weight.

is far more common among females than among males (Bruch, 1973; Garfinkel & Garner, 1983; Herzog, 1988).

Both obese and anorexic young people often lack a clear sense of their own identity as separate and distinct individuals capable of setting and achieving their own goals. Anorexia is a particularly puzzling condition because the adolescent has such a distorted perception of her own body. Many anorexic females who appear to neutral observers as little more than an emaciated bundle of skin and bones continue to express concern about putting on too much weight. We still have much to learn about this condition, which, while still relatively rare, seems to be increasing in frequency, especially among affluent youth. Biological factors (possibly an impairment of the functioning of the anterior pituitary gland at the base of the brain) may play some role, but psychological factors appear to be of primary importance.

Parents are often surprised by the onset of anorexia because their child has always seemed so "normal." As children, anorexic adolescents typically seemed almost "too good"—quiet, obedient, always dependable, eager to please. Most have been good students. When one looks more closely, however, the picture is not as bright. At least unconsciously, most anorexic young people feel that they have been exploited and prevented from leading their own lives and that they have been unable to form a strong personal identity. Perhaps in reaction, they are likely to display an obsessional need to be in control of every aspect of their life, particularly bodily functions. They may also feel incapable of meeting the demands of sexual maturity. Severe undereating, which can interrupt menstruation and make secondary sex characteristics less prominent, may be—at least unconsciously—a way of avoiding growing up.

Studies of the parents of female anorexic adolescents indicate that the parents have frequently exerted such firm control and regulation during childhood that the girl had difficulty establishing a sense of identity and gaining confidence in her ability to make decisions for herself. These parents are also likely to have encouraged their children to become perfectionistic overachievers (Minuchin, Rosman, & Baker, 1978).

Still another eating disorder, *bulimia*, has shown a dramatic increase among female adolescents and young women (Herzog, 1988; Russell, 1985; Striegel-Moore, Silberstein, & Rodin, 1986). In this disorder, which combines elements of both anorexia and obesity, binge eating (gorging) alternates with forced purging through self-induced vomiting or laxative abuse. Although health is likely to be impaired by this disorder, often seriously, normal weight may be maintained, making the disorder more difficult to detect. Bulimic individuals characteristically are afraid that they will be unable to stop this eating pattern (which they recognize as abnormal). They typically report a depressed mood and self-deprecating thoughts following the eating binges. Nearly three-fourths acknowledge that their abnormal eating pattern has adverse effects on their physical health (Johnson, C., 1982; Johnson, C., Lewis, & Hagman, 1984).

Bulimic practices, as well as the condition of being greatly over- or underweight, can cause serious, sometimes life-threatening physiological problems. Specialized medical care is essential in such cases. Over the long term, however, skilled psychological treatment is important. And because disturbed parent-child relationships (including problems related to the development of independence and sexual maturation) typically play an important part in eating disorders, a well-designed therapeutic program for adolescents almost always requires active involvement on the part of the parents (Minuchin et al., 1978).

Treatment of Adolescents

To work successfully with adolescents, whether individually or in groups, a therapist must have specialized training. Regardless of the therapist's particular theoretical orientation, certain personal qualities contribute to success or failure. Adolescents, even more than children, have a particular talent for spotting phoniness—and exploiting it. If the therapist is straightforward, neither minimizing his or her qualifications nor retreating into professional pomposity, the adolescent will usually develop a feeling of trust and respect while still making it clear that he or she isn't awed by "shrinks."

The effective adolescent psychotherapist is flexible and can move easily from listening to questioning to reassurance to clarification to interpretation—even to arguing—and, when necessary, to setting limits (Conger, 1977b; Holmes, 1964). Emotionally disturbed adolescents "need externally imposed limits because, as a result of their confused state, they are not able to set their own limits. They seek a fence beyond which they cannot go, within which they can experiment and by trial and error and accidental success find a self-concept with which they can feel satisfied" (Josselyn, 1971, p. 146). At the same time, the therapist must keep in mind that the establishment of independence is a critical developmental task of adolescence. Like the wise parent, the therapist must be on guard against the seductive tendency to try to substitute his or her own identity for that of the young person, or to prolong therapy unduly (Conger, 1977a). Although their roles inevitably differ in important respects, an effective parent and an effective therapist share some essential characteristics. Neither job is an easy one, but both are less difficult for adults who genuinely like adolescents, which probably means adults who have come to terms with their own adolescence.

SUMMARY

Although young people generally feel reasonably happy, positive about themselves, and optimistic about their futures, there remain significant minorities for whom life is not going well. These include young people who are alienated from society. *Alienation* is a profound rejection of the values of society or a deep feeling of isolation from other people. For some, alienation has its roots in personal developmental experiences, such as disturbed parent-child relationships; for others, specific social concerns, such as racial or economic discrimination, play a dominant role. For still others, there is an overall rejection of society and its current values. A "new" form of adolescent alienation is characterized by feelings of loneliness, difficulty in achieving intimacy, feelings of rootlessness, a decreased sense of purpose and direction, and a diffuse sense of self.

Drug use is not limited to adolescents, and the majority of adolescents do not become serious, high-risk drug users. Nevertheless, rates of drug use among American adolescents remain high. Those who work with adolescents believe that the youth in the greatest danger is the one who turns to drugs in order to cope with insecurity, stress, and similar problems. Repeated escapes into the world of drugs leave such young people ill prepared to meet the demands of adulthood.

Adolescents use drugs for a variety of reasons. These include peer pressure, poor parent-child relationships, desire to escape from the pressures of life, emotional disturbance, and alienation or societal rejection.

Each year more than 1 million young people run away from home, and perhaps half return after a few days or weeks. Those who do not return become homeless and face a variety of risks. Typically, they come from families characterized by conflict and lack of communication, and often by problems such as parental alcoholism, family violence, physical and sexual abuse, chronic neglect, and outright rejection. As a result of these conditions, runaways are often characterized by low self-esteem, mistrust, lack of social competence, suicidal impulses, and other psychological and psychophysiological problems.

Lacking money, food, or shelter, adolescent runaways are ready candidates for exploitation. They may become involved in prostitution and the production of pornographic films and magazines. In addition, they are often robbed, assaulted, underfed, and lured into drug use and dealing. Temporary shelters attempt to protect and assist runaways, but they tend to be understaffed and underfunded.

The term *juvenile delinquent* refers to a young person who engages in behavior that is punishable by law. Such behavior includes *status offenses* that are illegal only when committed by young people. Although the overall delinquency rate reached a peak in 1980, since 1960 the incidence of serious offenses by young people has been rising at a faster rate than the rate of delinquency in general. Boys outnumber girls in juvenile arrests, particularly for serious offenses.

In the United States and other highly industrialized nations, current high rates of delinquency appear to be related at least in part to changes in the structure of society such as increased mobility and population shifts. Poverty also contributes to delinquency. Increases in delinquency appear to be most likely in situations in which a sense of community solidarity and the integrity of the extended family have been seriously disrupted.

As a group, delinquents score somewhat lower on IQ tests and have a slightly higher-than-average incidence of mental retardation. However, low intelligence by itself does not appear to be a primary factor in delinquency. More important are personality characteristics; delinquents are more likely than nondelinquents to be socially assertive, defiant, lacking in achievement motivation, hostile, suspicious, destructive, and lacking in self-control. Numerous studies suggest that efforts to defend against low self-esteem and an uncertain sense of self are important in the development of delinquency.

Within a social-class group, family relationships are the best single predictor of delinquency. Lax or overly strict discipline, usually involving physical punishment, and weak parental supervision are associated with delinquency. Delinquents' relationships with their parents often lack intimate communication, mutual understanding, and affection. Instead, there is mutual hostility and parental rejection, indifference, dissension, or violence.

A variety of approaches have been employed in efforts to prevent or treat delinquency, but they have not been very successful. Imprisonment in correctional institutions also does little to solve the problem. Currently, behavioral methods appear to show the greatest promise for the treatment of delinquency.

Adolescents are going through a period of dramatic physical, cognitive, and social change, which may increase vulnerability to psychological and psychophysiological disturbances. Among those disturbances are anxiety reactions, depression, suicide, schizophrenia, brief reactive psychosis, and eating disorders such as anorexia nervosa and bulimia. Effective treatment of adolescents with these disorders requires skilled, trained professionals who are flexible and genuinely like young people.

REVIEW QUESTIONS

1. What is meant by alienation? How do patterns of adolescent alienation today differ from those of the 1960s?

2. Briefly describe current trends in adolescent drug use.

3. Why do adolescents use drugs?

4. What causes adolescents to run away from home?

5. What social and individual factors contribute to juvenile delinquency?

6. What approaches are used in efforts to prevent or treat delinquency? How effective are they?

7. How is depression manifested during adolescence?

8. Why do adolescents attempt suicide? How can suicide attempts be predicted?

9. Why is it sometimes difficult to diagnose adolescent schizophrenia?

10. What kinds of eating disorders sometimes occur among adolescents?

GLOSSARY

alienation   A profound rejection of the values of society or isolation from other people.

juvenile delinquent   A young person, generally under 18 years of age, who engages in behavior that is punishable by law.

status offense   An act that is illegal only when committed by young people.

SUGGESTED READINGS

Bachman, J. G., Johnston, L. D., & O'Malley, P. M. (1987). *Monitoring the future: Questionnaire responses from the nation's high school seniors.* Ann Arbor, MI: Institute of Social Research, University of Michigan. Recent edition of a series, published annually since 1975, that shows national trends among high school seniors in drug use, social values, and attitudes toward education, work, sex roles, interpersonal relationships, and other topics. (Senior authorship varies from year to year.)

Curran, D. K. (1987). *Adolescent suicidal behavior.* Washington, DC: Hemisphere. This well-balanced, comprehensive discussion of the problem of adolescent suicidal behavior in contemporary society corrects a number of popular—and dangerous—misconceptions.

Janus, M. D., McCormack, A., Burges, A. W., & Hartman, C. (1987). *Adolescent runaways: Causes and consequences.* Lexington, MA: Lexington Books. This book on the results of a study of 149 adolescent runaways demonstrates that running away typically has its roots in dysfunctional family relationships. It also shows how much more dangerous running away is today than it was in an earlier era, and discusses ways to help runaways.

Rutter, M., & Giller, H. (1984). *Juvenile delinquency: Trends and perspectives.* New York: Guilford. A clear, well-written summary and evaluation of the current status of research on the causes, prevention, and treatment of delinquency.

Weiner, I. B. (1980). *Psychopathology in adolescence.* In J. Adelson (Ed.), *Handbook of adolescent psychology.* New York: Wiley. A good introduction to the psychological disturbances most often associated with the adolescent years.

No author. (1981). *Teenage Pregnancy: The problem that hasn't gone away*. New York: The Alan Guttmacher Institute.

Abel, E. L. (1980). Fetal alchohol syndrome: Behavioral teratology. *Psychological Bulletin*, 87, 29–50.

Achenbach, T. M., & Edelbrock, C. S. (1981). Behavioral problems and competencies reported by parents of normal and disturbed children aged four through sixteen. *Monographs of the Society for Research in Child Development*, 46, Serial No. 188.

Ackerman, B. P. (1986). Children's sensitivity to comprehension failure in interpreting a non-literal use of an utterance. *Child Development*, 57, 485–497.

Adams, G. R., Abraham, K. G., & Markstrom, C. A. (1987). The relations among identity development, self-consciousness, and self-focusing during middle and late adolescence. *Developmental Psychology*, 23, 292–297.

Adams, G. R., & Gullota, T. (1983). *Adolescent life experiences*. Monterey, CA: Brooks/Cole.

Adams, G. R., & Munro, G. (1979). Portrait of the North American runaway: A critical review. *Journal of Youth and Adolescence*, 8, 359–373.

Adams, L. T., & Worden, P. E. (1986). Script development and memory organization in preschool and elementary school children. *Discourse Processes*, 9, 149–166.

Adamson, L. B., Bakeman, R., Smith, K. B., and Walters, A. S. (1987). Adults' interpretations of infants' acts. *Developmental Psychology*, 23, 383–387.

Adamsons, K. (1987). The effects of drugs and other substances on the fetus. In R. A. Hekelman, S. Blatman, S. B. Friedman, N. M. Nelson, & H. M. Seidel (Eds.), *Primary pediatric care* (pp. 437–447). St. Louis: C. V. Mosby.

Adelson, J. (1971). The political imagination of the young adolescent. *Daedalus*, 100, 1013–1050.

Adelson, J. (1982, Summer). Rites of passage: How children learn the principles of community. *American Educator*, 6 ff.

Ahlstrom, W. M., & Havighurst, R. J. (1971). *400 losers*. San Francisco: Jossey-Bass.

Ainsworth, M. D. S., Blehar, M. C., Waters, E., & Wall, S. (1978). *Patterns of attachment: A psychological study of the strange situation*. Hillsdale, NJ: Erlbaum.

Albarran, L. (1987). *Recognition memory in infants*. Unpublished manuscript.

Alejandro-Wright, M. N. (1985). The child's conception of racial classification: A socio-cognitive developmental model. In M. B. Spencer, G. K. Brookins, & W. R. Allen (Eds.), *Beginnings: The social and affective development of black children* (pp. 185–200). Hillsdale, NJ: Erlbaum.

Allen, M. C. (1984). Developmental outcome and followup of the small for gestational age infant. *Seminars in Perinatology*, 8, 123–133.

Allport, G. (1937). *Personality: A psychological interpretation*. New York: Holt, Rinehart and Winston.

Almquist, E. M., & Angrist, S. S. (1971). Role model influences on college women's career aspirations. *Merrill-Palmer Quarterly*, 71, 263–279.

Almy, M., Monighan, P., Scales, B., & Van Hoorn, J. (1983). Recent research on playing: The perspective of the teacher. In L. Katz (Ed.), *Current topics in early childhood education* (Vol. 5). Norwood, NJ: Ablex.

Alwitt, L. F., Anderson, D. R., Lorch, E. P., & Levin, S. R. (1980). Preschool children's visual attention to attributes of television. *Human Communication Research*, 7, 52–67.

American Psychiatric Association (1987). *DSM III R: Diagnostic and statistical manual of mental disorders* (3rd rev. ed.). Washington, DC: The Association.

American Psychological Association, Committee on Ethical Standards in Psychological Research (May, 1972). Ethical standards for research with human subjects. *APA Monitor*, I–XIX.

Ames, L. B. (1937). The sequential patterning of prone progression in the human infant. *Genetic Psychology Monographs*, 19, 409–460.

Anastasi, A. (1987). *Psychological testing* (6th ed.). New York: Macmillan.

Anderson, C. W., Nagel, R. J., Robert, W. A., & Smith, J. W. (1981). Attachment to substitute caregivers as a function of center quality and caregiver involvement. *Child Development*, 52, 53–61.

Anderson, D. R., Choi, H. P., & Lorch, E. P. (1987). Attentional inertia reduces distractibility during young children's television viewing. *Child Development*, 58, 798–806.

Anderson, D. R., & Collins, P. A. (1988). *The impact on children's education: Television's influence on cognitive development*. Washington DC: U.S. Department of Education.

Anderson, D. R., & Field, D. E. (1983). Children's attention to television: Implications for production. In M. Meyer (Ed.), *Children and the formal features of television*. Munchen: K. G. Saur.

Anderson, D. R., & Lorch, E. P. (1983). Looking at television: Action or reaction? In J. Bryant & D. R. Anderson, (Eds.), *Children's understanding of television: Research on attention and comprehension*. New York: Academic Press.

Anderson, D. R., Lorch, E. P., Field, D. E., & Sanders, J. (1981). The effects of TV program comprehensibility on preschool children's visual attention to television. *Child Development*, 52, 151–157.

Anglin, J. M. (1977). *Word, object, and conceptual development*. New York: Norton.

Apgar, V., & Beck, J. (1974). Is my baby all right? New York: Pocket Books.

Applegate, J. L., Burke, J. A., Burleson, B. R., Delia, J. G., & Kline, S. L. (1983). Reflection-enhancing parental communication. In I. E. Sigel (Ed.), Parental belief systems: The psychological consequences for children. Hillsdale, NJ: Erlbaum.

Arbuthnot, J., Gordon, D. A., & Jurkovic, G. J. (1987). Personality. In H. C. Quay (Ed.), Handbook of juvenile delinquency (pp. 139–183). New York: Wiley.

Arend, R., Gove, F. L., & Stroufe, L. A. (1979). Continuity of individual adaptation from infancy to kindergarten: A predictive study of ego resiliency and curiosity in preschoolers. Child Development, 50, 950–959.

Areshansel, C. S., & Rosen, B. C. (1980). Domestic roles and sex differences in occupational expectations. Journal of Marriage and the Family, 42, 121–131.

Armstrong, J. S. (1980). The relationship of sex-role identification, self-esteem, and aggression in delinquent males. Dissertation Abstracts International, 40(b), 3900.

Aronfreed, J. (1968). Conduct and conscience: The socialization of internalized control over behavior. New York: Academic Press.

Aronson, E., Blaney, N., Stephen, C., Sikes, J., & Snapp, M. (1978). The jigsaw classroom. Beverly Hills, CA: Sage.

Asher, S. R. (1978). Referential communication. In G. J. Whitehurst & B. J. Zimmerman (Eds.), The functions of language and cognition. New York: Academic Press.

Asher, S. R., & Hymel, S. (1981). Children's social competence in peer relations: Sociometric and behavioral assessment. In J. D. Wine & M. D. Smys (Eds.), Social competence. New York: Guilford.

Asher, S. R., & Renshaw, P. D. (1981). Children without friends: Social knowledge and social skill training. In S. R. Asher & J. M. Gottman (Eds.), The development of children's friendships. New York: Cambridge University Press.

Asher, S. R., Singleton, L. C., & Taylor, A. R. (1982). Acceptance versus friendship: A longitudinal study of racial integration. Paper presented at the Annual Meeting of the American Educational Research Association, New York.

Astin, A. W., Green, K. C., & Korn, W. S. (1987). The American freshman: Twenty year trends. Los Angeles: Higher Education Research Institute, University of California at Los Angeles.

Astin, A. W., Green, K. C., Korn, W. S., & Schalit, M. (1986). The American freshman: National norms for fall 1986. Los Angeles: American Council on Education and Graduate School of Education, University of California at Los Angeles.

Avery, A. W. (1982). Escaping loneliness in adolescence: The case for androgyny. Journal of Youth and Adolescence, 11, 451–459.

Babson, S. G., Pernoll, M. L., & Benda, G. I. (1980). Diagnosis and management of the fetus and neonate at risk. St. Louis: Mosby.

Bacas, H. (1986, August). Where are the teenagers? Nation's Business, pp. 18–25.

Bachman, J. G. (1970). Youth in transition (Vol. 2): The impact of family background and intelligence on tenth-grade boys. Ann Arbor, MI: Institute for Social Research, University of Michigan.

Bachman, J. G., & Johnston, L. D. (1979). Fewer rebels, fewer causes: A profile of today's college freshmen. Ann Arbor, MI: Survey Research Center, Institute for Social Research, University of Michigan.

Bachman, J. G., Johnston, L. D., & O'Malley, P. M. (1987). Monitoring the future: Questionnaire responses from the nation's high school seniors: 1986. Ann Arbor, MI: Institute for Social Research, University of Michigan.

Bachman, J. G., Johnston, L. D., O'Malley, P. M., & Humphrey, R. H. (1988). Differentiating the effects of perceived risks, disapproval, and general life style factors. Journal of Health and Social Behavior, 29, 92–112.

Bacon, M. K., & Ashmore, R. D. (1986). A consideration of the cognitive activities of parents and their role in the socialization process. In R. D. Ashmore & D. M. Brodzinsky (Eds.), Thinking about the family: Views of parents and children. Hillsdale, NJ: Erlbaum.

Baer, D. M. (1970). An age-irrelevant concept of development. Merrill Palmer Quarterly, 16, 238–245.

Banducci, R. (1967). The effect of mother's employment on the achievement aspirations, and expectations of the child. Personnel and Guidance Journal, 46, 263–267.

Bandura, A. (1969). Principles of behavior modification. New York: Holt, Rinehart and Winston.

Bandura, A. (1977). Social learning theory. Englewood Cliffs, NJ: Prentice-Hall.

Bandura, A. (1981). Self-referent thought: A developmental analysis of self-efficacy. In J. H. Flavell & L. Ross (Eds.), Social cognitive development: Frontiers and possible futures. New York: Cambridge University Press.

Bandura, A. (1982). Self-efficacy mechanism in human agency. American Psychologist, 37, 122–147.

Bandura, A., & Huston, A. C. (1961). Identification as a process of incidental learning. Journal of Abnormal and Social Psychology, 63, 311–318.

Bandura, A., Grusec, J. E., & Menlove, F. L. (1967). Vicarious extinction of avoidance behavior. Journal of Personality and Social Psychology, 5, 16–23.

Bandura, A., & Mischel, W. (1965). Modification of self-imposed delay of reward through exposure to live and symbolic models. Journal of Personality and Social Psychology, 2, 698–705.

Bane, M. J. (1986). Household composition and poverty. In S. H. Danziger & D. H. Weinberg (Eds.), Fighting poverty: What works and what doesn't (pp. 209–231). Cambridge, MA: Harvard University Press.

Bank, S., & Kahn, M. D. (1975). Sisterhood-brotherhood is powerful: Sibling subsystems and family therapy. Family Process, 14, 311–337.

Barnes, G. M. (1984). Adolescent alcohol abuse and other problem behaviors: Their relationships and common parental influences. *Journal of Adolescence and Youth*, 13, 329–348.

Barnes, H., & Olson, D. H. (1985). Parent-child communication and the circumplex model. *Child Development*, 56, 438–447.

Barnes, K. E. (1971) Preschool play norms: A replication. *Developmental Psychology*, 5, 99–103.

Barnett, M. A. (1987). Empathy and related responses in children. In N. Eisenberg & J. Strayer (Eds.), *Empathy and its development*. New York: Cambridge University Press.

Bar-Tal, D. (1978). Attributional analysis of achievement-related behavior. *Review of Educational Research*, 48, 259–271.

Bar-Tal, D., & Raviv, A. (1979). Consistency of helping- behavior measures. *Child Development*, 50, 1235–1238.

Baruch, G. K. (1972). Maternal influences upon college women's attitudes toward women and work. *Developmental Psychology*, 6, 32–37.

Baruch, G. K., & Barnett, R. C. (1986). Fathers' participation in family work and children's sex-role attitudes. *Child Development*, 57, 1210–1223.

Bates, E., Benigni, L., Bretherton, I., Camaioni, L., & Volterra, V. (1979). *The emergence of symbols: Cognition and communication in infancy*. New York: Academic Press.

Bates, E., Bretherton, I., & Snyder, L. (1988). *From first words to grammar*. New York: Cambridge University Press.

Bates, J. E. (1982). *Temperament as part of social relationships: Implications of perceived infant difficultness*. Paper presented at the International Conference on Infant Studies, Austin, Texas.

Bates, J. E., & Petit, G. S. (1981). Adult individual differences as moderators of child effects. *Journal of Abnormal Child Psychology*, 9, 329–340.

Battaglia, F. C., & Simmons, A. (1978). The low-birth-weight infant. In F. Falkner & J. Tanner (Eds.), *Human growth* (Vol. 2): *Postnatal growth* (pp. 507–556). New York: Plenum.

Baumrind, D. (1967). Child care practices anteceding three patterns of preschool behavior. *Genetic Psychology Monographs*, 75, 43–88.

Baumrind, D. (1968). Authoritarian vs. authoritative control. *Adolescence*, 3, 255–272.

Baumrind, D. (1971). Note: Harmonious parents and their preschool children. *Developmental Psychology*, 4, 99–102.

Baumrind, D. (1973). The development of instrumental competence through socialization. In A. D. Pick (Ed.), *Minnesota symposia on child psychology* (Vol. 7). Minneapolis: University of Minnesota Press.

Baumrind, D. (1975). Early socialization and adolescent competence. In S. E. Dragastin & G. H. Elder, Jr. (Eds.), *Adolescence in the life cycle: Psychological change and social context*. New York: Wiley.

Baumrind, D. (1978). A dialectical materialist's perspective on knowing social reality. In W. Damon (Ed.), *New directions in child development: Moral development*. San Francisco: Jossey-Bass.

Baumrind, D. (1988). *Familial antecedents of social competence in middle childhood*. Unpublished manuscript.

Behrman, R. E., & Vaughn, V. C. (1987). *Nelson textbook of pediatrics*. Philadelphia: Saunders.

Bell, A. P. (1969). Role modeling of fathers in adolescence and young adulthood. *Journal of Counseling Psychology*, 16, 30–35.

Bell, A. P., & Weinberg, M. S. (1978). *Homosexualities: A study of diversity among men and women*. New York: Simon & Schuster.

Bell, A. P., Weinberg, M. S., & Hammersmith, S. K. (1981). *Sexual preference: Its development in men and women*. Bloomington: Indiana University Press.

Bell, R. (1980). *Changing bodies, changing lives: A book for teens on sex and relationships*. New York: Random House.

Bell, R., & Wildflower, L. Z. (1983). *Talking with your teenager*. New York: Random House.

Bell, R. Q. (1979). Parent, child, and reciprocal influences. *American Psychologist*, 34, 821–826.

Bell, R. Q., & Harper, L. V. (1977). *The effect of children on parents*. Hillsdale, NJ: Erlbaum.

Belsky, J. (1984). The determinants of parenting: A process model. *Child Development*, 55, 83–96.

Belsky, J., Lerner, R. M., & Spanier, G. B. (1984). *The child in the family*. Reading, MA: Addison-Wesley.

Belsky, J., & Rovine, M. (1987). Temperament and attachment security in the Strange Situation. *Child Development*, 50, 787–792.

Bem, S. L. (1974). The measurement of psychological androgyny. *Journal of Consulting and Clinical Psychology*, 42, 155–162.

Bem, S. L. (1981). Gender schema theory: A cognitive account of sex typing. *Psychological Review*, 88, 352–364.

Bem, S. L. (1989). Genital knowledge and gender constancy in preschool children. *Child Development*, 60, 649–662.

Bender, B. G., Linden, M. G., & Robinson, A. (1987). Environmental and developmental risk in children with sex chromosome abnormalities. *Journal of the American Academy of Child and Adolescent Psychiatry*, 26, 499–503.

Benedict, H. (1979). Early lexical development: Comprehension and production. *Journal of Child Language*, 6, 183–200.

Berndt, T. J. (1979). Developmental changes in conformity to peers and parents. *Developmental Psychology*, 15, 606–616.

Berndt, T. J. (1982). The features and effects of friendship in early adolescence. *Child Development*, 53, 1447–1460.

Berndt, T. J., & Bulleit, T. N. (1985). Effects of sibling relationships on preschoolers' behavior at home and at school. *Developmental Psychology*, 21, 761–767.

Berndt, T. J., Hawkins, J. A., & Hoyle, S. G. (1986). Changes in friendship during a school year: Effects on children's and adolescents' impressions of friendship and sharing with friends. *Child Development*, 57, 1284–1297.

Bernstein, A. C. & Cowen, P. A. (1981). Children's conceptions of birth and sexuality. In R. Bibace & M. E. Walsh (Eds.), *New directions for child development*: Vol. 14. *Children's conception of health, illness, and bodily functions*. San Francisco: Jossey-Bass.

Bernstein, B. (1970). A sociolinguistic approach to socialization: With some reference to educability. In F. Williams (Ed.), *Language and poverty: Perspectives on a theme*. Chicago: Markham.

Berry, G. & Mitchell-Kernan, C. (Eds.), (1982). *Television and the socialization of the minority child*. New York: Academic Press.

Bersoff, D. N. (1981). Testing and the law. *American Psychologist, 36*, 1047–1056.

Bertenthal, B. I., Proffitt, D. R., & Cutting, J. E. (1984). Infant sensitivity to figural coherence and biomechanical motions. *Journal of Experimental Child Psychology, 37*, 213–230.

Bertenthal, B. I., Proffitt, D. R., Kramer, S. J., & Spetner, M. B. (1987). Infants' coding of kinetic displays varying relative coherence. *Developmental Psychology, 23*, 171–178.

Bertoncini, J., Bijelac-Babic, B., Jusczyk, P. W., Kennedy, L. J., & Mahler, J. (1988). An investigation of young infants' perceptual representations of speech sounds. *Journal of Experimental Psychology: General, 117*, 21–33.

Bhatia, V. P., Katiyar, G. P., & Apaswol, K. N. (1979). Effect of intrauterine nutritional deprivation on neuromotor behaviour of the newborn. *Acta Paedriatrica Scandinavica, 68*, 561–573.

Bigner, J. J. (1974). Second born's discrimination of sibling role concepts. *Developmental Psychology, 10*, 564–573.

Bijou, S., & Baer, D. (1961). *Child Development I: A systematic and empirical theory*. Englewood Cliffs, NJ: Prentice-Hall.

Biller, H. D. (1971). *Father, child, and sex role*. Lexington, MA: Heath.

Bishop, J. E. (November 18, 1986). Genetic omen: Chromosome impairment linked to mental impairment raises abortion issue. *The Wall Street Journal*, pp. 1, 31.

Bixenstine, V. E., DeCorte, M. S., & Bixenstine, B. A. (1976). Conformity to peer-sponsored misconduct at four grade levels. *Developmental Psychology, 12*, 226–236.

Blasi, A. (1980). Bridging moral cognition and moral action: A critical review of the literature. *Psychological Bulletin, 88*, 1–45.

Blasi, A. (1983). Moral cognition and moral action: A theoretical perspective. *Developmental Review, 3*, 178–210.

Blasi, A. (1984). Moral identity: Its role in moral functioning. In W. M. Kurtines & J. L. Gewirtz (Eds.), *Moral behavior, and moral development* (pp. 128–139). New York: Academic Press.

Blass, E. M., Ganchrow, J. R., & Steiner, J. E. (1984). Classical conditioning in newborn humans 2–48 hours of age. *Infant Behavior and Development, 7*, 223–235.

Bliss, D. C. (1977). The effects of the juvenile justice system on self-concept. *Criminal Justice Abstracts, 10*, 297–298.

Block, J. H. (1984). *Sex role identity and ego development*. San Francisco: Jossey-Bass.

Block, J. H., & Block, J. (1980). The role of ego-control and ego-resiliency in the organization of behavior. In W. A. Collins (Ed.), *Minnesota symposium on child psychology*: Vol. 13. *Development of cognition, affect, and social relations*. Hillsdale, NJ: Erlbaum.

Block, J., & Block, J. H. (1973). *Ego development and the provenance of thought: A longitudinal study of ego and cognitive development in young children*. (Progress report for National Institute of Mental Health).

Bloom, L. M., Hood, L., & Lightbown, P. (1974). Imitation in language development: If, when, and why. *Cognitive Psychology, 6*, 380–420.

Bloom, L., Lahey, L., Hood, L., Lifter, K., & Fiess, K. (1980). Complex sentences: Acquisition of syntactic connectives and the semantic relations they encode. *Journal of Child Language, 7*, 235–261.

Bloom, L., Rocissano, L., & Hood, L. (1976). Adult-child discourse: Developmental interaction between linguistic processing and linguistic knowledge. *Cognitive Psychology, 8*, 521–552.

Blum, R. H., et al. (1972). *Horatio Alger's children*. San Francisco: Jossey-Bass.

Blyth, D., Hill, J., & Thiel, K. (1982). Early adolescents' significant others: Grade and gender differences in perceived relationship with familial and non-familial adults and young people. *Journal of Youth and Adolescence, 11*, 425–440.

Blyth, D. A., Simmons, R. G., Bulcroft, R., Felt, D., VanCleave, E. F., and Bush, D. M. (1981). The effects of physical development on self-image and satisfaction with body-image for early adolescent males. In R. G. Simmons (Ed.), *Research in Community and Mental Health, 2*, 43–73.

Bogatz, G. A., & Ball, S. (1971). *The second year of "Sesame Street": A continuing evaluation* (Vols. 1 & 2). Princeton, NJ: Educational Testing Service.

Bohman, M., Sigvardsson, S., & Cloninger, R. (1981). Maternal inheritance of alcohol abuse. *Archives of General Psychiatry, 38*, 965–969.

Borek, E. (1973). *The sculpture of life*. New York: Holt, Rinehart and Winston.

Bornstein, M. H., Kessen, W., & Weiskopf. (1975). The categories of hue in infancy. *Science, 191*, 201–202.

Borow, H. (1976). Career development. In J. F. Adams (Ed.), *Understanding adolescence*. Boston: Allyn & Bacon.

Bouchard, T. J., Jr., & McGee, M. G. (1981). Familial studies of intelligence: A review. *Science, 212*, 1055–1059.

Bourne, E. (1978a). The state of research on ego identity: A review and appraisal (Part 1). *Journal of Youth and Adolescence, 7*, 223–251.

Bourne, E. (1978b). The state of research on ego identity: A review and appraisal (Part 2). *Journal of Youth and Adolescence, 7*, 371–392.

Bowerman, M. (1978). Systematizing semantic knowledge. *Child Development, 49*, 977–987.

Bowerman, M. F. (1981). Cross-cultural perspectives on language development. In H. C. Triandis (Ed.) *Handbook of cross-cultural psychology*. Boston: Allyn & Bacon.

Bowlby, J. (1969). *Attachment and loss*. New York: Basic Books.

Boxer, A. M., & Petersen, A. C. (1986). Pubertal change in a family context. In G. K. Leigh & G. W. Peterson (Eds.), *Adolescents in families* (pp. 73–103). Cincinnati: South-Western Publishing Company.

Brackbill, Y. (1976). Long-term effects of obstetrical anaesthesia on infant autonomic function. *Developmental Psychobiology, 9*, 353–358.

Brackbill, Y. (1979). Obstetrical medication and infant behavior. In J. Osofsky (Ed.), *Handbook of infant development* (pp. 76–125). New York: Wiley.

Bradley, R. H., & Caldwell, B. (1984). The relation of infants' home environments to achievement test performance in first grade: A follow-up study. *Child Development, 55*, 803–809.

Bradley, R. H., Caldwell, B. M., & Elardo, R. (1977). Home environment, social class, and mental test performance. *Journal of Educational Psychology, 69*, 697–701.

Braine, M. D. S. (1963). The ontogeny of English phrase structures: The first phase. *Language, 39*, 1–13.

Brainerd, C. J. (Ed.). (1983). *Recent advances in cognitive-developmental theory: Progress in cognitive development research*. New York: Springer-Verlag.

Braithwaite, J. (1981). The myth of social class and criminality reconsidered. *American Sociological Review, 46*, 36–57.

Brand, D. (1987, August 31). The new whiz kids. *Time*, pp. 42–51.

Brandt, I. (1978). Growth dynamics of low-birth-weight infants with emphasis on the perinatal period. In F. Falkner & J. Tanner (Eds.), *Human growth: Vol. 2. Postnatal growth*. New York: Plenum.

Brannigan, M. A. (1986, September 2). Shortage of youths brings wide changes to labor market. *The Wall Street Journal*, pp. 1, 22.

Braukmann, C. J., Ramp, K. K., Tigner, D. N., & Wolf, M. M. (1984). The teaching family approach to training group-home parents. In R. F. Dangel & R. A. Polster (Eds.), *Parent training: Foundations of research and practice* (pp. 144–161). New York: Guilford.

Bregman, J. D., Dykens, E., Watson, M., Ort, S. I., & Leckman, J. F. (1987). Fragile-X syndrome: Variability of phenotypic expression. *Journal of the Academy of Child and Adolescent Psychiatry, 26*, 463–471.

Brennan, T. (1980). Mapping the diversity of runaways: A descriptive multivariate analysis of selected social psychological background conditions. *Journal of Family Issues, 1*, 189–209.

Brennan, T. (1982). Loneliness at adolescence. In L. A. Peplau & D. Perlman (Eds.), *Loneliness: A sourcebook of current theory, research, and therapy*. New York: Wiley.

Brennan, T., Huizinga, D., & Elliott, D. S. (1978). *The social psychology of runaways*. Lexington, MA: D. C. Heath.

Brent, R. L., & Harris, M. I. (1976). *Prevention of embryonic, fetal, and perinatal disease* (Vol. 3). Fogarty International Center Series on Preventive Medicine.

Bretherton, I. (1987). New perspectives on attachment relations. In J. D. Osofsky (Ed.), *Handbook of infant development*, (2nd ed) (pp. 1061–1100). New York: Wiley.

Bretherton, I., Fritz, J., Zahn-Waxler, C., & Ridgeway, D. (1986). Learning to talk about emotions: A functionalist perspective. *Child Development, 57*, 529–548.

Brim, O. G. (1958). Family structure and sex role learning by children. *Sociometry, 21*, 1–16.

Brinkley, J. (1986, October 1). Drug use held mostly stable or lower. *The New York Times*, p. 10.

Brittain, C. V. (1966). Age and sex of siblings and conformity toward parents versus peers in adolescence. *Child Development, 37*, 709–714.

Brittain, C. V. (1969). A comparison of rural and urban adolescents with respect to parent vs. peer compliance. *Adolescence, 13*, 59–68.

Brody, G. H., Pellegrini, A. D., & Sigel, I. E. (1986). Marital quality and mother-child and father-child interactions with school-aged children. *Developmental Psychology, 22*, 291–296.

Broman, S. H., Nichols, P. L., & Kennedy, W. A. (1975). *Preschool IQ: Prenatal and early developmental correlates*. Hillsdale, NJ: Erlbaum.

Bronfenbrenner, U. (1970). *Two worlds of childhood: U.S. and U.S.S.R.* New York: Russell Sage.

Bronfenbrenner, U. (1979). *The ecology of human development: Experiments by nature and design*. Cambridge, MA: Harvard University Press.

Bronfenbrenner, U. (1986). Ecology of family as a context for human development: Research perspectives. *Developmental Psychology, 22*, 723–742.

Bronfenbrenner, U., Alvarez, W., & Henderson, C. R., Jr. (1984). Working and watching: Maternal employment status and parents' perceptions of their three-year-old children. *Child Development, 55*, 1362–1378.

Bronfenbrenner, U., & Crouter, A. (1981). *Work and family through time and space*. Unpublished manuscript, 1981. A report prepared for the Panel on Work, Family and Community, Committee on Child Development Research and Public Policy. National Academy of Sciences, National Research Council.

Bronson, W. (1975). Peer-peer interactions in the second year of life. In M. Lewis & L. A. Rosenblum (Eds.), *Friendship and peer relations*. New York: Wiley.

Brook, J. S., Lukoff, J. F., & Whiteman, M. (1980). Initiation into adolescent marijuana use. *Journal of Genetic Psychology, 137*, 133–142.

Brooks-Gunn, J., & Ruble, D. N. (1983). The development of menstrual-related beliefs and behaviors during early adolescence. *Child Development*, 53, 1567–1577.

Brooks-Gunn, J., & Ruble, D. N. (1984). The experience of menarche from a developmental perspective. In J. Brooks-Gunn & A. C. Petersen (Eds.), *Girls at puberty: Biological, psychological, and social perspectives*. New York: Plenum.

Brophy, J. (1985). Interactions of male and female students with male and female teachers. In L. C. Wilkinson & C. B. Barett (Eds.), *Gender influences in classroom interaction* (pp. 115–142). New York: Academic Press.

Brown, A. L. (1975). The development of memory: Knowing, knowing about knowing, and knowing how to know. In H. W. Reese (Ed.), *Advances in child development and behavior* (Vol. 10). New York: Academic Press.

Brown, A. L., Bransford, J. D., Ferrara, R. A., & Campione, J. C. (1983). Learning, remembering, and understanding. In P. H. Mussen (Series Ed.), J. H. Flavell & E. M. Markman (Eds.), *Handbook of child psychology: Vol. 3. Cognitive development* (4th ed.) (pp. 77–166). New York: Wiley.

Brown, B. B., Clasen, D. R., & Eicher, S. A. (1986). Perceptions of peer pressure, peer conformity, dispositions, and self-reported behavior among adolescents. *Developmental Psychology*, 22, 521–530.

Brown, G. E., Wheeler, K. J., & Cash, M. (1980). The effects of a laughing versus a nonlaughing model on humor responses in preschool children. *Journal of Experimental Psychology*, 29, 334–339.

Brown, G. W., Harris, T. O., & Bifulco, A. (1986). In M. Rutter, C. E. Izard, & P. B. Read (Eds.), *Depression in young people: Developmental and clinical perspectives* (pp. 251–296). New York: Guilford.

Brown, R. (1958). How shall a thing be called? *Psychological Review*, 65, 14–21.

Brown, R. (1973). *A first language: The early stages*. Cambridge, MA: Harvard University Press.

Brown, W. T., Jenkins, E. C., Friedman, E. et al. (1982). Autism is associated with the fragile X syndrome. *Journal of Autism and Developmental Disorders*, 12, 303–307.

Bruch, H. (1973). *Eating disorders*. New York: Basic Books.

Bruner, J. S. (1975). From communication to language: A psychological perspective. *Cognition*, 3, 255–287.

Bruner, J. S., Jolly, A., & Sylva, K. (1976). *Play: Its role in development and evolution*. London: Kenwood.

Brunnquell, D., Crichton, L., & Egeland, B. (in press). Maternal personality and attitude in disturbances of childrearing. *Journal of Orthopsychiatry*.

Brunswick, A. F., & Boyle, J. M. (1979). Patterns of drug involvement: Developmental and secular influences on age of initiation. *Youth and Society*, 11, 139–162.

Brunswick, A. F., & Meseri, P. A. (1984). Origins of cigarette smoking in academic achievement, stress, and social expectations: Does gender make a difference? *Journal of Early Adolescence*, 4, 353–370.

Bryant, B., & Crockenberg, S. (1980). Correlates and discussion of prosocial behavior: A study of female siblings with their mothers. *Child Development*, 51, 529–544.

Bryant, B. J. (1982). Sibling relationships in middle childhood. In M. E. Lamb & B. Sutton-Smith (Eds.), *Sibling relationships*. Hillsdale, NJ: Erlbaum.

Brynner, J., O'Malley, P., & Bachman, J. (1981). Self-esteem and delinquency revisited. *Journal of Youth and Adolescence*, 10, 407–441.

Bullinger, A., & Chatillon, J. F. (1983). Recent theory and research of the Genevan school. In P. H. Mussen (Series Ed.), J. H. Flavell & E. M. Markman (Eds.), *Handbook of child psychology. Vol. 3: Cognitive development* (4th ed.) (pp. 231–262). New York: Wiley.

Burchard, J. D., & Harig, P. T. (1976). Behavior modification and juvenile delinquency. In H. Leiternberg (Ed.), *Handbook of behavior modification and behavior therapy* (pp. 405–452). Englewood Cliffs, NJ: Prentice-Hall.

Burgess, R. L., & Conger, R. D. (1978). Family interaction in abusive, neglectful and normal families. *Child Development*, 49, 1163–1173.

Burt, M. R. (1986). Estimating the public costs of teenage childbearing. *Family Planning Perspectives*, 18, 221–226.

Buss, A. H., & Plomin, R. (1984). *Temperament: Early developing personality traits*. Hillsdale, NJ: Erlbaum.

Byrne, D., & Griffitt, W. B. (1966). A developmental investigation of the law of attraction. *Journal of Personality and Social Psychology*, 4, 699–702.

Cairns, R. B. (1983). An evolutionary and developmental perspective on aggressive patterns. In C. Zahn-Waxler, E. M. Cummings, & R. Iannotti (Eds.), *Altruism and aggression*. New York: Cambridge University Press.

Calvert, S. L., & Huston, A. C. (1987). Television and children's gender schemata. In L. Liben & M. Signorella (Eds.), *New directions in child development: Vol. 38. Children's gender schemata: Origins and implications* (pp. 75–88). San Francisco: Jossey-Bass.

Campbell, A. (1984). *The girls in the gang*. Oxford: Basil Blackwell.

Campbell, S. (1979). Mother-infant interaction as a function of maternal ratings of temperament. *Child Psychiatry and Human Development*, 10, 67–76.

Campbell, S. B. (1983). Developmental perspectives on child psychopathology. In T. H. Ollendick & M. Hersen (Eds.), *Handbook of child psychopathology* (pp. 13–40). New York: Plenum.

Campbell, T. A., Wright, J. C., & Huston, A. C. (1987). Form cues and content difficulty as determinants of children's cognitive processing of televised educational messages. *Journal of Experimental Child Psychology*, 43, 311–327.

Campos, J. J., Barrett, K. C., Lamb, M. E., Goldsmith, H. H., & Stenberg, C. (1983). Socioemotional development. In P. H. Mussen (Series Ed.), M. M. Haith, & J. J. Campos (Eds), *Handbook of child psychology*: Vol. 2. *Infancy and developmental psychobiology* (pp. 783–916). New York: Wiley.

Campos, J., Hiatt, S., Ramsay, D., Henderson, C., & Svejda, M. (1978). The emergence of fear on the visual cliff. In M. Lewis & L. Rosenblum (Eds.), *The origins of affect*. New York: Plenum.

Campos, J. J., Langer, A., & Krawitz, A. (1970). Cardiac responses on the visual cliff in prelocomotor human infants. *Science*, 170, 196–198.

Campos, J., Svejda, M., Bertenthal, B., Benson, N., & Schmid, D. (April, 1981). *Self produced locomotion and wariness of heights*. Paper presented at the Biennial Meeting of the Society for Research in Child Development, Boston.

Cancro, R. (1983). History and overview of schizophrenia. In H. I. Kaplan & B. J. Sadock, *Comprehensive textbook of psychiatry* (Vol. 1, pp. 631–642). Baltimore: Williams and Wilkins.

Cann, A., & Newbern, S. R. (1984). Sex stereotype effects on children's picture recognition. *Child Development*, 55, 1085–1090.

Canter, R. J. (1982). Family correlates of male and female delinquency. *Criminology*, 20, 149–160.

Cantor, J., & Sparks, G. G. (1984). Children's fear responses to mass media: Testing some Piagetian predictions. *Journal of Communication*, 34, 90–103.

Cantor, J., & Wilson, B. J. (1984). Modifying fear responses to mass media in preschool and elementary school children. *Journal of Broadcasting*, 28, 431–443.

Caparulo, B., & Zigler, E. (1983). The effects of mainstreaming on success expectancy and imitation in mildly retarded children. *Peabody Journal of Education*, 60, 85–98.

Caplow, T., & Bahr, H. M. (1979). Half a century of change in adolescent attitudes: Replication of a Middletown survey by the Lynds. *Public Opinion Quarterly*, 1–17.

Carlson, G. A., & Cantwell, D. P. (1980a). A survey of depressive symptoms, syndrome and disorder in a child psychiatric population. *Journal of Child Psychology and Psychiatry*, 21, 19–25.

Carlson, G. A., & Cantwell, D. P. (1980b). Unmasking masked depression in children and adolescents. *American Journal of Psychiatry*, 137, 445–449.

Carmichael, L., Hogan, H. P., & Walter, A. A. (1932). An experimental study of the effect of language on reproduction of visually perceived form. *Journal of Experimental Psychology*, 15, 73–86.

Caro, F. G. (1966). Social class and attitudes of youth relevant for the realization of adult goals. *Social Forces*, 44, 492–498.

Carpenter, C. J. (1983). Activity structure and play: Implications for socialization. In M. B. Liss (Ed.), *Social and cognitive skills: Sex roles and children's play*. New York: Academic Press.

Case, R. (1986). The new stage theories in intellectual development: Why we need them; What they assert. In M. Perlmutter (Ed.), *Minnesota symposia on child psychology*: Vol. 19. *Perspectives on intellectual development* (pp. 57–96). Hillsdale, NJ: Erlbaum.

Catz, C., & Yaffe, S. J. (1978). Developmental pharmacology. In F. Falkner & J. M. Tanner (Eds.), *Human growth*: Vol. 1. *Principles and prenatal growth*. New York: Plenum.

Caudill, W., & Frost, L. A. (1973). A comparison of maternal care and infant behavior in Japanese-American, American, and Japanese families. In W. Lebra (Ed.), *Youth, socialization, and mental health*. Honolulu: University Press of Hawaii.

Cavior, N., & Dokecki, P. R. (1973). Physical attractiveness, perceived attitude similarity, and academic achievement as contributors to interpersonal attraction among adolescents. *Developmental Psychology*, 9, 44–54.

CDF Reports, January, 1988, 9, No. 8, p. 1.

Ceci, S. J., Toglia, M. P., & Ross, D. F. (Eds.) (1987). *Children's eyewitness memory*. New York: Springer-Verlag.

Cerra, F. (1980, May 11). Study finds college women still aim for traditional jobs. *The New York Times*.

Challman, R. C. (1932). Factors influencing friendships among preschool children. *Child Development*, 3, 146–158.

Chandler, M. J. (1973). Egocentrism and antisocial behavior: The assessment and training of social perspective-taking skills. *Developmental Psychology*, 9, 326–332.

Chapman, M. (1977). Father absence, stepfathers, and the cognitive performance of college students. *Child Development*, 48, 1152–1154.

Charlesworth, W. (1966). *Development of the object concept*. Paper presented at a meeting of the American Psychological Association, New York.

Cheyne, J. A., & Rubin, K. H. (1983). Playful precursors of problem solving in preschoolers. *Developmental Psychology*, 19, 577–584.

Chi, M. R. H. (1978). Knowledge structures and memory development. In R. Siegler (Ed.), *Children's thinking: What develops?* Hillsdale, NJ: Erlbaum.

Children's Defense Fund. (1987). *A children's defense budget*. Washington DC: Children's Defense Fund.

Chilman, C. S. (1983). *Adolescent sexuality in a changing American society: Social and psychological perspectives* (2nd ed.). Washington, DC: U.S. Government Printing Office.

Ching, W. (1982). The one-child family in China: Need for psychosocial research. *Studies in Family Planning*, 13, 208–312.

Chomsky, N. (1957). *Syntactic structures*. The Hague: Mouton.

Chomsky, N. (1959). (Review of verbal behavior by B. F. Skinner). *Language*, 35, 26–58.

Christensen, H., & Gregg, C. (1970). Changing sex norms in America and Scandinavia. *Journal of Marriage and the Family*, 32, 616–627.

Chudley, A. (1984). Behavior phenotype. In A. Chudley & G. Sutherland (Eds.), Conference Report: International Workshop on the Fragile X Syndrome and X-Linked Mental Retardation. *American Journal of Medical Genetics*, 17, 45–53.

Cicirelli, V. G. (1972). The effect of sibling relationship on concept learning of young children taught by child-teachers. *Child Development*, 43, 282–287.

Cicirelli, V. G. (1973). Effects of sibling structure and interaction on children's categorization style. *Developmental Psychology*, 9, 132–139.

Cicirelli, V. G. (1975). Effects of mother and older sibling on the problem-solving behavior of the younger children. *Developmental Psychology*, 11, 749–756.

Clark, E. V. (1973). What's in a word? On the child's acquisition of semantics in his first language. In T. E. Moore (Ed.) *Cognitive development and the acquisition of language*. New York: Academic Press.

Clark, E. V., & Anderson, E. S. (1979). *Spontaneous repairs: Awareness in acquiring language*. Paper presented at a meeting of the Society for Research in Child Development, San Francisco.

Clarke-Stewart, K. A., & Hevey, C. M. (1981). Longitudinal relations in repeated observations of mother-child interactions from 1 to 2 and one-half years. *Developmental Psychology*, 17, 127–145.

Clary, E. G., Miller, J. (1986). Socialization and situational influences on sustained altruism. *Child Development*, 57, 1358–1369.

Clasen, D. R., & Brown, B. B. (1985). The multidimensionality of peer pressure in adolescence. *Journal of Youth and Adolescence*, 14, 451–468.

Clausen, J. A. (1975). The social meaning of differential physical and sexual maturation. In S. E. Dragastin & G. H. Elder, Jr. (Eds.), *Adolescence in the life cycle: Psychological change and social context*. New York: Wiley.

Cleary, T. A., Humphreys, L. G., Kendrick, S. A., & Wesman, A. (1975). Educational use of tests with disadvantaged students. *American Psychologist*, 36, 15–41.

Clingenpeel, W. G., & Segal, S. (1986). Stepparent-stepchild relationships and the psychological adjustment of children in stepmother and stepfather families. *Child Development*, 57, 474–484.

Cloringer, C. R. (1987). Genetic principles and methods in high-risk studies of schizophrenia. *Schizophrenia Bulletin*, 13, 515–523.

Cloward, R. A., & Ohlin, L. E. (1960). *Delinquency and opportunity: A theory of delinquent gangs*. New York: Free Press.

Clymer, A. (1986, September 2). Public found ready to sacrifice in drug fight. *The New York Times*, pp. 1, 16.

Cohen, D. J., Dibble, E., & Grawe, J. M. (1977). Fathers' and mothers' perceptions of children's personality. *Archives of General Psychiatry*, 34, 480–487.

Cohler, B. J., & Boxer, A. M. (1984). Settling into the world: Person, time and context in the middle-adult years. In D. Offer & M. Sabshin (Eds.), *Normality and the life cycle*. New York: Basic Books.

Cohn, J. F. & Tronick, E. Z. (1987). Mother-infant face-to-face interaction. *Developmental Psychology*, 23, 68–77.

Coie, J. D., & Dodge, K. A. (1983). Continuities and changes in children's social status: A five-year longitudinal study. *Merrill-Palmer Quarterly*, 29, 261–282.

Colby, A., Kohlberg, L., Gibbs, J., & Lieberman, M. (1983). A longitudinal study of moral judgment. *Monographs of the Society for Research in Child Development*, 48, (Serial No. 200).

Cole, N. S. (1981). Bias in testing. *American Psychologist*, 36, 1067–1077.

Coleman, J. C. (1980). *The nature of adolescence*. London: Methuen.

Colletta, N. D. (1981). *The influence of support systems on the maternal behavior of young mothers*. Paper presented at the meeting of the Society for Research in Child Development, Boston.

Colletta, N. D. (1983). At risk for depression: A study of young mothers. *Journal of Genetic Psychology*, 142, 301–310.

Collins, W. A. (1982). Cognitive processing in television viewing. In D. Pearl, L. Bouthilet, & J. Lazar (Eds.), *Television and behavior: Ten years of scientific progress and implications for the eighties*. Washington DC: U.S. Government Printing Office.

Colombo, J. (1986). Recent studies in early auditory development. *Annals of Child Development*, 3, 53–96. JAI Press.

Committee to Study the Health-Related Effects of Cannabis and its Derivations (1982). National Academy of Sciences, Institute of Medicine. *Marihuana and health*. Washington, DC: National Academy Press.

Comstock, G., & Cobbey, R. E. (1978). Television and the children of ethnic minorities. *Journal of Communication*, 29, 104–115.

Conger, J. J. (1973). *Adolescence and youth: Psychological development in a changing world*. New York: Harper & Row.

Conger, J. J. (1976). Roots of alienation. In B. Wolman (Ed.), *International encyclopedia of neurology, psychiatry, psychoanalysis, and psychology*. New York: McGraw-Hill.

Conger, J. J. (1977a). *Adolescence and youth: Psychological development in a changing world* (2nd ed.). New York: Harper & Row.

Conger, J. J. (1977b). Parent-child relationships, social change, and adolescent vulnerability. *Journal of Pediatric Psychology*, 2, 93–97.

Conger, J. J. (1979). *Adolescence: Generation under pressure*. New York: Harper & Row.

Conger, J. J. (1980). A new morality: Sexual attitudes and behavior of contemporary adolescents. In P. H. Mussen, J. J. Conger, & J. Kagan (Eds.), *Readings in child and adolescent psychology: Contemporary perspectives*. New York: Harper & Row.

Conger, J. J. (1981). Freedom and commitment: Families, youth, and social change. *American Psychologist, 36,* 1475–1484.

Conger, J. J. (1987). Behavioral medicine and health psychology in a changing world. *Child Abuse and Neglect, 11,* 443–453.

Conger, J. J. (1988). Hostages to fortune: Youth, values, and the public interest. *American Psychologist, 43,* 291–300.

Conger, J. J. (in press). *Adolescence and youth: Psychological development in a changing world* (4th ed.). New York: Harper & Row.

Conger, J. J., & Miller, W. C. (1966). *Personality, social class, and delinquency.* New York: Wiley.

Conger, J. J., & Petersen, A. C. (1984). *Adolescence and youth: Psychological development in a changing world* (3rd ed.). New York: Harper & Row.

Conger, R., Burgess, R., & Barrett, C. (1979). Child abuse related to life change and perceptions of illness: Some preliminary findings. *Family Coordinator, 28,* 73–78.

Congressional Budget Office (1988). *Trends in family income: 1970–1988.* Washington DC: Congressional Budget Office.

Connolly, J., Doyle, A. B., & Ceschin, F. (1983). Forms and functions of social fantasy play in preschoolers. In M. B. Liss (Ed.), *Social and cognitive skills: Sex roles and children's play* (pp. 71–92). New York: Academic Press.

Conway, E., & Brackbill, Y. (1970). Delivery medication and infant outcomes: An empirical study. In W. A. Bowes, Y. Brackbill, E. Conway, & A. Steinschneider (Eds.), The Effects of obstetrical medication on fetus and infant. *Monographs of the Society for Research in Child Development, 35*(4), 24–34.

Cook, T., Goldman, J., & Olczak, P. (1978). The relationship between self-esteem and interpersonal attraction in children. *Journal of Genetic Psychology, 132,* 149–150.

Cook, T. D., Appleton, H., Conner, R. F., Shaffer, A., Tabkin, C., & Weber, S. J. (1975). *"Sesame Street" revisited.* New York: Russell Sage.

Cooper, C. R. (March, 1977). *Collaboration in children: Dyadic interaction skills in problem solving.* Paper presented at the Biennial Meeting of the Society for Research in Child Development, New Orleans.

Cooper, C. R., & Ayers-Lopez, S. (1985). Family and peer systems in early adolescence: New models of the role of relationships in development. *Journal of Early Adolescence, 5,* 9–21.

Cooper, C. R., & Grotevant, H. D. (1987). Gender issues in the interface of family experience and adolescents' friendship and dating identity. *Journal of Youth and Adolescence, 16,* 247–264.

Cooper, C. R., Grotevant, H. D., & Condon, S. M. (1983). Individuality and connectedness in the family as a context for adolescent identity formation and role-taking skill. In H. D. Grotevant and C. R. Cooper (Eds.), *Adolescent development in the family* (pp. 43–60). San Francisco: Jossey-Bass.

Cooper, H. M. (1979). Pygmalion grows up: A model for teacher expectation communication and performance influence. *Review of Educational Research, 49,* 389–410.

Corah, N. L., Anthony, E. J., Painter, P., Stern, J. A., & Thurston, D. (1965). Effects of perinatal anoxia after 7 years. *Psychological Monographs, 79,* 1–34.

Corby, D. G. (1978). Aspirin in pregnancy: Maternal and fetal effects. *Pediatrics, 62,* 930–937.

Cordua, G. D., McGraw, K. O., & Drabman, R. S. (1979). Doctor or nurse: Children's perceptions of sex-typed occupations. *Child Development, 50,* 590–593.

Corrigan, R. (1978). Language development as related to stage 6 object permanence development. *Child Language, 5,* 173–179.

Corsaro, W. (1981). Friendship in the nursery school: Social organization in a peer environment. In S. R. Asher & J. M. Gottman (Eds.), *The development of children's friendships.* Cambridge: Cambridge University Press.

Costanzo, P. R. (1970). Conformity development as a function of self-blame. *Journal of Personality and Social Psychology, 14,* 366–374.

Costanzo, P. R., Coie, J. D., Grumet, J. F., & Farnill, D. (1973). A reexamination of the effects of intent and consequence on children's moral judgments. *Child Development, 44,* 154–161.

Costanzo, P. R., & Shaw, M. E. (1966). Conformity as a function of age level. *Child Development, 37,* 967–975.

Covington, M., & Omelich, C. (1979). Effort: The double-edged sword in school achievement. *Journal of Educational Psychology, 71,* 169–182.

Crandall, V. C. (1969). Sex differences in expectancy of intellectual and academic reinforcement. In C. P. Smith (Ed.), *Achievement-related motives in children* (pp. 11–45). New York: Russell Sage.

Crandall, V. C. (1978, August). *Expecting sex differences and sex differences in expectancies.* Paper presented at the Annual Meeting of the American Psychological Association, Toronto.

Cravioto, J., & DeLicardie, E. R. (1978). Nutrition, mental development, and learning. In F. Falkner & J. M. Tanner (Eds.), *Human growth: Vol. 3. Neurobiology and nutrition.* New York: Plenum.

Cressey, D. R., & Ward, D. A. (1969). *Delinquency, crime, and social process.* New York: Harper & Row.

Crockenberg, S. (1981). Infant irritability, mother responsiveness, and social support influences on the security of infant-mother attachment. *Child Development, 52,* 857–865.

Crockett, L. J., & Petersen, A. C. (1987). Pubertal status and psychosocial development: Findings from the early adolescent study. In R. M. Lerner & T. T. Foch (Eds.), *Biological and psychosocial interactions in early adolescence: A life-span perspective* (pp. 173–188). Hillsdale, NJ: Erlbaum.

Cross, W. E., Jr. (1985). Black identity: Rediscovering the distinction between personal identity and reference group orientation. In M. B. Spencer, G. K. Brookins, & W. R. Allen (Eds.), *Beginnings: The social and affective development of black children* (pp. 155–172). Hillsdale, NJ: Erlbaum.

Curran, D. K. (1987). *Adolescent suicidal behavior*. Washington, DC: Hemisphere Publishing Corporation.

Curran, J. W., Jaffee, H. W., Hardy, A. M., Morgan, W. M., Selik, R. M., Dondero, T. J., & Fareir, A. S. (1988). Epidemiology of HIV infection and AIDS in the United States. *Science, 239*, 610–616.

Curtiss, S. (1977). *Genie: A psycholinguistic study of a modern-day "wild-child"*. New York: Academic Press.

Daehler, M. W., & Bukatko, D. (1985). *Cognitive development*. New York: Knopf.

Dale, P. (1976). *Language development structure and function* (2nd ed.). New York: Holt, Rinehart and Winston.

Damon, W. (1977). *The social world of the child*. San Francisco: Jossey-Bass.

Damon, W. (1983). *Social and personality development*. New York: Norton.

Damon, W., & Hart, D. (1982). The development of self-understanding from infancy through adolescence. *Child Development, 53*, 841–864.

Daniels, D., Dunn, J., Furstenberg, F. F., & Plomin, R. (1985). Environmental differences with the family and adjustment differences within pairs of siblings. *Child Development, 56*, 764–774.

Darville, D., & Cheyne, J. A. (1981). *Sequential analysis of response to aggression: Age and sex effects*. Paper presented at the Biennial Meeting of the Society for Research in Child Development, Boston.

David, A., DeVault, S., & Talmadge, M. (1961). Anxiety, pregnancy, and childbirth abnormalities. *Journal of Consulting Psychology, 25*, 74–77.

Davis, J. M., Rovee-Collier, C. K. (1983). Alleviated forgetting of a learned contingency in eight week old infants. *Developmental Psychology, 19*, 353–365.

Davitz, J. R. (1955). Social perception and sociometric choice in children. *Journal of Abnormal and Social Psychology, 50*, 173–176.

Dawson, D. A. (1986). The effects of sex education on adolescent behavior. *Family Planning Perspectives, 18*, 162–170.

de la Cruz, F. (1985). Fragile X syndrome. *American Journal of Medical Genetics, 23*, 573–580.

de Villiers, J. A., & de Villiers, P. A. (1978). *Language acquisition*. Cambridge, MA: Harvard University Press.

Dean, R. A. (1982). Youth: Moonies' target population. *Adolescence, 17*, 567–574.

Deemer, D. (in press). *Life experiences and moral judgment development*. Doctoral dissertation. Minneapolis: University of Minnesota.

DeFries, J. C., & Plomin, R. (1978). Behavioral genetics. *Annual Review of Psychology, 29*, 473–515.

Detera-Wadeigh, S. D., Berrettin, W. H., Goldin, L. R., Boorman, D., Anderson, S., & Gershon, E. S. (1987). Close linkage of c-Harvey-ras-1 and the insulin gene to affective psychosis is ruled out in three North American pedigrees. *Nature, 325*, 806–808.

Diamond, A. (1985). Development of the ability to use recall to guide action, as indicated by infants' performance, on AB. *Child Development, 56*, 868–883.

Diener, C. I., & Dweck, C. S. (1978). An analysis of learned helplessness: Continuous changes in performance, strategy, and achievement cognitions following failure. *Journal of Personality and Social Psychology, 36*, 451–462.

Diener, C. I., & Dweck, C. S. (1980). An analysis of learned helplessness: II. The processing of success. *Journal of Personality and Social Psychology, 39*, 940–952.

Dietz, W. H., Jr., & Gortmaker, S. L. (1985). Do we fatten our children at the television set? Obesity and television viewing in children and adolescents. *Pediatrics, 75*, 807–812.

Dix, T. H., & Grusec, J. E. (1985). Parent attribution processes in the socialization of children. In I. E. Sigel (Ed.), *Parental belief systems: The psychological consequences for children*. Hillsdale, NJ: Erlbaum.

Dixson, M. C., & Wright, W. E. (1975). *Juvenile delinquency prevention programs: An evaluation of policy-related research on the effectiveness of prevention programs*. Nashville, TN: Office of Education Services, Peabody College for Teachers.

Dlugokinski, E. L., & Firestone, I. J. (1974). Other centeredness and susceptibility to charitable appeals: Effects of perceived discipline. *Developmental Psychology, 10*, 21–28.

Dobbing, J. (1976). The later development of central nervous system and its vulnerability. In A. V. Davison & J. Dobbing (Eds.), *Scientific foundations of Pediatrics*. London: Heinemann.

Dodge, K. A. (1980). Social cognition and children's aggressive behavior. *Child Development, 51*, 162–170.

Dodge, K. A. (1985). A social information processing model of social competence in children. In M. Perlmutter (Ed.), *Minnesota symposia on child psychology: Vol 18. Cognitive perspectives on children's social and behavioral development*. Hillsdale, NJ: Erlbaum.

Dodge, K. A. (1986). Social information-processing variables in the development of aggression and altruism in children. In C. Zahn-Waxler, E. M. Cummings, & R. Iannotti (Eds.), *Altruism and aggression: Biological and social original*. New York: Cambridge University Press.

Dodge, K. A., Murphy, R. R., & Buchsbaum, K. (1984). The assessment of intention-cue detection skills in children: Implications for developmental psychopathology. *Child Development, 55*, 163–173.

Dollard, J., Doob, L. W., Miller, N. E., Mowrer, O. H., & Sears, R. R. (1939). *Frustration and aggression*. New Haven: Yale University Press.

Donaldson, M. (1978). *Children's minds*. New York: Norton.

Donaldson, S. K., & Westerman, M. A. (1986). Development of children's understanding of ambivalence and causal theories of emotions. *Developmental Psychology*, 22, 655–662.

Donovan, J. M. (1975). Ego identity status and interpersonal style. *Journal of Youth and Adolescence*, 4, 37–56.

Dore, J. (1979). Conversation and preschool language development. In P. Fletcher & M. Gorman (Eds.), *Language acquisition*. Cambridge: Cambridge University Press.

Dornbusch, S. M., Ritter, P. L., Leiderman, P. H., Roberts, D. F., & Fraleigh, M. J. (1987). The relation of parenting style to adolescent school performance. *Child Development*, 58, 1244–1257.

Dorr, A. (1985). Contexts for experience with emotion, with special attention to television. In M. Lewis & C. Saarni (Eds.), *The socialization of emotion* (pp. 55–85). New York: Plenum.

Dorr, A. (1986). *Television and children: A special medium for a special audience*. Beverly Hills, CA: Sage.

Douvan, E., & Adelson, J. (1966). *The adolescent experience*. New York: Wiley.

Dudgeon, J. A. (1976). Infective causes of human malformations. *British Medical Bulletin*, 32, 77–83.

Duncan, G. J. (1984). *Years of poverty, years of plenty*. Ann Arbor, MI: Survey Research Center, University of Michigan.

Duncan, O. D., Featherman, D. L., & Duncan, B. (1972). *Socioeconomic background and achievement*. New York: Seminar Press.

Dunn, J. (1983). Sibling relationships in early childhood. *Child Development*, 54, 787–811.

Dunn, J. (1988). *The beginning of social understanding*. Cambridge, MA: Harvard University Press.

Dunn, J., & Kendrick, C. (1979). Interaction between young siblings in the context of family relationships . In M. Lewis and L. A. Rosenblum (Eds.), *The child and its family*. New York: Plenum.

Dunn, J., & Kendrick, C. (1980). The rival of a sibling. *Journal of Child Psychology and Psychiatry*, 21, 119–132.

Dunn, J., & Kendrick, C. (1981). Social behavior of young siblings in the family context: Differences between same-sex and different-sex dyads. *Child Development*, 52, 1265–1273.

Dunn, J., & Kendrick, C. (1982). Siblings and their mothers: Developing relationships within the family. In M. C. Lamb & B. Sutton-Smith (Eds.), *Sibling relationships*. Hillsdale, NJ: Erlbaum.

Dweck, C. S., & Elliot, E. S. (1983). Achievement motivation. In P. H. Mussen (Series Ed.) & E. M. Hetherington (Eds.), *Handbook of child psychology*: Vol. 4. *Socialization, personality, and social development* (pp. 643–692). New York: Wiley.

Dweck, C. S. (1975). The role of expectations and attributions in the alleviation of learned helplessness. *Journal of Personality and Social Psychology*, 31, 674–685.

Easson, W. M. (1977). Depression in adolescents. In S. Feinstein & P. Giovacchini (Eds.), *Adolescent psychiatry* (Vol. 5). New York: Aronson.

East, B. A. (1976). Cross-age tutoring in the elementary school. *Graduate Research in Education and Related Disciplines*, 8, 88–111.

Eccles, J. (1983). Expectancies, values, and academic behaviors. In J. T. Spence (Ed.), *Achievement and achievement motives* (pp. 75–146). San Francisco: Freeman.

Eccles, J., Adler, R., & Meece, J. L. (1984). Sex differences in achievement: A test of alternate theories. *Journal of Personality and Social Psychology*, 46, 26–43.

Eckerman, C. O., Whatley, J. L., & Kutz, S. L. (1975). The growth of social play with peers during the second year of life. *Developmental Psychology*, 11, 42–49.

Edelbrock, C. (1980). Running away from home: Incidence and correlates among children and youth referred for mental health services. *Journal of Family Issues*, 1, 2, 210–228.

Edelman, M. W. (1987). *Families in peril: An agenda for social change*. Cambridge, MA: Harvard University Press.

Edwards, C. P. (1981). The development of moral reasoning in cross-cultural perspective. In R. H. Munroe, R. L. Munroe, & B. B. Whiting (Eds.), *Handbook of cross-cultural human development*. New York: Garland Press.

Egeland, B., Breitenbucher, M., & Rosenberg, D. (1980). Prospective study of the significance of life stress in the etiology of child abuse. *Journal of Consulting and Clinical Psychology*, 48, 195–205.

Egeland, J. A., Gerhard, D. S., Pauls, D. L., Sussex, J. N., Kidd, K. K., Allen, C. R., Hostetter, A. N., & Housman, D. E. (1987). Bipolar affective disorders linked to DNA markers on chromosome 11. *Nature*, 325, 783–787.

Egeland, B., & Sroufe, L. A. (1981). Attachment and early maltreatment. *Child Development*, 52, 44–52.

Eggers, C. (1978). Course and prognosis of childhood schizophrenia. *Journal of Autism and Childhood Schizophrenia*, 8, 21–36.

Eifermann, R. R. (1970). Cooperativeness and egalitarianism in kibbutz children's games. *Human Relations*, 23, 579–587.

Eimas, P. D. (1975). Developmental studies of speech perception. In L. B. Cohen & P. Salapatek (Eds.), *Infant perception*. New York: Academic Press.

Eisenberg, N., & Miller, P. (1987). Empathy, sympathy, and altruism: Empirical and conceptual links. In N. Eisenberg & J. Strayer (Eds.), *Empathy and its development*. New York: Cambridge University Press.

Eisenberger, R., Mitchell, M., & Masterson, F. A. (1985). Effort training increases generalized self-control. *Journal of Personality and Social Psychology*, 49, 1294–1301.

Elder, G. H., Jr. (1980). *Family structure and socialization*. New York: Arno Press.

Elder, G. H., Jr., & Caspi, A. (1988). Economic stress in lives: Developmental perspectives. *Journal of Social Issues*, 44(4), 25–46.

Elkind, D. (1968). Cognitive development in adolescence. In J. F. Adams (Ed.), *Understanding adolescence*. Boston: Allyn & Bacon.

Elkind, D. (1978). *A sympathetic understanding of the child: Birth to sixteen* (2nd ed.). Boston: Allyn & Bacon.

Elkind, D. (1981). Giant in the nursery—Jean Piaget. In E. M. Hetherington & R. D. Parke (Eds.), *Contemporary readings in child psychology* (2nd ed.). New York: McGraw-Hill.

Elliot, A. J. (1981). *Child language*. Cambridge: Cambridge University Press.

Elliott, D. S., Ageton, S. S., Huizinga, D., Knowles, B. A., & Canter, R. J. (1983). *The prevalence and incidence of delinquent behavior, 1976–1980*. Boulder, CO: Behavioral Research Institute.

Elliott, D. S., Hinzinga, D., & Ageton, S. S. (1985). *Explaining delinquency and drug use*. Beverly Hills, CA: Sage Publications.

Ellis, M. J. (1973). *Why people play*. Englewood Cliffs, NJ: Prentice-Hall.

Emde, R., Harmon, R., & Good, W. (1986). Depressive feelings in children: A transactional model of research. In M. Rutter, C. E. Izard, & P. B. Read (Eds.), *Depression in young people: Developmental and clinical perspectives* (pp. 135–162). New York: Guilford.

Emler, N. P., & Rushton, J. P. (1974). Cognitive-developmental factors in children's generosity. *British Journal of Social and Clinical Psychology, 13*, 277–281.

Emmerich, W. (1966). Continuity and stability in early social development: II. Teacher's ratings. *Child Development, 37*, 17–27.

Enright, R. D., Lapsley, D., & Shukla, D. (1979). Adolescent egocentrism in early and late adolescence. *Adolescence, 14*, 687–695.

Epstein, S. (1973). The self-concept revisited. *American Psychologist, 38*, 404–416.

Erikson, E. H. (1956). The problem of ego identity. *Journal of the American Psychoanalytic Association, 4*, 56–121.

Erikson, E. H. (1963). *Childhood and society* (2nd ed.). New York: Norton.

Erikson, E. H. (1968). *Identity: Youth and crisis*. New York: Norton.

Erikson, E. H. (1983). Obstacles and pathways in the journey from adolescence to parenthood. In M. Sugar (Ed.), *Adolescent psychiatry: Developmental and clinical studies* (Vol. XI). Chicago: University of Chicago Press.

Ernhart, C. B., Graham, F. K., & Thurston, D. (1960). Relationship of neonatal apnea to development at three years. *Archives of Neurology, 2*, 504–510.

Eron, L. D. (1987). The development of aggressive behavior from the perspective of a developing behaviorism. *American Psychologist, 42*, 435–442.

Eron, L. D., & Huesmann, L. R. (1984). The control of aggressive behavior by changes in attitudes, values and the conditions of learning. In R. J. Blanchard & C. Blanchard (Eds.), *Advances in the study of aggression* (Vol. 2). New York: Academic Press.

Eron, L. D., Walder, L. O., & Lefkowitz, M. M. (1971). *Learning of aggression in children*. Boston: Little, Brown.

Ervin-Tripp, S. M. (1972). Children's sociolinguistic competence and dialect diversity. In I. J. Gordon (Ed.), Early childhood education. *The 71st Yearbook of the National Society for the Study of Education. Part II* (pp. 123–160). Chicago: University of Chicago Press.

Ervin-Tripp, S. (1976). Speech acts and social learning. In K. H. Basso & H. Selby (Eds.), *Meaning in anthropology*. Albuquerque: University of New Mexico Press.

Ervin-Tripp, S. (1977). Wait for me, rollerskate. In C. Mitchell-Kernan & S. Ervin-Tripp (Eds.), *Child discourse*. New York: Academic Press.

Estrada, P., Arsenio, W. F., Hess, R. D., & Holloway, S. D. (1987). Affective quality of the mother-child relationship: Longitudinal consequences for children's school-relevant cognitive functioning. *Developmental Psychology, 23*, 210–215.

Evans, R. B. (April 1971). Parental relationships and homosexuality. *Medical Aspects of Human Sexuality*, 164–177.

Fabricius, W. V., Sophian, C., & Wellman, H. M. (1987). Young children's sensitivity to logical necessity in their inferential search behavior. *Child Development, 58*, 409–423.

Fagen, J. F., Yengo, L. A., Rovee-Collier, C. K., Enright, M. K. (1981). Reactivation of a visual discrimination in early infancy. *Developmental Psychology, 17*, 266–274.

Fagot, B. I. (1974). Sex differences in toddlers' behavior and parental reaction. *Developmental Psychology, 10*, 554–558.

Fagot, B. I. (1977). Consequences of moderate cross-gender behavior in preschool children. *Child Development, 49*, 902–907.

Fagot, B. I. (1978). Reinforcing contingencies for sex-role behaviors: Effect of experience with children. *Child Development, 49*, 30–36.

Fagot, B. I. (1985). Beyond the reinforcement principle: Another step toward understanding sex role development. *Developmental Psychology, 21*, 1097–1104.

Fagot, B. I., & Hagan, R. (1982). *Hitting in toddler groups: Correlates and continuity*. Paper presented at the Annual Meeting of the American Psychological Association, Washington, DC.

Falbo, T., & Polit, D. F. (1986). Quantitative review of the only child literature: Research evidence and theory development. *Psychological Bulletin, 100*, 176–189.

Falkner, F., & Tanner, J. M. (Eds.) (1978a). *Human growth: Vol. 1. Principles and prenatal growth*. New York: Plenum.

Falkner, F., & Tanner, J. M. (1978b). *Human growth* (Vol. 2): *Postnatal growth*. New York: Plenum.

Farel, A. M. (1982). *Early adolescence and religion: A status study*. Carrbro, NC: Center for Early Adolescence.

Farmer, H. S. (1985). The role of typical female characteristics in career and achievement motivation. *Youth and Society, 16*, 315–334.

Farrington, D. P. (1981). The prevalence of convictions. *British Journal of Criminology, 21*, 123–135.

Farrington, D. P. (1987). Epidemiology. In H. C. Quay (Ed.), *Handbook of juvenile delinquency* (pp. 33-61). New York: Wiley.

Farrington, D. P., Biron, L., & LeBlanc, M. (1982). Personality and delinquency in London and Montreal. In J. C. Gunn & D. P. Farrington (Eds.), *Abnormal offenders: Delinquency and the criminal justice system*. New York: Wiley.

Faust, M. S. (1960). Developmental maturity as a determinant in prestige of adolescent girls. *Child Devleopment, 31*, 173–184.

Faust, M. S. (1977). Somatic development of adolescent girls. *Monographs of the Society for Research in Child Development, 42*, No. 1, 1–90.

Faust, M. S. (1984). Alternative constructions of adolescence and growth. In J. Brooks-Gunn & A. C. Petersen (Eds.), *Girls at puberty: Biological, psychological, and social perspectives*. New York: Plenum.

Fein, G. G. (1981). Pretend play: An integrative review. *Child Development, 52*, 1095–1118.

Feinstein, S. C., & Miller, D. (1979). Psychoses of adolescence. In J. D. Noshpitz (Ed.), *Basic handbook of child psychiatry*, Vol. II. Disturbances in development (pp. 708–722). New York: Basic Books.

Feld, S., Rutland, D., & Gold, M. (1979). Developmental changes in achievement motivation. *Merrill-Palmer Quarterly, 25*, 43–60.

Fennema, E., & Peterson, P. (1985). Autonomous learning behavior: A possible explanation of gender-related differences in mathematics. In L. C. Wilkinson & C. B. Marrett (Eds.), *Gender influences in classroom interaction* (pp. 17–36). Orlando: Academic Press.

Fenson, L., Cameron, M. Z., & Kennedy, M. (1988). Role of perceptual and conceptual similarity in category matching at age two years. *Child Development, 59*, 897–907.

Feshbach, N. D. (1978). Studies of empathic behavior in children. In B. A. Maher (Ed.), *Progress in experimental personality research* (Vol. 8). New York: Academic Press.

Feshbach, N. D., & Feshbach, S. (1982). Empathy training and the regulation of aggression: Potentialities and limitations. *Academic Psychology Bulletin, 4*, 399–413.

Feshbach, S. (1970). Aggression. In P. H. Mussen (Ed.), *Carmichael's manual of child psychology* (Vol. 2, 3rd ed., pp. 159–259). New York: Wiley.

Fischer, M., Rolf, J. E., Hasazi, J. E., & Cummings, L. (1984). Follow-up of a preschool epidemiological sample: Cross-age continuities and predictions of later adjustment with internalizing and externalizing dimension of behavior. *Child Development, 55*, 137–150.

Fiske, S. T., & Taylor, S. E. (1984). *Social cognition*. Reading, MA: Addison-Wesley.

Fitts, W., & Hammer, W. (1969). *The self-concept and delinquency*. Nashville: Counselor Recordings and Tests.

Flavell, J. H. (1963). *The developmental psychology of Jean Piaget*. Princeton, NJ: Van Nostrand.

Flavell, J. H. (1977). *Cognitive development*. Englewood Cliffs, NJ: Prentice-Hall.

Flavell, J. H. (1982). On cognitive development. *Child Development, 53*, 1–10.

Flavell, J. H. (1985). *Cognitive development* (2nd ed). Englewood Cliffs, NJ: Prentice-Hall.

Flavell, J. (1986). The development of children's knowledge about the appearance-reality distinction. *American Psychologist, 41*, 418–425.

Flavell, J. H., & Ross, L. (Eds.) (1981). *Social cognitive development*. New York: Cambridge University Press.

Flavell, J. H., Botkin, P. T., Fry, C. L., Wright, J. W., & Jarvis, P. E. (1968). *The development of role-taking and communication skills in children*. New York: Wiley.

Flavell, J. H., Shipstead, S. G., & Croft, K. (1978). *What young children think they see when their eyes are closed*. Unpublished report. Stanford University.

Flodereus-Myrhed, B., Pedersen, N., & Rasmuson, I. (1980). Assessment of heritability for personality, based on a short form of the Eysenck Personality Inventory: A study of 12,898 twin pairs. *Behavior Genetics, 10*, 153–162.

Flynn, J. R. (1987). Massive IQ gains in 14 nations: What IQ tests really measure. *Psychological Bulletin, 101*, 171–191.

Folger, M., & Leonard, L. (1978). Language and sensorimotor development during the early period of referential speech. *Journal of Speech and Hearing Research, 21*, 519–527.

Forbes, G. B. (1978). Body composition in adolescence. In F. Falkner & J. M. Tanner (Eds.), *Human growth: Vol 2. Postnatal growth*. New York: Plenum.

Ford, M. E. (1982). Social cognition and social competence in adolescence. *Developmental Psychology, 18*, 323–340.

Foremen, G. E., & Hill, F. (1980). *Constructive play: Applying Piaget in the preschool*. Monterey, CA: Brooks/Cole.

Forsterling, F. (1985). Attributional retraining: A review. *Psychological Bulletin, 98*, 495–512.

Fowler, J. W. (1981). *Stages of faith: The psychology and human development and the quest for meaning*. New York: Harper & Row.

Fraiberg, S. (1975). The development of human attachments in infants blind from birth. *Merrill Palmer Quarterly, 21*, 325–334.

Fraser, F. C., & Nora, J. J. (1986). *Genetics of man*. Philadelphia: Lea & Febiger.

Freedman, R., Adler, L. E., Baker, N., Waldo, M., & Mizner, G. (1987). Candidate for inherited neurobiological dysfunction in schizophrenia. *Somatic Cell and Molecular Genetics, 13*, 479–484.

Freeman, R. N. (1986, July 20). Cutting black youth unemployment. *The New York Times*.

Freud, A. (1969). Adolescence as a developmental disturbance. In G. Caplan & S. Lebovici (Eds.), *Adolescence: Psychosocial perspectives*. New York: Basic Books.

Freud, S. (1964). *An outline of psychoanalysis*. Standard edition of the works of Sigmund Freud, London: Hogarth Press.

Fuller, J. L., & Clark, L. D. (1968). Genotype and behavioral vulnerability to isolation in dogs. *Journal of Comparative and Physiological Psychology, 66*, 151–156.

Furrow, D., Nelson, K., & Benedict, H. (1979). Mothers' speech to children and syntactic development: Some simple relationships. *Journal of Child Language*, 6, 423–442.

Furstenberg, F. J., Jr., Brooks-Gunn, J., & Morgan, S. P. (1987a). Adolescent fertility: Causes, consequences and remedies. In L. Aiken & D. Mechanic (Eds.), *Applications of social science to clinical medicine and health policy*. New Brunswick, NJ: Rutgers University Press.

Furstenberg, F. J., Jr., Brooks-Gunn, J., & Morgan, S. P. (1987b). *Adolescent mothers in later life*. New York: Cambridge University Press.

Furstenberg, F. F., Nord, C. W., Peterson, J. L., & Zill, N. (1983). The life course of children of divorce: Marital disruption and parental contact. *American Sociological Review*, 48, 656–668.

Furth, H. G. (1966). *Thinking without language*. New York: Free Press.

Gagne, R. M. (1968). *The conditions of learning*. New York: Holt, Rinehart and Winston.

Gagne, R. M., & Smith, E. C. (1964). A study of the effects of verbalization on problem solving. *Journal of Experimental Psychology*, 63, 12–18.

Galanter, M. (1980). Psychological induction into the large group: Findings from a contemporary religious sect. *American Journal of Psychiatry*, 137, 1574–1579.

Gallup, G. (1978, January 15). Gallup youth survey. *Denver Post*, p. 50.

Gallup, G. (1979, November 20). Gallup youth survey. *Denver Post*, p. 36.

Gallup, G., & Polling, D. (1980). *The search for America's faith*. New York: Abington.

Garbarino, J. (1986). Can we measure success in preventing child abuse? Issues in policy, programming and research. *Child Abuse and Neglect*, 10, 143–156.

Garbarino, J., & Plantz, M. C. (1986). Child abuse and delinquency: What are the links? In J. Garbarino, C. J. Schellenbach, & J. M. Sebes (Eds.) *Troubled youth, troubled families: Understanding families at risk for adolescent maltreatment* (pp. 27–39). New York: Aldine de Gruyter.

Garbarino, J., & Sherman, D. (1980). High-risk neighborhoods and high-risk families: The human ecology of child maltreatment. *Child Development*, 51, 188–198.

Garbarino, J., Wilson, J., & Garbarino, A. (1986). The adolescent runaway. In J. Garbarino, C. J. Schellenbach, & J. M. Sebes (Eds.), *Troubled youth, troubled families: Understanding families at-risk for adolescent maltreatment*. New York: Aldine de Gruyter.

Garfinkel, I., & McLanahan, S. S. (1986). *Single mothers and their children: A new American dilemma*. Washington DC: The Urban Institutes Press.

Garfinkel, P. E., & Garner, D. M. (1983). *Anorexia nervosa: A multidimensional perspective*. New York: Brunner/Mazel.

Garmezy, N. (1985). Stress-resistant children: The search for protective factors. In J. E. Stevenson (Ed.), *Recent research in developmental psychopathology* (pp. 213–233). New York: Pergamon.

Garmezy, N. (1986). Developmental aspects of children's responses to the stress of separation and loss. In M. Rutter, C. E. Izard, & P. B. Read (Eds.), *Depression in young people: Developmental and clinical perspectives* (pp. 297–324). New York: Guilford.

Garmezy, N. (1987, November 12). Disadvantaged children: Strategies of their resilience under stress. *Proceedings of the Third Annual Rosalynn Carter Symposium on Mental Health Policy* (pp. 22–32). Atlanta, GA: Carter Presidential Center.

Garrett, C. J. (1984). *Meta-analysis of the effects of institutional and community residential treatment on adjudicated delinquents*. Unpublished doctoral dissertation, University of Colorado.

Garrett, C. J. (1985). Effects of residential treatment on adjudicated delinquents: A meta-analysis. *Journal of Research on Crime and Delinquency*, 22, 287–308.

Garvey, C. (1975). Requests and responses in children's speech. *Journal of Child Language*, 2, 41–63.

Garvey, C. (1977). *Play*. Cambridge, MA: Harvard University Press.

Gelman, R. & Baillargeon, R. (1983). A review of some Piagetian concepts. In J. H. Flavell & E. M. Markman (Eds.), P. H. Mussen (Series Ed.), *Handbook of child psychology: Vol. 3. Cognitive development* (pp. 167–230). New York: Wiley.

Gelman, R., & Gallistel, C. R. (1978). *The child's understanding of number*. Cambridge, MA: Harvard University Press.

Gelman, S. A., Collman, P., & Maccoby, E. E. (1986). Inferring properties from categories versus inferring categories from properties: The case of gender. *Child Development*, 57, 396–404.

George, C., & Main, M. (1979). Social interaction of young abused children: Approach, avoidance and aggression. *Child Development*, 50, 306–318.

Gerson, R. P., & Damon, W. (1978). Moral understanding and children's conduct. In W. Damon (Ed.), *New directions in child development: Moral development*. San Francisco: Jossey-Bass.

Gesell, A. (1945). *The embryology of behavior*. New York: Harper & Row.

Gesell, A., & Amatruda, C.S. (1941). *Developmental diagnosis: Normal and abnormal child development*. New York: Hoeber.

Gessell, A., Halverson, H. M., Thompson, H., Ilg, F. L., Costner, B. M., & Amatruda, C. S. (1940). *The first five years of life: A guide to the study of the preschool child*. New York: Harper & Row.

Gewirtz, J. L. (1965). The cause of infant smiling in four child-rearing environments in Israel. In B. M. Foss (Ed.), *Determinants of infant behavior* (Vol. 3). London: Metheun.

Gilligan, C. (1982). *In a different voice*. Cambridge, MA: Harvard University Press.

Gilligan, C., & Belenky, M. F. (1982). A naturalistic study of abortion decisons. In R. Selman & R. Yando (Eds.), *Clinical-developmental psychology*. San Francisco: Jossey-Bass.

Ginsburg, H. P., & Opper, S. (1979). *Piaget's theory of intellectual development* (2nd ed). Englewood Cliffs, NJ: Prentice-Hall.

Ginsburg, H. P. & Russell, R. L. (1981). Social class and racial influences on early mathematical thinking. *Monographs of the Society for Research in Child Development, 46*, (Serial No. 193).

Ginzberg, E. (1972). Toward a theory of occupational choice: A restatement. *Vocational Guidance Quarterly, 20*, 169–176.

Glass, D. C., Neulinger, J., & Brim, O. G. (1974). Birth order, verbal intelligence, and educational aspiration. *Child Development, 45*, 807–811.

Gleitman, L. R., Gleitman, H., & Shipley, E. F. (1972). The emergence of the child as grammarian. *Cognition, 1*, 137–164.

Glick, P. C. (1984). Marriage, divorce, and living arrangements: Prospective changes. *Journal of Family Issues, 5*, 7–26.

Glucksberg, S., & Krauss, R. M. (1967). What do people say after they have learned how to talk? *Merrill-Palmer Quarterly, 13*, 309–316.

Gnepp, J. & Hess, D. L. R. (1986). Children's understanding of verbal and facial display rules. *Developmental Psychology, 22*, 103–108.

Gold, D. & Andres, D. (1978a). Comparisons of adolescent children with employed and nonemployed mothers. *Merrill-Palmer Quarterly, 24*, 243–254.

Gold, D., & Andres, D. (1978b). Developmental comparisons between ten-year-old children with employed and nonemployed mothers. *Child Development, 49*, 75–84.

Gold, D., & Andres, D. (1978c). Relations between maternal employment and development of nursery school children. *Canadian Journal of Behavioral Science, 10*, 116–129.

Gold, D., Andres, D., & Glorieux, J. (1979). The development of Francophone nursery-school children with employed and nonemployed mothers. *Canadian Journal of Behavioral Science, 11*, 169–173.

Gold, M. (1978). Scholastic experiences, self-esteem, and delinquent behavior: A theory for alternative schools. *Crime & Delinquency, 24*, 290–308.

Gold, M. (1987). Social ecology. In H. C. Quay (Ed.), *Handbook of juvenile delinquency* (pp. 62–105). New York: Wiley.

Gold, M., & Mann, D. (1972). Delinquency as defense. *American Journal of Orthopsychiatry, 42*, 463–479.

Gold, M., & Petronio, R. J. (1979). Delinquent behavior in adolescence. In J. Adelson (Ed.), *Handbook of adolescent psychology*. New York: Wiley.

Goldberg, W. A., & Easterbrooks, M. A. (1984). Role of marital quality in toddler development. *Developmental Psychology, 20*, 504–514.

Goldfarb, J. L., Mumford, D. M., Schum, D. A., Smith, P. B., Flowers, C., & Schum, D. (1977). An attempt to detect "pregnancy susceptibility" in indigent adolescent girls. *Journal of Youth and Adolescence, 6*, 127–144.

Goldsen, R., Rosenberg, M., Williams, R., & Suchman, I. (1960). *What college students think*. New York: Van Nostrand.

Goldsmith, H. H. (1983). Genetic influences on personality from infancy to adulthood. *Child Development, 54*, 331–355.

Goldsmith, H. H. (1984). Continuity of personality: A genetic perspective. In R. N. Emde & R. J. Harmon (Eds.), *The development of attachment and affiliative systems*. New York: Plenum.

Goldsmith, H. H., & Campos, J. J. (1982). Genetic influence on individual differences in emotionality. *Infant Behavior and Development, 5*, 99.

Goldsmith, H. H., & Gottesman, I. I. (1981). Origins of variation in behavioral style. *Child Development, 52*, 91–103.

Goldsmith, R., & Radin, N. (1987, April). *Objective versus subjective reality: The effects of job loss and financial stress on fathering behaviors*. Paper presented at the meeting of the Society for Research in Child Development, Baltimore.

Goldstein, A. (1981). *Psychological skill training*. New York: Pergamon.

Goldstein, K. M., Caputo, D. V., & Taub, H. B. (1976). The effects of perinatal complications on development at one year of age. *Child Development, 47*, 613–621.

Goldstein, M. J. (1987). The UCLA high-risk project, 1962–1986. *Schizophrenia Bulletin, 13*, 505–514.

Goldstein, M. J., Baker, B. L., & Jamison, K. R. (1980). *Abnormal psychology: Experiences, origins, and interventions*. Boston: Little, Brown.

Goodchilds, J. D., & Zellman, G. L. (1984). Sexual signaling and sexual aggression in adolescent relationships. In N. M. Malamuth & E. D. Donnerstein (Eds.), *Pornography and sexual aggression*. New York: Academic Press.

Goodman, G. S., Aman, C., & Hirshmani, J. (1987). Child sexual and physical abuse: Children's testimony. In S. J. Ceci, M. P. Toglia, & D. F. Ross (Eds.), *Children's eyewitness memory* (pp. 1–23). New York: Springer-Verlag.

Goodnow, J. J. (1985). Change and variation in ideas about childhood and parenting. In I. E. Sigel (Ed.), *Parental belief systems: The psychological consequences for children*. Hillsdale, NJ: Erlbaum.

Gopnik, A., & Meltzoff, A. (1987). The development of categorization in the second year and its relation to other cognitive and linguistic developments. *Child Development, 58*, 1523–1531.

Gottesman, I. I., & Shields, J. (1967). A polygenic theory of schizophrenia. *Proceedings of the National Academy of Science, U.S.A., 58*, 199–205.

Gottesman, I. I., & Shields, J. (1982). *Schizophrenia: The enigmatic puzzle*. New York: Cambridge University Press.

Gottman, J. M. (1977). Toward a definition of social isolation in children. *Child Development, 48*, 513–517.

Gottman, J. M. (1983). How children become friends. *Monographs of the Society for Research in Child Development, 48*, (Serial No. 201).

Grace, W. C., & Sweeney, M. E. (1986). Comparison of the P>V sign on the WISC-R and WAIS-R in delinquent males. *Journal of Clinical Psychology*, 42, 173–176.

Graham, F. K., Matarazzo, R. G., & Caldwell, B. M. (1956). Behavioral differences between normal and traumatized newborns. *Psychological Monographs*, 70(5).

Graham, P., & Rutter, M. (1985). Adolescent disorders. In M. Rutter and L. Hersov, *Child and adolescent psychiatry*. Oxford: Blackwell Scientific Publications.

Graham, S. (1984). Communicating sympathy and anger to black and white children: The cognitive (attributional) consequences of affective cues. *Journal of Personality and Social Psychology*, 47, 40–54.

Green, R. (1974). *Sexual identity conflict in children and adults*. New York: Basic Books.

Green, R. (1980). Homosexuality. In H. I. Kaplan, A. M. Freedman, & B. J. Sadock (Eds.), *Comprehensive textbook of psychiatry* (Vol. 2) (3rd ed., pp. 1762–1770). Baltimore: Williams and Wilkins.

Green, R. (1987). *The "sissy boy syndrome" and the development of homosexuality*. New Haven, CT: Yale University Press.

Greenberg, B. S. (1972). Children's reactions to TV blacks. *Journalism Quarterly*, 5–14.

Greenberg, B. S. (1986). Minorities and the mass media. In J. Bryant and D. Zillmann (Eds.), *Perspectives on mass media effects* (pp. 165–188). Hillsdale, NJ: Erlbaum.

Greenberger, E., & Steinberg, L. (1986). *When teenagers work: The psychological and social costs of adolescent employment*. New York: Basic Books.

Greenough, W. J., Black, J. E., & Wallace, C. S. (1987). Experience and brain development. *Child Development*, 58, 539–555.

Greif, E. B., & Ulman, K. J. (1982). The psychological impact of menarche on early adolescent females: A review of the literature. *Child Development*, 53, 1413–1430.

Grossman, F. K., Eichler, L. S., Winikoff, S. A., & Associates. (1980). *Pregnancy, birth, and parenthood: Adaptations of mothers, fathers, and infants*. San Francisco: Jossey-Bass.

Grossman, K., Grossman, K. E., Huber, F., & Wartner, Y. (1981). German children's behavior toward their mothers at 12 months and their fathers at 18 months in the Ainsworth Strange Situation. *International Journal of Behavioral Development*, 4, 157–181.

Grossman, K., Thane, K., & Grossman, K. E. (1981). Maternal tactual contact of the newborn after various post-partum conditions of mother-infant contact. *Developmental Psychology*, 17, 158–169.

Grotevant, H. D., & Cooper, C. R. (Eds.). (1983). *Adolescent development in the family*. San Francisco: Jossey-Bass.

Grumbach, M. M. (1978). The central nervous system and the onset of puberty. In F. Falkner & J. M. Tanner (Eds.), *Human growth*: Vol. 2. *Postnatal growth*. New York: Plenum.

Grusec, J. E., Saas-Kortsaak, P., & Simutis, Z. M. (1978). The role of example and moral exhortation in the training of altruism. *Child Development*, 49, 920–923.

Guidubaldi, J., Perry, J. D., & Cleminshaw, H. K. (1983). The legacy of parental divorce: A nationwide study of family status and selected mediating variables on children's academic and social competencies. *School Psychology Review*, 2, 148.

Guilford, J. P. (1979). *Cognitive psychology with a frame of reference*. San Diego: Edits Publishers.

Gump, P. V. (1980). The school as a social situation. *Annual Review of Psychology*, 31, 553–582.

Gump, P. V., & Ross, R. (1977). The fit of milieu and programme in school environments. In H. McGurck (Ed.), *Ecological factors in human development*. New York: Elsevier North-Holland.

Gunter, N. C., & LaBarba, R. C. (1980). The consequences of adolescent childbearing on postnatal development. *International Journal of Behavioral Development*, 3, 191–214.

Gupta, D., Attanasio, A., & Raaf, S. (1975). Plasma estrogen and androgen concentrations in children during adolescence. *Journal of Clinical Endocrinology and Metabolism*, 40, 636–643.

Guttmacher, A. F., & Kaiser, J. H. (1986). *Pregnancy, birth, and family planning*. New York: New American Library.

Haan, N., Smith, B., & Block J. (1968). Moral reasoning of young adults. *Journal of Personality and Social Psychology*, 10, 183–201.

Haas, A. (1979). *Teenage sexuality: A survey of teenage sexual behavior*. New York: Macmillan.

Hack, M. (1983). The sensorimotor development of the preterm infant. In A. A. Fanaroff, R. J. Martin, & J. R. Merkatz (Eds.), *Behrman's neonatal-perinatal medicine*. St. Louis: Mosby.

Haith, M. M. (1987). *Expectations and the gratuity of skill acquisition in early infancy*. Unpublished manuscript.

Haith, M. M. (1980). *Rules that babies look by*. Hillsdale, NJ: Erlbaum.

Hall, G. S. (1891). The content of children's minds on entering school. *Pedagogical Seminary*, 1, 139–173.

Hall, V. C., & Kaye, D. B. (1980). Early patterns of cognitive development. *Monographs of the Society for Research in Child Development*, 45, (Serial No. 184).

Hallinan, M. T. & Teixeira, R. A. (1987). Opportunities and constraints: Black-white differences in the formation of interracial friendships. *Child Development*, 58, 1358–1371.

Halpern, D. F. (1986). *Sex differences in cognitive abilities*. Hillsdale, NJ: Erlbaum.

Hamburg, D. A., & Trudeau, M. B. (1981). *Biobehavioral aspects of aggression*. New York: Alan R. Liss.

Hamilton, S. F., & Crouter, A. C. (1980). Work and growth: A review of research on the impact of work experience on adolescent development. *Journal of Youth and Adolescence, 9*, 323–338.

Hansen, R. D. & O'Leary, V. E. (1986). Sex-determined attributions. In V. E. O'Leary, R. K. Unger, & B. S. Wallston (Eds.), *Women, gender, and social psychology* (pp. 67–100). Hillsdale, NJ: Erlbaum.

Hanson, J. W. (1977). Unpublished paper, cited in A. Clarke-Stewart & S. Friedman (1982) *Child development: Infancy through adolescence* (p. 127). New York: Wiley.

Harkness, S., & Super, C. M. (1985). Child-environment interactions in the socialization of affect. In M. Lewis & C. Saarni (Eds.), *The socialization of emotions* (pp. 21–36). New York: Plenum.

Harlow, H. F., & Harlow, M. K. (1966). Learning to love. *American Scientist, 54*, 244–272.

Harlow, H. F., & Suomi, S. J. (1970). The nature of love-simplified. *American Psychologist, 25*, 161–168.

Harris, L. (1971, January 8). Change, yes — upheaval, no. *Life*, pp. 22–27.

Harris, L. (1987). *Inside America*. New York: Vintage.

Harris, P. L. (1985). What children know about the situations that provoke emotion. In M. Lewis & C. Saarni (Eds.), *The socialization of emotions* (pp. 161–186). New York: Plenum.

Harris, P. L., Donnelly, K., Guz, G. R., & Pitt-Watson, R. (1986). Children's understanding of the distinction between real and apparent emotion. *Child Development, 57*, 895–909.

Harrison, A., Serafica, F., & McAdoo, H. (1984). Ethnic families of color. In R. D. Parke (Ed.), *Review of child development research*: Vol. 7. *The family*. Chicago: University of Chicago Press.

Harter, S. (1982). The perceived competence scale for children. *Child Development, 53*, 87–97.

Harter, S. (1983). Developmental perspectives on the self-system. In P. H. Mussen (Series Ed.) & E. M. Hetherington (Ed.), *Handbook of child psychology*: Vol. 4. *Socialization, personality, and social development* (4th ed., pp. 275–386). New York: Wiley.

Harter, S. (1985). Competence as a dimension of self-evaluation: Toward a comprehensive model of self-worth. In R. Leahy (Ed.), *The development of the self*. New York: Academic Press.

Hartup, W. W. (1970). Peer interaction and social organization. In P. H. Mussen (Ed.), *Carmichael's manual of child psychology* (Vol. 2). New York: Wiley.

Hartup, W. W. (1974). Aggression in childhood: Developmental perspectives. *American Psychologist, 29*, 336–341.

Hartup, W. W. (1983). Peer relations. In E. M. Hetherington (Ed.), & P. H. Mussen (Series Ed.), *Handbook of child psychology*: Vol. 4. *Socialization, personality, and social development* (4th ed., pp. 103–196). New York: Wiley.

Hartup, W. W., Brady, J. E., & Newcomb, A. F. (1981). *Children's utilization of simultaneous sources of social information: Developmental perspectives*. Unpublished manuscript, University of Minnesota.

Haskins, R. (1985). Public school aggression among children with varying day-care experience. *Child Development, 56*, 689–703.

Hauser, S. T., Book, B. K., Houlihan, J., Powers, S., Weiss-Perry B., Follansbee, D., Jacobson, A. M., & Noam, G. G. (1987). Sex differences within the family: Studies of adolescent and parent family interactions. *Journal of Youth and Adolescence, 16*, 199–220.

Hawkins, R. P. (1977). Behavioral analysis and early childhood education: Engineering children's learning. In H. L. Hom & P. A. Robinson (Eds.), *Psychological processes in early education*. New York: Academic Press.

Hay, D. F. (1979). Cooperative interactions and sharing among very young children and their parents. *Developmental Psychology, 15*, 647–653.

Hayes, C. D. (Ed.). (1987). *Risking the future: Adolescent sexuality, pregnancy, and childbearing* (Vol. 1). Washington, DC: National Academy Press.

Hayes, D. S. (1978). Cognitive bases for liking and disliking among preschool children. *Child Development, 49*, 906–909.

Hearold, S. (1986). A synthesis of 1043 effects of television on social behavior. In G. Comstock (Ed.), *Public Communication and Behavior* (Vol. 1: pp. 66–133). New York: Academic Press.

Heath, D. B. (1977). Some possible effects of occupation on the maturing of professional men. *Journal of Vocational Behavior, 11*, 263–281.

Heibeck, T. H., & Markam, E. M. (1987). Word learning in children: An examination of fast mapping. *Child Development, 58*, 1021–1034.

Hermans, H. J. M., Ter Laak, J. J., & Maes, P. C. (1972). Achievement motivation and fear of failure in family and school. *Developmental Psychology, 6*, 520–528.

Herr, E. L., & Cramer, S. H. (1979). *Career guidance through the life span: Systematic approaches*. Boston: Little, Brown.

Herzog, A. R., Bachman, J. G., & Johnston, L. D. (1979). *Paid work, child care, and housework: A national study of high school seniors' preferences for sharing responsibilities between husband and wife*. Ann Arbor, MI: Survey Research Center, Institute for Social Research, University of Michigan.

Herzog, D. P. (1988). Eating disorders. In A. M. Nicholi, Jr. (Ed.), *The new Harvard guide to psychiatry* (pp. 434–445). Cambridge, MA: Harvard University Press.

Hess, R. D. (1970). Social class and ethnic influences on socialization. In P. Mussen (Ed.), *Carmichael's manual of child psychology* (Vol. 2, 3rd ed.). New York: Wiley.

Hess, R. D., Holloway, S. D., Dickson, W. P., & Price, G. G. (1984). Maternal variables as predictors of children's school readiness and later achievement in vocabulary and mathematics in sixth grade. *Child Development*, 55, 1902–1912.

Hess, R. D. & McDevitt, T. M. (1984). Some cognitive consequences of maternal intervention techniques: A longitudinal study. *Child Development*, 55, 2017–2030.

Hetherington, E. M. (1967). The effects of familial variables on sex typing, on parent-child similarity, and on imitation in children. In J. P. Hill (Ed.), *Minnesota symposia on child psychology* (Vol. 1). Minneapolis: University of Minnesota Press.

Hetherington, E. M., & Camara, K. A. (1984). Families in transition: The processes of dissolution and reconstitution. In R. D. Parke (Ed.), *Review of child development research: Vol. 7. The family.* Chicago: University of Chicago Press.

Hetherington, E. M., Camara, K. A., & Featherman, D. L. (1983). Achievement and intellectual functioning of children from one-parent households. In J. T. Spence (Ed.), *Achievement and achievement motives.* San Francisco: Freeman.

Hetherington, E. M., Cox, M., & Cox, R. (1979). Family interaction and the social, emotional and cognitive development of children following divorce. In V. Vaughan & T. B. Brazelton (Eds.), *The family: Setting priorities.* New York: Science and Medicine Publishing.

Hetherington, E. M., Cox, M., & Cox, R. (1982). Effects of divorce on parents and children. In M. Lamb (Ed.), *Nontraditional families.* Hillsdale, NJ: Erlbaum.

Higgins, A., Power, C., & Kohlberg, L. (1984). The relationship of moral atmosphere to judgments of responsibility. In W. M. Kurtines & J. L. Gewirtz (Eds.), *Morality, moral behavior, and moral development.* New York: Wiley.

Hill, J. P., & Holmbeck, G. (1987). Disagreements about rules in families with seventh grade boys and girls. *Journal of Youth and Adolescence*, 16, 221–246.

Hill, J. P., & Palmquist, W. (1978). Social cognition and social relations in early adolescence. *International Journal of Behavioural Development*, 1, 1–36.

Hill, K. T. (1980). Motivation, evaluation, and educational testing policy. In L. J. Fyans (Ed.), *Achievement motivation: Recent trends in theory and research.* New York: Plenum.

Hill, K. T. & Sarason, S. B. (1966). The relation of test anxiety and defensiveness to test and school performance over the elementary school years: A further longitudinal study. *Monographs of the Society for Research in Child Development*, 31, Serial No. 104.

Hilton, I. (1967). Differences in the behavior of mothers toward first and later born children. *Journal of Personality and Social Psychology*, 7, 282–290.

Hinshaw, S. P. (1987). On the distinction between attentional deficits/hyperactivity and conduct problems/aggression in child psychopathology. *Psychological Bulletin*, 101, 443–465.

Hirsch, S. P. (1974). Study at the top: Executive high school internships. *Educational Leadership* 32, 112–115.

Hirschi, T. (1969). *Causes of delinquency.* Berkeley, CA: University of California.

Hirschi, T., & Hindelang, M. J. (1977). Intelligence and delinquency: A revisionist review. *American Sociological Review*, 42, 571–587.

Hock, E. (1980). Working and nonworking mothers and their infants: A comparative study of maternal caregiving characteristics and infant social behavior. *Merrill-Palmer Quarterly*, 26, 79–101.

Hock, E., & Clinger, J. B. (1981). Infant coping behaviors: Their relationship to maternal attachment. *Journal of Genetic Psychology*, 138, 231–243.

Hodgkinson, S., Sherrington, H. G., Gurling, H., Marchbanks, S. R., Mallet, J., Petursson, H., & Bynjolfsson, J. (1987). Molecular genetic evidence for heterogeneity in manic depression. *Nature*, 325, 805–806.

Hodgson, J. W., & Fischer, J. L. (1978). Sex differences in identity and intimacy development in college youth. *Journal of Youth and Adolescence*, 7, 333–352.

Hodgson, J. W., & Fischer, J. (1979). Sex differences in identity and intimacy development in adolescence. *Journal of Youth and Adolescence*, 8, 37–50.

Hofferth, S. L., Kahn, J. R., & Baldwin, W. (1987). Premarital sexual activity among U.S. teenage women over the past three decades. *Family Planning Perspectives*, 19, 46–53.

Hoffman, L. W. (1972). Early childhood experiences and women's achievement motives. *Journal of Social Issues*, 28, 129–155.

Hoffman, L. W. (1973). The professional woman as mother. *Annals of the New York Academy of Sciences*, 208, 211–216.

Hoffman, L. W. (1980). The effects of maternal employment on the academic attitudes and performance of school-aged children. *School Psychology Review*, 9, 319–336.

Hoffman, L. W. (1984). Work, family, and the socialization of the child. In R. D. Parke (Ed.), *Parent-child interaction and parent-child relations in child development. The Minnesota Symposium on Child Psychology* (Vol. 17, pp. 101–128). Hillsdale, NJ: Erlbaum.

Hoffman, L. W. (1986). Work, family, and the child. In M. S. Pallak, & R. O. Perloff (Eds.), *Psychology and work: Productivity, change, and employment.* Washington, DC: American Psychological Association.

Hoffman, L. W. (1989). Maternal employment. *American Psychologist*, 34, 859–865.

Hoffman, L. W., & Nye, F. I. (1974). *Working mothers.* San Francisco: Jossey-Bass.

Hoffman, M. L. (1967). Moral internalization, parental power, and the nature of the parent-child interaction. *Developmental Psychology*, 5, 45–57.

Hoffman, M. L. (1970). Moral development. In P. Mussen (Ed.), *Carmichael's manual of child psychology* (Vol. 2, 3rd ed.). New York: Wiley.

Hoffman, M. L. (1975). Developmental synthesis of affect and cognition and its implications for altruistic motivation. *Developmental Psychology*, 11, 607–622.

Hoffman, M. L. (1980). Moral development in adolescence. In J. Adelson (Ed.), *Handbook of adolescent psychology*. New York: Wiley.

Hoffman, M. L. (1981). Development of the motive to help others. In J. P. Rushton & R. M. Sorrentino (Eds.), *Altruism and helping*. Hillsdale, NJ: Erlbaum.

Hoffman, M. L. (1983). Affective and cognitive processes in moral internalization. In E. T. Higgins, D. N. Ruble, & W. W. Hartup (Eds.), *Social cognition and social behavior: Developmental perspectives*. New York: Cambridge University Press.

Hoffman, M. L., & Saltzstein, H. D. (1967). Parent discipline and the child's moral development. *Journal of Personality and Social Psychology*, 5, 45–47.

Holinger, P. C. (1978). Adolescent suicide: An epidemiological study of recent trends. *American Journal of Psychiatry*, 135, 754–756.

Hollenbeck, A. R., & Slaby, R. G. (1979). Infant visual and vocal responses to television. *Child Development*, 50, 41–45.

Holmes, D. J. (1964). *The adolescent in psychotherapy*. Boston: Little, Brown.

Honzik, M. P., Macfarlane, J. W., & Allen, L. (1948). The stability of mental test performances between two and eighteen years. *Journal of Experimental Education*, 17, 309–324.

Horn, J. M. (1968). Organization of abilities and the development of intelligence. *Psychological Review*, 75, 242–259.

Horn, J. M. (1983). The Texas adoption project: Adopted children and their intellectual resemblance to biological and adoptive parents. *Child Development*, 54, 268–275.

Horn, J. M. (1985). Bias? Indeed! *Child Development*, 56, 779–780.

Hornick, J. P., Doran, L., & Crawford, S. H. (1979). Premarital contraceptive usage among male and female adolescents. *Family Coordinator*, 28, 181–190.

Horowitz, F. D. (1987). *Exploring developmental theories: Toward a structural/behavioral model of development*. Hillsdale, NJ: Erlbaum.

Horowitz, F. D., & Paden, L. Y. (1973). The effectiveness of environmental intervention programs. In B. M. Caldwell & H. N. Ricciuti (Eds.) *Review of child development research* (Vol. 3). Chicago: University of Chicago Press.

Horwitz, R. A. (1979). Psychological effects of the "open classroom". *Review of Educational Research*, 49, 71–86.

House Committee of Education and Labor, Subcommittee of Human Resources, Juvenile Justice, Runaway Youth and Missing Children's Act amendments 98th Cong., 2nd sess., 7 March 1984, Y4.E8.1:J 98/15.

Householder, J., Hatcher, R., Burns, W. J., & Chasnoff, I. (1982). Infants born to narcotic-addicted mothers. *Psychological Bulletin*, 92, 453–468.

Howes, C. (1988). Relations between early child care and schooling. *Developmental Psychology*, 24, 53–57.

Howes, C., & Stewart, P. (1987). Child's play with adults, toys, and peers: An examination of family and child-care influences. *Developmental Psychology*, 23, 432–430.

Huesmann, L. R. & Eron, L. D. (Eds.) (1986). *Television and the aggressive child: A cross-national comparison*. Hillsdale, NJ: Erlbaum.

Huesmann, L. R., Eron, L. D., Lefkowitz, M. M., & Walder, L. O. (1984). The stability of aggression over time and generations. *Developmental Psychology*, 20, 1120–1134.

Huesmann, L. R., Lagerspetz, K., & Eron, L. D. (1984). Intervening variables in the television violence-aggression relation: Evidence from two countries. *Developmental Psychology*, 20, 746–775.

Hughes, D., Johnson, K., Rosenbaum, S., Simons, J., & Butler, E. (1987). *The health of America's children: Maternal and child health data book*. Washington, DC: Children's Defense Fund.

Humphrey, L. L. (1984). Children's self-control in relation to perceived social environment. *Journal of Personality and Social Psychology*, 46, 178–188.

Hunt, M. (1974). *Sexual behavior in the 1970s*. Chicago: Playboy Press.

Huston, A. C. (1983). Sex typing. In E. M. Hetherington (Ed.), & P. H. Mussen (Series Ed.), *Handbook of child psychology*: Vol. 4. *Socialization, personality, and social development* (4th ed., pp. 387–467). New York: Wiley.

Huston, A. C. (1984). *Do adopted children resemble their biological parents more than their adoptive parents? No. A note on the study of behavioral genetics*. Unpublished manuscript, University of Kansas.

Huston, A. C., & Carpenter, C. J. (1985). Gender differences in preschool classrooms: The effects of sex-typed activity choices. In L. C. Wilkinson & C. B. Barett (Eds.), *Gender influences in classroom interaction* (pp. 143–166). New York: Academic Press.

Huston, A. C., Carpenter, C. J., Atwater, J. B., & Johnson, L. M. (1986). Gender, adult structuring of activities, and social behavior in middle childhood. *Child Development*, 57, 1200–1209.

Huston, A. C., & Wright, J. C. (1983). Children's processing of television: The informative functions of formal features. In J. Bryant & D. R. Anderson (Eds.), *Children's understanding of television: Research on attention and comprehension*. New York: Academic Press.

Huston, A. C., Wright, J. C., Rice, M. L., Kerkman, D., & St. Peters, M. (1987, April). *The development of television viewing patterns in early childhood: A longitudinal investigation*. Paper presented at the Meeting of the Society for Research in Child Development, Baltimore.

Huston, T., & Ashmore, R. D. (1986). Women and men in personal relationships. In R. D. Ashmore & F. K. Del Boca (Eds.). *The social psychology of female-male relations*. Orlando: Academic Press.

Huston-Stein, A., Friedrich-Cofer, L., & Susman, E. J. (1977). The relation of classroom structure to social behavior, imaginative play, and self-regulation of economically disadvantaged children. *Child Development, 48,* 908–916.

Hutchings, B., & Mednick, S. A. (1974). Registered criminality in the adoptive and biological parents of registered male adoptees. In S. A. Mednick, F. Schulsinger, J. Higgens, & B. Bell (Eds.), *Genetics, environment and psychopathology* (pp. 215–227). Amsterdam: North-Holland.

Iannotti, R. J. (1985). Naturalistic and structured assessments of prosocial behavior in preschool children: The influence of empathy and perspective taking. *Developmental Psychology, 21,* 46–55.

Ilg, F. L., & Ames, L. B. (1955). *Child Behavior.* New York: Harper & Row.

Illingworth, R. S. (1987). *The development of the infant and young child: Normal and abnormal.* Edinburgh: Churchill Livingstone.

Inamdar, S. C., Siomopoulos, G., Osborn, M., & Bianchi, E. C. (1979). Phenomenology associated with depressed moods in adolescents. *American Journal of Social Psychiatry, 136,* 156–159.

Ipsa, J. (1981). Social interactions among teachers, handicapped children, and nonhandicapped children in a mainstreamed preschool. *Journal of Applied Developmental Psychology, 1,* 231–250.

Izard, C. (1982). *Measuring emotions in infants and children.* New York: Cambridge University Press.

Izard, C. E., Hembree, E. A., Dougherty, L. M., & Spizzirri, C. C. (1983). Changes in two to nineteen month infants' facial expressions following acute pain. *Developmental Psychology, 19,* 418–426.

Jacobs, J. (1971). *Adolescent suicide.* New York: Wiley.

Jacobson, S. (1979). Matching behavior in the young infant. *Child Development, 50,* 425–431.

James, W. (1892/1961). *Psychology: The briefer course.* New York: Harper & Row.

Janus, M. D., McCormack, A., Burgess, A. W., & Hartman, C. (1987). *Adolescent runaways: Causes and consequences.* Lexington, MA: Lexington Books.

Jensen, A. R. (1969). How much can we boost IQ and scholastic achievement? *Harvard Educational Review, 39,* 449–483.

Jessor, R. (1984). Adolescent development and behavioral health. In J. D. Matarazzo, S. M. Weiss, J. A. Herd, N. E. Miller, & S. M. Weiss (Eds.), *Behavioral health: A handbook of health enhancement and disease prevention* (pp. 69–90). New York: Wiley.

Jessor, R., & Jessor, S. L. (1975). Adolescent development and the onset of drinking: A longitudinal study. *Journal of Youth and Adolescence, 36,* 27–51.

Jessor, R., & Jessor, S. L. (1977). *Problem behavior and psychosocial development: A longitudinal study of youth.* New York: Academic Press.

Jiao, S., Ji, G., & Jing, Q. (1986). Comparative study of behavioral qualities of only children and sibling children. *Child Development, 57,* 357–361.

Joffe, J. M. (1969). *Prenatal determinants of behavior.* Oxford: Pergamon.

Johnson, B., & Moore, H. A. (1968). Injured children and their parents. *Children, 15,* 147–152.

Johnson, C. (1982). Anorexia nervosa and bulimia. In T. J. Coates, A. C. Petersen, & C. Perry (Eds.), *Adolescent health: Crossing the barriers.* New York: Academic Press.

Johnson, C., Lewis, C., & Hagman, J. (1984). The syndrome of bulimia. *Psychiatric Clinics of North American, 7,* 247–274.

Johnson, R. P. (1977). Social class and grammatical development. *Language and Speech, 20,* 317–324.

Johnson, W. F., Emde, R. N., Pannabecker, R., Stenberg, C., & Davis, M. (1982). Maternal perception of infant emotions from birth through 18 months. *Infant Behavior & Development, 5,* 313–322.

Johnston, F. E. (1978). Somatic growth of the infant and preschool child. In F. Falkner & J. M. Tanner (Eds.), *Human growth: Vol. 2. Postnatal growth.* New York: Plenum.

Johnston, J. & Ettema, J. S. (1982). *Positive images: Breaking stereotypes with children's television.* Beverly Hills, CA: Sage.

Johnston, L. D. (1988, January 13). Summary of 1987 drug study results. Press release available from News and Information Service, University of Michigan.

Johnston, L. D., Bachman, J. G., & O'Malley, P. M. (1986). *Monitoring the future: Questionnaire responses from the nation's high school seniors:* 1985. Ann Arbor, MI: Survey Research Center, Institute for Social Research, University of Michigan.

Johnston, L. D., Bachman, J. G., & O'Malley, P. M. (in press). *National trends in drug use and related factors among American high school students and young adults, 1975–1987.* U.S. Department of Health and Human Services. Washington, DC: National Institute on Drug Abuse.

Johnston, L. D., & O'Malley, P. M. (1986). Why do the nation's students use drugs and alcohol? Self-reported reasons from nine national surveys. *The Journal of Drug Issues, 16,* 29–66.

Johnston, L. D., O'Malley, P. M., & Bachman, J. G. (1984). *Highlights from drugs and American high school students, 1975–1983.* (National Institute on Drug Abuse). Washington, DC: U. S. Government Printing Office.

Johnston, L. D., O'Malley, P. M., & Bachman, J. G. (1987). *American high school students and young adults, 1975–1986.* U. S. Department of Health and Human Services. Washington, DC: National Institute on Drug Abuse, DHHS Publication No. (ADM) 87–1535.

Jones, C. P. & Adamson, L. B. (1987). Language use and mother-child-sibling interactions. *Child Development, 58,* 356–366.

Jones, E., Forrest, J. D., Goldman, N., Henshaw, S. K., Lincoln, R., Rosof, J. I., Westoff, C. F., & Wulf, D. (1985). Teenage pregnancy in developed countries: Determinants and policy implications. *Family Planning Perspectives, 17,* 53–63.

Jones, H. E. (1946). Environmental influence on moral development. In L. Carmichael (Ed.), *Manual of child psychology*. New York: Wiley.

Jones, H. E. (1954). The environment and mental development. In L. Carmichael (Ed.), *Manual of child psychology* (2nd ed.). New York: Wiley.

Jones, K. L., Smith, D. W., Ulleland, C. N., & Streissguth, A. P. (1973). Patterns of malformation of offspring of chronic alcoholic mothers. *Lancet*, 1, 1267–1271.

Jones, M. C. (1957). The later careers of boys who were early or late maturing. *Child Development*, 28, 113–128.

Josselyn, I. M. (1968). *Adolescence*. Washington, DC: Joint Commission on Mental Health of Children.

Josselyn, I. M. (1971). *Adolescence*. New York: Harper & Row.

Kacerguis, M., & Adams, G. (1980). Erikson's stage resolution: The relationship between identity and intimacy. *Journal of Youth and Adolescence*, 9, 117–126.

Kagan, J. (1981). *The second year*. Cambridge, MA: Harvard University Press.

Kagan, J. (1984). *The nature of the child*. New York: Basic Books.

Kagan, J., Hans, S., Markowitz, A., Lopez, D. (1982). Validity of children's self-reports of psychological qualities. In B. A. Maher & W. B. Maher (Eds.) *Progress in experimental personality research* (Vol. 11). New York: Academic Press.

Kagan, J., Kearsley, R., & Zelazo, P. (1978). *Infancy: Its place in human development*. Cambridge, MA: Harvard University Press.

Kagan, J., Klein, R. E., Finley, G. E., Rogoff, B., & Nolan, E. (1979). A cross-cultural study of cognitive development. *Monographs of the Society for Research in Child Development*, 33, (4 Serial No. 120).

Kagan, J., & Moss, H. A. (1962). *Birth to maturity*. New York: Wiley.

Kagan, J., Reznick, J. S., Davies, J., Smith, J., Sigal, J., & Miyake, K. (1986). Selective memory and belief: A methodological suggestion. *International Journal of Behavioral Development*, 9, 205–218.

Kagan, J., Reznick, S., & Snidman, N. (1988). Biological bases of childhood shyness. *Science*, 240, 167–171.

Kail, R. (1988). Developmental functions for speeds of cognitive processes. *Journal of Experimental Child Psychology*, 45, 339–364.

Kaitz, M., Meschulach-Sarfarty, O., Auerbach, J., & Eidelman, A. (1988). A reexamination of newborns' ability to imitate facial expressions. *Developmental Psychology*, 19, 62–70.

Kamerman, S. B., Kahn, A. J., & Kingston, P. (1983). *Maternity policies and working women*. New York: Columbia University Press.

Kamii, C. K. (1985). *Young children reinvent arithmetic: Implications of Piaget's theory*. New York: Teachers College Press.

Kandel, D. B. (1978). Similarity in real-life adolescent friendship pairs. *Journal of Personality and Social Psychology*, 36, 306–312.

Kandel, D. B. (1980). Drug and drinking behavior among youth. *Annual Review of Sociology*, 6, 235–285.

Kantner, J. F., & Zelnik, M. (1973). Contraception and pregnancy: Experience of young unmarried women in the United States. *Family Planning Perspectives*, 5, 21–35.

Kantrowitz, B. (1986, March 31). A mother's choice. *Newsweek*, pp. 46–51.

Kaplan, H. & Dove, H. (1987). Infant development among the Ache of Eastern Paraguay. *Developmental Psychology*, 23, 190–198.

Kaplan, H. B. (1980). *Deviant behavior in defense of self*. New York: Academic Press.

Karlsson, J. L. (1981). Genetics of intellectual variation in Iceland. *Hereditas*, 95, 283–288.

Karmiloff-Smith, A. (1979). Language development after five. In P. Fletcher & M. Gorman (Eds.), *Language acquisition*. Cambridge: Cambridge University Press.

Karniol, R. (1978). Children's use of intention cues in evaluating behavior. *Psychological Bulletin*, 85, 76–85.

Katchadourian, H. A. (1985). *Fundamentals of human sexuality* (4th ed.). New York: Holt, Rinehart & Winston.

Katz, M., Keusch, G. T., & Mata, L. (Eds.) (1975). Malnutrition and infection during pregnancy: Determinants of growth and development of the child. *American Journal of Diseases of Children*, 29, 419–463.

Katz, P. A. (1976). The acquisition of racial attitudes in children. In P. A. Katz (Ed.) *Towards the elimination of racism*. New York: Pergamon.

Kauffman, J. M. (1985). *Characteristics of children's behavior disorders* (3rd ed.). Columbus: Charles E. Merrill.

Kaufman, I. R. (1979, October 14). Juvenile justice: A plea for reform. *New York Times Magazine*, 42–60.

Keating, D. P. (1975). Precocious cognitive development at the level of formal operations. *Child Development*, 46, 276–280.

Keating, D. P. (1980). Thinking processes in adolescence. In J. Adelson (Ed.), *Handbook of adolescent psychology*. New York: Wiley.

Keating, M. B., McKenzie, B. E., & Day, R. H. (1986). Spatial localization in infancy: Position constancy in a square and circular room with or without a landmark. *Child Development*, 57, 115–124.

Keil, F. (1979). *Semantic and conceptual development*. Cambridge, MA: Harvard University Press.

Kelley, K. (1979). Socialization factors in contraceptive attitudes: Roles of affective responses, parental attitudes, and sexual experience. *Journal of Sex Research*, 15, 6–20.

Kempe, R. S., & Kempe, C. H. (1978). *Child abuse*. Cambridge, MA: Harvard University Press.

Kendall, P. C., Lerner, R. M., & Craighead, W. E. (1984). Human development and intervention in childhood psychopathology. *Child Development*, 55, 71–82.

Kendler, K. S., Gruenberg, A. M., & Strauss, J. S. (1981). An independent analysis of the Copenhagen sample of the Danish Adoption Study of Schizophrenia. I. The relationship between anxiety disorder and schizophrenia. *Archives of General Psychiatry*, 38, 937–977.

Kendrick, C. & Dunn, J. (1983). Sibling quarrels and maternal responses. *Developmental Psychology*, 19, 62–70.

Keniston, K. (1968). *The uncommitted: Alienated youth in American society*. New York: Harcourt Brace Jovanovich.

Kerman, G. L. (1978). Affective disorders. In A. M. Nicholi, Jr. (Ed.), *The Harvard guide to modern psychiatry*. Cambridge, MA: Harvard University Press.

Kermoian, R., & Campos, J. J. (1987). *Self produced locomotor experience: A facilitator of spatial search performance*. Unpublished manuscript.

Kerr, P. (1986, November 17). Anatomy of an issue: Drugs, the evidence, the reaction. *The New York Times*, pp. 1, 12.

Kessel, F. S. (1970). The role of syntax in children's comprehension from ages six to twelve. *Monographs of the Society for Research in Child Development*, 35 (6, Whole No. 139).

Kessler, S. S. (1975). Psychiatric genetics. In D. A. Hamburg & K. Brodie (Eds.), *American handbook of psychiatry: Vol. VI. New psychiatric frontiers*. New York: Basic Books.

Kessler, S. S. (1980). The genetics of schizophrenia: A review. *Schizophrenia Bulletin*, 6, 404–416.

Kety, S. S., Rosenthal, D., Wender, P. H., Schulsinger, F., & Jacobsen, B. (1975). Mental illness in the biological and adoptive families of adoptive individuals who have become schizophrenic: A preliminary report based on psychiatric interviews. In R. Fieve, D. Rosenthal, & H. Brill (Eds.), *Genetic research in psychiatry*. Baltimore: Johns Hopkins University Press.

Kety, S. S., Rosenthal, D., Wender, P. H., Schulsinger, F., & Jacobsen, B. (1978). The biological and adoptive families of adopted individuals who became schizophrenic: Prevalence of mental illness and other characteristics. In L. C. Wynne, R. L. Cromwell, & S. Matthysse (Eds.), *The nature of schizophrenia: New approaches to research and treatment*. New York: Wiley.

Kiell, N. (1967). *The universal experience of adolescence*. Boston: Beacon.

King, L. J., & Pitman, G. D. (1971). A follow-up of 65 adolescent schizophrenic patients. *Diseases of the Nervous System*, 32, 328–334.

King, M. K., & Yuille, J. C. (1987). Suggestibility and the child witness. In S. J. Ceci, M. P. Toglia, & D. F. Ross (Eds.), *Children's eyewitness memory* (pp. 24–35). New York: Springer-Verlag.

Kinnert, M. D., Campos, J., Sorce, J. F., Emde, R. N. & Svejda, M. J. (1983). Social referencing. In R. Plutchik & H. Kellerman (Eds.), *The emotions in early development*. New York: Academic Press.

Kinsey, A. C., Pomeroy, W. B., & Martin, C. E. (1948). *Sexual behavior in the human male*. Philadelphia: Saunders.

Kinsey, A. C., Pomeroy, W. B., Martin, C. E., & Gebhard, P. H. (1953). *Sexual behavior in the human female*. Philadelphia: Saunders.

Kirby, D. (1985). School-based health clinics: An emerging approach to improving adolescent health and addressing teenage pregnancy. Report prepared for the Center for Population Options.

Kirigin, K. A., Wolf, M. M., Braukman, C. J., Fixsen, D. L., & Phillips, E. L. (1979). A preliminary outcome evaluation. In J. S. Stumphauzer (Ed.), *Progress in behavior therapy with delinquents* (pp. 118–145). Springfield, IL: Chas C Thomas.

Klaus, R. A., & Gray, S. W. (1968). The early training project for disadvantaged children: A report after five years. *Monographs of the Society for Research in Child Development*, 33 (4, Serial No. 120).

Klebanoff, M. A., Gronbard, B. I., Kessel, S. S., & Berendes, H. W. (1984). Low birth weight across generations. *Journal of the American Medical Association*, 252, 2423–2427.

Klein, J. R., & Litt, I. F. (1984). Menarche and dysmenorrhea. In J. Brooks-Gunn & A. C. Petersen (Eds.), *Girls at puberty: Biological, psychological, and social perspectives*. New York, Plenum.

Klein, M. W. (1979). Deinstitutionalization and diversion of juvenile offenders: A litany of impediments. In N. Morris & M. Tonry (Eds.), *Crime and justice: An annual review of research*, Vol 1 (pp. 145–201). Chicago: University of Chicago.

Klerman, G. L. (1988). Depression and related disorders of mood (affective disorders). In A. M. Nicholi, Jr., (Ed.) *The new Harvard guide to psychiatry* (pp. 309–336). Cambridge, MA: Harvard University Press.

Kliegman, R. M., & King, K. C. (1983). Intrauterine growth retardation: Determinants of aberrant fetal growth. In A. A. Fanaroff, R. J. Martin, & J. R. Merkatz (Eds.), *Behrman's neonatal-perinatal medicine*. St. Louis: Mosby.

Kligman, D., Smyrl, R., & Emde, R. (1975). A non-intrusive longitudinal study of infant sleep. *Psychosomatic Medicine*, 37, 448–453.

Klinnert, M. D., Campos, J., Source, J. F., Emde, R. N., & Svejda, M. J. (1983). Social referencing. In P. Plutchik and H. Kellerman (Eds.), *The emotions in early development*. New York: Academic Press.

Knoblock, H., & Pasamanick, B. (1966). Prospective studies on the epidemiology of reproductive casualty: Methods, findings, and some implications. *Merrill-Palmer Quarterly of Behavior and Development*, 12, 27–43.

Koch, H. L. (1960). The relation of certain formal attributes of siblings to attitudes held toward each other and toward their parents. *Monographs of the Society for Research in Child Development*, 25, (4, Whole No. 78) 1–134.

Kohlberg, L. (1963). The development of children's orientations toward a moral order: I. Sequence in the development of human thought. *Vita Humana*, 6, 11–33.

Kohlberg, L. (1964). Development of moral character and moral ideology. In M. L. Hoffman & L. W. Hoffman (Eds.), *Review of child development research* (Vol. 1). New York: Russell Sage, 1964.

Kohlberg, L. (1969). Stage and sequence: The cognitive-developmental approach to socialization. In D. A. Goslin (Ed.), *Handbook of socialization theory and research*. Chicago: Rand McNally.

Kohlberg, L. (1976). Moral stages and moralization: The cognitive-developmental approach. In T. Lickona (Ed.), *Moral development and behavior*. New York: Holt, Rinehart and Winston.

Kohlberg, L. (1978). Revisions in the theory and practice of moral development. In W. Damon (Ed.), *Moral development: New Directions for Child Development*, No. 2. San Francisco: Jossey-Bass.

Kohlberg, L. (1984). *Essays on moral development*: Vol. II. *The psychology of moral development*. New York: Harper & Row.

Kohlberg, L., & Gilligan, C. (1972). The adolescent as a philosopher: The discovery of the self in a postconventional world. In J. Kagan & R. Coles (Eds.), *12 to 16: Early adolescence*. New York: Norton.

Kohn, M. L. (1959a). Social class and the exercise of parental authority. *American Sociological Review*, 24, 352–366.

Kohn, M. L. (1959b). Social class and parental values. *American Journal of Sociology*, 64, 337–351.

Kohn, M. L. (1969). *Class and conformity: A study in values*. Homewood, IL: Dorsey Press.

Kohn, M. L., & Schooler, C. (1978). The reciprocal effects of the substantive complexity of work and intellectual flexibility: A longitudinal assessment. *American Journal of Sociology*, 84, 24–52.

Kohn, M. L., & Schooler, C. (1982). Job conditions and personality: A longitudinal assessment of their reciprocal effects. *American Journal of Sociology*, 87, 1257–1286.

Kohn, M. L., & Schooler, C. (1983). *Work and personality: An inquiry into social stratification*. Norwood, NJ: Ablex.

Konopka, G. (1976). *Young girls: A portrait of adolescence*. Englewood Cliffs, NJ: Prentice-Hall.

Koop, C. E. (1986). *Surgeon General's report on acquired immune deficiency syndrome*. Washington, DC: U. S. Department of Health and Human Services.

Kopp, C. B., & Parmelee, A. H. (1979). Prenatal and perinatal influences on infant behavior. In J. Osofsky (Ed.), *Handbook of infant development*. New York: Wiley.

Korones, S. B. (1986). *High risk newborn infants*. St. Louis: Mosby.

Kosslyn, S. N. (1980). *Image and mind*. Cambridge, MA: Harvard University Press.

Kotelchuck, M., Schwartz, J., Anderka, M., & Finison, K. (1983). *1980 Massachusetts Special Supplemental Food program for Women, Infants, and Children (WIC) evaluation project*. Prepublication manuscript.

Kovach, J. A., & Glickman, N. W. (1986). Levels and psychosocial correlates of adolescent drug use. *Journal of Youth and Adolescence*, 15, 61–78.

Kovacs, M., Feinberg, T. L., Crouse-Novak, M. A., Paulauskas, S. L., & Finkelstein, R. (1984). Depressive disorders in childhood. I.: A longitudinal prospective study of characteristics and recovery. *Archives of General Psychiatry*, 41, 229–237.

Kozol, J. (1988). *Rachel and her children*. New York: Crown Press.

Krauss, R. M., & Glucksberg, S. (1969). The development of communication: Competence as a function of age. *Child Development*, 40, 255–266.

Krebs, D., & Sturrup, B. (1982). Role-taking ability and altruistic behavior in elementary school children. *Journal of Moral Education*, 11, 94–100.

Kreutzer, M. A., & Charlesworth, W. R. (1973). *Infants' reaction to different expressions of emotion*. Paper presented at the Society for Research in Child Development, Philadelphia.

Kuchuk, A., Vibbert, M. & Bornstein, M. H. (1986). The perception of smiling in its experiential correlates in three month old infants. *Child Development*, 57, 1054–1061.

Kuczynski, L. (1983). Reasoning, prohibitions, and motivations for compliance. *Developmental Psychology*, 19, 126–134.

Kuczynski, L., Zahn-Waxler, C. & Radke-Yarrow, M. (1987). Development and content of imitation in the second and third year of life. *Developmental Psychology*, 23, 276–282.

Kuhl, P., & Meltzoff, A. (1982). The bimodal perception of speech in infancy. *Science*, 218, 1138–1141.

Kunkel, D., & Watkins, B. (1987). Evolution of children's television regulatory policy. *Journal of Broadcasting and Electronic Media*, 31, 367–389.

Kurdek, L. A. (1981). An integrative perspective on children's divorce adjustment. *American Psychologist*, 36, 856–866.

Kurdek, L. A., & Krile, D. (1982). A developmental analysis of the relation between peer acceptance and both interpersonal understanding and perceived social self-competence. *Child Development*, 53, 1485–1491.

Laboratory of Comparative Human Cognition (1983). Culture and cognitive development. In P. H. Mussen (Series Ed.) & W. Kessen (Ed.), *Handbook of child psychology*: Vol. 1. *History, theory, and methods* (pp. 295–358). New York: Wiley.

Labov, W. (1970). The logic of nonstandard English. In F. Williams (Ed.), *Language and poverty: Perspectives on a theme*. Chicago: Markham.

Lamar, J. V., Jr. (1986, September 27). Rolling out the big guns: The first couple and Congress press the attack on drugs. *The New York Times*.

Lamar, J. V., Jr. (1988, May 9). Kids who sell crack. *Time*, pp. 20–33.

Lamb, M. E. (1982). Sibling relationships across the lifespan. In M. E. Lamb & B. Sutton-Smith (Eds.), *Sibling relationships*. Hillsdale, NJ: Erlbaum.

Lamb, M. E., Hwang, C. P., Frodi, A. M., & Frodi, M. (1982). Security of mother and father infant attachment and its relation to sociability with strangers in traditional and nontraditional Swedish families. *Infant Behavior and Development*, 5, 355–368.

Lambert, B. (1988, January 13). Study finds antibodies for AIDS in 1 in 61 babies in New York City. *The New York Times*, pp. 1, 34.

Landau, R., & Gleitman, L. (1985). *Language and experience*. Cambridge, MA: Harvard University Press.

Langlois, J. H., & Downs, A. C. (1980). Peer relations as a function of physical attractiveness: The eye of the beholder or behavioral reality? *Child Development*, 51, 1237–1247.

Langlois, J. H., Roggman, L. A., Casey, R. J., Ritter, J. M., Rieser-Danner, L. A., & Jenkins, V. Y. (1987). Infant preference for attractive faces: Rudiments of a stereotype. *Developmental Psychology*, 23, 363–369.

Largo, R. H., & Schinzel, A. (1985). Developmental and behavioral disturbances in 13 boys with fragile-X syndrome. *European Journal of Pediatrics*, 143, 269–275.

Larson, L. E. (1972a). The influence of parents and peers during adolescence. *Journal of Marriage and the Family*, 34, 67–74.

Larson, L. E. (1972b). The relative influence of parent-adolescent affect in predicting the salience hierarchy among youth. *Pacific Sociological Review*, 15, 83–102.

Lasch, C. (1979). *The culture of narcissism: American life in an age of diminishing expectations*. New York: Norton.

Lavine, L. O. (1982). Parental power as a potential influence on girls; career choice. *Child Development*, 53, 658–661.

LaVoi, J. C. (1973). Punishment and adolescent self-control. *Developmental Psychology*, 8, 16–24.

Lazar, I., & Darlington, R. (1982). Lasting effects of early education: A report from the Consortium of Longitudinal Studies. *Monographs of the Society for Research in Child Development*, 33 (Serial No. 120).

Lee, V. E., Brooks-Gunn, J., & Schnur, E. (1988). Does Head Start work? A 1-year follow-up comparison of disadvantaged children attending Head Start, no preschool, and other preschool programs. *Developmental Psychology*, 24, 210–222.

Lefkowitz, M. M., Eron, L. D., Walder, L. O., & Huesmann, L. R. (1977). *Growing up to be violent*. New York: Pergamon.

Leighton, K., & Peleaux, R. (1984). The effects of temporal predictability on the reactions of one year olds to potentially frightening toys. *Developmental Psychology*, 20, 449–458.

Leiman, B. (1978, August). *Affective empathy and subsequent altruism in kindergartners and first graders*. Paper presented at the meeting of the American Psychological Association, Toronto.

Lemann, N. (1986, June). The origins of the underclass. *The Atlantic*, pp. 31–55.

LeMare, L. J., & Rubin, K. H. (1987). Perspective taking and peer interaction: Structural and developmental analyses. *Child Development*, 58, 306–315.

Lemish, D., & Rice, M. L. (1986). Television as a talking picture book: A prop for language acquisition. *Journal of Child Language*, 13, 251–274.

Lempers, J. C., Flavell, E. R., & Flavell, J. H. (1978). The development in very young children of tacit knowledge concerning visual perception. *Genetic Psychology Monographs*, 95, 3–53.

Lempert, H. (1984). Topic: A starting point for syntax. *Monographs of the Society for Research in Child Development*, 49 (Serial No. 208).

Lennon, R., Eisenberg, N., & Carroll, J. (1986). The relation between nonverbal indices of sympathy and preschoolers' prosocial behavior. *Journal of Applied Developmental Psychology*, 7, 219–224.

Leonard, L. B. (1976). *Meaning in child language*. New York: Grune & Stratton.

Lepper, M. R. (1981). Intrinsic and extrinsic motivation in children: Detrimental effects of superfluous social controls. In W. A. Collins (Ed.), *Minnesota symposia on child psychology* (Vol. 14). Hillsdale, NJ: Erlbaum.

Lepper, M. R. (1983). Social control processes, attributions of motivation, and the internalization of social values. In E. T. Higgins, D. N. Ruble, & W. W. Hartup (Eds.), *Social cognition and social behavior: Developmental perspectives*. New York: Cambridge University Press.

Lerman, R. I. (1986). Unemployment among low-income and black youth: A review of causes, programs and policies. *Youth and Society*, 17, 237–266.

Lerner, R. M., & Knapp, J. R. (1975). Actual and perceived intrafamilial attitudes of late adolescents and their parents. *Journal of Youth and Adolescence*, 4, 17–36.

Lerner, R. M., & Lerner, J. (1977). Effects of age, sex and physical attractiveness on child-peer relations, academic performance, and elementary school adjustment. *Developmental Psychology*, 13, 585–590.

Lesser, G. S., & Kandel, D. (1969). Parent-adolescent relationships and adolescent independence in the United States and Denmark. *Journal of Marriage and the Family*, 31, 348–358.

Leung, E. H. L., & Rheingold, H. L. (1981). Development of pointing as a social gesture. *Developmental Psychology*, 17, 215–220.

Levine, L. E. (1983). Mine: Self definitions in two year old boys. *Developmental Psychology*, 19, 544–549.

Levy-Shiff, R. (1982). Effects of father absence on young children in mother-headed families. *Child Development*, 53, 1400–1405.

Lewine, R. R. J. (1980). Sex differences in age of symptom onset and first hospitalization in schizophrenia. *American Journal of Orthopsychiatry*, 50, 316–322.

Lewis, C. C. (1981). The effects of parental firm control: A reinterpretation of findings. *Psychological Bulletin*, 90, 547–563.

Lewis, M., & Brooks-Gunn, J. (1979). *Social cognition and the acquisition of self*. New York: Plenum.

Lewis, M., & Saarni, C. (Eds.) (1985). *The socialization of emotions.* New York: Plenum.

Liben, L. S., & Signorella, M. L. (Eds.). (1987). *New directions in child development: Vol. 38. Children's gender schemata.* San Francisco: Jossey-Bass.

Liebert, R. M., & Baron, R. A. (1972). Some immediate effects of televised violence on children's behavior. *Developmental Psychology, 6,* 469–475.

Liebert, R. M., & Sprafkin, J. (1988). *The early window: Effects of television on children and youth* (3rd ed.). New York: Pergamon.

Lindsay, J. W. (1985). *Teens look at marriage: Rainbows, role, and realities.* Buena Park, CA: Morning Glory Press.

Linn, M. C., & Petersen, A. C. (1985). Emergence and characterization of sex differences in spatial ability: A meta-analysis. *Child Development, 56,* 1479–1498.

Linn, S., Reznick, J. S., Kagan, J., and Hans, S. (1982). Salience of visual patterns in the human infant. *Developmental Psychology, 18,* 651–657.

Linton, T. (1973). Effects of grade displacement between students tutored and student tutors. *Dissertation Abstracts International, 33,* 4091–4092A.

Lipsitt, L., & LeGasse, L. (1989). Avidity and attachment. In J. S. Reznick (Ed.), *Perspectives on behavioral inhibition.* Chicago: University of Chicago Press.

Little, G. A. (1987). The fetus at risk. In R. A. Hekelman, S. Blatman, S. B. Friedman, N. M. Nelson, & H. M. Seidel (Eds.). *Primary pediatric care* (pp. 397–410). St. Louis: Mosby.

Little, J. K. (1967). The occupations of non-college youth. *American Educational Research Journal, 4,* 147–153.

Livesley, W. J., & Bromley, D. B. (1973). *Person perception in childhood and adolescence.* London: Wiley.

Livson, N., & Peskin, H. (1980). Perspectives on adolescence from longitudinal research. In J. Adelson (Ed.), *Handbook of adolescent psychology* (pp. 47–98). New York: Wiley.

Llublinskaya, A. A. (1957). The development of children's speech and thought. In B. Simon (Ed.), *Psychology in the Soviet Union.* Stanford, CA: Stanford University Press.

Loehlin, J. C., & Nichols, R. C. (1976). *Heredity, environment, and personality.* Austin: University of Texas Press.

Londerville, S., & Main, M. (1981). Security of attachment and compliance in maternal training methods in the second year of life. *Developmental Psychology, 17,* 289–299.

London, P. (1970). The rescuers: Motivational hypotheses about Christians who saved Jews from the Nazis. In J. Macaulay and L. Berkowitz (Eds.), *Altruism and helping behavior.* New York: Academic Press.

Lorch, E. P., Bellack, D. R., & Augsbach, L. H. (1987). Young children's memory for televised stories: Effects of importance. *Child Development, 58,* 453–463.

Lorenz, K. Z. (1981). *The foundations of ethology.* New York: Springer-Verlag.

Lorion, R. P., Tolan, P. H., & Wahler, R. G. (1987). Prevention. In H. C. Quay (Ed.), *Handbook of juvenile delinquency* (pp. 383–416). New York: Wiley.

Lubchenco, L. O. (1976). *The high risk of infants.* Philadelphia: Saunders.

Lubchenco, L. O., Searls, D. T., & Brazie, J. F. (1972). Neonatal mortality rate: Relationship to birth weight and gestational age. *Journal of Pediatrics, 81,* 814–822.

Luce, J. (1970, November 8). End of the road. *San Francisco Sunday Examiner and Chronicle,* pp. 8–10.

Lutz, C. (1985). Cultural patterns and individual differences in the child's emotional meaning system. In M. Lewis & C. Saarni (Eds.), *The socialization of emotions* (pp. 37–55). New York: Plenum.

Lyles, M. R., Yancey, A., Grace, C., & Carter, J. H. (1985). Racial identity and self-esteem: Problems peculiar to biracial children. *Journal of the American Academy of Child Psychiatry, 24,* 150–153.

Lynd, H. (1966). *On shame and the search for identity.* New York: Science Editions.

Lytton, H. (1977). Do parents create, or respond to, differences in twins? *Developmental Psychology, 13,* 456–459.

McCabe, M. P., & Collins, J. K. (1979). Sex role and dating orientation. *Journal of Youth and Adolescence, 8,* 407–425.

McCall, R. B., Appelbaum, M. I., & Hogarty, P. S. (1973). Developmental changes in mental performance. *Monographs of the Society for Research in Child Development, 38* (Serial No. 150).

McCall, R. B., Parke, R. D., & Kavanaugh, R. D. (1977). Imitation of live and televised models by children one to three years of age. *Monographs of the Society for Research in Child Development, 42*(5).

McCarthy, D. (1946). Language. In L. Carmichael (Ed.), *Manual of child psychology.* New York: Wiley.

McCartney, K., Scarr, S., Phillips, D., & Grajek, S. (1985). Day care as intervention: Comparisons of varying quality programs. *Journal of Applied Developmental Psychology, 6,* 247–260.

Maccoby, E. E. (1980). *Social development: Psychological growth and the parent-child relationship.* New York: Harcourt Brace Jovanovich.

Maccoby, E. E. (1984). Middle childhood in the context of the family. In W. A. Collins (Ed.), *Development during middle childhood—The years from six to twelve.* Washington, DC: National Academy Press.

Maccoby, E. E., & Jacklin, C. N. (1974). *The psychology of sex differences.* Stanford, CA: Stanford University Press.

Maccoby, E. E., & Jacklin, C. N. (1980). Sex differences in aggression: A rejoinder and reprise. *Child Development, 51,* 964–980.

Maccoby, E. E., & Martin, J. A. (1983). Socialization in the context of the family: Parent-child interaction. In P. H. Mussen (Series Ed.) & E. M. Hetherington (Ed.), *Handbook of child psychology*: Vol. 4. *Socialization, personality and social behavior* (4th ed., pp. 1–102). New York: Wiley.

Maccoby, E. E., & Jacklin, C. N. (in press). Gender segregation in childhood. In H. Reese (Ed.), *Advances in child behavior and development*. New York: Academic Press.

Maccoby, E. E., Snow, M. E., & Jacklin, C. N. (1984). Children's dispositions and mother-child interactions at 12 and 18 months: A short-term longitudinal study. *Developmental Psychology, 20*, 459–472.

McGhee, P. E. (1979). *Humor: Its origin and development*. San Francisco: Freeman.

McGuire, W. J. & McGuire, C. V. (1986). Differences in conceptualizing self versus conceptualizing other people as manifested in contrasting verb types used in natural speech. *Journal of Personality and Social Psychology, 51*, 1035–1043.

McGuire, W. J., McGuire, C. V., Child, P., & Fujioka, T. (1978). Salience of ethnicity in the spontaneous self-concept as a function of one's ethnic distinctiveness in a social environment. *Journal of Personality and Social Psychology, 36*, 511–520.

McLoyd, V. C. (1989). Socialization and development in a changing economy: The effects of paternal job and income loss on children. *American Psychologist, 44*, 293–302.

Madden, J., Payne, R., & Miller, S. (1986). Maternal cocaine abuse and effects on the newborn. *Pediatrics, 77*, 209–211.

Madsen, M. C. (1967). Cooperative and competitive motivation of children in three Mexican sub-cultures. *Psychological Reports, 20*, 1307–1320.

Madsen, M. C., & Shapira, A. (1970). Cooperative and competitive behavior of urban Afro-American, Anglo-American, Mexican-American, and Mexican village children. *Developmental Psychology, 3*, 16–20.

Magsud, M. (1979). Resolution of moral dilemmas by Nigerian secondary school pupils. *Journal of Moral Education, 7*, 40–49.

Main, M., & George, C. (1979). Social interaction of young abused children: Approach, avoidance, and aggression. *Child Development, 50*, 306–318.

Main, M., & George, C. (1985). Responses of abused and disadvantaged toddlers to distress in agemates: A study in the daycare setting. *Developmental Psychology, 21*, 407–412.

Main, M., Weston, D. R., & Wakeling, S. (1979). "Concerned attention" to crying of an adult actor in infancy. Paper presented at the meeting of the Society for Research in Child Development, San Francisco.

Mandler, J. M. (1983). Representation. In J. H. Flavell & E. M. Markman (Eds.), P. H. Mussen (Series Ed.), *Handbook of child psychology*: Vol. 3. *Cognitive development* (pp. 420–494). New York: Wiley.

Marantz, S. A., & Mansfield, A. F. (1977). Maternal employment and the development of sex-role stereotyping in five- to eleven-year-old girls. *Child Development, 48*, 668–673.

Marcia, J. E. (1980). Identity in adolescence. In J. Adelson (Ed.), *Handbook of adolescent psychology*. New York: Wiley.

Marcus, J., Hans, S. L., Nagler, S., Auerbach, J. G., Mirsky, A. P., & Aubrey, A. (1987). Review of the NIMH Israel Kibbutz-city study and the Jerusalem infant development study. *Schizophrenia Bulletin, 13*, 425–438.

Marcus, R. F. (1975). The child as elicitor of parental sanctions for independent and dependent behavior: A simulation of parent-child interaction. *Developmental Psychology, 11*, 443–452.

Marini, M. M. (1978). Sex differences in the determination of adolescent aspirations: A review. *Sex Roles, 4*, 723–753.

Marsh, H. W. (1985). Age and sex effects in multiple dimensions of preadolescent self-concept: A replication and extension. *Australian Journal of Psychology, 37*, 167–179.

Marsh, H. W., Smith, I. D., & Barnes, J. (1985). Multidimensional self-concepts: Relations with sex and academic achievement. *Journal of Educational Psychology, 77*, 581–596.

Marshall, W. A. (1978). Puberty. In F. Falkner & J. M. Tanner (Eds.), *Human growth*: Vol. 2. *Postnatal growth*. New York: Plenum.

Marshall, W. A., & Tanner, J. M. (1970). Variations in the pattern of pubertal changes in boys. *Archives of Disease in Childhood, 45*, 13.

Marsiglio, W., & Mott, F. L. (1986). The impact of sex education on sexual activity, contraceptive use and premarital pregnancy among American teenagers. *Family Planning Perspectives, 18*, 151–162.

Martin, B. (1975). Parent-child relations. In F. D. Horowitz, E. M. Hetherington, S. Scarr-Salapatek, & G. M. Siegel (Eds.), *Review of child development research* (Vol. 4). Chicago: University of Chicago Press.

Martin, C. L., & Halverson, C. F., Jr. (1981). A schematic processing model of sex typing and stereotyping in children. *Child Development, 52*, 1119–1134.

Mash, E. J., & Johnson, C. A. (1982). A comparison of the mother-child interactions of younger and older hyperactive and normal children. *Child Development, 53*, 1371–1381.

Mash, E. J., Johnston, J. L., & Kovitz, K. A. (1982). A comparison of the mother-child interactions of physically abused and nonabused children during play and task situations. *Journal of Clinical Child Psychology, 1982*.

Mason, W. A. (1978). Social experience and primate cognitive development. In G. M. Burghardt and M. Bekoff (Eds.), *The development of behavior*. New York: Garland Press.

Masters, W. H., & Johnson, V. E. (1970). *Human sexual inadequacy*. Boston: Little, Brown.

Masters, W. H., Johnson, V. E., & Kolodny, R. C. (1988). *Human sexuality* (3rd ed.). Glenview, IL: Scott, Foresman.

Matheny, A. P., Jr. (1983). A longitudinal twin study of stability of components from Bayley's Infant Behavior Record. *Child Development*, 54, 356–360.

Matheny, A. P., Jr., Wilson, R. S., Dolan, A. B., & Krantz, J. Z. (1981). Behavior contrasts in twinships: Stability and patterns of differences in childhood. *Child Development*, 52, 579–588.

Mednick, S. A., Parnas, J., & Schulsinger, F. (1987). The Copenhagen high-risk project. *Schizophrenia Bulletin*, 13, 485–495.

Medrich, E. A., Rosen, J., Rubin, V., & Buckley, S. (1982). *The serious business of growing up: A study of children's lives outside of school*. Berkeley, CA: University of California Press.

Meltzoff, A. N. (1988). Infant imitations and memory: Imitation by nine-month-olds in immediate and deferred tests. *Child Development*, 59, 217–225.

Meltzoff, A. N., & Borton, R. W. (1979). Intermodal matching by human neonates. *Nature*, 282, 403–404.

Meltzoff, A. N., & Moore, M. K. (1977). Imitation of facial and manual gestures by human neonates. *Science*, 198, 75–78.

Menken, J. (1980). The health and demographic consequence of adolescent pregnancy and childbearing. In C. Chilman (Ed.), *Adolescent pregnancy and childbearing: Findings from research* (pp. 000-000). Washington, DC: U.S. Department of Health and Human Services.

Messaris, P., & Hornik, R. C. (1983). Work status, television exposure, and educational outcomes. In C. Hayes & S. B. Kamerman (Eds.), *Children of working parents: Experiences and outcomes* (pp. 44–72). Washington, DC: National Academy Press.

Metcoff, J. (1978). Association of fetal growth with maternal nutrition. In F. Falkner & J. M. Tanner (Eds.), *Human growth: Vol. 1. Principles and prenatal growth*. New York: Plenum.

Michalson, L., & Lewis, M. (1985). What do children know about emotions and when do they know it? In M. Lewis & C. Saarni (Eds.), *The socialization of emotions* (pp. 117–140). New York: Plenum.

Millar, W. S., & Watson, J. S. (1979). The effect of delayed feedback on infant learning reexamined. *Child Development*, 50, 747–751.

Miller, H. C. (1922). *The new psychology and the parent*. London: Jarrolds.

Miller, M. L., Chiles, J. A., & Barnes, V. E. (1982). Suicide attempters within a delinquent population. *Journal of Consulting and Clinical Psychology*, 50, 490–498.

Miller, P. H., Haynes, V. F., DeMarie-Dreblow, D., & Woody-Ramsey, J. (1986). Children's strategies for gathering information in three tasks. *Child Development*, 57, 1429–1439.

Miller, P. Y., & Simon, W. (1980). The development of sexuality in adolescence. In J. Adelson (Ed.), *Handbook of adolescent psychology*. New York: Wiley.

Miller, S. M., & Green, M. L. (1985). Coping with stress and frustration: Origins, nature, and development. In M. Lewis & C. Saarni (Eds.), *The socialization of emotions* (pp. 263–314). New York: Plenum.

Miller, W. B. (1976, May 1). Report to the Law Enforcement Assistance Administration, Department of Justice.

Minuchin, P. (1985). Families and individual development; Provocations from the field of family therapy. *Child Development*, 56, 289–302.

Minuchin, P. P., & Shapiro, E. K. (1983). The school as a context for social development. In P. H. Mussen (Series Ed.) & E. M. Hetherington (Ed.), *Handbook of child psychology: Vol. 4. Socialization, personality and social development* (4th ed., pp. 197–274). New York: Wiley.

Minuchin, S., Rosman, B. L., & Baker, L. (1978). *Psychosomatic families: Anorexia nervosa in context*. Cambridge, MA: Harvard University Press.

Mischel, W. (1966). Theory and research on the antecedents of self-imposed delay of reward. In B. A. Maher (Ed.), *Progress in experimental personality research* (Vol. 3). New York: Academic Press.

Mischel, W. (1968). *Personality and assessment*. New York: Wiley.

Mischel, W. (1970). Sex typing and socialization. In P. H. Mussen (Ed.), *Carmichael's manual of child psychology* (Vol. 2, 3rd ed). New York: Wiley.

Mischel, W. (1974). Processes in the delay of gratification. In L. Berkowitz (Ed.), *Advances in experimental social psychology* (Vol. 7). New York: Academic Press.

Mischel, W., & Ebbesen, E. B. (1970). Attention in delay of gratification. *Journal of Personality and Social Psychology*, 16, 329–337.

Mischel, W., & Metzner, R. (1962). Effects of attention to symbolically presented rewards upon self-control. *Journal of Abnormal and Social Psychology*, 64, 425–431.

Mischel, W., & Patterson, C. J. (1978). Effective plans for self-control in children. In W. A. Collins (Ed.), *Minnesota symposia on child psychology* (Vol. 11, pp. 199–230). Hillsdale, NJ: Erlbaum.

Mishkin, M., & Appenzeller, T. (1987). The anatomy of memory. *Scientific American*, 256, 80–89.

Miyake, K., Chen, S., & Campos, J. J. (1985). Infant temperament, mother's mode of interaction and attachment in Japan: An interim report. In I. Bretherton and E. Waters (Eds.), *Monographs of the Society of Research in Child Development*, 50 (Serial No. 209, Nos. 1–2), 276–297.

Mohr, D.M. (1978). Development of attributes of personal identity. *Developmental Psychology*, 14, 427–428.

Moir, J. (1974). Egocentrism and the emergence of conventional morality in preadolescent girls. *Child Development*, 45, 299–304.

Mondell, S., & Tyler, F. (1981). Parental competence and styles of problem solving/play behavior with children. *Developmental Psychology*, 17, 73–78.

Monighan-Nourot, P., Scales, B., Van Hoorn, J., with Almy, M. (1987). *Looking at children's play: A bridge between theory and practice.* New York: Teachers College Press.

Montemayor, R. (1985). Maternal employment and adolescents' relations with parents, siblings, and peers. *Journal of Youth and Adolescence*, 13, 543–557.

Montemayor, R., & Eisen, M. (1977). The development of self-conceptions from childhood to adolescence. *Developmental Psychology*, 13, 314–319.

Moore, B. S., & Eisenberg, N. (1984). The development of altruism. In G. Whitehurst (Ed.), *Annals of child development* (pp. 107–174). Greenwich, CT: JAI Press.

Moore, D., & Schultz, N. R., Jr. (1983). Loneliness at adolescence: Correlates, attributions, and coping. *Journal of Youth and Adolescence*, 12, 95–100.

Moore, E. G. J. (1986). Family socialization and the IQ test performance of traditionally and transracially adopted black children. *Developmental Psychology*, 22, 317–326.

Moore, K. L. (1982). *The developing human: Clinically oriented embryology* (3rd ed.). Philadelphia: Saunders.

Moore, T. W. (1975). Exclusive early mothering and its alternatives. *Scandinavian Journal of Psychology*, 16, 256–272.

Morgan, M. (1982). Television and adolescents' sex role stereotypes: A longitudinal study. *Journal of Personality and Social Psychology*, 43, 947–955.

Morgan, M., & Gross, L. (1982). Television and educational achievement and aspiration. In D. Pearl, J. Bouthilet, & J. Lazar, (Eds.), *Television and behavior: Ten years of scientific progress and implications for the eighties* (Vol. 2) Washington, DC: U.S. Government Printing Office.

Morganthau, T. (1986, March 17). Kids and cocaine. *Newsweek*, pp. 58–65.

Morrison, D. M. (1985). Adolescent contraceptive behavior: A review. *Psychological Bulletin*, 98, 538–568.

Moss, H. A., & Susman, E. J. (1980). Longitudinal study of personality development. In O. G. Brim & J. Kagan (Eds.), *Constancy and change in human development*. Cambridge, MA: Harvard University Press.

Mueller, E., & Brenner, J. (1977). The origin of social skills in interaction among play group toddlers. *Child Development*, 48, 854–861.

Mueller, E., & Lucas, T. (1975). A developmental analysis of peer interaction among toddlers. In M. Lewis & L. A. Rosenblum (Eds.), *Friendship and peer relations*. New York: Wiley.

Mulhern, R. K., & Passman, R. H. (1981). Parental discipline as affected by sex of parent, sex of the child, and the child's apparent responsiveness to discipline. *Developmental Psychology*, 17, 604–613.

Munsinger, H. (1975). Children's resemblance to their biological and adopting parents in two ethnic groups. *Behavior Genetics*, 5, 239–254.

Murphy, L. (1937). *Social behavior and child personality*. New York: Columbia University Press.

Murray, J. P., & Kippax, S. (1978). Children's social behavior in three towns with differing television experience. *Journal of Communication*, 28(1), 19–29.

Mussen, P. H., Conger, J. J., & Kagan, J. (1980). *Essentials of child development and personality* (5th ed.). New York: Harper & Row.

Mussen, P. H., & Jones, M. C. (1957). Self-conceptions, motivations, and interpersonal attitudes of late and early maturing boys. *Child Development*, 28, 243–256.

Nash, S. C. (1979). Sex role as a mediator of intellectual functioning. In M. A. Wittig & A. C. Petersen (Eds.), *Sex-related differences in cognitive functioning*. New York: Academic Press.

National Assessment of Educational Progress (1981). *Reading, thinking, and writing: Results from the 1979–80 national assessment of reading and literature*. Denver: Education Commission of the States.

National Center for Juvenile Justice, Unpublished data, 1975–1979. Pittsburgh, PA.

National Commission on Excellence in Education (1983). *A nation at risk: The imperative for educational reform*. Washington, DC: Congressional Budget Office.

Neimark, E. D. (1975a). Intellectual development during adolescence. In F. D. Horowitz (Ed.), *Review of Child Development Research* (Vol. 4). Chicago: University of Chicago Press.

Neimark, E. D. (1975b). Longitudinal development of formal operations thought. *Genetic Psychology Monographs*, 91, 171–225.

Nelson, C. A., & Dolgin, K. G. (1985). The generalized discrimination of facial expressions in seven month old infants. *Child Development*, 56, 58–61.

Nelson, C. A., & Salapatek, P. (1986). The electrophysiological correlates of infant recognition memory. *Child Development*, 57, 1483–1497.

Nelson, K. (1975). Individual differences in early semantic and syntax development. In D. Aaronson & R. W. Rieber (Eds.), *Developmental psycholinguistics and communication disorders. Annals of the New York Academy of Science*, 263, 132–139.

Nelson, K. (1981). Social cognition in a script framework. In J. Flavell & L. Ross (Eds.), *Social cognitive development* (pp. 97–118). Cambridge: Cambridge University Press.

Nemiah, J. C. (1988). Psychoneurotic disorders. In A. M. Nicholi, Jr. (Ed.), *The new Harvard guide to psychiatry* (pp. 234–258). Cambridge, MA: Harvard University Press.

New York Times (1977, November 14), p. 20.

Newport, E. L., Gleitman, H., & Gleitman, L. R. (1977). Mother, I'd rather do it myself: Some effects and non-effects of maternal speech style. In C. E. Snow & C. A. Ferguson (Eds.), *Talking to children*. Cambridge: Cambridge University Press.

Nicholi, A. M., Jr. (1988). The adolescent. In A. M. Nicholi, Jr. (Ed.), *The new Harvard guide to psychiatry* (pp. 637–664). Cambridge, MA: Harvard University Press.

Nicholls, J. G. (1978). The development of the concepts of effort and ability, perception of academic attainment, and the understanding that difficult tasks require more ability. *Child Development, 49,* 800–814.

Nicholls, J. G., & Miller, A. T. (1985). Differentiation of the concepts of luck and skill. *Developmental Psychology, 21,* 76–82.

Nichols, R. C. (1978). Heredity and environment: Major findings from twin studies of ability, personality, and interests. *Homo, 29,* 158–173.

Nilsson, L., Furuhjelm, M., Ingelman-Sundberg, A., & Wirsen, C. (1981). *A child is born*. New York: Dell (Delacorte Press).

Ninio, A., & Bruner, J. (1976). *The achievement and antecedents of labelling*. Unpublished paper, Hebrew University, Jerusalem.

Nisan, M., & Kohlberg, L. (1982). Universality and variation in moral judgment: A longitudinal and cross-sectional study in Turkey. *Child Development, 53,* 865–876.

Norback, C. (Ed.), (1980). *The complete book of American surveys*. New York: New American Library.

Norman, J., & Harris, M. (1981). *The private life of the American teenager*. New York: Rawson, Wade.

Novey, M. S. (1975). The development of knowledge of others' ability to see. Unpublished doctoral dissertation. Harvard University.

Nucci, L., & Nucci, M. (1982). Children's social interactions in the context of moral and conventional transgressions. *Child Development, 53,* 865–876.

Nucci, L., & Turiel, E. (1978). Social interactions and the development of social concepts in preschool children. *Child Development, 49,* 400–407.

Nurnberger, J. I., & Gershon, E. S. (1981). Genetics of affective disorders. In E. Friedman (Ed.), *Depression and antidepressants: Implications for courses and treatment*. New York: Raven.

O'Brien, M., & Huston, A. C. (1985). Development of sex-typed play behavior in toddlers. *Developmental Psychology, 21,* 866–871.

O'Connell, J. C. & Farran, D. C. (1982). Effects of day care experience on the use of intentional communicative behaviors in a sample of socioeconomically depressed infants. *Developmental Psychology, 18,* 22–29.

Oden, S. & Asher, S. F. (1977). Coaching children in social skills for friendship making. *Child Development, 48,* 95–506.

Offer, D. (1975). Adolescent turmoil. In A. H. Esman (Ed.), *The psychology of adolescence*. New York: International Universities Press.

Offer, D., & Offer, J. (1975). *From teenage to young manhood*. New York: Basic Books.

Offer, D., Ostrov, E., & Howard, K. (1981). The mental health professionals' concept of the normal adolescent. *Archives of General Psychiatry, 38,* 149–152.

Olweus, D. (1979). Stability of aggressive reaction patterns in males: A review. *Psychological Bulletin, 86,* 852–875.

Olweus, D. (1980). Familial and temperamental determinants of aggressive behavior in adolescent boys: A causal analysis. *Developmental Psychology, 16,* 644–660.

Orlofsky, J. L. (1978). Identity formation, achievement, and fear of success in college men and women. *Journal of Youth and Adolescence, 7,* 49–62.

Orlofsky, J., Marcia, J., & Lesser, I. (1973). Ego identity status and the intimacy versus isolation crisis of young adulthood. *Journal of Personality and Social Psychology, 27,* 211–219.

O'Rourke, D. H., Gottesman, I. I., Suarez, B. K., Rice, J., & Reich, T. (1982). Refutation of the general single-locus model for the etiology of schizophrenia. *American Journal of Human Genetics, 34,* 630–649.

Orvaschel, H., Weissman, M. M., & Kidd, K. K. (1980). Children and depression. *Journal of Affective Disorders, 2,* 1–16.

Osipow, S. H. (1986). Career issues through the life span. In M. S. Pallak & R. O. Perloff (Eds.), *Psychology and work: Productivity, change and employment* (pp. 141–168). Washington, DC: American Psychological Association.

Osofsky, J. D., & O'Connell, E. J. (1972). Parent-child interactions: Daughter's effects upon mothers' and fathers' behavior. *Developmental Psychology, 7,* 157–168.

Osterrieth, P. A. (1969). Adolescence: Some psychological aspects. In G. Caplan & S. Lebovici (Eds.), *Adolescence: Psychosocial perspectives*. New York: Basic Books.

Ostrov, E., & Offer, D. (1978). Loneliness at adolescence: Correlates, attributions, and coping. *Journal of Youth and Adolescence, 12,* 95–100.

Page, D. C., Mosher, R., Simpson, E. M., Fisher, E. M. C., Mardon, G., Pollack, J., McGillivray, B., de la Chapelle, A., & Brown, L. G. (1987). The sex-determining region of the human chromosome encodes a finger protein. *Cell, 51,* 1091–1094.

Page, E. W., Villee, C. A., & Villee, D. B. (1981). *Human reproduction: Essentials of reproductive and perinatal medicine* (3rd ed.). Philadelphia: Saunders.

Papousek, H. (1967). Experimental studies of appetitional behavior in human newborns and infants. In H. W. Stevenson & H. L. Rheingold (Eds.), *Early Behavior*. New York: Wiley.

Parke, R. D. (1977). Punishment in children: Effects, side effects, and alternative strategies. In H. L. Hom & P. A. Robinson (Eds.), *Psychological processes in early education*. New York: Academic Press.

Parke, R. D., Berkowitz, L., Leyens, J. P., West, S., & Sebastian, R. J. (1977). Some effects of violent and nonviolent movies on the behavior of juvenile delinquents. In L. Berkowitz (Ed.), *Advances in experimental social psychology* (Vol. 10). New York: Academic Press.

Parke, R. D., & Collmer, C. W. (1975). Child abuse: An interdisciplinary analysis. In E. M. Hetherington, J. W. Hagen, R. Kron, & A. H. Stein (Eds.), *Review of child development research* (Vol. 5). Chicago: University of Chicago Press.

Parke, R. D., & Slaby, R. G. (1983). The development of aggression. In E. M. Hetherington (Ed.) & P. H. Mussen (Series Ed.), *Handbook of child psychology: Vol. 4. Socialization, personality, and social development* (4th ed., pp. 547–642). New York: Wiley.

Parke, R. D., & Tinsley, B. R. (1981). The father's role in infancy: Determinants of involvement in caregiving and play. In M. E. Lamb (Ed.), *The role of the father in child development*. New York: Wiley.

Parry-Jones, W. L. L. (1985). Adolescent disturbance. In M. Rutter & L. Hersov (Eds.) *Child and adolescent psychiatry: Modern approaches* (2nd ed.) (pp. 584–598). Oxford: Blackwell Scientific Publications.

Parsons, J. E., Adler, T. F., & Kaczala, C. M. (1982). Socialization of achievement attitudes and beliefs: Parental influences. *Child Development, 53*, 310–321.

Parsons, J. E., Kaczala, C. M., & Meece, J. L. (1982). Socialization of achievement attitudes and beliefs: Classroom influences. *Child Development, 53*, 322–339.

Parten, M. (1932). Social participation among pre-school children. *Journal of Abnormal Psychology, 27*, 243–268.

Pascual-Leone, J. (1970). Mathematical model for the transition rule in Piaget's developmental stages. *Acta Psychologica, 63*, 301–345.

Passman, R. H., & Blackwelder, D. E. (1981). Rewarding and punishing by mothers: The influence of progressive changes in the quality of their son's apparent behavior. *Developmental Psychology, 17*, 614–619.

Pastor, D. L. (1981). The quality of mother-infant attachment and its relationship to toddlers' initial sociability with peers. *Developmental Psychology, 17*, 326–335.

Patterson, C. J., Massad, C. M., & Cosgrove, J. M. (1978). Children's referential communication: Components of plans for effective listening. *Developmental Psychology, 14*, 401–406.

Patterson, G. R. (1976). The aggressive child: Victim and architect of a coercive system. In L. A. Hamerlynck, L. C. Handy, & E. J. Mash (Eds.), *Behavior modification and families: I. Theory and research*. New York: Brunner/Mazel.

Patterson, G. R. (1979). A performance theory for coercive family interactions. In R. Cairns (Ed.), *Social interaction: Methods, analyses, and illustrations* (pp. 119–162). Hillsdale, NJ: Erlbaum.

Patterson, G. R. (1980). The unacknowledged victims. *Monographs of the Society for Research in Child Development, 45*, (5, Serial No. 18b).

Patterson, G. R. (1981). Some speculations and data relating to children who steal. In T. Hirschi & M. Gottfredson (Eds.), *Theory and fact in contemporary criminology*. Beverly Hills, CA: Sage.

Patterson, G. R. (1982). *Coercive family process*. Eugene, OR: Castalia Press.

Patterson, G. R., Littman, R. A., & Bricker, W. (1967). Assertive behavior in children: A step toward a theory of aggression. *Monographs of the Society for Research in Child Development, 32* (5, Serial No. 113).

Payne, F. (1980). Children's prosocial conduct in structured situations and as viewed by others. *Child Development, 51*, 1252–1259.

Pea, R. D. (1980). The development of negation in early child language. In D. R. Olson (Ed.), *The social foundations of language and thought: Essays in honor of Jerome S. Bruner*. New York: Norton.

Pearce, J. (1978). The recognition of depressive disorder in children. *Journal of the Royal Society of Medicine, 71*, 494–500.

Pearce, J. (1982). Personal communication, March, 1982. (Cited in Graham, P., & Rutter, M., Adolescent disorders.) In M. Rutter, & L. Hersov (Eds.), *Child and adolescent psychiatry: Modern approaches* (pp. 351–367). Oxford: Blackwell Scientific Publications.

Peevers, B. H., & Secord, P. F. (1973). Developmental changes in attribution of descriptive concepts to persons. *Journal of Personality and Social Psychology, 27*, 120–128.

Pellegrini, A. D. (1985). Social-cognitive aspects of children's play: The effects of age, gender, and activity centers. *Journal of Applied Developmental Psychology, 6*, 129–140.

Penner, S. G. (1987). Parental responses to grammatical and ungrammatical child utterances. *Child Development, 58*, 376–384.

Pepler, D. J., Abramovitch, R., & Corter, C. (1981). Sibling interaction in the home: A longitudinal study. *Child Development, 52*, 1344–1347.

Peskin, H. (1967). Pubertal onset and ego functioning. *Journal of Abnormal Psychology, 72*, 1–15.

Peskin, H. (1973). Influence of the developmental schedule of puberty on learning and ego functioning. *Journal of Youth and Adolescence, 2*, 273–290.

Petersen, A. C. (1984). Menarche, Meaning of measures and measuring meaning. In S. Golub (Ed.), *Menarche: An interdisciplinary view*. New York: Springer-Verlag.

Petersen, A. C. (1988). Adolescent development. *Annual review of psychology, 39*, 583–608.

Petersen, A. C., & Boxer, A. (1982). Adolescent sexuality. In T. Coates, A. Petersen, & C. Perry (Eds.), *Adolescent health: Crossing the barriers*. New York: Academic Press.

Petitto, L. (1983). From gesture to symbol. Unpublished doctoral dissertation, Harvard University.

Petti, T. (1983). Depression and withdrawal in children. In T. H. Ollendick & M. Hersen (Eds.). *Handbook of child psychopathology* (pp. 293–322). New York: Plenum.

Pezdek, K. (1987). Memory for pictures: A life-span study of the role of visual detail. *Child Development, 58,* 807–815.

Phillips, D. A. (1987). Socialization of perceived academic competence among highly competent children. *Child Development, 58,* 1308–1320.

Phillips, D., McCartney, K., & Scarr, S. (1987). Child-care quality and children's social development. *Developmental Psychology, 23,* 537–543.

Piaget, J. (1965, original published 1932). *The moral judgment of the child.* New York: Free Press.

Piaget, J. (1926). *The language and thought of the child.* London: Routledge & Kegan Paul.

Piaget, J. (1951). *Play, dreams, and imitation in childhood.* New York: Norton.

Piaget, J. (1954). *The construction of reality in the child.* New York: Basic Books.

Piaget, J. (1967). Language and thought from the genetic point of view. In D. Elkind (Ed.), *Six psychological studies.* New York: Random House.

Piaget, J. (1970). Piaget's theory. In P. H. Mussen (Ed.), *Carmichael's manual of child psychology* (Vol. 1) (3rd ed.). New York: Wiley.

Pinard, A. (1985). Metacognition and meta-Piaget. In C. J. Brainerd & V. F. Reyna (Eds.), *Developmental psychology* (pp. 233–246). Amsterdam: Elsevier Science Publishers.

Pinon, M. F., Huston, A. C., & Wright, J. C. (1989). Family ecology and child characteristics that predict young children's educational television viewing. *Child Development* 60, 846–856.

Pittel, S. M., & Miller, H. (1976). *Dropping down: The hippie then and now.* Berkeley, CA: Haight Ashbury Research Project, Wright Institute.

Plato (1953). *The dialogues of Plato* (Vol. 4): Laws (4th ed.) (B. Jewett, trans.). Oxford: Clarendon Press.

Plomin, R. (1986). *Development, genetics, and psychology.* Hillsdale, NJ: Erlbaum.

Plomin, R., & DeFries, J. C. (1985). A parent-offspring adoption study of cognitive abilities in early childhood. *Intelligence, 9,* 341–356.

Plomin, R., & Foch, T. T. (1980). A twin study of objectively assessed personality in childhood. *Journal of Personality and Social Psychology, 39,* 680–688.

Plomin, R., Willerman, L., & Loehlin, J. C. (1976). Resemblance in appearance and the equal environments assumption in twin studies of personality. *Behavior Genetics, 6,* 43–52.

Pomeroy, W. B. (1969). *Girls and sex.* New York: Delacorte Press.

Potts, R., & Collins, W. A. (in press). Affect and children's processing of television narrative. In A. Dorr (Ed.), *Television and affect.*

Potts, R., Huston, A. C., & Wright, J. C. (1986). The effects of television form and violent content on boys' attention and social behavior. *Journal of Experimental Child Psychology, 41,* 1–17.

Powell, G. J. (1973). *Black Monday's children: A study of the effects of school desegregation on self-concepts of Southern children.* Englewood Cliffs, NJ: Prentice-Hall.

Powell, G. J. (1985). Self-concepts among Afro-American students in racially isolated minority schools: Some regional differences. *Journal of the American Academy of Child Psychiatry, 24,* 142–149.

Prescott, P. S. (1981). *The child savers.* New York: Knopf.

Pressley, M. (1979). Increasing children's self-control through cognitive intervention. *Review of Educational Research, 49,* 319–370.

Puig-Antich, J. (1986). Psychobiological markers: Effects of age and puberty. In M. Rutter, C. E. Izard, & P. B. Read (Eds.), *Depression in young people: Developmental and clinical perspectives* (pp. 341–382). New York: Guilford.

Pulkkinen, L. (1983). Finland: The search for alternatives to aggression. In A. P. Goldstein & M. H. Segal (Eds.), *Aggression in a global perspective.* (pp. 104–144). New York: Pergamon.

Putallaz, M. (1987). Maternal behavior and children's sociometric status. *Child Development, 58,* 324–370.

Putallaz, M., & Gottman, J. (1981). Social skills and group acceptance. In S. Asher & J. Gottman (Eds.), *The development of friendship: Description and intervention.* New York: Cambridge University Press.

Quay, H. C. (1987a). Intelligence. In H. C. Quay (Ed.), *Handbook of juvenile delinquency* (pp. 106–117). New York: Wiley.

Quay, H. C. (1987b). Patterns of delinquent behavior. In H. C. Quay (Ed.), *Handbook of juvenile delinquency* (pp. 118–138). New York: Wiley.

Quay, H. C. (1987c). Institutional treatment. In H. C. Quay (Ed.), *Handbook of juvenile delinquency* (pp. 244–265). New York: Wiley.

Radke-Yarrow, M., & Zahn-Waxler, C. (1984). Roots, motives, and patterns in children's prosocial behavior. In E. Staub, D. Bar-Tal, J. Karylowski, & J. Reykowski (Eds.), *Development and maintenance of prosocial behavior: International perspectives on positive development.* New York: Plenum.

Radke-Yarrow, M., Zahn-Waxler, C., & Chapman, M. (1983). Children's prosocial dispositions and behavior. In P. H. Mussen (Series Ed.) & E. M. Hetherington (Ed.), *Handbook of child psychology: Vol. 4. Socialization, personality and social development.* (4th ed., pp. 469–546). New York: Wiley.

Rakic, P., Bourgeois, J. P., Eckenhoff, M. F., Zecevic, M. & Goldman-Rakic, P. S. (1986). Concurrent over production of synapses in diverse regions of the primate cerebral cortex. *Science, 232,* 232–235.

Ramey, C. T., Yeates, K. O., & Short, E. J. (1984). The plasticity of intellectual development: Insights from preventive intervention. *Child Development, 55,* 1913–1925.

Reed, E. W. (1975). Genetic anomalies in development. In F. D. Horowitz (Ed.), *Review of child development research* (Vol. 4). Chicago: University of Chicago Press.

Renshaw, P. D., & Asher, S. R. (1983). Children's goals and strategies for social interaction. *Merrill-Palmer Quarterly, 29,* 353–374.

Reschly, D. J. (1981). Psychological testing in educational classification and placement. *American Psychologist, 36,* 1094–1102.

Resnick, H. L. P. (1980). Suicide. In H. I. Kaplan, A. M. Freedman, & B. J. Sadock (Eds.), *Comprehensive textbook of psychiatry* (Vol. 2) (pp. 2085–2097). Baltimore: Williams & Wilkins.

Rest, J. R. (1983). In J. Flavell & E. Markman (Eds.), P. H. Mussen (Series Ed.) *Handbook of child psychology:* Vol. 3. *Cognitive development* (4th ed., pp. 556–629). New York: Wiley.

Rest, J. R. (1986). *Moral development: Advances in research and theory.* New York: Praeger.

Reznick, J. S. (1982). The development of perceptual and lexical categories in the human infant. Unpublished doctoral dissertation, University of Colorado.

Rheingold, H. L., Hay, D. F., & West, M. J. (1976). Sharing in the second year of life. *Child Development, 47,* 1148–1158.

Rholes, W. S., Blackwell, J., Jordan, C., & Walters, C. (1980). A developmental study of learned helplessness. *Developmental Psychology, 16,* 616–624.

Rice, M. E., & Grusec, J. E. (1975). Saying and doing: Effects on observer performance. *Journal of Personality and Social Psychology, 32,* 584–593.

Rice, M. L. (1980). *Cognition to language.* Baltimore: University Park Press.

Rice, M. L. (1983). Cognitive aspects of communicative disorders. In R. H. Schiefelbusch & J. Picka (Eds.), *Communicative competence: Acquisition and integration.* University Park, MD.: University Park Press.

Rice, M. L., Huston, A. C., Wright, J. C., & Truglio, R. (1988). *Words from Sesame Street: Learning vocabulary while viewing.* Unpublished manuscript, Center for Research on the Influences of Television on Children, University of Kansas, Lawrence, KS 66045.

Richman, N., Graham, P., & Stevenson, J. *Preschool to school: A behavioral study.* London: Academic Press.

Richmond, J. B. (1982, November 29). *Health needs of young children.* Paper presented at the John D. and Catherine MacArthur Foundation conference on child care: Growth-fostering environments for young children. Chicago.

Riese, M. A. (1987). Temperament stability between the neonatal period and 24 months. *Developmental Psychology, 23,* 216–221.

Rijit-Plooij, V., Hitt, C., & Plooij, F. Z. (1987). Growing independence, conflict, and leaving in mother-infant relations in free-ranging chimpanzees. *Behavior, 101,* 1–86.

Rist, R. C. (1973). *The urban school: A factory for failure.* Cambridge, MA: MIT Press.

Ritchie, D., Price, V., & Roberts, D. F. (1987). Television, reading, and reading achievement: A reappraisal. *Communication Research, 14,* 292–315.

Robins, L. (1966). *Deviant children grow up: A sociological and psychiatric study of sociopathic personality.* Baltimore: Williams & Wilkins.

Robins, L. (1978). Sturdy childhood predictors of adult antisocial behavior: Replications from longitudinal studies. *Psychological Medicine, 8,* 611–622.

Roche, A. F. (1978). Bone growth and maturation. In F. Falkner & J. M. Tanner (Eds.), *Human growth:* Vol. 2. *Postnatal growth.* New York: Plenum.

Rode, S. S., Chang, P., Fisch, R. O., & Stroufe, L. A. (1981). Attachment patterns of infants separated at birth. *Developmental Psychology, 17,* 188–191.

Rodin, J. (1985). Insulin levels, hunger, and food intake: An example of feedback loops in body weight regulation. *Health Psychology, 4,* 1–24.

Roff, M., Sells, S., & Golden, M. (1972). *Social adjustment and personality development in children.* Minneapolis: University of Minnesota Press.

Roffwarg, H. P., Muzio, J. N, & Dement, W. C. (1966). Ontogenetic development of the human sleep dream cycle. *Science, 152,* 604–619.

Rosenberg, M. (1985). Identity: Summary. In M. B. Spencer, G. K. Brookins, & W. R. Allen (Eds.), *Beginnings: The social and affective development of black children* (pp. 231–236). Hillsdale, NJ: Erlbaum.

Rosenhan, D. (1969). Some origins of concern for others. In P. Mussen, J. Langer, & M. Covington (Eds.), *Trends and issues in developmental psychology.* New York: Holt, Rinehart and Winston.

Rosenthal, D. (1970). *Genetic theory and abnormal behavior.* New York: McGraw-Hill.

Rosenthal, D., Wender, P. H., Kety, S. S., Schulsinger, F., Welner, J., & Rieder, R. O. (1975). Parent-child relationships and psychopathological disorder in the child. *Archives of General Psychiatry, 32,* 466–476.

Rosenthal, R. (1976). *Experimenter effects in behavioral research* (2nd ed.). New York: Irvington.

Rosenthal, R., & Jacobson, L. (1968). *Pygmalion in the classroom: Teacher expectation and pupils' intellectual development.* New York: Holt, Rinehart and Winston.

Ross, R. J. (1973). Some empirical parameters of formal thinking. *Journal of Youth and Adolescence, 2,* 167–177.

Rothbart, M. K. (1971). Birth order and mother-child interaction in an achievement situation. *Journal of Personality and Social Psychology, 17,* 113–120.

Rothbart, M. K., & Derryberry, D. (1981). Development of individual differences in temperament. In M. E. Lamb & A. L. Brown (Eds.), *Advances in developmental psychology* (Vol. 1), Hillsdale, NJ: Erlbaum.

Rovee-Collier, C. K., Sullivan, M., Enright, M., Lucas, D., & Fagen, J. (1980). Reactivation of infant memory. *Science, 208,* 1159–1161.

Rubin, K. H., Fein, G. G., & Vandenberg, B. (1983). Play. In P. H. Mussen (Series Ed.) & E. M. Hetherington (Ed.), *Handbook of child psychology:* Vol. 4. *Socialization, personality, and social development* (4th ed., pp. 693–774). New York: Wiley.

Rubin, K. H., Watson, K. S., & Jambor, T. W. (1978). Free-play behaviors in preschool and kindergarten children. *Child Development, 49,* 534–536.

Rubin, S. (1980). *It's not too late for a baby: For women and men over 35.* Englewood Cliffs, NJ: Prentice-Hall.

Rubin, S., & Wolf, D. (1979). The development of maybe. *New Directions for Child Development, 6,* 15–28.

Ruble, D. N., Boggiano, A. K., Feldman, N. S., & Loebl, J. H. (1980). Developmental analysis of the role of social comparison in self-evaluation. *Developmental Psychology, 16,* 105–115.

Ruble, D. N., & Brooks-Gunn, J. (1982). The experience of menarche. *Child Development, 53,* 1557–1566.

Ruble, D. N., Parsons, J. E., & Ross, J. (1976). Self-evaluative responses of children in an achievement setting. *Child Development, 47,* 990–997.

Rugh, R., & Shettles, L. B. (1971). *From conception to birth: The drama of life's beginnings.* New York: Harper & Row.

Rushton, J. P. (1975). Generosity in children: Immediate and long term effects of modeling, preaching, and moral judgment. *Journal of Personality and Social Psychology, 31,* 459–466.

Rushton, J. P., & Weiner, J. (1975). Altruism and cognitive development in children. *British Journal of Social and Clinical Psychology, 14,* 341–349.

Russell, G. F. M. (1985). Anorexia and bulimia nervosa. In M. Rutter & L. Hersov (Eds.), *Child and adolescent psychiatry: Modern approaches* (pp. 625–637). Oxford: Blackwell Scientific Publications.

Russell, J. A., & Bullock, M. (1986). On the dimensions preschoolers use to interpret facial expressions of emotion. *Developmental Psychology, 22,* 97–102.

Rutter, M. (1977). Brain damage syndromes in childhood: Concepts and findings. *Journal of Child Psychology and Psychiatry, 18,* 1–21.

Rutter, M. (1979a). Maternal deprivation, 1972–1978: New findings, new concepts, new approaches. *Child Development, 50,* 283–305.

Rutter, M. (1979b). Protective factors in children's responses to stress and disadvantage. In M. W. Kent & J. Rolf (Eds.), *Primary prevention of psychopathology,* Vol. III: *Social competence in children* (pp. 49–74). Hanover, NH: University Press of New England.

Rutter, M. (1980). *Changing youth in a changing society: Patterns of adolescent development and disorder.* Cambridge, MA: Harvard University Press.

Rutter, M. (1981). *Maternal deprivation reassessed* (2nd ed.). New York: Penguin.

Rutter, M. (1986). The developmental psychopathology of depression. In M. Rutter, C. E. Izard, & P. B. Read (Eds.), *Depression in young people: Developmental and clinical perspectives* (pp. 3–30). New York: Guilford.

Rutter, M., & Garmezy, N. (1983). Developmental psychopathology. In P. H. Mussen (Series Ed.) & E. M. Hetherington (Ed.), *Handbook of child psychology:* Vol. IV. *Socialization, personality and social development* (pp. 775–911). New York: Wiley.

Rutter, M., & Giller, H. (1984). *Juvenile delinquency: Trends and perspectives.* New York: Guilford.

Rutter, M., Graham, P., Chadwick, O. F. D., & Yule, W. (1976). Adolescent turmoil: Fact or fiction? *Journal of Child Psychology and Psychiatry, 17,* 35–56.

Rutter, M., Izard, C. E., & Read, P. B. (1986). *Depression in young people: Developmental and clinical perspectives.* New York: Guilford Press.

Rutter, M. & Quinton, D. (1984). Long term follow-up of women institutionalized in childhood. *British Journal of Developmental Psychology, 2,* 191–204.

Rutter, M., Tizard, J., & Whitmore, K. (1970/1981). *Education, health and behavior.* Huntington, NY: Krieger. (Original work published 1970, London: Longmans).

Ryan, N. D., Puig-Antich, J., & Ambrasini, P. (1987). The clinical picture of major depression in children and adolescents. *Archives of General Psychiatry, 44,* 854–886.

Sackett, G. P., Ruppenthal, G. C., Fahrenbruch, C. E., Holm, R. A., & Greenough, W. T. (1981). Social isolation rearing effects in monkeys vary with genotype. *Developmental Psychology, 17,* 313.

Sagi, A., Lamb, M. E., & Gardner, W. (1985). Relations between Strange Situation behavior and stranger sociability among infants in Israeli kibbutzim. *Infant Behavior and Development.*

Sagotsky, G., Patterson, C. J., & Lepper, M. R. (1978). Training children's self-control: A field experiment in self-monitoring and goal-setting in the classroom. *Journal of Experimental Psychology, 25,* 242–253.

St. Clair, S., & Day, H. D. (1979). Ego identity status and values among high school females. *Journal of Youth and Adolescence, 8,* 317–326.

Salomon, G. (1977). Effects of encouraging Israeli mothers to co-observe "Sesame Street" with their five-year-olds. *Child Development, 48,* 1146–1151.

Salomon, G. (1979). *Interaction of media, cognition, and learning.* San Francisco: Jossey-Bass.

Salomon, G. (1983). Television watching and mental effort: A social psychological view. In J. Bryant & D. R. Anderson (Eds.). *Children's understanding of television: Research on attention and comprehension* (pp. 181–198). New York: Academic Press.

Sameroff, A. J., Seifer, F., & Zax, M. (1982). Early development of children at risk for emotional disorder. *Monographs of the Society for Research in Child Development, 47,* (7).

Sameroff, A. M., & Zax, M. (1973). Perinatal characteristics of the offspring of schizophrenic women. *Journal of Nervous and Mental Diseases, 157,* 191–199.

Sampson, E. E., & Hancock, F. T. (1967). An examination of the relationship between ordinal position, personality, and conformity: An extension, replication, and partial verification. *Journal of Marriage and the Family, 36,* 294–301.

Sandoval, J., & Millie, M. P. W. (1980). Accuracy of judgments of WISC-R item difficulty for minority groups. *Journal of Consulting and Clinical Psychology, 48,* 249–253.

Sanson, A., Prior, M., Garino, E., Oberkaid, F. & Sewell, J. (1987). The structure of infant temperament. *Infant Behavior and Development, 10,* 97–104.

Santrock, J. W. (1970). Influence of onset and type of paternal absence on the first four Eriksonian developmental crises. *Developmental Psychology, 6,* 273–274.

Santrock, J. W. (1975). Father absence, perceived maternal behavior, and moral development in boys. *Child, Development, 46,* 753–757.

Santrock, J. W. (1984). *Adolescence: An introduction.* Dubuque, IA: Wm. C. Brown Puplishers.

Santrock, J. W. (1987). *Adolescence: An introduction* (3rd ed.). Dubuque, IA: Wm. C. Brown.

Santrock, J. W., & Warshak, R. A. (1979). Father custody and social development in boys and girls. *Journal of Social Issues, 35*(4), 112–135.

Santrock, J. W., Warshak, R., Lindbergh, C., & Meadows, L. (1982). Children's and parents' observed social behavior in stepfather families. *Child Development, 53,* 472–480.

Sarason, I. G. (1978). A cognitive social learning approach to juvenile delinquency. In R. Hare & D. Schalling (Eds.), *Psychopathic Behavior: Approaches to Research* (pp. 299–317). New York: Wiley.

Sarason, I. G., & Ganzer, V. J. (1973). Modeling and group discussion in the rehabilitation of juvenile delinquents. *Journal of Counseling Psychology, 20,* 442–449.

Sarason, S. B., Hill, K. T., & Zimbardo, P. C. (1964). A longitudinal study of the relation of test anxiety to performance on intelligence and achievement tests. *Monographs of the Society for Research in Child Development, 29,* (No. 7).

Scaife, M., & Bruner, J. S. (1975). The capacity for joint visual attention in the infant. *Nature, 253,* 265–266.

Scarr, S. (1981). *Race, social class, and individual differences in* IQ. Hillsdale, NJ: Erlbaum.

Scarr, S., Caparulo, B. K., Ferdman, B. M., Tower, R. B., & Caplan, J. (1983). Developmental status and school achievements of minority and non-minority children from birth to 18 years in a British Midlands town. *British Journal of Developmental Psychology, 1,* 31–48.

Scarr, S., & Carter-Saltzman, L. (1979). Twin method: Defense of a critical assumption. *Behavior Genetics, 9,* 527–542.

Scarr, S., & Kidd, K. K. (1983). Developmental behavior genetics. In M. Haith & J. Campos (Eds.), P. H. Mussen (Series Ed.), *Handbook of child psychology: Vol. 2. Infancy and developmental psychobiology* (pp. 345–435). New York: Wiley.

Scarr, S. & McCartney, K. (1983). How people make their own environments: A theory of genotype $\rightarrow$ environment effects. *Child Development, 54,* 424–435.

Scarr, S., & Weinberg, R. A. (1976). IQ test performance of black children adopted by white families. *American Psychologist, 31,* 726–739.

Schacter, F. F. (1981). Toddlers with employed mothers. *Child Development, 52,* 958–964.

Scheintuch, G., & Lewin, G. (1981). Parents' attitudes and children's deprivation: Child rearing attitudes of parents as a key to the advantaged-disadvantaged distinction in preschool children. *International Journal of Behavioral Development, 4,* 125–142.

Scheirer, M. A. & Kraut, R. E. (1979). Increasing educational achievement via self-concept change. *Review of Educational Research, 49,* 131–150.

Schiff, M., Duyme, M., Dumaret, A., & Tomkiewicz, S. (1982). How much could we boost scholastic achievement and IQ scores: A direct answer from a French adoption study. *Cognition, 12,* 165–196.

Schiff, M., Duyne, M., Dumaret, A., Stewart, J., Tomkiewicz, S., & Feingold, J. (1978). Intellectual status of working-class children adopted early into upper-middle-class families. *Science, 200,* 1503–1504.

Schindler, P. J., Moely, B. E., & Frank, A. L. (1987). Time in day care and social participation of young children. *Developmental Psychology, 23,* 255–261.

Schmidt, G. (1975). Male-female differences in sexual arousal and behavior during and after exposure to sexually explicit stimuli. *Archives of Sexual Behavior, 1*, 353–364.

Schomberg, S. F. (1978). Moral judgment development and freshmen year experiences. *Dissertation Abstracts International, 39*, 3482A (University Microfilms no. 7823960).

Schorr, L. B. (1988). *Within our reach: Breaking the cycle of disadvantage and despair.* New York: Doubleday/Anchor.

Schultz, T. R., & Horibe, F. (1974). Development of the appreciation of verbal jokes. *Developmental Psychology, 10*, 13–20.

Schunk, D. H. & Cox, P. D. (1986). Strategy training and attributional feedback with learning disabled students. *Journal of Educational Psychology, 78*, 201–209.

Schunk, D. H., Hanson, A. & Cox, P. D. (1987). Peer-model attributes and children's achievement behaviors. *Journal of Educational Psychology, 79*, 54–61.

Schwartz, J. C., Schrager, J. B., & Lyons, A. E. (1983). Delay of gratification by preschoolers: Evidence for the validity of the choice paradigm. *Child Development, 54*, 620–625.

Schweder, R., Turiel, E., & Much, N. (1981). The moral intuitions of the child. In J. H. Flavell & L. Ross (Eds.), *Social cognitive development: Frontiers and possible futures.* New York: Cambridge University Press.

Scott, R. M. (1980). Coordinating services for runaway youth: The case of New York City. *Journal of Family Issues, 1*, 308–312.

Sears, R. R. (1975). Your ancients revisited: A history of child development. In E. M. Hetherinton (Ed.), *Review of child development research* (Vol. 5). Chicago: University of Chicago Press.

Sears, R. R., Maccoby, E. E., Levin, H. (1957). *Patterns of child rearing.* New York: Harper & Row.

Sebald, H., & White, B. (1980). Teenagers divided reference groups: Uneven alignment with parents and peers. *Adolescence, 15*, 579–984.

Sechrest, L., & Rosenblatt, A. (1987). Research methods. In H. C. Quay, (Ed.), *Handbook of juvenile delinquency* (pp. 417–450). New York: Wiley.

Seeman, M. (1975). Alienation studies. In A. Inkeles, J. Coleman, & N. Smelser (Eds.), *Annual review of sociology* (Vol. 1). Palo Alto, CA: Annual Reviews.

Segal, N. L. (1985). Monozygotic and dizygotic twins: A comparative analysis of mental ability profiles. *Child Development, 56*, 1051–1058.

Seligman, M. E. P., & Peterson, C. (1986). A learned helplessness perspective on childhood depression: Theory and research. In M. Rutter, C. E. Izard, & P. B. Read (Eds.), *Depression in young people: Developmental and clinical perspectives* (pp. 223–250). New York: Guilford.

Selman, R. L. (1976). Social cognitive understanding: A guide to educational and clinical practice. In T. Likona (Ed.), *Moral development and behavior: Theory, research, and social issues.* New York: Holt, Rinehart and Winston.

Selman, R. L. (1980). *The growth of interpersonal understanding.* New York: Academic Press.

Selman, R. L. (1981). The child as a friendship philosopher. In S. R. Asher & J. M. Gottman (Eds.), *The development of children's friendships.* New York: Cambridge University Press.

Senate Committee of the Judiciary, Subcommittee to Investigate Juvenile Delinquency, Hearings on Protection of Children against Sexual Exploitation, 95th Cong., 1st sess., 27 May 1977, 2.

Senate Committee of the Judiciary, Subcommittee of Juvenile Justice Exploitation of Children, 96th Cong., 2nd sess., 5 November 1981, Y4.J892:J-97-78, 35.

Serbin, L. A., Connor, J. M., & Citron, C. C. (1981). Sex differentiated free play behavior: Effects of teacher modeling, location, and gender. *Developmental Psychology, 17*, 640–646.

Serbin, L. A., Conner, J. M., Burchardt, C. J., & Citron, C. C. (1979). Effects of peer presence on sex-typing of children's play behavior. *Journal of Experimental Child Psychology, 27*, 303–309.

Serbin, L. A., & Sprafkin, C. (1986). The salience of gender and the process of sex typing in three- to seven-year-old children. *Child Development, 57*, 1188–1199.

Serbin, L. A., Tonick, I. J., & Sternglanz, S. H. (1977). Shaping cooperative cross-sex play. *Child Development, 48*, 924–929.

Sex education and sex related behavior (1986). *Family Planning Perspectives, 18*, 150, 192.

Shaffer, D. (1985). Depression, mania, and suicidal acts. In M. Rutter & L. Hersov (Eds.), *Child and adolescent psychiatry: Modern approaches* (2nd ed.) (pp. 698–719). Oxford: Blackwell Scientific Publications.

Shaffer, D. (1986). In M. Rutter, C. E. Izard, & P. B. Read (Eds.), *Child and adolescent psychiatry: Modern approaches* (pp. 283–396). New York: Guilford.

Shah, F., & Zelnik, M. (1981). Parent and peer influence on sexual behavior, contraceptive use, and pregnancy experience of young women. *Journal of Marriage and the Family, 43*, 339–348.

Shannon, L. W. (1981). *Assessing the relationship of adult criminal careers to juvenile careers.* Washington, DC: National Institute of Juvenile Justice and Delinquency Prevention.

Shantz, C. U. (1983). Social cognition. In P. H. Mussen (Series Ed.), J. H. Flavell & E. M. Markman (Eds.), *Handbook of child psychology: Vol. 3. Cognitive development* (pp. 495–555, 4th ed.). New York: Wiley.

Shapira, A., & Madsen, M. C. (1974). Between- and within-group cooperation and competition among Kibbutz and non-Kibbutz children. *Developmental Psychology, 10,* 140–145.

Sharabany, R., Gershoni, R., & Hoffman, J. E. (1981). Girlfriend, boyfriend: Age and sex differences in intimate friendship. *Developmental Psychology, 17,* 800–808.

Shatz, M., & Gelman, R. (1973). The development of communication skills: Modifications in the speech of young children as a function of the listener. *Monographs of the Society for Research in Child Development, 38* (Serial No. 152).

Sheldrick, C. (1985). Treatment of delinquents. In M. Rutter and L. Hersov (Eds.), *Child and adolescent psychiatry: Modern approaches* (pp. 743–752). Oxford: Blackwell Scientific Publications.

Sherman, J. (1971). Imitation and language development. In H. W. Reese & L. P. Lipsitt (Eds.), *Advances in child development and behavior*. New York: Academic Press.

Shibley-Hyde, J., & Linn, M. C. (1986). *The psychology of gender: Advances through meta-analysis*. Baltimore: Johns Hopkins University Press.

Shinn, M. (1978). Father absence and children's cognitive development. *Psychological Bulletin, 85,* 295–324.

Shiono, P. H., Klebanoff, M. A., Granbard, B. I., Berendes, H. W., & Rhoads, G. G. (1986). Birth weight among women of different ethnic groups. *Journal of the American Medical Association, 255,* 48–52.

Shweder, R., & Bourne, E. J. (1984). Does the concept of the person vary cross-culturally? In R. A. Shweder & R. A. LeVine (Eds.), *Cultural theory: Essays on mind, self, and emotion*. Cambridge: Cambridge University Press.

Siegal, M., & Storey, R. M. (1985). Day care and children's conceptions of moral and social rules. *Child Development, 56,* 1001–1008.

Siegler, R. S. (1983). Information processing approaches to development. In P. H. Mussen (Series Ed.), W. Kessen (Volume Ed.), *Handbook of child psychology: Vol. 1. History, theory, and methods* (pp. 129–212). New York: Wiley.

Siegler, R. S. (1986). Unities across domains in children's strategy choices. In M. Perlmutter (Ed.), *Perspectives on intellectual development. The Minnesota symposia on child psychology* (Vol. 19, pp. 1–48). Hillsdale, NJ: Erlbaum.

Sigel, I. E. (1986). Reflections on the belief-behavior connection: Lessons learned from a research program on parental belief systems and teaching strategies. In R. D. Ashmore & D. M. Brodzinsky (Eds.), *Thinking about the family: Views of parents and children*. Hillsdale, NJ: Erlbaum.

Signorella, M. L., & Liben, L. S. (1984). Recall and reconstruction of gender-related pictures: Effects of attitude, task difficulty, and age. *Child Development, 55,* 393–405.

Silbert, M., & Pines, A. (1981). *Runaway prostitutes*. Unpublished paper, Delancey Street Foundation, San Francisco.

Simmons, R. G., Blyth, D. A., & McKinney, K. L. (1983). The social and psychological effects of puberty on white females. In J. Brooks-Gunn & A. C. Petersen (Eds.), *Girls at puberty: Biological and psychological perspectives* (pp. 229–272). New York: Plenum.

Simmons, R. G., Blyth, D. A., VanCleave, E., & Bush, D. (1979). Entry into early adolescence: The impact of school structure, puberty, and early dating on self-esteem. *American Sociological Review, 44,* 948–967.

Simmons, R. G., & Rosenberg, F. (1975). Sex, sex roles, and self-image. *Journal of Youth and Adolescence, 4,* 229–258.

Simpson, R. L. (1962). Parental influence, anticipatory socialization, and social mobility. *American Sociological Review, 27,* 517–522.

Sinclair, H. (1971). Sensorimotor action patterns as a condition for the acquisition of syntax. In R. Huxley & E. Ingram (Eds.), *Language acquisition: Models and methods*. New York: Academic Press.

Singer, J. L. (1973). *The child's world of make believe*. New York: Academic Press.

Singer, J. L., & Singer, D. G. (1980). *Imaginative play in preschoolers: Some research and theoretical implications*. Paper presented at the meeting of the American Psychological Association, Montreal.

Singleton, L. C., & Asher, S. R. (1979). Racial integration and children's peer preferences: An investigation of developmental and cohort differences. *Child Development, 50,* 936–941.

Siono, P. H., Klebanoff, M. A., Granbard, B. I., Berendes, H. W., & Rhoads, G. G. (1986). Birth weight among women of different ethnic groups. *Journal of the American Medical Association, 255,* 48–52.

Skinner, B. F. (1938). *The behavior of organisms: An experimental analysis*. New York: Appleton-Century-Crofts.

Skodak, M., & Skeels, H. M. (1949). A final follow-up of one hundred adopted children. *Journal of Genetic Psychology, 75,* 85–125.

Slavin, R. E. (1987). Developmental and motivational perspectives on cooperative learning: A reconciliation. *Child Development, 58,* 1161–1167.

Slobin, D. I. (1971). *Psycholinguistics*. Glenview, IL: Scott, Foresman.

Smetana, J. (1981). Preschool children's conceptions of moral and social rules. *Child Development, 52,* 1333–1336.

Smith, N. W. (1976). Twin studies and heritability. *Human Development, 9,* 65–68.

Smith, P. K. (1977). Social and fantasy play in young children. In B. Tizard & D. Marvey (Eds.), *Biology of play*. London: William Heinemann Medical Books.

Smith, P. K. (1982). Does play matter? *Behavioral and Brain Sciences, 5,* 139–184.

Smith, P. K., & Connolly, K. J. (1980). *The ecology of preschool behavior*. Cambridge: Cambridge University Press.

Smith, R. E. (Ed.). (1979). *The subtle revolution: Women at work*. Washington, DC: Urban Institute.

Smith, R., Anderson, D. R., & Fischer, C. (1985). Young children's comprehension of montage. *Child Development, 56,* 962–971.

Smith, S. R. (1975). Religion and the conception of youth in seventeenth-century England. *History of Childhood Quarterly: the Journal of Psychohistory*, 2, 493–516.

Smoking and health: A report of the Surgeon General (1979). (DHEW Publication No. (PHS) 79-50066, U.S. Department of Health, Education and Welfare.) Washington, DC: U.S. Government Printing Office.

Snow, C. E. (1974). *Mother's speech and research: An overview.* Paper presented at the Conference on Language Input and Acquisition, Boston.

Snyder, J., & Patterson, G. (1987). Family interaction and delinquent behavior. In H. C. Quay (Ed.), *Handbook of juvenile delinquency* (pp. 216–243). New York: Wiley.

Society for Research in Child Development. (1973). Ethical standards for research with children. *SRCD Newsletter*, (Winter), 3–4.

Sodian, B., & Wimmer, H. (1987). Children's understanding of inference as a source of knowledge. *Child Development*, 58, 424–433.

Sontag, L. W. (1944). War and fetal maternal relationship. *Marriage and Family Living*, 6, 1–5.

Sontag, L. W., Baker, C. T., & Nelson, V. L. (1958). Mental growth and personality: A longitudinal study. *Monographs of the Society for Research in Child Development*, 23, (Serial No. 68).

Sorensen, R. C. (1973). *Adolescent sexuality in contemporary America: Personal values and sexual behavior ages 13–19.* New York: Abrams.

Spence, J. T. (1977, May). *Traits, roles, and the concept of androgyny.* Paper presented at the Conference on Perspectives on the Psychology of Women, Michigan State University.

Spence, J. T. (1985). Gender identity and its implications for concepts of masculinity and femininity. In T. B. Sonderegger (Ed.), *Nebraska symposium on motivation: Psychology and gender* (Vol. 32). Lincoln: University of Nebraska Press.

Spence, J. T., & Helmreich, R. L. (1978). *Masculinity and femininity: Their psychological dimensions, correlates, and antecedents.* Austin: University of Texas Press.

Spence, J. T., Helmreich, R. L., & Holahan, C. K. (1979). Negative and positive components of psychological masculinity and femininity and their relationships to self-reports of neurotic and acting-out behaviors. *Journal of Personality and Social Psychology*, 37, 1673–1682.

Spickelmier, J. L. (1983). College experience and moral judgment development. Doctoral dissertation. Minneapolis: University of Minnesota Press.

Sroufe, L. A., & Wunsch, J. P. (1972). The development of laughter in the first year of life. *Child Development*, 43, 1326–1344.

Standley, K. (1979). Personal communication. Cited in Y. Brackbill. Obstetrical medication and infant behavior. In J. Osofsky (Ed.), *Handbook of infant development.* New York: Wiley.

Stein, A. H., & Bailey, M. M. (1973). The socialization of achievement orientation in females. *Psychological Bulletin*, 80, 435–366.

Stein, A. H., & Friedrich, L. K. (1975). Impact of television on children and youth. In E. M. Hetherington (Ed.). *Review of child development research*: Vol. 5 (pp. 183–256). Chicago: University of Chicago Press.

Steinberg, L. D. (1985a). *Adolescence.* New York: Knopf.

Steinberg, L. D. (1985b). Psychotic and other severe disorders in adolescence. In M. Rutter & L. Hersov (Eds.) *Child and adolescent psychiatry: Modern approaches* (2nd ed.) (pp. 567–583). Oxford: Blackwell Scientific Publications.

Steinberg, L. D. (1981). Transformation in family relations at puberty. *Developmental Psychology*, 17, 833–840.

Steinberg, L. D., Catalano, R., & Dooley, D. (1981). Economic antecedents of child abuse and neglect. *Child Development*, 52, 975–985.

Steinberg, L. D., & Hill, J. P. (1978). Patterns of family interaction as a function of age, the onset of puberty, and formal thinking. *Developmental Psychology*, 14, 683–684.

Steinberg, L. D., & Silverberg, S. B. (1986). The vicissitudes of autonomy in early adolescence. *Child Development*, 57, 841–851.

Steinschneider, A. (1975). Implications of the sudden infant death syndrome for the study of sleep in infancy. In A. D. Pick (Ed.), *Minnesota Symposia on Child Psychology* (Vol. 9). Minneapolis: University of Minnesota Press.

Stenberg, C., & Campos, J. J. (1983). The development of the expression of anger in human infants. In M. Lewis & C. Saarni (Eds.), *The socialization of affect.* New York: Plenum.

Stephenson, S. P. (1979). From school to work: A transition with job-search implications. *Youth and Society*, 11, 114–133.

Stern, W. (1930). *Psychology of early childhood.* (6th ed.) (A. Barwell, trans.) New York: Henry Holt.

Sternberg, R. J. (Ed.). (1984). *Mechanisms of cognitive development.* New York: W. H. Freeman.

Sternberg, R. J. (1985). *Beyond IQ: A triarchic theory of human intelligence.* Cambridge: Cambridge University Press.

Sternberg, R. J., & Powell, J. S. (1983). The development of intelligence. In P. H. Mussen (Series Ed.), J. H. Flavell & E. M. Markman (Eds.), *Handbook of child psychology: Vol. 3. Cognitive development* (pp. 341–419, 4th ed.). New York: Wiley.

Sternberg, R. J., & Suben, J. G. (1986). The socialization of intelligence. In M. Perlmutter (Ed.), *Perspectives on intellectual development. The Minnesota symposia on child psychology* (Vol. 19, pp. 201–236). Hillsdale, NJ: Erlbaum.

Sternglanz, S. H., & Serbin, L. A. (1974). Sex role stereotyping in children's television programs. *Developmental Psychology*, 10, 710–715.

Stevenson, H. W., & Newman, R. S. (1986). Long-term prediction of achievement and attitudes in mathematics and reading. *Child Development*, 37, 646–659.

Stevenson, H. W., Parker, T., Wilkinson, A., Bonnaveaux, B., & Gonzalez, M. (1978). Schooling environment and cognitive development: A cross cultural study. *Monographs of the Society for Research in Child Development*, 43, (No. 175).

Stevenson, H. W., Stigler, J. W., Lee, S., Lucker, G. W., Kitamura, S., & Hsu, C. (1985). Cognitive performance and academic achievement of Japanese, Chinese, and American children. *Child Development, 56,* 718–734.

Stewart, R. B. (1983). Sibling attachment relationships: Child-infant interactions in the strange situation. *Developmental Psychology, 19,* 191–199.

Stigler, J. W., Lee, S., & Stevenson, H. W. (1987). Mathematics classrooms in Japan, Taiwan, and the United States. *Child Development, 58,* 1272–1285.

Stilwell, R. (1983). Social relationships in primary school children as seen by children, mothers, and teachers. Unpublished doctoral thesis, University of Cambridge.

Stipek, D., & McCroskey, J. (1989). Investing in children: Government and workplace policies for parents. *American Psychologist, 44,* 434–440.

Stoller, R. J. (1980). Gender identity disorders. In H. I. Kaplan, A. M. Freedman, & B. J. Sadock (Eds.), *Comprehensive textbook of psychiatry* (Vol. 2) (3rd ed.). Baltimore: Williams & Wilkins.

Stone, L. J., & Church, J. (1973). *Childhood and adolescence: A psychology of the growing person* (3rd ed.). New York: Random House.

Stoneman, Z., Cantrell, M. L., & Hoover-Dempsey, K. (1983). The association between play materials and social behavior in a mainstreamed preschool: A naturalistic investigation. *Journal of Applied Developmental Psychology, 4,* 163–174.

Strain, P. S. (1985). Programmatic research on peers as intervention agents for socially isolate classmates. In B. H. Schneider, J. E. Ledingham, & K. H. Rubin (Eds.), *Children's peer relations: Issues in assessment and intervention.* New York: Springer-Verlag.

Stratton, P. (Ed.). (1982). *Psychobiology of the human newborn.* New York: Wiley.

Strayer, F. F., Waring, S., & Rushton, J. P. (1979). Social constraints on naturally occurring preschool altruism. *Ethology and Sociobiology, 1,* 3–11.

Strayer, J. (1986). Children's attributions regarding the situational determinants of emotion in self and others. *Developmental Psychology, 22,* 649–654.

Streissguth, A. P., Barr, H. M., & Martin, D. C. (1983). Maternal alcohol use and neonatal habituation assessed with the Brazelton Scale. *Child Development, 43,* 1109–1118.

Streissguth, A. P., Martin, D. C., Barr, H. M., Sondman, B. M., Kirchner, G. L., & Darby, B. L. (1984). Intra-uterine alcohol and nicotine exposure: Attention and reaction time in 4-year-old children. *Developmental Psychology, 20,* 533–541.

Striegel-Moore, R. H., Silberstein, L. R., & Rodin, J. (1986). Toward an understanding of risk factors for bulimia. *American Psychologist, 41,* 246–263.

Stuckey, M. F., McGhee, P. E., & Bell, N. J. (1982). Parent-child interaction: The influence of maternal employment. *Developmental Psychology, 18,* 635–644.

Stunkard, A. J. (1980). Obesity. In H. I. Kaplan, A. M. Freedman, & B. J. Sadock (Eds.), *Comprehensive textbook of psychiatry* (Vol. 2), (3rd ed.) (pp. 1872–1882). Baltimore: Williams & Wilkins.

Sulloway, F. (1972). *Family constellations, sibling rivalry, and scientific revolutions.* Unpublished manuscript, Harvard University, Cambridge, MA.

Sully, (1896). *Studies of childhood.* New York: Appleton.

Super, C. M. (1976). Environmental effects on motor development: The case of African infant precocity. *Developmental Medicine and Child Neurology, 18,* 561–567.

Super, D. E. (1967). *The psychology of careers.* New York: Harper & Row.

Super, D. E. (1980). A life span, life space approach to career development. *Journal of Vocational Behavior, 16,* 282–298.

Sutton-Smith, B., & Rosenberg, B. G. (1968). Sibling consensus on power tactics. *Journal of Genetic Psychology. 112,* 63–72.

Sutton-Smith, B., & Rosenberg, B. G. (1970). *The sibling.* New York: Holt, Rinehart and Winston.

Sutton-Smith, B., Rosenberg, B. G., & Landy, F. (1968). The interaction of father absence and sibling presence on cognitive abilities. *Child Development, 39,* 1213–1221.

Swope, G. W. (1980). Kids and cults: Who joins and why? *Media and Methods, 16,* 18–21.

Sylva, K., Bruner, J. S., & Genova, P. (1976). The role of play in the problem solving of children three to seven years old. In J. S. Bruner, A. Jolly, & K. Sylva (Eds.), *Play: Its role in development and evolution.* London: Kenwood, 1976.

Tabachnick, N. (1980). The interlocking psychologies of suicide and adolescence. *Adolescent Psychiatry, 9,* 399–410.

Tanner, J. M. (1970). Physical growth. In P. H. Mussen (Ed.), *Carmichael's manual of child psychology* (Vol. 2) (3rd ed.). New York: Wiley.

Tanner, J. M. (1971). Sequence, tempo, and individual variation in the growth and development of boys and girls aged twelve to sixteen. *Daedalus, 100*(4), 907–930.

Tapp, J. L., & Levine, F. J. (1972). Compliance from kindergarten to college: A speculative research note. *Journal of Adolescence and Youth, 1,* 233–249.

Taylor, A. R., Asher, S. R., & Williams, G. A. (1987). The social adaptation of mainstreamed mildly retarded children. *Child Development, 58,* 1321–1334.

Taylor, A., III (1986, August 18). Why women managers are bailing out. *Fortune,* pp. 16–23.

Teicher, J. (1973). A solution to the chronic problem of living: Adolescent attempted suicide. In J. C. Schoolar (Ed.), *Current issues in adolescent psychiatry*. New York: Brunner/Mazel.

Templin, M. C. (1957). Certain language skills in children. *Institute of Child Welfare Monographs*, (Serial No. 26). Minneapolis: University of Minnesota Press.

Thatcher, R. W., Walker, R. A., & Giudice, S. (1987). Human cerebral hemispheres develop at different rates and ages. *Science*, 236, 1110–1113.

Thomas, A., & Chess, S. (1977). *Temperament and development*. New York: Brunner/Mazel.

Thomas, A., Chess, S., & Birch, H. G. (1968). *Temperament and behavior disorders in children*. New York: New York University Press.

Thomas, N. G., & Berk, L. E. (1981). Effects of school environments on the development of young children's creativity. *Child Development*, 52, 1153–1162.

Thompson, R. A., Lamb, M. E., & Estes, D. (1982). Stability of mother-infant attachment and its relationship to changing life circumstances in an unselected middle-class sample. *Child Development*, 53, 144–148.

Thompson, V. D. (1974). Family size: Implicit policies and assumed psychological outcomes. *Journal of Social Issues*, 30, 93–124.

Thorndike, R. L., Hagen, E. P., & Sattler, J. M. (1986). *The Stanford-Binet Intelligence Scale: Fourth edition. Guide for administering and scoring*. Chicago: Riverside Publishing.

Tienari, P., Sorri, A., Lahti, I., Naarla, M., Wahlberg, J. M., Pohjola, J., & Wynne, L. C. Genetic and psychosocial factors in schizophrenia: The Finnish adoptive family study. *Schizophrenia Bulletin*, 13, 477–484.

Tinbergen, N. (1951). *The study of instinct*. Oxford: Oxford University Press.

Tittle, C. K. (1980, September). *Life plans and values of high school students*. Paper presented at the annual meeting of the American Psychological Association, Montreal.

Tittle, C. K. (1981). *Careers and family: Sex roles and adolescent life plans*. Beverly Hills, CA: Sage Publications.

Tobin-Richards, M., Boxer, A., & Petersen, A. C. (1984). The psychological impact of pubertal change: Sex differences in perceptions of self during early adolescence. In J. Brooks-Gunn & A. C. Petersen (Eds.), *Girls at puberty: Biological, psychological, and social perspectives*. New York: Plenum.

Toder, N. L., & Marcia, J. E. (1973). Ego identity status and response to conformity pressure in college women. *Journal of Personality and Social Psychology*, 26, 287–294.

Tomlinson-Keasy, C., & Keasy, C. B. (1974). The mediating role of cognitive development in moral judgment. *Child Development*, 45, 291–298.

Toner, I. J., Moore, L. P., & Emmons, B. A. (1980). The effect of being labeled on subsequent self-control in children. *Child Development*, 51, 618–621.

Torgersen, A. M., & Kringlen, E. (1978). Genetic aspects of temperamental differences in infants: A study of same-sexed twins. *Journal of the American Academy of Child Psychiatry*, 17, 433–444.

Trasler, G. (1987). Biogenetic factors. In H. C. Quay (Ed.), *Handbook of juvenile delinquency* (pp. 139–183). New York: Wiley.

Trevarthen, C. (1974). Conversations with a two-month-old. *New Scientist*, 62, 230–233.

Trevarthen, C. (1977). Descriptive analyses of infant communicative behavior. In H. R. Schaffer (Ed.), *Studies in mother-infant interaction*. London: Academic Press.

Turiel, E. (1983). Interaction and development in social cognition. In E. T. Higgins, D. N. Ruble, W. W. Hartup (Eds.), *Social cognition and social development*. New York: Cambridge University Press.

Turiel, E., Edwards, C. P., & Kohlberg, L. (1978). Moral development in Turkish children, adolescents, and young adults. *Journal of Cross-Cultural Psychology*, 9, 75–86.

Turkle, S. (1984). *The second self: Computers and the human spirit*. New York: Simon & Schuster.

Tyack, D., & Ingram, D. (1977). Children's production and comprehension of questions. *Journal of Child Language*, 4, 211–224.

Ugurel-Semin, R. (1952). Moral behavior and moral judgment of children. *Journal of Abnormal and Social Psychology*, 47, 463–474.

U. S. Commission on Civil Rights. (1977). *Window dressing on the set: Women and minorities on television*. Washington, DC: U. S. Government Printing Office.

U.S. Bureau of the Census (1981). *Statistical abstract of the United States: 1981*. Washington, DC (102 ed.).

U.S. Bureau of the Census. (1986a). *Marital status and living arrangements: March 1985*. Current Population Reports. Washington, DC: U.S. Government Printing Office.

U.S. Bureau of the Census (1986b). *Statistical abstract of the United States: 1987* (107th ed.). Washington, DC: U.S. Government Printing Office.

U.S. Bureau of the Census (1987). *Statistical abstract of the United States, 1988*. Washington, DC: U.S. Government Printing Office.

U.S. Department of Labor, Bureau of Labor Statistics (1986, February). *Wives' and mothers' labor force activity includes those with infants*. Monthly Labor Review.

U.S. Department of Labor, Bureau of Labor Statistics (1986). *Occupational projections and training data*. Washington, DC: U.S. Government Printing Office.

U.S. Department of Labor, Women's Bureau (1984). *Time of change: 1983 handbook on women workers.* Bulletin 298. Washington, DC: U.S. Government Printing Office.

U.S. Federal Bureau of Investigation. *Crime in the United States, annual.*

Van Doorninck, W. J., Caldwell, B. M., Wright, C., & Frankenburg, W. K. (1981). The relationship between 12-month home stimulation and school achievement. *Child Development, 52,* 1080–1083.

Van Ijzendorn, M. H., & Kroonenberg, P. M. (1988). Cross-cultural patterns of attachment: A meta-analysis of the Strange Situation. *Child Development, 59,* 147–156.

Vandell, D. L., & Corasaniti, M. A. (1988). The relation between third graders' after-school care and social, academic, and emotional functioning. *Child Development 59,* 868–875.

Vandell, D. L., Henderson, V. K., & Wilson, K. S. (1988). A longitudinal study of children with day-care experiences of varying quality. *Child Development, 59,* 1286–1292.

Vandell, D. L., Wilson, K. S., & Whalen, W. I. (1981). Birth order and social experience differences in infant peer interaction. *Developmental Psychology, 17,* 438–445.

Vandenberg, S. G., Singer, S. M., & Pauls, D. L. (1986). *The heredity of behavior disorders in adults and children.* New York: Plenum.

Vatter, M. (1981). Intelligenz und regionale Herkunft. Eine Langsschnittstudie im Kanton Bern. In A. H. Walter (Ed.), *Region und Sozialisation* (Vol. 1). Stuttgart: Frommann-Holzbook.

Vaughn, C. E., Snyder, K. S., Freeman, W., Jones, S., Falloon, T. R. A., & Libeman, R. P. (1982). Family factors in schizophrenia relapse. *Schizophrenia Bulletin, 8,* 425–428.

Veroff, J. (1969). Social comparison and the development of achievement motivation. In C. P. Smith (Ed.), *Achievement-related motives in children.* New York: Russell Sage.

Visher, C. A., & Roth, J. A. (1986). Participation in criminal careers. In A. Blumstein, J. Cohen, J. A. Roth, & C. A. Visher (Eds.), *Criminal careers and "career criminals"* (Vol. 1) (pp. 211–291). Washington, DC: National Academy Press.

Vogel, S. R., Broverman, I. K., Broverman, D. M., Clarkson, F. E., & Rosenkrantz, P. S. (1970). Maternal employment and perception of sex roles among college students. *Developmental Psychology, 3,* 384–391.

Vollmer, F. (1986). The relationship between expectancy and academic achievement—How can it be explained? *British Journal of Educational Psychology, 56,* 64–74.

Voorhies, T. M., & Vanucci, R. C. (1984). Perinatal cerebral hypoxia-ischemia: Diagnosis and management. In H. B. Sarnot (Ed.), *Topics in neonatal neurology.* New York: Grune & Stratton.

Vorster, J. (1974). Mother's speech to children: Some methodological considerations. *Publications of the Institute for General Linguistics* (No. 8). Amsterdam: U.S. Department of Amsterdam.

Vygotsky, L. S. (1962). *Thought and language.* New York: Wiley.

Wachs, T. D. (1979). Proximal experience and early cognitive intellectual development: The physical environment. *Merrill-Palmer Quarterly, 25,* 3–41.

Wagatsuma, H. (1977). Some aspects of the contemporary Japanese family: Once Confucian, now fatherless. In The Family, *Daedalus, 106,* 181–210.

Wagner, S., Winner, E., Cicchetti, D., & Gardner, H. (1981). Metaphorical mapping in human infants. *Child Development, 52,* 728–731.

Walker, E., & Emory, E. (1985). Commentary: Interpretive bias and behavioral genetic research. *Child Development, 56,* 775–778.

Walker, L. J. (1984). Sex differences in development of moral reasoning: A critical review. *Child Development, 55,* 677–691.

Wallerstein, J. S., & Kelly, J. B. (1980). *Surviving the breakup: How children and parents cope with divorce.* New York: Basic Books.

Wartella, E., & Hunter, L. (1983). Children and the formats of television advertising. In M. Meyer (Ed.), *Children and the formal features of television* (pp. 144–165). Munchen: K. G. Saur.

Waterman, A. S. (1982). Identity development from adolescence to adulthood: An extension of theory and a review of research. *Developmental Psychology, 18,* 341–358.

Waterman, A. S. (1984). Identity formation: Discovery or creation? *Journal of Early Adolescence, 4,* 329–341.

Waterman, A. S., & Waterman, C. K. (1974). A longitudinal study of changes in ego identity status during the freshman to the senior year in college. *Developmental Psychology, 10,* 387–392.

Waters, E., Wippman, J., & Stroufe, L. A. (1979). Attachment, positive affect, and competence in the peer group. *Child Development, 50,* 821–829.

Watson, J. B. (1928). *Psychological care of infant and child.* New York: Norton.

Watson, J. B. (1967) (Originally published, 1930). *Behaviorism.* Chicago: University of Chicago Press.

Watson, J. D., & Crick, F. H. C. (1953). Molecular structure of nucleic acids: A structure for deoxyribose nucleic acid. *Nature, 171,* 737–738.

Waxman, S. (1987, April). *Linguistic and conceptual organization in 30-month-old children.* Presented at a meeting of the Society for Research in Child Development, Baltimore.

Webb, P. A., & Abrahamson, A. A. (1977). Stages of egocentrism in children's use of "this" and "that": A different point of view. *Journal of Child Language, 3,* 349–367.

Webb, T. P., Bundey, S. E., Thake, A. I., & Todd, J. (1986). Population incidence and segregation ratios in the Martin-Bell Syndrome. *American Journal of Medical Genetics, 23,* 573–580.

Weiner, B., & Handel, S. J. (1985). A cognition-emotion-action sequence: anticipated emotional consequences of causal attributions and reported communication strategy. *Developmental Psychology, 21,* 102–107.

Weiner, I. B. (1970). *Psychological disturbance in adolescence.* New York: Wiley.

Weiner, I. B. (1980). Psychopathology in adolescence. In J. Adelson (Ed.), *Handbook of adolescent psychology* (pp. 447–471). New York: Wiley.

Weiner, I. B., & del Gaudio (1976). Psychopathology in adolescence: An epidemiological study. *Archives of General Psychiatry, 33,* 187–193.

Weiner, I. B., & Elkind, D. (1972). *Child development: A core approach.* New York: Wiley.

Weinraub, M., & Wolf, B. M. (1983). Effects of stress and social supports on mother-child interactions in single and two-parent families. *Child Development, 54,* 1297–1311.

Weinstein, C. S. (1979). The physical environment of the school: A review of the research. *Review of Educational Research, 49,* 577–610.

Weisberg, D. K. (1985). *Children of the night: A study of adolescent prostitution.* Lexington, MA: Heath.

Weiss, R. J. (1982). Understanding moral thought: Effects on moral reasoning and decision-making. *Development Psychology, 18,* 852–861.

Weissman, M. M., & Boyd, J. H. (1983). Affective disorders: Epidemiology. In H. I. Kaplan & B. J. Sadock (Eds.), *Comprehensive textbook of psychiatry,* Vol. I. (pp. 764–768). Baltimore: Williams and Wilkins.

Weissman, M. M., Gershon, E. S., Kidd, K. K., Brusoff, B. A., Leckman, J. F., Dibble, E., Hamovit, J., Thompson, W. D., Pauls, D. L., & Guroff, J. J. (1984). Psychiatric disorders in the relatives of probands with affective disorders. *Archives of General Psychiatry, 41,* 13–21.

Wellman, H. M., & Lempers, J. D. (1977). The naturalistic communicative ability of two-year-olds. *Child Development, 43,* 1052–1057.

Werker, J. F., & Tees, R. C. (1984). Cross-language speech perception: Evidence for a perceptual reorganization during the first year of life. *Infant Behavior and Development, 7,* 49–64.

Werner, E. E. (1979). *Cross-cultural child development.* Monterey, CA: Brooks-Cole.

Werner, E. E., Bierman, J. M., & French, F. E. (1971). *The children of Kauai: A longitudinal study from the prenatal period to age ten.* Honolulu: University of Hawaii Press.

Werner, E. E., & Smith, R. S. (1982). *Vulnerable but invincible.* New York: McGraw-Hill.

Wessel, (1986, September 22). Growing gap: U.S. rich and poor gain in numbers. *The Wall Street Journal,* pp. 1, 20.

West, D. J. (1982). *Delinquency: Its roots, careers and prospects.* London: Heinemann Educational.

West, D. J., & Farrington, D. P. (1973). *Who becomes delinquent?* London: Heinemann Educational.

Weston, D., & Turiel, E. (1980). Act-rule relations: Children's concepts of social rules. *Developmental Psychology, 16,* 417–424.

Wetzel, R. (1976). Hopelessness, depression, and suicide intent. *Archives of General Psychiatry, 33,* 1069–1073.

Whaley, L. F. (1974). *Understanding inherited disorders.* St. Louis: Mosby.

White, C. B., Bushnell, W., & Regnemer, J. L. (1978). Moral development in Bahamian school children: A three-year examination of Kohlberg's stages of cognitive development. *Developmental Psychology, 14,* 58–65.

Whiting, B. B., & Whiting, J. W. M. (1973). Altruistic and egotistic behavior in six cultures. In L. Nader & T. W. Maretzki (Eds.), *Cultural illness and health: Essays in human adaptation.* Washington, DC: American Anthropological Association.

Whiting, B. B., & Whiting, J. W. M. (1975). *Children of six cultures: A psychocultural analysis.* Cambridge, MA: Harvard University Press.

Wilks, J. (1986). The relative importance of parents and friends in adolescent decision making. *Journal of Youth and Adolescence, 15,* 323–334.

Willerman, L. (1979). Effects of families on intellectual development. *American Psychologist, 34,* 923–929.

William T. Grant Foundation Commission on Work, Family, and Citizenship (1988). *The forgotten half: Non-college youth in America: An interim report on the school-to-work transition.* Washington, DC: The Commission.

Williams, P. A., Haertel, E. H., Walberg, H. J., & Haertel, G. D. (1982). The impact of leisure-time television on school learning: A research synthesis. *American Educational Research Journal, 19,* 19–50.

Williams, T. M. (Ed.). (1986). *The impact of television: A natural experiment involving three towns.* New York: Academic Press.

Wilson, H. (1980). Parental supervision: A neglected aspect of delinquency. *British Journal of Criminology, 20,* 203–235.

Wilson, R. S. (1972). Twins: Early mental development. *Science, 175,* 914–917.

Wilson, R. S. (1975). Twins: Patterns of cognitive development as measured on the Wechsler Preschool and Primary Scale of Intelligence. *Developmental Psychology, 11,* 126–134.

Wilson, R. S. (1977). Twins and siblings: Concordance for school-age mental development. *Child Development, 48,* 21–216.

Wilson, R. S. (1983). The Louisville twin study: Developmental synchronies in behavior. *Child Development, 54,* 298–316.

Wilson, R. S. (1985). Risk and resilience in early mental development. *Developmental Psychology, 21,* 795–805.

Wilson, R. S., & Harpring, E. B. (1972). Mental and motor development in infant twins. *Developmental Psychology, 7,* 277–287.

Winn, M. (1987). *Unplugging the plug-in drug.* New York: Penguin.

E. (1988). *The point of words.* Cambridge, MA: Harvard University Press.

r, G. (1975). Heredity in the affective disorders. In E. Anthony & T. Benedek (Eds.), *Depression in human existence.* Boston: Little,
own.

Wittig, M. A., & Petersen, A. C. (Eds.) (1979). *Sex-related differences in cognitive functioning.* New York: Academic Press.

Wohlford, P., Santrock, J., Berger, S., & Liberman, D. (1971). Older brothers' influence on sex-typed, aggressive, and dependent behavior in father-absent children. *Developmental Psychology,* 4, 124–134.

Wolensky, R. P. (1977). College students in the fifties: The silent generation revisited. In S. C. Feinstein & P. L. Giovacchini (Eds.), *Adolescent psychiatry: Developmental and clinical studies* (Vol. 5). New York: Aronson.

Wolf, D. P., & Grollman, S. H. (1982). Ways of playing. *Contributions to Human Development,* 6, 46–63.

Wolf, D. P. (1984). Repertoire, style and format. In P. Smith (Ed.), *Play in animals and humans* (pp. 175–193). Oxford: Basil Blackwell.

Wolfe, D. A., Katell, A., & Drabman, R. S. (1982). Parents' and preschool children's choices of disciplinary child-rearing methods. *Journal of Applied Developmental Psychology,* 3, 167–176.

Wolff, P. H. (1987). *The development of behavioral states and the expression of emotions in early infancy.* Chicago: University of Chicago Press.

Wood, W. (1987). Meta-analytic review of sex differences in group performance. *Psychological Bulletin,* 102 53–71.

Wooden, K. (1976). *Keeping in the playtime of others.* New York: McGraw-Hill.

Wright, J. C., & Huston, A. C. (1983). A matter of form: Potentials of television for young viewers. *American Psychologist,* 38 835–843.

Wright, P. H., & Keple, T. W. (1981). Friends and parents of a sample of high school juniors: An exploratory study of relationship intensity and interpersonal rewards. *Journal of Marriage and the Family,* 43 559–570.

Wright, R. (1945). *Black boy: A record of childhood and youth.* New York: Harper & Row.

Wroblewski, R., & Huston, A. C. (1987). Televised occupational stereotypes and their effects on early adolescents: Are they changing? *Journal of Early Adolescence,* 7, 283–298.

Wynne, L. C., Singer, M. T., Bartko, J.J., & Toohey, M. (1976). Schizophrenics and their families: Recent research on parental communication. In J. M. Tanner (Ed.), *Psychiatric research: The widening perspective.* New York: International Universities Press.

Yando, R., Seitz, V., & Zigler, E. (1978). *Imitation in developmental perspective.* Hillsdale, NJ: Erlbaum.

Yankelovich, D. (1969). *Generations apart.* New York: CBS News.

Yankelovich, D. (1974). *The new morality: A profile of American youth in the 1970s.* New York: McGraw-Hill.

Yankelovich, D. (1981). *New rules: Searching for self-fulfillment in a world turned upside down.* New York: Random House.

Yarrow, M. R., & Waxler, C. Z. (1976). Dimensions and correlates of prosocial behavior in young children. *Child Development,* 47, 118–125.

Yarrow, M. R., Scott, P. M., & Waxler, C. Z. (1973). Learning concern for others. *Developmental Psychology,* 8, 240–260.

Younger, B. A., & Cohen, L. B. (1986). Developmental changes in infants' perception of correlations among attributes. *Child Development,* 57, 803–815.

Youniss, J. (1980). *Parents and peers in social development: A Sullivan-Piaget perspective.* Chicago: University of Chicago Press.

Youniss, J. (1983). Social construction of adolescence by adolescents and parents. In H. D. Grotevant and C. R. Cooper (Eds.), *Adolescent development in the family* (pp. 93–109). San Francisco: Jossey-Bass.

Youniss, J., & Smollar, J. (1985). *Adolescent relations with mothers, fathers, and friends.* Chicago: University of Chicago Press.

Zabin, L. S., Kantner, J. F., & Zelnik, M. (1979). The risk of adolescent pregnancy in the first months of intercourse. *Family Planning Perspectives,* 11, 215–222.

Zahn-Waxler, C., Radke-Yarrow, M. & King, R. A. (1979). Child rearing and children's pro-social initiation toward victims of distress. *Child Development,* 50, 319–330.

Zelazo, N. A., Zelazo, P. R., & Kolb, S. (1972). *Science,* 176, 314–315.

Zelnik, M., & Kantner, J. F. (1977). Sexual and contraceptive experience of young unmarried women in the United States, 1976 and 1971. *Family Planning Perspectives,* 9, 55–71.

Zelnik, M., & Kantner, J. F. (1980). Sexual activity, contraceptive use, and pregnancy among metropolitan-area teenagers: 1971–1979. *Family Planning Perspectives,* 12, 230–237.

Zigler, E. (1980). Controlling child abuse: Do we have the knowledge and/or the will? In G. Gerbner, C. J. Ross, and E. Zigler (Eds.), *Child abuse: An agenda for action.* New York: Oxford University Press.

Zigler, E., & Valentine, J. (Eds.). (1979). *Project Head Start: A legacy of the war on poverty.* New York: Free Press.

Zigler, E., Abelson, W. D., & Seitz, V. (1973). Motivational factors in the performance of economically disadvantaged children on the Peabody Picture Vocabulary Test. *Child Development,* 44, 294–302.

Zigler, E., Abelson, W. D., Trickett, P. K., & Seitz, V. (1982). Is an intervention program necessary in order to improve economically disadvantaged children's IQ scores? *Child Development,* 53, 340–348.

Zill, N. (1985). *Happy, healthy and insecure.* New York: Doubleday.

Zillman, D., Williams, B. R., Bryant, J., Boynton, K. R., & Wolf, M. A. (1980). Acquisition of information from educational television programs as a function of differentially paced humorous inserts. *Journal of Educational Psychology,* 72, 170–180.

Zimmerman, B. J. (1984). Children's development of associative memory: A social learning view. In C. J. Brainerd & V. F. Rayne (Eds.), *Developmental psychology* (pp. 259–270). Amsterdam: Elsevier Science Publishers.

NAME INDEX

Abel, E. L., 73
Abelson, W. D., 360
Abraham, K. G., 621
Abramovitch, R., 497
Achenbach, T. M., 415, 438, 677
Adams, G. R., 607, 621, 644
Adams, L. T., 306, 385
Adamson, L. B., 138, 251
Adamsons, K., 74
Adelson, J., 605, 621, 622, 642, 643
Adler, L. E., 54
Adler, R., 348
Adler, T. F., 363
Adolescent Pregnancy, 596, 597
Ageton, S. S., 662, 667
Ahlstrom, W. M., 672
Ainsworth, Mary D. S., 156, 157, 162, 165
Alan Guttmacher Institute, 69, 594
Albarran, L., 115
Alejandro-Wright, M. N., 403
Allen, L., 344
Allen, M. C., 80, 558
Allport, Gordon, 38
Almquist, E. M., 634
Almy, M., 427, 437
Alvarez, W., 506
Aman, C., 319
Amatruda, C. S., 104, 106
American Psychiatric Association, 55, 682
American Psychological Association, 27, 28
Ames, L. B., 15, 104
Anastasi, A., 338, 342, 345, 346
Anderka, M., 72
Anderson, D. R., 288, 315, 321, 542, 546, 547
Anderson, E. S., 228, 238
Andres, D., 506, 634
Angrist, S. S., 634
Anthony, E. J., 79
Apaswol, K. N., 72
Apgar, V., 62, 67, 73, 75, 77, 79, 81
Appelbaum, M. I., 344
Appenzeller, T., 121
Applegate, J. L., 480
Arbuthnot, J., 671
Arend, R., 163
Areshansel, C. S., 630, 631
Aristotle, 568
Armstrong, J. S., 671
Aronfreed, J., 486

Aronson, E., 532
Arsenio, W. F., 363
Asher, S. R., 437–439, 533
Ashmore, R. D., 479, 480, 620
Astin, A. W., 585, 636, 637, 645
Attanasio, A., 569
Atwater, J. B., 396
Auerbach, J., 190
Augsbach, L. H., 318
Avery, A. W., 602
Avery, Oswald, 39
Ayers-Lopez, S., 603, 605

Babson, S. G., 75
Bacas, H., 626, 638, 640
Bachman, J. G., 586, 600, 606, 629, 631, 632, 636, 637, 643, 645, 647, 654–656, 662, 671
Bacon, M. K., 479, 480
Baer, D. M., 262, 302
Bahr, H. M., 643
Bailey, M. M., 349, 353, 356, 363
Baillargeon, R., 284, 285
Bakeman, R., 138
Baker, B. L., 601
Baker, C. T., 344
Baker, L., 684
Baker, N., 54
Baldwin, W., 588, 590
Ball, L., 619
Ball, S., 370
Banducci, R., 634
Bandura, Albert, 17, 349, 385, 387, 444, 538
Bank, S., 495
Barnes, G. M., 662
Barnes, H., 601
Barnes, J., 349
Barnes, K. E., 427
Barnes, V. E., 678
Barnett, K. C., 413
Barnett, M. A., 461
Barnett, R. C., 402
Baron, R. A., 24
Barr, H. M., 74
Barrett, C., 507
Bar-Tal, D., 350, 458
Bartko, J. J., 601
Baruch, G. K., 402, 634

Bates, E., 226, 232
Bates, J. E., 469, 478
Battaglia, F. C., 80, 81
Baumrind, Diana, 363, 456, 458, 464, 491–495, 599, 600
Beach, F., 590
Beck, A. T., 678
Beck, J., 62, 67, 73, 75, 77, 79, 81
Behrman, R. E., 73–75
Belensky, M. F., 642
Bell, Alan P., 590–592, 633
Bell, N. J., 506
Bell, R., 574, 577, 578, 584, 585, 588, 592, 606, 607
Bell, R. O., 481
Bellack, D. R., 318
Belsky, J., 164, 170, 478
Bem, Sandra L., 394, 395, 399–401, 623, 624
Benda, G. I., 75
Bender, B. G., 53
Benedict, H., 226, 251
Benson, 671
Berenedes, H. W., 80
Berger, S., 498
Berk, L. E., 526
Berko, Jean, 235
Berkowitz, L., 25
Berndt, T. J., 437, 497, 603–605
Bernstein, Anne, 327
Bernstein, B., 252
Berry, G., 549
Bersoff, D. N., 361
Bertenthal, B. I., 108
Bertoncini, J., 223
Bhatia, V. P., 72
Bianchi, E. C., 678
Bias, Len, 657
Bierman, J. M., 78
Bifulco, A., 680
Bigner, J. J., 497
Bijou, S., 262
Biller, H. D., 501
Binet, Alfred, 267, 341
Birch, H. G., 469
Biron, L., 671
Bishop, J. E., 53
Black, J. E., 104
Blackwelder, D. E., 488
Blackwell, J., 353
Blaney, N., 532

Blasi, A., 456, 642
Blass, E. M., 123
Blehar, M. C., 156
Bliss, D. C., 671
Block, J., 444, 457, 458
Block, Jeanne H., 364, 444, 600, 623, 624
Bloom, L. M., 229, 234, 236, 243, 254
Blum, R. H., 600
Blyth, D. A., 574, 579, 580, 607
Bogatz, G. A., 370
Boggiano, A. K., 353
Bonnaveaux, B., 338
Borek, E., 39
Bornstein, M. H., 101, 110
Borow, H., 625, 628
Borton, R. W., 112
Botkin, P. T., 286
Bouchard, T. J., Jr., 47
Bourgeois, J. P., 104
Bourne, E., 621
Bowerman, M. F., 228, 246, 310
Bowlby, John, 153, 156–158
Boxer, A. M., 570, 573, 574, 577, 580,
    600
Boyd, J. H., 677, 682
Boyer, M., 619
Boykin, A. W., 359
Boyle, J. M., 662
Boynton, K. R., 547
Brackbill, Y., 74
Bradley, R. H., 362, 365
Brady, J. E., 438
Braine, M. D. S., 230
Brainerd, C. J., 284
Braithwaite, J., 669, 670
Brand, D., 635
Brandt, I., 80
Brannigan, M. A., 640
Bransford, J. D., 265, 317
Braukman, C. J., 302, 675
Brazelton, T. B., 91
Brazie, J. F., 80
Bregman, J. D., 51, 53
Breitenbucher, M., 507
Brennan, T., 602, 664
Brenner, J., 189
Brent, R. L., 75
Bretherton, I., 158, 226, 232, 408, 411,
    413
Bricker, W., 537
Brim, O. G., 210, 496
Brinkley, J., 656
Brittain, C. V., 604
Brody, G. H., 481
Broman, S. H., 356–358
Bromley, D. B., 433
Bronfenbrenner, Urie, 481, 506, 552–553,
    633, 634
Bronson, W., 426
Brook, J. S., 662, 663
Brooks-Gunn, Jeanne, 200, 202, 365, 577,
    595, 596
Brophy, J., 531

Broverman, J. K., 634
Broverman, M. D., 634
Brown, A. L., 265, 326, 583
Brown, A. W., 317
Brown, B. B., 603, 604
Brown, G. E., 540
Brown, G. W., 680
Brown, Harold (Peewee), 674–675
Brown, Roger, 218, 232, 246
Brown, W. T., 53
Brownstone, J. E., 603
Bruch, H., 684
Bruner, Jerome S., 186, 226, 253, 383
Brunnquell, D., 507
Brunswick, A. F., 662
Bryant, B. J., 497
Bryant, J., 547
Brynner, J., 671
Buchsbaum, K., 417
Buckley, S., 438
Bulleit, T. N., 497
Bullinger, A., 283
Bullock, M., 411
Bundey, S. E., 53
Burchard, J. D., 675
Burgess, A. W., 663, 664, 666
Burgess, R., 507, 508
Burke, J. A., 480
Burleson, B. R., 480
Burns, W. J., 74
Burt, M. R., 595
Bushnell, W., 453
Buss, A. H., 56
Butler, E., 559
Byrne, D., 437

Cairns, R. B., 465
Caldwell, B. M., 79, 362, 365
Calvert, S. L., 403, 549
Camera, K. A., 502, 504
Cameron, M. Z., 115
Campbell, A., 670
Campbell, S., 480
Campbell, S. B., 419
Campbell, T. A., 288
Campioine, J. C., 317
Campione, J. C., 265
Campos, J. J., 56, 142, 143, 161, 413
Cancro, R., 681
Cann, A., 399
Canter, R. J., 667, 672
Cantor, Joanne, 409–410
Cantrell, M. L., 523
Cantwell, D. P., 677
Caparulo, B. K., 358, 439
Caplan, J., 358
Caplow, T., 643
Caputo, D. V., 74
Carey, S., 227
Carlson, G. A., 677
Carmichael, L., 249

Caro, F. G., 627
Carpenter, C. J., 396, 526
Carroll, J., 462
Carter-Saltzman, L., 49
Case, R., 300
Cash, M., 540
Caspi, A., 555
Catalano, R., 508
Catz, C., 73
Caudill, W., 477
Cavior, N., 439
Ceci, S. J., 319
Cerra, F., 630
Ceschin, F., 292
Chadwick, O. F. D., 681
Challman, R. C., 437
Chandler, M., 619
Chandler, M. J., 431
Chang, P., 166
Chapman, M., 204, 502
Chapman, R. S., 229
Charlesworth, W. R., 128, 138, 383
Chasnoff, I., 74
Chatillon, J. F., 283
Chess, Stella, 147–150, 469, 480
Cheyne, J. A., 321, 465
Chi, M. R. H., 289
Child, P., 404
Children's Aid Society, 665
Children's Defense Fund, 519, 554, 597
Chiles, J. A., 678
Chilman, C. S., 585, 586, 589, 590, 592, 597,
    598
Ching, W., 500
Choi, H. P., 315
Chomsky, Noam, 244, 257
Chudley, A., 53
Church, J., 578, 605
Cicchetti, D., 112
Cicirelli, V. G., 498
Citron, C. C., 530
Clark, E. V., 228, 229, 238, 256
Clark, L. D., 147
Clarke-Stewart, K. A., 163
Clarkson, F. E., 634
Clary, E. G., 463
Clasen, D. R., 603, 604
Clausen, J. A., 579, 580
Cleary, T. A., 361
Cleminshaw, H. K., 501
Clingenpeel, W. G., 505
Cloringer, C. R., 54
Cloward, R. A., 670
Clymer, A., 656
Cobbey, R. E., 548
Cohen, D. J., 56
Cohen, L. B., 115
Cohler, B. J., 600
Coie, J. D., 438, 446
Colby, A., 453, 641
Cole, N. S., 361
Coleman, J. C., 603
Coletta, N. D., 478, 482

Collins, J. K., 607
Collins, P. A., 546
Collins, W. A., 414, 548
Collman, P., 308
Collmer, C. W., 487, 507
Colombo, J., 102
Comstock, G., 548
Condon, S. M., 599, 601, 620
Conger, J. J., 69, 72, 568, 574, 578, 579,
    581, 582, 585–590, 592, 595–602, 604–
    606, 614, 618, 619, 622, 623, 625, 626,
    629, 637, 640, 641, 643–647, 654, 655,
    659, 662, 663, 669–671, 678, 681, 682,
    685
Conger, R., 507–509
Congressional Budget Office, 554
Conner, J. M., 530
Connolly, J., 292
Connolly, K. J., 522, 526
Conway, E., 74
Cook, A. H., 439, 556
Cook, T. D., 370
Cooper, C. R., 438, 599, 601, 603, 605, 620,
    621
Cooper, H. M., 531
Corah, N. L., 79
Corby, D. G., 73
Cordua, G. D., 399
Corsaro, W., 437
Corter, C., 497
Cosgrove, J. M., 255, 325
Costanzo, P. R., 446, 603
Couter, A., 634
Covington, M., 351
Cowan, Philip, 327
Cox, M., 501, 503
Cox, P. D., 351, 541
Cox, R., 501, 503
Craighead, W. E., 417
Cramer, S. H., 626
Crandall, V. C., 349, 353
Cravioto, J., 72
Crawford, S. H., 597
Cressey, D. R., 672
Crichton, L., 507
Crick, Francis, 39
Crissey, Marie Skodak, 13–14
Crockenberg, S., 17, 482, 497
Crockett, L. J., 580
Cross, W. E., Jr., 644
Crouse-Novak, M. A., 677
Crouter, A. C., 626, 633
Cummings, L., 419
Curran, D. K., 678–681
Curran, J. W., 76
Curtiss, S., 245
Cutting, J. E., 108

Damon, W., 388, 389, 429, 433–435, 446,
    457, 485, 488, 489, 491
Darlington, R., 367

Darville, D., 465
Darwin, Charles, 496
David, A., 77
Davies, J., 477
Davis, J. M., 117
Davis, M., 144
Davitz, J. R., 437
Dawson, D. A., 589
Day, H. D., 621, 622
Day, R. H., 121
Dean, R. A., 644
DeClark, Georgia, 279
Deemer, D., 642
DeFries, J. C., 50
de la Cruz, F., 53
del Gaudio, A. C. D., 676
Delia, J. G., 480
DeLicardie, E. R., 72
DeMarie-Dreblow, D., 320
Dement, W. C., 92
Derryberry, D., 148, 150
Detera-Wadeigh, S. D., 54
DeVault, S., 77
de Villiers, J. A., 236–238, 245
de Villiers, P. A., 236–238, 245
Diamond, A., 120
Dibble, E., 56
Dickson, W. P., 364
Diener, C. I., 351
Dietz, W. H., Jr., 545
Dix, T. H., 478, 479
Dixson, M. C., 676
Dlugokinski, E. L., 463
Doane, J. A., 682
Dobbing, J., 71
Dodge, K. A., 417, 419, 438, 468
Dokecki, P. R., 439
Dolan, A. B., 56
Dolgin, K. G., 110
Dollard, J., 464
Donaldson, Margaret, 272, 285–286
Donaldson, S. K., 413
Donnelly, K., 413
Donovan, J. M., 621
Doob, L. W., 464
Dooley, D., 508
Doran, L., 597
Dore, J., 253
Dornbusch, S. M., 364
Dorr, A., 414, 545
Dougherty, L. M., 144
Douvan, E., 605, 621, 622, 643
Dove, H., 106
Downs, A. C., 538
Doyle, A. B., 292
Drabman, R. S., 399, 487
Dudgeon, J. A., 75
Dumaret, A., 50
Duncan, B., 437
Duncan, G. J., 555
Duncan, O. D., 437
Dunn, J., 197, 204, 209, 430, 497, 498
Duyme, M., 50, 358

Dweck, C. S., 350, 351
Dykens, E., 51, 53

Easson, W. M., 678
East, B. A., 540
Easterbrooks, M. A., 481
Ebbesen, E. B., 442
Eccles, Jacquelynne, 347–349
Eckennoff, M. F., 104
Eckerman, C. O., 426
Edelbrock, C. S., 415, 438, 664, 677
Edelman, A., 190
Edelman, Marian Wright, 72, 595–597, 669
Edwards, C. P., 452
Egeland, B., 507, 508
Egeland, J. A., 54
Eggers, C., 682
Eichler, L. S., 481
Eifermann, R. R., 430
Eimas, P. D., 223
Einstein, Albert, 248
Eisen, M., 619, 620
Eisenberg, N., 458, 462
Eisenberger, R., 444
Elardo, R., 362, 365
Elder, G. H., Jr., 555, 599, 600
Elkind, D., 266, 583, 584, 643, 682
Elliot, E. S., 350, 351
Elliott, D. S., 244, 662, 664, 667, 669
Ellis, M. J., 429
Emde, R. N., 92, 144, 161, 677
Emler, N. P., 458
Emmerich, W., 466
Emmons, B. A., 443
Emory, E., 50
Enright, M. K., 117
Enright, R. D., 584
Epstein, Seymour, 202
Erikson, Erik H., 90, 91, 156, 174, 606, 614–
    618, 620–622, 624, 647, 655
Ernhart, C. B., 79
Eron, L. D., 22, 23, 26, 363, 466, 467, 469,
    551
Ervin-Tripp, Susan, 236, 359
Estes, D., 163
Estrada, P., 363
Ettema, J. S., 550

Fabricius, W. V., 321
Fagen, J. F., III, 100, 117
Fagot, B. I., 396, 465, 523, 530, 538, 540
Fahrenbruch, C. E., 147
Falbo, T., 498
Falkner, F., 46, 570
Family Planning Perspectives, 589
Falloon, I. R. H., 682
Farel, A. M., 643
Farmer, H. S., 630
Farnill, D., 446

Farrington, D. P., 667, 669, 671, 672
Faust, M. S., 570, 573, 574, 580, 581
Featherman, D. L., 437
Fein, G. G., 292, 427, 428
Feinberg, T. L., 677
Feinstein, S. C., 682
Feld, S., 346–347, 353
Feldman, N. S., 353
Fennema, E., 347
Fenson, L., 115
Ferdman, B. M., 358
Ferrara, R. A., 265, 317
Feshbach, N. D., 430, 465
Feshbach, N. S., 462
Field, D. E., 288, 542
Fiess, K., 234
Finison, K., 72
Finkelstein, R., 677
Finley, G. E., 265
Firestone, I. J., 463
Fisch, R. O., 166
Fischer, C., 321
Fischer, J. L., 607, 622
Fischer, M., 419
Fiske, S. T., 384
Fitts, W., 671
Fixsen, D. L., 675
Flavell, E. R., 285
Flavell, John H., 127, 202, 247, 267, 272, 285, 286, 291–293, 323, 382, 581–583
Flodereus-Myrhed, B., 56
Foch, T. T., 150
Forbes, G. B., 572
Ford, M. E., 583
Foreman, G. E., 427
Forrest, J. D., 593
Forsterling, F., 351
Fowler, J. W., 643
Fraiberg, Selma, 140
Fraleigh, M. J., 364
Frank, M., 556
Frank, A. L., 520
Frankenburg, W. K., 362
Fraser, F. C., 39, 41, 46n, 51
Freedman, R., 54
Freeman, R. N., 640
Freeman, W., 682
French, F. E., 78
Freud, Sigmund, 16, 19, 90, 91, 153–156, 174, 266, 442, 490, 568, 615
Friedman, E., 53
Friedrich, L. K., 552
Friedrich-Cofer, L., 526
Fritz, J., 408
Frodi, A. M., 165
Frodi, M., 165
Frost, L. A., 477
Fry, C. L., 286
Fujioka, T., 404
Fuller, J. L., 147
Furrow, D., 251

Furstenberg, F. F., Jr., 505, 595, 596
Furuhjelm, M., 59

Gagne, R. M., 301
Galanter, M., 644
Gallistel, C. R., 284
Gallup, G., 606, 644
Gamble, T. J., 170
Ganchrow, J. R., 123
Ganzer, V. J., 675
Garbarino, A., 663
Garbarino, J., 508, 663, 664, 672
Gardner, H., 112
Gardner, W., 167
Garfinkel, I., 557
Garfinkel, P. E., 684
Garino, E., 150
Garmezy, N., 53, 676, 678
Garner, D. M., 684
Garrett, C. J., 675
Garvey, Catherine, 181, 254, 292, 426, 428
Gebhard, P. H., 589
Gelman, R., 254, 284, 285, 383
Gelman, S. A., 308
Genova, P., 186
George, C., 509
Gershon, E. S., 55
Gershoni, R., 607
Gerson, R. P., 457
Gesell, A., 66, 104, 106
Gesell Institute of Child Development, 15
Gewirtz, J. L., 145
Giller, H., 670, 672, 673, 675, 676
Gilligan, C., 449, 642
Ginsburg, H. P., 269, 271, 280, 360
Ginzberg, E., 626
Giudice, S., 290
Glass, D. C., 496
Gleason, J. B., 235, 237
Gleitman, H., 238
Gleitman, L. R., 238
Glick, P. C., 505
Glickman, N. W., 662
Glorieux, J., 506
Glucksberg, S., 255
Gold, D., 506, 634
Gold, M., 346–347, 670, 671
Goldberg, W. A., 481
Golden, M., 438
Goldfarb, J. L., 598
Goldman, J., 439
Goldman, N., 593
Goldman-Rakic, P. S., 104
Goldsen, R., 637
Goldsmith, H. H., 56, 150, 413
Goldsmith, R., 555
Goldstein, A., 467
Goldstein, K. M., 74
Goldstein, M. J., 54, 601, 682
Gonzalez, M., 338
Good, W., 677

Goodchilds, J. D., 597
Goodman, G. S., 319
Goodnow, J. J., 477, 479, 480
Gordon, D. A., 671
Gortmaker, S. L., 545
Gottesman, I. I., 54, 150
Gottman, J. M., 435, 439
Gove, F. L., 163
Grace, W. C., 670
Graham, F. K., 79, 79
Graham, P., 498, 676, 681
Grajek, S., 520
Grawe, J. M., 56
Gray, S. W., 368
Green, K. C., 585, 636
Green, M. L., 414
Green, R., 591, 623
Greenberg, B. S., 549
Greenberger, E., 626, 627
Greenfield, P. M., 246
Greenough, W. J., 104, 147
Greif, E. B., 577
Griffitt, W. V., 437
Grollman, S. H., 184
Gronbard, B. I., 80
Gross, L., 547
Grossman, F. K., 481
Grossmann, K., 164, 166
Grossmann, K. E., 164, 166
Grotevant, H. D., 599, 601, 620
Grubb, W. N., 557
Gruenberg, A. M., 54
Gruendel, M. M., 229
Grumbach, M. M., 569
Grumet, J. F., 446
Grusec, J. E., 464, 478, 479
Guidubaldi, J., 501, 502, 504
Guilford, J. P., 338, 339
Gullota, T., 644
Gump, P. V., 523
Gunter, N. C., 69
Gupta, D., 569
Guttmacher, Alan F., 69
Guz, G. R., 413

Haan, N., 457
Haas, A., 589
Hack, M., 80
Haertel, E. H., 546
Haertel, G. D., 546
Hagan, R., 465
Hagen, E. P., 342
Hagman, J., 684
Haith, M. M., 122
Hala, S., 619
Hall, G. Stanley, 14–15, 568
Hall, Tony, 619
Hall, V. C., 358
Hallinan, M. T., 532
Halpern, D. F., 356
Halverson, C. F., Jr., 399

Hamburg, D. A., 586
Hamilton, S. F., 626
Hammer, W., 671
Hammersmith, S. K., 590, 591
Hancock, F. T., 496
Handel, S. J., 413
Hans, S., 101, 391
Hansen, R. D., 356
Hanson, A., 541
Hanson, J. W., 74
Harig, P. T., 675
Harkness, S., 410
Harlow, Harry F., 26, 157
Harlow, M. K., 157
Harmon, R., 677
Harper, L. V., 481
Harpring, E. B., 48, 56
Harris, L., 587–589, 644, 647
Harris, M., 75, 585, 590
Harris, P. L., 412, 413
Harris, T. O., 680
Harrison, A., 477
Hart, D., 388, 389
Harter, S., 389, 391, 404, 619
Hartman, C., 663, 664, 666
Hartup, W. W., 438, 465, 541, 602, 603, 605
Hasazi, J. E., 419
Haskins, R., 520
Hatcher, R., 74
Hauser, S. T., 620
Havighurst, R. J., 672
Hawkins, J. A., 437
Hawkins, R. P., 484, 486
Hay, D. F., 430, 458
Hayes, C. D., 69, 437, 590, 592, 593
Haynes, V. F., 320
Heath, D. S., 482
Heibeck, T. H., 228
Helmreich, R. L., 394, 623, 624
Hembree, E. A., 144
Henderson, C., 143
Henderson, C. R., Jr., 506
Henderson, V. K., 522
Henshaw, S. K., 593
Hermans, H. J. M., 364
Herr, E. L., 626
Herzog, D. P., 631, 684
Hess, R. D., 363–365, 480
Hetherington, E. M., 491, 501–505
Hevey, C. M., 163
Hiatt, S., 143
Higgins, A., 454, 455
Hill, F., 427
Hill, J. P., 579, 598, 599, 607, 619
Hill, Kennedy T., 353, 354
Hindelang, M. J., 670
Hirschi, T., 670, 672
Hirschman, J., 319
Hock, E., 507
Hodgkinson, S., 54
Hodgson, J. W., 607, 622
Hoffereth, S. L., 588, 590, 592

Hoffman, L., 170
Hoffman, L. W., 460, 480, 506, 630, 633, 634
Hoffman, Martin L., 463, 488, 489, 642, 643
Hofman, J. E., 607
Hogan, H. P., 249
Hogarty, P. S., 344
Holahan, C. K., 624
Holinger, P. C., 678
Hollenbeck, A. R., 542
Holloway, S. D., 363, 364
Holm, R. A., 147
Holmbeck, G., 599
Holmes, D. J., 685
Honzik, M. P., 344
Hood, L., 234, 243, 254
Hoover-Dempsey, K., 523
Horibe, F., 239
Horn, J. M., 50, 338, 362
Hornick, J. P., 597
Hornik, R. C., 544
Horowitz, F. D., 365
Horowitz, S. B., 370
Horwitz, R. A., 524
House Committee of Education and Labor, 663, 666
Householder, J., 74
Howard, K., 568
Howes, C., 521
Hoyle, S. G., 437
Huber, F., 164
Hudson, W. H., 614
Huesmann, L. R., 22, 23, 26, 363, 466, 469, 551
Hughes, D., 559
Huizinga, D., 662, 664, 667
Humphrey, L. L., 444
Humphrey, R. H., 656
Humphreys, L. G., 361
Hunt, M., 590
Hunter, L., 552
Huston, A. C., 17, 50, 288, 356, 370, 396, 398, 402, 403, 501, 506, 523, 526, 528, 539, 544, 547, 549, 550, 623, 624, 634
Huston, T., 620
Huston-Stein, A., 526
Hutchings, B., 671
Hwang, C. P., 165
Hymel, S., 439

Iannotti, R. J., 462
Ilg, F. L., 15
Illingworth, R. S., 73, 75
Inamdar, S. C., 678
Ingelman-Sundberg, A., 59
Inhelder, Barbel, 282
Iowa Child Welfare Research Station, 12, 13
Izard, C. E., 54, 144, 677

Jacklin, C. N., 148, 189, 356, 396, 398, 465, 488, 528

Jacobs, J., 678
Jacobsen, B., 54
Jacobson, L., 531
Jacobson, S., 190
Jaeger, E., 170
Jambor, T. W., 427
James, William, 388
Jamison, K. R., 601
Janus, M. D., 663, 664, 666
Jarvis, P. E., 286
Jenkins, E. C., 53
Jensen, Arthur, 358
Jessor, R., 600, 662
Jessor, S. L., 600, 662
Ji, G., 500
Jiao, S., 500
Jing, Q., 500
Joffe, J. M., 77
Johnson, B., 507
Johnson, C., 684
Johnson, K., 559
Johnson, L. M., 396
Johnson, V. E., 585
Johnson, W. F., 144
Johnston, C. A., 481
Johnston, F. E., 103
Johnston, J., 550
Johnston, J. L., 507
Johnston, L. D., 586, 606, 629, 631, 632, 636, 645, 656, 657, 662
Jolly, A., 186
Jones, C. P., 251
Jones, E., 593
Jones, H. E., 49, 579
Jones, K. L., 74
Jones, M. C., 579, 580
Jones, S., 682
Jordan, C., 353
Jossely, I. M., 678
Josselyn, I. M., 568
Jurkovic, G. J., 671

Kacerguis, M., 607
Kaczala, C. M., 363
Kagan, Jerome, 56, 101, 112, 140, 150, 181, 183, 184, 188, 189, 193, 196, 209, 226, 265, 303, 320, 337, 391, 466, 477
Kahn, A. J., 172, 558
Kahn, J. R., 588, 590
Kahn, M. D., 495
Kail, R., 317
Kaiser, J. H., 69
Kaitz, M., 190
Kamerman, S. B., 172, 558
Kamii, Constance, 278–279
Kandel, D. B., 437, 600, 662, 663
Kantner, J. F., 574, 588–590, 593
Kantrowitz, B., 631
Kaplan, H., 106
Kaplan, H. B., 671

Karnioil, R., 446
Katchadourian, H. A., 585, 586
Katell, A., 487
Katiyar, G. P., 72
Katz, M., 71, 72
Katz, P. A., 403, 404
Kauffman, J. M., 415
Kaufman, Irving R., 673
Kavanaugh, R. D., 184
Kaye, D. B., 358
Kearsley, R., 112
Keasy, C. B., 454
Keating, D. P., 581, 582
Keating, M. B., 121
Keil, F., 383
Kelley, K., 598
Kelly, J. B., 504, 505
Kempe, C. H., 507
Kempe, R. S., 507
Kendall, P. C., 417
Kendler, K. S., 54
Kendrick, C., 204, 209, 430, 497, 498
Kendrick, S. A., 361
Keniston, K., 654
Kennedy, M., 115
Kennedy, W. A., 356
Keple, T. W., 599
Kerkman, D., 544
Kerr, P., 655
Kessel, F. S., 229
Kessel, S. S., 80
Kessen, W., 101
Kessler, S. S., 54
Ketterlinus, R. D., 620
Kety, S. S., 54
Keusch, G. T., 71
Kidd, K. K., 45, 46, 48, 51, 55, 56, 478
Kiell, N., 568
King, K. C., 75
King, L. J., 682
King, M. K., 319
King, Martin Luther, Jr., 448
King, R. A., 138, 461
Kingston, P., 172
Kinnert, M. D., 161
Kinsey, A. C., 589, 590
Kippax, S., 545
Kirby, D., 596
Kirigin, K. A., 675
Klaus, R. A., 368
Klebanoff, M. A., 80
Klein, J. R., 578
Klein, M. W., 672
Klein, S. L., 480
Kleinman, D., 675
Klerman, G. L., 54, 55, 677, 678
Kliegman, R. M., 75
Klien, R. E., 265
Kligman, D., 92
Kniesel, P. M., 602
Knoblock, H., 71
Knowles, B. A., 667
Koch, H. L., 210

Kohlberg, Lawrence, 398–399, 420, 447–457, 471, 641
Kohn, M. L., 482, 633
Kolb, S., 106
Kolodny, R. C., 585
Konopka, G., 605
Koop, C. Everett, 76
Kopp, C. B., 51, 69, 71, 74, 79, 80
Korn, W. S., 585, 636
Korones, S. B., 62, 67, 74, 79, 80
Kosslyn, S. N., 308
Kotelchuck, M., 72
Kovach, J. A., 662
Kovacs, M., 677
Kovitz, K. A., 507
Kozol, J., 483
Kramer, S. J., 108
Krantz, J. Z., 56
Krauss, R. M., 255
Kraut, R. E., 349
Krawitz, A., 142
Krebs, D., 458
Kreutzer, M. A., 138, 383
Krile, D., 438
Kringlen, E., 56
Kroonenberg, P. M., 162, 164
Kuchuk, A., 110
Kuczynski, L., 192, 489
Kuhl, P., 112
Kurdek, L. A., 504
Kurkek, L. A., 438
Kutz, S. L., 426

LaBarba, R. C., 69
Laboratory of Comparative Human Cognition, 338
Labov, W., 244
LaGasse, L., 164
Lagerspetz, K., 22, 23
Lahey, L., 234
Lamar, J. V., Jr., 655, 659–661
Lamb, M. E., 163, 165, 167, 413, 495, 506
Lambert, B., 76
Landy, F., 498
Langer, A., 142
Langolis, J. H., 538
Lapsley, D., 584
Largo, R. H., 53
Larson, L. E., 604
Lasch, Christopher, 655
Lavine, L. O., 491
LaVoi, J. C., 486
Lazar, I., 367
Lazerson, M., 557
LeBlanc, M., 671
Leckman, J. F., 51, 53
Lee, S., 357
Lee, V. E., 365
Lefkowitz, M. M., 466, 467, 469
Leiderman, P. H., 364
Leiman, B., 462
Lemann, N., 640

LeMare, L. J., 430
Lemish, D., 545
Lempers, J. C., 285
Lempert, H., 237
Lennon, R., 462
Leonard, L. B., 227
Lepper, M. R., 443, 484–486
Lerman, R. I., 631
Lerner, J., 439
Lerner, R. M., 417, 439, 478
Lesser, G. S., 600
Lesser, I., 607, 622
Leung, E. H. L., 458
Levenstein, Phyllis, 187
Levin, G., 479
Levin, H., 156
Levine, F. J., 642
Levine, L. E., 203
Lewin, Kurt, 14
Lewine, R. R. J., 681
Lewis, C. C., 600, 684
Lewis, Michael, 200, 202, 408, 410, 411, 414
Leyens, J. P., 25
Liben, L. S., 399, 400
Liberman, D., 498
Liberman, R. P., 682
Liebert, R. M., 24, 542, 547, 550–552
Lifter, K., 234
Lightbown, P., 243
Lincoln, R., 593
Linden, M. G., 53
Lindsay, J. W., 606
Linn, M. C., 101, 111, 398
Linton, T., 540
Lippitt, Ronald, 13–14
Lipsitt, L., 164
Litt, I. F., 578
Little, G. A., 75
Little, J. K., 627
Littman, R. A., 537
Liublinskaya, A. A., 250
Livesley, W. J., 433
Livson, N., 580, 581
Locke, John, 6, 128, 208
Loebl, J. H., 353
Loehlin, J. C., 49
Londerville, S., 163, 167
London, P., 463
Lopez, D., 391
Lorch, E. P., 288, 315, 318, 547
Lorenz, Konrad, 157
Lorian, R. P., 672
Lubchenco, L. O., 62, 64, 67, 75–77, 79–81
Lucas, D., 117
Lucas, T., 426
Luce, J., 663
Lukoff, J. F., 662
Lutz, C., 410
Lynd, H., 618
Lyon, A. E., 442
Lytton, H., 49

McCabe, M. P., 607
McCall, R. B., 184, 344
McCarthy, D., 15
McCartney, K., 520, 526
Maccoby, E. E., 148, 156, 189, 308, 356, 396, 398, 465, 478, 480, 484, 488, 528
McCormack, A., 663, 664, 666
McCrosky, J., 554, 559
McDevitt, T. M., 364
Macfarlane, J. W., 344
McGee, M. G., 47
McGhee, P. E., 239, 506
McGill, C. W., 682
McGraw, K. O., 399
McGuire, C. V., 390, 404
McGuire, W. J., 390, 404
McKenzie, B. E., 121
McKinney, K. L., 574, 580
McLanahan, S. S., 557
McLoyd, V. C., 555
Madden, J., 73, 74
Madsen, M. C., 458
Maes, P. C., 364
Magsud, M. C., 452
Main, M., 163, 167, 461, 509
Mandler, J. M., 306, 307
Mann, D., 670, 671
Mansfield, A. F., 395
Marantz, S. A., 395
Marcia, J. E., 607, 620–622, 624
Marcus, J., 682
Marini, M. M., 630
Markman, E. M., 228
Markowitz, A., 391
Markstrom, C. A., 621
Marsh, H. W., 349, 392
Marshall, W. A., 569, 570, 574
Marsiglio, W., 588, 589
Martin, B., 469
Martin, C. E., 589, 590
Martin, C. L., 399
Martin, D. C., 74
Martin, J. A., 484
Mash, E. J., 481, 507
Mason, W. A., 143
Massad, C. M., 255, 325
Masters, W. H., 585
Masterson, F. A., 444
Mata, L., 71
Matarazzo, R. G., 79
Matheny, A. P., Jr., 56
Meadows, L., 505
Mednick, S. A., 54, 671, 682
Medrich, E. A., 438
Meece, J. L., 348
Meltzoff, A. N., 112, 190
Menken, J., 69
Merrill, Maude, 341
Meschulach-Safarty, O., 190
Messaris, P., 544
Metcoff, J., 71, 72
Metzner, R., 442
Michaelson, L., 411

Miklowitz, D. J., 682
Millar, W. S., 484
Miller, A. T., 353
Miller, D., 682
Miller, H., 663
Miller, J., 463
Miller, M. L., 678
Miller, N. E., 464
Miller, P., 462
Miller, P. H., 320
Miller, P. Y., 585, 586
Miller, S., 73, 74
Miller, S. M., 414
Miller, W. B., 670
Miller, W. C., 671
Millie, M. P. W., 360
Minuchin, Patricia, 510, 511, 518, 524, 531, 532
Minuchin, S., 684, 685
Mischel, W., 10, 325, 401, 442–444
Mishkin, M., 121
Mitchell, M., 444
Mitchell-Kernan, C., 549
Miyake, K., 164
Mizner, G., 54
Moely, B. E., 520
Mohr, D. M., 389
Moir, J., 454
Mondell, S., 478
Monighan, P., 437
Monighan-Nourot, P., 427–428
Montemayor, R., 619, 620, 634, 635
Moore, B. S., 458
Moore, D., 602
Moore, E. G. J., 358, 364
Moore, H. A., 507
Moore, K. L., 39, 46, 59, 71, 73–75
Moore, L. P., 443
Moore, M. K., 190
Moore, T. W., 634
Morgan, M., 547
Morgan, S. P., 595, 596
Morganthau, T., 659
Morrison, D. M., 597
Mortimer, J. T., 633
Moss, H. A., 148, 150, 209, 466
Mott, F. L., 588, 589
Mowrer, O. H., 464
Much, N., 456
Mueller, E., 189
Mueller, R., 426
Mulhern, R. K., 488
Munro, G., 664
Munsinger, H., 50
Murphy, L., 458
Murphy, R. R., 417
Murray, J. P., 545
Murrow, Ed, 14
Mussen, P. H., 579
Muzio, J. N., 92

Nash, S. C., 623

National Assessment of Educational Progress, 627
National Center for Juvenile Justice, 670
National Commission on Excellence in Education, 627
NBC Monitor, 666
Neimark, E. D., 289, 581, 582
Nelson, C. A., 110
Nelson, K., 228, 251, 252
Nelson, V. L., 344
Nemiah, J. C., 676
Neulinger, J., 496
Newbern, S. R., 399
Newcomb, A. F., 438
Newport, E. L., 250
New York Times, 666
Nicholi, A. M., Jr., 677, 678
Nicholls, J. G., 353
Nichols, P. L., 356
Nichols, R. C., 48, 49
Nilsson, L., 59, 63
Ninio, A., 226
Nisan, M., 453
Nolan, E., 265
Nora, J. J., 39, 41, 46n, 51
Norback, C., 644
Nord, C. W., 505
Norman, J., 585, 590
Novey, M. S., 203
Nucci, L., 456
Nucci, M., 456
Nurnberger, J. I., 55
Nye, F. I., 506

Oberkaid, F., 150
O'Brien, M., 396
Offer, D., 568, 622
Offer, J., 622
Ohlin, L. E., 670
Olczak, P., 439
O'Leary, V. E., 356
Olson, D. H., 601
Olweus, D., 466, 469, 672
O'Malley, P. M., 586, 606, 629, 631, 645, 656, 662, 671
Omelich, C., 351
Opper, S., 269, 271, 280
Orlofsky, J. L., 607, 621, 622
O'Rourke, D. H., 54
Ort, S. I., 51, 53
Orvaschel, H., 478
Osborn, M., 678
Osipow, S. H., 624, 626
Osterrieth, P. A., 583, 584
Ostrov, E., 568

Paden, L. Y., 365
Page, D. C., 46
Page, E. W., 74
Painter, P., 79

Palmquist, W., 619
Pannabecker, R., 144
Papousek, H., 123
Parke, R. D., 25, 167, 184, 465, 469, 486–488, 507–509
Parker, J. G., 438
Parker, T., 338
Parmelee, A. H., 51, 69, 71, 74, 79, 80
Parnas, J., 54
Parry-Jones, W. L. L., 680
Parsons, J. E., 353, 363, 528
Parten, M., 15, 427
Pasamanick, B., 71
Pascual-Leone, J., 317
Passman, R. H., 488
Pastor, D. L., 163, 167
Paterson, P., 347
Patterson, C. J., 255, 325, 443
Patterson, Gerald R., 443, 467, 469–470, 488, 537, 538, 671, 672, 675
Paulauskas, S. L., 677
Pauls, D. L., 46, 51, 54
Payne, F., 458
Payne, R., 73, 74
Pea, R. D., 253
Pearce, J., 677
Pederson, N., 56
Peevers, B. H., 433
Pellegrini, A. D., 481, 523
Penner, S. G., 251
Pepler, D. J., 497
Pernoll, M. L., 75
Perry, J. D., 501
Peskin, H., 580, 581
Petersen, A. C., 356, 570, 573, 574, 577, 578, 580–582, 585, 586, 600, 602, 622, 623, 626, 637, 643, 644, 663, 670
Petersen, J. L., 505
Peterson, C., 678
Petit, G. S., 478
Petitto, L., 202
Petronio, R. J., 671
Petti, T., 416
Pezdek, K., 306
Phillips, D. A., 170, 363
Phillips, E. L., 675
Phillips, D., 520
Piaget, Jean, 9, 17, 90, 91, 125–130, 246, 248, 253, 257, 263, 265–295, 300, 301, 303, 304, 311, 326, 327, 384, 409, 419, 430, 446–447, 449, 471, 552, 581, 582
Pines, A., 664
Pitman, G. D., 682
Pittel, S. M., 663
Pitt-Watson, R., 413
Plato, 568
Platz, M. C., 672
Plomin, R., 48–50, 54–56, 150
Polit, D. F., 498
Polling, D., 644
Pomeroy, Wardell B., 578, 589, 590
Postman, N., 545

Potts, R., 414, 523, 547
Powell, G. J., 403, 404
Power, C., 454
Prescott, P. S., 673
Pressley, M., 443
Price, G. G., 364
Price, V., 547
Prior, M., 150
Proffitt, D. R., 108
Puig-Antich, J., 54, 677, 678
Pulkkinen, L., 672
Putallaz, M., 39, 437

Quay, H. C., 670–672, 675

Raaf, S., 569
Radin, N., 555
Radke-Yarrow, M., 138, 192, 204, 460, 461
Rakic, P., 104
Ramey, C. T., 171, 368
Ramp, K. K., 302
Ramsay, D., 143
Rasmuson, I., 56
Raviv, A., 458
Read, P. B., 54, 677
Reed, E. W., 51
Regnemer, J. L., 453
Reich, T., 229
Renshaw, P. D., 438, 439
Reschly, D. J., 345
Rescorla, R., 121
Resnick, H. L. P., 680
Rest, J. R., 446, 456, 641, 642
Reznick, J. S., 56, 101, 115, 226, 477
Rheingold, H. L., 430, 458
Rhoades, G. G., 80
Rholes, W. S., 353
Rice, M. E., 464
Rice, M. L., 247, 370, 544, 545
Richman, N., 498
Richmond, J. B., 81
Ridgeway, D., 408
Riese, M. A., 150
Ritchie, D., 547
Ritter, P. L., 364
Roberts, D. F., 364, 547
Robins, L., 419, 671, 672
Robinson, A., 53
Roche, A. F., 573
Rocissano, L., 254
Rode, S. S., 166
Rodin, J., 682, 684
Roff, M., 438
Roffwarg, H. P., 92
Rogers, Don, 657
Roggman, L. A., 170
Rogoff, B., 265
Rolf, J. E., 419
Rosen, B. C., 630, 631
Rosen, J., 438

Rosenbaum, S., 559
Rosenberg, B. G., 496–498
Rosenberg, D., 507
Rosenberg, F., 574
Rosenberg, M., 404, 637
Rosenblatt, A., 672
Rosenhan, D., 463
Rosenkrantz, P. S., 634
Rosenthal, D., 54
Rosenthal, R., 531
Rosman, B. L., 684
Rosof, J. I., 593
Ross, D. F., 319
Ross, J., 353
Ross, R., 523
Ross, R. J., 581, 583
Roth, J. A., 669
Rothbart, M. K., 148, 150
Rousseau, Jean Jacques, 6
Rovee-Collier, C. K., 117
Rovine, M., 164
Rubin, K. H., 292, 321, 427–430
Rubin, Z., 71, 184, 434, 435, 437, 438
Ruble, D. N., 353, 577
Rugh, R., 59, 63, 71
Ruppenthal, G. C., 147
Rushton, J. P., 458, 464
Russell, G. F. M., 684
Russell, J. A., 411
Russell, R. L., 360
Rutland, D., 346–347
Rutter, M., 53, 54, 169, 482, 601, 670, 672, 673, 675–677, 681
Ryan, N. D., 677

Saarni, C., 408, 410
Saas-Kortsaak, P., 464
Sackett, G. P., 147
Sagi, A., 167
Sagotsky, G., 443
St. Clair, S., 621, 622
St. Peters, M., 544
Salapatek, P., 110
Salomon, G., 544
Saltzstein, H. D., 463
Sameroff, A. J., 163
Sameroff, A. M., 77
Sampson, E. E., 496
Sanders, J., 288
Sandoval, J., 360
Sanson, A., 150
Santrock, J. W., 456, 498, 501, 505, 597, 600
Sarason, I. G., 675
Sarason, S. B., 353, 354
Sattler, J. M., 342
Scaife, M., 383
Scales, B., 427, 437
Scarr, Sandra, 45, 46, 48–51, 55, 56, 358, 520, 526
Schacter, F. F., 506
Schalit, M., 636

Scheintuch, G., 479
Scheirer, M. A., 349
Schiff, M., 50, 358
Schindler, P. J., 520
Schinzel, A., 53
Schmidt, G., 585
Schnur, E., 365
Schomberg, S. F., 642
Schooler, C., 482, 633
Schorr, L. B., 69, 557, 596
Schrager, J. B., 442
Schulsinger, F., 54
Schultz, N. R., Jr., 602
Schultz, T. R., 239
Schunk, D. H., 351, 541
Schwartz, J., 72
Schwarz, J. C., 442
Schweder, R., 456
Scott, P. M., 462
Scott, R. M., 666
Searls, D. T., 80
Sears, R. R., 12, 156, 464
Sebald, H., 604
Sebastian, R. J., 25
Sechrest, L., 672
Secord, P. F., 433
Seeman, M., 654
Segal, N. L., 48
Segal, S., 505
Seifer, F., 163
Seitz, V., 192, 360
Seligman, M. E. P., 678
Sells, S., 438
Selman, R. L., 619
Selman, Robert L., 389, 430–434
Senate Committee of the Judiciary,
   663
Serbin, L. A., 400, 530, 539
Sewell, J., 150
Shaffer, D., 677–680
Shah, F., 593
Shannon, L. W., 667
Shantz, C. U., 353, 431, 433
Shapira, A., 458
Shipiro, E. K., 518, 524, 531, 532
Sharbany, R., 607
Shatz, M., 254
Shaw, M. E., 603
Sheldrick, C., 672
Sherman, D., 508
Sherman, J., 241
Sherman, J. A., 301
Shettles, L. B., 59, 63, 71
Shibley-Hyde, J., 398
Shields, J., 54
Shinn, M., 502
Shiono, P. H., 80
Shipley, E. F., 238
Short, E. J., 171, 368
Shukla, D., 584
Shure, Myrna B., 440, 441
Siegal, M., 520
Siegel, L. S., 105

Siegler, Robert, 289, 310
Sigel, I. E., 479, 481
Signorella, M. L., 399, 400
Sikes, J., 532
Silberstein, L. R., 684
Silbert, M., 664
Silverberg, S. B., 603, 604
Simmons, A., 80, 81
Simmons, R. G., 574, 579–581
Simon, W., 585, 586
Simons, J., 559
Simpson, R. L., 633, 635
Simutis, Z. M., 464
Sinclair, H., 246, 248
Singer, D. G., 429
Singer, J. L., 429
Singer, M. T., 601
Singer, S. M., 46, 51, 54
Singleton, L. C., 437, 533
Siomopoulos, G., 678
Skeels, M. H., 13, 50
Skinner, B. F., 262, 300, 484
Skodak, M., 50
Slaby, R. G., 465, 469, 508, 509, 542
Slavin, R. E., 532
Slobin, Dan I., 241, 246
Smetana, J., 456
Smith, B., 457, 458
Smith, D. W., 74
Smith, I. D., 349
Smith, K. B., 138
Smith, N. W., 48
Smith, P. K., 180, 438, 522, 526
Smith, R., 321
Smith, R. E., 629, 631, 634, 637
Smith, R. S., 78, 81, 373
Smith, S. R., 568
Smollar, J., 598, 599, 602, 605, 606, 620
Smryl, R., 92
Snapp, M., 532
Snidman, N., 56
Snow, C. E., 250
Snow, M. E., 148
Snyder, J., 671, 672, 675
Snyder, K. S., 682
Snyder, L., 226, 232
Society for Research in Child Development,
   14n, 27, 28
Sodian, B., 323
Sontag, L. W., 77, 344
Sophian, C., 321
Sorce, J. F., 161
Sorensen, R. C., 586, 588–590, 592, 643
Spanier, G. B., 478
Spelke, E., 383
Spence, J. T., 394, 623, 624
Spetner, M. B., 108
Spickelmier, J. L., 642
Spitz, René, 19
Spivak, George, 440, 441
Spizzirri, C. C., 144
Sprafkin, C., 400
Sprafkin, J., 542, 547, 550–552

Sroufe, L. A., 145, 163, 166, 508
Standley, K., 74
Stein, A. H., 349, 353, 356, 363, 552
Steinberg, L. D., 508, 579, 598, 603, 604,
   607, 626, 627, 676, 681, 682
Steiner, J. E., 123
Steinschneider, A., 92
Stenberg, C., 143, 144, 413
Stephan, C., 532
Stephenson, S. P., 628
Stern, J. A., 79
Sternberg, L. D., 346
Sternberg, R. J., 339, 359, 583
Sternglanz, S. H., 530
Stevenson, H. W., 338, 357
Stevenson, J., 498
Stewart, P., 521
Stewart, R. B., 498
Stigler, J. W., 357
Stilwell, R., 498
Stipek, D., 554, 559
Stoddard, G. D., 13
Stoller, R. J., 623
Stolz, H. and L. M., 581
Stone, L. J., 578, 605
Stoneman, Z., 523
Storey, R. M., 520
Strain, Philip, 418
Stratton, P., 92
Strauss, J. S., 54
Strayer, F. F., 458
Strayer, J., 409
Streissguth, A. P., 74
Striegel-Moore, R. H., 684
Stuckey, M. F., 506
Stunkard, A. J., 682
Sturrup, B., 458
Suben, J. G., 339, 359
Suchman, I., 637
Sullivan, M., 117
Sulloway, F., 496
Sully, James, 199, 208
Suomi, S. J., 26
Super, C. M., 106, 410
Super, D. E., 626
Susman, E. J., 148, 526
Sutton-Smith, B., 496–498
Svejda, M., 143, 161
Sweeney, M. E., 670
Swope, G. W., 644
Sylva, K., 186

Tabachnick, N., 681
Talmadge, M., 77
Tanner, James M., 46, 570, 572, 574, 579
Tapp, J. L., 642
Taub, H. B., 74
Taylor, A., III, 631
Taylor, A. R., 437, 533
Taylor, S. E., 384
Teenage Pregnancy, 589, 596

Tees, R. C., 223
Teicher, J., 680
Teixeira, R. A., 532
Templin, M. C., 252
Ter Laak, J. J., 364
Terman, Lewis, 341
Thake, A. I., 53
Thane, K., 166
Thatcher, R. W., 290
Thiel, K., 607
Thomas, Alexander, 147–150, 469, 480
Thomas, N. G., 526
Thompson, J. R., 229
Thompson, R. A., 163
Thompson, V. D., 498
Thorndike, R. L., 342, 345
Thurston, D., 79
Tienari, P., 54, 682
Tigner, D. N., 302
Tinbergen, Nikko, 157
Tinsley, B. R., 167
Tittle, C. K., 631
Tizard, J., 677
Tobin-Richards, M., 574, 580
Todd, J., 53
Toder, N. L., 622
Toglia, M. P., 319
Tolan, P. H., 672
Tomkiewicz, S., 50
Tomlinson-Keasy, C., 454
Toner, I. J., 443
Tonick, I. J., 530
Toohey, M., 601
Torgeson, A. M., 56
Tower, R. B., 358
Trasler, G., 671
Trevarthen, C., 383
Trickett, P. K., 360
Trudeau, M. B., 586
Truglio, R., 370
Turiel, E., 452, 456
Turkle, Sherry, 384
Tyler, F., 478

Ugurel-Semin, R., 458
Ulleland, C. N., 74
Ulman, K. J., 577
U.S. Bureau of the Census, 69, 500, 629, 638, 640, 669, 670, 678
U.S. Commission on Civil Rights, 549
U.S. Department of Labor, 506, 629, 637, 641
U.S. Federal Bureau of Investigation, 670
U.S. Office of Education, 549
U.S. Public Health Service, 29

Valentine, J., 365, 366
Vandell, Deborah Lowe, 521–522
Vandenberg, B., 292, 427
Vandenberg, S. G., 46, 51, 54

Van Doorninck, W. J., 362
Van Hoorn, J., 427, 437
van IJzendorn, M. H., 162, 164
Vanucci, R. C., 79
Vatter, M., 483
Vaughan, V. C., 73–75
Vaughn, C. E., 682
Veroff, J., 349
Vibbert, M., 110
Villee, C. A., 74
Villee, D. B., 74
Visher, C. A., 669
Vogel, S. R., 634
Vollmer, F., 349
Voorhies, T. M., 79
Vorster, J., 250
Vygotsky, L. S., 238

Wachs, T. D., 362
Wagatsuma, H., 208
Wagner, S., 112
Wahler, R. G., 672
Wakeling, S., 461
Walberg, H. J., 546
Walder, L. O., 466, 467
Waldo, M., 54
Walker, E., 50
Walker, L. J., 456
Walker, R. A., 290
Wall, S., 156
Wallace, Alfred, 496
Wallace, C. S., 104
Wallerstein, J. S., 504, 505
Walter, A. A., 249
Walters, A. S., 138
Walters, C., 353
Ward, D. A., 672
Waring, S., 458
Warshak, R. A., 501, 505
Wartella, E., 552
Wartner, Y., 164
Waterman, A. S., 614, 621, 622
Waterman, C. K., 621
Waters, E., 156, 163, 461
Watson, J. S., 484
Watson, James, 39
Watson, John B., 16, 38, 153, 413
Watson, K. S., 427
Watson, M., 51, 53
Waxler, C. Z., 458, 462
Waxman, S., 249
Webb, T. P., 53
Weinberg, M. S., 590–592
Weinberg, R. A., 50, 358
Weiner, B., 413
Weiner, I. B., 676, 681, 682
Weiner, J., 458
Weinraub, M., 170, 482
Weinstein, C. S., 524
Weisberg, D. K., 666
Weiskopf, S., 101
Weiss, R. J., 642

Weissman, M. M., 54, 478, 677
Wellman, H. M., 321
Wender, P. H., 54
Werker, J. F., 223
Werner, E. E., 78, 81, 373, 477
Wesman, A., 361
Wessel, 631
West, D. J., 482, 671, 672
West, M. J., 430 ,
West, S., 25
Westerman, M. A., 413
Westoff, C. F., 593
Weston, D. R., 456, 461
Wetzel, R., 680
Whaley, L. F., 41
Whatley, J. L., 426
Wheeler, K. J., 540
White, B., 604
White, C. B., 453
Whiting, B. B., 458, 464
Whiting, J. W. M., 458, 464
Whitman, M., 662
Whitmore, K., 677
Wildflower, L. Z., 606
Wilkinson, A., 338
Wilks, J., 604
Willerman, L., 49, 50
Williams, B. R., 547
Williams, P. A., 546
Williams, R., 637
Williams, T. A., 547
Williams, T. M., 545
William T. Grant Foundation, 626
Willis, R. H., 603
Wilson, H., 672
Wilson, J., 663
Wilson, K. S., 522
Wilson, R. S., 48, 56, 81
Wimmer, H., 323
Winickoff, S. A., 481
Winn, M., 545
Winner, E., 112, 229
Winokur, G., 54
Wippman, J., 163
Wirsen, C., 59
Wittig, M. A., 356
Wohlford, P., 498
Wolensky, R. P., 637
Wolf, B. M., 482
Wolf, D. P., 183, 184
Wolf, M. A., 547
Wolf, M. M., 302, 675
Wolfe, P. H., 487
Wolff, P. H., 144, 145
Wooden, K., 673
Woody-Ramsey, J., 320
Worden, P. E., 306, 385
Wright, C., 362
Wright, J. C., 288, 370, 523, 544, 547
Wright, J. W., 286
Wright, P. H., 599
Wright, Richard, 405–406

Wright, W. E., 676
Wroblewski, R., 550
Wulf, D., 593
Wunsch, J. P., 145
Wynne, L. C., 601

Yaffe, S. J., 73
Yando, R., 192
Yankelovich, D., 636, 637, 643, 644, 646, 647, 655
Yarrow, M. R., 458, 462, 463

Yeates, K. O., 171, 368
Yengo, L. A., 117
Younger, B. A., 115
Youniss, J., 433, 598, 599, 601, 602, 605, 606, 620
Yule, W., 681
Yullie, J. C., 319

Zabin, L. S., 574
Zahn-Waxler, C., 138, 192, 204, 408, 460, 461, 463
Zax, M., 77, 163

Zecevic, M., 104
Zelazo, N. A., 106
Zelazo, P. R., 106, 112
Zellman, G. L., 597
Zelnik, M., 574, 588–590, 593
Zieman, 671
Zigler, E., 170, 192, 360, 365, 366, 439, 509, 556
Zill, N., 501, 505
Zillmann, D., 547
Zimbardo, P. C., 353
Zimmerman, B. J., 288

SUBJECT INDEX

Abused children, 507–509
  as runaways, 665–666
Acceptance, in friendships, 438–440
Accommodation, in Piaget's theories, 272–273, 294
Achievement, 354–355
  developmental patterns and, 352–353
  individual differences in
    early intervention in, 365–370
    home environment in, 361–365
    interaction of biology and environment in, 370–373
    in IQ scores, 344–345
    cultural and environmental influences in, 355–360
  motivation for, 346–351, 374
  television viewing and, 545–547
  test anxiety and, 353–354
Active versus passive nature of children, 8–9
Adaptation
  in Piaget's theories, 270–273
  in triarchic theory of intelligence, 340
Adolescence
  alienation in, 654–655, 685–686
  cognitive development during, 581–584
  delinquency during, 667–669, 686–687
    personality and parent-child relationships in, 670–672
    prevention and treatment of, 672–676
    social change and, poverty and, 669–670
  drug use in, 655–663, 686
  moral development values during cognitive growth and, 641–643
    current adolescent values, 644–647
    religious beliefs in, 643–644
  parent-child relationships during, 598–601
  peer relationships during, 600–601, 610
    conformity in, 602–603
    friendships and identity development in, 605–606
    with opposite sex, 606–608
    parents versus, 603–605
  physical development during, 572, 608
    growth spurt in, 570–571
    hormones in, 569
  pregnancy in, 69
  psychological and psychophysiological disturbances during
    anxiety reactions, 676–677

brief reactive psychosis, 682
  depression, 677–678
  eating disorders, 682–685
  schizophrenia, 681–682
  suicides, 678–681
  treatment of, 685
  psychological effects of maturation during
    erections, ejaculations, and nocturnal emissions in males, 578
    menstruation in females, 577–578
    timing of, in females, 580–581
    timing of, in males, 579–580
  runaways and, 663–666, 686
  sense of identity during, 614–615
    developing, 617–621
    ego identity in, 622
    Erikson's stages of, 615–617
    gender and sex-role identity in, 623–624
    identity foreclosure and identity confusion in, 621
    variations in formation of, 622
  sexuality during, 584–585
    changing attitudes and behavior in, 586–589
    homosexual behavior and orientation in, 590–592
    pregnancy and contraception in, 592–598
    premarital intercourse and, 589–590
    sex differences in, 585–586
    variations in attitudes and behavior in, 592
  sexual maturation during, 609
    in females, 574
    in males, 573–574
    normal variations in, 574–577
  vocational choice during, 624–626
    by females, 628–632
    parental influences on, 632–635
    prospects for, 637–641
    socioeconomic influences in, 626–628
    values and social change in, 635–637
Adoption studies
  of delinquency, 670–671
  of IQ scores, 49–50, 358, 362
  of schizophrenia, 54
Adulthood
  in Erikson's stage theory, 617
  timing of maturation and, 580
Advertising, 552

Affection, 362–363
Age
  changes in religious belief with, 643
  in cognitive learning theories, 301–302
  developmental changes with, 326–329
    emotions, 409
    memory, 317–318
  IQ scores changing over, 344
  of mother, in prenatal development, 69
Aggression, 464–465
  causes of, 468–470
  patterns of, 465–468
  peer relationships and, 537–538
  punishment and, 481, 487–488
  sexual, 586
AIDS (acquired immune deficiency syndrome), 76
Aid to Families with Dependent Children (AFDC), 555
Alcohol, fetal alcohol syndrome and, 74
Alienation, 654–655, 685–686
  drug use and, 663
Altruism, 462–464
Amniocentesis, 69–71
Anal stage, 156
Androgens, 569
Androgyny, 394, 623–624
Animal studies, 26–27
  of ethology, 157–158
Anorexia nervosa, 682–684
Anoxia, 77–79
Anxiety, 676–677
Apgar scores, 370–371
Applied research, 18
Aptitude, 265
  in IQ scores, 344–345
Arithmetic, 278–279
Aspirin, 73
Assimilation, in Piaget's theories, 272, 294
Associative play, 426
Attachment, in infants, 174–175
  to caregivers, 158–161
  measurement of, 162–165
  parental practices and, 165–167
  variations in quality of, 167–172
Attention, 313–314
  to television, 547
Attentional inertia, 313, 315
Attributions, 349–351

Attribution theory, 385
  on emotions, 413
Authoritarian parenting style, 364, 495, 600
Authoritative parenting style, 363–364, 493–495, 599–600
Autocratic parenting style, 600
Autonomous standards, 349
Awkwardness, during adolescence, 572

Babbling, 223–224
Basic research, 18
Bayley Scale of Infant Development, 105
Behavior
  in childhood
    bidrectionality principle on, 480–481
    child care quality and, 521–522
    gender-typed, 396–398
    imitation, 190–195
    learned from peers, 537–538
    play, 181–189
    problems in, 415
    punishment and, 208–209, 486–488
    self-awareness in, 200
    standards of, 196–197, 199
    teachers and, 528–530
  delinquent, 667–669
    personality, parent-child relationships and, 670–672
    prevention and treatment of, 672–676
    social change, poverty and, 669–670
  experimental analysis of, 300–301
  gender typing in, 401
  of infants
    inferring emotions from, 138–143
    temperamental differences in, 147–152
  inferring thought from, 262–263
  parental, toward adolescents, 599–601
  of parents, 491–495
  prosocial, 458–464
    learned from peers, 537–538
    portrayed on television, 552
    training for, 462–464
  sexual
    changes in, 586–589
    homosexual, 590–592
    premarital intercourse and, 589–590
    variations in, 592
  social, 470–472
    aggression, 464–470
    friendships in, 433–440
    moral development in, 445–457
    peer relationships in, 426–433
    self-control in, 441–445
    training in skills of, 440–441
Behavior analysis, 300
Behaviorism, 16, 262
  learning theory and, 300–302, 329–331
  on social and emotional development of infants, 156–157
  in treatment of delinquency, 675
Bidirectionality principle, 151–152, 174, 480–481

parental behavior and, 495
punishment and, 487
Biology. *See also* Genetic factors in development; Heredity
  in causes of depression, 677–678
  environment versus, 6
  in intellectual development, 370–373
  in Piaget's theories, 268
  in reflexes, 94–95
  in schizophrenia, 681
  in teaching about gender, 400–401
  in theories of behavior
    of aggression, 468–469
    of empathy, 459
  in theories of infancy, 91, 154–156
Bipolar (manic-depressive) disorder, 54, 55, 678
Birth. *See* Childbirth
Birth defects, 100
  amniocentesis to detect, 70–71
  anoxia and, 77–79
  developmental disabilities, 51
  fetal alcohol syndrome and, 74
  phenylketonuria (PKU), 46
Birthweight, 92
  in prematurity, 80
Blacks
  group identity in, 404–406
  infant mortality among, 72–73
  integration of, 532–534
  IQ scores of, 358–360
    court rulings on test bias and, 361
  sexual attitudes and behavior of, 592
  stereotypes of, 549
Blastocysts, 58
Blood, Rh factor in, 76–77
Bonding, 165–167
Boys. *See* Males
Brain. *See also* Nervous system
  of infants, 104
    cognitive development and, 107–108
    event-related potentials in, 110
    sudden infant death syndrome and, 92–94
  language development and, 244
Bulimia, 684

Carolina Abecedarian Project, 368, 370
Categories, 113–115
  hierarchical relationships among, 278–280
  in information-processing approach, 308–310
  symbolic, 222
Cerebral palsy, 79
Cheating, 457
Child abuse, 507–509
  runaways and, 665–666
Childbirth, 67
  children's concepts of, 327–328
  complications of, 77–79
  drugs taken during, 74
  prematurity and, 80–81

Child care. *See also* Day care
  parental employment and, 556–557
  quality of, 521–522
Childhood years
  achievement in, 354–355
    developmental patterns in, 352–353
    individual differences in, 360–373
    motivation for, 346–351
    test anxiety and, 353–354
  child-rearing and disciplinary practices during, 481–484
    children's personality and behavior in, 480–481
    imitation and identification in, 489–491
    inductive techniques in, 488–489
    parental characteristics and beliefs in, 478–480
    punishment in, 486–488
    reinforcement in, 484–486
  cognitive development in
    age-based changes in, 326–329
    empirical findings in, 283–293
    issues in study of, 262–265
    learning theory and behaviorism on, 300–302
    Piaget on, 265–283
  emotions in, 407–414
  family interactions in, 205–210
  family socialization during, 511–513
    child abuse and, 507–509
    family structure in, 500–507
    parental behavior in, 491–495
    siblings in, 495–500
    systems approach to, 509–511
  imitation in, 190–195
  individual and social development in
    Erikson's stages of, 615–617
    ethnic group and identity in, 403–406
    gender typing and identity in, 392–403
    problems in, 414–419
    self-concept in, 619
    sense of self in, 388–392
    theories of, 382–388
  information-processing approach to
    assumptions in, 303
    cognitive processes in, 311–321
    cognitive units in, 303–311
    metacognition in, 321–326
  intelligence in
    cultural context of, 336–337
    dimensions of, 338–340
    individual differences in, 360–373
    limitations on tests of, 343–345
    measurements and tests of, 341–343
    as single versus multiple abilities, 337–338
    use of tests of, 345–346
  language in
    cognition and, 248–250
    for communication and conversation, 253–255
    environmental influences on, 250–253
    functions of, 220–222

Childhood years (*continued*)
  pragmatics in, 238–240
  semantics in, 226–230
  speech components for, 222–226
  syntax in, 230–238
  theories of acquisition of, 240–248
  moral development in, 445–446
    Kohlberg's theory of, 447–456
    moral judgments in, 446–447, 454–457
    standards and, 195–198
  self-awareness in, 198–204
  social behavior in, 470–472
    aggression, 464–470
    friendships in, 433–440
    peer relationships in, 426–433
    prosocial behavior in, 458–464
    self-control in, 441–445
    training in skills of, 440–441
  socialization in, 560–561
    in day care and school, 518–535
    governmental and economic influences
      on, 552–559
    peers in, 535–541
    television in, 542–552
  symbolic functioning in, 180–181
    functions of play in, 184–186
    play with other children in, 187–189
    symbolic play in, 181–184
  theories of, 6
Child rearing
  children's personality and behavior and,
    480–481
  cultural context of, 172–173
  emotional and social effects of, 165–167
  empathy and, 460–461
  external community and, 482–483
  imitation and identification in, 489–491
  inductive techniques in, 488–489
  infant attachment and, 159–161
  infant inhibitions and, 151
  nonsexist, 400–401
  parental characteristics and beliefs in,
    478–480
  parenting styles in, 363–364
  punishment in, 486–488
  reinforcement in, 484–486
  in second and third years, 205
  social context of, 481
Children
  abused, 507–509
  conceptions of ethnic groups of, 403–404
  with employed mothers, 506–507
  as eyewitnesses, 318–319
  homeless, 483
  in poverty, 554–555
  reproduction concepts of, 327–328
  in single-parent families, 501–502
  television viewing by, 542–544
    parents' influence on, 544–545
    understanding of, 547–548
China, 499–500
Chinese children, 357
Chromosomes, 39

amniocentesis and, 70–71
developmental disabilities and, 51
  maternal age and, 69
  in reproduction, 43
  sex chromosomes, 45–46
Classical (respondent) conditioning, 121,
  123, 300, 385
Cocaine, 73, 74, 656–657
  crack, 660–661
Cognition, 262
Cognitive development
  in adolescence, 581–583
    hypothetical thinking in, 583
    moral development and, 641–643
    personality development in, 584
    timing of maturation and, 579–580
  in childhood
    age-based changes in, 326–329
    distinguishing people from objects in,
      383–384
    empirical findings in, 283–293
    gender typing in, 398–399
    issues in study of, 262–265
    of language, 246–250
    learning theory and behaviorism on,
      300–302
    Piaget on, 265–283, 288–289
    play and, 186–187
    television and, 548
  in current theories, 17
  in infants, 107–108
    learning theory and conditioning in,
      121–125
    recognition of information in, 108–121
  information-processing approach to
    assumptions in, 303
    cognitive processes in, 311–321
    cognitive units in, 303–311
    metacognition in, 321–326
Cognitive-development theory
  on emotions, 411–413
  on gender typing, 398–399
  on language development, 246–247
  on social development, 382–385
Cognitive learning theories, 301–302
Cognitive processes, 311
  attention, 313–314
  inference, 320–321
  in intelligence
    tests based on, 342–343
    in triarchic theory, 339
  memory, 314–320
  metacognition and, 321–326
  perception, 311–313
  problem solving, 321
  television viewing and, 545–547
Cognitive structures, 271
Collaborative Perinatal Project, 148–150
Collective monologues, 253
Color, infants' perception of, 101
Commercials, 552
Communications. *See also* Language; Speech
  conversation, 253–255

within family, during adolescence, 601
  language for, 220–221
Competence, 263–265, 345
Computers, 383–384
Conception, 56–58
  children's concepts of, 327–328
  sexual maturation and, 574
Concepts, in information-processing
  approach, 308–310, 330
Concrete operations
  stage of, 276–280
    emotions in, 409–410
  training in, 284
Conditioning, 16, 121–123, 300, 385
  classical, 123
  instrumental, 123–125
Conformity, 602–605
Conservation, Piaget's theory of, 276–277,
  284
Contraception, 593
  failure to use, 596–598
Conversation, 253–255
Cooperation
  in behavior, 458–459
  in learning, 531–532
  in play, 426–427
Correctional institutions, 672–673
Correlational studies, 22–23
Correlations, 22
Crack (cocaine), 657, 659–661
Crawling, 104
Creeping, 104
Crime. *See* Delinquency
Critical periods, 157
Criticism, in schools, 528–530
Cross-cultural studies, 26
Crossing-over (in germ cells), 45
Cross-sectional studies, 2–23
Cross-species studies, 26–27
Crystallized abilities, 338, 373
Cults, 644
Culture(s)
  adolescence in, 569
  child rearing in, 172–173
  development independent of, 4–5
  facial expressions constant across, 413
  family in, 557–558
    in China, 499–500
    social policies on, 558–559
  infant day care and, 170–172
  in infant physical development, 106
  infants' separation fear and, 140–141
  in intelligence and achievement, 336–337,
    355–360
  language to transmit, 221
  moral development in, 199, 456
  perinatal stress and, 78
  Piaget's stages in, 289
  play and
    cognitive development and, 186–187
    symbolic, 182–183
  prosocial behavior in, 458–459
  sense of self in, 338

strange situation and reactions to, 164
studies across, 26
Custody (in divorce), 501
stepparents and, 505–506

Darwinism, 91
Dating, 606–607
Day care
educational, 368
for infants, 170–172
quality of, 521–522
social development in, 519–520
Deaf children
babbling by, 224
language in, 237
Deaths
from AIDS, 76
of fathers, 501–502
infant mortality and, 69, 72–73
prematurity and, 80
from sudden infant death syndrome, 92–94
suicides, 678–681
Decentration, 276
Deictic words, 236–237
Delinquency, 667–669, 686–687
personality, parent-child relationships and, 670–672
prevention and treatment of, 672–676
sex differences in, 669
social change, poverty and, 669–670
Dependent variables, 23
Depression
in adolescence, 677–678
in childhood, 416
genetic factors in, 54–55
Desegregation, 532–534
Development, 4
continuity versus discontinuity in, 9–10
ethical issues in study of, 27–29
history of study of, 12–18
research on, 18–20
Developmental changes, 314
with age, 326–329
in memory, 317–318
in self-concept, 388–389
in understanding emotions, 411
Developmental disabilities, 51
Developmental psychology, 12
Differential Aptitude Test, 341–342
Difficult temperament in infants, 148, 149
Dimorphism, 569
Discipline. *See also* Child rearing
parental characteristics and beliefs in, 478–480
punishment and, 486–488
reinforcement in, 484–486
Discrepancy principle, 108–112
Diseases
during pregnancy, 75–76
prenatal, amniocentesis to detect, 70–71
Dishabituation, 111

Divorce, 502–505, 555
by adolescent mothers, 595
single-parent families after, 501–502
stepparent-stepchild relationships after, 505–506
Dizygotic (fraternal) twins, 47–49.
See also Twin studies
DNA (deoxyribonucleic acid), 39–41
Dominant genes, 46
Down's syndrome, 51, 69
Drawings, by children, 183–184
Drugs
adolescent use of, 655–659, 662–663, 686
crack, 660–661
AIDS and, 76
in prenatal environment, 73–75

Easy temperament in infants, 148
Eating disorders, 682–685
Ecology, 5
Economy, 554–555
Education. *See also* School; Schools
academic organization of, 523–526
classroom organization in, 531–535
employment and
in high school, 627
joint programs in, 626–627
prospects for, 640–641
shifts in goals for, 636–637
Head Start programs in, 365–368
moral development and, 642
physical environment for, 522–523
sex education, 587–589
teachers in, 526–531
Educational television, 369–370, 544–545, 547
Ego, 442
Egocentric speech, 253
Egocentrism
in adolescence, 584
in Piaget's theories, 274, 283, 285–286, 384
Ego control, 444, 445
Ego identity, 622
Ego resilience, 445
Ejaculations, 578
Electroencephalograms (EEGs), 290
Elementary schools, 523. *See also* School
Embryonic period, 58–64
maternal diseases during, 75
Emotional disturbances, 416–419, 687
anxiety reactions, 676–677
brief reactive psychosis, 682
community and, 482–483
depression, 54–55, 677–678
drug use and, 662–663
eating disorders, 682–685
schizophrenia, 54, 681–682
suicides and 678–681
Emotions
in childhood, 407–411
development of, 411–414

empathy, 430
in imitation, 194–195
peer relationships and, 540
problems and disturbances in, 414–419
in infancy, 136–138
attachment to caregivers and, 158–161
cultural context of child rearing and, 172–173
inferring from behavior, 138–143
inferring from facial expressions, 143–147
measurement of attachment and, 162–165
parental practices and, 165–167
quality of attachment and, 167–172
temperamental differences in, 147–152
theories of, 153–158
intimacy in, 607
Empathy, 203–204, 430, 459–462
Employment
child-rearing practices and, 482
in high school, 627
of mothers, 506–507, 555–557
infant day care and, 170–172
sex-role concepts of children of, 402
unemployment and, 555
vocational choice and, 624–626, 648–649
parental influence on, 632–635
prospects for, 637–641
socioeconomic influences in, 626–628
values and social change in, 635–637
of women, 628–632
Encoding, in memory, 316, 330
English (language), 222–223
Environmental influences
in aggressive behavior, 469
biology versus, 6
in cognitive learning theories, 301
in development, 5
in experimental psychology, 16–17
in infant temperament, 154
institutional and depriving, 169
in intelligence and achievement, 50, 355–360, 374
early intervention in, 365–370
home environment in, 361–365
interaction between biology and, 370–373
in IQ scores, 344
in language, 250–253
prenatal, 67
drugs in, 73–75
maternal age in, 69
maternal diseases and disorders in, 75–76
maternal nutrition in, 69–72
maternal stress in, 77
radiation in, 75
Rh blood factor in, 76–77
on sex chromosome abnormalities, 53
on twins, 48–49
Equilibration, 272
Erections, 578

Estrogen, 569, 574
Ethical issues in research, 27–29
Ethnic groups
  children's conceptions of, 403–404
  differences in intellectual performance by, 356–360
    court rulings on test bias and, 361
  group identity with, 404–406
  integration of, 532–534
  stereotypes of, 548–549
Ethology, 157–158
Event-related potentials, 110
Event schemata (scripts), 306–307, 384
Executive processes, 323–325, 331
  in intelligence tests, 343
Expectancies, of teachers, 531
Experience
  in cognitive learning theories, 301–302
  emotional, 410–411
  infant temperament and, 147, 154
  in information-processing approach, 303
  IQ scores and, 360
  in Piaget's theories, 268
  traumatic, 319
  in triarchic theory of intelligence, 340
Experimental methods, 23–25
  in analysis of behavior, 300–301
Experimental psychology, 16–17
Externalizing syndromes, 416, 419
Extinction (of reinforcement), 485
Eye color, 46
Eyewitnesses, children as, 318–319

Facial expressions
  across cultures, 413
  emotions in, 410, 411
  infants' reactions to, 383
  inferring infants' emotions from, 143–147
Family
  adolescents and
    communications in, 601
    in sense of identity, 620–621
  aggressive behavior and, 469–470
  childhood interactions with, 205–210
  child-rearing and disciplinary practices in, 481–484
    children's personality and behavior in, 480–481
    imitation and identification in, 489–491
    inductive techniques in, 488–489
    parental characteristics and beliefs in, 478–480
    punishment in, 486–488
    reinforcement in, 484–486
    social context of, 481
  in China, 499–500
  effect on intelligence and achievement of, 362
  income loss by, 555
  other social systems and, 557–558
  socialization in, 511–513

  child abuse and, 507–509
  family structure and, 500–507
  parental behavior in, 491–495
  siblings in, 495–500
  systems approach to, 509–511
  social support for, 554
Family day care, 519–520
Family therapists, 510–511
Fathers
  adolescents' vocational choices and, 633
  child custody by, 501
  divorced, 503
  infants' attachments to, 167
Fears, 136
  anxiety reactions and, 676–677
  in childhood, 409
  in infancy, 138–139, 141–143
    of separation, 140–141
    of strangers, 139–140
  test anxiety, 353–354
Feeding, 156–157
Females
  as adolescents
    delinquency among, 669
    gender identity and sex role identity in, 623–624
    growth spurt in, 570, 572
    puberty in, 569
  gender identity of, 394–395
  as girls
    with employed mothers, 506
    gender typing by peers of, 538–539
    in mother-custody homes, 501
    sibling relationships of, 497, 498
  sex chromosomes in, 45
    fragile-X syndrome in, 53
  sexual development in, 574
    menstruation in, 577–578
    timing of, 580–581
  sexuality of, 585–586
    pregnancy and contraception in, 592–598
    premarital intercourse and, 590
    prostitution and, 666
  television portrayals of, 549, 550
  work and, 628–632
Fertility rates, 69
Fetal alcohol syndrome, 74
Fetal period, 58, 64–67
  amniocentesis during, 70–71
  maternal diseases during, 75
  maternal stress during, 77
Field experiments, 25
Field studies, 23
Figurative language, 229–230
Firstborn children, 495–496
  sibling relationships of, 496–498
Fixations, 155, 156
Fluid abilities, 338, 373
Formal operations, stage of, 280–283, 581–582
Fragile-X syndrome, 51–53
France, 558

Fraternal (dizygotic) twins, 47–49.
  See also Twin studies
"Freestyle" (television series), 549–550
Friendships, 433–435. *See also* Peer relationships
  acceptance and rejection in, 438–440
  in adolescence, 605–606
    with opposite sex, 606–608
  forming, 435–437
  maintaining, 437
  peer relations and group structure in, 437–438
  training in social skills for, 440–441
Frustration-aggression hypothesis, 464, 471–472

Games, 429–430
  moral judgments in, 446
Gangs, 438, 670
Gender
  aggressive behavior and, 465
  differences in intellectual performance by, 356
  fetal development of, 64–65
  genetic determination of, 46
  in Kohlberg's theory of moral development, 456
  in school environment, 526
Gender constancy, 395
Gender identity, 393–395, 623–624
Gender salience, 399–400
Gender typing, 392–394
  causes of, 398–403
  development of, 394–398
  by peers, 538–539
  teachers and, 528–531
Genes, 39–41, 51
Genetic factors in development, 6
  amniocentesis to detect disorders linked to, 70–71
  chromosomes and genes in, 38–41
  determining extent of, 46–56
  in infants' temperament, 148–150
  in intellectual development
    interaction between environment and, 370–373
    in IQ scores, 344, 358
  mechanisms of, 42–44
  sex chromosomes in, 45–46
  of siblings, 44–45
Germ cells, 43–45
Germinal period, 58, 59
Girls. *See* Females
Goals, vocational, 626
  shifts in, 636–637
  women's work and, 629–631
"Going steady," 606–607
Government, 553–557
  family policies of, 558–559
Graham-Rosenblith behavioral test, 100
Grammar
  as innate, 244

syntactic rules of, 231–232
Grammatical morphemes, 232–234
Gratification, delay of, 442–444
Group identity, 404–405
Groups
  in friendships, 437–438
  moral judgment and atmosphere of, 454–455
Growth spurt, during adolescence, 570–572

Habituation-dishabituation method, 111–112
Handicapped children, 418
  mainstreaming of, 534–535
Head Start programs, 365–368, 375, 519
Health, television viewing and, 545
Hearing, by infants, 102
Hemophilia, 70
Heredity. *See also* Genetic factors in development
  chromosomes and genes in, 38–41
  in early child development theories, 15
  extent of genetic influences in, 46–56
  infant temperament and, 147
  in intelligence tests, 344
  mechanisms of, 42–44
  of reflexes, 94–95
  in schizophrenia, 681
  sex chromosomes in, 45–46
  in siblings, 44–45
Herpes, 75
Heterosexuality, 590–592
Higher-order operations, 280–281
Home environment, 361–365, 374
Homelessness, 483
  runaways and, 664
Homosexuality, 590–592
Hormones, 569, 586
Humor, 239
Hypothetical thinking, 583

Id, 442
Identical (monozygotic) twins, 44, 47–49.
  See also Twin studies
Identification, 489–491
Identity
  in adolescence, 614–615, 647–648
    cognitive aspects of, 584
    development of sense of, 617–621
    ego identity, 622
    friendships and, 605–606
    gender and sex-role identity, 623–624
    identity foreclosure and confusion in, 621
    variations in formation of, 622
    vocational, 624–625
  in childhood
    ethnic group and, 403–406
    gender (sex), 392–403
    self-concept in, 388–390
    self-esteem in, 391–392
  Erikson's eight stages of, 615–617

Identity confusion, 621
Identity foreclosure, 621
Images, in information-processing approach, 307–308, 330
Imitation
  in childhood behavior, 190–195, 210
  in child rearing, 489–491
  in language acquisition, 240–243
  in observational learning, 385–387
  in Piaget's theories, 274
Imprinting, 157
Income loss, effects of, 555
Independent variables, 23
Induction, 463–464
Inductive techniques, 488–489
Infancy
  aggressive behavior in, 469
  cognitive development in, 107–108
    distinguishing people from objects in, 383–384
    early intervention in, 368
    learning theory and conditioning in, 121–125
    recognition of information in, 108–121
  emotional and social relationships with adults in
    attachment to caregivers in, 158–161
    cultural context of child rearing and, 172–173
    measuring attachment in, 162–165
    parental practices in, 165–167
    quality of attachment and, 167–172
    theoretical perspectives on, 153–158
  emotions in, 136–138
    inferring from behavior, 138–143
    inferring from facial expressions, 143–147
    temperamental differences in, 147–152
  empathy in, 459
  imitation in, 190
  language development in, 223–224
  newborns, 92
    perceptions of, 95–102
    premature, 66–67, 80–81
    reflexes of, 94–95
    sudden infant death syndrome of, 92–94
    physical growth and maturation in, 103–106
    Piaget on, 128–129
      object permanence in, 127–128
      sensorimotor period in, 126–127
      sensorimotor schemes in, 125–126
    play in, 188–189
    theories of, 90–91
Infantile autism, 53
Infant mortality, 69, 72–73
  prematurity and, 80
  from sudden infant death syndrome, 92–94
Inference, 320–321
Information-processing approach, 329–331
  on adolescence, 583

  assumptions in, 303
  cognitive processes in, 311–321
  cognitive units in, 303–311
  on gender typing, 399–400
  metacognition in, 321–326
  on social cognition, 384–385
Inhibitions, in infants, 150–151, 164
Institutionalized children, 169
Instrumental (operant) conditioning, 121, 123–125, 300, 385
Integration, 532–534
Intellectualization, 584
Intelligence, 373
  cultural context of, 336–337
  dimensions of, 338–340
  heredity and, 47–51
  individual differences in
    early intervention in, 365–370
    home environment in, 361–365
    interaction of biology and environment in, 370–373
  of infants, testing of, 100, 105
  measurements and tests of, 341–343
    cautions on use of, 345–346
    limitations of, 343–345
  play and, 186–187
  role-taking ability correlated with, 431
  as single versus multiple abilities, 337–338
Intelligence quotients (IQs), 336, 373–375
  court rulings on, 361
  cultural and environmental influences in, 358–360
    by gender, 356
    by nationality, social class, and ethnic group, 356–358
  of delinquents, 670
  individual differences in
    early intervention and, 365–370
    home environment in, 361–365
    interaction of biology and environment in, 370–373
  measurements of, 341–343
    limitations on, 343–345
    use of, 345–346
  nature versus nurture controversy on, 6
  stability over time of, 10
  teacher expectations and, 531
  test anxiety and, 353–354
Intercourse
  attitudes toward, 585–586, 592
  contraception and, 593, 596–598
  pregnancy and, 594–597
  premarital, 589–590
  during puberty, 574
Internalizing syndromes, 416–417
Intimacy, 607
Irony, 230
Irritability, in infants, 150

Japan, 357, 477
Juvenile delinquency. *See* Delinquency

Kaufman A-B-C tests, 342
Klinefelter's syndrome (XXY), 51
Knowledge, in triarchic theory of intelligence, 339–340
Kramer vs. Kramer (film), 555–556

Labeling, self-control and, 443
Laissez-faire parenting style, 600–601
Language. *See also* Communications; Speech
    cognition and, 248–250
    for communication and conversation, 253–255
    components of, 222–226
    in emotional experiences, 410
    environmental influences on, 250–253
    functions of, 220–222
    pragmatics in, 238–240
    semantics in, 226–230
    syntax in, 230–238
    theories of acquisition of, 240–248
Language acquisition device (LAD), 244
Learned helplessness, 351
Learning. *See also* Education; School
    active versus passive theories of, 8–9
    activity in, 288
    conditioning in, 300
    cooperation in, 531–532
    of emotions, 413–414
    in infants, schemata for, 113
    observational, 385–387
    from peers, 537–541
    self-monitoring in, 324
    from television, 548–552
Learning theory, 300–302, 329–331
    conditioning in, 121–122
        classical conditioning, 123
        instrumental conditioning, 123–125
    on emotions, 411, 413–414
    on empathy, 460–461
    on gender-typed behavior, 401–403
    on language acquisition, 240–243
    on self-control, 442
    on social and emotional development
        in childhood, 385–388
        in infants, 156–157
Libido, 91, 154–156
Locomotion of infants, 104–106
    fear of visual cliffs and, 143
Longitudinal studies, 23
Long-term (permanent) memory, 316, 330
Love
    in adolescence, 607
    in second and third years, 206

Mainstreaming handicapped children, 418, 439, 534–535
Males
    as adolescents
        delinquency among, 669
        gender identity and sex role identity in, 623–624

growth spurt in, 570, 572
    puberty in, 569
    as boys
        aggressive behavior by, 465
        with employed mothers, 506
        in father-custody homes, 501
        punishment of, 488
        sibling relationships of, 498
    gender identity of, 394–395
    sex chromosomes in, 45–46
        fragile-X syndrome in, 53
    sexual development in, 573–574
        erections, ejaculations, and nocturnal emissions in, 578
        timing of, 579–581
    sexuality of, 585–586
        contraception and, 597–598
        premarital intercourse and, 590
        prostitution and, 666
    unemployed, 555
    working lives of, 482
Marijuana, 656
Marriage, 595
    women's work and, 631–632
Masturbation, 578, 586–589
Mathematical abilities, 347–348
    sexual stereotypes in, 356
Maturation
    age-based developmental changes in, 326–329
    in cognitive learning theories, 301
    in infants, 103–106
    in information-processing approach, 303
    in Piaget's theories, 268, 283–284
Mean length of utterance (MLU), 232, 256
Meiosis, 43–44
Memory
    in adolescence, 582
    in infants, 115–121
    in information-processing approach, 314–320, 330–331
    language and, 249–250
    metacognition and, 321–322
    metamemory and, 323
    schemata in, 305
Men. *See* Males
Menarche, 575
Menstruation, 577–578
Mental disorders. *See also* Emotional disturbances
    genetic factors in, 53–55
Mental retardation
    chromosome abnormalities and, 51
    fragile-X syndrome and, 53
    phenylketonuria (PKU) and, 46
Metabolic diseases, 70–71
Metacognition, 321–326, 331
Metacognitive processes, 339, 343
Metalinguistic awareness, 238
Metamemory, 323, 331
Methods, 20–21
    cross-cultural studies, 26

cross-sectional and correlational studies, 22–23
cross-species studies, 26–27
experimental, 23–25
habituation-dishabituation, 111–112
longitudinal studies, 23
Minimum-sufficiency principle, 485, 486
Mitosis, 38, 43
Models
    for prosocial behavior, 462–463
    teachers as, 530–531
Monozygotic (identical) twins, 44, 47–49.
    See also Twin studies
Moral development, 445–446. *See also* Self-control
    in adolescence
        cognitive growth and, 641–643
        current trends in, 644–647
        religious beliefs in, 643–644
    in childhood, 195–199
    Kohlberg's theory of, 447–454
        criticisms of, 456
    moral judgments in, 446–447
        behavior and, 456–457
        democratic atmosphere and, 454–455
Moral realism, stage of, 446
Moral relativism, stage of, 446–447
Moro reflex, 95, 99, 100
Morphemes, 224–226, 256
    grammatical, 232–234
Motherese, 250–251
Mothers. *See also* Parent-child relationships
    adolescents as, 595–596
    bonding between newborns and, 166–167
    divorced, 503
    employed, 170–172, 506–507, 555–557
        adolescents' vocational choices and, 633–635
        high-school seniors' views of, 631–632
    infants' attachment to, 158–161
    infants' fear of separation from, 140–141
    monkey experiments on infant contact with, 157
    prenatal development in, 56–67
    prenatal environment in, 67
        age and, 69
        diseases and disorders and, 75–76
        drugs in, 73–75
        nutrition in, 69–72
        radiation in, 75
        Rh blood factor in, 76–77
        stress in, 77
    as single-parents, 501
Motivation, 346–351, 374

Nationality, differences in intellectual performance by, 356–361
Nativist theory, 243–244
Nature versus nurture controversy, 6
    in language acquisition, 240, 243
Negatives (in language), 237
Neonates. *See* Newborns

Nervous system. *See also* Brain
actions, knowledge and emotions located
in, 136
anoxia and, 77–79
embryonic development of, 63
of infants, 104
Newborns, 92. *See also* Infants
bonding between mothers and, 166–167
facial expressions in, 143–144
perceptions in, 95–102
premature, 66–67, 80–81
reflexes in, 94–95
siblings of, 497
sudden infant death syndrome in, 92–94
Nicotine, 74
Nocturnal emissions, 578
Nonsexist child rearing, 400–401
Number skills, 284, 278–279
Nutrition
during adolescence, 570–571
in prenatal environment, 69–72
eating disorders and, 682–685

Obesity, 682
Objectivity, 21
Object permanence, 127–128
Observation
of gender-typed behavior, 401–403
in learning emotions, 414
in prosocial behavior, 462–463
Observational learning, 385–387
Only children, 498–499
in China, 499–500
Open education, 523–525
Operant (instrumental) conditioning, 121,
123–125, 300, 385
Operations (in Piaget's theories), 271
Oral stage, 91, 155
Organization
in long-term memory, 316
in Piaget's theories, 270–273
Orphanages, 15, 169
Ova, 58
Overcontrol, 444–445
Overextensions (in language), 228–229

Parallel play, 426, 427
Parent-child relationships
in adolescence, 598–601
delinquency and, 670–672
drug use and, 662
eating disorders and, 684–685
peers versus, 603–605
vocational choice and, 632–635
aggressive behavior and, 469–470
bidirectionality in, 151–152
child abuse in, 507–509
in developing prosocial behavior, 463
divorce and, 503
effect on intelligence and achievement of,
362–365

emotional and social effects of, 165–167
gender-typing in, 402
as models for friendships, 435–437
parental behavior in, 491–495
parental characteristics and beliefs in,
478–480
in second and third years, 205
stepparent-stepchild, 505–506
strange situation to measure, 162–165
Parenting styles, 363–364, 491–495. *See also*
Child rearing
during adolescence, 599–601
Parents
abusive, 507–509
children's imitation of, 192
children's television viewing and, 544–545
divorce of, 503–505
employed mothers, 506–507, 555–557
infants' attachment to, 158–161
infants' temperament and, 148
peers versus, 536–537
sex education by, 588
single, 500–502, 557
stepparents, 505–506
Peer relationships
in adolescence, 601–602
conformity and, 602–603
drug use and, 662
friendships and identity development
in, 605–606
with opposite sex, 606–608
parents versus, 603–605
vocational choice and, 635
in moral judgments, 454–455
perceptions of others in, 431–433
play in, 426–430
role taking in, 430–431
in socialization, 535–536
parents versus, 536–537
social learning from, 537–541
Perceived self-efficacy, 349
Perception
in information-processing approach, 311–
314, 330
in newborns, 95–102
of phonemes, 223
of others, 431–433
Performance, 263–265
on IQ tests, 345
cultural and environmental influences
in, 355–360
standards of, 348–349
Perinatal stress, 78
Permanent (long-term) memory, 316, 330
Permissive parenting style, 206–208, 364
Personality
in child-rearing practices
of children, 480–481
of parents, 478–480
cognitive development and, 584
delinquency and, 670–671
Freud's components of, 442
genetic factors in, 55–56

sex stereotypes for, 395
sexuality in, 585–586
Petting, 589
Phenylketonuria (PKU), 46
Phonemes, 222–224
Physical development
in adolescence, 572, 608–609
erections, ejaculations, and nocturnal
emissions, in males, 578
female sexual development, 574
growth spurt in, 570–571
hormones in, 569
male sexual development, 573–574
menstruation, in females, 577–578
normal variations in, 574–577
sexuality in, 584–598
timing of, in females, 580–581
timing of, in males, 579–580
in infants, 103–106
Physical fitness, 545
Pituitary gland, 569
Placenta, 59–62
Planned Parenthood Federation, 596
Planning, 323–324
Play
assimilation in, 272
cognitive development and, 292
developmental stages in, 291
functions of, 184–186
gender-typed, 396
with other children, 187–189
peer relationships in, 426–430
symbolic, 181–184
Pollution, 73
Polygenetic inheritance, 46–47
Popularity, 438–440
Possessiveness, 200–203
Post-traumatic stress disorder, 664
Posture, of infants, 104–106
Potential competence, 265
Poverty, 554–555
delinquency and, 669–670
Pragmatics (in language), 238–240
Praise, 528–530
Pregnancy. *See also* Prenatal development
in adolescence, 593–598
prenatal environment during, 67–77
stages of, 56–67
Premarital intercourse, 586, 589–590
Premature infants, 66–67, 80–81
Prenatal development
from conception, 56–58
embryonic period in, 59–64
environment during, 67
drugs in, 73–75
maternal age and, 69
maternal diseases and disorders in, 75–
76
maternal nutrition in, 69–72
maternal stress in, 77
radiation in, 75
Rh blood factor in, 76–77
fetal period in, 64–67

Prenatal development (*continued*)
  germinal period in, 59
Preoperational stage, 273–275
  emotions in, 409
Preschool programs, 365–368
  social development in, 519–523
Prescription drugs, 656
Pretend play, 428, 429
Primary circular reactions, 126
Primary Mental Abilities Test, 341–342
Primary reinforcers, 124, 156
Problem solving, 321
Progestins, 569
Project Head Start, 365–368, 375, 519
Propositions, in information-processing
  approach, 310–311, 330
Prosocial behavior, 458–462
  peer relationships and, 537–538
  portrayed on television, 552
  training for, 462–464
Prostitution, 666
Psychoanalytic theory, 16, 19
  on adolescence, 568
  on self-control, 442
  on social and emotional development in
    infants, 154–156
Psychological and psychophysiological dis-
    turbances, 687
  anxiety reactions, 676–677
  brief reactive psychosis, 682
  depression, 677–678
  eating disorders, 682–685
  schizophrenia, 681–682
  suicides, 678–681
  treatment of, 685
Psychosis, 682
Psychosocial reciprocity, 615
Psychotherapy, 685
Puberty, 569, 572
Punishment, 208–209, 469, 486–488

Questions
  in children's conversation, 254–255
  in language development, 236

Racial integration, 532–534
Radiation, 75
Random assignment, 24
Reading, 547
Reasoning, 222
Recall memory, 117–120, 316–317, 331
Recessive genes, 46
Recognition, 316–317, 331
Reflexes, of newborns, 94–95, 99, 100
Reinforcement, 123–125
  in child rearing, 484–486
  of gender-typed behavior, 401
  in language acquisition, 240, 241
  by peers, 537–540
  by teachers, 528–530
Reinforcing stimuli, 301

Rejections, in friendships, 438–440
Relational thinking, 278
Religious beliefs, 643–644
REM sleep, 92
Reproductive system
  children's concepts of, 327–328
  fetal development of, 64–65
Research on child development, 18–19
  ethical issues in, 27–29
  methods of, 20–27
Respondent (classical) conditioning, 121,
    123, 300, 385
Restrictive child rearing, 206–208
Retrieval, in memory, 316, 330
Rewards, 484–485. *See also* Reinforcement
Rh blood factor, 76–77
Role models, 206
Role taking, 430–432
Rubella (German measles), 63–64, 75
Rules
  for games, 429–430, 446
  prescriptive and proscriptive, 441
  punishment and, 486
Runaways, 663–666

Schemata, 108, 180
  for categories, 113–115
  discrepancy principle and, 108–112
  for gender typing, 399–400
  in information-processing approach, 304–
    307, 330
  language and, 222
  memory and, 115–121
  in play among children, 188
  senses and, 112–113
  in social cognition, 384–385
Schematic prototypes, 108
Schemes, 125
Schizophrenia, 54, 681–682
School
  achievement in, 354–355
    developmental patterns and, 352–353
    motivation for, 346–351
    test anxiety and, 353–354
  employment and, 635
    in high school, 627
    joint programs in, 625–626
    shifts in goals for, 636–637
  friendships in, 437
  Head Start programs and, 365–368
  mainstreaming handicapped children in,
    418, 439
  sex education in, 587–589
  social development in
    academic organization in, 523–526
    classroom organization in, 531–535
    in day care and preschool, 519–522
    physical environment in, 522–523
    teachers in, 526–531
Scripts (event schemata), 306–307, 384, 548
Secondary circular reactions, 126–127
Secondary reinforcers, 124, 156

Sects, 644
Self-awareness, 198–204
Self-concept, 388–390
  of ability, 349
  in adolescence, 619–620
  self-esteem distinguished from, 391
Self-control, 441–442. *See also* Moral de-
    velopment
  measuring and developing, 442–444
  over- and undercontrol, 444–445
Self-esteem, 349, 391–392
  group identity in, 404–405
  popularity and, 439
  timing of maturation and, 579–581
Semantics, 226–230
Senses of infants, 111–113
Sensorimotor coordination, 125
Sensorimotor schemes, 125–126, 271
Sensorimotor stage, 126–127, 273
Sensory memory, 315, 330
Sentences
  complex, 234–236
  first, 230–231
  passive, 237
Separation, fear of, 140–141
Seriation, 277–278
"Sesame Street" (television program), 369–
    370, 544–545, 547
Sex. *See* Gender
Sex chromosomes, 39, 45–46
  abnormalities of, 51, 53
    amniocentesis to detect, 70–71
    fragile-X syndrome and, 51–53
Sex differences
  in adolescent physical development, 572
  in adolescent sexuality, 585–586
  in aggression, 465
  in delinquency, 669
  in intellectual performance, 356
  in Kohlberg's theory of moral develop-
    ment, 456
Sex education, 587–589
Sex role adoption, 394, 396–398
Sex role identity, 394, 623–624
  women's work and, 629–631
Sex role preferences, 394–396
Sex stereotypes, 395, 401
  in mathematical abilities, 356
  in peer relationships, 538–539
  on television, 402–403
    changing, 549–550
  on women's work, 629
Sex typing. *See* Gender typing
Sexuality
  in adolescence, 584–585
    changing attitudes and behavior in,
      586–589
    homosexual behavior and orientation
      in, 590–592
    personal values on, 645
    pregnancy and conception in, 592–598
    premarital sexual intercourse in, 589–
      590

sex differences in, 585–586
variations in attitudes and behavior, 592
in Freud's theory, 91
prostitution and, 666
Sexually transmitted diseases, 592–593
Sexual maturation
in females, 574
in males, 573–574
normal variations in, 574–577
psychological aspects of
of erections, ejaculations, and nocturnal emissions, in males, 578
of menstruation, in females, 577–578
timing of, in females, 580–581
timing of, in males, 579–580
Shame, 136
Short-term (working) memory, 115–117, 315, 330
Shy children, 416–417
Siblings, 495–499
hereditary transmission in, 43–45
infant temperament and, 154
twins, 47–49
of two and three-year-olds, 209–210
Sign language, 237
Single-parent families, 500–502, 555, 557
Sitting, 104
Sleep, by infants, 92
Slow-to-warm-up temperament in infants, 148
Smiling, 144–146
Smoking, 74
Social behavior, 470–472
aggression, 464–470
friendships in, 433–435
acceptance and rejection in, 438–440
forming friendships, 435–437
maintaining friendships, 437
with peers and groups, 437–438
moral development in, 445–447
in adolescence, 641–647
in childhood, 195–199
Kohlberg's theory of, 447–457
peer relationships in
perceptions of others in, 431–433
play and, 426–430
role taking in, 430–431
prosocial behavior, 458–462
training for, 462–464
self-control in, 441–445
theories of, 385–388
training in skills of, 440–441
Social change
delinquency and, 669–670
vocational choice and, 635–637
Social cognitions, 17
Social cognition theories, 382–385
Social-comparison standards, 349
Social development. *See also* Socialization
in childhood
classroom organization and, 531–535
in day care and preschool, 519–522

emotions in, 407–414
ethnic group and identity in, 403–406
gender typing and identity in, 392–403
imitation in, 193–194
problems in, 414–419
in school, 522–526
sense of self in, 388–392
teachers' influence on, 526–531
theories of, 382–388
in infancy
attachment to caregivers and, 158–161
cultural context of child rearing and, 172–173
measuring attachment in, 162–165
parental practices and, 165–167
quality of attachment and, 167–172
theories of, 153–158
Social groups, 438
Socialization, 476–477, 560–561
in adolescence
parent-child relationships in, 598–601
peer relationships in, 601–608
sexuality and, 584–598
child-rearing and disciplinary practices in, 481–484
children's personality and behavior and, 480–481
imitation and identification in, 489–491
inductive techniques in, 488–489
nonsexist child rearing in, 400–401
parental characteristics and beliefs in, 478–480
punishment in, 486–488
reinforcement in, 484–486
social context of, 481
in day care and preschools, 518–522
external society in, 552–553
social trends and policy in, 553–557
in family, 511–513
child abuse and, 507–509
family structure and, 500–507
parental behavior in, 491–495
siblings in, 495–500
systems approach to, 509–511
family in
cultural context of, 558–559
relations between other social systems and, 557–558
by gender, 356
peers and, 535–536
parents versus, 536–537
social learning from, 537–541
in school, 522–523
academic organization of, 523–526
classroom organization in, 531–535
teachers in, 526–531
in second and third years, 206–209
television in, 542–544
children's understanding of, 547–548
learning from, 548–552
no television versus, 545–547
parents' influence on, 544–545
Socialized speech, 253

Social knowledge, 548
Social learning
from peers, 537–541
Social-learning theory
on emotions, 411, 413–414
on empathy, 460–461
on gender-typed behavior, 401–403
on language acquisition, 247–248
on self-control, 442
on social and emotional development
in childhood, 385–388
in infants, 156–157
Social policy, 553–557
Social referencing, 161
Social skills, training in, 440–441
Social trends, 553–557
Social withdrawal, 416–417
Socioeconomic influences
in child abuse, 508
in child-rearing practices, 480
in delinquency, 669–670
in friendships, 437
in infant physical development, 103
in intelligence, 50–51, 356–358, 374
Head Start programs and, 365–368
on language, 252–253
in poverty, 554–555
in premature births, 80, 81
on sexual attitudes and behavior, 592
on television viewing, 542
achievement and, 546
on vocational choice, 626–628
parental influence in, 632–633
prospects for, 640
Solitary play, 426, 427
Speech. *See also* Communications; Language
morphemes and words in, 224–226
phonemes in, 222–224
semantics in, 226–230
syntax in, 230–238
Sperm cells, 57
Stage theories of development, 9–10, 300
Erikson's, 615–617
Freud's, 16
of infancy, 91
of social and emotional development, 156
of moral development
Kohlberg's, 447–456, 641
Piaget's, 446–447
Piaget's
of childhood, 273–283, 294–295
empirical findings and, 283–293
of infancy, 125–129
Standards. *See also* Moral development
in childhood, 195–199
of performance, 348–349
Standing, 105–106
Stanford-Binet IQ tests, 341–343
Status offenses, 667, 673
Stepparents, 505–506
Stereotypes. *See also* Gender typing
learned from television, 548–549

Stereotypes (*continued*)
  sex, 395, 401–403
    changing, 549–550
    in mathematical abilities, 356
    in peer relationships, 538–539
Strangers, fear of, 139–140
Strange situation, 162–165, 170
Strategies, in memory, 318–320
Stress
  child abuse and, 508
  infant temperament and, 154
  maternal, during pregnancy, 77
  perinatal, during childbirth, 78
  traumatic experiences as, 319
Sudden infant death syndrome (SIDS), 92–94
Suicides, 678–681
Superego, 442
Symbolic categories, 222, 308
Symbolic functioning, 180–181
  functions of play in, 184–186
  in Piaget's theories, 274
  play with other children in, 187–189
  symbolic play in, 181–184
Symbolic play, 181–184
Synapses, 104
Syntax, 230–238
Syphilis, 76
Systems approach, 509–511

Taiwan, 357
Talking
  babbling, 223–224
  conversation, 253–255
  sentences, 230–238
  words, 224–226
Teachers
  influence upon children of, 526–531
  methods used by, 525–526
  peers as, 540–541
Teaching
  of arithmetic, 278–279
  of language, 250–252
  by parents, 364
  prosocial behavior, 462–464
  social skills, 440–441
Teaching Family Model, 302
Teenagers. *See also* Adolescence
  pregnancy in, 69, 593–598

Television
  children's emotional reactions to, 409–410
  educational, 369–370
  sex stereotypes on, 401–403, 549–550
  socialization by, 542–544
    children's understanding of, 547–548
    learning from, 548–552
    no television versus, 545–547
    parents' influence on, 544–545
Temperament, in infants, 147–148, 174
  activity level and, 148–150
  aggressive behavior and, 469
  early experiences and, 154
  reactions to unfamiliarity and, 150–151
    bidirectionality principle and, 151–152
  strange situation and, 164
Tertiary circular reactions, 127
Test anxiety, 353–354
Test bias, 360, 361
Testimony, by children, 318–319
Testosterone, 468–469, 586
Thalidomide, 73
Theories of child development, 12–18
Thinking. *See* Cognition; Cognitive development
"Time outs," 486
Tobacco, 74
Toilet training, 615
Tomexia of pregnancy, 76
Toys, 187, 274, 426, 523
  gender typing and, 539–540
Training. *See* Teaching
Traumatic experiences, 319
Triarchic theory of intelligence, 339–340
Trophoblast, 59
Trust, 91, 156, 605
Twins, 44
  monozygotic and dizygotic, 47–49
Twin studies, 48–49
  of infants' temperament, 148–150
  of personality, 55–56
  of schizophrenia, 54

Ultrasound pictures (sonographs), 70–71
Umbilical cord, 59
Undercontrol, 444–445
Underextensions (in language), 229
Unemployment, 555, 637

Values. *See also* Moral development
  in adolescence
    cognitive growth and, 641–643
    current trends in, 644–647
    religious beliefs in, 643–644
  effect on intelligence and achievement of, 363
  sexual, 586
  vocational, 635–637
    on women's work, 629–631
Variables, 23–24
Violence. *See also* Aggression
  delinquency and, 673–675
  portrayed on television, 550–551
Vision, in newborns, 95–101
Visual cliffs, 141–143, 161, 174
Vocational choice, 624–626, 648–649
  parental influence on, 632–635
  prospects for, 637–641
  socioeconomic influences in, 626–628
  values and social change in, 635–637
  of women, 628–631
    marriage and, 631–632

Walking, 105–106
Wechsler Intelligence Scales, 341
Whites, integration and, 532
Withdrawn children, 416–417
Women. *See* Females
Words, 224–226
  semantics of, 226–230
  syntax of, 230–238
Work. *See* Employment; Vocational choice
Working (short-term) memory, 115–117, 315, 330

X chromosomes, 45–46
  abnormalities of, 51
  fragile-X syndrome and, 51–53
  hemophilia and, 70
  mental disorders and, 54
X-rays, 75

Y chromosomes, 45–46

Zygotes, 58